Sociology

Experiencing Changing Societies

Seventh Edition

Economy Version

Kenneth C. W. Kammeyer
The University of Maryland

George Ritzer
The University of Maryland

Norman R. Yetman
The University of Kansas

ALLYN AND BACON

Boston   London   Toronto   Sydney   Tokyo   Singapore

Editor in Chief, Social Sciences: Karen Hanson
Editorial Assistant: Jennifer Jacobson
Executive Marketing Manager: Joyce Nilsen
Editorial Production Service: MARBERN HOUSE
Manufacturing Buyer: Megan Cochran
Cover Administrator: Linda Knowles

Library of Congress Cataloging-in-Publication Data
Kammeyer, Kenneth C. W.
    Sociology, experiencing changing societies : economy version /
Kenneth C. W. Kammeyer, George Ritzer, Norman R. Yetman. – 7th ed.
        p.   cm.
    Includes bibliographical references and index.
    ISBN 0-205-16801-9 (alk. paper)
    1. Sociology.   2. Social change.   3. United States–Social
conditions.   I. Ritzer, George.   II. Yetman, Norman R., 1938–
III. Title.
HM51.K27   1997
301–dc20   96-8755
                                                                    CIP

Printed in the United States of America
10 9 8 7 6 5 4 3 2 1   01 00 99 98 97 96

CONTENTS

PART III   Social Institutions

11   Family   359

12   Education   396

13   The Economy and Work   423

14   Health and Medicine   457

PREFACE

In every edition of this book since the first, now nearly twenty years ago, we have tried to remain faithful to our original objective, that is, to present sociology in an orderly, consistent, and integrated manner. However, as we point out in the first chapter, this is not an easy task because sociology is not as orderly, consistent, and integrated as we would like it to be.

On the other hand, because sociology is not a monolithic whole, and because of its diversity, it continues to be interesting. Sociology represents many different approaches to a diversity of subjects. In the pages ahead readers are introduced to different sociological theories and widely different kinds of research. Theoretical and methodological diversity are found throughout the book. When theories are useful for increasing understanding, we use them, and, when research methods, of whatever type, produce interesting and meaningful data and information, we present them.

We also continue to be faithful to our original view that sociological principles, concepts, and ideas must be related to personal experience. Whenever possible, we use personal accounts of people describing their own experiences. We are also increasing our attention to contemporary events, because sociology often provides a useful way of analyzing what is happening in the everyday world.

To highlight the applicability of sociology to the news events of the day we are continuing a feature we call **In the News.** Sometimes these featured boxes call attention to what sociologists are doing that is newsworthy—such as the box in Chapter 2 that recounts the experiences of a sociology graduate student who actually spent time in jail rather than testify before a grand jury and reveal information he had learned in confidence while studying animal-rights groups.

Sociology is also part of the contemporary scene in the way it is now using computers for communication. Cyberspace, as it is called, is a realm of computer communication among people who may never see each other face to face. These communicators in cyberspace share interests in an infinite variety of subjects, and therefore it is not surprising that cyberspace communications about sociology have emerged in the last few years (see Chapter 1, Sociology on the Internet).

The continuing emphasis on contemporary events is only one way in which we have been faithful to our belief that sociology must show the dynamic character of social life. We repeatedly point out that societies and cultures are constantly changing, and in this edition we are more than ever aware of the importance of human agency at work in the change. We point out, as we always have, that, although social structures and other, more static aspects of society are important, human beings in our society, and every other, have the ability to change and modify the social systems in which they live. The source of societal change is, in a fundamental sense, brought about by the actions of individuals.

Of course, the accumulated actions of individuals often bring on changes in major processes at what is called, in the first chapter, the *macroscopic level.* For many years, industrialization, urbanization, and bureaucratization have been the processes that have changed the nature of societies. As we have just noted, we are seeing more and more signs that the computerization of society is now a major social process that is transforming societies.

We also continue, as we have for a number of editions, to stress the importance of cross-cultural and cross-national perspectives. These materials are found in the text and in boxes with those titles. **Cross-national** and **Cross-cultural Perspective** boxes present materials from other societies and cultures; some of these materials are historical, some are anthropological (perhaps describing small, non-literate societies), but often they are descriptions of contemporary societies. For example, in Chapter 16 we describe the (possible) political breakup of the United States's northern neighbor, Canada, or, in Chapter 13, the changing Chinese economy. The discussion of cross-national and cross-cultural issues plays an important part in broadening our sociological perspectives.

Organization

The text is divided into four parts. Part One serves as an introduction to the fundamental ideas of sociology. In the first two chapters we present key theories and research methods of sociology. The major sociological theories and classical theorists are introduced in Chapter 1 and then referred to when appropriate throughout the text. The chapters that follow introduce the concepts of *culture, interaction, groups, organizations, society, socialization,* and *deviance.* Chapter 4, "Forms of Social Life: Interaction, Groups, Organizations, and Societies," covers small and large units of society.

The final chapter of Part One—Chapter 7, "Sexual Behavior from a Sociological Perspective"—is a unique feature both to this book and to other introductory sociology texts. Here, we turn our attention to sexual behavior, a topic that is inherently interesting to most people. In this featured chapter we show how a sociological perspective can be usefully applied to this universal and fascinating human behavior. Our aim is to use the core sociological concepts presented in the first six chapters to illustrate how these basic sociological ideas can be applied to the study of sexual behavior and, by implication, to any other human behavior.

Part Two is concerned with the basic dimensions of inequality in societies. Again, whenever possible we introduce materials from other societies to supplement examples derived from the United States. Chapter 8 is concerned with socioeconomic stratification. Notable in this chapter is a discussion of the declining middle class, a relatively new social phenomenon not traditionally covered by introductory sociology texts. Chapter 9 explores race and ethnic inequality, and Chapter 10, gender and age stratification and inequality. In these chapters we discuss societal inequalities in Africa, Canada, China, and India, along with many other societies.

Part Three describes and analyzes in six chapters the basic institutions of societies—family, education, economy and work, health and medicine, religion, and politics. Once again the illustrative cases come from societies, both modern and preliterate, around the world. Part Four contains two chapters. One combines two societal features that have been especially important in the twentieth century: population growth and urbanization. This chapter presents succinctly an appropriate amount of introductory material on demography and urban sociology. The final chapter, Chapter 18, covers social change, collective behavior, and social movements.

Pedagogical Aids

At the end of each chapter, Critical Thinking questions challenge you to probe more deeply into your sociological understanding. The questions can serve as a springboard for classroom discussion or as home assignments. Each chapter has an introduction designed to draw you into the subject of the chapter. At the end of each chapter, a summary allows you to briefly review chapter content. Each major sociological concept is printed in boldface. A complete glossary of all major terms appears at the end of this book.

A Study Guide is also available for this book. It contains learning objectives, chapter outlines, key terms and definitions, key people, and self-tests. Your bookstore can assist you in ordering this if your instructor has not done so already.

Acknowledgments

Once again a number of people gave us help, guidance, and information as we prepared this edition. We especially want to thank Bob Antonio, Bill Falk, Jan Geeson, Elhum Haghighat-Bakhshai, Lee Hamilton, Ramon Henkel, Janet Hunt, Larry Hunt, Joan Kahn, Sunita Kishor, Steve Lankenau, Stanley Presser, Debra Reinfeld, Arlene Saluter, David Segal, Mady Segal, Jay Teachman, Reeve Vanneman, Barbara Wilson, Rita Wood, Doug Yetman, and Jeremy Yetman-Michaelson. Among the staff members in the Kansas and Maryland sociology departments, we have received help from Dorothy Bowers, Cindy Mewborn, Cass O'Toole, Gerry Todd, Agnes Zane, Penny Fritts, Pam Johnson, and Pam Levitt. We especially want to thank Jill Yetman-Michaelson for constructing the index. Eden Rome, too, deserves special credit for her assistance and substantive contributions.

For many years now, through the six previous editions of this book, we have benefited from the advice and suggestions of dozens of college teachers who have read and used our textbook. While the names and colleges of these many sociologists cannot be listed here, we wish to note that the traces of their suggestions can still be found throughout the seventh edition. There are a few people who have been especially helpful in the most recent revisions, including this one, and we would like to acknowledge their help here: Carole Campbell, University of California-Long Beach; William Flanagan, Coe College; Chris Hurn, University of Massachusetts-Amherst; Charles Hurst, the College of Wooster; Carol Poll, Fashion Institute of Technology; Wade Roof, University of California-Santa Barbara; and Beth Anne Shelton, SUNY-Buffalo. We asked JoAnn DeFiore to give us her suggestions for this edition, since she was using the sixth edition and was also familiar with the authors' objectives. She made a number of excellent suggestions, although not all could be carried out in this edition. We sincerely thank her.

Finally, we want to thank the publishing professionals at Allyn and Bacon for their assistance and their general good humor when we were less than perfect about meeting deadlines and carrying out tasks. We especially want to thank again our long-time editor Karen Hanson who continues to be supportive and helpful. Her assistants in the home office, have been excellent to work with, especially the last, Jennifer Jacobson, who is always delightfully cheerful. Once again Marjorie Payne has provided her special blend of personal and professional guidance through the production process. We thank her for being helpful, efficient, and a good long-distance friend.

Part I   Introduction to Sociology

1

A Brief Introduction to Sociology

What Is Sociology?

Sociology is the study of the social world in which we live. To see the potential usefulness of sociology, we need only pick up a major newspaper or listen to a television broadcast. The news headlines of any day will describe events that reflect important sociological issues. Here are a few typical headlines and some of the sociological issues that they raise.

Black Couple Murdered by Racists from the 82nd Airborne
Three white soldiers are alleged to have selected an African American couple walking down a street in Fayetteville, North Carolina, and, without provocation, murdered them. The soldiers were known by their army buddies to be neo-Nazi skinheads who held virulent racist attitudes. The sociological issues in this incident include racism, crime, and a deviant counterculture, all topics that will be considered in this book.

War-weary People of Former Yugoslavia Face Uncertain Future
Since 1991 the ethnic–religious populations in the former Yugoslavia have carried out a brutal war that has led to the deaths of thousands of people. News reports from this war have repeatedly described atrocious acts of killing, rape, incarceration, and starvation. These terrible acts have been perpetrated by all sides in this struggle and reflect the existence of ancient hatreds among these ethnic and religious groups. The cultures and

subcultures of ethnic and religious groups and intergroup relations will be the focus of several chapters.

Corporate Welfare More Difficult to Cut Than Welfare for the Poor
Political leaders at all levels of government have been vigorously attacking welfare for the poor. The Congress and the Administration have been considering various ways of cutting welfare for the poor in order to reduce federal budget deficits. However, the federal government also has welfare programs for the wealthier segments of society, both corporations and individuals, and these programs have been more difficult to cut. People and business interests with economic resources have more power and influence in the government and are usually able to retain their economic benefits. Power and influence and inequalities among economic segments of the society will be frequently discussed in the chapters ahead.

Racism, crime, countercultures, ethnic and religious conflict, power, influence, and inequality are but a few examples of the sociological issues that can be found in any day's news. The full range of sociological issues is reflected in a definition of sociology.

Sociology is the systematic study of

A.   the social behavior of individuals;
B.   the workings of social groups, organizations, cultures, and societies; and
C.   the influence of social groups, organizations, cultures, and societies on individual and group behavior.

Although some people believe that sociology is concerned only with social groups and societal behavior, the definition above calls attention to the fact that sociologists are also interested in the social behavior of individuals. By using the word *social* to modify behavior, we are simply signalling that sociologists have a special interest in the behavior of individuals as it is influenced by social groupings. The definition shows also that sociologists are interested in the way various kinds of social groupings work, and especially how their workings influence human behavior.

Sociology and Other Sciences of Human Behavior

A number of sciences, in addition to sociology, are concerned with human behavior. Most of these are social sciences, including anthropology, economics, political science, and psychology. But history—one of the humanities—also involves the study of human behavior, and at least a part of biology—a natural science—is concerned with the study of human behavior.

When compared with the other social sciences, sociology is unique because it is the only one that covers the entire spectrum of human behavior, while the rest are relatively focused on one aspect of human behavior. Furthermore, sociology includes an interest in these same behaviors. Anthropologists are primarily concerned with the cultures of people; one of the specialties of sociology is *cultural sociology.* Economists are almost exclusively interested in economic behavior; sociology includes *economy and society* as a specialty, as well as the *sociology of work, occupations, and professions* (Kalleberg, 1995). Psychologists are mainly interested in individual behavior, but sociology, as we emphasized in our discussion of the definition of sociology, is also interested in individual behavior (Thoits, 1995). Political scientists focus on the political institution; sociology includes the specialty *political sociology* (Hicks, 1995).

Historical studies are done by a number of sociologists, including those who identify with the *history of social thought* specialty and others who do historical comparative research (see Chapter 2) (Griffin, 1995). And, finally, the biological bases for human behavior are being studied by sociologists in the *biosociology* specialty (Udry, 1995).

Because sociology encompasses the interests of all these other social sciences, as well as parts of history and biology, it is in a unique position with respect to the study of human behavior (Gove, 1995). Sociology has the potential to be an integrative discipline, bringing together the knowledge gained by all the other disciplines into a more comprehensive understanding of human behavior (Gove, 1995).

Sociology also benefits from the work of these other fields of study and can, at least potentially, contribute to them. Sociology does often use the research conducted in these other fields, but the other disciplines do not seem to use much of the sociological work that is available to them (Gove, 1995).

This brief discussion of the relationship between sociology and other fields of study underlies how varied sociology is. The variety found in sociology is seen by some as a disadvantage, because sociology tries to do everything and has no essential core (Cole, 1994; Davis, 1994). But, as we will point out in the next section, the variety found in sociology may have some advantages, especially for the beginning student.

The Different Kinds of Sociology

Sociology is a wide-ranging way of studying human behavior (Gove, 1995). While sociologists generally accept the definition offered above, there are many different kinds kinds of sociologists, and their approaches to the field are often very different (Ennis, 1992; Cappel and Guterbock, 1992). It is important to understand that *there is no one sociology; there are many sociologies.* To show this clearly, we will identify next some of the most important differences among sociologists, beginning with their specialties.

Sociological Specialties

Sociologists often ask each other, "What kind of sociologist are you?" or "What are your sociological interests" when they want to know another's specialty. Specialties generally focus on some type of human behavior (crime), some part of society (the political institution), or ways of studying these things (statistics). Sociologists currently recognize about fifty different specialties (Ennis, 1992). Table 1–1 provides a list of the specialties most commonly identified by sociologists. At the present time the most popular specialty is social psychology, which is concerned primarily with the way individual behavior is influenced by social contexts. The next five most popular specialties are family and marriage, sociological theory, sociology of gender, statistical and mathematical methodology, and medical sociology (Ennis, 1992, p. 260).

To give you an idea of the variety of sociological specialties and the range of topics that might be studied, consider the following examples:

- *Sociology of aging (also called social gerontology)*—Topics: The economic conditions of the elderly, relations between the elderly and their middle-age children (or their grandchildren), sex lives of the elderly, or the political behavior of the elderly.

- *Criminology*—Topics: The changing crime rates of the society, the causes of violent crime, or the deterrents of crime.

- *Sociology of emotions*—Topics: The management of emotions in the workplace, men's emotions compared to women's emotions, ways of expressing love, or trust and distrust between friends.

- *Medical sociology*—Topics: The distribution of AIDS in the population, the organization of medical systems, the different medical problems of racial groups, or the relationship between doctors and patients.

- *Sociology of religion*—Topics: The relative importance of religion in different societies, the role of women in religious organizations, the characteristics of religious programs on television, or the nature of religious experiences.

- *Urban sociology*—The movement of people toward urban places, the organization of cities, or the negative and positive features of city life.

These are just a few of the sociological specialties and a small sample of the topics studied by sociologists in these specialties. Throughout this book, you will be introduced to many others.

Theoretical Preferences

Some sociologists identify strongly with particular theories of sociology. Later in this chapter we will present four of the major theoretical approaches in sociology today. One is named *symbolic interactionism,* so some sociologists might answer by saying, "I'm a symbolic interactionist." Symbolic interaction theory is one of

Table 1–1   Major Specialties of Sociology

Aging, sociology of or social gerontology	Mass communication and public opinion
Applied sociology and social policy	Medical sociology
Art and literature, sociology of	Mental health, sociology of
Biosociology	Metatheory
Collective behavior and social movements	Methodology, qualitative approaches
Comparative or cross-national sociology	Methodology, statistics, and mathematical
Computers and sociology	sociology
Criminology and criminal justice	Military sociology and sociology of war
Cultural sociology	Occupations, work, and professions, also
Demography or population studies	industrial sociology
Development or modernization, the	Organizations, social, formal, complex
sociology of	Political sociology
Deviant behavior and social	Political economy
disorganization	Race and ethnicity, sociology of
Economy and society	Religion, sociology of
Education, sociology of	Rural sociology
Emotions, sociology of	Science, sociology of
Environmental sociology	Small groups, sociology of
Ethnomethodology/phenomenology	Social change
Family and marriage, sociology of	Social control
Gender, sociology of and women,	Social psychology
sociology of	Socialization
History of social thought	Sociological theory
Human ecology	Sociology of knowledge
Language, sociology of, and social	Stratification, mobility and social class
linguistics	Urban sociology and community sociology
Law and society	World conflict and world systems,
Leisure, sports and recreation, sociology of	sociology of

the basic theories associated with the subfield of social psychology (Charon, 1992; Rosenberg and Turner, 1990a). You will learn some key features of this theory later, but for now it is enough to know that when a sociologist claims to be a symbolic interactionist it means that he or she attaches a special importance to the words and symbols that people use when they interact with each other (Fine, 1990; Stryker, 1990).

Many sociologists do not limit themselves to one theory. They can see the usefulness and validity of different theoretical approaches, depending on what issue or problem is being studied. In this book we will not limit our discussions to one theoretical approach but will employ different theories as they reflect the field of sociology.

Research Preferences

Some sociologists identify with particular ways of doing sociological research. You have probably often read or heard about the results of social surveys (for example, surveys on how people feel about their work or about their religion). Some sociologists who are expert in conducting social surveys may describe themselves as "survey researchers." Other sociologists may gather data primarily by observing behavior in some particular context, such as a school, hospital, or street gang (Ambert et al., 1995; Denzin and Lincoln, 1994). Observers often try to be as inconspicuous as possible while they observe what people do in their natural everyday activities. In Chapter 2 we will introduce the major research methods used by sociologists and provide a fuller description of surveys and observation, as well as other data-gathering procedures. These alternative research methods differentiate sociologists, just as the different specialties and theories do.

With respect to research, sociologists can also be classified according to whether they prefer quantitative research techniques or whether they favor a more qualitative approach. **Quantitative research** emphasizes numerical measurement and statistical analysis as a way of conducting sociological studies. **Qualitative research** relies more on verbal descriptions and analysis. Sociologists who prefer the quantitative approach often see the natural sciences as a model for sociology. Sociologists who prefer the qualitative approach emphasize that the subject matter of sociology cannot be easily reduced to mathematical formulae and statistical techniques. Although there are strong advocates of both the quantitative and qualitative approaches, many sociologists believe that both approaches are useful. Which approach is preferable at any given time is determined by the nature of the problem under study.

Microscopic and Macroscopic Sociology

There is another major way that sociologists are differentiated, but usually this distinction is not so much a matter of personal identity. Sociologists can be classified according to the level of analysis that they use in their sociological work (Cappel and Guterbock, 1992; Mouzelis, 1992; Ritzer, 1991). In the above definition of sociology we mentioned individuals, groups, organizations, cultures, and societies. These are all points along a continuum that extends from the smallest units of sociological analysis, individuals, to the largest units, societies. The smallest units are at the microscopic end of the social continuum; the largest are at the macroscopic end.

The terms *microscopic* and *macroscopic* are borrowed from the physical world, where microscopic objects are the smaller units of nature, for example, molecules, viruses, and so on. Macroscopic objects of the physical world are the large units such as continents, planets, and galaxies. **Microscopic sociology** refers to the study of the smallest social units, that is, individuals and their thoughts and actions. **Macroscopic sociology** focuses on larger social units such as groups, organizations, cultures, and societies.[1]

Between microscopic social units and macroscopic units there are many different social phenomena, such as families, small groups (bowling teams), large groups (religious congregations), and organizations (the U.S. Navy). For convenience we can divide the range of social phenomena into the microscopic and macroscopic realms, but we should recognize that many social phenomena fall in the middle of the continuum and are difficult to categorize as strictly microscopic or macroscopic.

To sum up the differences among sociologists: first, differences are based on their specialties or subfields, but differences may also exist in their preferred theories or in their ways of doing sociological research and scholarship. Differences are also noticeable in the social levels in which they work. While it is true that differences exist among sociologists, it is necessary at the same time to note that sociologists generally agree about many aspects of their field. We will focus on these fundamental ideas of sociology in a moment.

The Advantages of Sociological Variety

At first, the diversity of sociology may seem a bit overwhelming, but it is also an advantage (Gans, 1992). Sociology can deal with all aspects of society and human behavior and is not limited in the same way as, say economics, which is focused on money and economic issues. As new societal problems or issues arise, sociologists can study them. This adds to the excitement of the field (Gans, 1992).

Sociology's diversity and variety also have an advantage for you as a student. Since there are many different parts of sociology (specialties, theories, methods, and topics), it is almost a certainty that some of these parts will be especially interesting to you. The truth is that all sociologists have personal preferences. As individual sociologists, we think some specialties are more interesting than others, some theoretical approaches are more significant than others, and some kinds of research and scholarship are more important than others. Some of us prefer to work at the micro level of social life, while others of us prefer the macro level. Throughout this book we invite you to sample the range and diversity of sociology and to discover some, perhaps many, features of sociology that will interest and engage you.

---

[1]Sociologists often use the shortened terms, *micro* and *macro,* to refer to these different levels of sociological analyses.

In the News

Sociology on the Internet

Bill Gates, the computer guru and billionaire founder of Microsoft, appeared on the covers of virtually every major news magazine in the country after the recent publication of his book *The Road Ahead* (Gates, 1995). In this book, Gates offers his vision of how computers will influence our lives in the future. He sees a time when it will be possible to receive information on any subject almost instantly. Gates looks beyond the currently popular Internet and the World Wide Web and sees a time when many people will be able to receive information on wireless communication devices, even smaller and much more flexible than today's portable computers. The vision of Bill Gates provides a glimpse into the *information age,* an age in which information on virtually any subject can be instantaneously available to us.

Today, the Internet and the World Wide Web are the principal systems that provide information to many Americans. Internet enthusiasts claim that even today virtually any imaginable information can be found someplace in cyberspace. So what is there for sociologists on the Internet? The following are some current examples, and the list grows daily (McMillan, Dittemore, and Kem, 1995).

General

- **Berkeley Sociology Gopher.** This source identifies journals, data archives, Internet directories, and guidebooks. Access: gopher://infolib.lib.berkeley.edu/11/resdbs/soci

- **Yahoo Sociology.** Yahoo stands for: Yet Another Hierarchical Officious Oracle. The Yahoo group identifies and systematizes Internet resources for sociologists. Access: http://www.yahoo.com/social_science/sociology

- **Sociology Departments.** It is possible to connect to thirty-five or more sociology departments and receive information on their programs. Access: http://www.shu.edu/~brownsam/v1/institut.html

- **WWW Sociology Virtual Library.** Lists scholarly and professional organizations, academic departments, and research centers related to sociology. Access: http://www.w3.org/hypertext/DataSources/bySubject/Sociology/Overview.html

Special Topics in Sociology

- **H-Durkheim.** Focuses on the work of this key figure in the early development of sociology. (Durkheim is discussed in this chapter.) Access: LISTSERV@UICVM.CC.UIC.EDU

- **McDonaldization.** Discussion and critiques of George Ritzer's book *The McDonaldization of Society.* (See Chapter 3 for a description of McDonaldization.) Access: http://www.UMD.edu/~allen/macdonald.html

- **Sportsoc-L.** A discussion list on the sociology of sports. Access: LISTSERV@V,/TEMPLE.EDU

Subjects of Interest to Sociologists

- **The Deviant Society.** An organization of people who intentionally go against the norms of the surrounding culture. (See Chapter 3.) Access: http:/www.csv.warwick.ac.uk/%Ephumc/index.html

- **Sex.** Along with Star Trek, sex is one of the most popular topics on net discussion groups. (See Chapter 7 for a further discussion of sex on the Internet.)

These net sites are just a few examples of how sociology is part of the content of the information highway.

McMILLAN, GARY A., DITTEMORE, MARGARET R., and KEM, CAROL RITZEN. "Internet Resources for Sociology," *College and Research Libraries News,* Vol. 56, 1995.

Some Fundamental Ideas of Sociology

Since we have called attention to the variety and diversity of sociological views, it is important to emphasize the points on which almost all sociologists agree. Most agree that the actions and behaviors of humans create social settings and social rules, but that these same settings and rules, in turn, influence the way humans act. This idea is both simple and complex, and it is certainly important enough to consider more fully.

Societies and Other Social Settings Are Humanly Created

The social settings in which people live and the social rules by which they live have all been humanly created. We know, of course, that the customs and practices of our society today are not the same as those of the past. Changes have occurred; those changes have been the products of human actions.

We have only to look at the changes that have occurred in United States history to see how human actions can change the practices and customs of society. American women were not considered qualified to vote by the men who wrote the Constitution. After more than a century of effort by many women and some men, women in the United States did achieve the right to vote.

Fifty years ago, many Americans simply assumed that African Americans should be excluded from many parts of American life—neighborhoods, schools, voting, sports, entertainment events, hotels, and restaurants; and they were. African Americans had to work and fight in many ways to gain at least a degree of equal treatment and equal opportunity in the United States. When, in 1955, Rosa Parks of Atlanta, Georgia, refused to give up her seat on the bus to a white man, she was helping to change American society.

During the last half of the twentieth century, African Americans, along with many other citizens, have used boycotts, civil disobedience, the courts, and the political process in order to get voting rights, congressional representation, school integration, employment opportunities, and housing equality. Today, even though various forms of discrimination persist, most Americans do not question the right of African Americans to participate equally in all aspects of societal life.

The general sociological point is that, every day, people affirm or challenge the society in which they live. Through their affirmations they keep the society as it is; through their challenges they often modify and change the society. Whenever modifications and changes are made, resistance usually arises from those who benefit from the existing social arrangements. Sociology is concerned with the way individuals affirm and maintain their societies or challenge and change them.

Social Influences on Human Behavior

A second fundamental view of sociology is that, even though people perpetuate and create society, they are at the same time influenced and constrained by that society. To understand the operation of this view, we may go back to an individual's early years of life when parents (or a parent) introduced the child to the social world. Through parents or parent surrogates, children learn the basic attitudes, values, and rules that correspond more or less to those of the larger society. Later in life, teachers, friends, and others, along with the mass media, continue to influence the way people behave in matters large and small.

We can illustrate this point by continuing to focus on African Americans in American society. In the early part of this century, many Americans would have had no reluctance to speak of black Americans in derogatory terms and, without thinking, deny them access to many parts of American life. Today, most Americans, even those who may hold racist views, do not usually express such views and would acknowledge that black Americans have the same rights as all others in the society. Again, this is not to say that prejudice and discrimination against African Americans do not exist, but simply that the behavior and even attitudes of most people are influenced by the changes that have occurred in the society.

Agency and Structure.   Throughout this book we will see examples of how society influences people's behavior, and yet, at the same time, individuals and groups are capable of acting in ways that show that they are not totally constrained by the society in which they live. Sociologists use the term *agency* to signify this independence of action by members of society. Their actions can and often do run counter to the existing *structures* of the society (Archer, 1988; Giddens, 1984; Bourdieu and Wacquant, 1992; Habermas, 1987).

How Can Sociology Be Useful to You?

Since you are just beginning your first course in sociology, we want to tell you about the benefits you may derive from your study of sociology, even if this introductory course is the only one you ever take. Other benefits, such as jobs and careers in sociology, can be attained only if you go on to take other work and perhaps even advanced degrees (a masters or doctorate) in sociology. But let us begin with what you may gain from this course alone.

Facts and Information

Sociologists, through scientific research and study, accumulate and relate facts and information about social behavior and the society in which we live (as well as other societies). They often have a preference for facts that are not widely known or facts that run contrary to popular beliefs. Therefore, both in this book and in your class, you will learn a few things about human behavior that you did not know before. Suppose you were presented with the following statements and asked whether you believed them to be true or false. What would you say?

- At the beginning of this century Americans married at an early age, often in their teens.

- The rate of suicide is higher among teenagers than any other age group in the society.

- The percentage of the United States population that is African American has doubled since 1970 and is now about 25 percent of the total.

- The murder rate in the United States is higher in the 1990s than it was in the 1980s.

What is your reaction to these statements? Are they true or false? Every one of these statements is *false*, although they are widely believed to be true.

- At the beginning of the twentieth century, men were about 26 years old at the time of their first marriages; women were about 22 years old. Perhaps it is surprising that these ages are similar to the ages at which men and women marry today. The median age for males today is 26.5 and for females it is 24.5 (U.S. Bureau of the Census, 1994).

- In the United States the rate of suicide for 15- to 19-year-olds is *lower* than for any other age group in the adult population. The suicide rate for people over 65 is nearly twice as high as the suicide rate for 15- to 19-year-olds. (U.S. Bureau of the Census, *Statistical Abstract of the United States: 1995*, p. 100.)

- African Americans constitute about 12.6 percent of the total U.S. population, only slightly higher than the 1970 percentage of 11.5 percent (U.S. Bureau of the Census, 1995b, p. 14). Polls show that most Americans believe the percentage is about twice as high. Interestingly, African Americans give the highest estimates at over 25 percent (Morin, 1995).

- The murder rate in the 1990s has been consistently lower than it was in the 1980s. In 1980 the murder rate in the United States was 10.2 per 100,000 people; by 1994 it had decreased to 9.0 (U.S. Bureau of Justice Statistics, 1995b, p. 13).

Facts about marriage age, suicide, population, and murder are statistical facts. Because statistical facts are fairly easy to obtain (often in government publications), the truth or falsity of such statements can be easily checked (although it is generally recognized that even statistical facts can sometimes be misleading). While sociologists try to document their statements of fact with statistics or research results, some statements of fact, including many in this book, are based on other kinds of data and observations. In Chapter 2 we will describe the different research methods used by sociologists to establish social facts.

Knowledge and Awareness of Other Societies

Sociologists have always had a great interest in societies other than their own. Early sociologists were especially intrigued by the work of anthropologists (and others) who described remote societies and their cultures—often small, non-Western societies with unusual and exotic customs. It was both fascinating and instructive to learn how differently societies could be organized, and how much the beliefs and values of people could differ from one society to another.

Sociologists today continue to be interested in the small nonliterate societies, because there are still lessons to be learned and insights to be gained from such cases. The reports and descriptions of these and other distinct cultures have traditionally been called **cross-cultural studies,** and throughout this book we will be using them frequently to highlight or illustrate sociological points.

Today an even greater need exists for sociologists to understand other societies around the world. No longer are nations and societies on the other side of the earth simply regarded as unusual and exotic places with no relevance for our personal lives. Travel and commerce among all nations of the earth are now commonplace.

For sociologists, this means that we are now able to obtain information, both quantitative and qualitative, from nations previously closed to sociological scrutiny. We must know about other societies, not just because they are sociologically instructive, but because we live in an interdependent global society.

In contemporary times it is just as important for Americans to learn, for example, about political, economic, and social developments in Russia as it is to know about those in the United States. Even though the Cold War is over, Russia is still a major country in world affairs, and occurrences there can still affect Americans.

United States military personnel continue to be sent to all parts of the world, where they encounter people and cultures that are unfamiliar to them. When, in 1995, U.S. peacekeeping forces were sent to Bosnia, most Americans were still only vaguely aware of the causes of the prolonged war in that region of Europe. Because of the importance of knowing about other societies, we have purposely illustrated many sociological issues with examples from other nations of the world. These examples will supplement the many examples coming from U.S. society.

Many times the examples of sociological issues in other societies and cultures will be in boxes. These boxes will be of two types: *Cross-cultural Perspectives* will offer examples from historical societies or the more traditional anthropological studies of small, non-Western societies; *Cross-national Perspectives* will present research and analysis coming from one or more contemporary nations.

An Understanding of Human Behavior and Societal Life

As human beings we are always trying to understand ourselves, the people around us, and the events occurring in our society (or the world). One of the implicit promises of sociology is that it will offer some insights into human behavior and societal life that will improve your understanding of contemporary issues. Furthermore, the insights offered by sociology are not limited to any specific case, but should be useful to you far beyond the questions of the day. You should be able to use sociological insights for problems and issues of the future, ones that we may not even be able to imagine now.

Throughout this book you will be introduced to many different sociological concepts (the technical terms of sociology). It is necessary in sociology, just as it is in economics or biology or physics, to learn the vocabulary of the field. We will alert you to the most important sociological concepts by providing a definition immediately after the concept is printed in **boldface.** These terms will also be defined fully at the end of the book. We believe that you will often find many of the terms and concepts applicable and useful, long after you have finished this course.

As an example, the word bureaucracy is already likely to be a familiar term. You may have complained about the frustrations of having to deal with a bureaucracy, such as the government or your college or university. Later in this chapter and more fully in Chapter 4, you will be introduced to the term *bureaucracy* as a sociological concept. You will become familiar with bureaucracy's characteristics, its shortcomings, and, yes, even its beneficial features. Since you will probably be dealing with many different bureaucracies during the rest of your life, it may be useful for you to understand this form of social organization in a more objective way. This understanding of bureaucracies may be helpful to you in many circumstances that you will encounter in the years ahead.

In addition to concepts, we will also introduce you to a number of sociological theories. As we present these theories, we will show you how they can be useful tools for understanding current issues and problems. But equally important, these theories will provide the basis for understanding many issues and problems that will appear long after you have finished this college course in sociology. The usefulness of sociological theories is parallel to the way in which the theoretical principles of economics, biology, or physics can help you understand particular problems that you encounter in the economic, biological, or physical worlds. Thus, one of the important benefits of studying sociology is the general applicability of sociological theories to your personal and social worlds, in both the present and future.

To begin, then, we will use the final section of this chapter to introduce you to the historical beginnings of sociology and to some of the major scholars who have shaped the field. We will close by presenting the major sociological theories that currently prevail.

The Beginnings of Sociology

No precise date can be given for the founding of sociology, but its beginning dates back to the early 1800s. Most scholars agree that the work of the French scholar Auguste Comte (1798–1857) gave sociology its name and an identity that eventually led to its status as a scholarly discipline (Heilbrun 1990; Ritzer,1996b). Of course, long before the term *sociology* was coined, intellectuals and philosophers theorized about the social bases of human behavior (Erikkson, 1993).

Harriet Martineau, a nineteenth-century English sociologist, deserves credit for bringing Comte's ideas to the attention of English-speaking scholars by translating his work (Hill, 1995). Since Martineau also published her own sociological treatise, one that predated the main work of Comte, some scholars say she, along with Comte, deserves credit for founding sociology (Ritzer, 1996b, p. 442).

Auguste Comte

Like many scholars of the nineteenth century, Auguste Comte was influenced by the rapid changes occurring in European societies. During the years of Comte's young adulthood, French society had continued to experience repercussions from

Cross-national Perspectives

Sociology in China

Sociology in China dates back to the beginning of the twentieth century, when Chinese scholars who had studied in Europe and the United States returned to their homeland with the ideas of this new field. Through the early decades of this century the Chinese scholars translated into Chinese a number of the classic American and European sociological studies, including Durkheim's *Division of Labor* and Herbert Spencer's *Study of Sociology*. Through the first 50 years of the twentieth century, Chinese sociology grew steadily. Chinese sociologists were interested in both sociological theory and sociological research. The Chinese had a special interest in the study of social problems such as poverty, overpopulation, problems of rural life, and social welfare. In this respect, Chinese sociology had many of the same interests as American sociology.

However, things changed dramatically after the Communists came to power in 1949. By 1952, sociology had been labeled a *pseudoscience* and was abolished. All teaching and research activities in sociology were banned.

There were several reasons why the study of sociology was banned in China. First, in the early years of the revolution the Soviet Union was taken as a model by the Chinese. Since sociology was insignificant in the Soviet Union, the Chinese concluded that it was unimportant for them also. Second, the Chinese believed that Marxian theory could take the place of conventional Western sociology (as late as the 1950s Marxian theory was not strongly represented in American sociology). Third, the Chinese decided that their revolution would solve existing social problems, therefore, sociological studies were not needed.

In 1957, a Chinese population scholar tried to revive a part of sociology by setting up an institute to study population problems, but that effort was also crushed. All sociology, including the study of population, was labeled a plot against the Communist party. The result was a total ban on sociology, although a few sociologists did find refuge in other academic settings, such as history.

However, with the death of Mao Zedong and the defeat of his allies, the country moved in a more liberal direction. In 1979, a symposium was held in which the president of the Chinese Academy of Social Sciences announced that sociology had been "rehabilitated." The next day the Chinese Sociological Association was founded. However, those who sought to rebuild sociology faced a difficult task since almost all work in the field had been discontinued since 1952. Almost three decades of sociological development throughout the world was unknown in China. Most of the sociologists who practiced in 1952 were either dead or too old to begin learning all the new developments in the field. Young people who were gravitating toward sociology faced a shortage of well-trained faculty, facilities, and written materials.

Through most of the 1980s, Chinese sociology made dramatic strides. A number of foreign universities developed formal and informal arrangements with Chinese universities. Foreign sociologists were routinely brought to China to teach and do research. Many foreign works in sociology, both classic and contemporary, were translated into Chinese. Most important, many Chinese students began studying sociology abroad, especially in the United States, and this promised to create in China a whole new crop of professors who were knowledgeable about the latest developments throughout the world. Finally, native Chinese sociologists were creating their own distinctive brand of theory and sociological research.

The events of May 1989, when the Chinese government crushed the emergent democratic movement in Tiananmen Square, led to some temporary repression of sociology. But since then, sociology has been thriving in China. Fifteen universities and colleges have set up departments of sociology, and there are over thirty research institutes and offices. Nonetheless, the history of sociology in China reveals how an authoritarian government can be an immanent threat to sociology at all times.

HANLIN LI, FANG MING, WANG YING, SUN BINGYAO, and QI WANG. "Chinese Sociology, 1898–1986," *Social Forces* 65, 1987.
KEJING, DAI. "The Vicissitudes of Sociology in China." *International Sociology,* 8, 1993.

---

the French Revolution, which had started in 1789. The Revolution had brought about a considerable amount of chaos and disorder in France, and Comte viewed these developments negatively. Although Comte knew that a return to pre-Revolutionary conditions was impossible, he was looking for a way to bring greater order and tranquility to French society.

Comte thought that order could be restored if it were possible to understand more fully the way in which society worked. The fact that he lived in an age when the scientific approach had proved useful for understanding the physical world prompted Comte to put his faith in science. He rejected theological and philosophical approaches and concluded that the scientific approach was the way to achieve a better understanding of society. Comte originally called this new science of society *social physics,* but later switched to *sociology* because a Belgian scholar named Adolphe Quetelet had already used the term social physics (Lazarsfeld, 1961).

Comte's work is important primarily because it advanced the idea that there could be (and should be) a science of society. He gave sociology a position among the other sciences of his time, and although it required the work of later scholars to solidify that position, Comte's pioneering effort deserves recognition. Also important in Comte's work is the idea that, as a science, sociology could solve social problems such as war, revolution, crime, and poverty. This idea continues to be a significant feature of sociology today.

As we move beyond the work of Comte and the beginnings of sociology, we encounter several major figures who either shaped the development of sociology as an academic discipline or had a major impact on the field. We will briefly examine their contributions to contemporary sociology, beginning with Emile Durkheim (Ritzer, 1996b).

Emile Durkheim

After Comte, no sociologist worked more diligently to give sociology a place among the established scholarly disciplines than the French scholar Emile Durkheim (1858–1917). In the scholarly and intellectual communities of Europe in the late nineteenth and early twentieth centuries, sociology was by no means completely accepted. Durkheim made it a personal crusade to advance sociology and sociological explanations of human behavior.

Durkheim often wrote in an argumentative style in which he first rejected non-social explanations of human behavior, especially those based on biological or psychological reasoning. He used this approach in one of his major works, *Suicide* (Durkheim, 1897/1951), in which he sought to demonstrate the importance of social factors in explaining what seemed to be distinctively individual behavior. Even today our normal first reaction to a report of suicide is to try to understand and explain this event in individual, usually psychological, terms. Durkheim, however, demonstrated that the social contexts in which people live can explain variations in the frequency of suicide. For example, he collected and analyzed statistical data on suicide rates in various European countries, and found that suicide rates went up during periods of social upheaval and change. He reasoned that, during times of revolution, war, or economic depression, the conventional rules of conduct would be in flux and, therefore, unclear. Durkheim called this societal condition *anomie*. **Anomie** literally means normlessness; it refers to situations in which individuals are uncertain about the norms of society. Suicide rates that go up during times of social upheaval (and thus presumed normlessness) illustrate what Durkheim called anomic suicide. Durkheim went on to identify other societal conditions that also led, in different ways, to variations in suicide rates.

Durkheim's analysis of suicide is also an excellent demonstration of sociology as a science. Durkheim used suicide statistics that allowed him to do his analyses and report his findings in a quantitative form. The statistical analysis of social data has become a prominent feature of sociology. The second reason for holding up Durkheim's work on suicide as a sociological ideal is that he used social factors (in this case, societal conditions) to explain a behavior that is usually thought of in only individual terms. Durkheim demonstrated a basic sociological premise, which is that human behavior can be explained in social terms.

Even though Durkheim fought successfully to establish sociology as a legitimate science of human behavior, he is not without his contemporary critics. His work on suicide is still being debated today, nearly 100 years after its original publication (Lester, 1994). Many scholars believe Durkheim did not pay enough attention to social change and social conflict. He has also been criticized for emphasizing the social influences on human behavior, but neglecting the importance of individual action—what we previously called agency (Ritzer, 1996b, p. 98). A recent feminist critic has pointed out that Durkheim saw men as "the product of society" and women as "the product of nature," a view that is considered sexist today (Lehman, 1995a; 1995b, p. 576).

Max Weber

The German sociologist Max Weber[2] (1864–1920), like Durkheim, saw problems in the way European societies were changing (Ritzer, 1996b). The key change, according to Weber, was the increase of rationality as the basis of human behavior. **Rationality** is a form of human action in which goals and objectives are set, and then achieved in the most efficient way possible. The choice of a behavior is based on how quickly and easily it will allow a person to reach a chosen goal or objective. Weber believed that, over the course of several centuries, the Western world had come to emphasize rationality so completely that it dominated every aspect of modern social life. Although rationality has obvious benefits, Weber also considered it a negative development in human societies. Furthermore, he believed that the trend toward an ever-greater emphasis on rationality would continue. For Weber, the problems of the modern world, with its emphasis on rationality, were like an "iron cage" from which there was no hope of escape (Mitzman, 1969).

We can illustrate Weber's concern with an example that will be familiar to anyone who has gone through the American educational system. Most large high schools and many colleges and universities are based to a great degree on the principles of rationality. That is, they are set up to process the largest number of students (to give them an "education") in the most efficient way possible. Often U.S. college students receive their educations in large, mass-production-like classes. By assembling large numbers of students in a single lecture class, using multiple-choice or other objective examinations (often machine graded), only a

---

[2]Sociologists use the German pronunciation for Weber, which is roughly *Vay-ber.*

relatively small amount of time will be required from one professor. Hundreds of students can earn credit for a course with a minimum of professorial effort. The emphasis on efficiency in systems of mass education is highlighted by comparing mass education with the undergraduate education in an elite British school, where a student may spend hours in discussion with a professor and where a personal relationship often develops between teacher and student. A mass education system makes it almost impossible for college professors to know more than a few of their many students personally. And the students usually know their professors in only a most superficial and impersonal way.

The most visible symbol of rationality and efficiency to Weber (and to many Americans) was the bureaucracy. A large university, of the type just described, is one type of bureaucracy, but many other organizations are equally familiar examples (Rothstein, 1996). In a bureaucracy, the standards of rationality and efficiency reign supreme; work is carefully divided into simple precise steps and made routine. The emphasis is only on speed and efficiency, with little regard for whether the work is meaningful for individual workers. We will examine bureaucracies more in Chapter 4, where we will note, as did Weber, that although it is easy to criticize the bureaucracy, many tasks can be accomplished with precision, speed, and continuity within a bureaucratic organization (Weber in Gerth and Mills, 1958, p. 214).

Karl Marx

The German-born social philosopher and social analyst Karl Marx (1818–1883) has a somewhat different place in sociology's history than has either Durkheim or Weber (Ritzer, 1996b). Although he lived and did much of his writing before either of them, and therefore influenced the work of both, Marx was not a part of any effort to establish sociology as an academic or scholarly discipline. Marx was not a sociologist and did not consider himself to be one. He was an analyst and a critic of society, and as such, he and his ideas have had a profound effect on contemporary sociology.

Through his ideas, Marx has also had a significant impact on the events of world history—an influence that continues to the present. For Marx, as is well known, was not only an analyst of society; he was also a political activist. He believed that his ideas about society should play a part in solving the problems that he identified. It is important to recognize and keep in mind the distinction between Marx as the social theorist and Marx as the political activist.

In his role as a political activist, Marx advocated and expected the revolutionary overthrow of capitalism and the emergence of communist states. In view of the collapse of many communist regimes in recent years, one might ask if Marx's ideas still have relevance to sociology (Aronson, 1995; Hudelson, 1993). The answer is that Marx's sociological ideas, his understandings of important societal processes, are still relevant. Marx offered a "sociological theory that can be used to analyze *any* society, not just capitalistic societies and their economic systems" (Ritzer, 1996b, p. 42).

When Marx examined the societies of his time, he was struck by the inequities that prevailed between the masses of people who were at the bottom of the society and those who were at the top. In societies that had a capitalist/industrial form of economic organization, the workers—the **proletariat**—sold their labor to the owners of the means of production. The owners of the means of production were the **capitalists,** the social class that owned the raw materials, the factories, the machines, and the equipment. Marx saw the relationship between the capitalists and the proletariat as one of struggle and conflict. The capitalists had the advantage in this struggle because they controlled not only the means of production but also the ideas, the values, and information that prevailed in society.

While contemporary societies are too complicated to be analyzed in terms of the proletariat and the capitalists, a critically important part of Marx's view of society is that there is always an ongoing struggle between those who have power and those who do not. In particular, Marxian theory points out that power often resides primarily in the hands of those who have economic dominance in a society. Throughout this book, but especially in our consideration of social stratification systems (Chapter 8), we will see the pervasive importance of this Marxian emphasis—how those who control economic resources have a special ability to influence, and be the beneficiaries of, educational systems, health care and medical systems, and many other parts of the society. For this reason, any societal analysis that employs a Marxian perspective is likely to look first at the economic system, and especially at the class structure.

In the next section we will see that a general sociological theory, called **conflict theory,** is built on the principle that social groups and societies are composed of units that are often engaged in some kind of struggle for power. Thus, conflict theory can be identified as a direct descendant of Marxian theory.

To a lesser degree some of the other pioneers of sociology have a connection with contemporary sociological theories. Durkheim, with his emphasis on the importance of social factors and the structure of society, was a forerunner of structural–functional theory, which will also be discussed below. Weber, in much of his work, emphasized the importance of ideas in shaping the direction and nature of societies. This emphasis is closely connected with some of the fundamental features of symbolic interaction theory, which will be discussed next.

Sociological Theories

A **theory** is a set of ideas that provides explanations for a broad range of phenomena. By extension, **sociological theories** are those that explain a wide range of human behavior and a variety of social and societal events. A sociological theory designates those parts of the social world that are especially important, and offers ideas about how the social world works. Every sociological theory has special words or terms that are unique to that theory.

Certain sociological theories are related to the microscopic level of sociological analysis. These theories are not inevitably bound to the microscopic level, but sociologists concerned with the behavior, actions, and interactions of individuals tend to use them. Two of these theories are symbolic interactionism and social exchange theory.

Symbolic Interactionism

Symbolic interactionism deals primarily with the interaction between individuals at the symbolic level (Charon, 1992; Rosenberg and Turner, 1990; Stryker, 1990). **Symbols** are the words, gestures, and objects that communicate meaning between people. In any given society, people share a common understanding of these symbols. Words are the most important symbols from a symbolic interactionist viewpoint. If someone were to walk into the room where you are reading and shout "Fire!" no further description or detail would be necessary. That single word would convey the message that something significant is burning, and is possibly dangerous to you. Of course, the expression on the person's face might also convey a message, and we have learned to read messages in the faces, hands, and bodies of other people. If a friend were to describe the actions of another person and simultaneously roll his or her eyes skyward, you would understand that the friend is saying something like, "Can you believe that?" That facial gesture might not be understood by people from another society; however, it is a symbol that we have learned to interpret in a particular way.

Spoken and written words, as well as facial and bodily gestures, are important for symbolic interactionists. Human beings have an exceptional, and perhaps unique, ability to use words, and people make connections with other people through these words, or symbols.

Research on human infants during the last 20 years has convinced many developmental psychologists that, even under the age of 2, babies have a remarkable ability to distinguish vocal sounds (Boodman, 1992). Many now accept the theory of linguist Noam Chomsky that infants are biologically "hardwired" to learn language. Human infants, in Chomsky's view, have an innate ability to comprehend the structure of language systems (Chomsky, 1972, 1980). Infants learn the particular language of their culture through the people in their environment.

There can be no doubt that humans have a tremendous capacity for learning words. By the age of 7, an average child has command of 8000 words (Pfeiffer, 1985). Children at an early age learn words that stand for concrete things such as *cat* and *ball*. Gradually, children learn more abstract symbols—symbols that indicate not just things but evaluations as well (for example, naughty puppy, pretty kitty, dirty garbage). Obviously, most of the evaluations that children learn are those held by family members, especially parents. Parents and other family members are referred to as **significant others** because their views have such a great influence on young children. Later in life, friends, schoolmates, marriage partners, fellow workers, religious and political leaders, and others will also be significant others.

In the process of learning language and symbols, children learn evaluations of themselves, just as they learn evaluations of other objects. In the same way that parents might convey the idea that "garbage is dirty," they might also convey the idea that "Doug is a good boy" when he plays nicely with his baby sister. It is through this process of learning symbols about themselves that children develop what symbolic interactionists call a **self-concept,** that is, an individual's thoughts or feelings about himself or herself (Gecas and Burke, 1995; Rosenberg, 1979, 1990). Symbolic interactionism is, therefore, a theory that has something to say about how individuals think about themselves and thus how they act as individual human beings.

But symbolic interactionists also stress that the symbols people learn govern their responses to all other human beings and things. If someone were to show us a painting and say it was by Pablo Picasso, we would probably be in awe. We would probably respond as much to the name Picasso (a symbol) as to the painting itself. This example also illustrates how most members of any given society share a wide variety of symbols. The commonality of shared symbols at any given time gives symbolic interactionism a macroscopic dimension, as well as its predominant microscopic focus (Fine, 1990).

In summary, symbolic interactionists pay special attention to the symbols individuals use to interpret and define themselves, the actions of other people, and all other things and events. By understanding the meanings that people give to these things through the use of words and symbols, it is possible to understand much of human behavior.

Social Exchange Theory

A second important sociological theory is **social exchange theory** (often simply called *exchange theory*), which focuses on the relations between individuals or groups and is based on the assumption that rewards and costs motivate all human behavior (Molm and Cook, 1995). Every human action is seen as having some cost, and therefore, if carried out, it must have a reward. On the other hand, if an action is costly but unrewarded in some way, the individual will not likely repeat it (Blau, 1964; Cook et al., 1990; Ekeh, 1974; Homans, 1974).

As a simple example of the principles of social exchange theory, suppose you were to see an elderly man, with his arms full of packages, struggling to open a door. You might take the time to help him, even though you are in a hurry. The cost of your action is your time and energy. Your reward might be the thanks of the man, or perhaps the smiles of other people who were passing by and saw how helpful you had been. According to exchange theory principles, you would more likely aid the next person who needs help because you received a reward for your actions. On the other hand, if the elderly man were to tell you, "Stop interfering and mind your own business!" you would probably have felt punished for your action, and you would not be as likely to repeat it in a similar circumstance.

Following these principles of reward and cost, social exchange theorists have been able to demonstrate that human relationships are formed and maintained because actors provide equal, or nearly equal, benefits to each other (Molm and Cook, 1995, p. 211). The exchange of benefits reflects the concept of reciprocity.

Reciprocity is the socially accepted idea that if you give something to someone, that person must give something of equal or near equal value in return (Gouldner, 1960). If a fellow student asks you for your class notes or solutions to some problems the night before an exam, and you give them, you will normally expect that person to give you something in return. Once again, what you receive in return need not be the same thing. Your fellow student may give you some concert tickets, invite you to a party, or simply tell other people what a generous and smart person you are. If you do not feel you have received an adequate reward (reciprocity), you are likely to feel slighted, and you will probably not be as generous if you are asked again.

The rules of reciprocity can be found at many levels of social life. We try to give people gifts that are similar in value to the ones they give to us; married couples try to entertain their friends in about the same way as they expect to be, or have been, entertained; friendly nations try to maintain a balance in their trading relations with imports roughly equal to exports. When there are violations of the principle of reciprocity, with one side returning less than it is receiving, relations between individuals, groups, or nations are apt to become strained. Too great a violation of reciprocity may result in anger and hostility and a breaking off of the relationship.

Although social exchange theory might have some applicability to the level of groups and societies, it is most often applied at the micro level of individuals. We will turn now to two theories that apply primarily to the macro level (groups, organizations, cultures, and societies): structural-functionalism and conflict theory.

Structural–Functional Theory

Structural–functional theory, often called *functional theory* or *functionalism,* emphasizes that every pattern of activity (that is, every structure) in a society makes some positive or negative contribution to that society (Alexander and Colomy, 1990; Colomy, 1990; Maryanski and Turner, 1991; Ritzer, 1996b). The two key words of structural–functional theory are *structure* and *function.* The term *structure* is used in this case as shorthand for social structure, which is a very basic sociological concept. A **social structure** is a regular pattern of social interaction or persistent social relationships. Examples of social structures include the socioeconomic status system of a society (the social class structure will be considered fully in Chapter 8), the patterned social relationships between races and ethnic groups (Chapter 9), or the patterns of family organization (Chapter 11). These and other patterned social relationships are the structural features of a society.

Structural–functionalists are interested in why certain structures exist in a society and especially what purpose, or function, they serve. A **function,** according to structural–functionalists, is a positive purpose or consequence—one necessary for the continued existence of a society (or some other social system). With regard to the family system in a society, the functions might include producing children, caring for them when they are young, and training them in the ways of the society. If a society does not have a fairly persistent structure for producing new members, caring for them, and socializing them, the society is not likely to survive.

Early structural–functional theorists believed that every structure of a society had a function, that is, made a positive contribution to the continuation of the society (Malinowski, 1925/1955). Modern-day functionalists still look for the positive contributions that various structures provide, but they also emphasize that some structures are detrimental to the survival of the society. When a social structure has a detrimental effect or consequence for the existence or well-being of a society it is said to be **dysfunctional.**

To illustrate a possible dysfunction, we consider again the example of marriage and family systems that produce children for the society. Throughout most of human history the death rates for infants and children were extremely high. In addition, many mothers died in pregnancy and childbirth. As a consequence, most societies developed marriage and family systems that encouraged people to have children, as many as they could. A marriage and family system that could produce many children under high-death-rate conditions was probably functional for most societies. However, in the twentieth century, the infant, childhood, and maternal death rates were greatly reduced in many countries. Nonetheless, the marriage and family structures continued to produce large numbers of children, who, consequently, had to be cared for and fed. The marriage and family system that had previously been functional was now viewed by many observers to be dysfunctional. The large numbers of children were seen as a threat to the survival of the society.

Structural–functionalists are also inclined to compare the obvious functions of social structures with the less obvious functions. The **manifest function** is the intended and well-recognized purpose of some social structure. The less obvious, unanticipated, or unexpected purpose of a social structure is called a **latent function.** To illustrate, we may ask the question, "Why do we have organized crime in the United States?" At the level of manifest function, the purpose of organized crime is for criminals to make money from illicit activities. But what is the latent function, the function that is less obvious? To answer this question, we must look for the less obvious, unanticipated, or unexpected consequences of organized crime.

Functional theorists would ask if organized crime serves a purpose for someone other than the criminals or for the society as a whole. For starters, organized crime is allegedly involved in providing illegal drugs, prostitution, and gambling. The users of these "services" are generally involved in an illegal activity, but many think of themselves as "law-abiding." (Most people who bet illegally on sports events consider this activity a part of everyday life.) Organized crime is also said to distribute most of the pornography in the society—again, a "service" that many citizens are willing to pay for without asking too many questions.

Recent news reports describe how organized crime, in years past, served the function of "keeping the peace" in the city of Las Vegas (Heath, 1995). For many years, the Mafia owned the gambling casinos of Las Vegas and therefore had an interest in keeping the gambling public safe from armed robbers and thefts. The crime bosses, using their own strong-arm methods, made the city unattractive for hoodlums and thieves. However, in the last two decades the casinos have been purchased by legitimate corporations and organized crime has departed. One result is that today Las Vegas is being terrorized by about 100 warring youth gangs who roam the streets, selling drugs, robbing stores, and shooting at each other. Many local citizens and businesses are now realizing that it was the Mafia that kept their streets safe, and some are wishing for a return of the old days (Heath, 1995).

This functionalist analysis of organized crime helps to answer the otherwise perplexing question: "Why does organized crime persist in our society, even though most members of government, most law enforcement agencies and agents, as well as most citizens claim to want it stopped?" The answer is that organized crime, viewed as a structural feature of our society, provides a variety of services that are wanted and used by the rest of the society. It is in this sense that organized crime (as a structure) is functional.

The final major theory, conflict theory, also applies primarily to macroscopic analysis, that is, the analysis of larger social units such as social groups, social organizations, and societies.

Conflict Theory

In our discussion of Karl Marx we noted that his work sensitized sociologists to the fact that, in any kind of social group or system, from families to entire societies, inequities exist in the amount of power and resources held by the participants. Furthermore, these power and resource inequities are likely to persist over time. As we saw earlier, Marx believed that in a capitalist society the holders of the means of production are likely to have a persistent edge over the workers. Conflict theory is an extension of this idea, and thus as a general theory it emphasizes that in any social group, social organization, or society, certain positions (or statuses) are endowed with greater power than other positions or statuses. The incumbents of these positions, those with greater power and resources and those with less, are, according to conflict theory, engaged in a more or less continuous struggle. Those who have greater power and resources do not give them up voluntarily, and therefore those with less power and fewer resources try to wrest those resources from those who hold them (Collins, 1990; Coser, 1956; Dahrendorf, 1959; Ritzer, 1996b).

As an example of how conflict theory can be applied, we turn again to the family. Even though we usually think of the family as a highly cooperative social unit, one where feelings of love and affection exist between the members, the principles of conflict theory are clearly applicable (Collins, 1971; Scanzoni, 1972). In our society (and in most others) two family statuses almost always have more power and control more resources: adults (compared to children and adolescents) and males (compared to females). The adult male in the family is therefore usually able to exercise power over other members of the family, which means that he can make other family members do (or not do) what he wants.

A simple, and probably familiar, example of the way the family members who are in the subordinate status struggle to get more power is found in the relations between adolescent children and their parents. Until adolescence the power of parents over their children is usually unquestioned by both parties. However, adolescence in our society is often a period of considerable conflict between parents and their children because the adolescents are striving to have a greater voice in deciding what they can and cannot do. A 16-year-old or 17-year-old is likely to want greater freedom and independence than parents are willing to give. Outright conflict sometimes results, but disobedience and subversion are more commonly the tactics of adolescents as they push for greater personal autonomy.

If there are conflicts and struggles for power in the family (and we have said nothing about husbands and wives), then clearly the same is apt to be true of other social groups, social organizations, and societies. Conflict theory can also be useful for the analysis of sororities and fraternities, schools, religious organizations, majority–minority relations, the politics of nations, and, of course, the relations between nations. In later chapters many examples will be provided of the inequities between those who have power and resources and those who do not, as well as descriptions of the conflict that ensues when the group with less power and fewer resources struggles for greater equity.

Summary

Sociology is the systematic study of the social behavior of individuals; the workings of social groups, organizations, cultures, and societies; and the influence of these on individual and group behavior. Sociology is one of the sciences of human behavior, but it differs from the other social sciences such as anthropology, economics, and political science by covering the whole spectrum of human behavior. Sociology also overlaps with parts of history and biology and benefits from all these other fields of study.

There is no single sociology, however; there are many sociologies. Sociological specialties focus on some part of human behavior and/or some aspect of social life. Sociologists have different theoretical preferences, research preferences, and levels of analysis (microscopic or macroscopic).

Although sociologists differ on a number of issues, they generally share some fundamental ideas and views. One is that societies and other social settings are humanly created. Every day, people affirm and modify their social settings, but these same social settings, in turn, influence and constrain human behavior.

Sociology can be useful in a number of ways. It provides a wide range of statistical and substantive facts about social conditions and trends. Sociology also provides an awareness and knowledge of cross-cultural and cross-national information. Through sociological concepts and theories, sociology can aid in understanding many issues and problems beyond the subject immediately under study.

The beginnings of sociology can be dated to the early 1800s, when the work of Auguste Comte gave sociology its name and its place among other scholarly disciplines. Among the other pioneers of sociology, the most famous are Emile Durkheim and Max Weber. Karl Marx was an early analyst and critic of society whose ideas have had a profound effect on contemporary sociology.

There are four contemporary theories that dominate sociology. Symbolic interaction theory is oriented toward the interaction between individuals, especially at the symbolic level. The symbols that individuals learn through interaction govern their responses to other human beings, to things, and to themselves. Social exchange theory emphasizes the fact that the motivations for human behavior are found in the costs and rewards of human actions. Humans will continue actions and interactions that are rewarded, and will discontinue those that are not. Structural–functional theory focuses on macroscopic levels of analysis and emphasizes that every pattern of activity (structure) in a society makes some kind of positive or negative contribution to that society. Structural–functional theory also calls attention to less obvious functions of social structures; these are called latent functions. Conflict theory, which is an extension of some basic Marxian ideas, emphasizes that, in any social group, social organization, or society, positions of unequal power probably exist. The struggle for power is a source of conflict in these social groupings.

Appendix: Occupations and Careers That Use Sociology

In this first chapter you have been given a brief introduction to the field of sociology, but the emphasis has been mostly on the nature of sociology—its fundamental principles, its founders, and its major theories. You have seen that sociology can be useful to you, primarily through the facts and principles you will be learning. Little, however, has been said about the more practical applications of sociology, especially the occupational and career opportunities sociology offers. In this brief appendix we will focus more directly on how the study of sociology can lead to occupations and careers.

What you might be able to do with training in sociology depends greatly on the academic degree or degrees you earn. With an undergraduate degree in sociology you can pursue a number of fields of advanced study. A bachelor's degree in sociology can be a basis for careers in social work, law, education, journalism, politics, public relations, business, or public administration. Sociology can also prepare one for graduate or professional schools, such as social work, law, education, counseling, or one of the health professions.

The training that is part of a typical undergraduate degree program in sociology can also be useful for going directly into positions in government, research, marketing and sales, and human resources (personnel work). In addition, the skills learned in social research methods (see Chapter 2) and statistical data analysis are skills often sought by businesses, research organizations, national and state associations and interest groups, and governmental agencies at all levels.

If you continue beyond the bachelor's degree and earn an advanced degree in sociology (master's or doctorate), the range of opportunities includes all those listed above as well as the role of professional sociologist. The most common career for professional sociologists is teaching, generally at the college level, from community and junior colleges to the largest and most prestigious universities. Some college teaching positions at the community and junior-college level may be held with a master's degree, but the Ph.D. degree is almost always required for positions at any college beyond the 2-year level.

More and more nonteaching jobs have become available for those with advanced degrees in sociology, especially for those with doctorates. Holders of these advanced degrees are often highly trained in research, data analysis, and in the analysis of organizational and governmental policies (Iutcovich and Iutcovich, 1987). Governmental agencies employ sociologists to carry out surveys and analyze data. Prominent federal agencies with sociologists on their staffs include the National Institutes of Health, the Census Bureau, the Civil Rights Commission, the National Science Foundation, and many others. Private organizations and businesses also hire sociologists who have been trained to design and carry out social research and policy analysis. Sociologists are employed by radio and television broadcasting companies, insurance companies, advertising agencies, and other businesses that must have valid information on public needs and interests.

If you would like further information about careers and occupations in sociology, you may wish to obtain a copy of *Careers in Sociology* (4th edition), 1995, published by the American Sociological Association, 1722 N Street NW, Washington, D.C. 20036.

CRITICAL THINKING

1. Select two of the specialties of sociology given in Table 1–1 and try to anticipate some of the issues that the sociologists of these specialties might study.
2. Skim the table of contents of this book and find three topics that you believe will be especially interesting to you. What would you hope to learn about these topics.
3. Suppose a sociologist wanted to study education in the United States. What could be the focus of a microscopic study of education? What would be the subject of a macroscopic study?
4. Look for examples from your own life experiences that would illustrate how social settings have influenced your behavior.
5. Why do many people believe, erroneously, that teenagers have a higher suicide rate than other age groups?
6. In what ways do you think sociology will be useful to you in your personal life or in your future (or present) occupation.
7. Give examples of important symbols on your college campus.
8. Assume the beliefs of a social exchange theory sociologist. How would the idea of reciprocity apply to your relationship with your parents?
9. Give some examples to support the following statement: "By understanding the meanings that people give to words and symbols we can understand their behavior."

2

Sociological Research

William Foote Whyte is one of the best known sociological researchers of the twentieth century. Whyte's most famous sociological work, *Street Corner Society,* was originally published in 1943 and has been published three times since, most recently in 1993. He has called it "The Book That Would Not Die" (Whyte, 1994, p. 319). The method of research he used in that study, participant observation, is so closely associated with his name that he titled his autobiography *Participant Observer* (Whyte, 1994).

Street Corner Society is a study of the social life of what was, in the 1930s, an Italian slum neighborhood in Boston's North End. When Whyte started his study, he had no idea of how to get acquainted with the people who lived there. However, he met a Harvard economics instructor who described his technique, which was to drop in at local bars where he would strike up an acquaintance with unaccompanied young women. Whyte thought that sounded like an excellent idea and describes what happened when he tried to carry it out.

> With some trepidation, I climbed the stairs to a bar and entertainment area and looked around. There I encountered a situation for which no advisor had prepared me. There were women present all right, but none of them was alone. Some were there with men, and there were two or three pairs of women together. I pondered the situation briefly. I had little confidence in my skill at picking up women, and it seemed inadvisable for me

to tackle two at the same time. Still, I was determined not to admit defeat without a struggle. I looked around again and now noticed a threesome: one man and two women. It occurred to me that here was a maldistribution of females that I might be able to rectify. I approached the group and opened with something like this, "Pardon me. Would you mind if I joined you?" There was a moment of silence while the man stared at me. He then offered to throw me downstairs. I assured him that this would not be necessary and demonstrated as much by walking right out of the bar (Whyte, 1994, p. 66).

Fortunately for sociology, Whyte did not let this early setback deter him, and he went on to conduct many other studies in the United States, as well as in Peru, Venezuela, and Spain (Whyte, 1994). During most of his career, he focused on work settings and especially the perspectives of workers.

Participant observation, which involves the researcher directly in the lives and activities of the people being studied, is only one way to do sociological research. There are many other ways, including some in which researchers have no direct contact with people at all. There is some irony in the fact that sociologists today can do research simply by using data stored in computers and thus have no contact with people; the irony stems from the fact that most sociologists are attracted to the field because of their interest in people.

We will begin our consideration of sociological research by first examining some of the basic ideas of science. We will then describe some of the ethical issues that are especially associated with social research. After describing the research process, we will undertake a review of the most important research techniques used by sociologists.

A Scientific Approach to Knowledge

Sociology, as we noted in Chapter 1, is one of the sciences of human behavior. All sciences have some characteristics in common, and yet the sciences of human behavior are different in some ways from sciences like physics, microbiology, or genetics. We will begin our consideration of sociological research by considering some basic elements of the scientific approach, while at the same time noting how the scientific approach must be modified to fit the subject matter of sociology.

Empirical Observation

One word that is critical for understanding the essence of a scientific approach is **empiricism,** which is the act of experiencing something with one's senses. Empiricism contrasts sharply with imagination and speculation, even though these two activities are also important parts of the scientific approach. We can imagine how some aspect of the social world will be, but we will not know what it is really like until we make some observations, or obtain information, either directly or indirectly.

Objectivity and Sociological Research

The central importance of empiricism in science leads directly to a consideration of a second feature of the scientific method—objectivity. **Objectivity** in science means, in general terms, that scientists conduct their research in such a way that their personal, subjective views do not influence the results of their research. This general statement may seem an easy rule to follow, but, for sociologists, objectivity poses some special problems.

Objectivity has two dimensions. Objectivity is first an attitude of the scientist who must try to keep his or her personal views, beliefs, and values from influencing either the conduct or the conclusions of the research. The second dimension of objectivity is the use of research procedures described in sufficient detail so that other scientists may, if they choose, repeat (or replicate) a study. The attitudinal dimension of objectivity is much more difficult to achieve and maintain than is the procedural dimension, and we will deal with that first.

Objectivity as an Attitude. Scientists are expected to be objective about the subjects of their research. However, in everyday experience, scientists in all fields find it difficult to remain "value free." All scientists have personal views, attitudes, and values that could potentially affect the selection of particular problems for study, the conduct of the research, and the interpretation of the results.

In sociology, as well as in other social and behavioral sciences, special problems occur with this aspect of objectivity. Sociology often deals with issues, questions, and problems that are personally important in the lives of the sociologists conducting the research. Consider, for example, the issue of the death penalty for major crimes. One sociologist might be personally in favor of the death penalty, while another might be opposed. Will they likely ask the same research questions and carry out the same research? In an ideal world these two scientists with different views would not allow those views to influence the planning and execution of their research. However, in the real world these scientists might ask different research questions and reach different conclusions.

While some sociologists argue that all sociologists must be objective and value free at all times, others hold a more realistic view. This more realistic view acknowledges that sociologists have personal values, and, at least in some stages of their professional research, they may be allowed to use these values to influence their selection of issues and the types of questions they ask (Seubert, 1991). For example, a sociologist might support the idea that women have a right to enter and succeed in occupations that have been previously male dominated. Such a sociologist could design a study to learn if women entering male-dominated occupations are treated and evaluated fairly. But, for validity, the study would have to be done fairly and the results reported honestly.

Attitudinal objectivity requires scientists to maintain an attitude of fairness and honesty when planning and conducting their research. Researchers cannot intentionally design their studies in such a way that the results will be predetermined to support their views. They cannot design the questions or measures in such a way as to influence the outcome of the research. They certainly cannot interpret their results in a biased or dishonest manner in order to obtain the results they desire. An objective attitude must be rigorously maintained in the conduct of research, or one of the fundamental elements of science is sacrificed.

Objectivity as a Procedure. **Procedural objectivity** refers to the performing and reporting of all research tasks in such a way that any interested person will know exactly how the research was conducted. The research procedure cannot include any methods of observation that other qualified scientists are unable to repeat. For example, if an astronomer claimed to have heard a message from intelligent beings coming from outer space but then asserted, "The messages can only be heard on my recording instruments, and no one else may use my instruments," such a report, no matter how interesting, could not be accepted by other scientists or, for that matter, by the public. To be scientific, the methods of observation must be reported in such a way that other scientists will be able to use those same methods. Only then can other scientists verify or reject the results of the original research.

Although this standard is widely accepted by scientists and the public alike for the natural and biological sciences, a tendency exists to hold the social sciences to a less rigorous standard. But the standards of scientific inquiry should be uniformly applied. If, for example, a sociologist were to report that a "sample of 200 adults completed a questionnaire" and then reported the results of the research without providing any additional information about the sample, we should be skeptical about the report. As a minimum requirement, any interested person should be able to ask for information as to where and how the sample was selected.

Sociological researchers must also report, or be prepared to provide more details about, the specific questions asked in interviews or on questionnaires. If questions have been combined in certain ways so as to create general measures, these steps would also have to be described. Finally, any statistical procedures used to analyze the data must be reported.

Some sociological research methods do not involve samples, questionnaires, or statistical analyses, but rather involve the observation of individuals or groups in natural social settings. With these methods the precise research procedures are often more difficult to document, but the researchers are nonetheless obligated to provide full reports of their methods if they are to measure up to the standards of procedural objectivity.

Ethical Issues of Social Research

When sociologists carry out research projects they may cause problems for, or even do harm to, the people they study. This possibility makes it necessary for sociologists to consider the ethical implications of their research. The basic question that any social researcher must ask is: If I carry out this research, will it harm the participants or other people in some way? There are several types of potentially harmful or negative consequences that may come from social research.

Physical Harm

Although relatively rare, it is possible that a researcher's actions can cause physical harm to the people being studied. As an example, a social psychologist named Muzafer Sherif once conducted a field experiment with 12-year-old boys at a summer camp, and the final stages of the experiment had to be curtailed because the boys were in danger of being seriously hurt (Sherif, 1953). In this study the boys were divided into two groups, and then, through the manipulations of the researchers, the groups were brought into competition and conflict. For a number of days the conflict was limited to apple-throwing fights and to raids on each other's cabins, but in a final severe confrontation in the dining hall the two groups of boys faced off and the situation became dangerous. Some of the boys started to throw silverware and plates. The researchers quickly stepped in and stopped the hostilities (and that phase of the field experiment).

One of the objectives of Sherif's study was to observe how competition between groups could lead to conflict and then to learn about reducing conflict between those groups. Although that goal is surely desirable, it may have been outweighed in this case by the possible dangers to the subjects of the study.

Psychological Harm

The actions of a social researcher could possibly cause psychological harm as well, although anticipating when and how this might occur is often difficult. Researchers today frequently ask respondents about sensitive and personal issues, including questions about alcohol use, criminal acts, heterosexual or homosexual experiences, child or spouse abuse, deaths of relatives, mental illness, physical handicaps, and so on. For most people questions on these and similar subjects will not likely cause any psychological distress, but the possibility always exists that some respondents will suffer psychological harm. An example comes from a study of psychological depression in which interviewers asked subjects about an array of life's tragedies and about their symptoms of mental illness. The trained interviewers who conducted the pretest interviews reported that some of the interviewees were showing clear signs of depression after being questioned about these topics. The research directors became concerned that their interview was actually *causing depression.* Before the study could continue, the questions were broadened to include some more positive and "upbeat" topics (Converse and Presser, 1986).

Intrusions into Private Lives

Sometimes sociologists collect information on the private (even secret) lives of individuals and thereby raise ethical questions about the research. Sociologists occasionally study people whose behavior is immoral, improper, or illegal; when they do, the information they obtain could be damaging to the people being studied (Adler and Adler, 1993). The now-classic example of this type of research (and the ethical problems it raises) is a study of the homosexual activities of men in public restrooms (Humphreys, 1975). To study these men, Humphreys posed as a "watch-queen," a lookout who signals those engaged in homosexual acts that a stranger, or worse, a police officer, is approaching. Only a few of the men he studied knew that he was a sociological researcher. Although Humphreys took great care to disguise and protect the identity of the men he studied, a number of sociologists believed that, by deceiving the men under study, he was violating the ethical standards of social research. Humphreys subsequently reported that if he were to repeat the study he would spend more time "cultivating and expanding the [number] of willing respondents..." (Humphreys, 1975, pp. 229–231).

The Humphreys study is an extreme example of a concern that nearly every social researcher must have when collecting research data: How much must the researcher tell the respondents about the nature of a study in order to get their cooperation?

Researchers who study drug dealers and drug users face similar ethical problems since they often find themselves witnessing crimes. A group of researchers who studied the distribution and sale of crack cocaine report having contact with over 300 different crack distributors (Williams et al., 1992). But this group, because its research was federally funded, received a Certificate of Confidentiality from the Department of Health and Human Services. Eloise Dunlop, one of the researchers, has described how, as soon as she makes contact with drug dealers, she explains that their identities will be concealed and interview materials will never be available to police or law-enforcement agencies (Williams et al., 1992, p. 349).

While the courts have upheld the confidentiality of information obtained by these drug researchers, this guarantee is not as certain in other research on illegal activities (Leo, 1995; Scarce, 1994). When sociologists study illegal behavior of any kind (date rape, shoplifting, domestic violence, and so on), it often raises questions about the rights of the people who are being studied. For an example of one sociologist's experience with the legal system and what he had to do to avoid giving up his research data, see the In the News Box on the next page.

Today most sociological research is conducted under rules of *informed consent,* which means that, when people are asked to participate, they are told in a general way about the nature and purpose of the study and of any sensitive or dangerous aspects of the study (Presser, 1995). Of course, it must be clear that participation in the study is voluntary, and that the identities of participants will remain confidential. Most sociologists agree that, although it is sometimes inconvenient

In the News

Sociological Research and Privileged Information

Sociologists routinely assure the subjects of their studies that the information that they provide will be held in confidence; in fact, they are often required to do so because of federal guidelines. But sometimes researchers collect information that later becomes relevant for criminal or civil court cases. Then police, prosecutors, grand juries, or the courts may demand that the researcher reveal what he or she knows. There have been a number of such cases, but one that has received the most attention recently is that of Rik Scarce, a Ph.D. candidate at Washington State University (Scarce, 1994). Scarce spent 5 months in jail because he refused to testify before a federal grand jury about the activities of the animal rights activists that he was studying (Scarce, 1994).

As part of his graduate work at Washington State University, Rik Scarce was doing research on radical social movements. Among the groups that he was studying was an animal rights group called the Animal Liberation Front (ALF). In August, 1991, ALF raided a federally funded animal research laboratory at Washington State University, where they released the research animals, vandalized computers, and caused damage estimated at $100,000 (Scarce, 1994, p. 124).

Nine months after the break-in, a police officer at Washington State University, along with an FBI agent, questioned Scarce about his knowledge of the animal rights activists who might have committed the acts. Scarce refused to answer questions about the members of the animal rights group that he had interviewed, claiming that he could not be made to do so under First Amendment rights (specifically, freedom of the press). After his refusal, the FBI agent handed Scarce a federal grand jury subpoena.

When Scarce appeared before the grand jury, he again refused to answer any questions that he believed would violate the promises of confidentiality that he had given to his research subjects. Scarce based his refusal on the First Amendment, claiming that research scholars needed to gather information in order to do their research and that promises of confidentiality, once given, cannot be broken. This is in accord with the Code of Ethics of the American Sociological Association. Scarce further told the court that he feared for his ability to earn a living as a sociologist if he were compelled to testify, because research subjects would be unwilling to talk to him, and institutions would not be willing to hire him after he had behaved unethically (broken his promise of confidentiality) to research subjects.

The federal court judge, however, did not accept Scarce's argument and found him in contempt of court for refusing to answer the questions of the grand jury. The penalty for refusing to answer questions in a grand jury proceeding can be up to 18 months in jail. After a number of delays, one of

which was granted so that Rik Scarce could complete his doctoral examinations in sociology at Washington State University (which he did successfully), the judge's sentence was imposed. At 8:00 A.M. on May 14, 1993, U.S.
marshals handcuffed Scarce and transported him to the Spokane County
jail. He remained incarcerated for 159 days, until October 19, when the
judge finally signed a motion made by Scarce's lawyers for his release
(Scarce, 1994).

Rik Scarce did not break his promise of confidentiality to his research
subjects, but he paid a heavy price for his principled decision. In addition to
the time he spent in jail, he went through more than 2 years of stress and
uncertainty, and there can be no doubt that his education and professional
advancement were negatively affected. Yet, despite his sacrifice, the rights
of social researchers remain as ambiguous as ever. The courts today do not
give social researchers the same rights of privileged communication traditionally enjoyed by lawyers, medical doctors, and the clergy.

Reflecting on his own experience, Scarce has said that social researchers will continue to be in jeopardy until federal legislation clarifies the rights
of scholars and researchers. However, there is no immediate prospect that
any such legislation will be passed, since none is currently in the offing. In
the meantime, researchers must understand that whenever they give
research subjects promises of confidentiality they may someday be called
on to honor that commitment, perhaps at the cost of their own freedom (Leo,
1995).

Leo, Richard. "Trial and Tribulations: Courts, Ethnography, and the Need for Eviden-
tiary Privilege for Academic Researchers." *The American Sociologist,* Vol. 26, 1995.
Scarce, Rik. "(No) Trial (But) Tribulations." *Journal of Contemporary Ethnography,*
Vol. 23, 1994.

to go through the informed-consent procedures (and occasionally a study is
changed or impeded because of them), it is better to err on the side of safety and
to avoid problems of questionable ethics.

Research Questions and Hypotheses

All research starts with a question, but the questions may come from very different sources. Sociologists may study a question because it reflects a long tradition
in sociology, or because it reflects a current societal development, or simply
because it has a special importance in their personal lives.

As an example of a long sociological tradition there is the work of Emile
Durkheim, some of whose ideas were introduced in Chapter 1. As you will recall,
Durkheim studied the ways in which suicide is related to social conditions.

(Anomie, or normlessness, was one such condition.) Durkheim also speculated (or theorized) that social integration would be related to suicide. He defined **social integration** as belonging to, or being a part of, social groups or the society. Using data from various nineteenth-century European countries, Durkheim found that the more socially integrated segments of populations had lower suicide rates. Married people, for example, were presumed to be more socially integrated because of marriage and family ties, and married people had lower rates of suicide (Durkheim, 1897/1951).

Durkheim's theoretical insight—that the level of social integration can influence social behavior—has continued to stimulate research and analysis among present-day sociologists (Booth et al., 1991; Zimmerman, 1991). Contemporary studies still show that social integration, as represented by marriage, reduces suicide (Breault, 1986). Or, looked at from the opposite point of view, being divorced—and thus having a lower level of social integration—is associated with higher suicide rates. Research in the United States (Stack, 1990a), Canada (Trovato, 1987), and Denmark (Stack, 1990b) supports the Durkheimian idea that low social integration leads to higher levels of suicide.

Researchers have also found social integration to be related in some ways to divorce. In a study that involved three interviews conducted between 1980 and 1988 with a sample of married couples (called a *panel* or *longitudinal study*), their level of social integration was measured. This was done by asking questions about their number of friends, number of organization memberships, number of shared friends, and whether they had friends or relatives who were divorced. While this study found some measures of social integration to be related to lower divorce, the relationships were not strong enough or consistent enough to say that social integration (or the lack of it) explains divorce rates (Booth et al., 1991, p. 222).

These research results supporting Durkheim's theory of social integration can lead to other research hypotheses. A **hypothesis** is a statement about how various phenomena are expected to be related to each other. Since social integration (or the lack of it) has been found to be related to both suicide and divorce, other, new hypotheses may be suggested. A researcher might hypothesize that violence in the family (wife abuse, child abuse, elder abuse) would occur more often among families with low levels of social integration. The research literature on abuse lends some support to this hypothesis, because it has been found that when parents are more isolated (few friends, little contact with other relatives) they are more likely to abuse their children (Garbarino and Sherman, 1980). Research has also shown that cohabitating couples are more likely to experience physical aggression than married couples because they are less socially integrated (Stets, 1991).

Theoretical Concepts and Research Variables

A theoretical idea such as social integration is called a concept. A **concept** is a word or phrase that summarizes some meaningful part of the social world. An important part of social research consists of translating key concepts into observable phenomena. For example, to translate the concept of social integration into an observable phenomenon, Durkheim used the percentage of the population that was married. Of course, being married is not the only indication of social integration. As we have just seen, social integration is also reflected in the number of friends a person has or the number of organization memberships a person has. These observable phenomena are called **indicators**—in this case, indicators of the degree to which people are socially integrated.

When concepts are observed through the use of indicators, researchers often refer to the indicators as variables. **Variables** are defined as objects or phenomena that can change from one size, state, or degree to another. Levels of social integration are variable because some people, or some groups, are more socially integrated than others.

Independent and Dependent Variables

Social researchers divide variables into two basic classes: independent variables and dependent variables. **Independent variables** are those that are thought to produce a change in some other variable. Durkheim expected, on the basis of his theory, that the independent variable, social integration, would produce changes in suicide rates, the dependent variable. **Dependent variables** are those that are changed or influenced by independent variables. In everyday terms, independent variables are the presumed *causes* of changes; they produce *effects* on dependent variables. A researcher who wants to test the hypothesis that a low level of social integration will produce higher levels of child abuse would call social integration the independent variable and child abuse the dependent variable.

We have reviewed some of the basic elements of scientific research and turn now to the major research methods used in sociology. As we consider these research methods, further illustrations and elaborations will be given of the principles and processes already introduced.

Major Sociological Research Methods

Experiments

Experiments are typically set up in such a way that the independent variable is under the control of the researcher and its impact on a dependent variable can be observed directly. Experiments are ideally suited for assessing causality (Meeker and Leik, 1995). Experiments are sometimes conducted in laboratories and other times in more natural settings. The latter are called *field experiments.* In both laboratory and field experiments, groups of subjects are randomly assigned to receive a treatment of some kind (independent variable) to see what its effect will be on the dependent variable.

In a classic **laboratory experiment,** two groups of subjects are assembled through random selection. One group is designated as the **experimental group,** and this group is exposed to the experimental independent variable. The second group, called the **control group,** is not exposed to the independent variable. The experimental and control groups are then compared to see if the dependent variable is different between the two groups. If a difference in the dependent variable is observed, it is assumed that the experimental variable was the cause.

Laboratory experiments in sociology generally involve bringing subjects into a room or laboratory where they are asked to engage in some activity or task (solve a problem or write a story, for example). The experimenter will then administer different experimental treatments to randomly selected groups of the subjects. An experiment designed by Johnson (1994) can serve as an illustration. She created a simulated organization in a laboratory and assigned male and female subjects randomly to different conditions. In some groups females were managers, while in others males were. The experiment sought to learn if gender or organizational position most influenced verbal and nonverbal behavior (dependent variables). One conclusion coming from this experiment was that organizational position was more important than gender in determining verbal patterns (Johnson, 1994). This experiment does not support the view popularized by Tannen (1990) that men and women speak in fundamentally different ways.

The laboratory experiment has the advantage of giving the researcher close control over experimental variables, but it is a research method that sees only limited use in sociology. Even in social psychology, the subfield of sociology where experiments have been used most, the experiment is not often used. In the words of two sociologists who are social psychologists, "the experimental method remains the strongest model of scientific proof in science. Its chief limitation, from the [sociological] perspective is that it is poorly adapted to deal with many of the substantive questions of interest to sociologists." (Rosenberg and Turner, 1990, p. xi.)

Further, laboratory experiments are often highly artificial, unnatural, and contrived. Subjects are often asked to do tasks in the laboratory that they would not be likely to do in real life. Therefore, the results of laboratory experiments may be questioned for their applicability to real-life situations.

A distinction is often made between applied and basic research. **Applied research** is research designed and conducted to answer a specific practical question or to solve a particular social problem. **Basic research** tests hypotheses derived from theories, such as the test of Durkheim's social integration hypothesis discussed earlier. Applied research can be done with surveys and other research methods, but field experiments are often used to evaluate and assess the effectiveness of social programs or to test the desirability of proposed government policies that are designed to solve some social problem (Saxe and Fine, 1981).

Field Experiments

Field experiments, as we have noted, share characteristics with the laboratory experiment, but are conducted in more natural settings where activities are relatively normal. An illustration of a field experiment is found in the work of Sherman and Berk (1984) on domestic violence.

In 1981, the police department in Minneapolis, Minnesota, agreed to participate in an experimental study that sought to determine the best way of dealing with domestic abuse cases. The procedure of this field experiment required that the police, when responding to a misdemeanor domestic violence call, randomly apply one of three responses: (1) arrest the suspect, (2) threaten the suspect with arrest and make him or her leave the home, or (3) give some form of advice, counseling, or mediation (give the suspect a "talking to"). The action to be taken by the police in any given case was randomly determined through a color-coded pad of report forms. The color of the top sheet determined the officer's action. If, for example, the top sheet was blue, the officer arrested the offender; if it was yellow, the officer administered the lecture.

To determine if arresting the suspect had a deterrent effect, the researchers (1) monitored police records for 6 months to see if the suspect's name appeared again in a case of domestic violence and (2) interviewed the original victims by telephone over a 6-month period to find out if there had been a repeat incident with the same suspect. The evidence coming from this experiment showed that suspects who were arrested and temporarily incarcerated were less likely to be involved in later incidents of domestic violence (Sherman and Berk, 1984).

Largely on the basis of this original field experiment, many police departments around the United States adopted the policy of routinely making arrests in cases of domestic violence (Sherman and Cohn, 1989). By 1991, laws making arrests mandatory in domestic violence cases had been passed in 15 states (Zorza, 1992). Since this study was so influential, the National Institute of Justice agreed to check the validity of the Minneapolis study by funding similar field experiments in six other U.S. cities (Berk et al., 1992; Pate and Hamilton, 1992; Sherman and Smith, 1992).

Replication: The Importance of Repeating Research

Repeating the Minneapolis field experiment in six other cities is an example of **replication,** which is the redoing of studies or experiments to see if the findings of the original study can be duplicated.

Results from most of the replication studies do not support the simple conclusion that arrests deter all people from repeating their offenses (Berk et al., 1992). In fact, in three of these cities, arrests were related to *increases* in subsequent arrests (Sherman and Smith, 1992). Further analysis shows that certain suspects are deterred from repeating their offenses, but others are not. When arrested suspects are employed, for example, they are less likely to repeat their offenses at a later date. But those who are unemployed are *more likely* to repeat the offense (Pate and Hamilton, 1992). It seems that being employed makes people more "socially bonded" (Sherman and Smith, 1992, p. 681) or, to use the concept of Durkheim, more socially integrated. Persons who are more socially bonded (or integrated) seem to have much more to lose by being arrested. Having been arrested once, they may wish to avoid the risk of being arrested again. Those persons who are not employed, by contrast, are less socially bonded or integrated, and another arrest may have fewer social consequences for them. An arrest not only does not deter them, it may actually lead them to further arrests.

These field experiments on domestic violence demonstrate the importance of replication in science. The original field experiment in Minneapolis produced results that were strong enough to convince most people of their validity. Now, after the new studies in different cities, it is clear that changes in police policies, especially those making arrests mandatory in domestic violence cases, may have been premature. The arrests of certain suspects may even have exacerbated the problem of violence in some cases (Berk et al., 1992; see also Buzawa and Buzawa, 1996).

Observational Studies

There is a long tradition of sociological research based on the observation of human behavior (Adler and Adler, 1993). **Observational studies** are systematic and purposive observations of human behavior in natural settings. In the most basic observational studies researchers station themselves in public places (bus depots, airports, restaurants, theaters, libraries, or parks) and observe the behaviors of people as they go about the business of everyday life (Lofland, 1989; Wolfinger, 1995). The observer in this case is nonintrusive and generally unnoticed by the people being observed (Adler and Adler, 1993).

An example of basic observational research is found in studies of fathering behavior in public settings (Mackey, 1986). Observers stationed themselves in public places, such as parks, public squares, and shopping centers, in the United States and 17 other countries where they systematically observed and recorded the interaction between adult males and their apparent children. The observers recorded the proximity of the adult to the child (or children), group size and composition, physical contact during a designated 30-second period, and whether or not the adult looked directly at the child. These data were assembled and analyzed for the various countries, making it possible to determine levels and amounts of "fathering" behavior (Mackey, 1986). Mackey concluded, on the basis of these observations, that fathers in all cultures have a natural affinity to bond with their children.

At the beginning of this chapter we described the work of William Foote Whyte, who did much of his research with a method called participant observation. Sociologists who do **participant observation** collect data by involving themselves directly in the lives and activities of the people they are studying. Participant observers hear and see what people say and do in the normal course of their regular activities. Sometimes researchers may go beyond observation and ask the subjects about what they are doing and thinking. They may also collect documents and other artifacts. Participant observers typically make extensive notes on what they see and hear, sometimes in the presence of the subjects, but often when they are alone (Simmons and McCall, 1985).

Participant observation is closely associated with the research method of anthropologists called *ethnography,* or sometimes simply *fieldwork* (Atkinson and Hammersley, 1994). With both methods the researcher is closely involved with the people being studied.

The degree to which participant observers become involved in the same activities as their subjects can vary greatly from one study to the next. For example, a sociological observer may actually be a member of some group of people (in an office or on an assembly line) and still observe what is happening from a sociological perspective. Sociological observers in these cases are called *insiders* (Burgess, 1984).

One sociologist did participant observation where he was clearly an insider, by studying the hospital where he was confined with tuberculosis (Roth, 1963). Using his sociological training to observe the actions of doctors, staff, and other patients, he kept detailed notes on conversations, routines, and activities. Even though he was like other patients, he was also acting in his role as a sociologist. After his recovery, he continued doing research by studying other hospitals, but as an *outsider* (Roth, 1963).

A second form of participant observation, more common than that involving true insiders, occurs when sociologists *act as if* they are bona fide members of the setting they are studying. A few people in the setting may be aware that sociological observations are being made, but most participants are not.

When sociologist Douglas Harper (1982) studied the lives of hoboes and tramps, he hitched rides on the railroad freight cars and participated as fully as possible in their way of life. He slept in hobo jungles and camps and shared food and company with those he met there. Although he did occasionally reveal his identity as a writer and photographer, to most of the people he met in the tramp world he was one of them. By being accepted as a real hobo, he could observe their normal, everyday behavior.

In the third (and by far the most common) form of participant observation, sociologists approach the people to be observed and openly declare their intentions of doing a sociological study. Using this approach, they are clearly recognized as outsiders and, because they are outsiders, the researchers must gain the confidence of those being observed. They do so by involving themselves in the activities of the group so that they will become both familiar and nonthreatening to group members.

Sociologist Gary Fine (1987), who conducted participant observation research among Little League preadolescent boys, has reported how he first obtained permission from the league president to make his observational study. He described his research in general terms, explaining that he wanted to observe the behavior of preadolescent boys as they participated in Little League baseball and in their leisure time. When he was introduced to the coaches, and later to the boys, he made a similar statement. He informed the boys that he might eventually write a book, which gave him credibility and respect. In fact, the boys saw him as a kind of official chronicler and historian of the team, and occasionally asked him if some event were "going to be in the book."

Fine handled the issue of informed consent by telling the coaches that he would not study their teams unless they agreed. The boys were told that they did not have to answer his questions (including a questionnaire he handed out) or have anything to do with him if they did not want to. Each boy was given a letter to take to his parents that explained the central focus of the research; it invited the parents to ask questions, and informed them that if they had any objections he would respect their wishes. (Only two parents objected to the study.)

Sociological observers who are open about the aims and intentions of their research are often helped immeasurably by some members of the group who act as informants and interpreters (Johnson, 1990; Trice, 1970; Wax, 1971). When Fine studied the boys on Little League baseball teams, he soon earned the trust of several boys who became his confidants. They interpreted events for him and alerted him when something special was occurring. On one occasion, a young boy sidled up to him and said, "Moons are shining tonight," which was a signal that several of the boys were at the edge of the baseball park, "mooning" the passing traffic. It was at this point that sociologist Fine knew that he had gained the confidence of the boys.

Qualitative Interviews

Qualitative interviews, also called **in-depth interviews,** are questions asked in face-to-face situations in which the interviewer uses an interview guide, or a loosely organized list of questions to elicit information (Mutchnick and Berg, 1996). Qualitative interviews may be used in conjunction with participant observation methods or as the exclusive data-gathering method of a study (Weiss, 1995).

Gilgun (1995) used qualitative, in-depth interviews when she studied eleven incest perpetrators (10 men and 1 woman). Her sample was small, as it often is with qualitative interview research, but she interviewed each person an average of six times for an average interview time of 12 hours (Gilgun, 1995, p. 269). These interviews revealed that perpetrators of incest, incredibly, define their acts as caring and loving and their behavior as considerate and fair. These violators of one of society's strongest taboos knew that they were breaking it, but they were able to create an account of their actions that gave these actions a degree of legitimization in their own minds. This research finding could probably only have been uncovered with in-depth, qualitative interviews (Ambert et al., 1995).

Social Surveys

The research method most strongly associated with sociology is the social survey. A **social survey** is a method of collecting information from a sample of people by means of questionnaires or interviews. **Questionnaires** are written sets of self-administered questions that are delivered to respondents by hand or through the mail. **Interviews** are questions asked by an interviewer or researcher, either in person or on the telephone.

Survey research has two basic objectives: description and explanation. **Descriptive surveys** are designed to obtain some basic information about a population, the simplest being public opinion polls and market surveys. Public opinion polls, now routinely conducted and reported, are familiar parts of contemporary U.S. life. Although such polls are sometimes conducted by sociologists and the results are of interest to sociologists, they are not a primary form of sociological research. The same holds true for marketing surveys, which are usually conducted by organizations specifically set up for the purpose of determining public tastes—for example, television viewing habits.

Sociologists conduct other types of descriptive surveys, often with the objective of identifying typical patterns of behavior or the distribution of attitudes in some population. For example, each year since 1975 the Institute for Social Research at the University of Michigan has conducted a survey among high school seniors in the United States. The reports of these surveys provide descriptive accounts of the life-styles, values, and attitudes of young people in their last year of high school. Among other things, this survey has asked high school seniors since 1975 about their use of marijuana. (The survey is funded in part by the National Institute of Drug Abuse.) Figure 2–1 shows the percentage of high school seniors who reported marijuana use during the preceding year. These data make it clear that marijuana use among high school seniors reached a peak in 1979 (50.8 percent) and declined until 1992, when it reached a low of 21.9 percent. Since then each year's survey has shown increases in marijuana use among high school seniors, moving to 34.7 percent in the 1995 survey (University of Michigan, 1995).

Descriptive surveys often raise questions about causes. What, for example, accounts for the recent increase in marijuana use among high school seniors? This kind of question leads to explanatory surveys. **Explanatory surveys** attempt to find independent variables that will be related to and possibly account for differences in behaviors and attitudes (as dependent variables).

Earlier analysis by the researchers who conduct this survey of high school students showed that students' attitudes about the dangers of drug use were consis-

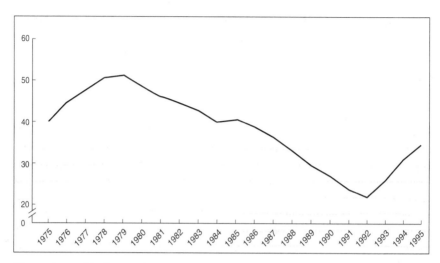

Figure 2–1. Marijuana Use among High School Seniors, 1975–1995. (*Source:* Johnson et al., 1989; University of Michigan, 1995.)

tently associated with actual drug use. The steady declines in marijuana use during the 1980s were associated with increasing concerns among students about the *risks* of using marijuana (Bachman et al., 1988). Now, in the 1990s, the percentage of students who think that regular marijuana use puts users at risk has been declining (University of Michigan, 1995). This decline in perceived risks corresponds with increases in marijuana use and therefore provides one level of explanation for the recent increase in use. Of course, this survey does not explain *why* the perceived risks of marijuana use have declined among young people, but the researchers speculate there are more positive messages about drugs (from music groups and the lyrics of their songs) and fewer negative messages from parents and the mass media (University of Michigan, 1995).

Samples for Social Surveys.   The respondents questioned in social surveys are sometimes loosely referred to as the sample. However, a careful use of this term requires that the people who are questioned be drawn in some random way from a specified population (or universe of people). For example, to draw a **random sample** of the adult population of the United States, researchers would have to use a sampling procedure that would give each adult in the population an equal chance of being selected in the sample. Methods for drawing random samples have been well developed and are used regularly by major survey–research organizations, public-opinion polling organizations, and the federal government.

While random samples are highly desirable, many researchers in sociology use respondents who have not been randomly selected. The resulting sample is called a **convenience sample,** that is, research subjects who are conveniently available to complete questionnaires or respond to interviews. (College classes often serve as convenience samples.) Convenience samples are usually justified on the grounds that the research is exploratory.

Secondary Analysis

Much sociological research today is based on the reanalysis of data collected by earlier surveys, a method called **secondary analysis.** Researchers who do secondary analysis often study issues that are very different from those studied by the original collectors of the data. One great advantage of secondary analysis is that it is relatively inexpensive and thus is an excellent way for beginning researchers to get involved in sociological research.

The importance of secondary analysis in contemporary sociology can be illustrated by the National Survey of Families and Households, which was conducted in 1987–1988 (Sweet et al., 1988). This survey, supported by a federal government agency, the National Institute of Child Health and Human Development, produced personal interviews with a random sample of 13,017 individuals aged 19 and older. The interviews in this survey asked the respondents about their family histories as they were growing up and about their personal histories of cohabitation and marriage. The data from this survey have now led to more than 150 published research articles, most of which are the product of secondary analysis (Center for Demography and Ecology, University of Wisconsin, Madison, 1995).

A few examples of the conclusions reached by secondary analysis researchers will illustrate the usefulness of this research method.

- Premarital childbearing reduces the chances of marriage (Bennett et al., 1995).

- The "gender gap" in housework (women doing more than men) is greater in married couple households than in other types of households (South and Spitze, 1994).

- A mother's employment has a substantial positive effect on her children's educational attainment (Kalmijn, 1994).

- Employed mothers who are near the poverty level receive less social support from friends, relatives, and neighbors than do more affluent employed women (Benin and Keith, 1995).

Government Archives for Secondary Analysis.   The federal government of the United States conducts surveys and censuses of various types on a regular basis, and data from these are available to researchers. When the population of the United States is counted every ten years through a national census, the information obtained goes far beyond a simple count of men, women, and children. The census collects information on jobs, income, housing, marital status, childbearing, and many other aspects of U.S. life. These data are available to the public and provide the raw material for many sociological studies.

The Historical–Comparative Method

Sociological researchers who use the **historical–comparative method** examine the events and histories of whole societies, or the events and histories of major components of societies (for example, religious systems, economic systems, governmental systems). The historical–comparative method is concerned with macroscopic types of social phenomena, to use the terminology introduced in Chapter 1. This method also includes a comparative dimension, meaning, for example, that one society may be compared to itself at different historical periods or two or more societies may be compared to each other. Often the goal is to understand how historical events and conditions in different societies have led to different societal outcomes. Sometimes this method is used to explain why a society has changed in certain ways. To do this, researchers might study how conditions and events at one time in history led to different conditions at a later time. This study can be most effective when comparisons among two or more societies are made.

A classic example of historical–comparative research is the work of Max Weber, one of the pioneering sociologists introduced in Chapter 1. Weber, as we saw, was interested in rationality, that is, human action based primarily on the criterion of efficiency. He was especially interested in why the Western world, primarily Europe and the United States, had come to place so much emphasis on rationality. Using a historical–comparative research strategy to study this question, Weber compared the cultures of India and China with those of European countries. He was looking for historical factors that might have led to an acceptance of rationality in the West and that might have inhibited its acceptance in non-Western societies. Weber concluded that the rise of Protestantism and the acceptance of its belief system in Europe was a key factor that led to an emphasis on rationality and efficiency and a striving for material success. When Weber examined the religious ideas of Eastern societies he found none that encouraged rationality in the same way that Protestantism had in Europe. Indeed, some Eastern religions inhibited rational approaches (Weber, 1904–1905/1958).

One of the foremost contemporary historical–comparative researchers is S. N. Eisenstadt (Grosby, 1995). His recent historical analysis of Japan confirms that the Japanese have gone through many of the same transitions as European countries and the United States, but they have nonetheless retained their cultural distinctiveness (Eisenstadt, 1995). While the Japanese have borrowed elements from many other cultures, they have typically "Japanized" them. One example that is

Cross-national Perspectives

The Gender–Poverty Gap in Eight Industrial Countries

The poverty gap between American men and women is well established. For example, in 1991, women in the United States were 30 percent more likely to be poor than men. (Casper et al., 1994). But what is not well known is whether the United States is unusual in this regard. Cross-national research can reveal whether the United States is different from other countries and also, perhaps, help to explain what produces a gender–poverty gap.

Research by Casper et al. (1994) used data from eight industrialized countries—the United States, Canada, Australia, the United Kingdom, West Germany (before unification), Sweden, Italy, and the Netherlands—to study the gender–poverty gap.

The Luxembourg Income Study provided the data for this analysis. This study, originally conducted in 17 countries, provided data on household income, as well as information on household members. The seven countries used in this analysis were selected because the data on marriage, parenthood, and employment were most complete, and they are similar to the United States in terms of economic development.

Poverty, in this study, was defined as having an income that is less than 50 percent of the median income for the nation. (A median income means that half the population has higher and half has lower income; see the section Statistics and Social Research later.) Thus, if the median household income for a nation is $36,000, a household with less than $18,000 income would be considered poor. This is a relative measure of poverty, because it gives an indication of household income "relative to the common standard of living in [the country]" (Casper et al., 1994, p. 596).

The poverty gap in the eight countries is depicted graphically in Figure 2–2 by percent of men and women in poverty and the ratio of women's to men's poverty rates. The United States, for example, has a ratio of 1.41, which means that women in the United States are 41 percent more likely than men to live in poverty. In Australia, with a ratio of 1.34, women are 34 percent more likely than men to live in poverty. As Figure 2–2 shows, the United States has a higher gender–poverty gap than any of the other seven countries. In Sweden, women are *less* likely than men to live in poverty.

Further analysis by these researchers reveals that employment, parenthood, and marital status are the most important factors accounting for the gender–poverty gap in these eight countries. The more that women participate in the labor force, the less the gender–poverty gap. In Sweden, for

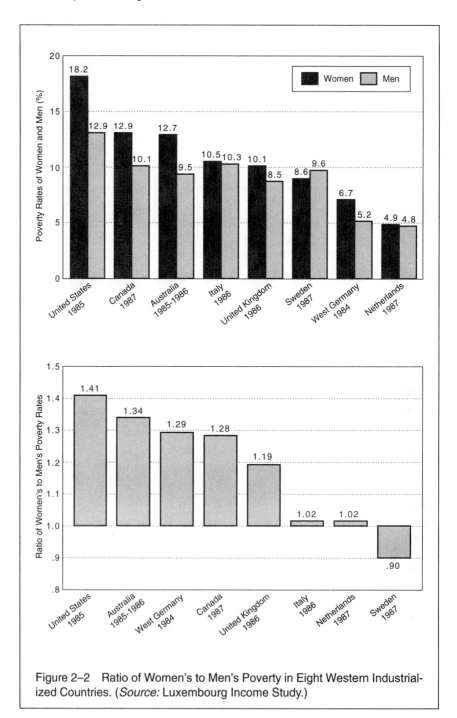

Figure 2–2   Ratio of Women's to Men's Poverty in Eight Western Industrial-ized Countries. (*Source:* Luxembourg Income Study.)

example, women are employed nearly as often as males, and there is no poverty gap. Parenthood, especially unmarried parenthood, also contributes greatly to the gender–poverty gap. With children, women are more likely to be out of the labor force, and thus their potential incomes are lost to the household. Marriage reduces the gender–poverty gap because incomes of two people are more likely to be pooled. Italy, for example, has a relatively low difference in male and female poverty, because the rate of marriage is very high (Casper et al., 1994).

The higher gender–poverty gap in the United States is produced by the same factors as other countries with relatively high gaps: relatively lower employment levels of women, more children, and higher rates of nonmarriage.

Casper, Lynne M., McLanahan, Sara S., and Garfinkel, Irwin. "The Gender–Poverty Gap: What We Can Learn from Other Countries." *American Sociological Review,* Vol. 59, 1994.

familiar to many American sports fans is the game of baseball, which the Japanese borrowed from the United States, but then transformed to fit their cultural ways. Americans who play baseball in Japan must learn that individual performance is not as highly valued as teamwork and team success.

Because the historical–comparative method of social research requires an extensive knowledge of historical conditions in different societies, it is not widely used in contemporary sociology. A similar approach that puts less emphasis on historical processes and more emphasis on collecting quantitative data from different societies is called *cross-national research* (Kohn, 1989a, 1989b).

Cross-national Research

Cross-national research is the collecting of similar kinds of data in two or more nations for comparison. A major example of cross-national research is found in the work of Melvin Kohn and his research associates (Kohn, 1977; Kohn and Schooler, 1983; Miller-Loessi, 1995). Survey research studies of a similar nature were conducted over several years in the United States, Poland, Japan, Italy, and Taiwan. These studies showed that, in each country, the people who were higher in the social stratification system (more education, better jobs, higher incomes) were more likely to value self-direction. In raising their children, they tended to emphasize autonomy and to deemphasize simple obedience to rules. Since similar results were found in several different countries, these researchers concluded that a consistent relationship exists between social stratification and values that adults hold, especially with respect to rearing their children (Kohn, 1989b). (This study will be discussed more fully in Chapter 5.)

Statistics and Sociological Research

Statistics are techniques used to process the numbers produced by research and measurement. Statistics should always help us in some way; if they do not explain or clarify, they are of no use. Basically, statistics will do one of two things: (1) make the communication of information easier or simpler; (2) help us to make certain kinds of decisions. Statistics that help us communicate information about numerical data are called **descriptive statistics.** Statistics that help us to make decisions are called inferential statistics.

Descriptive Statistics

Some of the most useful statistics are those that convey information about many numbers in a simple way—often with only a single number. When an instructor returns an examination to a class and says, "The average grade on the test was 92," he or she is using a single number to convey something about the scores of all the people who took the examination. The class is being told what the mean, the numerical average, is. The **mean** is calculated by adding all the scores together and dividing the sum by the number of people who took the examination. The mean is one type of statistic that is frequently used to say something about the central tendency of a group of numbers.

A second common measure of central tendency is the median. The **median** of the class's examination scores is the score in the center, or middle, of the distribution of scores. Roughly speaking, half of the students in the class would have scores that were higher than the median score, and half would have scores that were lower.

A third, less widely used, measure of central tendency is the mode. The **mode** on a set of examination scores would be the one single score received by the largest number of students.

Measures of Association and Correlation.   Sociologists, as we have seen, are often interested in how different parts of the social world are related to each other. A number of statistical techniques show relationships between variables, and simple percentages are frequently used for this purpose. Let us suppose that, in a study of the relationship between level of education and divorce, we found that 21 percent of the women with less than a high school education had been divorced, but only 10 percent of women with college degrees had been divorced. This comparison of percentages would suggest that level of education is related to divorce.

   Statisticians (some of whom are sociologists) have developed other statistics to summarize, often in a single number, whether and how much two variables are related. A widely used, but fairly complex, measure of relationships is called correlation. **Correlation** is a measure of how much two variables are co-related. When two different variables are measured numerically, they can be correlated. In the example of educational level and divorce, the former can be measured numerically by using the number of years of completed education. Divorce cannot technically be measured numerically because it is an "all or nothing" characteristic. (Sociologists will, however, sometimes use the correlation technique for analyzing this relationship by arbitrarily assigning numbers 0 and 1 to the divorced and nondivorced states, respectively.) Educational level could also be correlated with another measure, such as number of months engaged before marriage. A sample of married people could provide information on their educational level and the length of their engagement before marriage. Every person would then have two measures: number of years of education and number of months engaged.

   We will not go into the complex statistical calculation for correlation here except to say that the product of the appropriate mathematical procedures is a single number. This number can range from -1.00 to $+1.00$. Usually it will be a two-digit decimal fraction preceded by a sign (for example, $-.43$ or $+.61$). This number, called a *correlation coefficient,* will conveniently summarize the degree and the direction of the relationship for anyone who understands correlations, even minimally. For example, if the correlation between educational level and length of engagement is .00 (or near zero), one would probably conclude that no relationship or association exists between these two variables. On the other hand, if the correlation is $+.53$ or $+.61$, one would say that the two variables are positively correlated. An interpretation would be that those people with higher numbers on one of the variables would also generally have higher numbers on the other variable. Persons with long engagements are likely to have high levels of education. Notice that nothing is said about cause and effect. We might reasonably say that people with higher levels of education have longer engagements before marriage because they are more likely to wait until they finish college before marrying, but the correlation value alone does not provide conclusive proof of this assumption. The correlation technique tells us only whether two things are related (co-related) and the direction and degree of that relationship.

Inferential Statistics

Inferential statistics are techniques that assist researchers in making decisions about whether, on the basis of a sample, statements can be made about the population from which the sample was drawn. For example, suppose we find a relationship between two variables in a sample of respondents in a social survey. Although the relationship holds for the sample, there is no certainty that it holds for the total population from which the sample was drawn. Even a randomly drawn sample may not *exactly* reflect the population. This is where statistical tests of inference become useful.

Some statistical tests will provide us with a probability statement that might, in a particular case, tell us something like the following: the chances are 99 out of 100 that the relationship found between two variables in our sample will also be found in the total population. If this probability is the result of the statistical test, we feel confident making an inference about the total population, even if we have studied only a sample from it. We could conclude that the relationship found in the sample is probably true of the total population, since the chances are only 1 in 100 that it would not be.

Summary

Although the research methods used by sociologists are varied and thus reveal the diversity of sociology, all are based on the idea that human behavior can be studied by using a scientific approach. A key element in the scientific approach is empiricism, a reliance on experiencing something with one's senses. Objectivity, a second key element, is both an attitude of value neutrality and a clear description of the research procedures used.

When carrying out social research, sociologists must be concerned about the possible harm they may do to their subjects. In extreme cases they may do physical harm, but the more likely danger is psychological harm. Ethical considerations demand caution when intruding into the lives of research subjects.

The social research process begins with a question. Research questions may come from the personal interests of researchers, current societal developments, or sociological theories. Research hypotheses are derived from reports of previous research or from theories. Concepts are measured by indicators that can be empirically observed. When concepts have been converted into measures they are called variables. Independent variables are those that are thought to produce change in dependent variables.

Experiments are research techniques that are ideally suited for assessing causality. Sociological experiments are classified as field experiments or laboratory experiments. Field experiments are often used to test the effectiveness of social programs or the desirability of proposed government policies. Field experiments are more closely connected with the real world, but laboratory experiments are under the closer control of the researchers.

Replication is the scientific practice of redoing studies and experiments to see if the findings of an original study can be duplicated. A 1981 field experiment on domestic violence, which received wide attention and acceptance, was replicated in other cities, and the results of the replication studies were only partially supportive of the original. This example attests to the importance of replication.

Observational studies, the systematic and purposive observation of human behavior in natural settings, have a long tradition in sociological research. At its most basic level, observational researchers are unnoticed by the people being studied. Participant observation is a form of observational study in which researchers interact with and observe the behavior of those whom they are studying. Participant observers may be involved to varying degrees in the groups and social settings they are studying, sometimes as full-fledged participants, or insiders, but more commonly as outsiders.

Qualitative interviews, or in-depth interviews, are questions asked in face-to-face situations, but are loosely organized and allow the interviewer to probe for new information.

Social surveys often involve random samples of populations. The people selected in samples are questioned, either with questionnaires or through interviews. The two basic forms of surveys are descriptive and explanatory.

Secondary analysis is the use of data collected by other researchers for new and often very different kinds of research questions. Data collected by the government (for example, the census) are often used for secondary analysis.

Historical–comparative research examines the histories of societies and compares either different periods in the history of a single society or the histories of several societies. Cross-national research is the use of survey data collected from two or more nations so that the results can be compared. Cross-national research is more quantitative than classic historical–comparative studies.

Statistical methods used by sociologists are descriptive or inferential. Descriptive statistics convey information about the central tendencies of numerical data and associations or correlations between measures. Inferential statistics are tools that help researchers make decisions about their data when they have drawn samples from larger populations.

Appendix: Statistical Tables

Reading a Statistical Table

Many adolescents engage in risky behavior, a cause for great concern among adults, and especially the parents of teenagers. Risky behaviors include driving while drunk, using drugs, engaging in unprotected sex, having multiple sex partners, carrying firearms, or attempting suicide.

A national sample of 11,631 U.S. high school students has been surveyed and asked about their involvement in risky behaviors (Sosin et al., 1995). Table 2–1 presents data from this study, showing the relationship between having been in one or more fights during the previous 30 days and engaging in risky behaviors. We are using this table as a way of illustrating the proper procedure for reading and understanding a statistical table (Mutchnick and Berg, 1996).

Table 2–1   Percentage of High School Students Reporting Risky Behaviors: All Students and Students Fighting During the Last 30 Days

Risky Behaviors	All Students	Students in One or More Fights in Last 30 Days
Carried a firearm in last 30 days	4.1	25.6
Used cocaine in last 30 days	2.1	13.0
Drunk driving in last 30 days	16.8	38.7
Multiple sex partners during last 3 months	11.6	40.5
Nonuse of condom during last sex	29.1	44.9
Attempted suicide in past 12 months	8.3	24.0

Source: Sosin *et al.,* 1995

The first and most important rule for reading a table is to read the title carefully. Even experienced table readers can get confused if they fail to take the moment necessary to see what the title says. The title of this table first tells us that we will be getting information on the "Percentage of High School Students Reporting Risky Behaviors." Notice that the numbers in the body of the table do not have percentage symbols because the title establishes that these are percentages. The second part of the title informs us that the risky behaviors of two sets of students will be presented: all students and those who report being in one or more fights during the past 30 days.

The second rule for reading a table is to begin at the left side and examine the column headings. The first heading, "Risky Behaviors," identifies the nature of the items listed below it: "Carried a Firearm . . .," "Used Cocaine . . .," and so on. It is customary to call these categories on the left *stubs.*

Moving across the top of the table we see the headings for the columns of percentages in the body. As the title has already informed us, the two headings are for "All Students" and those "Students [who have been] in One or More Fights in the Last 30 Days."

We are now ready to turn to the information in the body of the table. The first number tells us that 4.1 percent of all students carried a firearm in the last 30 days. The next number in the first row tells us that 25.6 percent of the students who had been in a fight had carried a gun in the last 30 days. Students who have been in a fight were six times more likely to carry a gun than all students combined. We can now follow the same procedure for all the other risky behaviors, and a consistent pattern is obvious. Students who engage in fighting are much more likely to engage in various kinds of risky behavior. Fighting, it might be said, is a *marker* for students who are likely to engage in risky behaviors of all types.

An added piece of information can be obtained from this table: the percentage of high school students who engage in various types of risky behavior. Very few students use cocaine (2.1 percent), while not using a condom is much more common (29.1 percent).

CRITICAL THINKING

1. What are the key features of a scientific approach? Why are they important in the study of sociology?
2. Sociologists must retain their objectivity about subjects that they study. If you were a sociologist, about which topics might you have difficulty maintaining a degree of objectivity?
3. Why should social sciences be held to the same rigorous standards of procedural objectivity as natural or biological sciences?
4. Discuss several ethical issues that need to be considered by sociologists when constructing research projects. Assume you are a sociologist interested in researching sexual behavior. Give examples of what you would consider to be ethical and unethical research practices for that topic.
5. Should social researchers be given the same rights of communication confidentiality with their research subjects as lawyers and doctors are given with their clients?
6. Suppose you were a sociologist beginning a research project on race relations in the United States. Develop several hypotheses that you might choose to test. What research methods would be most effective in testing these hypotheses?
7. Why must sociologists, and those who use sociological research, be wary of the statistics they use and see?

3

Culture

In the mountains of the northeastern part of India, there is an area inhabited by 26 native tribes. The 858,000 inhabitants who live in this remote area are so isolated that it takes 7 or 8 days on foot to reach them (Moore, 1992). Few outsiders have been allowed into this area, and the tribes themselves are so separated from each other that they have different languages. In the contemporary world there are relatively few such isolated societies remaining because most have already been changed by the outside world. Even the tribes in this isolated part of the world are starting to change because some of their young people are leaving to be educated in the schools of India. Further changes are being made because satellite-dish antennas are picking up broadcasts from New Delhi and Bombay and bringing them to the people of this region.

But the traditional ways of life persist for many of these people, and their cultures remain, for the time being, intact. In the village of Balek, the people live in bamboo huts built on stilts along the mountain side. They brew an alcoholic beverage that is a cross between beer and cider, and their favorite delicacy is a "crunchy, hard-shelled bug the size of a thumbnail that is eaten alive" (Moore, 1992, p. A23). The religion of these people involves the sacrifice of animals and the worship of the sun and moon. The village has a central meeting and worship hall where the village hunters hang the heads of the animals they have killed. In the past, some of these tribes engaged in head-hunting, and the rows of skulls of some of their victims are still on display.

The central village hall may not be entered by women of the village when they are menstruating. The cultural custom of isolating menstruating women has been found in many societies around the world. The reason for this widespread custom is still being debated, but some scholars believe it is a way of asserting male superiority over females, or simply to emphasize the separate social spheres of men and women (Sanday, 1981).

In this chapter, we will examine the nature of culture as a key feature of social life. While there are some similarities from one culture to another (as with the menstrual taboo), this chapter will also show that every society has its own special customs, its standards of acceptability, its way of life. These reflect what the people of that society believe is acceptable, desirable, and proper. The way of life of a society, or its culture, is a key element of social life, and is the subject of this chapter.

The Importance of Culture

The Meaning of Culture

Culture is the entire complex of ideas and material objects that the people of a society (or group) have created and adopted for carrying out the necessary tasks of collective life (Berger, 1995). As this definition suggests, cultures are human creations, but, of course, people inherit much of their culture from those who created it. In other words, every culture has a history. When children are born into a society they learn the elements of their culture, and they in turn pass them on, probably in some modified form, to those who follow them. Cultures, therefore, are also capable of change.

One convenient way to think about culture is to recognize that the people of every society have an array of tasks to perform and problems to solve. All people must have ways of providing food, clothing, and shelter, ways of producing and caring for children, and ways of solving disputes between members. Perhaps most important, all people must have a way of making life orderly and predictable.

We will present a fuller analysis of the components of culture later in this chapter, but two aspects of culture are important enough to introduce them here. They are *values* and *norms*.

Cultural values can be defined as the standards of desirability, of rightness, and of importance in a society. Among the tribes of northern India described above, the older people tend to value the old traditional ways of doing things, but some of the younger people who have been exposed to modern ways no longer value the old ways. They value progress and change. One young man, who had graduated from college and returned to his village, said, "We don't want to be wild any more" (Moore, 1992, p. A23). **Cultural norms** are rules for what should and should not be done in given situations. In the northern Indian villages, the rule prohibiting women from entering the village hall during menstruation is an example of one of their norms.

A Cultural Explanation of Human Behavior

Culture offers an explanation of human behavior. The people in different societies have different beliefs and customs, and these influence their behavior. An example from Japanese society will illustrate how cultural beliefs influence behavior. Many Japanese believe that a person's blood type influences character and behavior (Sullivan, 1995).

Most Americans do not even know their blood type (A, B, O, or AB), but most Japanese do, and many believe it is an important piece of information about a person. Indeed, it is viewed with some suspicion if a person does not know or will not reveal his or her blood type (Sullivan, 1995). The significance of blood type for many Japanese is perhaps roughly equivalent to the way Americans view astrological signs. Some people believe wholeheartedly, many find it an amusing pastime, while the rest think of it as a superstition.

Among the Japanese, blood types are associated with character traits. For example, type A people are thought to be orderly, law-abiding, fastidious, soft-spoken, fashionable, and calm. On the negative side, type A people are considered picky, selfish, secretive, pessimistic, inflexible, and reckless when drunk. Type A people are best suited to be accountants, librarians, economists, novelists, computer programmers, and gossip columnists (Sullivan, 1995, p. F6).

In Japan, both mate selection and product marketing are often based on blood types. Young people may make some of their decisions about members of the opposite sex on the basis of blood type. One young woman says that she finds out her date's blood type within the first 2 hours, because if he is the wrong type there is no need to waste further time (Sullivan, 1995).

Many products in Japan are marketed with an eye toward blood types. For example, one company marketed soft drinks that came in several flavors according to blood type; type AB was banana flavored and was supposed to reduce stress among the hyperactive AB personality. Recently, a condom maker produced different colors and styles of condoms for different blood types. At least one Tokyo hair salon asks its customers about their blood types in order to cut and style their hair accordingly. In addition, there are key chains, chewing gum, calendars, magazines, and books built around blood types. Merchandisers may be using blood types as a somewhat playful sales gimmick, but the belief in their significance is widespread in Japan and influences a wide array of behavior.

This is but a small example of how a culture can influence human behavior, but throughout this chapter we will see many other examples. First, we will consider some opposing views of human behavior.

Two Competing Views of Human Behavior

Two alternative explanations of human behavior compete with the cultural explanation. First, *human nature* is believed by some people to explain why people do what they do. Second, *sociobiology,* a scientific theory rooted in evolutionary biology, claims that much of human behavior is genetically determined. We will describe each of these alternative explanations of human behavior and show why a cultural explanation is preferable.

Human Nature

Many times one hears people say, "It's just human nature to be selfish, ... or jealous, ... or compassionate, ... or aggressive." Speakers who make these statements seem to believe that these traits, or others, are found in all humans, and thus they explain behavior.

But how useful is human nature as an explanation of behavior? It seems to be a very weak explanation because it is difficult to find any human trait that is universal. Too much variety is found among the people in different societies. Often, it is possible to find societies in which the behavior of people is very different and even completely opposite. An example of extreme differences can be found in an examination of two societies, the Quakers of the United States and the Yanomamo of South America.

Quakers believe in nonviolence and generally behave nonviolently. Their lives are built around these principles, and they rarely engage in aggressive or violent behavior. The Yanomamo, who live in the Amazon rain forest, have such a violent life-style that they have been called "the fierce people" (Chagnon, 1968).

The violent ways of the Yanomamo can be found in all phases of their lives. They are constantly warring with neighboring villages and fighting among themselves. According to data gathered by anthropologists, 44 percent of the Yanomamo men over the age of 25 have killed someone (Rensberger, 1988). In the Yanomamo family, husbands often punish their wives brutally and children are routinely abused.

It is difficult to imagine how a single "human nature" explanation can cover both the Quakers and the Yanomamo. But a second view of human behavior is not dispensed with so easily, for it rests on an established scientific base. Over the last two decades, a biological–evolutionary view of human behavior, called *sociobiology,* has emerged (Wilson, 1975).

Sociobiology.   There is a long history of scientists claiming that biological characteristics influence human behavior (Degler, 1991). The theories have been of various sorts, but in recent decades the theory that has had the most impact is sociobiology. The fundamental idea of **sociobiology** is that human behavior reflects genetically inherited traits. Sociobiologists argue that humans are very much like other species of animals, that is, that human characteristics and behaviors are products of the Darwinian notions of natural selection and evolution. **Natural selection** is the idea that the fittest of any species will survive and spread its favored traits throughout the population (Gould, 1977).

According to this theory, we humans who are alive today have inherited the genetic characteristics that increased the chances of survival among our ancestors. The reasoning of sociobiology goes this way: if a specific trait appeared at some time in the genes of early humans, and that genetic trait made it more likely for the carrier and its offspring to survive, then that trait would more likely be passed on to the next generation. In the long run, through the process of natural selection, the traits that improved chances of survival would be found in the human population. Traits that detracted from survival, or were less advantageous for survival, would disappear or become rare. Sociobiologists conclude from this that any widely observed human behavior must have been beneficial for survival and, therefore, have been passed down genetically (Lumsden and Wilson, 1983).

As an example of the sociobiological approach, we have an attempt to explain the predisposition for human beings to feel love. The basic hypothesis was: "the great majority of women and men are born with a genetic capacity and need for forming durable attachments of an emotional character [love]" (Mellen, 1981, p. 139).

The sociobiological explanation for the human tendency to feel love is stated as follows: When early humans lived by hunting and gathering food, they had to cover a wide geographic area in pursuit of game and in search of other food. Hunting, especially, required speed and mobility. During the time when females were pregnant or were caring for their young, they were relatively immobile and needed assistance. The males, not similarly restricted, could range over large areas in search of food and game. If women and their children were to survive under these conditions, the males had to return with some food for them. Sociobiologists reason that males who were selfish might not return with the food, but if a male were born with a tendency to feel an attachment for the female who bore his child (a tendency to feel love), he would return to the female and child to share his food. If he did so, the child carrying his genes (perhaps including the gene that made him capable of feeling love) would be more likely to survive.

Or consider the opposite scenario—a male who did not have the genetic tendency to feel love for a female. Because this male would probably not return as often to the female and her child, this child might die from lack of food, and the male's genes would not survive to the next generation. In this way, in the course of hundreds of thousands of years, the genes that produced a capacity for love would have survived in the human species (Mellen, 1981).

Many features of this sociobiological description are not proved facts; many may be unprovable. In fact, no one has actually isolated a gene that gives people the capacity to love. We also know very little about the lives of prehistoric humans, so much of the scenario above is simply conjecture. Nevertheless, suppose it were all true. We are still left with the question, "Does it make any difference in our attempt to understand human behavior?" Perhaps all humans do have the capacity for love, but what difference does it make when love is viewed so differently in different cultures? According to an anthropological account, one Yanomamo woman said her husband must care for her because he beat her over the head so often (Harris, 1974). A beating on the head is hardly considered an expression of love in American society.

Furthermore, although Americans believe in entering marriage on the basis of love, many societies consider love before marriage to be irrelevant. Often the bride and groom hardly know each other at the time of marriage, so they would not likely be in love. Why do the cultures of some societies emphasize love as a basis for marriage and other cultures deemphasize or ignore it? This interesting sociological question is one that the sociobiological point of view cannot address. Even if the sociobiological explanation were true (and that is by no means certain), sociobiology often misses interesting and important questions and issues such as why the people in different societies adopt such widely different behaviors (Bock, 1980).

Another way of seeing the power of culture is to observe how the people of every society tend to believe that their way of life is best. We will examine this view next, as we discuss ethnocentrism.

Ethnocentrism

When the ancient Greeks heard people speaking in other languages, the sounds they heard seemed meaningless. To the Greeks, such talking sounded like "bar, bar, bar, bar." Thus they called people with other languages *barbarians* (Ciardi, 1980, p. 18). The Greeks applied this word to all people who came from other societies whom they regarded as uncivilized.

People in all societies tend to think of themselves as the chosen people or, at the very least, as those at the center of humanity. From this view, it is understandable that people of any society would think their ways of doing things were the right ways, and the ways of other people were less right. This attitude is labeled *ethnocentrism*. **Ethnocentrism** is a view held by the people of a society that says that *they* are of central importance in the universe and therefore their way of doing things is the "right" way (Sumner, 1906).

Obviously, not every group of people can be right, since often the customs of one group are totally different from the customs of another. Also, if we had been born into another society, we obviously would have grown up thinking that the norms of that society were right and proper. It is the culture itself that makes things "right."

Cultural Relativism

The study of diverse cultural traditions often helps us to see how different customs can be equally acceptable. This view is the key to an important idea called *cultural relativism.* **Cultural relativism** is an approach that evaluates the behavior of the people of another society, not on the basis of the evaluator's culture but on that culture's own terms.

In an extreme version of cultural relativism, there are no rights and wrongs, only different cultural values and norms. A more moderate version emphasizes the fact that cultures vary, and other people's patterns of behavior are best judged in the context of their own culture. The following example illustrates the point.

Staphorst is a small town in the Netherlands (Newton, 1978). If you were to drive into Staphorst you would find a picturesque community where the people still dress in traditional Dutch clothing, reminiscent more of the time of Rembrandt than of the twentieth century. You might be tempted to photograph these people but, if it were a Sunday, it would be better to refrain, since the people of Staphorst are very religious and dislike having their photographs taken on their special day of worship. Indeed, the Staphorst people take Sunday so seriously that males and females do not spend time together on that day. They even separate their male and female farm animals on Sunday (Newton, 1978).

If you were to stay around Staphorst for a while, you would learn that their Sunday behavior is only a minor reflection of their conservative religious views. The people of Staphorst are 95 percent Protestant (75 percent Calvinist and 20 percent Dutch Reformed). They follow a conservative religious tradition and believe strongly in a literal heaven and hell. They are conservative in other ways, also, rejecting most of the ways of modern Dutch life. (Polio vaccine was resisted until 1971, when the town experienced an epidemic.)

If you were to delve into the courtship and marriage patterns of the people of Staphorst, however, you might be surprised at some of the customs (Gibney, 1948). When a young man of Staphorst becomes interested in a young woman, he gives her a signal by trying to snatch the rain cape she keeps tied to her waist. If the young woman is interested, she probably helps him succeed. The actual courtship begins when the young man starts coming to the young woman's house (which he will do on Monday, Wednesday, and Friday evenings) after she has retired to her bedroom. Even though the young woman's parents are in a nearby room and can obviously hear what is going on, the young man will crawl through her bedroom window. He will spend the night with her but leave before morning. Quite understandably, this practice often leads to the young woman's becoming pregnant. When this happens, it is time for the two young people to marry, which they do shortly thereafter.

To summarize the courtship system of Staphorst, young people *must* have premarital sex and the young woman *must* be pregnant before marriage is possible. In our society and in many others, premarital pregnancy is typically viewed as an

Cross-cultural Perspectives

American Culture as a Foreign Culture

It is very difficult to see one's own culture as an outsider might see it. Many generations of American students in anthropology and sociology classes have had an outsider's glimpse of their own culture when they were asked to read a classic essay by Horace Miner on "body rituals" practiced in the *Nacirema* culture (Miner, 1956). Miner described the practices and rituals of the Nacirema with respect to the body. For example, he described a daily ritual associated with the mouth as follows:

> The daily body ritual performed by everyone includes a mouth-rite.... It was reported to me that the ritual consists of inserting a small bundle of hog hairs into the mouth, along with certain magical powders, and then moving the bundle in a highly formalized series of gestures (Miner, 1956, p. 504).

Miner described other rituals performed by the men and women of the Nacirema, beginning with a ritual practiced only by the males: "This part of the rite involves scraping and lacerating the surface of the face with a sharp instrument," And one practiced by the females: "Special women's rites are performed only four times during each lunar month, but what they lack in frequency is made up in barbarity. As part of this ceremony, women bake their heads in small ovens for about an hour" (Miner, 1956, p. 505).

Miner's essay goes on to describe other strange customs of the Nacirema in a similar fashion, until almost every reader eventually guesses that the name *Nacirema* when spelled backward is *American*. The customs described above are the American customs of brushing one's teeth, shaving, and having one's hair done.

This essay on the *Nacirema* allowed readers to look at their own culture as outsiders, even if only for a few moments. But there are many Americans today who have the actual experience of seeing their native culture as if they were outsiders. These are the Americans who have, for one reason or another, lived in a foreign country for a long and continuous period of time. When they reenter American society they often see this culture from a new perspective; for them, American culture is like a foreign culture (Austin, 1986).

Many Americans have occupations requiring them to live in other countries for extended periods of time. Included are foreign service and military personnel, United Nations specialists, employees of multinational corporations, members of the Peace Corps, relief organizations, religious groups, and educators. Even students who study abroad may be gone long enough to experience some "reentry" experience and reactions.

Many people who have lived in other countries for long periods of time report experiencing stress and a period of readjustment when they return to their home culture.

One problem for the reentrants stems from the fact that cultures change while one is gone, even for a relatively short period of time. Cultures are not static, especially that part called *popular culture.* Popular culture includes entertainment and entertainers, television shows, movies, music, clothing styles, and even language (slang is a special part of popular culture). Many details of popular culture are likely to be different from when one left, even a year or so earlier.

When they return to their home culture, people may feel "left out," not even fully understanding conversations among their friends and family. "'We didn't feel as though we understood what was happening...sometimes we felt as if we had returned from outer space!'" (Koehler, 1986, p. 91).

Many people who spend time in another culture find themselves more critical of their native culture when they return home. "When you come back from overseas you see America as a foreigner does. You view America through a sharper lens, and are able to pick up the strengths and weaknesses of the country more clearly" (Sobie, 1986, p. 97). In the words of one returnee from Germany, "'When I came back to the states, I found Americans shallow and plastic...'" (Sobie, 1986, p. 97). Another woman describes her feelings about American wastefulness: " 'We had a water shortage on Okinawa and it disturbed us greatly to see how water was wasted here'"(Koehler, 1986, p. 91).

When returning Americans see their own culture as a foreign culture, they are likely to lose some ethnocentrism. Having seen their culture more objectively, they are less likely to believe that their way of life is the right way.

Austin, Clyde N. (ed.). *Cross-cultural Reentry: A Book of Readings.* Abilene, Tex.: Abilene Christian University Press, 1986.
Koehler, Nancy. "Re-entry Shock." In Clyde N. Austin (ed.), *Cross-cultural Reentry: A Book of Readings.* Abilene, Tex.: Abilene Christian University Press, 1986.
Miner, Horace. "Body Ritual Among the Nacirema." *American Anthropologist, 58,* 1956.
Sobie, Jane Hipkins. "The Culture Shock of Coming Home Again." In Clyde N. Austin (ed.) *Cross-cultural Reentry: A Book of Readings.* Abilene, Tex.: Abilene Christian University Press, 1986.

unfortunate occurrence. Indeed, often people who are most religious are especially apt to be upset by a premarital pregnancy. Yet here we find the people of Staphorst, who are extremely religious, actually requiring pregnancy before marriage.

It would be difficult to argue that the acceptance of premarital sex and pregnancy by the people of Staphorst makes them "immoral." Judged by their standards, this practice is accepted as both moral and appropriate. Viewed from the perspective of cultural relativism, we as outsiders would accept the customs of the Staphorst people as part of their particular way of life.

The Staphorst example shows us that, if we take the time to look at the cultural traditions of other people, we can be more sensitive to the integrity of other cultures. In other words, we will be more inclined toward cultural relativity and less inclined toward ethnocentrism.

Cultural relativism, however, does not suggest that one must invariably accept the practices of other people regardless of what they might be. For example, when the Nazi government of Germany in the 1930s put into slavery or killed entire categories of people (Jews, gypsies, and the mentally retarded), one could not regard this phenomenon as just another example of cultural diversity. The idea of cultural relativity implies greater tolerance for cultural differences but not a blind acceptance of all forms of human behavior.

The Components of Culture

Earlier we defined culture as the entire complex of ideas and material objects shared by the people of a society. We are now ready to look more systematically at the major components of culture. We begin with a consideration of symbols.

People who live in the same culture generally understand each other, because they share the same symbols. **Symbols** are words, gestures, and objects that communicate meaning when people agree on and recognize what they represent. Every symbol has a social character because a group of people agrees on the symbol's meaning (Charon, 1988; Meltzer, 1978). As we noted in our consideration of symbolic interaction theory in Chapter 1, shared symbols are used by the people of any given society to communicate with each other and to create a certain order and predictability in daily life. Symbols can be divided into two types: nonverbal and verbal.

Nonverbal Symbols

In historical movies, when the Lord and Lady of the Manor ride through the village in their carriage, the tradesmen and shopkeepers often tip their caps and bow slightly. The symbolism of tipping one's hat to someone of high status is unmistakable: the lower-status person is showing respect for the high-status person. This act is an illustration of a **nonverbal symbol,** a physical display that has social meaning.

In a time when men wore hats, they used to tip their hats when meeting women acquaintances on the street; this gesture was a nonverbal symbol of their respect. Tipping the hat as an act of respect is rarely seen today, but a vestige of this custom can still be seen in some instances. When the president of the United States steps out of his helicopter, he usually exchanges salutes with the military personnel in attendance. The military salute is an evolved version of tipping one's hat and is initiated by the lower-status person and returned by the higher-status person. It is a nonverbal symbolic act, a sign of respect for someone in a higher social position.

Another example of using nonverbal symbols to show respect for people of higher status can be seen among students in many military settings (for example, West Point), who come to attention when their instructors enter the room. They are seated only when told to do so. Coming to one's feet in the presence of someone of a higher status is a common display of respect found in many societies.

However, the meanings of nonverbal symbols are by no means the same from one society to another. Nonverbal symbols can sometimes have exactly opposite meanings in two different societies. In the United States, audiences and fans will often show their approval of performances by whistling. In Europe, however, audiences and fans whistle as a way of demonstrating disapproval and dissatisfaction.

The kiss, another nonverbal symbol, also varies widely in its meaning and use from one society to another. American male political leaders often have to brace themselves when they meet political leaders from the Middle East, some European countries, or Russia, because a common greeting among men in these countries is to exchange kisses on the cheeks. In U.S. society, kisses on the cheek between men and women are used as a way of greeting friends and acquaintances, but men do not usually exchange kisses unless they are close relatives—fathers and sons and brothers may kiss after having been separated for some time.

The kiss on the lips between lovers is not as natural as it may seem. The lip kiss is said to have been invented by the people of ancient India, although the earliest Indian records (about 2000 B.C.) indicate that their prior custom was a nose or "sniff" kiss (Pike, 1976). By the time the famous Indian manual of sex and love, the *Kama Sutra,* was written in the fourth century, the lip kiss was well established. The practice of kissing with the lips spread westward to Persia, Syria, Greece, Italy, and eventually to the countries that make up Northern Europe. For Americans, who inherited their culture from these European countries, the lip kiss between romantic partners has always been an expression of love and affection. In many societies, however, lip kissing between lovers was unknown until it was introduced by explorers, traders, and missionaries from the West. According to reports from these observers, the people of most African societies did not kiss on the lips, nor did the New Zealand Maoris, the Australian aborigines, the Papuans, Tahitians, or other South Sea Islanders. It is said that the Chinese considered kissing vulgar because it reminded them of cannibalism. Among Eskimo tribes of the Arctic, the custom was for lovers to rub their noses together (Pike, 1976).

In contemporary Japan, kissing in public, even a greeting kiss, is still considered inappropriate by many people (Reid, 1994). The traditional greeting for friends, spouses, or lovers in Japan is a smile and polite bow. Kissing in a public place, especially if the kiss is passionate, is considered by many Japanese to be shameful or a sign of weakness (Reid, 1994, p. A13). Nonetheless, the young people of Japan are breaking away from the traditional prohibitions, and kissing in public is becoming more common.

Lip kissing has spread to most societies from its Indo-European origins. This spread of a cultural custom from one society to another is called **cultural diffusion.**

Nonverbal symbols include many other things besides the physical acts performed by people. Many physical objects are also endowed with symbolic meaning. Flags, emblems, insignias, and coats-of-arms are some familiar examples of objects that have special meaning for people (Gusfield and Michalowicz, 1984). These objects are displayed on homes, automobiles, and clothing as a way of conveying messages to other people. In recent years the makers of clothing have adopted the practice of placing their names, logos, and trademarks on the outside of clothing. The successes of clothing lines carrying these symbols suggest that aesthetics is not the only reason for a brand name to be written on the outside of one's shirt, blouse, or pants. It takes only a little sociological imagination to see that recognizable names, logos, or trademarks send out a social message for the observers. Indeed, many different types of clothing convey messages to observers. Scientists, some of whom never go near a laboratory, nonetheless don their laboratory jackets as a symbol of their status as scientists (Joseph, 1986).

Verbal Symbols and Language

Although the nonverbal symbols of a culture are often interesting, it is the verbal symbols that have the most sociological significance. **Verbal symbols** are any verbal utterances that are part of the spoken or written language of a society. The language system shared by the people of a society serves as one of its most important social bonds. But more than that, language influences the way people of the same culture perceive reality.

The ability to learn and use verbal symbols is undoubtedly the most extraordinary ability that human beings possess, and using words and language is a critical element in people's social and cultural lives. At an early age, humans can learn hundreds—and then thousands—of different symbols and can use them to communicate with other people. Not only do humans learn words, but they also learn the rules of grammar and sentence structure that are characteristic of their particular language. English-speaking children, even as toddlers, learn to add an *s* to the end of a noun when they want to speak of more than one object. We find it humorous when small children say "mouses" instead of mice, but they are simply following a generalized rule that, in all likelihood, no one has explicitly taught them.

In the News

The Importance of Symbols in Politics

The verbal and nonverbal symbols of politics have always been important. In the United States, the donkey symbolizes the Democratic party and the elephant the Republican, even though the origins of these animal symbols have long since been forgotten by all but a few Americans.

Each political campaign produces a new set of symbols by which the parties and candidates attempt to influence the voters. Television has been particularly important in the regard. Many people believe that Barry Goldwater's bid for the presidency in the 1960s was thwarted by a television commercial that implied that he would blow up the world with nuclear weapons if he were elected president. The television image seen by American voters was that of a little girl picking a flower while a mushroom cloud appeared in the background. In the 1980s, a similar fate befell presidential candidate Michael Dukakis when a television commercial depicted a criminal being released from prison. The narrative described how a prisoner named Willie Horton was released from prison in Dukakis's state, and how this paroled criminal went on to terrorize and rape a woman in Maryland.

But words are even more important than visual symbols in political campaigns. Politicians have probably always tried to associate positive words with their own campaigns and negative words with those of their opponents. In the past, the best politicians probably used intuition and good judgment in their selection of effective words and symbols, but today this is not always left to chance.

A recent news story describes how the Republican members of Congress were carefully schooled in their use of words as they prepared for a congressional debate on Medicare (Weisskopf and Maraniss, 1995). As part of the Republican plan to balance the federal budget, they wanted to reduce Medicare expenditures by $270 billion over the following 7 years. Yet the Republicans had to be careful about their rhetoric, since Medicare provides health care for 33 million elderly Americans, an age group that regularly votes and might be expected to oppose any cuts in their benefits. Therefore, the Republican leadership enlisted Linda DiVall, a political consultant, who advised their members about what kinds of words could and could not be used in the upcoming debate.

DiVall told the Republicans, "Do not say *changing* Medicare" (Weisskopf and Maraniss, 1995, p. A26), because her research had found that elders got nervous about the word *change.* Further words that should be avoided in discussions about Medicare were *cut, cap,* and *freeze,* again because older citizens viewed these words as negative. On the other hand, focus groups with the elderly found that they felt much more comfortable with the word *preserve,* and DiVall suggested that the legislation be called the Medicare

Preservation Act (Weisskopf and Maraniss, 1995, p. A26). After carefully testing a variety of words, the Republican leadership settled on three words and urged their members to say that "Republicans want to preserve, protect, and improve Medicare" (Weisskopf and Maraniss, 1995, p. A26). For maximum impact, these words were to be said in precisely that order.

The Republicans' second word-use strategy emerged out of the annual report of the Medicare board, which concluded that Medicare's hospital trust fund faced bankruptcy by the year 2002. This allowed Republicans to say that their proposed cuts in Medicare "were saving Medicare from bankruptcy" (Weisskopf and Maraniss, 1995, p. A26). Throughout the congressional debate and in numerous news conferences, this statement was made again and again.

The Democrats, on the other hand, developed a similar litany, which they too invoked at every opportunity. President Clinton said time and again that he would not approve a budget bill that harmed "children, the elderly, the environment, or education." Probably, these words were also selected because they had been found to resonate positively with citizens. These examples show the importance of symbols and emphasize that in contemporary politics the selection of words and symbols has become a highly developed art.

Weisskopf, Michael, and Maraniss, David. "Republican Leaders Win Battle by Defining Terms of Combat." *Washington Post,* Oct. 29, 1995.

Small children hear the plural form used for many nouns and then, quite reasonably, adopt the rule as a way of using the language properly.

The capacity to learn symbols, as well as the rules for using them, allows humans to store and transmit information, thoughts, and ideas with great ease. This ability gives language its particular importance as a carrier of culture. Through language we share not just the names for things but also the rules and values that shape and influence how we relate to these things. An example of this principle can be found in some recent controversies surrounding the rights and responsibilities of biological fathers.

In American society the term *biological father* is important; a biological father has certain rights and responsibilities with regard to any children he produces. However, in recent years new reproductive technologies have allowed women to conceive babies by being impregnated with the sperm of male donors. This practice has raised questions and created problems in some cases about the rights of the "biological father." In some cases the sperm donors have claimed their rights as biological fathers. For Americans this raises a perplexing question because sperm donors would not ordinarily have rights to a child, but a biological father (which the donor seems to be) does (Edwards, 1991).

In some societies the notion of a biological father does not have the same meaning and significance as it does for Americans. For example, a few societies exist where two or more men are married to the same woman.[1] In such a case, there is often no way to determine which husband is the biological father. In one such society in the foothills of the Himalayas, the lack of concern about the biological father extends to cases where wives become pregnant while visiting their home villages. The pregnancy is accepted (even welcomed) by the woman's husbands, and the infant is considered theirs. Apparently, the biological father is of no importance and has no rights to the child (Zorsa, 1982).

Americans might have a difficult time understanding how these Himalayan people could be unconcerned about the actual biological father and about his rights and responsibilities. But again, the reason is that Americans cannot easily ignore the social meanings attached to the term *biological father.* The words and symbols shared by the people of a society are important not simply because they convey information but also because they carry social rules and values.

The Sapir–Whorf Hypothesis. The words of any language seem to be symbols for elements that exist in the physical and social worlds. Clouds exist in the physical world, so a word has to be created so that we can refer to them. But another way to see the relationship between words and the physical and social worlds is to regard language as *shaping and influencing* what we see and perceive.

The idea that language shapes our perception of reality was developed by Edward Sapir and his student Benjamin Whorf in the 1930s; it is usually referred to as the **Sapir–Whorf hypothesis** (McCurdy and Spradley, 1979). This idea can be illustrated by observing how the people of some societies give to certain objects in their environment many different names with precise and detailed meanings. Among the Eskimos the constant presence of snow and its importance in their lives is reflected in their language. The Kobuk Eskimos of northeastern Alaska have many different words for types and conditions of snow, including *snow falling on the ground, falling snow, swirling or drifting snow, and snow that collects horizontally on trees* (Boas, 1911; Williams and Major, 1984).

When a language system has many different words to represent variable aspects of the same object, it enables people to have much more complicated perceptions of that part of reality. Most of us have only one word for snow, and thus we do not usually make distinctions among different types of snow. However, avid skiers do make distinctions between *powder* and *machine-made* snow, and they also have special words for various snow surfaces. These words make skiers more sensitive to variations in snow, supporting the hypothesis that language shapes our perception of reality.

---

[1]This form of marriage is called *polyandry.* For a more complete description of marriage, including polyandry, see Chapter 11.

An even more exotic language system has developed in the surfing world, where an entire language system called "surfspeak" has evolved (Bishop, 1991). While the language of surfers includes novel words for everyday nonsurfing matters, the language becomes especially exotic when the focus is on the surf and waves. Surfers have many terms to describe waves according to their size, character, and qualities. A "double-overhead," for example, is a wave that looks from the shore as if it is twice the height of someone riding it. In actuality, a double-overhead is usually about 8 feet high. A triple-overhead is 10 feet (Finnegan, 1992, p. 51). While these surfer terms for wave heights are relatively clear and meaningful, even to an outsider, only surfers are likely to understand terms such as "gnarly," "suckout," and "funkdog" (Finnegan, 1992, p. 44).

Knowledge and Beliefs

Knowledge and beliefs, taken together, constitute a body of information created by the people of a society that influences behavior. Knowledge is presumed to be verifiable information, while beliefs are presumed to be difficult to verify. In practice, however, these forms of information are frequently interchangeable. Consider, for example, the following four statements about the sun:

- The sun is a god and should be worshipped.
- The sun is our primary source of heat and light.
- Sunbathing, which leads to a deep tan, is healthy for humans.
- Direct exposure to the sun over a period of time may produce skin cancer.

Which of these statements are knowledge and which are beliefs? Most of us would agree that the first statement is a belief, while the second is a factual statement and, therefore, knowledge. Statements 3 and 4, however, are more troublesome. Some of us think that three is knowledge and four is only a belief, while others think the opposite is true. Furthermore, a true believer in a sun god would think it ridiculous to doubt the validity of the first statement. Knowledge and beliefs are not as easy to disentangle as one might suppose. An analysis of our reactions to this series of statements about the sun reveals the cultural nature of knowledge and beliefs. Those statements that we believe to be valid or true will influence how we behave. From a cultural viewpoint, knowledge and beliefs are accepted by substantial numbers of people in a society, and therefore shape general behavior. If we are to judge from the number of people who seek out beaches and swimming pools each summer, working assiduously at getting suntans, most Americans still seem to believe that a suntan is healthy (or at least attractive).

However, knowledge and beliefs in every society undergo continuous change. As knowledge and beliefs change, behavior also changes. Even today, some people have modified their views about suntanning and have changed their suntanning practices. It is ironic that, if Americans begin to shield themselves from the sun at the beach or the swimming pool, their behavior will parallel the behavior of Americans a century ago. In that era, women in particular kept their faces, arms, and legs shielded from the sun, not because of a fear of skin cancer but because a tanned skin was associated with laborers and peasants whose work exposed them to the full day's sun.

We return now to what many regard as the key or primary component of culture: cultural values, or simply values. In comparison with knowledge and belief that focus on *what is,* values are related to what *should be.*

Values

We noted earlier that values are a society's standards of desirability, of rightness, and of importance. Values are expressions of what is good or bad, beautiful or ugly, pleasant or unpleasant, appropriate or inappropriate. Cultural values are shared by a substantial number of people in a society and therefore influence the behavior of most people. The social rules governing behavior (called norms) are generally consistent with, or reflections of, cultural values.

Although it is possible to identify cultural values, not everyone in a society holds exactly the same values. Individual variation suggests the notion of personal values. **Personal values** are the values individuals use to make decisions about their personal lives and about the ways in which they respond to public issues. Personal values, like cultural values, deal, not with the trivia of life, but with fundamental and important aspects of our social lives. It is not a value to prefer the music group U2 or the movies of Jodie Foster, although selecting any of them could perhaps reflect a more basic value. Personal values are likely to influence our occupational choices, our decisions about marriage mates (or about marriage itself), and our views about politics. Personal values influence our reactions to public issues: for example, our choice of a political party or our views on international relations, the environment, medical practices, and so on.

Values are not neutral; they are positively or negatively charged. Cultural and personal values can also vary in degree from very strong to very weak. Some values are more important, more pervasive, and more influential than others. Later, in our discussion of American cultural values, we will look for our most important ones.

Values vary from society to society. What one group of people considers desirable may be viewed as undesirable by another group. For example, in our society a high value is placed on youth, beauty, and vigor. Many people make strenuous efforts to remain youthful in appearance. Health clubs, weight-loss spas, cosmetic surgery facilities, the clothing industry, and many related businesses thrive on the desire of Americans to stay young looking. In other societies, youth is not so highly valued. In many societies around the world, older people are considered wise and valued advisors.

Engaging in competition in order to win is another value not shared by the people of all societies. Americans generally believe that winning is much better than losing, and that it is inappropriate to play a game without trying to win. However, among the Tangu people of New Guinea, winning is not the object of their game, *Taketak*. *Taketak* involves spinning around dried fruit rinds ("tops") into masses of stakes that have been driven into the ground. Players from each of two teams take turns spinning the tops in the palms of their hands and throwing them into the masses of stakes, trying to hit as many stakes as possible. Stakes that have been touched are removed. The object of the game is not to have one team "win" by hitting all the stakes, but to have both teams hit exactly the same number of stakes, at which time the game ends. Ending in a tie expresses one of the primary values of the Tangu culture—the notion of moral equality among all persons (Burridge, 1957).

While we have already touched on some American cultural values, we now examine more systematically the dominant values in American society.

Dominant Values of American Society

Observers and social analysts have tried since the earliest days of American history to identify the dominant values of the people who settled on the land that is now the United States (de Tocqueville, 1961; de Crevecoeur, 1782/1981). The effort continues into the present, as contemporary sociologists try to isolate dominant values held by most people in the United States today (Bellah et al., 1985; Berger, 1994; Gans, 1988). It is interesting to note that some of the dominant American values observed in the earliest days of this society still prevail today. The most prominent among these is the way Americans value individualism.

Individualism. **Individualism** is the concept behind the special importance that Americans attach to the rights, freedoms, and responsibilities of every person. Individual rights and freedoms and individual responsibility are key features of the U.S. political philosophy that has its roots in the Judeo-Christian religious tradition. Americans believe that individuals have a fundamental responsibility for their own lives, and their successes or failures result from their own efforts and actions. This *belief* in individual responsibility leads directly to the *value* of individualism—the freedom of every person to do, think, say, and believe what he or she wants. Naturally, no individual has a right to harm other people or to infringe on their rights, but aside from those limitations, individuals have the freedom to lead their lives as they wish.

The spirit of American individualism is expressed in the words of a California man, a top-level manager in a large corporation:

> I guess I feel like everybody on this planet is entitled to have a little bit of space . . . one of the things that makes California such a pleasant place to live, is people by and large aren't bothered by other people's value systems as long as they don't infringe upon your own. . . . if you've got the money, honey, you can do your thing as long as your thing doesn't destroy someone else's property, or interrupt their sleep, or bother their privacy, that's fine. (Bellah, 1985, pp. 6–7).

Personal Control.   Also a part of individualism, and closely related to personal freedom, is the notion of personal control. **Personal control** means that individuals cannot be made to do things they do not want to do by social, political, or economic forces. In concrete terms, a person has

> the right to be neighborly or to ignore the people next door. It is the ability to be distant from incompatible relatives and to be with compatible friends instead; to skip unwanted memberships in church or union; to vote for candidates not supported by parents or spouses or not to vote at all; and to reject unwelcome advice or demands for behavior change from spouses, employer, or anyone else (Gans, 1988, p. 3).

Americans value the right to be in control of their own lives.

Not only do Americans believe they have a right to control their lives, but they are confident that they can do so and are optimistic about meeting and overcoming every challenge (Spindler and Spindler, 1983). Again this idea is expressed in the words of the California corporation manager who said, "Given open communication and the ability to think problems out, most problems can be solved" (Bellah et al., 1985, p. 7).

Hard Work, Success, and Personal Achievement.   Americans also place a high value on work, personal achievement, and success. These values are certainly found in the occupational world, where most people (especially males in our society) act them out. The emphasis on work and success often becomes so important that people sometimes forget why they are working and striving to succeed. These three powerful values are pervasive in American life. Indeed, they extend into many areas of life beyond the work world. Some observers note that Americans work even when they are engaging in leisure-time activities (Kando, 1980; Gunter and Gunter, 1980). Sports are no longer games but highly organized, serious competitions. Travel becomes a ceaseless driving marathon to see how many miles can be covered in a day, how many "points of interest" can be seen in a week. Childrearing is often measured more in terms of success and achievement than experienced as the joy of being with a child. Parents feel that they have "done a good job" when their children achieve good grades, win the most-popular-student award, make the football team or cheerleading squad, or graduate with honors.

Closely related to success is the value of materialism. **Materialism** is a preoccupation with acquiring more and more possessions and property. Sometimes the emphasis on acquiring cars, houses, video and sound systems, and recreational equipment is simply called greed. But material things are acquired for reasons other than the pleasure they give; possessions are also an indication of status. The term **conspicuous consumption** (Veblen, 1899) is often used to describe the American tendency to acquire things simply to display them.

Rationality.   One important additional value of American society is rationality (Kalberg, 1980; Ritzer, 1983; Brubaker, 1984). **Rationality** as a value emphasizes the importance of setting goals and objectives and then achieving these goals in the most efficient way possible. Rationality reaches its peak when it is possible to calculate exactly which procedure will achieve an objective most quickly and with the least expenditure of effort.

Although the value of rationality has characterized much of the Western world in the last several centuries, it has a special prominence in the United States. Almost every part of life in the United States is in some way marked by an emphasis on efficiency and effectiveness. As a result, nearly everything is produced with an eye toward minimizing time and cost, and maximizing output and productivity.

McDonaldization: Rationality in Action.   There is no better way to see the importance of rationality in our everyday lives than to look closely at a familiar part of our society: the McDonald's fast-food restaurant chain. McDonald's is built on the principles of rationality—*efficiency, predictability, control,* and *quantification* (Ritzer, 1996a).

The McDonald's system offers us efficiency by getting us from being hungry to being satisfied (or at least no longer hungry) in the shortest period of time. Because both the customers and the management value the speed with which food can be delivered and eaten, the restaurants offer a limited, simple menu with food prepared and served in assembly-line fashion. While not noted by most customers, the speedy service offered is even more important for the restaurant than for the customer. It is in the restaurant's interests to move the customers in and out as rapidly as possible. To ensure this efficiency, the seating is made intentionally hard so that customers will not linger after finishing their meal (Luxenberg, 1985). Some McDonald's establishments go beyond that subtle encouragement, however, and post signs stating that customers may spend no longer than 20 minutes in a booth or at a table.

Predictability is also an aspect of the McDonald's system. Customers know almost exactly how they will be greeted at McDonald's or any other familiar fast-food restaurant. For years, the customers at Roy Rodgers' restaurants heard "Howdy partner" when they approached the counter (Ritzer, 1996a). In almost every other fast-food restaurant, the counter staff is well rehearsed to deliver a welcoming script.

More importantly, it is the food in fast-food restaurants that is predictable. The Big Mac or Egg-McMuffin we get in Kansas City will be the same as the one we get in downtown Miami, or in a shopping mall in Portland, Oregon (or, for the international traveler, in downtown Amsterdam or Moscow). The Big Mac or Egg McMuffin may not be gourmet eating, but it will be dependably acceptable as food. The predictability of McDonald's food is a result of the high level of control exercised over the preparation of the food and the routine measurement and quantification of all aspects of the process.

Control is another principle of rationality and, in the case of McDonald's, refers especially to the *substitution of nonhuman technology for human judgment.* One of the earliest technological developments at the McDonald's restaurants was a French-fry machine that determined precisely when the fries were done to perfection. The cooking of the French fries was not to be left to the judgment of a busy or disinterested worker. In any McDonald's (as well as in most other fast-food restaurants) the soft-drink and milkshake dispensers automatically measure the precise, predetermined amounts that go into the paper cups.

Quantification, the exact measurement of every aspect of the process, is another feature of a completely rationalized system. When you eat a McDonald's hamburger you can be quite sure that exactly 19 percent of it will be fat, or, if you order the new "light" burger, it will be only 9 percent fat. Potatoes will be sliced so that each french fry is exactly nine thirty-seconds of an inch wide. Thirty-two slices of cheese, no more, no less, will be cut from a pound of cheese. Everything is measured and timed in the McDonald's system; the numbers are precise and unvarying.

The success of the McDonald's system, has, of course, been imitated by fast-food restaurants throughout the food-service industry (Hardees, Arby's, Pizza Hut, Taco Bell, and many others). More important, the principles of rationality as employed by the McDonald's system have now become pervasive throughout businesses and the service industries of society. The vice chairman of Toys "Я" Us wants to be thought of "as a sort of McDonald's of toys." Jiffy-Lube, Midas Muffler, H & R Block, Pearle Vision Centers, Kampgrounds of America (KOA), Kinder Care, and Nutri-System all reflect the principles of rationality so successfully introduced by McDonald's. Even the services of lawyers and doctors (McDocs) can be obtained from an efficient, rationalized system.

The principles of rationality, as exemplified by McDonald's, have now been adopted throughout U.S. society and in many other societies of the world. For this reason, one of the authors of this text has labeled this phenomenon the "McDonaldization of society" (Ritzer, 1996a).

Norms

As we have previously noted in this chapter, norms are another major component of culture. While values are the general guidelines for evaluating behavior in society, norms deal with more specific situations and circumstances. We have defined norms as the rules for what one should or should not do in given situations (Williams, 1970, p. 442).

William Graham Sumner (1906) was one of the earliest sociologists to address the norms, or rules, of society. Sumner made the distinction between folkways and mores. **Folkways** are rules that generally govern everyday conduct. Violations of those rules usually bring no serious repercussions. The eating rules of a society often fall into the category of folkways. For example, eating an entire dinner with a spoon would be considered odd behavior for an adult, but it would not be a violation that calls for punishment.

Mores (pronounced *mor-ays*), by comparison, are rules relating to much more serious behaviors. Mores involve the moral standards of the society. Thus violations of the mores will result in severe punishments (often called **sanctions**) for violators. Stealing, robbing, killing, and espionage are considered to be immoral acts and are often punished severely.

Frequently, the rules that a society considers important are written into **laws** by the government. When norms are made into laws, the government takes on responsibilities for enforcing the rules. Many laws reflect the mores of the society.

An illustration of the relationship between mores and laws can be found in the many towns and counties in the United States where business is prohibited on Sundays. These laws, called *blue laws,* reflect a time when Sunday business was considered immoral. Today, some of these laws remain in effect, although most Americans do not consider shopping on Sunday immoral. This example shows that laws often reflect the norms of a society, but not invariably.

Variations in Following Norms. Although norms are the rules of behavior in a society, not everyone follows the norms at all times. One reason is simply a *lack of knowledge* about certain norms. Some people might not know what the rules are. Such is often the case with newcomers to a society, as illustrated by the immigrants in Israel who were unfamiliar with the norms that surround bus riding there. An Israeli bus driver described their plight:

> They don't know how to behave. They don't know what it means to stand in line; they haggle about the fare as if they were in the market; sometimes they even jump through the windows. (Toren, 1973, p. 103)

Faced with such violations of the norms, the driver may take the role of teacher, educating the immigrants about the norms of bus riding:

> The driver may have to convince these passengers that it is not customary to cook and eat on the bus. Less dramatic is the need to explain the basic rules of the game—that fares are fixed and have to be paid, that buses run according to a time schedule, and that the driver has to comply with traffic regulations. (Toren, 1973, p. 109)

Sometimes people are familiar with a norm, but they *do not accept it or choose not to follow it.* For example, although the norm of tipping for service in restaurants is generally understood in the United States, some people tip only when they consider the service to be of high quality. They do not accept the norm of routine tipping. (Some norms are easier to reject than others because penalties for rejection are not always severe.)

Ideal versus Real Culture

Sociologists also make a distinction between the ideal and real cultures, (Berger, 1995). The **ideal culture** reflects the values and norms that most people of a society are aware of and accept. The **real culture** reflects what people actually do in the conduct of their everyday lives, even though it may differ from the ideal culture.

An illustration of the distinction between the ideal and real cultures concerns a dominant American value discussed earlier: individualism. This value is undoubtedly supported by the vast majority of Americans, and it does influence behavior in the society. However, there are limits to how much individualism is allowed in the real world, even by those who accept the ideal of individual freedom. If an individual who is suffering from a fatal illness wishes to commit suicide, many people object strongly. Dr. Jack Kevorkian has been the subject of public outrage and state legislation because he has openly assisted people who want to end their lives. Americans place a value on individualism, as an ideal, but in real-life situations, most do not give an individual the right to end his or her life.

Material Culture, Technology, and Cultural Lag

The definition of culture presented earlier included both the "ideas and material objects that the people of a society have created. . . ." So far we have devoted most of our attention to cultural ideas, but now we will focus directly on the material objects of culture. **Material culture** includes all the artifacts, objects, and tools that are used in some way by the members of a particular society. In the United States, homes, cars, appliances, clothing, and works of art are all part of the material culture, as are the highways and roads, the machines that produce agricultural products and manufactured goods, television and radio networks and stations, and energy-producing facilities.

The concept of technology is closely related to the material culture, but the two terms are not synonymous. Technology includes machines and production systems that are, of course, material things, but there is more to technology than machines. **Technology** is the interplay of machines, equipment, tools, skills, and procedures for carrying out tasks. This broader view, especially with the inclusion of procedures, allows us to see that a technology exists for running churches, providing medical care, or conducting political campaigns. For example, today's political campaigns combine the technology of television with the technology of public relations. Political candidates are instructed by their staffs what to say, as well as how to say it and where and when to say it, in order to maximize their coverage on the evening news (see Chapter 16). In this case, the technology of media management is more important than the material aspects of television (cameras, videotape, transmission lines, and so on).

Technology in the contemporary world often changes very rapidly, usually much faster than social and cultural systems. Technological changes often make existing social practices or cultural forms obsolete, irrelevant, or even dangerous. Members of the society may not recognize the obsolescence of certain social or cultural practices and may continue to follow them. **Cultural lag** exists when social and cultural practices are no longer appropriate for prevailing technological conditions (Ogburn, 1922/1964).

For example, cultural lag exists between the level of productivity possible with modern machines and automated production systems and the expectations that most people have about working. In contemporary developed societies, fewer people are required to produce things (cars, wheat, bricks, household appliances, and so on). Yet we cling to the ideas that everyone should work and that their work should produce "things" (although increasingly we consider services, such as tax consulting, public relations advising, or beauty counseling useful and productive). We also tend to think that everyone should work productively at least 40 hours a week. As machines take over even more tasks of production (and services), we will have to give people economic rewards for what we now consider "nonwork." Perhaps someday people will be routinely paid for creating artistic works, traveling, thinking, meditating, or having therapy. If this idea strikes us as strange or impossible, we might recognize our own reaction as an example of cultural lag.

Another example of cultural lag is found in the use of computers as a means of communication. Online bulletin board systems allow computer users to communicate with others on a wide range of topics, including some that may violate the norms (or even the laws) of society. The most prominent example is the exchange of sexual material that violates sexual norms or laws (Durkin and Bryant, 1995). Law enforcement agents today often monitor these online systems, but online users are claiming that the police have no right to spy on their personal communications (Bowles, 1996). Computer communication is a new and widely used technology; however, the cultural norms about the privacy of these communications are lagging behind the technology.

Cultural Diversity

Up to now we have generally treated cultures as wholes, although we have occasionally noted that there may not be complete agreement about cultural norms and values. Clearly, there may be diversity within cultures. Sociologists, in comparison with anthropologists, have been especially inclined to look for cultural diversity in societies (Berger, 1995). In this final section we will look at three types of diversity: cultural war, subcultures, and countercultures.

A Cultural War: The Orthodox versus Progressives

Some sociologists believe that there is a cultural war going on between the adherents of two major ideological belief systems in the United States (Hunter, 1991; 1994). The two opposing cultural camps are called the *orthodox* and the *progressive*—or, in political terms, the *conservatives* and *liberals* (Hunter, 1991).

The orthodox cultural view is supported by "evangelical and fundamentalistic Protestants, traditional Catholics, Conservative Jews, and so-called neoconservative intellectuals" (Woolfolk, 1995, p. 488). The progressive view is espoused by "many mainstream Protestants, liberal Catholics, Reform Jews, and so-called secular humanists" (Woolfolk, 1995, p. 488).

The most prominent issues that divide these two cultural camps include abortion, homosexuality and other forms of sexual license, male and female gender roles, multiculturalism and sex education in the schools, and school prayer (Hunter, 1994; Shehan and Scanzoni, 1988). The orthodox–conservatives typically oppose abortion, resist changes in traditional family forms and male–female behavior, criticize sexual openness and variety, and emphasize the centrality of religion in American life. The progressive–liberals generally accept abortion, are open to changes in traditional family forms and male–female behavior, support sexual freedom and variety, and support the separation of church and state.

Not all sociologists agree that the split between the orthodox and progressive groups in the United States is severe enough to be called a cultural war. While recognizing the differences in opinions between the two groups, many sociologists believe that both sides nonetheless subscribe to many of the basic American cultural values that we discussed earlier (materialism, individualism, rationality, and so on).

Subcultural Groups

Another kind of cultural diversity is found in subcultural groups. A **subcultural group,** or simply a **subculture,** is a group that accepts much of the dominant culture, but also has some culturally significant characteristics that set it apart from the dominant culture (Zellner, 1995). The Amish and Hasidic Jews, both religious groups, are two classic examples of subcultures in the United States. While these two examples are religious groups, there are other examples of subculture that are not based on religion. The Cuban community in Miami Florida is a subculture, as are Native Americans in many parts of the United States.

The Amish. The Amish are a religious group who came to this country from Europe and settled on the Mid-Atlantic coast around the year 1700 (Kephart and

Zellner, 1991). The Amish today are generally prosperous farmers who work hard, have many children, and practice their austere religion.

Several features of Amish life set them off from the rest of the population. They dress in dark and plain clothing. The bearded men wear broad-brimmed hats, while the women wear long dresses and lacy white caps that rest neatly on their straight, pulled-back hair. They travel by horse and buggy and do all their farm work with draft horses. In general the Amish avoid modern conveniences, including electricity. Although the Amish are deeply religious people they do not have regular churches. Services are conducted in members' homes (Zellner, 1995).

The Amish interact as little as possible with the outside world, as they try to maintain their distinctive cultural ways. Yet, because the Amish are not at war with the culture of the larger society, most Americans do not see the Amish as a cultural threat. Indeed, many Americans admire the Amish for their hard work, prosperity, and devotion to family and religion (Zellner, 1995). Because the Amish have a distinctive culture and yet hold views that are consistent with many larger cultural values, they epitomize the concept of a subculture (Zellner, 1995).

Hasidic Jews.   Hasidic Jews had their beginnings in Poland in the early eighteenth century (Harris, 1986). Hasidism was innovative "in the way it redefined traditional Jewish values by placing prayer, mysticism, dancing, singing, storytelling, and the sanctification of daily life on an equal footing" with the study of traditional law (Harris, 1985a, p. 42). There are about 250,000 Hasidim in the world today (about one-fifth of the number that existed at the turn of the century); 200,000 live in the United States, half of them in Brooklyn. The Hasidim are divided into a number of groups, or "courts," the largest of which is the Lubavitchers (named after the city in Belorussia that was its original home). Despite many similarities among all Hasidim (for example, all adult males are bearded), some differences exist (for example, Lubavitcher men do not wear *peyes,* or long sidelocks of hair).

The Lubavitchers live in the Crown Heights section of Brooklyn. They live in a well-defined area characterized by synagogues, kosher butcher shops, and ritual bath houses. They follow a number of notable customs:

- Husbands and wives are forbidden to kiss or embrace each other in public.

- No physical contact between the sexes is permitted outside of the family.

- Few men attend college and work is not seen as an end itself, but rather as a means to earn a living so that they can follow a religious existence.

- After they marry, women cut off most of their hair and wear wigs.

- Most families do not own television sets or go to the movies.

- Women are not allowed to sing in the presence of men.

- Boys and girls go to separate schools and men and women are separated in synagogue.

- A woman may not have any physical contact with her husband during menstruation or for a week afterwards. At the end of this period the woman is required to have a ritual bath at the *mikveh* before resuming sexual relations with her husband.

The Lubavitchers live in an enclave in Brooklyn completely surrounded by a mostly black population, many of whom are of Caribbean origin (Duke, 1992). Over the years the two groups lived side-by-side, in relative peace, with the Lubivitchers separating themselves not only from blacks but also from more mainstream Jews. However, the peace between the two groups was severely ruptured in 1991 when a car from the motorcade of the leader of the Lubavitchers "accidently struck and killed one black child and seriously injured another" (Duke, 1992, p. A6). This led to street violence in which a Jewish rabbinical student was allegedly killed by a black youth. At a subsequent trial the black youth was acquitted, which angered the Hasidic community. On two subsequent occasions groups of Jewish men allegedly attacked black men they suspected of committing crimes. The strife between Hasidic Jews and blacks in the Crown Heights section of Brooklyn has probably been heightened by the high degree of insulation and separateness between these two culturally different groups.

Countercultures

Often, in a society, groups emerge that are not just different in their ways, but are consciously in opposition to the widely accepted norms and values of the dominant culture. This type of group is known as a **counterculture** (Yinger, 1960; Zellner, 1995).

Many different groups in the United States have been called countercultures, including the beatniks of the 1950s, the hippies of the 1960s, the Ku Klux Klan, skinheads, neo-Nazis, Satanists, survivalists, Hell's Angels, and even some religious groups, such as the Church of Scientology and the Unification Church (Zellner, 1995).

Most counterculture groups explicitly demonstrate their rejection of dominant cultural values. Both the beatniks and the hippies made it clear, through their lifestyles and their words, that they rejected conventional morality about sex, drugs, and work. The Ku Klux Klan has openly rejected the cultural value of equal treatment for all Americans, singling out for special vilification African Americans and Jews, although immigrants, Catholics, union members, and communists have also been among their targets (Zellner, 1995).

The 1995 bombing of the federal building in Oklahoma City focused attention on a loosely knit counterculture that has recently emerged in the United States.

The term *militia groups* has been applied to these quasi-military organizations, all of whom are highly critical of the federal government, claiming that it is repressive, corrupt, and evil. There have been a number of specific versions of this counterculture, including the Aryan Nations, The Order, Posse Comitatus, and the Covenant, Sword, and Arm of the Lord (Zellner, 1995). These groups claim to be patriotic and defenders of the country, but they see the government itself as the major threat to the American way of life. One widespread belief is that the federal government will soon turn over control of the country to a foreign army, led by the United Nations, Zionists, or some other non-Americans (Wills, 1995).

The militia groups (sometimes calling themselves survivalists) are often heavily armed and carry out their own self-styled military training exercises. Others of these antigovernment groups have committed robberies, assassinations, bombings, and other acts of terrorism (Wills, 1995; Zellner, 1995). Thus, they clearly meet the criteria of countercultural groups.

Summary

Culture is the entire complex of ideas and material objects that the people of a society (or group) have created and adopted for carrying out the necessary tasks of collective life. Cultural rules give the people of a society a guide for behavior and make their behavior relatively predictable.

As an explanation of human behavior, culture offers an alternative to a "human nature" explanation. The extensive differences in the behavior of people in different societies supports the importance of culture as an explanation.

Sociobiology offers another alternative explanation. It stresses that human behavior is influenced by genetically inherited tendencies. A major criticism of sociobiology is that it does not allow for cultural factors to override whatever genetically inherited tendencies humans might have.

Most people think of their own cultural practices as the best and right way—a perspective called *ethnocentrism.* The study of different cultures allows us to see that particular cultural practices are best judged in the context of the culture in which they occur—a view called *cultural relativism.*

The most important components of culture include the verbal and nonverbal symbols of a people. The verbal symbols, or language system, of a culture tend to shape people's perceptions of the real world (the Sapir–Whorf hypothesis). Knowledge and beliefs are also components of culture. Values, the standards of desirability within a culture, are centrally important for understanding culture. In the United States the most prominent value is individualism. Closely related is the importance placed on personal control of one's life. Other significant American values are hard work, personal success, personal achievement, materialism, and rationality. *McDonaldization* refers to a form of rationalization that has been adopted by businesses and service industries throughout the society.

Norms are the general guidelines for evaluating behavior in society. Folkways are norms that govern everyday conduct, while mores are norms that reflect the moral standards of the society. Norms are not observed uniformly by all people in a society.

An ideal culture does exist, which contrasts with the real culture—what people actually do in the conduct of their everyday lives.

Material culture and technology are also important elements. When the material culture and technology change, a cultural lag often results as other parts of the culture become obsolete or irrelevant.

Subcultural groups (or, simply, subcultures) are groups with identifiable cultural characteristics that set them apart from the dominant culture. Subcultures often get changed and influenced by the dominant culture through a process of cultural assimilation. To retain its distinctive ways, a subcultural group must make an effort to remain separate from the dominant culture. Groups with cultural characteristics that are consciously in opposition to the dominant culture are called *countercultures.*

CRITICAL THINKING

1. In what ways can knowledge of the concept of culture be practical in business and travel?
2. Why (or why not) is a cultural explanation of human behavior more useful and significant than an explanation based on human nature or sociobiology?
3. Review the definition of ethnocentrism given in the chapter. Can you think of examples of American humor about peoples and cultures that are based on ethnocentrism?
4. The authors state that in order to be a cultural relativist one need not blindly accept all forms of human behavior. Give examples of human behavior (historical or other) that you feel are beyond the limits of tolerance. To what extent are your beliefs based on your culture's views of right and wrong?
5. Give examples of *nonverbal* symbols that you use or see others use.
6. Give an example of how a new technology has produced new verbal symbols for everyday life. For example, what new words have computers added to our language?
7. If Americans place such a high value on individualism and freedom, why is there so much opposition to suicide? Especially assisted suicide?
8. What norms govern your behavior as a college student? Would you classify these norms as folkways, mores, or laws?
9. Give one or two examples of discrepancies between our notion of the ideal culture and the real culture. How do you explain such discrepancies?
10. Can you name any subcultures or countercultures in American society other than those described in the text? How do these groups differ from the dominant American culture?

4

Forms of Social Life: Interaction, Groups, Organizations, and Societies

Human behavior is not random; it is patterned. Regularity and order can be found in the actions of all humans, whether they are Nepalese living in Katmandu, aborigines living in the outback of Australia, or New Yorkers living on the Upper East Side of Manhattan. Average people living anywhere will know how to relate to the people with whom they come in contact in their daily lives. Imagine what would happen, however, if we were to take a person from any one of these places and put him or her in another society. The results would vividly reveal how the patterns of behavior in a society must be learned.

Because many of the social patterns of our own society are so familiar, we often give them little attention. In this chapter we will examine a wide range of different patterns of social relations. We will begin with a general concept that sociologists often use when describing a pattern of social relationships (social structure). Then, beginning at the microscopic level, we will see how interaction between individuals produces patterned behavior even in a two-person relationship. Next we will move to the level of groups and then to organizations. The chapter will conclude with a discussion of societies.

Social Structures

Social structures are regular patterns of social interaction and persistent social relationships. Social structures are constructed by the ongoing interaction of people, but at the same time, by observing these patterns of interaction, we can identify social structures. Social structures can be observed at any social level from the interaction between two people, through groups and organizations, to entire societies. To illustrate how a social structure is created through interaction, and, simultaneously, how social structures are observable in the regularities of everyday interaction, we will consider a familiar example.

Imagine a number of college students who come together at the beginning of a school year to live on the same corridor of a dormitory. When they first move in they are probably strangers, or perhaps they know each other only casually. Over a period of time, however, through their interaction, they will start sorting themselves into sets of people who spend time together. These sets of people will talk, go to meals together, help each other with homework, and so on. Some of the emerging groups are apt to have special interests and activities—sports, dorm politics, partying, practical jokes, or studying. Using the words of the social structure definition, we can say that regular patterns of social interaction and persistent social relationships will occur among these students.

When anthropologist Michael Moffatt (1989) lived among the residents of a dormitory at Rutgers University in New Jersey, he was able to observe the social structures that emerged during the first two months of the school year. He reports: "By late October, the residents of the floor had connected themselves together in the complex network of friendship [groups]" (Moffatt, 1989, p. 95). He describes some of the larger friendship groups and cliques, identifying their leaders, their special activities, and their differing styles. He also notes that there were some two- and three-person groups (see "Dyads and Triads," p. 95) that were either outside the larger groups, or in some cases connecting two different groups. Also, some first-year students "floated between this clique and others on the floor" (Moffatt, 1989, p. 96). These patterns of interaction (social structures) on a single dormitory floor were clearly identifiable after only two months of interaction. One can be quite certain that at the beginning of each academic year similar structures will emerge in dormitories and residence halls at every other college.

Because of the patterned nature of social structures, they can typically be sketched in diagrammatic form. For example, Figure 4–1 is a partial depiction of Moffatt's diagram of the student social structure that emerged on the dormitory floor where he made his observations. In Figure 4–1, the lines drawn between individuals are based on mutual friendship choices as expressed on a questionnaire that Moffatt gave to the residents of the floor in late October.

Because social structures are created by people, they can change over time. But structures tend to have some persistence, and when sociologists speak of social structures they are talking about patterns of interaction and social relationships that persist over time. Included would be the major social structures found in societies, for they generally do not change rapidly. Very often structures reflect patterned inequalities by which some people are treated as more important than others; some have more privileges and power than others (Ridgeway and Walker,

1995). Examples in American society, to be examined later, are the socioeconomic-status system with its different social classes (Chapter 8) and the major racial and ethnic groups (Chapter 9). These stratification systems are, of course,

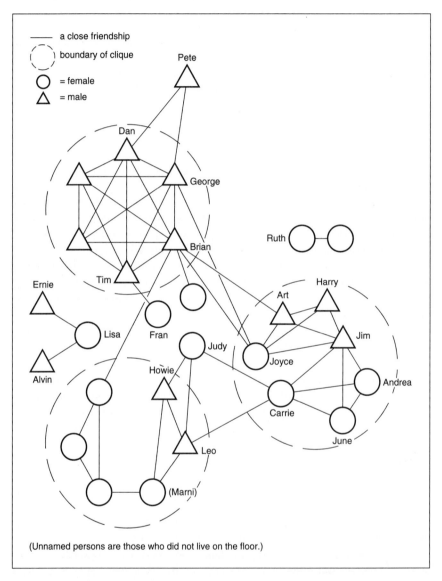

Figure 4–1.   Student Social Structure on a Dormitory Floor. (*Source:* Michael Moffatt, *Coming of Age in New Jersey,* copyright © 1989 by Rutgers, The State University. Reprinted by permission of Rutgers University Press.

social structures. The social class structure of the society is observable through the way people interact with each other, and these patterns of interaction do not change much over time. The same is true with respect to the relationships between racial and ethnic groups in the United States. Racial discrimination, for example, which places blacks and other racial minorities in disadvantaged positions, has existed for centuries and persists today.

Throughout this chapter we will be describing social structures at the various levels of social life. We will begin with the interaction between individuals and then move on to groups and organizations. We will conclude, at the macroscopic end of the social continuum, with a consideration of societies.

Interaction

The ability of humans to meet and interact with other humans is a high-level skill, but most of the time we do it with ease. In an average day a person typically interacts with a wide variety of people, including friends, relatives, lovers, acquaintances, and strangers. As long as we share the same language with these people, we can negotiate almost any kind of situation, whether it is friendly or hostile, comfortable or awkward, casual or formal.

As we saw in our consideration of symbolic interaction theory in Chapter 1, the human mind, with its ability to understand and use symbols (both verbal and nonverbal), makes interaction possible between people. People interact primarily through verbal symbols, or words, not only with others but with themselves. By using symbols to interact with themselves, people are able to evaluate other people and situations, and decide what actions to take. Again, this is an important principle of symbolic interaction theory.

When interaction occurs between two people, two things happen, almost simultaneously. Each person in an interaction situation is *sending* words and cues and *receiving and processing* words and cues as they come in from the other person. The important feature of any interaction is the way people use their minds to interpret the words and cues of another person, deduce their meaning, and respond accordingly.

This abstract description of interaction makes it seem complex and unfamiliar, but if we take an everyday situation we can see how the process of interaction works. Consider a hypothetical yet commonplace situation in which a male and a female college student are getting acquainted. If they are in college and happen to sit next to each other in a class, over a period of time they may have a series of interactions that could ultimately result in their dating and becoming romantically involved. Their early interaction is important in this process. Two people seated side by side may rarely talk with each other at first. Gradually, however, they may start to interact. Of course, the very act of engaging in conversation when it is not necessary is in itself a symbolic act. When two people find themselves engaged in conversation they may recognize that their interaction could imply a mutual attraction. Even as they talk about something as mundane as the sociology professor or the next test, the young man might reflect to himself that he is attracted to the young woman and that she might be attracted to him.

As this interaction continues, different things might be happening at different levels simultaneously. Noncommittal ideas may first be exchanged, as the students talk about the professor or about studying for the next examination. The young woman may say she doesn't have anyone with whom to study, but if she makes this remark, the young man must interpret what it means. He has only a second or two to decide if she is saying that it might be pleasant for the two of them to get together outside of class, ostensibly to do some studying. At the same time, as he is assessing what her words really mean, he is formulating his response. If he responds to her objective statement inappropriately, he may look foolish. If he treats it as a suggestion that they get together outside of class and she did not mean it that way, he may be embarrassed. The young man must quickly select from his many possible choices: "I don't have anyone to study with either," or "I always find it helps to study with someone just before the test," or "Why don't we get together before the test?"

If the young man made the last of these statements, the young woman would have to decide exactly what his words mean. He could be asking for a date, or he could simply be suggesting that they study together. The woman must weigh all the evidence, again in just a second or two, and make some appropriate response. As a rule, a person in this situation will reply in such a way that the response will be appropriate regardless of the real intent of the statement. Or the young woman could simply say, "Are you asking me for a date or do you want to get together to study?" However, before doing so she will have to weigh the consequences of this response. Will the young man be shocked by her directness? Will her statement have the effect of acknowledging the previously unstated attraction between them?

The interaction just described goes on within the context of the cultural values and the social norms we discussed in the last chapter. In some societies, the norms of courtship would make it totally inappropriate for two young people to make a date of any kind. Often parents would have to be consulted and a chaperon obtained before two young people of the opposite sex could spend any time together. We can see from these normative constraints why human behavior is not random but is, as we said, patterned. The interaction between two people who are getting acquainted is partially open to their own creativity and inventiveness, but it is also patterned by the norms that prevail in a society.

But there is another important social constraint on the interaction between the young man and woman we have been describing. Both people have social statuses, or positions, and attached to these statuses are social roles. Status and role are important sociological concepts because they reveal why there is a great amount of regular and patterned social behavior.

Status and Role

The words and actions of the young man and woman described above will certainly be influenced and shaped, especially in the early interaction, by the fact of their genders. Many American young people still believe it more appropriate for males to initiate invitations for dates than for females to do so. This view is changing, but many young women still say, "I think it is fine for a woman to ask a guy for a date, *but I wouldn't do it.*" This statement tells us that although some young women do not see anything wrong with a woman initiating a date, many still feel that it might be inappropriate behavior. But why is it viewed as inappropriate? To understand why someone would feel this way and why this feeling is shared by many other people—young and old, female and male—we have to examine the importance of the sociological concepts of status and role.

A **status** is a socially recognized position in a social system. A **role** is the behavior generally expected of one who occupies a particular status. Again we can use gender as an example of status and role. In all societies, males and females have socially recognized positions, with certain expectations, about what one will and will not do. However, males and females are not expected to act in the same way in every society. In Chapter 10 we will examine some societies in which men and women are expected to act in ways that are very different from those traditionally expected of them in U.S. society. But—and here is the important point—gender is always a status that carries with it some expected behaviors. Roles are always connected with gender.

Statuses can be of two types: ascribed and achieved. An **ascribed status** is one into which individuals move or are placed, irrespective of their efforts or capacities. Examples of ascribed statuses include being male or female, young or old, black or white, son or daughter. We have little control over our ascribed statuses. (An example of an effort to control ascribed status would be a person who undergoes a sex change.) In contrast, an **achieved status** is one that people acquire through their own efforts. Examples include becoming a college graduate, getting married, having children, becoming an astronaut, or even becoming a bank robber.

A related concept is that of master status. A **master status** refers to a position so important that it dominates and overrides all other statuses, both for the person and all other people. For example, a study of male college basketball players at a major university demonstrated that the status of being on the men's basketball team overwhelmed all other statuses of these young men (Adler and Adler, 1991). Even if these men wished to be seen as more than simply basketball players, everyone else on campus identified them in this way. For them, *basketball player* became a master status that overrode all other statuses.

Often in our society, a master status is related to one's occupation. A person who is a Supreme Court Justice, a nun, a college president, or an opera singer is likely to be seen primarily in terms of his or her major occupational role—a master role.

Another point about statuses and roles is that they have a reality of their own; they exist irrespective of the persons who fill them. Whoever occupies the status of the president of the United States, or is the center-fielder on a baseball team, or the anchorperson on a television news show must attend to certain expectations that accompany the status. In general, the people who fill a status understand the expectations and follow the behavior expected of them.

However, not everyone in a particular status behaves in exactly the same way. There are two reasons for this. First, the role expectations connected with a status are not fully detailed. Role expectations are not so precisely stated or understood that every detail of expected behavior is clear. Second, individuals who hold statuses may have their own orientations toward the role. Let us deal with each of these issues separately.

Roles do not specify every exact behavior that a person in a given status must follow. In fact, roles often have only broad requirements within which a person must operate. Airline pilots, for example, are expected to be competent to fly planes in all kinds of conditions and handle difficult and emergency situations in a calm and collected way. When pilots speak to the passengers, they generally present themselves as steady, serious, and relaxed, even though they may not always feel that way. However, some pilots will occasionally inject humor, irritation (with delays, for example), or other emotions into their public presentations. When they are not within hearing or sight of the passengers, their behavior may be even more at odds with the general role expectations for airline pilots. Behind the scenes they are able to introduce their unique, personal characteristics and still fulfill the role expectations connected with a status. In other words, people do not simply conform to role expectations; they also actively modify their roles. This ability of individuals to modify (at least to some degree) their own roles has been called **role making** (Hewitt, 1984, p. 81).

Another way to see how individuals can vary their performance of a role is to note that the dominant view about what is expected of people in a given status need not be universal. Different orientations toward a role can exist. The college student role has broad outlines—enrolling, going to class, studying, taking exams—but different students might emphasize different features of the student role. These different emphases are called **role orientations.** Some students might emphasize the academic and intellectual aspect of the student role. With this orientation they would take advantage of college to become involved in intellectual pursuits. Their role orientation toward their college-student status has been called the *academic–intellectual* role orientation. In comparison, other college students are more oriented toward the vocational or professional training they receive in school. They see student life as an opportunity to learn a profession and gain entry into it. This orientation has been called the *vocational* role orientation.

Some students see their college experience as an opportunity to engage in an active social life or to learn social skills. For them, college is a learning ground for their future social lives. The fraternity–sorority scene may be a forerunner of the country club life that they expect to enter later. This has been called the *social life* role orientation (Bolton and Kammeyer, 1967).

As we have seen, the roles connected with statuses do not make individuals in the same status behave in the same way, but enough similarity is evident in role performance to produce some general patterns of behavior. These patterns, found among males and females, airline pilots, and students, and a vast array of other statuses, are sufficiently consistent to produce identifiable patterns in social life. However, statuses and roles can always be modified and changed over time, through the continuing actions and interactions of people.

Dyads and Triads

When two people engage in interaction, it is called a **dyad.** When a third person is introduced into the interaction, it is called a **triad.** While both dyads and triads involve interaction, and both can be seen as groups, there are some interesting differences between two-person and three-person interaction. From a sociological and practical point of view, the triad is a much more complicated social arrangement (Simmel, 1950).

A dyad has only one relationship, but a triad has three (A and B, A and C, B and C). That in itself makes the triad more complicated. Consider, for example, the common situation of a husband and wife dyad becoming parents of a new baby, thus becoming a triad. The relationship between the husband and wife becomes more complicated because each will now have a relationship with the baby. It is a fairly common occurrence for a new mother to devote so much attention to her relationship with the baby that her husband feels neglected. A substantial amount of research shows that satisfaction with marital relationships declines when married couples have children. Part of the reason can probably be attributed to the changes in interaction when a married-couple dyad becomes a triad.

Similar problems often emerge in three-person friendship groups. Although three-person groups can maintain a cohesive "three-musketeers" relationship, a balance is difficult to maintain. All pairs of relationships in a triad must be about equal in time spent together, displays of friendship, conversation, and so on. If this equality is not maintained, then one of the pairs will dominate, leaving the third person relatively isolated. Many people who have been in three-person friendship groups have had the experience of two members drawing closer together and shutting out the third.

Although dyads and triads are frequent forms of social interaction, the social group brings us to a more purely sociological level. We turn to this level next.

Social Groups

While the word *group* is used in various ways in everyday speech, and even in sociology, the technical sociological meaning focuses our attention on some important features of social life. A **group** may be defined as a relatively small number of people who interact with one another over time and thereby establish patterns of interaction, a group identity, and rules or norms governing behavior.

One key feature defining a group is the interaction among all members. A larger entity such as a society (for example, U.S. society) differs from a group in that all the members of a society cannot possibly interact with each other because of their large number.

Although a large number of people cannot technically constitute a social group, a small number of people will not necessarily constitute a group either. Several people who meet briefly on an elevator are not a group, because they lack a group identity and because they do not interact on the basis of patterns they have established.

In-groups and Out-groups

According to our definition, a basic characteristic of a group is that the interacting individuals have a group identity. Therefore, to qualify as a group, the people who compose it must define themselves as members and, conversely, those outside the group must be defined as outsiders. The emphasis on group identity leads to the distinction between *in-groups* and *out-groups* (Sumner, 1904). An **in-group** is one that members are involved in and with which they identify, while an **out-group** is one to which outsiders belong. The importance of this distinction is the tendency for people to believe in the rightness and desirability of the in-group, and to reject the ways of the out-group. The in-group, out-group distinction usually takes on its greatest significance when two or more groups are in close proximity. Members of fraternities and sororities on a college campus may view members of other fraternities and sororities as out-groups. This can lead to an attitude of "us" against "them." In extreme cases, in-group, out-group attitudes may lead to conflict between groups. (See the box In the News, on pages 98–99.)

Primary and Secondary Groups

Sociologists also differentiate between primary groups and secondary groups. The concept of **primary groups** was developed by Cooley (1909) to describe groups "characterized by intimate face-to-face association and cooperation." Primary groups are typically small and close-knit. The relationships among the members are very personal. They strongly identify with each other as well as with the group as a whole. As a result of the closeness of the relationships, the primary group often has a profound effect on its members. As examples of primary groups, Cooley cites the family, play groups of children, and neighborhood or community groups.

Secondary groups, in contrast to primary groups, are typically large and impersonal. Members do not know each other as intimately or completely as do the members of a primary group. Members' ties to a secondary group are typically weaker than the ties to primary groups. Secondary groups have a less profound impact on members. They are usually formed for a specific purpose, and the members rarely interact with each other outside of the activities that are oriented toward the group goal. The members of a local Parent–Teacher's Association or a labor union are examples of secondary groups.

Reference Groups

Another sociological perspective on groups is revealed by thinking of how groups (both primary and secondary) serve as reference groups. **Reference groups** are any groups that a person takes into account when evaluating his or her actions or characteristics. As humans we are always trying to evaluate ourselves and our behavior. Am I attractive? Am I doing a good job? Should I wear these clothes tonight? One way we answer these questions for ourselves is to refer to the performance or the qualities of the members of some group. Although individuals often use groups of which they are members as reference groups, a person does not necessarily have to be a member of a group in order to use it as a reference group. Take, for example, a woman who is making reasonably good career progress and, after some years, becomes a manager in a major corporation. If this woman's reference group is made up primarily of the circle of friends with whom she went to high school, she will probably have positive feelings about her career progress. Many of her high school friends have probably not gone on to jobs in the corporate world; compared to them she is doing well. On the other hand, if this same woman manager takes as her reference group the fastest-rising executives in her own corporation, she will evaluate her career success more negatively.

As this example shows, a reference group can be used to make comparative evaluations about oneself and one's performance. But reference groups can also provide a normative function by supplying an individual's norms and values. Thus, a young manager may not yet be a member of top management, but the latter can be his or her reference group, supplying the aspiring executive with the relevant standards of behavior. For example, if an aspiring young female manager notices that the successful female executives wear tailored suits and silk blouses, she too might stock her wardrobe with these items.

In the News

Street Gangs and Group Identity

There are thousands of known street gangs in the United States. A systematic survey of police departments has found that between 800 and 1,100 cities and towns have some street gang activity; these cities and towns report a total of 2,600 gangs (Klein, 1995). Los Angeles county alone has an estimated 800 street gangs, with more than 90,000 members (Lacy, 1991). Police in adjacent Orange county report 200 street gangs (Klein, 1995).

Gangs are generally found in poverty areas of cities and towns; slums and ghettos are the breeding grounds for gangs (Jankowski, 1991; Klein, 1995; Padilla, 1992). Particular gangs are likely to be of one racial, ethnic, or nationality group. There are gangs whose members are African American, Hispanic (Chicano, Puerto Rican, Dominican), Asian, and white (Armenian and Irish, for example) (Jankowski, 1991; Klein, 1995).

Gangs have group identities that are displayed through their names, symbols, and activities. Often individual gangs will have a distinct type of clothing that sets them apart from other gangs. These symbols of identity give gang members a strong sense of in-group feeling, which commonly leads to hostility toward out-groups. In Los Angeles, two major groups who are arch rivals are the Bloods and the Crips. The identifying color of the Bloods is red; the Crips color is blue. The Bloods and the Crips are actually two major categories, with each having many neighborhood groups subsumed under their general labels, for example, the Grape Street Crips of Watts, the Hoover Street Crips, or the Inglewood and Avenue Piru Bloods (Rheinhold, 1988).

In areas of Los Angeles where gangs thrive, a gang member who strays into the neighborhood of a rival gang or is found in the street wearing the wrong color clothing might get beaten up or even killed. Because of the dangers associated with wearing the colors of the Bloods and Crips, many Los Angeles-area schools have, for years, enforced dress codes that prohibit students from wearing either red or blue bandanas, shoelaces, or belts (Lacey, 1991). But the gangs have a new clothing fad—the wearing of professional sports team jackets and hats—that is now endangering the lives of nongang members living in Los Angeles (Lacey, 1991).

In some Los Angeles schools, administrators have banned students from wearing clothes that symbolize gang membership (Klein, 1995). Even some athletic jackets, representing popular professional sports teams, have been banned because of their close association with gangs (Lacy, 1991). School administrators justify this action because innocent students may be taken for gang members if they wear athletic jackets that are associated with gangs. But, in addition, by suppressing gang-related clothing, school officials hope to suppress recruitment to gangs (Klein, 1995).

JANKOWSKI, MARTIN SANCHEZ. *Islands in the Street: Gangs and American Urban Society.* Berkeley: University of California Press, 1991.

KLEIN, MALCOLM W. *The American Street Gang: Its Nature, Prevalence, and Control.* New York: Oxford University Press, 1995.
LACEY, MARC. "Danger Links for Fans as Gangs Adopt Pro Attire." *Los Angeles Times,* March 20, 1991.
PADILLA, FELIX M. *The Gang as an American Enterprise.* New Brunswick, N.J.: Rutgers University Press, 1992.

Religious group membership often provides an important reference group that has a profound influence on individual behavior. A study of U.S. adults has shown that membership in different religious groups influences attitudes toward premarital sex, birth control, and abortion (Bock et al., 1983). Research evidence also reveals that religions as reference groups influence alcohol use (Cochran et al., 1988).

A person will likely have a number of reference groups, and those groups will probably change over time. Many college students have reference groups that include students who are socially popular figures, varsity athletes, and campus leaders. After graduation some of the characteristics and qualities of these types may seem superficial and irrelevant. Whatever one's reference groups are while in college, they are likely to change dramatically when one leaves the campus and enters the business or professional world.

Conformity: Three Classic Experiments

As the discussion of reference groups suggests, individual behavior is influenced by the groups to which one belongs and the groups to which one aspires. The tendency of individuals to respond to social groups and to allow them to influence behavior is one of the most intriguing aspects of human behavior. As we saw in the last chapter, Americans place great value on their individualism, and yet there is ample evidence that individuals have a tendency to *conform* to the behavior of other members of a group, even when no explicit demands are made to do so. That is, people seem to want to go along with the majority of group members even when those group members do not explicitly pressure them to conform.

The Sherif Experiment. An important study in this line of research is Muzafer Sherif's (1935) famous experiment, "A Study of Some Social Factors in Perception." Sherif was interested in studying what people would do when presented with an ambiguous phenomenon—one lacking in stable reference points. The phenomenon Sherif presented to his subjects was a single point of light in a completely dark room. Because no other objects in the room could be seen, there were no reference points, and the light appeared to move (even though it was not moving). This phenomenon is known as the *autokinetic effect.* In one part of this study individuals were first shown the light alone and then again in the presence of a group of people. When individuals alone were presented with the light, each established a sense of the distance that the light had moved. When those individuals were then placed in the same situation with a group of people, each individual's judgment of the distance that the light moved tended to converge with the judgment of the group. It appears from this experiment that individuals prefer to be closer to the standards of the group; they preferred to be in conformity.

The Asch Experiment.   In another classic experiment, Solomon Asch (1952) studied groups of seven to nine college students to examine the effect of group pressure on individuals. In each group, all but one of the members (the subject) were confederates of the researcher. The group was shown pairs of cards—the first card with a single vertical line and the second with three vertical lines. One of the lines on the second card was equal in length to the line of the first card. The other two lines were sufficiently different that, when asked to match lines on the two cards, the vast majority of people making decisions alone chose the correct line.

In the crucial experiment, Asch had his confederates choose an incorrect line on the second card. These choices were made out loud, within hearing of the subjects, who were positioned toward the end of the group. Responding in turn, subjects showed that they were experiencing group pressure, even to the extent of making the same incorrect choice. In about one-third of the cases the subjects sided with the majority and made the incorrect choice. This tendency to conform to the majority opinion appeared even when the subjects apparently knew that they were making incorrect judgments. Although this experiment demonstrates the pressure to conform to group opinions, it is important to remember that in about two-thirds of the cases the subjects resisted the majority and made the correct decision.

The Milgram Experiment.   An experiment conducted by Stanley Milgram (1974) focused on a somewhat different aspect of conformity. He was able to demonstrate that many people will comply with the orders of someone who appears to be in a position of authority in an organization (the social form we will consider next). In the Milgram experiments subjects were asked to work with other individuals who, unknown to the subjects, were paid by Milgram to act out prearranged parts. The subjects always found themselves in the position of "teacher" in the study, while the confederates served as "learners." The learners were strapped into chairs and hooked up to electrodes. The teacher-subjects were placed in another room with a fake shock generator. Labels on the generator indicated the increasing intensity of its charge—from "Slight Shock" at the low end to "Danger: Severe Shock" and, finally, "XXX" at the other end. The shocks were not real, but the teacher-subjects did not know it. They were instructed to give the learner-confederates an electric shock for every wrong answer (intentional on the part of the confederate) and to increase the amount of shock each time. Learner-confederates reacted with screams, as if pained by the shocks. Almost two-thirds of the subject-teachers continued to administer shocks to the point marked "XXX"—a level they believed was potentially lethal. The researcher, dressed in white coat and projecting an aura of scientific respectability, was perceived by most subjects as an authoritative figure whose instructions were to be followed regardless of the resulting harm to other people.

Before the study, almost all of the subjects said they would never be able to bring themselves to inflict severe pain on someone in any foreseeable circumstances. The Milgram study indicates that, under certain conditions, many people, especially if they receive orders from authority figures, will violate their own moral norms and inflict pain, perhaps even at lethal levels, on other human beings.

These experimental studies reveal how people are influenced by the behavior of other members of groups and by authority figures in organizations. Furthermore, these reactions were produced in experimentally created groups and organizational settings. It is possible that the real groups and organizations to which individuals belong (families, friendship groups, schools, workplaces, and so on) may have even more influence on member behavior. Clearly, groups and organizations can and do exert an influence on the behavior of individuals.

We are now ready to take a closer look at organizations and how they work. Of special importance is the bureaucratic form of organization that is so pervasive today.

Organizations and Bureaucracies

We live in a world that is increasingly characterized by large-scale organizations. Most of us were born in large hospitals or multipurpose medical centers; we have been educated in large school systems, have often worked for major corporations or businesses, and have dealt with complex governmental systems. Major portions of our lives are spent dealing with and working in large-scale organizations. We recognize increasingly that we cannot understand the society in which we live if we do not understand how organizations work and how the many different kinds of organizations—political, economic, and social—relate to each other (Clark, 1988).

To see just how enmeshed we are with large-scale organizations, we have only to open our wallets or purses. We carry social security cards, identification cards, registration cards, driver's licenses, medical insurance cards, credit cards, and a variety of other membership cards that verify that we belong to organizations. In other words, we live in an "organizational society" (Presthus, 1978).

Sociologists use the term **organization** to describe a deliberately constructed collectivity aimed at achieving specified goals with clearly delineated statuses, roles, and rules. Thus, the U.S. Postal Service is an organization of managers, supervisors, postal clerks, mail carriers, and many others whose task it is to deliver the mail. Handgun Control is an organization established to reduce the number of handguns in U.S. society. Any neighborhood improvement association, with officers, members, and meetings, is an organization created to do something positive for a neighborhood.

These three examples show that many different types of organizations exist. Some are government agencies; some are private enterprises. Organizations may focus on causes or have special interests and may be national or local in scope.

Another way to make distinctions among types of organizations is on the basis of how control is exerted over people who exist at or near the bottom of the organization, called the *lower participants*. Three types of organizations have been identified on this basis (Etzioni, 1961).

Coercive Organizations

A **coercive organization** uses force to control those at the bottom of the structure. The major examples of coercive organizations are prisons and custodial mental hospitals. The lower participants in such organizations are prisoners and mental patients—people who have no personal commitment to these organizations. Because they are not deeply committed to the organization and, in fact, probably have negative feelings toward it, coercion is needed to get them to do what the organization wants.

A special name given to a certain extreme type of coercive organization is the total institution (Goffman, 1961). A **total institution** is an organization that is cut off from the rest of society, forming an all-encompassing social environment to meet all the needs of its members. Not all coercive organizations are total institutions; for example, some prisons and mental institutions allow inmates considerable flexibility (for example, weekend leaves, conjugal visits, open doors). On the other hand, some total institutions may not have the key characteristics of coercive organizations. For example, many large naval ships remain at sea for weeks and even months, providing the personnel on board everything they need for a full and complete life (food, personal and medical services, entertainment and recreation, religious services, and so on). Although these ships are total institutions, the people on board are not absolutely coerced into being there. We will have more to say about total institutions in Chapter 5.

Utilitarian Organizations

A second type of organization is the **utilitarian organization** that uses money to control the people at the bottom. Industries and businesses are the most common types of utilitarian organizations. All employees and workers, but especially those at the bottom (clerks and those who do menial labor), are in the organization primarily for the wages they receive. Such workers are not likely to be highly committed to their organizations, although they tend to have a higher level of commitment than the lower participants in coercive organizations. They do what the organization expects of them because they are paid for it.

Normative Organizations

Finally, in **normative** or **voluntary organizations,** participants are controlled by the norms and values of the organization. Mothers Against Drunk Drivers, which was founded in 1980 by Candy Lightner of Fair Oaks, California, after her 13-year-old daughter was killed by a hit-and-run driver, is an example of a normative organization (Weed, 1990, 1991). MADD chapters appeared all around the United States because people in many communities shared a concern about the needless deaths caused by drunk driving and sought to do something about the problem. MADD and a similar organization, RID (Remove Intoxicated Drivers), have had some success, especially in raising the legal drinking age to 21 (Wolfson, 1995).

Many of the normative organizations are part of larger social movements. For example, Greenpeace is part of the environmental movement, and the Animal Liberation Front is part of the animal rights movement. Many politically oriented organizations (Young Democrats and Young Republicans) are also examples of normative organizations. In all cases, members are motivated to participate by some value or belief.

The Cultures of Organizations

Organizations, like societies, have cultures (Mohan, 1993; Pheysey, 1993; Trice and Beyer, 1993). Any organization will have many of the same elements of culture that we considered in Chapter 3. Organizational cultures have symbols, beliefs, values, and norms, just like societal cultures. Researchers of organizations are increasingly paying attention to these organizational cultures, because understanding the culture helps us to understand how an organization works.

While all organizations have cultures, the elements of such cultures can be seen vividly in some of the well-known direct-selling organizations (these include familiar names such as Amway, Avon, Mary Kay Cosmetics, and Tupperware). Direct-selling organizations often place a special emphasis on symbols, and these are very likely to reflect their values.

The Mary Kay Cosmetics organization, for example, uses the color pink as one of its primary symbols, perhaps because it is associated with femininity and, by extension, the use of cosmetics. The values of ambition and enthusiasm are expressed at Mary Kay meetings when the members sing special songs, such "I've Got That Mary Kay Enthusiasm" (sung to the tune of "I've Got That Old-time Religion"). The theme of financial success is also highlighted by frequent awards ceremonies at which top sellers are presented with gold and diamond pins, fur stoles, and the ultimate symbol of success, the pink luxury automobile (Trice and Beyer, 1993).

Every organization's culture is in some ways different from every other organization's culture. But almost all organizations, especially as they grow in size, tend to become bureaucracies. The bureaucracy has become the most common form of organization in contemporary life. Although the term is often used in a negative or derogatory way, it is necessary to take a more neutral and objective look at this form of organization.

What Is a Bureaucracy?

A **bureaucracy** is an organization with a special set of characteristics:

1. A division of labor among the members, with everyone having specialized duties and functions;
2. A well-defined rank order of authority among members;
3. A system of rules covering the rights and duties of all members in all positions;
4. Rules and procedures for carrying out all tasks;
5. Impersonality in the relations among members;
6. Selection for membership, employment, and promotion based on competence and expertise.

These typical features of a bureaucracy are what sociologists call an ideal type. An ideal type is not, as it might seem, a best possible form of something. Rather, an **ideal type** is a logical, exaggerated, and "pure" model of some phenomenon that one wishes to study or analyze. It is a methodological tool developed by the German theorist Max Weber, whom we discussed in Chapter 1 (Weber, 1903–1917/1949). Weber developed the ideal type as a tool for analyzing and studying real bureaucracies. By specifying the characteristics of the ideal-type bureaucracy, it is possible to see if, and to what degree, actual organizations are bureaucratic.

As an ideal type, a bureaucracy consists of a hierarchy of positions, with each position under the control and supervision of the one above it. Each position is assigned the task of performing a set of official functions, and procedures in each position are defined by a set of official rules. The individual in each position is granted the authority to carry out the functions of that position, but that authority does not extend beyond it.

For bureaucrats to apply the rules attached to their positions, they must receive specialized training. In general, only those who are formally qualified through specialized training are entitled to hold positions within a bureaucracy. Bureaucrats do not own the means of production—the offices, desks, and machines; the organization owns them and provides them to the bureaucrats as needed. Bureaucrats are not self-employed; they are employees. The written word is the hallmark of a bureaucracy because administrative acts, decisions, and rules are all put into writing.

Only the highest authority within a bureaucracy can obtain his or her position without going through bureaucratic selection procedures such as testing or presenting certain educational credentials. Often in the federal government the heads of departments or agencies are political appointees, perhaps chosen more for their special relationship with the president than for their specialized skills. Although such appointees may obtain their positions through nonbureaucratic means, their authority, like that of those below them in the bureaucracy, is limited by the position they hold.

People become bureaucrats by their own choice, not because they have inherited a position in a bureaucracy. Bureaucrats are paid a salary, which is usually directly related to their positions in the bureaucratic hierarchy. The work associated with the official title is the sole, or at least the primary, occupation of the bureaucrat and is looked upon as a career. This opens up the possibility of moving to ever-higher positions within the organization. Upward mobility is based on merit and seniority. Promotion is determined by superiors within the organization.

Remember that this ideal–typical description may not pertain to any particular organization, but it should describe the characteristics that appear to some degree in any large organization (Blau and Meyer, 1987). One of these characteristics—the authority that is invested in the positions of a bureaucracy—requires some special attention.

Authority refers to "legitimate" power; it is the exercise of power that is accepted by those over whom it is exerted. It probably seemed quite natural when we stated above that people in the higher positions of an organization have authority over those in positions below them. But why is this true? How does a position in an organization give someone power over others in that organization? To understand the answer to this question we must examine how authority becomes legitimate (Weber, 1921/1968).

Legitimation of Authority.   In earlier times authority came primarily from the positions into which people were born. Kings and other royal family members in times past (and even in some places today) believed they were born with the *right* to exercise power over their subjects. But equally important is the fact that the people they ruled considered it their *duty* to obey the ruler's demands. This kind of authority is legitimized by **tradition**—the way things have been done for a long time in a society or social group. While traditional authority was more common in the past, tradition can also produce legitimacy for authority in some organizations today. Subordinates accept the position of a traditional leader because they have accepted it for a long period of time or their parents and grandparents accepted it.

A second way authority can be legitimized is by the charisma a leader claims—and is believed by followers to possess. **Charisma** is the extraordinary, sometimes supernatural, qualities of a person. Leaders of revolutionary social, political, and religious movements frequently derive their authority from their charismatic qualities. Examples of charismatic political leaders are Hitler, Mao Zedong, Castro, and Gandhi. Charismatic religious leaders include Jesus, Mohammed, and Reverend Sun Myung Moon of the Unification Church. Even some entertainment stars are sometimes believed by their fans to have charisma or a larger-than-life quality that gives them extraordinary power. Charisma is derived more from the beliefs of the followers than from the actual qualities of leaders. As long as a person believes he or she has special qualities, or it is believed by followers, authority can be derived from charisma.

Charisma is a very short lived form of authority, generally limited to the life span of the charismatic leader and perhaps a short while thereafter. Attempts are frequently made to extend a leader's charisma beyond his or her own lifetime. This process, called the **routinization of charisma,** is accomplished when the qualities originally associated with a charismatic individual are passed on and incorporated into the characteristics of a group or organization. As an example, even after the death of Martin Luther King, the civil-rights movement in the United States was able to keep his charismatic qualities alive in order to advance the movement's objectives. Once charismatic leadership is translated into an organizational form, however, it eventually evolves into either a traditional or a rational-legal form of authority (Weber, 1921/1968).

In a system of **rational–legal authority,** leaders are legitimized by the rule of law. They derive their authority from the rules and regulations of the system rather than from their personal qualities or from tradition. For example, the office of president of the United States is legitimized by the Constitution, which defines the president's rights and responsibilities. The president's authority generally does not stem from his personal charismatic qualities or from tradition, although it may in some cases. Presidential power is legitimized because people accept the rule of law and therefore accept the president's right to exercise the power of that office.

These ideas on the sources of authority relate closely to our concern with bureaucracy. Weber argued that each form of authority would manifest itself through some form of organizational structure. Rational–legal authority, with its emphasis on adherence to carefully defined rules and regulations, is conducive to the development of bureaucratic organization, while the other forms of authority spawned other types of organizational structures. Bureaucratization is the organizational form of rational–legal authority. Weber believed that as societies become increasingly rationalized, rational–legal authority would increasingly triumph over traditional and charismatic authority. In other words, the modern world would become increasingly bureaucratized.

In the early years of this century, before bureaucratic tendencies had reached nearly the proportions they have today, Max Weber predicted the triumph of bureaucracy in the modern world. His sociological prediction proved to be correct, but he would not have been pleased. He deplored the move toward bureaucratization, saying that we were creating an "iron cage" from which there would be no escape (Mitzman, 1969). Weber thought that individuality and creativity would disappear in the face of the inexorable advance of bureaucratization. In Weber's view of the future: "Not summer's bloom lies ahead of us, but rather a polar night of icy darkness and hardness..." (in Gerth and Mills, 1958, p. 128).

The Realities of Bureaucracy

In the preceding section we have examined the ideal–typical features of bureaucracies: features that can be viewed as a rational system for accomplishing large numbers of tasks or great amounts of work. Indeed, bureaucracies do exactly that. Each year in the United States billions of pieces of mail are delivered, billions of checks are processed, and millions of student grade reports are placed on college transcripts. All these tasks and many billions of others are accomplished by the people and computers of bureaucratic organizations. These monumental amounts of work are completed because the people and machines of bureaucracies apply precise rules and procedures in a uniform manner to every case processed. Also, because of the high degree of specialization, each person in a bureaucracy is doing a limited range of things in a highly repetitive manner. These features of the bureaucracy make it efficient in dealing with large numbers of tasks.

As everyone who has encountered a bureaucracy knows, however, bureaucracies are not very good at handling unusual or unique cases. The customer, or client, or student who has an out-of-the-ordinary situation or case nonetheless has the rigid rules of the bureaucracy applied, even though they are inappropriate or inapplicable. Under such circumstances many people become frustrated with bureaucracies and find them unfair as well as inefficient. But this reality of bureaucracies is just one of many that conflict with the organizational model of rationality and efficiency. We will consider a few others next.

The Impersonal Treatment of Clients. The ideal bureaucrat is supposed to perform in a formal and impersonal manner. When bureaucrats come into contact with clients, however, the clients often perceive this behavior style as disinterest or even hostility. The impersonal treatment of clients has been called "service without a smile" (Hummel, 1987, p. 27). The client feels like a nonperson in the face of this impersonal bureaucratic treatment. Of course, now that much bureaucratic work is done by computers there is literally no live person with whom the client can interact.

Paperwork and Red Tape.   As noted earlier, the written word is the hallmark of bureaucracies. Not only is this true for the bureaucrats who must maintain written records of their actions, but it is also true for the clients of bureaucracies. Clients are frequently asked to complete various elaborate and detailed forms. Anyone who has ever applied for admission to a college, applied for a credit card, or visited a doctor knows that the first step is to fill out an application. Bureaucracies ask for many different kinds of personal information, and through their computers they are easily able to retain files on massive numbers of people. Every adult in contemporary society has left a paper trail of his or her activities through encounters with bureaucracies.

Rules and Regulations.   Bureaucracies have exact rules that are supposed to cover all situations and cases. The rules are to be followed precisely so that clients and cases will be uniformly treated. In this way the bureaucracy does not engage in favoritism and special treatment. However, sometimes the rules of the organization actually get in the way of what the organization is supposed to accomplish. The following account of an incident in a post office illustrates this point:

> I overheard a clerk telling a customer that he couldn't rent a post-office box unless he had a permanent address.

> "But the reason I need a box is because I don't have a permanent address," the man explained. "When you get a permanent address," the clerk politely explained, "you can get the box." "But, then I won't need it . . ." (Greenberg, 1979).

This example may be called a "Catch 22," a term first used in the title of a novel by Joseph Heller (1955). In this novel about military life during World War II, the protagonist, a bomber pilot named Yossarian, wanted to be excused from flying any more bombing missions by having the doctor declare him crazy. But the doctor explained that, even though there was a rule stating that a flier could be grounded if he were crazy, there was another rule—number 22—stating that anyone who wanted to get out of combat was not really crazy. This is the origin of the phrase "Catch 22."

The term **Catch 22** has become a part of the English language and is used for a wide range of encounters with bureaucracies. Generally, the term is applied to situations in which the rules of an organization make it impossible to do what these same rules require.

The Bureaucratic Personality.   Closely related to the issue of rules is the term **bureaucratic personality,** which is the tendency for bureaucrats to conform in a slavish manner to the rules of the organization. The person with a bureaucratic personality treats the rules as more important than the task or the objective of the organization. By adopting a bureaucratic personality, the bureaucrat can avoid guilt and personal conscience in dealing with clients (Hummel, 1987). The clerk who will not accept your check because the "company policy forbids accepting checks" can avoid personal blame or guilt when turning you down.

The Informal System.   According to the ideal-type characterization, bureaucratic organizations are built on the principle of impersonal relations among members. Members are supposed to be judged on the basis of objective measures of their performances, and relationships are based on rational principles. However, in reality, bureaucratic organizations always contain personal relationships and often close-knit social groups—primary groups of the type we discussed earlier. Some of the classic studies of sociology have shown how the informal groups in organizations, such as manufacturing plants, employment agencies, and the U.S. Army, influence behavior in ways that either subvert or override the objectives of the organization (Roethlisberger and Dickson, 1939/1964; Blau, 1963; Little, 1970).

The Thickening of Bureaucracy.   While no one doubts the increasing numbers of bureaucracies in contemporary society, a recent study of the federal government has uncovered a new phenomenon: the federal bureaucracy, at the top, is "thickening." This term is used to describe the increasing number of administrators at the top levels of the federal bureaucracy, for example, the various assistants to cabinet secretaries (Light, 1995).

Between 1960 and 1992, the layers of managers in federal bureaucracies increased from 17 to 32 (Light, 1995). The number of upper-level managers in the federal government increased during this 32-year period from 451 to 2,393. With this many managers, it is possible that "no one anywhere in government is accountable for what goes right or wrong" (Barr, 1995, p. A17).

The Tendency toward Oligarchy

Although positions in bureaucratic organizations, including leadership positions, are supposedly based on competence and expertise, such is not always the case. Even democratic organizations have a tendency to end up being undemocratic, or oligarchic. An **oligarchy** is characterized by a small group of people at the top of the organization having almost all the control and power. An early sociologist formulated the "iron law of oligarchy" to depict this tendency (Michels, 1915/1962).

To test out his thesis, Michels focused on the most unlikely places for oligarchies to arise—socialist political parties and labor unions. He felt that if he found oligarchical tendencies in such seemingly democratic organizations, he would find them anywhere and everywhere. In fact, Michels did find the existence of oligarchy in such organizations and concluded that the tendency toward oligarchy must be an "iron law" (Michels, 1915/1962, p. 50).

Michels attributed the oligarchic tendencies of organizations, in part, to the resources that come naturally to the people in positions of leadership, The leaders have higher-quality information and more information than is held by the membership. Leaders also control the flow of information throughout the organization, through the organization's news media and by an agenda they choose to present to the organization's membership. Leaders are also likely to have and develop a higher level of political skill—making speeches, writing editorials, and organizing group activities. Michels argued that leaders of organizations place their need to continue in a dominant position over the needs, interests, and values of the organization. In other words, power becomes more important to organizational leaders than does democracy. This means that the leaders of such organizations are perfectly willing to subvert the basic democratic principles of the organization in order to maintain their power.

Conflict in Organizations

The ideal–typical description of bureaucracy does not include conflict between individuals or groups within organizations. Yet conflict within organizations is pervasive. Of course, much conflict in organizations occurs between individuals, perhaps because they have incompatible personalities or because they are in competition for some scarce goal or resource. However, sociologists are often more interested in conflict that grows out of the characteristics of the organizations themselves (Clark, 1988; Perrow, 1986).

A major form of conflict within bureaucracies occurs when professionals such as physicians, lawyers, and scientists are employed in bureaucratic organizations. Professionals generally assume that their actions and performances should be judged and controlled only by other professionals. However, professionals employed in bureaucratic organizations are often subject to the supervision of nonprofessional superiors.

One study of Canadian doctors employed by large companies found the doctors in conflict with managers over various medical and health issues. For example, preemployment physical examinations were given to prospective employees, and the doctors were pressed by the company to disqualify any doubtful cases, even for minor medical reasons. The company wanted to minimize future risks, but this created conflicts with doctors who felt they were being pressured to violate their medical ethics. A number of other areas—plant safety, pressures on workers to return to work after injuries, and compensation for illnesses and injuries—revealed management interests that were in conflict with the medical autonomy of company doctors (Walters, 1982).

We have presented only one of many instances in which individuals or a sector of an organization has a nearly inevitable conflict with some other sector. For example, conflict almost always exists between sales and production people in industrial firms, between administrators and faculty in colleges, between doctors and nurses and administrators in hospitals, and between treatment and custodial staffs in prisons (Perrow, 1986).

Can Bureaucracy Be Eliminated?

While Max Weber was one of the first to fear and dislike the advance of bureaucracy, he was certainly not the last. Other scholars and intellectuals, as well as politicians and average citizens, have criticized the ever-larger bureaucracies and lamented the increasing number of bureaucrats (Blau and Meyer, 1987, pp. 194–195). Most contemporary observers, however, think that the clock cannot be turned back. "As much as we may wish otherwise, . . . large organizations operating on bureaucratic principles will remain part of the social landscape for some time to come" (Blau and Meyer, 1987, p. 195).

Another view of the future of bureaucratic organizations, however, sees profound changes occurring (Hage, 1988; Heydebrand, 1989). According to this view, the mindless rigidity of large bureaucracies is being replaced by smaller organizations characterized by informality and flexibility. Even though large organizations may continue to exist, their working subunits will be smaller, less formal, and more democratically organized. These working units will be mission or task oriented. A quarter-century ago, Toffler (1970) coined the word *ad-hocracies* to suggest the idea of temporary work groups composed of a wide variety of highly skilled workers brought together to solve specific, nonroutine problems.

An example of an ad-hocracy can be seen in the way a movie might be produced by a group of creative and highly skilled people. Few rigid rules would guide their behavior, because most of the time they would be dealing spontaneously with emerging problems and questions. Some people believe that more and more circumstances will occur where these more informal and flexible work groups will emerge because they are best suited for the tasks at hand (Heydebrand, 1989; Toffler, 1970).

Although some social analysts foresee a future in which bureaucratic forms of organization will decline, the fact remains that the bureaucratization of life continues to expand. In the schools where we are educated, the organizations in which we work, and in virtually every other organization we encounter in our everyday lives, the form of organization is bureaucratic (Blau and Meyer, 1987; Meyer et al., 1985). On a worldwide basis the lives of more and more people are undoubtedly touched by governments and organizations that are increasingly bureaucratic. The bureaucratic form of organization may be modified, but it will not disappear in the foreseeable future.

Organizations of the type we have been considering are parts of larger social units called institutions. Institutions will be introduced briefly at this point and discussed in Part 3 of this book.

Institutions

An **institution** is a set of groups and organizations with norms and values that center around the most basic needs of a society. The major institutions are the family, education, the economy, health and medicine, and the polity. All these institutions are found in one form or another in all societies because they carry out necessary societal tasks. As an example, societies must have some orderly way of ensuring that males and females produce enough offspring and care for them well enough so that a sufficient number will survive and the society can continue. The institution that accomplishes these tasks is, of course, the family. Following the definition offered above, the family as an institution has identifiable groups (families and kinship units); there are norms associated with the family (for example, rules specifying how many spouses one can have); and there are values associated with the family (loyalty to family members).

Descriptions of the major institutions help to define the nature of a society. Indeed, all of the institutions, taken together, give a fairly clear view of a society. We are now ready to consider this major social unit, the society.

Society

Although sociologists sometimes focus on large portions of the world (Chirot, 1985) or on the relationships between parts of the world (Arrow and King, 1990; Sklair, 1991; Wallerstein, 1974, 1980; Waters, 1995), the largest social entity typically studied by sociologists is the society. A society typically is the most complete, the most all-encompassing unit of sociological analysis. A **society** is a population living in a given territory, with a social structure, and sharing a culture.

This definition covers a wide range of actual societies and therefore encompasses considerable diversity. For example, the population size of a society can vary greatly. With a 1994 population of approximately 260 million people, the United States is a society, but other societies in the world have only a few thousand people (the Yanomamo described in Chapter 3), and some have only a few hundred. Even China, with its population of over a billion people (1.3 billion in 1994), is described as a society, although great cultural differences exist from one part of China to another.

Societies are most commonly described in terms of their economic systems. The long history of human existence has had only a few basic types of economic arrangements. We will summarize them briefly:

Hunting and Gathering Societies

Through hundreds of thousands of years of human existence, until about 7000 B.C., all humans lived by hunting and gathering their food. They hunted wild game

Cross-national Perspectives

When Societies Collapse

When societies are functioning relatively smoothly, as they usually do, it is easy to overlook the importance of social order. But when societies collapse, the necessity for social order is vividly revealed. In recent years several societies, in various places, have come to the world's attention because they reached a state of utter disorder.

Americans became especially aware of one case of a collapsed society in 1992, when newspaper photographs and television pictures from Somalia started to reveal the plight of the people there. The images of starving Somalian children and adults, huddled in refugee camps, waiting in vain for relief supplies of food, touched the conscience of Americans and many others throughout the world.

Somalia at its chaotic and anarchic worst provided a glimpse of what life is like when organized society fails. The only order that existed there was based on raw firepower—rifles, grenades, and small artillery pieces (Gregory, 1992).

Eventually, American military forces were sent to Somalia as part of an effort to restore some semblance of order and allow emergency food shipments to reach the starving people of that country. News reports from Somalia today indicate that some societal order has been restored and at least the people are not living in famine conditions.

Today, however, a number of other African countries, this time in Western Sub-Saharan Africa, seem to be on the verge of collapse. Sierra Leone, for example, is beset by all types of political, social, economic, and medical ills that have led one observer to describe it as a "failed society" (Kaplan, 1996). In Sierra Leone, a country of 4.5 million people, there are 400,000 displaced people who have left their homes. Another 380,000 have fled to nearby countries. The government controls only part of the country's territory, despite a policy of considerable brutality. The people of Sierra Leone have only occasional electricity, and their contact with the outside world is limited to short-wave radios. Virtually all the people of Sierra Leone suffer from malaria, but only the most severe cases receive medical treatment. Crime is so commonplace that the few well-off members of the society need continuous protection by private guards. For example, when the elite go to dinner at a restaurant, they hire armed youths to protect their cars in the parking lot. The police in Sierra Leone are nearly completely ineffectual after dark (Kaplan, 1996).

Robert Kaplan, a journalist who has recently visited and reported on the countries of Sierra Leone and its neighbors, has found similar societal chaos in other countries of the world (Kaplan, 1996). For example, Cambodia, in Southeast Asia, a country that has been torn by warfare and internal killing for more than 30 years, was, for him, "eerily similar" to Sierra Leone. Cambodia, too, has "random crime, mosquito-borne disease [malaria], a government army that is more like a mob, and a countryside that is ungovernable because of guerilla insurgents" (Kaplan, 1996, p. 411).

Extreme cases of societal collapse, illustrated by Somalia, Sierra Leone, and Cambodia, are testaments to the importance of societal order. When societies collapse, the people often live under terrible conditions where their very survival is at stake.

GREGORY, SOPHFRONIAS S. "How Somalia Crumbled." *Time,* December 14, 1992.
KAPLAN, ROBERT. *The Ends of the Earth: A Journey to the Dawn of the 21st Century.* New York: Random House, 1996.

or fished and gathered wild fruits and plants. Hunting and gathering societies were not permanently fixed in one place, because when the supply of food declined in a particular area it was necessary to move on to another. Only a few small hunting and gathering societies still survive in the world today. One, for example, is the !Kung[1] in the Kalahari Desert of Africa, a society that has been of great interest to anthropologists. The !Kung offer anthropologists an opportunity to study a hunting and gathering society and thereby gain insights into what the lives of prehistoric peoples might have been.

Horticultural Societies

Beginning about 9000 years ago (7000 B.C.), some humans started growing part of their own food rather than gathering foods growing wild. In horticultural societies, food is typically grown in gardenlike plots, which may be somewhat temporary in nature. When people started to grow their own food, they also established more permanent communities and were not as likely to be nomadic.

Horticultural societies can still be found in the world today, as, for example, the Gahuku people of the New Guinea Highlands (Read, 1980). The Gahuku people have small personal garden plots that they cultivate with digging sticks. They

---

[1]The exclamation mark before the name Kung reflects the fact that the !Kung uses a clicking sound in their language that does not exist in English.

raise mostly sweet potatoes, taro, and corn, though banana trees and other wild-growing fruits also provide food. These horticultural people also raise pigs, which provide food, especially for special ceremonial occasions.

Agrarian Societies

Agrarian societies appeared in about 3000 B.C. (5000 years ago). These societies differed from the horticultural societies by their larger scale of food production. Crops were regularly planted and harvested, often with the aid of plows pulled by draft animals. Generally, the production of foods in agrarian societies was at a subsistence level, which means that the farm produce of one growing season was consumed during that year. As agricultural methods improved, however, some surpluses were produced, allowing some people in the society to engage in other kinds of productive activity. Since communities in agrarian societies could grow to larger sizes, the first cities emerged during this era.

The most prominent, early agrarian societies were in ancient Egypt, the Middle East, and China, and later in medieval Europe. Agrarian societies exist today wherever most of the people rely on agriculture for their livelihood and subsistence.

Industrial Societies

Industrial societies are those in which the predominant economic activity is the production of manufactured goods. The Industrial Revolution, which opened the way for industrialization, is usually placed in the last half of the eighteenth century. England led the way by introducing a variety of machines, powered by steam, that produced manufactured goods in factories. Agricultural production must, of course, continue in industrial societies, but in the most highly industrialized societies only a small proportion of the population is engaged in agriculture. In the United States today, the figure is about 2 percent.

Postindustrial Societies

A recently introduced term for describing the economic base of a society is *postindustrial society* (Bell, 1973). The **postindustrial society** describes a society that was formerly industrial but is now primarily engaged in producing services and information rather than manufactured goods. In the United States today, most people in the labor force are providing services of some kind instead of producing things. The postindustrial economy will be discussed more fully in Chapter 13.

A Sociological Classification of Societies

While the economic systems of societies have been widely used as a basis for classification, the classic sociological way describes societies in terms of the social relationships that predominate. A question that can be asked about societies is, How do people generally relate to one another? Or, looked at historically, Do people relate to each other differently in contemporary society (especially the large urban-industrial—or postindustrial—societies) than they did in societies of the past? A nineteenth-century German sociologist named Ferdinand Toennies suggested that the relationships between people are different in modern societies than in societies of the past. He labeled historical societies *gemeinschaft* and modern societies *gesellschaft* (Toennies, 1887/1957).

Gemeinschaft societies are characterized by very personal face-to-face relationships such as those that exist in families, in rural villages, and perhaps in small towns. These highly personal relations between people are valued for their intrinsic qualities, not for their usefulness.

Gesellschaft societies are characterized by relationships that are impersonal and distant. People interact with each other only in limited ways. The relationships are entered into only for what they might provide. Social relationships in a *gesellschaft* society are seen as means to ends.

Obviously any modern, industrial society today has both *gemeinschaft* and *gesellschaft* relationships. No society exists in which close personal relationships are totally absent. Similarly, in historical, traditional societies, people did enter some relationships for self-interested reasons. Toennies's distinction calls attention to the *prevailing* or *predominant* patterns of social relations in a society.

Summary

The way the people of any society relate to each other and organize their social lives is not random but patterned. Social structures are regular patterns of interaction and persistent social relationships. At a societal level, structures often reflect distributions of wealth, power, or authority, but structures can also be described along ethnic or racial lines.

Interaction between individuals is a complex process, but people do it with ease in their everyday lives. Although interaction has a creative and spontaneous dimension, it is patterned to some degree by cultural values and social norms.

Patterns of behavior are also produced by the statuses and roles that people occupy. Statuses are positions, and roles are the expected behaviors for a person occupying a position. However, people do not simply conform to a rigid set of role expectations, but may actively modify their roles.

Two people engaging in interaction is a dyad. When a third person is added, the dyad becomes a triad, making relationships much more complicated.

A key feature of social groups is that they are composed of a number of people who interact over time and thereby establish patterns of interaction, a group identity, and norms. Identifying with a group often produces in-group attitudes maintaining that the ways of one's own group are right and those of out-groups are wrong. Primary groups are intimate, face-to-face groups, while secondary groups are larger and more impersonal. Reference groups are groups that people take into account in evaluating their behavior, even when they are not members of those groups. Experimental studies have shown that people tend to conform to the ways of groups they are in.

Organizations and bureaucracies are increasingly important in contemporary life. Organizations, divided according to how they control the members at the bottom, can be classified as coercive, utilitarian, and normative–voluntary. Bureaucracies are organized along rational-legal lines, and in an ideal–typical sense are characterized by a division of labor, rank-ordered authority, a system of rules, impersonality, and membership based on competence or expertise.

The realities of bureaucracy include impersonal treatment of clients, paperwork and red tape, scrupulous observance of rules, a tendency toward oligarchy, and conflict. Although bureaucracies are often viewed negatively, they are not likely to disappear; however, the future may see modifications and changes in bureaucratic organization.

Institutions, such as the family, education, the economy, health and medicine, and the polity, are found in all societies. It is through the institutions that necessary societal tasks are accomplished.

Societies, the largest social entity typically studied by sociologists, are commonly distinguished by their economic systems: hunting and gathering, horticultural, agrarian, industrial, and postindustrial. Sociologically, societies can be described as *gemeinschaft* or *gesellschaft* types.

CRITICAL THINKING

1. Draw a diagram of the social structure of some set of people you know (or have known). The people could be in your living unit, in your community, or in your high school class, for example.
2. What statuses do you hold in life? Give an example of an expected behavior associated with each.
3. Are the following statuses achieved or ascribed: teacher, grandparent, female, judge, baby, nurse? How do you make the determination?
4. Give examples of groups that illustrate primary or secondary groups. Explain how the classification is made.
5. What reference groups are most important in your life? Explain how these groups may or may not influence your behavior.
6. Describe the Sherif, Asch, and Milgram experiments. What does each show us about human behavior in groups?
7. Use today's newspaper to identify two or three *organizations* (using the term *organization* as sociologists would define it). Classify each organization as coercive, utilitarian, or normative.
8. The authors agree that the modern world is becoming increasingly bureaucratized. Give examples from this chapter and from your own life to support or refute this idea.
9. Give examples of both *gemeinschaft* and *gesellschaft* relationships in contemporary society.

5

Socialization

The late Bruno Bettelheim, a world-famous psychologist, once told an anecdote that illustrates the importance of the topic of socialization. Bettelheim's story involves a familiar parenting experience, getting a reluctant young child (say, a boy) to eat his vegetables. An American parent might say, "You must eat your vegetables, they are good for you and will make you strong." A Japanese mother, by contrast, would be more likely to say, "How do you think it makes the man who grew these vegetables feel? He grew them for you to eat and now you reject them." Or "How do you think it makes the carrots feel? They grew so you could eat them, but now you will not" (paraphrase of Bettelheim, 1985, p. 58).

Thus, the Japanese teach even their young children to be sensitive to the feelings of others. In contrast, the admonition of the U.S. parent ("It will make you grow") emphasizes how the child himself will benefit from eating the vegetables. When the Japanese mother stresses how important it is for the child to be sensitive to the feelings of others, she is paralleling the notion of social responsibility and group loyalty found in the Japanese culture. Similarly, in the United States when the parent stresses the well-being of the individual child, she is reflecting her culture's concern with individual self-interest.

Arnett (1995) makes a distinction between *broad* and *narrow* cultural socialization. "Cultures characterized by broad socialization tend to encourage individualism, independence, and self-expression" (Arnett, 1995, p. 617). By contrast, cultures with narrow socialization emphasize the importance of obedience and conformity and discourage deviation from cultural norms. Socialization in the United States, especially in the schools and through the mass media, tends to be broader than in countries like Japan (Arnett, 1995).

In this chapter we will examine the socialization process in detail, exploring how people learn about their cultures from peers, schools, and the mass media, as well as from their parents. But, first, we will see how socialization produces human qualities and the personalities of children.

The Nature of Socialization

Socialization is the process by which a person learns and generally accepts the established ways of a particular social group or society. The principal purpose of socialization is to make sure that the new members will do things in about the same way as they are currently being done. In other words, societies, groups, and organizations maintain a certain amount of continuity over time because of the socialization of new members. Generally, new members accept what is taught to them as the right and proper way of doing things.

In a similar way, from a cultural perspective, socialization passes on the values and norms to the new members, which allows norms and values to persist from one generation to the next. Even when the new members of a society are not born into that society but come in as immigrants, various forms of socialization initiate these newcomers into the culture of the new society.

In addition to its significance at the level of the society and culture, socialization also contributes to the process of producing the characteristics and personality of the individual. The socialization that occurs early in life, in infancy and early childhood, is especially critical in this regard. Often called **primary socialization,** it is usually provided by the parents or other caregiver(s) and lays the foundation for personality development. In this process infants become social beings. The early stages of socialization nurture a tendency for the human infant to want and need interaction with other people—a tendency that generally endures.

Socialization continues throughout the lifetime of every individual. As people move into new jobs, organizations, communities, and even new life stages they will learn the values, norms, and behaviors expected of them in these settings. Later in this chapter we will turn to the socialization that occurs during adolescence, adulthood, and old age, but first we focus on the critically important socialization that occurs in infancy and early childhood.

The importance of socialization during infancy and early childhood can be understood by considering what human beings would be without contact with other humans. At this fundamental level we are not focusing on socialization per se, although some socialization is occurring, but simply on the contact and interaction between infants and other human beings.

Acquiring Human Qualities

Human babies cannot care for themselves when born; they must have some other human present to give them food and keep them warm, or they will not survive. Although babies in these early days of life seem to be very limited and almost entirely biological in their nature, increasing evidence shows that they are already orienting toward the humans in their environment. Video camera observations have shown that infants, even in the first hours after birth, have a "quiet–alert stage" when they are attentive to their environment, especially to people. In the first few days or weeks of life infants will make eye contact with a parent and will respond to a parent's facial expressions and voice sounds. This research on very young infants seems to show that the physical dependence infants have on other humans is augmented by an early tendency to be attracted to their primary caregivers.

Since the human infant begins responding to other humans at such an early stage of life, we might too easily assume that many social and personal qualities normally found in humans are also inborn or inherent. But the evidence is to the contrary for, although human infants might have the tendency toward sociability, they must have sustained contact with other human beings or it will not develop. We can never know with complete certainty how an infant would develop if it were kept alive without contact with other humans, but a few documented cases of isolated children provide some insights. These substantiated cases of infants who have been raised in nearly complete isolation reveal all too clearly that, without human contact, the qualities we associate with humanness can be almost completely lost.

Children Isolated from Human Contact

Mythological stories have been told of children who were reared by animals instead of human beings, and some cases of children who were allegedly found living in the wild with animals have been minimally documented. (They are called **feral,** meaning *wild children.*) In one such case in India, two children were found living with wolves. They were brought to an orphanage where they were cared for, observed, and photographed over a period of years. Long after they were found, these children continued to display animal-like behavior, such as walking on all fours, eating food with their mouths, and preferring to play with dogs (Singh and Zingg, 1942).

The reported cases of feral children are generally not as trustworthy as the cases of children who lived in human settings but were kept virtually isolated from human contact (Curtiss, 1977; Davis, 1940, 1947). In each known case a family member placed the child in some isolated part of the home, providing only enough food and water to keep the child alive but offering no human contact. When found, the children did not talk, nor did they show the range of emotions that humans usually display (crying, smiling and laughing, responding to human gestures of friendship, and the like).

One such case occurred in Temple Hills, California, where a father locked his daughter in a room from age 2 until she was discovered (in 1970) at age 13 (Curtiss, 1977; Rymer, 1993). The girl (called Genie) was placed by her father in a restraining harness, seated on a potty chair during the day, and placed in a strait-jacket at night. The mother of this girl, terrorized by her brutal husband and further limited by blindness, had almost no contact with Genie after infancy. When Genie was finally found she was unable to speak, because during her formative years her father had not allowed her to make any sounds. Even with intensive training after her discovery, Genie was unable to use language at more than a rudimentary level. The professionals who worked with her did not believe she was mentally retarded, because she showed a quick mind in nonverbal ways and had especially good spatial skills. Genie was eager to communicate, but it was nearly impossible for her to master pronouns, tenses, and the meanings of familiar terms of social intercourse. "She could not learn to say 'Hello' in response to 'Hello,' [and] could not grasp the meaning of 'Thank you'" (Rymer, 1992, p. 57).

Efforts to socialize her were only partially successful; long after she was found she persisted in behaviors that went beyond normal acceptability. One of Genie's teachers, who developed a close relationship with her, described how this 14-year-old girl "had many distasteful mannerisms and her behavior was often disconcerting and unpalatable" (Curtiss, 1977, p. 20). Genie would spit and blow her nose on everything and everyone around her. She also had a special fondness for plastic things and certain items of clothing or accessories:

> If anyone she encountered in the street or in a store or other public place had something she liked, she was uncontrollably drawn to him or her, and without obeying any rules of psychological distance or social mores, she would go right up to the person and put her hands on the desired item (Curtiss, 1977, p. 20).

Genie also masturbated whenever and however she could. Any object that she could use for masturbation attracted her. For more than four years after her discovery the professionals working with her were unable to limit this socially unacceptable form of behavior.

Genie has spent most of her adult years in institutions. Now in her thirties, she lives in a home for the retarded (Rymer, 1992). Despite her apparent innate intelligence, she was never able to overcome the early years of isolation and live a normal social life.

The information provided by Genie and the limited number of other cases of extreme isolation demonstrate that human beings do not become "human" if they do not have at least some human contact. Furthermore, there seems to be a critical formative period when infants and children need human contact and interaction or the effects upon their personalities are devastating and largely irreversible.

Early Socialization: "Getting Hooked on People"

How does a baby become human and develop personal traits? Most human infants eventually approximate the human qualities that are prominent in the particular group into which they happen to be born. To understand how this happens, we must go back to our earlier discussion of the human infant who cannot survive on its own.

Because a baby absolutely needs adults for comfort and survival, adults control the situation. Although most parents first respond by freely gratifying their baby's every need, they do not do so for long. Eventually, adults start to assert their power. Parents continue to give what a child needs, but they start exacting a price. Mothers and fathers will feed and change the diapers of the baby, but eventually they want something in return, even if it is only a smile. If they get the smile, they may give something else—a hug, a cuddle, or a tickle. If the baby responds again, more comforting rewards are given.

This is the beginning of socialization for the norm of reciprocity (Gouldner, 1960). The **norm of reciprocity** calls for two interacting people to give one another things of equal or almost equal value. People want to continue to interact with one another if they are receiving something roughly equal in value to what they are giving.

Reciprocity in interaction is probably the earliest social lesson. Campbell (1975) describes reciprocity from the point of view of what is happening to the infant:

> The human infant is both highly dependent and pleasure seeking. Put these two things together, and it follows clearly that he must have the help of others in securing his own gratification. This simple fact is the root-source of a process that we shall call, quite unscientifically, "getting hooked on people" (Campbell, 1975, p. 17).

By "getting hooked on people," Campbell means that after a while the baby needs more than the food and the dry diapers that the adult provides. The baby also needs the smiles, the attention, the hugs, and the comforting words of the adult who delivers the other necessities.

At first adults will give warmth and comfort freely—but not forever. Adults soon start demanding more and more from their babies for what they provide. Thus babies must slowly give up their totally selfish ways. They have to start doing some things that they do not want to do and stop doing other things. Eating solid foods instead of warm milk, especially milk from the mother's warm body, comes just one step before sitting on the cold potty—and so the process of making a responsible member of society begins. Later, adults bestow smiles, praise, and affection for brushing teeth, keeping a room clean, sitting quietly during religious services, bringing home good grades on report cards, or writing thank-you letters promptly.

Parents and other adults also use negative sanctions, which they have at their disposal by virtue of their powerful position. They may augment their reward system by scolding, spanking, withholding desserts, or "grounding" to get the child or adolescent to do what is "right."

The use of reward and punishment to produce acceptable social behavior is not the only way to accomplish socialization; it is only a basic mechanism that is part of the larger process of socialization. Something else happens in this process that cannot be explained by the simple idea of rewarding good behavior and punishing bad behavior. Children do what their parents and others expect of them, even when their parents are not around to see what they are doing. Children will generally do the "right" things without constant reward or punishment. The following discussion explores how and why this happens.

Symbolic Interaction and the Social Self

In Chapter 1 we introduced a theory called symbolic interactionism, and we noted that through symbols infants and children acquire an understanding of the world and themselves. Especially important is the way a child develops a sense of self through the process of interaction with significant others (Gecas and Burke, 1995). **Significant others** are those people in an individual's life who shape the individual's self and provide definitions for other social objects (Mead, 1934/1962). Usually, parents are the most important significant others in the early stages of life. The recognition by symbolic interactionists that the self is essentially a social creation is probably the single most important insight of this perspective (Fine, 1990).

One of the early symbolic interactionists, Charles Horton Cooley, emphasized the social nature of the self with his concept of the **looking-glass self** (Cooley, 1902). This concept conveys vividly the notion that every child develops a self-image that reflects how others respond to her or him. Both as children and adults, we can see ourselves mostly through the responses and reactions of others.

While Cooley's term, the looking-glass self, is descriptive, most sociologists today simply use the term *self,* or *social self,* which is the totality of all an individual's thoughts and feelings that make up her or his definition of self (Gecas and Burke, 1995).

Interacting with others gives people the ability to put themselves in the place of another person. As adults we do it almost constantly. If we are stopped by the police for a minor traffic violation, we try to decide quickly how to talk to the officer. Should we be flippant, aggressive, or humble? How will the officer respond to each of these approaches? Often we try to run through a scene as it might develop from these different approaches. We are not always successful in choosing the best strategy, but we try to anticipate how other persons will respond by putting ourselves in their places. The ability to respond to ourselves as objects, much as others respond to us, and the ability to anticipate how others will respond to our behavior or actions indicate a fairly high level of social being.

But one more step remains in the socialization process. We ultimately evaluate ourselves not only according to how specific individuals respond to us but also according to how others in general will respond. We consider what people will think if we do this or that. We want general social approval for what we do, not just approval from specific others.

Developmental Stages.   George Herbert Mead (1934/1962), an originator of symbolic interaction theory, first described how children arrive at the point where they are concerned about how others *in general* will respond to their behavior. Mead postulated a three-stage developmental process during childhood. In the first stage, the **preparatory stage,** young children engage in a primitive form of interaction with adults. The baby, for example, may utter a random vocalization and the parent responds to it, perhaps imitating the child's sound. This may encourage the child to respond again in a similar way. The adult and child thus carry on a verbal interaction, but the utterances they make have no clear symbolic meaning; in everyday terms, the parent and child are talking "baby talk." In the second stage, the **play stage,** the child learns the symbols of the language system, which gives him or her a *self-consciousness.* Children in the play stage use language to put themselves in another person's place. Last is the **game stage,** during which children assume the roles of a number of other people simultaneously and respond to the expectations that these people have. During the game stage children acquire a sense of, and seek the approval of, what Mead called the *generalized other.*

The **generalized other** is the internalization of the norms of the larger social group or the society. As an example, most students will not cheat on an examination—even when there is no chance of being caught—because they have learned and internalized the idea that it is best to be honest. In a sense, they are rewarding themselves for living up to a standard they have learned and accepted. When people accept the ways of the society and generally behave in conformity to those ways, even when no specific punishment or reward will result from their conformity, then they are fully socialized.

To summarize, children learn to evaluate all objects (both abstract and concrete and including the self) largely from the people with whom they interact. Furthermore, their learning is not just superficial or calculated to get other people to bestow social rewards and approval. Nor is the learning of a society's ways done only to avoid punishment or penalty. The process starts there, but eventually humans internalize the ways of the society. They accept them as right for themselves and others, and they provide their own rewards when they conform to them.

This acceptance of societal ways does not mean that an effective social system will produce a society of conforming robots. People do cheat on tests; they also cheat in business deals and on marriage partners. Socialization to norms and values is never totally effective and certainly is not uniform throughout society. The rules and values of a society are themselves never universal or absolute. There is plenty of room for individual variation. Our description of early socialization explains why we have as much order and regularity in society as we do, and why it is possible to have a society at all. Although childhood socialization does not explain every individual's behavior, it does show how every individual is, to a great degree, a social product.

Agents of Socialization

Socialization is generally initiated by the people who are already members of a social system; they are called the agents of socialization, and they have the task of socializing new members. In the case of infants being born into families, the first socializing agents are the parents, but as children grow older, other agents of socialization also become important. Included among the other socializing agents are children's peers (often including siblings), teachers, and the mass media (Arnett, 1995). We will begin with the most important early socializing agents, the parents.

Parents as Socializing Agents

Almost all parents recognize the responsibility of teaching their children the skills necessary to get along in life. From a sociological perspective, parents are responding to the social role of being a parent. Most adults learn the parental role through their own socialization.

Many parents also feel responsible for *shaping* the personalities of their children. Many contemporary parents have accepted the basic sociological and psychological view that personalities of children are shaped by environmental influences in general, and especially by parental influences on the child. However, parents cannot consciously set out to produce a certain kind of child and succeed in getting what they want.

Many young, modern, and well-educated parents seem to conceive of shaping the personalities of their children as a process of direct, straightforward teaching: "If I want my child to be independent, I will teach independence, and my child will be independent. If I want my child to be frugal or neat, I will teach those things." This naive view of the socialization process often causes parents to wonder "where they went wrong" when their children do not mature exactly according to their expectations.

Several factors explain why socialization is not a process of direct teaching. First, socialization is more complex than the direct-teaching idea suggests. To begin with, socialization usually involves two parents (or parent figures). Two socializing parents may send quite different messages to the child, and the result of mixed messages in the child's development cannot be anticipated. Even when parents are consistent, children often turn out differently from what their parents wish.

Second, the direct-teaching notion of socialization fails to take into account how pervasive and subtle socialization is. Socialization occurs as much by example as by direct verbal means. A father may tell his children to try to get along with other people and be friendly, but if he frequently engages in disputes with his neighbors and coworkers, the children get a different message. This father is socializing his children as much by his behaviors as by his words.

Furthermore, socializing agents other than family members influence a child. At a fairly early age children begin to be socialized by the communication media, especially television. Somewhat later, playmates and friends, the schools, and the print media (magazines, newspapers, and books) play a part in a child's socialization.

One final influence, biological inheritance, contributes an additional unpredictable factor. Although sociologists do not generally view personality characteristics as genetically inherited, the possibility does exist that certain natural endowments might moderate and interact with the socialization process (Dunn and Plomin, 1990; Rose, 1979).

Because socialization is complex, pervasive, and subtle, and because outside socializing agents compete with familial ones, parents cannot expect to shape their children exactly as they desire. The scientific analysis of socialization and the experiences of many parents do not support the notion of socialization as a process of direct teaching.

Parental Differences in Socialization

The parents in any particular society will usually be in accord on a wide range of things they teach their children to do and not do. (Almost no parent, for instance, will consciously teach a child to lie, cheat, or use profanity.) But despite this general agreement, substantial differences exist in what the parents value in one part of the society, compared to the parents in another. Parents coming from different subcultural, ethnic, or religious groups, different social classes, and different critical historical periods will have differing notions of what they should teach their children (Peterson and Rollins, 1987).

The most extreme variations from mainstream socialization values typically occur in cases where parents are zealous about some cause or belief system. Recent newspaper accounts of certain fundamentalist Christians reveal how some parents will take extreme measures to socialize their children into the ways of their religious beliefs. Two fathers gave nearly identical accounts of how they terrorized their 5-year-old children with a fear of going to hell so they could be assured that the children would be obedient and God-fearing.

In the words of one of these fathers:

> My daughter is 5 years old and—people say how inhumane—I let my daughter lay and cry herself to sleep for a week straight about the flames of hell. See my daughter personally lay at night and said, 'I don't want to go to hell, I don't want to go to hell,' and she'd be laying there crying.
>
> I could have ran right in there and gave her the Gospel and she could have made a profession of salvation, but I let it get deep into her memory. Know what I mean? That there is a hell. And that will affect her whole life. That's why she is an obedient child (Naughton, 1988).

As a rule, parents try to teach their children lessons that they themselves have found to be useful or important in life. This rule has been most thoroughly documented with regard to the differences among socialization values of parents who are at different levels in the class structure (Kohn, 1977; Gecas, 1990; Miller-Loessi, 1995).

Cross-national Findings.   Studies conducted in the United States, Italy, Taiwan, Poland, and Japan have documented that parents at different levels of the class structure have different values that they communicate when they socialize their children (Kohn et al., 1983; Slomczynski et al., 1981; Naoi et al., 1985). The major findings of these studies can be briefly summarized: parents who are in the middle-class and upper-middle-class levels of the stratification structure (those with above average education and white-collar, managerial, or professional jobs) tend to value autonomy, creativity, and self-direction; by comparison, parents in the working class (especially those with blue-collar occupations) tend to value conformity to the rules and respect for external authority. In everyday terms, working-class parents are more likely to value obedience.

When parents engender in their children the value of autonomy and self-direction, they are portraying the world as a place that can be influenced by individuals who take initiatives. In contrast, parents who place a greater value on their children's obedience are reflecting their view of the world as a place of many rules and regulations and where people in authority give orders. To make one's way in this world, a person must learn obedience to the rules of those in authority.

When socializing their children, middle-class and upper-middle-class fathers wanted their children to be considerate of others, interested in how things happen, responsible, and self-controlled. These fathers were less likely to emphasize that their children should be well mannered, neat, clean, obedient, honest, and studious. These latter traits, however, were exactly the ones that the lower-class fathers strongly desired in their children.

Cross-cultural Perspectives

Some Alternative Views of Children's Personalities

While Americans tend to believe that parents shape the personalities of their children, the people of certain other societies have distinctly different views. The Irish and the Hindus of India (to take examples from two very different cultures) place much more emphasis on the inherited characteristics of children. However, as we will see, there are other distinctive differences in the views of the Irish and the Hindus.

Irish parents do recognize that they play an important role in bringing up their children and especially in teaching them right from wrong. They are likely to say, "Beware of the habit you give them" (Scheper-Hughes, 1979). But they also see a child's basic personality, talents, abilities, and nature as largely inherited. The Irish word that expresses this view is *dutcas*. *Dutcas* is translated as *blood, stock,* or *breeding,* but more specifically it refers to the personality characteristics one inherits from one's ancestors. Thus, when a mother throws up her hands in despair over her unruly sons, saying, "They're too full of their father's *dutcas*" (Scheper-Hughes, 1979), she is saying that the wildness of her sons is a trait they have inherited from their father.

An Irish child's *dutcas* does not have to come from an immediate parent, for the Irish believe that the characteristics of any ancestor can appear in the personality of a child. Thus, a daughter may be said to inherit her thriftiness from a particular grandmother, while a son may be seen as getting his laziness from a ne'er-do-well uncle.

A different view of inherited personality traits can be found among the Hindus of India (Kaker, 1979). Indian religious, medical, and folk beliefs hold that life begins at conception. It is here that the spirit from the body of someone who has lived previously is joined with the fertilized ovum. Thus, a major portion of the personality of a child comes not from immediate ancestors but from an already existing spirit that has lived in another body at a previous time. For the Hindu mother there is, however, an opportunity to modify the spirit while the fetus is still in the womb. The critical period for influencing the psychological development of the baby comes in the third month of pregnancy. According to Indian tradition, it is in that month that the feelings and wishes of the fetus, which come from its previous life, are transmitted to the mother. These are revealed to the mother in the form of cravings for particular foods. These cravings, which are really the wishes of the fetus, are not to be denied, for their fulfillment will ensure the proper psychological development of the child.

The personality of the Indian child is thought to be largely determined by the spirit from a previous life, though this might have been modified while in the womb. With this view in mind, it is not surprising that Indian parents are highly indulgent with their children. Mothers do not try to mold their children into a particular desired image. They are inclined to follow rather than lead the child in its development (Kaker, 1979).

These beliefs about the inherited personality traits of children, coming from the Irish and Hindu people, are not entirely unfamiliar to Americans. The personality traits of a child are sometimes seen as reflections of the personality of a particular family member—"She is just like her grand-mother in her love of animals." There is also a long-standing folk belief in the United States that what a mother does during her pregnancy will affect the character of her baby. This parallels the Hindu belief described above. One American proponent of this view has collected cases that have led him to conclude that, from the sixth month of pregnancy, a fetus can begin to learn, and respond emotionally to its mother (Verny and Kelly, 1984). In one such case, a young musical conductor knew the entire score of a musical number, even though he had never seen it before. This is alleged to have occurred because his mother had played this piece of music while she was pregnant.

KAKER, SUDHIR. "Childhood in India: Traditional Ideals and Contemporary Reality." *International Social Science Journal* 31, 1979.
SCHEPER-HUGHES, NANCY. "Breeding Breaks Out in the Eye of the Cat: Sex Roles, Birth Order, and the Irish Double-Bind." *Journal of Comparative Family Studies* 10, 1979.
VERNY, THOMAS and KELLY, JOHN. *The Secret Life of the Unborn Child.* New York: Dell, 1984.

Because of these different orientations, parents in the middle and lower social classes disciplined their children differently. Lower-class mothers punished their children directly or immediately after the child misbehaved, without asking questions. Middle-class mothers were more likely to punish or not punish their children according to how they interpreted the child's intention when committing the act. Middle-class parents judged the child's misbehavior by considering whether it seemed to violate the long-range goal that their child be able to demonstrate self-direction and individual responsibility. Working-class parents punished misbehavior if it violated some rule. They wanted obedience from their children—obedience to the rules that they had set down and obedience to the rules of the larger society.

In socializing their children, why do the middle classes value autonomy and the working classes value obedience to the rules? What is the relationship between position in the class structure and socialization values? According to the research of Kohn (1983) and his associates, the crucial factor is the occupational setting or work experience of the father. Middle-class fathers are typically employed in occupations that reward individual initiative and responsibility—autonomous behavior. The more they take initiatives, assume responsibility, and act independently, the more they are rewarded. In comparison, working-class fathers are typically employed in work settings where they must do exactly what they are told and where individual initiative is not especially valued or rewarded. People working on the assembly lines understand that they must do the work in the way they have been instructed if they want to keep their jobs.

Middle-class parents expect, at least implicitly, that their children will enter the occupational world at levels where they will be expected to show individual responsibility and self-direction. They socialize their children with this idea in mind, so that they will get along best and most successfully when they enter the white-collar, managerial, and professional occupations. Working-class parents have experienced a different kind of work world, one where they do what they are told, when they are told to do it. They assume that their children will enter the same kind of world, so they teach their children the importance of obedience in order that they will survive in that world. One might say that the arbitrary, absolute, and sometimes unfair demands for obedience that are often attributed to working-class fathers might be a way of forewarning their children about adult life. People in the lower strata of society are often treated arbitrarily by their superiors in the work world, as well as by other agents of authority (including police, the courts, and school personnel).

This line of research also shows how socialization is a contributor to the perpetuation of the existing class structure of a society. This socialization process may be *one* mechanism that pushes the children of working-class parents toward working-class occupations, whereas the children of middle-class parents move toward middle-class occupations. The different socializing influences that working-class and middle-class parents exert on their children actually help to keep the social class system more or less intact. As will be discussed in Chapter 8, a relatively consistent and orderly continuation of the basic class structure persists from one generation to the next, perhaps due in part to class differences in parental socialization.

Reverse Socialization: Children Influencing Parents

Socialization is often viewed as a one-way process. In the case of parents and children the focus is primarily on the way the parents socialize their children. However, there is increasing recognition of the fact that children also influence their parents (Peters, 1985; Peterson and Rollins, 1987). Children's acting to change the behaviors, attitudes, or values of their parents is an example of **reverse socialization.** In general terms, reverse socialization occurs when people who are normally the ones being socialized are, instead, doing the socializing.

Reverse socialization in the family probably occurs most prominently after children have reached their teenage years. At this age the children are attuned to the mass media, where they learn about recent changes and innovations. The children can then serve as sources of information in the areas where the parents are not as attentive (clothing styles, slang, music, movies, and so on). Reverse socialization from children to parents is apt to be found in societies that are changing rapidly (Mead, 1970).

A contemporary example of reverse socialization occurs in the case of immigrant families living in the United States. Often the children of these families learn English before their parents do, so the children have to act as interpreters for their parents (Dell'Angela, 1995). The children, often as young as 10 years, must translate and explain government regulations, commercial transactions, and the news on television. Many immigrant parents, especially those from Asian, Latin American, and Eastern European countries, find themselves in a very different power relationship with their children than is customary in their home countries (Dell'Angela, 1995).

Peers as Socializing Agents

At a very early age, children begin to learn about their social world from playmates and nursery school companions. One sociologist who has studied nursery school children intensively contends that, once children move outside the family and start to have peer cultures, the nature of adult–child socialization is transformed radically (Corsaro, 1992). This researcher claims that "with the creation of an initial peer culture [even in nursery school], other children become as important as adults in the socialization process" (Corsaro, 1992, p. 162).

As children move into elementary school, socialization by their peers is clearly in evidence. In Chapter 10 we will see how children at the elementary school level learn about traditional gender role characteristics from their classmates (Adler et al., 1992).

A study of preadolescent boys in Little League baseball also shows vividly how intense peer-group socialization can be (Fine, 1987). Boys in this age group apparently feel free to discuss many topics with their peers that they would not discuss with adults. This freedom enhances the importance of peer-group socialization. Once again, since the boys' social world is one they have created and is separate from the adult world, it is taken seriously by the boys (Fine, 1987, p. 79).

In a Little League setting young boys are often learning traditional male behavior from their peers. Through the reactions and words of their peers they learn how to control and channel their behavior in ways that are consistent with the male gender role. The sociologist who observed hundreds of preadolescent boys over three years says explicitly that, through socialization by peers, "Boys learn to act like men" (Fine, 1987, p. 86). The socialization is effective and may, in some cases, run counter to the child-rearing goals of the boys' parents.

As young people move into adolescence, there is evidence that peer socialization is even more likely to be in conflict with socialization messages coming from other sources, especially parents and the schools (Arnett, 1995). Alcohol use, reckless driving, and other risk-taking behaviors are commonly learned from adolescent peers (Arnett, 1992).

The Mass Media as Socializing Agents

The media of mass communication, especially television, movies, and radio, but also magazines and newspapers, convey thousands of visual, aural, and verbal messages each day. These messages are embedded in dramas, comedies, news reports, music lyrics, comics, cartoons, news stories, and commercial advertising. In myriad ways these messages are defining social life for people of all ages. From childhood to old age, the media of communication are continuing the process of socialization.

While all the media of communication are important, television has undeniably overtaken all others in reaching and influencing people. In American households television sets are on more than 7 hours each day (Liebert and Sprafkin, 1988).

Television as a Socializing Agent for Children

An average 6-month-old infant in the United States will be in front of a television set 1.5 hours a day. By 3 years of age, most children will be selecting their favorite television shows (Liebert and Sprafkin, 1988, p. 5). Television viewing continues to increase until it reaches a peak at about 11 years of age, when an average child watches more than 4 hours a day.[1] Teenagers still average 3 hours of television per day (Vobejda, 1992). "It has been estimated that by the age of 18 a child ... will have spent more time watching television than in any single activity besides sleep" (Liebert and Sprafkin, 1988, p. ix). This massive exposure suggests that television is an important socializing agent for the children of contemporary society.

Research on the influence of television on children and adolescents has focused special attention on violence (Huston et al., 1992) and gender roles (Kimball, 1986; Liebert and Sprafkin, 1988). See the related In the News box on the next page.

---

[1]The reported *average* amount of television watching by children obscures the fact that substantial differences exist among children with different backgrounds. Children in the lower social classes and from minority backgrounds watch much more than middle-class white children (Liebert and Sprafkin, 1988).

In the News

Talk Shows and Rap Music Are Charged with Subverting the Values of America's Youth

William Bennett has been called America's "Morality Guru" (Kurtz, 1995), in part because he is the author of a best-selling book on virtues. Bennett, also a former secretary of education and federal drug czar, is dismayed by the decline of morality in the United States. He finds many causes for this decline, including, as we will see, the failure of parents to raise their children in a morally responsible manner. But more recently he has been speaking out against music lyrics—especially rap music—and the daytime talk shows—Sally, Ricki, Jenny, Montel, Rolanda, Geraldo, and the rest.

Bennett has not been alone in his attacks on music lyrics and television talk shows. Several years ago, Tipper Gore, before her husband became the vice-president, launched a campaign against popular music lyrics. When she testified before a congressional committee, she said she deplored the sex and violence found in contemporary music lyrics and the harm that they may do to America's children.

Bennett was joined in his more recent attack on music lyrics by C. Delores Tucker, an African American and liberal Democrat. They focused their attack on the lyrics of rap-music groups distributed by the Time Warner Corporation. Senator Robert Dole, who was then a candidate for president, joined in this attack (Kurtz, 1995), as did Kathie Lee Gifford, herself a television talk show host.

The recent attack on television talk shows centers around the way guests openly discuss their abnormal romantic, marital, and family relationships and their often bizarre sexual behavior. Bennett and his staff have compiled a list of some of the most sordid topics that have been featured on these shows: a husband who has been patronizing a prostitute for 2 years reveals this to his wife on the show (Jenny Jones). Another husband reveals to his wife that he has been having an affair and the woman who is his lover appears on stage (Jerry Springer). On one Sally Jessy Raphael show, the topic was "My Daughter Is Living as a Boy." Montel Williams featured a 17-year-old girl who claimed to have slept with more than 100 men. On the Rolanda show, a maid of honor tells the bride that she slept with the groom only a week before the wedding (Kurtz, 1995).

The moral criticism of these television shows—and music lyrics—is that they convey distorted views about sex, relations between men and women, marriage, and family life. The critics of contemporary music and television are especially concerned about the effect that they may have on impressionable young people.

There are two counterreactions to these criticisms. The first is an empirical question of whether music lyrics or television talk show topics do, in fact, change people's values, even the values of young people. Senator Joseph Lieberman, also a critic of television talk shows, has said, "These talk shows really take the abnormal and make it acceptable, and in doing so degrade the culture" (Kurtz, 1995, p. C8). Even though this argument seems plausible, it is not necessarily true. There is almost no concrete evidence to prove that people who listen to music lyrics or watch talk shows are influenced sufficiently to modify their basic values.

The second criticism relates to the political issue of how much communication, and especially the artistic forms, can be censored in a free society. Television talk shows attract about 4.5 million listeners, and as talk show host Sally Jessy Raphael has asked, "Are we going to tell them you can't watch my show anymore, you should watch what *he* [Bennett] thinks you should watch?" (Kurtz, 1995, p. C8).

The talk show supporters also argue that, while their main purpose is entertainment, they also have some educational value. Again, Raphael defends talk shows, saying that talk show television grapples with important topics, such as "incest, AIDS, drug addiction, breast implants, and teenage pregnancy" (Kurtz, 1995, p. C8). Speaking of her own show, Raphael says, "The purpose of the show is very much a morality play" (Kurtz, 1995, p. C8).

KURTZ, HOWARD. "Morality Guru Takes on Talk TV." *Washington Post,* October 26, 1995.

Violence.   Even a casual viewing of television reveals that violence is the mainstay of many programs: killing, fighting, verbal abuse, and threats are pervasive. These kinds of violence are found on Saturday morning cartoons and other children's programs, as well as in police and crime dramas, military and war stories, and space adventures. Even music videos have their share of stylized violence and aggression.

A recent study, conducted by researchers at four universities, scientifically sampled about 2,500 hours of television programming and found that 57 percent of programs contained some violence (Farhi, 1996). Nearly three-fourths of the perpetrators of violent acts go unpunished, and nearly half show no harm to the victims. The researchers believe that television viewers, especially young ones, will conclude that violence has no consequences, either for the perpetrators or the victims. This study has added to calls for limitations of the amount and availability of violence on television.

Even though some studies have shown that seeing violence on television increases violent behaviors (Joy et al., 1986), the question still remains as to why a connection exists. Several possible explanations have been offered (Liebert and Sprafkin, 1988):

1. *Observational learning:* Children might, for example, see a Kung Fu kick on television and copy this method when fighting.
2. *Reduced social constraints:* Children who see violence used in many different situations might feel fewer social constraints against using violence.
3. *Arousal of aggressive tendencies:* Some children may have aggressive tendencies that may be aroused by seeing violence (or other exciting events) on television.

Gender Roles.   Television programming and commercials persistently show females in traditional and stereotypic ways (Davis, 1990; Signorielli, 1989). Women occupy only one-quarter to one-third of the parts on entertainment programs, and, when they are shown, they are usually in lower-status jobs or are unemployed. The personalities of women on television are generally passive, deferential, emotional, and weak. In comparison, men are usually active, dominant, rational, and powerful. Television commercials also show women less than men, and males are seen much more in dominant, forceful, and active roles (Kimball, 1986; Liebert and Sprafkin, 1988).

There is general agreement that television programs for young children, especially those shown on Saturday morning, are very traditional in their treatment of gender roles (Carter, 1991). Saturday morning programs on the commercial networks are dominated by cartoons and other shows in which males are in the dominant roles. The reason seems to be, in part, that girls will watch shows with male leads, but boys will not watch programs that have females as the leading characters (Carter, 1991).

Adolescent and Adult Socialization

Socialization does not end with childhood, but continues throughout life, as we will see in the remainder of this chapter. Some adult socialization occurs in connection with changes expected from one life stage to the next, changes that come largely from the process of aging, such as adolescence, for instance, and old age. Other life transitions come unexpectedly and often with suddenness, such as the loss of one's job, or getting divorced, or being widowed. Other adult socialization occurs in connection with entering occupations or professions, organizations, work settings, or institutions.

Adolescent Socialization

Adolescence, a period of life between childhood and adulthood, is recognized as a specific life stage in the United States and many other contemporary countries. There are, however, two interesting questions related to the idea of adolescence as a distinct life stage: (1) Is adolescence universal, that is, is adolescence found in all societies? (2) Is adolescence a clearly defined number of years, closely associated with the onset of puberty and the 3 to 5 years immediately thereafter? The answer to both of these questions is, at least partially, no.

Social historians and anthropologists have looked for an adolescent life stage in different societies, and there are enough disagreements in what they have found for us to conclude that adolescence, at least as we currently define it, is not universal. Even when adolescent life stages have been found in societies, there are wide differences about when it is supposed to have started and when it typically ends. Describing the research of social historians, one writer says, adolescence "could start not at all or at seven, at twelve, at fourteen, at sixteen, at eighteen, or at twenty and end anywhere from seven, twelve, fourteen, and so on" (Hanawalt, 1992, p. 342).

From a sociological view, we can say that adolescence is a socially defined life stage that is found in some, but not all societies. The social definition in any particular society, if it recognizes adolescence at all, will cover a specified period of time and will often include some behaviors expected during that life stage. The currently most widely accepted American definition of adolescence describes it as a period after childhood, associated with the onset of puberty, that lasts until about 18 years of age. This American definition of adolescence usually includes a number of characteristic behaviors that are likely to be manifested (erratic, unpredictable, moody, uncommunicative, and so on).

If adolescence is socially defined, and therefore socially created, it probably serves a useful societal purpose. In developed societies that purpose is likely to be related to economic needs. Young people in many contemporary societies need formal education beyond childhood. By defining an adolescent period of life, young people are not obligated to enter into adult responsibilities until they have acquired the skills necessary for a highly technological and bureaucratic economic system.

People often learn what will be expected of them in a given status before they enter that status. Called **anticipatory socialization,** this process typically occurs in each stage of the life cycle. For example, young people learn, even before they reach the teenage years, that they will become adolescents. They learn that when they reach this stage their behavior and feelings will probably differ from the behavior and feelings of their childhood years. The words *adolescence* and *teenage years* become symbols with a self-fulfilling reality. In contemporary society, the economic system, augmented by mass advertising, sells the teenage years—a very lucrative market.

Teenagers are sensitized to the idea that they should like things that are clearly distinguished from childish and adult (or parental) things. Adolescents want to be clearly set apart from children and clearly set apart from parents and "old people." What adolescents define as their special domain is constantly being invaded by older and younger members of society. When preteen children start to idolize

a music star first cultivated by teenagers, the teenagers quickly move on to someone else.

Adult Socialization

A number of important occasions arise in adult life when socialization occurs
with special intensity. The term **adult socialization** refers to occasions in life
when adults learn the new behaviors expected of them as they enter new occupations, professions, organizations, work settings, institutions, or life stages.

Socialization in Professional and Graduate Schools

When students enter professional or graduate schools, their primary task is to
master the knowledge in their field of study. Certainly, law students are learning
the law, medical students are learning medicine, physics graduate students are
learning physics, and sociology graduate students are learning sociology. But
learning the subject matter of a field is only one part of a professional or graduate
education. Students are also learning a view of the world from the perspective of
their future profession. Law students, for example, "acquire distinctive modes of
perception, thinking and practice. Such dispositions influence the way students
learn to . . . relate to the world (Granfield, 1992, p. 15).

Many studies of professional education have shown how students have idealistic views when they enter professional schools and then, through the course of
their education, abandon those ideals. Medical students who enter medical school
with the ideal of learning all there is to know about medicine give up that notion
in the face of an overwhelming, nearly crushing, workload (Becker and Geer,
1958). In a more specific case, law students who enter Harvard Law School are
often planning to go into public interest law (helping disadvantaged groups in the
society), but by the time they finish their educations, many have given up this
ideal (Granfield, 1992).

The socialization that occurs in a professional or graduate school has been
called the *informal curriculum* (Granfield and Koenig, 1992, p. 504). The informal curriculum at one of the country's most prestigious law schools, Harvard Law
School, begins almost as soon as the new students reach the campus (Granfield,
1992; Granfield and Koenig, 1992). The students who are admitted to Harvard
Law are almost all very intelligent, highly motivated, and aggressively competitive in academic matters. They have succeeded in their previous academic work
because they were highly competitive, and that is also why they were admitted to
the school. When they arrive at Harvard, they generally expect to continue, or
even increase, their aggressive, competitive style. But the message they receive,
beginning in the very first week, is that "competition is not the key to law school

success" (Granfield and Koenig, 1992). Instead, the socialization message is that it will be solidarity and cooperation with their fellow students that will contribute to their success at Harvard Law.

Orientation meetings for new students are led by second- or third-year students who tell the newcomers that cooperation and camaraderie are the behaviors expected of them, not aggressive competitiveness. Later, fellow students will punish those who persist in being too competitive and individualistic.

This is the purpose of a game called *turkey bingo,* which is designed to ridicule those students who persist in being overly competitive in classes. The game uses a bingo card with the names of aggressive students instead of numbers. When one of these students talks in class, his or her name is checked off on the card. When a "bingo" is attained, the winning card holder answers a professor's question with a prearranged code word to inform the rest of the class. The aggressive students generally tone down their behavior when they realize they are being ridiculed (Granfield, 1992, p. 81).

New students at Harvard Law are also socialized to understand that they are now entering an institution that has great historic eminence and they are moving toward becoming a part of that elite group. The new students are taught that their status will come primarily from the *collective eminence* of being Harvard Law graduates and not so much from their own individualistic achievements as a student. Students are socialized to submerge their individual interests and to become a part of the collective eminence of Harvard Law (Granfield and Koenig, 1992).

The socialization of Harvard Law students requires them to make a radical personal transformation, from being highly individualistic and competitive to adopting a collective identity and being cooperative. Most students make this transformation, even though their earlier competitiveness might have been considered a deeply embedded personality characteristic. The changes most students make illustrate how influential socialization can be.

Socialization in Occupations and Work Settings

There is more to be learned in a new job or organization than the specific tasks that one is assigned. One must also learn the norms and the expected role behaviors of the work setting or organization. Anyone who enters a large office, an academic department, a service agency, an industrial shop, or any other work group enters an ongoing social system. Every social system, in addition to norms and roles, will have—as we saw in the last chapter—a social structure (prevailing patterns of interaction). The social structure will include friendship patterns as well as patterns of privilege, deference, and respect among members. Newcomers must be sensitive to these features of the group they are joining.

Some occupations and professions feature intense training at the time of entry; often this training is a conscious effort at socializing new members.

Military organizations are especially likely to begin this socialization as soon as new recruits arrive. A less well known but striking example of early training–socialization is found in the way the airline industry trains flight attendants (Hochschild, 1983).

The training of flight attendants extends far beyond the technical aspects of their work. Equally important is the socialization that flight attendants receive on how to present themselves to the flying public. Above all, they must perform their duties in a way that makes them seem friendly, helpful, cheerful, and composed at all times. Flight attendants, especially the females, must smile easily and often. They are taught to display a friendly and cheerful presence, even when they are hurrying to complete their work, are being harassed by demanding and unruly passengers, or are facing a crisis.

The socialization of flight attendants begins even before they are hired. In an airline publication for prospective flight attendants, candidates are told how to conduct themselves at the hiring interview. This book tells candidates to be sincere, modest, and to display a friendly smile. Interviewees are also told to be enthusiastic, but with calmness and poise, to be "vivacious but not effervescent" (Hochschild, 1983, p. 96).

After flight attendants have been hired they are sent to an airlines' school where, in addition to learning the fundamental skills and tasks of the job, they are drilled intensively on proper behavior and demeanor. Airlines often have strict rules about what flight attendants may and may not do. In the Delta Air Lines school, flight attendants are told they may not drink alcohol while in uniform or for 24 hours before flight time. While on flights they may not knit, read, or sleep (Hochschild, 1983, p. 99).

But the most important aspect of the socialization of flight attendants is that they must learn to control their real emotions and display the emotions that the airline demands. They must "manage" their feelings and emotions because they are being paid by the airlines to do so. Hochschild has called this behavior *emotion labor* (1983, p. 7). While we all learn to manage our emotions through the normal socialization processes, flight attendants are taught that managing theirs is part of their work. They are taught to deal with difficult passengers, and they are coached and drilled on how to control their anger.

Even though it is taboo to express anger toward passengers, flight attendants sometimes reach a breaking point. One flight attendant described an incident in which she finally did give vent to her anger toward a female passenger who had steadily complained about all the services and then attacked one of the co-worker flight attendants with a racial slur. In the flight attendant's words:

> Then she began yelling at me and my co-worker who happened to be black. "You nigger bitch!" she said. Well that did it. I told my friend not to waste her pain. This lady asked for one more Bloody Mary. I fixed the drink, put it on a tray, and when I got to her seat, my toe somehow found a piece of carpet and I tripped—and that Bloody Mary hit that white pants suit! (Hochschild, 1983, p. 114)

Of course, this kind of incident is an exception, and most successful airline flight attendants are able to control and manage their emotions, even under very adverse circumstances. Most are thoroughly and effectively socialized to provide the "emotional labor" that the airline requires of them.

Even though this type of formal socialization occurs in various occupations, equally important informal socialization occurs when new employees begin working. Older members of the group take on the task of training newcomers, which they accomplish both by example and direct instruction. Often the socialization message of veterans differs from that in the formal training process. Such was the case in the police department studied by sociologist Jennifer Hunt (1985). When rookie police officers went on active duty, they were quickly taught by veteran officers that it was permissible to use force, and even violence, when dealing with citizens. The veterans were quite aware that a discrepancy existed between police academy training about force and violence and the advice they were offering to rookies. Veterans often said, "It's not done on the street the way that it's taught at the academy."

Veteran street police quickly informed rookie officers that the weapons and nightsticks they had been issued were not adequate for the job on the street. Rookies quickly replaced their wooden batons with the more powerful plastic nightsticks. In the police academy recruits had been taught to avoid hitting people on the head or neck because blows there could cause serious injury or death. In contrast, on the street the standard was to hit wherever it would do the most damage in order to avoid danger to oneself.

Veteran police officers carried out their socialization by showing their approval and support when rookie officers used force. One female officer was upset when she learned that she was the object of a brutality suit, and she was reluctant to face her male colleagues. When she did report for work, however, the men greeted her with a standing ovation. Their support also included a sexist compliment when they told this woman officer, "You can use our urinal now" (Hunt, 1985, p. 319). Thus, by praise and support as well as by example, rookie police officers learn that it is acceptable to use "normal" force on the street, even though the level of violence often exceeds what is legally permissible.

Both formal and informal socialization are likely to occur whenever one enters a new profession, organization, or work setting. Even when a person enters an organization or work setting in a position of authority, some socialization occurs. A new office manager or department head must usually take some time to learn the existing social system before making dramatic changes in working procedures (Gouldner, 1954).

Resocialization in a Total Institution

Some instances of socialization in adulthood are so intense and pervasive that they can be called resocialization. **Resocialization** is the process of unlearning old norms, roles, and values, and then learning new ones required by the new social environment. In the most extreme cases of resocialization the social self of the incoming person is stripped away or destroyed, so that the individual becomes dependent on the institution for a new self. This extreme often occurs when an adult enters a total institution such as a mental hospital or prison (Goffman, 1961).

As we saw in Chapter 4, a total institution is usually cut off from the rest of society and forms an all-encompassing social environment that meets all the needs of the members. Prisons and mental institutions are prominent examples of total institutions. Total institutions are miniature societies, with all of the characteristics of societies: they have a cultural system with values and norms, as well as a social structure with statuses and roles. Another distinct feature of total institutions is the almost complete control they exert over the lives of people who exist within them. A total institution requires an extensive reorganization of the life of the entering individual. Because the old rules and roles of life can no longer apply completely in a prison or mental institution, resocialization must take place.

Jean Harris, a former headmistress of an elite girls' school who was convicted of murdering the best-selling diet-book author, Dr. Herman Tarnower, has vividly described her resocialization in a women's prison. One of the first things Harris learned is that prison discipline "has little to do with wrongdoing. It has a great deal to do with how people feel about you, or how fearful the staff is of the people who complain about you" (Harris, 1986, p. 201). In other words, discipline is often meted out arbitrarily. The same behavior by two different inmates will get different reactions from the guards. Harris describes how she received a misconduct charge for absentmindedly leaving her government-issued coat in the exercise yard (the charge was "not taking care of government property"). In contrast, another inmate, sitting only 7 feet from one of the guards, cut up her coat and made it into a vest. The guard said nothing.

Harris also describes the complex daily routine of obtaining an antidepressant medication. If an inmate needs medication she must go to the dispensary for each administration. However, it is no simple task to get there because the round trip requires getting through eight locked doors. The guards stationed at each of these doors often keep the inmates waiting for considerable lengths of time before allowing them to pass through. Inmates requiring medication three times a day spend a considerable part of their day making these trips to the dispensary. In prison, even the simple task of taking a pill requires learning an intricate procedure and coping with a variety of complications and frustrations.

Resocialization for life in prison means that inmates must learn both a formal and an informal social system. The formal rules are made and enforced by the administrators and guards. The informal social system of a prison is controlled by the inmates. A sociological study of a women's prison, conducted by Heffernan (1972), shows how a new inmate must learn the informal system quickly or risk getting into trouble with the more powerful inmates. In the bathrooms, certain sinks and showers are reserved for women with the highest status. When movies are shown in the recreation room, the best seats are available only to these high-status women. In the words of the women inmates, "Some can, some can't." Should a new and unaware inmate accidentally select one of these preferred places, the result is a verbal or sometimes physical attack. New inmates in a total institution have few options; they must learn the rules of the new system (both formal and informal) and abide by them. The socialization is generally quick and effective.

Since total institutions are also places of work for many people, it is not surprising that there is also an informal social system that influences staff members as well. A young woman who had recently been a youth counselor at an institution for delinquent girls describes what she learned about making changes in the institution:

> When I first began to work here I was fresh out of college. You have all these ideas about all the changes you're going to make—to apply all the things you learned in college to rehabilitate. You try to express your views to the rest of the staff—that other ways of doing things might be more effective. But after you're here a while, you become institutionalized [socialized]. You find out that's not what's wanted. People who have been here a long time are the ones that make the decisions. They're the ones who call the shots. They really don't want change. . . . After a while you change. You do things just like they've always been done here (Giallombardo, 1974, p. 107).

The lesson is the same for the new inmate and the new staff member: the ongoing social system of rules and arrangements must be learned when one enters a total institution. What distinguishes total institutions from other groups and organizations is that total institutions influence all aspects of a person's life, and the influence is continuous. In other settings, one must adapt to the norms and rules of a new place of work, for example, but one can escape for many hours each day. In a prison, mental institution, nursing home, or monastery, or aboard a ship, such escape is not possible, and therefore the socialization is both more intense and more pervasive.

Socialization for Death

The ultimate and universal stage in the life cycle is death. Social systems, then, must have mechanisms for preparing people for death. Anticipatory socialization is an especially appropriate concept in this case, since preparation for death must occur before the actual event (Prigerson, 1992).

Funeral services, for example, are increasingly common occurrences as people grow older. For the elderly, the deaths of family members and friends become regular reminders of their own impending deaths. The rituals connected with death legitimize death; people learn to accept the deaths of others and also their own (Berger and Luckmann, 1967, p. 10).

A sociological study of a community of very elderly people (average age was 80) revealed that much of the social organization of the community centered around death (Marshall, 1980). Residents of the community were repeatedly made aware of the fact that death was more or less imminent both for themselves and others around them. The administration of the community repeatedly urged residents to plan the arrangements for their deaths—the disposition of their bodies, bequests, and other details. The residents did not treat death as a major philosophical issue but as a normal and expected occurrence (Marshall, 1980).

This example of socialization reveals again that social systems do not leave unattended the important passages from one life-cycle stage to another. Instead, the people in the system are prepared (socialized) to accept their movement into the next stage, even if that stage is death itself.

Summary

Socialization is the process by which a person learns and accepts the ways of a particular social group or society. Every social system makes sure that new members joining the system learn the accepted ways of doing things. Socialization is also important in producing the characteristics and personality of the individual.

The process of socialization begins in the very early stages of life, and through this process human qualities are acquired. Infants who are isolated from human contact during the early years of life do not show the characteristics we normally associate with human nature. Human infants develop reciprocal relationships with adults in which they learn to satisfy their basic needs by behaving in the way adults want them to. Through socialization, a child develops a social self, that is, the learned perception that a person has about his or her qualities and attributes. People learn to evaluate themselves through interaction with others, just as they learn to evaluate all other social objects. Social objects include the values, norms, and roles that prevail in the society.

Parents are important primary socialization agents, and many parents take very seriously the responsibility of shaping the personalities of their children. However, socialization is too complex and subtle for parents to achieve exactly what they desire in the socialization of their children.

Research on childhood socialization has shown that working-class families socialize their children differently from middle-class, white-collar families. Working-class families socialize their children to be obedient and to observe social rules. Middle-class parents socialize their children to take initiatives and to participate in decision making (autonomy). These two forms of behavior are related to the kinds of roles that children from different social classes are likely to play in the adult work world. Reverse socialization occurs when children socialize their parents. Empirical evidence shows that children teach their parents about some aspects of contemporary life.

Peers are important socializing agents for young children, and often the socialization of peers runs counter to that of parents. The mass media, especially television, are pervasive socializing forces in contemporary society. Children spend much of their time watching television, and evidence reveals that they are influenced by violence and by male and female characterizations seen there.

Adolescents and adults are also socialized by television, which is just one aspect of adult socialization. Adolescents receive anticipatory socialization for the adolescent stage of life. Adult socialization occurs when people receive graduate and professional training or enter new occupations, organizations, work settings, institutions, or life stages. The total institution provides a particularly vivid example of adult socialization; this socialization is so extensive that it is referred to as resocialization. Death is the final stage of life, and the elderly and terminally ill are socialized to prepare for dying.

CRITICAL THINKING

1. Why is socialization important for the continuation of a culture? What would happen to a culture if all socialization ceased?
2. Explain how the socialization process in your culture taught you the following: how to say goodbye, proper table manners, and appropriate dress for religious occasions.
3. What evidence supports the claim that primary socialization is important to our "humanness"?
4. What is the norm of reciprocity? Give examples from your own life that illustrate this principle.
5. How do some of the values of middle-class and lower-class parents differ with regard to the socialization of their children? What accounts for this difference in values? How might this explain the perpetuation of the class structure in American society?
6. Explain how reverse socialization can take place between parents and children.
7. Evaluate some television shows in light of the information about violence and male–female roles presented in the chapter.
8. What evidence supports the notion that adolescence is a socially created stage in the life cycle rather than a biologically created one?
9. What is adult socialization? What changes in a person's life might cause such socialization to occur?
10. Under what conditions is resocialization likely to occur?

6

Deviance and Social Control

Ask a group of ordinary people to provide examples of deviance or deviant behavior, and you are apt to get an amazing array of responses. Indeed, when one sociologist asked people to do just that, he received 252 different descriptions. Among them, the following examples were offered:

> Movie stars, junior executives, perverts, perpetual bridge-players, psychiatrists, drug addicts, political extremists, conservatives, career women, prostitutes, liars, prudes, girls who wear make-up, priests, atheists, liberals, communists, alcoholics, the retired, criminals, divorcees, reckless drivers, and know-it-all professors (Simmons, 1965).

As we look at this list, we might wonder how the respondents could describe some of these examples as deviant. The fact that they did illustrates that deviant behavior is not as clear-cut and obvious as we might suppose, nor is deviant behavior as fixed and unchanging as we sometimes think. To arrive at a sociological understanding of deviant behavior, we must first see that deviance is *socially defined,* and that social definitions of deviance differ from one society or social group to another.

The Social Nature of Deviance

To say that **deviance** is socially defined means that whenever most of the people of a given society, or social group, consider a behavior deviant, *it will be deviant.* As a result, a vast array of behaviors have been and are considered deviant in different societies. Even within the same society, significant changes often occur in what people consider deviant behavior. Cross-cultural and historical evidence provides many examples of the shifting nature of deviant behavior, showing clearly that it is socially defined.

For example, among many Arabs the use of alcohol was prohibited, but smoking hashish was more likely to be accepted. An Arab who preferred alcohol to hashish would have been considered deviant by his own people, and yet most people in the United States would see the situation in exactly the opposite way (Simmons, 1965).

The Changing Nature of Deviance

The fact that deviance is socially defined becomes abundantly clear when we examine some recent changes in what Americans think of as deviant behavior. Some behaviors that, only a decade or so ago, were not considered deviant are now viewed as deviant. The reverse is also true.

From Acceptability to Deviance.   Two centuries ago in the United States, for instance, being fat was considered good; it was certainly not considered deviant (Schwartz, 1986). But in the contemporary United States, many people consider obesity a form of deviance (Hughes and Degher, 1993; Smith, 1995c). To be fat today is to have a blemish on one's appearance and to be a social disgrace. Fatness is considered to be a morally reprehensible condition (Millman, 1980).

Smoking, especially in public places, is a behavior that has undergone a rapid transformation in the United States in a short span of years. By the end of World War II, smoking had reached a peak of popularity in the United States. Cigarette smoking was viewed as glamorous and sophisticated behavior. The tobacco industry even advertised that cigarette smoking was healthy ("as an aid to digestion," "to calm nerves," and "to control weight"). Smoking in public, even in closely confined places such as planes, cars, and restaurants, was perfectly acceptable behavior.

Personal attitudes about smoking began to change when the Surgeon General of the United States issued a report in 1963 showing that smoking was related to a number of illnesses, especially cancer and heart disease. Although many individuals decided to stop smoking, the social attitude toward public smoking did not change. Public smoking, even in confined spaces, continued to be acceptable behavior. Only gradually in the 1970s, and then rapidly in the 1980s and 1990s, did the *social* definition of smoking in public change.

During the 1980s and 1990s, more and more nonsmokers openly contested the rights of smokers to smoke wherever they pleased. The problem of passive smoking came into existence (Jackson, 1994). Today, the social definition of smoking is almost completely the opposite of what it was several decades ago. Smokers who "light up" in the presence of nonsmokers will likely be told in very strong terms that their behavior is unacceptable. Smokers now often complain that their rights are being violated because they are made to feel like "criminals" when they smoke.

The changing attitudes toward smoking is reflected in the growing ban on smoking on airplanes. For most of the history of aviation, passengers were free to light up on planes, but in April 1988, smoking was prohibited on domestic flights of two hours or less. On February 25, 1990, that ban was extended to domestic flights of 6 hours or less (Reinhold, 1990). Thus, virtually all domestic flights, except for a few flights to Alaska and Hawaii, are now smoke-free. In 1995, legislation was introduced to ban smoking on international flights to and from the United States (Oberstar, 1995).

The attitudes toward smoking have not changed as much in other nations as they have in the United States. Asians are smoking in record numbers (Agence France Presse, 1994), and there are few signs of a reduction in smoking throughout much of Europe where, in many places, people smoke far more heavily than Americans ever did (Kaplan, 1994). The case of France is highly instructive. On November 1, 1992, a tough new law took effect in France banning smoking in airports, subway stations, hotels, government buildings, and many places in offices and factories. In addition, smoking was banned in cafes and restaurants, where smoking is considered by many to be integral to drinking and dining (Riding, 1992). The French government has been almost totally resistant to imposing the law out of a fear of the reaction of the many dedicated smokers in the nation. As of this writing, the French law against smoking is almost totally ignored (Agence France Presse, 1995). However, the fact is that over 50,000 people die each year in France from tobacco-related ailments. As the former health minister in charge of drafting the restrictive legislation said, "More than 50,000 people die here every year from smoking.... If 200 Boeings crashed every year in France, would you still fly in planes?" (Riding, 1992, p. A4). Apparently, given their continued smoking, the French (as well as many other people in Europe, Asia, and much of the rest of the world, including the United States) would continue to fly under such conditions.

Drunk driving may be defined as "all driving that occurs when skills and abilities are significantly impaired by alcohol" (Ross, 1992, p. 12). It is almost impossible to estimate precisely the extent of drunk driving, but one study showed that about 20% of U.S. drivers, or 33 million people, drive while illegally impaired at least once a year, and the number would be far greater if we use the above definition and include those who are "legally impaired." More damningly, it is estimated that of the 40,000 plus highway deaths per year, slightly less than half involve crashes in which at least some alcohol was involved. However, it should be pointed out that included in the preceding estimates are drivers who had consumed negligible amounts of alcohol as well as victims who had been drinking.

Although driving a vehicle while under the influence of alcohol has always been illegal, and thus a somewhat deviant act, recent changes in social definitions have clearly made drunk driving more deviant. In the past, most people hardly gave a second thought to driving after they had had a few drinks or more. Now, with growing concern about death and injury caused by drinking drivers, especially when innocent bystanders are killed or hurt, the social definitions are changing. Active campaigns against drunk driving by organizations such as Mothers Against Drunk Driving (MADD) and Students Against Drunk Driving (SADD) have heightened public awareness that driving after drinking is now apt to be considered a deviant act. While it is unclear how much of the drop can be attributed to MADD's activities, alcohol-related traffic deaths have been reduced by 40 percent since the formation of the organization in 1980 (Field, 1995).

In fact, the courts, too, are treating the offense of "driving under the influence" as a more serious crime, and jail sentences are not uncommon—especially for multiple offenders and in cases where innocent people are killed or injured. In 1982, twenty-seven states passed new, stiffer laws against driving under the influence of alcohol (and drugs), and in the mid-1990s, many states moved to strengthen their drunk-driving laws (Field, 1995). Among other things, penalties were made more severe, and the certainty of punishment was increased (Kingsnorth and Jungsten, 1988). However, some questions have been raised about increasingly severe punishments for drunk driving infractions. For example, mandatory jail terms or unusually long license revocations may have the unanticipated consequence that they will not be invoked by judges who regard them as too severe for the crime (Ross, 1992).

While smoking and drinking are relatively common forms of behavior that are more likely to be considered deviant in recent years, it is worth noting that a similar fate has befallen a far less common form of behavior—dirt eating! (Forsyth and Benoit, 1989). Yes, eating dirt, usually fine clays, occurs in many parts of the world, including the rural United States. The dirt may be eaten "raw" or cooked with seasonings and vinegar. Those who eat dirt do so because they have done it since childhood, because it makes them feel healthier (it supposedly relieves stomach cramps), and because they enjoy it as a "snack." Said one dirt eater about dirt as a snack: "I don't know it is just crunchy, its satisfying, its like a craving or something you get used to like a candy bar. . . there is nothing else that will surpass that taste" (Forsyth and Benoit, 1989, p. 64). However, as rural residents have moved into urban areas, dirt eating has grown to be perceived as more deviant, even by those who engage in it. Those who still practice dirt eating generally conceal it from the public and even family members.

However, not all efforts to have a once-accepted type of behavior be seen as deviant are successful—take the case of "battered husbands." Lucal (1995) wonders why husband-battering has not come to be considered a social problem equivalent to wife-beating. She identifies three factors. First, the battered women's movement worked in conjunction with the women's movement, while there was no significant men's movement to support the effort to have husband-beating seen as a problem. Relatedly, the battered women's movement, fearful of losing support and resources, has tended to oppose the claims of battered men. Second, battered men have not received the kind of professional and media attention accorded to battered women. Finally, traditional gender roles have worked for the battered women's movement and against the parallel men's movement; it is hard for most people to imagine men being victimized by women. To put this another way, it is hard for most people to see women as deviants who batter their husbands.

From Deviance to Acceptability.   Just as some behavior becomes more deviant over time, other behavior becomes less deviant, or more acceptable. Cohabitation before marriage is a case in point. In the 1950s and early 1960s, some couples lived together without being married, but most people regarded their behavior as unacceptable. Such couples were commonly described as "living in sin." If an unmarried couple remained together long enough, and especially if they had children, the label *common-law marriage* was applied, always carrying a negative stigma, however. Couples involved in common-law marriages were looked down upon by most people in the community and were clearly regarded as deviants. Now, just a few decades later, many Americans accept cohabitation as a natural stage between dating and marriage. Even people who would not accept cohabitation for themselves do not attach much of a negative stigma to those who do.

The open discussion of sexual behavior is no longer taboo. Part of this change is born of necessity, in response to the AIDS crisis. In large measure, however, candor in discussing sex reflects changing norms. For example, only a few years ago, condoms would never have been discussed openly, especially on television or in public settings. Since the spread of AIDS has become a national public concern, it has become acceptable, if not praiseworthy, to urge the use of condoms. Today, they are displayed, discussed, and demonstrated in a wide range of public forums. In the late 1980s the Surgeon General of the United States stood before a high school audience and demonstrated the proper use of a condom. Less than 10 years ago that act would have been considered deviant.

However, it would be a mistake to think that sexual discussion is completely open. For example, Joycelyn Elders, former Surgeon General under President Clinton, was fired in late 1994, at least in part, for suggesting that it might be worth considering teaching about masturbation in the schools (August, 1994).

Deviant Behavior as Defined by Specific Groups

Even within the same society, different social groups often define deviance differently. Groups of people who share the same norms and values will develop their own rules about what is and what is not deviant behavior. Their views may not be shared by members of the larger society, but the definitions of deviance will apply to group members. For example, the students in any high school will establish their own codes for dress, hairstyles, and behavior. Although not everyone has to have the same appearance, when an individual strays too far from the current fashion, that person is likely to be considered deviant.

The importance of group definitions of deviance among high school students can be illustrated by the case of gifted students (Margolin, 1993) who consider themselves deviant. One such student described all gifted students as "not really trying to get along with others, a little obnoxious about being smart" (Huryn, 1986, p. 178). Not only did gifted students consider themselves to be deviant, but 77 percent of them felt that their peers at school regarded them as deviants. While the larger society, especially the adults, might view gifted students as the ideal for young people, the gifted students themselves may be considered deviant in their own social environments.

These illustrations indicate clearly that deviance is profoundly influenced by the society or social group in which the behavior or act occurs. Although deviance is often associated with individual behavior (individuals are considered bad, weak, corrupt, dishonest, or evil when they commit deviant acts), the sociological view emphasizes that deviance is a social phenomenon. We can only understand deviant behavior if we first recognize that societies and social groups define what is deviant, and what is not. Therefore, the sociological definition of **deviance** is any behavior that members of a society or social group consider a violation of group norms.

The Social Functions of Deviance

As we saw in Chapter 1, structural–functionalists look for the way societal structures (defined as regular patterns of interaction) may have some positive purpose for the ongoing functioning of the society. However, structural–functionalists also recognize that some social structures can have negative results (dysfunctions) for a society. At first glance, it would seem that most deviant behavior in a society (crime and other forms of unacceptable behavior) would be socially dysfunctional. However, since the work of Emile Durkheim (1895/1964), sociologists have recognized that deviant behavior can have positive functions for society. This paradoxical relationship can be explained by the fact that when a deviant behavior occurs, society's norms are reaffirmed. The deviant act serves to clarify the existing standards of social conduct. Without periodic violations of the standards of conduct, the standards would become less clear and thus less strongly held (Dentler and Erikson, 1959; Jensen, 1988).

Sociological Theories of Deviance

Sociologists are concerned with why some people in a society engage in behaviors that violate, or run counter to, norms. Why do some people steal, rob, kill, and commit other illegal and antisocial acts? Theories of deviance attempt to answer these questions.

Strain Theory

The **strain theory** of deviant behavior approaches deviance from the level of cultures and social structures (in other words, at the macroscopic level). According to strain theory, a discrepancy, or a lack of congruence, exists between cultural values and the means of achieving them. The strain can be thought of as a pressure that occurs when the culture values one thing, but the structure of the society is such that not everyone can realize the values in a socially accepted way. As we saw in Chapter 3, the culture of the United States places a value on material or economic success. The structure of our society, however, does not give everyone the same chance for economic success. Many people in the lowest social classes have almost no chance to succeed economically. The result is that they may accept the cultural goal of "getting rich" but reject the socially accepted means of doing so. (Chapter 8 investigates the inequality inherent in the socioeconomic system.)

In the poor and minority areas of many U.S. cities, many youngsters are pressured into deviant behavior because the conventional means for achieving economic success (education and careers) are both difficult and remote. For these youths, illegal activities represent other ways of achieving economic success, even extraordinary success. For example, selling drugs can be a means of making money. Many young men are willing to risk their lives selling "crack" and other drugs because in return they often make thousands of dollars a week.

As we will see later, however, deviance is also present in the upper levels of society. Wall Street traders and stock manipulators have made huge sums of money through a variety of illegal activities. In these cases, the cultural value of economic success has won out over prohibitions against breaking the law.

Merton's Typology. Strain theory does not excuse illegal behavior among the poor or the wealthy. Rather, it emphasizes that there are different ways of responding to cultural values (or goals), and some of the responses are deviant behaviors.

Sociologist Robert Merton (1938, 1957; Farnsworth and Leiber, 1989; Menard, 1995; Snell et al., 1994), who formulated strain theory, provides a typology of the different ways in which people respond to cultural values or goals. Merton labeled as **conformist** people who accept the cultural goals (achieving economic success) and who also accept the conventional or institutionalized means of achieving these goals (getting an education, working hard, and so on). In Merton's typology, conformists clearly are not deviants.

People who accept the cultural goals (economic success) but reject the conventional or institutional means of achieving them are called **innovators.** When large-scale cocaine dealers make great sums of money, they are innovators because they come up with new ways of achieving the cultural goal of economic success.

Those resigned to being unable to achieve cultural goals such as wealth and recognition, but who nonetheless slavishly adhere to conventional rules of conduct, are called **ritualists.** Ritualists continue to work at bureaucratic or dead-end jobs even though they have given up on any significant advancement in life. Because they have abandoned cultural goals, they, too, are in some degree deviant.

The **retreatist** rejects both the cultural goals *and* the conventional, institutionalized means. The retreatist response can be found among people who have given up on the system completely. They have no interest in economic success and thus have no reason to involve themselves in hard work or any other conventional, institutionalized means. Such people are almost always seen as deviant.

A fifth type of response to cultural goals and institutional means is the rejection of both and the substitution of new cultural goals and means. These are the **rebels,** illustrated by revolutionaries who want to create a new type of society. The new society might have entirely new cultural goals (harmony and cooperation rather than individual economic success) and new institutional means (meditation, communing with the spirit world, and the like).

The different responses to cultural goals and institutional means are summarized in Table 6–1.

To give this discussion some substance, let us look at a study of Chinese students in American colleges and universities and the applicability to them of Merton's five responses to anomie, innovation in particular (Situ et al., 1995). Among the innovative behaviors undertaken by Chinese students, given difficulties in obtaining undergraduate and graduate degrees, are illegally taking off-campus employment without a permit in order to earn additional money, falsifying documents such as tax returns, offering sexual favors in return for money, or even engaging in violence. In terms of the latter, in one well-known (but highly atypical) case, a Chinese doctoral student shot four professors and another Chinese student before turning the gun on himself.

Strain theory is most effective in showing how deviant behavior can be a product of the relationship between cultural goals and the structural characteristics of

Table 6–1   Typology of Modes of Conformity and Deviance

		Culture Goals *(getting rich, etc.)*	*Institutionalized Means* *(working hard, etc.)*	
I.	Conformity	Acceptance	Acceptance	Nondeviance
II.	Innovation	Acceptance	Rejection	
III.	Ritualism	Rejection	Acceptance	
IV.	Retreatism	Rejection	Rejection	Types of Deviance
V.	Rebellion	Rejection and substitution	Rejection and substitution	

Source: Adapted from Robert K. Merton, *Social Theory and Social Structure,* rev. ed., p. 140. Copyright 1957 by The Free Press.

a society. As a theory of deviance, it is most closely associated with structural–functional theory (see Chapter 1). Strain theory shows how some structural features of society (social classes, the poor, racial minorities) can be dysfunctional by keeping many people from realizing important cultural goals. Deviant behavior is often the result.

Strain theory is less effective as an explanation for deviance among those who are members of advantaged groups. As we noted earlier, when deviant behavior occurs among Wall Street brokers, it cannot be attributed to their position in the social structure. Their position in the social structure has not blocked their paths to success. Thus, the explanation for their choosing deviant behavior lies elsewhere (Akers and Cochran, 1985).

Deviance as Learned Behavior

As we saw in Chapter 5, people learn both norms and values through socialization. We also saw that the norms and values that people learn vary greatly. Values and norms depend on the society in which one lives and the social groups of which one is a member. Two theories of deviance are built on the idea that some people learn values and norms that lead to deviant behavior.

Differential Association Theory.   Edwin Sutherland (1947), who originated this theory, saw deviant behavior as the result of socialization. **Differential association theory** emphasizes that individuals may be socialized by a group of people who engage in and accept deviant behavior. The name of the theory reflects the idea that what people do is influenced by the differences in the people with whom they associate (Warr, 1993). This argument is akin to a folk belief about the dangers of "keeping bad company." People learn to be drug addicts, alcoholics, or car thieves by keeping company with others who engage in or admire such behavior.

In a classic sociological study, Howard S. Becker (1963) pointed out the importance of friendship groups in the process of learning to smoke marijuana. When people start using marijuana, they usually rely on their friends to supply the drug until they are relatively experienced users. Furthermore, people *learn* how to enjoy the effects of marijuana from their friends.

It is widely held in the drug culture that people who say they cannot get high on marijuana have been improperly instructed in how to smoke it, and that people who say they do not enjoy being high did not smoke with people they like or trust. Research has confirmed the importance of social support for marijuana use (Akers and Cochran, 1985; Goode, 1969).

Subcultural Theory.   These studies are consistent with a second, and closely related, theory of deviant behavior, which is also based on learning deviant behavior from a social group. This second theory is called the *subcultural theory of deviance* (Cohen, 1955; Cloward and Ohlin, 1960; Campbell and Muncer, 1989). **Subcultural theory** puts the emphasis on the carrier of deviant ideas and identifies subcultures that have norms and values quite different from those of the larger society (Forsyth and Marckese, 1993). Therefore, deviant behavior is really conformity to a set of norms and values accepted and taught by a particular social group. But when these norms and values are not held by the majority of people, the resulting behavior will be frowned on and labeled deviant by the dominant groups in society.

One of the pioneering studies using this approach was Cohen's (1955) analysis of a gang of delinquent boys. Considering this group as a deviant subculture, Cohen found that the group held values that constituted a sort of "anti-culture" or negative reflection of the "straight" middle-class world. The boys in the gang held other people's property in contempt and expressed their feelings by acts of wanton destruction and vandalism. They also seemed to derive malicious satisfaction out of making "straight" people feel uncomfortable. They were "negativistic" in that they often turned middle-class values upside down. Thus Cohen sought to establish that the deviant group he studied was a particular kind of antiestablishment subculture. He also generalized the idea that most deviant groups are simply negative reflections of the majority culture.

Lasley (1995) has recently studied the middle-class, suburban, graffiti-writing subculture and compared it to a similar lower-class, urban subculture. While there are a number of similarities and differences between the two subcultures, they are largely distinct from one another; the graffiti subculture has *not* simply been transplanted from lower- to middle-class areas. While lower-class graffiti artists might be more rebellious than their middle-class counterparts, who both accept and reject the dominant culture, the members of the two groups share an interest in achieving fame through their graffiti.

Deviant subcultures are very similar to the countercultures described in Chapter 3. We noted there that in the United States many groups have held values and subscribed to norms that were in opposition to the most widely held values and norms. Various kinds of bohemian groups from beatniks to hippies to punks to skinheads have been considered deviant because they held values and accepted norms that were at odds with the majority. Examples of deviant subcultures can be found in every large society, for example, the violent subculture of British soccer fans (Dunning et al., 1986).

Conflict Theory of Deviance

In Chapter 1 we saw that conflict theory rests on the premise that, in any society, inequalities in resources and power will exist. When focusing on deviant behavior, conflict theorists emphasize the ways in which a society is organized to serve the interests of the rich and powerful members, often at the expense of other members of the society. To many conflict theorists, the ultimate source of deviance in U.S. society is the capitalist economic system (Gordon, 1981). This view is well summed up by the title of a book, *The Rich Get Richer and the Poor Get Prison* (Reiman, 1979). Since inequality is built into the very basis of the system, many conflict theorists hold that the only real solution lies in the system's total overhaul—a replacement by a much more equitable system in which the gap between the "haves" and the "have-nots" will be minimized.

Although deviance is found at every level of society, the nature, rate, and punishment of deviance are frequently related to the social-class position of the deviant individual (Berk et al., 1980; Braithwaite, 1981). Generally, those from the upper strata of society—the wealthy, the powerful, the influential—play a major role in defining what is, or is not, deviant. These individuals are able to influence the moral and legal definition of deviance in numerous legal ways, including lobbying, making financial contributions to political campaigns, selecting candidates for office, and participating in various policy-making bodies. The result is that a society's moral and legal system reflects the interests of the powerful. The behavior of those whose interests are not represented is therefore much more likely to be defined as deviant. For instance, upper-class people are seldom, if ever, likely to be caught for, and charged with, vagrancy—an illegal behavior for which lower-class persons are frequently caught, charged, and convicted. As Anatole France (1922) once sarcastically commented, "The law, in all its majestic equality, forbids the rich as well as the poor to sleep under bridges on rainy nights, to beg on the streets, and to steal bread."

Elite Deviance.   Although deviance is usually equated with acts such as vagrancy, burglary, robbery, kidnapping, and assault—for which members of the lower classes are more likely to be convicted—as we have seen, society's elites also break laws and deviate from the accepted morality (Simon and Eitzen, 1990). Conflict theorists have a special interest in **elite deviance,** or the deviant and criminal acts committed by the wealthy and powerful. Cases of elite deviance are often much more costly in economic terms than other types of crime, yet punishment is more lenient.

Elite deviance can take many different forms and may range from unethical or immoral acts to criminal acts punishable by fines and imprisonment. Stock manipulation and individual embezzlement of company funds, for example, are clearly illegal. However, a public official who lies to his constituency or gives special favors to friends may be called immoral or unethical yet may be immune from prosecution. Some elite deviant acts result in personal economic gains (such as a senator's accepting a bribe). Other acts result in economic gain for a business or corporation (as in the case of price fixing or kickbacks or bribes to secure business contracts). A major recent example of this is the "collective embezzlement" of large sums of money by a number of banks and bank executives (Calavita and Pontell, 1991). So much money was embezzled, so many banks went broke as a result, and the government had to bail so many of them out with such large infusions of public money that this came to be known as the *savings and loan scandal*. While elite deviance is generally less visible, dramatic, and overtly violent than other forms of deviance, it may still be injurious to the public's health, safety, or financial well-being. For example, in 1967 the President's Crime Commission estimated that the nation's annual loss to white-collar crime was 27 to 42 times as great as the loss through traditional property crime (robbery, burglary, larceny, and forgery) (Thio, 1978, p. 355). In the early 1970s, a Senate panel put the yearly cost of corporate crime at between $174 billion and $231 billion. A study done in the mid-1980s showed that the average cost of a corporate offense that involved sentencing of a federal court was $565,000, whereas it was only $1000 for each burglary and $400 for each larceny (Simpson, 1992). Even when criminal convictions are obtained, the penalties for elite deviance are often relatively light (Simpson, 1992). When the E. F. Hutton company, a major financial institution, was caught in a fraudulent check "kiting" scheme, a crime for which ordinary citizens would generally be penalized, no company officials were criminally indicted. Even though the company officials were systematically writing checks when they had insufficient funds in bank accounts, and were therefore fraudulently taking the bank's money, the U.S. Justice Department did not choose to prosecute.

In the 1980s a scandal occurred on Wall Street involving the illegal buying and selling of stocks on the basis of inside or advance information about stocks that were going to rise in value. This is called *insider trading,* and it is illegal. The insider trading case that rocked Wall Street in 1986 centered around Ivan Boesky (nicknamed "Ivan the Terrible," or "Piggy" because he was so greedy). Boesky was a multimillionaire stock market speculator who ultimately admitted that his unbelievable economic successes (for which he was greatly admired) were the result of advance information he had acquired about corporate takeover deals. With this information Boesky was able to buy into the companies before their stock prices rose, and he could therefore make great profits. By the time these illegal dealings came to light, Boesky had amassed a huge fortune.

When his crimes were uncovered, Boesky agreed to help the government find others who were involved in insider trading. He eventually agreed to pay $100 million in penalties and was banished for life from professional stock trading. In exchange, the government allowed Boesky to sell $440 million in stock he controlled *before* the announcement of his penalties was made. In other words, Boesky was allowed to sell his stock before the price was to plummet *because* of the announcement of his penalties. Boesky was clearly treated quite gently by the authorities and emerged from the scandal with a significant portion of his fortune intact.

Boesky was also sentenced to a 3-year prison term (he ultimately served only 2 years) at the prison of his choice; he chose the minimum security facility in Lompoc, California. The California climate is gentle, and the prison is set on 44,000 acres of rolling hills and manicured lawns. It offers the inmates a gym, tennis courts, a weight-lifting room, and an outdoor track. It is hard to imagine a burglar or robber who has stolen hundreds of millions of dollars being given such preferential treatment and such a light sentence in a "country-club" prison.

Another prominent figure in the Wall Street scandals was Michael Milken, the pioneer of "junk bonds." Milken was involved with Boesky and, in fact, it was Boesky who, in order to aid his own case, wore a "wire" and helped gather the information that led to Milken's arrest (Kempton, 1990). Milken was eventually convicted of securities fraud and other business crimes and was sentenced to 10 years in prison, a surprisingly harsh sentence for a white-collar crime. Prior to his conviction, Milken had agreed to pay a $200 million fine and a $400 million penalty. In spite of the forfeit of $600 million, it was estimated that Milken was left with a fortune of $700 million. Attorney General Richard Thornburgh said that Milken's conviction strongly suggests "that law enforcement has upped the ante considerably for 'crime in the suites' committed by the white-collar criminal" (McCartney, 1990, p. A22). However, Representative John Dingell said of the sentence that "its apparent harshness is more illusion than reality" (McCartney, 1990, p. A22).

In August 1992, supposedly because of his cooperation with the Securities and Exchange Commission (SEC), Milken's sentence was reduced so that in the end he, too, served only 2 years in prison. This in spite of the fact that the SEC claimed that Milken had been of little or no help to them. A congressman described the sentence reduction as "outrageous," sending "exactly the wrong signal to Wall Street" (Sullivan, 1992, p. D17). Milken emerged from prison a very wealthy man. While barred from the securities industry, Milken remains active today in the business-world (Peers, 1995), as well as in various other kinds of activities, including helping to find a cure for prostate cancer from which he suffers.

Conflict theorists argue, as we have noted, that elite deviants commit much larger crimes and receive lighter punishments than average citizens. This viewpoint can be illustrated by comparing the Boesky-Milken case (or the E. F. Hutton case) with that of William J. Rummel. Rummel was convicted of three offenses by the courts of Texas. His crimes were the following:

1. Forging a check for $28.36
2. Obtaining $80 by fraudulent use of a credit card
3. Taking a check for $120.75 in return for a false promise to repair an air conditioner

Although none of these crimes involved physical injuries to the offended parties, these convictions all happen to be felonies, and under Texas law conviction for a third felony carries a mandatory sentence of life imprisonment. The constitutionality of the law was sustained by the Supreme Court (*New York Times,* 1980a, p. A24). Thus, for crimes involving a total of $229.11, William Rummel faces a life behind bars.

Conflict theory emphasizes the inequalities of power and money in societies. Many conflict theorists, following Marxian theory, see the inequalities as growing out of a capitalist economic system. However, other conflict theorists have noted that inequalities in power and authority also exist in countries with other economic systems (Dahrendorf, 1959).

We will turn next to a theory of deviance that shares with conflict theory the view that inequalities between groups of people in a society can influence who is and who is not considered deviant. Called *labeling theory,* it is associated with symbolic interaction theory (Chapter 1) because it places great emphasis on the symbolic labeling of people as deviants.

Labeling Theory

Labeling theory focuses on the social nature of the process by which some individuals in the society are able to label other individuals as deviant. Also of interest is how the labeled person accepts or adopts the deviant label for himself or herself (Dotter and Roebuck, 1988; Gove, 1980; Walsh, 1990).

Labeling theory is concerned with which people will be labeled "alcoholics," "drug addicts," "mentally ill" (Link et al., 1989), "juvenile delinquents" (Matsueda, 1992; Zhang and Messner, 1994) or as possessing childhood disabilities (Gill and Maynard, 1995). When such labels are applied, the labeling process begins. It involves a person or group doing the labeling (the labeler) and a person or group to whom the label is applied (the labelee). Those who do the labeling are social control agents. Often these agents, such as the police or psychiatrists, label as part of their official functions. Labeling also occurs in very informal contexts, such as when a family member or friend labels someone a drunk or a liar. Those who are labeled in this process are the deviants. Thus, from a labeling perspective, a deviant is someone to whom a deviant label has been successfully applied (Becker, 1963, p. 9).

The process of becoming deviant usually begins when people perform acts that are disapproved of by certain members of society. Some people rape, steal, or become mentally ill. These forms of deviance may be due to personality problems, a particular kind of home life, community conditions, peer-group influence, or other factors. Although some sociologists focus on the causes of deviance that lie within individuals or their environments, many have come to focus on the official and unofficial social control agents and the labels they create and apply. If no deviant labels were created by social control agents, then there would be no deviance. According to labeling theorists, in order for behavior to be considered deviant, it must be labeled as such:

> [S]ocial groups create deviance by making the rules whose infraction constitutes deviance and by applying these rules to particular people and labeling them as outsiders. From this point of view, deviance is not a consequence of the act the person commits, but rather a consequence of the application by others of rules and sanctions to an "offender" (Becker, 1963, p. 9).

In other words, no specific behavior is inherently deviant; behavior becomes deviant only when others define it as such.

As we have shown, the deviant label is not applied uniformly. The poor, minority groups, and the disadvantaged are more likely to be labeled deviant for a given act than are more advantaged individuals who behave in the same way. In cases of extreme offenses, such as murder, the community's selectivity in labeling people as deviant is not as clear, but it is quite clear in less extreme forms of deviance: "Some men who drink too much are called alcoholics and others are not; some men who act oddly are committed to hospitals and others are not; some men who have no visible means of support are hauled into court and others are not" (Erikson, 1964, pp. 11–12). These realities have led observers to argue that people are more likely to be labeled mentally ill when they are poor, work in low-status occupations, or are in similarly devalued circumstances (Goffman, 1959a). A person in a more advantageous social situation often escapes being labeled deviant, despite manifestations of the same forms of behavior.

Labeling theory has also been used to help us to understand deviance from the perspective of the victim of deviant acts. In cases where husbands have abused their wives, it is frequently the woman, the *victim,* who is labeled as the deviant (Carlson, 1987). The abusing husband will often successfully label his wife as deviant, charging her with being inadequate, perhaps not living up to the expectations of some ideal female role. Many abused wives report that their husbands convinced them, often for years, that *their* inadequacies were the cause of the beatings. Second, if an abused wife tries to do something about the violence, she is likely to be labeled as deviant by the larger society for revealing that her home and marriage are "defective." Thus, labeling contributes to violence against wives and to their reluctance to do anything about it. The abusive husband may ultimately be labeled as a deviant, but before that occurs, the female victim is likely to have acquired that label.

Primary versus Secondary Deviance. When deviance is viewed from a labeling perspective, the focal concern is not individual, isolated acts of deviance. Labeling theorists are not concerned with explaining why previously "straight" people steal their first orange from a fruit stand, embezzle their first dollar from their employer, or assault their first victim. Such early, nonpatterned acts of deviance are called **primary deviance.**

Virtually everyone commits some acts of primary deviance. In a study of 1689 adults in New York City, Wallerstein and Wyles (1947) found that 91 percent of the respondents in the study admitted that they had broken a law after their sixteenth birthday. Sixty-four percent of the men and 29 percent of the women could have been convicted of a felony. Between 80 percent and 90 percent of all the men and women studied had stolen something. One-fourth of the men admitted to having stolen an automobile, and one out of ten had committed a robbery. Thus, isolated acts that would be labeled deviant by social control agents are widespread.

Labeling theorists, however, are chiefly concerned with **secondary deviance,** which refers to forms of deviance that persist in individuals and that cause them to organize their lives and personal identities around their deviant status. Labeling theorists focus on the process whereby individuals become labeled as criminals, and the label comes to override all other definitions of self.

Although the labeling approach focuses on the degree to which others label an individual, it is also possible for individuals to label themselves (Thoits, 1985). For example, persons who are sick label themselves as ill in the hope that others will recognize this label and respond appropriately—by expressing sympathy, curing the illness, or excusing the sick person from normal activities and responsibilities. Deviants, then, sometimes label themselves before anyone else does and proceed to act in accordance with that label (Lorber, 1967).

Although a number of criticisms have been leveled against labeling theory, it persists as a powerful sociological perspective on deviance (Bazemore, 1985; Klein, 1986; Sommer et al., 1988; Ward and Tittle, 1993). Much of the following discussion, in fact, is a reflection of the insights of labeling theory.

The Process of Social Control

Having defined deviance (and various theories of deviance), we now come to the problem of analyzing the reciprocal process of social control, which is an important part of labeling deviants. **Social control** refers to the process whereby a group or society enforces conformity to its demands and expectations. Social control involves those with power who seek (often successfully) to label as deviant those who do not conform. Those who develop labels and engage in the labeling process are the social control agents. Those successfully labeled are the deviants. (It is also possible to use positive labels (for example, beautiful or handsome) in order to control people (Margolin, 1993).) From the perspective of labeling theory, deviants and social control agents cannot exist without each other. We also can differentiate between two broad types of social control agents: rule enforcers and rule creators (Becker, 1963).

Acting as Rule Enforcers

When we think of rule enforcers, we generally think of the formal agents involved in the social control process—the police, the courts, prisons, even parents (Birenbaum and Sagarin, 1976). Arrest by police, conviction and imprisonment by the courts, and punishment by parents are all examples of the exercise of social control through rule enforcement. Each of these social control agents is clearly implicated in the labeling process. Arrest and incarceration serve to label an individual as a murderer, thief, or rapist. Even parental admonishments can label a child lazy, dumb, or mean. **Rule enforcers** attempt to maintain social control and order through the threat or actual application of undesirable social labels.

Although most of us think of formal agencies when we think of rule enforcement, we are somewhat less likely to think of ourselves as rule enforcers. All of us, however, act as rule enforcers on a fairly regular basis in our day-to-day activities. If people around us violate a social norm, we act in a variety of ways to indicate that they have done so, in an effort to bring them back into line. We are likely to act as rule enforcers when we observe someone spitting on the floor, cutting in at the head of a line, or hassling an innocent passerby. Even a raised eyebrow, a grimace, or a frown can serve the function of social control. We can also engage in more extreme forms of rule enforcement such as a raised voice, a clenched fist, or even a blow to the head. Such interpersonal social control devices, both subtle and blatant, are far more widespread than the formal means employed by the police, the courts, and other social control agencies.

Rule Creators and Social Change

The **rule creator** devises the rules, norms, or laws (Ryan, 1994). Without rule creators, we would have no deviance, since we would have nothing from which to deviate. This is what we mean when we say that deviance is created by social control agents who establish a society's normative system. While some laypersons may believe that norms, rules, and laws represent eternal and incontrovertible truths, sociologists see these rules as generally produced to protect the vested interests of the rule creators and those they represent.

A number of studies have shown that social rules are the product of the vested interests of social control agents. One illustration is found in Chambliss's analysis (1964) of the history of vagrancy laws—laws that came into being when feudalism was breaking up. Medieval landowners needed a large pool of cheap labor when they could no longer depend upon serfs to carry out their work. Vagrancy laws provided this cheap labor by forcing people to work in order to avoid being arrested for vagrancy.

This has come to be broadened to what is known as a social constructionism. That is, social problems do not simply occur, but are actively constructed by those with an interest in having certain issues be seen as problems (Miller and Holstein, 1993). For example, Beckett (1994) has addressed the issue of increasing public concern over the relationship between street crime and drugs. She found that the state played a central role and the media a somewhat lesser role in creating this concern among the public.

A somewhat different process occurred in the recent criminalization of computer abuse. **Computer abuse** is the unauthorized entry into someone else's computer data for the purposes of altering, stealing, or sabotaging them (Hollinger and Lanza-Kaduce, 1988). Initially, computer abuse was likely to take the form of hackers breaking into large computer systems more to show that it could be done than for any personal gain (Takahashi, 1995). In the most famous case of this kind, in 1988 a Cornell University graduate student created a virus (a program, or set of instructions, that replicates itself from computer to computer) and succeeded in injecting it into a national network of interlinked computers. The virus spread rapidly through the system, ultimately crippling 6000 computers in government agencies and laboratories, companies, and universities (Markoff, 1988).

What seems to be increasing rapidly today is criminals using computers not to break into a computer system just for kicks, or to demonstrate that it can be done, but rather "to steal valuable information, software, phone service, credit card numbers and cash" (Flanagan and McMenamin, 1992, p. 184). Although hard to gauge precisely, the FBI estimates that computer crimes like these now cost the nation between $500 million and $5 billion per year.

The first law against computer crime was passed in Florida in 1978. In this case, the law came about not so much because of pressure from interest groups, but because new social conditions had arisen that required new legislation (Hollinger and Lanza-Kaduce, 1988). In the mid-1990s, there is increased pressure to pass national legislation, and some nations (Italy, for example) have already passed such legislation, outlawing things like damaging public information systems, possessing and disseminating illegally obtained passwords, and spreading computer viruses (*Computer Audit Update,* 1994).

An interesting new issue is emerging in this realm—the existence of pornography on the Internet and the efforts to limit its distribution, especially to children (*Los Angeles Times,* 1995). More generally, this new technology has helped to create a whole new series of forms of deviant sexual behavior—"log-on sex"—

including obtaining information about deviant sexual behavior, arranging meetings in order to have sex (especially of a deviant kind), and misrepresenting the writer's sexual orientation (Durkin and Bryant, 1995).

The Personal Experience of Deviance

Becoming Deviant

Although some people come to be labeled deviant without having committed a deviant act, we begin our discussion with the assumption that some act has been committed that some rule-enforcement agents consider deviant. Some people who commit a deviant act once or twice may never commit another; others will proceed only part way through the process of becoming deviant; still others move from primary deviance to secondary deviance (Lemert, 1967).

If an act of primary deviance is observed, the person committing it may be punished by rule-enforcement agents. Despite punishment, some people commit additional acts of primary deviance. If these acts are observed by social-control agents, further and probably more severe punishments will occur. Although punishment may deter some people, others will engage in still further acts of deviance and possibly develop hostility and resentment toward those who punish them. This leads to a crisis level in the community's ability to tolerate more deviance. The most likely result is some formal action by social-control agents that labels the individual. For some, this strengthens their deviant identity and increases their deviant conduct. Ultimately, the individual who moves through the entire process comes to accept deviant social status and attempts to adapt to it. The end product is secondary deviance, or a person whose life and identity are organized around a deviant label.

Although some people consciously enter into a deviant career, most seem to simply respond to circumstances and situations in which they find themselves (Lemert, 1972, p. 80).

Coping with Deviance: Goffman's Theory of Stigma

More than anyone else, Erving Goffman has contributed to our understanding of how people, having been labeled deviant, cope with their own deviance. Goffman's work was done primarily in the tradition of symbolic interaction theory. He was especially interested in the way people interacted with each other, and in the messages they were sending by their words and gestures. In one of his most influential books, he studied people with certain characteristics that others would find unusual, unpleasant, or deviant (Goffman, 1963). Goffman called these characteristics *stigmas,* and he was particularly concerned with how people who have stigmas cope with them.

Goffman's analysis begins with physically stigmatized people and gradually introduces a wide array of other stigmas (e.g., being on welfare; see Rogers-Dillon, 1995). In the end, readers realize that they have not been reading about a remote person who has a physical deformity, but about themselves. As Goffman (1963, p. 127) says: "The most fortunate of normals is likely to have his half-hidden failing, and for every little failing there is a social occasion when it will loom large, creating a shameful gap."

Goffman deals with two basic types of stigmatized individuals. The first type, the individual with a **discredited stigma,** "assumes his differentness is known about already or is evident on the spot." The second type, the individual with a **discreditable stigma,** assumes that his stigma "is neither known about by those present nor immediately perceivable by them" (Goffman, 1963, p. 4). Discredited or discreditable stigmas can take the form of physical deformities, as when a person has lost a limb; character blemishes, as when a person has a prison record or a history of mental illness; or membership in an ethnic or racial group that is often viewed negatively by others (gypsies, for example).

In Goffman's view, people with discredited stigmas (readily visible) face different problems from those with discreditable stigmas (not immediately obvious). With a discredited stigma, the person, for example, a topless dancer (Thompson and Harred, 1992) or a funeral director (Thompson, 1991), can be prepared for some expected (often hostile) responses in social interaction with other people. On the other hand, persons with discreditable stigmas often try to manage interaction so that others will not learn of their characteristic. Concealment often becomes cumbersome. For example, there is the case of Mrs. G., whose husband was in a mental hospital. To keep the neighbors from discovering what she believed to be a stigma, she told them that he was in the hospital because of a suspected cancer. Every day she would rush to get the mail before her neighbors picked it up for her as they used to do. She abandoned second breakfasts at the drug store with the women in the neighboring apartments to avoid their questions. Before inviting her neighbors in, she hid any material that identified the hospital, and so on (Yarrow et al., 1955, cited in Goffman, 1963, p. 89). This case also illustrates that is is not just the afflicted person who is stigmatized; relatives (and others) are also likely to be stigmatized. To take another example, Gray (1993) found that parents of autistic children felt stigmatized by their children's disease.

AIDS and Stigma. A major example of stigma in the United States today is AIDS. There is great fear of the disease and, at least in some segments of American society, substantial hostility toward those with AIDS. In the early stages of the disease, AIDS patients have a discreditable stigma, since there are usually not any overt signs of the disease. Victims will then often attempt to manage information so that others do not learn that they have AIDS. However, as the disease progresses, concealment of the stigmatized characteristics becomes increasingly difficult. AIDS victims are likely to lose substantial amounts of weight, look unwell, require frequent hospitalization, and perhaps develop the visible skin lesions of Kaposi's sarcoma. In Goffman's terms, AIDS victims in the later stages of the disease have discredited stigma; their disease is very visible. Rather than concealing information, AIDS victims come to focus on managing the tension produced by people who know that they have the dreaded disease. They may be shunned by friends, may lose their jobs, and may be badly treated by health personnel. The social aspects of having AIDS are easily understood as a contemporary example of Goffman's insightful analysis of stigma (Tewksbury, 1994).

Recently, Leiker et al. (1995) studied factors related to the stigmatization of those with AIDS. Key to the study was the distinction among four causes of AIDS: homosexual sex, IV drug use, heterosexual sex, and blood transfusions. The issue was whether there are differences in the degree of stigmatization of AIDS victims based on differences in causes. The least stigmatized condition was AIDS traceable to a blood transfusion, followed by contracting the disease as a result of heterosexual sex. The most stigmatizing causes, and to an almost equal degree, were homosexual sex and IV drug use. Leiker et al. (1995, p. 345) explain that those "who develop AIDS as a result of homosexual behavior or IV drug use bear the additional burden of a great moral stigma being attached to their deviant lifestyles and behavior." They are, in effect, doubly stigmatized. Interestingly, homophobia was related to the stigmatization of AIDS victims under all four conditions, even those that had nothing to do with homosexuality. This reflects the degree to which AIDS continues to be identified with homosexuality in our society.

Female Athletes, Lesbianism, and Stigma.   Female athletes, especially professional golfers (Rotello, 1995), are often assumed to be lesbians and are, as a result, frequently stigmatized. In an interview study of women athletes, Blinde and Taub (1992) were interested in the way in which they coped with the stigma. Since the fact that they were athletes, let alone lesbians (and most claimed they were not lesbians), was not immediately obvious to outsiders, they were faced with a discreditable stigma, which they handled by three strategies of information management. First, they sought to *conceal* their stigma by, for example, self-segregating themselves from nonathletes, "passing" as nonathletes, and using various disidentifiers like dresses and makeup to disassociate themselves from the image people have of female athletes (and lesbians) (Blinde and Taub, in Bedell, 1995). Second, the women sought to *deflect* attention from their status as athletes by accentuating another of their roles, for example, their student role. Finally, the women could directly confront their stigma and try to *normalize* it by, for example, seeking to educate others about female athletes and/or their relationship, or lack thereof, to lesbianism.

Fatness and Stigma.   Hughes and Degher (1993) studied the ways in which members of a national weight reduction organization cope with the stigma of obesity. They identified five basic coping strategies:

1. *Avoidance* involves either not thinking about one's fatness or avoiding situations in which being fat might pose a problem. In terms of the former strategy, one respondent said

   > You know, most of the time I am pretty happy. I don't even think about being fat. It is only when something happens, like having to fly and not being able to fit in the seats and having to ask for a seat belt extension, that I start to think about it again. If I had to think about it all the time, I think I would kill myself (Hughes and Degher, 1993, p. 302).

2. *Reaction formation* involves rejecting or even reversing the general definition of acceptable behavior by, for example, eating even more and getting even fatter.

3. *Compensation.* People may compensate for being fat by overachieving in other situations (for example, becoming the leader of an organization).

4. *Compliance* can take the form of either complying with the expectations that others have of fat people (accept being the butt of fat jokes, for one) or with the expectation that they diet, even though they are not really committed to such action.

   > My husband paid for me to go to a hypnotist, one who specialized in weight reduction. He gave me a posthypnotic suggestion that would keep me away from food. It never took, but every time Jim (my husband) was around I pretended to hate food. When he left I raided the refrigerator (Hughes and Degher, 1993, p. 306).

5. *Accounts* are stories, including those that serve as excuses, explaining why one has become fat ("it's genetic"; "it's the fault of circumstances or of others," especially family members), as well as those that explain why the individual continues to be fat (the result of a personal tragedy, and so on).

Leaving the Deviant Role

Once imposed, the deviant label is difficult and sometimes impossible to remove. However, many deviants do manage to shed the label and leave the deviant role. Our concern in this section is not with those who can escape the deviant label relatively easily (such as someone defined as slightly overweight, who can go on a diet), but rather with those whose label is difficult to remove. Although we will focus on alcoholics and criminals, the same points apply to many other deviant roles.

The problems of leaving a deviant role are illustrated by sociological studies of Alcoholics Anonymous (AA) (Trice and Roman, 1970; Denzin, 1986, 1987). In AA, one finds examples of successful **delabeling,** that is, cases in which alcoholics were able to shed their deviant label and replace it with a socially acceptable one, "recovering alcoholic."

Alcoholics Anonymous uses various methods to help alcoholics shed their deviant label. AA believes that alcoholics have a biological predisposition to become alcoholics. This interpretation of the causes of alcoholism counters the alternate belief that alcoholics are responsible for their actions or that alcoholism is a form of mental illness. To help further in the delabeling process, AA argues that since alcoholics' deviance stems from their drinking, once they stop drinking, their deviant status ends. AA also has constructed a rather unusual repentant role. By admitting that they are alcoholics, alcoholics will supposedly embark on the road to delabeling and acquiring the new "more respectable role" of ex-alcoholic. AA also stresses the degradation of drinking. By showing how far down some alcoholics have descended, they set the stage for stories of glorious comebacks.

Although AA is more successful than most organizations in helping people leave a deviant role, few hard data are available on its success ratio. AA has been a middle-class organization with little attraction for individuals from the lower classes. Also, it could be argued that voluntary membership makes AA successful because those who decide to join AA are the ones most motivated to solve their drinking problem. AA, however, does help some people modify or change their deviant label.

As a transition to the next section, let us close with a discussion of "desistance," or ceasing criminal activity. Sommers et al. (1994) have recently studied this process in the case of female street criminals. They discovered a lengthy and complex process involving three basic stages:

1. *Resolving to stop.* Rather than drifting back toward conventional behavior, all the women in this study made a conscious decision to stop their criminal behavior. This decision was usually triggered by some sort of shock or the delayed impact of deterrence. It was generally motivated by the difficulties of life on the street, the fear of dying as a result of street activities, and the feeling that life was going nowhere.

2. *Breaking away from the life.* Commitment to stop criminal activities is only a first step. Needed next is a public announcement that one is leaving the criminal life and a redefinition of "economic, social, and emotional relationships that were based on a deviant street culture" (Sommers et al., 1994, pp. 141–142). The female criminals need to become reintegrated into conventional life, and they often need help of some kind in order to do so.

3. *Maintaining a conventional life.* The initial steps toward reintegration need to be sustained and expanded. The women need to develop a stake in their conventional lives that is incompatible with their street lives. This serves to reinforce both their commitment to leave a life of crime and their identities as noncriminals.

Crime: A Major Form of Deviance

In this final section we turn our attention to a significant aspect of deviant behavior: crime. **Crime** is deviant behavior that violates the law and is subject to formally sanctioned punishment by the larger society (U.S. Bureau of Justice, 1983, p. 2). The study of crime, criminal behavior, and the treatment of criminals is a subfield of sociology called **criminology.**

Types of Crime

One way of differentiating crimes is to distinguish between crimes against people and crimes against property. **Crimes against people** (or **violent crimes**) involve the threat of injury, or threat (or use) of force, against victims. Violent crimes include four major types:

1. Murder and nonnegligent homicide (all willful homicides as distinguished from deaths caused by negligence, suicide, accident, and so on);
2. Forcible rape (including assault to rape, threat of force, and attempted rape);
3. Robbery (stealing or taking anything of value by force or threat of force);
4. Aggravated assault (assault with intent to kill or to do great bodily harm) (U.S. Department of Justice, 1992a).

Property crimes do *not* involve the threat of injury, or the threat (or use) of force, against victims; the objective is to gain or destroy property unlawfully. The following are the major types of property crime:

1. Burglary (unlawful entry into a structure with the intent to commit a felony or theft—includes attempts);
2. Larceny-theft (unlawful taking of another's property without force, violence, or fraud—excludes embezzlement and forgery);
3. Motor vehicle theft (theft or attempted theft of a motor vehicle);
4. Arson (willful and malicious burning of, or attempt to burn, houses, buildings, vehicles, personal property, and the like, of another person).

The FBI calls all eight of these violent crimes and property crimes **index offenses.** They are also often called **street crimes,** a term used frequently in the mass media.

Another important way to differentiate crimes reflects the ways they are handled by the criminal justice system. **Felonies,** more serious crimes (for example, homicide, rape, and robbery), are punishable by a year or more in prison. **Misdemeanors,** minor offenses (for example, drunkenness, shoplifting, and disturbing the peace), are punishable by imprisonment for less than a year.

Although this section focuses on street crimes, at least five other major types of crime can be identified. As discussed earlier, a major social problem is **white-collar crime** (Braithwaite, 1985), or crime usually committed by upper-status people in the course of their occupations (for example, computer data theft, embezzlement, consumer fraud, and bribery). Another type is **political crime,** which is misconduct and crime committed within or against a political system. As a result of government scandals such as Watergate, the Iran–*Contra* affair, and other questionable behavior of a variety of government officials (for example, illegal campaign contributions and "influence peddling"), political crime is an issue of growing importance. Another facet of political crime is terrorism, which is an act carried out to influence or change existing governments. **Organized crime** refers to "those self-perpetuating, structured, and disciplined associations of individuals, or groups, combined together for the purpose of obtaining monetary or commercial gains or profits, wholly or in part by illegal means, while protecting their activities through a pattern of graft and corruption" (U.S. Bureau of Justice Statistics, 1983, p. 3). We usually think of the Mafia when we think of organized crime. In **victimless crime** (Schur, 1965) it is difficult to identify a victim: the participants choose to be involved in the activities (for example, selling and buying pornography, prostitution). Finally, **juvenile delinquency** refers to illegal or antisocial behavior on the part of a minor.

Official Crime Statistics

The best-known crime statistics in the United States are gathered from official law enforcement agencies and collated and published by the FBI as the *Uniform Crime Reports* (U.S. Bureau of Justice Statistics, 1994). Local police agencies send the FBI monthly and annual summary reports on crimes in their jurisdictions, which provide the basis for the *Uniform Crime Reports* statistics. These reports include data on the number of offenses discovered by, or reported to, these law-enforcement agencies.

For 1993, according to the FBI, 14.14 million criminal offenses were reported to the police in the United States. (Of course, there were many more crimes that were never reported.) Of these, about 12.22 million (about 86 percent) were *property* crimes: burglary, larceny, motor vehicle theft, and arson. The 1.92 million *crimes against people* (violent crimes) included 24,526 homicides, 104,806 forcible rapes, 659,757 robberies, and 1,135,099 aggravated assaults. It is clear that the vast majority of crimes in the United States are crimes against property and *not* crimes against people (U.S. Bureau of Justice Statistics, 1994).

The great volume of crime in the United States is revealed by the frequency of various crimes. On the basis of the crimes reported in the *Uniform Crime Reports,* the FBI has prepared a Crime Clock, which is shown in Figure 6–1. Among other

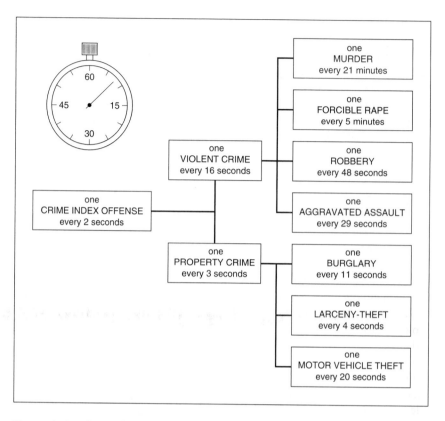

Figure 6–1.   Crime Clock, 1993. The Crime Clock should be viewed with care. Being the most aggregate representation of UCR data, it is designed to convey the annual reported crime experience by showing the relative frequency of occurrence of the Index Offenses. This mode of display should not be taken to imply a regularity in the commission of Part I Offenses; rather, it represents the annual ratio of crime to fixed time intervals. (*Source:* United States Bureau of Justice Statistics, 1994.)

facts, this clock shows that in the United States one violent crime is committed every 16 seconds and one crime against property, every 3 seconds.

Murder in the United States.   The Crime Clock reveals that in the United States a murder is committed every 21 minutes. Compared to other countries, the United States has an exceptionally high homicide rate. For example, in 1980, 23,000 murders were committed in the United States. This number of murders was committed by a U.S. population of 227 million people. As a comparison, the combined populations of Denmark, the Federal Republic of Germany, Greece,

Japan, and Poland had populations totaling 230 million. Yet these countries had only slightly more than 2300 murders (U.S. Bureau of the Census, 1984, p. 181). In 1980 the United States had a murder rate that was *ten times* higher than these widely dispersed nations of the world. However, it should be pointed out that since 1980 the murder rate in the United States has not increased appreciably. In fact, in the first half of 1995, murders reported to the police dropped 12 percent in comparison to the same period in 1994, the largest such drop in 35 years (*Washington Post,* 1995a, p. A4). It is likely, therefore, that at the minimum the differential between the United States and these other nations has not increased.

Crime in Urban and Rural Areas

In 1993, U.S. cities had a violent-offense rate of 354.9 per 100,000 (that is, there were 354.9 arrests for every 100,000 people living in cities), whereas the comparable rate in rural areas was 163.6 per 100,000. In the same year, cities had a property-offense rate of 995.4 per 100,000, whereas the comparable rate in rural areas was 384.9 per 100,000 (U.S. Bureau of Justice Statistics, 1995). These figures underscore the extent to which crime is disproportionately an urban problem. Violent crimes are more than twice as likely to occur in cities than in rural areas, and the likelihood of property crimes in cities is more than two and one-half times that in rural areas.

One probable reason for the higher crime rates in urban areas is the greater likelihood of drug use in cities. An increasing body of evidence shows that drug sales and use are related to crime rates, which is discussed later.

Women and Crime

Over the last two decades there has been an increase in the number of women arrested for crime (Simon and Landis, 1991). In 1963, 11.4 percent of those arrested for all crimes were women; in 1987 that had increased to 17.7 percent, and by 1993 it was up to almost 23 percent. Quite striking was the increase in women arrested for violent crimes, rising 81.5 percent between 1984 and 1993. In the past, almost all the increase in female crime involved property offenses (especially larceny); there was very little increase in violent crime (homicide, aggravated assault, and robbery) committed by females. However, this has changed dramatically in the last decade (English, 1993). Between 1984 and 1993, the largest increases in specific categories were a 109.1 percent increase in motor vehicle theft (a property crime) and a 94.8 percent increase in aggravated assaults (a violent crime). Rapes by females grew by 52 percent, although the absolute numbers remain minuscule (380 in 1993). Interestingly, in spite of the overall increase in violent crime committed by females, the number of murders perpetrated by females *declined* by 10.8 percent between 1984 and 1993 (U.S. Bureau of Justice Statistics, 1995a).

How do we account for this dramatic increase in female arrest rates? Four basic explanations have been offered. The first is the *masculinity thesis,* which argues that as women have become liberated, they have been freed to assert themselves in typically male ways—including crime. The second, or *opportunity thesis,* contends that, as women gain more education, enter the labor force in greater numbers, and assume positions of greater authority, they will have more opportunity to commit crimes, especially white-collar property offenses. The third position is the *economic marginalization thesis,* which maintains that because women still have poorer occupational and income opportunities than men, there is a greater need for them to commit crime. Finally, there is the *decline of chivalry thesis,* which asserts that while in the past chivalry served to hold down female arrest rates, such chivalry has disappeared, with the result that female criminals are now more likely to be treated like their male counterparts. While Simon and Landis (1991) find support for the opportunity thesis, it seems likely that all these factors are involved in the increase in female arrest rates. In addition to the four factors mentioned, one must also add increasing drug-related problems as a factor in the rise of female criminality (Biron et al., 1995).

Drugs and Crime

There is a strong linkage between drug use and crime (McBride and McCoy, 1993). The number of arrests for drug-abuse violations increased by 56 percent between 1982 and 1993 (U.S. Bureau of Justice Statistics, 1995a). Furthermore, drug abusers, especially heroin addicts, commit other crimes in order to support their costly habits (Kowalski and Faupel, 1990). In fact, many addicts become skilled criminal entrepreneurs in order to support their drug needs. Heroin addicts tend to specialize in a particular type of crime, which they refer to as their "main hustle." For males the most common main hustle is drug sales, while for females it is shoplifting and prostitution. As they specialize, they become increasingly adept at their particular crimes with the result that they will probably avoid arrest for committing the crime. This gives us one reason why the crime statistics on drug addicts, while still high, are probably greatly underestimated (Faupel, 1986).

Particularly worrisome is the linkage between drugs, most notably cocaine and especially crack, and criminal violence. By one estimate, over half of the murders in New York City in the late 1980s may have been drug related (Goode, 1992). Crack cocaine was involved in 32% of the homicides and powdered cocaine in another 12%. By way of contrast, heroin was involved in less than 1 percent of the homicides.

The drug–crime linkage is rocking many American cities; in fact, it is disrupting many of the world's cities. Several Latin American countries are increasingly under the control of drug dealers. (See the box on Colombian drug traffickers, "Drugs and Political Power: The Case of Colombia.") Although the United States as a whole is not in the grip of drug gangs, certain areas of a number of our major cities are controlled by heavily armed drug gangs (with the Uzi machine gun as the weapon of choice) which deal viciously with those who seek to cut in on their territories.

To deal with the increasing problems produced by drugs, a number of law enforcement and political leaders such as Kurt Schmoke, the mayor of Baltimore, and Joycelyn Elders, the former U.S. Surgeon General, have urged decriminalization of drugs (MacCoun et al., 1993). Decriminalization means that using drugs would not be a crime, and some agency of the government would dispense drugs to those who wanted them (perhaps even free of charge). Those who support decriminalization do not usually support the *legalization* of drugs, which would allow private business to sell drugs that are now illegal (for example, cigarette companies could sell marijuana cigarettes).

The interest in decriminalizing drugs stems from a belief that little can be done at the moment about the seemingly insatiable demand for drugs in the United States. Slogans such as "Just say no" are not likely to have much of an impact on hardcore drug abusers. Furthermore, it is impossible to completely seal off the borders of the United States in order to cut off the supply of drugs. Therefore, with little to be done about demand or supply, decriminalization might be tried.

Decriminalization would squeeze the criminal element out of the business because, if the government dispensed drugs at no cost, or at a nominal cost, the profits would be taken from the illegal drug business. The presumption is that illegal drug dealers would lose interest in supplying drugs to addicts if they could not make enormous profits.

Decriminalizing Drugs: European Experiences.   Those who advocate decriminalization cannot take much heart from the experience of the Netherlands. The Dutch have had a very liberal attitude toward drugs; the use of soft drugs was decriminalized in 1976. Drugs are viewed as a health problem rather than a criminal matter. One positive consequence of this policy is the waning of the AIDS epidemic among intravenous drug users in Amsterdam because of the free dispensation of clean needles by drug clinics (*AIDS Weekly*, 1995). Designated shops legally dispense up to 30 grams of marijuana or hashish. Amsterdam has a city-owned houseboat where cocaine and heroin are openly used. Specially designed buses travel around the city and dispense methadone at regular locations. In spite of this liberalness, or perhaps because of it, crime in Amsterdam has risen dramatically, with hard drug users blamed for the vast majority of the crimes. Drug abusers from many nations have gravitated toward Amsterdam because of its liberal policies. Neighboring countries have been angered by the fact that their citizens are bringing drugs back from the Netherlands. Some businesses have been hurt, and the city's image as a tourist attraction has been tarnished. As a result, the

Cross-national Perspectives

Drugs and Political Power: The Case of Colombia

One of the most ominous developments in the area of drugs is the degree to which Latin American countries (Peru, Bolivia, and especially Colombia) are involved in the international drug trade and controlled by drug lords (Drozdiak, 1991). Government officials who stand up to, and attempt to arrest and prosecute, the drug kingpins have often found themselves in grave danger, and many have been killed for their efforts. In their attempts to control drug sellers, many hundreds of members of the police and the military have been killed.

Colombian officials struck back with a plan not supported by the United States. The Colombian government offered a deal to the drug lords—turn yourselves in and you will not be extradited to the United States. They were promised that they would be tried in Colombia and that they would receive a reasonable sentence.

To avoid being extradited to the United States, Pablo Escobar surrendered to Colombian authorities in June 1991. He flew to a mountaintop "prison" built especially for him where his "cell" was larger than the warden's room. Escobar's private prison came "complete with a soccer field, Jacuzzis, 60-inch television sets and banquets at which prison guards served as waiters" (Farah; 1996a). He selected six of his top lieutenants, including his older brother, to serve "time" with him. They protected Escobar inside the prison, while outside 40 guards shielded him from enemies, including the local police who blamed him and his organization for the deaths of 250 of their peers. A lawyer who is close to Escobar said that the prison "is not designed to keep Escobar in . . . but to keep his enemies out" (Post and Farah, 1991, p. 34). In fact, a little over a year later, Escobar seemed to tire of his country-club prison and "escaped" (French, 1992).

Pablo Escobar was killed by government security officers in December 1993. However, this has had little or no effect on the exportation of drugs to the United States (UPI, 1995). The Medellin cartel that Escobar headed was reeling for a time, but there is talk that it is being revived. More importantly, the Medellin cartel was supplanted after Escobar's death by the Cali cartel under the leadership of Gilberto Rodrigues Orejuela. That cartel is said to now control 80 percent of the world's cocaine business (Torchia, 1995). The Cali cartel is not nearly as brutal as the Medellin cartel, but it is perhaps more dangerous. Instead of guns and hit men, it relies primarily on its economic and political power and a battery of lawyers, public relations people, computer experts, and accountants. It is believed to have corrupted the government at various levels. In fact, Colombia has come to be called a "narco-democracy" (Luft, 1995).

In mid-1995, Orejuela was captured and placed under arrest. However, it is unclear whether he will be tried and convicted and, even if he is, how harshly he will be punished. In fact, Orejuela has unrestricted visits from females, who often, among other things, smuggle in cellular phones so that he can continue to run the drug business. Another leader of the Cali cartel escaped in early 1996, prompting Colombia's leading antidrug prosecutor to exclaim, "'Corruption has triumphed'" (Farah, 1996a). In the meantime, the Colombian drug business continues unfazed by changes in its leadership. And the by-products of that business continue, as well. For example, in mid-1995 a bombing killed 20 people in Medellin, and the head of Colombia's counterintelligence service was murdered, probably by drug traffickers.

The current president of Columbia, Ernesto Samper, has long been linked to drug barons and drug money. In the early 1980s, when campaigning as a presidential candidate, Samper was accused of taking $300,000 from Pablo Escobar. When Samper denied taking the money, Escobar said, "'The reality in this dispute with Dr. Samper is the hypocrisy of denouncing certain types of financial assistance and, at the same time, accepting the money'" (Farah, 1996d). Shortly before he was inaugurated as the president of Colombia, Ernesto Samper was accused of taking $6 million from the Cali cartel in his 1994 campaign. Those charges took on renewed importance in early 1996 when the charges were reiterated by a one-time friend, campaign manager, and defense minister. As a result, at least one political analyst believes that Colombians are finally recognizing what outsiders have told them for years—that the nation is corrupt. They are beginning to undertake the painful process of examining the "cesspool" that is their political system. (Farah, 1996c).

Columbia has another, related problem—Marxist guerrillas (Farah, 1996b). A public opinion poll conducted at the end of 1995 indicated that far more Colombians considered guerrilla violence (38 percent), rather than drug trafficking (16 percent), to be the country's most severe problem. The murder rate (per 100,000 people) in 1994 in Colombia (77.5) was almost ten times the rate in the United States (8) (whose rate, in turn, is almost twice as high as that of France). However, the guerrilla problem is not unrelated to the drug problem. In fact, in the 1990s the largest source of income for the guerrillas was from drug trafficking. They are often employed by the drug cartels to guard remote drug laboratories and hidden airstrips.

Drozdiak, William. "Europe Finds Colombian Cartels Well Ensconced." *Washington Post,* April 11, 1991.

Farah, Douglas. "Colombia's Jailed Drug Barons Said to Carry On Business." *Washington Post,* January 13, 1996a.

Farah, Douglas. "New Focus: Political Violence." *Washington Post,* January 15, 1996b.

Farah, Douglas. "Colombians Demand Samper's Resignation." *Washington Post,* January 24, 1996c.

FARAH, DOUGLAS. "Officials Say U.S. Long Ago Mistrusted Colombia's Samper." *Washington Post,* February 4, 1996d.
FRENCH, HOWARD W. "Bogota Is Criticized over Drug Baron's Prison Escape." *New York Times,* July 24, 1992.
LUFT, KERRY. "For Busted Drug Lord, Terror too Crass." *Chicago Tribune,* June 15, 1995.
POST, TOM, and FARAH, DOUGLAS. "10 Acres, Valley Vu: A Drug Lord's Jail." *Newsweek,* July 1, 1991.
TORCHIA, CHRIS. "Cali Drug Arrest Leaves Much Work to Be Done." *Fresno Bee,* June 11, 1995.
UPI. "Police Seize $92 Million in Cocaine." October 5, 1995.

Dutch are considering placing a variety of additional restrictions on drug use. However, there is some evidence that, contrary to what one might expect, marijuana use has declined, as has heroin addiction among young people (Drozdiak, 1995). In addition, drug-related crime has declined in the 1990s (Salome, 1994).

In Zurich, Switzerland, a similar, albeit more limited, effort at decriminalizing drug use has apparently ended in failure (Cohen, 1992). For years, the city has been allowing drug addicts to use a public park, Platzspitz, as an open drug market where clean syringes and the help of health officials were available to addicts. This was based on the idea that the major problem was the illegality associated with drugs, not the drugs themselves. However, the park became a magnet for European addicts, and the number of regular users of the park rose from a few hundred in 1987 to about 20,000, many of whom came from foreign countries. The closing was prompted by such things as the doubling of drug-related deaths to 81 in 1991 and the fact that health personnel, including five doctors, were assigned to the park to, among other things, resuscitate on average a dozen people a day (some days as many as 40 people required resuscitation). One drug addict said of the park, "too many kids were getting hooked too easily" (Cohen, 1992, p. A10).

The drug addicts who once frequented the park were scattered around the streets of Zurich. Said another addict, "This is a crazy decision, we'll be in the whole city now" (Cohen, 1992, p. A10). Swiss police are trying to at least get those addicts who do not come from Zurich to leave the city. In spite of the failures, the city's chief medical officer remains opposed to legal efforts to try to halt the sale and consumption of drugs: "I believe and most Swiss experts believe that prohibition does a lot of damage" (Cohen, 1992, p. A10). A second drug zone opened in an abandoned train station, but it, too, was closed down in early 1995 (Kabel, 1995; *Swiss Review of World Affairs,* 1994).

Just as the Swiss were moving away from their lenient policy toward drug use, there were signs that Germany was moving toward a more lenient policy, at least toward the use of marijuana and hashish. In March 1992, a German judge ruled that laws outlawing the possession of those two drugs were unconstitutional. In April 1994, the German Supreme Court recommended that police not arrest people caught with up to .3 ounce of hashish (Gedye, 1994). Some political leaders have urged that Germany adopt the Dutch model and allow the sale of such soft drugs in coffee shops. Said one government official, "It is high time to take cannabis products out of the zone of illegality," while another contended, "I would look positively on any policy that decriminalizes the use of soft drugs" (Kinzer, 1992, p. A5).

The American Justice and Penal Systems

Americans today expect that people who have been convicted of crimes will spend time in jail or prison; however, it has not always been that way. During the colonial period most convicted criminals were fined, whipped, or confined in stocks. If their crimes were serious enough, they were hanged. The colonists did not conceive of imprisoning criminals for a specified period of time (Rothman, 1971). Only after colonial times did the idea of imprisoning criminals become an accepted practice.

Prison Overcrowding.   In the United States today, the overcrowding of prisons has become a serious problem (Crouch and Alpert, 1992; McCown, 1994). The population of state and federal prisons in mid-1995 was over 1.1 million (*Washington Post,* 1995b). The U.S. prison population in 1995 was more than five times larger than it was in 1970, an increase of 450 percent (see Figure 6–2 for the growth of prison inmates since the 1920s). In the words of one recent book, the United States is on an "imprisonment binge" (Irwin and Austin, 1994).

A good example of prison overcrowding and its consequences can be found in Maine, which currently has 44% *more* inmates than the institutions were designed to hold (LaFraniere, 1992, pp. A1, A12). (Even more extremely, federal prisons were at 166% of capacity in 1991.) In the Maine State Prison, inmates were doubled up in 6 by 7-foot cells (about the size of a walk-in closet) for 23 hours a day. Were it not for this doubling up, Larry Richardson would probably be alive today. He was found hanging from a twisted sheet in his cell, after he "had been tortured for four nights by his cellmate, who pounded out one of his teeth against a toilet bowl and kicked him in the groin until the bruises reached from Richardson's thighs to his waistline" (LaFraniere, 1992, p. A1). Said an attorney, "The only difference between this and what happens all the time is the poor guy died" (LaFraniere, 1992, p. A12). An even more extreme example is a prison outside Harrisburg, Pennsylvania, which housed 2600 inmates even though it was designed to hold 1800. During a two-night rampage in 1989, the prison was set ablaze and 146 people were injured.

Much of the increase in the prison population is related to increases in incarceration for drug law violations (Chambliss, 1994). And many of those arrested for drug law violations (more that 40 percent) are black; young black males (15 to

34) make up 14 percent of the American population, but more than 40 percent of the prison population. Two-thirds of state prison inmates convicted for drug law violations are black. However, studies have tended to show that whites are far

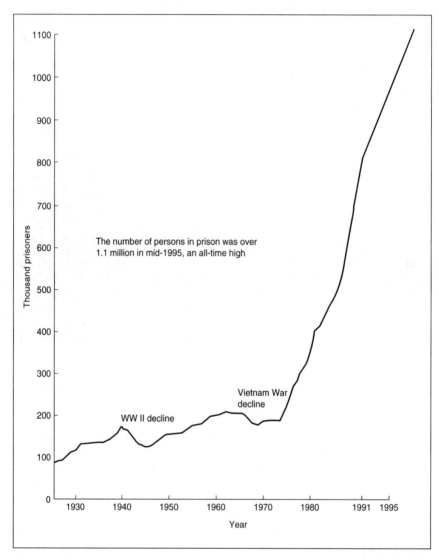

Figure 6–2. Number of Persons in Prison: 1930–1995. (*Sources:* U.S. Bureau of Justice Statistics, *Report to the Nation on Crime and Justice* (Washington, D.C.: U.S. Department of Justice, 1983), p. 81; U.S. Bureau of Justice Statistics, *Prisoners in 1991* (Washington, D.C.: U.S. Department of Justice, May 1992B; *Washington Post,* 1995b, p. A4.)

more likely to use drugs (except crack cocaine) than blacks. Chambliss attributes at least part of the overrepresentation of blacks among those incarcerated for drug violations to the far more intensive police surveillance of black communities than of white communities. A more general cause is the definition of "the problem of crime generally, and drug use in particular, as a problem of young black men" (Chambliss, 1994, p. 183).

Overcrowding and the high cost of imprisonment are causing some governors to rethink imprisonment for nonviolent offenders. Support is growing for such alternatives as supervised probation, halfway houses, and home confinement. The governor of Virginia said of the estimated $25 billion a year spent on all prisons in the United States, "It is absolutely insane the amount of money we spend on corrections" (Hinds, 1992, p. A17). Costs are likely to accelerate not only because of inflation, but also because courts are increasingly mandating that over-crowding be reduced. States can respond to the latter either by building new, even more costly prisons or by finding alternative punishments for some types of crime. The states are also motivated by the fact that many of the alternatives seem more "humane" than imprisonment, although humanity seems to run a distant second to cost-cutting as the major motivation.

Prison overcrowding is not only a problem in itself, but is related to a series of other problems in the prison. For one thing, while prisons have long had gangs, a whole new series of gangs has developed, leading to more splintered and conflict-laden relationships. For another, there is a new generation of younger prisoners who are more violent than the older prisoners and are unwilling to show them the desired respect. The result of such changes, as one older prisoner pointed out, is a much more uncertain and unpredictable prison:

> since there are so many children and kids in prison it is hard to do time now. It is not like it used to be where you can wake up one morning and know what to expect. But now you wake up and you don't know what to expect, anything might happen (Hunt et al., 1993, p. 406).

It is worth noting that the incarceration rate in the United States at the end of 1994 was the highest in the world. While the rate of imprisonment in Russia was almost as high, the U.S. rate was eight to ten times higher that the incarceration rate in the industrialized nations of western Europe (*Washington Post,* 1995b).

Females in Prison.   The number of female prisoners is growing dramatically. In 1994, the number of female inmates grew by 10.6 percent (compared to an 8.5 percent increase for males). As of December 31, 1995, there were 64,403 women in state and federal prisons, 6.1 percent of all prisoners. Between 1980 and 1993, the number of black and white female prisoners grew at higher rates than those for black and white male inmates (National Criminal Justice Reference Service, 1996). The increase in female prisoners is attributable mainly to the increase in drug use and more stringent drug penalties, as well as to mandatory sentencing laws that treat males and females equally. Said one observer, "There used to be a disparity between the ways judges looked at women and men. . . . Now the feeling is if you're going to play the game, you're going to go to prison" (Applebome, 1992, p. A10).

One problem that is exacerbated by the increase in women in prison is an increase in children whose home lives are disrupted by the imprisonment. More than three-fourths of female prisoners had children, the vast majority less than 18 years old. Only 22 percent of women reported that their children were now living with the father, while male prisoners with children reported that 90 percent of them were living with the mother (Greenfeld and Minor-Harper, 1991). Thus, it is clear that female imprisonment is far more disruptive to children than male imprisonment.

The High Cost of Imprisonment. The custody of the increasingly large and diverse prison population is extremely expensive; more and more money is being spent on criminal justice, or what Christie (1993) has called the "crime industry." Chambliss (1994) details a long list of ways in which expenditures on criminal justice have increased dramatically in the last few decades (for example, between 1972 and 1988 the increase in expenditures on criminal justice were three time the increases in expenditures on education; spending on corrections [prisons, and so on] doubled in the 1980s).

Chambliss asks why we are experiencing this enormous increase in expenditures on prisons and other elements of the criminal justice system. The major reason that is generally given is the increase in crime, but Chambliss argues that the best available data (victim surveys) show that crime has *not* increased significantly in the last two decades. Chambliss also reports data that contradict the idea that the increase is traceable to an increase in the seriousness of crime. Nor does he see it as a result of pressure from public opinion. Chambliss points the blame at conservative politicians, the media, and the crime control industry for furthering their own interests by creating a "moral panic" in the public over the crime issue.

Arrest and Imprisonment as Deterrents to Crime. The threat of imprisonment is supposed to serve as a deterrent to crime. We can differentiate between two types of deterrence. In **specific deterrence** the actual punishment of an individual is supposed to deter him or her from committing other crimes in the future. **General deterrence** involves the threat of punishment and the idea that people will not commit crimes because they fear they will be caught and sent to prison (Simpson, forthcoming; Miranne and Gray, 1987).

The question posed by specific deterrence is whether an offender will be more or less likely to commit another crime after arrest or punishment. A recent study shows that arrested offenders will be less likely to commit a future crime than offenders who are released by the police. This was true for novice (first-time) offenders, but it was especially true of experienced offenders (Smith and Gartin,

1989). Persons who are arrested for criminal acts are less likely to commit a crime at a later date than those persons who are released by the police.

Although arrests seem to deter people from future criminal acts, the same is not true for imprisonment. One study has shown that the severity of punishment (imprisonment) does not reduce the likelihood of a return to crime; being imprisoned actually *increases* the likelihood of another criminal offense (Shannon, 1980). Other studies have shown that about one-third of the people who serve time in prison, and are released, return to prison at a later date. This is called **recidivism** (Waldo and Griswold, 1979). If one-third of the people who spend time in prison are not deterred from further crime, it suggests that something about the prison experience may lead to further crime for some people. Moreover, even though it might be supposed that prison would be a special deterrent for white-collar crime, a recent study has suggested that even white-collar criminals are not deterred from future crime by prison sentences (Moore, 1987).

Alternatives to Deterrence.   Given the failures discussed above, several scholars have recently questioned the utility of deterrence in preventing crime. For example, Simpson (forthcoming) has discussed deterrence as it relates to corporate (white-collar) criminals and argued that deterrence through the operation of the formal legal system (detection, arrest, and punishment, including incarceration) is likely to be less effective than informal sanctions employed by corporate personnel. For example, corporate officials can use such tools as threatening a white-collar offender's reputation, current position, future career prospects, or personal and professional relationships. Such informal sanctions may be more likely to deter corporate crime than formal legal sanctions.

Ross has raised the issue of the efficacy of deterrence in terms of drunk driving infractions. While deterrence may be effective if it is "swift and certain," as pointed out earlier in the case of drunk driving, severe penalties may backfire since judges may be unwilling to impose them. Given this weakness, Ross raises a larger issue about the way in which we deal with drunk driving.

Ross argues that the conventional approach to drunk driving, and the one that stands behind the use of deterrence, is to blame the problem on the irresponsible driver. However, Ross argues for a new approach that focuses on viewing drunk driving as an "understandably predictable product of social institutions," especially the institutions of "recreation and transportation" (Ross, 1992, pp. 170–171). That is, drunk driving is linked to the widespread use of the automobile for transportation, the extensive use of alcohol in leisure and recreation, and the interrelationship between the two, since so much leisure and recreation take place outside the home.

Given this perspective, Ross argues that we should focus on changing these institutions. For example, on recreational drinking, Ross urges such steps as raising the minimum drinking age so that it will be harder for young people (who are overrepresented among drunk drivers) to drive drunk, raising the taxation on alcoholic

In the News

The Rise of Rent-a-Cops

A trend of some note and considerable sociological significance is the increasing use of private police officers. Businesses of various types (corporate offices and shopping malls, for example) have employed their own police officers for some time, but what is new in recent years is the growing number of private, usually affluent, residential neighborhoods and communities employing their own police officers. The statistics on the increase in private police are striking.

- Private protection is already a $52-billion-a-year business.
- It is growing at a rate of 8 percent per year.
- The private protection industry now employs about 1.5 million people.
- It already employs 2.5 times as many people as are employed in public law enforcement (Munk, 1994).

The major factors in the rise of private police are the public perception that crime is increasing dramatically (although the statistics do not support this view) and that the public police force is unable to provide adequate protection. Among other things, the public police are seen as undermanned, dispirited, operating with outmoded equipment, and often outgunned by the criminals.

The existence and growth of private police forces raise a number of interesting and important sociological issues:

1. *The issue of fairness.* Should those who are more affluent have better police protection than those who are less well-to-do? In fact, it is those who are least likely to be crime victims, the affluent, who are best able to afford the additional private police protection. In contrast, the poor, most likely to be victimized by criminals, are the least likely to be able to afford private protection. Said one citizen, "Personal security is one of the first functions of government, just like the country's national defense.... It's wrong for citizens with a little more means to have a greater level of personal safety" (Munk, 1994).

2. *Economic support for public police.* There is fear that those who pay for private police might be unwilling to pay taxes to support the public police force. If this were to occur, it would adversely affect funding for the public police. In addition, it is possible that this could be extended to other domains that the well-to-do prefer to finance on their own (schools, for example). There is a potential threat here to public services in general.

3. *Physical danger.* There is the danger posed by armed private police officers, hired often on the basis of limited screening and frequently the recipients of limited training, who might constitute a physical threat to innocent private citizens.

4. *Civil rights.* These private officers might also be a threat to the civil rights of citizens (Spayd, 1994).
5. *Vigilantism.* There are those who see the growth of private police forces as a type of vigilantism. Instead of taking matters into their own hands, wealthy citizens are hiring others to do it for them.

In spite of the problems, the use of private police is likely to grow in coming years. For one thing, there is at least some anecdotal evidence that it leads to reductions in the crime rate (Wheeler, 1994). For another, many people seem to feel safer, whatever the actual situation. According to one Washington, D.C., neighborhood leader, "'Most residents are scared to walk in Georgetown at night.... Now we are feeling more comfortable. We are getting closer to our goal of a safer community'" (Wheeler, 1994).

While some people favor private police because of frustration with the ability of the public police to accord them adequate protection, others recognize the inherent limitations of the public police, as well as the need for communities to look after their own interests: "'People have to be responsible for their neighborhood and themselves.... We can't look to government to do everything. We do pay high taxes but the city is in difficult financial straits. There are limits as to what the city can do'" (Wheeler, 1994).

MUNK, NINA. "Rent-a-cops." *Forbes,* October 19, 1994.
SPAYD, LIZ. "Willing to Pay a Price for Safety: Area's Boom in Private Security Raises Questions." *Washington Post,* May 29, 1994.
WHEELER, LINDA. "In Georgetown, Private Guard Patrols Buy Peace of Mind." *Washington Post,* March 29, 1994.

beverages making them harder to afford, and regulating sales and serving practices by, for example, limiting "happy hours" and training servers to better recognize impairment. Similarly, in terms of reforms of transportation, Ross urges such things as increases in the minimum drinking age, in designated driver programs, in the minimum driving age, and in subsidies to taxi companies to transport those who are inebriated. Finally, in terms of the linkage between drunk driving and death in auto accidents, Ross suggests such things as engineering cars so that they are easier to drive (so that even someone who is impaired could drive), better highway guardrails and breakaway utility poles, and improved emergency medical services so that more lives can be saved after accidents occur. There is evidence that some of these changes have been made (Field, 1995).

Thus, one way to approach drunk driving, and indeed all crimes, is through deterrence (Field, 1995); but another way is through changing the social institutions that support and encourage it and make it more dangerous. Ross (1992, p. 193) argues, "If we are going to save lives currently lost to drunk driving, it will not be enough to redouble our efforts to deter it.... We will have to accept the need to modify social institutions, especially recreation and transportation." However, even if deterrence is combined with all the steps suggested by Ross, we will never eliminate drunk driving, or most other crimes, in our society.

Although many sociologists and criminologists are critical of deterrence, it would be premature to reject the idea entirely. A series of recent studies of the deterrent effect of arrest in cases of family violence is relevant here (Sherman and Smith, 1992; Pate and Hamilton, 1992; Berk et al., 1992). In general, these studies show that formal arrests do *not* have a strong and direct effect in deterring subsequent incidents of family violence. However, arrests *do* have a deterrent effect when they interact with other factors, especially those relating to the background of the offender. In other words, arrest *does* deter some types of criminals.

Three Strikes and You're Out

In an effort to deal with the perception, if not the reality, of a rising crime rate, there have been wide-scale efforts to get "tough on crime," to wage a "war on crime." One notable example of this is the passage by the federal government and several states of "three strikes and you're out" laws (Lewis, 1994). Although there are variations in these laws, the basic premise is that a third felony conviction leads to a mandatory sentence of life in prison. The idea is that if discretion as to sentencing is taken away from judges and if criminals are sure that a third offense will lead to life in prison, they will be far less likely to commit that offense (but see the earlier discussion of deterrence). However, these laws have a series of unforeseen negative consequences, such as juries and judges being unwilling to convict people of a third offense, as well as exacerbating the problem of prison overcrowding.

Capital Punishment.   Capital punishment is increasingly popular (Bedau, 1994). Between 1977, the year executions were resumed after a nearly 10-year lull due to unresolved legal issues, and January 1993, there were 184 executions in the United States. There were 119 more executions in the ensuing 3 years, which reached a peak of 54 executions in 1995 (Kirkland, 1995). As of April 30, 1995, 3009 people were under sentence of death, more than have ever been on death row in the history of the United States (Paternoster, 1991; Paternoster, personal communication; U.S. Bureau of Justice Statistics, 1995a). In executing people the United States stands in opposition to nations such as France, Canada, and the United Kingdom, which have outlawed capital punishment. On the other hand, the United States shares the death penalty with such repressive nations as Iraq and the People's Republic of China.

Much of the support for the death penalty in the United States stems from the belief that it serves as a deterrence against major crimes. There is little question that it serves as a specific deterrence—the person executed will never commit a crime again. However, there is a real question as to whether capital punishment serves as a better general deterrent than imprisonment. In fact, most research shows a pattern of nondeterrrence in the relationship between capital punishment and murder (Bailey and Peterson, 1994). For example, a substantial body of research shows that homicide rates in states with the death penalty are *not* lower than the rates in states that have abolished the death penalty. One study showed that publicized executions led to an *increase* in the incidence of homicides (Stack, 1994).

Not only does capital punishment fail as a form of general deterrence, but it is also discriminatory, especially toward blacks. Blacks are more likely to be executed for murder than whites, and they are far more likely than whites to be executed for rape, especially if the victim is white.

Thus, while a number of people have been executed in recent years, and many more are in jeopardy of capital punishment, the fact is that there are real questions about the efficacy of the death penalty as a deterrent as well as about its fairness to minority groups. The result is that there is a strong anti-death penalty movement in the United States (Haines, 1992).

Summary

Deviance is socially defined, which means that whenever most of the people in a given society or social group consider a behavior deviant, it will be deviant. It can be shown that many behaviors that were at some time acceptable are now deviant; similarly, many behaviors that were deviant at an earlier time are now acceptable. Deviant behavior can often serve to define for the society what is and is not acceptable behavior.

A number of theories of deviance exist: strain theory, deviance as learned behavior (differential association and subcultural), conflict theory, and labeling theory. Each one has a different perspective on deviant behavior.

From a social control perspective, there are attempts to keep most people in conformity with the prevailing norms of the society. Although the most powerful people in the society are most likely to define acceptable and deviant behavior, everyone at some time or another acts as rule enforcer and rule creator.

Three different stages of a career of deviance can be defined. The first stage is becoming deviant, the second is coping with deviance, and the third is leaving the deviant role. Important social aspects are involved in all three of these stages.

Crime is the most attention-getting aspect of deviant behavior. Several distinct types of crime can be defined, including crimes against people (violent crimes), property crime, white-collar crime, political crime, organized crime, victimless crime, and juvenile delinquency. Most crime in the United States is crime against property, but this country also has a high murder rate, especially compared to other nations. Crime is higher in urban areas than in rural areas, and this is probably attributable in part to the extensive use of drugs in today's society. The number of women arrested for crimes has increased substantially. Drugs in general are linked to crime, and cocaine, especially crack, is particularly related to violent crime. Drug abuse has become such a serious problem in the United States that some law-enforcement officials and political leaders have suggested decriminalizing drugs. However, attempts in Europe to decriminalize drugs, while they have many merits, have recently run into serious problems.

Persons convicted of crimes in the United States are expected to spend time in jail or prison. As a result, the U.S. prison system has been charged with managing ever-larger numbers of inmates; overcrowding has become an increasing problem. Larger numbers of females are being imprisoned, with dire implications for their children. Prisons are extremely expensive, and costs have risen dramatically, even though the crime rate has not shown a parallel increase. Serious questions have been raised about whether arrest and punishment deter individuals from further crime. As a result, some experts have been exploring alternatives to imprisonment for various crimes. Others have sought to put more people in prison for longer periods of time through such mechanisms as "three strikes and you're out" laws. After a lull, capital punishment is once again employed in the United States. However, there are serious questions about how well it performs as a general deterrent, and it is clearly practiced in a discriminatory fashion.

CRITICAL THINKING

1. Use examples from the chapter to illustrate that deviant behaviors are socially defined behaviors that may vary from group to group.
2. What determines the nature of deviant behavior in a society or social group?
3. According to the structural–functionalists, how might deviant behavior have a positive societal function?
4. Depending on your cultural group, how might certain behaviors represent both conformity and deviance?
5. Use examples from the chapter to explain how conflict theorists explain deviant behavior. From the perspective of conflict theory, how does social class influence society's response to deviance?
6. How would a labeling theorist respond to a mother's statement that "her young son was just naturally naughty?" Would the sociologist consider her son's behavior an example of primary or secondary deviance?
7. In what ways have you acted as a rule enforcer in your day-to-day activities?
8. Give examples of rules that are produced to protect the vested interests of the rule creators in the following social organizations: U.S. Congress, high schools, prisons.
9. Use a daily newspaper to identify examples of the following types of crimes: property crimes, misdemeanors, white-collar crime, political crime, and organized crime. Compare society's punishments for each of these types of offenses.
10. What is the relationship between drugs and various types of crime? What can be done about this relationship?
11. What are the various dimensions of today's prison crisis? What steps can be taken to alleviate the problem?
12. What is drunk driving? Discuss the pros and cons of the various approaches to dealing with the problem.
13. What do you think of current efforts to get tough on crime, such as the "three strikes and you're out" laws and the increased use of capital punishment?

7

Sexual Behavior from a Sociological Perspective

A NOTE FROM THE AUTHORS: *This chapter on sexual behavior has a special purpose at this point in the book. The first six chapters have introduced you to some fundamental concepts and ideas of sociology. Throughout the rest of the book, many of the concepts you have learned, such as values, norms, roles, reference groups, and so on, will help you to analyze and understand various aspects of social life. Similarly, the sociological ideas introduced in the preceding chapters will continue to provide insights about human social behavior in the remaining chapters. As an example, a fundamental sociological idea is that human behavior is influenced by cultural values, by social norms, by membership in groups and organizations, and by the verbal and nonverbal symbols that we share with other people. This chapter on sexual behavior will present applications of many of the basic concepts and fundamental ideas of sociology.*

Sexual behavior is a strategic area to choose for applying sociological concepts because it is explained so frequently by biological characteristics or psychological mechanisms. Although both biology and psychology are important in understanding sexual behavior, we will show that sociological concepts and ideas are also significant. With this approach we hope to strengthen your understanding of these concepts and ideas and, most important, give you the experience of seeing how helpful and relevant a sociological perspective can be.

- Sexuality is a basic human characteristic.
- Sexual behavior is universal, found in every society.
- Sexual behavior at its most fundamental level is a physical and biological act.

These facts are nearly indisputable, and as such they seem to suggest that a sociological perspective might have little relevance to sexuality and sexual behavior. Yet in Chapter 3 we considered the people of Staphorst, who insisted that their children have premarital sex before marriage; this case reveals how important cultural customs can be in determining sexual behavior. To demonstrate more fully the importance of cultural norms and values, we begin this chapter with a brief examination of how much sexual behavior, and even sexuality, varies from one society to another. These cultural variations will make it clear that we learn much of our sexual behavior from the cultures of the societies in which we live (Reiss, 1986).

Sexual behavior undoubtedly has a biological basis in human beings, just as it has in every other animal species, but biology alone does not explain sexual behavior. This is obvious if we consider the cultural differences in sexual behavior among people in different societies.

There are societies, for example, in which a brother and sister eating at the same table is considered a mildly *sexual* act, and therefore they are prohibited from eating together (Davenport, 1977). In the United States, of course, there is nothing sexual about a brother and sister eating a meal together, even if they are alone. This illustration is but one example of the way in which sexual behavior is culturally defined and regulated.

Through the culture of a society, people learn what is acceptable sexual behavior and what is not acceptable (Irvine, 1994). They learn when sex is appropriate or inappropriate and with whom it is acceptable or not acceptable. The very meaning of sex changes from one society to another. In some societies, sex is a pleasurable, nearly recreational, activity, while in others it is "dirty," and shameful, and rarely spoken of at all. There are some societies in which sex is a hostile battleground between the sexes, and other societies where sex is only for the purpose of reproduction.

To get a sense of how much sexual behavior is influenced by societal and cultural differences, we will first consider some cross-cultural and historical examples of sexual behavior. As we examine these variations in sexual behavior we should remind ourselves that we too learn appropriate sexual behavior from our own culture, in our time.

Cultural Differences in Sexual Behavior

One of the most unusual examples of sexual behavior comes from the classical period of Greek history (500 to 300 B.C.). During this period it was customary for many Greek men to have sexual relations with young boys. Often these men were teachers or military men, and the boys were their students or apprentices. Many of the men had wives and had fathered children, obviously having had heterosexual relations, but that fact did not preclude sexual relationships with boys as well (Flaceliere, 1962).

Although the practice of having sexual relations with young boys was widespread in classical Greece, it was not accepted universally. Aristotle, for example, one of the great philosophers of that era, thought that men who engaged in such relationships were depraved.

A similar cultural pattern has been observed among the Azande people of the Southern Sudan in Africa, where the men also routinely had sexual relations with young boys. Among the Azande the unmarried warriors had young boys who lived with them as personal aides. A boy would take care of the daily needs of his "husband," which included the soldier's sexual needs (Evans-Prichard, 1970).

Another cultural variation in sexual behavior is found in the way husbands and wives relate to each other during sexual intercourse. In Chapter 3 we saw that among the Yanomamo people of the Amazon Valley, violence is common between husbands and wives, and this violence extends into their sexual relations. Similarly, the Gusii of southwestern Kenya define sexuality as a hostile and antagonistic relationship between men and women. Both sexes regard intercourse as a situation in which the man overcomes the natural resistance of the woman. Women are expected to frustrate men with sexual taunts and insults. Gusii men are said to experience greater sexual gratification when women protest and cry during intercourse (Davenport, 1977).

The Gusii view of sexuality is taught to the children when they are young and is especially emphasized at the time of puberty rituals. If girls display any signs of sexuality when they are young, they are punished; signs of sexuality among young boys, however, are both encouraged *and* punished. When these youngsters of the Gusii reach adolescence, they are taught sexual antagonism through the puberty rituals. The adolescent boys are circumcised at a secret initiation ceremony, after which the adolescent girls are brought to where the boys are. The girls are naked and perform erotic dances, while making negative remarks about the boys' mutilated genitals. The girls' dances are supposed to arouse the boys sexually, giving them erections, which will cause them pain since they have just been circumcised (Davenport, 1977). It is little wonder, then, after these childhood and adolescent experiences, that the Gusii think of sexual relations in the context of antagonism and hostility.

In contemporary Islamic societies, sexual relations between husbands and wives are greatly influenced by interpretations of female sexuality based on the *Koran*. Women's sexual needs are seen as very strong, and husbands must meet these needs if their wives are to remain virtuous. Female sexuality is often viewed as dangerous because women, if not under strict control, can be "fatal attractions" for men. A married man can too easily be distracted from his social and religious obligations by a woman other than his wife. Therefore, all women must be kept secluded in their homes, and when they enter public places their faces should be veiled and their bodies completely covered with clothing (Mernissi, 1987).

Cultural Definitions of What Is Sexual

Not only does sexual behavior vary from one culture to another, but definitions of what is considered "sexy" differ as well. For example, in the United States, popular magazines often publish articles that claim to reveal which parts of the male and female anatomy are most sexy. Females are often said to favor the buttocks as the sexiest part of a male.

The newspaper *USA Today* has on occasion awarded honors for the best buttocks seen in movies (Beefiest Butt, Meanest Butt, and so on). Actors such as Mel Gibson and Arnold Schwarzenegger have been recently honored for their posteriors (Kurtz, 1991).

As for males, they too are said to be attracted by the buttocks as one of the sexiest parts of a woman, but breasts and legs also evoke some favor. Apparently, almost no American males select the armpits as one feature of a woman that arouses them sexually. Fewer still choose the neck as sexually exciting. Yet there are males in different parts of the world who would select these as the sexiest parts of a woman's body. Indeed, they would think it strange that men in other societies would not consider them sexy. For instance, among the Abkhasians, a group of people living in the southern part of the former Soviet Union, the female's armpit is especially exciting sexually (Benet, 1974). It would be unthinkable among the Abkhasians for a woman to allow a man other than her husband to see her armpits. Japanese males, on the other hand, consider a woman's neck as a particularly sexual part of her body. They are especially attracted to a long, swanlike neck. For many years the late Hollywood film actress Audrey Hepburn was very popular among Japanese men, precisely because one of her most striking features was a long, slim neck. Although this feature might have appealed to some American males, it is doubtful that very many would have seen it as sexually arousing.

Women's breasts are considered objects of sexual attraction and erotic stimulation in almost every society, even those where the breasts are normally uncovered. However, among the Mangaia of Polynesia, women's breasts have no sexual significance. Because the males of this society do not find them erotic, women's breasts have no place in heterosexual foreplay or in sexual communication (Davenport, 1977).

History provides other examples of diversity regarding what was considered sexual. In Hawaii, before the influence of Western cultural ideals, extremely obese women were viewed as highly erotic, especially among the aristocrats and members of royalty (Davenport, 1977). In the United States, as recently as the beginning of this century, if one were to judge from the photographs of women who were considered sexually appealing, the ideal woman's body was much heavier and more well rounded than the ideal body of today. The beginning of the twentieth century was also a time when women wore floor-length dresses, which made the sight of a woman's ankle or calf sexually arousing to males.

Although the sexual attractions of females are most often noted by contemporary Western people, sometimes the males of a society are the objects of sexual attention. Among the Wodaabe, a nomadic tribe in Central Africa, young males are the center of attraction, especially during ceremonies held several times a year. Dances are performed by the young males, who compete with each other to be chosen the most beautiful and charming (Beckwith, 1983). Their costuming and makeup, along with the parading and performing before tribe members, are comparable to a Miss America contest in the United States. The most handsome young men of the tribe stand in a kind of chorus line where their attractiveness is judged largely on the basis of their exaggerated facial expressions. An observer describes the scene as follows: "Eyes roll; teeth flash; lips purse, part and tremble; cheeks, inflated like toy balloons, collapse in short puffs of breath" (Beckwith, 1983, p. 508).

These facial features, especially the large rolling eyes, are particularly alluring to the women of the tribe, who may cry out in ecstasy when a man performs well. The charm and magnetism of these facial gestures may bring multiple wives to the most handsome young men of the tribe. American women would probably not find these facial gyrations sexually attractive, but the Wodaabe women clearly do.

These examples of cultural variations in sexual practices illustrate some of the many ways in which sexual behavior is culturally defined. Variations in definitions can also be seen in the context of a single society *over time,* when there are changing definitions of sexuality. As an example, definitions of sexuality and norms governing sexual behavior have changed dramatically in the United States throughout its history, as a brief review will reveal.

Historical Views of Sexuality in the United States

The historical evidence we have about the sexual lives of nineteenth-century married couples in the United States comes from diaries, journals, reports of doctors and midwives, folk songs, sayings, stories, and poems. As we will see later in this chapter, social research on sexual behavior, especially the systematic use of interviews and questionnaires (social surveys), were not undertaken until well into the twentieth century. Although the qualitative historical evidence we have must therefore be accepted cautiously, it does give us some insight into the views of many men and women in earlier times.

Social historians believe that marital sex was very different in the United States a century or two ago. In the nineteenth century the authority and supremacy of the husbands and fathers in many families (called **patriarchy**) dominated most of family life. In regard to sex, patriarchy meant that many husbands simply dictated when they would have sexual intercourse with their wives. In this powerful position, men often showed little regard for either the feelings of their wives or the physical repercussions of their actions (Shorter, 1982).

This example of the attitudes prevailing in the nineteenth century about marital sex shows one way in which sociological theories can be important in understanding sexual behavior. Conflict theory, which was introduced in Chapter 1, emphasizes the importance of power and conflict in any social group, including the family. Power differences between husbands and wives, which were especially pronounced in this patriarchal era, made marital sexual relations an area of conflict within the family.

The indifference that many nineteenth-century husbands displayed to the physical and emotional well-being of their wives is shown in the words of one social historian who said, "intercourse in the traditional family was brief and brutal, and there is little evidence that women derived much pleasure from it" (Shorter, 1982, p. 9). Evidence reveals that many husbands did not abstain from having sex with their wives either during pregnancy or immediately after the birth of a child. Despite warnings of doctors and midwives that the health of women would be endangered during these periods, especially by infections, many wives reported with embarrassment that their husbands paid "no heed" (Shorter, 1982).

Of course, not every pretwentieth-century man behaved in this brutish and insensitive way. Certainly there were loving and considerate husbands who were sensitive to the emotional and physical feelings of their wives. We are describing only a general condition that prevailed in many marriages of that era.

And how did pretwentieth-century women regard sex? Many probably viewed it with fear because sexual intercourse often meant another pregnancy. Most women of the nineteenth century, especially those living in rural areas, had no knowledge of contraception or even of a safe period during their menstrual cycles. For women of a childbearing age, the only preventions against pregnancy were being pregnant already and—maybe—breastfeeding. An average married woman in the nineteenth century typically had seven or eight pregnancies, and perhaps as many as six live births. In addition to the difficulties of pregnancy itself, the very real danger of death during childbirth always existed. In the light of all these dangers, added to the insensitivity of many husbands, it is understandable that many married women would view sexual intercourse with apprehension and probably dread.

Another indication of the way definitions of sexuality have changed over time comes from the marriage manuals of the nineteenth and early twentieth centuries. One main theme found in marriage manuals of the 1800s was the belief that women have very little sexual desire. Women had sex with their husbands primarily because it was their wifely duty. An 1869 marriage manual asserted the following:

> As a general rule, a modest woman seldom desires any sexual gratification for herself. She submits to her husband, but only to please him and but by the desire of maternity... (Hayes, 1869, quoted in Gordon and Shankweiler, 1971, p. 460).

A second theme of nineteenth-century marriage manuals is also reflected in the statement above—the claim that women are interested in sex only because of a desire for maternity. This is often called the **procreative view of sex**—sex for reproduction only.

Writers of this period, including many who were doctors, also tended to see sex as a "draining," "exhausting," and "debilitating" activity. Men, especially, were thought to have a "loss of vital body fluids" when they had sexual intercourse, leading to negative effects on health and vitality. The view that men lose strength and vital fluids from having sex is a widely held notion in other cultures around the world. Many Hindus in contemporary India believe that men are born with a fixed amount of semen, which must be conserved if a man is to live to an old age (Harris, 1981).

Not until the twentieth century did marriage manuals start to acknowledge that women as well as men could have sexual desires, and that they, too, could enjoy the physical pleasure of sex. In the nineteenth century, this idea was only grudgingly admitted, and women who revealed their sexual desires too openly were often labeled mentally ill or deviant. Deviant behavior, as we saw in the last chapter, depends on what people, at a particular time, consider deviant. Thus, although a woman of the nineteenth century who was actively interested in sex was considered deviant, in contemporary American society a woman who claimed to have *no* sexual desire would probably be the one considered deviant (Barker-Benfield, 1976).

As we consider these changing historical definitions of sexuality and different norms for appropriate sexual behavior, we should note that views about sexuality and sexual behavior are in some way a reflection of the general characteristics of the society in which they are found. The place of women in the nineteenth-century United States was subordinate to that of the patriarchal male, so it is not surprising that sexual life would reflect this societal feature. But other general characteristics of society may also influence the nature of sexual behavior. We will consider this possibility next.

A Societal Perspective on Sexual Behavior

A basic sociological premise holds that the general nature of a society will shape and influence all types of behavior, including sexual behavior (Schur, 1988). In the case of the United States, it can be argued that sexual relations, as a reflection of the characteristics of the society generally, have become *depersonalized, commercialized,* and increasingly *coercive* and *aggressive.*

Depersonalization of Sex

Many social analysts have observed that social relations in modern society have become more and more impersonal. In Chapter 4 we saw how the early sociologist Toennies used the term *gesellschaft* as a label for a type of contemporary society in which personal relations tend to be impersonal and based primarily on individual self-interest. A parallel feature of contemporary society is that many people are given much more personal freedom than are people who live in more close-knit traditional societies (Simmel, in Wolff, 1950). If these characteristics (impersonality, self-interest, and personal freedom) describe life in contemporary U.S. society, and there is considerable evidence that they do, we might expect that they would also be found in sexual relations. Thus, the **depersonalization of sex** is defined as sexual interaction that is impersonal and self-interested.

The depersonalization of sex was especially glorified in the 1970s, when many people viewed sex as a recreational activity. Sex was just one of many pleasurable activities and had little meaning beyond the immediate experience. This may still be true for some people today, but because of concerns about AIDS, recreational sex seems to be less popular.

A current-day manifestation of the depersonalization of sex is the vast amount of sexual material that is posted on computer networks (Durkin and Bryant, 1995). Apparently many online users get sexual pleasure from their participation on chat lines on which a variety of sexual practices are discussed. While the private communications between two online users may be limited to lighthearted flirting, they often move on to "hot chatting" (Durkin and Bryant, 1995, p. 186). This form of sex, called cybersex, is a clear example of the depersonalization of sex, since the participants have no actual physical contact and their sexual activity does not occur in the context of a personal relationship.

Commercialization of Sex

Commercialization prevails when everything can be bought and sold, when everything has a monetary value and can be purchased if one has the money to pay. The **commercialization of sex** refers to the fact that sex is bought and sold just like any other commodity in the marketplace. Americans are accustomed to purchasing their recreation, and since sex is seen by many as a form of recreation, it follows that sex is something to be purchased. Some obvious ways in which sex is purchased are prostitution, soft- and hardcore pornography, erotic telephone services, R-rated and X-rated movies and videos, and subscriptions to sexually oriented television networks.

X-rated films and videos are, today, at the apex of the pornography industry (Faludi, 1995). The pornographic film business has exploded with the advent of VCRs and cable television. Pornographic films today are of two types. One type is the soft-porn variety that can be seen on cable television, and the second is the raw, often violent, artless sex film found in video stores and pornography shops.

One irony of the pornographic movie industry is that women are the highly paid "stars," while most of the men command much lower salaries (Faludi, 1995).

The females who become stars in the pornographic film industry often return to "table- and lap-dancing stripper clubs," where some "make as much as ten thousand dollars a week" (Faludi, 1995, p. 69).

At a different level, the commercial side of sex includes the sale of sexually oriented clothing and other sexual paraphernalia that are widely advertised and displayed. Almost all of these sex-related products and services can be legally purchased (the only exceptions being some extreme forms of pornography and prostitution).[1] It is estimated that the legal "sex industry" adds up to $5 billion yearly (Schur, 1988).

Another dimension to the commercialization of sex goes beyond the obvious commercial transactions for sex or sexually related materials. A widely held view exists that says that women are often "purchased" and displayed as the sexual property of men. Sociologist Randall Collins has said that, "With male dominance, the principal form of sexual property is the male ownership of females" (Collins, 1971, pp. 7–8). Even in dating situations, when males pay for meals and entertainment, there is often the implicit assumption that the females owe something in return. That something may be sex.

Sexual Coercion

The third aspect of sexual behavior in American society is **sexual coercion,** which is forced sex, or rape. Rape is alarmingly widespread. Official statistics on rape reflect only reported cases, and the record shows 104,810 attempted or actual rape cases in the United States in 1993 (U.S. Bureau of the Census, 1995b). Some people maintain that a level of "sexual terrorism" exists in contemporary U.S. society that allows males to frighten, and therefore dominate, females. Sexual terrorism makes it necessary for women to ask themselves "whether to go to the movies alone, where to walk or jog, whether to answer the door or telephone" (Sheffield, 1987, p. 171).

Official statistics on rape undoubtedly understate the case, however, since many instances of rape are not reported to authorities. Many women are forced to have sex against their will by men they know, such as acquaintances, friends, former boyfriends, and former husbands, as well as current dates and romantic partners (Brownmiller, 1975). Of women who have been the victims of rape, more than 80 percent knew their attackers, and more than half reported that the rape happened on a date (Warshaw, 1988).

The prevalence of rape (or sexual coercion) in the United States in not known with precision because there is no completely agreed upon definition of these

---

[1]Even prostitution is legal in a few Nevada counties.

terms. However, every contemporary study finds that more than 20 percent of women report having experienced sexual coercion.

A survey of American college women at 32 institutions of higher learning (Koss et al., 1987) found that 27.5 percent had experienced legally defined rape or attempted rape (Fonow et al., 1992, p. 109). An additional 12 percent said they had experienced sexual coercion, meaning that they "had given in to sexual intercourse because of intimidation by someone in authority or because of verbal pressure or argument" (Fonow et al., 1992, p. 109).

In a recent national survey, one that focused on all sexual experiences of American adults, women respondents were asked, "Have you ever been forced by a man to do something sexual that you did not want to do?" (Laumann et al., 1994, p. 334). Twenty-two percent of the women said they had been forced to do something sexual by a man. As the researchers note, not every woman will have interpreted this question in the same way, but more than one in five acknowledge that they have experienced some form of sexual coercion.

According to Schur's societal analysis of sex in American society, both the society at large and sexual behavior in particular are characterized by depersonalization, commercialization, and coercion–aggression. The fundamental assumption of this view is that the characteristics of a society will be reflected in the sexual realm. Although the resulting depiction of sex in American society may not be accepted by everyone (it is controversial), it does shed some light on contemporary American sexual patterns.

The Sexual Norms of Societies

All societies have rules and norms about sexual behavior. These norms sometimes require people to act in certain ways (have sexual intercourse if they marry, for instance); but more often, norms relating to sex prohibit certain behaviors. We will focus on two of the most widely recognized sexual norms: the incest taboo and the double standard.

The Incest Taboo

Every known *contemporary society* has a norm (almost always supported by laws) that prohibits sexual relations (and, of course, marriage) between close kin members—an *incest taboo*. In every case the norm prohibits sex between parents and children and between siblings. With regard to other relatives, the rules are much less consistent. In many societies, first cousins are prohibited from marrying and thus from having sexual relations. However, in every country of Europe and in 20 states in the United States, first cousins may marry (Ottenheimer, 1990). In many of the societies studied by anthropologists, marriage between cousins is actually preferred.

Cross-cultural Perspectives

Societal Reactions to Erotica and Pornography

The people of prehistoric times produced artifacts, drawings, and paintings showing their keen interest in the sexual features and sexual acts of males and females. Most of the major historical cultures of the world—Greece, Rome, India, China, Japan, Africa—have produced art or writing that depict sexual behavior and sexuality. In the contemporary world there is a continuing outpouring of paintings, sculptures, photographs, films, and writing about sexuality and sexual behavior. Despite the universality of interest in sexuality and sexual behavior, the societal responses to sexual representations and descriptions are extremely varied, and often the source of great controversy.

The very words used to describe visual representations and written descriptions of the human body and sexual acts indicate how differently people react to sexual subjects. It is common to hear people speak of *dirty pictures* and *dirty books,* words that often reflect the speaker's negative feelings. The word *pornography* also carries a negative connotation about sexually explicit materials. On the other hand, the word *erotica* is apt to indicate a neutral, or even positive, reaction to sexual images, objects, or writing.

Sociologist Ira Reiss (1986) defines *erotica* as any material designed predominantly for sexual arousal. *Pornography* is the term applied to erotic material that is distasteful or obscene to the person who uses the label. From this perspective erotica is a more general, neutral, or less judgmental term, while pornography indicates that certain material is considered beyond a societal or personal standard of acceptability.

The differences and changes in the social acceptability of erotica is a sociologically interesting issue, because the standards and the justifications for acceptability are so varied. When Michelangelo, the Italian Renaissance artist, was asked by Pope Clement VII to paint a biblical scene on the wall behind the altar of the Sistine Chapel (25 years after he had completed the ceiling paintings) he painted all the figures, including Christ and the Virgin Mary in the nude. The Pope, however, considered these paintings objectionable, and, although he first wanted the paintings destroyed, he later agreed to have another painter (nicknamed by the Italians the *breechesmaker*) add clothing to the figures (Bullough, 1976; Lewinsohn, 1958). Indeed, over the next 200 years other painters continued to add clothing to the figures in Michelangelo's painting.

Late in his life Michelangelo painted *Leda and the Swan* for an Italian duke. This painting also depicted a nude woman, and if it had survived it would be invaluable today. It was ultimately burned, however, because the authorities of the time considered it objectionable (Bullough, 1976; Lewinsohn, 1958).

In India, many of the ancient temples of the Hindu religion are adorned with sculptures of a sexual nature. These sculptures do not simply show nude human figures, but depict males and females engaging in sexual intercourse. In fact, these Indian temple sculptures are noted for the variety of sexual positions of the participants.

In contemporary times, in many societies, sculptures and paintings of male and female bodies and people engaged in sexual acts continue to be produced and displayed. Especially important today are the erotic materials produced by photographers and the motion picture industry. Often, this form of erotic material makes no claim to being art, but is openly aimed at sexual stimulation. Reiss (1986) has called this form of sexual material *commercial erotica.* In the late 1960s Denmark and Sweden were among the first countries to change their laws about erotic materials, making them easily available. In these countries it has been possible for many years to purchase virtually any kind of visual or literary erotic material.

Many countries of the world, including the United States, have followed the lead of the Scandinavian countries and have made commercial erotica available to the public. The major exceptions are the Islamic and Communist countries (China and Cuba, for example), where erotic materials are severely restricted.

In the United States the widespread availability of erotic materials is opposed and decried by several groups who consider such material pornographic. Among the most vocal opponents are religious leaders and political conservatives whose objections are on religious and moral grounds. But feminists, also, have raised an important challenge to pornographic materials, claiming that they perpetuate the subjugation, objectification, and debasement of women (Kaminer, 1992; Reiss, 1986).

Bullough, Vern L. *Sexual Variance in Society and History.* New York: John Wiley & Sons, 1976.

Kaminer, Wendy. "Feminists Against the First Amendment." *Atlantic,* November 1992.

Lewinsohn, Richard. *A History of Sexual Customs: From Earliest Times to the Present.* New York: Harper & Row, 1958.

Reiss, Ira L. *Journey into Sexuality: An Explanatory Voyage.* Englewood Cliffs, N.J.: Prentice Hall, 1986.

The prohibition of sex between close relatives has been nearly universal, but in a number of historical circumstances it has been allowed (Hopkins, 1980; Middleton, 1962). Generally, such exceptions to the rule permitted members of royal families to marry each other in order to retain royal power. In the Egyptian, Incan, and Hawaiian royal families, marriages between immediate family members kept the royal bloodline "pure" and retained privilege and power in the family. In one documented historical period, however, marriage between brothers and sisters, as well as fathers and daughters, occurred frequently among commoners. When the Romans ruled Egypt during the first to the third centuries A.D., such marriages were widely recorded. By allowing marriage between family members, Egyptians prevented family wealth and property from being confiscated by the Roman authorities through inheritance laws (Hopkins, 1980).

The exception to the incest taboo among the Egyptians shows once again how variable sexual behavior can be, but that should not obscure the fact that virtually every other society prohibits sex (and marriage) among close family members. One sociological explanation for the near-universal incest taboo is that it would be too disruptive to family relationships if sex were allowed between close family members. If such sexual relations were possible, they would probably lead to jealousies and alliances between some family members against others, which would produce family instability.

The Double Standard

After the incest taboo, one of the most pervasive sexual norms, found in many societies besides the United States, is the double standard of sexual behavior. The **double standard** is a set of norms that gives males more sexual freedom than females. The *traditional* double standard includes the following specifics:

- Men may have sexual intercourse before marriage; women should not.

- Men may have sexual intercourse with women even when there is no emotional feeling or commitment; women may have sexual intercourse when they are in love, or when there is a mutual commitment.

- Men may have multiple sexual partners; women should not have multiple partners.

- Men may have sexual intercourse with women who are much lower in social status, or are "immoral" women; if a woman were to have sexual intercourse with a man of lower status, it would be viewed even more negatively than with a man of her own status.

- Men may have sexual intercourse for recreation or to gain sexual experience and expertise; women are not allowed to have these motives or objectives.

Because of the undeniable liberalization of sexual norms in the United States over the last several decades, some of these standards may have been somewhat relaxed. Perhaps among some individuals as well as in certain groups in the society, the double standard is not as rigidly enforced as it once was, but researchers continue to uncover evidence showing that significant aspects of the double standard are still with us.

One place the double standard can still be found is in the labels applied to males and females who are very active sexually. Males are given a great latitude in their sexual behavior before negative labels are applied. For example, among young people the word *gigolo* is sometimes applied to a male who has many different sexual partners, but it is only partially negative. If a female has many different sexual partners she is called a *slut,* which is unquestionably negative (Rubin, 1990). Sometimes young women today use the word *stud* in a sarcastic or hostile way when they refer to males who try to have sex with as many females as possible, but the term does not seem to have the same damaging force as the word *slut.*

Even preadolescent boys frequently use these negative terms to refer to girls. Sociologist Gary Fine, who spent a summer observing preteenage boys who were in Little League baseball, frequently heard these boys refer to girls as "sluts" and "prosties" (apparently a reference to prostitutes). After listening to and observing these preadolescent boys, Fine concluded: "boys generally wish to be seen as sexually potent, whereas girls lose status by having the same reputation—the double standard is very much in existence in preadolescence" (Fine, 1987, p. 107).

Another kind of evidence for the persistence of the double standard is an experimental study conducted among college students. The researchers asked the subjects to evaluate a specific person on the basis of his or her sexual behavior. (The person was fictitious, but the subjects were led to think it was a real person.) As one aspect of the experiment, subjects were asked to evaluate either a male or a female who had a first sexual intercourse experience in a casual relationship at age 16. Both male and female subjects gave more negative evaluations to a female than to a male who had done so. The researchers concluded that some aspects of the double standard still exist (Sprecher et al., 1987).

Two other experimental studies support the continued existence of the double standard (Oliver and Sedikides, 1992). These experiments, conducted at the University of Wisconsin in 1990, revealed that males preferred sexually permissive women *in noncommitted relationships* (for example, blind dates), but did not prefer sexually permissive women in more committed relationships. Women, by contrast, preferred men who were less sexually permissive in both types of relationships. From the perspective of males, the most desirable women for committed relationships were those who were less sexually permissive (Oliver and Sedikides, 1992).

When Moffatt (1989) lived in the dormitory with Rutgers University students, he found students saying that no one should feel guilty about his or her sexual behavior. In actuality, however, these students, by their words and actions, still revealed their adherence to the traditional double standard. The men in particular still divided the women into the "good women" and the "sluts."

In her interviews with teenage women, Rubin (1990) found many who were reluctant to pass judgment on the sexual behaviors of other women. This appears to be a change from former times, when women were as severe as men in their condemnation of women who were sexually liberal. Today, young women with female friends who have casual or recreational sex are inclined to say that it is "none of their business" (Rubin, 1990, p. 70). While young women recognize that men can (and do) still apply negative labels to women's sexual behavior, they themselves try to be tolerant.

Sexual norms, such as the double standard, are learned through the process of socialization. In the next section we will examine how sexual socialization occurs and how it shapes sexual attitudes and behaviors, especially of young people.

Socialization for Sex

Most Americans say that children should learn about sex from their parents. The general assumption is that if parents take responsibility for the socialization of their children regarding sex, the values of the children will be healthier and their behavior will be more responsible. The alternatives to parental socialization about sex are formal sex education programs in the schools, learning about sex from peers, and learning about sex (either directly or indirectly) from the mass media—especially movies, magazines, music, and television.

Although most people believe that children *should* learn about sex from their parents, the fact is that parents do a very poor job of teaching their children about sex (Fox, 1980; Fox and Inazu, 1980; Roberts et al., 1978). To the extent that the sexual socialization of young people does occur in U.S. families, it is largely left to mothers, and the greatest amount of communication about sex is between mothers and daughters. Mothers are as likely as fathers (and some studies have shown them to be more likely) to discuss sex with their sons (Aldous, 1983; Fox and Inazu, 1980; Kahn, 1994).

Adolescents receive a considerable amount of socialization about sex from their friends. When sociologist Gary Fine (1987) observed 11-year-old and 12-year-old Little League boys, he found that sexual topics ranked with aggression as the two major themes of their discussions. Boys of this age have relatively little sexual experience—apparently kissing and limited petting are the major activities of the most active boys—but their interest level is high. When they talk about it, they are trying to show that they are interested and knowledgeable about heterosexual relations. Through the talk, banter, joking, and teasing about sexual matters, the "boys learn what is expected of them by their peers" (Fine, 1987, p. 110).

While these preadolescent boys talk a great deal about heterosexual relations, they also make frequent references to homosexual topics. This often takes the form of derogatory expressions such as "God, he's gay," "He's the biggest fag in the world," and "What a queer." Although these phrases are not generally used to refer to actual homosexual behavior and are often used among friends in a good-natured way, the rhetoric of homosexuality is a flexible and abusive part of the preadolescent's language (Fine, 1987, p. 115). Probably this negative use of homosexual terminology is a way in which many boys are trying to define their own sexual identity.

Socialization by the Mass Media

In the early 1960s the word *pregnant* was not allowed on television, and movies and television did not show married couples in the same bed (twin beds were the standard). However, in recent years the amount of sexual content in the mass media—especially television, movies, and magazines—has increased dramatically. Today television and movies are important sources of information and values about sexual matters for many children and adolescents. As early as 1977, a religiously oriented group that was concerned about the amount of sexuality on television monitored the networks and found 2.81 references to sex per hour of prime-time viewing. Their calculation was that over the course of a year television "viewers would be exposed to 9230 scenes of suggested sexual intercourse or sexually suggestive comments" (quoted in Liebert and Sprafkin, 1988, p. 199). Although much of the sexuality on television in the 1970s was verbal, it is now much more likely that actual sexual behavior will also be shown (Liebert and Sprafkin, 1988). Perhaps most important, couples shown on television having sex are not usually married. Unmarried sexual intercourse "occurs five times as often as married intercourse on the prime-time series adolescents watch most often" (Liebert and Sprafkin, 1988, p. 201).

There is little doubt that television programs and movies are providing children and adolescents with information and normative standards about sexual behavior. Studies have shown that even young adolescents can understand the sexual talk and innuendos on prime-time television. When public opinion pollster Louis Harris asked youngsters themselves about the relative importance of prime-time television as a source of information about sex, they ranked friends, parents, and courses in school as more important; but, of course, the messages of television sex may be more subtle and indirect than adolescent viewers recognize.

Sex before Marriage

In American society, sex has traditionally been associated with marriage. The cultural ideal, which is still preferred by some people, is for young people to refrain from sex until they are married, to "save oneself for marriage." The evidence, as we will see shortly, indicates that this ideal is not widely held in the contemporary United States. Furthermore, historical data show that from the earliest days of American history premarital chastity has been far from universal.

Before the Twentieth Century

The Puritan period of American history is noted for its religious strictness and the close community scrutiny of all citizens' personal lives, and yet, even during that period, some couples had sex before marriage. A study by Calhoun (1945) found that approximately one-third of Puritan brides confessed to their ministers that they had sex before marriage. Most of them confessed because they were already pregnant and wished to have their babies baptized. Other brides, who might have had sexual intercourse but were not pregnant, might not have felt as compelled to confess (Reiss and Lee, 1988).

Other historical evidence also shows that premarital sexual intercourse occurred at significant levels early in American history (Smith, 1978). Church records of marriages and baptisms from the eighteenth and nineteenth centuries reveal that many first-born children were probably conceived before marriage (for example, a first child born within 9 months of a marriage was probably conceived premaritally). One study that used this method and collected data from various New England communities shows that before 1700 about 11 percent of all births may have been premaritally conceived. This was, in fact, the lowest percentage found over the next 200 years. The highest percentages of premarital conceptions came in the period between 1761 and 1800, when slightly over one-third of the births were very possibly premaritally conceived. The data from this study suggest that in pre-twentieth century America about one in five first births was conceived before marriage (Smith, 1978; see also D'Emilio and Freedman, 1988, pp. 22–23).

Again, these figures only reflect premarital pregnancies, not premarital sexual intercourse. There are two reasons why premarital pregnancies are underestimates of premarital sexual intercourse. First, it is unlikely that all women who became pregnant while unmarried went on to marry. Some might have intentionally aborted their pregnancies, had spontaneous miscarriages, or had children without marrying. These cases would not be reflected in the births occurring within 9 months of marriage. Second, some couples might have had sexual intercourse while unmarried and yet not have conceived a child. This could have been the result of sterility on the part of either the man or the woman, the use of some elementary form of birth control (for example, withdrawal), or having intercourse at a time when conception was not possible. If all these considerations are taken into account, it is possible to estimate from these data that at least one-fourth and perhaps as many as 40 percent of American young women had sexual intercourse before they were married. The percentages for young men were probably higher, because they were generally given more sexual liberty.

When we examine trends in the twentieth century, the source of information changes, but the evidence still shows that premarital sex was prevalent.

Premarital Sex in the Twentieth Century

The twentieth century saw the beginnings of social research that used interviews and questionnaires as primary data-gathering methods. The researcher whose name is linked most closely to the earliest studies of sexual behavior is Alfred C. Kinsey, a biologist by training. Kinsey and his associates conducted interviews with 5300 males and nearly 6000 females. The Kinsey interview was designed to provide the complete sexual life history of each respondent. Kinsey published his studies of male and female sexual behavior in the late 1940s and early 1950s.

The Kinsey studies showed that a substantial number of women (and men) who reached adulthood in the twentieth century had sex before marriage. Among women born before 1900, about one-fourth revealed to the interviewer that they had premarital sexual intercourse. Among women born after 1900, more than half said they had sex before marriage (adapted from Reiss, 1980, p. 170).

Although the percentages show that sex before marriage did occur during the first part of the twentieth century, the actual numbers must be accepted with caution. Kinsey's samples were large, but they were notoriously biased toward the better-educated, higher-status, segment of the population and generally overrepresented women who were more willing to talk about their sex lives (Laumann et al., 1994). The sample bias was toward those women who reported having premarital sex more often.

Even so, the findings of the Kinsey studies, along with the earlier historical research, leave little doubt that a significant number of women and men, throughout our history, have had premarital sex. That having been said, however, we must add quickly that there have been some dramatic changes in premarital sexual behavior in the last 25 years. The percentage of unmarried young people who have sexual intercourse has increased greatly, the age at which young people start having intercourse has declined, the social relationships and social contexts in which sex occurs have changed, and attitudes about sex before marriage have changed. All these changes will be considered in the next section.

Sexual Activity among Contemporary American Adolescents

Since the 1960s there has been a number of surveys of sexual behavior among adolescents and high school students showing that premarital sexual intercourse, especially among young women, has increased greatly (Vener and Stewart, 1974; Reiss, 1967; Zelnik and Kantner, 1980). The most rapid early increases occurred in the 1970s, but the percentages have continued to go up since that time (Billy et

al., 1993; Hofferth et al., 1987; Kahn et al., 1988; Forrest and Singh, 1990; Laumann et al., 1944; *Morbidity and Mortality Weekly,* 1992; Mott and Haurin,
1988).[2]

Some of the major findings coming from a national sample of high school students are the following:

- Of all students, grades 9–12, 54.2% said they had had intercourse at least
  once; 39.4% said they had intercourse sometime during the preceding 3
  months.

- Male students were significantly more likely than female students to have
  had sexual intercourse at least once (60.8% and 48.0%, respectively).

- Male students were also more likely than female students to have had
  sexual intercourse during the preceding 3 months (42.5% and 36.4%,
  respectively).

- Black students were significantly more likely than white or Hispanic
  students to have had sexual intercourse (72.3%, 51.6%, and 53.4%,
  respectively).

Figure 7–1 shows the percentage of white, Hispanic, and black high school
students, by gender, who have had sexual intercourse. Figure 7–2 shows the percentage of high school students by gender and grade in school who have had sexual intercourse.

Figure 7–2 shows that, by the time high school students reach the twelfth
grade, two-thirds of the females and nearly three-fourths of the males have had
sexual intercourse. More than half of these twelfth-graders are sexually active, as
indicated by the percentage who have had sexual intercourse in the 3 months prior
to the survey. Among twelfth-grade females, 53% said that they had had sexual
intercourse in the preceding 3 months; among twelfth-grade males, 57% reported
that they had had sex during that period (*Morbidity and Mortality Weekly Report,*
1992).

By the time American women reach age 20, more than two-thirds of them
report having had sexual intercourse, and some studies have found the percentage
over 70 percent (Laumann et al., 1994). Surveys of males produce more varied
numbers, but on the basis of the results of different studies it can be said that over
three-fourths of males, and probably as many as 80 percent, have had sexual intercourse by the time they reach 20. One survey found the percentage to be as high
as 86 percent for 19-year-old males (Sonenstein et al., 1989).

---

[2]Some surveys have studied high school students only, others have been random samples from
metropolitan areas only, and others have sampled from the total U.S. population. Some surveys studied only women.

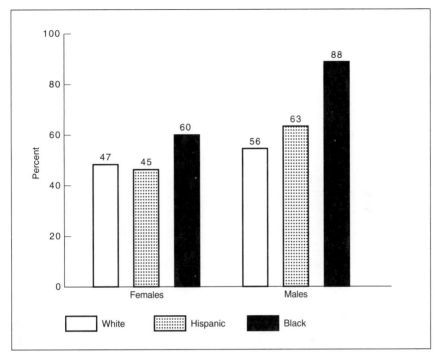

Figure 7–1.   Percentage of High School Students Reporting Having Had Sexual Intercourse, by Race and Gender, 1990. (*Source:* "Sexual Behavior among School Students," *Morbidity and Mortality Weekly Report,* Vol. 40, 1992, p. 885.)

Males also report having sex at earlier ages than females. One study, for example, found that at age 17 nearly half of the males (48.4 percent) but only one-third of the females (33.2 percent) had experienced sexual intercourse (Mott and Haurin, 1988). It is interesting that in two Scandinavian countries (Sweden and Norway) exactly the opposite pattern prevails (Sundet et al., 1992). At age 17, for example, 60 percent of Norwegian females had experienced sexual intercourse, but only 47 percent of the Norwegian males (Traeen and Lewin, 1992).

Factors Associated with Early Sexual Experience[3]

Race and ethnicity, socioeconomic status, educational experiences, religious beliefs, and family contexts, as well as the use of alcohol, cigarettes, and drugs, are all associated with how soon young people begin to have sex.

---

[3]In the following section the data will be presented on both males and females whenever possible. Often, however, data are only available for females, apparently because the sexual activities of young unmarried females are still considered more significant than the sexual activities of young males.

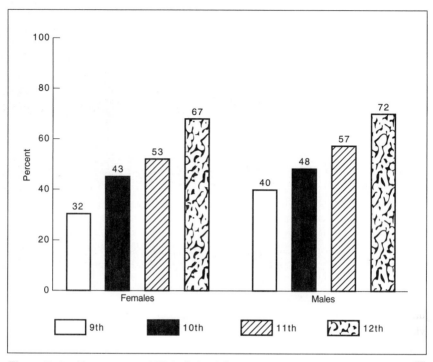

Figure 7–2. Percentage of High School Students Reporting Having Had Sexual Intercourse, by Grade and Gender, 1990. (*Source:* "Sexual Behavior among School Students," *Morbidity and Mortality Weekly Report,* Vol. 40, 1992, p. 885.)

Race is one of the most important factors associated with the beginning of sexual activity (Rosenbaum and Kandel, 1990, p. 784). African American adolescents, especially males, start having sex much earlier than whites and Hispanics (Kahn et al., 1988; Rosenbaum and Kandel, 1990). Black males are three times more likely to have sex before age 15 than white and Hispanic males (Rosenbaum and Kandel, 1990). African American females also begin to have sex earlier than white and Hispanic females, but the differences are much less than for males; by age 17, about 40 percent of African American females have had sex, compared to about 30 percent of white and Hispanic females (Rosenbaum and Kandel, 1990).

Having lower socioeconomic status is also related to starting sex early (Furstenberg et al., 1987; Kahn et al., 1988), as is dropping out of high school (Mott and Haurin, 1988). Adolescents who have higher academic performance and educational aspirations are less likely to have sexual intercourse early.

Teenagers who are more religious are also less likely to have sex as teenagers. Those who attend religious services more often have more negative attitudes about premarital sex and are less likely to have premarital sex (Thornton and

Camburn, 1989). American teenagers who belong to fundamentalist Protestant and Baptist churches are the most likely to be opposed to premarital intercourse. In general terms, young people have sex later if they have a "commitment to conventional values and institutions" (Rosenbaum and Kandel, 1990).

Earlier sexual activity is also related to characteristics of the families of teenagers. In particular, when young people come from single-parent homes they are more likely to start having sex earlier. Teenage girls in particular are more likely to have sex if they live in single-parent homes. Since sexual activity usually requires a degree of privacy, girls in single-parent homes may have more opportunity to have intercourse because they are less closely supervised (Miller and Bingham, 1989). Privacy in the home is not likely to be the only influential factor, however, since young people who come from large families are also more likely to have sex as teenagers (Rosenbaum and Kandel, 1990).

Adolescents who begin to use alcohol, cigarettes, and drugs at an early age are also more likely to start having sex early (Mott and Haurin, 1988; Rosenbaum and Kandel, 1990). For both males and females, the use of these substances before age 16 is strongly associated with having sexual intercourse when younger. Males who use alcohol and/or cigarettes before 16 are 40 percent more likely to have sex before 16 than boys who do not use alcohol and/or cigarettes. If males use marijuana before age 16, they are almost three times more likely to have sex than boys who do not.

For females, the importance of early cigarette, alcohol, and drug use is even greater. Early use of alcohol and/or cigarettes increases the chances of early sex by 80 percent. Early marijuana use makes early sex 3.45 times more likely, while use of other illicit drugs makes sex 5 times more likely (Rosenbaum and Kandel, 1990). The strong relationship between sex and early cigarette, alcohol, and drug use does not mean that drugs *cause* sexual activity. The research done thus far has only shown that these behaviors are associated in the lives of teenagers.

First Sexual Intercourse Experience

While surveys of sexual behavior can tell us when, how many, and which adolescents have sex, these surveys do not tell us much about how the young people themselves define and interpret the experience. What motivates them to have sex? What is the first sexual experience like for most adolescents? For answers to these questions we must turn to qualitative studies, in which young people describe their sexual experiences.

Gender Differences.   Research evidence consistently shows that at the time of first sexual intercourse the *relationship* with one's partner is very different for males and females. A recent national survey of American adults asked about the nature of the respondent's relationship with his or her first sex partner and found that 75 percent of women were married to or in love with their first sexual partner. Only 41 percent of the men said they were married to or in love with their first sexual partner (Laumann et al., 1994). This is consistent with studies of teenagers and college students, which found that females were much more likely than males to say that their first sexual partners were persons with whom they had a serious or committed relationship (DeLameter and MacCorquodale, 1979; Sprecher et al., 1995; Zelnik and Shah, 1983).

These differences in the relationships of males and females with their first sexual partners are very likely a product of the different meanings that sex has for adolescent males and females. Females are more likely to associate sex with feelings of love and affection for their partners. Young males, on the other hand, are much more likely to focus on sex as a physical activity. For boys, the objective is often simply to experience sex. Sex for them is an achievement, and they may care very little about who their partner is.

When adult men recall their first sexual experience, they often use terms that show how important it was for their masculinity. In the words of one researcher: "They [men] characterized the experience as an 'important accomplishment' a 'landmark achievement.' For them, it was a rite of passage, a crucial step on the road to manhood—a step in which they exulted. . . ."(Rubin, 1990, p. 43).

For young men, then, the first sexual experience is usually a measure of achievement, but for young women, it is more likely to be an expression of love.

Negative Reactions. Although young men might be pleased by the accomplishment of their first sexual experience, they do not necessarily enjoy it. In fact, Rubin concluded, on the basis of her in-depth interviews with 75 teenagers and 300 adults, both males and females, that the overwhelming majority of both sexes look back on their first sexual intercourse as a neutral or negative experience. In her interviews, the most common words used to describe the experience were "'overrated,' 'disappointing,' 'a waste,' 'awful,' 'boring,' 'stupid,' 'empty,' 'ridiculous,' 'awkward,' 'miserable,' 'unmemorable'" (Rubin, 1990, p. 43).

Once again, however, the disappointments that the males may have had with the actual experience, were overshadowed by their "exhilaration of achievement" (Rubin, 1990, p. 44). The females had more complicated reactions, often tied to ambivalence about what was acceptable sexual behavior for females. It is noteworthy that women who had the most positive reactions to their first sexual experience were the ones who had sex with men that they had known for a long time and cared deeply about.

A New Openness among Adolescent Women. Young women are now more open in their discussions about their sexual desires and their early sexual experiences than they once were (Tolman, 1994). Many now talk about their reactions to sex with their female friends, much as boys have always done with their male friends. It is apparently a staple in the conversations of teenage women to describe "My first time" (Thompson, 1990). But stories about "My first time" have two different themes: The first emphasizes how the first experience was one of physical pain, discomfort, or general unpleasantness; theme two describes the pleasure and excitement of the first sexual experience (Thompson, 1990). In interviews, approximately 75 percent of young women reflect the first theme, which is consistent with the earlier description of most people remembering their first sexual experience in negative terms.

Not only do many young women describe their first sexual experience negatively, but they are also often unsure about what actually happened. They tell of not knowing what was going to happen until it was over. These young women are not sure whether they had sex because they wanted it or because their boyfriends forced them into it (Thompson, 1990). In a recent survey of adult Americans, at least one-fourth of women respondents said their first sexual intercourse experience was not something that they wanted, but something they "just went along with" (Laumann et al., 1994, p. 328).

Many young women describe to their friends the fear and pain that they experienced when they first had sexual intercourse. But some recount the experience with a kind of bravado to show their "superiority over other girls who don't have what it takes to be women" (Thompson, 1990). One girl bragged,

> I really didn't feel nothing special. Most girls say, 'Oh, God, it really hurt,' and like that. It was nothing to me (Thompson, 1990, p. 348).

But there is another set of young women, about one-fourth of Thompson's sample, who describe their first sexual experience positively. It may be that their positive experience stems from the positive way in which they learned about sex, especially from their mothers (Thompson, 1990).

Unlike the young women who tell the negative stories, these girls have a sexual memory that goes back to a time before their first sexual intercourse experience. They describe how they had looked forward to sex, often for a long time. Many of them discovered masturbation at an early age and see their sexuality as a very desirable personal quality. These girls also report experimenting sexually with boys, even in their prepubertal years (Thompson, 1990).

These adolescent women who had pleasurable first-sex experiences frequently describe how they related openly with their mothers about sex. Their mothers often talked openly about sex and their own sexual lives and often in a natural and positive way. One daughter described her mother in this way:

> Mom had always talked very casually about sex. I mean, I have sat at the dinner table and discussed with mom what contraceptive she used when she was, uh uh, you know, having an affair with my dad for the year before she married him. And, uhm, actually we have discussed what sex was like with my father and what she did in—in the way of fooling around before she got married (Thompson, 1990, p. 354).

Adolescent women today are talking more openly with their friends about their sexual lives, especially their first sexual experience. Most young women describe their first sexual experience in negative terms, but some do not. The ones who report having pleasurable first experiences are those who had, for some years, been sensitive to their sexuality and knowledgeable about it. In many cases, these young women had mothers who treated sex as a natural and pleasurable part of life.

AIDS and Sexual Behavior

Acquired immune deficiency syndrome (AIDS) was first recognized in the United States in 1981. Although there was some early confusion about who could contract the disease, it was soon recognized as a major threat to public health in general.

A person is most likely to get the AIDS-producing virus (human immunodeficiency virus, abbreviated HIV) when the blood or semen from an infected person enters his or her bloodstream. Sexual intercourse, therefore, is a principal way of passing the virus from one person to another. The virus can also be transmitted through contaminated hypodermic needles (as is often the case among intravenous-drug users), by blood transfusions when a person receives infected blood, or by infected mothers to their unborn babies.

Sexual transmission of HIV is most probable when lesions or cuts are present through which infected semen or blood can enter the bloodstream. Thus, for example, a woman who has active herpes will be in greater danger of infection from a diseased partner, since the herpes lesions will admit the infected semen. Similarly, anal intercourse, which has a high likelihood of tearing rectal tissue, will lead to a higher rate of HIV transmission.

The Centers for Disease Control estimates that about 1 million people in the United States are HIV positive (CDC National AIDS Clearinghouse, telephone communication, 1995). The 1 million number is simply the midpoint within a range of estimates, with a low of 800,000 to a high of 1.2 million. These are only estimates, since only 26 states now have confidential reporting systems for HIV-positive cases, and none of the high-incidence states (especially New York, California, and Florida) are included.

The distribution of the AIDS virus in the population is highly skewed toward males. It is estimated that 1 in every 100 men and 1 in every 800 women in the population is HIV positive (CDC National AIDS Clearinghouse, telephone communication, 1995).

The numbers of people who have the AIDS disease is known with reasonable accuracy, because all medical personnel are required to report new AIDS cases to the Centers for Disease Control. The summaries of these reports are published in the *HIV/AIDS Surveillance Report* (Centers for Disease Control, 1995). Statistical data on AIDS cases in the United States, through June 1995, are shown in Table 7–1.

Table 7–1   AIDS Cases among Adults and Adolescents (13 and over) by Exposure Category, Cumulative Number of Cases from 1981 through June 1995, and New Cases between July 1994 and June 1995

Exposure Category	New Cases from July 1994 to June 1995		Cumulative Cases from 1981 to June 1995	
	Number	Percent	Number	Percent
Men who have sex with men	32,448	(43)	244,235	(52)
Injecting drug use	20,149	(27)	118,694	(25)
Men who have sex with men and inject drugs	3,609	(5)	31,024	(7)
Hemophilia/coagulation disorder	453	(1)	3,872	(1)
Heterosexual contact	8,178	(11)	35,683	(8)
Blood transfusion	687	(1)	7,128	(2)
Other/risk not reported or identified	10,301	(14)	29,652	(6)
Totals	75,825	(100)	470,288	(100)

Source: Centers for Disease Control. *HIV/AIDS Surveillance Report,* Vol. 7, 1995, p. 8.

Table 7–1 shows clearly that sexual relations continue to be the primary way in which AIDS is acquired. Forty-three percent of the most recent year's new cases were the result of men having sex with men and another 5 percent were from men having sex with men who inject drugs. Heterosexual contact accounted for 11 percent of the last year's new AIDS cases. (It should be noted that AIDS typically takes years to develop after the virus has been acquired). Nearly 60 percent of the newest AIDS cases are associated with sexual behavior.

Knowledge about AIDS

There has been an extraordinary effort to inform the American people about AIDS and the transmission of HIV. In the 1980s, the Surgeon General of the United States mailed an informational brochure on AIDS to every address in the United States, describing how the HIV is transmitted from one person to another, discussing the dangers of unsafe sex, and explaining what precautions should be taken. The federal government maintains a 24-hour, toll-free hotline that provides free and confidential information about AIDS (1-800-342-AIDS). Magazines and newspapers have addressed the AIDS story many times in a variety of ways. Schools throughout the United States have initiated AIDS-education programs, sometimes beginning as early as elementary school.

Efforts to inform the American people about AIDS and how it is transmitted have been extremely successful. A national survey of 100,000 American adults conducted periodically to determine the extent of their knowledge about AIDS has shown that there is nearly universal knowledge of the disease and a very high level of understanding of the three major modes of transmission. Eighty-seven percent of adults know that the HIV is transmitted through sexual contact, 85 percent know that the virus can be transmitted from a pregnant woman to her baby, and 95 percent know that needle sharing by intravenous drug users is a means of transmission.

The most common misconceptions about AIDS pertain to its transmission. Some people still believe it can be contracted from casual contact with someone who has the disease (shaking hands) or from toilet seats, doorknobs, or insect bites. Within the adult population, those who have the lowest levels of knowledge are "the elderly, minorities, people with low levels of education, and those for whom English is a second language" (Russell, 1991, p. 7).

While this survey of American adults reveals a significant level of knowledge about AIDS and its transmission, it also shows that most Americans do not consider themselves at risk of contracting the disease. Eighty percent of adult Americans believe that there is no chance that they have been infected with HIV. "Fifteen percent said they thought there was a slight chance. Fewer than 1 percent said they thought they had a high chance of being infected now or in the future" (Russell, 1991, p. 7).

Since Americans know about AIDS and understand that it is transmitted sexually, one would expect some significant changes in sexual behavior. On the other hand, since the vast majority of Americans believe that there is little or no likelihood that they will contract the disease, there would be little reason for them to change their sexual behavior. This leads to the obvious question: Have Americans changed their sexual behavior (and attitudes) since the beginning of the AIDS outbreak?

Has AIDS Changed Sexual Behavior?

For the population at large, about one-fourth or more say that they have changed their sexual behavior. The federal government's survey of adults found that nearly 25 percent of those who said that they were sexually active had reduced their number of sexual partners and/or used condoms (Russell, 1991). Another recent national survey of adults found that 30 percent say that they have changed their behavior in response to AIDS (Laumann et al., 1994). Men are more likely than women to have changed their behavior, and younger people are more likely to have changed than older people. Members of the 18- to 24-year-old group are more likely to have changed their behavior than any other age group (42.9 percent). Another encouraging note from the national survey is that those people who are most at risk (those with multiple partners and males with same-sex partners) are most likely to have changed their sexual behavior (Laumann et al., 1994).

These survey findings support qualitative evidence that gay men, especially in the major urban centers where the earliest concentration of AIDS cases occurred (San Francisco and New York), did modify their behavior considerably. After an initial resistance, the gay community in San Francisco, for example, recognized that social and behavioral changes had to be made. The gay baths in San Francisco—where impersonal sex was the standard—were closed with the support of the gay community (Fineberg, 1988).

A 1988 national survey of adolescent males reached somewhat similar conclusions with regard to condom use (Sonenstein et al., 1989). These young men were asked a series of questions to determine their knowledge about AIDS. They proved to be very knowledgeable about how AIDS was transmitted and indicated that they did not take the threat of AIDS lightly. Seventy-nine percent of these males "disagreed a lot" with the statement, "Using condoms to prevent AIDS is more trouble than it's worth." An even higher percentage (82 percent) "disagreed a lot" with the statement, "Even though AIDS is a fatal disease, it is so uncommon that it's not a big worry." Given these views, it is not too surprising that more than half (55 percent) said that they used a condom the first time they had intercourse, and 57 percent reported that they had used a condom the last time they had intercourse (Sonenstein et al., 1989). In a similar survey conducted in 1979, only 21 percent of adolescent males had used a condom the last time they had intercourse. Clearly, the campaign to instruct young people about the importance of using condoms to prevent the spread of AIDS has had an effect.

This 1988 study, however, found that the young men who were most likely to use condoms were those whose behaviors put them at the lowest risk for contracting AIDS. The researchers divided the sample into high-risk, moderate-risk, and low-risk groups on the basis of their sexual and drug-use behaviors. The criteria for determining the high-, moderate-, and low-risk groups are shown in Table 7–2, along with the percentage in each risk group who used condoms at the time of their last sexual intercourse experience.

Table 7–2 shows that the low-risk group was most likely to use condoms; two-thirds reported using a condom the last time they had sexual intercourse. The moderate-risk group had the lowest percentage using condoms, 45 percent. The high-risk group had a somewhat higher percentage using condoms, 51 percent. Condom use among the high-risk young men varied greatly by the type of high-risk behavior that they reported. Those who engaged in homosexual behavior (3 percent of the sample) were very likely to have used a condom (66 percent). But the intravenous drug users and those who reported having sex with a prostitute had very low percentages using condoms (21 and 17 percent, respectively) (Sonenstein et al., 1989).

Although not shown in Table 7–2, this study also found that young men who had the *most* sexual partners during the last year were the *least* likely to use a

Table 7–2   Percentage of Never-Married, Sexually Active Males Aged 15 to 19 Who
Had Used a Condom at the Time of Last Sexual Intercourse, by Risk Group

	Used a Condom at the Time of Last Intercourse
High-risk Group (9 percent of the total)	51%
(One or more of the following behaviors:	
had engaged in homosexual activity,	
had had a sexually transmitted disease,	
had ever had sex with a prostitute,	
had used intravenous drugs,	
had a partner who used IV drugs.)	
Moderate-risk Group (38 percent of the total)	45%
(Not in the high-risk group, but had engaged in	
one or more of the following:	
had sex with a stranger,	
had five or more partners in the last year,	
had sex with someone who had had many partners.)	
Low-risk Group (54 percent of the total)	66%
(Reported none of the behaviors of the high- and	
moderate-risk groups.)	

condom; those who had the *fewest* partners were the *most* likely to use a condom (Sonenstein et al., 1989).

The results of this study are encouraging on the one hand, since many more sexually active young men are using condoms than in the past, but discouraging because many of those at greatest risk are the least likely to use condoms. The small percentage of young men who are engaging in homosexual behavior is the exception. The high percentage who used a condom at the time of last intercourse is further evidence that gay males are modifying their sexual behavior as precaution against AIDS.

A Study of University Women.   Random samples of the national populations are important for an understanding of changing sexual behavior, but smaller studies of specialized populations can also be revealing. Such is the case with a survey of Brown University women who were given a questionnaire about their sexual behavior in 1989 that was nearly identical to ones completed by Brown University women in 1979 and 1986.

The 1989 survey showed, once again, that the educational campaign recommending the use of condoms has had some impact. In 1975, 6 percent of the Brown women said that condoms were used as their "usual method of birth control." In 1986, the percentage had risen to 14 percent, and in 1989, the percentage was up again, to 25 percent.

With regard to sexual activity, however, the Brown women have made few changes since 1975. In both 1975 and 1989, about 88 percent of these women, who averaged about 21 years of age, were sexually active. In 1975, the pre-AIDS era, about 22 percent of the women reported that they had had more than six sexual partners in their lifetimes and more than three partners in the year preceding the survey. In 1989, after having been told for nearly a decade that multiple sex partners may increase one's risk for getting AIDS, almost exactly the same percentage (21 percent) reported having had more than six sexual partners in their lifetimes and more than three in the past year. The percentages who said they engaged in oral or anal sex had also remained at about the same levels between 1975 and 1989 (DeBuono et al., 1990).

Deviant Sexual Behavior

In our consideration of deviant behavior in Chapter 6, we saw that almost every behavior has been defined as deviant by the people of some society at some time. We also saw that virtually every kind of behavior has been socially acceptable at one time or another. Thus, when we ask, "What is deviant sexual behavior?" we should be prepared to find that it depends upon who is defining the behavior and when.

The sexual abuse of children, for example, has become clearly recognized as deviant behavior, but it has not always been so (Okami, 1992). Over the last 25 years the recognition of, and research on, child sexual abuse has increased dramatically. While adults who engage in sexual relations with children are considered deviant, what if children themselves are the "perpetrators" of sexual acts with other children? When and under what circumstances are such children engaging in deviant behavior, and when are they engaged in normal childhood sexual experimentation? Some experts claim that children, too, can be sexual abusers of other children (Johnson, 1988, 1990), while others are reluctant to identify such behaviors as deviant (Okami, 1992). The social definition of children as sexual abusers is still ambiguous and not completely accepted among the people at large in American society.

To understand which sexual behaviors are deviant and which are not deviant in any particular society, we need some measures or indicators. Several ways have been suggested for evaluating whether a sexual behavior is deviant in a society (Bryant, 1982).

One measure of deviance is whether a particular sexual act is *against the legal statutes* of a nation or state. Acts that are illegal are presumably deviant to some degree. The problem with using the law as a measure of deviance is that laws often remain on the books for many years, even when they are no longer enforced.

Cross-national Perspectives

Gays and Lesbians as a Silent Minority: The Case of China

Gays and lesbians in many countries of the world, especially in the United States, Europe, and other Western countries, have "come out of the closet," but in other parts of the world openness about homosexuality is still severely limited (Miller, 1992). In Argentina, Hong Kong, Japan, South Africa, and Uruguay, gays and lesbians are making tentative steps toward coming into the open, but doing so is still fraught with difficulties and sometimes dangers (Miller, 1992). An extreme case is China, where gays and lesbians are far from being open about their sexual preferences. In fact, officially, Chinese authorities deny the existence of homosexuality. One result of this is that there are no laws or regulations in China dealing with homosexuality. Thus, the average Chinese citizen has little or no awareness of homosexuality. Yet it is estimated that a minimum of 2% of the Chinese population is gay. Since the Chinese population is currently about 1.3 billion, that means that there are at least 25 million homosexuals and lesbians in the country. That represents an extremely large minority group. As one Chinese sociologist says, " 'This society should not overlook such a large proportion of people'" (Sun, 1992a, p. A44).

Homosexuals in China were not always so invisible. In fact, references to homosexuality in Chinese literature go back almost 46 centuries. Various emperors, aristocrats, and merchants throughout the history of China were widely known to have engaged in homosexual behavior. One emperor Ai Di (6 B.C. to A.D. 1) awoke to find the sleeve of his gown caught beneath his sleeping male lover. Rather than awaken him, the emperor cut the sleeve from his gown. To this day in China, the term "cut sleeve" is synonymous with homosexuality. However, when the Communists came to power in 1949, the situation confronting gays changed dramatically. While they were not repressed or physically assaulted, gays came to be treated as "nonpersons"; they simply did not exist as far as the Communist authorities were concerned.

While officially nonexistent, the authorities and the public have always had to deal with homosexuals. For example, authorities tend to ignore homosexual activities in public parks, but they may be forced to act if complaints are made. When complaints are made, and since homosexuals do not exist publicly, they are almost always accused of "hooliganism." Nevertheless, reflective of an undercurrent of deep hostility toward gays, such hooligans may be given stiff jail terms, sometimes being sentenced to as many as 7 or 8 years in prison.

It is not unusual for doctors to define homosexuality as mental illness. While doctors no longer use shock therapy as they once did to treat homosexuality, many do inject homosexuals caught by the police with drugs designed to make them vomit. The hope is that the nausea will help discourage them from having erotic thoughts about same-sex partners in the future.

The larger public, while it too is largely ignorant about homosexuality, has a deep reservoir of disgust and hostility toward homosexuals. The result is that most homosexuals must keep silent about their sexual preferences. They often marry in order to conceal their true sexual preference, as well as to have an heir, since to not have an heir is considered an insult to one's parents. They must hide their homosexuality from spouses and parents. If they are discovered to be homosexual, they are likely to lose the respect of family and friends. They may also lose "their jobs, their housing, their Communist Party membership, and become social pariahs" (Sun, 1992a, p. A39). Said one homosexual of his fear of discovery:

> If you are caught, it will be all over.... You can't work, you can't face your parents, the police will tell the neighborhood committee and then the whole neighborhood will know. Then you can't live there anymore (Sun, 1992a, p. A44).

More extremely, some homosexuals have committed suicide or been forced to leave the country.

The general ignorance about homosexuality in China has various consequences. On the one hand, people are very naive about the nature of homosexuality. For example, one man described the scene after his first homosexual experience: "We were lying on the bed, and I asked him, 'What we just did, is this homosexuality?' And he said, 'What do you ... think you are anyway?' Then I thought, how can I become like this?" (Sun, 1992b, p. A39). On the other hand, the lack of public awareness and the lack of official legal restrictions against homosexuality makes China, at least in some ways, "'a paradise for gays'" (Sun, 1992a, p. A44). Various kinds of liaisons are made easier by the fact that the vast majority of people are unlikely to suspect that homosexual behavior is taking place.

Of course, things are changing in China in various ways, and this includes homosexuality. There are some signs that the impact of the West is being felt here, too, and that homosexuals are increasingly being treated as normal people, rather than as lawbreakers or psychiatric cases. But, of course, the major impact from the West is a growing awareness in China of AIDS and of the relationship between homosexual behavior and the disease. Thus, AIDS prevention workers have been distributing safe-sex pamphlets in Beijing and there is now an active AIDS hotline in that city. While the infection rate is low, it is increasing fast, and as it does one can expect even more public and government attention to AIDS and to homosexuality. But, it is still unclear whether gays will receive more sympathy and understanding or be subject to further disapproval and repression.

MILLER, NEIL. *Out in the World.* New York: Random House, 1992.
SUN, LENA H. "Gay Millions: China's Silent Minority." *Washington Post,* November 4, 1992a.
SUN, LENA H. "One Man's Story 'What We Just Did, Is This Homosexuality?'" *Washington Post,* November 4, 1992b.

For example, many states have laws against fornication, prohibiting sexual intercourse between people who are not married. A law against fornication would make almost every cohabiting couple lawbreakers. In the state of Virginia a cohabiting couple attempted to get the state's law against cohabitation declared unconstitutional, but Virginia's court of appeals rejected their lawsuit. From the legal perspective, the most important consideration is whether violations of a law are prosecuted. In the case of cohabitation, in Virginia as well as other states, it is unlikely that the laws prohibiting sexual intercourse between unmarried individuals will be enforced against cohabiting couples.

A second indication of sexual deviance is the *statistical frequency of some act.* If a particular sexual act is widespread, involving large numbers of people, it is not likely to be considered deviant. Again, the case of cohabitation is instructive, since the number of cohabiting-couple households in the United States now exceeds 3 million. A second example is adultery, which is contrary to existing social norms as well as against the law in most places. However, estimates are that at least 40 to 50 percent of all married men and more than 20 percent (Lauman et al., 1994) of all married women have adulterous sex. Among high-income men—those earning $60,000 or more a year—an estimated 70 percent have extramarital affairs. Many of the women who are the mistresses of such men do not consider themselves deviant; they accept these affairs as a normal part of their lives (Richardson, 1985).

A third standard that can be used to evaluate the deviance of a sexual act is the degree to which *one person is a victim.* Being a victim indicates that one person in a sexual act is coerced or forced to do something against his or her will. Homosexual behavior, for example, almost always occurs between consenting adults, which leads some people to conclude that no deviance is involved. Similarly, prostitution is a sexual act that involves two people who agree, through a commercial transaction, to engage in sex. However, since many female prostitutes are addicted to drugs, have no other means of making a living, or are under the control of a male pimp, some question does arise about whether they are free in making their decisions.

Several sexual acts clearly involve victims. One obvious case is rape, in which one person, through force or threat, makes another person perform a sexual act. Closely related are all cases when children are sexually abused. The sexual abuse of children can occur either in the family or outside it. Inside the family, the most common circumstance is for a young girl to be sexually abused by either a father, brother, or other male relative living in the home. It is also possible for young boys to be sexually molested in similar circumstances, but the incidence is considerably lower. Even if the sexual abuse occurs outside the family, the aggressor is typically either a relative or friend of the family, or someone who has been charged with responsibility for the child. The results of a study conducted among college students at the University of New Hampshire showed that 19.2 percent of female students and 8.2 percent of male students had been "sexually victimized" sometime during childhood (Finkelhor, 1979).

Many kinds of sexual deviance, including some of those discussed above, depend to some degree on the situation or context in which they occur. For example, exhibitionism is the act of showing one's body in a public place, and yet people who go to nudist camps or nude beaches often emphasize that their action is neither sexual nor deviant (Bryant, 1982).

This sociological analysis of sexual deviance leads us back to where we started. Sexual behavior, both that which is acceptable and that which is deviant, is determined to a considerable degree by the norms, values, and roles of the particular society in which people live.

Summary

Sexuality is a basic human characteristic, sexual behavior is universal, and sex is a biological act; but many societal and cultural differences exist in sexual behavior and sexuality. All these variations and differences, including historical changes from one period to another, indicate that sexual behavior is influenced as much by social factors as it is by biological factors.

A number of societal characteristics of the contemporary United States are reflected in sexual behavior. These characteristics include the depersonalization of sex, the commercialization of sex, and coercive and aggressive sex.

Sexuality is normatively controlled in every society. The most nearly universal norm is the prohibition of sex between closely related individuals—the norm prohibiting incest. However, the norms vary from one society to another, and there are historical exceptions to even the most widely held prohibitions—parent–child and sibling sexual relations.

The double standard is a complex of norms that gives males greater freedom in their sexual behavior than females. Although the rigidity of the double standard of sexual behavior might have lessened, it is still very much alive in American society today.

Children learn about sex through the socialization process. Although there is widespread agreement that children should learn about sex from their parents, evidence reveals that most parents communicate to their children very little information about sex. Children and adolescents learn about sex from their peers and the mass media, especially television and movies.

The traditional cultural ideal of not having sex before marriage has never been fully complied with in American society. Premarital pregnancies indicate a considerable amount of premarital sexual activity among young people prior to the twentieth century. Research by Kinsey and others in the first half of the twentieth century also revealed substantial numbers of young people having sex before marriage, but during the last 25 years the numbers have increased greatly.

Sex at an early age is associated with race–ethnicity, academic performance, family settings, religiosity, and tobacco, alcohol, and drug use. The first sexual intercourse for males is associated with achievement; for females it is often an expression of love. In recalling their first sexual intercourse experience the majority of males and females describe it in negative terms. Young women today are discussing their sexual experiences more openly than in the past.

AIDS has introduced a new factor into the sexual behavior of people in the United States. More open discussions are held now about sexual matters, and awareness of sexual issues has increased. The chances of contracting AIDS can be reduced by certain modifications of sexual behavior, which most Americans understand, but, except for some gay males, and a general increase in condom use, there have been only moderate changes in sexual behavior.

Sexual deviance, like all other forms of deviance, is socially defined. Sexual deviance can be defined by the laws of a society, but the laws may fall into disuse. The frequency of a sexual behavior also indicates whether it is deviant; previously deviant acts often become more commonplace and thus less deviant. Deviance is also indicated by the degree to which a sexual behavior victimizes another person. In the final analysis, deviant sexual behavior, as well as acceptable sexual behavior, is determined by the norms, values, and roles of a society.

CRITICAL THINKING

1. Why is sexual behavior a good subject to demonstrate how fundamental human behavior is influenced by culture?
2. Why do our beliefs about sexuality reflect the general characteristics of our society? Give contemporary and historical examples to support your answer.
3. Do the ideas of sexual coercion, commercialization, and depersonalization find support in any recent movies you have seen? Give examples.
4. In your view, are there still norms about sexual behavior that support a double standard for males and females? How do you explain the existence of such a standard?
5. What differences exist between the ideal roles and real roles of parents in socializing their children about sex? What other sources of socialization influence a person's sexual behavior and beliefs?
6. How do changes in the ability of sociologists and other researchers to gather data about sexual behavior reflect changing views about sex in society at large?
7. What do you think accounts for the fact that younger siblings have sex earlier than older siblings?
8. Two major modifications in sexual behavior have been suggested as a result of the AIDS epidemic. To your knowledge, to what extent has behavior changed to comply with these suggestions?
9. What standards might be employed in determining whether a particular sexual behavior is deviant?

Part II Inequality

8

Stratification: Living with Social Inequality

All societies face the basic problem of how to distribute scarce and desirable resources and social rewards—money, power, influence, and respect—among their members. Seldom, if ever, are they distributed equally; differences in social rank appear in virtually all human societies, even those that claim to be egalitarian. Throughout human history, some people have possessed greater wealth, prestige, and power than others, regardless of the society in which they lived, and this phenomenon shows no sign of disappearing. **Social stratification** refers to the structure of social inequality in each society—the manner in which scarce resources and social rewards are distributed among different social categories.

An individual's position in a system of stratification affects **life chances,** a term referring to the likelihood of realizing a certain standard of living or quality of life. For example, in American society the life chances of the poor for education, nutrition, health, life expectancy, quality of housing, and treatment by the criminal justice system differ dramatically from those of the rich. This chapter will be concerned with the nature and consequences of social inequality and social ranking: wealth and poverty, power and powerlessness, dominance and subordination, prestige and degradation, and the ways in which advantages and disadvantages are passed from one generation to another.

Although social stratification is virtually universal, societies differ in the ways in which they allocate scarce resources. Therefore, forms of stratification systems vary widely. Even though most societies have been stratified in some way, this does not necessarily mean that a society must be stratified. "A system of ranks does not form part of some natural and invariable order of things, but is a human contrivance or product, and is subject to historical changes" (Bottomore, 1966b, p. 10). In other words, social stratification is not "natural" or inevitable. A classless society is a possibility, if not a probability.

Social stratification is a *social* phenomenon. A system of stratification in any group or society is *not* determined by the biological characteristics of individuals or by supernatural laws. It results from human actions in both the present and the past. Earlier generations create a system of stratification that influences each succeeding generation. Throughout their lives people learn the structure of, and their places in, their society's stratification system.

Dimensions of Stratification

In a complex society such as exists in the United States, determining one's position in its stratification system is frequently difficult because several criteria may be used—wealth, prominence, prestige, influence, and ancestry. Although wealth is obviously an important determinant of one's place in the American stratification system, it is not the only one. People are evaluated differently depending on how their wealth is attained. For example, members of the U.S. House of Representatives have annual salaries of $133,600. However, they have a different location in the stratification system from a professional baseball player, a cocaine dealer, a plumber, a lottery winner, a small-town business owner, or a playboy whose annual incomes are the same or much higher. Each of these different sources of income carries differences in prestige and power which, in addition to wealth, must be considered in evaluating how people are distributed in a system of stratification.

Because social stratification in modern societies is influenced by different factors, Max Weber distinguished among three basic dimensions: class, status, and power. **Class** is a social ranking made on the basis of economic factors. **Status** in the context of stratification refers to a social ranking on the basis of *prestige,* that is, the esteem, honor, and social approval accorded an individual or group. **Power** is a social ranking based on the ability to make others do what you want them to do.

Class

Although Weber recognized wealth as an important dimension of stratification, it was Karl Marx who especially emphasized the role of economic factors in determining social ranking. He identified two basic social classes, which are distinguished by their relationship to property. The dominant class—composed of landowners, slaveowners, and factory and business owners—owns and controls the means of production (such as land, machines, and tools). The subordinate class includes industrial laborers, peasants, serfs, and slaves who work for the dominant class.

In a capitalist society, industrial laborers (the **proletariat**) are forced to sell their labor to those who own the means of production (the **capitalists**). To achieve profits, capitalists exploit workers by paying wages that are less than the value of the goods the workers produce. As capitalists compete with each other and seek to achieve ever-greater profits, they try to cut costs by reducing wages paid to the workers. Marx described different ways—among them, employing children and lengthening the work days—in which capitalists in the nineteenth century sought to increase their profits.

Post–World War II industrial capitalism differs greatly from capitalism in Marx's day, and critics have argued that his analysis no longer applies. Dahrendorf (1959), for example, contended that Marx focused too narrowly on the idea of the ownership of property. The distinctive feature of capitalism in the postwar era was the modern corporation, which is owned by hundreds of thousands of shareholders, not by one or even a handful. Such corporations, however, are controlled and run by a small number of people—corporate managers and executives. Therefore, *control,* not *ownership,* of the means of production has become the factor that distinguishes classes in modern capitalist societies.

As we will discuss more fully in Chapter 13, in the past quarter-century the American economy has changed dramatically, producing a "permanently new economy" (Ritzer, 1989). Numerous writers and social critics from a wide range of political perspectives (e.g., Bluestone, 1995; Hernnstein and Murray, 1994; Lasch, 1995; Lind, 1995; Reich, 1992, 1995) have suggested that these changes are contributing to the emergence of a new system of social inequality in the United States and other industrialized countries. The primary feature of this new class structure is that income, wealth, and power are increasingly becoming concentrated in an **overclass** comprised of what Reich (1992, 1995) has termed "symbolic analysts"—people as diverse as research scientists, management and political consultants, investment lawyers, design engineers, writers and editors, or public relations and advertising executives—who do not own property but are highly educated and whose work focuses on "problem solving, problem-identifying, and strategic brokering activities." Members of the overclass are distinguished by their highly technical and specialized skills, and they are involved in the manipulation of information and professional expertise. Because they possess skills and expertise that are critical to success in an increasingly globalized economy, members of the overclass are linked with their elite counterparts in other countries throughout the world.

In the News

The Overclass: Economic Restructuring and the Rise of the New Elite Class

During the first half of the 1990s, a growing inequality of income and wealth in American society, coupled with almost daily news accounts of corporate downsizing, has, for many Americans, called into question the perception of the United States as a middle-class society and a land of opportunity. Although the United States has experienced economic expansion, relatively low inflation, and relatively low unemployment since 1991, a majority of Americans are pessimistic about their economic futures and do not expect their children's generation to have a higher standard of living than they do.

In addition to eliciting comments from economists and politicians, this trend toward widening economic inequality has been prominently featured in the news. For example, in a cover story, "Inequality: How the Gap Between Rich and Poor Hurts the Economy," *Business Week* referred to the "explosion of income equality..., the widest rich-poor gap since the Census Bureau began keeping track in 1947." Similar stories in daily newspapers and popular magazines such as *Newsweek, Harpers,* and *The Atlantic Monthly* have examined this trend, provided explanations for its causes, and speculated on its implications for the future of American society.

Although most experts agree that economic inequality has recently increased in the United States, they disagree over the reasons why it has occurred. Critics of the Reagan-Bush administrations of the 1980s contend that the economic policies they implemented favored the rich and widened the economic gap. However, most economists argue that broader social and economic factors—the deindustrialization and increasing globalization of the American economy, the increasing role of technology and the premium placed on highly skilled training, and changes in social norms—are more compelling explanations. Most important have been technological changes that have dramatically changed the skills needed in today's global economy, which places a premium on *very highly* skilled and technologically sophisticated workers—that Reich has termed *symbolic analysts.*

However, new technologies also enable a smaller number of individuals to dominate a particular field or market—whether in entertainment, sports, and the professions—and to command much higher salaries. This has led to what Frank and Cook have characterized as the "winner-take-all" society. Reflecting these trends, *Newsweek* recently ran a cover story entitled "The Overclass," that asked, "Is a new elite of high-tech strivers pulling away from the rest of America?" It then proclaimed, "We are witnessing an epochal moment in American sociology, the birth of a new class. . . . They are a new American elite." To celebrate its own ingenuity in disseminating the term *overclass* to a mass, popular audience, *Newsweek* featured what it dubbed the "Overclass 100"—an "unscientific list...of the country's comers, the newest wave of important and compelling people," which included the "Today" show's Katie Couric, movie producer Wayne Wang, financier Robert Rosenkrantz, Baltimore mayor Kurt Schmoke, Vice President Al Gore, and United Way president Elaine Chao. The basic credential for membership in the overclass, *Newsweek* contended, is merit, especially in fields that require imagination, creativity, and highly sophisticated, technical, and specialized training.

FRANK, ROBERT H. and COOK, PHILLIP J. *The Winner-Take-All Society.* New York: The Free Press, 1995.
"Inequality: How the Growing Gap Between Rich and Poor in America is Hurting the Economy." *Business Week,* August 15, 1994.
LIND, MICHAEL. "To Have and Have Not." *Harpers,* June 1995.
"The Overclass: Is a New Elite of Highly Paid, High-tech Strivers Pulling Away From the Rest of America?" *Newsweek,* July 31, 1995.
REICH, ROBERT B. *The Work of Nations.* New York: Random House, 1992.

Status

Although Max Weber did not ignore the special significance that Marx attributed to property and economic factors, he believed that stratification was based on prestige and power as well as on economic factors. Whereas one's class position is determined by wealth and income, Weber argued, one's status is based on the prestige that attaches to the positions that people occupy in society. Usually one's status position is intimately related to one's class position, but it is possible for individuals to be ranked differently on these two dimensions. Status, therefore, according to Weber, refers to groups of people who share similar life chances resulting from social estimation of honor or prestige.

For example, despite a popular egalitarian ideology, one source of status in American society is lineage or family background. Considerable prestige is connected with membership in such hereditary societies as the Daughters of the American Revolution, the Society of Mayflower Descendants, the United Daughters of the Confederacy, and the National Society of Colonial Dames. Although many such organizations tend to draw their membership primarily from those with considerable wealth, the primary criterion is ancestry. Similarly, inclusion in the *Social Register,* a published listing of about 65,000 families and single adults that has been used by sociologists as an index of the upper class in the United States, is based on social standing, not on wealth alone.

Power

Weber argued that a third dimension of stratification exists—power—that is different from class and status. Power refers to the ability to get others to do what you want, even against their own will. The nature and distribution of power and the struggle among groups vying for power have been among the central concerns of sociologists. Although class, status, and power are closely related, Weber felt that they were theoretically separate—that is, there are situations in which those wielding the greatest power in a society do not necessarily possess great economic resources or prestige. Thus power is a crucial part of any system of social inequality. The president of the United States, for example, has extraordinary power, both in this country and throughout the world, but he is not necessarily wealthy. We would not argue that basketball star Michael Jordan, pop star Michael Jackson, or even the wealthiest American—billionaire William Gates, founder of the Microsoft Corporation, the leading software company—are as powerful or are accorded prestige equal to that of the president of the United States. We will examine the nature and distribution of power more fully in Chapter 16.

How Are Stratification Systems Justified?

Stratification systems are systems of inequality, and it is important for the stability of such systems that the majority of people accept that inequality. The people in privileged positions generally can accept the inequality easily, but even they can feel more comfortable if something justifies their position. People lower in the system must have some basis for accepting the inequalities they experience. For these reasons stratification systems usually have an ideology. An **ideology** is a set of ideas that explains reality, provides directives for behavior, and expresses the interests of particular groups. An ideology is used to legitimize and justify the existing social order and to maintain the inequalities in wealth, power, and prestige. The ideology, which contains a set of rules that explain how and why the society's resources are distributed as they are, frequently becomes accepted by those in subordinate as well as dominant positions. Different stratification systems have developed different kinds of ideologies, which may include religious, political, economic, or "scientific" elements.

Religion has frequently provided an ideology to support social inequalities. American slaveholders, for example, maintained that the Bible supported slavery—that blacks were condemned to eternal servitude by the curse of Ham. Similarly, the Indian caste system, characterized by a system of rigidly defined social ranks and an extremely high degree of social inequality that has endured for thousands of years, is justified by the Hindu religion. Hindu belief emphasizes the importance of reincarnation—the process whereby one's soul is reborn in another person after one's death. However, whether one's soul is reincarnated in a person higher or lower in the caste system depends on how faithfully one has accepted and observed one's duties in the previous life. Failure to observe the rules of the caste system could condemn someone to be reincarnated as an "outcaste," the lowest and most despised position in the system.

Science has also been widely used to justify social ranking. In American society for more than a century, so-called scientific findings have shaped views on race. In the nineteenth century, scientists conducted numerous studies to prove the existence of a racial hierarchy in brain size, and therefore intelligence, with northern Europeans highest on the scale and blacks lowest. Early in the twentieth century, intelligence testing replaced such anatomical studies as a way of "scientifically" validating the "natural" superiority of socially dominant groups. Today, the controversy over the use of IQ tests has been revived. In *The Bell Curve,* Herrnstein and Murray (1994) argue that IQ is destiny, determining the position of both individuals and social groups in the hierarchy of power and privilege and that little can be done to change the structure of social inequalities in the United States (see box on pages 301–303).

Intelligence testing has played an important role in the development of a **meritocratic ideology,** which today has become used as a way of justifying social inequalities in American society. The basic belief in this ideology is equality of opportunity—that all people in the United States have equal chances to achieve success and that inequalities in the distribution of income, wealth, power, and prestige reflect the qualifications or merit of individuals in each rank in society. In other words, in a meritocratic society, all people are perceived to have an equal opportunity to succeed or fail—to go as far as their talents will take them—and the system of social ranking that develops is simply a "natural" reflection of each person's abilities or merit. Affluence is perceived to be a result of the personal qualities of intelligence, industriousness, motivation, and ambition, while poverty exists because the poor lack those attributes. Therefore, in this aristocracy of talent, those in the upper strata deserve the power, prestige, and privileges that they enjoy, while those lower in the social ranking system are placed according to their ability. Thus, many Americans accept the idea that those at the top of the economic pyramid are meritorious and deserve to be there, and they attribute the responsibility for poverty to the qualities of the poor themselves, not to factors outside their control (Huber and Form, 1973; Bobo and Kluegel, 1993). Ryan (1971) labels this explanation of poverty "blaming the victim," because it fails to recognize the ways in which the distribution of affluence and poverty are affected by the structure of opportunities available to people in different socioeconomic statuses.

Structural–Functional and Conflict Theories of Social Stratification

Sociologists have developed two broad theories to account for social stratification: structural–functional theory and conflict theory. These competing conceptions of social inequality have generated considerable controversy.

Structural–functionalists are inclined to see social stratification as an expression of common values in society. Therefore, because American society values economic success, it accords those with more money higher status in the stratification system. Since the stratification system supports basic American values, it contributes to societal integration and stability. In contrast, conflict theorists view stratification as an expression of conflicting group interests. The various strata are seen as emerging from the conflict over scarce, valued resources.

The *functional theory* of stratification views the stratification system as equitable because people get what society seems to say they deserve (Jeffries and Ransford, 1980). Those at the top are seen as deserving greater power, prestige, and life chances than those at the bottom, who deserve much less of each. Functionalists see inequality in the distribution of rewards as beneficial to both individuals and society because society's tasks are accomplished by the best-qualified people. Conflict theorists, on the other hand, view the existing distribution of rewards as unjust and detrimental to most people as well as to society as a whole.

To structural–functionalists, power and coercion do not play a central part in maintaining a system of rewards and privileges. In their view, the system is maintained because most of a society's members believe in and accept common values. Once again, conflict theorists disagree. They do not believe that most people in the United States accept the fact that some have a right to greater rewards. We accept it, they say, because those in power have forced us to, perhaps by propagandizing us into believing in their greater rights.

Structural–functionalists contend that the major function of stratification is to motivate the relatively few capable people to occupy higher-level, more prestigious positions in society. To encourage people to want to occupy these more "important" positions, Davis and Moore (1945) argue, they must be offered greater rewards, in the forms of more money, power, and prestige. Therefore, a society must not only be stratified, but it must be stratified in such a way that the higher a person rises in the system, the greater are the rewards attached to a position. So, the argument goes, if we want the most talented people to become physicians, politicians, or business managers, we must offer them greater rewards. If we do not, the structural–functionalist says, then not enough of the most talented people will enter these positions.

Conflict theorists ridicule this idea. They argue that these positions will prove intrinsically attractive to many people, with no need to offer greater rewards. Conflict theorists argue that since members of the upper classes occupy these positions in large numbers, they have a vested interest in attaching great rewards to them. They contend that the functional theory of stratification simply perpetuates the privileged position of people who already have power, prestige, and money. The functional theory also can be criticized for assuming that simply because a social structure has existed in the past, it must continue to exist in the future. Possibly future societies can be organized in other, nonstratified ways.

Critics of functionalism also challenge the idea that positions vary in their importance to society. Are garbage collectors really less important to the survival of society than advertising executives? Despite the lower pay and prestige of the garbage collectors, they may actually be more important for the survival of the society.

Even in cases where one position obviously serves a more important function for society, greater rewards do not necessarily accrue to that position. The registered nurse may be more important to society than the movie actor, but the registered nurse has far less power, prestige, and income than the actor.

Other critics question whether there really is a scarcity of people capable of filling high-level positions. In fact, evidence suggests that many people who may possess ability are prevented from obtaining the training needed to achieve prestigious positions. Moreover, formal educational credentials may themselves be unrelated to job performance and, therefore, serve to exclude capable people from jobs that they could effectively perform (Persell, 1977, pp. 158–163). In general, many able people may never get a chance to show that they, too, can handle high-ranking positions.

Finally, functionalists see the U.S. stratification system as open, with the ability to rise in it generally dependent on personal talent and motivation. This expresses the American belief that those with ability and ambition can make it to the top. Conflict theorists reject this notion as well. They argue that ability and motivation are insignificant; what really matters is being born into the upper strata where people have greater access to educational facilities, the best universities, and the "right" contacts. Conflict theorists hold that status in the U.S. stratification system is often ascribed, rather than achieved. That is, more people remain in the position into which they are born than achieve higher positions through personal effort.

Social Inequalities in the United States

Describing American society in 1830, the French aristocrat, Alexis de Tocqueville, began his classic book, *Democracy in America,* by saying, "Nothing struck me more forcibly than the general equality of condition among the people" (Tocqueville, 1835/1954, p. 3). The perception of the United States as a society characterized by a "general equality of condition" among a broad middle class and by the relative absence of extreme poverty and extreme wealth has persisted to the present as an article of faith for both Americans and foreign observers alike. The ideal of middle-class America was nowhere more prominently reflected than in President Bill Clinton's 1992 presidential campaign, which was primarily an appeal to the American middle class, which, he maintained, had been "forgotten." We turn now to examine whether the "general equality of condition" that Tocqueville described in 1830 can be found in the United States today.

Inequalities of Class

As noted, *class* refers to social ranking based on economic factors. Therefore, in examining class inequalities in the United States today, we will focus primarily on how the economic "pie" is divided, how economic resources are distributed and concentrated.

In examining economic inequalities, we must first distinguish between wealth and income. **Wealth** refers to the total economic resources that people have, while **income** refers to how much money people obtain during a specified period of time, usually a year. Although there is frequently a close relationship between the two, an individual could possibly have substantial wealth and little income, or vice versa. For example, wealthy landowners might be *land poor;* that is, they may own a considerable amount of real estate but derive little income from it. On the other hand, some people might have a very high income, but spend or lose most of it and thus have accumulated little wealth. In the discussion that follows, we will examine data on trends in the distribution of income and wealth in the United States.

Income. Income is specifically the wages, salaries, dividends, interest, and rents received each year by individuals or family units. Median family income in the United States in 1993 was $36,959 (U.S. Bureau of the Census, 1995y). This means that half the families earned more than that amount and half earned less. However, this figure is somewhat misleading, because it tells nothing about the range of incomes above $36,959. Much more room exists at the top for high incomes than at the bottom for low incomes, as the annual earnings of many corporate executives, professional athletes, and entertainers demonstrate. In other words, the incomes of the bottom half of American families range from $0 to $36,959 annually, but the incomes of the upper half range from $36,959 to over $1 billion. However, the earnings of most American families are far closer to the figure of $36,959 than to the huge sums earned by the superrich.

Trends in Income Distribution. During the quarter-century after World War II, Americans experienced unprecedented prosperity and increases in family income. Average weekly earnings rose by 50 percent, and real median family income nearly doubled, increasing from $18,098 in 1947 to $36,893 in 1973 (in 1993 dollars). Moreover, during this period, income became more equitably distributed. In 1950 the bottom 20 percent of American families received 4.8 percent of the nation's income and the top 20 percent received 42.2 percent. By 1970, the share of the bottom 20 percent had increased to 5.5 percent, while the share of the top one-fifth had declined to 40.9 percent (see Figure 8–1). Widespread prosperity and more equitable distribution of income supported the image of the United States as a middle-class society. It also reinforced the widespread belief among Americans that the quality of their lives would always improve over that of their parents and that the quality of their children's lives would exceed theirs.

However, since the early 1970s the economic position of the U.S. middle class has stagnated. Since 1973, real median family income, which achieved an all-time high of $36,893 (in 1993 dollars), has failed to maintain the growth that occurred

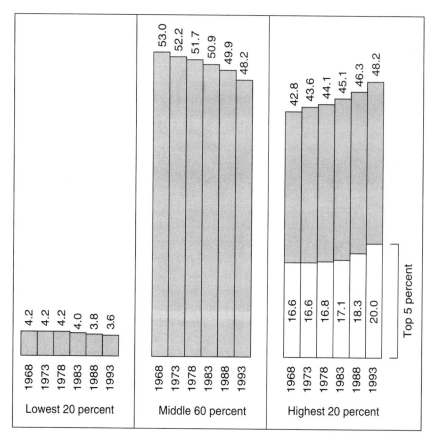

Figure 8–1.   Share of Aggregate Household Income, by Quintile: 1968 to 1993 (in percent). (*Source:* U.S. Bureau of the Census, *Current Population Reports,* Series P-60, No. 188, 1995.)

during the 1950s and 1960s. Real median family income for 1993 ($36,959) was virtually the same as in 1973 ($36,893). This stagnation in family income occurred despite a dramatic increase in married-couple families in which both spouses were in the paid labor force. In 1973, about half (49.7 percent) of wives did not hold jobs in the paid labor force; by 1994, this proportion had declined to about one-fourth (28 percent) (Crispell, 1994, p. 34). Indeed, the incomes of the bottom 80 percent of married couples with children would have declined during the 1980s without the increased earnings of wives (Mischel and Bernstein, 1992, pp. 32–36). The period of rising U.S. prosperity had ended.

In general, the trend over the past quarter-century has been toward increasing income inequality. The gap between the rich and the poor increased substantially;

the rich grew richer and the poor poorer. The data in Figures 8–1 and 8–2 show the changes in distribution of income in the United States between 1968 and 1993. Figure 8–1 shows the share of income that was received by each quintile (one-fifth) of the population. The share of national income of the poorest fifth of American households declined from 4.2 percent in 1968 to 3.6 percent in 1993, the lowest it had been since the early 1950s. On the other hand, the 48.2 percent of income received by the richest one-fifth equaled the amount obtained by the middle three-fifths and represented an all-time high.

However, focusing on the top one-fifth of the population masks the increasing concentration of income at the very top. In 1993, the top 5 percent of households (those with incomes above $113,182) received 20 percent of all income, far more than the total income for the entire lowest 40 percent of U.S. families. These recent increases in income inequality are reflected in the second measure of income inequality, an index of income concentration (technically called the *Gini* index), which ranges from 0, perfect equality, in which everyone receives the same share, to 1, perfect inequality, in which all the income is received by one individual. As income is distributed more equally, the index declines; as income inequality increases, so does the index. Although the index of income concentration has been characterized by periodic fluctuations, it declined between 1950 and 1970 and then has risen steadily, in 1993 reaching its highest level (.447) in the post–World War II period (see Figure 8–2).

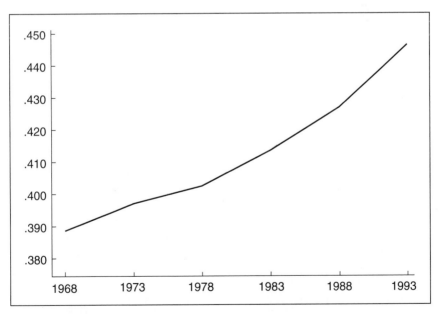

Figure 8–2.   Index of Income Concentration, 1968–1993 (*Source:* U.S. Bureau of the Census, *Current Population Reports,* Series P-60, No. 188, 1995.)

In the News

"In-Your-Face Capitalism": CEO Compensation, Corporate Downsizing, and the Wage Gap

During the past two decades, income and wealth in the United States have become increasingly unequally distributed; the rich have gotten richer and the poor have become poorer. One of the most visible manifestations of this growing disparity has been the compensation of corporate executives. For example, in 1991, Robert C. Goizueta, the CEO (chief executive officer) of Coca-Cola, received a compensation package valued at $81 million; Time Warner's CEO, Steven Ross, received more than $78 million; Paul B. Fireman of Reebok International received $33 million; and Rand V. Araskog of ITT received more than $11 million. Since 1991 this trend had accelerated. A survey of 76 of the 150 largest U.S. corporations found that the compensation of major corporate CEOs increased 9 percent annually during the first 5 years of the 1990s while the rise in workers' wages and salaries never exceeded 4 percent. In 1995 alone, the total compensation of these CEOs increased by 31 percent, to nearly $5 million annually.

These astronomical levels of compensation occurred during a period in which worker salaries stagnated, resulting in an increasing economic chasm between American top executives and workers. In 1990, for example, while the country was mired in the midst of a recession, worker layoffs were increasing, and corporate profits were weak, the pay for CEOs increased by 8 percent, more than any other group of salaried workers. Although general economic conditions had not improved, the number of CEOs at the nation's 800 largest companies who earned more than $1 million increased from 386 in the year 1990 to 407 in 1991. Overall, the average ratio of the CEO compensation to that of the typical worker increased from 30-to-1 during the 1960s to more than 100-to-1 by 1995.

These rising levels of CEO pay have been made even more dramatic by well-publicized examples of corporate downsizing—the reduction in company workforce—during the first half of the 1990s at the same time that CEO compensation was escalating. For example, in 1991, GM laid off 74,000 workers; in 1993, Sears laid off 50,000; and, in 1996, AT&T laid off 40,000 (bringing its total for the 1990s to 123,000). Indeed, one of the explanations for CEO pay increases is precisely because downsizing reduces payrolls and, therefore, increases a company's stock prices—an outcome for which CEOs are handsomely rewarded. This is a phenomenon that *Newsweek* writer Allan Sloan has dubbed "in-your-face capitalism." However, surveys of 1994 and 1995 data showed little or no relationship between CEO compensation levels and company performance.

American CEOs are much more highly paid than are their counterparts in any other major industrial nation. While major CEOs in the United States averaged $3.2 million in 1991, major corporate heads in Britain made $1.1 million; in Germany, $800,000; and in Japan, $525,000. According to Congressional testimony, whereas, in 1991, the CEO of a large U.S. corporation received 110 times the annual wages of workers in their companies, the top executives in comparable Japanese companies earned about 17 times their average worker; in Germany the gap was 23 times.

One explanation for the rising levels of CEO pay is that their compensation is not determined by shareholders but rather by boards of directors that are often selected by the CEOs themselves. Moreover, CEOs frequently serve on the boards of directors of other corporations, resulting in "board room backscratching." A recent study of 89 companies found that, although CEOs could achieve "modest" raises by improving the company's performance, the most effective way for CEOs to obtain a substantial pay increase was "to appoint to the compensation committee a highly paid fellow chief executive officer." Thus, in 1991 the CEO of Goodrich helped set the $890,000 pay of the head of the Kroger Company, who, in turn, was on the committee that recommended that the Goodrich CEO receive $905,000.

Increasingly, these skyrocketing American CEO pay levels have led legislators, stockholders, workers, and critics of American corporate competitiveness to call for limits on executive compensation and to ensure shareholders a greater role in determining it.

COHEN, ROGER. "Steve Ross Defends His Paycheck." *New York Times,* March 22, 1992.
COWAN, ALISON LEIGH. "Coke's Chief Paid a Million Shares in '91." *New York Times,* March 19, 1992.
COWAN, ALISON LEIGH. "Board Room Back-Scratching?" *New York Times*, June 2, 1992.
DOBRZYNSKI, JUDITH H. "Getting What They Deserve?" *New York Times,* February 22, 1996.
KITCHEN, STEVE, and HARDY, ERIC S. "Putting It in Perspective." *Forbes,* May 15, 1992.
LOHR, STEVE. "Recession Puts a Harsh Spotlight on Hefty Pay of Top Executives." *New York Times,* January 20, 1992.
New York Times. "Bill to Check Executive Pay." June 5, 1991.
New York Times. "Good Guys, Bad Guys." February 2, 1992.
New York Times. "Executive Pay at New Highs." May 11, 1992.
SLOAN, ALLAN. "The Hit Men." *Newsweek,* February 16, 1996.
UCHITELLE, LOUIS. "No Recession for Executive Pay." *New York Times,* March 18, 1991.
UCHITELLE, LOUIS. "1995 Was Good for Companies, and Better for a Lot of C.E.O.'s." *New York Times,* March 29, 1996.
UCHITELLE, LOUIS, and KLEINFIELD, N. R. "The Downsizing of America." *New York Times,* March 3, 1996.

Thus, since the mid-1970s, income inequality has steadily increased in the United States, with the more affluent sectors of the population, not the broad middle class, receiving a greater percentage of the nation's income. One striking index of this increase in income inequality since the mid-1970s is the percentage of full-time, year-round workers whose earnings fell below the government's official poverty level. As Figure 8–3 shows, the proportion of full-time, year-round

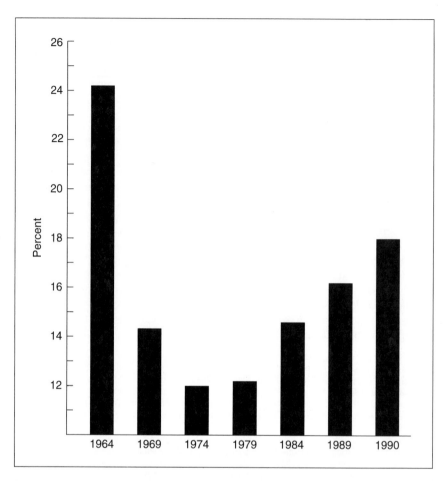

Figure 8–3. Percentage of American Workers with Low Annual Earnings, 1964–1990. (*Source:* U.S. Bureau of the Census, "Workers with Low Earnings, 1964 to 1990." *Current Population Reports,* Series P-60, No. 178, 1992, p. 3.)

workers with low wages declined dramatically between 1964 and 1974 and remained relatively stable throughout the 1970s. However, during the 1980s, a period of economic expansion that brought prosperity to the affluent, the proportion of low-wage workers increased nearly 50 percent, growing from 12.1 percent of American workers in 1979 to 18.0 percent in 1990, when a total of 14.4 million full-time, year-round workers earned wages that placed them below the poverty level (U.S. Bureau of the Census, 1992g). Similarly, income changes have increasingly become linked to education and skill levels. Between 1979 and 1989, males with less than 4 years of college saw their wages fall, while only those with postgraduate education experienced income gains. These data reflect the trend noted previously toward greater income polarization between an overclass of highly educated and technically sophisticated "symbolic analysts" and the declining economic fortunes of the less educated and skilled (Bluestone, 1995; Reich, 1992).

The growing inequalities of income and wealth in the United States are especially striking when compared to other countries. The most recent and comprehensive studies available have demonstrated that by the mid-1980s the gap between rich and poor was wider in the United States than in any Western industrialized country. The data in Figure 8–4 provide a measure of income inequality by showing the ratio of the per capita income of the richest tenth of the adult population compared to the per capita income of the poorest tenth. Thus, the income disparity ratio in the United States, 5.9, was far greater than for any other country

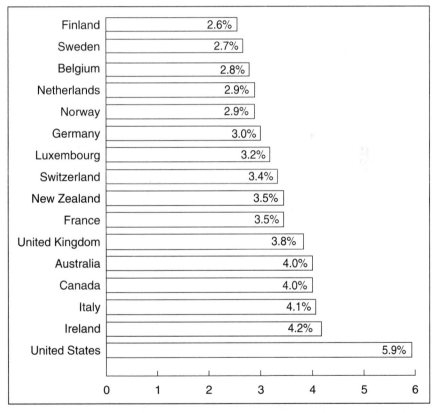

Figure 8–4.   Income Disparity Ratio: Per Capita Income of Richest Tenth of the Adult Population Compared to Per Capita Income of the Poorest Tenth, by OECD Country. (*Source:* Anthony B. Atkinson, Lee Rainwater, and Timothy M. Smeeding, *Income Distribution in OECD Countries.* Paris: Organisation for Economic Cooperation and Development, 1995, p. 40.)

and more than double that of Finland, Sweden, Belgium, Netherlands, and Norway (Atkinson et al., 1995, p. 40).

Income and the Tax Burden. Studies of economic inequality that focus on income distribution have been criticized because they generally focus on pretax income and therefore do not consider the effect of taxes on net income. The tax burden in any society may be distributed in three different ways: progressively, proportionately, or regressively. **Progressive taxes** are based on the ability to pay—the percentage of income paid in taxes *increases* as income increases; the wealthier are taxed at higher rates than the poor. **Proportional** (or flat) **taxes** place the same percentage of burden on all income levels; in other words, all incomes are taxed at the same rate. In a system of **regressive taxes,** the percentage of income paid in taxes *decreases* as income increases; the poor are taxed at higher rates than the wealthy.

The most familiar progressive tax in the United States is the federal income tax, which was established by the 13th Amendment to the Constitution in 1913. Precisely how high tax rates should be on different levels of income has been a perennial source of political controversy. One of the most dramatic changes in tax policy in the twentieth century occurred during the presidency of Ronald Reagan, when the rates for upper-income categories were reduced substantially. Between 1981 and 1988, taxes on those in the highest tax brackets fell from 70 to 28 percent. When the decrease in taxes paid by the highest income categories is combined with the increase in other federal taxes (for example, Social Security, a regressive tax), the impact of the federal tax changes of the 1980s was that the overall tax burden for all but the richest 10 percent of the population increased (Phillips, 1990, pp. 76–82).

While federal income taxes were becoming less progressive during the 1980s, state and local governments resorted with increasing frequency to regressive taxes as their primary sources of revenue. These regressive taxes included residential, business, and personal property taxes, sales taxes, and gasoline and cigarette excise taxes. A study of tax policies found that, because state and local governments rely heavily on regressive taxes, poor and middle-income families are taxed at rates significantly higher than the richest Americans, and the percentage of income paid in state and local taxes declines significantly as income increases. Thus, in 1991 a four-member family with an income in the poorest quintile (one-fifth) annually paid 13.8 percent of their $12,700 annual earnings in state and local taxes; the second-lowest one-fifth (with an average income of $26,800) paid 10.7 percent; the middle fifth (averaging $39,100) paid 9.5 percent; the second highest fifth (averaging $54,000) paid 8.4 percent; and the richest 1 percent, (whose incomes average over $875,000), paid only 6 percent. Moreover, there was considerable variation among the states. California, Delaware, Maine, and Vermont were the only states in which the rich paid a greater share of income than middle-income families, while Nevada, Texas, Florida, Washington, South Dakota, Tennessee, Wyoming, and New Hampshire taxed middle-income families at nearly twice the rates as the richest families. Poor families in Nevada, Texas, Florida, Washington, and South Dakota were taxed at five times the rate of the rich (Citizens for Tax Justice, 1991).

Wealth. Measures of income inequality alone do not adequately measure a society's stratification system. To gain an accurate picture of the distribution of a society's economic resources, we must also examine wealth, which includes savings, investments, homes, and property. Wealth represents accumulated assets or "stored-up" purchasing power.

Historical trends in the distribution of wealth show that the Colonial and immediate post-Revolutionary periods were the most egalitarian in U.S. history (Smith, 1984; Williamson and Lindert, 1980). In other words, wealth was more equally distributed during this period than at any other time. Between the early nineteenth century and the beginning of the Great Depression in 1929, economic inequalities increased. During the Great Depression and World War II, the distribution of wealth became significantly more equal. From the end of World War II to 1963, an overall increase occurred in the concentration of wealth; but then it declined, so that by 1976, for the first time in the twentieth century, the wealthiest 1 percent of Americans owned less than one-fifth (19 percent) of the nation's total assets (Wolff, 1992a). However, the most recent data available indicate that during the 1980s the trend toward more equitable distribution of wealth was dramatically reversed (Kennicknell and Shack-Marquez, 1992; Wolff, 1995a, 1995b). By 1989, wealth had become more heavily concentrated at the top than at any time since 1929; the wealthiest 1 percent of American families accounted for 39 percent of the nation's total wealth, or more than double what their share had been in 1976. This increasing concentration was especially pronounced among the very richest families, the top one-half of 1 percent, which accounted for 31 percent of the total. Indeed, these superrich families were the only category to increase their wealth during the 1980s; the percentage of wealth held by even the next richest one-half of one percent declined (Wolff, 1992b).

Thus, wealth is much more unequally distributed and heavily concentrated in the upper extremes than is income. Whereas the highest fifth of the population received 44.6 percent of the nation's income in 1989, the wealthiest quintile of families accounted for 83.6 percent of the nation's net worth (U.S. Bureau of the Census, 1990b; Wolff, 1992b).

The unequal distribution and concentration of wealth in American society is even more apparent if one distinguishes between net worth and financial wealth or net financial assets. Most studies of the distribution of wealth have relied on measures of **net worth,** which refers to the difference between a household's assets and its liabilities.

However, the net worth of most Americans who have accumulated some wealth is held almost exclusively in the investments that they have in their homes and automobiles. Oliver and Shapiro (1989) have therefore argued that the most accurate measure of the concentration of wealth in the United States should exclude equity in homes and vehicles, since these can seldom be converted to other purposes (such as financing a college education, establishing or expanding a business, or paying for emergency medical expenses). The term **net financial assets (NFA)** refers to household wealth after the equity in homes and vehicles has been deducted. If this measure of wealth (rather than net worth) is used, figures on the overall distribution of wealth in American society change dramatically. Oliver and Shapiro (1989) found that, although the overall household median net worth in 1984 was $32,609, household median net financial assets were only $2,599 (slightly less than enough for a family of four to live at the poverty level for only 3 months). Moreover, one-third of all U.S. households had zero net worth; that is, their debts outweighed their financial assets.

In more recent studies, Wolff (1992a, 1992b, 1995a, 1995b) examined 1989 data to determine whether these extreme inequalities in wealth had changed during the 1980s. Using a measure (financial wealth) similar to net financial assets, he found that between 1983 and 1989 the financial wealth of 80 percent of American households actually declined; in 1989, the typical American household had fewer disposable financial resources than they had had in 1983. However, during this same period, which was characterized by sustained economic expansion, the increase in the nation's wealth was experienced almost exclusively by the wealthiest Americans; the top 1 percent of American families accounted for nearly two-thirds (66.2 percent) of the nation's total increase in household financial wealth between 1983 and 1989. During the 1980s, the concentration of wealth became more extreme than at any time since the 1920s. By 1989, the top 1 percent owned 48 percent of the nation's financial wealth (compared to 43 percent in 1983); the top half of 1 percent (which Wolff termed the "superrich") owned 40 percent (compared to 34 percent in 1983). Thus, net financial assets (financial wealth) are even more highly concentrated and their distribution more unequal than income and net worth. Whereas the top 20 percent of American households earned over 49 percent of all income in 1989, they held 85 percent of net worth and 94 percent of all net financial assets (Wolff, 1992b, 1995a, 1995b). Although Americans have long perceived of themselves as a society characterized by a "general equality of condition," recent studies suggest that the inequalities in wealth in the United States, as described, are greater than in other western industrialized countries (Great Britain, Sweden, and France) for which comparable data are available. "By the late 1980s, [there was] a much higher concentration of wealth in the United States than in Europe. Europe now appears the land of equality" (Wolff, 1995a, p. 21).

The Shrinking Middle Class

As these recent trends indicate, then, both income and wealth are unequally distributed in American society, and, during the past two decades, these inequalities have increased substantially. The economic fortunes of an extremely well educated and technically skilled and sophisticated *overclass* have improved substantially at the same time that those of the poorly educated, relatively unskilled, and extremely poor *underclass* have deteriorated. Simultaneously, the political and economic forces underlying this growing polarization of the haves and have-nots have produced a decline in the size of the American middle class.

These trends were observed in a recent study by Duncan et al. (1992), who followed a nationally representative sample of families for more than 20 years (1968–1989) to determine how their mobility was affected by broad economic changes during this period. Using two different measures, they found that the proportion of American adults who could be broadly defined as middle class declined from 78 percent in 1978 to 67 percent in 1986. Some of the decline occurred because some people moved into upper-income categories. However, an even greater percentage dropped out of the middle class and joined America's poor. The 1980s "were simultaneously a time of enhanced upward mobility [especially for the college educated] and more frequent downward mobility.... The probability of falling from middle-income to lower-income status increased significantly after 1980" (Duncan et al., 1992, pp. 36, 38). Moreover, they contend that, given the underlying conditions producing these trends, the recession of 1990–1992 should have greatly enhanced the increase in upper-middle-class opportunity, but further reinforced the probability of downward mobility for lower-income members of the middle class.

The implications of these changes in the distribution of wealth and income in American society have been noted by writers from a variety of political and scholarly perspectives (Bluestone, 1995; Hernnstein and Murray, 1994; Lasch, 1995; Lind, 1995; Reich, 1992, 1995), who have voiced concern over growing social inequality in American society. Commenting on these trends, especially the erosion of the middle class, which he characterizes as "one of America's greatest crises," Phillips (1993) foresees that disenchantment and growing alienation as a result of these changed living standards will provide the underlying basis for the politics of the 1990s.

Poverty. In most complex societies throughout human history, the vast majority of people were propertyless. The existence of sharp disparities between a small elite class comprised of wealthy property holders and a huge propertyless underclass was so common a feature of most complex societies that poverty was simply taken for granted and perceived to be inevitable. This perception was reinforced by the Bible: "For ye have the poor always with you" (Matthew 26:11) and "The poor shall never cease out of the land" (Deuteronomy 15:11). However, in modern American society, the most affluent in human history, the existence of poverty appears as an anomaly, a glaring contradiction and one that has been the subject of considerable debate (Murray, 1984; Harrington, 1984; Sandefur and Tienda, 1988; Jencks and Peterson, 1991).

Obviously, poverty is a relative concept. Many people would argue that the lives of extremely poor people in rural Mississippi or in New York City are considerably better than those of impoverished families in Calcutta, India, who are forced to live, eat, sleep, and die on the street. Similarly, poor families in the United States live better lives than most families did in preindustrial times.

However, Americans do not live hundreds of years ago or in Calcutta today. We live in a society that takes for granted many gains in the quality and security of life. We find it intolerable that people should live on the streets or die at an early age of minor ailments (as they did in preindustrial times). Nevertheless, even in the United States today, the poor suffer from hunger, inadequate shelter, and premature death.

The most widely used definition of poverty in the United States is based on the idea of *income sufficiency,* the amount of money needed to purchase the basic necessities of life. Although several standards might be used to determine what level of income is sufficient, the measure used by the Social Security Administration has become the official government index of poverty. The **poverty index** utilizes the U.S. Department of Agriculture estimates of the cost of a minimal food budget, adjusted to the size of the family. The per person daily food budget is multiplied by 3 to determine the approximate level of funds needed for all other living costs: housing, clothes, medical care, heat, electricity, and other necessities. Therefore, in 1993 the index classified as poor all families of four with an income of less than $14,763 (U.S. Bureau of the Census, 1995, p. 21). By this measure, 39.3 million Americans, 15.1 percent of the population, lived below the poverty level in 1993.

Who are America's poor? Many Americans think of them as the "dregs" of society, its most disreputable members. The poor are often visualized as skid-row winos, "bag ladies," able-bodied adults who prefer welfare to working, and so on. However, the reality is that the poor do not fit our stereotypes so easily. For one thing, there are large numbers of working people who earn so little from their work that their income is below the poverty level. In the post-World War II era until the mid-1970s, poverty was primarily the result of not having a job, but increasingly people in poverty are working full-time, but hold jobs that do not provide a living wage (Reich, 1992, p. 203). As noted previously, in 1990 14.4 million full-time workers received wages that were insufficient to lift a family of four from poverty (U.S. Bureau of the Census, 1992i).

Recent data from the U.S. Bureau of the Census (1992g; 1995) indicate these characteristics of the poor:

- The poverty rate for African American (33 percent) and Hispanic (31 percent) families is more than three times that of non-Hispanic whites (9.9 percent). However, two-thirds (67 percent) of the poor are white.

- Many poor people live in two-parent families. However, one striking recent trend in the United States has been the *feminization of poverty,* the increasing percentage of impoverished families that are headed by women. In 1993, more than half (53 percent) of families in poverty were headed by women. Moreover, although in most countries women are more likely than men to be poor, a recent cross-national comparison of poverty rates by gender showed that women in the United States were 41 percent more likely to live in poverty than men—the greatest difference between male and female poverty rates in any of the eight Western countries examined (Casper et al., 1994).

- Of the 39.3 million poor Americans, 40 percent (15.7 million) were children under 28 years of age; of those poor 16 to 24 years of age, more than 40 percent were students.

- More than half (53.2 percent) of poor adults were high school graduates and about one-sixth (18.7 percent) had completed one or more years of college.

- About 10 percent of the poor (3.8 million) were aged 65 and older.

- Of those poor over 16 years of age, nearly one-fifth (19 percent) were disabled.

- More than one-fourth (27 percent) of the population living below the poverty level received no governmental assistance whatsoever; less than half of the poor received public assistance payments.

This profile of poverty in the United States shows that the stereotypical portrait of the poor is overly simplistic. First, many of those living in poverty are doing so because of economic conditions beyond their control. For example, thousands of blue-collar workers in "smokestack" industries have lost their jobs as manufacturing plants have shut down or moved; thousands of family farmers, caught between rising production costs and falling prices for their products, have been forced into bankruptcy. Second, nearly 40 percent of those living in poverty are working or seeking more stable work. Third, many of those included in the categories mentioned—children under 18, some people over 65, the handicapped or disabled—are unable to work. Finally, the poverty category contains a disproportionate number of single mothers. Therefore, whereas some people are poor because employment is not available or because their employment does not pay a living wage, a great many poor people are unemployable under existing conditions rather than unemployed. The vast majority of the poor did not create their condition of poverty and are virtually powerless to change it on their own.

During the past quarter-century, changes have occurred in the extent of poverty in the United States. In 1959, the first year for which comparable data were collected, 39.5 million people, or 22.4 percent of the population, were below the poverty line. Those figures declined steadily throughout the 1960s until, by 1973, they reached low points of 23.0 million people, or 11.1 percent of the population. The major decline occurred during the middle 1960s, when poverty programs initiated by the Kennedy and Johnson administrations were in full-scale operation. This was the same period during which real family incomes rose dramatically and the distribution of income and wealth became more equal.

The **poverty rate** (the percentage of the population below the poverty line) remained fairly stable through the 1970s until the recession late in that decade, when it began to rise (see Figure 8–5). This increase was further spurred by substantial cuts by the Reagan administration in social welfare assistance programs. The number of people in poverty continued to climb until 1984, when the poverty rate fell to 14.4, its first decline since 1978. Since the late 1980s the poverty rate

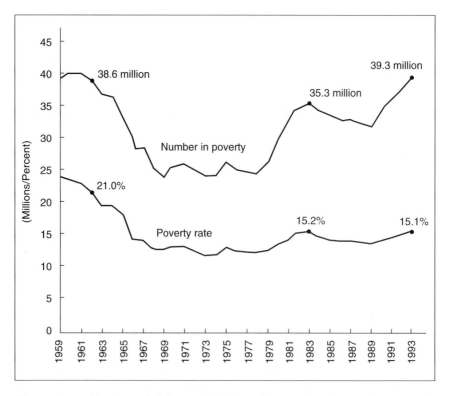

Figure 8–5. Number of Poor and Poverty Rate, 1959–1993. (*Source:* U.S. Bureau of the Census, "Income, Poverty and Valuation of Noncash Benefits: 1993." *Current Population Reports,* Series P-60, No. 188, 1995.)

has continued to rise again, in 1993 standing at 15.1, about the same level that it had been in 1983.

The poverty rate provides us with an annual snapshot of the percentage of people experiencing poverty at one point in time; for example, in 1991 about one-seventh (14.2 percent) of the U.S. population lived below the poverty level. Such figures convey the impression of a permanent and well-defined group of "poor people." However, these figures obscure the turnover among the low-income population. An intensive study of U.S. families between 1968 and 1978 revealed that one-quarter of the U.S. population lived below the poverty level for at least 1 year during that period, but only slightly more than half of those living in poverty in 1 year were still poor the next year (Duncan et al., 1984). Similarly, a recent Census Bureau study that examined transitions into and out of poverty showed that about one-fourth of those who were poor in 1987 were not poor in 1988 (U.S. Bureau of the Census, 1992e, p. xix). However, several recent studies have shown that poverty was somewhat more enduring in the 1980s than it had been in the 1970s (Jencks, 1991, pp. 35–36) and, as noted previously, that upward mobility for lower-income people has become increasingly difficult (Duncan et al., 1992). Finally, Browne (1995) has found evidence of a cohort effect in poverty. Among whites born during and, especially, after the baby boom, "every successive generation of family heads . . . faces an increasingly greater chance of being born poor" (1995, p. 1072). She argues that this generational increase in poverty is *not* simply a result of changes in household structure (that is, an increase in female-headed families), but is rather a broader structural pattern that is growing with each successive generation.

The Underclass.   Although a substantial minority of the U.S. population lives in poverty at some point in life, for most of the poor this condition is not permanent. However, numerous scholars have recently begun to describe the lives of the most impoverished segment of American society, those who not only are economically marginal but are also concentrated in extreme poverty areas and are socially isolated from the rest of society. They contend that this social category at the very bottom of the social pyramid, referred to as the **underclass,** represents a steadily increasing and persistent form of poverty in the United States. Found primarily in the nation's inner cities, the underclass is characterized by high rates of joblessness, out-of-wedlock births, families headed by females, welfare dependency, school drop-outs, and serious crime. Although the underclass is disproportionately black and Hispanic, it also includes a substantial number of whites.

The concept of an underclass has been raised most prominently by Wilson (1987, 1989a, 1991), who has argued that the growth of the urban underclass—the "truly disadvantaged"—results from major economic changes in U.S. society that have caused extremely high levels of inner-city unemployment. Earlier in the twentieth century, relatively uneducated and unskilled native and immigrant workers were able to find stable employment and income in manufacturing. However, today, as a result of changes in the global economy, manufacturing jobs have moved from inner cities to the suburbs, the Sun Belt, or overseas; and the jobs created in the cities demand credentials that most inner-city residents do not possess. Thus, inner-city residents find themselves without prospects for work. Moreover, as many stable working-class and middle-class residents with job qualifications have moved from the inner cities into better residential neighborhoods, the stability of neighborhood social institutions (for example, churches, schools, and recreational facilities) has been undermined, and the social fabric of community life has deteriorated. The underclass has become increasingly isolated, socially and economically.

The notion of an underclass has been the subject of considerable debate (Wilson, 1989b; Jencks and Peterson, 1991). Some critics contend that the term *underclass* should be abandoned. For example, Gans (1990) has argued that the term has become a highly ideological and value-laden buzzword; people included in the underclass have been perceived as disreputable, the "undeserving poor," who could and should earn a living for themselves. Thus, the underclass has come for many people to refer not to a category of people made jobless by faults in the economy, but rather by moral faults in the jobless themselves.

Moreover, critics have charged that the term is analytically imprecise and tends to lump together under a single rubric several different characteristics assumed to be found among all members of the underclass. For example, Jencks (1991) argued that there are several kinds of underclasses, including an impoverished underclass, a jobless underclass, an educational underclass, a violent underclass, and a reproductive underclass. He found that, while some conditions (for example, job opportunities for those without higher education and the incidence of single-parent families) deteriorated during the 1970s and 1980s for those on the bottom of the social pyramid, on a number of other indicators—high school drop-out rates, teenage pregnancy rates, and violent crime—conditions improved. Given these contradictory trends, Jencks argues that the idea of a single, uniform, and growing underclass actually obscures, rather than helps to understand, what is actually happening to those at the very bottom of U.S. society.

Homelessness

One of the most visible manifestations of extreme poverty, especially pronounced in urban areas of the United States today, is the increasing numbers of homeless people. The homeless have existed throughout U.S. history. However, homelessness became especially acute during the Great Depression of the 1930s. As unemployment rates soared, some people were forced to "take to the road" in search of employment. Some became hobos, unemployed wanderers who illegally used the railroads as their means of transportation. The struggles, sorrows, and desperation of these people were shared by folksong writer and singer Woody Guthrie (1912–

1967), who traveled with the homeless and recorded their lives in such songs as "The Hobo's Lullaby."

The homeless today, however, are different from those in Guthrie's time, because homelessness then was more likely to be either a chosen life-style or a temporary condition based on the extreme economic conditions of the 1930s. Today, homelessness is a more serious problem because few people freely choose such a life, and it is far more likely to be a permanent condition. Moreover, unlike the homeless in the past, who were generally confined to a city's skid-row section, today it is difficult for most urban dwellers to escape contact with the homeless, who are increasingly likely to be found near the homes and office buildings of the most affluent members of society. People living and sleeping in makeshift cardboard shelters in city parks, huddled over steam grates on city pavements, and panhandling or berating pedestrians—these are part of the reality that intrudes on the lives of most urban residents and visitors today. Thus, the problem of homelessness is glaringly apparent "in the very midst of day-to-day urban existence" (Rossi, 1992, p. 14).

Who are the homeless and where do they come from? How widespread is homelessness in the United States? There has been considerable controversy over both these questions. Estimates of the numbers of the homeless people nationally range from 250,000 to 500,000 to between 1.5 and 3 million at any specific time (White, 1991; Giamo and Grunberg, 1992, p. 9; Rossi, 1989, p. 17; Burt, 1992). The lower figures are derived from several detailed studies; the higher figures have been advanced by advocates for the homeless. The discrepancy between these estimates is reflected by a systematic study of Chicago's homeless in 1985 by Rossi (1989), who found about 2,700 homeless people on an average night (4,600 to 7,000 different individuals during the course of a year), a striking contrast to the figure of 15,000 to 20,000 claimed by advocates for the homeless (Rossi, 1989; Giamo and Grunberg, 1992, pp. 8–9). However, federal government estimates placed the number of people who were homeless at some time between 1985 and 1990 at 7 million (Jencks, 1994a). Whatever the correct figure, there is agreement that the number of homeless during the past decade is significantly higher than in the past.

In addition to their increasing numbers and visibility, the *new* homeless of the 1980s and 1990s can be distinguished in several ways from the *old* homeless of the past.

- Whereas the old homeless were overwhelmingly unattached men, in recent years there has been a significant increase in the percentage of homeless women and homeless families. Studies conducted during the 1980s found that women comprised between one-tenth and one-third of the homeless (Rossi, 1989, p. 20). Similarly, Bassuk and associates (1986) estimated that families comprised over 20 percent of the homeless population in 1985. Because these families are almost always headed by women, there has been an increasing feminization of homelessness that is a reflection of the broader feminization of poverty in the United States.

- The homeless today are much younger than in the past; few elderly are found among the new homeless, whose median ages tend to be in the mid-thirties (Rossi, 1989, p. 20).

- Whereas the old homeless were overwhelmingly white, homeless people today are disproportionately black, Hispanic, and Native American. "Minorities are consistently overrepresented among the new homeless" (Rossi, 1989, p. 21).

- The new homeless are much less likely to be employed, and they have less income than homeless people in the past. "Today's homeless are clearly among the poorest of the poor" (Rossi, 1989, p. 20). Their meager income places the cost of even the cheapest housing beyond the means of most homeless people, leaving them dependent on the services provided by charitable organizations.

- The homeless suffer disproportionately from both physical and mental illnesses, and their average age of death is only slightly over 50. Although the estimates of mental illness among the new homeless vary significantly, most studies report that about one-third of the homeless have severe mental disorders, a figure about double the estimates of mental illness among the old homeless. Many of the homeless are among the chronically mentally ill who have been *deinstitutionalized,* that is, released from the mental institutions where they had in many instances been involuntarily held. Moreover, the number of homeless has been increased by those who are mentally ill but who have either rejected or been rejected for care by mental hospitals. Jencks (1994c) agrees with Rossi's conclusions that "The de- and noninstitutionalization processes of the past three decades have significantly contributed to the increased presence of the chronically mentally ill among today's homeless" (Rossi, 1989, p. 23).

- Similar to the old homeless, the homeless today disproportionately suffer from the effects of alcohol and substance abuse. In Rossi's Chicago homeless study, one-third of those interviewed reported having been in a detoxification unit at least once (Rossi, 1989, p. 25). Moreover, after having reviewed a wide range of literature, Jencks argues that a major factor contributing to the rise in homelessness during the 1980s was an increase in heavy drug use, especially of crack. The result was that marginally employable adults become even less employable, money for food and rent was used to support their habit, and friends and relatives were less likely to shelter them (Jencks, 1994c, p. 26).

Explanations for the New Homeless.   The preceding discussion has focused on the personal and social characteristics of the homeless population, but it provides little explanation for the existence of homelessness today. Such a description tends to explain homelessness as a consequence of the personal failings of the homeless people themselves and to ignore the manner in which social policies and economic and political changes in the structure of the larger society may have contributed to its growth. In other words, are such character traits as alcoholism, drug abuse, and mental illness a cause of homelessness, or, rather, a consequence of the circumstances of extreme poverty and deprivation in which homeless people find themselves?

From a broader sociological perspective, therefore, the existence of homelessness reflects the distribution of power and resources in American society. Specifically, the increase in homelessness has been affected by the decline of inexpensive housing in urban America. Jencks argues that, although federal subsidies for low-cost housing actually increased during the 1980s, only one-third of eligible low-income households received such subsidies. Moreover, in many cities, housing once occupied by the very poor, such as skid-row flophouses (called "cubicle hotels" or "lodging houses") has been destroyed and in some cases replaced by accommodations for the affluent (Jencks, 1994a; Rossi, 1989; Kozol, 1989). In other situations, gentrification of inner-city housing (see Chapter 17) has displaced the poor from the cheapest housing without providing alternative housing for them to occupy. Thus, the greater the availability of housing in a city is, the lower the rate of homelessness.

Rossi (1989) points out that the decline of affordable low-cost housing has both a direct and an indirect impact on homelessness, both of which reflect the impact of poverty on homelessness.

> The direct effect is obvious; if one's income is only three or four dollars a day and the cheapest possible place to live costs seven or eight dollars a day, then even the alternative is more subtle but no less important: the loss of low-income housing pushes more and more poverty households into carrying high rent burdens, which in turn leaves them with proportionately less income with which to help their dependent adult members. If housing alone eats up 50 percent to 70 percent or more of the monthly income, then tough choices must be made in order to survive on the income that remains. One choice would be to turn out household members who, in better circumstances, could be allowed to stay...(Rossi, 1989, p. 33).

A second structural factor that has contributed to the increase in homelessness is the decline in opportunities for unskilled labor that has accompanied the shift from an industrial to a service economy and a rise in unemployment, especially for young male workers. As our discussion of the underclass indicated, each of these factors has diminished the earnings prospects of the poor and has had the effect of pushing many of the most disadvantaged into a situation of homelessness (Blau, 1992; Jencks, 1994c).

Thus, the situation of the homeless is inextricably linked with the structure of the American economy and with public policies. In the public mind the homeless are usually perceived as responsible for their own fate: they are on the streets primarily because they are mentally ill, alcoholics, drug addicts, or deviant in some other respect. These characteristics are, indeed, found disproportionately among the homeless. However, Wright (1989, p. 108) estimates that, because these problems often occur together, a majority of the homeless do not suffer from these disabilities. Rather, most of the homeless are unskilled workers (and their families) who have gone in and out of the job market in dead-end, low-paying jobs that do not enable them to get off the streets. These people are trapped in poor economic conditions that lead to further poverty and despair.

Inequalities of Status

The importance of status as a key dimension of stratification in U.S. society was demonstrated in one of the classic studies in sociology. Analyzing a New England community he called "Yankee City," W. Lloyd Warner began his research on the community's stratification system with the assumption that economic factors would be the most important in determining stratification (Warner and Lunt, 1941). But he found that the prestige of people's social backgrounds and life-styles (for example, neighborhoods in which they lived, clubs to which they belonged), as well as their income levels, determined where they were ranked by others in the stratification system.

One of the most frequently used indices of status in modern societies is occupational prestige. Table 8–1 shows the prestige ratings given to various occupations in American society. The most prestigious occupations are usually compensated by substantial incomes, but they frequently require highly technical skills or are associated with political power. Thus, occupational categories with low prestige can possibly have incomes exceeding those with higher prestige. In many areas of the country the incomes of plumbers exceed that of college professors, despite the higher prestige associated with being a professor. In most cases, however, a close relationship exists between class and status positions.

One striking feature of the studies on occupational prestige is that occupational rankings in American society have shown little change since the first such studies were conducted in 1947. Moreover, considerable research has demonstrated that strong similarities exist in the occupational prestige rankings in most industrial countries and industrializing societies, such as China, as well (Inkeles and Rossi, 1956; Treiman, 1977; Lin and Xie, 1988). Finally, there is considerable cross-national agreement that low status jobs (for example, an unskilled worker or bus driver) should earn less than higher-status occupations (for example, a physician), although there are social class and national differences on how much the wage inequalities between the high- and low-status jobs should be. On

Table 8–1   Occupational Prestige Rankings, 1989

Occupation	Score
Physician	86
Department head in a state government	76
Lawyer	75
College professor	74
Physicist	74
Computer scientist	74
Architect	73
Chemist	73
Biologist	73
Judge	72
Dentist	72
Aeronautical engineer	72
Mayor of a large city	70
Geologist	70
Clergy	69
Civil engineer	69
Psychologist	69
Pharmacist	68
Medical technician	68
Secondary school teacher	66
Registered nurse	66
Accountant	65
Professional athlete	64
Elementary school teacher	64
Economist	63
Veterinarian	62
General manager of a manufacturing plant	62
Airline pilot	61
Journalist	60
Police officer	59
Musician in a symphony orchestra	59
Actor	58
Superintendent of a construction job	57
Statistician	56
Librarian	54
Artist	53
Firefighter	53
Farmer (owner–operator)	53
Ballet dancer	53
Social worker	52
Urban planner	52
Electrician	51
Funeral director	49
Manager of a supermarket	48
Real estate agent	49

Continued

Table 8–1   Continued

Occupation	Score
Machinist	47
Mail carrier	47
Insurance agent	46
Musician	46
Secretary	46
Photographer	45
Plumber	45
Jewelry maker	45
Bank teller	43
Postal clerk	42
Welder	42
Travel agent	41
Automobile mechanic	40
Carpenter	39
Longshoreman	37
Barber	36
Hairdresser	36
Bricklayer	36
Shoe repairer	36
Child-care worker	36
Assembly-line worker	35
Butcher	35
House painter	34
Housekeeper in a private home	34
Cook in a restaurant	34
Cashier in a supermarket	33
Bus driver	32
Logger	31
Truck driver	30
Gardener	29
Taxicab driver	28
Waiter or waitress	28
Garbage collector	28
Bartender	25
Bill collector	24
Farm laborer	23
Cleaning person in a private home	23
Janitor	22
Gas station attendant	21
Newspaper peddler	19
Car wash attendant	19

Source: Keiko Nakao and Judith Treas. "Computing 1989 Occupational Prestige Scores." *General Social Survey Methodological Report Number 70.* Chicago: National Opinion Research Center, 1990.

the one hand, high SES groups support higher pay for elite occupations (although they do not favor lower pay for low-status jobs). On the other hand, communist countries favor a much more egalitarian wage distribution than capitalist countries, and, among capitalist countries, Americans support substantial wage inequalities between high- and low-status jobs, while Australians are the most egalitarian (Kelley and Evans, 1993).

As Warner suggested, however, status is not determined solely by occupation. Ancestry, religious affiliation, place of residence, life-style, amount of education, and many other factors have all been associated with an individual's status. There may be contradictions among these different factors: for example, sex and race might affect the prestige attached to occupants of a particular occupation. Acker (1980) found that predominantly female ("pink-collar") jobs have a lower average prestige than traditionally male occupations. This finding was reinforced by Bose and Rossi (1983), who found a substantial overall difference in the prestige ratings of traditionally women's jobs (for example, housekeeper, dental assistant, private secretary, registered nurse) and predominantly men's jobs (for example, garbage collector, electrical engineer, building construction contractor, plumber).

Some Consequences of the U.S. Stratification System

During the 1988 presidential campaign, Republican candidate George Bush asserted that class is "for European democracies or something else—it isn't for the United States of America. We are not going to be divided by class" (quoted in DeMott, 1990). President Bush's sentiments reflect a widespread tendency among Americans to deny the objective reality of class in the United States. However, such a tendency is not restricted to residents of the United States. In a study of six western democratic societies, Kelly and Evans (1995) found that most people subjectively perceive themselves as middle-class, regardless of their objective position in the social hierarchy, and they also perceive little class conflict in their particular society.

In this section we focus on the effects or consequences of one's place in the system of stratification. We will concentrate on the differences in life-style and life chances for people in various strata, especially the poor. We have already mentioned that life chances—the likelihood of realizing a certain standard of living or quality of life—are influenced by position in the social hierarchy. Numerous factors, including life expectancy, cause of death, and mental and physical health, are all related to people's positions in the stratification system. Conversely, people's places in the system affect their life-styles: tastes, fashions, preferences, and other ways in which they lead their lives. Life-styles may include such items as one's type of home, vacations, leisure-time activities, reading habits, and sexual behaviors.

Health

As we will see more fully in Chapter 14, economic inequalities are significantly related to physical and mental health. In the United States and most other societies, people in the lower classes are more likely to suffer from poor physical and mental health than those in the higher socioeconomic groups (Syme and Berkman, 1981; Rainwater, 1968; Hollingshead and Redlich, 1958; Cockerham, 1986). For example, a disproportionate number of poor people suffer the disabling effects of chronic illnesses. In fact, the rates of disability among the poor for the major chronic illnesses—heart disease, arthritis and rheumatism, back and spine ailments, impairments of the legs or hips, and hypertension—are nearly double those of the nonpoor (Newacheck et al., 1980).

On the basis of their systematic review of the relationship between income and illness, Newacheck and colleagues conclude that there is "a substantial health gap between 'poor' and 'nonpoor' families in the United States" (Newacheck et al., 1980, p. 143). Summarizing a considerable body of research dealing with the impact of social class factors on health, Cockerham (1986) comes to a similar conclusion: "On nearly every measure, membership in the lower classes carries health penalties. . . . To be poor is by definition to have less of the things (including health care) produced by society" (Cockerham, 1986, p. 49).

Nevertheless, Navarro (1990, 1991) maintains that there has been a "deafening silence" in the United States on how class affects public health, and he points out that the United States is the only Western developed nation that does not collect mortality statistics by class (Navarro, 1990, p. 1238). Instead, U.S. data focus on differences in racial patterns of disease and mortality rates. However important racial factors are in determining how people live, get sick, and die, researchers such as Navarro argue that the focus on the substantial racial disparities in health has masked how closely linked class factors are to patterns of death and disease among Americans.

For example, the impact of class factors on health has been increasingly apparent in America's inner cities, where poverty and inadequate medical services have contributed to dramatic increases in the incidence of tuberculosis, hepatitis A, gonorrhea, measles, mumps, whooping cough, ear infections, and AIDS. So severe is the crisis in health and medical care in poverty areas of the country that medical experts compare conditions in these areas with underdeveloped countries. For example, the New York City region has a worse record of immunization against a range of childhood diseases, including measles, tuberculosis, tetanus, polio, diphtheria, and whooping cough, than many Third World countries. Only 40 percent of children in New York had completed the recommended series of vaccinations by age 2. In contrast, 98 percent of children in Cuba, Chile, Antigua, and North Korea; 89 percent in Algeria; 77 percent in Uganda; and 76 percent in El Salvador had been vaccinated (Lee, 1991, p. B12). As a consequence, as one physician remarked, "We're seeing scenes straight out of underdeveloped countries, diseases that haven't been seen in the United States since the turn of the century" (Rosenthal, 1990, p. A1).

Numerous researchers, while acknowledging the impact of race, contend that class is a more important factor than race in predicting health. For example, one of the few studies in the United States that included information on class concluded that mortality rates for heart disease were strongly related to class: people with less education, less income, and blue-collar occupations were 2.3 times more likely to die of heart disease than managers and professionals, and these differences were far greater than black–white mortality differences (Navarro, 1991, pp. 3–4). Similarly, researchers found that class differences in morbidity (illness) were more substantial than race differences. People with annual family incomes of less than $14,000 were nearly 4.5 times more likely to assess their health as fair or poor than those making over $50,000 (National Center for Health Statistics, 1992, p. 23). Similarly, people making less than $10,000 were 4.6 times more likely to report having been sick than those earning over $35,000, while blacks reported getting sick 1.9 times as frequently as whites. Thus the racial difference was less than half the class difference (Gladwell, 1990; Navarro, 1990). Moreover, a 1991 study by the National Cancer Institute found that the most important factors influencing the incidence of cancer were low income and poor living conditions (Okie, 1991).

Another critical way in which class affects health is the availability of medical care. The United States spends a greater share (12.4 percent in 1990) of its gross domestic product on health care than any other major industrialized country (Canada had the second largest share, 9.0 percent). Despite this massive allocation of resources to health care, the United States today is the only major industrialized country except South Africa without a program of national health care; as a consequence, at any one time in 1996, 42 million people (one-sixth of the population under 65) had no medical insurance; 58 million were without such insurance at some time during the year (Eckholm, 1994, p. A7).

However, those lacking medical insurance coverage are not randomly distributed throughout the population; access to health care is closely affected by one's class position. Therefore, the increasing disparities between the rich and the poor that characterized the American class structure during the 1980s and into the 1990s are reflected in changes in medical insurance coverage. In 1980, 31 percent of Americans under 65 with incomes of less than $14,000 had no medical coverage, compared with 4 percent of those with incomes over $50,000. However, by 1989, reflecting the restructuring of the American economy and, especially, the declining middle class, more than 39 percent of those with incomes of less than $14,000 had no medical insurance coverage, while only 3 percent of those with $50,000 or more did not have it (National Center for Health Statistics, 1992a, p. 291).

Central to this crisis of health care is that in the United States, unlike most other countries, health care benefits are provided primarily through employers and the workplace. Increasingly, as occupational restructuring and inequalities in wealth and income have increased, so also have the numbers of Americans who have no health benefits coverage. Moreover, for many Americans who do have health care coverage, their benefits have been reduced and the costs of their medical care increased. Finally, the absence of medical insurance is not restricted to those who do not work or work only part time. In 1992 more than half of those who lacked health insurance were employed full time (Eckholm, 1994).

Life Expectancy

Life expectancy refers to the average number of years that people in a particular demographic or social category will live. The effect of social class on life expectancy is dramatically illustrated by the fate of passengers on the luxury liner *Titanic,* which sank in 1912. Of the 143 first-class female passengers on board, only four perished, and of those four, three chose to remain with the ship. Of the 93 second-class female passengers, 15 perished. However, 81 of the 179 third-class female passengers died as the ship went down (Lord, 1955). On the *Titanic,* as in society in general, life expectancy is related to one's position in the social hierarchy.

In a survey of a number of studies on the relationship between social rank and life expectancy, Antonovsky (1967) found that socioeconomic position has a significant effect upon life expectancy. In societies in which overall death rates are either very low or very high, only small differences exist between classes. Low death rates reflect great achievements in the battle against death, while high death rates reflect people's helplessness. In these extreme cases, position in the stratification system makes little difference. However, in societies where moderate progress has been made in reducing the death rate, differences are likely to be great because relatively scarce resources (such as new drugs and new medical techniques) are more available to members of the upper strata.

Studies conducted in the United States for more than 50 years have consistently supported Antonovsky's conclusions (Daugherty and Kammeyer, 1995). Two national studies, one conducted in the 1960s and the other in the 1970s, found that when educational level is used as a measure of social class position, those with higher educational attainment have much lower mortality rates than those with lower educational attainment (Kitagawa and Hauser, 1968; Rosen and Taubman, 1979). Rosen and Taubman's study, which was limited to the white population, found that the least-educated people had death rates that ranged from 40 to 60 percent higher than the most-educated people (Rosen and Taubman, 1979). A pronounced difference was also noted when family income was used as a measure of social class. The death rate for the lowest income groups was 2.75 times higher than for the highest income groups. A study of the causes of the deaths of over 48,000 white Oregon residents between 1976 and 1984 found that residents of the poorest census tracts had the highest mortality rates for all causes of death; the wealthiest had the lowest. The greatest difference between the poorest and wealth- iest groups was found in deaths attributed to alcoholism, in which the lowest income group's index of potential life lost was 11.7 times higher than the index for the most wealthy group (United States Centers for Disease Control, 1988).

The higher death rates of people in lower social classes may be the result of a variety of factors. Since the economic resources of the middle and upper classes are greater, they may put their resources toward better environmental conditions or more extensive health care. The lower classes may have little money left for medical care after they provide for the necessities of food, clothing, and shelter (Rosen and Taubman, 1979).

People are also becoming increasingly aware that the occupations of members of the lower social strata are directly related to their higher mortality rates. One reason for the lower prestige of certain occupations is that they are more danger- ous to health and life. Occupations such as underground mining, lumbering, oil drilling, and construction all have a greater chance of leading to accidental deaths. But although accidents may cause some deaths, evidence has also shown that con- ditions of the workplace may have delayed effects on health, thus reducing the length of life. Coal miners and cotton mill workers are known to have a high inci- dence of respiratory diseases (black and brown lung diseases) that lead to higher mortality rates. The long-term effects of working with asbestos materials, lead, and various petrochemicals are almost certainly injurious to health, and probably produce higher death rates (Fox and Adelstein, 1978).

Criminal Justice

The impact of social class on life chances is strikingly apparent in the area of criminal justice. The sociological literature on the relationship between social class and criminal behavior, however, has produced contradictory findings. On the basis of an extensive review of studies examining this relationship, Tittle, Villemez, and Smith conclude that "class and criminality are not now, and proba- bly never were related, at least not in the recent past" (Tittle et al., 1978, p. 652). However, Braithwaite (1981), who conducted a review of studies of social class and juvenile crime, concluded that there is an inverse relationship between social class and crime; lower-class people commit more crimes against people, which are more likely to come to the attention of the police, than middle-class people do. Finally, depending on how social status is defined, Thornberry and Farnsworth (1982) found that social class background is not related to criminal behavior by juveniles. Among adults, however, an individual's educational attainment and job stability are both inversely related to criminal behavior; those with low educa- tional attainment and unstable jobs have higher rates of criminal behavior.

However, most studies analyzing the relationship of social class and criminal behavior have not dealt with white-collar crime (including embezzlement, fraud, and bribery), which is almost exclusively an upper-class and upper-middle-class phenomenon. It is also more lucrative than other forms of crime. For example, the U.S. Chamber of Commerce estimates that white-collar crime costs over $40 billion annually, over 250 times the amount of all bank robberies, and more than ten times the annual amount in thefts (Reiman, 1979, p. 106). Yet the rates of arrests and convictions and lengths of sentences for white-collar crime are nowhere near as severe as those for index offenses, or street crimes.

The poor are disadvantaged in their relationship to the criminal justice system in several ways. First, they are much more likely to be victims of violent crimes. Moreover, they are more likely to be suspected of crimes by the police, and as a result, they are more likely to be arrested and charged with crimes. Higher-class individuals arrested for the same offenses are more apt to be released without being charged (Reiman, 1979). Once arrested, the poor are less able to afford bail. Often they must stay in jail until they are tried, which limits their ability to gather information for their defense. Because they probably cannot afford a private lawyer, they are forced to use overworked public defenders, who often lack the resources of private lawyers. In court they are likely to appear guilty because their dress, manner, and speech differ from that of judges and jury members, who are usually members of the middle or upper classes. If they are convicted, the poor cannot often afford to appeal their cases. When they do get out of jail, their poverty and their jail records prevent them from getting good jobs or perhaps any jobs at all. This situation, of course, leads some people into a vicious cycle of crime and incarceration that lasts a lifetime.

Education

In our society education is a crucial factor in determining one's chances of success in virtually every realm of life. College, postgraduate, and professional degrees are essential to occupational and economic success in our credential-oriented society, and socioeconomic factors have a strong influence on the level and quality of education that an individual is able to attain. Several studies have demonstrated that students with the same academic records but varying social-class backgrounds have different probabilities of obtaining education past high school. For example, Sewell (1971) found an extremely strong relationship between parents' socioeconomic status (SES) and college attendance: "the lower the SES group, the more limited the opportunities at each level" (Sewell, 1971, p. 795). He found that a student from a high SES background has almost 2.5 times as much chance as a low SES student *with the same academic ability* to attend some kind of post-high school educational institution. The advantage was 4 to 1 for access to college, 6 to 1 for graduation from college, and 9 to 1 for attaining a graduate or professional education. Similarly, Bowles and Gintis (1976) found that children from the lowest tenth in socioeconomic status are only one-twelfth as likely to complete college as those in the highest 10 percent. However, Stolzenberg's recent research (1994) has suggested that, although SES affects the ability of people to attend and graduate from college, it does not have a significant impact on the likelihood that college graduates will pursue postgraduate degrees (for example, law, medicine, and business) and graduate.

A variety of factors related to SES may influence educational attainment. As Kozol (1991) has recently argued in *Savage Inequalities,* the unequal distribution of educational resources dramatically affects the quality of education available to rich and poor students; the quality of public elementary and high school education available to the poor is generally inferior to that available to middle and upper class children. Focusing on the vast disparities in the quality of facilities, programs, and curricula that typically distinguish urban and suburban schools, Kozol found that what was most glaringly apparent were the dramatic financial inequities among schools serving poor and affluent students, often in neighboring school districts; schools attended by poor students were invariably the most poorly funded, while those attended by students from affluent backgrounds had the highest per-pupil expenditures.

> A study... of 20 of the wealthiest and poorest districts of Long Island [New York], for example, matched by location and size of enrollment, found that the differences in per-pupil spending were not only large but had approximately doubled in a five-year period. Schools in Great Neck, in 1987, spent $11,265 for each pupil. In affluent Jericho and Manhasset the figures were, respectively, $11,325 and $11,370. In Oyster Bay the figure was $9,980. Compare this to Levittown, also on Long Island but a town of mostly working-class white families, where per-pupil spending dropped to $6,900. Then compare these numbers to the spending level in the town of Roosevelt, the poorest district in the county, where the schools are 99 percent nonwhite and where the figure dropped to $6,340. Finally, consider New York City, where in the same year $5,590 was invested in each pupil—less than half of what was spent in Great Neck. The pattern is almost identical to that [in the Chicago metropolitan area] (Kozol, 1991, p. 120).

Such dramatic differences in the allocation of educational resources implicitly answers the question "Who shall be educated?" Moreover, because the state requires school attendance but does not allocate its resources equally, Kozol contends that it "effectively requires inequality. Compulsory inequality, perpetuated by state law, too frequently condemns our children to unequal lives" (Kozol, 1991, p. 56).

SES also affects the ability of parents to provide the economic resources necessary to obtain education (for example, to send their children to college). Many lower-class children either cannot afford to start college or are forced to drop out before they finish because they must go to work to support themselves and their families. Even when those from lower- and working-class backgrounds do attend college, they are much more likely to attend two-year community colleges or four-year colleges of lesser quality and prestige (Cohen and Brawer, 1982). Finally, there may be social class differences in educational aspirations; higher

SES families are more likely to emphasize the value of educational attainment (Alexander et al., 1976).

Open and Closed Systems of Stratification

Societies differ in the extent to which they permit and encourage **social mobility**— the movement of persons from one social class to another. An **open class system** of stratification is one in which few obstacles exist for people who are changing their social positions; success is unaffected both by the constraints of disadvantaged social origins or by the privileges of advantaged social class backgrounds. All people, regardless of birth (sex, race, religion, ethnicity, social background), have genuinely equal opportunity to change positions and move up or down in the stratification system. The greater the degree of social mobility, the more open the class system is. In an open class system emphasis is placed on achievement.

By contrast, a completely closed stratification system allows virtually no social mobility. A **closed class system** is one in which children inherit their parents' social position. In a closed class system people's places in a social hierarchy are fixed or ascribed (that is, based on qualities such as race, ethnicity, social background, or sex, over which they have no control). In a closed class system little possibility exists for social mobility. People are born into a position and cannot, under normal circumstances, move out of it.

The most rigid and closed of all stratification systems is a **caste system.** A caste system is endogamous, which means that people must marry within their own caste. A person who does not marry within his or her caste will probably be punished severely. Intimate contact, such as eating with someone of a different caste, is prohibited. Typically elaborate systems of rituals and customs are developed to limit interaction between caste members. As an example of a completely closed system, we will consider the traditional caste system of India.

The traditional Indian caste system, the basis for organizing Indian society since the fifth century B.C., is the classic example of caste. The system can be divided into five broad strata, each of which contains thousands of internal distinctions based primarily on occupation. At the top of the hierarchy stand the Brahmans, the priests, scholars, and teachers of basic religious principles, who provide religious support for the social order (Mayer and Buckley, 1970). Occupying the lowest and most despised position are the *Harijans,* a term meaning "people of God," which was popularized by Gandhi. These people are the outcastes, whom Indians believe fall outside the caste system. They are frequently called "untouchables" because the outcastes are not permitted to touch members of the upper castes. Indians believe that they can be contaminated even if an outcaste's shadow touches their clothing, food, or person. Outcastes are so despised that in rural areas they are frequently barred from the villages during the early or late part of the day when they cast long shadows and are therefore more likely to contaminate other villagers.

Since 1949, discrimination on the basis of caste has been outlawed, and the coming of modernity to India has undermined and disrupted the traditional caste system, especially in large metropolitan areas. In the modern Indian world of bureaucracies, factories, and schools, contact among castes has increased. Despite these changes, however, the Indian caste system persists, especially in the rural areas, where 75 percent of the Indian population lives. In rural villages people still find it unthinkable to marry someone from another caste. How deeply the caste system is rooted and how harshly its rules are enforced is illustrated by a recent incident in a rural Indian village in which a 16-year-old girl, her 18-year-old lover, and a friend who had tried to help them elope were lynched by relatives and neighbors. The young woman was a *Jat*, the dominant caste in the region, while the young men were outcastes. The deaths of all three were decreed by the *Jat*-dominated village council after the young woman refused to give up her lover (Crossette, 1991, p. 60).

A caste system is not unique to India. For example, in Japan members of a caste called *Burakumin* are economically and socially discriminated against and are considered mentally inferior by the rest of Japanese society; marriages between the *Burakumin* and the upper caste are considered a tragedy (by upper-caste members) and are strongly discouraged. (For a further discussion of the *Burakumin*, see "Japan's Outcastes: The Burakumin" in the Cross-national box.) As we will discuss more fully in Chapter 9, the structure of relations between blacks and whites in the United States historically has resembled a caste system. Hereditary factors (skin color, hair texture, lip form) were used as the criteria for determining opportunities for full participation in society. African Americans were relegated to an inferior status, and their access to politics, education, jobs, and housing was restricted. Moreover, throughout the South, interpersonal relations between black and white were governed by what was known as the "etiquette of race relations," which required patterns of deference by blacks to whites. Although the legal basis for the caste system has been eliminated by judicial rulings and by federal legislation, the issue still remains controversial as to how closely black–white relations today resemble a caste system.

In the same way that a genuinely classless society probably has never existed, pure caste and class systems probably do not exist either. No stratification system is totally closed or totally open. Virtually all societies display ascription and achievement in some form, and thus fall somewhere between the two extremes.

The Sociological Analysis of Mobility

Lee Iacocca is one of the most prominent and celebrated businessmen in contemporary society. Born of parents who had immigrated to the United States from

Cross-national Perspectives

Japan's "Invisible Race": The *Burakumin*

The term *caste* refers to an extreme case of a closed system of stratification that is characterized by a hierarchy of social statuses into which people are born and must remain throughout their lives. The case of the Japanese *Burakumin,* Japan's "invisible race," reflects the continuing impact of a caste system in one of the world's most modern, rational, and technologically advanced nations. Physically indistinguishable from other Japanese, the *Burakumin* are acknowledged to be completely Japanese, but of such lowly social origins that they are constantly subjected to prejudice and discrimination.

The contemporary *Burakumin* are descendants of the untouchable *eta* caste. The degree to which the *eta* were despised by the rest of Japanese society is revealed in the name itself: *eta* means "filth abundant." Under the feudal system of Tokugawa, Japan, from the seventeenth to the nineteenth centuries, the *eta* occupied an outcaste status below the four superior castes (the ruling caste of warriors and administrators, the peasants, artisans, and merchants) that constituted Japanese society. The *eta* were discriminated against in every aspect of their lives, and a number of laws were enacted to reinforce their inferior status. For example, as outcastes they were restricted to the dirtiest, most defiling, and least desirable occupations (for example, butchers, leatherworkers, grave tenders, and executioners). They were legally segregated from the rest of the Japanese people and forced to live in isolated ghettos, the locations of which were deliberately omitted from maps. Moreover, they were required to walk barefoot and to wear special clothing that identified them as *eta.* Because they were considered innately inferior and "impure," their marriages were restricted to other *eta;* intermarriages with non-*eta* were virtually nonexistent.

The *eta* were legally "emancipated" during the mid-nineteenth century, at about the same time as U.S. slaves were freed, and the laws that had formerly restricted their lives and discriminated against them were formally abolished. Although emancipation provided legal freedom, discrimination against the outcastes (subsequently known as *Burakumin,* or "village people") persisted, and *Burakumin* continued to be viewed as "mentally inferior, incapable of high moral behavior, aggressive, impulsive, and lacking any notion of sanitation or manners" (Wagatsuma, 1976, p. 245).

Today there are an estimated 1 to 3 million *Burakumin* living in Japan, a nation of 123 million. During the past quarter century the status of the *Burakumin* has begun to change. The Japanese government has enacted legislation to end discrimination against them, and it has invested heavily in social programs designed to improve *Burakumin* neighborhoods. As a consequence, *Burakumin* are no longer restricted to their traditional occupations, and their access to housing outside traditional neighborhoods has increased.

Despite such signs of improvement, the socioeconomic status of Burakumin lags considerably behind the rest of the Japanese population. *Burakumin* family income is only 60 percent of the national average; single parent households are twice as common as in the nation as a whole; and *Burakumin* welfare rates are 7 times those of the overall population. *Burakumin* children are characterized by lower IQ scores than are non-*Burakumin,* and their rates of college attendance are only about half of other Japanese. And they are still likely to live in overcrowded slumlike ghettoes.

Moreover, although deeply ingrained prejudices against the *Burakumin* have begun to decline, traditional negative stereotypes persist. The power of such stereotypes is reflected in the importance attached to family registration records, which certify "proper" social backgrounds. Until recently, such records were frequently required in connection with applications for jobs, loans, and admission to schools. Above all, it was not unusual for families to undertake exhaustive investigations of the lineages of their children's prospective spouses to ensure that their families would not be "contaminated" by *eta* origins. Although such searches have declined in recent years, few public figures are today willing to admit to having had *Burakumin* ancestry.

During the twentieth century, the *Burakumin* have organized social movements to protest the discrimination they have encountered in employment, education, and housing. Recently, the militant *Burakumin* Liberation League has become a potent political force by using techniques of direct harassment and intimidation against those who do not share its views of the *Burakumin* plight. As a consequence, the publishers of Japanese books, magazines, and newspapers, fearful of disruptions of their offices and homes by *Burakumin* "direct action" squads, have adopted an unwritten policy of not mentioning the *Burakumin* in their publications.

DeVos, George and Wagatsuma, Hiroshi. *Japan's Invisible Race: Caste in Culture and Personality.* Berkeley: University of California Press, 1966.

Fallows, James. "Japan's Hidden Race Problems." *New York Times,* October 14, 1990.

Kristoff, Nicholas D. "Japanese Outcasts Better Off Than in Past but Still Outcast." *New York Times,* November 30, 1995.

Wagatsuma, Hiroshi. "Political Problems of a Minority Group in Japan: Recent Conflicts in Buraku Liberation Movements." In Willem A. Veehoven and Winifred Crum Ewing (eds.), *Case Studies on Human Rights and Fundamental Freedoms.* Vol. III. The Hague: Martinus Nijhoff, 1976.

Italy, he experienced the hard times of the Great Depression as he grew up in Allentown, Pennsylvania. He worked his way through college, and, through the classic virtues of hard work, ingenuity, and industriousness, became president of two of the nation's largest corporations, the Ford Motor Company and, later, the Chrysler Corporation (which he rescued from near bankruptcy and transformed into a once-again prosperous company). His name has been prominently mentioned as a possible presidential candidate.

In 1984 Iacocca published his autobiography, *Iacocca.* Although books describing how to achieve success appear frequently on the best-seller list, *Iacocca* remained on the list for more than 2 years, a phenomenal feat for any book. One reason for the book's sensational success is that Iacocca's life story epitomizes the American dream. His is the classic success story—humble origins, an unquenchable desire to gain an education, a commitment to hard work, and a meteoric rise to the top of the U.S. corporate world. Well publicized success stories such as Iacocca's reinforce the widespread belief among Americans that their society provides great opportunities for social mobility (Huber and Form, 1973).

Two types of social mobility can be described. One is **horizontal mobility,** which refers to movement from one social position to another of equal rank. Iacocca's shift from the presidency of the Ford Motor Company to the same position at Chrysler exemplifies this type.

However, popular interest in, and sociological research on, social mobility has centered on **vertical mobility,** which refers to movement upward or downward in the stratification system. Iacocca's rise to fame, fortune, and power is an example of upward vertical mobility; an example of downward vertical mobility would be if the son of a lawyer were to spend his career as a carpenter.

In analyzing the nature of social mobility, sociologists have focused on two main types: intragenerational mobility and intergenerational mobility. **Intragenerational or career mobility** refers to the movement of individuals in the stratification system during their lifetimes. Studies of this type of mobility focus on the life span of individuals, examining where people begin their careers and where they finish them. Someone who starts as a laborer and ends as a lawyer has clearly experienced upward mobility. On the other hand, someone who ends up on skid row after beginning as a physician has experienced downward mobility.

Intergenerational mobility refers to differences between the social class position of children and the social class position of their parents. Studies of this type of mobility compare the social class of parents with those of their children, most often the social class positions of fathers and sons. If the children have more money or education or occupy a higher status than their parents, they have experienced upward mobility. If they are lower than their parents on any of these dimensions, they have experienced downward intergenerational mobility.

Any assessment of the extent to social mobility in U.S. society must consider the effects of **structural mobility**—mobility occurring as a result of changes in a society's occupational structure. Structural mobility is caused by large-scale structural changes in the society as a whole. Among the structural changes that have had a profound effect on the class structure of many countries, including the United States, are technological innovations, wars, economic fluctuations (for example, depressions or recessions), and urbanization. If the nature of the economy and the occupational structure change over time, for example, if the number of white-collar workers increases over blue-collar workers, then the possibility of upward social mobility blue-collar to white-collar occupations will be increased because more higher-status jobs will be available. Between 1940 and 1990, professional and technical jobs in the United States increased by more than 300 percent, while farm jobs declined by 75 percent, thus creating an occupational structure with substantially greater opportunities for high-status positions in 1990 than in 1940 (Gilbert and Kahl, 1993, p. 150).

On the other hand, these data over half a century obscure a recent countertrend: the recent restructuring of the American economy diminished structural opportunities for mobility during the 1980s. Moreover, if an increasing percentage of the population has earned college degrees, the proportion of their children who can achieve mobility through college education will decrease. Thus Hout found that the frequency of changes between social origins and current occupations recently declined for both men and women. "[The] origins and destinations of workers in the early 1980s are more similar than were the origins and destinations of workers in the early 1970s" (Hout, 1988, p. 1382). This was especially true in high-status salaried professional and management occupations, where workers in the 1980s were more likely to have had fathers with those occupations than was the case in the 1970s. These factors combined to create an overall decline in social mobility, especially among the youngest workers, in the 1980s (Gilbert and Kahl, 1993, p. 155).

Patterns of Social Mobility in the United States

How much social mobility is there in the United States? Some general conclusions can be drawn from the large body of sociological research on social mobility. First, most previous social mobility research has focused on men, a fact that itself reflects the significant role that gender plays in the American stratification system (see Chapter 10). Until very recently, little attention was devoted to patterns of social mobility for women, whose social status and class position were typically inferred from their relationships to men, either husbands or fathers. However, Gilbert and Kahl (1993) conclude that, in general, "women's occupational achievement, like men's, is powerfully influenced by their occupational origins" (1993, p. 143).

Second, there is considerable movement, both up and down, within the American system of stratification. Gilbert and Kahl (1993) recently compared the occupational mobility patterns of working-age men since the 1960s. Their analysis showed that approximately one-third of all sons were found at the same broad occupational level as their fathers. Nearly half (44 to 49 percent) experienced upward mobility, while between one-fifth (20 percent) and one-sixth (16 percent) moved down (see Table 8–2). However, during the 1980s the rate of upward occupational mobility declined, while downward mobility increased.

Third, although there is considerable intergenerational occupational mobility in the United States, the social mobility that does occur is modest; it usually occurs in steps between adjacent strata—for example, from the lower middle class to the middle class, rather than in dramatic leaps from the lower class to the upper class; the classic rags-to-riches story is the exception, not the rule. For example, Solon (1992) recently studied the correlation between the 1984 incomes of a sample of men born during the 1950s with their fathers' incomes in 1967. He found that sons whose fathers' incomes were in the bottom 5 percent of earners had one chance in twenty of reaching the top 20 percent of income, one chance in four of rising above the median income level, but two chances in five of staying in the lowest 20 percent of income (Solon, 1992, p. 404). Therefore, social mobility does occur, but it is limited; "those born wealthy or poor usually stay so" (Nasar, 1992a, p. A1).

Fourth, occupational inheritance is greatest at the top and at the bottom of the occupational structure. Men from upper-middle-class and unskilled blue-collar backgrounds are most likely to have occupations similar to their fathers, and children whose fathers had occupations between these two extremes are most likely to experience mobility. Studies of the highest levels of American society indicate that recruitment for the most powerful corporate positions is largely restricted to individuals from upper-class and upper-middle-class origins. A recent study of the chief executive officers of 243 major corporations in 1986 showed that nearly two-thirds had been raised in upper-middle-class or upper-class families (Boone et al., 1988; see also Kerbo, 1983; Tumin, 1985).

Fifth, patterns of social mobility in the United States have not changed dramatically over time. Although most historical studies of social mobility are limited to cities and do not represent the nation as a whole, such studies tend to show that

Table 8–2   Changes in Occupational Status by Sons Compared with Fathers

	Up	Stable	Down	Total
1962	49	34	17	100
1973	49	32	19	100
1972–1980	50	35	16	100
1982–1990	44	36	20	100

Source: Dennis Gilbert and Joseph A. Kahl. *The American Class Structure: A New Synthesis,* 4th ed., 1993. Belmont, Calif.: Wadsworth, p. 154.

patterns of social mobility at the turn of the twentieth century and at mid-century were roughly the same as today. In other words, opportunities for social mobility in the United States were no greater in the past than they have been in the last half of the twentieth century; historical studies of business elites show patterns of recruitment from the upper class similar to the contemporary elite (Kerbo, 1983, pp. 346–348). However, as noted above, changes in the occupational opportunity structure and in the distribution of household income during the 1980s, especially for younger workers, suggest that these patterns of social mobility, in which those experiencing upward mobility were far more common than those experiencing downward mobility, may not be continued in the future (Gilbert and Kahl, 1993; Duncan et al., 1992).

Finally, the overall rates of social mobility in the United States do not differ substantially from those in other Western industrialized countries. Although differences do exist in the historical experiences and occupational structures of the sixteen countries they studied, Grusky and Hauser concluded that "industrialized societies share a common pattern of mobility" (Grusky and Hauser, 1984, p. 35). Similarly, Kerckhoff and co-workers (1985) found substantial similarities in the amount of intergenerational occupational movement of men in Great Britain and the United States. Consistent with the findings cited earlier, both studies found the greatest degree of inheritance of occupational position among the highest-status and lowest-status occupations, with the greatest mobility occurring among those in between. "The picture that emerges is one of severe immobility at the two extremes of the occupational hierarchy and considerable fluidity in the middle" (Grusky and Hauser, 1984, p. 35). Such studies contradict the notion that the United States is more open in terms of social mobility than other nations and points to strong similarities in people's expectations of their position within the social hierarchies of western democratic societies.

Summary

Social stratification, or structured social inequality, is a universal feature of human societies. Social inequalities and social ranking are usually justified by reference to an ideology, a set of ideas used to explain and justify the inequalities. The inequalities in American life are justified by a meritocratic ideology that emphasizes an ideal of equality of opportunity.

Sociologists have distinguished three basic dimensions of social stratification: class, status, and power. Class is an economic variable strongly emphasized by Marx as the determinant of social stratification. However, Weber argued that status, or prestige, and power were also important dimensions in a system of social stratification. An examination of the American stratification system reveals that, despite an egalitarian ideology, considerable inequality exists in contemporary American society. Inequalities in the concentration of wealth and income in the

United States have been substantial throughout the nation's history, and they have become more pronounced during the 1980s and 1990s. Inequality is also manifested in differences among the social classes in both life chances and life-styles.

Stratification systems differ in the extent to which they are open or closed. An open class system is one in which there are few obstacles to social mobility, which is the movement between positions in a system of stratification. In a closed class system little possibility exists for mobility; people's positions in a social hierarchy are determined almost completely by birth. The most closed of all stratification systems is a caste system, which is exemplified by traditional Indian society.

There are different types of social mobility. Vertical mobility can be either upward or downward. Horizontal mobility involves the movement between comparable positions in the social structure. Sociologists have examined both intragenerational, or career, mobility and intergenerational mobility, in which parents' occupational positions are compared with those of their offspring. In general, studies of social mobility suggest that, despite a widespread belief that the United States has provided unique opportunities for social mobility, upward social mobility is no greater in the United States than in other Western industrialized nations.

CRITICAL THINKING

1. The authors state that a "classless society is a possibility, if not a probability." What conditions need to exist in order for such a society to be possible? Which existing society comes closest to this ideal?
2. Review the definitions of class, status, and power presented in the text. To what extent does each affect the following occupations in American society: judge, nurse, firefighter, mechanic, janitor?
3. Meritocracy has been a predominant ideology in American society. What are the basic tenets of this ideology? Review the data presented in the chapter to determine the validity of this ideology. Does it justify the existing social order? How did you learn about this ideology as you grew up? Give examples.
4. Explain the key differences between the structural-functional and the conflict interpretations of social inequality. What evidence presented in the chapter supports each theory?
5. How do the income data in the chapter support the contention that dominant and subordinate classes exist in the United States?
6. The United States has been stereotyped as a "middle-class society" in which each generation is more successful than the previous one. Does the evidence in the chapter support this idea? How has the distribution of income been affected by America's move to a postindustrial society?
7. How can you explain the existence of an underclass in the United States?
8. How are our lives (health, education, life expectancy, and so on) affected by social stratification?
9. What characteristics does a closed class system have? To what extent is American society closed?
10. Examine the experience of a grandparent, parent, and yourself to assess the intragenerational and intergenerational mobility in your family. In addition, assess each individual's horizontal and vertical mobility. Does your family's experience tend to prove or disprove the authors' main conclusions?

9

Racial and Ethnic Inequality

The arrest, trial, and acquittal of former football star and media celebrity O.J. Simpson, charged with the brutal murder of his ex-wife, Nicole, and Ron Goldman, was one of the most sensational in all of American history. As on many other issues, race influenced the reporting and conduct of the case and divided Americans in their responses to it. For example, a *USA Today*/CNN/Gallup poll taken soon after Simpson's arrest found that 68 percent of whites but only 15 percent of blacks believed that the charges against him were true; conversely, 60 percent of blacks said he was innocent, whereas only 24 percent of whites did. Sixty-four percent of blacks but only 41 percent of whites said that Simpson would not be able to get a fair trial (Walker, 1994, p. 1A). Polls taken immediately after the case was concluded indicated that 85 percent of African Americans agreed with the jury verdict, while only 32 percent of whites did (*Newsweek,* October 15, 1995b). "As blacks exulted at Simpson's acquittal, horrified whites had a fleeting sense that . . . blacks really were strangers in their midst" (Gates, 1995, p. 56).

In many ways the O.J. Simpson case dramatically symbolizes the divisive role that race has played—and continues to play—in American life; race and ethnicity have been among the critical issues defining American social and political life throughout the nation's history, and, as we approach the twenty-first century, they

274

remain critical to understanding the structure of social inequality in American society.

As we saw in Chapter 8, social inequalities are a universal feature of human societies. Although a wide range of factors has been used to place people into social categories of superiority and inferiority and dominance and subordination, race and ethnicity have been used throughout history as criteria for ranking a society's members into categories of unequal wealth, power, and prestige.

Prejudice and discrimination and conflict and violence based on racial and ethnic distinctions are found throughout the world today—among black, white, colored, and Indian in South Africa, between Hutu and Tutsi in Rwanda and Burundi, between English-speaking and French-speaking people in Canada, between East Indians and blacks in Guyana, between Kurds and Iraqis in Iraq, between Tamils and Sinhalese in Sri Lanka, between Chinese and Malays in Malaysia, or between the Tivs and Junkuns in Nigeria, to name only a few. In the last few decades more people have died in ethnic conflicts around the world than in the Korean and Vietnam wars combined.

Indeed, the ferment that led to the end of the Cold War and unleashed dramatic political changes throughout eastern Europe since the late 1980s was fed by and resulted in a resurgence of ethnic and national rivalries and antagonisms. The disintegration of the Soviet Union was reinforced by interethnic and nationalistic conflicts, such as those between Armenians and Azerbaijanis, as well as by the demands for independence from numerous other nationalities, such as Lithuanians, Latvians, Estonians, Georgians, Moldavians, and Ukrainians. Even after the breakup of the Soviet Union, Russia has continued to be the site of numerous ethnic conflicts—involving more than 180 ethnic clashes in 1992 alone and, from 1994 to 1996, a bloody war to prevent Chechen rebels in the province of Chechnya from declaring their independence.

Slavic nationalism, which earlier in the twentieth century had provided the spark that ignited World War I, resurfaced with a vengeance. In Yugoslavia, conflicts among that country's several nationalities—Slovenes, Croatians, Serbs, Bosnians, Montenegrins, Macedonians, and Albanians—led to the nation's dissolution and to one of the most bitter and deadly conflicts among European ethnic groups in the post-World War II era, resulting in the deaths of 250,000 people and the displacement of more than 2 million (Cohen, 1994). Since 1992, Bosnian Serbs have used a reign of terror, including rape, murder, torture, and intimidation, to forcibly expel hundreds of thousands of Croats and, especially, Muslims from their homes and villages in Bosnia-Herzegovina. They characterized their efforts to eliminate non-Serbians from territories under their control as "ethnic cleansing," thereby adding a new term to the vocabulary of human ethnic conflict. Czechoslovakia split along ethnic lines into two separate nations—the Czech Republic and Slovakia. Prior to the fall of the Rumanian strongman Nicolae Ceausesçu in 1989, approximately 2 million Hungarians living in Rumania were subject to forced assimilation, the closing of Hungarian schools and social organizations, the suppression of the Hungarian language, and discrimination against those Hungarians who tried to retain their Hungarian identity. Similar accusations of forced assimilation were raised by the Turkish minority in Bulgaria, where ethnic tensions led to the forced removal of thousands of Muslim Turks to Turkey.

These examples demonstrate how widespread ethnic conflict is throughout our world today. In this chapter we consider the dynamics of racial and ethnic relations, especially in the United States. We will focus on how different patterns of racial and ethnic relations are achieved and maintained.

Ethnic and Racial Groups

The word *ethnic* is derived from the Greek word *ethnos,* meaning "people." **Ethnic group** refers to a group that is socially defined on the basis of its cultural characteristics. **Ethnicity,** the sense of belonging to a particular ethnic group, thus implies the existence of a distinct culture or subculture in which group members feel themselves bound together by common history, values, attitudes, and behaviors. Other members of the society may also regard them as distinctive. Ethnic groups may differ in cultural characteristics as diverse as food habits, family patterns, sexual behavior, modes of dress, standards of beauty, political orientations, economic activities, and recreational patterns. In its broadest sense, the term *ethnic* implies a sense of common peoplehood. In the United States, Chicanos, Italians, Jews, Poles, Filipinos, and white Anglo-Saxon Protestants, among others, can all be considered ethnic groups.

The terms *race* and *ethnicity* are often used interchangeably, but they should be distinguished. An ethnic group is socially defined and constructed on the basis of its *cultural* characteristics; the term **race** refers to groups that are socially defined on the basis of *physical* characteristics. A group is defined as a race when certain physical characteristics are selected for special emphasis by members of a society.

The term *race* is meaningless in a biological sense, because there are no "pure" races; the racial categories found in each society are social constructs or conventions. The crucial aspect of any definition of a group as ethnic or racial is that the characteristics that distinguish it are *socially defined* and *constructed.* Thus, the criteria selected to make racial distinctions in one society may be overlooked or considered insignificant or irrelevant by another society. In much of Latin America, skin color and the shape of the lips—important differentiating criteria in the United States—are much less important than hair texture, eye color, and stature. A person defined as black in Georgia or Michigan might be considered white in Peru. Among the Tutsi (where men average a height of over 6 feet) and the Hutu (who stand slightly over 4 feet) peoples of central Africa, the physical characteristic of height is the basis for group distinctions. Therefore, the recent conflict between these two peoples in Rwanda and Burundi, which resulted in the murders of thousands of the minority people, is racial.

The South African system of **apartheid,** or racial separation, provided one of the most vivid examples of the way in which racial classifications are social, not biological, categories. Under apartheid, which was established in 1950 and formally abolished in 1991, all people were required to be classified into one of four legally defined racial groups—white, black, colored, and Indian. The racial categories into which people were (often arbitrarily) placed determined whether they could vote or own land; the jobs they could hold; the schools they could attend; where they could live, eat, or play; and whom they could love and marry.

The principle that racial differences are socially defined is vividly shown by laws in the United States that prohibited interracial marriages. Until recently, many states stipulated that any person with one-fourth or more black[1] ancestry (that is, with one black grandparent) was legally defined as "black" and therefore prohibited from marrying someone "white." However, some states enacted more restrictive definitions of race. A recent example of this enactment occurred in Louisiana, when Susie Guillory Phipps, a light-skinned woman with Caucasian features and straight black hair, found that her birth certificate classified her as "colored." Mrs. Phipps, who contended that she had been "brought up white and married white twice," challenged a 1970 Louisiana law declaring that anyone with at least one-thirty-second "Negro blood" was legally classified as black. Under this law an individual who had *one* great-great-great grandparent who was black (and thus had only one-thirty-second "black" and thirty-one thirty-seconds "white" ancestry) was legally defined as black. Although the state's lawyer conceded that Mrs. Phipps "looks like a white person," the state strenuously maintained that her racial classification was appropriate (Trillin, 1986).

The arbitrary, socially constructed nature of racial and ethnic categories and identities is also revealed by circumstances in which individuals change categories, which is exemplified by the story of Gregory Howard Williams, the dean of the Ohio State University School of Law. Williams grew up in Virginia believing that he was white. He was 10 when his parents' marriage and his father's businesses failed and he and his brother moved with their father to his hometown of Muncie, Indiana. On the bus ride to Muncie, his father told him and his brother,

---

[1]Reflecting the dynamic, fluid, and socially defined nature of racial and ethnic categories, both the categories and terms used to identify them frequently change. For example, over the last 200 years, a variety of terms—colored, Negro, Afro-American, black—have been used to refer to Americans of African descent. Recently, many black leaders have urged adoption of the term *African American.* However, although that term has gained increasing acceptance among both black and white Americans, when this book was written, no consensus on terminology had emerged. Therefore, we will use both *African American* and *black American* in this chapter and the more customary *black American* in the remainder of the book. Similarly, there is no consensus today concerning the appropriate terminology for two other important racial and ethnic categories in the United States: American Indian or Native American, on the one hand, and Hispanic or Latino, on the other. In each case we will use the terms interchangeably.

"Life is going to be different from now on. In Virginia you were white boys. In Indiana you're going to be colored boys" (Williams, 1995 p. 33). In Muncie he was thrust into the black segment of a racially segregated community, and his book describes the difficulties he encountered trying to negotiate "life on the color line" between black and white (Williams, 1995).

Although racial categories are arbitrary, most of us are placed in a specific racial category—both by public perceptions and, more formally, by the categories (for example, Asian, Native American, black, white, and Hispanic) used by government and even by discussions such as this one. However, as the United States grows increasingly more racially diverse, the arbitrary, irrational, and socially constructed nature of such racial distinctions is becoming increasingly recognized and questioned. For example, in a recent cover story titled "What Color Is Black?" *Newsweek* answered that "it is every conceivable shade and hue from tan to ebony—and suddenly a matter of ideology and identity as much as pigmentation" (1995, p. 64). Moreover, increasing numbers of Americans, especially those with multiracial backgrounds, are rejecting requirements that they choose one single racial category on census forms, school enrollment forms, and job, loan, and mortgage applications. Increasingly people are calling for either the elimination of official racial distinctions altogether or for the creation of a "multicultural" category that will not force individuals to choose between two or more racial identities (Wright, 1994).

Although racial categories are arbitrary, because American consciousness of race is so pronounced, most of us are placed in a specific racial category—both by public perceptions and, more formally, by the categories (for example, African American, Hispanic, Asian, American, Indian, European) used by the government and even by discussions such as this one.

What Is a Minority Group?

Sociologists usually use the terms *majority* and *minority* to refer to social relations in which racial and ethnic criteria are employed in the society's system of stratification. The distinctive feature of a **minority group,** or **subordinate group,** is that it occupies a *subordinate* or inferior position of prestige, wealth, and power in a society. A minority group is typically excluded from full participation in a society and is the object of discrimination by the majority group.

The term *minority* does not refer to the numerical size of a group. For example, in South Africa today, blacks are a numerical majority (69 percent) of the total population, yet they are systematically excluded from full social, economic, and political participation. Numerical superiority, therefore, does not necessarily ensure that a group will be dominant.

The crucial variable in majority–minority relations is *power*—the ability of one group to realize its goals and interests, even in the face of resistance. Power may be based on the superior population size, weaponry, technology, property, education, or economic resources of the dominant group. Superior power is crucial to the establishment of a system of ethnic or racial stratification. Moreover, having achieved power, a **majority group,** or **dominant group,** is reluctant to give it up voluntarily, but instead usually strives to maintain and perpetuate its privileged position.

Race and Ethnicity in the American Experience

The United States, which has been called a "nation of nations," is one of the most racially and ethnically diverse societies in the world (Table 9–1). Despite an ideology formally committed to human equality, racial and ethnic criteria have frequently determined social status in American society. Figure 9–1 presents data on the distribution of major racial and ethnic groups in the United States. Presently, members of the largest racial and ethnic minorities (African Americans, Hispanics, Asians, and American Indians) comprise more than one-quarter of the population.

One of the most prominent features of the American experience is the competition among numerous racial and ethnic groups for economic, social, and political dominance. Moreover, in the future the impact of racial and ethnic factors will probably be even more pronounced. By the year 2000, one-third of all school-age children will be either Hispanic, African American, Asian, or American Indian (American Council on Education, 1988). Furthermore, in some states (for example, California) the *majority* of working-age adults in 2000 will be members of these minorities (California Assembly Office of Research, 1986). These minority peoples will affect the nation's prosperity more substantially than ever before in U.S. history. In this section we sketch some key features of ethnic and racial relations in the American experience, beginning with the earliest inhabitants—Native Americans—and concluding with a discussion of some characteristics of contemporary immigration to the United States.

Native Americans/American Indians

The first Americans migrated from Asia 12,000 to 60,000 years ago, slowly dispersing throughout North, Central, and South America. Characterized by widely different levels of technology and cultural complexity, Native American peoples developed a great diversity of cultures, which persist to the present, despite the popular perception of North American Indians as a single, distinct ethnic group. A good index of this cultural diversity is the number of languages, about 200, spoken today among American Indians. Although Indians represent less than 1 percent of the American people, the number of languages found among them is equal

Table 9–1   Racial Populations in the United States, 1970–1990

| | Number (thousands) | | | Percent of the population | | |
	1970	1980	1990	1970	1980	1990
Total	203,212	226,546	248,710	100.0	100.0	100.0
White	177,749	188,341	199,686	87.5	83.2	80.3
Black	22,580	26,488	29,986	11.1	11.7	12.1
American Indian, Eskimo, and Aleut	827	1,418	1,959	0.4	0.6	0.8
Asian and Pacific Islander	1,539	3,501	7,274	0.8	1.5	2.9
Chinese	435	806	1,645	0.2	0.4	0.7
Filipino	343	775	1,407	0.2	0.3	0.6
Japanese	591	701	848	0.3	0.3	0.3
Asian Indian	NA	362	815	—	0.2	0.3
Korean	69	355	799	0.0	0.2	0.3
Vietnamese	NA	262	615	—	0.1	0.2
Hispanics[a]	9,073	14,609	22,354	4.5	6.4	9.0
Mexican-American	4,532	8,740	13,496	2.2	3.9	5.4
Puerto Rican	1,429	2,014	2,728	0.7	0.9	1.1
Cuban	544	803	1,044	0.3	0.4	0.4
Other Hispanic	2,566	3,051	5,086	1.2	1.3	2.0

NA, not available.
[a]Hispanics are also included in "White," "Black," and "Other Hispanic."
Sources: U.S. Bureau of the Census, *U.S. Census of the Population, 1970,* vol. 1, Part I: *Characteristics of the Population,* Summary Section 2, Washington, D.C.: U.S. Government Printing Office, 1973; U.S. Bureau of the Census, *U.S. Census of the Population. 1970,* Subject Reports PC(2)-1G; *Japanese, Chinese, Filipinos,* Washington, D.C.: U.S. Government Printing Office, 1973; U.S. Bureau of the Census, *1980 Census of the Population,* vol. 1: *Characteristics of the Population,* chap. D, "Detailed Population Characteristics, Part I: U.S. Summary," PC80-1-D1-A, Washington, D.C.: U.S. Government Printing Office, 1984; U.S. Bureau of the Census, *Census and You,* Washington, D.C.: U.S. Government Printing Office, 1991.

to the number of those spoken among the remaining 99 percent of the population combined (Hodgkinson, 1990, p. 1).

The European invasion of North America had a permanent impact on American Indian peoples and cultures. From the 1600s onward, the insatiable European demand for land became the primary source of conflict with Native Americans. The process of European expansion westward involved the expulsion of Indians from their tribal lands. Although Indians resolutely resisted domination, the advance of white settlement eventually overwhelmed Indian resistance. Armed with superior military technology and bolstered by increasing numbers, whites moved inexorably westward. Native peoples were forced to retreat as the lands that they had formerly occupied came under the control of Europeans. Their land base, which initially had been over 2 billion acres, dwindled to 155 million acres in 1871 and 90 million acres in 1980 (Dorris, 1981). Diseases such as smallpox, scarlet fever, measles, and cholera were fatal to large numbers of Indian peoples, who for centuries had been physically isolated from the Old World and had developed little or no resistance to these diseases. Moreover, substantial numbers of American Indians died as a result both of warfare with Europeans and the deliberate extermination of Indians by European invaders. The Native American population, which had numbered between 5 and 6 million when Columbus arrived in the New World, dwindled to 237,000 by 1900 (Thornton, 1987, p. 32). Traditional Indian cultures and patterns of authority were undermined as their economic resources were eroded, their numbers plummeted, and Indian affairs became controlled by whites.

By the turn of the twentieth century, whites believed that American Indians were a vanishing race and that the few remaining Indians should be forced to assimilate—to give up their cultural heritages and to adopt the white values of

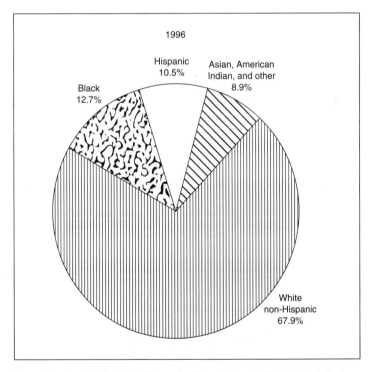

Figure 9–1.   Racial and Hispanic Population of the United States, 1996. (*Source:* U.S. Bureau of the Census, *Statistical Abstract of the United States: 1995.* Washington, D.C., 1995, p. 14); U.S. Bureau of the Census, Internet Home Page, 1996.

rugged individualism, competition, and private enterprise. To ethnocentric whites, these values represented more "civilized" forms of behavior.

Nevertheless, a striking feature of American Indian life in the twentieth century has been an ability to endure. Despite strong pressures to assimilate into the mainstream of American society, American Indians have clung tenaciously to their cultures. In 1990 nearly 2 million people identify themselves as American Indian, an increase of 40 percent over 1980, and Census Bureau projections estimate an American Indian population of 4.6 million in 2050 (1.2 percent of the population) (Day, 1993; Harris, 1994b).

During the nineteenth century, American Indians were removed to isolated areas not then coveted by Europeans, and their relationships with whites were defined by solemn treaties signed with the U.S. government. These treaties, involving special water, fishing, and territorial agreements, guaranteed that Indians would retain the rights granted to them (including sovereignty over the remaining lands) in perpetuity—"as long as the grass shall grow and the rivers shall run." These treaties form the basis of the unique legal and political status of Native Americans today. In contrast to other American racial and ethnic minorities, American Indian tribes "are due certain privileges, protections, and benefits [for] yielding some of their sovereignty to the United States" (Dorris, 1981, p. 54). Among these rights are the obligations of the federal government to protect their lands and to provide Indians with social, medical, and educational services.

Although the lands held by American Indians today represent only a small portion of those guaranteed in treaties, they include vast and extremely valuable agricultural, water, timber, fishing, and energy resources. However, Indians have seldom received significant amounts of income from these lands because the resources have been developed for and exploited primarily by non-Indian interests. For example, Indian reservations have provided water for the extensive urban development of the Southwest and have received almost nothing in return. Similarly, because of leases signed by the Bureau of Indian Affairs on their behalf, in 1981 the Navajo received 15 to 38 cents a ton for coal that was sold by American suppliers to foreign buyers for $70 a ton (Snipp, 1986).

Native Americans are among the poorest and least educated groups in American society. In 1989, Indian median household income was less than two-thirds (64 percent) that of whites; nearly one-third (31 percent) of Native Americans lived below the poverty level. The problems of poverty are especially acute on Indian reservations—the lands to which Native peoples have title and over which they exercise sovereignty—where from one-third to one-half of all families have incomes below the poverty level; on some reservations the unemployment rates exceed 80 percent. By 1990, less than two-thirds (66 percent) of all Indians age 25 and older had completed high school, compared to four-fifths (80 percent) of whites. The percentage of Indians at that age category (9.3 percent) who had graduated from college was less than half the percentage of whites (21.5 percent) (U.S. Bureau of the Census, 1992b).

In response to the exploitation and depletion of their resources, Native Americans are increasingly challenging their political and economic domination by outsiders and are seeking to exert Indian control over reservation resources. In response to congressional legislation and a 1987 Supreme Court decision that exempted American Indian tribes, as sovereign nations, from most gambling regulations, over 90 tribes have opened gambling casinos that they anticipate will begin to address some of the economic problems of Indian peoples. Indian activists have mounted legal challenges to ensure that the U.S. government honors the terms of the treaties that it has made with Indian tribes. Indian activism has also been reflected in their efforts to develop organizations to advance Indian economic interests by resisting external exploitation of their resource base, including timber, water, and, especially, minerals. One of the most prominent of these has been the Council of Energy Resource Tribes (CERT), which was formed to promote Indian economic interests in the substantial coal, gas, oil, and uranium reserves that are found on Indian lands (Snipp, 1986). Moreover, rather than lease their lands to drill for oil or gas or mine for coal, several tribes have formed their own high-technology mining ventures that enable them, rather than large energy companies, to retain the profits from these enterprises (Johnson, 1994c). As the powerful economic and political pressures intensify over increasingly scarce and valuable Native resources, it seems inevitable that conflicts will increase in the future (Erdrich and Dorris, 1988).

European Americans

The first European immigrants to settle permanently in what is now the United States were almost exclusively English. The economic, legal, and political traditions that English settlers brought established the English character of American institutions, language, and culture. Ethnic groups who migrated later were forced to adapt to the cultural and social systems that the English had created.

Although the English composed the greatest proportion of the early colonial population, the middle colonies (New York, New Jersey, Pennsylvania, and Delaware) were settled by substantial numbers of Germans, Dutch, Scots-Irish, Scots, Swedes, and French Huguenots. Here the idea of America as a melting pot, in which diverse cultures come together to form a new people, was first formulated.

Immigration to the United States was greatest in the century between 1820 and 1920, when more than 30 million immigrants entered the country. Between 1820 and 1895, immigrants were drawn principally from countries of northern and western Europe—from Germany, Ireland, Great Britain (England, Scotland, and Wales), and Scandinavia (Norway, Sweden, and Denmark). With the exception of the Catholic Irish, the **"old" immigration** (as the immigration from these countries became known) was heavily Protestant.

Immigration to the United States reached its peak between 1890 and the outbreak of World War I in 1914, and those who entered were drawn from countries different from those of the old immigrants. The **"new" immigration**—including Greeks, Croatians, Italians, Russians (primarily Jewish), Poles, Hungarians, Czechs, and Lithuanians—hailed from southern and eastern Europe. Unlike the old immigration, which was heavily Protestant and followed agricultural pursuits in the United States, new immigrant groups were overwhelmingly Catholic or Jewish and were attracted primarily to the economic opportunities in the nation's rapidly expanding cities.

Native-born whites held deep-seated prejudices against the new immigrants, believing that they were innately inferior to previous immigrants. The U.S. Commissioner of Immigration described the new immigrants as "beaten men from beaten races; representing the worst failures in the struggle for existence. They have none of the ideas and aptitudes which fit men to take up readily and easily the problem of self-care and self-government" (quoted in Saveth, 1948, p. 40).

Such beliefs in the racial and cultural inferiority of new immigrants provided the foundation for American immigration policy from 1917 to 1965, which was designed precisely to discriminate against new immigrants by restricting their numbers while still permitting substantial numbers of old immigrants to enter.

Despite fears that they were undesirable and unassimilable and that they represented a threat to American society, the descendants of the new immigrants, today referred to as **white ethnics,** have achieved considerable socioeconomic success (Model, 1991). Greeley (1976) has characterized their socioeconomic achievements as the "ethnic miracle." By the 1970s, Jews had attained the highest income levels of all European ethnic groups in American society, and they were followed by Irish, German, Italian, and Polish Catholics, not by white Anglo-Saxon Protestants. Moreover, when parental educational levels are held constant, Catholic ethnics show higher educational achievement than any other European groups except Jews. Yet, despite their economic and educational achievements, many white ethnics still retain a sense of cultural identity with their ethnic and national roots (Waters, 1990).

In 1996 about two-thirds (67.9 percent) of the American people were identified by the U.S. census as non-Hispanic whites (see Figure 9-1). However, primarily because of lower fertility and immigration rates, the white population is projected to decline to substantially less than two-thirds of the total population in 2020 and to about only one-half of the American people by 2050 (Day, 1993).

African Americans

From the earliest settlement to the present, the principal racial division in American society has been between white and black; no other minority group has experienced discrimination so intense, pervasive, and enduring as African Americans.

Numbering nearly 33 million—more than 12.5 percent of the total population—African Americans are today the largest racial minority in American society. Their numbers total more than the entire population of Canada or of the Scandinavian countries of Sweden, Denmark, Norway, Finland, and Iceland combined. Only Nigeria, Ethiopia, and Zaire have larger black populations than the United States. Moreover, the black population is expected to double in the first half of the twenty-first century, reaching 62 million, or about one-sixth of the American population by 2050 (Day, 1993).

Slavery and Caste.   During the first 200 years of their existence in American society, the lives of African American people were defined primarily by their role as slaves, a status in which individuals are involuntarily placed in perpetual servitude, are defined as property, and are denied rights generally given to other members of society.

Equally important in understanding the dynamics of race relations in the United States is that even those African Americans who were free during the slavery era (more than one-tenth of the black population) did not have the same rights and privileges as whites and were not accepted into society on an equal basis. In contrast to slaves in many other societies, slaves in the United States were subject to *racial* discrimination as well as legal servitude. Therefore, the most distinctive and enduring feature of black–white relations in the United States has been that African Americans—slave or free—have occupied a lower caste status, both during the more than 200 years of slavery and long after it was legally abolished in 1865.

The Aftermath of Slavery.   Bolstered by passage of the 13th Amendment, which abolished slavery; the 14th Amendment, which extended to them the equal protection of the law; and the 15th Amendment, which guaranteed the right to vote, African Americans actively sought to realize the opportunities and responsibilities of freedom. However, freed blacks were formally given freedom but not the means (that is, economic, political, and educational equality) to realize it. Through intimidation, violence, lynching, and terrorism, African Americans were kept in a subordinate status and subjected to systematic racial discrimination long after slavery had been legally abolished.

To ensure that European dominance would be perpetuated, whites created the Jim Crow system of racial segregation, which excluded African Americans from the economic, political, and educational opportunities available to whites. During the late nineteenth century, southern legislatures passed a variety of laws requiring racial separation and exclusion of African Americans from the political, legal, economic, and social opportunities available to most other Americans. This system of white domination was justified by the 1896 Supreme Court decision of *Plessy* v. *Ferguson,* which provided legal support for the "separate but equal" doctrine, but it was ultimately maintained through the use of violence and intimidation.

From Plantation to Ghetto.   In response to these oppressive conditions, African Americans began to leave the South during the early twentieth century. They migrated primarily to northern urban areas, where their settlement was both legally and informally restricted to areas in which other blacks lived. This migration out of the rural South has been one of the most significant aspects of the African American experience and one of the most important demographic changes in American history. In 1900, almost 90 percent of the black population lived in the South; by 1990 the percentage was only slightly more than one-half (53 percent). In 1900, African Americans were primarily rural residents, with only 22.7 percent living in urban areas. By 1990, nearly nine-tenths (87.2 percent) of the African American population lived in urban areas, indicating that blacks have become a more urbanized population than whites. Although a substantial portion of this increase in urban blacks occurred in the North, many southern blacks also moved into cities. Table 9–2 shows the percentage of the African American population residing in major American cities for the years 1920, 1950, 1970, 1980, and 1990.

The massive migration of African Americans out of the South was one of the most important factors underlying the protest movement that swept the nation during the 1950s and 1960s. Although discrimination against African Americans in education, employment, housing, and the administration of justice also prevailed in the North, greater opportunities were available for them in northern urban areas than in the South. Especially after World War II, an educated and

Table 9–2   African American Population as Percentage of the Total Population of the 10 Largest U.S. Cities,[a] 1920, 1950, 1980, and 1990

	1920[b]	1950[b]	1970	1980	1990
New York	2.7	9.8	21.1	25.2	28.7
Los Angeles	2.7	10.7	17.9	17.0	14.0
Chicago	4.1	14.1	32.7	39.8	39.1
Houston	24.6	21.1	25.7	27.6	28.1
Philadelphia	7.4	18.3	33.6	37.8	39.9
San Diego	1.2	4.5	7.6	8.9	9.4
Detroit	4.1	16.4	43.7	63.1	75.7
Dallas	15.1	13.2	24.9	29.4	29.5
Phoenix	3.7	6.0	4.8	4.8	5.2
San Antonio	8.9	6.7	7.6	7.3	7.1

Sources: U.S. Census of 1920; U.S. Census of 1950; U.S. Bureau of the Census, *Negroes in the United States, 1920–1932,* Washington, D.C.: U.S. Government Printing Office, 1935; "Characteristics of the Population," *Statistical Abstract of the United States, 1972,* pp. 21–23; *Statistical Abstract of the United States, 1984,* pp. 28–30; U.S. Department of Commerce News Releases, Bureau of the Census, February 1991.

[a]These were the 10 largest cities in the United States in 1990.

[b]Figures pertain to "nonwhite" population, of which over 90 percent was black.

articulate black middle class played an important part in legal challenges to the southern Jim Crow system. These actions culminated in the Supreme Court's 1954 *Brown* v. *Board of Education* decision that segregated schools were unconstitutional. The *Brown* decision, which overturned the Court's 1896 "separate but equal" doctrine, symbolized the beginning of an era in which the legal basis for the caste system would crumble.

The Changing Status of African Americans.   During the late 1950s and early 1960s, African Americans employed numerous forms of direct protest—such as nonviolent sit-ins, boycotts, and voter registration drives—to effect changes in the existing system of race relations. During the 1960s, federal, state, and local governments and private organizations made efforts to eliminate black inequality. The Civil Rights Act of 1964 substantially reduced public discrimination in restaurants, hotels, and business establishments. It also provided the impetus for substantial integration of public school systems in the South and for affirmative action efforts to ensure nondiscriminatory job hiring. The Voting Rights Act of 1965 enabled African Americans throughout the South to exercise their right to vote. Finally, the Civil Rights Act of 1968 banned discrimination in the sale or rental of housing.

The effects of these and other changes were most marked in politics and education. Between 1964 and 1994, the number of African Americans elected to public office increased from 103 to over 8400 (still, however, less than 2 percent of all elected public officials) (Joint Center for Political Studies, 1996). Moreover, the number of African American mayors increased from *none* in 1964 to more than 400 in 1994. Many major American cities now have black mayors, including Baltimore, Seattle, St. Louis, Kansas City, Detroit, Atlanta, Denver, San Francisco, and Washington, D.C.

Despite these electoral changes, in 1994 African Americans represented less than 2 percent of the elected officials in the United States. In the South, where blacks accounted for more than 20 percent of the population, in 1992 only 3 percent of elected officials were black. Moreover, in many instances the political power that black elected officials have is limited. Given the exodus of middle-class residents and businesses to the suburbs, African Americans often find that they have gained access to political offices without adequate financial resources to provide the jobs and services (educational, medical care, police and fire protection) that their constituents urgently need (Joint Center for Political Studies, 1992).

During the 1950s and 1960s, African Americans also achieved educational gains, but those gains were not sustained throughout the late 1970s and early 1980s. In 1976, college participation rates for whites and blacks were virtually the same; about one-third (33 percent) of high school graduates of both races attended college. However, between 1976 and 1985, the college participation rate for black high school graduates declined dramatically, from 33.5 percent to 26.1 percent, while the white participation rate remained virtually unchanged. This decline in black college participation rates resulted in a decline in the percentage of bachelor's degrees awarded to African Americans, from 6.4 percent in 1976 to 5.9 percent in 1985. On the other hand, between 1985 and 1992, participation rates for both whites and blacks increased: whites reached an all-time high (42.2 percent), while blacks returned to the level (33.8 percent) that they had achieved in 1976; only by 1992 did the percentages of bachelor's degrees earned by African Americans return to 1976 levels. Moreover, while the overall enrollment of black students in graduate and professional schools increased during the mid-1980s and 1990s, the percentage of advanced degrees awarded to African Americans declined. The percentage of master's degrees awarded to African Americans declined from 6.6 percent in 1976 to 5.2 percent in 1992, while the number of doctoral degrees awarded to blacks declined from 1032 in 1982 to 951 in 1992 (Carter and Wilson, 1995).

Moreover, the overall economic status of African Americans has shown little improvement since the early 1970s. The economic recovery of the 1980s did little to enhance black population income. Although many individual blacks have experienced socioeconomic mobility during the past decade, African Americans remain underrepresented in high-status professional, technical, and managerial positions and overrepresented in service occupations, traditionally recognized as low-status jobs in American society (Farley and Allen, 1987). Furthermore, an enormous gap still separates black and white family incomes. As Figure 9–2 shows, since 1950 income levels for both African American and white families have risen substantially. White median family income more than doubled, increasing from $19,000 (in 1993 dollars) in 1950 to $39,300 in 1993. The median family income for blacks increased more than 108 percent, reaching $21,542 by 1993. Although the gap between black and white incomes tended to narrow slightly during the 1960s, since 1970 this gap has increased (see Figure 9–2). In 1970, black median family income was 61 percent of white family income. By 1993 it stood at 55 percent (U.S. Bureau of the Census, 1992c; 1995a).

An even greater disparity between blacks and whites is revealed in the distribution of wealth (accumulated assets or stored-up purchasing power). As we noted in Chapter 8, a Census Bureau survey of the net worth of American households showed that in 1991 white households had a median net worth of $44,408, while the median net worth of black households was $4,604. As a result of all the economic inequities between blacks and whites, both past and present, white households average about ten times greater net worth than black households (Eller, 1994).

Inequalities in economic status are also reflected in substantial racial differences in poverty, in the increasing concentration and isolation of the poor, and in the increasing severity of their poverty. In 1993, the poverty rate for black families (33 percent) was nearly three times that for white families (12 percent) (U.S. Bureau of the Census, 1995a).

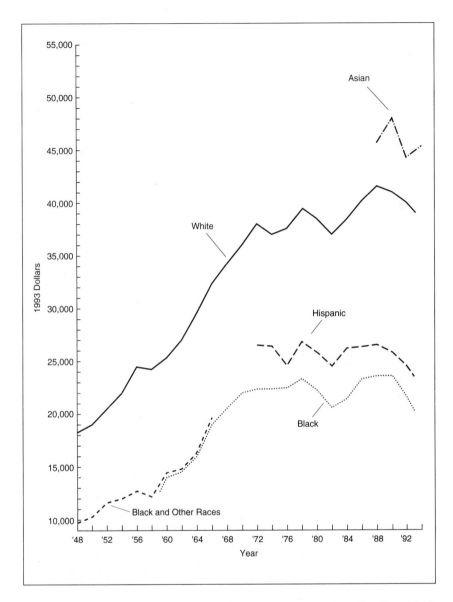

Figure 9–2. Median Income of Black, White, Asian, and Hispanic Families, 1948–1993 (in 1993 U.S. dollars). (*Source:* U.S. Bureau of the Census, *Current Population Reports,* Series P-60, 1964–1991; U.S. Bureau of the Census internet home page, 1996.)

The gap separating African Americans from the mainstream of American life is also reflected by the extreme residential segregation—the "American apartheid"—that they experience. Despite federal legislation outlawing discrimination in the sale of housing and despite a modest decline in the residential segregation of blacks during the 1970s and 1980s (especially in younger southern and western metropolitan areas with recent housing construction), blacks and whites remained highly segregated in 1990, especially in older, large northeastern and midwestern metropolitan areas with older housing stock. Historically, this segregation has been primarily a result of racial discrimination, not class differences; even affluent blacks have lived in predominantly black neighborhoods. Although there is some indication that during the 1980s middle- and upper-income African Americans were better able than in the past to obtain housing commensurate with their incomes, other American racial and ethnic minorities—notably Asians and Hispanics—do not experience levels of housing segregation comparable to those of blacks (Massey and Denton, 1987, 1988, 1993; Farley and Frey, 1994).

The patterns of discrimination responsible for black residential segregation include efforts by some people in the housing industry who discourage blacks from buying homes in white neighborhoods and organized neighborhood resistance to proposals for low-income and moderate-income housing. Another crucial source of housing discrimination involves home loans. A study that analyzed over 10 million applications for home loans from every savings and loan association in the country between 1983 and 1988 showed that black applications were rejected more than twice as often as the applications by whites. Moreover, the applications of high-income blacks were rejected more often than those of low-income whites (Dedman, 1989). Similarly, a Federal Reserve Board study of 5.3 million mortgage applications received by 9300 bank and lending institutions in 1990 found that whites within the same income group were nearly twice as likely as blacks to get home loans (Canner and Smith, 1991). These findings were reinforced by a 1992 Federal Reserve Board study of racial difference in denials of mortgage applications in the Boston metropolitan area, which found that "even after controlling for financial, employment, and neighborhood characteristics, black and Hispanic mortgage applicants...are 60 percent more likely to be turned down than whites" (Munnell et al., 1992). Thus the substantial differences separating black and white Americans economically, educationally, and residentially have not been eliminated, and in some respects they have widened during the past decade.

Hispanic Americans

Hispanic Americans constitute one of the largest and most rapidly growing ethnic categories in the United States today. During the 1980s the Hispanic, or Latino, population grew nearly five times faster than the rest of the population, reaching a total of more than 26 million, or 10 percent of the total population, by 1995.

Recent projections suggest that the Hispanic population will surpass the African American population by 2010 and total nearly 90 million, or 22 percent of the population, by 2050 (Day, 1993).

The recent growth of the Latino population has produced some dramatic changes in the ethnic composition of many American cities. By 1994, Hispanics outnumbered blacks in four of the nation's ten largest cities—Los Angeles, Houston, Phoenix, and San Antonio, as well as such other major cities as Miami, El Paso, Pittsburgh, and San Francisco. And, given their higher growth rates, Hispanics are projected to exceed blacks in New York City in the very near future.

The overall economic status of Hispanics is only slightly higher than that of African Americans. In 1993, Hispanic median family income was only 60 percent of white income; nearly a third (31 percent) of Hispanic families lived in poverty. Reflecting the interrelated impact of class, gender, and ethnicity, more than half (52 percent) of poor Hispanic families were headed by women (compared to 29 percent of non-Hispanic white families in poverty (U.S. Bureau of the Census, 1995a). One-third of all Hispanic children lived in poverty, and during the 1980s childhood poverty increased more rapidly among Hispanics than among any other racial or ethnic group (Huckshorn, 1991). Finally, in 1991 the median net worth of Hispanic households was $5,345, less than one-eighth the net worth of non-Hispanic white households (Eller, 1994).

Since 1970, the educational attainments of Hispanic Americans have improved substantially. The proportion of adult Hispanics with less than a fifth grade education declined. The proportion who were high school graduates increased from less than one-third (32 percent) in 1970 to more than half (53 percent) in 1993; similarly, the proportion who were college graduates doubled, increasing from less than one-twentieth (4.5 percent) in 1970 to nearly one-tenth (9.4 percent) of the adult Hispanic population in 1992 (U.S. Bureau of the Census, 1993; 1994). Nevertheless, Hispanics still lag considerably behind the educational attainments of non-Hispanic whites, Asians, and African Americans. In 1992, slightly over half of 18- to 24-year-old Hispanics had graduated from high school, compared to nearly three-fourths (74.6 percent) of blacks and five-sixths (83.3 percent) of non-Hispanic whites. Moreover, only 21 percent of 18- to 24-year-old Latinos were enrolled in college, compared to 35 percent of non-Hispanic whites and 25 percent of African Americans (Carter and Wilson, 1994, 1995).

Latino political representation in some respects parallels the situation of African Americans. Reflecting the impact of the 1965 Voting Rights Act and the rapidly increasing Hispanic population, in the past two decades Hispanics have gained political strength; by 1995, nearly 5459 Hispanics held public office in the United States. Nevertheless, Hispanics still accounted for only about 1 percent of all elected officials, far below the 10 percent of the population that they represent (Brimhall-Vargas, 1994). One reason for the relatively small number of Hispanic political figures is that, because the Hispanic population is very young and includes many recent immigrants, Latinos comprise a disproportionately small share of the electorate. However, as Hispanic youth achieve voting age and immigrants obtain citizenship, it is likely that the power of Hispanic voters will increase.

Although Latinos are more likely than the rest of the population to be Spanish speaking, Catholic, and poor, they do not constitute a single ethnic category; there are widely diverse cultural, historical, and geographic backgrounds among them. The category of Hispanics includes representatives from more than 20 Latin American and Caribbean nations, as well as from Spain and Portugal. More than three-fourths of Hispanic Americans are of Mexican, Puerto Rican, or Cuban descent, but there are also substantial communities from the Caribbean, Central America, and South America—for example, Salvadorans, Dominicans, Colombians, Guatemalans, Nicaraguans, Ecuadorians, and several other Latin nationalities—in the United States (U.S. Bureau of the Census, 1993). We focus here on the three largest Hispanic ethnic groups: Mexicans, Puerto Ricans, and Cubans.

Mexican Americans (or Chicanos) are the largest Hispanic group and (after blacks) the second largest minority group in American society. More than 17 million Chicanos live in the United States, about 90 percent of them in the southwestern states of Texas, New Mexico, Arizona, Colorado, and California. The earliest Mexican Americans became a minority through the annexation of Mexican lands by the United States in the nineteenth century. However, most Mexican Americans are descended from immigrants who came to the United States in the twentieth century. Mexican immigration is still a major factor in American society; today Mexicans are the largest national category of both legal and illegal immigrants to the United States. The proximity of Mexico to the United States enables Mexican Americans, even in the third and fourth generations, to maintain close ties with their families in Mexico, reinforcing their cultural identity and language.

Several indicators reveal that Mexican Americans lag considerably behind the mainstream of American society in socioeconomic status. Despite some evidence of improvement among younger generations, Mexican American educational attainment is less than that of both whites and African Americans. Long stereotyped as primarily rural farm workers, today Mexican Americans are overwhelmingly urban residents. However, they tend to be found primarily in low-paying blue-collar and semiskilled occupations that have been especially hard hit by the decline of manufacturing and the downsizing of economic sectors, such as military-related jobs, that have contributed to rising Hispanic unemployment during a period of economic growth (1992–1995) in which overall unemployment declined (Hershey, 1995). As Table 9–3 indicates, in 1993 median family income for Mexican Americans was only 59 percent of white median family income; nearly one-third (32 percent) of Mexican American families had incomes below the poverty level (U.S. Bureau of the Census, 1995).

Other Spanish-speaking peoples have immigrated primarily to urban areas on the East Coast, particularly since the end of World War II. Although the number of immigrants from countries throughout the Caribbean and Central and South

Table 9–3   Median Family Income in 1993

	Income ($)	Percent of White Income
All races	36,959	
White	39,300	
Black	21,542	55
Hispanic	23,670	60
Mexican	23,361	59
Puerto Rican	19,687	50
Cuban	27,038	69
Central and South American	25,324	64
Other Hispanic[a]	25,059	64

[a]Includes those who identified themselves as from Spain or as Hispanic, Spanish, Spanish-American, Hispano, or Latino.

Sources: U.S. Bureau of the Census, "Income, Poverty, and Valuation of Noncash Benefits: 1993," *Current Population Reports,* Series P60-188. Washington, D.C.: U.S. Government Printing Office, 1995; U.S. Bureau of the Census, "Statistical Tables for the Hispanic Origin Population From the March 1994 Current Population Survey," September, 1995.

America has increased markedly during this period, Puerto Rico and Cuba have been the two primary sources.

Puerto Ricans, who, unlike other immigrants, are American citizens, began migrating to the mainland primarily after World War II. Today, nearly two-thirds of the more than 2 million mainland Puerto Ricans live in New York City, which has been the principal magnet for Puerto Rican immigrants. This migration to the mainland has been prompted primarily by economic pressures among the impoverished lower strata of Puerto Rican society. Consequently, Puerto Rican immigrants have been concentrated in blue-collar, semiskilled, and unskilled occupations, and their income level (50 percent of white median family income) is the lowest and their poverty rate (38 percent) among the highest for American ethnic groups.

Cuban immigrants have been primarily political refugees. Approximately 750,000 Cubans have entered the United States since Castro's rise to power in 1959, and today they number more than 1 million. In contrast to most previous immigrations to the United States, early Cuban immigrants tended to be drawn mainly from the upper social and economic strata of Cuban society. With these backgrounds, they brought skills (educational, occupational, business, and managerial), entrepreneurial values, and substantial amounts of financial capital that enabled them to achieve rapid socioeconomic success. Assisted by federal government programs that facilitated their adjustment to American society, in the 30 years since their initial migration, Cubans have become the most affluent of all Hispanics and are an integral part of the economies of a number of American cities, especially Miami, Florida, which they have transformed into a major commercial center with ties throughout Latin America. Nevertheless, in 1992 Cuban family income was still only 69 percent of white income, and the Cuban poverty rate was 20 percent compared to the overall white rate of 12 percent (U.S. Bureau of the Census, 1995).

Asian Americans

Asian Americans are an extremely diverse category that includes Chinese, Japanese, Filipinos, Koreans, Asian Indians, Vietnamese, Cambodians, Laotians, and several other national or ethnic groups. Some have resided in the United States for generations; others have arrived very recently. Compared to the millions of Europeans who have immigrated to the United States, Asian immigration has historically been slight; as late as 1970, Asians were just 0.7 percent of the total population. However, as a result of changes in U.S. immigration laws, which before 1965 had virtually excluded them, Asians today are proportionately the nation's fastest growing racial category. During the 1980s, Asians constituted more than two-fifths (42 percent) of all legal immigrants, and the Asian population increased by 107 percent (compared to increases by Hispanics of 53 percent, by American Indians of 40 percent, and by African Americans of 13 percent). By 1990, Asians numbered 7.3 million, which represented 2.9 percent of the American people (U.S. Commission on Civil Rights, 1992, p. 15).

This rapid growth of the Asian American population is expected to continue during the twenty-first century, reaching 12 million by 2000 and 41 million (or about 10 percent of the population) by 2050 (Day, 1993). Although almost all states experienced substantial increases in their Asian populations during the 1980s, almost 40 percent of all Asian Americans live in California, where they represent nearly 10 percent of the state's population (Min, 1995, p. 20).

Historically, the Chinese, Japanese, and, later, Filipinos have been the most prominent Asian groups; Asian Indians, Koreans, Vietnamese, Cambodians, and Laotians are more recent arrivals. The initial migration of Chinese, who were the first Asians to immigrate to the United States, began in the 1850s and reached its peak from 1873 to 1882. Initially welcomed as a source of labor, the Chinese soon became perceived as an economic threat to native labor, and they were subjected to various forms of discriminatory legislation as well as to discrimination at the hands of individuals. In 1882, Congress passed the Chinese Exclusion Act, the first law to restrict a specific nationality from immigrating to the United States.

Anti-Asian sentiment was revived when many Japanese began immigrating to the mainland of the United States in the early twentieth century. Although the Japanese represented an extremely small proportion of the total population, their presence generated intense hostility from whites. Like the Chinese before them, the Japanese were the object of legislation specifically designed to harass them and diplomatic efforts by the American government to prevent their further immigration. In 1924, all Asian immigration to the United States was restricted, and it remained limited until 1968, when a new immigration law went into effect.

Despite intense anti-Asian discrimination, which was exemplified by the evacuation and internment of over 110,000 Japanese Americans (nearly two-thirds of them American citizens) during World War II, Asians have made significant socioeconomic gains. By 1990, 37 percent of the Asian population over age 25 had completed at least 4 years of college, which was nearly double the figure (22 percent) for non-Hispanic whites (Mar and Kim, 1994, p. 38). So extraordinary have Asian educational attainments been that charges have been raised that many of the nation's most prestigious universities have placed limitations on the percentage of Asian students that they admit.

Similarly, the income levels of Asian Americans are slightly higher than those of whites; in 1990, more than one-third (35 percent) of Asian American households had incomes of $50,000 or more, compared to 26 percent of white households (U.S. Bureau of the Census, 1992b *Minority Economic Profiles*). By 1993 Asian American median households income was 116 percent of white households (compared to 59 percent for black and 69 percent for Hispanic households). These achievements have led many observers to praise Asians as "model minorities," who, as *Time* magazine recently reported, "have parlayed cultural emphases on education and hard work into brilliant attainments" (*Time,* 1993, p. 55).

However, the public perception of educational and economic success among Asians masks continued discrimination against them (Kuo, 1995). Asians generally earn less than do non-Hispanic whites of the same age and educational characteristics, and studies have demonstrated that Asians gain 21 percent less than non-Hispanic whites from each year of schooling. Moreover, the high levels of Asian household income may reflect the greater number of Asian household members who work (U.S. Bureau of the Census, 1992b; O'Hare and Felt, 1991). Similarly, during the 1980s the poverty rate for Asians actually increased, and by 1989 it was nearly 50 percent higher than the rate for non-Hispanic whites (Lee, 1994). Finally, focusing on overall income and educational attainments obscures substantial differences among Asian ethnic groups. Although Indian, Japanese, Chinese, and Filipinos have incomes above those of whites, Vietnamese and Koreans earn less (Lee and Edmonston, 1994). Poverty rates also vary considerably among Asian ethnic groups and are especially pronounced among recent Asian immigrants who lack proficiency in English: poverty was highest among Laotians and Cambodians, nearly double white rates among Chinese, Vietnamese, and Koreans, but below white rates among Asian Indians and Filipinos (Lee, 1994, pp. 549–550).

Contemporary Immigration

During the early 1980s a *Time* cover story entitled "The New Ellis Island," concerning the dramatic influx of immigrants into Los Angeles, proclaimed, "Los Angeles is being invaded" (*Time,* June 13, 1983). Fears of an immigrant "invasion" have been voiced frequently throughout American history, especially during periods of heavy immigration and economic stagnation, often by representatives of ethnic groups that had previously been feared. Such sentiments have emerged again during the past quarter-century, during which patterns of immigration into the United States have been transformed. This new immigrant wave promises to produce the most dramatic and far-reaching changes in the ethnic composition of the United States since the influx of "new" immigrants at the turn of the twentieth century. First, the number of immigrants to the United States has increased substantially. During the 1980s, the number averaged over 633,000 annually, compared to 282,000 in the decade prior to 1965 (see Figure 9–3). During the first five years of the 1990s, the number of immigrants averaged 1.2 million, the highest total for any 5-year period in American history. In 1991 alone, more than 1.8 million immigrants were admitted. Moreover, experts estimate that there is an additional net annual increase of about 300,000 illegal immigrants (U.S. Immigration and Naturalization Service, 1994), resulting in the permanent addition of about 1 million new immigrants annually.

The changes in the national origins of contemporary immigrants are as dramatic as their increasing numbers. Until the late 1960s, immigration to the United States was overwhelmingly European, ranging from a high of 96 percent of all immigrants for the decade 1891–1900 to 53 percent between 1950 and 1960. Today, as a result of changes in the global economy and in U.S. immigration laws, only a small percentage (10 percent during the 1980s) of immigrants come from Europe. The predominant sources of immigration are Third World nations in Asia, Central and South America, and the Caribbean. Of the ten leading countries from which the United States received immigrants in 1993, only three—the states of the former Soviet Union combined, Poland, and the United Kingdom—were European. There were more immigrants from Iran than from Ireland, more from Ghana than from Sweden, more from Guatemala than from Germany, more from Trinidad and Tobago than from Italy and the Netherlands combined, and nearly double the number from India as from the United Kingdom (U.S. Immigration and Naturalization Service, 1994). Given the declining birth rate of the U.S. population, some demographers estimate that, if current trends in birth rates and immigration rates continue, by 2050 Hispanics and Asians will comprise nearly one-third (32 percent) of the total population and non-Hispanic whites will represent only a slight majority (53 percent) (Day, 1994). The impact of these immigration trends has been to create a genuinely multiracial, multicultural, cosmopolitan society— what Wattenberg (1991) has characterized as the "first universal nation."

The settlement patterns of today's immigrants differ from previous flows into the United States. Whereas previous immigrants settled primarily in the industrial states of the Northeast and Midwest (New York, Illinois, New Jersey, and Pennsylvania), immigrants today are much more dispersed regionally, but they tend to be highly concentrated in a small number of states. In 1990, six states (California, New York, New Jersey, Florida, Texas, and Illinois) accounted for three-fourths of

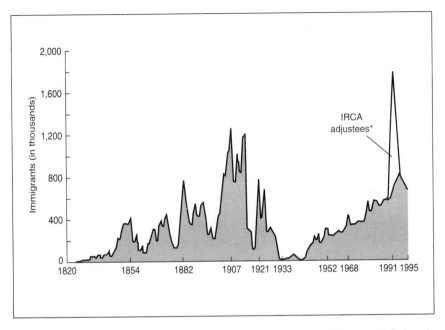

Figure 9–3.   Immigration to the United States, 1821–1995 (*Source:* U.S. Immigration and Naturalization Service. *Statistical Yearbook of the Immigration and Naturalization Service, 1993.* Washington, D.C.: U.S. Government Printing Office, 1994. 1994 and 1995 data provided by Immigration and Naturalization Service internet home page, 1996.)

IRCA adjustees refers to a special category of immigrants—illegal aliens who, under the provisions of the Immigration and Control Act of 1986 (IRCA), were permitted to apply for regular permanent resident status in the United States. By 1994 virtually all those eligible for permanent residence had achieved that status.

the foreign-born population; over one-third lived in California alone, and Los Angeles has become the largest immigrant city in the world, with 2.9 million foreign-born residents (which represented one-third of its population).

When Americans think of immigrants to the United States, they often have an image of "huddled masses" who are poor, unskilled, and uneducated. Changes in U.S. immigration laws since 1965 have affected the occupational and educational composition of the present immigrant population. On the one hand, whereas a substantial proportion of immigrants to the United States during the first two decades of the twentieth century were unskilled, blue-collar workers, post-1965 immigration laws have established preferences for immigrants with skills needed in the United States. Physicians, nurses, scientists, architects, artists, entertainers, engineers, and others with highly technical skills have contributed to a "brain drain," first from Europe and later from Third World nations and to the profile of contemporary immigrants as highly educated and technically skilled. For example, today, the overall educational level of foreign-born in the United States is similar to that of the native-born. 20.3 percent of native-born U.S. adults aged 25 and over have completed college, while 20.4 percent of immigrants have done so. Immigrants from Africa and Asia are especially well educated; in 1990 almost half (47 percent) of African and more than one-third (38 percent) of Asian immigrants had completed college (Rumbaut, 1994, p. 607).

On the other hand, because the overwhelming majority of recent immigrants entered the U.S. under preferences or family reunification, a substantial proportion are also unskilled, poor, and relatively uneducated. Indeed, although immigrants are disproportionately represented among the nation's most highly educated people, they are also more likely than native-born Americans to be among the most poorly educated. Moreover, immigrants are also more likely than natives to be poor and to be the recipients of public assistance (Rumbaut, 1994, 606–614). Moreover, Borjas (1994) has argued that over the past two decades overall immigrant skill levels have actually declined.

The preferences for immigrants with skills has meant that, unlike the situation for most of American history prior to 1965, it has become almost impossible for unskilled workers to enter the United States legally unless they can claim a close family relationship or refugee status. Because recent immigration laws established a preference for those with occupational skills, increasingly the less skilled have resorted to illegal means of entering the U.S. Despite increased efforts to restrict the numbers of "undocumented aliens," in 1993, 1.3 million illegal immigrants from over 100 countries were apprehended, the vast majority from Latin America, especially Mexico (U.S. Immigration and Naturalization Service, 1994). Although, as we noted earlier, the estimated annual net increase from illegal immigrants is substantially lower than from legal immigrants, the U.S. Immigration and Naturalization Service estimates that the total number of undocumented aliens living in the United States is about 3.3 million (U.S. Immigration and Naturalization Service, 1994, p. 183).

As was the case in the early part of the twentieth century, concern over the political, cultural, and, especially, economic impact of immigration has created a growing sense of alarm among many native-born Americans that these new immigrants will have a negative impact on American society, draining economic resources, taking jobs from American citizens, and transforming (for some undermining) American culture and social institutions. Immigration restrictionist sentiments have historically increased during and been exacerbated by periods of economic recession and anxiety, and this relationship has recently been most glaringly apparent in California. In 1994, in the throes of a recession greatly influenced by substantial reductions in military spending, Californians overwhelmingly supported Proposition 187, a ballot referendum that denies state-supported health and educational services to illegal immigrants and their children. The success of that referendum galvanized restrictionist advocates in the United States Congress to "take control of our borders" by adopting further measures not only to curtail illegal immigration but to further limit levels of legal immigration as well. And it provided a powerful vehicle in 1994 for the re-election campaign of California governor Pete Wilson and in 1996 for the presidential campaign of Republican Pat Buchanan, who advocated a moratorium on immigration for five years.

Explanations of Racial and Ethnic Inequality

Inevitably, questions arise as to why racial and ethnic inequalities exist. Why have some groups been able to "make it" while other groups have not? Explanations of differences in income levels, education, and occupational success among American ethnic groups can be divided into two broad categories: those that emphasize qualities and characteristics *internal* to an ethnic group and those that emphasize factors *external* to an ethnic group, forces over which members of the group have no control.

Internal Explanations

Internal explanations of social inequality attribute racial and ethnic inequality to each group's abilities and characteristics. Each ethnic group is believed to possess distinctive qualities that determine its economic, political, and social status. Dominant groups have achieved their status because they possess desirable qualities; the economic, political, and social status of subordinate groups is attributed to their deficiencies. Therefore, in this view, racial and ethnic groups are responsible for their own fate.

Biology. One of the oldest internal explanations is that racial groups have different *biological* endowments, innately different mental, emotional, and moral characteristics that are genetically transmitted from generation to generation. Such explanations flourished during the late nineteenth and early twentieth centuries, when differences between the political, social, and economic institutions of Anglo-Saxon and non-Anglo-Saxon peoples were attributed to biologically transmitted—that is, "racial"—traits. During this period the ideology of racism gained respectability. **Racism** involves a belief in the inherent superiority of one racial group and the inherent inferiority of others. Its primary function is to provide a set of ideas and beliefs that can be used to explain, rationalize, and justify a system of racial domination.

For more than a century the ideology of racism has been shaped and justified by "science." Early in the twentieth century, studies of cranial capacity—brain sizes and structures—became fashionable. Assuming that brain size and intelligence are related, scientists established a racial hierarchy of intelligence, with northern Europeans highest and Africans lowest. Recalculation of the data in many of these studies has shown that the procedures that were used simply supported the scientists' prejudices; these procedures amounted to "advocacy masquerading as objectivity" (Gould, 1981). Although the studies were far from scientific, they were used to prove the biological superiority of northern and western Europeans and justify social policies of racial domination.

Early in the twentieth century, intelligence testing replaced anatomic studies as a way of scientifically validating the "natural superiority" of socially dominant groups. Intelligence tests have continued to play a crucial role in reinforcing the belief that racial and ethnic inequalities result from innate qualities.

Since the 1910s and 1920s, intelligence tests have been widely administered and have had a direct impact on public policy. The poor performances of southern and eastern European immigrants were frequently cited in the congressional debates that resulted in the discriminatory immigration quotas established during the 1920s. Moreover, racial differences in intelligence test results provided the justification for racial segregation, vastly unequal school systems for blacks and whites, and the virtual exclusion of blacks from higher education (Gould, 1981; Weinberg, 1983).

By the mid-twentieth century, as criticisms of these tests and their uses mounted, the notion of racial differences in intelligence found little support in the scientific community. However, after the Supreme Court's 1954 *Brown* decision, the issue of racial differences in intelligence was revived and became a prominent argument in the southern campaign of "massive resistance" to school desegregation.

The alleged genetic component in interracial IQ differences became the subject of international debate in 1969 with the publication of an article by Arthur R. Jensen in the *Harvard Education Review.* Jensen distinguished between two types of learning: *associative* (involving memory and rote learning) and *conceptual* (involving problem solving and the use of abstractions). He contended that, while all children possess associative learning abilities, poor and minority children are deficient in conceptual learning abilities and that these differences are "genetically conditioned" (Jensen, 1969).

A quarter-century later, *The Bell Curve,* a book by Richard Herrnstein and Charles Murray (1994), has once again raised the claim that certain groups in American society—especially African Americans—are intellectually inferior because they generally have lower scores on standardized intelligence tests. Equally important, Herrnstein and Murray claim that the stratification system of the United States is a direct reflection of the differential intelligence of individuals and groups and that intelligence is primarily inherited or genetic. Their argument is presented in a massive (845 pages) volume, filled with statistics and graphs, that, for all its scholarly sophistication, simply represents another effort to demonstrate "scientifically" that some groups are intellectually inferior to others and to justify the inequalities among them.

Jensen's and Herrnstein and Murray's arguments were in each instance greeted by an avalanche of criticism from psychologists, sociologists, and geneticists, who attacked their logic, methods, and evidence and, above all, the implications that differences in intelligence test scores should influence public and educational policy. (See *"The Bell Curve:* The Legitimization of the Status Quo" on page 302.)

Culture.   Today, biological explanations of racial and ethnic inequality enjoy little scientific support. One of the changes in the study of human behavior in the twentieth century has involved an understanding of the process by which behavioral characteristics are transmitted. Traits that once were considered to be "instinctual," innate, genetic, and biologically inherited, are today thought to be learned, a product not of the genes but of socialization, the process by which a person learns and accepts the ways of a particular social group. Therefore, the most commonly heard internal explanation today is a **cultural explanation of social inequality** that emphasizes racial and ethnic differences in cultural characteristics: the values, attitudes, beliefs, customs, and habits learned in the family and the community. In this view, the ethnic groups that have succeeded have done so because they possess values and behaviors that make for success in American society: high achievement motivation, industriousness, perseverance, orientation to the future, ability to postpone immediate gratification, and so forth. By contrast, a group's low socioeconomic status can be attributed to the fact that its cultural inventory does not include the requisite values, attitudes, and personal qualities.

For example, cultural factors have frequently been cited to explain the extremely high educational, occupational, and income attainments of Jews, whose values and cultural norms are perceived as being compatible with the dominant American values. Jewish immigrants, reflecting traditional Orthodox Jewish culture, emphasized education, learning, and scholarly inquiry (Strodtbeck, 1958; Steinberg, 1989). By contrast, the disadvantaged position of African Americans, Hispanics, and American Indians today is simply a consequence of cultural characteristics incompatible with a modern industrial society (Sowell, 1980).

Therefore, an ethnic group's value system and social institutions—especially the family—are seen as the sources of its success or failure. By implication, groups that have been less successful can enter the American mainstream by becoming more fully culturally assimilated by simply adopting the cultural values of the dominant group.

However, the argument that *values* explain the relative success of different ethnic groups has been criticized for ignoring differences in social class backgrounds among racial and ethnic groups and the different resources that social class position confers. Social class factors include both financial capital (money and property) and human capital (skills, education, and knowledge). Steinberg has pointed out that the social class characteristics of different American ethnic groups have

In the News

The Bell Curve: The Scientific Legitimization of the Status Quo

Throughout the twentieth century, one of the most prominent, recurring, and bitterly contested explanations for social inequality in American life is that socioeconomic, ethnic, and racial groups differ in intellectual abilities. Early in the twentieth century, intelligence (IQ) tests were developed to provide a "scientific" way of measuring intelligence and, since the 1910s and 1920s, have been widely administered and have had profound impact on public policy. The poor performances of southern and eastern European immigrants were frequently cited in the congressional debates that resulted in the discriminatory immigration quotas established during the 1920s. Moreover, racial differences in intelligence test results provided the justification for the Jim Crow system of racial segregation that included vastly unequal school systems for blacks and whites (Weinberg, 1983; Gould, 1981).

In *The Bell Curve,* Richard Herrnstein and Charles Murray have presented a massive (845 pages), detailed, and painstaking defense of that proposition. The authors argue that intelligence ("a person's capacity for complex mental work") describes a real attribute of humans that is "substantially" (60 percent) inherited and remains stable over a person's lifetime. Moreover, they assert that intelligence "can be measured with accuracy and fairness by any number of standardized mental tests, [which] are not biased against socioeconomic, ethnic, and racial groups." Numerical intelligence test (IQ) scores thus reflect individual and group intelligence levels. Examining a great amount of data, they maintain that in American society today measured intelligence (IQ) is positively correlated with success, as measured by educational and occupational attainment and overall socioeconomic status, and is negatively correlated with poverty, unemployment, single-parent families, and criminality. They conclude that the class structure of contemporary American society reflects the distribution of intelligence; the upper classes are comprised of members of the "cognitive elite," while the less intelligent are overrepresented in the lower classes. Moreover, they contend that races differ in intelligence and that the lower IQ test performance of blacks and Latinos indicates that they are less intelligent than whites and Asians. Finally, they find that many modern social problems—poverty, unemployment, poor parenting, single-parent families, welfare dependency, and crime—result from low intelligence and, as a consequence, social and educational programs (for example, Head Start) designed to improve and remedy such conditions are ineffective.

However, critics have vigorously opposed Herrnstein and Murray's basic assumptions, procedures and methods, interpretations, and conclusions; they argue that, despite the wealth of data Herrnstein and Murray cite, the two authors ignore, omit, misrepresent, or use selectively evidence that contradicts their basic argument. *The Bell Curve,* according to one reviewer is "clearly the most incendiary piece of social science to appear in the last decade or more."

First, numerous critics challenge Herrnstein and Murray's assumption that intelligence is a single, primarily inherited trait that can be accurately measured by IQ tests; rather they argue that intelligence involves multiple and distinctly different attributes—language skills, mathematical skills, musical ability, interpersonal skills, artistic ability, and spatial relations abilities, for example—that cannot be reduced to a single overall measure. Moreover, they reject the magnitude of Herrnstein and Murray's estimates of the genetic inheritance of intelligence, which are based on inferences drawn from studies of pairs of biological relatives (that is, different IQ correlations between identical twins, fraternal twins, siblings, and first cousins). Such studies measure not only genetic factors but also the effect of environmental factors, which Herrnstein and Murray minimize. "The more similar a pair is biologically, then the more similar they are as well in their environment"— even among twins separated early in life and raised in different environments. Thus, performance on IQ tests depends not simply on an individual's innate "intelligence," but on what a person has previously learned (Hanson, 1995).

Critics also contest Herrnstein and Murray's contention that, because intelligence is substantially genetic, it changes little in the lives of individuals or the histories of racial and ethnic groups. Contrary to Herrnstein and Murray's objections that programs such as Head Start have failed to enhance educational performance, the American Psychological Association released a press statement that "there is a wealth of research evidence showing that early educational interventions are effective in raising performance and achievement levels for disadvantaged groups." Similarly, after recalculating data used by Herrnstein and Murray, Hauser (1995) and Nisbitt (1995) independently showed that improvements in black test scores between 1969 and 1990 undermine notions of the immutability of intelligence over time. Similarly, conservative economist Thomas Sowell has noted that the test performances of numerous American ethnic groups (Jews, Italians, Poles) have improved dramatically over the course of the twentieth century.

The reliability of IQ tests themselves have been questioned. Taylor (1995) rejects Herrnstein and Murray's assertion that such tests are free of cultural bias and argues that the authors selectively ignored evidence of such cultural bias in some of the studies that they themselves cite. Moreover, Wolfe (1995) challenges the notion that IQ predicts later career success, contending that there is no evidence that IQ test performance is related to job performance or income attainments. Finally, assertions of intelligence differences between racial groups ignores the arbitrary, socially constructed nature of such categories. In American society the categories of "white," "black," and

"Asian" are not real "biological" entities, but rather are comprised of people with a wide range of biological characteristics. In order for inferences to be drawn about racial characteristics, it would be necessary to have distinct, "pure" biological pools, which, given the extraordinary ethnic diversity of the American people, obviously is not the case in the United States.

Herrnstein and Murray conclude *The Bell Curve* with a discussion of the public policy implications of their findings. Critics charge that the real objective of *The Bell Curve* is to advance and provide justification for the authors' conservative policy agenda; although they cloak their argument in mantle of "science," the authors' real objective is to attack a number of public policies, including welfare, affirmative action, and immigration.

FRASER, STEVEN, ed. *The Bell Curve Wars.* New York: Basic Books, 1995.

GOULD, STEPHEN J. "Curveball." In S. Fraser (ed.), *The Bell Curve Wars.* New York: Basic Books, 1995.

GOULD, STEPHEN J. *The Mismeasure of Man.* New York: Norton, 1981.

HANSON, H. ALLAN. "Testing, *The Bell Curve,* and the Social Construction of Intelligence." *Tikkun,* 10:1, 1995.

HAUSER, ROBERT M. Review of *The Bell Curve. Contemporary Sociology* 24:2, March 1995.

HERRNSTEIN, RICHARD J., and MURRAY, CHARLES. *The Bell Curve: Intelligence and Class Structure in American Life.* New York: Free Press, 1994.

NISBITT, RICHARD. "Race, IQ, and Scientism." In S. Fraser (ed.), *The Bell Curve Wars.* New York: Basic Books, 1995.

SOWELL, THOMAS. "Ethnicity and IQ." In S. Fraser (ed.), *The Bell Curve Wars.* New York: Basic Books, 1995.

TAYLOR, HOWARD F. Review of *The Bell Curve. Contemporary Sociology* 24:2, March 1995.

WEINBERG, MEYER. *The Search for Quality Integrated Education.* Westport, CT: Greenwood Press, 1983.

WOLFE, ALAN. "Has There Been a Cognitive Revolution in America? The Flawed Sociology of *The Bell Curve.* In S. Fraser (ed.), *The Bell Curve Wars.* New York: Basic Books, 1995.

critically influenced their adaptation to American society and especially the socioeconomic status of their descendants.

For example, Jews experienced much more rapid social mobility than did other European immigrant groups, not because of their cultural values but because they came to the United States equipped with superior skills and higher levels of education (Steinberg, 1989). Social class factors have also had an impact on the different ways in which various Hispanic and Asian immigrants have adapted to the United States. Cubans, the most affluent Hispanic group, have been drawn disproportionately from the upper classes of Cuban society and have brought with them not only substantial amounts of financial capital, but, equally important, relatively high levels of education and skills useful in a modern American society. Puerto Rican immigrants, by contrast, have been relatively poor and unskilled. Among

Asians, Japanese immigrants to the United States were typically more highly edu-cated and skilled than other Asian groups; today the Japanese have the highest educational and income levels of all Asian groups.

External Explanations

External explanations of social inequality emphasize the external constraints, disabilities, limitations, and barriers to which a group is subjected and that serve as obstacles to achievement. Some groups (for example, African Americans) have been confronted with substantial barriers that have limited the resources available to them and precluded their free and equal participation in American society.

Because most American ethnic groups had to overcome hardships and barriers of some sort, cultural interpretations tend to minimize the impact of external bar-riers in limiting group opportunities. Even when past discrimination is acknowl-edged, its impact on contemporary American society is minimized (Sowell, 1980). A cultural perspective therefore assumes that American society provides a relatively level playing field for all racial and ethnic groups.

Moreover, a cultural argument generally views culture as fixed and unalter-able, rather than dynamic. Critics of the cultural perspective see a group's behav-iors, values, and attitudes—its culture—as an adaptive phenomenon, something that changes constantly in response to external conditions. For example, in explaining differences among ethnic groups in school performance, John Ogbu has distinguished between the experiences of "voluntary" or "immigrant" and "involuntary" or "castelike" minorities. *Voluntary* minorities entered American society believing that the quality of their lives would be enhanced, and their per-ceptions of American institutions are likely to be optimistic and positive. *Involun-tary* minorities, by contrast, have been incorporated into American society against their will and perceive the dominant group—European Americans—and Ameri-can institutions as a source of oppression rather than opportunity. Thus, the edu-cational inequalities of involuntary minorities—African Americans, Puerto Ricans, American Indians, and Chicanos—have not been caused simply by the absence of a cultural emphasis on education; rather, their poor academic perfor-mance is a product of their perception that academic achievement will not be rewarded because of the economic, social, and political barriers that they have experienced. In other words, the absence of high educational aspirations, high motivation for academic achievement, and an orientation toward the future is a coping mechanism, a response to their realistic perception that their job opportu-nities are extremely restricted (Ogbu, 1990). Lower school performance is merely a symptom of the way in which external factors shape cultural characteristics.

From an external perspective, therefore, it is the opportunity structure, not cul-tural characteristics, that accounts for racial and ethnic inequalities. Conse-quently, it is the opportunity structure, the range of occupational opportunities, not minority cultures, that must be changed to reduce the inequalities of American life.

Therefore, the assumptions of a cultural explanation of inequality have been challenged by people who contend that the barriers confronting Chicanos, Puerto Ricans, American Indians, and, in particular, African Americans have been qualitatively different from those encountered by European immigrants or even by Asians. External explanations focus on the role of prejudice and discrimination in creating and maintaining racial and ethnic inequality.

Prejudice and Discrimination

Prejudice and discrimination are important elements in all majority–minority relations. The term *prejudice* (derived from two Latin words, *prae,* before, and *judicum,* judgment) denotes a judgment before all the facts are known. **Prejudice** refers to a set of rigidly held negative attitudes, beliefs, and feelings toward members of another group. **Discrimination,** on the other hand, involves unfavorable treatment of individuals because of their group membership. Unlike prejudice, which is an attitude and an internal state, discrimination involves overt action or behavior.

Clearly, however, a close relationship frequently exists between prejudice and discrimination. Because they are related, an extensive amount of research has been carried out concerning the nature and causes of prejudice. Attitude surveys conducted since the 1940s have shown a significant decline in antiblack prejudice; increasingly, white Americans have come to support broad principles of racial integration and equal treatment in public accommodations, employment, public transportation, schools, and housing. For example, in 1942, 32 percent agreed that whites and blacks should attend the same schools; by 1982 this figure was 90 percent. In 1944, 45 percent thought that blacks should have as good a chance as whites to get any kind of job and, by 1972, 97 percent agreed. The percentage approving integration in public transportation rose from 46 percent in 1942 to 88 percent in 1970. Moreover, whites have indicated increasing willingness to participate personally in desegregated settings (Schuman et al., 1985). Illustrative is the decline in opposition to residential integration. In 1963 almost half of whites (45 percent) said they would move if black people moved next door, but by 1990 only 5 percent indicated that they would (Gallup and Hugick, 1990, p. 27). These changes are a result of two factors. First, they reflect attitude changes among individuals over their lifetimes. Second, younger people generally exhibit less racial prejudice than their elders, and as younger, more tolerant, cohorts have replaced older, more prejudiced ones, overall racial prejudice has declined (Firebaugh and Davis, 1988).

However, the same striking agreement does not appear among Americans on how to combat discrimination or segregation (Jaynes and Williams, 1989). Although today white Americans endorse broad principles of nondiscrimination and desegregation in important areas of American life, they are much less likely to support specific policies for translating these principles into practice. For example, despite their strong support of the principle of integrated education, the percentage of whites who felt that the federal government should ensure that black and white children attend the same schools declined between the 1960s and the 1980s. Moreover, widespread white opposition was raised to busing as a means of desegregating schools (Schuman et al., 1985).

The substantial gap between people's support for broad principles of equality and their support for specific programs to implement these principles indicates the complexity of racial attitudes. The relationship between prejudicial attitudes and discriminatory behavior is equally complex. Although prejudice is frequently seen as the cause of discrimination, it does not always produce discrimination. An individual can be prejudiced without *acting* in a discriminatory manner. Whether prejudice is expressed in discriminatory *acts* is strongly influenced by the social context in which the prejudice occurs. Discrimination is much more likely to occur in a social environment in which acts of ethnic and racial bias are accepted or not strongly condemned.

This principle, which has been established from numerous social psychological studies, was recently underscored in a study at Smith College, where in 1989 racial tensions erupted after four black students received anonymous hate messages. Researchers asked students walking across campus how they felt about these incidents. Before the student could answer, a confederate, arriving at precisely the same time, would respond, by either strongly condemning or strongly justifying the incidents. The researchers found that students' opinions were strongly influenced by those expressed by the confederates. Hearing others express strongly racist opinions produced similar sentiments, whereas students who first heard expressions more accepting of racism offered "significantly less strongly anti-racist opinions produced similar sentiments, whereas students who first heard expressions more accepting of racism offered "significantly less strongly anti-racist opinions" (Blanchard et al., 1991, p. 104). Clearly, the social climate strongly affects whether personal prejudices are translated into discriminatory acts.

Because sociologists are primarily concerned with understanding human behavior, the primary focus in or analysis of racial and ethnic inequality is on discrimination, which is the means of preserving the inferior social, economic, and political position of minorities and the power and privileges of the majority. Discrimination can range from mild slights (ethnic jokes and slurs, for instance) to systematic oppression (slavery) to violence (lynching, pogroms, ethnic cleansing, and genocide). We can distinguish two interrelated and mutually reinforcing types of discrimination: attitudinal and institutional.

Attitudinal discrimination refers to discriminatory practices that stem from prejudicial attitudes. The discriminator either is prejudiced or acts in response to the prejudices of others. Attitudinal discrimination is usually direct, overt, blatant, and visible. Despite increasing verbal acceptance by whites of principles of nondiscrimination and racial integration, African Americans especially have been confronted with attitudinal discrimination in virtually every public aspect of their lives. Many of the discriminatory acts encountered by blacks appear inconsequential to white observers—a white couple crossing the street to avoid walking past a black male; a "hate stare"; receiving poor service in restaurants, stores, hotels, or business services. Many whites also trivialize the discrimination resulting from racial slurs and epithets. Incidents of this kind are seldom reported in the press, but they are demeaning realities to which African Americans of all social classes are consistently exposed (Feagin, 1991; Feagin and Sikes, 1994; Cose, 1993).

Much more dramatic incidents of discrimination have been reported in the news media (although many such incidents go unreported). For example, the 1991 brutal beating of Rodney King by members of the Los Angeles Police Department was captured on videotape, was widely publicized, and drew widespread attention to the vulnerability of blacks to police harassment. Yet the King incident was only one of 15,000 complaints of police brutality filed with the federal government between 1985 and 1991 (Lewis, 1991, p. 1). Moreover, during the 1980s hundreds of incidents of intimidation, harassment, vandalism, and attacks occurred against racial and religious minorities, including more than 200 on college campuses between 1986 and 1988 alone (*Time,* 1987; Ehrlich, 1990; U.S. Commission on Civil Rights, 1990).

In a study involving interviews with African Americans from throughout the United States, Feagin found that, despite antidiscrimination legislation and changing white attitudes, even middle-class blacks remain vulnerable targets for discrimination and that incidents of discrimination against them are far from isolated; they are cumulative—that is, a black person's encounters with discrimination are best described as a "lifelong series of such incidents" (Feagin, 1991, p. 109). One informant, a professor at a major university, described the constant tension that these experiences and the anticipation of them created.

> [One problem with] being black in America is that you have to spend so much time thinking about it. I worry when I get pulled over by a cop. I worry because the person that I live with is a black male, and I have a teen-aged son. I worry what some white cop is going to think when he walks over to our car, because he's holding on to a gun. And I'm very aware of how many black folks accidentally get shot by cops. I worry when I walk into a store, that someone's going to think I'm in there shoplifting. And I have to worry about that because I'm not free to ignore it. And so, that thing that's supposed to be guaranteed to all Americans, the freedom to just be yourself, is a fallacious idea. And I get resentful that I have to think about things that a whole lot of people, even my very close white friends whose politics are similar to mine, simply don't have to worry about (Feagin, 1991, p. 114).

Similarly, despite the enactment of antidiscrimination legislation and contrary to white perceptions that discrimination has been eradicated and that minorities receive preferential treatment in hiring, recent "bias studies" have demonstrated that African Americans and Hispanics continue to experience discrimination in employment. Pairs of white and black men with identical qualifications applied for 476 jobs advertised in Washington and Chicago newspapers. Whereas 15 percent of the white applicants received job offers, only 5 percent of the black applicants did. Moreover, white applicants advanced further in the hiring process and in the Washington area were much less likely to report receiving rude, unfavorable, or discouraging treatment than their black counterparts. These findings were similar to an earlier study of the hiring experiences of Hispanics and Anglos in Chicago and San Diego, in which whites were three times as likely both to advance farther in the hiring process and to receive job offers as were the Hispanic applicants (Turner et al., 1991).

Attitudinal discrimination does not always occur in so blatant or so obvious a manner. It can be manifested less dramatically merely by the adherence of members of the dominant group to social definitions of traditional subordinate group roles. Malcolm X, the charismatic black protest leader who was assassinated in 1965, recalled how his well-meaning white high school English teacher, Mr. Ostrowski, was bound by cultural norms concerning the "proper" caste roles for blacks.

> I know that he probably meant well in what he happened to advise me that day. I doubt that he meant any harm. . . . I was one of his top students—but all he could see for me was the kind of future "in your place" that almost all white people see for black people. . . . He told me, "Malcolm, you ought to be thinking about a career. Have you been giving it thought?". . . The truth is, I hadn't. I never have figured out why I told him, "Well, yes sir, I've been thinking I'd like to be a lawyer." Lansing certainly had no Negro lawyers—or doctors either—in those days, to hold up an image I might have aspired to. All I really knew for certain was that a lawyer didn't wash dishes, as I was doing.
>
>   Mr. Ostrowski looked surprised, I remember, and leaned back in his chair and clasped his hands behind his head. He kind of half-smiled and said, "Malcolm, one of life's first needs is for us to be realistic. Don't misunderstand me, now. We all here like you, you know that. But you've got to be realistic about being a nigger. A lawyer—that's no realistic goal for a nigger. You need to think about something you can be. You're good with your hands—making things. Everybody admires your carpentry shop work. Why don't you plan on carpentry? People like you as a person—you'd get all kinds of work" (Malcolm X, 1966, p. 36).

Institutional Discrimination.   The structure of opportunity may be limited by attitudinal discrimination, which is motivated by prejudice against racial and ethnic minorities. **Institutional discrimination,** on the other hand, refers to rules, policies, practices, procedures, and laws that appear to be race (or gender) neutral but have a discriminatory effect on minorities. Unlike attitudinal discrimination, institutional discrimination is not intentional or a consequence of prejudice, but it still has a disproportionately adverse impact on a minority group. Therefore, institutional discrimination is usually much more subtle, more complex, and less readily visible than attitudinal discrimination. Because it does not result from the motivations or intentions of specific individuals, but rather from policies that appear race neutral, institutional discrimination is more impersonal than attitudinal discrimination, and its effects are more easily denied, ignored, or overlooked. Consider the following examples:

- An employer may be genuinely willing to hire individuals of all races but may rely solely on word-of-mouth recommendations to fill job vacancies. If Hispanics were previously excluded from such employment, they would be unlikely to be members of a communications network that would allow them to learn about such vacancies.

- Jury selection is supposedly color-blind in most states, with jurors randomly selected from lists of registered voters. However, because they are more likely to be poor and geographically mobile (and thus ineligible to vote), blacks are less frequently selected as jurors.

- City commissions are selected on either an at-large or a district basis. In at-large elections, all voters select from the same slate of candidates. By contrast, when elections are conducted on a district basis, the city is divided into geographically defined districts and a resident votes only for candidates within his or her district. When an ethnic or racial group constitutes a numerical minority of a city's population, its voting power is likely to be diluted, and its representation in city government is likely to be lower than its proportion of the population under an at-large system of voting. Thus, under an at-large system, a city with a population that is 40 percent black could have no black representation on the city commission if voting went along racial lines. Because of patterns of residential segregation, this would be much less likely in a system organized on a district basis.

- In Minnesota a judge ruled unconstitutional a law that punished possession of crack more severely than possession of comparable amounts of powdered cocaine. Testimony indicated that crack is used mainly by blacks, while whites are much more likely to use cocaine. She therefore ruled that, because there was inadequate evidence to show that crack was "significantly more deadly or harmful than cocaine," the practical effect of the law was discriminatory. (See the Box, "Institutional Discrimination in the War on Drugs".)

Institutional discrimination is central to one of the most controversial interpretations of recent American race relations. In *The Declining Significance of Race* (1978) and *The Truly Disadvantaged* (1987), William J. Wilson argued that, in the past, attitudinal discrimination was the major factor responsible for the unequal economic, political, and social status of African Americans. He acknowledges that in many areas of American life, such as housing, education, and municipal politics, attitudinal discrimination is still pervasive and serves as a barrier to black participation in the mainstream of American society today.

However, Wilson contends that the overall economic position of urban blacks has recently deteriorated not only because of instances of attitudinal discrimination such as those just cited; it has also occurred because of impersonal economic changes that have little to do with race. These include "the shift from goods-producing to service-producing industries, the increasing polarization of the labor market into low-wage and high-wage sectors, technological innovations, and the relocation of manufacturing industries out of the central cities" (Wilson, 1987, p. 39). Relatively unskilled blacks concentrated in the nation's central cities are especially vulnerable to the relocation of manufacturing jobs that in the past provided economic opportunities for several generations of relatively unskilled workers—native and foreign, black and white. The economic opportunities of the African American underclass, who lack the educational and occupational skills necessary for the highly technological jobs being created in the cities today, are therefore rapidly diminishing.

Although the African American underclass's lack of educational and occupational skills reflects a legacy of historic attitudinal discrimination, institutional factors—broad structural changes in the economy—play a crucial role in sustaining black economic inequality. Even if all racial prejudice were eliminated, the African American underclass would still lack the necessary qualifications to participate in the mainstream of the economy and would continue to be found primarily in the unskilled sector, where unemployment is extremely high and wages very low. In other words, in the economic sphere, institutional discrimination has become an important source of continuing African American inequalities. Many of these institutional conditions that Wilson has described—the decline of manufacturing, the flight of both job opportunities and working- and middle-class families from the cities, and the increasing concentration of poverty, especially among African Americans and Hispanics—characterized south-central Los Angeles, which in 1992 was the scene of massive destruction and violence following the acquittal of four police officers in the Rodney King case (Barringer, 1992).

Whereas Wilson's analyses have focused primarily on the black underclass, Zinn has pointed out that similar institutional conditions have affected Hispanics, especially Puerto Ricans and Mexicans. Increases in Hispanic poverty have been most pronounced in those regions (such as the "rustbelt" Northeast and Midwest) in which broad structural changes in the economy have occurred. "The association between national economic shifts and high rates of social dislocation among Hispanics provides further evidence for the structural argument that economic conditions rather than culture create distinctive forms of racial poverty" (Zinn, 1989, p. 871).

Institutional discrimination is thus more subtle, more complex, and less visible than attitudinal discrimination. Because it does not result from the motivations or intentions of specific individuals, it is more impersonal than attitudinal discrimi-

In the News

Institutional Discrimination in the War on Drugs

If all racial prejudice were suddenly and miraculously eliminated from the hearts and minds of Americans, would racial discrimination disappear as well? If discrimination is invariably rooted in prejudice, the answer would be yes. However, if we adopt the perspective that institutional discrimination plays a crucial role in maintaining racial inequalities in American society, then the answer is no.

A controversial ruling in 1991 by Judge Pamela Alexander of Minnesota's Hennepin County District Court provides an excellent example of institutional discrimination in the nation's war on drugs. Judge Alexander ruled unconstitutional a Minnesota law that punished the possession of crack more severely than comparable amounts of powdered cocaine. Similar laws calling for stiffer penalties for crack possession than cocaine possession have been widely enacted by the Federal government and by many states.

The case involved five black defendants charged with possession of crack, a crime punishable by a four-year jail term for first-time offenders. On the other hand, the sentence for conviction of possession of the same amount of cocaine was simply probation. Testimony in the case indicated that crack is used mainly by blacks, while whites and Hispanics are much more likely to use cocaine. For example, in 1995 powdered cocaine offenders in Federal prisons were overwhelmingly white (32 percent) or Hispanic (39 percent), while better than 90 percent of those convicted of crack possession were black.

At issue was whether the difference in the severity of the sentences for possession of the two illicit drugs was justified. The Minnesota legislature had enacted the crack possession law in 1989 only after hearing considerable anecdotal testimony that crack was more addictive and harmful than cocaine. However, Judge Alexander maintained that there was insufficient scientific evidence on the effects of the two drugs to justify the dramatic disparity in the penalties for their possession. Although there was general agreement that the Minnesota legislature had enacted the penalties for the two crimes without any intent of targeting a specific minority group, Judge Alexander contended that the absence of racial prejudice or negative intent in the law's enactment was less relevant in considering the constitutionality of the crack law than whether it affected blacks disproportionately. "There had better be a good reason for any law that has the practical effect of disproportionately punishing members of one racial group. If crack was significantly more deadly or harmful than cocaine, that might be a good enough reason. But there just isn't enough evidence that they're different enough to justify the radical difference in penalties" (Quoted in London, 1991, p. B9).

> The issue posed by Judge Alexander's ruling concerning the racial disparities in sentencing for crack and powdered cocaine has become a hotly contested part of the national debate over mandatory federal sentences for drug offenses. Despite a recommendation by the independent U.S. Sentencing Commission that Congress scrap laws that establish dramatically harsher sentences (by a ratio of 100-to-1) for possession of crack than for possession of cocaine, in 1995 both the Clinton Administration and Congress refused to modify the disparate sentences given for possession of the two drugs. By the spring of 1996 at least one case addressing the legal ramifications of the issue had been heard by the Supreme Court.
>
> GREENHOUSE, LINDA. "Justices Hear Case on Disparity in Cocaine Sentences." *New York Times,* February 27, 1996.
> JONES, CHARISSE. "Crack and Punishment: Is Race the Issue?" *New York Times,* October 25, 1995.
> LONDON, ROBB. "Judge's Overruling of Crack Law Brings Turmoil." *New York Times,* January 11, 1991.
> MORLEY, JEFFERSON. "Crack in Black and White." *Washington Post,* November 19, 1995.

nation. Nevertheless, it has the same discriminatory consequences for minority group members. In examining institutional discrimination, therefore, we must consider the *effect* of a particular policy or practice on a minority group, rather than the motivations of the majority group.

Patterns of Racial and Ethnic Relations

The efforts of dominant groups to create and maintain their positions of power have been expressed in many different patterns of racial and ethnic relations, ranging from violent conflict to peaceful coexistence. The following discussion reviews the range of patterns of racial and ethnic relations. The patterns are not mutually exclusive; a majority group may adopt more than one of these policies at the same time or at different times. For example, as our discussion of Indian–white relations indicated, Native Americans at different times have been subjected to policies ranging from extermination to expulsion to forced assimilation.

Extermination

The most repressive and destructive dominant-group pattern of majority–minority relations is **extermination,** or **genocide,** which denies the subordinate group's very right to live. According to William O'Brien, genocide refers to actions intended "to destroy, in whole or in part, a national, ethnic, racial, or religious group." His definition includes:

> (a) killing members of the group; (b) causing serious bodily or mental harm to members of the group; (c) deliberately inflicting on the group conditions of life calculated to bring about its physical destruction...; (d) imposing measures intended to prevent births within the group; (e) forcibly transferring children of the group to another group (cited in O'Brien, 1968, p. 516).

Although examples of genocide are not confined to the twentieth century, some of the most notorious examples have occurred relatively recently in human history. In 1915, 1.5 million Armenians were massacred by the Turks. Between 1935 and 1945, the Nazis exterminated more than 6 million Jews and other "non-Aryan" groups (such as Gypsies). In the small African country of Burundi, members of the Hutu minority have been periodically systematically murdered by the dominant Tutsi people; in 1972, more than 100,000 Hutu were killed, and the wholesale slaughter of the Hutu population was renewed in clashes that erupted with increasing frequency between 1988 and 1995. In 1994 the tables were turned in the neighboring country of Rwanda, where an estimated 750,000 Tutsi were systematically annihilated in just a few months and over 1 million refugees fled to neighboring countries (Smith, 1995b). (Refer to the Cross-national box, "African Genocide: Tutsi-Hutu Strife in Burundi and Rwanda," for further discussion of this topic.)

Because genocide violates the sanctity of human life, an ideology of racism is often used to justify genocidal actions. As noted previously, racism involves a belief in the inherent superiority of one racial group and the inherent inferiority of others. By denying that a racial minority has human qualities or by depicting it as subhuman or destructive of human values and life, the minority's extermination is made morally justifiable and acceptable. For example, in 1876 an Australian writer defended efforts to annihilate the native people of New Zealand (Maoris), Australia, and Tasmania: "When exterminating the inferior Australian and Maori races... the world is better for it.... [By] protecting the propagation of the imprudent, the diseased, the defective, the criminal... we tend to destroy the human race" (quoted in Hartwig, 1972, p. 16).

Expulsion and Exclusion

The objective of extermination is to reduce or eliminate contact between majority and minority, and to create an ethnically (or racially) homogeneous society. A similar rationale underlies the process of **expulsion**, that is, the ejection of a minority group from areas controlled by the dominant group. Expulsion can be of two types: direct and indirect (Simpson and Yinger, 1985, pp. 19–20). **Direct expulsion** occurs when minorities are forcibly ejected by the dominant majority, often through military or other governmental force. The policy of direct expulsion was at no time more pronounced in American history than during the nineteenth century, when thousands of American Indians were removed from the East to areas beyond the Mississippi River. During World War II, 110,000 Japanese Americans, most of them United States citizens, were forcibly removed from their homes and placed in detention camps in remote areas of the country.

Indirect expulsion occurs when harassment, discrimination, and persecution of a minority becomes so intense that members "voluntarily" choose to emigrate. Harassment and persecution of minorities, particularly religious minorities, led many groups to seek refuge in the United States. Persecuted Protestant sects were among the earliest European immigrants to the American colonies, and the tradition of the United States as an asylum for the oppressed has continued into the present. Since the early Christian era, Jews periodically have been forced, either directly or indirectly, to leave the lands in which they have settled. The most dramatic emigration in modern Jewish history occurred in the late nineteenth and early twentieth century when millions (more than one-third of all Eastern European Jews) fled czarist Russia. Recently the persecution of Jews has revived in the Soviet Union and other former Soviet-bloc countries in Eastern Europe, forcing Jews by the thousands to seek refuge in other countries.

Several noted instances of expulsion have occurred throughout the world in the past decade. In 1989 more than 310,000 Bulgarians of Turkish descent (of a Bulgarian Turkish community estimated at between 900,000 and 1.5 million), whose ancestors had lived in Bulgaria for generations, fled to Turkey (Haberman, 1989). Similarly, at the end of the 1991 Middle East war, an estimated 2 million Kurds from northern Iraq fled to Iran and Turkey to escape Iraqi violence and terror. Turkish officials interpreted the massive exodus as a result of Iraqi leader Saddam Hussein's longstanding effort to empty Iraq of this troublesome minority (Haberman, 1991). In 1983, Nigeria expelled about 2 million immigrants from the neighboring countries of Ghana, Cameroon, Benin, Chad, and Niger. In 1985, another 700,000 people were forced to leave (*The Economist,* 1985). In Israel, Meir Kahane, a U.S.-born rabbi, gained considerable political support for his proposal to resolve Arab–Jewish tensions in that country by forcibly removing all Arabs from Israel and its occupied territories and making Israel into an exclusively Jewish state (Friedman, 1985).

However, the most dramatic recent example of expulsion has occurred in the former nation of Yugoslavia, which since its dissolution in 1991 has been the scene of brutal ethnic violence that has driven more than 2.3 million people from their homes and villages. Formerly one of the Yugoslav republics, Bosnia and Herzegovina was the home of three ethnic groups—Slavic Muslims (44 percent), Serbs (31 percent), and Croats (17 percent). After Bosnia declared its independence in early 1992, Serbian militiamen embarked on a campaign to create ethnically homogeneous enclaves by forcibly removing and displacing non-Serbs, especially Muslims. The Serbian campaign took many forms: arson, rape, and terror against civilian populations; executions; imprisonment and torture in concen-

Cross-national Perspectives

African Genocide: Tutsi-Hutu Strife in Burundi and Rwanda

Ethnic conflict and violence are not restricted to Western countries. During the past quarter century there have been several violent interethnic conflicts in Africa. In the process, thousands have died and many thousands more have been forced to flee their homes, creating in Africa one of the world's largest refugee populations. In Nigeria, conflict among Yoruba, Ibo, and Hausa peoples resulted in a bloody civil war that, between 1968 and 1970, cost 1 million lives, and ethnic divisions continue to be a major source of social and political instability in that country. In Uganda, dictator Idi Amin slaughtered more than 100,000 Ugandans, mostly members of the Buganda, Langi, and Acholi tribes. Within the past decade bitter conflicts have been waged along ethnic lines in many other African countries, including Ethiopia, the Sudan, Benin, Ivory Coast, Liberia, and Angola. But the most horrific of these conflicts have taken place in the two small east African countries of Burundi and Rwanda, which in the past quarter century have experienced two of the largest ethnic massacres since the atrocities of Nazi Germany.

Burundi and Rwanda are neighboring landlocked countries of central Africa, situated between the republics of Zaire, Uganda, and Tanzania. During their colonial periods, which ended in 1962, both were controlled by the Belgians. As in several other African countries, independence from European colonialism brought deep-rooted ethnic rivalries to the surface. In 1972, a wave of government-sponsored violence swept through Burundi. An estimated 100,000 Hutus—3.5 percent of Burundi's population—were killed in 1972 and more than 100,000 more in subsequent massacres in 1988 and 1993 by its Tutsi dominated government. But the numbers killed in Burundi pale in comparison to the slaughter that occurred in neighboring Rwanda in 1994, where more than 750,000 people—nearly 10 percent of all Rwandans—were murdered by the Hutu-dominated Rwandan government and over a million more were made homeless.

The genocide in Burundi and Rwanda reflects the rivalry of these two countries' major ethnic groups: the Tutsi and the Hutu. The Tutsi, originally a tall and slender people, make up only 15 percent of Burundi's population and less than 10 percent of the population of Rwanda. For centuries before the arrival of European colonial powers, the Tutsi had held the Hutu, a people of shorter stature, in a form of serfdom (the term *Hutu* itself means "subject" or "servant"). During the colonial period the Belgians magnified and exaggerated the social divisions of a Tutsi aristocracy and a Hutu servant class. When independence was achieved in 1962, many Hutu were hopeful that, since they represented the overwhelming numerical majority of the populations of both countries, the promise of majority rule would bring an end to Tutsi domination. However, Hutu frustration in Burundi grew in the years following independence as the more politically powerful Tutsi effectively blocked Hutu efforts to change the status quo. In 1972, the Tutsi-dominated government of Burundi responded with a wave of violence to allegations of a Hutu revolt against their control. In many villages all Hutu of any wealth, community influence, or educational level above grade school were systematically shot or beaten to death. The killing was selective, aimed at all influential Hutu. The objective of the annihilation of the Hutu elites was to crush any Hutu threat to Tutsi power. The Tutsi sought to eliminate "not only the rebellion but Hutu society as well, and in the process lay the foundation of an entirely new social order" (Lemarchand, 1975).

In Rwanda, on the other hand, freedom from colonial Belgian rule in 1959 led to a bloody but successful Hutu-led revolt against Tutsi political domination. But exiled Tutsi leaders continued to seek to regain political power, and, fearful that they would succeed, Hutu extremists in the Rwandan government used Rwandan president Haabyarimana's death in a plane crash in April 1994 as a pretext to begin their campaign of genocide. Government-sponsored death squads roamed the country, using guns, clubs, and machetes to annihilate all opposition—primarily Tutsi but including any Hutus who protected Tutsi or protested against government policies. The result was one of the most savage massacres of people since the Holocaust implemented by Nazi Germany.

Although numerous writers have argued that racial and ethnic distinctions did not *cause* the waves of genocide that have swept Burundi and Rwanda, the savage conflict between Tutsi and Hutu in these two troubled countries does demonstrate how ethnic and racial divisions continue to provide the basis for bloodshed and violence throughout the modern world.

Cohen, Andrew Jay. "On the Trail of Genocide." *New York Times,* September 7, 1994.

Friedman, Thomas L. "The Next Rwanda." *New York Times,* January 24, 1996.

Lemarchand, Rene. "Ethnic Genocide." *Society,* 12, 1975.

Murray, James. "Rwanda's Bloody Roots." *New York Times,* September 3, 1994.

Smith, David N. "The Genesis of Genocide in Rwanda: The Fatal Dialectic of Class and Ethnicity." *Humanity and Society* 19:4, November 1995.

tration camps and prisons; removal and confinement to ghetto areas for non-Serbs; and forcible deportation. Moreover, non-Serbs were intimidated by the Serbian reign of terror into signing "voluntary" letters giving up their property and possessions in return for being "permitted" to leave Bosnia (Human Rights

Watch, 1992). The terms that the Serbs used to describe their objectives—"ethnic cleansing" and "ethnic purification"—epitomize the quest for ethnic homogeneity and exclusivity that underlies a policy of expulsion.

Achieving or retaining ethnic homogeneity is also attained when a host society refuses to permit another group entrance because that group is perceived as a threat to the society's basic social institutions. When countries have policies that refuse to admit culturally different groups it is called **exclusion.** As we noted earlier, between 1917 and 1965 American immigration policy was based on the assumption that immigration from southern and eastern Europe and Asia should be substantially or completely restricted. This assumption was embodied in the 1924 immigration legislation, which established numerical quotas for each nation. More than four-fifths of the quotas were assigned to those nations of northern and western Europe whose ethnic characteristics most closely coincided with those of the "original" settlers of the country. Although Great Britain had an admissions quota exceeding 65,000, Italy was allocated less than 6000, and Hungary, less than 1000. Asians were almost completely excluded. This policy remained virtually intact until its repeal in 1965.

Oppression

Oppression involves the exploitation of a minority group by excluding it from equal participation in a society (Turner, Singleton, and Musick, 1984, pp. 1–2). Oppression "depends on exclusiveness rather than exclusion" (Bonacich, 1972, p. 555). Unlike extermination, expulsion, or exclusion, a system of oppression accepts the existence of minorities but subjugates them and confines them to inferior social positions. The majority group uses its power to maintain its access to scarce and valued resources in a system of social inequality.

Slavery, in which the slave's labor was a valuable resource exploited by the slave owner, was an example of oppression in American society. Even after slavery was legally abolished, the Jim Crow system of racial segregation that ensued was organized to exploit blacks for the benefit of the dominant whites. After taking a tour of the South at the turn of the century, a journalist remarked upon the exploitative nature of black–white relations:

> One of the things I saw in the South—and I saw it everywhere—was the way in which the people were torn between their feelings of race prejudice and their downright economic needs. Hating and fearing the Negro as a race (though often loving individual Negroes), they yet want him to work for them; they can't get along without him. In one impulse a community will rise to mob Negroes or to drive them out of the country because of Negro crime or Negro vagrancy, or because the Negro is becoming educated, acquiring property and "getting out of his place;" and in the next impulse laws are passed or other remarkable measures taken to keep him at work—because the South can't get along without him (Baker, 1964, p. 81).

A classic contemporary example of oppression was the South African system of *apartheid,* or "separate development," which functioned to maintain the privileged position of whites, who have enjoyed one of the highest standards of living in the world but who represent only 15 percent of the country's population. On the other hand, South African blacks, who comprise more than two-thirds (69 percent) of the population, were excluded from genuine participation in the nation's political system and were legally confined to rural reserves, or "homelands," that represented only 13 percent of the land. However, black labor has provided a cheap labor supply for South African mines, farms, manufacturing, and domestic help that is essential to the South African economy and the system of white privilege. Therefore, the entire system of state controls restricting black political power, residence, and education was designed to perpetuate the system of white privilege (Cohen, 1986).

Assimilation

In general, the majority group's response to ethnic minorities in America has been to seek their assimilation. **Assimilation** involves efforts to integrate or incorporate a group into the mainstream of a society. As with other majority group policies previously discussed, the objective of assimilation is a homogeneous society. In American society two distinct conceptions of assimilation have existed: Anglo-conformity and the melting pot.

Anglo-conformity.   The principal assimilationist model in the American experience has emphasized conformity by minority groups to dominant-group standards. In the United States this has been termed *Anglo-conformity.* **Anglo-conformity** assumes that ethnic minorities should give up their distinctive characteristics and adopt those of the dominant group (Cole and Cole, 1954). It can be expressed by the formula $A + B + C = A$, in which A is the dominant group and B and C represent ethnic minority groups that must conform to the values and life-styles of the dominant group if they want to achieve positions of importance and prestige in the society (Newman, 1973, p. 53).

A policy of Anglo-conformity not only seeks a homogeneous society organized around the idealized cultural standards, institutions, and language of the dominant group; it also assumes the inferiority of the cultures of other ethnic groups. Many Americans retain vivid and painful recollections of the ridicule of their cultural ways and the pressures for them to become "Americanized." Many tried to rid themselves of their traditional beliefs and practices. A daughter of Slovenian immigrant parents recalls her childhood:

> In the 9th grade, a boy said to me, "You talk funny." I wondered what he meant. I listened to my friends, and I did not think they "talked funny." Then, that great American

experiment, the public high school, opened my ears. I heard the English language spoken as I had never heard it spoken.... I began to hear that I did indeed pronounce my words differently, and so did my friends. I practiced [English] in secret, in the bathroom, of course, until I could pronounce properly the difficult "th" sound, which seemed the most distinctive and, therefore, the most necessary to conquer. How superior I felt when I had mastered this sound...! Alas, however, I refused to speak Slovenian (Prosen, 1976, pp. 2–3).

The Melting Pot.   Like Anglo-conformity, the ultimate objective of a melting pot policy is a society without ethnic differences. More tolerant than a policy of Anglo-conformity, the **melting pot** sees ethnic differences as being lost in the creation of a new society and a new people—a synthesis unique and distinct from any of the different groups that formed it. Unlike Anglo-conformity, none of the contributing groups is considered to be superior; each is considered to have contributed the best of its cultural heritage to the creation of something new. The melting pot ideal can be expressed by the formula $A + B + C = D$, in which A, B, and C represent the different contributing groups and D is the product of their synthesis (Newman, 1973, p. 63). As Ralph Waldo Emerson expressed it in the mid-nineteenth century,

> in this continent—asylum of all nations—the energy of Irish, Germans, Swedes, Poles, and Cossacks, and all the European tribes—of the Africans, and of the Polynesians—will construct a new race, a new religion, a new state, a new literature...(quoted in Gordon, 1964, p. 11).

Cultural Assimilation and Structural Assimilation.   To what extent has ethnic assimilation actually occurred in American society? Milton Gordon (1964) pointed out that assimilation is not a single phenomenon but involves several processes. The two most important of these are cultural assimilation and structural assimilation. Most of the previous discussion has concerned **cultural assimilation,** or **acculturation**—that is, the acquisition of the *cultural* characteristics of the dominant group, including its values, beliefs, language, and behaviors. But many ethnic groups have become fully acculturated to the dominant American culture and still have not been able to achieve full *social* participation in the society. Sharing the same language, norms, and culture does not ensure access to informal social organizations, clubs, cliques, and friendship groups.

Structural assimilation occurs when there is social interaction among individuals of different ethnic backgrounds. Two types can be distinguished: secondary and primary. Secondary structural assimilation refers to the ethnic integration of social situations characterized by impersonal secondary relationships: jobs, schools, political organizations, neighborhoods, and public recreation. However, even sharing membership in such secondary groups does not necessarily involve primary-group associations—informal social organizations, friendships, and, ultimately, intermarriage. Primary structural assimilation is achieved when these kinds of interethnic associations occur.

Considerable research has recently focused on measuring rates of assimilation among different U.S. racial and ethnic groups who have been compared in terms of educational attainment, income levels, occupational characteristics, residential distribution, and intermarriage (Model, 1991). These data show that, overall, European ethnic groups and Asians have experienced considerable socioeconomic, educational, residential, and marital assimilation in American society. However, these patterns of assimilation are not duplicated among Hispanics, American Indians, and African Americans (Yetman, 1991).

Pluralism and Separatism

Pluralism refers to a system in which different cultures can coexist and be preserved. According to this notion, the strength and vitality of American society is derived from its ethnic diversity. Belonging to a "nation of nations," each group should be permitted to retain its unique qualities while affirming its allegiance to American society. This ideal can be expressed by the equation $A + B + C = A + B + C$, in which A, B, and C are each ethnic groups that maintain their distinctiveness over time (Newman, 1973, p. 67).

Pluralism is more tolerant of diversity than any of the policies we have previously considered, for it implies recognition of cultural equality among ethnic groups, not the superiority of one. It accepts and encourages—even celebrates—cultural differences but generally assumes that different ethnic groups will coexist within a common political and economic framework. As we point out in Chapter 16, American religion has consistently been characterized by denominational pluralism, in which more than 1200 different religious organizations coexist. Members of most religious groups participate in the political and economic life of the country.

However, a number of groups, many of them religious—such as the Amish, the Hutterites, or Hasidic Jews—have sought to preserve their cultural identity by remaining both socially and geographically separate from the rest of the society. Groups who, in addition to retaining their cultural distinctiveness, refrain from extensive participation in the political, economic, and social life of the broader society in order to maintain their own subsocieties are examples of **separatism,** or self-segregation, which differs from pluralism primarily in the degree of geographic and social separation it emphasizes.

In the American experience pluralism and separatism have seldom been advocated by the majority; the primary advocates of each stance have been minority spokespersons. The basic difference between a policy of separatism and one of exclusion is that under separatism the minority is relatively autonomous and may voluntarily choose to place itself apart, whereas under a policy of exclusion the separation is dictated by the majority group. Under separatism the majority does not require separation of ethnic, religious, or racial groups; it simply permits it.

Minority-Group Responses to Dominant Group Pressures

How do minorities experience and respond to demands of the dominant group? The previous discussion has emphasized the role of the dominant group in setting the limits within which minority groups may function. Minorities, however, are not simply passive recipients of dominant-group policies; they actively respond in a variety of ways to majority pressures for subordination.

Sociologists have distinguished three broad and general categories of minority-group responses: acceptance, resistance, and avoidance. Acceptance involves the minority's moving toward the majority. Avoidance and resistance involve a rejection of, or moving away from, the majority. Depending on the situation, individual or group responses may change from one of these responses to another.

Acceptance and Acquiescence

A minority may accept the dominant group's definition of its subordinate status. Given the majority's superior power, acquiescence may be necessary for survival. The Southern caste system was for many years relatively stable because most blacks, at least on the surface, accepted the elaborate system of racial etiquette and segregation. The most severe violence against blacks—lynchings and terrorism— was committed when blacks made, or whites perceived them to have made, an effort to reject the traditional subordinate roles ascribed to them. Alvin Poussaint, a prominent African American psychiatrist, graphically recounted how he was forced to accept the traditional role of black submissiveness and deference toward whites.

> Once last year [1967] as I was leaving my office in Jackson, Miss. with my Negro secretary, a white policeman yelled, "Hey, boy! Come here!" Somewhat bothered, I retorted: "I'm no boy!" He then rushed at me, inflamed, and stood towering over me, snorting, "What d'ja say, boy?" Quickly he frisked me and demanded, "What's your name, boy?" Frightened, I replied, "Dr. Poussaint. I'm a physician." He angrily chuckled and hissed, "What's your first name, boy?" When I hesitated he assumed a threatening stance and clenched his fists. As my heart palpitated, I muttered in profound humiliation, "Alvin."
>
> He continued his psychological brutality, bellowing, "Alvin, the next time I call you, you come right away, you hear? You hear?" I hesitated. "You hear me, boy?" My voice trembling with helplessness, but following my instincts of self-preservation, I murmured, "Yes, sir." Now fully satisfied that I had performed and acquiesced to my "boy status," he dismissed me with, "Now, boy, go on and get out of here or next time we'll take you for a little ride down to the station house!" (Poussaint, 1971, p. 349).

The Southern caste system placed African Americans in a position of permanent subservience. Most European ethnic groups, however, were not so rigidly proscribed from seeking equal status with "native" whites. Nevertheless, the pressures of Anglo-conformity frequently led ethnic minorities to accept dominant-group standards. These standards included degrading perceptions of their own cultures, which caused them to feel ambivalent about their background and sometimes to reject it. The son of Italian immigrant parents describes his childhood in the following way:

> I enter the parochial school with an awful fear that I will be called Wop.... I begin to loathe my heritage....
>
> I am nervous when I bring friends to my house; the place looks so Italian. Here hangs a picture of Victor Emmanuel and over there is one of the cathedrals of Milan, and next to it, one of St. Peter's, and on the buffet stands a wine-pitcher of medieval design; it's forever brimming, forever red and brilliant with wine. These things are heirlooms belonging to my father, and no matter who may come to our house, he likes to stand under them and brag.
>
> So I begin to shout at him. I tell him to cut out being a Wop and be an American once in a while. Immediately he gets his razor-strap and whales hell out of me, clouting me from room to room and finally out the back door. I go into the woodshed and pull down my pants and stretch my neck to examine the blue slices across my rump. A Wop! That's what my father is. Nowhere is there an American father who beats his son this way (Fante, 1966, pp. 391–394).

Some minority-group members have shown a willingness to lose their ethnic identity and adopt the characteristics of the majority group. The eagerness and intensity with which assimilation was sought are exemplified in Abraham Cahan's classic novel of immigrant adjustment, *The Rise of David Levinsky*. To enhance his ability to function in American society, Levinsky, a Russian Jewish immigrant, enrolls in an evening English class, where his teacher becomes one of his first American role models.

> At first I did not like him. Yet I would hang on his lips, striving to memorize every English word I could catch and watching intently, not only his enunciation, but also his gestures, manners, and mannerisms, and accepting it all as part and parcel of the American way of speaking.... If I heard a bit of business rhetoric that I thought effective I would jot it down and commit it to memory. In like manner I would write down every new piece of slang, the use of the latest popular phrase being, as I thought, helpful in making oneself popular with Americans ... (Cahan, 1917/1966, pp. 129, 292–293).

Resistance and Confrontation

Some minority-group members respond to majority-group pressures by refusing to accept majority-group definitions of their status. Resistance may include boycotts, strikes, legal action, political activity, nonviolent mass protest, and violence. Each of these techniques has been used by American minority groups to achieve greater equality in American life.

Despite murder, lynching, terrorism, and harassment—the tactics whites have used to enforce black subordination—African Americans have an enduring tradition of resistance to the caste system and discrimination. This spirit of resistance is typified by the following account by Fred Shuttlesworth, an African-American minister and leader of efforts to end racial segregation in Birmingham, Alabama, during the late 1950s and the 1960s. Shuttlesworth barely escaped death when his house was demolished by more than a dozen sticks of dynamite. Shuttlesworth recalls the experience:

> That house was about fifty years old, all that black dust and stuff, dynamite smoke and stuff, and I came out. On the way from around the back of the house, this Klans—this policeman who was a Klansman—said to me,. . . I think it shook him, he said, "I know some people. I know some people in the Klan. They're really after you." He said, "If I was you I'd get outa town as quick as I could."
>
> I said, "Well, you tell them that I'm not going out of town." I said, "You see all this I've come through?" I said, "If God could save me through this, then I'm gon' stay here and clear up this." I said, "I wasn't saved to run . . ." (quoted in Raines, 1978, p. 166).

Throughout the twentieth century the black protest movement has used the legal process to resist a minority status. Most noteworthy among these was the historic 1954 Supreme Court decision of *Brown* v. *Board of Education,* which declared segregated schools unconstitutional. Bolstered by the knowledge that segregation was unconstitutional, during the Civil Rights Movement of the 1950s and 1960s African Americans used a variety of tactics—public confrontations, boycotts, picketing, and civil disobedience—to bring about social change. Since the 1970s civil rights issues have more frequently been pursued through traditional political channels. Moreover, as Feagin's (1991) study of their responses to public discrimination indicated, today middle-class blacks especially no longer respond with the "deference rituals" expected in the Southern caste system. Instead, utilizing the resources (for example, money, personal connections, knowledge of the law) that their middle-class status affords them, they vigorously contest, challenge, and confront such discrimination with increasing frequency and effectiveness.

The black protest movement has been instrumental in generating resistance among other racial and ethnic minorities. Although American Indians have for generations resisted pressures for assimilation, they have recently used many of the tactics of direct protest (such as sit-ins) employed by African Americans. Indians are also effectively using the legal system to challenge past and present treaty violations by whites. Resistance among Chicanos increased as well. One of the most dramatic manifestations of increased Chicano militancy was the armed confrontation of the charismatic Reies Tijerina, who advanced claims for millions of acres of Mexican land guaranteed to Mexican-American residents under the 1848 Treaty of Guadalupe Hidalgo. On another front, Cesar Chavez led agricultural workers, primarily Mexican Americans, in a struggle to improve their status. Such efforts have made apparent the political impact of the nation's 26 million Hispanics. Given their rapidly increasing numbers, Hispanics have become an important political factor, particularly because of their concentration in such key electoral states as California, New York, Texas, and Florida. Moreover, because Hispanics represent the nation's youngest population group, their political influence is likely to be even greater in the future (Gonzalez, 1991).

Avoidance and Withdrawal

Another response to minority status is avoidance, or withdrawal, in which the minority neither accepts nor resists the dominance of the majority. Rather, they seek to set themselves apart from the majority and to keep contact minimal. Such a stance shields minority group members from prejudice and discrimination by the majority group and enables them to preserve their own culture and social institutions with minimal outside interference.

Throughout the American experience many ethnic groups have tried to avoid the pressures of their minority status by embracing a form of ethnic pluralism or separatism as the most appropriate means of adjusting to American society. The adjustment of the immigrant Irish during the nineteenth century was typical of numerous other ethnic groups. Although the objects of discrimination by Protestant Americans, the Irish avoided much of the hostility directed toward them by creating a society within a society, a separate institutional system centered around the Roman Catholic Church. The institutional system that developed around the church—its schools, hospitals, orphanages, asylums, homes for the aged, charitable and athletic organizations, and informal groups—integrated the Irish community and served to maintain Irish-American solidarity and identity.

The most extreme form of avoidance is *separatism,* in which little, if any, interaction occurs with the majority. The impulse for separatism frequently has been created by conflict with the majority group and a desire to avoid a recurrence of the discrimination or oppression that a group has encountered. In other instances it is based on a resurgence or emergence of ethnic identity and a desire to form social institutions around it. Within the past decade the appeal of separatism has increased dramatically in numerous countries. This has been especially apparent in three eastern European countries—Czechoslovakia, Yugoslavia, and the Soviet Union—where decades of Communist-enforced unity disintegrated under the pressures for ethnic autonomy and independence.

The idea of separate ethnic areas or states has been advocated by spokespersons of a number of different ethnic groups in the United States—by African Americans, American Indians, and German Americans, among others. Moreover, as we noted above, the idea of separatism has long appealed to religious groups seeking to protect their unique identity from the influences of the larger society. Today the value of racial and ethnic separatism is being hotly debated throughout the United States. This is especially apparent in the area of higher education. First, although the Supreme Court's 1954 *Brown* decision ruled that segregated public schools were illegal, enrollments in historically black public universities increased dramatically during the late 1980s and early 1990s. And, as traditionally white campuses have become more ethnically diverse, separate ethnic dormitories, ethnic studies departments, and even separate graduation ceremonies have emerged as ways of enabling minority students to adjust to the pressures of functioning in an overwhelmingly white student body. (For a sensitive discussion of such dilemmas experienced by a Chicano student at Harvard, see Navarrette, 1993).

Summary

Societies are frequently stratified by ethnic or racial categories. The terms *majority* or *dominant* refer to a group's relative power—its ability to realize its own objectives and interests. A *minority group,* in contrast, is subordinate to the majority group and is relatively powerless. An *ethnic group* is identified on the basis of its cultural characteristics. A *racial group,* on the other hand, is distinguished by its physical characteristics. Both racial and ethnic phenomena are socially defined—that is, the same racial or ethnic group may be perceived and responded to differently in different societies.

From its very inception, American society has been a multicultural society. American Indians, the first Americans, are culturally and linguistically extremely diverse and, despite a substantial decline in their numbers from the sixteenth to the early twentieth century, have in recent years been increasing. The ethnic diversity of the American people has been reinforced by the acquisition of territory containing both Indians and Mexicans and by the migration of European, African, Asian, and Latin American peoples during the past three and one-half centuries. The greatest period of immigration to the United States occurred between 1820 and 1920. The *old immigration,* composed of peoples from northern and western Europe, occurred primarily prior to 1895. Immigrants from southern and eastern Europe—the *new immigrants*—came primarily between 1890 and 1920. The descendants of most African Americans, the largest racial minority in contemporary American society, were involuntary migrants to the United States. Despite considerable changes brought about by the enactment of federal, state, and local laws barring discrimination, African Americans still remain considerably outside the mainstream of American society. Asian immigration, initially from China and Japan and more recently from Korea and Southeast Asia, has occurred primarily during the late nineteenth and twentieth centuries. During the twentieth century, Spanish-speaking peoples entered the United States in increasing numbers. The largest number of these have been Mexican Americans, who entered in substantial numbers prior to the Great Depression of the

1930s and since World War II. Puerto Rican and Cuban migrations are essentially post-World War II phenomena.

Two broad explanations—internal and external—have been used to explain racial and ethnic inequalities in American society. *Internal* explanations, which focus on factors within the minority group, include biological (racist) arguments that attribute a group's status to innate and inherited mental, emotional, and moral qualities. Cultural arguments see a group's position as a consequence of that group's own qualities, but consider them to be learned, that is, socially but not genetically inherited. *External* explanations focus primarily on factors outside of minority groups over which they have little or no control. *Prejudice* refers to attitudes and beliefs, while *discrimination* involves behavior or acts by individuals, groups, organizations, and institutions. There are two forms of discrimination: attitudinal and institutional. *Attitudinal* discrimination emanates from the prejudicial attitudes of the majority, while *institutional* discrimination involves policies and practices that appear to be neutral, but unintentionally have a disproportionate impact on a particular racial or ethnic group.

The adaptation of ethnic groups is influenced by both the policies of the majority groups and the characteristics of the minority group. Among the range of majority-group policies toward racial and ethnic minorities, *extermination,* or *genocide,* is the most repressive. *Expulsion* and *exclusion* also aim for an ethnically homogeneous society but do not systematically resort to genocide to achieve their goal. A system of *oppression* accepts the existence of ethnic differences but excludes minorities from full and equal participation in the society. *Assimilation* involves the integration or incorporation of a minority into the mainstream of a society. In the United States this assimilation took either the form of *Anglo-conformity,* in which there was an insistence upon conformity to the majority's cultural standards, or the form of the *melting pot,* in which diverse peoples each contributed to the creation of a new culture and society. Finally, *pluralism* and *separatism* involve a system in which different ethnic groups coexist equally and preserve their own cultural characteristics.

Minorities also respond actively and differently to majority policies, and their responses influence their adaptation. *Acceptance* involves acquiescence to the dominant group's definition of their status. *Resistance* may involve direct protest and action. *Avoidance* involves neither acceptance nor resistance; instead, minority people seek to separate themselves from contact with the majority. Its most extreme form is *separatism.*

CRITICAL THINKING

1. What is the difference between an ethnic and a racial group? Give examples to show that the characteristics of each of these types of groups are socially defined.
2. Give examples of majority and minority groups in American society. Does a majority group need to be numerically superior in order to be dominant? Give at least one example to support your ideas.
3. Why is the migration of African Americans from the rural South to the urban North an important demographic trend in American society?
4. Explain how legal decisions have changed the status of African Americans. Have laws produced true equality for African Americans in society? What would?
5. Compare and contrast the experience of Hispanic Americans and Asian Americans with that of African Americans. How do you explain the similarities and differences that you see?
6. Speculate about the impact of the population growth of minority groups on American society. Does an increase in numbers necessarily mean an increase in power? Explain.
7. Give examples of at least three ethnic groups in American society. How do the cultural characteristics of these groups differ? Which ethnic group do you feel is dominant in American society? Why?
8. In what ways are majority and minority groups in our society stereotyped? How do these stereotypes help perpetuate the existing social order?
9. Compare and contrast the power basis of the majority groups in the United States and South Africa.
10. How do dominant groups maintain control of subordinate groups? List the policies explained in this chapter and give an example of each.
11. How do minorities respond and adapt to majority policies?

10

Gender and Age:
Stratification and Inequality

We are born either male or female, and, except for a tiny number of people who take the dramatic step of changing their sex, there is little we can do about it. The sex of a person is determined by certain physical characteristics, including the reproduction organs by which the sexes are biologically identified. Age is also a biological characteristic, but unlike sex, which is relatively stable, the process of aging goes on continuously. These two biological characteristics—sex and age—are part of our makeup at all times. What makes sex and age sociologically important is that every society attaches social significance to these biological characteristics.

Sociologists today generally use the word gender, not sex, when speaking of the social nature of being male and female. **Gender** emphasizes that males and females are socially defined, and these social distinctions influence the positions of males and females in society and their behaviors. Gender, therefore, like other aspects of the society, is *socially constructed* (Thompson and Walker, 1995). Since gender is socially constructed, it is not fixed, but variable—from one society to another and one time to another (Osmond and Thorne, 1993). An additional underlying theme of this chapter is that "gender carries undue importance in the social world, and its salience tends to reinforce men's power over women" (Coltrane, 1994, p. 43).

Age is also socially constructed and, like gender, the social definitions of different ages determine the place of people in society and influences their behavior (Hooyman and Kiyak, 1991; Riley et al., 1988).

The organization of societies around gender and age distinctions are of considerable importance because, as the title of this chapter suggests, the result is often one of inequities, or systems of inequality. We have already seen in Chapter 8 on social stratification and Chapter 9 on race and ethnic groups how inequalities exist in wealth, power, and access to many of society's opportunities. In this chapter we examine how being male or female, or being young or old, leads to different social arrangements and social behaviors. Although these differences do not inevitably lead to negative results, we will see that gender and age distinctions often produce inequalities.

We will begin by considering the positions of males and females, both in American society and in societies around the world. Later in the chapter we will focus on age groups, especially the elderly and the young.

Gender Stratification

In Chapter 8, we examined the social stratification system with its emphasis on class (economic resources), status (prestige and honor), and power. Gender stratification is a subset of the social stratification system, which emphasizes the importance of gender in the hierarchical arrangement of societies (Huber, 1991; Blumberg, 1991; Osmond and Thorne, 1993). There are three key dimensions in gender stratification: power, division of labor, and gender roles (Chafetz, 1991). **Power** is the ability to impose one's will upon others, even if they resist. Power can exist only when there is a relationship between individuals, between groups, or between classes of people. In this chapter we are interested in the power relationship between sexes—males and females.

Division of labor is also a general sociological term, commonly used to describe how the occupations of a society are specialized so that any individual has only one major occupation or task. When we use the term *division of labor* in connection with *gender,* we refer to the society-wide assignment of different work tasks to males and females. We will refer to this as **division of labor by gender.**

Gender roles are the expectations that prevail in a society about the activities and behaviors that may and may not be engaged in by males and females. These expectations are widely understood and produce social pressures such that people feel the need to comply with them. These role expectations are socially learned through the process of socialization.

These three concepts—power, division of labor, and gender roles—are closely related to each other. They also reflect inequalities between different groups of people. With regard to power, obviously if one set of people has power over another, inequality results. With regard to division of labor and gender roles, the inequality is not as immediately obvious, but a closer examination will show how each concept leads to inequality between males and females. We will begin by looking at differences in male and female power in different societies.

Power and Gender

In most societies around the world, males have greater power than females, both in the personal and public spheres. For example, males have generally been the political leaders, historically (for example, classical Greece, Imperial China, and the Roman Empire) and in contemporary modern societies. There have been a few notable women leaders in recent decades (Great Britain's Margaret Thatcher, the Philippines' Corazon Aquino, the late Golda Meir of Israel, and Indira Gandhi of India), but these women constituted only a tiny percentage of the world's national leaders. The male dominance of political leadership is also the standard among the vast majority of nonliterate societies on which we have ethnographic information.

At the private level the picture is almost identical. In the family, for example, males almost always have greater power than females (Osmond and Thorne, 1993). Much of the power of males within the family comes directly from a patriarchal tradition. Patriarchy means that a husband or father has unquestioned authority or dominance over other family members. Also, an organization—or, indeed, an entire society—may be based on the principle of patriarchy. In the case of Western societies, including the United States, support for patriarchy can be found prominently in the sacred writings of the Judaic and Christian religious traditions. Although these sources of male power might have diminished somewhat in recent years, their influence has certainly not disappeared.

In non-Western cultures the basis for male power in the family is also found in religious and ideological systems (Bernard, 1987; Giele, 1977, 1988). In the Islamic world males are given ultimate authority, both within their families and in the larger society where they predominate (Mernissi, 1987). Hinduism also gives primary power to males, again both inside the home and in the public world.

It is worth noting, however, that there have been some societies, as shown by anthropological and historical records, in which women have had power that was equal to, or perhaps even exceeded, the power of men. The key contributing factor has usually been the economic contribution of women. When economic or historical circumstances make men dependent on the activities of women, men are more likely to share power (Sanday, 1981).

For example, among the African tribe called the !Kung, who live in the Kalahari Desert, food supplies depend upon hunting animals and gathering vegetation from the "bush." The !Kung women do the gathering, which requires that they go far out in the bush. From this activity alone they provide between 60 percent and 80 percent of the tribe's food. The !Kung women also assist, in various ways, when men do the hunting. The !Kung society is essentially egalitarian, as are other societies where the economic contribution of women is significant compared to that of men (Draper, 1975; Sanday, 1981).

A cross-national study of 111 contemporary societies confirms anthropological studies showing the importance of women's economic contributions (South, 1988). This study shows that the more that women participate in the labor force, the less males are able to exercise power over them. Specifically, men are less able to restrict women to traditional roles (early marriage, high fertility, and illiteracy) if women participate in the labor force (South, 1988).

Similar conclusions about the importance of women's economic contributions have been reached by studying families in the United States. As a woman's income increases relative to her husband's income, his share of the household work increases (Huber, 1986; Ross et al., 1983).

In the *public* sphere, however, there are only limited indications that women gain very much public or political power in societies where they make greater economic contributions. American women, for example, are contributing greatly in the economic realm, but, as we will see later in this chapter, their positions of power in the political or economic realms are still very limited.

Despite the existence of societies in which women exercise power at least equal to that of men, in the overwhelming majority of societies males have had dominance over females.

Therefore, the question that needs to be addressed is, Why do males so often have greater power than females? Biology is often used to account for the greater power and prestige of males (Goldberg, 1973). *Sociobiologists,* who look for evolutionary explanations of human behavior, argue that males evolved as the hunters and food providers, while females evolved as specialists in having and caring for babies and in taking care of the home (Tiger, 1969). The related assumption is that the male activities are more important, and thus they receive greater power and prestige. One major flaw in this argument is that it is not supported by the facts we have about food sources in hunting and gathering societies. In the hundreds of thousands of years before the development of agriculture, humans had to get their food by hunting animals and gathering edible vegetation. We know from contemporary hunting and gathering societies that women typically get most of the food (just as we saw in the case of the !Kung above). If preagricultural hunting and gathering societies were at all similar, it is hard to see how females could have been genetically programmed to leave the "breadwinning" activities exclusively to males (Collins, 1988).

One of the early economic theories of male domination goes back to the work of Friedrich Engels (1884/1972). The key to most economic explanations of male dominance lies not in who does the work, but in who controls the means of production (for example, land, tools, machines). Contemporary scholars who advance the economic hypothesis point out that the power of women has usually been less in agrarian societies where women have not typically been the owners of the land (Blumberg, 1984, 1991). Women's power is especially low in societies where the inheritance system passes land from fathers to sons and where, at marriage, a woman must leave her home and live in her husband's family residence.

Division of Labor by Gender

In societies around the world, men and women are usually assigned different work tasks, which is another way of saying that labor is typically divided by gender. Exactly why a division of labor is so commonplace is a matter of considerable discussion. Some argue that certain tasks are assigned to men because of their greater physical strength. Whatever the validity of this explanation, it cannot account for all differences in gender-related work. An analysis of 50 types of work in 186 societies identified only two tasks invariably assigned to men: (1) the hunting and butchering of large animals, and (2) the processing of hard and tough materials, such as mining and quarrying rocks and minerals, smelting metal ores, and doing metalwork (Murdock and Provost, 1973). Women, on the other hand, were most likely to be responsible for grinding grain, carrying water, and cooking. At first glance, it would appear that this division of labor is based purely on physical strength, but carrying water—a woman's task—requires considerable physical strength. Furthermore, women in many societies carry heavy loads including—in addition to water—firewood, food, and various other products. According to reports, African women, who often carry heavy loads by balancing them on their heads, can carry as much as 70 percent of their body weight. This means that a woman weighing 140 pounds could carry nearly 100 pounds on her head (Rensberger, 1986).

In addition, there are more societies in which women are responsible for erecting and dismantling shelters than there are societies in which men have this responsibility. Women are responsible just as often as men for preparing the soil and planting seed, as well as for tending and harvesting crops (Murdock, 1937).

Evelyn Reed (1971) has argued that when agriculture was done primarily with a digging stick, this task was left most often to women. With the taming of animals and the development of the plow, agriculture was taken over by men. But farming done with a digging stick must have been just as backbreaking as farming done with draft animals and the plow. Physical strength alone, therefore, does not account for variations in the division of labor by gender.

Some scholars have suggested that differences in male and female work may reflect a desire, especially by men, to establish a clear male identity. Many people define themselves as male or female on the basis of what they do. For females, childbearing (and nursing) is unarguably their exclusive responsibility: "Perhaps because women have ways of signaling their womanhood, men must have ways to display their manhood" (Sanday, 1981, p. 78). From this point of view, men in all societies must have a way of demonstrating maleness in an activity prohibited to females. One activity frequently reserved for males is fighting battles and waging wars (Collins, 1988). There is an ironic symmetry in this idea: women are responsible for producing life, while men are responsible for taking life (Sanday, 1981).

We have now seen how power and the division of labor vary from one society to another, but at the same time generally favor men. We are now ready to turn our attention to the third dimension of gender stratification: gender roles.

Gender Roles

Feminist sociologists have become increasingly critical of the concept of gender roles (Thompson and Walker, 1995). They are critical because the concept of gender roles implies that all members of the society, including women, accept the legitimacy of gender expectations and their inequalities (Anderson, 1993; Ferree, 1990; West and Fenstermaker, 1993). Some critics object to the implication that individuals learn gender roles early in life, which thereafter remain fixed and unchangeable (West and Fenstermaker, 1993). This view of gender roles, they believe, puts the emphasis on individual learning and obscures the social nature of gender (Stacey and Thorne, 1985).

Our view of gender roles is similar to that of Komarovsky (1992). We believe that social roles in general, and gender roles in particular, are shaped by and reflect structural and cultural features of societies and cultures. We also concur with Thompson and Walker (1995), who point out that a gender role approach can be useful for several purposes: (1) to point out conflicts, discontinuities, or contradictions in traditional roles; (2) to show the link between culture and behavior; (3) to demonstrate how interaction creates gender roles; or (4) to reveal the inequality of male and female roles (Thompson and Walker, 1995, p. 851).

Cultural Differences in Gender Roles

Cultural differences in gender roles were described many years ago by Margaret Mead (1935) in her now classic study of three New Guinea tribes. The cultures of the three tribes Mead studied happened to have dramatic differences in gender roles, thus demonstrating how gender roles are learned from the culture in which one lives.

Mead first studied the *Arapesh,* a society in which both the males and females generally behaved in ways that are associated with the traditional gender roles of females in Western societies. Both sexes among the Arapesh were passive, gentle, unaggressive, and emotionally responsive to the needs of others. In contrast, Mead found that in another New Guinea group, the *Mundugumor,* both the males and the females were characteristically aggressive, suspicious, and, from a Westerner's view, excessively heartless and cruel, especially toward children. The striking feature of these two cultures is that males and females were expected to be very alike, and they were.

Mead then studied a third New Guinea tribe, the *Tchambuli.* In this group, the gender roles of the males and females were almost exactly reversed from the roles traditionally assigned to males and females in Western society. Mead reported in her autobiography that "among the Tchambuli the expected relations between men and women reversed those that are characteristic of our own culture. For it was Tchambuli women who were brisk and hearty, who managed the business affairs of life, and worked comfortably in large cooperative groups" (Mead, 1972, p. 214). The children also exhibited these characteristics. Girls were the brightest and most competent, and displayed "the most curiosity and the freest expression of intelligence." The Tchambuli boys "were already caught up in the rivalrous, catty and individually competitive life of the men" (Mead, 1972, p. 214). Mead reported also that while the women managed the affairs of the family, the men were engaged differently: "Down by the lake shore in ceremonial houses the men carved and painted, gossiped and had temper tantrums, and played out their rivalries" (Mead, 1972, p. 215).

This cross-cultural examination of gender roles shows vividly how the behavior and the seemingly "natural" personal attributes of the sexes can vary greatly.

Stereotyped Personality Traits and Gender Roles

Although we have been using the general term gender roles, it is possible to make a distinction between stereotyped personality traits and the expected behavior associated with gender (Kammeyer, 1964). We will distinguish between these two closely related ideas next.

Stereotyped Personality Traits

Many people believe that certain personality traits are inherently related to being either male or female, that males and females are born with distinguishing tendencies and characteristics. This way of thinking creates stereotypes. A **stereotype** is a belief that a certain category of people has a particular set of personal characteristics. Stereotypes exist for racial groups, religious groups, ethnic groups, and, in the case at hand, males and females.

For example, females are often stereotyped as emotional, whereas males are believed to be unemotional. Males are believed to be less affected by things that would deeply touch females. Males are thought to be more aggressive, and women are seen as more passive. Many people believe that these and other personality traits come with the biological makeup of males and females. Refutations of these stereotypes are all around us, but the beliefs persist. Consider the following poignant statement by a young man describing an event with his girlfriend.

There was an occasion when I went to Susan's one night, a happy man, and left feeling like a disheartened boy. She wanted to know why I didn't make a move on her and why I wasn't aggressive.... I know I'm not as aggressive as other men are or as I "should be" but I told her that it shouldn't matter.... I took her in my arms and asked her if she knew I loved her and she said she didn't know. I know she said it in disgust but it really hurt me. I began to cry. Man, I just about ran out of the door because I didn't want her to see me cry. I was not a man: I wasn't aggressive and I didn't hide my emotions and I really felt bad (Forisha, 1978, p. 160).

It is clear from this young man's reactions to his own behavior how deeply embedded the stereotyped views are of male personality traits. He shows shame and even disgust at his own characteristics and behavior. He feels that he failed by not being as aggressive as men are supposed to be, and he compounded the sin by displaying his emotions in front of his girlfriend.

A number of other personality traits are associated with being either male or female. Women are thought to be followers rather than leaders. Women are thought to be more sympathetic, sensitive, compassionate, and concerned about others. They are portrayed as more inclined toward artistic and aesthetic activities. They are assumed to be less inclined toward mathematics, science, and even intellectuality. Women are often thought to be more moral, more religious, or, in some cultures, "purer" than men.

Men are thought to be better leaders, more objective, aggressive, independent, active, dominant, competitive, logical, scientific, calculating, tough, strong, and unsentimental.

Believing in the stereotyped personality traits of males and females serves as a support or justification for many kinds of gender inequality. If males are believed to be better leaders and decision makers, it would, of course, follow that men should be given positions of leadership. If women, on the other hand, are thought to be more sensitive, compassionate, and concerned for others, then they would "naturally" fit better into the tasks and jobs that call for these skills (caring for children, the ill, or the elderly, for example). But the occupations so often reserved for women have much less prestige than the leadership jobs allocated to men.

Beliefs about Gender Stereotypes

Gender stereotypes continue to be surprisingly persistent, with many Americans still believing that the basic personality traits of males and females are very different. Data collected by Harris (1994) from 1500 females and 1500 males[1] revealed that most people think it is desirable for males to have certain personality traits

---

[1]The 3000 adults who participated in this study were "randomly selected" from persons visiting Chicago area shopping malls. Thus, despite the size of the sample, it is not a probability sample of the United States or even of the Chicago population.

and females others. Both men and women believed that it was best for males to be *aggressive, ambitious, competitive, independent, and self-sufficient; to have leadership abilities; to defend their own beliefs; to be willing to take a stand; and to have strong personalities* (Harris, 1994, p. 254). By comparison, according to both men and women, the most desirable personality traits for females include being *compassionate, gentle, sympathetic, tender, and warm, and they should love children* (Harris, 1994, p. 254). The African Americans in this study, both males and females, were less likely to accept the traditional gender stereotypes than were Anglo-Americans and Hispanics (Harris, 1994).

Contemporary public opinion polls also continue to show adults holding oversimplified descriptions of females and males. A 1990 Gallup poll found that a majority of Americans (58 percent) believe that women and men are different in terms of their personalities, interests, and abilities (DeStefano and Colasanto, 1990). Men are most often described—by women as well as men—as aggressive, strong, proud, disorganized, courageous, confident, and independent. Women, on the other hand, are most often described as emotional, talkative, sensitive, affectionate, patient, romantic, and moody (DeStefano and Colasanto, 1990).

In general, a belief in stereotyped male and female personality traits is found among people who prefer a traditional allocation of tasks between the sexes. Most important, men are more likely to believe in stereotyped personality traits than women are. Studies have found also that age is related to beliefs about stereotyped personality traits, which means that older people believe in the stereotypes more than younger people do. Also, better educated people are less likely to believe in stereotyped personality traits, while religious people are more likely to do so (Mirowsky and Ross, 1987).

Expected Behaviors of Males and Females

The prescriptions for male and female behavior, according to the traditional gender roles, fit the stereotyped personality traits like a glove fits a hand. As we previously noted, whenever people hold stereotyped views of male and female personality characteristics, they are likely to hold traditional expectations about male and female behavior (Komarovsky, 1992).

Although traditional gender-role expectations are found in almost every sphere of life, they are revealed most clearly in the family. According to the traditional feminine role, women are expected to perform supportive tasks within the family, and in general are expected to be subordinate to men. Women have the primary responsibility of taking care of home and children. Recent studies, conducted in Sweden and the United States, continue to find that men generally do between 20 and 30 percent of the housework, even when both husband and wife are employed. This pattern prevailed across social classes in both countries (Wright et al., 1992).

The traditional expectation for men is that they will provide for and, if necessary, defend their families. Although these traditional female and male role expectations may seem exaggerated and even out of date, they still exist for substantial numbers of people in contemporary society. For example, in a modern-day family (with or without young children) it would still be acceptable for a wife to remain in the home while her husband was the sole wage earner. However, it would be considered very unusual if a husband stayed at home while his wife was the sole breadwinner.

Attitudes about Gender Roles

Traditional views about the feminine and masculine roles have been undergoing significant changes since the feminist movement began in the 1960s. The reduced support for the traditional gender roles that occurred during the late 1960s and early 1970s has been described as a "revolution in attitudes" (Mason and Lu, 1988, p. 39). Changes in attitudes have continued to move in the feminist direction since then. In 1985, a national sample of American adults expressed more profeminist views than a similar sample had in 1977. Both men and women, in every age group from 18 to over 65, showed less acceptance of the traditional feminine role in 1985 than they had less than a decade earlier (Mason and Lu, 1988).

While both men and women have modified their attitudes about gender roles, virtually all studies show that males are more likely than females to hold traditional attitudes about the feminine role. Recent studies find that even among young people males continue to have more traditional views than females. This pattern has been found among students at a public university in Virginia (Willets-Bloom and Nock, 1994), high school and college students in Michigan (Jackson et al., 1994), and college students at a large urban university in Pennsylvania (Morinaga et al., 1993).

Studies in other countries have also found that males have more traditional gender role attitudes than females. This is true of high school students in New Zealand (Tuck et al., 1994) and college students in Japan and Slovenia (Morinaga et al., 1993).

Socialization for Gender Roles

To document the ways in which girls are socialized to exhibit female personality traits, and boys, male personality traits, is much like trying to document the ways in which people learn how to talk or use proper sentence structure. This socialization is such a continuous and ever-present experience that examples are both obvious and subtle.

Gender roles can be learned in a variety of ways, including direct training. Direct training occurs when significant others, especially parents, in the child's environment reward the child for behaviors that are consistent with traditional gender roles. If a 3-year-old boy falls and skins his knee, his parent might say, "Oh, you are such a brave little man, you won't cry. Will you? If you don't cry we will let the puppy in the house." If significant others respond one way to boys and another way to girls, and if their responses reinforce the expected gender-role behaviors, then male and female behavior will likely be shaped and modified accordingly.

While everyday observations lead us to believe that such gender-role reinforcement does go on, it has not been easy to document this reinforcement in scientifically controlled observational studies (Losh-Hesselbart, 1987; Maccoby and Jacklin, 1974). What is demonstrable is that parents and others respond to children on the basis of their gender. Parents often provide toys and clothes that are consistent with their expectations of how children of each sex should behave. In one study, the homes of 120 infants were visited by researchers who compared the number and types of toys, the colors and types of clothing, and the colors and motifs of the children's rooms. Twenty baby girls and boys in each of three age groups—5 months, 13 months, and 25 months—were included in the study (Pomerleau et al., 1990).

The researchers found that boys were provided with more sports equipment, tools, and large and small vehicles, while girls had more dolls, fictional characters, child's furniture, kitchen appliances and utensils, typewriters, and telephones. Girls' clothing was pink and multicolored more often, while boys' clothing was more often blue, red, and white. The color of girls' bedrooms was varied (not necessarily pink), but the bedrooms of boys were often decorated in blue (Pomerleau et al., 1990).

The tendency to identify infant males and small boys more often with stereotypic colors has also been found in other studies. When mothers in public places were asked if strangers had made mistakes about their two-year-olds' gender, 70 percent of the mothers of girls said mistakes had been made, while only 30 percent of the mothers of boys said so. Parents of boys appeared to be more concerned that boys be seen as males and took more care to dress them and cut their hair so they would not be mistaken for females (McGuire, 1988).

This greater concern that boys be identified as boys indicates that adults consider it more serious when boys are misidentified, or in some way slip over into the female gender. It has often been noted that there is more adult tolerance for "tomboy" behavior in girls than feminine behavior in boys. Some observers have reasoned that this is true because "male-type" behavior is more highly valued in our society. Perhaps this is why it seems more tolerable when a girl behaves like a boy than when a boy behaves like a girl. At least, the reasoning goes, the tomboy female is aspiring to a "higher-status" position, while the boy who is more "feminine" is actually "lowering" himself. Perhaps this is why young girls can more successfully deviate from the traditional gender role. They cannot safely do so, however, much beyond the age of 10 or 11.

One additional indication of how parents treat their sons and daughters differently is found in the names they give them (Lieberson and Bell, 1992; Rossi, 1965). A recent study has shown that parents are more likely to give boys traditional names and girls more fashionable names. Traditional boys' names often reflect family, Western culture, and religion (Michael, Christopher, John, David, for example), while girls names are more likely to be fashionable, novel, and decorative (Jennifer, Nicole, Tiffany, and Jessica, for example). The implication of these naming patterns is that boys are seen as more important in terms of "historical continuity and stability—boys are taken more seriously..." (Lieberson and Bell, 1992, p. 548).

Modeling is a second way in which traditional gender roles may be learned. **Modeling** occurs when children observe significant others of the same sex (again, often parents) engage in a behavior and then imitate that behavior. For example, girls see their mothers (and other females) applying makeup and may imitate that behavior in play. Of course, modeling is based on the assumption that children can determine which sex they belong to and thus which behavior to model. This process may be aided by parents and significant others who will make it clear which sex is the appropriate or inappropriate model. If a boy begins to apply lipstick in imitation of his mother, he may be told that "little boys do not wear lipstick."

The mass media, and especially television, may also serve as important gender-role models for children. Evidence shows that children respond to television portrayals of the sexes, in that children who watch the most television are more likely to hold gender stereotypes (Losh-Hesselbart, 1987).

A Theory of Gender-Role Learning

In addition to acquiring appropriate gender-role behavior through social rewards, children also acquire gender roles as a result of the organization of the ideas and experiences they have encountered in early life (Kohlberg, 1966). The mental organization of ideas and experiences is a fundamental learning process and is actually an extension of the idea of the self-concept discussed in Chapter 5. Children develop a sense of self from interacting with other persons. They learn that they are *boys* or *girls* because they are so identified by parents and significant others. Kohlberg describes this extension of the self for a boy:

> The...basic sexual self-concept (his categorization as a boy...) becomes the major organizer and determinant of many of his activities, values, and attitudes. The boy in effect says, "I am a boy, therefore I want to do boy things," therefore the opportunity to do boy things (and to gain approval for doing them) is rewarding (Kohlberg, 1966, p. 89).

Kohlberg's view of gender-role development starts with the idea that children organize their worlds as simply and efficiently as possible. Gender is already a part of most children's understanding by the age of 3 and is firmly fixed by the age of 5 or 6. Once children have an idea of their gender, they tend to build their values and attitudes around this basic dimension. Parents start this process of gender-role differentiation, and normal developmental processes characteristic of all children then complete the process of acquiring a gender identity. **Gender identity** is a recognition of one's gender and an acceptance of characteristics typically associated with that gender.

Learning gender identity depends on symbolic communication with others, especially with significant others. At first children simply learn labels for themselves, much as they learn any other label for any other object. More than half of 2½-year-old children do not give the correct answer when they are asked their gender. By the time they are 3 years old, however, from two-thirds to three-fourths of children will answer the question correctly.

Although young children may recognize that *boy* or *girl* applies to them, they do not necessarily recognize that these words apply to entire categories of people. A young girl named Susan may know that she is both Susan and a girl, but she may not recognize that *girl* is a word that can be applied to a whole set of young females. At the age of two or three, children usually focus on superficial social characteristics, such as clothing styles and hairstyles, not on genital or other gender-related physical differences. This focus is reflected in the anecdote about the 3-year-old who came home and announced to her mother that she had seen a new baby at her friend's house. When asked if the baby was a boy or a girl, she said she didn't know because "it wasn't wearing any clothes."

Kohlberg argues that the structuring of a child's world goes on at the same time as gender-role stereotypes are being learned. The male child recognizes not only that he is a boy but also that *boy* is a general category of people of which he is a part. Furthermore, he learns that boys are part of the general category called males and men. Girls learn the same kinds of things. When boys and girls begin to identify with their respective categories, they begin to value characteristics that are associated with their category.

Children tend to value things that are the same as, or similar to, things they already know and like. A boy, for example, learns to value certain games, toys, and active and sometimes aggressive behaviors because they are consistent with being a boy. Thereafter the boy will look for, and be interested in, activities that are associated with his already accepted malelike behavior. The same process occurs for girls.

There is a steady interweaving of the mental development of the child and the social learning that occurs with socialization. Through this process, males and females learn, and generally accept as appropriate, the major dimensions of the gender roles of their society. Through the remainder of this chapter we examine the ways gender roles continue to influence the behavior of males and females.

Gender Roles among Elementary School Children

Traditional gender roles are also reinforced in the elementary schools. The importance of traditional gender role characteristics has been shown by a participant-observation study of kindergarten through sixth-grade children enrolled in two public schools in middle- and upper-middle-class neighborhoods in a large, mostly white, university community (Adler et al., 1992).

This study found that the popularity of boys at this age is based on very different characteristics and behaviors than is the popularity of girls. The characteristics and qualities needed for popularity, even at this young age, seem to reflect the traditional roles of males and females and anticipate the adolescent and adult roles of the genders.

Boys' popularity among elementary school aged children is based on athletic ability, "coolness," toughness, social sophistication, and, by the fourth and fifth grades, being able to relate to girls. For boys, high academic performance is negatively related to popularity, unless it is clearly counterbalanced by athletic ability. On the other hand, low academic ability is also a negative factor in determining the popularity of boys.

Even in the early elementary school grades, the most popular boys are identified as the best athletes. Even when the athletic boys are also mean and boastful, they are still judged the most popular.

Being cool and tough are also characteristics that make boys popular. Coolness is largely a matter of self-presentation. It includes wearing the right clothes and shoes and presenting them in a stylish way (Nike Air Jordans or Reeboks left open and untied, for example). Toughness, especially in the upper elementary school grades, means defying adult authority, challenging the rules, and acting belligerent. The boys who are tough are often in trouble with the teachers because of their insolence or clowning in the classroom, but it makes them the center of attention and admiration.

The popularity of elementary school aged girls is importantly related to family background. Girls who come from high socioeconomic status families, which provide them with clothes and other material possessions, are attractive as friends. Girls are also more popular if they come from families that do not supervise them closely or restrict them in their activities.

The popularity of girls is also related to their physical appearance, which includes their good looks, but also their clothes and makeup. A kindergarten girl described the most popular girl in her class by saying, "It's just that she has a lot of money but we don't, so it's like that's why she has the prettiest clothes and, you know, the prettiest makeup" (Adler et al., 1992, p. 179).

Another factor related to the popularity of elementary school girls is their level of social development. This is comparable to the sophistication factor among boys. The girls who are the most precocious with respect to social relations and especially in their relations with boys are among the most popular.

Academic performance for girls is not a negative factor in the way it is for boys. Girls do not have to get good grades to be popular, but it doesn't count against them if they do.

This study of schoolchildren finds them being rewarded by their peers for having characteristics associated with the traditional gender roles. Girls' status is based on grooming, clothes, and makeup, as well as social sophistication, romantic success, and material possessions. Boys gain their status from behaviors and characteristics closely related to the traditional male role. They are most popular when they distance themselves from authority and academic effort and emphasize athletics, toughness, trouble-making, coolness, and dominance (Adler et al., 1992).

Teachers and Gender

Studies of elementary and junior high schools have shown that males and females are treated differently by the teachers (Sadker and Sadker, 1985; Chira, 1992). Even though teachers claim that boys and girls are treated the same, observational studies of classroom behavior have shown that boys dominate communication in the schools. Even in language arts and English classes, where girls traditionally outperform boys, the boys still command more of the teacher's attention when they speak. In part, this male dominance in communication comes from boys' being more assertive, but, in addition, teachers respond differently to boys than they do to girls (Sadker and Sadker, 1985).

When boys call out answers without raising their hands, teachers are likely to accept their responses. However, when girls call out their answers, teachers have a greater tendency to reprimand them for not raising their hands. Teachers also give more attention to boys and praise them more often when they answer questions. The following dialogue illustrates a typical pattern in the classroom:

TEACHER:	What's the capital of Maryland? Joel?
JOEL:	Baltimore.
TEACHER:	What's the largest city in Maryland, Joel?
JOEL:	Baltimore.
TEACHER:	That's good. But Baltimore isn't the capital. The capital is also the location of the U.S. Naval Academy. Joel, do you want to try again?
JOEL:	Annapolis.
TEACHER:	Excellent. Anne, what's the capital of Maine?
ANNE:	Portland.
TEACHER:	Judy, do you want to try?
JUDY:	Augusta.
TEACHER:	OK (Sadker and Sadker, 1985, p. 56).

This classroom interchange illustrates how males often receive support, which helps them move toward the right answers, and they receive praise when they answer correctly. Girls, on the other hand, are given less information about the quality of their answers and less praise (Sadker and Sadker, 1985).

The communications patterns in the schools, which are also found in the family, reinforce the same general pattern. Female contributions are less highly valued than those of the male. If we think of how these patterns can make important differences in college, in organizations, in political groups, and in the work world, we will realize that they are not trivial or inconsequential. When what men say is considered more important than what women say (perhaps by both men and women in many instances), then men will have an advantage in obtaining job positions, being promoted, and receiving career rewards. In the political world men will be more successful in running for office and getting elected. We turn now to the public world to see how women have fared in the worlds of politics, occupations, and careers.

Men and Women in the Public World

It is not difficult to document the dominance of men in all realms of public life. The political and occupational worlds are major areas in which males are greatly overrepresented in leadership positions. Using income as a measure of the positions people hold, or as a reward for their work, men have consistently had the advantage. The world of politics provides an excellent example of the underrepresentation of women in leadership positions of the U.S. system of government.

The Political Arena

When the Constitution and the Declaration of Independence were being written and were adopted, substantial debate centered on the inalienable rights of "men." When the founders of the new country used the word *men,* they may or may not have been using it to refer to *all* people, both men and women. Perhaps they were, but in fact they set up a form of government in which women (as well as slaves and Native Americans) were denied the right to vote. Not until the ratification of the Nineteenth Amendment to the Constitution in 1920—a century and a half later—did women finally receive the vote.

Although the United States was not the first nation in the world to grant women the vote, it was certainly not the last. On a worldwide basis, New Zealand was the first country to grant women suffrage, in 1893. Other countries that preceded the United States in giving women the vote include Australia (1902), Finland (1906), Denmark (1915), the Soviet Union (1917), England (1918), and (in 1919) Luxembourg, the Netherlands, and Austria (Giele, 1988). Some European countries gave women the vote much later (France, 1944; Hungary, 1945; Yugoslavia, 1946; Italy, 1947; Belgium, 1948; and Switzerland, 1971). Japan did not allow women to vote until 1945. A number of countries, especially in the Islamic Third World, still have not given women the vote (Giele, 1988).

Even though more women are entering political life in the United States, they are still woefully underrepresented in Congress. Among the 100 members of the Senate in 1995, there were 8 women. In the House of Representatives, in 1995, 47 of the 435 members were women (U.S. Bureau of the Census, 1995b). Among these national lawmakers, slightly over 10 percent were women, although over 50 percent of the population is female.

The World of Work

Women and men are treated differently in the occupational world in two ways. The first is **sex segregation,** which is the unequal allocation of occupations and professions to men and women (Figure 10–1); the second is the **gender gap** in wages, which gives women lower monetary rewards than men even when they are in the same occupational categories (Peterson and Morgan, 1995).

Sex Segregation in Occupations.   The unequal allocation of occupations and professions to men and women—sex segregation—seems to reflect discrimination at the point of training or hiring. Importantly, the jobs women get tend to pay less than the jobs men get, which therefore produces the gender gap in wages. Analysis of both blue- and white-collar workers in sixteen U.S. industries and ten professional and administrative occupations found that women earn less than men because of sex segregation in the labor force (Peterson and Morgan, 1995).

A similar pattern was found in a study of federal government employees. This study is especially important because federal law makes it illegal to discriminate by sex, and we might suppose that the law would be more faithfully followed in the federal workforce. However, that proved not to be the case, since female federal employees were generally hired at lower levels than male. Newly hired women were concentrated in female-dominated jobs in the lower tier of the job ladder, precisely the ones that offered the least opportunity for advancement. Even more important, women in the middle grades of federal workers were promoted at lower rates than men. This study also found that the most difficult kind of promotion for women was from the middle-level ranks to supervisory and managerial jobs (DiPrete and Soule, 1988).

Some alternative explanations have been offered for the widespread existence of sex segregation in occupations (England et al., 1988). One alternative has been offered by economists, who argue that women intentionally select occupations that are easy to get into and out of, while still providing moderately good incomes. An extension of this economic argument is that women also select occupations that allow them to take time out when they want to have children and remain at home. Obviously, this economic explanation is in line with the view that

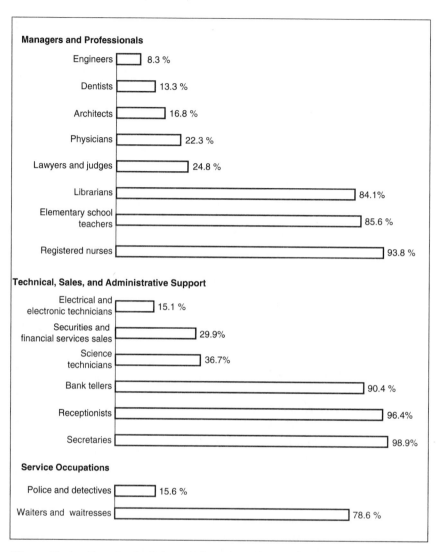

Figure 10–1. Females in Selected Occupations, as a Percent of the Total, 1994. (*Source:* U.S. Bureau of the Census, *Statistical Abstract of the United States,* 1995. Washington, D.C.: U.S. Government Printing Office, 1995, Table 649, pp. 411–413.)

women *choose* to be in sex-segregated occupations. Although this economic theory sounds plausible, a national sample of male and female workers did not find support for its major assertions (England et al., 1988).

The results of this study and many others suggest a more sociological explanation for sex segregation of occupations and the accompanying lower wages for women. This explanation first emphasizes the mutual or two-way influence between gender-role socialization and discrimination by employers. Traditional gender-role socialization leads many women to the view that certain jobs are more appropriate and available for them. Employers conclude from this that women do not want certain male-dominated jobs. This may feed their already existing belief that women are "by nature" not suited to certain jobs (England, et al., 1988). The general view that one sex is inherently superior to the other sex is called **sexism.** Sexism often serves as the basis for overt discrimination against women in the occupational world, keeping occupations sex segregated and, as we will see, women's pay less than men's pay.

Even in the absence of overt discrimination by employers, structural or institutional factors act to keep women in sex-segregated (and often lower-paying, lower-status) jobs. These structural or institutional impediments to promotion and higher pay have been called *institutional sexism.* **Institutional sexism** is defined as the day-to-day operations, rules, and policies of organizations and institutions that result in the discriminatory treatment of women. An important aspect of institutional sexism is that it can operate without individuals being prejudiced against women or intentionally discriminatory. However, when organizations and institutions have rules or policies that directly or indirectly impede or limit women, the effect can be just as important as when prejudice is blatant and discrimination intentional.

An example of institutional sexism may be found in the practice of having female jobs in organizations that lead only to other female jobs—jobs that have relatively low pay and status. Other such institutional practices that work to the disadvantage of women include giving preferences to military veterans (which favor many more men than women), limiting public advertising for jobs (which might give the male friends of already employed men a better chance of being hired), and designing machines and tools for the average height and strength of men rather than women (England et al., 1988). As an example of the latter, some female police candidates in training programs are unable to use large caliber firearms effectively and are therefore unable to meet the training requirements. In actual police work, however, smaller-caliber weapons are often used by officers.

Another example of institutional sexism stems from employee policies about child care, which may have a significant effect on female employees. Few American employers provide child-care services in the work setting. (Employers in societies like Sweden are far more likely to provide adequate child-care facilities.) Since the traditional feminine role expectation is that women will care for children, women with children are apt to face more problems and strains than men working for the same employer. The employer cannot be blamed personally for creating the problems of their female employees with children, and the employer certainly cannot be charged with prejudice. The point remains that a company policy that does not provide adequate child-care services does affect some women adversely.

The Gender Gap in Wages. Among full-time, year-round workers, women earn about 71 percent of what men earn (U.S. Bureau of the Census, 1995b). In 1967, women earned 62 percent of what men earned, revealing thus that, over the last quarter-century, women's economic gains relative to men have been modest. Most of the gains for women came in the 1970s and 1980s, but even some of this gain was produced by the worsening of men's earnings (Bernhardt et al., 1995). Figure 10–2 shows the median incomes of men and women in selected occupational categories.

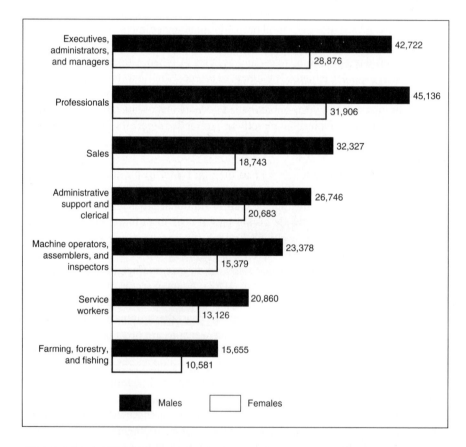

Figure 10–2. Median Incomes of Males and Females in Selected Occupational Categories. (*Source:* U.S. Bureau of the Census, *Statistical Abstract of the United States,* 1995. Washington, D.C.: U.S. Government Printing Office, 1995, Table 679, p. 435.)

Age Stratification and Inequality

Societies are stratified by age, just as they are stratified by economic status, race, ethnicity, and gender. Age is used to divide a population into different categories, which are then treated differently. Different age groups are given different rights, opportunities, rules, and limitations. Often the old or the young age groups, since they tend to be dependent on the rest of the adult population, are at a disadvantage and therefore receive unequal treatment in the society. Although every society makes some distinctions on the basis of age, the nature of age stratification systems differs from one society to another and has changed from one historical period to another (Riley et al., 1988).

Children and Society

Since childhood appears to be a normal and natural stage of life, it is interesting to find that for much of Western history, childhood was not thought of as a distinct life stage. This, at least, is the view of social historian Philippe Ariés (1962), who assembled evidence to support the thesis that in the Middle Ages a child went from infancy directly into a kind of adulthood. The most common image of the medieval child, as Ariés found in the paintings of that period, was that of a kind of miniature adult. Obviously, if parents did not recognize a stage of life that we recognize as childhood, they were likely to treat their children differently than they are treated today.

Children at a very early age were expected to participate in productive work. Because of their size they could not do all things that adults could do, but they were not allowed to spend their time in frivolous play. In the nineteenth century in the United States, children of poor and working classes were expected to contribute to the family income and production by working. Even in the twentieth century, children of farm families often left elementary school to help with farm tasks.

Today, the situation is quite different, with children rarely entering the work force until at least high school age. Again the exceptions are likely to be on family farms, or other farm labor, and family businesses. Usually children are not expected to work, but they are also denied a wide range of rights and privileges. Children and adolescents in contemporary families are usually rather closely controlled and limited by parents. The assumption is that their immaturity makes it imprudent to give them too much freedom. Although some agitation has occurred for greater children's rights, no significant social movement has emerged (Farson, 1974).

Some rights that were earlier granted to adolescents and young adults have been withdrawn in recent years. Many high schools adopted liberalized policies of dress and behavior in the 1970s, which have since been retracted. Smoking, for example, was often allowed in specified areas of high schools, but in recent years many schools have discontinued this privilege. In a similar way, many states and localities in the 1970s lowered the age for drinking alcoholic beverages to 18. More recently, the laws have been changed, raising the legal drinking age in most places to 21.

Again, these changes illustrate how the social definitions of age groups can change from one time to another, even in the same society. When age categories are socially defined, certain rights and limitations will be attached to the people in that category. This system is referred to as **age stratification.**

The attitude that limitations and restrictions can be based on age is called **ageism.** Although the term *ageism* is applied primarily to the treatment of the elderly, it can generally refer to any instance when an individual's age is the primary basis for evaluating and dealing with that person. An example of ageism would be a 63-year-old worker's being released from a job, while younger workers who are no more productive are retained. But ageism could also be illustrated by a brilliant teenager who has been denied entry into college simply because of age.

In the next section we will turn our attention to the elderly, a growing and increasingly important part of the population. Much of our discussion will reflect the work being done in a field of study called *social gerontology.* **Social gerontology** is the study of the impact of social and cultural conditions on the process of aging, and also the social consequences of age changes in the population of a society (Hooyman and Kiyak, 1991).

The Elderly Population

Old age cannot be precisely defined in terms of years of life, because just as the meaning of childhood has changed, so also has the meaning of old age. In the United States it is both the legal and social custom to use the 65th birthday as the beginning of old age. When the Social Security Act was passed in 1935, age 65 was set as the age when retirement benefits could be received. Thus, in the public mind, 65 became linked with old age. However, the laws have changed periodically, and for several decades Americans have had the option of receiving partial Social Security benefits at age 62. Beginning in the year 2000, the age at which full benefits can be received will increase in gradual steps from age 65 to 67. Furthermore, as a way of combatting age discrimination in the occupational world, Congress passed legislation that allows most workers to work until age 70, if they wish.

Even though this legislation gives older people the right to remain in the labor force until they are well past 65, the actual trend in retirement has been in the opposite direction. For the last 100 years American workers have been retiring at younger and younger ages. In 1890, 70 percent of males over the age of 65 were still in the labor force. Today, about 12 percent of Americans over 65 are employed or seeking employment (Treas, 1995). By ages 62 to 64 less than half of all males are still in the labor force (Soldo and Agree, 1988). Although some older people may be out of the labor force because they are unable to get work, the majority have probably retired voluntarily.

Who Are the Elderly Today?

The legal and social trends just discussed are indications of who the elderly are in our society, but some of these indicators are providing different pictures. If time of retirement means old age, then old age is coming earlier than ever before; yet the laws governing Social Security benefits, and prohibiting mandatory retirement, suggest that old age is coming later. Obviously, any definition of old age is very arbitrary, depending on the way in which age is socially defined. In the contemporary United States, many people still view age 65 as the beginning of old age, but new definitions are emerging, particularly from the older people themselves. Often people at age 65 and even older do not think of themselves as old because they have a level of health and a style of life that they do not associate with old age (Treas, 1995).

To reflect the changing conditions of older people, it has been suggested that we think in terms of the *third quarter of life*. The **third quarter of life** is defined as beginning at about age 50 and continuing until about 75 (Pifer and Bronte, 1986). Clearly, this concept minimizes the significance of reaching age 65 and emphasizes the fact that most people today continue to live active lives until age 75. The age of 50 is chosen in part because many people make important changes in their lives at that point—usually their children have established independent lives, their occupations and careers (and incomes) have often reached about the highest level that will be attained, and retirement emerges as a serious consideration. Age 75 is suggested as an upper limit for the third quarter of life because many people begin then to experience significant declines in physical and mental abilities (Pifer and Bronte, 1986).

Obviously a third quarter of life would have to be followed by a **fourth quarter of life,** the years between 75 and 100 years of age. The idea that an average person could live to 100 is not as extraordinary as it may sound. The life span (the maximum length of human life) has long been over 100 years, although only a few people in most populations reach this maximum. However, some scientists, especially those who put their faith in new preventive therapies that will avert or treat degenerative diseases, foresee a life expectancy of over 100 years; some speculate that life expectancy could reach 125 years or more (Manton et al., 1991).

Another refinement on the definition of the elderly is found in the already widely accepted terms *young-old* and *old-old.* The **young-old** are people aged 65 through 74, while the **old-old** are aged 75 and older. Again, the young-old category is a recognition of the fact that many people over 65 are still vigorous, healthy, and active; the old-old category of 75 and older marks the beginning of, in many cases, physical and mental decline, although some people are still independent and active well beyond that age.

The Size of the Older Population in the United States

In 1995, about 34 million Americans were 65 years of age or older (Treas, 1995). This number is about 13 percent of the total population. At the beginning of the century, only 4 percent of the population was 65 or older, but by the year 2030, the percentage will be over 20 percent (Treas, 1995). The past and future growth of the population 65 and over and 85 and over is shown in Figure 10–3.

Economic Condition of the Elderly

Just as the physical lives of many older people have been improving, so have their economic lives. There is definitely a bright side to the economic condition of the elderly population today, but there is also a dark side. We will deal with the bright side first, because it probably reflects the majority of the elderly. We have already seen an indication of the improved economic conditions of the elderly in the his-

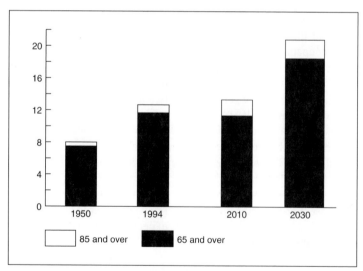

Figure 10–3.   Older Population as Percentage of Total U.S. Population: 1950–2030. (*Source:* From Soldo, Beth J. and Agree, Emily. "America's Elderly." (Population Bulletin, Population Reference Bureau) Vol. 43, 1988, p. 8; U.S. Bureau of the Census, 1995b.)

torical trends in retirement. We saw that, in 1890, 70 percent of all males 65 and over were still employed, while today about 15 percent of men and less than 10 percent of women 65 and over are employed. The United States is not unusual in the trend toward earlier retirement. A comparative study of Australia and Japan found earlier retirement in those societies, too (Schultz et al., 1991).

The high percentages of early retirement among men today probably reflects the fact that they are economically able to retire. In fact, it is said that "No generation of U.S. elderly has enjoyed as high a standard of living as today's older Americans" (Treas, 1995, p. 22). Elderly people's incomes come partly from Social Security, which accounts for about 40 percent of the total, and a slightly larger percentage comes from pensions and assets. Older Americans also receive noncash benefits in the form of Medicare and Medicaid.

Annual income is not the only economic resource of the older population, however. The majority of older people have some economic resources in real estate, savings, and investments. Over three-fourths of elderly householders own their own homes, which, in most cases, are mortgage free. Among elderly *couples,* 88 percent own their own homes, but only 65 percent of elderly females *living alone* own their own homes. Although the health care costs for the elderly are greater than for other age groups, Medicare now covers the major portion of their medical costs. In many cases taxes (both personal income and state and local property taxes) are reduced for people over 65. With these economic resources, many of today's elderly are able to live relatively comfortably, but certainly not in affluence (Soldo and Agree, 1988; Treas, 1995).

But now we turn to that part of the elderly population where the economic picture is much darker. Some people have reached old age who are perhaps in poor health and with physical disabilities, who do not own homes, and who have no savings or other assets. Often, their monthly rent takes a substantial part of their only money income—Social Security benefits. These elderly people live in very precarious economic conditions, often in poor, dilapidated housing. They are truly the impoverished elderly.

In 1993, according to the federal government's poverty standard, 12 percent of the elderly were living in poverty—with the old-old having a higher percentage in poverty than the young-old (U.S. Bureau of the Census, 1995b). However, the most serious poverty exists among elderly women and elderly minorities (Harel et al., 1990; Soldo and Agree, 1988). Elderly women have a significantly higher level of poverty (15 percent) than elderly men (8 percent). Elderly blacks have a much higher poverty level than elderly whites (31 percent compared to 11 percent), while elderly Hispanics are at an intermediate level (22.5 percent). The most seriously impoverished are elderly black women who live alone; a full 60 percent of these women are below the poverty level. These official poverty levels may actually be missing some of the poorest people in the society, for some elderly may be so poor that they live with relatives and thereby may reside in households that are not below the poverty level (Soldo and Agree, 1988).

In the News

Are America's Elderly Being Pampered?

In the U.S. Congress, the budget debates of the mid-1990s often focused on the large amount of money being spent for "entitlements," which are government payments that go largely to the elderly. Often those who argued for a balanced federal budget claimed that cuts were necessary in the major entitlement programs—Social Security, Medicare, and Medicaid—in order to make progress in balancing the budget. They further claimed that if these cuts were not made the younger generation would be saddled with an unbearable national debt in the future. In essence, the elderly were being blamed for taking up too much of the federal budget, while others in the society were paying the price.

More and more critics are accusing elderly Americans of being pampered, selfish, and greedy members of the society. Two such critics, for example, tried to brand the elderly with the label *whoopies*. This acronym was supposed to stand for "well-off older people" and carried the unflattering implication that many older Americans are living very well at the expense of the rest of the American population (Marotta and Marotta, 1989). Fortunately, the label whoopies did not catch on, but the criticism of older Americans as a pampered part of the population continues to be heard (Samuelson, 1990).

The increase in negative feelings about the elderly is a relatively recent phenomenon. A quarter-century ago, almost all Americans were concerned about the elderly, and for good reason. In 1970, one-quarter of all people over age 65 were living below the poverty level. Many more were surviving just above the poverty level. Before the advent of Medicare in 1966, many older citizens were constantly in danger of losing all their meager resources if they encountered a serious health or medical problem.

But over the last 25 years the economic status of elderly Americans has improved greatly. The post-World War II economy provided relatively good incomes for many people, allowing them to purchase homes, accumulate savings, make investments, and participate in private pension programs. These resources, augmented by Social Security and Medicare, give today's elderly a higher standard of living than any generation in history (Treas, 1995).

However, the well-being of older Americans should not be exaggerated. Even today, 40 percent of all income received by elderly Americans comes from Social Security, with monthly payments averaging about $650. Those older Americans who do not have paid-for homes or who pay a monthly rent are often hard pressed to live on their monthly Social Security payments. If these elderly people have high medical and drug costs not covered by Medicare, they can be thrown into severe poverty. The economic condition of many Americans, especially minorities and women, is often quite precarious.

Despite the economic plight of some older Americans, there is a widening perception that too many elderly are living in very comfortable circumstances and are, at the same time, getting government monies that are desperately needed for other purposes. Many people are especially concerned that, if the older part of the population continues to receive such a large proportion of the federal budget, the national debt will rise, and the young people of today will ultimately be hurt. Today's younger generation will not only be paying for the enormous costs of the baby-boom generation— now reaching age 50—but will also be saddled with interest on the federal debt, which will have grown even larger.

The elderly, for their part, often feel that they have contributed to the economy through their work and their tax contributions, and now it is their turn to receive what is due to them. The views of older people are often politically important because they vote more than any other age group, and elected officials are sensitive to their demands.

Whether older people will continue to get what they want will depend greatly on the perception of the rest of the population. If younger age groups increasingly see the elderly as pampered and privileged (and even greedy), their support for the elderly may diminish rapidly. This is a trend in public opinion that should be watched closely.

MAROTTA, JUNE, and MAROTTA, GEORGE. "Shame on the Whoopies." *Washington Post,* August 22, 1989.
SAMUELSON, ROBERT J. "Pampering the Elderly." *Washington Post,* October 24, 1990.
TREAS, JUDITH. "Older Americans in the 1990s and Beyond." *Population Bulletin,* Vol. 50, May 1995.

Economic Comparisons between the Elderly and Children

Although many elderly in the United States are poor, even more poverty exists among the children of the society. In 1993, 22 percent of all children under 18 years old were living in households where incomes were below the poverty level (U.S. Bureau of the Census, 1995b). Among black children the percentage was 46 percent; among Hispanic children it was 40 percent. Since we have already seen that only about 12 percent of the elderly have incomes below the poverty level, clearly these children as a group are more disadvantaged than old people, especially because children (and their parents) are not likely to have the economic assets of many older people (homes, savings, investments).

The disturbing trend in the United States is that, while poverty levels for the elderly have been going down, the poverty rate for children has been going up (Hernandez, 1995). Government expenditures for the elderly have been increasing, while programs for children have been going down. The major program for children (Aid to Families with Dependent Children) has not kept up with inflation since 1970 (Johnson et al., 1991). Public and political opposition to welfare in the 1990s threatens even more cuts in welfare programs for children.

Why are Americans choosing to devote more of their government expenditures to the dependent elderly than to dependent children? One explanation can be found in the competing voter interest groups, which have different levels of political power. In a democratic society the decisions that allocate different levels of resources to the dependent parts of the population are made by voters. Which groups of voters are more likely to support expenditures for the elderly? The elderly themselves would be justified in looking out for their own economic interests. As a group, the population over age 65 votes more than any other age category (U.S. Bureau of the Census, 1995b). The elderly are now a significant voting block in the United States, and through organized interest groups, such as the American Association of Retired Persons, they are becoming stronger (Cockerham, 1991). But the middle-aged voting population is also likely to support expenditures for the elderly, for two self-interested reasons. The first is that, if the government does not support their elderly parents, it will fall to them to do so. The second is that the adults in the population, especially those who are middle-aged, may be looking ahead to when they reach old age, and they prefer to have governmental programs in place for their own support.

In contrast, none of these adult voting groups, except the parents of children, have a direct interest in supporting children. The matter has been put succinctly in the following statement:

> Children don't vote; and adults don't vote on behalf of their own children, which is water over the dam. I daresay that if we passed through life backwards, adults would insist that conditions in childhood be made far more appealing (Preston, 1984, p. 385).

Summary

Every society is organized to some degree on the basis of gender and age categories, and often the results are inequities or systems of inequality. The inequalities between males and females, the gender stratification system, can be analyzed in terms of three separate but closely related concepts: power, division of labor by gender, and gender roles.

In most societies males tend to have greater power and more privileges than females, but some exceptions are notable. Women have greater power in societies where they carry out activities on which men are dependent. In societies around the world, men and women are typically assigned to different work. The division of labor by gender often finds men doing heavy and dangerous work, but there are many instances when females, too, are assigned heavy and arduous tasks.

Cross-cultural evidence shows that the gender role differences familiar in American society are not universal and therefore are not inborn characteristics of the sexes. Anthropological studies give evidence that gender roles are learned through the socialization process.

The stereotyped personality traits associated with males and females attribute certain traits (emphasizing achievement and action) to males and other traits (emphasizing emotional support and comfort) to females. Therefore, traditional feminine and masculine roles in American society emphasize that females should participate in activities that are supportive and expressive, while males should participate in ones that are active and instrumental.

Attitude studies among Americans show that traditional gender-role attitudes have been reduced; but many Americans, especially those with fundamentalist religious beliefs, still hold to some traditional expectations, especially for women.

The socialization for gender roles occurs through social rewards provided by significant others and by models provided by males and females in the child's environment. Also, children themselves develop a gender identity and actively adopt the behaviors and attitudes associated with the different genders.

Traditional gender roles are reinforced by classmates in the schools, beginning as early as kindergarten and the elementary grades. Teachers also respond to the genders differently, giving greater recognition and advantage to the males.

In the public world, especially in political and economic life, women are underrepresented in the more prestigious positions. Sex segregation in occupations, produced in large part by sexism and institutional sexism, continues to leave women less rewarded in the work world.

In the stratification of society by age, the elderly and children are the most disadvantaged. Children and young adults are defined by the rest of the society as being less than mature, and thus limitations are placed on their rights.

The definition of old age is changing in the United States because of the improving health and economic positions of many people over age 65. The elderly population is growing rapidly, and will continue to increase in numbers and as a proportion of the population. Many elderly people today are reaching old age with considerably greater economic resources than in the past. However, elderly women who live alone, especially if they are members of minority groups, have much higher than average levels of poverty than other categories of the elderly.

When the poverty levels of the elderly and children are compared, higher rates of poverty are found among children.

CRITICAL THINKING

1. What relationship exists between economic contributions, power, and gender in our society?
2. How do Margaret Mead's studies of gender roles in New Guinea societies show that such roles are the result of society rather than biology?
3. List some common gender-related stereotypes. How are these stereotypes reinforced in the mass media?
4. Give examples of gender-role expectations in your family.
5. Give examples from your own childhood of how you learned the gender roles expected of you in society.
6. Is sexism and gender stereotyping likely to decrease in the future? Explain, using information from the chapter as well as your own ideas.
7. Compare and contrast the rights and restrictions associated with old age and childhood.
8. Give examples of inequalities in our society related to gender and/or age.

Part III   Social Institutions

11

Family

In the election year of 1996, politicians frequently expressed concern over the condition of the family in the United States. The signs of decline seemed to be coming from all sides: A young couple abandoned their toddler son in a California shopping mall, while they went on to a Grateful Dead concert; deadbeat parents (those who fail to make child-support payments) were being tracked down and threatened with all sorts of dire consequences to make them provide for their children; a historically high percentage of women were having children outside of marriage; family violence and child abuse were reported daily in the news; and divorces continued to break up marriages, leaving children in broken families and women, often, in poverty.

These stories about the family do seem discouraging, but it might put matters in a clearer perspective if we recognize that laments and predictions of the demise of the family have been with us for a long time. One of the earliest sociologists of the family, Frederic LePlay (1855), who studied the French family in the 1850s, was convinced that the decline of the patriarchal, extended family would lead to the disorganization of society. In the United States, in the early part of the twentieth century, there were similar concerns about the declining importance of the family (Ogburn, 1922).

While there are certainly reasons to be concerned about some aspects of contemporary family life, the fact is that most Americans marry and have children, and they do the best they can to rear their children properly. The family is still a valued institution and the majority of people believe in its importance.

We can get a better perspective on the American family by looking at the most recent figures on American households. A household is not necessarily a family, since "households are defined as all persons who occupy a housing unit such as a house, apartment, single room, or other space intended to be living quarters" (Ahlburg and De Vita, 1992). Therefore, some households may be composed of families (of different types) and others may not. Figure 11–1 shows American households in terms of marital and family characteristics. To see what changes have occurred in the last quarter-century, Figure 11–1 presents the characteristics of households in 1970 and 1994.

Figure 11–1 shows that, in 1970, 70 percent of American households were composed of married couples (some with children, some without). In 1970, 5 percent of the households were single-parent households, and 6 percent were other types of family households, for example, siblings living together. The remaining 19 percent were nonfamily households. Nonfamily households are those in which a person lives alone or with unrelated persons. Cohabiting couples would be included among these nonfamily households, as would gay and lesbian households without children.

In 1994, the household composition of the U.S. population had changed from what it was in 1970, but not completely. Fifty-five percent of all households were still married-couple households, while single-parent households increased to 9 percent. Other types of family households made up 7 percent, and the percentage of nonfamily households increased to 29 percent (Rawlings and Saluter, 1995).

Nonfamily households have clearly increased most over the last 30 years, but most of these households (over 80 percent) are made up of men or women who live alone, many of whom are elderly. Even though someone lives in a single-person household it does not mean that they have no families or family relationships. Many elderly, for example, live alone, but they do so by preference, and they often have close relationships with their children and grandchildren.

These figures tell us that, while the family in the United States may be changing, it has certainly not disappeared as an important institution. Throughout this chapter we will examine the ways in which marriage and family life are changing and, whenever possible, explain why these changes are occurring.

One indication of family change is found in the activities, tasks, or functions of the family. In many societies, both historically and in the contemporary world, it is the family that performs many important societal tasks. These tasks are often called the functions of the family, reflecting the structural–functional theory discussed in Chapter 1. In general, the family in contemporary society performs fewer functions than the family has historically. More and more tasks have been taken over by other institutions, but some basic functions are still largely handled

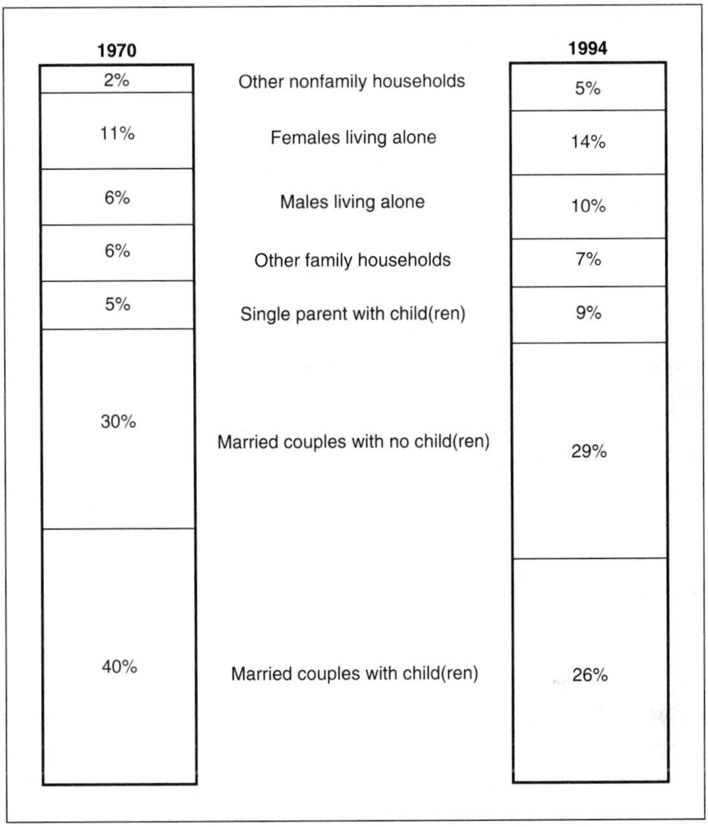

1970		1994
2%	Other nonfamily households	5%
11%	Females living alone	14%
6%	Males living alone	10%
6%	Other family households	7%
5%	Single parent with child(ren)	9%
30%	Married couples with no child(ren)	29%
40%	Married couples with child(ren)	26%

Figure 11–1.   Households in the United States by Family and Non-family Types, 1970 and 1994. (*Source:* U.S. Bureau of the Census, *Current Population Reports,* "Household and Family Characteristics: March 1994," P-20, No. 483, 1995.)

by families. In the next section we will examine some major functions of the family, beginning with those that are found most widely and moving toward those that are found less often or with diminishing importance.

Functions of the Family

An analysis of family functions will show that, while the family often carries out or controls important societal tasks, there is almost nothing the family does that cannot be done outside the family. As we have said, the functions of the family often seem to be diminishing. This will be apparent as we examine the most important traditional functions, many of which are now changing or are declining in importance.

Reproduction.   For a society to continue, replacements must be provided for the members who die, a task accomplished primarily through childbearing. (Sometimes the reproduction function is called *replacement*.) In almost every society, men and women who are married are the preferred producers of children. But there are societies in which many children are produced by couples who are not formally married; they have **de facto unions** because they have cohabited for extensive periods of time. In addition, children in many societies are born to unmarried women, and in these cases, even with the fathers absent, mothers and their children are usually accepted as family units. In the United States today, 30 percent of all births are to unmarried women. In Sweden, 50 percent of all births are to unmarried women, although many of these women are in stable, long-term domestic relationships (Morin, 1995). In Japan, by contrast, only 1 percent of the births are to unmarried women (U.S. Bureau of the Census, 1995b).

Care and Nurturance of Children.   As we have previously noted, the human infant is incapable of caring for itself. It must be given physical care or it will not survive. We also recognize more and more that the human infant must have emotional support and nurturance. Family sociologist Ira Reiss, who has searched for the universal family functions, has concluded that every family system, regardless of form, provides emotional support and nurturance for its children (Reiss and Lee, 1988).

Socialization.   If some degree of order and continuity is to exist in a society from one generation to the next, infants must also be taught the society's cultural and social ways. In Chapter 5 we discussed the importance of parents' socializing their children, but we also noted that in many societies the mass media and schools are also significant socializers.

Meeting Economic Needs.   The family is a societal unit in which members cooperate to satisfy their common economic needs. Generally, family members share their resources and the fruits of their labor with all other family members. There are alternative structures of economic cooperation, such as communes and *kibbutzim,* although they are not nearly as common as the family. Also, as we have already noted, many individuals in the United States today live alone, and while their families may provide some economic support, many are economically self-sufficient.

In many societies, however, the family has been, and continues to be, both an economic-producing unit and a consuming unit. Production within the family, through farming, a family business, or family handicrafts, has been most common through history. However, in contemporary, economically developed societies, the family is primarily integrated through its consumption, not its production.

Intergenerational and Kin Support.   Long after childhood, physical, economic, and emotional support continues between generations within families. Parents continue to help and support their adult children in a variety of ways, and adult children reciprocate by giving help, respect, and attention to their parents. In the United States and many other societies, social contacts between generations are maintained by the women of the middle generation. Middle-aged women, according to a recent study, are most likely to maintain contact with their children and parents more than their siblings or in-laws (Waite and Harrison, 1992).

Regulation of Sexual Behavior.   Marriage is often a way of controlling sexual behavior. Many societies have norms prohibiting sex before marriage, as well as having strong prohibitions against extramarital sex. In restricting sex to marriage, these norms regulate sexual behavior. However, in such societies the restrictions are often imposed on women more than on men—again, an example of the double standard of sexual behavior. Furthermore, in Chapter 7 we saw that, in the United States and many other societies, the norms prohibiting premarital sex are not very effective. Although marriage systems can be, and often are, strong regulators of sexual behavior, many exceptions also exist.

Social Placement.   In many societies, the family is a mechanism for placing new members into the existing structure of the society. In rigidly stratified societies, the family into which one is born will determine for life one's place in the society's structure. Obviously, in more open societies, this social placement function of families is much less determinant, but even when upward (or downward) mobility is possible, one still starts from the level of one's family of birth.

Reproduction, care and nurturance of children, provision of economic necessities, kin support, regulation of sexual behavior, and social placement, then, are the major functions of family systems; although other functions have been identified, such as education, religious training, and recreation, they are much less widespread and significant. The family system of every society will carry out at least some of these tasks, and in many societies the family performs most of them.

Even though the same functions are performed by the family systems of many different societies, the actual family structure may vary greatly from one society to another. We will consider next some of the major differences in family types.

Two Basic Family Types

The simplest distinction of forms of the family differentiates between nuclear families and extended families.

Nuclear Family.   When a family unit is made up of a husband, wife, and children living in the same house, it is called a **nuclear family.** The primary bond of loyalty in the nuclear family is between the husband and wife.[1]

Most people are members of two different nuclear families during their lifetimes. The nuclear family into which one is born is one's **family of orientation.** (This is the family that gives a person his or her orientation, or socialization.) The nuclear family that one creates by marrying and having children is one's **family of procreation.**

Extended Family.   When a family unit is made up of three or more generations living in the same household or very close together, it is an **extended family.** An extended family thus includes first-generation parents, their married sons or daughters, their spouses, and their children. Extended family units have a high degree of economic cooperation across all generations, and primary loyalty is usually given to the oldest generation.

Table 11–1 provides the names and descriptions for other major variations in family norms and structures.

The Family and Social Change

The preceding section and Table 11–1 have shown that family systems can take many different forms, the norms that govern family relations can vary greatly, and the functions of the family differ from society to society, from one time to another. All these facts indicate that the family is not a fixed and unchanging social arrangement, but that it can and does change. This statement raises the question about how and why the family changes from one time to another.

Because the family is widely accepted as a basic social institution of the society, it is often thought that the family shapes or influences the rest of the society. Although that can be true in some instances, it is usually the case that the alternative is true—the family as an institution is often shaped and changed by the rest of the institutions of the society. For this reason the family is appropriately called an *adaptive institution.* The family typically adapts, or makes adaptive changes, when some other part of the society changes.

The most familiar case of the family as an adaptive institution is found in the way the family adapts to changing economic conditions. History provides many examples: when economic times are bad—times of depression, for instance—

---

[1]This description, and other family structures and norms, are *ideal types.* In Chapter 4 an ideal type was described as a logical, exaggerated, and "pure" model of some phenomenon that we wish to study or analyze. A nuclear family could still exist if a husband and father were living in another place (for example, on military active duty) or were no longer alive.

Table 11–1   Family Types

Rules of Descent		
Matrilineal	*Patrilineal*	*Bilineal*
Descent comes from mother and her kin.	Descent comes from father and his kin.	Descent comes equally from mother's and father's family.
Inherits property from, and owes primary allegiance to, that family	Inherits property from, and owes primary allegiance to, that family	Allegiance is shared.

Rules of Residence		
Matrilocal	*Patrilocal*	*Neolocal*
Newly married couples live with wife's family.	Newly married couples live with husband's family.	Newly married couples establish new, separate household.

Authority		
Matriarchy	*Patriarchy*	*Egalitarian*
Authority held by oldest female, usually mother.	Authority held by oldest male, usually father.	Husbands and wives share authority equally.

Number of Marriage Mates		
Monogamy	*Polygamy*	
One partner at a time	Two or more partners (either husbands or wives) at a time	
	Polygyny	*Polyandry*
	A husband having more than one wife	A wife having more than one husband

families typically cut back on the number of children they have. In the United States, during the depression of the 1930s, people cut back on their childbearing, and this was before the time when contraception was easily and widely available. The birth rate was lower during that period, in part because people postponed marriage (an adaptation in itself), and if they were married, they had fewer children.

Ireland experienced a devastating famine in the middle of the nineteenth century (which killed more than a million of their 8 million people), and the people of Ireland thereafter completely reorganized their family system. Instead of allowing their children to marry early, as they had done before the famine, the Irish started using a system of inheritance and dowries that kept their children from marrying until they were quite old (men were often in their thirties or older).

This new system also kept as many as a quarter of the Irish from marrying at all (Kammeyer, 1976).

These are but two examples of the ways family systems adapt to changing external conditions. But the family also adapts to many political actions as well. Family systems are changed by immigration laws, tax laws, abortion laws, military conscription, social security systems, housing regulations, and many other government actions and policies. Overall, the family is an institution that is more apt to adapt to changes in other parts of society than it is to produce basic social changes.

The Processes of Marriage and Family Life

To examine the marriage and family systems we can consider some typical processes that people experience as they enter marriage, have children, and, in many cases, divorce and remarry. We know that all people do not follow the same steps in the same order—some people have children before marriage, some married couples do not have children, spouses sometimes die at an early age, and, of course, not every married couple divorces. Nonetheless, a review of some of the typical processes, from courtship through remarriage, can reveal much about current-day marriage and family life.

Choosing Marriage Mates

In many countries of the world today, young people have almost complete responsibility for finding and selecting a mate for marriage. It is certainly true of mate selection in the United States today, and it has been so since the earliest days of the American experience. Even in colonial times Americans gave their children considerable freedom and autonomy in the selection of their marriage mates. Young people were allowed to spend time together in recreational settings where they could enjoy each other's company. Many European visitors in the eighteenth and nineteenth centuries believed that Americans, especially young women, were given far too much freedom.

The mate-selection system in the United States has almost always been based on the idea of romantic love, or mutual attraction. The people of every society recognize that two people can develop an intense emotional attachment, but they often do not consider this emotion a sound basis for choosing a marriage mate. In fact, many societies regard it as foolish to select a mate on the basis of this heightened emotional state. Marriage is too important and serious an institution to be based on an emotion that will almost certainly diminish (Goode, 1959).

Nevertheless, the idea that romantic love should be a precondition of marriage did take root and thrive in the United States (Goode, 1959). It can be said that choosing one's marriage mate on the basis of attraction and love is consistent with the emphasis that early Americans placed on personal freedom and individual rights. The Declaration of Independence gave every individual the right to life, liberty, and the pursuit of happiness, a concept that was certainly consistent with choosing one's own marriage partner. Emphasizing romantic love as a basis for marriage gave participants great control over the selection of marriage mates in the past, just as it does today.

In contrast, most societies have had, and many continue to have, arranged marriages. In **arranged marriages** the parents select marriage partners for their children. Often the young people scarcely know each other, and it is not assumed that they will love each other at the time of marriage. In arranged marriage systems it is hoped that a couple will develop an affectionate and warm relationship after they are married, and that they will continue to have pleasant companionship for life.

Traditionalist support for arranged marriage is sometimes expressed in the slogan "Love matches start out hot and grow cold, while arranged marriages start out cold and grow hot" (Xiaohe and Whyte, 1990). The research on arranged marriages versus love marriages has not completely supported this slogan, however. In two separate studies, one conducted in Japan three decades ago, and the other a more recent replication in China, the husbands and wives of both types of marriage were studied. The results of these two studies were very similar. The husbands of arranged marriages did, after some years of marriage, have higher levels of love and marital satisfaction than husbands of love marriages, but the wives of arranged marriages had lower levels of love and marital satisfaction than either the wives of love marriages or, the husbands of either type of marriage (Blood, 1967; Xiaohe and Whyte, 1990).

Many Islamic societies use systems of arranged marriages. In Iran, for example, the parents of a young man often interview the families of some potentially marriageable young women. They will inquire about the general characteristics of the family (their standing in the community, economic resources, educational attainments, occupational levels, and the like), and they will ask about the qualities of the marriageable daughter. The parents of the young man will then make a recommendation to their son, and in most cases he will follow their advice. In societies where arranged marriage is the custom, the young people often consider it a very difficult and imposing task to select a marriage partner. Young people in these societies will often say that they are too inexperienced to make this decision, and they would prefer to have their parents do so because they are wiser and more knowledgeable.

Social Influences on the Selection of Marriage Mates

Marriages in any society are likely to occur between two people with similar social characteristics. This pattern is called **homogamy**—marriage between people with similar characteristics—such as religion, race, education, ethnicity, nationality, and social class.

Cross-cultural Perspectives

Polyandry: A Rare Marriage Type

Polygyny and polyandry are forms of marriage that involve more than one mate. Polygyny—the practice of having more than one wife or female mate at one time—is very common in societies around the world. About 75 percent of all the societies that have been studied by anthropologists and sociologists allow polygyny. By contrast, polyandry—the practice of having more than one husband or male mate at one time—is very rare. Only about 1 percent of the world's societies have practiced polyandry (Stephens, 1963).

The most fully documented polyandrous societies are the Toda (a non-Hindu tribe of India), the Marquesan Islanders in the South Pacific, and various groups in Tibet and the Himalayan region generally. The Nayar, on the basis of their pre-nineteenth-century practices, are also usually classified as polyandrous, because Nayar women typically had several lovers. These lovers, however, did not live in the woman's household, and this sets the Nayar apart from other polyandrous societies. These few examples of polyandry provide the bulk of the information we have about this unusual marriage form.

Often the polyandrous men who share wives are brothers. This was true of the Toda, where women understood that when they married a man they were also marrying his brothers. Even a brother who might be born after the marriage would be considered a woman's husband. Tibetan polyandry, also, is typically a case of two or more brothers married to the same woman. The Marquesan Islanders are an exception, however, since the co-husbands were apparently not brothers.

The ethnographic reports of polyandrous males insist that there is very little jealousy among husbands. Anthropologists were generally told that jealousy is a ridiculous idea, and that displays of jealousy would be socially disapproved. Of course, if a wife with two or more husbands became pregnant, there would be no way of knowing who the biological father was. The people of polyandrous groups consider this a special advantage, since every baby will have several fathers to give it special care and attention.

Often in areas where polyandry occurs, resources and land are limited. Polyandry may emerge in these places as a way of eking out a living from an inhospitable environment that requires the energies of several men to provide for one family unit. For example, in mountainous villages it can be advantageous if one husband cultivates the land, while another herds the sheep in a distant pasture. A third brother can gather wood, or cut grass for cattle food. Also, a wife in these places may be safer if at least one of her husbands is at home while others are away (Zorza, 1982).

One other economic advantage of polyandry is that the small parcels of land owned by a family do not have to be divided up among their sons. When two or more sons marry one wife and live in the same household, the land can remain intact from one generation to the next (Goldstein, 1978).

In societies where polyandry exists, some families move toward group marriage (multiple husbands *and* wives). If, for example, the family's resources allow, the husbands of a woman may take a second wife. Since sexual relations may occur between any pair of wives and husbands, the result is group marriage.

The dark side of polyandry is that it is frequently associated with female infanticide. Since the ratio of males to females is normally equal, or nearly so, there will be too many females for a polyandrous marriage system to work. In order to create an imbalanced ratio that has two or three times more males than females, polyandrous societies are apt to let some female children die in infancy.

The best theoretical perspective on polyandry is provided by structural–functional theory. Polyandrous marriage patterns can be functional in an environment with limited land and scarce resources. Polyandry allows all men to have sexual access to a woman and to experience parenthood. At the same time, this practice keeps the society's birth rate in balance with its resources, the family's land remains intact, and cooperating husbands have an easier time of providing for the needs of a family. The females who reach adulthood are likely to have an easier life with multiple husbands; in one polyandrous village the people said they pitied any woman who had only one husband (Zorza, 1982).

GOLDSTEIN, MELVYN. "Pahari and Tibetan Polyandry Revisited." *Ethnology* 17, 1978.
STEPHENS, WILLIAM N. *The Family in Cross-cultural Perspective.* New York: Holt, Rinehart and Winston, 1963.
ZORZA, VICTOR. "When Brothers Share Wives, Age Counts." *Washington Post,* May 2, 1982.

Marriages are apt to be homogamous, even in a society like the United States, where the selection of a mate is based on love and personal choice. Homogamous marriages are the result of many social influences on the selection of marriage partners. Parents today may not choose marriage mates for their children, but they do influence their children's choices—sometimes directly, sometimes subtly. Parents make inquiries about the dating partners and the opposite-sex friends of their children. They ask about the families they come from, and in particular they ask about religion, socioeconomic status, and perhaps about nationality and race.

Through such questions parents find out if their children are likely to be interested in someone coming from different social, cultural, racial, or economic origins. If these possible marriage mates are viewed as too different, and thus unacceptable, parents will often discourage the continuation of the relationship.

When children are still living at home, parents often try to influence the selection of mates by placing their children in social settings where they are less likely to meet members of the opposite sex who are "different." By selecting homes in neighborhoods with certain preferred characteristics, parents can reduce the chances of their children's meeting and ultimately wanting to marry someone of a different race, religion, ethnic group, or social class. Similarly, sending children to school, especially to college, may be done with an eye to the kind of young people their children are likely to meet. Whether or not parents fully recognize the significance of their actions, moving to a "nicer" neighborhood and sending the children to a "better" school makes it more probable that the children will meet, fall in love with, and want to marry someone who will be more acceptable to the parents.

Marriage to a person of the same (or similar) educational background—*educational homogamy*—has been studied over the last 50 years by Mare (1991). This study revealed that educational homogamy increased during most of that period (more men and women with similar educations married each other). In general, people who marry soon after leaving school (either high school or college) are most likely to marry someone with a similar educational background. People with higher levels of education also tend to marry someone with a similar educational background (Mare, 1991).

Religions and religious organizations frequently try to influence mate selection. Young members of most religions are encouraged by religious leaders to marry within their faith. Religious organizations often have rules that prohibit marriage to someone out of the faith, or procedures that must be observed if such a marriage is proposed. The religion's rules may require the nonmember to convert or to take religious instruction or training before the marriage is allowed.

Education and religion are both important factors influencing the selection of marriage mates, but there is some evidence that religion is decreasing in importance. According to a recent study, intermarriage between Protestants and Catholics has increased dramatically since the 1920s (Kalmijn, 1991). Similarly, Jews in the United States have increased their rate of marriage to non-Jews during the last three decades. The rate varies from community to community, often depending on the availability of Jewish marriage partners, but in some communities as many as 30 percent of Jews marry outside their religion (Judd, 1990).

There is evidence that in the twentieth century, as religious boundaries to marriage have diminished, they have been replaced by educational boundaries. The trend has been less intermarriage between people with educational differences and more intermarriage between people of different religions (Kalmijn, 1991).

Cohabitation as a Premarital Stage

In contemporary American society, as well as many other societies, **cohabitation,** that is, unmarried couples living together, has become for many people an expected stage of premarried life. Yet, only 30 years ago in the United States, cohabitation was relatively rare, and couples who did cohabit were engaging in behavior that was considered deviant. Often, cohabiting couples in the 1960s and earlier were people from the lower social strata of the society, or people who lived in some kind of Bohemian setting. In a fairly rapid transition, cohabitation became acceptable in the middle classes, and today cohabitation is found in every stratum of society.

In 1970, when the Census Bureau started collecting data on cohabiting couples in the United States, cohabiting households numbered slightly over a half-million. By 1994 the number of unmarried couples was over 3.6 million (U.S. Bureau of the Census, 1995). Among never-married persons aged 34 or younger, more than 40 percent report that they have cohabited at some time in their lives (Bumpass, Sweet, and Cherlin, 1991).

Cohabitation in Canada has followed the same pattern as in the United States, where it was also nearly nonexistent before 1970. Today, 10 percent of all couples are cohabiting couples, and over three-fourths of Canadians believe that cohabitation is acceptable for couples who "want to make sure that their future marriage will last" (Hall and Zhao, 1995, p. 421).

Cohabitation increases have contributed greatly to the downward trend in marriage rates and upward trend in marriage age (Bumpass, Sweet, and Cherlin, 1991). Young adults today are often substituting cohabitation for marriage; they "are setting up housekeeping with partners of the opposite sex at almost as early an age as they did before marriage rates declined (Bumpass, Sweet, and Cherlin, 1991, p. 924).

The trend of replacing marriage with cohabitation is even more pronounced in some other countries. In Sweden, for example, marriage rates have been going down rapidly since the mid-1960s, and the reduced number of marriages is directly related to the increase in long-term cohabitation (Popenoe, 1987). For some, but not all, Swedes, cohabitation has become a substitute for marriage.

Almost all Swedes who do marry cohabit first—estimates are variously placed at 98 or 99 percent. In Sweden today, becoming pregnant or having a child is no longer a reason for marriage. One Swedish couple described their "marital history" to a researcher in the following manner:

> They met in 1967, moved in together in 1969, exchanged rings in 1973 (this was around the time their first child was born and was for the purpose of "showing others that they were attached"), and married in 1977. When asked what anniversary they celebrated, they responded, "The day we met" (Popenoe, 1987, p. 176).

In contemporary Sweden, the customs, rituals, and ceremonies connected with marriage, if there is a marriage, have diminished in significance. Marriage ceremonies in most societies have social significance because they signal to the community, and to other social groups, that a couple is establishing a new relationship. Yet in Sweden the ceremonies and rituals connected with marriage are decreasing in importance. "Swedish young people today are merely drifting away from their families of orientation, usually in stages, and eventually settling down with someone else, all seemingly without any form of public or social recognition" (Popenoe, 1987, p. 176).

When individuals enter into marriage or cohabiting relationships without the involvement of family members or other social groups, the sociological implications are considerable. The involvement of family and community members in any couple relationship, whether cohabitation or marriage, serves to keep the couple together. When relationships are formed on an individual basis, without the benefit of these social supports, they tend to break up more easily. Again, the case of Sweden is instructive, for even among cohabiting couples who have a child, the rate of breakup is three times as high as the rate for comparable married couples (Popenoe, 1987).

Entering Marriage

A paradox of married life is that newly married couples often consider their first year or so together as the happiest and yet the most difficult. There are numerous adjustments to make in early weeks and months, even if a couple has previously cohabited. One type of adjustment is dealing with mismatched marital scripts.

Marital scripts are the expectations one has about what is proper and appropriate behavior for husbands and wives. Each partner has these expectations, but they are likely to be unconscious and unspoken (Broderick, 1989, 1979). During the early stages of marriage, husbands and wives may have arguments and hurt feelings because they have different (or conflicting) marital scripts. Family sociologist Carlfred Broderick, who developed the concept of the marital script, illustrates with a personal example how a married couple with mismatched scripts can experience disappointment and even anger over the resultant misunderstandings. Even though Broderick had known his wife since they were both in kindergarten and they had dated from the time they were in the tenth grade, he learned early in marriage that he and his wife had mismatched scripts regarding what happens when someone gets sick:

> Every right-thinking person knows what you should do when you get sick—you go to bed. That is your part. Then your mother, or whoever loves you, pumps you full of fruit juice.

Well, I married this woman I had known all my life, and in the natural course of events I caught the flu. I knew what to do, of course. I went to bed and waited. But nothing happened. Nothing, I couldn't believe it!

I was so hurt, I would have left if I hadn't been so ill. Finally, I asked about juice and she brought me some—in a little four-ounce glass. Period. Because, as I learned later, the only time they drank juice at her house was on alternate Tuesdays, when they graced breakfast with a drop in a thimble-size glass. My family's "juice glasses" held 12 ounces and there was always someone standing by to refill them.

It does not matter that an issue may seem foolish to an outsider, or that it may be solved simply. The point is that mismatched scripts can so easily derail a young couple (Broderick, 1979, p. 154).

Marital scripts, as can be seen from the illustration above, often come from unique family background experiences. Before we marry, the marriage relationship we have observed most closely is usually that of our parents. Whether that marriage was harmonious and idyllic or quarrelsome and stormy, we are likely to have picked up some deep-seated notions about the nature of the husband–wife relationship and of family life in general.

Marital Quality

Marital quality is a general term referring to an individual's satisfaction with a marriage and with the relationship between marriage partners (Johnson, Amoloza, and Booth, 1992). Sociologists who study marital quality may measure an individual's satisfaction by asking them to agree or disagree with statements such as "We have a good marriage," "My marriage with my partner is very stable," or "Our marriage is strong" (Norton, 1983). Other more elaborate measures of marital quality inquire into the degree of consensus about important matters such as philosophy of life, work and careers, or recreational activities. Marital quality can also be ascertained by asking a couple about the amount of affection they display, or how frequently they express their love. Conversely, low marital quality can be identified by asking how frequently they have arguments and fights (Spanier, 1976).

Studies of marital quality have consistently shown that despite the adjustment problems of couples during the early years of marriage, they are likely to see their marriage relationship as good. Couples who are recently married and do not yet have children are especially satisfied with their married lives. Most studies of marital quality have shown that at no time after the first years of marital life do couples express a higher level of satisfaction with marriage (Anderson et al., 1983).

Several personal characteristics are also associated with marital quality. Religiosity is one such characteristic; couples who are more religious are more likely to report being happily married (Shehan et al., 1990; Veroff et al., 1993). Higher levels of educational attainment, occupational status, and economic success are

In the News

Marriage for Gays and Lesbians

On March 25, 1996, 175 couples, some in wedding gowns, others in suits and tuxedos, gathered in a makeshift wedding hall in San Francisco where they were joined together as "domestic partners" (Boudreau, 1996). The couples were all gay or lesbian couples, and they were taking advantage of San Francisco's new same-sex marriage law.

The new law gives same-sex couples in San Francisco the right to a city-sanctioned marriage, much like heterosexual couples, but their marriages are largely symbolic, since they are not recognized by the state of California. Only Hawaii has passed a law that will give a state sanction to same-sex marriages, but even there the law will not take effect until 1998. And the Hawaii law is already being challenged in the courts. If the Hawaii law is upheld, it will have important implications for the rest of the country, because gay and lesbian marriages granted in Hawaii may have to be recognized when couples take up residence in other states.

Even without formal marriages, gay and lesbian couples have argued that they should be given the same rights as heterosexual married couples. Gays and lesbians claim that they are being deprived of their rights simply because of their sexual orientation.

In several cities besides San Francisco—Los Angeles, Denver, and Seattle, for example—municipal governments have debated whether they should extend the definition of marriage to include cohabiting homosexual and heterosexual couples. The Los Angeles city council has voted to extend sick leave to unmarried couples in order for an employee to care for a partner in the time of sickness or death. And five years before their recently enacted domestic partner marriage law, San Franciscans in homosexual unions were given the right to declare their domestic partnerships by filing documents with the city government. By doing so, city employees attained the rights to health care for their domestic partners, hospital visitation rights, and bereavement leave if a partner dies (Boudreau, 1996).

The debate about the legal definition of marriage has begun to move to states beyond Hawaii. In 1989, the New York State Supreme Court, in connection with a rent-control case, redefined marriage to include unmarried adults who have shown long-term financial and emotional commitments to each other. In this case, a man had shared an apartment with his homosexual lover for more than a decade, but after the lover died, the man was evicted. New York rent-control laws state that only "family members" can continue to live in rent-controlled apartments. Thus, the legal definition of marriage has practical ramifications, which in this case affects financial benefits.

But there are also countertrends. The Commonwealth of Virginia, in 1996, ruled that state funds would no longer be provided to unmarried couples

> for the purchase of a home. This ruling, which seems to have been directed largely toward gay and lesbian couples, also effectively excludes heterosexual cohabiting couples.
>
> Some countries of the world do recognize gay and lesbian marriages and have for some time. Czechoslovakia, for example, legalized gay and lesbian relationships between adults as early as 1961, and Denmark legalized same-sex unions in 1989 (Miller, 1992).
>
> BOUDREAU, JOHN. "Brides, Grooms and Partners." *Washington Post,* March 26, 1996. MILLER, NEAL. *Out in the World.* New York: Random House, 1992.

also associated with higher marital quality (Clark-Nicolas and Gray-Little, 1991). Couples who agree about their marital roles are likely to be more satisfied with their marriages. But when husbands hold traditional views about gender roles and their wives hold modern or feminist views, these couples are least happy with their marriages (Lye and Biblarz, 1993).

Parenthood and Marital Quality.   A marriage changes when couples become parents. Couples with a new baby experience a number of problems that tend to reduce their level of marital satisfaction. A most important factor is that they simply have less time together than they did before the arrival of the baby (White et al., 1986). Most new parents express some surprise about the sheer level of physical demands. One mother wrote in her diary when her daughter was a month old, "A month is only four weeks . . . but it has been an eternity for me. I'm a zombie. Four weeks of night feedings and little sleep. I haven't read a paper. I barely have time to shower and wash my hair" (Lowenstein and Lowenstein, 1983, p. 18). Among most new parents the overwhelming responsibility for caring for their baby falls to the mother. Most studies show that fathers carry less than 20 percent of the load in the routine tasks of infant care.

Naturally, if a new mother is too busy to take a shower and is not getting much sleep, a great many other aspects of married life are also being sacrificed, including a reduction in sexual activity because of decreased opportunities or fatigue (Sollie and Miller, 1980; LaRossa, 1983).

Married couples who have children when they are young and very shortly after they are married are particularly apt to experience feelings of dissatisfaction. A 28-year-old woman with three children describes her feelings:

One day I woke up and there I was, married and with a baby. And I thought, "I can't stand it! I can't stand to have my life over when I'm so young" (Rubin, 1976, p. 81).

A husband describes how his wife's pregnancy and the baby made him feel resentful and jealous:

When we were first married, I'd come home from work and she'd be kind of dressed up and fixed up, you know, looking pretty for me. Then she kept getting bigger and bigger, and she'd be tired and complaining all the time. I could hardly wait for her to finish being pregnant. And when that was over, she was too busy and too tired to pay me any mind.

I used to get mad and holler a lot. Or else I'd stay out late at night and get her worried about what I was doing. We had nothing but fights in those days because all she wanted to do was to take care of the baby, and she never had any time for me. It sounds dumb when I talk about it now—a man being jealous of a little kid, but I guess I was (Rubin, 1976, p. 82).

Marital Quality through the Later Stages of Marriage. Marital quality generally continues to decline after the first years of parenthood, especially after children reach school age (Anderson et al., 1983; Glenn, 1990). The negative effects of children are especially severe for lower-socioeconomic-status women who are employed (Schumm and Bugaighis, 1986). When children reach adolescence, the relationships they have with their parents are related to the marital relationship between their parents. Mothers who report having difficulties with their oldest daughters, and fathers who report difficulties with their oldest sons, are both more likely to be less satisfied with their marriages than parents who have fewer problems with their children (Steinberg and Silverberg, 1987). Many different studies show consistent evidence that children put a strain on parents and make their marital relationships less satisfying.

The negative effects that children have on marital happiness are shown in a study of what happens when the last child leaves home. At one time it was widely assumed that parents (especially mothers) would be upset and at "loose ends" when the last child left them in an "empty nest." But a study of parents who had "launched" their last child showed that this event clearly improved marital happiness, and under some circumstances it improved general life satisfaction as well (White and Edwards, 1990).

Since marital quality is high during the early years of marriage, is low during the childbearing years, and improves when children leave home, there is a curvilinear (U-shaped) relationship between stages of marriage and marital quality. This curvilinear relationship has been found in so many studies over the years that one sociologist has described it as "about as close to being certain as anything ever is in the social sciences" (Glenn, 1990, p. 823).

Power as a Dimension of Husband and Wife Relations

Power is the ability to impose one's will on someone else, and the exercise of power is found in the family just as it is in other social groups. In family decision making, power is partly a function of traditional male and female roles. In Chapter 10 we discussed the way women, especially married women, have traditionally been expected to play a subordinate role to men. When married couples accept the traditional gender-role prescription of the wife as a subordinate to her husband, then she clearly has less power than her husband. Most couples today claim to hold an egalitarian view of marriage; they emphasize that family decisions are made jointly and that neither husband nor wife has greater power. Despite these egalitarian ideals, however, other factors influence the exercise of power in marriages, and these factors also tend to give greater power to husbands.

One important theoretical formulation about family power, called **resource theory,** explains the distribution of power in terms of the resources brought into the marriage by each of the spouses (Blood and Wolfe, 1960). Resources include income-earning ability, education, and occupational prestige, which are all closely tied to the economic world outside the home, where men have a distinct advantage over women. Of course, there may also be noneconomic resources, such as companionship, emotional support, and social skills—attributes that have been more closely associated with women (Safilios-Rothschild, 1970).

Although noneconomic resources may give some advantage to women, the fact is that in American society greater weight is given to money, status, and occupational prestige. These latter characteristics are exactly what gives husbands in most marriages a distinct advantage over their wives. The larger society, in which all marriages are embedded, gives men distinct advantages in money earnings and occupational status and prestige (Szinovacz, 1987).

Research over the last 30 years on the power relations between husbands and wives has continued to show that husbands have greater power in marriages than their wives (Allen, 1984; Olsen and Cromwell, 1975; Scanzoni, 1979; Szinovacz, 1987). Despite the fact that many husbands and wives seek an egalitarian ideal, they do not always achieve it. In the next section we will see one major manifestation of the continuing marital power of males: despite ever-greater participation of married women in the labor force, they continue to do the greatest proportion of family work, such as cooking, cleaning, and child care.

The Family and Employment

A very important feature of marriage and family life today is the relationship between family and employment. There was a time, not many years ago, when the family and employment were viewed as two separate worlds. That may always have been a myth, but today, in a very real sense, the worlds of family and employment are closely linked.

Prior to the industrial revolution, work and family were closely tied together. In the United States when the economy was largely agricultural and other industries were at the craft level (shoemaking and tailoring, for example), almost all work was done by family units. However, when industries became mechanized and powered by water, coal, and steam, the places of employment moved out of the home. Men went out into the work world—factories and offices—and the concept of the breadwinner emerged. At the same time, women, especially in the middle and upper classes, remained in the home. This situation led to the glorification of women as homemakers, and the breadwinner–homemaker division of labor came into being. In the United States the transition to the breadwinner–homemaker system reached its peak at the beginning of the twentieth century. At that time only about 5 percent of married women were employed outside the home (Davis, 1984).

The nineteenth-century movement that separated women from the workplace and kept them in the home as homemakers was supported by a new set of cultural values about women, motherhood, and the home. Historians have called this new cultural image the "cult of true womanhood" (Lerner, 1969; Welter, 1966). This image stressed that women had a moral duty and responsibility to remain in the home and care for their families. The "natural" place for women was the home where they could attend to the physical and moral development of their children and give comfort to their husbands, who were facing the cruel and difficult outside world of work.

During the twentieth century the ideal of the breadwinner–homemaker system has remained firmly embedded in U.S. culture, but at the same time an objective reality emerged that deviated from it. The percentage of married women in the labor force started going up at the beginning of the century and continued to increase through each decade up to the present time (see Figure 11–2).

In 1994, the percentage of married women in the labor force reached 60.7 percent. A slightly higher percentage (61.7) of married women with children under 6 were in the labor force (U.S. Bureau of the Census, 1995b, p. 406).

Even though only a small percentage of American mothers are remaining at home as full-time homemakers, the role expectations embedded in the cultural ideal have not disappeared. Mothers rather than fathers are still expected to take primary responsibility for tasks related to children. Women also are expected to do much of the family work, such as cooking and cleaning (Heath and Bourne, 1995; South and Spitze, 1994).

The expectation that women are still primarily responsible for family work is borne out by the research evidence. For example, both men and women today report conflicts between their employment and family obligations; however, men experience the conflict as resulting from the excessive number of hours they work, while women experience the conflict as coming from scheduling difficulties. For women, the scheduling problems reflect their dual responsibilities: their jobs, on the one hand; home and children, on the other (Voydanoff, 1988).

With regard to housework, many studies have been conducted in recent years to see if husbands are taking a larger share of family work. The most consistent conclusion is that women, regardless of whether they are employed, are still doing the great majority of family work. In terms of the relative workloads, employed women perform approximately twice as much housework as their husbands, but, surprisingly, the majority of women believe that this is fair (Lennon and Rosenfield, 1994).

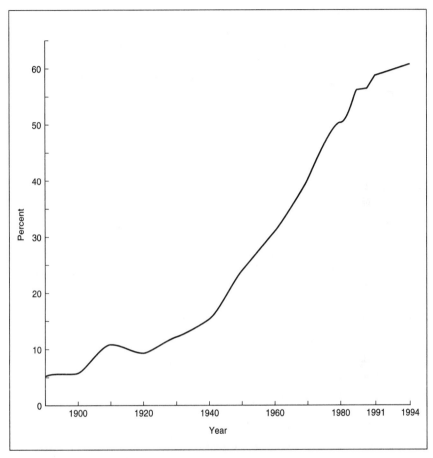

Figure 11–2. Percentage of All Married Women Who Are in the Labor Force, 1890–1994. (*Source:* U.S. Bureau of the Census, 1995b.)

Current estimates are that women still do about 80 percent of the laundry, shopping, and cooking and over 60 percent of the cleaning, dish washing, and child care. Men do about half the yard work, while women do about 40 percent (children do the remainder) (Goldschieder and Waite, 1991).

Conflict and Violence in the Family

The mass media have made most Americans aware of "abused children" and "battered wives." It is now well-known that violence occurs in families, although some confusion might still remain about its nature and frequency. Sociologists started examining the nature and extent of family violence in the 1970s, and as a result of their research, we now have a clearer and fuller understanding of this important social problem (Straus and Gelles, 1990; Steinmetz, 1987).

One misconception about family violence is that it is associated only with pathological or "sick" individuals. The most extreme and bizarre cases, often leading to serious injury and even death, are most widely reported; and on the basis of these cases, many people conclude that violence is the product of a mentally ill person. However, sociological studies have shown that violence is widely condoned as an acceptable way to deal with family problems, and is used frequently in "normal" or "average" families.

Many people in the United States accept the idea that it is legitimate to hit family members—under some circumstances. Marital partners, for example, often justify hitting a spouse, or being hit by a spouse, for one of two basic reasons: (1) the spouse is doing (or has done) something wrong in the eyes of the aggressor, or (2) the spouse "won't listen to reason" (Straus, 1980, p. 693). Both of these justifications can be found in interviews with a young married couple named Jennifer and Joe (LaRossa, 1980). Jennifer described herself as a strong-willed person who had been independent for much of her life and wanted to "run things" in her marriage. Her husband concurred in this evaluation, but he had opposing ideas about who should dominate the marriage. When the interviewer asked if Jennifer still wanted to run things, the following interchange occurred:

INTERVIEWER: Do you think you run things now?
JENNIFER: No, I tried, though!
JOE: She tries. One day we had a conflict and she more or less tried to run me and I told her no, and she got hysterical and said, "I could kill you!" And I got rather angry and slapped her in the face three or four times and I said, "Don't you ever say that to me again." And we haven't had any problems since (LaRossa, 1980, p. 160).

Joe analyzed his use of violence in the following way:

You don't use it until you are forced to. At that point I felt I had to do something physical to stop the bad progression of events. I took my chances with that and it worked (LaRossa, 1980, p. 160).

Later in the interview, Jennifer said:

Joe doesn't usually use force. That was the first and last time he'll ever do that. It was my fault. I was trying to dominate him, that's for sure (LaRossa, 1980, p. 161).

Joe, in this case, justified his use of violence by implying that Jennifer had gone too far in trying to dominate him. But, in addition, by saying that she was "hysterical," he was justifying what he had done on the grounds that she was beyond reason. For her part, Jennifer made it clear that it would be the last time he would hit her, but then she immediately added that it was her fault.

The case of Jennifer and Joe reveals that both the victim and the aggressor accepted violence under some circumstances. In this regard they are not unlike many other married couples. In a national sample of married couples, approximately one out of three husbands and one out of four wives agreed that it was at least "somewhat necessary," "somewhat normal," or "somewhat good" for couples to "slap each other around" (Straus et al., 1980, p. 47).

There have been two national surveys of family violence in the United States, one conducted in 1975 and the second in 1985 (Straus and Gelles, 1986). In these surveys, respondents provide self-reports on the amount and type of violence they have recently used against family members. The amount of violence thus reported may be less than the actual amount, but even so a substantial amount of violence is reported. Between 1975 and 1985, there was an apparent decrease in severe violence by husbands against wives (kicking, biting, hitting with fist, and other more extreme forms including the use of knives or guns). The rate of severe violence went from 38 cases per 1000 to 30 cases per 1000. While this reduction may seem modest, the researchers point out that for the United States population as a whole this reduction would mean 432,000 fewer beaten wives (Straus and Gelles, 1986). It is possible, of course, that as men become more sensitive to the stigma attached to wife abuse they may be more hesitant to admit their acts to an interviewer.

Survey research on violence in the family has often turned up the somewhat surprising finding that wives commit violent acts against their husbands at the same rate that husbands do against wives (Gelles and Cornell, 1990; Brush, 1990). This has been a very controversial finding, and has been debated vigorously in the social science literature. There are serious questions about whether survey research interviews can adequately measure the extent and severity of violent acts of men compared to the same types of acts by women (Brush, 1990; Dobash et al., 1992). Even though wives may say they have engaged in violent acts against their husbands, they very rarely *injure* their husbands. Males are bigger and stronger, and their blows do much more damage than those of females. Often wives are striking back after being hit or they are defending themselves (Saunders, 1986). Even when women are the aggressors (that is, commit the first act of violence), husbands often respond with more violent acts and are likely to strike the most damaging blows.

Another explanation is that there may be two different forms of husband-wife violence: patriarchal terrorism and common couple violence (Johnson, 1995).

Patriarchal Terrorism versus Common Couple Violence

Johnson (1995) argues that women who come to the attention of public agencies, especially through police or women's shelters, are the victims of what he calls patriarchal terrorism. **Patriarchal terrorism** is violence almost exclusively initiated by men as a way of gaining and maintaining total and absolute control over their women partners. The violence these men use may be frequent and severe or, in some cases, infrequent, but in either case, violence "reinforces the power of other tactics" (Pence and Paymar, 1993). Other control tactics include emotional abuse, threats, intimidation, blame, and isolation. Figure 11–3 shows

Figure 11–3. Power and Control Wheel. *Source:* Pence and Paymar: Education Groups for Men Who Batter, 1993. Copyright © Springer Publishing Company, Inc., New York 10012. Used by permission.

the types of control tactics battered women experience who men engage in patriarchal terrorism (Johnson, 1995; Pence and Paymar, 1993).

The victims of patriarchal terrorism are often the battered women who end up in women's shelters or hospitals or, in the most tragic cases, murdered. But they are not very likely to be respondents in random-sample surveys of the general population (Johnson, 1995). All surveys have nonrespondents who refuse to be interviewed, and men who terrorize their families are probably going to refuse to participate and are hardly likely to allow their wives to participate.

The family violence that social surveys uncover is probably the type Johnson calls **common couple violence,** which is the product of conflicts that occur in many couple relationships that sometimes "get out of hand" and often lead to violence (Johnson, 1995, p. 287). These are the violent acts that are more likely to be revealed by surveys and are as likely to be initiated by women as by men. Common couple violence may be mild or severe, but surveys are most likely to reveal the mild cases (Johnson, 1995). If or when perpetrators and victims of severe violence participate in surveys on violence, they are less likely to tell the truth.

382

The distinction between patriarchal violence and common couple violence may account for much of the difference in views about violence against women. Workers in women's shelters, leaders of educational programs for battered women, police, and medical personnel are likely to see the results of patriarchal terrorism. Survey researchers are more likely to uncover a different kind of domestic violence, and thus their data provide a different picture of its nature and intensity. Nonetheless, any form of violence between intimate partners is likely to be more damaging to women and be, to some degree, the product of male assumptions about their rights to control their partners.

Child Abuse and Maltreatment

Before 1960 public awareness of child abuse was low; that does not mean, however, that children were not abused in earlier times, for child abuse has a long and terrible history. One historian has said, "the history of childhood is a nightmare from which we have only recently begun to awaken. The further back in history one goes, the lower the level of childcare, and the more likely children are to be killed, abandoned, beaten, terrorized, and sexually abused" (deMause, 1974, p. 1).

Today, child abuse is recognized as being much more widespread than just occasional sensational stories of severe abuse. Child abuse is now understood as covering a range of behaviors, including physical abuse, sexual abuse, and physical neglect. Emotional abuse, which is much more difficult to define and detect, is also recognized for the harm it can do to children. However, even with this increase in public awareness, parents commit a variety of physical and verbal actions against their children in the name of discipline and normal punishment.

In the 1940s, Hollywood actress Joan Crawford reared her two children in a severe manner because she believed that, in this way, they would learn how to work and behave properly. When her daughter, as an adult, published an autobiographical account of the way she and her brother had been treated as children, many readers concluded that the children had been mistreated and abused (Crawford, 1978). And yet it seems that Miss Crawford's colleagues, friends, and visitors saw her only as a strict and demanding mother whose children always behaved perfectly. Even today, some people might discount the daughter's account as exaggerated and, in any case, give the benefit of the doubt to the parent.

The abuse and mistreatment of children in the family have been called a hidden problem because the public generally accepts that parents may use physical methods to punish children. Corporal punishment is defined as an act intended to inflict physical pain on a person. Exactly when this physical pain is excessive is difficult to ascertain. In the range of physical punishments, U.S. legal and informal norms allow parents to spank and slap a child, or to hit a child with an instrument such as a stick, hair brush, or belt.

In the United States, 80 percent of adults agree with the statement "it is sometimes necessary to discipline a child with a good, hard spanking" (Flynn, 1994,

p. 316). For differences in the acceptance of spanking by regions of the United States, see Figure 11–4.

Studies of family violence have shown consistently that families have a cycle of violence—violence in one generation is continued in the following generation. When children are treated with violence, they are more apt to become adults who see violence as a way of solving their problems. As adults they are more likely to

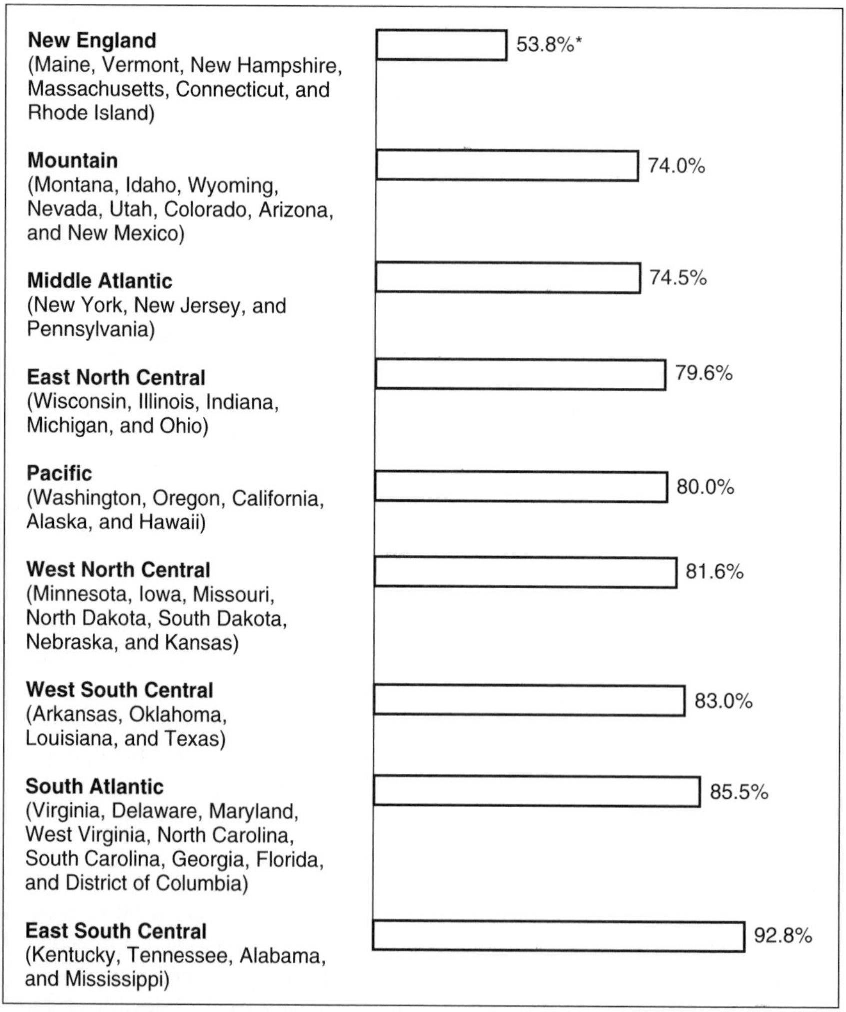

New England
(Maine, Vermont, New Hampshire, Massachusetts, Connecticut, and Rhode Island) — 53.8%*

Mountain
(Montana, Idaho, Wyoming, Nevada, Utah, Colorado, Arizona, and New Mexico) — 74.0%

Middle Atlantic
(New York, New Jersey, and Pennsylvania) — 74.5%

East North Central
(Wisconsin, Illinois, Indiana, Michigan, and Ohio) — 79.6%

Pacific
(Washington, Oregon, California, Alaska, and Hawaii) — 80.0%

West North Central
(Minnesota, Iowa, Missouri, North Dakota, South Dakota, Nebraska, and Kansas) — 81.6%

West South Central
(Arkansas, Oklahoma, Louisiana, and Texas) — 83.0%

South Atlantic
(Virginia, Delaware, Maryland, West Virginia, North Carolina, South Carolina, Georgia, Florida, and District of Columbia) — 85.5%

East South Central
(Kentucky, Tennessee, Alabama, and Mississippi) — 92.8%

*Percent who *Agree Strongly* or *Agree* that it is sometimes necessary to discipline a child with a good, hard spanking.

Figure 11–4. Regional Differences in Attitudes about Spanking Children. (*Source:* Flynn, 1994, p. 317.)

hit their spouses and their own children. And in a final irony, children who have been struck by their parents are more likely to strike these same parents when they reach old age. Because of the cyclical nature of family violence, the family provides the training ground for violence (Steinmetz, 1987).

Separation and Divorce

Any discussion of contemporary marriage and family life must consider the issue of divorce. The divorce rate in the United States is higher than any other country for which there are acceptable data. The most recent data show that the United States has a yearly divorce rate of 21 divorces per 1000 married couples. The next closest countries are Denmark, Sweden, and the United Kingdom with 13, 12, and 12, respectively. Japan's divorce rate is only 2 per 1000 married women (U.S. Bureau of the Census, 1995b, p. 852).

Percentage of All Marriages Ending in Divorce

The most often quoted divorce statistic is the percentage of all marriages ending in divorce. The most frequently heard number is that 50 percent of all marriages end in divorce. While this statistic seems straightforward and meaningful, it does not mean what most people think. Furthermore, the best current estimates are that approximately 40 percent of all recent marriages will end in divorce (Clarke and Wilson, 1994; Norton and Miller, 1992; Schoen and Weinick, 1993).

When researchers say that a certain percentage of marriages will end in divorce, they are making projections on the basis of data from marriages that occurred at least a decade or more ago. If we consider, for example, marriages that occurred over the last 3 years, we can easily see that, while some of these marriages will already have ended in divorce, it will be many years before we can know how many (and what percent) will finally end in divorce. If we go back to marriages that occurred 10 years ago, we will know more about how many of these marriages have ended in divorce, but we still will not have a complete record of the number that will end in divorce, because they still have many years to go before they have run their course (either ending in divorce or the death of one of the spouses).

The further back in time that we go to examine the divorce histories of marriages, the less confidence we can have that the couples marrying today are going to have divorce records similar to these couples of the past.

The most recent statistical analyses, which are more complicated than most people suppose, indicate that slightly over 40 percent of marriages that occurred *one, two, or more decades ago* will end in divorce (Clarke and Wilson, 1994; Norton and Miller, 1992; Schoen and Weinick, 1993).

The most realistic way to evaluate trends in divorce is to look at divorce rates, not the projected percentages of marriages that might end in divorce. A useful divorce rate can be obtained by determining the number of divorces in any year per 1000 marriages existing in the population. It is best to relate divorces to existing marriages, because any marriage in the population is "at risk" for a divorce. For the United States this divorce rate is shown in Figure 11–5, which covers the years 1925 to the present.

Divorce Rate Trends in the United States

During the twentieth century the overall trend in divorce has obviously been upward, although there have been some notable ups and downs in the divorce rate.

One obvious pattern in Figure 11–5 is the high peak of divorce in the middle 1940s. This peak corresponds with the end of World War II and probably reflects the way in which marriages were affected by couples being apart. The instability of marriages that were entered into hastily during the war is undoubtedly a factor here as well.

However, an even more dramatic increase in the divorce rate started in the 1960s and continued through most of the 1970s. During these two decades the divorce rate of the United States more than doubled. Since 1979, the U.S. divorce rate has declined slightly, although it still remains high compared to other countries. No one can say exactly why the divorce rate has declined, but probably the later age at marriage played a part, since people who marry later divorce less (Booth and Edwards, 1985; Martin and Bumpass, 1989).

The Separation and Divorce Experience

Separation and divorce are almost always stressful and disruptive events in people's lives. Even though both parties may agree that divorce is the correct course of action for them, it is nonetheless a wrenching personal experience. Divorce, by all accounts, is a confusing tangle of emotional experiences, uncertain decisions, and difficult actions.

In an attempt to sort out some of the complexities of the experience, Bohannan (1970) has identified six different "stations" of divorce. These are:

1. Emotional divorce: the recognition that the emotional relationship with one's spouse is deteriorating and the marriage is ending.
2. Legal divorce: the process of learning and going through the legal and procedural steps required by the state.
3. Co-parental divorce: the determination of the custody of children, visitation rights, and child support.

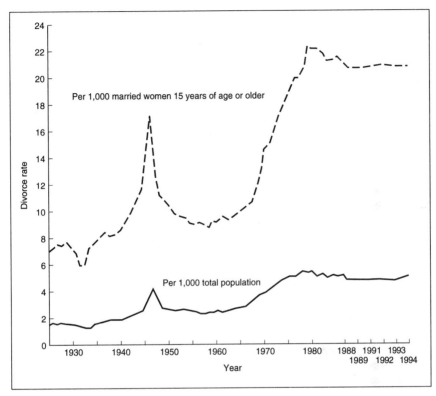

Figure 11–5. Divorce Rates for the United States, 1925–1995. *Source:* Singh, G. K., Mathews, T. J., Clarke, Sally. "Annual Summary of Births, Marriages, Divorces, Deaths, United States, 1994. *Vital Statistics Reports,* Vol. 43, No. 13. Hyattsville, MD: National Center for Health Statistics, 1995.

4. Economic divorce: the division of money and property, and the establishment of levels of economic support (alimony).
5. Community divorce: the changes necessary, because of the divorce, in relating to friends, relatives, and associates.
6. Psychic divorce: the process of regaining an individual identity and autonomy.

The emotional divorce, which is when individuals conclude that their marriage may actually end and they begin to act on that conclusion, is the most stressful stage of the divorce process. A divorce means the end of a relationship that one has entered into with the expectation that it will last a lifetime. Divorce means a refutation of one's earlier decision, which makes it very hard for most married people, even when the marriage has been unhappy.

The legal divorce has changed greatly since 1970 because since that time almost every state has adopted some form of "no-fault" divorce. When no-fault divorce is possible—or required, as it is in some states—an adversary divorce procedure, in which one spouse charges the other with some wrongdoing (adultery, cruelty, mental cruelty, and others), is no longer necessary. Today couples can usually get a divorce by claiming irreconcilable differences, irretrievable breakdown, or incompatibility.

As might be expected, the easier divorce process may increase the number of divorces. In 44 of the 50 states, divorces did go up in the years following the passage of the no-fault laws (Nakonezny et al., 1995). While this study does seem to show that more relaxed divorce laws may have contributed to increases in divorce, some additional points should be noted. First, the divorce rate in the United States had started its rapid increase in the 1960s *before* most states had changed their laws. Second, even though states passed no-fault divorce laws, it was still possible to use the adversary procedure, and many people did (Kitson, 1992). Finally, in the 1980s, when no-fault divorce laws were available in virtually all states, the divorce rate actually declined somewhat.

The economic divorce has become more costly for women during the last 20 years (Hoffman and Duncan, 1988; Kitson, 1992; Morgan, 1991; Weitzman, 1985). Changes in the divorce laws have made it possible for men to bounce back to their predivorce economic levels rather quickly, while women often drop to below their predivorce levels. In one of the earliest studies demonstrating how divorce affects women economically, Weitzman (1985) concluded that 1 year after a divorce the economic standard of living for men went up 42 percent, while the economic standard of living for women went down 73 percent (Weitzman, 1985). A reanalysis of her data indicates that the lowered income level for women may not have been quite as severe—perhaps only a decline of one-third—but the decline was still substantial (Hoffman and Duncan, 1988). Women who divorce in midlife, the age at which women are most affected by divorce, average a 39 percent loss of income after divorce (Morgan, 1991). These and other studies make it clear that the economic consequences of divorce are much more detrimental for women than for men.

A number of factors contribute to the detrimental economic effects of divorce on women, especially for women who have been married for 10 years or more and have minor children. The preeminent factor is that even when married women are employed they generally earn less than their husbands. Moreover, a substantial number of women, especially those with small children, are not in the labor force or are employed only part time. As long as these marriages remain intact, the nonemployment, partial employment, and even the lower pay of women can be viewed as advantageous for the family unit (Becker, 1991). Since husbands can generally earn more than their wives, it may seem rational for wives to withdraw from the labor force to care for young children. But the weakness of this arrangement is all too apparent at the time of a divorce. Then, wives, especially those who have been out of the labor force for years, are suddenly left without the income that had been provided by their husbands' jobs.

One way for women to retain some of that income is to receive alimony from their former husbands and, if they have children, child support as well. However, the liberalized no-fault divorce laws we have discussed, combined with other laws and court rulings, have reduced the amount and extent of alimony awards (Weitzman, 1985; Kitson, 1992). The courts now generally hold that alimony is to be used as an aid until the divorced person is self-supporting, not as a lifetime guaranteed income. The courts have also made it clear that alimony is not to be viewed as a punishment for the spouse who must pay it (Weitzman, 1985). With regard to child support, the amount paid by fathers is almost always inadequate and is frequently not received (Teachman, 1991).

The changing divorce laws have also negatively affected the property settlements that women receive in some states, especially through the adoption of community property laws. *Community property laws* hold that any earnings and any property accumulated during marriage are owned jointly by the couple (Weitzman, 1985). Community property laws were expected to work to the benefit of wives, especially those who were not employed, but studies in California after the community-property laws went into effect found that women received lower settlement awards than they had under the old law (Weitzman, 1985). Studies in Georgia and the state of Washington found some tendency for lower property settlements for women in Washington, but not in Georgia (Welsh and Price-Bonham, 1983).

Community-property laws also undercompensate women for the contributions that they have often made to their husbands' educations, professional degrees, and career advancements. Women who have sacrificed their own potential careers for their husbands' are often left with little to show for their efforts if their marriages end in divorce (Weitzman, 1985). The same is true of retirement funds, which are more likely to be in the husband's name.

Effects of Divorce on Children

Most parents, no matter how dissatisfied with their marriages, consider the impact that divorce will have on their children. Indeed, having children does decrease the likelihood of divorce (White et al., 1986). Children seem to be particularly effective in reducing divorce, at least in the first year after a child is born (Waite et al., 1985; White and Booth, 1985). Even the gender of children influences the likelihood of divorce. One study has shown that if the first child is male the parents are less likely to divorce than if the first child is female. Apparently, both fathers and mothers are more concerned about the absence of the father if the child is a male (Morgan et al., 1988).

Many parents, nonetheless, do divorce, which raises the question of how divorce affects the children. There are two popular beliefs about how divorce affects children. The first, and more general, is that when parents divorce the children are damaged psychologically and this will lead to various types of negative outcomes. The second is that children are not hurt any more by divorce than they would be by living in a home with parents who are constantly fighting. Each of these views, research has shown, has some degree of truth.

Research is not lacking on the effects of divorce on children, for there have been over 100 studies in the United States alone (Amato and Keith, 1991a, 1991b). Some studies focus on children in their childhood and adolescent years, while others study the long-term effects of divorce—into adulthood. Individual studies have produced varying results, with some, especially the qualitative and clinical studies, showing pervasive negative effects on children at the time of divorce and in the years immediately after (Wallerstein and Blakeslee, 1990). The long-term effects on children have been less conclusive, although, again, some individual studies have reported long-term negative outcomes. As an example, studies consistently show that children whose parents have divorced are more likely to divorce themselves.

Because there have been so many studies, it is possible to use the research method called meta-analysis, which we described earlier. Again, meta-analytic studies use the results of many individual studies to uncover the overall patterns of research findings. Two recent meta-analyses have been conducted, one on the effects of divorce on children and the other on the long-term effects on adults whose parents divorced (Amato and Keith, 1991a, 1991b).

The studies of children show that when parents divorce the children have lower academic achievement, more behavior problems, problems of psychological adjustment, lowered self-esteem, and poorer social relations (Amato and Keith, 1991a). However, these studies also show that the differences between children whose parents divorced and children whose parents did not *were not great* (Amato, 1993). These relatively small differences indicate that many children whose parents divorce do not experience negative outcomes, and many children whose parents remain married do. Thus, the average difference between the two groups is not great.

Furthermore, evidence from one major study using data from both the United States and Great Britain shows that some of the problems of children whose parents divorced existed *before* their parents divorced (Cherlin et al., 1991). This research calls attention to two points. First, if children manifested problem behavior before their parents divorced, it is illogical to claim that the divorce produced the problems. It is even possible that the psychological and behavioral problems of children might contribute to the marital troubles of parents. The second point is, however, the more important: that other kinds of parental and family behavior are associated with children's problems. Marital discord and a high level of conflict in the home can have just as negative an effect on children as if the parents divorce. This point is confirmed by a recent analysis showing that in 18 out of 21 studies parental conflict reduces the well-being of children (Amato, 1993).

A further point to be made about parental conflict is that it does not necessarily end with a divorce. When parents continue a high level of conflict during *and especially after* a divorce, negative outcomes are, once again, more likely for children. A meta-analysis of 28 studies found that in all but three, when parents continued their conflict after the divorce, the well-being of children was diminished (Amato, 1993).

We may summarize the effects of divorce on children (including adolescents) by making several points: (1) Probably all children whose parents divorce, except for those who are very young, feel pain and loss when their parents break up. (2) Some, but not all, children whose parents divorce will experience negative outcomes. (3) Parental conflict, whether it occurs in an ongoing marriage, during divorce, or after divorce, is likely to produce negative outcomes in children.

The long-term effects of divorce on children have been relatively harder to document with research, especially quantitative research. A number of major studies conducted in the 1970s concluded that in the long run there were no systematic impairments, either psychological or social, among children whose parents divorced (Kulka and Weingarten, 1979; Kurdek et al., 1981).

On the other side of the ledger, Judith Wallerstein, who followed a relatively small sample of children from the time of their parents' divorce until their adult years, has concluded that at least half of the children of divorce do display lasting negative effects (Wallerstein and Blakeslee, 1990). Wallerstein does acknowledge that "a lot of kids do manage to pull their lives together, albeit after much blood, sweat and tears and often therapy" (Brody, 1991, p. 9). Wallerstein's research is characteristic of the smaller-sample, qualitative studies of the children of divorce, which have, in general, found more long-term negative outcomes (Amato, 1993; Amato and Keith, 1991b).

A meta-analysis of 37 studies that focused on the long-term effects of divorce did show some negative outcomes for the children when they reached adulthood (Amato and Keith, 1991a). Parental divorce was associated with poorer psychological health (depression, lower life satisfaction), family problems (lower marital quality, more divorce), lower educational attainment, lower income and lower occupational prestige, and poorer physical health for the adult children (Amato and Keith, 1991a).

The relationship between parental divorce and negative adult outcomes was generally weak, which shows again that only some children of divorced parents showed negative outcomes in adulthood. Furthermore, some of these relationships may only be correlates of divorce. For example, if there is more divorce among lower socioeconomic status people, it would be understandable that the children of divorced parents would themselves have lower incomes, educational attainments, and occupational prestige.

Two additional points about the effects of divorce on children should be noted: First, more recent studies are less likely to show negative effects on children than earlier studies (Amato, 1991a). This suggests that as divorce became more common in the United States some of its negative impact on children diminished. Second, although divorce may have some negative effects on children, there are certainly other (sometimes correlated) family characteristics that are equally or more detrimental. These include, as we discussed, marital and family conflict. But, in addition, there are the pervasive and corrosive effects of poverty, neglect, abuse, and abandonment (Allen, 1993). These are "the real culprits in children's lives" (Allen, 1993, p. 48).

Family Relations after Divorce

Divorced parents with minor children usually continue to have regular contact. Children often live primarily with the parent who has custody, but they may often be spending some time in the home of the noncustodial parent as well. The concept of the **binuclear family** describes a family system made up of the two households of divorced parents, in which minor children move from one parent's home to the other (Ahrons, 1981). This family system requires a considerable amount of coordination and cooperation between divorced spouses (Masheter, 1991). When the relationship between them is relatively friendly (or not hostile), the task of coordinating activities that involve the children can usually be handled with minimal problems. However, if divorced spouses have unresolved conflicts, a high likelihood exists that children will be used as a way of hurting or gaining advantage over the former spouse (Ahrons and Rodgers, 1987; Weiss, 1979).

Remarriage

Most people who divorce eventually remarry. About five out of six men and two out of three women remarry after divorce (Cherlin, 1992, p. 157). Those who divorce when young are more likely to remarry; this is especially true for women, whose chances for remarriage diminish sharply with age. A woman who divorces under the age of 25 has nearly a 90 percent chance of remarrying, but this percentage goes down to 60 percent for those who divorce in their thirties, and to just over 30 percent for those who divorce at age 40 or older (Bumpass et al., 1990).

The generally high rates of remarriage have led to large numbers of remarried couple households. A **remarried couple household** is a household maintained by a married couple, one or both of whom have been previously married (Cherlin and McCarthy, 1985, p. 23). When one or both partners in a remarriage bring children to that marriage, the resulting family is often called a **blended,** or **reconstituted,** family (Duberman, 1975; Spanier and Furstenberg, 1987).

The families created by remarriage, especially when there are children involved (his, hers, or theirs), are filled with complexity, uncertainty, and problems. One source of problems is the incomplete institutionalization of remarriage (Cherlin, 1978). Remarriage is an incomplete institution because the roles and norms and even the legal aspects of remarriage have not yet evolved enough to give order to this new family form. One illustration of incomplete institutionalization is found in the shortcomings of our language. We do not have terms or names for many people who may be, in a sense, part of one's kin group—what does one call the parents of one's father's new wife?

The most common problem connected with the families of remarriage results from the fact that the boundaries of families have expanded to include many new people for whom there are no clear role relationships. Many complications are introduced into family life by these greater numbers of people for whom there are ambiguous obligations and relationships (Spanier and Furstenberg, 1987).

Summary

Many people today express concern about the condition of the family in the United States. But concerns about the family go back to the nineteenth century and yet the family is important to most Americans. The structure of American households has changed somewhat over the last quarter-century, but the majority of people still live in a family context. However, the functions that the family performs are fewer that those that the family performed historically.

The family can be organized in many different ways and still carry out a variety of functions that are both necessary and useful for the society. Some important functions of the family, found in most societies, are reproduction, care and nurturance of children, socialization, fulfillment of economic needs, provision of intergenerational and kin support, regulation of sexual behavior, and social placement. Many different types of family structures exist, as well as many different norms governing family life.

The family is an adaptive institution. Historical and contemporary examples support the idea that the family is likely to adapt to changes in other parts of the society, especially the economic system.

In many societies, including contemporary Iran, and to a lesser extent Japan, marriage is arranged by parents. However, in many Western societies the young people themselves choose their mates on the basis of mutual attraction and romantic love. The mate selection system of the United States has, throughout its history, been based primarily on romantic love. But, even when mate selection is left to young people, the family and other social groups can influence the process.

Cohabitation is now a stage of premarried life for many young people. The trend is more advanced in Scandinavia but is also prominent in the United States.

The early years of marriage are difficult in terms of adjustment, but these are also the years of high satisfaction with the marital relationship. Marital quality tends to decline with the arrival of children and continues to be negatively influenced by children throughout the later life stages. Most evidence shows that marital quality improves in the later years of marriage.

The relationship between family and work (both inside and outside the home) is the source of many complications and problems in contemporary family life. Despite the increase of women in paid employment, they still do most of the housework and child care.

Conflict and violence in marriage are more widespread than is often suspected. The major serious forms of violence are spouse abuse and child abuse. Two types of couple violence are patriarchal terrorism and common couple violence. It is the former that leads to the most serious harm to women. Child abuse covers a range of behaviors, including the uncertain area of physical and verbal actions that are accepted by many people as normal parental discipline.

The divorce rate of the United States is among the highest in the world. Divorces increased gradually after 1920 and more rapidly in the 1960s and 1970s. Since the peak in 1979, the divorce rate has declined somewhat. The declines may be due to later marriage.

Separation and divorce are stressful and complicated experiences. Six stations of divorce have been identified: emotional, legal, co-parental, economic, community, and psychic. Children do suffer when their parents divorce, but the long-range effects on children, while they exist, are not universal. As a result of divorce and remarriage, family relationships in contemporary society are becoming increasingly complex.

CRITICAL THINKING

1. What functions does the institution of the family commonly serve in societies? How relatively important is each of these functions in the United States today?
2. Is there a particular family form (nuclear or extended families, polygamy or monogamy, or others) that is better than others? Why?
3. Compare and contrast various methods for mate selection in different societies. To what extent do these methods reflect basic cultural values of the societies in which they are used?
4. How do you explain the emergence of cohabitation as a stage before marriage?
5. What is marital quality? How might marital scripts and parenthood affect marital quality?
6. What relationship exists between the family and work in contemporary society?
7. Describe the extent to which violence is a part of family life in American society. How do you explain this phenomenon?
8. How does statistical information about divorce and separation support the idea that the family is an adaptive institution?
9. How has divorce complicated the family structure in society? What other institutions in society have been affected by divorce?

12

Education

The current crisis in education is costing us the American Dream.

Wilson and Daviss, 1994

The "current crisis in education" is a theme heard so often that it is accepted unthinkingly by many Americans. But not everyone agrees that education is as bad as the critics claim. Some, such as psychologist Gerald Bracey, say, "I have researched the data on American education over the past century and have concluded that they show a record of almost continuous improvement" (Bracey, 1995). Researchers from the Rand Corporation, a respected independent research organization—with no apparent vested interest in the schools—have written a book titled, *The Manufactured Crisis: Myths, Fraud, and the Attack on America's Public Schools.*

And yet there are many serious critics of education who say that our schools are failing to do their job and are beset with problems. Still other critics say that the schools are not teaching the right things or are emphasizing the wrong things. Others complain about badly administered schools and weak teachers. Some critics point to violence and disorder in the schools and the need for greater discipline.

With this much disagreement about American schools, it is clear that this institution deserves sociological attention. But the sociology of education involves more than just an analysis of the U.S. school system. We will begin this chapter with a brief look at the history of education in the United States, and we will see that there are two different views of that history. Next we will consider sociological views of education, especially as reflected by functional and conflict theories, and once again we will see two different views. After taking a look at education in societies around the world, we will turn to the American school system, giving special attention to how well schools are performing and how fair they are. In the last part of the chapter we will focus on the social dimensions of schools and classrooms, with special attention to teacher–student relationships and violence and order in the schools.

A Brief Look at the History of Education in the United States

In the earliest settlements of colonial America, most youngsters were educated in the "real world" instead of the classroom. In 1647, however, more than a century before the American Revolution, the first mandatory school systems were established in the Massachusetts Bay Colony (Monroe, 1940). Education in the United States initially emphasized the four Rs: reading, 'riting, 'rithmetic, and *religion*. Later, schools were aimed more directly at the economic and occupational needs of the country.

Between colonial times and the 1870s, elementary education became more democratized, that is, more widely available to all children. Following the principles of universal education advocated by Thomas Jefferson, a free public school system emerged by the mid-1800s. The widespread education of girls at the elementary level also became a reality during this era. By the middle of the nineteenth century, the first public high schools had been founded.

The Traditional Historical View

The **traditional view of the *history* of American education** is that the United States was founded on democratic political principles, which required an educated and informed electorate. The United States also had a social and economic philosophy that was highly democratic. According to the ideal, every person, regardless of origins or social background, should have an equal opportunity to achieve and succeed. A school system that is available to all the children of the society, that is, a free and open system of mass education, is the major means by which equality is assured.

The traditional view of the history of American education still prevails today. Politicians, educators, and most citizens see the system of free and mass education as a way of ensuring that the society will have an informed citizenry, capable of making decisions in a democratic society. The educational system is also seen as the key to success and achievement in the United States. However, among historians of education, this view has been challenged by the revisionist view.

The Revisionist Historical View

The **revisionist view of the history of American education** emphasizes that the economic and social elites of the society will develop an educational system that meets their needs, not the needs of the masses of people. This view is a more critical, a less idealistic, perspective on education, based on the assumption that a fundamental conflict of interests always exists between the elites and masses of the society (Bowles and Gintis, 1976; Katz, 1968, 1987; Mennerick and Najafizadeh, 1987).

The revisionist historians of education contend that a major goal of mass education in the nineteenth century was to socialize the working-class and immigrant children so that they would be better workers in the nation's factories and businesses. The children were not learning the skills necessary for work as much as they were learning proper work habits. The educational system was teaching future workers the importance of punctuality, regular attendance, submission to authority, cleanliness, and order. Nowhere was the link between the needs of industrialization and those of the educational system more vividly revealed than in the Lancaster system.

The **Lancaster system,** named after its founder Joseph Lancaster, was a school system based on the principles of efficiency and order. Although the Lancaster system was found primarily in urban places, near industries and factories, it became the model for centralized and efficient school systems emerging around the country. In the Lancaster system, careful attention was devoted to every detail of student behavior and classroom procedures. Teaching in the classrooms of a Lancaster school was always conducted in precisely the same way: the emphasis was on rote memorization of facts and on strict discipline. The way in which students were seated and even the way in which they wore their hats were carefully regulated. The hats were to be attached by strings to shirt collars, slipped off at the proper signal, and left resting on the students' backs (Parelius and Parelius, 1978, p. 60).

As a way of increasing the efficiency of the system, the Lancaster schools made maximum use of a minimum number of teachers; only one teacher was assigned to every 400 to 500 students. To manage such large numbers of students, the system relied heavily on student "monitors" who had previously been taught the lesson by the teacher. The huge classes were divided into groups of ten, each of which was headed by a monitor.

Lancaster schools were like factories, except that their product happened to be students. It is easy to see how students who were often headed for work in factories were well prepared by a school system that was itself a factory. This interpretation is consistent with the revisionist view of education, since it would obviously be in the interests of factory owners to have well-socialized workers.

The traditional and revisionist views of the history of education resemble two competing sociological interpretations of education: functional and conflict theory. Functional theory offers an explanation of education that has some of the same elements as the traditional view. Conflict theory picks up key features of the revisionist view.

Functional Theory and Education

One aspect of functional theory emphasizes that societies are made up of separate institutions that are integrated and interdependent. Thus, in an urban, industrial society, where families are less able to socialize their children for the workforce, the educational system will take over some of the socializing functions. The educational system, according to functional theory, will ensure the social, political, and economic stability of the society. The schools can transform heterogeneous ethnic and religious groups into informed and productive citizens who have common values. Viewed in this way, the educational system contributes to an integrated, stable, and smooth-running society (Davies, 1995; Mennerick and Najafizadeh, 1987).

The functionalist perspective is very positive about education's role in commercial society. Schools are seen as a "benevolent but powerful force creating the social cohesion and unity" that commercial society requires (Rothstein, 1996, p. 17).

From a functionalist perspective, the schools perform more than an educational function; they provide a moral function as well. The **moral function** of the educational system is to teach children and young people the norms and values of the society. The norms and values are taught, in part, through the day-to-day activities of classrooms and schools, and, in part, through the content of what is taught to the young people. For example, even at the kindergarten level, children are being taught that they must conform to the expectations of those in authority and respect the rights of others. Kindergarten teachers organize the lives of the children in a way that prepares them for the order and conformity necessary at higher grades (Gracey, 1967).

Because schools transmit a society's norms and values, many students will internalize and accept as proper most of the values and rules that guide the larger society. For example, competition and achievement are two widely accepted American values. The school is instrumental in conveying the idea that it is fair to give different rewards for different levels of achievement (Parsons, 1959). Children soon learn that those who get their lessons done quickly and accurately will be praised and rewarded with good grades. Furthermore, and this is a very important lesson, the highest achievers will be given additional rewards—being allowed to carry out special errands for the teacher, becoming room monitors, engaging in recreational activities, and receiving honors and recognition. The winners not only get the intrinsic reward of accomplishing their school work but they get the additional external rewards as well.

This familiar classroom experience teaches a variety of lessons that apply again and again throughout life. The lesson that most activities are competitive is reinforced later in dating, making athletic teams, winning college scholarships, being admitted to the best colleges, getting into a professional or graduate school, and getting the best jobs.

Functional theorists view this part of the school's teaching in a positive light because it provides a shared set of values for all the people of the society who have gone through the school system. The moral function of the schools helps to integrate and stabilize the society.

However, functionalists also recognize that not every student will embrace the conventional values of the society. Some young people, especially those from the lower socioeconomic groups, may reject the values of individualism, achievement, and competitiveness (Davies, 1995). But their failure to do so is attributed to their rejection of the values and not to the failure of the schools.

Functional theory also emphasizes that an educational institution, especially one that rewards students for their ability and the quality of their work, provides an equal opportunity for every individual. The task of the schools is, therefore, to evaluate and sort the students according to their ability and performance (Mennerick and Najafizadeh, 1987).

Conflict Theory and Education

Conflict theory stresses that, in any social system or society, conflicts of interests will exist between different groups or categories of people. This theory also stresses that some groups will have more power than others and that the most powerful groups will take advantage of their position to maximize their interests. Thus, conflict theorists agree that the schools teach and gain acceptance for the prevailing norms and values of the society, but these are the norms and values that especially serve the needs of the advantaged and powerful people of the society.

When children in the schools learn that competition and achievement are the routes to economic rewards and high status, the positions of those who already have wealth and high status are legitimized. It is in the best interests of those who are already in advantaged and powerful positions to get the largest number of people agreeing that they have a right to be there. It is especially important that people who are in lower-status positions, and are likely to remain there, accept the legitimacy of a system of inequality.

Not only do children learn in school that competition and achievement are the routes to reward but, more important, they also learn to believe in the correctness of this method of obtaining rewards. For nearly everyone the method learned is so right that it seems natural or even instinctive. Even those who do not win the competition and thus do not get the rewards generally believe in and accept the system. Often losers blame themselves for not getting the rewards. Rarely do they question the legitimacy of the norms and values of the system (Sennett and Cobb, 1972).

Conflict theorists also see the educational system as organized to favor the interests of the most powerful members of the society in another way that is similar to the revisionist historical view of education: the educational system will produce the kinds of workers needed by the dominant economic interests of the society (Useem, 1986). The schools often do this, as we have seen, by providing well-socialized workers who have learned to be responsible and to carry out the assignments they have been given.

Another point of dispute between conflict and functional theorists concerns the fairness of the educational system. Conflict theorists see the schools as organized and operated in ways that give the children of the advantaged groups a better chance of succeeding, and thus the schools perpetuate inequalities in the social structure. The sharpest continuing dispute between conflict and functional theorists rests on this last point. Instead of an educational system that gives everyone equal opportunities for success, conflict theorists argue that the system favors the children of higher-status families and works against the lower-status youngsters (Bowles and Gintis, 1976).

The differences between the views of functional theorists and conflict theorists regarding the educational system may be summarized around three issues:

1. Functionalists view the teaching of cultural norms and values as an integrating function of schools; conflict theorists view these norms and values as favoring the already dominant groups in the society.
2. Functionalists see the educational system as providing the skilled and trained workers needed by the economy; conflict theorists see the educational system as providing a docile work force that will be used by the dominant economic interests.
3. Functionalists view the educational system as fair and equitable—a system that gives everyone a chance at success, based on individual ability, hard work, and diligence; conflict theorists see unfairness and inequity in the educational system—a system that operates to keep lower-status youngsters in their place at the bottom of the social structure and that gives the children of the advantaged groups a greater likelihood of success.

Throughout this chapter, as we examine different aspects of educational systems and schools, we will see these issues reflected at several points: at the elementary, secondary, and college levels, and in educational systems of the United States and other countries of the world.

Cross-cultural Perspectives

Why India Does Not Have Compulsory Education

India does not have compulsory education, even at the primary level, despite the fact that its constitution calls for it and many Indian states have passed laws that seem to require school attendance. With respect to compulsory education, India is different from every developed nation and from most developing nations; in most other nations, universal education at the elementary level is a reality. In India, fewer than half of the children (48 percent) between the ages of 6 and 14 attend school (Weiner, 1991). Indian girls are especially disadvantaged, with only 38 percent of those between the ages of 6 and 14 in school, while 58 percent of the boys in this age group are enrolled (Weiner, 1991).

A combination of forces conspire to keep most of the children of India out of school. It begins with the Indian social structure, which is rigidly divided into distinct social classes (or castes). Most Indians hold the strong belief that there are distinct categories of people and that their educational needs are very different. Middle- and upper-class Indians, especially, believe that children of the poor should learn to work with their hands and that for them schooling would only be a waste of time. Schools, they believe, should be primarily for the people who will work with their minds and who will later take on the responsibility of running the society (Weiner, 1991).

But the impediments to education for many Indian children also come from other sources. The parents of the children, especially the many millions who are extremely poor, see their children as economic assets. The children of India are often put to work at a very early age so that they can provide money for their families. The employers of children also have a vested interest in children being available for work. Children are a docile and cheap source of labor, especially in occupations that require low skill levels. The children of India are employed in many industries, including the highly dangerous fireworks and match-stick factories. They also make many of the inexpensive clothes that are sold in our own society. For example, many of the shirts, blouses, blue jeans, and jackets sold in Wal-Mart, Kmart, and other American chain stores come from India (Moore, 1995).

The children of India also work in restaurants and food stores and in households as domestic workers. They work in the fields and farms, where they plant and harvest crops, collect firewood, and tend cattle (Weiner, 1991).

India does have laws that prohibit the use of child labor, and there are sometimes convictions for violating these laws; but often government officials look the other way, because they believe that parents have the right to benefit from the labor of their children. Even when employers are arrested for hiring children, the fines are small—the equivalent of about $5. In fact, most observers admit that in India it is nearly impossible to enforce the laws prohibiting child labor because both parents and employers benefit from the employment of children. At the same time, these two groups also benefit when compulsory education laws are not enforced.

Even the educational establishment benefits when many children are absent from the schools. When fewer children are attending, the schools are able to use their economic resources on those children who do attend (Weiner, 1991).

The lack of compulsory education in India can be attributed to a number of forces and particular groups: the rigid class structure and the cultural belief that poor children do not need formal education, the economic interests of parents and employers, and the educational system, which benefits from having fewer children in schools. Most of the children of India are deprived of even the most elementary education because too many factors conspire against them.

MOORE, MOLLY. "Factories of Children." *Washington Post,* May, 21, 1995.
WEINER, MYRON. *The Child and the State in India: Child Labor and Education Policy in Comparative Perspective.* Princeton, NJ: Princeton University Press, 1991.

Education and Educational Systems Worldwide

The industrial nations of the world generally adopted mass education in the period between 1870 and 1940 and today have the most advanced and universally available systems (Meyer et al., 1992). However, even though modern industrial nations provide universal education, there is ample evidence from cross-national studies that children from lower socioeconomic classes attain lower levels of educational achievement (Ishida et al., 1995; Shavit and Blossfeld, 1993). Many educational theorists had assumed, following functional theory, that as countries became industrialized and modernized class differences in educational attainment would diminish, but that has not been demonstrated (Ishida et al., 1995).

In less developed countries, the inequities in education are even more pronounced. Many children in the developing world receive only minimal schooling, and national expenditures are inequitably distributed (Najafizadeh and Mennerick, 1988). Expenditures in these countries are often concentrated in the urban areas, and even then go largely to the social and economic elites.

In a study of ten selected Asian and Latin American countries, youths from the richest 20 percent of the population received from 38 to 83 percent of the educational subsidies (World Bank, 1988). Developing countries also use more of their economic resources to support students in higher education than they do for primary and secondary students. This policy, too, benefits the elites of these countries more than people in the lowest socioeconomic classes.

Females are especially disadvantaged in the developing countries of the world, where the gender differences begin at the primary level. In the world's developing countries, at the primary level, 86 percent of males are enrolled, compared to 71 percent of the females. At the secondary level, 35 percent of males are enrolled compared to 29 percent of the females (Najafizadeh and Mennerick, 1988).

From a worldwide perspective, in both the developed and developing countries, inequities in educational attainment are clearly evident. The social and economic elites and males benefit from education more than the lower classes, racial and ethnic minorities, and females (Davies, 1995). Cross-national studies of education support conflict theory more than functional theory (Ishida et al., 1995).

Who Succeeds in the American School System?

Functional theorists view the American educational system as fair and equitable, a system that gives everyone a chance at success. In an abstract way, it may be true that everyone enters the educational system with an equal opportunity, limited only by his or her intellectual ability and a willingness to work hard. But there is ample evidence that children from the disadvantaged strata in society do less well in the school system. One sociologist of education sums up the matter clearly:

> By almost any criterion, and with few exceptions, students from working class and ethnic/minority backgrounds do poorly in school. They drop out at a higher rate than do their middle-income and ethnic-majority contemporaries (Mehan, 1992, p. 3).

One way to examine the unequal success of American youth in educational attainment is to see how far the major racial and ethnic groups get in school. Table 12-1 shows what percentages of Americans (white, black, and Hispanic) aged 25 to 29 have completed various levels of education.

Ninety-one percent of white Americans complete high school, compared to 84 percent of African Americans and 60 percent of Hispanics. Among those who complete high school, the percentages who have some college (1 to 3 years) are about 63 percent for whites, but only about 50 percent for blacks and Hispanics. The percentages of high school graduates who complete college is about 30 percent for whites, but only 16 percent for blacks and 13 percent for Hispanics.

These statistics show that, for every 100 children in these racial and ethnic categories, about 27 whites, 14 African Americans, and 8 Hispanics graduate from college. It is clear from the numbers that, compared to white Americans, black Americans and Hispanics have a much smaller chance of succeeding in the American educational system.

Table 12–1   Schooling Completed among 25- to 29-Year Olds: Whites, Blacks, and Hispanics, 1994

		High school graduates completing:	
	Completed high school	*Some college*	*College degree*
Whites	91.1%	62.7%	29.7%
Blacks	84.1%	49.6%	16.2%
Hispanics	60.3%	51.5%	13.3%

Source: U.S. Department of Education, National Center for Educational Statistics. *The Condition of Education, 1995.* Washington, D.C., 1995.

Dropping Out of School

The differences in educational attainment shown in Table 12-1 are initially influenced by students dropping out of school before completing high school. Between 1978 and 1993, the dropout rate among American students has declined from 14.2 percent to 11.0 percent (McMillan et al., 1994). The dropout process begins even at the middle school level and increases during the high school years (Rumberger, 1995).

Middle School Dropouts.   In a study of 17,424 randomly drawn eighth grade students, race and ethnicity were related to dropping out of middle school: African American, Native American, and Hispanic students had higher than average dropout rates, while Asian students had significantly lower dropout rates (Rumberger, 1995).

This same study found that middle school students who came from lower socioeconomic backgrounds generally had higher than average dropout rates, but among black students socioeconomic status was not related to dropping out. Middle-school students who came from single-parent and step-parent homes and non-English speaking families also had significantly higher dropout rates. The more parents were involved in the school through PTA and volunteer work, the more they supervised the activities of their children, and the higher the expectations that they had for their children, the less likely students were to drop out at the middle-school level. Students who had been held back at some earlier grade were much more likely to drop out of middle school. These individual-level factors confirm the results of other studies (Rumberger, 1995).

However, this study also found that the type of school that students attend can also influence dropout behavior, above and beyond the characteristics of individuals. Students who attend schools with low socioeconomic populations and minority populations are more likely to drop out of middle school than students who attend higher-status, lower-percentage-minority schools (Rumberger, 1995).

High School Dropouts. The individual and family characteristics of students who drop out of high school are much the same as those of students who drop out of middle school. Socioeconomic status, race, ethnicity, family structure, parental practices, and previous academic performance are all related to dropping out of high school (Astone and McLanahan, 1991; Ensminger and Slusarcick, 1992).

Latino youth, as we saw above, have exceptionally low high school graduation rates; many leave school in the earliest years of high school (Rumberger, 1995). However, the educational attainment levels of the Latino population are substantially lowered by the Chicano (or Mexican) population, which constitutes nearly two-thirds of the total (Solorzano, 1995). The high dropout rates of Latino students, and especially Chicanos, is produced by a combination of their relatively low socioeconomic status, cultural and language obstacles, and the poor quality of the schools that they attend (Fernandez et al., 1989; Rumberger, 1991; Solorzano, 1995).

The dropout rates of African American students are also relatively high, especially when compared with white students. One long-term study in the Woodlawn area of South Chicago, a poor, 97 percent black community, followed more than 1100 students from the time that they were in the first grade. In 1982, the scheduled year of graduation for these students, only 43 percent of the males and 55 percent of the females graduated. This is a high dropout rate, but not greatly higher than the rates for Chicago as a whole in 1982 and dropout rates found in other studies of disadvantaged young people (Ensminger and Slusarcick, 1992).

Those who dropped out of school before graduating were more likely to have had certain personal and family characteristics when they were in the first grade, many years earlier. Dropouts, especially the boys who quit school before graduating, were more likely to have exhibited aggressive behavior and had poor grades in the first grade. They were also more likely to have come from poverty-level homes where the mother did not have a high school education.

Several family characteristics proved to be "protective factors," which means that they protected some of those students who had negative first-grade characteristics (poor grades and aggressive behavior). When males with poor grades in the first grade had mothers who had graduated from high school, they were more likely to graduate than other boys who had low grades. Being from a mother-father family was protective for girls who had early negative characteristics. Coming from a home with strict rules regarding school was also a factor that kept girls from dropping out, even when their early school grades were low (Ensminger and Slusarcick, 1992).

This study of school dropouts suggests that, even within a minority group, certain danger signs can be identified in the early years of a student's educational career. Furthermore, there are family characteristics that can counteract some of these early warning signs (Ensminger and Slusarcick, 1992).

Economic Background and College Attendance

Children from economically disadvantaged backgrounds are also less likely to succeed in the higher educational system. This can be seen in Figure 12-1, which shows a larger proportion of children from better-off families attending college.

The Importance of an "Elite" College Education

Today it is nearly a necessity to have a college education if one aspires to a high-status position in any relatively large corporate business in the United States. The

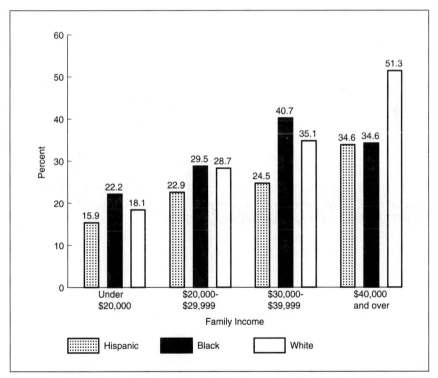

Figure 12–1.   Percentage of Households with at Least One Primary Family Member, 18 to 24 Years Old, in College, by Family Income, Race, and Origin. (*Source:* U.S. Bureau of the Census, *Current Population Reports,* Series P-20, No. 479, 1994, Table 16.)

same is true of the other developed societies of the world. However, not all colleges are equal because the degrees they grant are not considered equal. Colleges and universities in the United States are hierarchically ordered, with a small set of elite schools at the top that have the best reputations for academic excellence, distinguished faculties, and carefully selected, intellectually talented students. Disagreements may arise about the rank order of particular schools, but a typical list of elite colleges in the United States includes Harvard (also the oldest), Yale, Princeton, Columbia, and Stanford, just to name a few.

A question often asked by the public as well as by sociologists is "Does the college that one attends make a difference in one's career opportunities and occupational advancement?" The question is more complicated than it first seems, for several reasons. The college one attends is associated with a number of other characteristics that can also influence career opportunities and occupational advancement. These other characteristics include family background, personal ability, academic performance, and motivation to succeed (Alwin, 1974).

One study found that, even when all these factors were controlled, some independent effect of the college attended still prevailed (Alwin, 1974). Furthermore, a study conducted among Japanese males also found that the graduates of the most elite colleges of Japan attained higher lifetime incomes and higher positions in organizations than men who had graduated from less prestigious colleges. Although this study was not able to rule out family background as a contributing factor, the author argues that in Japan the status of the college from which one graduates does make a difference in the occupational careers of males (Miyahara, 1988).

In a study of over 2729 senior managers and executives of 208 major corporations in the United States, researchers tried to determine if getting a degree from one of the elite schools of the country influenced the chances of attaining the very topmost levels of corporate America (Useem and Karabel, 1986). The researchers were especially interested in whether the social (family) backgrounds of these top corporate leaders could account for their positions, or whether degrees from elite schools were more influential. The researchers considered not just bachelor's degrees but also master's of business administration degrees and law degrees. Thus, they came up with somewhat different lists of elite schools for each type of degree.[1]

---

[1] The elite schools for bachelor's degrees were Columbia, Cornell, Dartmouth, Harvard, Johns Hopkins, Massachusetts Institute of Technology, Pennsylvania, Princeton, Stanford, Williams, and Yale. Elite schools for master's degrees in business administration were Columbia, Dartmouth, Harvard, M.I.T., Northwestern, Stanford, California-Berkeley, California-Los Angeles, Chicago, Michigan, and Pennsylvania. Elite schools for law degrees were Columbia, Harvard, New York University, Stanford, California-Berkeley, Chicago, Michigan, Pennsylvania, and Yale.

This study concluded that the main portion of these 2729 senior managers and executives who made it to the very top of the corporate and business structure were helped by their educational credentials. Holding a bachelor's degree from a prestigious school made it more likely that a person would be chosen as a chief executive officer (CEO) of one of the major U.S. corporations. A bachelor's degree from an elite school made the chances of becoming a CEO twice as great as a noncollege graduate in this group. (About 15 percent of the 2729 corporate managers had not gone to college or had not completed college.) Master's degrees in business administration from elite business schools, and especially law degrees from one of the elite law schools, also gave these corporate managers a better chance of being selected for the top corporate positions (Useem and Karabel, 1986).

However, elite social background—coming from a family listed in the *Social Register* or attending one of the nation's exclusive prep schools—also aided in moving up in the higher levels of corporate management. In particular, an upper-class family background led more often to the boards of directors of corporations and to leadership positions in the top-level business associations. Of course, combining a high-status social background with an elite education made it even more likely that these highest levels of corporate management and leadership in the business world would be reached.

Since these managers were almost all middle-aged and older, and thus had received their college and professional degrees many years earlier, it is not clear why the status of their schools should continue to aid them in their careers. It seems unlikely that what they learned in college would still be an influential factor. It may be that their personalities or styles, which had been developed or cultivated in elite schools, gave them an advantage in the corporate world. It may also be that at the highest level of corporate management a great deal of uncertainty prevails, and trust is a critical factor. Thus, the top level of promotions go to people who are most like those already in power, both educationally and socially (Useem and Karabel, 1986, p. 198).

Getting a degree from an elite institution continues to be important at the level of graduate degrees (Ph.D.s, for example) and professional degrees (law and medicine). A study of Ph.D.s in psychology found that the best academic jobs, in the most prestigious research universities, went to the Ph.D. graduates who had gone to the most prestigious schools (Hurlbert and Rosenfeld, 1992). However, getting a Ph.D. from a prestigious school was only important for getting good first jobs and had no effect on the quality of later career jobs (Hurlbert and Rosenfeld, 1992).

An example of how important it can be to get a degree from an elite school is found in the case of Harvard Law School graduates (Granfield, 1992; Granfield and Koenig, 1992). By almost any objective standard (test scores or grades of students admitted, quality of the faculty, eminence of its graduates) and by its reputation, Harvard Law School is at or near the top of the elite law schools in the United States.

In their second and third years, the graduates of Harvard Law are heavily recruited by as many as 800 large, national law firms. Each student may have as many interviews with prospective employers as he or she wishes, since recruiters are required to meet with anyone who requests an interview. Some students report having as many as 90 interviews, but such a large number only reflects their stamina (Granfield and Koenig, 1992, p. 512).

As part of the recruitment process, Harvard Law students are often invited to visit the law firms recruiting them. These "fly-outs" are often very lavish and include eating in the best restaurants and staying in first-class hotels at the law firm's expense. Students describe their fly-out experiences in these words:

> On campus I had about 25 interviews. I flew out for about 15 of those. It was real cushy.

> I got a lot of fly-outs and spent a month on the road racking up frequent flyer points.

> It [recruiting] was beyond my wildest dreams (Granfield and Koenig, 1992, p. 513).

All Harvard Law School graduates, even those who do not graduate with top grades, expect and get the best and generally highest paying law jobs in the country. It is clearly a major benefit of graduating from an elite school.

Effects of Beginning at a Community College

At the opposite extreme from the elite colleges and universities are the community colleges of the United States. Nearly half of all college students at any given time are attending community colleges (Monk-Turner, 1990). The most likely students at community colleges are women, minorities, and students from working-class backgrounds. Many of these community college students go on to graduate from four-year colleges, but their occupational achievement is not as great as students who begin at four-year colleges (Monk-Turner, 1990).

Performance of the American School System

The task of the schools is to educate the children and young people of the society, and widespread concern exists about how the school system is performing its primary responsibility. The schools have many critics who have pointed to failures and shortcomings in various areas. In the early 1980s, a government report on the educational system was ominously titled *A Nation at Risk* (1983). The crux of this report emphasized that the American educational system was mediocre, and the threat that our schools posed for our national well-being and security was as great as any external threat.

In the remainder of this chapter we will see how well the school system is performing and what problems the educational system faces.

Performance on Achievement Tests

After the publication of *A Nation at Risk,* the Congress of the United States mandated that periodically the knowledge, skills, and attitudes of U.S. children and youth be assessed. Beginning in 1970–1971, schools initiated periodic assessments of U.S. students through a program called the National Assessment of Educational Progress. The program has measured reading achievement of 9-year-old, 13-year-old, and 17-year-old students six times since 1970–1971 (the latest in 1992).

Over the last 21 years, the reading scores of American students have varied over a small range, but remain virtually unchanged from their 1971 level (U.S. Department of Education, 1995). African American and Hispanic students have reading scores that are only 85 to 90 percent of white students' scores, but both minorities have closed the gap by about 5 percent since the reading tests were initiated. Over the entire testing period, females at ages 9, 13, and 17 have always had higher reading scores than males (U.S. Department of Education, 1995, p. 54).

This testing program started measuring mathematics proficiency in 1973, and there have been five subsequent tests. Since 1978, students at all ages, but especially 9- and 13-year-olds, have made modest improvements in their mathematics proficiency test scores (U.S. Department of Education, 1995). Males have slightly higher scores than females.

Writing proficiency has also been measured since 1973. In the 1992 test, fourth and eighth graders had slightly higher writing scores than 20 years earlier, but the scores of eleventh graders were lower (U.S. Department of Education, 1995).

Financial Disparities among Schools

American schools are financed largely through property taxes collected at the local level. Since the economic value of property varies greatly from one community to another, the quality of schools in affluent areas is substantially better than the schools in poor areas. With more financial resources, the children get better teachers, classrooms, laboratories, computers, libraries, and support personnel.

In his book *Savage Inequalities,* Jonathan Kozol (1991) has exposed the deplorable conditions that exist in some of the most impoverished school systems in the United States. In most of these schools the students are almost exclusively racial or ethnic minorities, and Kozol's descriptions make it clear that the obstacles to a good education are nearly insurmountable.

A more quantitative approach to the inequities among schools is provided by a comparison of suburban schools and urban schools (Strauss, 1994). A survey of the nation's 50 largest public school systems shows that the generally wealthier suburban school systems spend an average of $437 more per student than inner-city urban systems (Strauss, 1994). This is about a 10 percent difference, since the yearly average expenditure per student is $4422. Even this difference may not reveal all the inequality, because costs are probably higher in urban places.

Social Dimensions of Schools and Classrooms

Schools and their classrooms are not just places for teaching and learning; they are also social settings. As with all other social settings there are roles, norms, values, and status hierarchies. From a sociological perspective it is important to see how social factors influence what happens in schools and classrooms—both to the students and to the teachers. We will begin our consideration of social dimensions of schools by examining the most basic of all relationships—the relationship between teachers and students.

Teacher/Student Relationships

Without a doubt, the relationship between a teacher and a student can have a great influence on the student's academic performance and, ultimately, on his or her academic achievements. Many successful people are asked if any teachers influenced them, and usually they can recall one or two who had a significant effect on their lives. This anecdotal evidence showing that teachers "make a difference" is supported by research showing that teachers' attitudes and behavior can and do influence the academic performances of children.

Teachers in a school system may have expectations about how certain students or categories of students will perform even before they are directly responsible for them. Their expectations may influence their evaluations of the students. This phenomenon is called a **self-fulfilling prophecy:** an initial expectation, even one that is based on a false definition of the situation, can produce the behavior that makes the original expectation come true (Merton, 1968).

Teachers may base their expectations about particular students on reports from other teachers, or they may have expectations based on older siblings who have been in their classes. More harmfully, teachers may sometimes base their expectations on the racial, ethnic, or social class characteristics of their students. One outcome of these preconceptions is that students will be placed in different ability tracks (college preparatory, general, vocational), and once in these tracks they will be almost certain to stay there (Oakes and Guiton, 1995). Tracking will be discussed more fully later.

A somewhat different way of seeing the impact of teachers on the performances of their students comes from the study of a large and diverse sample of beginning first graders in the Baltimore, Maryland, public schools. Many of the

In the News

Two Current Educational Controversies

Americans take a keen interest in their schools, and by historical tradition they feel that they have the right to say what goes on in their schools. It is not therefore surprising that controversies are always boiling about how schools should be run and what schools should try to accomplish. In the United States today there are a number of controversies about schools, but the two that have received the most attention are school choice and multiculturalism.

School Choice

The fundamental feature of school choice is that parents (and their children) are given a choice about the school that the children will attend; children will not be required to attend the school in the district of their residence. Three prominent types of school choice are (1) students may attend any government school in their own school district, (2) students may attend any government school in their state, and (3) students may attend any school, including private or religious schools, and their parents will be given money (usually called vouchers) to pay any necessary tuition (Biggs and Porter, 1994; Cookson, 1994).

In many states and localities, different school-choice plans have already been tried. The most widespread experiment is the establishment of *magnet schools,* which are high-quality or specialty schools (music and the arts, for example) that are aimed at attracting students from anyplace in a school district. Magnet schools are intended to reduce the racial segregation of schools. Supporters believe that they have succeeded in reducing segregation, but not all research confirms this belief (Biggs and Porter, 1994).

The most controversial form of school choice is the voucher plan, which will allow parents to use vouchers to send their children to any school, including private schools.

Those who favor school choice generally use a marketplace model, which is based on the assumption that competition improves quality. In this view, the schools that provide the best education will attract the most students (and money), while the inferior schools will decline and perhaps disappear (Harmer, 1994).

The major argument against school choice is that the children who are the most economically advantaged will move to the best schools, leaving behind the disadvantaged students in the weakest and poorest schools (Walford, 1994). Another concern is that if many students (perhaps the most advantaged) use their vouchers to enroll in private schools, the public school system will go into decline because of a lack of financial support. A related issue is that if private schools are sponsored by religious groups the constitutional separation of church and state will have been breached. All these concerns have made many people apprehensive about the voucher system of school choice (Cookson, 1994).

Multiculturalism

The term *multiculturalism* reflects an educational movement that aims to broaden the curricula of American schools beyond their traditional focus on the writings, ideas, and accomplishments of European (and, by extension, American) white males. Stated in a positive way, a multicultural curriculum introduces students to the intellectual, social, and cultural contributions of people from non-European cultures—especially Asian and African—and women (Thompson and Tyagi, 1993).

Multiculturalism takes many forms. Many colleges and universities have included multicultural courses as part of their graduation requirements. Courses on African, Asian, and Latin cultures and courses on women, minorities, gays and lesbians, and other socially disadvantaged groups typically meet the multicultural requirements. Lists of core books that must be read by all students have been expanded beyond the classics written by European and American males and now include books by women and non-European scholars. In the process, some of the previous classics have been dropped from the lists, much to the dismay of traditionalists.

Multiculturalism is now making its way into the curricula of secondary and elementary schools, where it is often causing more controversy than it has at the college level. A case in point is the recently published National Standards for United States History (Gugliotta, 1994). These standards, which are simply a curriculum guide for elementary and secondary history courses, were developed over a 2½ year period by 35 national education organizations.

Everyone agrees that these new American history standards emphasize the accomplishments of minorities and women, often at the expense of males who were prominent in traditional American history courses. Lynne Cheney, former head of the National Endowment for the Humanities during the Bush administration and the official who approved the initial funding for the guidelines, is especially unhappy about the end product (Krauthammer, 1994).

Biggs, Donald, and Porter, Gerald. "Parental Choice in the U.S.A." In Mark Halstead, ed., *Parental Choice in Education.* Philadelphia: Kogan Page, 1994.

Cookson, Peter W., Jr. *School Choice: The Struggle for the Soul of American Education.* New Haven, CT: Yale University Press, 1994.

Gugliotta, Guy. "Up in Arms about the 'American Experience'," *Washington Post,* October 28, 1994.

Harmer, David. *School Choice: Why You Need It—How You Get It.* Washington, DC: Cato Institute, 1994.

Krauthammer, Charles. "History Hijacked." *Washington Post,* November 4, 1994.

Thompson, Becky W., and Tyagi, Sangeeta, eds. *Beyond a Dream Deferred: Multicultural Education and the Politics of Excellence.* Minneapolis: University of Minnesota Press, 1993.

Walford, Geoffrey. *Choice and Equity in Education.* New York: Cassell, 1994.

schools in this study are inner-city schools serving minority (primarily black) populations. This study set out to see if it makes a difference when the teachers and parents of a student have different attitudes about what constitutes "good" and "bad" student behavior (Alexander et al., 1987a). The main hypothesis of the study was that if a student's teacher and parent had the same notion of a good student (or bad student), the student would perform better in the first grade. This hypothesis was *not* supported by the research, but something equally important was found. *The values of the teachers were related to the performances of the students in their classes.*

The researchers were especially interested in the way teachers' values were negatively related to the report card grades of black first graders. The researchers speculate that "Teachers who place a premium on 'proper values' and on 'following the rules' may be especially frustrated when their expectations for how pupils ought to behave are not fulfilled in the context of predominantly black inner-city schools, and they may find themselves, whether consciously or not, grading these students down as a result" (Alexander et al., 1987a, p. 74).

In another analysis with this same sample of Baltimore first graders, the researchers found that minority students performed less well when their teachers were from high socioeconomic backgrounds. The same findings occurred among nonminority students who came from low-socioeconomic-status backgrounds. Both nonminority, low-status students and minority students had their greatest difficulties with teachers when the teachers had high-socioeconomic-status backgrounds. The high-status teachers were more apt to evaluate their students as less mature and to hold lower performance expectations for them. These high-status teachers were also the ones who had especially low scores when asked to evaluate the general climate of their schools. The picture that comes through is one of teachers who are not satisfied with their teaching settings and are, in the process, turning out low-achievement students. The sociological point of considerable significance is that the social origins of teachers can influence student academic achievement (Alexander et al., 1987a; Alexander et al., 1987b).

Long-term Effects of Elementary School Teachers

The early evaluations that teachers make of particular students may have a long-term impact on academic performance. In a follow-up study of students who had been first, second, and third graders some four to nine years earlier, evidence showed that the early influences of teachers (and parents) were continuing to affect academic performance. When these students were first studied in the early grades, their grades and achievement levels were found to be closely related to the influences of their teachers (for some students) or their parents (for other students). The teachers and parents influenced the performances of the students even when their cognitive or intellectual abilities were the same. Four to nine years later, these effects of "significant others" were still related to the school performances of these youngsters (again, among students with the same levels of cognitive ability).

Different interpretations might be made of these long-term effects of early experiences in school, but one possibility is that children incorporate as a part of their self-image a view given to them by their early teachers or by their parents. Furthermore, in school systems the grades earned one year may influence the grades earned the next year. In the researchers' words, "a 'paper person' is created that follows the child from grade to grade. Cumulative records that follow children through the school could support the children's high performance in later grades by affecting subsequent teachers' expectations" (Entwisle and Hayduk, 1988, p. 158).

Tracking and Later School Performance

One of the hotly debated topics of education is the impact that **tracking** (grouping children by ability level) has on the subsequent academic performances of students. The underlying assumption about tracking is that, when students with similar ability levels are placed in classes together, the academic gains for all students will be maximized. High-ability students will not be slowed down by the less competent students, while students with less ability will be taught at a level and pace that will be more appropriate and thus beneficial for them (Kerckhoff, 1986).

Tracking is used widely in the United States and many other countries, sometimes at the elementary school level, but especially at the junior and senior high school levels. The system appears to be widely accepted by teachers and administrators, but it has also developed a corps of critics (Oakes and Guiton, 1995). The critics build their case around three points: bias in the placement of students, inequalities in the different tracks, and the negative effects of tracking on some students.

Bias in Placement.   Studies of tracking systems have shown that minority and lower-class students are disproportionately placed in the lower tracks (Finley, 1984). In one study, white students were able to match their educational aspirations with the appropriate track better than black and Hispanic students (Kilgore, 1991). Also, once a student is in a lower track, there is very little chance of escaping. Oakes and Guiton (1995) found that almost all teachers and administrators see students' abilities, motivations, and aspirations as fixed and unchanging. This view makes it nearly impossible for students to move from one track to another once they have been placed.

Inequalities in Different Tracks.   The Oakes and Guiton study found that administrators and teachers provide the highest-quality courses for the students that they view as the most talented. They provide the richest curriculum when they view students as motivated and achievement oriented. On the other hand, when students are viewed as less motivated, the curriculum quality is lower. Courses and curricula are geared to accommodate the perceived abilities and needs of the students (Oakes and Guiton, 1995).

A participant observation study of tracking by Finley (1984) found that teachers defined the high-track classes as the most desirable classes to teach and competed for them. Teachers evaluated themselves on the basis of the ratio of high-track to low-track courses that they taught: the higher the ratio, the more positive they felt about themselves as teachers (Finlay, 1984).

Negative Effects of Tracking.   Students placed in low-ability tracks often come to define themselves as poor students, unable to do academic work, and consequently they will do poorly. In other words, the tracking system also tends to become a self-fulfilling prophecy (Eder, 1981); being placed in a high track tends to elicit high-quality performance, while being placed in a low track tends to produce poor academic performance. The following statement by a student illustrates the negative effects a tracking system can have:

> I felt good when I was with my class, but they went and separated us—that changed us. That changed our ideas, our thinking, the way we thought about each other and turned us into enemies toward each other—because they said I was dumb and they were smart (Schaefer, Olexa, and Polk, 1970, p. 12).

One interesting and perhaps surprising social psychological outcome of tracking is that some students who are placed in the high-ability tracks may experience declines in their academic self-concepts (Hoge and Renzulli, 1993). A recent Australian study found that students placed in gifted and talented programs experienced significant declines in their self-concepts in three areas of academic ability: reading, mathematics, and school generally (Marsh et al., 1995). The theoretical interpretation of this decline is that students are comparing their own academic ability to the academic ability of their more talented classmates, and some will thereby lower their own academic self-concept (Marsh et al., 1995, p. 290).

Other studies of students in different tracks have found that students in lower tracks were likely to be more alienated, distant, and punitive toward each other. Lower-track students also had more negative attitudes about themselves, were less attentive in classes, and were more negative about their futures. Lower-track classes were more apt to be disrupted, which contributed to lower reading levels. Teachers of lower-track students had lower expectations for their students (Oakes, 1982; Eder, 1981; Femlee and Eder, 1983).

The critical question about tracking is whether it does, in fact, improve the academic achievements of *all* students, as its supporters claim. Does it improve the academic performances and achievement levels of the students in the low-ability tracks as well as those in the high-ability tracks? On this question, studies coming from the United States, Great Britain, and Israel all support the same conclusion: students who are in the high-ability track generally improve their academic and intellectual performances over what they would otherwise be, but students in low-ability tracks are more likely to lower their performances (Kerckhoff, 1986; Rowan and Miracle, 1983; Shavit and Featherman, 1988).

In the Israeli study, these effects of tracking were found on cognitive intelligence tests administered to young males when they were tested for military service (Shavit and Featherman, 1988). This study finds that the experience of having been in a high-ability track in high school actually improved a person's cognitive *intelligence* level between ages 13 and 17. Students in high-track classes apparently had certain kinds of intellectual stimulation that raised their intelligence, while students in low-track classes did not. The measured intelligence of students in the low track remained the same at age 17 as it had been at age 13.

The impact of tracking on students in British schools was measured by achievement-test performances in both reading and mathematics. The evidence from this study left little doubt that students in the low-ability tracks lost ground when compared to students who had the same earlier academic performance but who were not placed in ability tracks. The opposite occurred for students in high-ability tracks: they increased their average performance level relative to comparable students in ungrouped schools. Thus, tracking improves the education of only the students who get in the high track, while it lowers the achievement levels of the students in the low track (Kerckhoff, 1986).

But the benefits of tracking, especially for those students who are placed in vocational tracks, can be evaluated in another way: Does vocational education reduce the risk of unemployment and improve the chances of entering skilled occupations (Arum and Shavit, 1995)? A sample of nearly 14,000 U.S. high school students has shown that vocational education does, in fact, reduce the risk of unemployment and increase the chances of employment in skilled occupations (Arum and Shavit, 1995). Vocational education improves the earnings and employment more for females than for males (Lewis et al., 1993).

Violence in the Schools

Stories about shootings, robbery, and rape in America's schools now appear with some regularity in the media. Many urban schools now routinely have metal detectors at the doors to deter students from bringing guns and knives into the building. Police officers and security guards patrol the halls of many schools in an effort to reduce crimes in the schools. Parents, politicians, and teachers, as well as many students, decry the apparent increases in violence in schools today (Furlong et al., 1995).

Many different kinds of violence occur in schools, ranging from thefts, physical assault, and robbery to rape and murder (Walker et al., 1995). Estimates of how often these various forms of violence occur in schools are typically based on victimization studies, in which students are asked about the violent acts that they have personally experienced (Bastian and Taylor, 1991; Furlong et al., 1995). One recent national study found that 9 percent of 12- to 19-year-old students reported being the victim of at least one crime in the 6 months prior to the survey (Bastian and Taylor, 1991).

School violence often involves victims and bullies, a form of violence defined as "the repeated physical and/or psychological harm perpetrated by one or more students on another student" (Furlong et al., 1995). Males are three times more likely than females to be the victims of school violence. African Americans are more likely to be victims of violence than white students, but generally the violence against either racial group comes from someone of the same race. Males are the most likely perpetrators of school violence (Furlong et al., 1995).

Violence in the schools by school bullies is not limited to the United States, as recent news stories from Japan demonstrate (Jordon and Sullivan, 1995; Jordon, 1996). The Japanese concern about school bullying was intensified recently when a 13-year-old boy committed suicide and left a note describing how he had been tormented by other students. At least 14 Japanese school children have committed suicide over the past year, claiming to be the victims of bullying. In Japan, bullying by schoolmates is often directed at someone who is unusual in some way; victims may be someone who is "too fat, short, quiet or even beautiful" (Jordon and Sullivan, 1995, p. A12). The Japanese tend to view negatively anyone who stands out from the group. Japanese culture generally stresses values such as self-denial, humility, and responsibility to the group over self-expression and individuality (Arnett, 1995).

Order and Control in the Classroom

One-third of American teachers say that discipline and order in the classroom is their biggest problem (Dworkin, 1987). Classroom order can be upset by student inattention, talking and laughing, classroom horseplay, or, in extreme cases, by fighting between students, or verbal and physical attacks on the teacher.

Teachers often feel nearly helpless in the face of classroom discipline problems. One researcher has concluded that "Regardless of what may be written in state law or school board regulations, the actual exercise of teacher authority is an uncertain, precarious enterprise" (Wegman, 1976).

One teacher response to potential discipline problems, especially at the high school level, has been labeled "defensive teaching" (McNeil, 1986, p. 157). Defensive teaching occurs when teachers reduce the difficulty of academic work in order to keep the support and goodwill of the students, and thus the harmony and control of their classrooms can be maintained. Another way to describe what happens in many classrooms is to see it as an implicit "bargain" between teachers and students. The teachers, on their side of the bargain, keep the academic demands low, while the students, in return, are reasonably well behaved and passive (Sedlak et al., 1986). By "spoon-feeding" easy academic material, teachers are able to keep peace in their classrooms and avoid behavior problems.

Different explanations may be given as to why defensive teaching is necessary in today's schools. One reason already given is that life for the teacher can be easier by striking a bargain with the students. If the material is simple and can be evaluated as right or wrong through objective examinations and quizzes, classroom teaching is easier. But probably a more important reason, one that most teachers quickly learn, is that if discipline is not maintained in one's classroom, the repercussions are serious. School superintendents and principals judge classroom performance largely on the absence of problems. As one observer has noted:

> A teacher will rarely, if ever, be called on the carpet or denied tenure because his [or her] students have not learned anything; he [she] will certainly be rebuked if his [her] students are talking or moving about the classroom, or—even worse—found outside the room...(Silberman, 1970, p. 140).

The obvious result of defensive teaching and the classroom bargain is that educational quality is lowered. Knowledge is sacrificed for control, and the students are sold short in their educations (McNeil, 1986; Sedlak et al., 1986).

Summary

Government-supported education on the American continent had its beginnings in 1647. The first formal schools were influenced by religious interests, but later occupational and economic factors became predominant influences. In the 1800s a universal education system emerged, a system, which, from a *traditional* view, was important for a democratic society and provided equal opportunities for all children. An alternative historical view, labeled *revisionist,* emphasizes that the economic and social elites of the society develop an educational system that meets their needs. The Lancaster system of education is an example of a system that produced workers suited for the industrial workplace.

Functionalist theory, paralleling the traditional view of education, emphasizes how education is an integrating institution. Education helps to socialize children coming from diverse backgrounds, presenting them with an ideal version of the society and culture. Functional theory takes a positive view of education, emphasizing how students are rewarded for their ability and hard work.

Conflict theory, recognizing the conflicts of interest among different groups and categories of people, stresses that powerful interest groups in the society will control the educational system for their own ends. The educational system serves the powerful by providing the workers needed by the economic interests of the society. Conflict theorists also see the educational system as favoring the children of the advantaged groups over the disadvantaged.

The worldwide picture with respect to education has improved dramatically since the 1950s. Although great advances have been made, some areas of the world, notably in Africa and parts of Asia, many children receive only minimal schooling, and educational funds are often inequitably distributed. In many countries, especially the less developed ones, females receive less education than males.

The educational system does not serve different groups in the population equally. Blacks, Hispanics, and students from lower socioeconomic backgrounds tend to succeed less often in the educational system than those from the dominant white population. A college education today gives a great advantage in the occupational world and therefore the economic world. An education from one of the elite colleges or universities is a key to top corporate management in both the United States and Japan. Graduate and professional degrees from the elite schools (Harvard Law School, for example) get the best and generally the highest paying jobs. By contrast, students who begin at community colleges are at a disadvantage in the job market.

In recent decades, many people have been critical of the performance of the U.S. educational system. Over 20 years, there has been no measurable improvement in reading proficiency among American students, although minorities did make some improvements. Mathematical proficiency did improve somewhat for the 9- and 13-year-olds, but not for 17-year-olds. Writing proficiency has not changed much since 1973.

American schools are inequitably financed. Generally, urban schools, especially those with minority students, are the least well supported financially, which means that their educational programs are inadequate.

A key social aspect of the educational system is the relationship between teachers and students. The evaluations that teachers make of students, even if based on false assumptions, can influence how they grade students. The values and social class origins of teachers also are related to how teachers grade students. The influence of teachers at elementary grade levels tends to be long-lasting.

Tracking students according to ability level is supposed to maximize the academic performances of all students, but the evidence shows that it has a positive effect on the high-track students and a negative effect on the low-track students.

Violence in American schools has become a serious problem. Violence by bullies is a serious problem both in the United States and Japan.

Order and control in schools and in the classrooms is an important problem in American education. Many teachers lower their educational standards as a way of maintaining control of the students in their classrooms.

CRITICAL THINKING

1. Compare and contrast the traditional view of the history of U.S. education with that of the revisionists. Which view does the Lancaster example support?
2. Assume, as the functionalists do, that the education system serves a moral function. Give examples of norms and values you have learned in school.
3. Compare and contrast the conflict and functional sociological interpretations of educational systems.
4. In the less developed countries, females are generally given less education than males. How would you explain this gender inequality?
5. How would you explain the fact that reading proficiency among American students has not increased in the last 20 years?
6. Does our educational system provide equal opportunity for all individuals in society? Use information from the chapter to support your conclusion.
7. In what ways might schools serve the needs of the advantaged and powerful people in society?
8. Does tracking perpetuate inequality? Use evidence from the chapter to support your conclusion.
9. What effect does defensive teaching have on the quality of education? What suggestions can you make to reverse this situation?

13

The Economy and Work

The **economy** is the social institution involved in the production and exchange of a wide range of goods and services. These activities are accomplished by various economic elements, including businesses, industries, corporations, markets for goods, labor markets, the banking system, labor unions, relevant government agencies, and occupations.

In this chapter we look at the economy, as well as many of its components. We begin with an examination of broad changes in the economy, including the Industrial Revolution and the changing nature of capitalism. Then we turn more specifically to the changing nature of the U.S. economy, as well as some of the problems being produced by these changes. We will also discuss and analyze a few of the possible solutions to America's economic problems. In the final section of this chapter, we will examine individual experiences in the work world.

Historical Changes in the Economy

Revolutionary changes in the economy have occurred during the last century, and the next century promises many more to come. Because much of the future of the U.S. economy will be shaped by past changes, we need to understand some of the major developments of the past as well as the dynamics of the present (Hearn, 1988).

The Industrial Revolution

To understand modern economies and the nature of work in the United States today, we must go back to the nineteenth century and the **Industrial Revolution,** which introduced the factory system of production. In this system, machines replaced hand tools, and steam and other sources of energy replaced human or animal power. The many workers who operated the machines ranged from the highly skilled to the almost totally unskilled. Because much of the needed skill was already built into the machine, skilled workers could be replaced by adults and children with little or no training, who worked long hours for low pay. The transformation of workers into machine tenders led to a decline in the use of skilled workers and a rise in the use of unskilled workers.

Another defining characteristic of this age was the elaborate division of labor whereby a single product went through the hands of a number of workers, each of whom performed a small step in the entire production process. Adam Smith depicted this development in his famous description of the new method of producing pins. Under the old system a single person producing a whole pin could produce only a few each day, but in the new division of labor a group of ten workers could produce almost 5000 pins each per day. He describes the division of labor:

> One man draws out the wire; another straights it, a third cuts it; a fourth points it; a fifth grinds it at the top for receiving the head; to make the head requires two or three distinct operations; to put it on is a peculiar business; to whiten the pin is another; it is even a trade by itself to put them into the paper; and the important business of making a pin is in this manner divided into about eighteen distinct operations, which in some manufactories are all performed by distinct hands (Smith, 1937, pp. 4–5).

The first factories were primitive affairs, but they gave way over the years to larger and more efficient entities geared to mass production. **Mass production** had a variety of characteristics: products were standardized; parts were made interchangeable; precision tools were used so that parts could be made to fit universally; the production process was mechanized to yield high volume; the flow of materials to the machine and products from the machine were synchronized; and the entire process was made as continuous as possible. This, of course, is the assembly-line type of production that continues today in such industries as automobile manufacturing. These systems reached their fullest application in the United States in the mid-twentieth century and spread throughout the world.

The Changing Nature of Capitalist Economic Systems

Capitalism is an economic system that emphasizes the private ownership of property and the means of production. The owners of property and especially the means of production are expected to strive for economic gains called *profits*. Capitalism is the guiding economic philosophy in many societies, including most prominently the United States, and is even coming to affect the economy of Russia (Burawoy and Krotov, 1992).

Karl Marx on Capitalism. As we saw in Chapter 8, social theorist Karl Marx offered a critical analysis and description of capitalist systems. He saw capitalist societies as divided into two social classes, one of which exploited the other. One class, the capitalist, owned the means of production, which included land, raw materials such as mines and forests, and factories with all their tools and machinery. The other class, the proletariat, was forced to sell its labor time to the capitalist class in order to have access to the commodities produced by the economic system. The capitalists pay the workers for their labor time, but, as Marx emphasized, the workers are paid *less* than the value of what they produce for the capitalist. The gap between the costs of labor and production and the worth of what is produced is called the profit.

Marx saw the capitalist system as exploitative of the proletariat because the workers were paid only enough for survival for themselves and their families. The capitalists, by contrast, could reinvest their profits and expand their businesses. The general success of the capitalist class is therefore derived from exploiting the work of the proletariat.

Writing in the mid-1800s, Marx was describing capitalism in its heyday. Over the years capitalism has changed tremendously, and many neo-Marxian scholars have attempted to adapt Marx's ideas to the changing realities of capitalist society. For example, the capitalism of Marx's day can be described as **competitive capitalism.** No one capitalist, or small group of capitalists, could gain complete and uncontested control over a market. Although it was Marx who foresaw the growth of monopolies, Baran and Sweezy (1966) designated modern capitalist society as **monopoly capitalism.** In this updated type of capitalism, one or a few capitalists control a given sector of the economy. Monopoly capitalism weakens competition and introduces changes in the control structure of capitalist enterprises. In competitive capitalism an enterprise tended to be controlled by a single capitalist–entrepreneur. In monopoly capitalism, however, the modern corporation is owned by a large number of stockholders, although often a few large stockholders own most of the shares in a given company. Although stockholders "own" the company, managers exercise the actual day-to-day control. Managers are crucial in monopoly capitalism, whereas the entrepreneurs were central in competitive capitalism. One by-product of this distinction is that Marx's simple model of opposition between capitalist and proletariat no longer applies. Who are the capitalists?

Are the millions of people who own a few shares of stock in General Motors capitalists? Are the managers of modern enterprises capitalists? Or are they members of the proletariat, since they are employees of the organization? These are just a few of the questions raised by changes in the capitalist system during the last century.

Another significant change in capitalism has been the growth of white-collar and service workers and the decline of the blue-collar workers whom Marx saw as the proletariat. Can Marx's theory of exploitation be extended to white-collar and service occupations? Making such an extension, Braverman (1974) argued that the concept of the proletariat describes not a specific group of people or occupations but a process of buying and selling labor power. Like blue-collar workers, white-collar and service workers are forced to sell their labor time to capitalists, although the impact of this exploitation and control is not yet as great as it has been on blue-collar occupations.

The Changing Nature of Worker Control.   Braverman recognized economic exploitation, which was Marx's focus, but he concentrated on the issue of managerial control over workers. (Smith, 1994; Bacharach and Bamberger, 1995; Edwards, 1979) sees control at the heart of the transformation of the workplace in the twentieth century. Following Marx, Edwards sees the workplace, both past and present, as an arena of class conflict—in his terms, a "contested terrain." Within this arena, dramatic changes have taken place in the way in which those at the top control those at the bottom. In nineteenth-century competitive capitalism, simple personal control was used. The "bosses exercised power personally, intervening in the labor process often to exhort workers, bully and threaten them, reward good performance, hire and fire on the spot, favor loyal workers, and generally act as despots, benevolent or otherwise" (Edwards, 1979, p. 19). Although this system continues to survive in small businesses, it has generally been undermined by the growth of large organizations. Simple **personal control** has been replaced by *impersonal technical* and *bureaucratic control.*

Technology is often used today as a way of controlling workers. The classic example is the assembly line found, for example, in the production of automobiles or farm machines, or in the processing of meat and other food. When workers are on an assembly line, their actions are controlled by the incessant demands of the moving line.

In today's industries and businesses many kinds of electronic automated equipment are used by management to increase control over workers. For example, telephone operators today do not have to be carefully watched and controlled by human supervisors because every operator's work is monitored by electronic equipment that records the exact amount of time an operator spends on each customer call. Operators know how long they should be spending to process each request, so there is no time for a friendly word before moving on quickly to the next caller. Technological control also diminishes the quality of the work experience (it is more boring, stressful, and the like) and demeans the lives of workers.

Many kinds of jobs do not take advantage of the distinctive human ability to think, create, and be inventive (Shaiken, 1986; Zuboff, 1988).

Still another modern form of control is revealed in Nicole Biggart's (1989) study of direct-selling organizations such as Mary Kay Cosmetics, Tupperware, and Amway. Those involved in direct selling work largely on their own and therefore cannot be controlled through direct personal supervision, technology, or bureaucracy. Biggart shows instead that direct-selling organizations use *morality* to control those who do the selling for them. For example, the organizations seek to instill in the sellers the idea that such work is more than a job—it is a total way of life encompassing not just the material world, but the spiritual and civic realms as well. Direct-selling organizations also often wrap what they are doing in cloaks of religiosity and patriotism. Overall, direct-selling organizations create an elaborate moral system that controls those who do the selling for them.

The Changing State of the U.S. Economy and the Problems Created by Those Changes

Given the preceding discussion of changes in the capitalistic system, we turn now to a more specific discussion of changes in the American economy, as well as the problems produced by these changes. These changes have become so omnipresent and so dramatic that one of the authors (Ritzer, 1989) has labeled this a "permanently new economy."

Changes in the Labor Force

Overall, the labor force in the United States will grow by over 26 million new jobs between 1992 and 2005, from 121.1 million to 147.5 million workers (Silvestri, 1993); the labor force was 131 million in 1994 (U.S. Bureau of the Census, 1994a, p. 399). Furthermore, there will continue to be major shifts within the labor force, changes that have been occurring throughout the twentieth century (see Table 13–1). The most dramatic of these, at least over the full course of the century, has been the decline in the number of people who work in farm-related occupations: agricultural, forestry, fishing, and related occupations. In 1900, just under 40 percent of the labor force was found in such occupations, but that percentage steadily declined throughout the twentieth century. Between 1992 and 2005, it is expected that there will be a slight increase in this category, but since this increase will be far less than that for any other category, its relative position will continue to erode. By the year 2005, only 2.5 percent of workers will be in farm-related occupations (Silvestri, 1993, p. 59). When we focus specifically on farmers, we find it is projected to be the occupation with *the* largest job decline between 1992 and 2005 (farm workers rank fourth in terms of projected job decline).

Table 13–1   Employment by Major Occupational Group, 1992 and Projected 2005, Moderate Alternative Projection, and Percent Change 1979–1992 and 1992–2005

	1992		2005		Percent change	
					1979–	1992–
Occupation	Number	Percent	Number	Percent	1992	2005
Total, all occupations	121,099	100.0	147,482	100.0	19.0	21.8
Executives, administrative, and managerial	12,066	10.0	15,195	10.3	50.4	25.9
Professional specialty	16,592	13.7	22,801	15.5	43.0	37.4
Technicians and related support	4,282	3.5	5,664	3.8	57.6	32.2
Marketing and sales	12,993	10.7	15,664	10.6	30.7	20.6
Administrative support, including clerical	22,349	18.5	25,406	17.2	15.0	13.7
Service	19,358	16.0	25,820	17.5	24.6	33.4
Agricultural, forestry, fishing and related occupations	3,530	2.9	3,650	2.5	–5.2	3.4
Precision production, craft, and repair	13,580	11.2	15,380	10.4	4.3	13.3
Operators, fabricators, and laborers	16,349	13.5	17,902	12.1	–10.3	9.5

(Number in thousands)

Note: The 1992 and 2005 employment data and the projected change 1992–2005 are derived from the industry–occupation employment matrices for each year. The data on 1979–1992 percent change were derived from the Current Population Survey (CPS) because a comparable industry–occupation matrix for 1979 is not available. The CPS data represent estimates of employed persons and exclude the estimates of persons with more than one job that are included in the industry–occupation employment matrices. The CPS exclusions of dual jobholders affects the employment levels and trends of some occupational groups more than others. Therefore, the resulting comparisons of change between 1979–1992 and 1992–2005 are only broadly indicative of trends.

Source: George Silvestri, "Occupational Employment: Wide Variations in Growth." *Monthly Labor Review,* November 1993, p. 59.

A number of social changes are implicated in the decline of farm work (Ilg, 1995). Technological changes such as improved farm equipment, fertilization, and irrigation have increased productivity and reduced the need for farm workers. Economies of scale have allowed fewer people to produce ever greater quantities of food. Increased costs of equipment and land have driven many people out of farming. Many of those who once worked in agriculture have been drawn off the farms by the new jobs being created in the service sector. Today, the independent farmer, in the process of being replaced by agribusiness, is on the verge of extinction.

Another occupational category undergoing a decline is operators, fabricators, and laborers. Many of those in this category are blue-collar workers associated with manufacturing industries. In fact, this category declined far more steeply between 1979 and 1992 than did agricultural workers. Technological advancement and the downsizing of these industries, as well as the movement of many of these jobs to other countries, have led to the decline in this occupational category. While these changes will continue, this occupational group will increase somewhat between 1992 and 2005, although also at a rate slower than that of the other occupational categories (except agricultural workers).

The percentage of the labor force in the professional specialty (Macdonald, 1995) almost quadrupled between 1900 and 1982. The category continues to undergo strong growth; by 2005, 15.5 percent of the labor force will be in the professions, compared to 13.7 percent in 1992. Major factors responsible for this rise include increasingly sophisticated knowledge, technologies that require more highly trained people (this also helps to account for the strong growth among technicians and related support), and increasing wealth and sophistication that allow us to want and afford a wide array of professional services.

The largest occupational category in 2005 will be service. This is reflective of the long-term change in the United States away from goods production and in the direction of service provision (Rosenthal, 1995). Included in this category would be food preparation workers, nursing aides, home health aides, and child care workers.

In recent years, the great growth has been in low-paying (for example, food service workers) and high-paying occupations (for example, professionals) (Rosenthal, 1995). This would seem to indicate a growth in income disparity in the coming years.

Fastest Growing Occupations.   In fact, it is service workers—home health aides, human service workers (many in health and human services), personal and home care aides—that are expected to be the fastest growing occupations between now and 2005 (see Figure 13–1). In part, this is a reflection of the aging of the American population and the growing demand for health and medical services. It is also linked to the high cost of medical care and the fact that it is often cheaper to care for people at home than in a hospital or nursing home. Finally, we have grown more accustomed to and able to afford having others do the things that people themselves, family members, and friends used to do. The growth in the next two fastest growing occupations—computer engineers and scientists and systems analysts—is obviously a reflection of the enormous increase in the importance of computers in our lives. These two computer-related occupations are followed by two more health-related occupations—physical and corrective therapy assistants and physical therapists. Thus, *all* the top seven occupations in terms of growth are directly related to dramatic social changes in health and computerization (Silvestri, 1993).

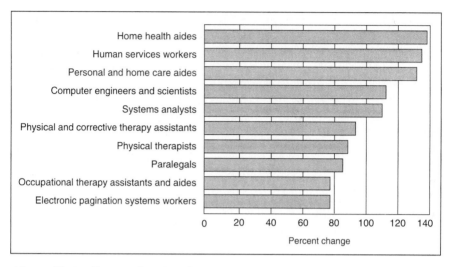

Figure 13–1.   Fastest Growing Occupations: 1992 to 2005. (*Source: Statistical Abstract of the United States: 1994* (114th edition). Washington, D.C.: U.S. Bureau of the Census, 1994, p. 394.)

Increasing Importance of Women in the Labor Force.   One of the most dramatic changes in the last few decades has been the increasing number of women in the labor force. In 1970, slightly more than a third of the labor force was female, but by 1992 women constituted 45.5 percent of the labor force. The projections are that by 2005 women will constitute 47.7 percent of the labor force (Fullerton, 1993). Between 1979 and 1992, the annual growth rate for women (2.1 percent) in the labor force was more than twice that for men (1.0 percent). Between 1992 and 2005, the projections are that the difference in the growth rates will narrow somewhat (1.7 percent for women and 1.0 percent for men). To put the overall change another way, the percentage of females in the labor force has risen from 43.3 percent in 1970 to a projected 63.2 percent in 2005 [by contrast the percentage of males is projected to decline from 79.7 percent in 1970 to 74.7 percent in 2005 (U.S. Bureau of the Census, 1995b, p. 399)]. Female participation in the labor force will continue to grow, but not as rapidly as it did in the 1970s and 1980s.

Although women appear to be doing quite well in the work world, many problems remain. For example, although there is much variation within occupations and organizations (Anderson and Tomaskovic-Devey, 1995), a stubborn pay gap (the percentage of male income earned by female workers) of between 60 and 70 percent (Ryscavage and Henle, 1990, p. 4) exists between female and male earnings, and women have a long way to go before achieving pay parity with men (Hodson and England, 1986). More generally, gender segregation has been declining, although interestingly it did not decline as much in the 1980s as it did in the 1970s (Cotter et al., 1995).

The occupational world continues to be sex-segregated (Reskin and Padovic, 1994), with "women's jobs" (for example, nurses) and "men's jobs" (for example, physicians) being the norm. However, the positions in which females predominate tend to be lower-paying and more likely to be dead-end positions with little likelihood of upward mobility (England, 1992; Jacobs, 1992). When females venture into male occupations, they tend to encounter structural disadvantages, while when men enter traditionally female occupations they tend to be advantaged structurally (Williams, 1989, 1992). Another continuing problem for women is the lack of adequate corporate child-care facilities (Fernandez, 1986; Wash and Brand, 1990). This need has become particularly pressing in the 1990s, since 60 percent of women are working by the time their children are four years of age. Approximately 28 million children are living in households in which the mother works for at least part of the day on a regular basis (Wash and Brand, 1990, p. 20). These difficult problems are among many others that remain for women despite their significant gains in the labor force.

Changing Labor Unions

In 1900, only 3 percent of the labor force of the United States belonged to unions, but the percentage grew to 23 percent by the end of World War II. A decline began in the early 1960s, and by 1994 the percentage had dropped to 15.5 percent (U.S. Bureau of the Census, 1995b, p. 433). Between 1979 and 1994, total union membership declined by almost 4.4 million (Williamson, 1994). Estimates indicate that the union movement will continue to decline for the foreseeable future (Lipset, 1987).

The situation is not quite as grim if we look at the membership of the largest conglomerate of unions in the United States, the AFL–CIO. Between 1979 and 1993, membership in the AFL–CIO decreased by only 322,000 members. Its 1993 membership of 13.3 million is not dramatically below its all-time high of 14.07 members in 1975 (U.S. Bureau of the Census, 1995b, p. 443; Swoboda, 1991). However, as is clear in Figure 13–2, membership in the AFL–CIO has failed dismally to keep pace with the overall growth in the labor force. Thus, while membership in the AFL–CIO has not changed dramatically since 1955, the American labor force has increased dramatically. One could say that by remaining more or less stable the AFL–CIO has lost significant ground. There have been a few bright spots for the AFL–CIO in recent years, but overall the future prospects are not good.

Not only have unions lost members, but they have shown evidence of decline in other ways as well. Although in the past many unions could often negotiate large wage increases for their members, in recent years wage increases have generally been small. In fact, in the 1990s pay raises for nonunion workers have generally outpaced those for union workers. In 1995, employer costs for nonunion

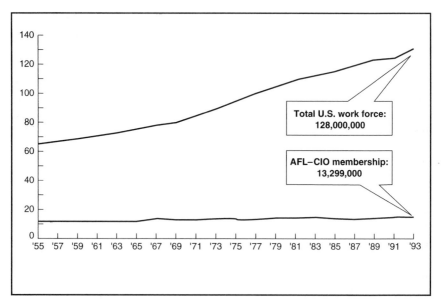

Figure 13–2.   Slow Union Gains: AFL–CIO Is Growing More Slowly Than the U.S. Work Force (in millions). (*Source:* U.S. Bureau of the Census, *Statistical Abstract of the United States, 1994.* Washington, D.C.: U.S. Government Printing Office, 1994, pp. 395, 438; Frank Swoboda, "AFL–CIO Membership Is Shifting." *Washington Post,* October 31, 1991, p. A17.)

workers rose by 2.9 percent, one-half percent *less* than those for union workers (Zachary, 1996). However, it should be pointed out that research has shown that the presence of unions leads to wage increases among nonunionized workers (Leicht et al., 1993). Employers often pay their nonunion employees a premium in the hope that higher wages will reduce their interest in joining a union. In addition, in order to get contracts with management, unions have been giving up rights and benefits they had won in previous contract negotiations (Katz, 1985). One of the most striking changes has been the decline in the use of the strike as a weapon in collective bargaining (Cimini, 1991). In the 1960s there were 300 or more strikes per year involving 1000 or more workers, but such strikes began declining in the mid-1970s and by 1994 there were only 45 such strikes in the United States. Afraid of losing even more jobs (and members) and fearful that strikes would push already marginal companies to close their doors altogether, unions are increasingly reluctant to use their most powerful weapon. "The strike has become, in effect, the nuclear device in labor's arsenal of weapons, something only to be used in total warfare when the union is willing to risk destruction ..." (Swoboda, 1992a, p. H1).

Another measure of the decline in union power is the growing weakness of one of its most powerful weapons, the picket line. During the heyday of unions, when a picket line was set up, large numbers of people refused to cross it. However, with the decline in union power, most people either do not identify with unions or are even hostile to them, with the result that they are much more likely to ignore picket lines. Picket lines retain some power in strong union cities like Pittsburgh and Detroit. But even in these cities, unions must make their case and convince the community; there is no longer an assumption among people that they will honor a picket line (Mehta, 1996). In a variety of ways, unions are weaker overall, including in their ability to negotiate with management. In numbers and in power, the U.S. labor movement is the weakest in the Western world.

Factors Involved in Union Decline.   Four key factors help to explain the decline in union membership: lack of competition among unions, worker resistance to unionization, management opposition to unions, and technological change. First, the union movement itself lost some of its dynamism because the internal competition between union organizations was reduced. The most notable case of reducing union competitiveness came when the two major unions, the AFL (American Federation of Labor) and the CIO (Congress of Industrial Organizations), combined to form the AFL–CIO, a single union organization.

Second, by the early 1950s, unions had already organized a large proportion of the group most receptive to unionization—blue-collar factory workers. When they had to look elsewhere for members, they found that other occupations proved resistant to union membership drives.

As one example, unions have not succeeded in organizing white-collar workers. Many white-collar workers are women, and females have historically been less likely to join unions, partly because of negative attitudes toward unions and partly because of their structural position in the work world. Among the structural factors is the fact that women are more apt to be in sectors of the economy (for example, bureaucracies rather than industries) where unionization is less common (Freeman and Medoff, 1984).

Unions have also failed to attract young people. As with the underrepresentation of women, the reason is not primarily a lack of desire to join unions but the result of a series of structural factors (Freeman and Medoff, 1984). For example, young people are often in temporary jobs, and temporary workers are clearly less interested in unions and more difficult to unionize than permanent employees.

It is also worth noting that unions have been historically underrepresented in the South, and unions continue to be largely unable to make inroads in that region of the country (Roscigno and Kimble, 1995).

The third factor in the decline of unions is management opposition (Goldfield, 1987; Fantasia, 1992). Management in the United States has never been favorably disposed to the union movement. (In other societies, especially in Western Europe, management has been much more accepting of unions.) In the earlier part of this century, management hired thugs and killers to keep unions out. More recently, most companies came to accept unions, even though grudgingly. But in the 1980s and 1990s management opposition to unions rose again. One successful move has been for companies to discontinue operations, or restructure the company, and thus break union contracts. Later the operations may be reestablished under a new name or different management, but the newly hired workers are non-union. Also, many company managers have stepped up their efforts to avoid unionization (Lawler and West, 1985).

The fourth factor in the decline of unions has been technological change that reduces jobs. Often the jobs eliminated are blue-collar jobs, which were most likely to have been unionized. A good example of this trend is in the printing industry, once one of the bastions of union strength. In the old days when type was set by skilled hands, a large proportion of the workers was unionized. However, manual typesetting has been replaced by computer technology, and virtually all of the skilled manual jobs have disappeared. With the disappearance of those jobs came a decline in union membership, and consequently the decline and disappearance of unions in the typesetting industry (Scott, 1987). More generally, new technologies such as computers and robots often cost jobs, and these lost jobs often translate into declines in union membership and union power.

Union Responses to Declines in Numbers.   Unions have tried to adapt to their new, reduced situation by concentrating on new groups of workers like government employees, health workers, and professional athletes. They have also tried to develop a series of new goals such as job guarantees for members, the prevention of the loss of American jobs to other countries, and new benefits for members (Cornfield, 1989).

Another way that unions have sought to adapt to their decline is through mergers with other unions. Mergers bring with them a variety of advantages by allowing the merged unions to "enhance bargaining and organizing power, achieve economies of scale, eliminate costly duplication of efforts, and increase financial and administrative resources" (Williamson, 1995, p. 24). On the other hand, there are costs, especially to the union, that have been absorbed as a result of the merger, including "an abandonment of history and tradition, and a loss of the institution's identity; and a loss of status for the leadership, and the need for the membership to adapt to the policies, practices, and philosophy of another organization" (Williamson, 1995, p. 24). In spite of the costs, we are likely to see more union mergers in an effort to deal with the new realities and difficulties facing the union movement.

In addition to the factors discussed above, union decline is also linked to the decline in U.S. heavy industry, where many unionized workers have been employed. As these industries have laid off workers, shut plants down, and "downsized," unions have lost large numbers of members. We turn now to a detailed discussion of this industrial decline, one that is often called **deindustrialization.**

Deindustrialization

While U.S. industry continues to dominate the capitalist world, it is not the powerful force it once was. Many U.S. industries, especially steel and automobiles, have declined—a process Bluestone and Harrison (1982) call "the deindustrialization of America."

A major manifestation of deindustrialization is the dramatic drop in employment in such key "smokestack" industries as steel (Hicks, 1992). In addition, many workers have been "dislocated," which in most cases means they have lost their jobs forever. They not only lose their jobs but they also may forfeit their benefits (health insurance, retirement, and the like). They are apt to be laid off with few skills and with few opportunities for the training needed for many of the high-tech occupations now being created by our economy. For many, their only options are jobs such as selling hamburgers in fast-food restaurants. Many blue-collar workers have lost their jobs, but increasingly managers and professionals are not immune to major reductions in force (*Fortune,* 1988a).

The Downsizing of American Industry.   As we will see in the accompanying In the News box, "Downsizing at AT&T (and Elsewhere)," downsizing is another major change taking place in work in America. Why are so many American companies cutting their work forces so dramatically?

First, technological change has eliminated the need for many jobs. It is often the case that because of technology fewer workers are needed, and in some cases the technology can do the job more or less on its own. Second, corporate mergers (discussed later) have created situations in which newly merged companies have more employees than they need. Third, many tasks are now being done overseas, making jobs in the United States unnecessary. Fourth, the highly competitive and changing marketplace has made many companies feel that they must be lean in order to compete successfully. Fifth, the increasing number of temporary workers makes it easier for companies to let full-time workers go and hire part-timers when there is a need for them. Sixth, the savings on labor cost tend to increase profits and to drive up the price of corporate stock. Finally, downsizing has become the corporate fad of the 1990s.

Thus, there are many reasons for corporate downsizing, and we are likely to see more of it for the foreseeable future.

Disinvestment, Mergers, and Takeovers.   Another aspect of the deindustrialization of America is the fact that many U.S. companies have stopped reinvesting substantial sums of money in their own growth and development (Bluestone and Harrison, 1982, p. 6). To maintain productivity as well as to stimulate growth, industries must invest in basic plant and equipment. This kind of industrial investment made the United States the world's greatest economic power. However, in recent years, money has been diverted from such productive investment. For example, instead of investing in new plants and equipment in the United States, corporations are investing in similar facilities in other countries.

Another major source of disinvestment is the merger and takeover mania that swept through the U.S. corporate world. Mergers between corporations cost money and, in themselves, produce no new factories, technologies, or jobs. Even more threatening are the huge multibillion dollar takeover efforts that have become commonplace in U.S. industry (and more recently in banking). In such efforts, one organization may borrow billions of dollars to take over another organization. Since the money is borrowed, it adds nothing to the productivity of the economy. In fact, in the case of takeovers, the economy may actually lose productive capacity as corporations that are taken over are dismantled and sold off in pieces in order to finance the takeover.

The Winner-Take-All Society.   Robert Frank and Philip Cook (1995) have recently described the emergence of what they call the "winner-take-all society" (see also, Pearlstein, 1995a). They see this as occurring at many different levels in society, but our interest is in its increasing occurrence within the economy. Basically, the free market is operating in such a way that those businesses and organizations with only a small advantage over competitors end up completely dominating a sector of the economy. A good recent example is Microsoft, which exercises control over the basic functions of the vast majority of computers in the world. Indeed, many recent mergers are aimed at gaining this kind of control over a sector of the economy.

This process is clearest and most obvious in the retail sector, where the so-called "category killers" have become increasingly dominant (Pearlstein, 1995a). These huge chains of specialized, nationwide (and increasingly international) superstores characterized by their enormous selection are driving many of their smaller competitors out of business. Included here would be chains like Border's (books), Circuit City and Best Buy (electronics), Staples (office supplies), and Toys Я Us. While small companies might still be able to find a niche for themselves, mid-sized companies find it almost impossible to compete with the category killers. They are likely to be driven out of business, leaving the category killers as the winners dominating much, if not all, of the market.

The U.S. Economy in the Coming Years

Although there have been problems in the recent history of the U.S. economy, there are a number of positive and hopeful signs. In the retail sector, U.S. chains are an increasing presence around the world. American financial institutions are preeminent in the world marketplace, most notably in the credit card business, where Visa, MasterCard and American Express are the credit cards of choice throughout the world (Ritzer, 1995). Then there is the American dominance of the Internet, as well as the businesses that are sprouting on and around it.

In the News

Downsizing at AT&T (and Elsewhere)

The long-term trend toward the downsizing of American corporations, especially large corporations, reached new heights in late 1995 when AT&T announced that it would lay off 40,000 employees (70 percent of them before the end of 1996). The number of people to be laid off is 13 percent of AT&T's worldwide work force of about 300,000 people. While the number to be let go is extraordinary, layoffs are not new phenomena at AT&T; in fact, the company has been laying off about 900 employees a month for over a decade. One is led to believe that this new round of huge layoffs must indicate that AT&T is experiencing great financial difficulties. Not so! AT&T earned almost $5 billion in 1994 and nearly $3 billion in the first nine months of 1995. The company is laying off tens of thousands of workers in the midst of a booming business. And the workers, who often feel that they made a significant contribution to that profitability, are, in the main, not happy about their predicament.

However, the company is not just throwing these people out onto the street. The layoff of 40,000 people includes about 7,500 managers who had previously accepted a reasonably generous buy-out offer from the company. Others in the group to be laid off will receive a lump sum payment of between 5 and 35 weeks of salary. In addition, many will receive money to help in retraining and relocation.

In spite of such efforts to ease the blow, the layoffs at AT&T (and many other companies) represent a major change in the way American companies relate to their employees. AT&T chairman Robert E. Allen acknowledged that both employees and the company used to have a lifelong commitment to one another. However, such a commitment is now a thing of the past. Furthermore, employees now recognize that diligence and commitment to the company no longer translate into job security for life (Church, 1996). AT&T now feels free to let employees, even those of long standing, go whenever they find it necessary, or even just desirable. For their part, employees tend to feel less and less allegiance to AT&T and most other companies.

Why did AT&T lay off so many employees? After all, it was enormously profitable even with all its employees. The company would argue that it did so in order to be able to continue to remain viable in what it perceives to be the increasingly competitive world of telecommunications. It would also argue that it did so to be responsive to and please its owners—the stockholders. In fact, AT&T stock went up $3 a share when the layoff was announced. While bad for the victims of downsizing, layoffs often increase the profitability of the company (through, among other things, labor-cost savings) and operate to the advantage of stockholders.

Of course, as we saw in the text, the downsizing at AT&T is just part of a very broad process occurring throughout American business. In 1995, plans were announced to cut almost 440,000 jobs in the United States. This represents a decline from 516,000 announced cuts in 1994 and the peak of

640,000 such cuts in 1993. However, it is worth noting that these are just announced cuts and do not include many other unannounced reductions in force made by many companies, both large and small (Mahoney, 1996). As a result, workers have had to rethink their relationships to their jobs and their employers. Employers are increasingly unlikely to think of having employees for life, and, for their part, workers are beginning to assume that they are going to change jobs and/or employers a number of times during their lifetimes. Victims of this process are coming to see the lack of job permanence as an inevitable fact of life in the 1990s.

Experts in the field of placing the newly unemployed know that a revolution is taking place. For those in marginal occupations, the situation is growing worse. Downsizing has a negative impact on two types of workers: those who lose their jobs feel betrayed because they believed their jobs were permanent; those who retain their jobs (at least for the moment), are in a permanent state of anxiety wondering when it will be their turns to lose their jobs (Mahoney, 1996).

As many companies are laying off thousands of full-time workers, a remarkable growth is taking place in temporary work. About 2 million temporary employees went to work each day in 1994. This represents a 69 percent increase over the amount of temporary work in 1994 (Mahoney, 1996). In fact, a striking statistic is that more people (600,000) are currently employed by one temporary agency, Manpower, Inc., than are employed by General Motors (375,000) (Mashberg, 1996).

One consequence of the loss of full-time jobs and the rise in part-time and temporary employment is growing income inequality. Clearly, temporary workers are going to have a more difficult time sustaining an affluent or even a decent lifestyle. There are likely to be periods of unemployment, sometimes of long duration, between temporary jobs. Furthermore, temporary workers are not going to have the health and life insurance coverage of full-time workers, as well as the other benefits that the latter type of workers has grown accustomed to. As a result, one economist concludes, "The Achilles' heel of the U.S. economy is that inequality is rising, that not everybody is sharing" (Reno, 1996). Those being laid off at AT&T and other American companies, many of whom will be lucky to get temporary work, are clearly among those who are not going to get what they assumed was going to be their share of the American dream.

Church, George J. "Disconnected: How AT&T Is Planning to Put 40,000 Members of Its Work Force Out of Service." *Time,* January 15, 1996.

Mahoney, Jerry. "Once Safe, Careers Now Hanging in the Balance; Downsizing, Restructuring or Whatever the Term, Capable People Are Losing Jobs." *Austin American-Statesman,* January 14, 1996.

Mashberg, Tom. "Mass. Middle Managers Cope with Job Loss; 'Downsizing' Forces Them to Be Creative; Changing Times Mean More Layoffs." *Boston Herald,* January 14, 1996.

Reno, Robert. "U.S. Economy Faces Double Whammy." *Sun-Sentinel* (Fort Lauderdale), January 18, 1996.

Many believe that manufacturing continues to be the key to the economic prosperity of the United States. While many of the problems discussed previously continue, there are a number of hopeful signs in this realm. Many American industries (most notably automobiles) have rebounded and become highly profitable once again, although this revival is traceable to some degree to the downsizing that led to lower costs as a result of smaller payrolls. Outside traditional areas of strength, other bright spots in U.S. industry include pharmaceuticals [for example, the drug t-PA that saves lives by dissolving clots that cause heart attacks and strokes (Brown, 1995); and "cosmeceuticals," for example, Retin-A to remove wrinkles and Rogaine to stimulate hair growth in those with male-type baldness (*Business Week,* 1988); and alpha-hydroxy acids to freshen the skin (Larcen, 1995)]. All these examples demonstrate strengths in the U.S. economy and considerable promise for the future.

The Postindustrial Economy

Many observers see the economy of the United States as moving beyond industrial capitalism into a stage called a **postindustrial society** (Bell, 1973). As noted in Chapter 4, a postindustrial society is one defined more by service industries than goods-producing industries. In 1940, 51.4 percent of the work force was in goods-producing areas like mining, construction, and manufacturing. In July 1992, about 21.6 percent of the work force was in those areas. On the other hand, in 1940, 48.6 percent of the work force was in service areas, but by July 1992 the percentage had increased to 78.4 percent (Kutscher, 1987; Plunkert, 1990; *Monthly Labor Review,* 1992, p. 63).

The projections for the year 2005 are even more striking. Between now and 2005, the number of workers in goods-producing areas is likely to increase slightly, while the number of people in service-producing areas is likely to increase dramatically (Kutscher, 1987); in fact, about 95 percent of the increase in all jobs will occur in the service sector (Franklin, 1993).

In addition to the growth in well-known service areas in recent years, a number of new service arenas have emerged. Many organizations now provide services to other businesses. For example, accounting, computing, and security services have boomed (Tschetter, 1987). Also in this category are the organizations that provide temporary help to business. Processing knowledge and information and providing it to those who need it have become major sectors of the service area. Some have argued that instead of calling it a "service society," it should be called an "information society" (Lyon, 1986).

However, all is not well with these new service and information jobs. Take the case of Omaha, Nebraska, which because of its location in the center of the country and its excellent telephone system has become a center of high-tech service industries such as telemarketing, telecommunications, and computer services

Cross-national Perspectives

The Changing Nature of the Chinese Economy

While China remains under the control, at least politically and militarily, of the Communist government, economically it is difficult to describe it as communist or socialist. Said a Shanghai journalist and dissident, "Preserving Communist Party rule is all that socialism means now. It's a game" (Kristof, 1992, p. A1). The New China News Agency argued that "the essence of socialism is to liberate and expand productive forces, eliminate poverty, avoid polarization in wealth distribution and finally acquire common prosperity" (Kristof, 1992, p. A6). This is clearly a highly elastic conception of socialism. China, today, might be described as a "socialist market economy"; that is, it is an economy that combines socialistic and capitalistic elements. Prior to economic reforms, virtually all Chinese industry was owned by the state. Many of these state industries continue to exist, but they have been supplemented by a large number of profit-making businesses, and it is the latter that are making the Chinese economy so dynamic. Overall, and in spite of the handicap of the sluggish state-owned businesses, the Chinese economy grew by 11.8 percent in 1994, down slightly from a 13.4 percent growth rate in 1993. However, the Chinese had the fastest and most consistently growing economy in the world over the decade ending in 1995 (Randall and Telesio, 1995). While a modest slowdown is projected to persist through 1996, China is expected to continue to be Asia's brightest economic star (Abbugao, 1995). In fact, part of the reason for the slowdown is a self-imposed austerity program designed to keep inflation from getting out of control.

At first, the heart of capitalistic industrial firms in China was in restricted coastal provinces, but in recent years such firms have spread to other, even remote, parts of the country. However, in spite of the growth of capitalist businesses and their spread throughout much of the country, the central government still exercises tight control over these businesses.

While China has undergone unprecedented economic growth, this growth has not been without its problems. There is, for example, the problem of the state-owned industries and what to do with them and the enormous number of people still employed by them. There is a large population of rootless people, displaced by economic development or in search of jobs, who are seeking new homes. While many people have grown wealthy, many more remain desperately poor. This income disparity has contributed to a rise in the crime rate. It also creates the potential for political unrest. Since there are few environmental protections and those that exist are often ignored, pollution is a serious problem (Endicott, 1995).

While American and other Western businesses have invested heavily in China, they remain concerned about the future of their investments and, more generally, of the Chinese economy. There are at least five scenarios about where China might be in the year 2010 (Randall and Telesio, 1995).

1. *The door will be shut.* In this scenario, the economic reforms currently underway are seen as failing, leading to civil disorder and then to the creation of an authoritarian military government to restore order. Openings to outsiders, especially in business, will be blamed for the problems, and contacts with the outside world will be severely curtailed. In this case, China reverts to being a less developed country dependent, primarily, on agriculture.

2. *The nation will fragment.* Here, because of large disparities in regional economic development and the weakness and division in Beijing, China is seen as breaking up into a series of semiautonomous regions. The rich coastal regions will prosper and engage in active commerce with the West, while the poorer interior regions, most of which have experienced little or no economic development, will fall farther behind economically.

3. *China will muddle through.* This is pretty much a continuation of the current situation. In spite of the ongoing conflict between those in favor of and those opposed to economic development, the country has been developing economically, and this scenario envisions a continuation of this process. Economic development will be solid, but not outstanding.

4. *China becomes an Asian power.* In this scenario, China is seen as becoming a major force in Asia. It is able to use its economic and military power, as well as the existence of Chinese enclaves throughout Asia, to exercise power throughout the continent. China becomes a leader in the Asian economy, and investments in China come primarily from other Asian nations. China, in this case, is a major regional player, but not nearly as important in the international arena.

5. *China becomes a global powerhouse.* In this case, China is seen as becoming a superpower by 2010. It is a major exporter, and its huge internal market fuels economic growth as well as the demand for imports. Citizens are granted increasing political freedom, and there are more guarantees of civil liberties. In this case, China has a greater industrial output than Japan and is the world leader in trade. Liberalized foreign investment has made it possible for foreigners to fully own businesses, at least in some sectors of the economy.

Clearly, there is an enormous range in these possible scenarios. Thus, while China continues to develop economically, it is far from clear where China will stand in the world economy in the near future.

ABBUGAO, MARTIN. "Economic Reforms to Continue in Post-Deng China." *Agence France Presse,* April 27, 1995.
ENDICOTT, WILLIAM. "Riding a Wild Dragon: China Grapples with Boom Times." *Sacramento Bee,* December 31, 1995.
KRISTOF, NICHOLAS D. "Chinese Communism's Secret Aim: Capitalism." *New York Times,* October 19, 1992.
RANDALL, DOUG, and PIERO TELESIO. "Planning Ahead: China's Economy." *China Business Review,* January, 1995.

(Swoboda, 1992b). As a result, 20,000 new jobs were created and unemployment is at about 3 percent, far less than the average for the nation. However, these are low-paid jobs with workers usually starting at $6 per hour and earning between $12,000 and $15,000 a year. In addition, health care and pension plans are either minuscule or nonexistent. Thus, while there are jobs in the service industries, they generally offer little more than a marginal standard of living.

The Declining Economic Fortunes of the Younger Generation

With all the changes occurring in the U.S. economy, many people in the younger generation will have a difficult economic future. Between 1945 and 1973, the wages of U.S. workers, adjusted for inflation, increased between 2.5 and 3.0 percent per year. But since 1973 wages have stagnated or even declined. People who were participating in the economy during the earlier time period generally developed quite comfortable lifestyles, which many continue today. They have job security through seniority, their housing costs remain stable because of fixed mortgages, and they have savings that grew dramatically during periods of high interest rates. In contrast, the generation coming into adulthood after 1973 has had a much more difficult time achieving the same lifestyle as their predecessors, and many are struggling economically. In order to achieve economic success, they will have to make many more sacrifices than the preceding generation. Many young U.S. couples today have both spouses working, and even so, they find it impossible to achieve what their parents did. Frequently they are unable to accumulate the capital necessary to purchase a home, and many incur great amounts of consumer debt. In addition, although many young couples want families, they must postpone or curtail having children because of economic considerations (Levy, 1987).

One measure of the declining fortunes of the younger generation is the plight of college graduates. In the 1960s, about only one in ten college graduates held lower wage, often dead-end, jobs that did not require a degree. In the 1980s and early 1990s, that number had doubled, and about 20 percent of college graduates were in positions that did not require college degrees. By the year 2005, it is projected that fully 30 percent of those who graduate from college will end up in such jobs (Nasar, 1992b).

The Rise of a Global Economy

While there are various things that American industry did to contribute to its decline, that descent is also traceable to a dramatic change in the world's economy. That is, the world is shifting from a nation-based economy to a global economy (Smith and White, 1992; see Chapter 18 for more on globalization). One leading spokesperson for this point of view is Robert Reich in his book *The Work of Nations*. In his view, in the coming century we will witness the end of such things as national economies, products, corporations, and industries. Instead, we will have a global economy in which all of the major factors of production—money, technology, factories, and equipment—will move easily back and forth across national boundaries. This change is not only affecting the United States, but every nation in the world. While other, less economically developed nations have had, and will have, much to gain from this change, the United States, because it entered the age of the global economy with so much, has already lost a great deal and will lose still more in the future.

Although it is impossible to give a precise date for the beginning of the global economy, Reich places great emphasis on the early 1970s, when America's business leaders discovered that "foreigners could undertake high-volume production of standard goods—cars, televisions, household appliances, steel ingots, textiles—and sell them in the United States more cheaply (and sometimes at a higher level of quality) than America's core corporations" (Reich, 1992, p. 69). This is the flip side of the causes within American society for the decline of its major, high-volume industries like automobiles, steel, and television sets. Other nations succeeded in these high-volume industries because their employees were willing to work for far less than their American counterparts, and this helped give them an enormous cost and price advantage. The industries of these nations also often had easier and less costly access to the raw materials needed to produce various goods. It soon proved to be the case that foreign executives were able to build and manage factories more effectively than their American counterparts. And increased efficiencies in international trade and communication, such as containerized cargo vessels and fax machines, made it possible for these new foreign firms to do their business internationally both cheaply and efficiently.

The rise of these foreign industries and the corresponding decline of their American counterparts led in relatively short order to the emergence of a global economy. Foreign industries were prepared to purchase raw materials, parts, and services wherever they could be obtained most cheaply and efficiently. And they were prepared to sell their products all over the world (including, and especially, in the United States with its huge consumer market), often at cut-rate prices in order to carve out new markets for themselves. For their part, after a slow start, American firms learned that they, too, needed to operate on a global basis. Instead of relying on indigenous factories, raw materials, parts, and services, American firms, like their foreign counterparts, began to do business wherever it could be done most cheaply and efficiently (Colclough and Tolbert, 1992). The result is that it is increasingly difficult to clearly define a product, or even an entire industry, as either American or foreign.

This brings us to another aspect of the globalization story, the increasing number of foreign companies like Honda, Toyota, and Nissan that are building plants in the United States. These companies are using American contractors to build their factories, hiring American workers and managers, and utilizing, at least to some degree, American suppliers of parts needed in the manufacturing process. In 1994, such factories represented an $11 billion investment, produced 1.8 million cars annually, employed 35,000 workers, and led to the creation of 200,000 additional jobs in supplier industries (PR Newswire, 1994).

Thus, these companies are making important contributions to the American economy, even though a large portion of the money and profits flow back to Japan. It is becoming increasingly difficult to think of a Honda manufactured in the United States as a Japanese car, just as it is difficult to think of the Ford Contour as an American car.

In fact, Honda, Toyota, Ford, and General Motors are now global, multinational companies with less and less connection to any single nation. Thus, the slogan, "What is good for General Motors is good for the country" is no longer (if it ever was) true. General Motors, like all global companies, will scour the world to find the means to lower costs and increase profits. If they can be found in the United States, then General Motors will do business there. If they can be found elsewhere, then General Motors will turn to those nations. The same holds true for Honda and all other truly global corporations.

While it is increasingly difficult to distinguish products on the basis of their nation of origin, it is still important to consider ways of improving America's position in the global economy. Let us close this section with Robert Reich's thoughts on what America can do to improve its position in that economy.

Reich's proposals are based on the idea that we must move from being a high-volume producer to a "high-value" producer. High volume characterizes the kind of industries (automobiles, steel) that made America rich, but that kind of production has been lost to other nations that can do it far more cheaply, but still as well as America can.

The issue today is not the production of volume, but the production of value, or the amount of value to be added to finished products. Thus, the issue for Reich is not the competitiveness of American industries or the American economy, but the competitiveness of the American *people.* It is a question of whether the American people can compete with the people of other societies in adding value to goods and services. Here is the way Reich puts the issue:

> The real economic challenge facing the United States in the years ahead—the same as that facing every other nation—is to increase the potential value of what its citizens can add to the global economy, by enhancing their skills and capacities and by improving their means of linking those skills and capacities to the world market (Reich, 1992, p. 8).

Thus, it is no longer a question of which nation owns what or in which nation a particular global corporation has its headquarters. Rather, it is a question of which nation has the most skilled and best-trained workers, because it is these workers who are capable of adding the most value to a product. Reich argues, therefore, that "the problem is not that American-owned corporations are insufficiently profitable; it is that many Americans are not adding sufficient value to the world economy to maintain or enhance their standard of living" (Reich, 1992, p. 168).

The question, then, is what do Americans need to do to enhance their ability to add value to the world economy? Most generally, what is needed is concentration on *training and education* so that the United States produces the kinds of highly skilled, highly trained workers who are able to contribute far more value than their less skilled, poorly trained peers in other nations. In terms of Reich's view of the labor force, this means that we need to concentrate on producing more of what he terms "symbolic analysts." People in these occupations, with advanced training and education, are the keys to America's competitive position in the world. Reich (1992, p. 184) argues that "the only true competitive advantage lies in skill in solving, identifying and brokering new problems." The symbolic analysts, according to Reich, are the ones who will be in the position to solve, identify, and broker the economic problems of the future.

Thus, instead of trying to blindly follow the model of Japan or South Korea or Germany, what the United States needs to do is to build on its own people and its own strengths. The base of America's economic rise was its creativity and inventiveness. It is this that has been lost and it is this that must be recovered. In Reich's (1992, p. 168) terms, "a nation's key technological assets" are "the skills and insights necessary to *continue* to invent." What is needed is a commitment to education and training that will allow Americans, especially the symbolic analysts, to be inventive. More generally, this creativity and inventiveness must be supported and nurtured at all levels throughout society.

Thus, Reich envisions a labor force and a society led by the creativity of its symbolic analysts. Because they are the ones who will be adding the most value to the nation's goods and services, the symbolic analysts will be in great demand and highly paid and will likely be doing work that they find highly satisfying. Unfortunately, this means that, because they add little value, large numbers of people in Reich's other two categories of the labor force—routine production and in-person services—are more likely to be unemployed or underemployed because they are not in great demand, are apt as a result to be poorly paid, and are likely to continue to be found in jobs (for example, assembly-line work or counterperson in a fast-food restaurant) that are largely unsatisfying.

Thus, Reich envisions a highly stratified society with a vast gulf between symbolic analysts and much of the rest of the labor force. What to do about this? For one thing, he argues that the symbolic analysts need to do what is necessary to improve the living standards of those in the other two categories in the labor force. This means developing a truly progressive income tax so that those in the top income brackets, primarily the symbolic analysts, pay far more in taxes, enough to allow the rest of society an adequate standard of living. Second, Reich contends that we need to be sure that any reasonably talented American is accorded the opportunity to become a symbolic analyst. In other words, we need to remove the barriers that prevent those in routine production or in-person services, or their children, from becoming symbolic analysts. Thus the United States needs to spend far more money on training, education, and the infrastructure needed to give everyone an equal opportunity to become symbolic analysts. The infrastructure most in need of vast increases in economic support is the educational system. In terms of the need for greater economic support, it should be noted that in 1985 the United States ranked fourteenth out of sixteen industrialized countries (beating out only Australia and Ireland) in terms of expenditures on education (Mishel and Frankel, 1991, p. 246).

Finally, Reich argues that it is not only necessary for the "haves" to help the "have nots" in the United States, but also around the globe. That is, it is the responsibility of the haves in America and in other nations to enhance the economy and culture of the world as a whole. Thus it appears that the fate of not only the United States, but the rest of the world, depends on the success of the most sophisticated and well-trained workers.

Experiences in the World of Work

Sociologists have studied the world of work in many different settings and occupations (Ritzer and Walczak, 1986; Reskin and Roos, 1990). While many people enjoy their work and get fulfillment from their jobs or careers, many other people experience stresses and conflict through their work. Conflict is a major factor in occupational life and is often built into the work role.

Role Conflict

Role conflict refers to a situation in which a person who holds a position is confronted with conflicting or contradictory expectations so that compliance with one makes compliance with the other difficult. We will consider four of the major forms of role conflict: role overload, interrole conflict, person–role conflict, and intersender role conflict.

Role Overload.   **Role overload** occurs when an individual in a role is confronted with a large number of expectations and finds it difficult, if not impossible, to satisfy all of them in a given time period. Because of the nature of their position at the top of organizations, executives are prone to virtually every form of role conflict and are particularly likely to be confronted with role overload.

Role overload is also illustrated by this school superintendent's comments: "There are times when I feel like I have about 15 balls in the air at one time, like a juggler. It's *so* many things. A committee working on this, a committee working on that, a dozen things going. Trying to keep abreast of all of them" (Blumberg and Blumberg, 1985, p. 151). Very often, as this example reveals, role overload is associated with the heavy time demands of high-status occupations and professions.

Interrole Conflict.   **Interrole conflict** occurs when the expectations attached to one role are in conflict with the expectations of another role. Women in the labor force are especially apt to experience interrole conflict because the demands of their jobs are in conflict with the expectations their family members have about their family responsibilities. The interrole conflict comes between the job and family roles (Wiersma, 1994; Thompson and Blau, 1993). Their bosses and fellow workers expect dedication to the job, while family members expect time and attention to their needs. Much has been written in the media about the "superwoman" who holds a high-prestige professional job and also fulfills relatively traditional family roles. However, as sociologist Myra Ferree (1987) points out, most women do not have jobs that conform to the media superwoman. The majority of employed women are employed as clerical workers, service workers, factory workers, or the relatively low-status professions of nursing and teaching. Despite the status level of these jobs, married women, especially those who have children, frequently experience interrole conflict between their employment and family roles. And it is worth noting that married mothers are much more likely to work full time than they did 20 years ago (Hayghe and Bianchi, 1994).

Person–Role Conflict.   **Person–role conflict** occurs when the expectations associated with a particular role violate a person's moral or personal values. This type of conflict is underscored in Robert Jackall's (1988) study of managers, *Moral Mazes*. [See also, Portello and Long's (1994) study of the way female managers deal with ethical (as well as interpersonal) conflict.] One of Jackall's findings is that what is right in organizational life is usually simply what one's boss wants. Thus, person–role conflict occurs when what one's boss desires conflicts with the manager's moral sense of what needs to be done. Most managers, if they want to survive, resolve this conflict by ignoring their own morality and doing what their superiors wish. However, there are some who resolve person–role conflict by rejecting the wishes of superiors and doing what they think is right. This is clear in the case of "whistle blowers," or those who reject what the boss wants because it is immoral and go public with their grievances against the organization. Although whistle blowers may satisfy their own morality, they often suffer adverse consequences within the organization for failing to conform to organizational norms and for publicly announcing their dissatisfaction with the organization.

Intersender Role Conflict. **Intersender role conflict** occurs when two or more people have conflicting expectations of a person in a given role. As one illustration, college professors often experience intersender role conflict because two important groups, students on the one hand and fellow professors on the other, place conflicting demands on them. These two groups have radically different expectations of the professor, who is literally caught in a crossfire between them. Students expect their professors to do a good job of teaching: they should remain up to date on relevant material, prepare carefully for class, and work hard at communicating what they know in an interesting and informative manner. Furthermore, professors are expected to prepare and grade exams carefully, being sure to give students feedback on their performance and to comment on how they could improve in the future. Professors should also be available to students during office hours and at other times of mutual convenience. This all seems quite reasonable from the students' perspective. It clearly takes a lot of the professor's time, but, after all, isn't that what professors are supposed to do with their time?

From the point of view of professional colleagues, that is *not* what professors are supposed to do with their time. Fellow professors generally expect their colleagues to put in a minimum amount of time teaching. The majority of their time is expected to be devoted to research, writing, giving papers at professional meetings, and engaging in an array of other professional activities. Professors expect their colleagues to contribute to their discipline, primarily through research and writing. Increases in salary and promotions generally go to professors who do the most high-quality research.

The conflict between the expectations of students and colleagues often forces individual professors to make a choice. Does the professor conform to the expectations of students and carefully prepare a lecture? Or does he or she conform to the expectations of colleagues and work on a research project? This is the intersender role conflict experienced by professors on a day-to-day basis.

Nandram and Klandermans (1993) studied intersender role conflict among those who occupied key positions within Dutch labor unions. They found that about 50 percent experienced conflict between the expectations of the union and their employer, and over a third faced conflict between expectations of co-workers and union members. Intersender conflict was related to emotional exhaustion among union leaders.

Conflict with Customers and Clients

People in service occupations often experience conflict with customers or clients (Peterson, Schmidman, and Elifson, 1982). Service occupations include, among many others, salespeople (Oakes, 1990), especially automobile salespersons, taxi drivers, airline flight attendants (Hochschild, 1983), maids (Romero, 1992), male and female prostitutes, and physicians in private practice. Direct and spontaneous conflict is always possible in occupations that serve customers, as is illustrated by the following examples of waitresses, flight attendants, and salespeople.

Table Servers.   Customers create all sorts of problems for waitresses (we focus here on female table servers), including complaints about service, belligerence, and drunkenness. Much conflict surrounds the waitresses' desire to be respected and the customers' propensity to act superior to them (Hall, 1993). Finally, the tip is significant to the waitress (as it is to the taxi driver), both as a symbol of success and as a source of income. The customer controls the size of the tip and, indeed, whether a tip is left. This is a continuing source of stress.

Hall (1993) found three major expectations of restaurant servers. First, they are expected to be friendly, to offer "service with a smile." Second, they are supposed to be subservient, with conflict arising here when servers feel as if they are being "treated like dogs." Finally, servers, especially waitresses, are expected to flirt with male customers, and conflict arises here when the waitresses feel they are victims of sexual harassment.

Flight Attendants.   Flight attendants have many of the same conflicts as waitresses; in fact, a good portion of their job involves the service of food and drink. However, airline attendants have other kinds of conflicts with their customers, the passengers (Hochschild, 1983). For example, airline attendants are expected to act as if the cabin of the airplane is their living room and the passengers are their guests. Conflict arises here because no such expectation exists for the passengers, who are free to treat airline attendants as workers who are there to provide them with services. In other words, airline attendants are expected to be "nice" to passengers, but passengers need not be nice to attendants. Thus, attendants are expected never to express anger at even the most obnoxious passengers, but the latter are perfectly free to express their hostility to airline attendants.

Salespeople.   The livelihood of all salespeople depends on their ability to make sales, and, as in all relationships between worker and client/customer, the situation produces a struggle for control. Salespeople seek to persuade the customer to make a purchase, while customers try to resist these efforts and retain control of the situation by not agreeing to a deal. In almost all cases, the resolution of the conflict involves the use of **dramaturgy** (Goffman, 1959b): performances by individuals (in this case, salespeople) aimed at manipulating situations in ways favorable to themselves.

A good example of the use of dramaturgy to resolve conflict between customer and client appears in Miller's (1964) study of people who sell used cars. The heart of the drama is the "pitch," which begins when customers have made it clear that they really are interested in buying a car. The pitch involves a social drama in which the salesperson tries to understand the customer and modify sales tactics to fit the customer's character. In discussing a trade-in, taking a test drive, and seeing the customer's old car, the salesperson is able to discover things about the customer that help in selling the car. The salesperson tries to find out what the customer is thinking at all times. He or she accomplishes this by taking the role of the customer, as well as by keeping the customer talking. At all times, the salesperson "desires to keep control, in fact, achieve mastery of his relationship with the customer" (Miller, 1964, p. 19).

Alienation

The concept of alienation continues to be an important and powerful idea for understanding occupational experiences. **Alienation** is a Marxian concept that refers to a breakdown of the natural connections between people and their work, other people, and the natural world. A number of sociologists have expanded upon this basic meaning in various ways (Blauner, 1964; Schwalbe, 1986; Silver, 1986; Zeffane and Macdonald, 1993; Rogers, 1995). For example, from a social-psychological perspective, alienation has four components. The first is **powerlessness,** or the domination of individuals by other persons or objects and the inability of individuals to reduce or eliminate that control. **Meaninglessness,** the second aspect of alienation, results from the inability of people to see their role in relation to other roles and to the purpose of their work. Third, alienated individuals suffer from **isolation:** they lack a feeling of belonging to the work situation and have little identification with the workplace. Alienation also involves a feeling of **self-estrangement,** which manifests itself in a lack of involvement in one's work. Self-estranged workers are unable to express their unique abilities, potentialities, or personalities (Blauner, 1964).

Experiencing and Coping with Alienation on the Assembly Line.   One occupation that epitomizes the characteristics of alienation is assembly-line work, where the major source of alienation is the relentless line itself. Assembly-line workers perform their assigned tasks at set intervals for eight hours every work day, with almost no variation allowed. In an automobile plant, a worker may tighten identical bolts hour after hour. In a poultry processing plant, a worker may stuff packages of giblets into turkey after turkey as they pass by on a conveyor belt. Respite comes only when the line breaks down, an event many workers hope for and sometimes contribute to by sabotaging the machinery.

Many assembly-line workers are almost totally powerless; they are unable to control the pace of the line, their superiors, or top management. This inability to control their own work pace is perhaps the most demoralizing aspect of the job. What distinguishes their work from virtually all other occupations is that both the rate of work and the kind of work are invariable and uncontrollable. Some degree of powerlessness exists in all occupations, but most workers can generally vary their own work pace and make their work more interesting by changing the tasks they perform.

Typically, assembly-line workers are unable to see what their specialized task has to do with the work of others on the line or at other levels in the organization. They are also unable to see what tightening a bolt has to do with the finished product (and, in many cases, they do not even know what the finished product is). The nature of the job contributes to a feeling of meaninglessness because it is so specialized, uninteresting, and unimportant that it is difficult for anyone to derive any satisfaction from the work.

The assembly-line workers' problems are compounded by their isolation. The noise and the demands of the line prevent interaction with coworkers on the job, making it difficult for an informal work group to develop. An assembly-line worker describes this phenomenon:

> You can work next to a guy for months without even knowing his name. One thing, you're too busy to talk. Can't hear. (Laughs) You have to holler in his ear. They got these little guys comin' around in white shirts and if they see you runnin' your mouth, they say, "This guy needs more work." Man, he's got no time to talk. (Quoted in Terkel, 1974, p. 165.)

Workers are also isolated from all levels of management because of the nature of their work and the desire of management to maintain what it considers to be proper distance. Assembly-line work is usually found in large plants, and their size also serves to inhibit the development of personal relationships.

Workers on the assembly line are particularly prone to self-estrangement. The work is so boring and anonymous that they derive little personal good feeling from it. Hence, workers spend a good part of their time daydreaming: "You dream, you think of things you've done. I drift back continuously to when I was a kid and what me and my brothers did. The things you love most are the things you drift back into" (quoted in Terkel, 1974, p. 160). Because no real skills or abilities are needed, assembly-line workers are unable to express themselves in their work.

Turning to coping mechanisms, one device often used by workers in alienating occupations is "working the system." In a participant observer study of a machine shop, Roy (1954) reports how the workers sought "to beat the system." "We machine operators did 'figure the angles,' we developed an impressive repertoire of angles to play and devoted ourselves to crossing the expectations of the formal organization with perseverance, artistry, and organizing ability of our own" (Roy, 1954, p. 257). For example, when a time study was being conducted to set piecework rates, the workers would take longer to do a job than they ordinarily would. They would run the machines at slower speeds or utilize extra movements such as "little reachings, liftings, adjustings, dustings, and other special attentions of conscientious machine operation and good housekeeping that could be dropped instantly with the departure of the time-study man" (Roy, 1954, p. 257). When the time-study person made a job difficult, the workers revised it to make it easier, even though the change might be harder on tools or reduce the quality of the product.

In another study, Roy (1959–1960) examined informal group practices that were not aimed against management but served to make work life more meaningful. Roy was interested in how machine operators prevented themselves from "going nuts." He was again a participant observer in a group of machine operators engaged in work that was repetitive and very simple and that required long hours and a six-day week. The following is Roy's description of the work:

> Standing all day in one spot beside three old codgers in a dingy room looking out through barred windows at the bare walls of a brick warehouse, leg movements largely restricted to the shifting of the body weight from one foot to the other, hand and arm movement confined, for the most part, to a simple repetitive sequence of place the die, punch the clicker, place the die, punch the clicker, and intellectual activity reduced to computing the hours to quitting time (Roy, 1959–1960, p. 160).

Roy focused on the social devices that machine operators used to find some meaning in an essentially meaningless occupation. First, the machine operators made a little game out of their work: they varied their activities by changing the colors of the material or the die shapes used. Informal group activities made the work day more interesting and pleasant. During the morning "peach time" was announced, and one worker took out two peaches and divided them among the four workers. Then there was "banana time." The same man who brought the peaches also brought a banana, which was for his own consumption. Regularly each morning one of the workers would steal the banana and consume it gleefully while yelling "banana time!" The person who brought the banana would regularly protest, and just as regularly another worker would admonish him for protesting so vociferously. As the day progressed, there was "window time," "lunch time," "pickup time," "fish time," and "Coke time." Through these contrived activities, workers in an essentially meaningless job endeavored to make their work life more meaningful.

Runcie (1980) and Houbolt (1982) describe other coping devices among assembly-line workers. For example, workers can withdraw by being absent. In fact, Runcie (1980, p. 109) found that "on many mornings the line could not start due to the shortage of workers. Often we would stand around waiting for the company to find people to fill the holes in the line." Both Runcie and Houbolt found that workers use drugs as a means of coping with alienation. Said one worker: "If

I smoke [marijuana], I can stare at a spot on the floor all day long and not get bored" (Runcie, 1980, p. 109).

Experiencing and Coping with Alienation in Temporary Office Work.   As we have seen, a growing trend in our society is the employment of temporary, rather than full-time, clerical workers. Rogers (1995) studied alienation among these workers and the ways in which they cope with (or, in Roger's terms, "resist") alienation.

Rogers identified three major forms of alienation. The first is alienation from work. Temporary workers are "doubly" alienated from the product of their work since they are alienated not only from the employer, but also from the temporary agency that recruits them and receives a fee for their services. Temporary workers are also alienated from the labor process because they often lack control over the conditions of their work and an understanding of the purpose of the tasks that they are performing. This alienation is exacerbated by the fact that temporary workers are frequently given the least desirable work to do, and they often find themselves with long periods during which they have little or nothing to do.

Second, temporary workers are alienated from others. For one thing, they have little or no interaction with those who work for the same temporary agency. For another, they are usually isolated at a particular work site, with full-time workers generally unwilling to put in the time and energy needed to get to know temporary workers who will soon be gone. Sometimes the temporary workers are almost literally isolated in locations like the "back room." Temporary workers are sometimes treated as "nonpersons" by full-time employees, that is, as if they are not even present.

Third, the temporary worker is alienated from her (all Rogers' subjects were women) self. For example, temps are often asked to put on, quite falsely, "happy faces" in quite unpleasant work settings. In addition, temporary workers had difficulty establishing their identities on the job; they were often treated as stereotypes, rather than as who they really were. They were often forced to change identities from one job to another and to hide certain characteristics that might hurt them on particular jobs.

Rogers outlines a number of ways in which temporary workers resist (or cope with) these types of alienation. In the case of monotonous work, temporary employees often focused on things other than work (for example, watching the comings and goings in the office). When there was too little work, they could "cruise" (work very fast so that they could take breaks), sleep during slack periods, play (computer games, for example), or do personal work. To deal with the alienation from others, temps took longer-term assignments when possible or limited their work to one or two agencies. When treated like "nonpersons," temporary workers could tell themselves that the situation is only temporary or even engage in office sabotage. Resisting alienation from self involved such things as taking "back office" jobs in order to avoid labor that forced them to behave in a false manner and, ultimately, leaving an agency or an assignment when such problems became intolerable.

While such techniques help, it should be noted that there are great limits to what temporary workers (indeed most workers) can do about their alienation. For example, ultimately they must please their agency if they are to get further assignments.

Unemployment

Unemployment has been a persistent reality in the U.S. economy. During the last 30 years the unemployment rate has rarely been below 5 percent of the labor force (Flaim, 1990). During the early 1980s the unemployment rate was near 10 percent for several years. In the 1990s, the unemployment rate has averaged between 5.5 and 7.4 percent (U.S. Bureau of the Census, 1994a, p. 420). Five or ten percent of the labor force translates into many millions of people out of work, many of whom are likely to be struggling economically and socially to survive. Traditionally, unemployment has plagued those in blue-collar, semi-skilled, and unskilled occupations. Although deindustrialization, downsizing, and restructuring have all served to increase the unemployment rate for white-collar and managerial workers, the rate for blue-collar workers still far outstrips that for white-collar workers. Other factors are highly related to unemployment. For example, those with less than a high school education have a far higher unemployment rate than college graduates. Race is also highly related to unemployment. Blacks since World War II have consistently had an unemployment rate that is double (or more) the rate for whites. For example, in 1994 the white unemployment rate was 5.2 percent, while for blacks it was 10.6 percent (U.S. Bureau of the Census, 1995b, p. 422). Interestingly, the black–white unemployment ratio is *higher* for college-educated men, leading one to question the idea that the solution to the black unemployment problem is more education (Wilson et al., 1995).

Unemployment is more than statistics; it involves highly personal effects on the people who are out of work (Burman, 1988). The most obvious problems for the unemployed person are the loss of income and the absence of a job in a society in which one is usually judged by one's occupation. The unemployed person must also learn how to structure the hours of the day that would normally be taken up by a job.

As symbolic interaction theory would suggest, an unemployed person is also likely to have some problems with his or her self-concept. Without work to think about, many of the unemployed have little to occupy their thoughts other than themselves: *"The only thing I have on my mind on these days is me. Nothing else"* (Burman, 1988, p. 188). More important, unemployment has a negative effect on self-esteem: *"On a bad day...I'll take it personally. Those are the days I feel incompetent, very unsure of myself"* (Burman, 1988, p. 200).

Obviously, structuring time and maintaining self-esteem are only two of the many difficulties facing those who are unemployed. The list is long, but the key point is that unemployment has a powerful impact on people. The unemployed are left to "kill time," and as a result end up in an endless process of "losing ground" occupationally, economically, and in a variety of other ways.

Summary

The economy is the social institution involved in the production, distribution, and exchange of the goods and services of a society. The major historical change in economic systems in the last 200 years was the Industrial Revolution. The factory system, an elaborate division of labor, and a system of mass production emerged during this era. Modern capitalism emerged concurrently as the dominant economic system in Western society. In the view of Karl Marx, capitalism is an economic system that exploits the proletariat. Since the nineteenth century, capitalism has evolved from being a competitive system to a monopoly system. Also, capitalism has shifted from being exploitative to being a system that manipulates and controls workers.

The U.S. economy is changing rapidly. Dramatic changes have occurred in the labor force, especially in the distribution of occupational categories and the increasing numbers of women. Labor unions have undergone substantial declines since mid-century. Deindustrialization in the United States—the reduced importance of manufactured goods—has changed the nature of work and wages. Downsizing, disinvestment, and mergers and corporate takeovers have become significant features of the U.S. economy. However, the U.S. economy, indeed any national economy, has become less important with the rise of the global economy. Within the new global economy, the United States faces difficulties (one of which will be the declining fortunes of the younger generation), but there are some bright spots, as well. A variety of possible solutions to America's economic problems exist, not the least of which is becoming a high-value producer.

While many workers get satisfaction from their jobs and careers, there are also many conflicts, stresses, and hazards in the world of work. Workers cope with the stresses and strains of their jobs in various ways. Conflicts are a normal part of the workworld: managers and officials are prone to role conflict, while customer/client conflicts are frequently experienced in service occupations. Alienation confronts those in low-status occupations, and workers have found various devices to cope with alienation. Unemployment is a persistent reality and poses grave difficulties for the millions who are out of work.

CRITICAL THINKING

1. Describe the major recent changes in capitalism.
2. What major changes in the labor force have occurred in American society since the turn of the century? How have these changes affected our life-styles?
3. Describe contemporary trends in the labor union movement in the United States. What general economic trends are partially responsible for the current state of U.S. labor unions? How have unions responded to change?
4. How has deindustrialization changed the U.S. economy? How has it benefitted overseas competitors?
5. What do we mean by the global economy? What are its implications for the American economy?
6. Are the economic changes in the United States benefitting or harming the economic status of the younger generation? What evidence in the chapter supports your viewpoint?
7. Assess the chances of the United States and its people becoming high-value producers.
8. Take each of the types of role conflict and apply them to your life as a student.
9. What forms does worker alienation take in modern industrial economies? What solutions would you suggest for this problem? What is the economic cost of these solutions?
10. Is unemployment an inevitable reality in the contemporary American economy?

14

Health and Medicine

The twentieth century has brought dramatic changes in types of illnesses, causes of death, and the nature of health care. The illnesses and diseases that caused most deaths at the beginning of this century are no longer the scourges they once were. In 1900 half of the leading causes of death were infectious diseases, with tuberculosis ranking first and pneumonia second. Influenza was another major killer. These are diseases caused by bacterial and viral agents, and their victims at the turn of the century were often children and young adults. By 1992, tuberculosis was far down the list as a cause of death, accounting for only 0.5 deaths for every 100,000 people in the United States. Pneumonia remained one of the top 10 causes of death, although it had dropped from second to sixth place. In addition, it was joined by another infectious disease, HIV (AIDS), which was the eighth leading cause of death in 1992. The resilience of pneumonia and the likely continued growth of AIDS make it clear that those who argued that the disappearance of infectious diseases is imminent were premature and misguided. Worse, growing resistance to antibiotics and the emergence of new strains of infectious diseases make it likely that such diseases will continue to undergo a resurgence (this is even clearer in the In the News box, *"Outbreak:* Dangers Posed by Infectious Diseases").

Now, noninfectious diseases such as heart disease, cancer, and cerebrovascular disease (for example, stroke) have become the leading causes of death. These three diseases accounted for almost two-thirds of all deaths in the United States in 1992 (National Center for Health Statistics, 1995b, p. 101). In contrast to the infectious diseases, noninfectious diseases are related in large part to life-style and the aging process. Among young people, injuries from accidents, suicides, and homicides are now the leading causes of death. Because all of today's major causes of death are connected to lifestyles and personal choices—in other words, social factors—sociologists have a keen interest in both health and medicine, as well as the medical profession itself.

Sociology of Health and Medicine

We may not be accustomed to thinking of sociology as a field concerned with health-related issues; these matters seem to fall within the exclusive province of physicians, biologists, and other health professionals. Yet the sociology of health and medicine, often called *medical sociology,* is one of the most popular specialties among sociologists.

The sociological study of health considers how human behavior contributes to disease and illness or detracts from good health. The sociological view is that both health and illness are not defined simply by physiological factors. Many social and cultural factors are involved, by serving as causes of illness, by influencing the course of an illness, or by affecting whether and how a person recovers from an illness. In addition, a powerful relationship exists between a person's health status and the social and cultural milieu in which the individual lives.

For example, consider how the food and dietary habits of the people in a society can influence their health. The Japanese prefer to eat fish, which has low levels of cholesterol, and they have very low rates of heart disease. In contrast, people in the United States have traditionally preferred red meat in their diet, which has a high level of cholesterol, and they have a relatively high rate of heart disease.

This comparison between the Japanese and U.S. dietary habits, and their apparently related heart-disease rates, illustrates an important aspect of medical sociology called **social epidemiology.** Social epidemiology is the study of the frequency and pattern of a disease within a particular population (Rockett, 1994; Wolinsky, 1988). Epidemiologists focus on the prevalence of specific diseases or illnesses in different populations and then try to determine if a distinguishing social or behavioral factor can be isolated that could account for the differences. One of the early, classic examples of social epidemiology occurred in the late 1700s when Sir Percival Potts discovered that chimney sweeps had a higher rate of scrotum cancer than other groups in the population. It seemed probable that something in the nature of their work caused chimney sweeps to suffer more from this form of cancer, and ultimately the cause was found to be the excessive amounts of soot to which they were exposed.

To illustrate social epidemiology in a more contemporary context, let us briefly examine the phenomenon of oral cancer. The statistics show that 40,000 new cases of oral cancer occur each year, and half of those diagnosed with the disease die within 5 years. The surgeon general of the United States predicts that if nothing changes we will see "a full blown oral cancer epidemic two or three decades from now" (Rich, 1992, p. A16).

Seventy-five percent of oral cancers are traceable to either smoking or the use of smokeless tobacco (chewing tobacco or snuff). Smokeless tobacco has a far higher concentration of carcinogens (nitrosamines, for example) than other types of tobacco. And it has more addictive nicotine, as well (Levine, 1995b). Since smoking is on the decline in the United States, it seems clear that the increase is due to greater use of smokeless tobacco. In fact, the number of pounds of smokeless tobacco sold and the revenues derived from those sales have been increasing dramatically.

The epidemiological aspect of this that is of interest and of great concern is that a large proportion of the users of smokeless tobacco are under 21, "many of them still playing Little League baseball" (Rich, 1992, p. A16). It is estimated that between three and four million teenagers use smokeless tobacco (Scott, 1995). And the tobacco companies have targeted teenagers through advertisements, giveaways, discounts, and sponsorship of events like auto racing that are likely to attract large numbers of young males. It is the utilization of smokeless tobacco by young males today that leads to the prediction of the epidemic of oral cancer a few decades from now.

That epidemic is made more likely by reactions like the following from a teenage tobacco chewer:

> "Amen to carcinogens and whatever else they put in this stuff that makes it taste so good....You've got to be a man and stand up to this kind of thing. I'm loving every chew I take" (Scott, 1995, npi).

Social Epidemiology and AIDS

Social epidemiology was a major tool in identifying how the AIDS virus was being transmitted. AIDS (acquired immune deficiency syndrome) was first reported in 1981, and it quickly became clear that the group in which AIDS was most prevalent was the homosexual male population. Early studies of gay men indicated that those who got the disease had engaged in sexual relations with a large number of partners. Therefore, it appeared that the sexual behaviors of these men were implicated in their contracting AIDS.

In 1982 further research revealed other high-risk groups in the population, indicating that the means of transmission could be other than sexual (Petrow,

1990). People who had received blood transfusions, especially hemophiliacs who need transfusions regularly, also had a high prevalence of AIDS. In addition, drug addicts who were taking their drugs intravenously appeared as a high-risk group. This evidence indicated that the virus was being transmitted by either infected blood or semen, and that victims were infected when the virus somehow entered the bloodstream. These facts were further confirmed when infants were born with the AIDS virus, which they were obviously getting from the infected blood of their mothers.

After these early facts were uncovered, it was clear that AIDS was not exclusively a disease of the gay population but could be contracted by anyone who had direct contact with the blood or semen of a person carrying the virus. The direct contact that most frequently transmitted the virus, however, involved the sexual practices of gay or bisexual males and intravenous (IV) drug use (apparently because users were sharing dirty hypodermic needles).

In 1993, gay and bisexual men and intravenous drug users accounted for over 88 percent of new diagnosed cases of AIDS. For women in 1993, almost 50 percent of the new cases were the result of IV drug use, while over one-third was traceable to heterosexual contact, often with IV drug users (National Center for Health Statistics, 1995, p. 149). The number of cases of AIDS traceable to heterosexual contact is increasing for both men and women. Between 1992 and 1993, the number more than doubled for men and women. However, it is also true that over the same period the number of cases of AIDS linked to homosexual contact more than doubled, to nearly 50,000 new cases in 1993. Some of the increases in 1993 were attributable to the expanded definition of AIDS that took effect on January 1 of that year.

Other Interests of Medical Sociology

Medical sociology involves much more than studies of social epidemiology, however. Sociologists are interested in how different sociocultural backgrounds affect people's "attitudes, beliefs and behavior concerning health, illness, and death" (Wolinsky, 1988, p. 39). Medical sociologists are also concerned with the nature of the relationship between physicians and patients and the changes that have taken place over the years in that relationship. Some sociologists direct their attention to the study of hospitals as bureaucratic organizations. Others focus on medical and health occupations (ambulance personnel, laboratory technicians) and professions (physicians, nurses, and pharmacists). A growing concern of sociologists is the overall organization of health care in society and the changes taking place within the health-care system. This brief description provides only a glimpse of the field of medical sociology, but many of these issues will receive fuller treatment throughout this chapter.

The Changing Nature of Health and Medicine

The infectious diseases that were the major killers at the beginning of the century (and are reemerging today to some degree) are called **communicable diseases.** Communicable diseases are diseases that can be transmitted to people in a variety of ways—by other people, by animals or other organisms, or from contaminated food or water that is ingested. Since, at the beginning of the twentieth century, there were few effective medicines or other techniques to combat these diseases, life expectancy was comparatively short (47 years in 1900 compared to almost 76 years in 1992); the infant mortality rate was high, and there was an ever-present likelihood of epidemics that could take massive numbers of lives in short periods of time. In many cases, contracting one of these infectious diseases had little to do with anything that people did or did not do. If a person happened to come into contact with the bacteria or virus, chances were that he or she would become ill. This point was proved most clearly in the case of the epidemics that swept through entire populations, often causing millions of deaths. [While these epidemics have all but disappeared in the United States, they continue to be problems in many other parts of the world. For example, in 1991 many countries in South America experienced a cholera epidemic (Okie, 1991).] People in the United States feared epidemic diseases in the earlier part of the century, but they had little fear of cancer. Cancer aroused less dread than tuberculosis, the greatest killer of that time (Patterson, 1987).

For an individual who lived at the turn of the century, contracting a disease and dying from it must have seemed largely a matter of chance or fate. Matters are quite different today. Most of the major diseases now prevalent can be traced to "problems of living" (for example, life-style, stress, environmental problems) rather than bacteria or viruses. In other words, diseases such as heart disease and cancer involve multiple causes, many of which are more closely related to the way people live than to strictly biological factors. To take just a few examples, eating foods high in cholesterol increases the likelihood of heart disease, smoking cigarettes is linked to lung cancer and emphysema, living in a community where pesticides are used heavily may contribute to a higher risk of cancer, and spending long hours sunbathing may lead to increased risk of contracting melanoma and other, less deadly, skin cancers. Diseases and illnesses today are apt to be tied to the actions we choose to take or not take. To a considerable degree, our individual chances of healthful living are much more in our own hands now than they were at the turn of the century.

In this context it is interesting to consider again the spread of AIDS. Like many of the infectious diseases that killed people at the turn of the century, AIDS is caused by a virus. Because the AIDS virus is not easily transmitted from one person to another, however, contracting the disease is closely linked to the choices people make in their actions and behavior. For example, people are more likely to get AIDS if they engage in male homosexual behavior, use drugs intravenously,

In the News

Outbreak: Dangers Posed by Infectious Diseases

The recent motion picture, *Outbreak,* has alerted large numbers of people to the dangers posed by infectious diseases. Ironically, it was little more than two decades ago that the surgeon general of the United States confidently proclaimed that it was "time to close the book on infectious disease" (Specter, 1992, p. 1). The surgeon general was talking only about the United States; infection continues to be the world's number one cause of death (Brown, 1995). However, some infectious diseases (tuberculosis, for example) have reemerged in the United States in recent years. More importantly, a number of new infectious diseases have begun to pose a threat to large numbers of people not only in poor and developing nations, but in the United States, as well. These include outbreaks of Ebola virus in Africa, hantavirus in the southwestern United States, *Escherichia coli* outside Seattle, cryptosporidiosis in Milwaukee, pneumonic plague in India, "flesh-eating bacteria" in many parts of the world, the better known flare-ups of Legionnaires' disease and Lyme disease, as well as the epidemic of AIDS.

The current thinking is that most, if not all, of these are not actually new diseases, but rather diseases that have broken out of their historically narrow ecological niches. Instead of a few people being infected in remote locales, there is now the possibility that large numbers of people in many parts of the world will be infected with these diseases (Henig, 1995). Furthermore, the global warming expected to occur over the next century promises an even greater increase in many of these diseases (especially tropical diseases like malaria), as well as their spread to areas that have previously been little affected by them (Brown, 1996).

Tuberculosis

The U.S. government began keeping statistics on TB in 1953, and it was in that year that an historic high of 84,300 new cases was reported. The number declined steadily and reached a low of 22,000 new cases in 1985. The number then began to rise, and there are now projections that the number of new cases will reach 50,000 per year by the end of the century. Said the president of the American Lung Association,

> I'm scared.... Here we are in 1992 with cure rates lower than countries like Malawi and Nicaragua. We can't keep track of our patients, and all evidence suggest that more and more of them have TB that is resistant to our best drugs. We have turned a disease that was completely preventable and curable into one that is neither. We should be ashamed (Specter, 1992, pp. 1, 44).

By 1992 the number of new cases had risen to almost 27,000. (However, it is worth noting that by 1993 the number of new cases had *declined* slightly to 25,287.)

Emerging Viruses

In most cases, it is not that viruses like Ebola are new and represent new threats to people, but rather that a number of social changes have helped to make them significant menaces for the first time:

- Technological developments that permit the movement of large numbers of people quickly and over long distances now enable diseases to spread widely and rapidly.
- More people are traveling through or moving into the tropical breeding grounds for many of these new diseases.
- Population growth has crowded people together and made it easier for these (and other) diseases to spread.
- More people can lead to the expansion of the animal populations that act to spread the diseases.
- Other social causes of the spread of the emerging viruses include destruction of the rain forest, other new technologies, and environmental pollution.

Also to be considered is another set of causes related more specifically to medical care. First, antibiotics have been overused, with the result that they have lost their effectiveness in the treatment of many diseases. Second, many children are not getting the vaccinations that they need in order to prevent diseases. Third, poor and declining health service, especially for those in poverty, threatens to leave that group, and ultimately the rest of society, more vulnerable to disease (Dietrich, 1995). Cutbacks in sanitation and in preventive measures like mosquito control also lead to the expansion of infectious diseases, especially among the poor. For example, in Latin America, in a situation similar to what happened in the case of tuberculosis in the United States, hundreds of thousands of cases of dengue fever were reported in the last half of 1995. This occurred in spite of the fact that the mosquitos that carry the disease were believed to have been nearly eliminated two decades before. The cause? Spraying to destroy the mosquitos had ceased. Ominously, the first case of dengue fever in the United States was reported in late 1995.

While most experts do not believe that these new infectious diseases represent a major threat to the world, and especially to the United States, a World Health official warns that these diseases are not contained by national borders. An outbreak in one country is a threat to many, perhaps all nations. Nations that are major destinations or hubs for international travellers are most at risk (Henig, 1995).

BROWN, DAVID. "Infectious Diseases Reemerging as Major Cause of U.S. Illness." *Washington Post,* October 16, 1992.
BROWN, DAVID. "Infection Is World's No. 1 Cause of Death." *Washington Post,* May 2, 1995.
BROWN, DAVID. "Infectious Disease May Rise as the World Gets Warmer." *Washington Post,* January 17, 1996.
DIETRICH, BILL. "'The Coming Plague': What Ordinary American Can Do about Newly Emerging Diseases. " *Seattle Times,* November 1, 1995.
GARRETT, LAURIE. *The Coming Plague: Newly Emerging Diseases in a World Out of Balance.* New York: Farrar, Strauss, and Giroux, 1994.
HENIG, ROBIN. "Old Ills in New Guises?; Scientists at Conference Ponder the Nature of Emerging Diseases." *Washington Post,* October 24, 1995.
NAVARRO, MIREYA. "Far Away from the Crowded City, Tuberculosis Cases Increase." *New York Times,* December 6, 1992.
ROSENTHAL, ELISABETH. "Doctors and Patients Are Pushed to Their Limits by Grim New TB." *New York Times,* October 12, 1992.
SPECTER, MICHAEL. "Neglected for Years, TB Is Back with Strains That Are Deadlier." *New York Times,* October 11, 1992.

and engage in heterosexual sex with high-risk partners. In addition, AIDS is tied to actions people fail to take, such as using condoms with a sex partner of whom they are uncertain, or using clean hypodermic needles when taking drugs intravenously. Thus, although AIDS is infectious, it is difficult to catch; the chances of being stricken with it are heightened by things that people do or don't do. People have much more control over this epidemic than they did over the epidemics that occurred in earlier times.

Individuals do not have complete control in all matters relating to their health, however, because illnesses are also influenced by the actions of other people and by societal conditions. For example, widespread use of chlorofluorocarbons in refrigerants, and in aerosol spray cans in many countries, is reducing the protective ozone layer in the atmosphere. This thinning of the ozone layer is linked to increases in skin cancer, including melanoma. Another example of an external threat to health is the use of pesticides and chemicals in the production and processing of foods. Most grains, fruits, vegetables, and meats today carry some residues of these chemicals and are adversely affecting the health of entire societies.

Historical Causes of Declining Death Rates

Many people assume that advances in medical practices and medical discoveries are responsible for the victory over the infectious diseases that historically plagued humankind. However, historical studies of disease and death have shown that declines in the major infectious diseases cannot be attributed to medical discoveries, treatments, and practices (McKeown, 1976, 1979). Studies have shown that death rates for most infectious diseases were on the decline long before the most effective medical intervention was discovered or developed. For example, studies of England have shown that the death rate due to tuberculosis was declining at least 30 years before the tubercle bacterium was discovered in 1882. These declines were not produced by the medical treatments of that day, since they were generally ineffective. In some cases medical treatment may even have been harmful to the patient, as it probably was in the case of President Andrew Jackson's wife, who was advised by her doctor to start smoking as a treatment for her tuberculosis (Remini, 1984). Not until 1947, with the introduction of streptomycin, was an effective chemotherapy for tuberculosis available. By that time, the death rate due to tuberculosis was only one-sixth of what it had been a century earlier (McKeown, 1976).

The reductions in deaths from most other infectious diseases have followed a similar pattern. In the United States in the nineteenth and twentieth centuries, McKinlay and McKinlay (1977) discovered that, for nine infectious diseases, the death rate was declining for eight of them *before* vaccines were created or treatment developed. (Polio was the exception.) What did bring the death rates down in these cases? *Death rates for infectious diseases declined because of changes in social and environmental factors rather than medical factors.* Such changes included better sanitation, housing, and nutrition—in other words, an overall improvement in the standard of living (McKeown, 1971, 1979).

None of this discussion is intended to argue that medical care does no good or that medical discoveries are not important. The development of inoculation procedures and vaccines have certainly had a long-term impact on the health of people around the world. In fact, when the medical discoveries of the Western world have been applied to much of the developing world during the last half of the twentieth century, they have been highly effective. These more recent medical successes should not, however, obscure the historical fact that declines in infectious disease did not result primarily from improved medical practices and treatments. In both Europe and the United States, social and environmental factors were more important in reducing death rates (McKinlay and McKinlay, 1977).

The Medicalization of Society

In this century we have witnessed an increase in the power of the medical profession, and the increasing dominance of the medical approach to health and illness. One manifestation of this dominance is the **medicalization of society,** defined as the tendency to exaggerate the importance of medicine and to "medicalize," or treat as an illness, things that are not normally considered illnesses (Conrad and Schneider, 1980; Conrad, 1986; Lowenberg and Davis, 1994). The process of medicalization has been obvious in the area of deviance, where people who exhibit behavior that is considered deviant have come to be labeled as sick and therefore in need of medical help. The most notable example is the way in which alcoholism is now nearly universally defined as a disease. In the past the excessive use of alcohol was generally viewed as a result of a person's lack of willpower. Now most people regard this form of substance abuse as stemming from a chemical imbalance in the body, genetically transmitted, in many cases. Other compulsive behaviors and disorders have been similarly reanalyzed.

A recent example is the medicalization of compulsive gambling. Described in the past as a personal weakness—a failure of will—compulsive gambling today is increasingly defined as a disease (Rosecrance, 1985), "the addiction of the '90s'" (Barbieri, 1992, p. D5). Various organizations such as the American Psychiatric Association and Gamblers Anonymous view gambling as a medical problem. Gambling is seen as analogous to drug addiction. According to the American Psychiatric Association, it is an "impulse control disorder." As such, it is supposed to give those involved "highs" as well as "withdrawal symptoms" when they are forced to quit. It is also seen as "behavior that compromises, disrupts, or damages personal, family, or vocational pursuits" (Marriott, 1992, p. 22). Here is the way one gambler described his addiction:

> Every waking thought was taken up with working out how I could gamble.... Then when I wasn't gambling I'd contrive a reason to gamble. I would conjure up an argument for no reason with my wife and storm out of the house as an excuse to get out, but really my objective was to gamble (Barbieri, 1992, p. D5).

Compulsive gambling is also associated with the development of problems such as drug abuse, attempts at suicide, and nonviolent crimes. Thus, a criminologist noted, "If this isn't a sickness, it sure mimics all the problems sicknesses have" (Marriott, 1992, p. 22).

However, others see in this a disturbing tendency to define anything that we regard as troublesome as a disease. While admitting that it was a "terrible problem," one sociologist said, "I don't think it is a disease" (Marriott, 1992, p. 22). There are powerful interests behind defining gambling as a disease, especially those who would set up centers for its treatment and seek payment from health insurers, who have thus far been highly reluctant to reimburse people for gambling-related treatment.

Previously, and for many decades, children who were overly active, impulsive, and aggressive would have been seen as disruptive youngsters who needed to be controlled or perhaps punished by parents and/or teachers. Later, and controversially, such children came to be labeled as hyperactive and seen as having a medical problem (Conrad, 1975). Recently, this controversy has taken on new intensity as hyperactivity acquired a medical label, attention deficit disorder (ADD), and millions of children (estimates range from 3 to 5 percent of the school-age population) have been defined as having the disease. In fact, it is now the most common behavioral disorder among children (Schmidt, 1995b). Definitions of the disease are growing more refined and, more recently, attention deficit hyperactivity disorder (ADHD) has been added to ADD. Those children who demonstrate three interrelated symptoms—hyperactivity, impulsivity, and inattention—are now defined as having ADHD. Even more striking is the fact that many of the children (and even some adults) diagnosed with ADD and ADHD are now increasingly being treated with drugs, especially Ritalin [use of this drug has doubled in the last 5 years (Guttman, 1995)]. While it seems to help many with the symptoms of ADD and ADHD, Ritalin is a powerful stimulant that can cause adverse side effects such as sleeplessness and loss of appetite, side effects that are particularly troublesome in children.

There are those, especially in the medical profession, who believe that ADD has physiological causes (for example, problems with the blood flow in the brain) that require drug therapy. According to at least some experts in the field, it is necessary for professionals in the educational sector to recognize that there is a range of such physiological causes of this disorder. However, there is no known biological marker for ADD. Lacking definitive tests, physicians must rely on examinations, interviews, scales that rate behavior, and psychological exams to try to determine whether a child is suffering from ADD (Schmidt, 1995a). Critics argue that what is for most children merely a behavioral problem has been redefined as a medical problem by physicians and educators (Armstrong, 1995). For example, the director of the Kaiser Permanente's Center for School Problems in San Diego believes that this is traceable to the fact that people in modern society are inclined to look for medical explanations for a child's failure to meet expectations. At the moment, ADD happens to be a popular explanation. However, at least this official believes that it is as if childhood has come to be defined as a diseased state (Schmidt, 1995a, b).

However, teachers and parents often welcome the definition of hyperactivity as a disease in need of drug therapy. In the view of one mother with two children diagnosed with ADD, the critics do not understand the situation because they do not have to deal with it on a daily basis (Schmidt, 1995b). This mother was confronted every day with uncontrollable behavior from her children. One of her children was highly impulsive, unable to sit still long enough even to watch a video tape on television. It was similarly impossible for the child to play games for very long with other children. The child was always on the move, constantly climbing over and under various things (Schmidt, 1995b). There are many parents who believe that the use of drugs has helped their hyperactive children. With medication, their children are able to concentrate on one thing at a time, and the impulses to try to do many things at once are reduced. However, there are some experts in the field of ADD who are beginning to have doubts about the diagnosis of ADD. They are happy that parents and educators are aware of ADD, but they are concerned that the ADD label is being overapplied. The ADD label was originally intended to apply to only a small proportion of children, but it has now come to be applied to many and, it is feared, to some children who are quite normal (Schmidt, 1995b).

A number of sociological factors help to explain the increased use of Ritalin and other drugs in the treatment of hyperactive children. First, there is greater acceptance today of physiological explanations of behavioral problems and therefore of medical treatment of these problems. Second, HMOs and other managed-care programs are willing to cover the cost of medication, with the result that physicians are more likely to prescribe them and parents are more likely to use them. Third, parents are more likely to be working or busy with other activities, with the result that they are apt to prefer quick fixes like drugs. Fourth, teachers, overwhelmed with large classes and myriad problems, are likely to see drugs as the easy solution to at least some of their difficulties.

Thomas Armstrong, a psychologist and author of *The Myth of the A.D.D. Child,* concludes:

> One of the biggest problems I have with the ADD myth . . . is that it creates an image of the child based on disease, damage, and deficiency—not on asset, affirmation, and advantage. We speak of the "ADD child" as if he had a little ADD virus running around in his brain, or an ADD tattoo somewhere hidden on his anatomy. Soon, the child begins to wear a kind of negative halo that others use to judge his character (Shaw, 1995, npi).

Thus, in addition to all the other problems discussed here, the increasing use of labels like ADD and ADHD lead to the kinds of problems discussed in Chapter 6 under the heading of labeling theory, such as stigmatization.

In addition to all this, some young people have taken to using Ritalin to get high (Stepp, 1996). Believing that it will improve their schoolwork and their social life, teenagers are increasingly using a drug some have come to call "Vitamin R," "R-Ball," or "the smart drug." Since the drug is legal, it is often obtained from friends or relatives. For those without ADD, Ritalin provides quick energy and perhaps even a sense of euphoria. Said one high school student after ingesting several times the normal dose, "I was happy all weekend long," but of the next weekend when she took an even larger dose, she said, "I felt like I was going to die" (Stepp, 1996, p. A6).

The medicalization process is not restricted to deviant behavior. Other examples include menstruation (Braunsen, 1992) and infertility (Becker and Nachtigall, 1992). Medicine has even come to define childbirth as a medical problem that must be handled by physicians in a hospital context (Arney, 1982). What was once a natural process dominated by family and midwives came to be seen as at least a potential medical problem (Wertz and Wertz, 1986). Of course, one factor that contributed to the medicalization of childbearing was the extremely high rate of death associated with the birth process. Recent years have brought a resurgence of midwives as a reaction against the medicalization of childbirth (Weitz and Sullivan, 1985). A greater interest has also arisen in natural childbirth, and a few people are choosing to have babies at home rather than in hospitals. Despite these trends, medicine continues to control the childbirth process as reflected in the extraordinarily high rate of births by cesarean section, a technique dominated by physicians.

Nor is the medicalization process restricted to the United States. For example, in Japan a number of extraordinary "diseases" have come to be defined as medical problems. For example, two diseases that now "strike" Japanese women are "kitchen syndrome" and "moving-day depression." A woman with kitchen syndrome might go on wild shopping sprees, while those suffering from moving-day depression might complain that the water in their new home does not agree with them. Japanese doctors have come to define these afflictions as diseases and treat them by counseling the "victims" as well as by prescribing medicines (Lock, 1987).

Variations in Health among Different Populations

In this section we will compare the health status of a number of populations or subpopulations in the United States, including differences between men and women and among races and social classes. As we proceed through the various comparisons between groups, we will rely heavily on the work of social epidemiologists, as described earlier.

Gender and Health

Historically, there have been significant differences between men and women in patterns of health, illness, and death (Verbrugge, 1989; this also holds, among other places, in Thailand [see Fuller et al., 1993]). Although some of these differences persist, indications are that greater similarities in the lives of men and women in the United States are producing more similarities in their mortality patterns.

Sex differences for some major causes of death have either stabilized, decreased, or are only slowly increasing (Verbrugge, 1985). Considerable speculation exists about the possible effects on female health of their increased participation in the labor force and changes in lifestyle, but it will be several years before these effects can be fully determined.

One important explanation for some equalization in death rates was the growing number of female smokers after World War II. As a former Secretary of Health, Education, and Welfare bluntly pointed out: "Women who smoke like men, die like men." In the 1980s and early 1990s, we saw increased lung cancer among women because greater numbers of women began smoking cigarettes in the 1940s. Lung cancer has almost overtaken breast cancer as the leading cause of cancer deaths among women. One measure of the increased risk to females is the fact that in 1965 only 4 percent of deaths among middle-aged women (35 to 69 years of age) were attributable to smoking. However, today 37 percent of the deaths in that age group can be blamed on smoking (Brown, 1992). Estimates show that smoking accounts for at least three-quarters of lung cancer deaths among females and slightly more (80 percent) among males (National Center for Health Statistics, 1992a, p. 16).

In spite of the increase in death rates due to lung cancer, women still have a higher life expectancy than men. Life expectancy for females born in 1993 was 78.9 years; for males, it was 72.1 years (U.S. Bureau of the Census, 1995b, p. 86). Male death rates generally exceed female death rates at all ages.

With respect to the two major causes of death, the male death rates due to heart disease and cancer are greater than the rates for women (at all ages). Women, on the other hand, tend to be sick more often, but their health problems are usually not as serious or as life threatening as those encountered by men. Women, for example, are eleven times more likely than men to have acute or short-term illnesses, such as infectious and parasitic diseases and digestive and respiratory conditions. But women, especially in later life, tend to die from the same causes as men. The difference is that men tend to develop these more serious illnesses much earlier in life and die from them at an earlier age (National Center for Health Statistics, 1988).

Some scholars suggest that women do not have more illnesses but are simply more sensitive to their bodily discomforts and more willing to report their symptoms. The best evidence indicates, however, that the differences in sickness are indeed real (Waldron, 1983). Verbrugge (1976, p. 401) observes, "females experience a less comfortable and satisfying life with regard to a cherished attribute"— feeling healthy (Ross and Bird, 1994). To summarize, women are sick more often but live longer. Men are sick less often but die sooner.

The longevity of men is less than that of women because of both biological and social–psychological factors. The lesser biological durability of males is evident in mortality rates from the prenatal and newborn stages of life onward. The chances of male fetuses dying before birth are about 10 percent higher than for female fetuses (McMillen, 1979). In the newborn stage, males continue to have higher death rates because a variety of respiratory, circulatory, and other disorders are more common among male babies (Cockerham, 1986). Females are less likely to get childhood leukemia, and they have a better chance of survival when they do. When they are adults, their female sex hormones may protect them to some degree from heart disease up to the time of menopause.

For adults, social–psychological effects on life expectancy appear more important than biological differences (Verbrugge, 1985). These effects are seen in the health risks associated with various social roles, occupations, and lifestyles. Males use more alcohol, illegal drugs, and cigarettes (despite the significant decline in male smokers), and they often have greater job-related stress. The lifestyle of the male business executive or professional, with its emphasis upon "career" and "success," is believed to contribute strongly to high rates of coronary heart disease. Among lower-class men, high levels of obesity and smoking, along with less leisure-time exercise and poor diet, join with the stress that accompanies a life of poverty to produce especially high rates of heart disease. The risk of dying from cancer is also higher than average for unemployed or underemployed men who live alone in poor, overcrowded, urban neighborhoods. They have less chance of early detection of cancer, and they are exposed to health conditions that make death more likely once cancer occurs (Jenkins, 1983).

The fact that accidents are also a major cause of death for males but not for females strongly suggests a difference in gender roles. Men are generally expected to be more aggressive than women in both work and leisure activities. High accident rates among males may be attributed to exposure to more dangerous activities, including jobs where the risk of death or injury is higher. Automobile accidents, too, kill or maim significantly more men than women, especially young adult males. Driving at high speeds is more common for males, as is participating in violent sports. Therefore, it would seem that the social psychology of the male gender role and male competitiveness are significant factors adversely affecting male longevity.

Women seem to take better care of themselves. They more readily admit that they are sick and more often consult with physicians. Whether women will assume the behavioral traits associated with the male role as they increasingly enter the same occupations as men is a question that sociologists will study with great interest in the years to come.

Women live longer than men, but the quality of their lives in old age appears to be lower than men in old age. On a variety of dimensions women aged 74 and over are *worse off* than their male counterparts. Women at this age are more likely to live alone than men are. Beyond age 74 about 70 percent of men are married, but only about one-fourth of women are married after that age. Since traditional gender roles are likely to prevail in this age group, males are apt to benefit from having wives who take care of them. Another factor is that older women are less likely to have adequate incomes. On medical issues, older women have higher cognitive impairment, and their health tends to be poorer than males of the same age. Finally, older women have less ability to perform the basic activities of daily living (Haug and Folmar, 1986).

Race and Health

The health of racial minority groups, as measured by life expectancy and infant mortality, has improved significantly during the twentieth century. Between 1900 and 1993, the life expectancy of black females increased from 33.5 years to 73.7 years; for black males, the increase for this period was from 32.5 to 64.7 years. (However, life expectancy for both groups, especially black males, has declined in the last few years.) Although the life expectancy of black males has risen dramatically in the United States since 1900, black males still lag behind their white counterparts. White females born in 1990 are projected to outlive black females by almost 6 years; white males will live more than 8 years longer than black males (U.S. Bureau of the Census, 1995b, pp. 86, 87) (See Figure 14–1). In terms of infant mortality, for blacks the rate declined from 43.9 (per 1000) in 1950 to 17.0 in 1990, while for whites it declined from 26.8 to 7.7. Despite the substantial decline in the rates for both races, the black infant mortality rate in 1990 was still more than double the rate for whites.

Although some diseases that are especially prevalent among blacks (such as hypertension and sickle cell anemia) appear to have a genetic basis, differences in life expectancy between the races for many other health problems can be attributed to the fact that racial minorities are also most likely to be poor. Low-income groups living in poverty show high rates of influenza and pneumonia, lead poisoning, rat-bite fever, ear infections, murder, alcoholism, drug addiction, and lung cancer.

Social Class and Health

Membership in the lower class is closely associated with health disadvantages (Dahl, 1994; House et al., 1994). The poor suffer more, not only from the infectious diseases that have been so devastating in the past, like influenza and tuberculosis, but also from the so-called "modern ills" like heart disease. In recent years the death rates from coronary heart disease have declined for all Americans, but more for the middle and upper classes than for the lower classes (Susser et al., 1983).

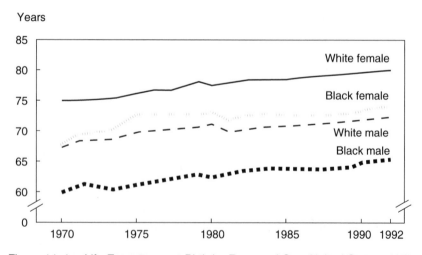

Figure 14–1. Life Expectancy at Birth by Race and Sex: United States, 1970–1992. (*Source: Health United States 1994 Sourcebook.* Hyattsville, MD: National Center for Health Statistics, 1995, p. 15.)

A study by the state of Maine further highlights the less favorable health situation of the poor. This study found that children from low-income families had higher death rates than children from more affluent families. Low-income children were ten times more likely to drown, 12 times more likely to die in fires, 16 times more likely to be murder victims, eight times more likely to die of disease, and four times more likely to be killed in automobile accidents (Cockerham, 1986).

Not only are the poor more apt to suffer ill health but they are also less able to afford to pay for needed health care. Because the poor are less likely to go to doctors, they are more likely than affluent people to come to hospitals for treatment of preventable conditions such as diabetes and bronchitis (Abramowitz, 1988). Even when they do go to doctors, the poor are apt to receive service that is inferior to that of their middle-class peers. This lower-quality care is related, in part, to the fact that middle-class patients are more actively involved in consultations with doctors, while lower-class patients tend to be more passive (Boulton et al., 1986).

The most important relationship between social class and health is the manner in which social class has an impact on the opportunities that a person has for a generally healthy life. Crowded living conditions, poor diet, inferior housing, low levels of income and education, exposure to violence, and alcohol and drug abuse combine to decrease the chances of a healthy life for the poor.

Changes in Health Care in the United States

The Problem of Escalating Costs

Health expenditures in the United States have increased dramatically. In 1956, U.S. citizens spent a total of $41.6 billion on health needs, as compared to 1993 expenditures of $884.2 billion (National Center for Health Statistics, 1995, p. 109). Between 1980 and 1993, the rise in spending for health was particularly dramatic, considerably more than tripling from $251.1 billion to $884.2 billion.

Two major factors contributing to higher costs of medical care are inflation and increased labor costs. Among the inflationary pressures have been the increased costs of medical equipment, supplies, and new construction, and these, in turn, have helped to intensify the demands of employees for higher wages. Labor represents a significant percentage, often in excess of 50 percent, of a hospital's total expenses; therefore, increased labor costs are a highly significant component of rising hospital expenses. Inflation and the higher costs of operation have resulted in an increase of almost 1000 percent in the cost per in-patient day since 1971. Also contributing to increasing medical costs is the increasing income of physicians.

More generally, the numbers tell the dramatic story of the rise in health care costs. The Consumer Price Index (CPI) for medical care has risen from 15.1 in 1950 to 158.2 in 1994. By way of comparison, the CPI for food rose from 25.4 in

1950 to 144.3 in 1994 (National Center for Health Statistics, 1995, p. 221). Looking at specific components of the health care bill, the CPI for physician services rose from 15.7 in 1950 to 199.8 in 1994, while for hospital rooms it increased from 4.9 in 1950 to a whopping 239.2 in 1994.

The High Cost of Prescription Drugs. Like all other aspects of health care, the cost of prescription drugs has risen dramatically. The CPI for prescription drugs increased from 43.4 to 230.6 between 1950 and 1994. In 1991, over $36 billion was spent on prescription drugs. Since 1980 the amount spent on prescription drugs has been increasing at a rate of almost 11 percent a year (National Center for Health Statistics, 1995, p. 251).

Drug prices in the United States are the highest in the world, 32 percent higher than in Canada, for example. Furthermore, high drug prices tend to have a dramatic effect on people since insurance plans are less likely to cover prescription drug costs than hospital stays or doctor visits. The drug companies claim that higher prices reflect increased research and development costs. Drug companies spend about $11 billion a year on R & D. It costs an average of about $231 million and 10 to 12 years to bring a new drug to market. Furthermore, in spite of the increases, drug companies argue that prescription drugs remain "the best bargain in health care" (Colburn, 1992a, p. 8). They point to an example like the antiulcer drug Zantac (which increased in price more than once a year between 1985 and 1991), which is estimated to have saved Medicaid as much as 70 percent a year on ulcer patients by keeping them out of the hospital and avoiding far more costly surgery.

Critics respond in various ways. For one thing, while drug companies spend $11 billion on R & D, they spend $1 billion *more* on marketing. Much of this is aimed at the private physicians who prescribe the drugs and who are, as a result, given free gifts and wined and dined, as well as given all the free samples they can handle. For another, a good portion of research money goes into producing drugs to compete with those being marketed by other drug companies and not into finding new drugs that constitute medical advances.

High drug prices are straining the federal budget, the health care insurers, and the budgets of private citizens. This is especially the case for older Americans, who are likely to be sicker and to require more, and more expensive, medications. For example, a retired Iowa couple (81 and 75 years of age) have combined Social Security payments of $1297, almost one-quarter of which (over $300) goes to pay for prescriptions. Other patients, unable to handle the cost, do without certain drugs. Said one physician, "We have patients who come to the hospital because they had a stroke—because they stopped taking their hypertension medicine. . . . They had medication prescribed for them, but they couldn't afford it—so they didn't take it" (Colburn, 1992a, p. 13).

Technology and Transplants. Another factor in the explosion of medical costs is the development and increasing use of new, highly expensive technologies such as CAT (computerized tomography), MRI (magnetic resonance imaging), and PET (positron emission tomography). MRI machines cost about $2 million and PET scanners currently cost about $4 million. A CAT scan costs the patient between $600 and $800.

Also very costly are the many new medical procedures. For example, heart bypass surgery accounts for about 20 percent of all health care costs in the United States (and for many people, such surgery does little good). Then there is the increasing frequency of organ transplants, of the heart and kidney, for instance. The cost of a heart transplant is about $200,000, and a liver transplant costs even more. The drugs that patients need to prevent them from rejecting the new organs are also expensive. Furthermore, attempts by the body to reject a new organ are not uncommon, which requires further hospitalization and additional expense (Kutner, 1987). Even though transplants are still comparatively rare, they do contribute disproportionately to the explosion in health-care costs.

With the cost of health care continuing to rise, government measures have been aimed at controlling health-care expenditures. In the early 1980s came the establishment of Diagnostic Related Groups by the federal government that placed a ceiling on how much the government would pay for specific services rendered by hospitals and doctors to Medicare patients. This action was bitterly contested by hospitals and the American Medical Association. The cost of health care continues to be one of our most serious societal problems and is a source of considerable public dissatisfaction.

Crisis in U.S. Health Care

An issue that has received a great deal of attention in the last few years, and one that is likely to lead to great change in the near future, is the widely acknowledged crisis in American health care (*Journal of the American Medical Association,* 1991; Light, 1992). This crisis has many dimensions, including the huge and rapidly growing cost of health care in the United States and the enormous drain this represents on the federal budget [health care now absorbs 13.9 percent of GDP (gross domestic product) in the United States]. Overall, as we have seen, almost $900 billion was spent on health in 1993 ($3,299 for every person in the United States) and that expenditure is rising rapidly (about $60 to $70 billion, or 8 percent) each year.

Another and particularly disturbing aspect of the crisis is that, despite the huge outlay of funds, 17.3 percent of Americans in 1993 (up from 15.7 percent in 1989), primarily from the lower social classes, lack health insurance of any kind (Seccombe and Amey, 1995). Those who are uninsured are less likely to receive state-of-the-art treatments and are more likely to die than those with private insurance. While only 4.6 percent of American families with incomes above $50,000 per year have no health insurance, 35.3 percent of families with incomes below

$14,000 per year are in this predicament (National Center for Health Statistics, 1994, p. 240). Furthermore, another 37 percent of the poor are covered by Medicaid, the health plan for the poor funded by the federal and state governments (only 26 percent of the poor have private health insurance). Medicaid coverage varies greatly by state, and many doctors, especially those at the top of their fields, will not accept Medicaid patients or will accept them only on a limited basis. The main reason is that Medicaid generally reimburses far less for a given procedure than the doctor's regular fee. For example, Medicaid reimbursement for a tonsillectomy is only 37 percent of the private fee for that operation. In spite of its problems, Medicaid is an enormous drain on the nation's resources. In 1992, over $90 billion was spent on federal and state programs.

Alternatives to the American System of Health Care: Canada, Germany, and Japan

Canada.   The Canadian national health insurance plan is one of the most comprehensive in the world (Rosenthal, 1991). Tax money is used to offer free health care to all Canadian citizens. Key to the success of the Canadian system is tight control on costs. There is a cap on the total amount that can be paid any single physician in a year ($450,000), hospital budgets are tightly controlled, there are far fewer surgical teams, and, as a result, the costs for major surgery are far lower, and there are far fewer high-tech and very expensive medical machines like MRIs and CATs. All Canadian citizens, rich and poor, are able to flash their insurance cards and virtually everything will be covered. And there is little of the enormous paperwork that hampers the U.S. system and adds enormously to the cost of health care.

However, there are problems with the Canadian system (Gladwell, 1992). There are sometimes long waits for medical procedures, even for people in need of such urgent procedures as heart bypasses. For example, while in Toronto you might need to wait 4 months for a bypass operation, "In Washington, if you can't get a bypass within a week, you probably need a new cardiologist" (Gladwell, 1992, p. C3). There are far fewer high-tech medical machines in Canada, with the result that there are long waits for them as well. Sometimes people are even completely unable to get access to them. For example, there are 35 MRI machines in the Washington, D.C., area, but only five in Toronto; there are between 75 and 100 CAT scanners in D.C. and just 21 in Toronto. Said the chairman of the Radiology Department at George Washington University Hospital, "We do 4000 scans a year, most of them head trauma. I suppose that some of them, you could say, well he got dinged but he'll probably be all right, and if he dies later of an epidural hematoma then you could say, well, I guess we had no way of knowing" (Gladwell, 1992, p. C3). Another problem with the Canadian system, at least as it would be applied to the United States, is that, since it is based on a payroll tax, middle- and upper-class Americans would end up paying far more for health insurance than they do now under the private system. For this reason, as well as the others discussed above, better-off U.S. citizens might balk at such a system, but the roughly 45 million people in the United States without health insurance would undoubtedly regard it as their salvation.

Germany.   The German system of health care would seem, on the surface, to be an even more attractive model to the United States because, unlike the Canadian system, it contains elements more familiar to Americans, such as private physicians and job-based private insurance. Some private insurers will even permit a free stay at a health spa every 2 or 3 years "to cure whatever ails you" (Fisher, 1992, p. A1). In addition, the system provides local government insurance for the unemployed with the result that all Germans, like all Canadians, are covered. In the German system, insured patients never see a medical bill. Furthermore, instead of being rushed in and out of hospitals, Germany's system encourages "long, leisurely hospital stays. Germans routinely check into the hospital for ten days for a normal birth or four days for a simple biopsy that is a one-hour outpatient procedure in the United States" (Fisher, 1992, p. A1). And health care costs in Germany are far less than in the United States (8% of GNP in comparison to the 13% in the United States). (See Figure 14–2 for a comparison of national health expenditures in the United States, Germany, Canada, and Japan.)

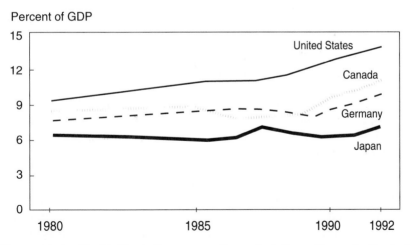

Percent of GDP

Figure 14–2.   Health Expenditures as a Percent of Gross Domestic Product: United States, Canada, Germany, and Japan, 1980–1992. (*Source: Health United States 1994 Sourcebook.* Hyattsville, MD: National Center for Health Statistics, 1995, p. 30.)

But the German system is not without its problems, and there are, in fact, ongoing efforts to reform it. For example, employee contributions are high in comparison to the United States; there is something of a two-tiered system since the wealthiest Germans can opt out of the public health system and purchase private insurance, which, in turn, gives them better health care; and costs are escalating out of control in Germany as they are in the United States, and this problem is likely to be exacerbated in the future as the German population ages. The government restricts access to hospital care and limits the number of high-tech machines, like CAT scanners and MRI machines, that each region of the country can have. The result is that there are the kinds of waits for access to these machines that one finds in Canada.

Japan.   The Japanese have what is described as "the most efficient universal health insurance system in the world" (Sterngold, 1992, p. A1). As in Germany, the Japanese system covers everyone with health insurance either through corporate or government plans. Because of their efficient health care system, as well as other factors, such as the nation's healthy diet, the Japanese are one of the healthiest societies in the world. As a result, life expectancy in Japan is the highest in the world. And, from the point of view of efficiency, it is done at comparatively low cost—Japanese companies pay about one-fifth of what American companies pay for health insurance. Patients do pay between 10 and 30 percent of their medical bills, although low-income people are heavily subsidized. Overall, the Japanese system costs even less than the German system, 6.8 percent of GNP.

But, of course, such a cost-efficient system has trade-offs—for example, once again, long waits. A 70-year-old man pedaled for 20 minutes to arrive at the hospital at 7:30 A. M., an hour before it officially opened. For his efforts, he was rewarded by being number 69 on the waiting list. This, in turn, meant that he would "only" need to wait until noon for a brief visit with the doctor (the typical private clinic physician sees 64 patients a day for an average of 5 minutes each), in which he was likely to receive little information and be allowed to ask few questions. For this, he pays $7.25 a month, no matter how many times he visits the hospital. Premiums are low because the government keeps a tight lid on medical costs and does not allow for variations in the reimbursement of different doctors or in different regions. Thus, for example, an appendectomy costs $388 wherever it is performed and whoever performs it. The clinics are likely to be crowded and dingy. Physicians tend to overprescribe medications, which they sell to patients to increase their restricted incomes. The result is that the Japanese take, on the average, 50 percent more medications than Americans. Furthermore, the physicians deign to tell their patients little or nothing about the drugs they are prescribing. A Japanese cancer specialist said, "The majority of patients in Japan know nothing about the drugs they are taking. . . . There are still plenty of doctors who clip off the name of the drug from the package given to patients. The attitudes are pre-modern" (Sterngold, 1992, p. A8).

Cross-national Perspectives

An International View of AIDS

The initial rapid growth of the AIDS epidemic, during the decade of the 1980s occurred in Sub-Saharan Africa, North America, and Western Europe. Now AIDS has spread and is threatening people on all continents (Bongaarts, 1996). The total number of AIDS cases worldwide is not known precisely, but the best estimates of the World Health Organization are that by 1994 17.2 million adults had been infected with the AIDS virus and nearly 3 million people have died of the disease. The yearly number of new HIV infections is now estimated at 2.4 million (Bongaarts, 1996).

While there is some uncertainty about the current numbers of HIV infections and AIDS cases, there is much more uncertainty about what will happen to those numbers in the future. In the early 1990s, some researchers made estimates that now are clearly excessive. For example, a group at the Harvard School of Public Health predicted a possible maximum of 110 million AIDS cases in the year 2000 (Altman, 1992). More realistic projections, based on World Health Organization data and careful demographic analysis, reveal much lower numbers, as can be seen in the accompanying table.

These projections are based on the fact that the yearly number of new HIV infections has already peaked in Africa, Latin America, North America, and Europe. Only Asia, with its enormous population, is expected to experience increases in yearly HIV infection rates in the years ahead (Bongaarts, 1996). In terms of worldwide numbers of AIDS cases in the future, Asia is certainly the largest unknown factor. But the potential dangers are obvious, as the case of India shows.

	HIV Infections (in millions)	
	Cumulative 1994	Cumulative 2005 (projections)
Sub-Saharan Africa	9.7	20.7[a]
Asia	3.5	19.1
North America	1.2	1.5
Latin America	2.0	4.6
Western Europe	0.7	0.9
World total	17.2	47.4

[a] These are the median projections by Bongaarts. High projections would be 50 percent higher and low projections would be 50 percent lower.

Source: Bongaarts, 1996.

A large and impoverished nation, India is experiencing a rapid increase in AIDS cases, caused by, among other things, widespread prostitution, the selling of blood on the black market in order to survive, and the ready availability of heroin (Anderson and Moore, 1992). The poorest people, with little education, do not understand where the disease comes from or how it can be prevented. The government, which is often ineffective, has been even more ineffectual in the case of AIDS because it has been "hampered by long-standing cultural taboos, the powerlessness of women and a general unwillingness to discuss sexual mores publicly" (Anderson and Moore, 1992, p. A20). One doctor, who founded the private Indian Health Organization in 1982, invades brothels trying to get customers to use condoms and drives around in a large van topped by a sign: "AIDS is too big to ignore" (Anderson and Moore, 1992, p. A20). But even he was forced to conclude, "A major catastrophe cannot be avoided. . . .The disease has already moved too fast and the country is too vast" (Anderson and Moore, 1992, p. A20).

At the present time, however, most of the attention with regard to AIDS is directed toward the United States and Sub-Saharan Africa where the disease is most common. Both social and economic factors are related to AIDS in these two areas and have produced important differences in the AIDS populations.

In general terms, AIDS is transmitted through sexual activity, blood, and prenatal contact. However, people in the United States and Africa get the disease in very different ways, which means that the distribution in the population also differs. In the United States the disease afflicts primarily homosexual men, and to a lesser, but increasingly important, degree, intravenous drug users. Since intravenous drug users are also more likely to be male, about 90 percent of the identified AIDS victims have been male (U.S. Bureau of the Census, 1990, p. 117). In Africa, by contrast, AIDS is widespread among heterosexuals, and thus there is a roughly 50–50 split between male and female cases (Makanjuola, 1991). These differences are traceable, in part, to differences in the sexual practices of the United States and Africa. For example, subordinate African women are unlikely to confront unfaithful husbands and they are not very apt to know about, or to be able to afford, condoms. In addition, many more Africans than Americans acquire AIDS through blood transfusions. In the United States, blood donors are now screened for the AIDS virus, but this is much less the case in Africa due to the lack of resources available for such procedures.

In the United States, in 1995 at least one-third of AIDS victims were intravenous drug users or persons who had had sex with intravenous drug users (Centers for Disease Control, 1995). By contrast, Africans are not as likely to get the disease through intravenous drug use because such drug use is virtually absent there. The intravenous drug users in the United States typically get AIDS by sharing contaminated needles with someone who has the disease, but Africans are likely to contract AIDS from other kinds of contaminated needles. For example, because of improper sterilization, AIDS is transmitted in Africa through medical injections for diseases such as malaria and diarrhea. In one study of AIDS patients in Kinshasa, the capital of Zaire, 80 percent reported that they had received medical injections before the symptoms of the disease appeared (Mann et al., 1986).

Also, because of the prevalence of heterosexual transmission of AIDS in Africa, about 2.5 million African women are infected with the AIDS virus; "82 per cent of women with AIDS worldwide have come from Africa" (Makanjuola, 1991, p. 6). African mothers are more likely to carry the virus than U.S. mothers. This means that there is a greater likelihood of newborn children getting the disease before, during, or shortly after birth in Africa.

Of course, there are important differences between the United States and Africa in the ability to deal with the disease. While it is a burden, the United States has the resources to care for its AIDS patients and to see that they receive the latest treatments. In Africa, there is little money to treat AIDS patients, given the continent's limited resources and its many other problems. Furthermore, although the United States and other nations such as Great Britain have gone to great lengths to inform and educate their populations about AIDS, such programs are likely to lag in Africa because of a lack of funds. Low levels of literacy in Africa reduce the effectiveness of such programs.

An interesting aspect of cross-national comparisons of AIDS is that, in different societies, different groups have come to be stigmatized as carriers of the disease. In the United States, homosexuals and intravenous drug users are most likely to be stigmatized. In Africa, female prostitutes have come to be stigmatized because they have an unusually high rate of the disease. In other nations, it is sometimes Americans and other times Africans who are stigmatized because of the prevalence of the disease in their countries.

ALTMAN, LAWRENCE K. "Researchers Report a Much Grimmer AIDS Outlook." *New York Times,* June 4, 1992.

ANDERSON, JOHN WARD, and MOORE, MOLLY. "AIDS Nears Epidemic Rate in India." *Washington Post,* September 14, 1992.

BONGAARTS, JOHN. "Global Trends in AIDS Mortality." *Population and Development Review,* Vol. 22, 1996.

CENTERS FOR DISEASE CONTROL. *HIV/AIDS Surveillance Report,* October 1995.

MAKANJUOLA, BOLA. "Living with AIDS." *West Africa,* January 14, 1991.

MANN, JONATHAN. "The Global AIDS Situation." *World Health,* June 1987.

MANN, J., FRANCIS, J. M., QUINN, T. et al. "Surveillance for AIDS in a Central African City: Kinshasa, Zaire." *Journal of the American Medical Association* 255, June 20, 1986.

Finally, as in Germany and the United States, the health care system in Japan is faced with spiraling costs, and it too is cutting back in various ways. While more successful in many ways than the U.S. system, the Japanese system has its problems and shares with the United States and Germany the problem of controlling skyrocketing costs in the future because, in part, of an aging population. Further reducing the viability of Japan as a model for the United States is the fact that the latter is able to deal with a fairly homogeneous, largely middle-class population, while the United States must create a system that distributes health care equitably within a far more stratified system with enormous pockets of poverty.

Thus, although the United States might learn some useful lessons from these other systems, the fact is that these systems have problems of their own, which are likely to grow in the coming years.

Organization of Health Care Systems in the United States

The Autonomy of Physicians

As of 1993, 670,300 medical doctors and 33,400 doctors of osteopathy actively practiced medicine in the United States (U.S. Bureau of the Census, 1995, p. 121). There were 1,853,000 registered nurses in the United States in 1992 (U.S. Bureau of the Census, 1994a, p. 121) (see Figure 14–3). Altogether, in 1994 over 9 million people were employed in a wide range of occupations within the health sector (by way of comparison, in 1980 there were only 5.3 million workers in this sector) (U.S. Bureau of the Census, 1995b, p. 121).

Although medical doctors constitute much less than 10 percent of the industry's total workforce, at present the entire health-care delivery system is subordinate to their professional authority. Physicians usually control not only the conditions of their own work but also the working conditions of other members of the health profession as well (Halpern, 1992). Consequently, the status and prestige awarded to the physician by the general public is recognition of the physician's monopoly of one of society's essential needs: health care.

Even though many changes in health care have occurred in recent decades, such as the increasing employment of physicians in for-profit hospitals, medical doctors continue to subscribe to a pattern of professional behavior that, in many ways, is based on an image of medical practice as it was around 1950. It is an image of the physician as an independent, fee-for-service, private practitioner. This image is of an entrepreneur completely free of lay control and totally in command of providing medical care. Medicine's autonomy rests on its supposed orientation of serving the public, its strong system of ethics, peer regulation, and professional expertise.

Number per 100,000 population

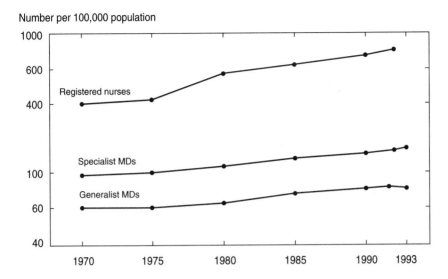

Figure 14–3. Active Doctors of Medicine and Registered Nurses: United States, 1970–1993. (*Source: Health United States 1994 Sourcebook.* Hyattsville, MD: National Center for Health Statistics, 1995, p. 29.)

In practice, these bases of medical autonomy have not worked as well as they should (Hafferty and Light, 1995). Peer regulation by physicians has generally been weak and ineffectual except in circumstances where errors and offenses have been blatant (Freidson, 1975; Millman, 1977; Bosk, 1979; Paget, 1988). Confronting a medical colleague is considered distasteful, even in private, and would be almost unthinkable in public. Freidson (1975) observes that rules of etiquette have restricted the evaluation of work and discouraged the expression of criticism. Millman (1977) contends that a "gentleman's agreement" exists among physicians, an unspoken agreement to overlook each other's mistakes, which grows out of a fear of reprisal and a recognition of common interests.

The American Medical Association has typically placed the self-interest of the medical profession over changes in public policy—especially when it comes to protecting the fee-for-service pattern of payment (Stevens, 1971). The medical profession in the United States has a consistent record of resisting social legislation that in any way reduces the authority, privilege, and income of physicians. As a group, the profession has opposed workmen's compensation, Social Security, voluntary health insurance, and health maintenance organizations (HMOs) in their initial stages. It has also opposed professional standards review organizations (intended to review the quality of medical work in federally funded programs), national health insurance, Medicare, Medicaid, and the Diagnostic Related Groups program. This has reduced societal confidence in medicine, since physicians in general are often viewed as placing the desire for financial profit ahead of the desire to help people (Laster, 1992).

A final example of the medical profession's self-serving position can be seen in the ways in which other health occupations have suffered because of the profession's manipulation. Chiropractors were at one time labeled *quacks* by the AMA, which continued its official efforts to discredit chiropractors until 1980. In 1987 a federal court decided that the AMA was guilty of unlawfully eroding the credibility of chiropractors (Shell, 1988). Physicians have also opposed acupuncturists; after they successfully drew acupuncture into the realm of medicine, they drastically limited its use (Wolpe, 1985).

The Subordinate Status of Nurses

Nursing is a major occupation in the health field. As physicians became the dominant profession in the United States, nurses have had great difficulty in achieving full professional recognition and, in fact, are usually considered by sociologists as semiprofessionals. They have never achieved anything close to the power, prestige, and income level attained by physicians. Because physicians have most of the formal, official power over patients in hospital settings, nurses' power is limited, although they may find ways of exercising informal power within this system. Nurses certainly enjoy less prestige than physicians, and there is no comparison between the incomes of the two occupations: the average net income for a physician in the United States in 1991 was almost $171,000 per year, while the average income of a full-time registered nurse in March 1992 was $37,738 (Aiken et al., 1995, p. 2).

How do we account for the failure of nurses to win full professional recognition? First, the overwhelming power of physicians within the health field makes it difficult for nurses to demonstrate their distinctive capabilities. Second, physicians have overtly opposed nurses' efforts to win professional recognition. Third, since nursing tends to be dominated by females (about 93.8 percent in 1994), males in general have opposed professional recognition for nursing. In fact, in male-dominated U.S. society, at least in the past, female-dominated occupations have found it impossible to win professional recognition. Finally, while physicians have generally assumed the high-status tasks (for example, brain surgery, open-heart surgery) for themselves, they have relegated nurses to the "dirty work" in hospitals (changing linen, emptying bed pans, etc.). Occupations that do dirty work are obviously hard-pressed to win professional recognition.

Doctor/Nurse Relationships

Traditionally, the work in medicine has been divided along gender lines. As mentioned earlier, doctors have been males and nurses have been females, and the authority of doctors has generally been unquestioned. Doctors make their medical decisions on the basis of medical histories, physical examinations, laboratory findings, and, sometimes, on the recommendations of other physicians who have been called in as consultants. Because nurses are often in close day-to-day contact with patients, they too, can give doctors useful information for making medical decisions. However, because doctors are supposed to be the medical authorities and decision makers, the advice given by nurses must be offered very carefully (Stein, 1974). When nurses advise doctors on appropriate medical treatments, they must do so without seeming to do so. For their part, doctors sometimes have to ask for the recommendations of nurses, but again without seeming to do so. This process has been called the "doctor–nurse game" (Stein, 1974, p. 202).

Hughes (1988) accepts Stein's views on the doctor–nurse game, but argues that it does not apply in all settings. Specifically, Hughes studied a casualty department in a British hospital. Although the formal authority for the sorting and initial diagnosis of acutely ill patients lies with doctors, in reality the need to make rapid decisions under great pressure falls mostly to nurses. The authority of the nurse is particularly clear in dealing with new doctors or with doctors recently returning to hospital work. Nurses in this setting often give doctors suggestions; they also reprimand doctors (especially young ones) and even question their competence.

Female Doctors

Although, as we have seen, medicine has often been divided along gender lines, changes are occurring. A particularly important development is the dramatic increase in female doctors. (It continues to be the case that relatively few males are entering nursing.) The increase in the number of women in medical schools is impressive: in 1971–1972, women made up only 10.9 percent of medical school students, but by 1992–1993 that percentage had almost quadrupled to 39.4 percent (National Center for Health Statistics, 1995, p. 210). Figure 14–4 shows the similarly impressive increase in medical degrees awarded to women. Less dramatic, but still indicative of a strong trend, is the fact that the percentage of female physicians increased from 10.8 percent in 1979 to 24 percent in 1993 (U.S. Bureau of the Census, 1995b).

Several accounts of women medical students and physicians detail the problems women have in gaining recognition as equal colleagues by male physicians and as "real" doctors by patients (Hammond, 1980; Lorber, 1984; West, 1984). But the trend is clear: women physicians will be commonplace in the future, and the impact should be significant. As more women enter the medical profession, there is the potential for a change in the relationship between doctors and nurses and, more important, between doctors and patients. With more women as doctors, improved communication is possible, along with a greater willingness to relate to patients as people. Lorber (1984) found that when male doctors assessed their accomplishments during their careers, they tended to talk of their skills and

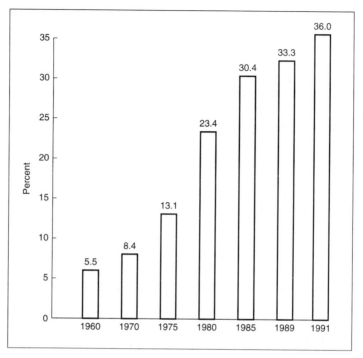

Figure 14–4. Percent of Medical Degrees Granted to Women, 1960–1989. (*Source:* U.S. Bureau of the Census, *Statistical Abstract of the United States, 1994,* p. 191.)

choices of appropriate treatment. The personal side of the physician–patient relationship was rarely mentioned. Women doctors, on the other hand, stressed their value to patients and did so using words like "help" and "care." As one woman physician put it, "I think the best thing that I do is simply taking care of patients and being a warm and caring physician" (Lorber, 1984, p. 106).

As women doctors in increasing numbers choose to work in specialties like internal medicine, family practice, and even surgery, instead of the usual choices of psychiatry, pediatrics, and pathology, they will be treating a wider range of patients and extending their influence. With a somewhat higher percentage of women doctors, sexist attitudes on the part of male physicians will likely diminish, since these doctors will have had exposure to competent and professional female counterparts in medical school and later in clinical practice (Halpern, 1988).

In spite of the gains being made by female physicians, however, they continue to lag behind male physicians in several ways. Most notable is the fact that male physicians earn, on the average, considerably more than female physicians (*Washington Post,* 1988b).

Emergence of the Business of Health Care

Important signs are now emerging that the professional dominance of the physician may be significantly reduced in the future. According to Cockerham (1986), three factors appear to account for this development. One is greater government involvement. Government intervention in health-care delivery remains limited at present, yet the evolving pattern is one of increased government regulation of medical practice. The second factor is the rise of consumerism in health care. More affluent and better educated people are attempting to take greater control over their health by making their own decisions about what medical services and health practices are best for them, and thereby interacting with physicians on a more equal basis.

The third challenge to the dominance of doctors is coming from a particularly powerful direction. A significant portion of the health market is being taken over by large business conglomerates (Starr, 1982; Ritzer and Walczak, 1988). Massive government funding of programs like Medicare and Medicaid has made health care a lucrative business. This fact has caused people to invest their money in private hospitals and nursing homes. Observing this trend, corporate chains began purchasing these facilities. This has been followed by a wave of mergers, acquisitions, and diversifications involving not only hospitals and nursing homes but a variety of enterprises such as hospital restaurants and supply companies, medical office buildings, emergency care centers, HMOs, health spas, and hospital management systems. The profit-making corporations expanded into markets that were underserved or into areas where they could compete successfully with nonprofit institutions by providing more attractive rooms, better food, a friendlier staff, and more efficient services.

In the context of corporate health care, the physician becomes an employee rather than an independent practitioner (Walsh, 1987). The doctor is bound to the rules, regulations, and procedures for practices established by the corporation, which, in all probability, is managed by people trained in business, not medicine. Hence, doctors who do corporate practice are not as likely to play the decisive role in decision making about policy, hospital budgets, capital investments, salaries, promotions, and personnel appointments. Work routines will undoubtedly be more regulated. Standards of performance will be developed, and the salaries of the doctors will be based on how well they perform. Physicians who do not meet these standards are apt to lose their jobs. Mistakes will also be closely scrutinized, not only to ensure quality care but also to avoid corporate liability for malpractice. In sum, the control of corporate medicine tends to be outside the immediate health care facility and in the hands of a management system that is primarily business oriented. Within this system, the doctor's autonomy will be significantly reduced. And as the twenty-first century approaches, the definition of medicine as a "sovereign profession" shows signs of being increasingly less accurate.

As a result of the changes discussed in this section, medicine is losing some of its luster. Physicians may be steering young people away from medical careers. As one physician said, "The realities of the new medicine are intruding on that relationship [between doctor and patient] and, for me and many others, are bringing this unique experience to an end" (Colburn, 1988, p. 9).

Patients and the Medical System

The Sick Role

The most influential theory explaining the behavior of sick persons in Western society is Talcott Parsons's (1951) concept of the sick role. It is based upon the assumption that being sick is undesirable, and the sick person wants to get well. However, because the sick are seen as unable to take care of themselves, they must seek medical treatment and cooperate with care providers. Therefore, sick persons have, in Parsons's view, a "duty to get well."

The **sick role** consists of four basic components: the sick person (1) is exempt from "normal" social roles, (2) is not responsible for his or her condition, (3) should try to get well, and (4) should seek technically competent help. Exemption from normal social roles because of illness is a temporary condition and is based on the premise that the sick person will try to get well. Therefore, the person who is excused from normal duties assumes an obligation to get well. This includes a further obligation to seek help from a technically competent practitioner, typically a physician. The physician, on the other hand, has an obligation to return the sick person to as normal a state as possible.

The merit of this analysis is that it describes a patterned set of expectations that defines the norms and values appropriate to being sick, both for the sick individual and for others who interact with that person. This pattern allows us to predict the behavior of the ill in certain circumstances, such as situations where people are excused from school or work to try to improve their condition, including a visit to a doctor if necessary. Consequently, Parsons's concept of the sick role describes the behavioral norms appropriate to being sick in Western society.

Situations do exist, however, where the sick role concept has limited value for explaining illness behavior. Not everyone behaves in the manner the sick role suggests. Some people deny being sick when they have symptoms of illness; others refuse to go to the doctor even when they know they should. Some do not cooperate with doctors when they receive medical advice; and others may not feel any particular obligation to get well, especially if they can benefit from illness by avoiding responsibilities such as work. The sick role applies best to illnesses that are temporary and can be overcome by a physician's help. But some diseases cannot be cured and are not temporary, and in this case becoming "well" is impossible. In addition, the sick role described by Parsons incorporates the middle-class assumptions that rational problem solving (seeking medical assistance for illness) is the most effective behavior possible, and effort will result in positive gain (health). The concept fails to take into account attitudes typical of an environment of poverty, where success is the exception.

Yet the sick role does provide a reasonably good explanation of the patient–physician relationship in terms of mutual obligations and expectations. (Both are expected to cooperate in improving the patient's health.) The concept also helps us understand the role of medicine in controlling deviant behavior. Taking a structural–functionalist approach, Parsons suggests that illness is a form of deviance, since it is abnormal to be sick. Illness is not only deviant but it is also dysfunctional for society as a whole because it interferes with the smooth functioning of a social system. If too many people were sick and not functioning properly, social systems would become unstable. This could lead to social breakdown because essential functions like growing food and educating the young could not be carried out.

The medical profession thus functions to offset the dysfunctional aspects of illness by curing, controlling, or preventing disease. Hence, medical practice becomes a mechanism by which a social system seeks to control the illnesses of its deviant sick by returning them to as normal a state as possible. Consequently, implicit in the concept of the sick role is the idea that medicine is an institution for the social control of deviant behavior and represents society in maintaining social stability. Whether medical procedures should be used to control a wide range of human behavior is a debatable topic, but the trend in modern society is to have medicine assume more and more responsibility for behavioral problems. (See our earlier discussion of the medicalization of society.) It has been argued, for instance, that there are few problems today that some group does not think of as a medical problem. Parsons helps us to see how medical practice operates as a form of social control.

Patients as Consumers

According to Reeder (1972), the concept of a person as a "health consumer" rather than a "patient" became established in the United States during the 1960s. In an age of consumerism, the traditional physician–patient relationship is significantly modified. Patients are expected to make demands and complain if those demands are not met (Nettleton and Harding, 1994). The patient exerts more control and assumes a more equal footing with the doctor in terms of status, decision making, and responsibility for outcomes. This is usually more characteristic of the middle and upper classes (Cockerham et al., 1986). Lower-class persons, in turn, may have a more passive orientation toward life and less willingness to take responsibility for their problems (Arluke et al., 1979).

An important counterinfluence on health consumerism, however, is medical technology. The development of a complex array of medical equipment and procedures has increasingly taken away the self-management of health from all patients, but especially from those at the bottom of society with their more limited levels of education and experience with technology. Although all patients are dependent upon physicians as experts, better educated persons are likely to be less in awe of medical "wonders."

Seeking Medical Care

Not everyone responds to the symptoms of illness in the same way, as mentioned earlier. Some people will consult with a doctor as soon as they feel sick, while others with similar symptoms will try self-treatment, ignore the symptoms, or perhaps simply wait to see what develops from them. Only about one-third of all symptoms that a person experiences will eventually be brought to the attention of a physician. The more uncertain someone is about the meaning of his or her symptoms, the more likely that person is to visit a doctor.

Typically, older people and females will see a physician about their health more readily than younger people and males. The aged visit doctors more often because, as a person becomes old, his or her bodily afflictions, even minor ones, tend to be more serious. Women visit physicians more often because they have more health problems. Even after subtracting doctor visits for conditions associated with pregnancy, women still show more visits to the doctor than men. Men visit doctors about four times a year, while women average over five visits annually (Cockerham, 1986).

Middle-class and upper-socioeconomic groups continue to maintain the highest levels of health and participate more in preventive care. Preventive care is intended to keep healthy people healthy and consists of regular physical examinations and the like. The lower class has more illness and disability, and visits physicians more for treatment of symptoms. However, when the affluent really have need of doctors, they have the financial resources to seek the services of the best doctors whenever they want.

Doctor/Patient Communications

The interaction that takes place between doctor and patient is an exercise in communication. As is the case in any other face-to-face situation, the effectiveness of this exercise depends upon the ability of the participants to understand each other. A major barrier to effective communication, however, rests in the differences between patients and physicians with respect to status (Fox, 1993; Meredith, 1993), education, professional training, knowledge (Hak, 1994), and authority.

Some doctors are very effective communicators, while others do poorly when it comes to communication with patients (Waitzkin, 1985).

Two groups in society, those with a poor education and women, have been identified as having the most communication problems with physicians. It has been found, for example, that poorly educated persons are the most likely to have their questions ignored and to be treated impersonally as a disease entity instead of an individual to be respected (Ross and Duff, 1982). Other studies show that physicians prefer upper-class and upper-middle-class patients and give them more personalized service (Link, 1983). A major reason is that doctors find these patients to be more like themselves; that is, higher strata patients reflect values, norms, and attitudes similar to those held by the doctor. Thus, doctors can be more comfortable in working with them. In contrast, Roth (1969) describes the way many physicians regard lower-class patients:

> They are considered the least desirable patients. The doctor has probably dealt with "their kind" during his years as a student and resident in outpatient and emergency clinics, and he has concluded that they are often dirty and smelly, follow poor health practices, fail to observe directions or meet appointments, and live in a situation which makes it impossible to establish appropriate health regimes (Roth, 1969, p. 227).

As for women, Fisher (1984; see also Todd, 1989) studied doctor–patient communication in a family practice clinic and found that many women patients were not satisfied with the explanations given them. Sometimes they did not believe they were being given the information needed to understand their health situation. "The women who called were often well educated and articulate, yet they did not feel they had enough information with which to make reasonable decisions or they felt they did not understand or could not trust the recommendation their physician made" (Fisher, 1984, p. 2).

Summary

In contemporary urban-industrial societies the major illnesses are no longer the infectious communicable diseases; instead they are chronic disorders. The major chronic diseases, heart disease and cancer, are importantly influenced by lifestyles.

The sociological specialty called *medical sociology* focuses on many different aspects of health and illness. Among the important parts of medical sociology is social epidemiology, which is the study of the frequency and pattern of disease within a particular population.

It is often assumed that medical discoveries and practices were responsible for the victory over infectious diseases, but social and environmental changes were far more important than developments in medicine.

The medicalization of society is a pattern of defining a variety of behaviors, often deviant behaviors, as medical problems. Alcoholism, compulsive gambling, and the treatment of hyperactive children are examples.

Males and females differ in their health problems and their responses to them. Women are sick more often, but live longer; men are sick less often, but die sooner. There are both biological and social psychological reasons for the earlier deaths of men. Smoking is increasing among females, however, which is bringing the female death rate for lung cancer closer to that of males.

The aging of the United States population is an increasingly important factor in the health problems of the country, even though the health of people reaching old age is better than it was in the past.

Black people in the United States have generally poorer health and higher mortality than the white population. The lower social classes of the society have higher rates of infectious disease, as well as higher rates of the "modern ills" like heart disease. The life-styles, economic limitations, and social environmental conditions of the poor contribute to their higher illness rates.

Health costs have escalated greatly in the last 20 years, primarily because of increased labor costs, rising costs of prescription drugs, new and expensive technologies, and inflation. Attempts to control costs have had only limited success.

There is a health care crisis in the United States that involves, among other things, a huge drain on the federal budget, 45 million largely poor Americans without health insurance, and the fragile state of many health insurance companies. The health plans of Canada, Germany, and Japan are functioning better and offer the United States many useful ideas, but they, too, are plagued with problems.

The health field has traditionally been dominated by the doctors, both individually and through their professional organizations. Nurses are another important part of the health field, but they have failed to win the power, status, and wealth accorded to physicians. In doctor–nurse relationships, doctors maintain a dominant position, even when they must rely on the greater knowledge of nurses. More and more women are becoming doctors, and their presence is likely to bring changes in the relationship between doctors and their patients.

Several changes are likely to reduce the dominance of physicians, including greater government involvement, increased consumerism among patients, and the rise of corporate health care.

The sick role is an undesirable role that carries with it both exemptions and expectations. The most important expectation is that patients will cooperate with medical practitioners in order to leave the sick role. People today are often thought of as "health consumers," who are expected to take an active responsibility for their health. Seeking medical care is one such responsibility that the more affluent, in the past, have been more likely to do. Those with greater economic resources could afford to get medical care because it caused them less financial hardship.

Communication between doctors and patients is largely controlled by the doctors. Some doctors communicate well and others, poorly. The quality of communication between doctor and patient is an important element in the treatment of disease.

CRITICAL THINKING

1. Explain how social epidemiology has been a useful tool in understanding the AIDS crisis in the United States.
2. How have the major causes of death in the United States changed since the beginning of this century? How do these changes move health even further into the realm of sociology?
3. How is the contraction of disease closely linked to people's actions and behaviors?
4. Give examples of the medicalization of U.S. society. Is this a positive or negative trend?
5. Compare and contrast the health status of various subpopulations in the United States. How important are gender, social class, age, and race in determining the quality of a person's health?
6. What are the major dimensions of the health care crisis in the United States?
7. What solutions to America's problems can be found in the health care systems of Canada, Germany, and Japan? What types of problems plague their health care systems?
8. Describe the traditional pattern of physician behavior in the United States. Upon what has physician status and prestige been based? What forces in the medical community may change this pattern?
9. Contrast the status of nurses and doctors in the United States. What accounts for the differences you see? How might the impending nursing shortage force change in this profession?
10. How is doctor behavior affected by patient expectations? Which groups in society have trouble communicating with doctors? Why?

15

Religion

One of the most striking features of the last quarter of the twentieth century has been the revival of religion throughout the world. Religious divisions have inspired bloody conflicts among Hindus and Sikhs and Muslims in India; between Catholics and Protestants in Northern Ireland; among Jews, Christians, and Muslims in the Middle East; between Shi'ite Muslims in Iran and Sunni Muslims in Iraq; and between Buddhists and Hindus in Sri Lanka. Equally as striking has been the prominence of religion and religious leaders in the momentous political changes that have engulfed countries throughout the former Soviet Union and its former satellites in Eastern Europe. For example, religious differences among Croatian Catholics, Serbian Eastern Orthodox, and Bosnian Muslims have been at the core of the savage conflict that has rent Bosnia–Herzegovina. Moreover, religious fundamentalism has swept through the Islamic world, has formed the basis of a major Hindu political party in India, and has asserted a vigorous presence in American political and cultural life. Thus, despite earlier predictions of its gradual decline, religion remains of vital importance in the modern world (see Table 15–1).

Religion, a universal feature of human existence, is one of the most dynamic, fascinating, varied, and complex of all human phenomena. Wallace (1966) has estimated that, from the earliest human history to the present day, humans have practiced about 100,000 different religions. Religions are intimately involved

Table 15–1. Estimated Adherents of the World's Principal Religions, Mid-1994

Religions	World	%
Christians	1,900,174,000	33.6
Roman Catholics	1,058,069,000	18.7
Protestants	391,143,000	6.9
Orthodox	174,184,000	3.1
Anglicans	78,038,000	1.4
Other Christians	199,707,000	3.5
Muslims	1,033,453,000	18.3
Hindus	764,000,000	13.5
Buddhists	338,621,000	6.0
Chinese folk religionists	149,336,000	2.6
New-Religionists	128,975,000	2.3
Tribal religionists	99,150,000	1.8
Sikhs	20,204,000	0.4
Jews	13,451,000	0.2
Shamanists	11,010,000	0.2
Confucians	6,334,000	0.1
Baha'is	5,835,000	0.1
Jains	3,987,000	0.1
Shintoists	3,387,000	0.1
Other religionists	20,419,000	0.4
Nonreligious	924,078,000	16.3
Atheists	239,111,000	4.2
Total Population	5,661,525,000	100.0

Source: David B. Barrett, "Worldwide Adherents of All Religions by Seven Continental Areas, Mid-1994." Reprinted with permission from *Britannica Book of the Year,* 1996. © 1996, Encyclopædia Britannica, Inc.

with the working of societies. On the one hand, religions often provide social stability and inhibit social change. On the other hand, religious inspiration has been a dynamic source of social change. Therefore, to comprehend fully the nature of human life, it is essential to understand the intimate relationship between religion and the functioning of human societies.

Religion has been a social institution of great interest to sociologists. Almost all of the classical social theorists—Marx, Weber, Durkheim, Simmel—and many of the most prominent sociologists today have been interested in the role of religion in human societies and, especially, in the emergence of modern society.

For example, in *The Protestant Ethic and the Spirit of Capitalism,* a study that has become one of the classics of sociological theory, Max Weber suggested that the development of the emphases on acquisitiveness, systematic calculation, and the work ethic that characterize the economic system of modern capitalism was closely linked to the spread of Protestantism throughout Western society. This relationship was especially pronounced among sects that had adopted the doctrines of John Calvin, a sixteenth-century Swiss theologian. Chief among Calvin's tenets was the idea of predestination, the doctrine that held that the fate of all people—whether they would be going to heaven or condemned to eternal hell when they died—was predetermined by God.

Calvinist religious doctrine eliminated the Catholic sacraments that guaranteed being saved, and ruled out good works and feelings as ways of determining whether God had selected them to go to heaven. Therefore, Calvinists could never know their fate with certainty. They were perpetually insecure and had to look elsewhere for signs that would indicate whether they might be among the "elect," those who were in God's favor and would escape the fires of hell. Having accepted Martin Luther's view that all earthly callings serve God, Calvinists came to believe that economic success in this life was a sign of salvation in the next. As a consequence, they struggled to accumulate wealth beyond their needs, and, in the process, they developed the character traits of hard work, self-discipline, and industriousness to achieve worldly success.

The Calvinist drive to achieve economic success was not simply a matter of personal greed but was rather an expression of a profoundly religious impulse. However, because Calvinists rejected worldly pleasures, they could not enjoy the fruits of their labors—the wealth that their hard work had enabled them to accumulate. Moreover, because they could never quite be sure whether they were saved, they could never relax. Instead, by reinvesting their profits and expanding their businesses, they were able to achieve additional worldly assurances of their otherworldly fate.

Eventually the religious basis of this constant quest for wealth was lost, and people came to seek the accumulation of profits, not as a sign of success in the next world, but as a measure of success in this world. However, the accumulation of profits was made legitimate by what Weber called the **Protestant ethic**—a system of beliefs and action involving a commitment to hard work, frugality, self-denial, and acquisitiveness. According to Weber, it was this legitimation (or justification) of the profit motive that contributed to the development of the values and personality traits that characterized the spirit of capitalism in the Western world and led ultimately to the development of the capitalist economic system (Weber, 1904–1905/1958).

The Sociological Perspective: Religion as a Social Phenomenon

A sociologist's perspective on religion differs from a theologian's or an adherent's. On the surface, a sociology of religion may seem to be a contradiction in terms. If sociologists are committed to an empirical and scientific analysis of social phenomena, how can they study something that is intimately related to the supernatural, which cannot be studied empirically?

Although we cannot scientifically study the supernatural, we can analyze the social phenomena that are related to the experience of the supernatural and are expressed as religious feelings. These include religious behaviors and practices, such as praying, missionary work, and observing religious holidays, and religious beliefs—for example, in a feminine God, in Satan or the Devil, in a Heaven populated by angels, in a Hell of eternal fire. In addition, the social roles (such as the clergy, theologians, denominational officials) connected with religion and the social organizations and institutions of religion (such as churches, synagogues, mosques, shrines, temples, sects, and denominations) are also frequent subjects of sociological investigation.

The **sociology of religion** examines the behaviors and practices, beliefs, roles, and organizational structures of the world's major religions, such as Islam, Christianity, Hinduism, Judaism, Buddhism, and Confucianism, as well as religious movements, such as Rastafarianism, santeria, Haitian voodoo, or the Hare Krishnas. In addition to focusing on the beliefs and practices associated with formal or "official" religious traditions and institutions, the sociology of religion also encompasses what has been termed *folk* or *popular* religion, which "exists alongside formal religious belief and practice [and refers to] the ways in which individuals take religious belief, interpret it in practical terms, and put it to work to do something that will give order and meaning to their lives" (Lippy, 1994, p. 2). Popular religion is present in numerous forms of popular culture, including rock music, film, television shows, theme parks, greeting cards, and literature. For example, Lardas (1995) has suggested that Graceland, the Memphis home of Elvis Presley, has become a shrine—"sacred space"—to which thousands of people annually make solemn pilgrimages that reflect deeply spiritual sentiments.

Thus, the sociology of religion is concerned with a wide variety of beliefs, symbol systems, and social practices, many of which are frequently not generally perceived or defined as "religious." For example, for many years communism served many people as a kind of religion that provided a set of doctrines for explaining and giving meaning to human existence, it provided policies for achieving a "heaven on earth," and it developed ceremonial rituals that united its followers into a community of believers. The dramatic changes that have accompanied the disintegration of the Soviet Union have led many to characterize communism as "the God that failed" (Marty, 1991).

Besides identifying political ideologies that assume a religious quality, some writers have suggested that for many people psychoanalysis and a variety of therapeutic techniques, groups, and support networks (for example, Alcoholics Anonymous) have become religious practices eliciting intense personal commitments from adherents (Glazer and Moynihan, 1963, p. 175; Lippy, 1994, pp. 231–232). Similarly, some commentators have argued that organized sport in contemporary society has taken on many religious characteristics (Rudin, 1972; Novak, 1976; Prebish, 1984; Hoffman, 1992).

The essential element uniting these diverse phenomena in the category of religion is that, to some extent, each has developed a sacred quality. In his classic study of religion, *The Elementary Forms of Religious Life,* Emile Durkheim (1912/1965) argued that at the heart of religion is the idea of the sacred, as contrasted with the profane. The **profane** refers to the ordinary, the everyday, the commonplace, the utilitarian, the mundane aspects of life. The sacred, on the other hand, elicits an attitude of reverence, respect, mystery, awe, and sometimes fear. The respect accorded to certain objects transforms them from the profane to the sacred. Although societies differ in what they define as sacred and profane, all societies make such distinctions. Often nonmaterial entities such as gods and spirits are defined as sacred, but "a rock, a tree, a spring, a piece of wood, a house—in a word, anything—can be sacred" (Durkheim, 1912/1965, p. 52). The **sacred** are those objects that people define and act toward with respect and reverence. Churches or temples are not merely buildings where religious meetings are held; they are also sacred places. They and their contents are treated with reverence and respect.

Above all, religion is a *social* phenomenon. First, religion involves aspects of human existence that are socially defined as sacred; what comprises the sacred varies among religious systems. Therefore, all religious systems are human phenomena, defined and constructed by people. Second, religion is fundamentally a shared, communal activity; it is expressed in communities of people who share common creeds, moral and ethical codes, and rituals. Thus religion is rooted in social processes, and its expression is shaped by the same factors—social class, ethnicity, technology, and language—that affect other social institutions. Sociologists are especially interested in examining how social conditions affect the expression of religious patterns.

Religion is a social phenomenon in still another sense; it is a socially defined way of interpreting and comprehending the realities of human existence, and of making them understandable. Religion provides a system of meaning, a definition and interpretation of life. **Religion,** then, involves those things that a society holds sacred; it comprises an institutionalized system of symbols, beliefs, values, and practices that deal with questions of ultimate meaning.

The Social Functions of Religion

Society and religion are closely interrelated. A useful way of viewing this interrelationship is to examine the functions and dysfunctions of religion for individuals and for the larger society. Such an examination underscores the social character of religion.

Meaning, Social Solidarity, and Social Control

Religion provides a source of personal comfort and consolation. A religious system offers emotional support for people that enables them to endure very difficult circumstances. Human existence, after all, is precarious and uncertain. Religion enables people to accept the unacceptable and the inevitable—the disappointments, frustrations, sufferings, tragedies, and inevitable death—that are inherent in human existence. Religion provides a source of strength and meaning in the face of the ever-present possibility of the unanticipated, unexpected, and unanswerable.

One of the objectives of Durkheim's classic study of suicide was to demonstrate the role of religion in providing the individual with strength in the face of adversity (Durkheim, 1893/1951). In the 1980s, Stack (1983) examined the relationship between religiosity and suicide rates in the United States. Using church attendance as his primary measure of religiosity, he found that the lower the rates of church attendance, the higher the rates of suicide. Indeed, the religious factor was more important than the unemployment rate in explaining suicide rates. He concluded that a decline in institutionalized religion will lead to a situation in which the individual is not integrated into a moral community and thus will be more isolated and more vulnerable to suicide.

A recent study by Pescosolido and Georgianna (1989) of differences among religious denominations in the United States confirmed the general proposition that religion influences the suicide rate. However, they found that suicide rates are influenced by the denominations found in a specific geographic area, and that some denominations exert a stronger "protective" influence (that is, have lower suicide rates) than others. Counties with higher percentages of Catholics and evangelical Protestants (Nazarenes, Evangelical Baptists, Seventh-Day Adventists, Churches of God) had lower suicide rates than counties where mainstream Protestant denominations (Episcopalian, Presbyterian, United Methodist, United Church of Christ, Lutheran) predominated. The authors' explanation for these denominational differences lies in the nature of the social bonds and the sense of community that each of these denominations creates. Catholics and evangelical Protestants are much more likely to have their religious membership result in ties that bind people to a religious community and create a sense of belonging. Thus, by integrating individuals into a moral community, religion provides a source of strength, security, and emotional support that sustains people during difficult times.

Social Control.   One of the basic problems for any society is to keep order and maintain social control. Society must deal with deviance and prevent those who have deviated from becoming fully alienated and thereby disrupting society. Religious ceremonies provide a source of social cohesion and unity for a society. Moreover, through various rites and ceremonies, such as the Catholic confessional or the Protestant communion, religion supplies ritualized ways in which those who have deviated from societal norms and values can rid themselves of their guilt. Religion provides an emotional release for the individual that also maintains the cohesion of the society. Religion thus serves as a means of social control, by which members of society accept and conform to dominant norms and values.

Religion not only provides psychological support for individuals; it also maintains the existing social order. Religions tend to support and to justify a society's norms and values, and to maintain the established and dominant groups within a society. Religion can also be used to legitimate the domination of one group by another. Although he had come to power as the leader of a secular Iraqi political movement, Saddam Hussein frequently employed traditional Islamic rhetoric to justify his 1990 invasion of Kuwait. Moreover, he denounced as "infidels" the U.S. and Western defense of Kuwait and characterized his military campaign against them as a *jihad* (holy war). Religion thus often functions to legitimate, that is, to provide ideological support or justification for, the status quo or particular economic or political policies. Berger (1967) has argued that this legitimating function is the primary and defining characteristic of religion.

An excellent example of the use of religious authority to support the traditional social order involves the widespread religious opposition to certain aspects of the women's movement. Pope John Paul II, for example, has said that motherhood is at the center of Christian beliefs and should be promoted. "I want to remind young women that motherhood is the vocation of women. It was that way in the past. It is that way now and it will always be that way. It is a woman's eternal vocation" (*Washington Post,* 1979).

By interpreting the existing social order as ordained by God, religion can mask the fact that all societies are constructed by people; it can make a society's norms, values, and social arrangements appear to be fixed, permanent, and immutable—beyond human control. In the process, religion may obscure the humanly constructed nature of society and social problems, especially for those at the bottom of the social hierarchy. By acting as a conservative force in supporting the status quo, religion can undermine and retard reform and change. This was the essence of Karl Marx's critique of religion. Marx argued that because religion deflects attention from the humanly created inequalities in a society, it serves as the "opiate of the masses."

From this perspective, religion offers temporary relief for the poor and the dispossessed, but it prevents them from acting to change the structure of society and thus dealing with the basic sources of their problems. It leads the poor to reject earthly rewards—which they cannot achieve—as valueless when compared with the rewards promised by their religious belief system. Individuals may not be a "success" in this earthly existence, but because they have accepted the "otherworldly" values of a religious system, their ultimate salvation is ensured.

In the News

"A Fundamental and Sacred Aspect of Life": Sexuality and Religious Ethics in Tension

Religion has never existed in a social vacuum; its form and content both shape and are shaped by the broader society. For example, organized religion has not escaped the impact of the sexual revolution that has recently liberalized expressions of sexuality in American society. Although numerous social issues (for example, race relations, women's rights, abortion) have recently been the subject of heated debates within religious bodies, none has been so divisive or has elicited greater turmoil than the issue of sexual morality. Christian and Jewish teachings have traditionally limited sexual relations to heterosexual relations within marriage and have excluded homosexuals from the clergy. Reflecting increased controversy over the issue, in 1990, the Roman Catholic Church reaffirmed its classic stand limiting sexual relations to heterosexual marriage partners. However, several prominent religious groups—the Presbyterian Church (U.S.A.), the United Methodist Church, the Episcopal Church, the Evangelical Lutheran Church in America, Reform Judaism, and Conservative Judaism—have recently issued studies that have begun to explore the implications of their restriction of sexuality to relations between married, heterosexual partners.

Among the Protestant denominations mentioned above, the Presbyterian Church (U.S.A.) has produced the most ambitious and comprehensive of the several denominational efforts to consider changes in their traditional stance on sexuality. The furor that greeted the 1991 publication of the Presbyterian task force report, "Keeping Body and Soul Together: Sexuality, Spirituality, and Social Justice," mirrors the controversy that the issue of human sexuality has aroused, even among more liberal religious bodies. Although public opinion polls showed Presbyterians overwhelmingly opposed to changes in church policy barring homosexuals from the ministry and declaring homosexual relationships sinful, the Presbyterian task force responsible for preparing the report heard extensive and often agonizing testimony from people—gays and lesbians, the aged, young unmarried people living together, the physically handicapped, women trapped in destructive marriages—who had been alienated from the church by its restriction of sexuality to heterosexual marital relationships. For example, 40 percent of adult Presbyterians are single, and adherence to the church's teaching would prevent them from experiencing sexual intimacy.

While the several denominational reports generally condemned adultery, sexual abuse, prostitution, pornography, and sexual exploitation, they also criticized the church's traditional notions of sexuality as being grounded on a patriarchal model that legitimates traditional gender roles and, especially, male gender privileges. As an alternative to the single sexual outlet that is currently sanctioned, the Presbyterian report (which reflected the perspective generally adopted by other denominations) emphasized the quality of commitments involved in sexual relationships rather than the genders or legal relationship of the partners. It called for "offering a diversity of responsible sexualities in the church, including the lives of gay men and lesbians, as well as new patterns among non-traditional families." Rather than fearing sexuality, the Presbyterian report (like those produced by the Methodists, Evangelical Lutherans, and Episcopalians) views it as a "divine gift" that can enhance the quality of life by bringing people into "loving, caring, mutual relations with others; sexual intimacy should be celebrated, not denied." The church's primary concern, therefore, "should not be focused in a limited way on rules about who sleeps with whom" or whether sexual activity is premarital, marital, or postmarital, but rather "whether the relation is responsible, the dynamics genuinely mutual, and the loving full of joyful caring. . . . What matters morally and ethically is how we live our lives as faithful people, regardless of our sexual orientation."

Criticism of these proposed changes in the Presbyterian Church's traditional stance toward sexuality was vehement and led ultimately (as in other religious bodies) to rejection of the report. However, the efforts among numerous religious groups to consider these issues demonstrates the intimate way in which religion is linked with the political and social controversies of the larger society. It also demonstrates the ways in which religion can act both as a conservative force that upholds and justifies the status quo and as a dynamic prophetic voice that critically challenges the existing social order.

CAREY, JOHN J. "Body and Soul: Presbyterians on Sexuality." *The Christian Century,* May 8, 1991.
"Churches in Change." *USA Today,* June 4, 1991.
FULKERSON, MARY MCCLINTOCK. "Church Documents on Human Sexuality and the Authority of Scripture." *Interpretation,* 49:1, January 1995.
The General Assembly Special Committee on Human Sexuality, Presbyterian Church (U.S.A.). "Keeping Body and Soul Together: Sexuality, Spirituality, and Social Justice." Reports to the 203rd General Assembly (1991), Baltimore, MD, 1991.
GITTINGS, JIM. "A Bonfire in Baltimore." *Christianity and Crisis,* May 27, 1991.
STEINFELS, PETER. "What God Really Thinks about Who Sleeps with Whom." *New York Times,* June 2,1992.
WATTS, GARY L. "An Empty Sexual Ethic." *The Christian Century,* May 8, 1991.
ZELIZER, GERALD L. "Conservative Rabbis, Their Movement, and American Judaism." *Judaism,* 44:3, Summer 1995.

Critical, or Prophetic, Function

Even though religion often legitimates an existing social order, it can also challenge and change it. Therefore, religion can also perform a critical, or prophetic, function. Religion performs a **prophetic function** when it provides the standards for critically examining, challenging, and changing the existing social order. This prophetic function has occurred throughout the history of Judaism and Christianity, and it exists in constant tension with religion's tendency to support the status quo.

Many radical social movements have been grounded in religion. One of the most visible in the world today has been the development of "liberation theology" that has emerged as a force for radical change, especially in Latin America. Liberation theology is committed to social justice for the poor and the dispossessed and to the elimination of the injustices created by systems of extreme social inequality (Candelaria, 1990; Smith, 1991; Levine, 1995).

The Changing Nature of Religion in the United States

Religion in the United States has been characterized both by relatively unchanging, stable features and by constant change. Religious organizations come and go; patterns of participation change; prevailing religious ideas vary from one generation to the next. At the same time, the basic patterns of commitment and participation are much as they were a century ago, and, despite evidence of a restructuring of American religion, the same broad religious communities (Protestant, Catholic, and Jewish) continue to be prominent features of American religious life. Here we examine three basic characteristics of American religion—its pervasiveness, its secularism, and its denominational pluralism—in light of its tradition of simultaneous continuity and change.

Pervasiveness of Religion

Religion has always been perceived to be a conspicuous part of American life. From the earliest European settlements, religious factors have been prominent in this society; the dominant trends in American religion have been "profoundly different" from those in Europe (Caplow, 1985, p. 101). Almost all available data indicate that "the United States has been among the most religious countries in the Christian world" (Lipset, 1963a, p. 150).

The extraordinarily religious character of the American people persists even today. Numerous surveys have shown that, among industrial nations, Americans are among the most religious people in the world. Public opinion surveys conducted over the past 40 years indicate that the vast majority of Americans (between 94 and 99 percent) believe in God or a universal spirit, a percentage greater than in any other Western industrial society (Princeton Religious Research Center, 1995, p. 1). In addition, when asked to rate, on a scale of 1 to 10, how important God is in their lives, the average rating of Americans is exceeded only by South Africans, with the highest rating reported by African Americans (see Figure 15–1).

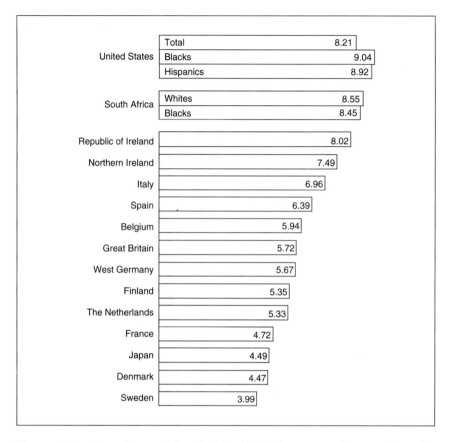

Figure 15–1.   Importance of God in Life (1981) (average ratings on ten-point scale). (*Source:* Gallup Opinion Index, "Religion in America: 50 Years: 1935–1985," Report No. 236, 1985, p. 50.)

Religious behavior among the American people—as measured by membership or participation in a religious community—has remained relatively stable during the past two decades. As Figure 15–2 indicates, church and synagogue membership among Americans has remained relatively unchanged since 1975, although, as we will note later, shifts have occurred in the religious groups with which people have been affiliated. The proportion of American adults who say that they are members of a church or synagogue rose to a peak of 76 percent in 1947 and gradually declined to 67 percent in 1972. Since then, church or synagogue membership has remained the same, standing at 69 percent in 1993 (Gallup and Newport, 1991; Princeton Religious Research Center, 1995, p. 6).

Americans are among the world's most active participants in formal religious services, ranking substantially behind Ireland, but only slightly behind Northern Ireland, Mexico, and South Africa (Campbell and Curtis, 1994). Church and synagogue attendance paralleled the decline in membership that occurred during the post-World War II period (see Figure 15–3), especially during the 1960s among

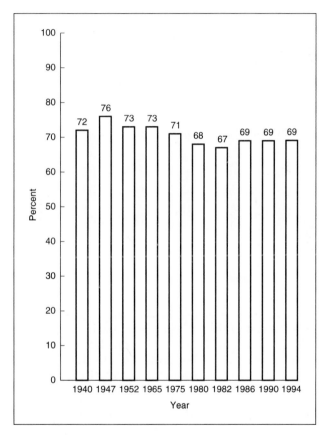

Figure 15–2. Church and Synagogue Membership as a Percentage of the U.S. Population. (*Source: The Gallup Report.* "Religion in America," Report No. 259, April 1987, p. 35; George Gallup, Jr., and Frank Newport, "More Americans Now Believe in a Power outside Themselves." *The Gallup Poll Monthly,* Report No. 297, June 1990, p. 37; Princeton Religious Research Center, "Religion in America: 1995 Supplement," p. 6.)

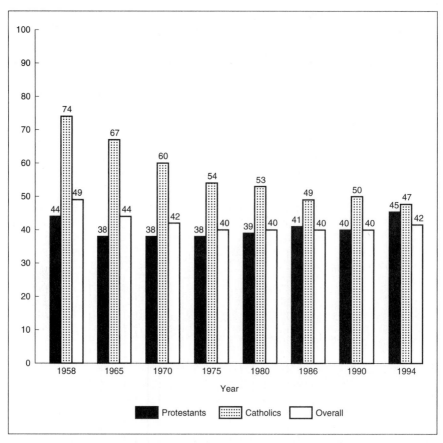

Figure 15–3. Percentage of Americans Attending Church during an Average Week. (*Source: The Gallup Report.* "Religion in America." Report No. 259, April 1987, p. 38; George Gallup, Jr., and Frank Newport, "More Americans Now Believe in a Power outside Themselves." *The Gallup Poll Monthly,* Report No. 297, June 1990, p. 37; Princeton Religious Research Center, "Religion in America: 1995 Supplement," p. 6.)

Roman Catholics who disagreed with Pope Paul VI's encyclical on "artificial birth control" (Hout and Greeley, 1987). Since 1975, however, religious participation has been relatively constant, with about 40 percent of Americans indicating that they regularly attend religious services. In 1994, this figure stood at 42 percent (McAneny and Saad, 1993, p. 4; Princeton Religious Research Center, 1995, p. 11).

Cross-national Perspectives

Population Growth in Islamic Nations

Sociologists have long been fascinated by the influence of religion on social life. For example, in his classic study of suicide, Durkheim compared suicide rates among Jews, Catholics, and Protestants. Similarly, Weber's classic, *The Protestant Ethic and the Spirit of Capitalism,* examined how the doctrines of Calvinism influenced the development of modern capitalism.

Many sociological studies have noted that religious affiliation tends to be associated with a variety of demographic factors, including fertility levels. In the United States, for example, Catholics have in the past generally had higher birth rates than Protestants and Jews, although these historic differences have recently changed (see Chapter 17). Because Muslim nations are among the world's most rapidly growing, we will examine whether Islam, today the world's second largest religion with nearly a billion adherents, influences population growth.

Islam was founded in the seventh century by the Prophet Muhammad in what is today Saudi Arabia, and it is characterized by considerable continuity with Jewish and Christian traditions. Muslims share with Christians and Jews a belief in the same God and in the Old Testament prophets, and they acknowledge Jesus as a prophet. However, they believe that the Prophet Muhammad was the messenger through whom God's final revelation was communicated and transcribed in Islam's sacred book, the *Qur'an.*

From its Middle Eastern Arab origins, Islam quickly spread to Europe, Africa, and Asia. Today Muslims live in every nation of the world, although Islam's primary strength is found in the Middle East, Southern and Southeastern Asia, and Northern and sub-Saharan Africa. Muslims are a majority of the population in forty nations, and in seven others they represent a significant minority (25 to 49 percent).

Like most major religions, Islam is characterized by considerable diversity. The major sectarian division in Islam—between the Sunnis and the Shi'is (Shi'ites)—emerged in a dispute over who should lead Islam after the death of the Prophet Muhammad. Although a majority of Muslims in the world today are Sunnis, Shi'ites represent a powerful minority that has become most visible to the West in Iran, where postrevolution social change led by the Ayatollah Khomeini reestablished religious authority over many aspects of life that had become increasingly secularized under the monarchy headed by the Shah. In addition to sectarian divisions, there is substantial ethnic, regional, economic, and other religious diversity among nations that have large proportions of Muslim citizens. These various factors must be considered when the social impact of the "religious" factor is assessed.

The primary source of Islam's dramatic population growth, which is expected to reach nearly 2 billion by the year 2020, is the extremely high fertility rates in Islamic countries, which average 6 children per woman, in contrast to a figure of 1.7 for developed countries. However, this average obscures considerable regional variations, from an average of 3.6 in Islamic nations of Southeast Asia (Indonesia, Malaysia, Brunei) to 6.6 for nations in sub-Saharan Africa (Somalia, Senegal, Gambia, Niger, Mali, Guinea, Sierra Leone).

These very high rates of childbearing are not a result of religious objections to contraception; "Islam itself prescribes no special barriers to the use of contraception" (Weeks, 1988). The frequency of contraceptive use among married Muslim women ranges from 45 percent in Southeast Asia to 5 percent in sub-Saharan Africa, but in each case contraceptive use is lower in Islamic nations than in non-Islamic nations in the same region. Regional differences are also pronounced in the frequency with which women marry at a young age in Islamic countries, thereby increasing the probable number of pregnancies. As many as 47 percent of women under age 19 are married in South Asia (Pakistan, Bangladesh, Afghanistan) compared to only 18 percent in Southeast Asia. Early marriage, like resistance to contraceptive use, is a practice prescribed by tradition, not by Islam. Therefore, as the variations in fertility rates among Islamic nations indicate, current and future fertility trends among Muslim peoples are not influenced by Islam but rather by broader social, economic, and political factors.

KELLY, MARJORIE. *Islam: The Religious and Political Life of a World Community.* New York: Praeger, 1984.
MUNSON, HENRY, JR. *Islam and the Revolution in the Middle East.* New Haven: Yale University Press, 1988.
WEEKS, JOHN R. "The Demography of Islamic Nations." *Population Bulletin* 43, December 1988.

Secularization

Paradoxically, another feature of American religion has been its secular quality. **Secularization** refers to the "diminishing social significance of religion" (Wallis and Bruce, 1991, p. 3). It involves a decline in the authority of religious institutions, beliefs, values, and practices and in the process by which religious institutions and symbols legitimate, support, and justify various aspects of society and culture. Secularization is one aspect of the massive transformation of Western society that has included industrialization, urbanization, bureaucratization, and rationalization.

Berger (1967) contends that secularization has occurred on three levels: societal, cultural, and individual. At the societal level, religious institutions no longer exercise substantial control or influence over the state or other important social institutions, such as education. Or, to put it another way, secularization involves the separation of other institutions from organized religion and religious ideas. To illustrate, we can point to the degree to which functions such as education, social welfare, and social control, once the responsibility of religious institutions, have become the responsibility of the state. In this sense, religious symbols and institutions have been relegated to a position in which their influence over the larger society has diminished (Wallis and Bruce, 1991; Lechner, 1991).

Patterns of secularization have also influenced various aspects of cultural life. As secularization proceeds, the arts, literature, and philosophy less frequently draw on religious sources for inspiration.

Finally, secularization also has a subjective, psychological aspect, involving the secularization of consciousness. "Put simply, this means that the modern West has produced an increasing number of individuals who look upon the world and their own lives without benefit of religious interpretations" (Berger, 1967, p. 107). In a presecular era, religious ideas were accepted as fundamental truths and were difficult, if not impossible, to question or to change. Today many people are no longer sure of traditional religion because its authority has been undermined. Even among those who consider themselves religious, religion influences less of their lives than was the case in the past (Wallis and Bruce, 1991, p. 18).

The basic tenets of secularization theory have been hotly debated. Critics contend that religion continues to play a vigorous role in modern societies. This is especially the case in the United States, where, as we will note more fully below, the American people are characterized by relatively high levels of religious belief and practice. Moreover, critics contend that secularization theory assumes a "golden age" that exaggerates the impact of religion in the past. From this perspective, the American people are more religious today—in their beliefs and in their membership and participation in religious organizations—than they were during a presecular era. For example, Finke and Stark (1992), contest the application of secularization theory to American society. They argue that the most striking feature of American religious history has been what they term the "churching of America," that is, increased church membership and growth from colonial times to the present (see also Warner, 1993). Finally, some critics argue that in many respects "religion" today assumes different forms than it has in the past and that what has occurred is simply a transformation, not a decline in religion. Thus, in addition to competing among themselves, supernatural religions today also compete with a variety of other forms of religious consciousness, sacred symbols, and meaning systems. In essence, "new" gods have replaced "old" ones. These new conceptions of the sacred are especially apparent in the religious consciousness and sacred symbols attached to nationalism (Crippen, 1988) and those offered by other meaning systems, such as science (Appleyard, 1992), psychoanalysis, or Marxism, each of which provides alternative ways of defining and interpreting the world. From this perspective, then, religion continues to play an extremely vital role in modern society.

However, defenders of secularization theory (Wallis and Bruce, 1991; Lechner, 1991) reject these arguments. They contend that to focus primarily on the pervasiveness of religious beliefs and practices of the American people obscures the declining authority of religion as a societal force and its relative lack of power over public policy outside the religious realm. They argue that religion is increasingly peripheral to the lives of even those who define themselves as religious and that it no longer has a substantial impact on social institutions such as education, politics, the economy, and social welfare. Finally, defenders of secularization theory dismiss their critics' suggestion of a transformation of religion from "old" supernatural gods to "new" modern gods, such as science, psychology, or Marxism. This transformation, they contend, is itself a rejection of traditional religious authority and therefore striking evidence of the impact of the secularization process (Lechner, 1991).

Selling God: The Marketing of Religion

The necessity of competing for followers requires that religion be "marketed." To compete in a pluralistic society, religious groups are forced to adapt their religious message to cultural themes intelligible to religious consumers and to adopt the characteristics of secular organizations in making their appeals. Therefore, modern supernatural religions, like other modern organizations, compete in the open market. In their drives to sell their product—their distinctive religious message—and to finance the organizations and enterprises that they have created to market their messages, religious organizations often resort to "hucksterism" and blatant commercial appeals. As religious organizations adopt commercial techniques and characteristics in order to survive and prosper, they become increasingly indistinguishable from nonreligious organizations and, in the view of secularization theorists, increasingly secularized.

R. Laurence Moore (1994) has recently argued that the marketing of religion in the United States is not a new phenomenon but was intimately associated with the rise of laissez-faire capitalism in the nineteenth century. "Much of what we usually mean ... by secularization," he writes, "has to do not with the disappearance of religion but its commodification, the ways in which churches have grown by participation in the market, or more specifically how religious influences established themselves in the forms of commercial culture..." (Moore, 1994, p. 5). For example, during the early nineteenth century, Protestant religious leaders began to produce and actively market religious publications, and they organized camp meetings that provided popular entertainment.

Today the marketing of religion has become most apparent in the development of television evangelism, which has dramatically changed the manner in which millions of people in the United States experience religion. In 1989 about half (49 percent) of American adults reported occasionally watching religious programs—a percentage greater than those reporting that they had attended religious services during the past week; about one-fifth (21 percent) said that they had watched religious programs on television during the preceding week (Colesanto and DeStefano, 1990, p. 18). Televangelists such as Jim and Tammy Bakker, Jimmy Swaggart, Oral Roberts, Pat Robertson, Jerry Falwell, and Robert Schuller have become national celebrities. The personal indiscretions of some of them have been sensationalized, and the scandals that have rocked the huge financial empires that they have created through television contributions have been closely scrutinized by the media, the Internal Revenue Service, the U.S. Congress, and the courts.

Today the "electronic church" has adopted the formats of the most successful commercial television shows and the most sophisticated marketing techniques to become a highly rationalized multimillion-dollar enterprise. Among the most prominent of the efforts to use television to market religion is Pat Robertson's Christian Broadcasting Network (CBN), the success of which has inspired several other religious network ventures among Christian conservatives. Moreover, religious ownership and management of television stations has increased dramatically throughout the United States (Kennedy, 1995, p. 100).

As a consequence, televangelism has become one of the most important political and cultural forces in modern American life (Frankl, 1987; Peck, 1993). Hadden and Shupe (1988) contend that the near monopoly of televangelism by evangelical and fundamentalist Christians has enabled them very effectively to mobilize religious and political conservatives into a powerful social movement. Not only has American religion been reshaped by television, but televangelists have had a substantial impact on the conservative movement of the 1980s and 1990s in American culture in general and American politics in particular. So effectively have religious conservatives used television to promote their social, political, cultural, and theological messages that an interfaith, interdenominational group of 29 religious organizations recently responded by establishing their own cable television network, Faith and Values Channel (F&V) (Kennedy, 1995).

However, Bruce (1990) has recently criticized much of the previous research on American televangelism and argues that its political and cultural impact has been exaggerated. Audiences for televangelists are not representative of a cross section of American society, but are typically comprised of women and people who are older, less educated, of lower socioeconomic status, and already religiously conservative. Watching religious television programming is "an infrequent activity of a small part of the American people.... not much televangelism is consumed by not many people" (Bruce, 1990, p. 112). Although the increasing visibility of conservative televangelists reflects the relative decline of "mainstream" Protestant denominations (which we will discuss below), he contends that, because there are great differences of belief among religious conservatives, a unified movement that would submerge those differences is unlikely. Therefore, the impact of conservative televangelism on broader cultural and political issues in the future will most likely not be greater than it was during its heyday during the 1980s.

Civil Religion

In the United States, people have historically regarded religion as a "good thing" and important for national well-being. Because of a strong tradition of religious pluralism and separation of church and state, a national church has never been established in the United States. However, numerous writers have argued that the pervasive acceptance of religion in the United States suggests the existence of a religious identity—*The* American Religion—that provides a common thread binding the American people together (Bloom, 1992). Transcending the doctrinal differences that distinguish the more than 1200 sects and denominations in the United States today, the American Religion is the underlying "culture-religion" (Herberg, 1955) that unites Americans around a cluster of sacred beliefs, symbols, and rituals. This common core of beliefs represents what Bellah (1967) has termed America's "civil religion," a public expression that reflects the nation's secular religiosity and serves as a source of cultural and social cohesion.

Civil religion refers to the set of symbols, beliefs, values, and practices about the ultimate meaning of life in a nation, including patriotic and political phenomena not typically associated with religion. Civil religion is an important part of almost all political events. God is mentioned in the pledge of allegiance to the flag; the motto "In God We Trust" is engraved on the nation's currency. Political events of all kinds, from political party conventions to sessions of Congress, begin with invocations, frequently by members of the clergy.

Presidential inaugural ceremonies, themselves ritual events that possess religious qualities, contain numerous elements that clearly reflect elements of American civil religion. In 1993, for example, in addition to attending a nonsectarian religious service on inaugural morning, Bill Clinton visited Arlington National Cemetery, where he placed a rose, knelt, and prayed before the grave of John F. Kennedy. And, as had virtually every other recent president in their inaugural addresses, Clinton invoked the existence and sought the blessings of God, ending his address with these words:

> From this joyful mountaintop of celebration we hear a call to service in the valley. We have heard the trumpets, we have changed the guard. And now each in our own way, and with God's help, we must answer the call (Clinton, 1993, p. A11).

Civil religion in the United States is more than belief in a nonsectarian God who is deemed to have a particular interest in the destiny of the United States. Its pantheon of saints includes George Washington and Thomas Jefferson, the revered "founding fathers." Among its martyred saints are Abraham Lincoln and John F. Kennedy. Like other religious systems, American civil religion has developed elaborate rituals, sacred symbols, and a sacred literature. The Declaration of Independence and the Constitution are the religion's sacred scriptures. Its holy days include the Fourth of July, Memorial Day, Veteran's Day, and, especially, Thanksgiving, each of which involves ritual celebrations that invoke the name and support of God for the nation. During its religious ceremonies, sacred hymns such as the "Star-Spangled Banner," "America the Beautiful," and "God Bless America" are played and sung. Finally, among the American Religion's sacred symbols are the U.S. flag and monuments such as the Statue of Liberty, the Lincoln Memorial, the Vietnam Veterans Memorial, and Arlington National Cemetery, each of which is perceived by Americans to possess a sacred quality that embodies the nation's basic values (Niebuhr, 1994).

The notion of civil religion has generated considerable research since Bellah's formulation in 1967 (Richey and Jones, 1974; Gehrig, 1979; Bellah and Hammond, 1980; Demerath and Williams, 1985). Empirical studies have demonstrated widespread belief among the American people in an American civil religion. However, some writers (including Bellah, who has been most closely identified with the term itself) have questioned whether its assumption of a cultural consensus, or unifying ideology embraced by most Americans, can accurately be applied today to a society that has become increasingly "fragmented, polarized, and fractured" (Demerath and Williams, 1985). Nevertheless, so prominent a part of American life are the nation's sacred symbols, rituals, and shrines that Bloom (1992) contends that they comprise an identifiable "national faith" that he has termed "The American Religion."

Denominational Pluralism

A civil religion is nonsectarian; it transcends denominational differences. Its symbols are uniquely American. It can be embraced by persons of all faiths and by people who have no formal religious affiliation. Civil religion is therefore consistent with one of the most distinctive features of religion in the United States, its *denominational pluralism*. Religious diversity has long been a feature of American life, but it is more apparent today than ever before. Melton (1987) has identified more than 1200 different religious organizations in the contemporary United States.

Recently, Finke and Stark (1992) have argued that the relatively high degree of religious belief and practice in the United States is a result of America's religious pluralism, in which a large number of religious bodies compete for followers. Competition among faiths makes available a much greater range of religious options to a people, and thus this diversity enhances the religious vitality of a society. On the other hand, societies with religious monopolies and without competition among different religious organizations tend to have extremely low levels of religious participation and commitment. "A single faith cannot shape its appeal to suit precisely the needs of one market segment without sacrificing its appeal to another" (Finke and Stark, 1992, p. 19). Therefore, the history of American religion is one of constant change and growth, as new religious organizations emerge in response to the changing demands of their environment.

Although only a small percentage of the adult population were members of religious congregations during the colonial era (Finke and Stark, 1992), the early pluralistic character of American religion was reflected in the marked denominational differences that existed among the colonies. Puritans were concentrated in New England; the Dutch Reformed, in New York; Quakers and German Moravians, Mennonites, and Lutherans, in Pennsylvania; Scots-Irish Presbyterians, along the western frontier; Swedish Lutherans, along the Delaware River; Roman Catholics, in Maryland; Anglicans, in Virginia; and French Huguenots, in South Carolina, to name only some of the diverse colonial religious groups. Despite this diversity, in only four of the thirteen colonies—Rhode Island, New Jersey, Delaware, and Pennsylvania—were there genuine religious liberty and toleration of religious dissent. Not until the 1830s was full religious liberty available in all the states (Hudson, 1973; Marty, 1985). The consequence of the disestablishment of official state churches and the establishment of religious toleration was to create "an unregulated free market religious economy," which during the nineteenth century resulted in the development and rapid growth of a wide range of "upstart" religious groups (Finke and Stark, 1992, p. 60).

As a consequence, religious diversity in the United States, which at its founding was overwhelmingly Protestant, became more pronounced during the nineteenth century. Rapid population growth, westward expansion, the dramatic growth of towns and cities, and massive European immigration provided the dynamic conditions in which diverse religious groups developed and flourished. Niebuhr (1929) has shown the important role that class, ethnic, and regional factors have played in creating and maintaining religious diversity in the United States.

Social Class, Ethnicity, and Religious Affiliation.   Claiming more than 94 million adult members, Protestant churches comprise the largest religious category in the United States today (Kosmin and Lachman, 1991). The two largest Protestant groups, Baptists and Methodists, increased their numbers dramatically during the nineteenth century, primarily because they were what Niebuhr (1929) termed "the churches of the disinherited." Neither emphasized ritual nor a highly intellectualized theology. They also did not require an ordained, educated, professional clergy. Consequently, they appealed to the common people both on the western frontier and in the towns and rural areas of the East. So significant was the growth of Methodism during the first half of the nineteenth century that Hatch has characterized it as "the most dramatic social movement [in the United States] between the Revolution and the Civil War" (Hatch, 1993, p. 16).

Another major source of growth among Protestant churches was immigration. Most immigrant groups brought distinctive religious traditions with them. For example, different strains of Lutheranism were imported by Scandinavians and by Germans, the largest immigrant group in the nineteenth century.

However, the most striking impact of nineteenth-century immigration upon the structure of American religion was the growth of the Roman Catholic church, which drew adherents from a great variety of ethnic backgrounds, including Irish, German, Italian, Polish, Czech, French, and Hungarian. German and especially Irish Catholics were prominent in the development of U.S. Catholicism during the nineteenth century. By 1900 membership in the Catholic church exceeded 12 million, and an elaborate Catholic institutional system of churches, schools, hospitals, and charities had been established. The "new" immigration from southern and eastern Europe and the later influx of Spanish-speaking immigrants from Mexico, Puerto Rico, Cuba, and Latin America further swelled the ranks of Catholics during the late nineteenth and twentieth centuries. By 1990 more than 46 million U.S. adults claimed membership in the Roman Catholic church, making it the largest single religious denomination in the country and the "wealthiest, most stable branch of world Catholicism" (Kosmin and Lachman, 1991; Duff, 1971, p. 73).

The growth of Judaism in the United States was also primarily a product of nineteenth- and early twentieth-century immigration. By 1880 about 250,000 Jews lived in the United States, most of them German Jews who emigrated in the mid-nineteenth century. The predominant influence on contemporary Judaism, however, was the wave of more than 2 million Eastern European Jews who entered the country between 1880 and 1924. Today more than 3 million adults in the United States identify themselves religiously as Jews (Kosmin and Lachman, 1991).

Another major source of America's religious pluralism has been the creation of new religious groups. Religious movements have frequently emerged during periods of intense religious enthusiasm. This was especially true during the Second Great Awakening, which took place in the first three decades of the nineteenth century. During this period of religious ferment several new religious movements appeared, emphasizing utopian ideals of community and religious brotherhood. Many utopian communes, such as the Oneida Community, were relatively short-lived. Other religious innovations, such as Christian Science, the Millerites (later known as Seventh-Day Adventists), the Campbellites (which later included both the Disciples of Christ and the Church of Christ), survived.

Most dramatic and vigorous of the movements that endured from that period is the Church of Jesus Christ of Latter-day Saints (the Mormons), which grew from an impoverished and persecuted cult in the 1840s into one of the most firmly established American religious groups. Until recently, the Mormon religious presence was restricted primarily to Utah and communities in adjacent states, where their doctrines and ideals provided the basis for a distinctive culture region. However, within the past few decades Mormon membership has increased dramatically, both in the United States and abroad. Today LDS membership stands at 4.6 million in the United States and 9.3 million worldwide (Shepherd and Shepherd, 1984; Barlow, 1991; Cornwall et al., 1994; Church of Jesus Christ of Latter-day Saints, 1995).

Recent Trends in Religion in the United States

During the 1950s several sociologists argued that the United States was undergoing a religious revival, a "surge of piety." Church attendance and membership reached all-time highs, and public professions of religious faith became fashionable. The apparent religiosity of the 1950s ended dramatically during the 1960s, when church attendance, particularly among Roman Catholics and the young, dropped sharply. Public opinion polls indicated a substantial decrease in the importance that Americans attributed to religion. During the 1960s, the authority of many traditional institutions, including the government, the family, schools, and religion, was challenged. Churches became deeply divided over political and social controversies, particularly over the civil rights of minorities and the Vietnam War. The counterculture that challenged the prevailing cultural values of the Protestant work ethic, materialism, and conventional sexual mores also threatened traditional religion. These issues produced a crisis in American religion that led not only to tension and division within and a defection from many established religious organizations but also to spiritual experimentation and to the creation of new religious movements (Pritchard, 1976; Roof and McKinney, 1987; Wuthnow, 1988b; Roof, 1993).

Neither the political movements nor the counterculture itself extended much beyond the 1970s, but the impact of that period on American religion today has been substantial. Religion in the United States has undergone several critical changes during the 1970s and 1980s.

Decline of Mainstream Protestantism

During the past half-century, religion in the United States has undergone several critical changes. Most prominently, the Protestant majority, the "religious establishment," declined substantially. Protestants comprised 69 percent of the American population in 1947 but only 59 percent in 1994 (see Table 15–2). This decline has occurred primarily among the larger mainstream Protestant denominations (Episcopal, United Methodist, Evangelical Lutheran, Presbyterian USA, United

Church of Christ, American Baptist, Disciples of Christ). During the last half-century, mainstream churches have stopped growing or experienced substantial membership losses and have experienced declines in participation and institutional support (Roof and McKinney, 1987; Finke and Stark, 1992). Between 1965 and 1985, membership in these mainstream denominations declined from 28.5 to 22.9 million, a decrease of 20 percent during a period in which the nation's population increased by over 20 percent (McKinney, 1991, p. 153). However, not all Protestant churches experienced these declines. During the same period, a new wave of religiosity has been especially pronounced among evangelical and conservative Protestant groups, such as the Assemblies of God, the Church of Christ, Pentecostal and Holiness groups, the Mormons, Seventh-Day Adventists, Jehovah's Witnesses, and Southern Baptists (Kelly, 1972; Hoge and Roozen, 1979; Roof and McKinney, 1987; Finke and Stark, 1992). Similarly, Roman Catholicism has recently experienced conservative movements (Dinges and Hitchcock, 1991), and Orthodox Judaism has grown more rapidly than either of Judaism's two more liberal branches, Reform and Conservative.

The conservative trend in American religious organizations was mirrored in the substantial percentages of Americans who report conservative religious beliefs. Among Protestants, 33 percent of adults described their faith as "evangelical" in 1988, but this figure increased to 38 percent in 1990 (Sullivan, 1991, p. 44). More than three-fourths (76 percent) of the American people agree that "the only assurance of eternal life is personal faith in Jesus Christ," nearly half (47 percent) reject evolution and accept a creationist view that God "created man pretty much in his present form . . . within the last 10,000 years," and more than one-third (35 percent) believe that the Bible is the "actual word of God and is to

Table 15–2   Religious Preferences in the United States, 1947–1993 (by percent)

Religion	1947	1957	1967	1977–1978	1986	1994
Protestant	69	66	67	60	59	59
Baptist	a	a	21	19	20	16
Methodist	a	a	14	11	9	8
Lutheran	a	a	7	6	5	5
Presbyterian	a	a	6	4	2	4
Episcopalian	a	a	3	2	2	2
Roman Catholic	20	26	25	29	27	24
Jewish	5	3	3	2	2	2
All others	1	1	3	1	4	7
No religious preference	6	3	2	8	8	8

[a]Data not available.

Source: The Gallup Report, 1987. Princeton Religious Research Center, "Religion in America: 1995 Supplement," pp. 3–6.

be taken literally, word for word" (Gallup and Newport, 1991; Newport, 1993). Not only has membership in conservative religious organizations been increasing, but these groups have become adept at using the electronic media—television in particular—to preach their doctrines. The most substantial impact of religious conservatism has been seen on American political life, where during the 1980s and 1990s the New Christian Right has had a powerful influence on debates over such issues as school prayer, abortion, gay rights, women's rights, and pornography (Liebman and Wuthnow, 1983; Hadden and Shupe, 1988).

Growth of the Roman Catholic Church

The Roman Catholic Church has grown in numbers and influence, increasing from 20 percent of the U.S. population in 1947 to 24 percent in 1994, making it the largest single religious denomination in the United States. Moreover, Catholics have increasingly become part of the social, political, and religious mainstream of American life (Davidson et al., 1995). However, Finke and Stark (1992) contend that, as American Catholics have become more socially and culturally assimilated, their religious commitment has declined. This has been especially apparent in the decline in lay participation in a wide range of Catholic activities, including attendance at mass and confession. Even more striking has been the sharp decline in the numbers of Roman Catholic men and women entering religious vocations. For example, between 1966 and 1994, the number of American candidates for the Roman Catholic priesthood declined from 43,000 to 4000. Consequently, the Catholic Church has increasingly imported clergy from other countries, resulting in a church that is visibly multicultural in its pastoral leadership (Tornquist, 1995).

Proliferation of New Faiths

In the past two decades, a wide array of new religious bodies, both Christian and non-Christian, has slowly begun to transform the American religious landscape. Especially as a consequence of changing patterns of immigration to the United States from Asia, the Middle East, and Africa, Eastern religious traditions (especially Islam, Buddhism, and Hinduism) have established substantial communities and become a visible presence in many American towns and cities, creating a new multireligious landscape far more diverse than ever before in American history (Eck, 1993). In 1994, 7 percent of the American population (more than 17 million) indicated identification with a faith outside the three religious categories of Protestantism, Catholicism, and Judaism. Observers have noted especially the rapid growth of Islam. In 1991, the largest and most comprehensive survey of religious affiliation yet undertaken placed the number of Muslims at 1.4 million, approximately the same size as the United Church of Christ or the Episcopal Church in America (Kosmin and Lachman, 1991). However, other observers have disputed the methods through which these data were obtained and have placed the number of Muslims in the United States as high as 8 million (Eck, 1993). Other scholars have placed the number between 3 and 4 million (Haddad, 1991, p. 8; Stone, 1991, p. 17; Bernstein, 1993). All would agree, however, that the Islamic population in the United States has been rapidly increasing.

Included among the new Christian groups are those with a fundamentalist Christian basis: the Children of God, Marantha Christian Ministries, the Way International, the Calvary Chapel Movement, and a host of local groups with no national affiliations. Like some religious groups drawn from Eastern religious traditions, some of these have been widely publicized and become highly controversial, for example, the Church of Scientology, which combines elements of popular psychology, folk wisdom, and spiritualism, and the Unification Church, founded by the Reverend Sun Myung Moon, who claims to be the prophet of a religion that fulfills traditional Christianity.

The Growth of Privatized Religion

Wallis and Bruce (1991) have suggested that one index of the increasing secularization of religion in modern societies is the extent to which religion has become primarily a private, individualistic, and deeply personal affair. Many people today fashion their own individual religious belief system without communal support and without participation in traditional institutionalized religious bodies.

> Privatized faith is common in contemporary America because it is very congenial with a highly differentiated society. Restricted largely to the spheres of family and personal life, it encroaches very little into the larger public world, which Americans increasingly define as off limits to religion. What one believes in private is one's own personal matter and hence off limits to religious institutions. With *believing* disjointed from *belonging,* it amounts to a "portable" faith—one that a believer can keep in the inner life and take along in life, having little contact with a religious institution or ascribed group (Roof, 1993, p. 200; italics in original).

Many of those embracing a private faith are apt to be nonaffiliates, people indicating no religious preference, whose number rose from 2 percent of the U.S. population in 1967 to 8 percent in 1994 (see Table 15–2). The primary goal of privatized religion is self-fulfillment, and the focus of such religious forms is therefore on the techniques—mystical, magical, social, psychotherapeutic, and technological—whereby fulfillment can be achieved.

This focus has been the common denominator of what has been termed the "New Age" movement, which includes a great number of consciousness-raising groups (such as est, Transcendental Meditation, Silva Mind Control, biofeedback,

Gestalt Awareness Training, and Lifespring) designed to heighten an individual's physical, social–psychological, and spiritual awareness and to enhance individual self-discipline and personal effectiveness. Although the publicity that they have received has tended to exaggerate their numbers (Kosmin and Lachman, 1993), what these diverse New Age groups have in common is their "belief in a cosmic destiny for [humankind], which individuals pursue mainly through mystical examination of the self; and in a 'new age' of existence that will be peopled by superior beings who have undergone a process of inner 'transformation'" (Bordewich, 1988, p. 38).

"Baby Boomer" Religion: A "Generation of Seekers"

Members of the "baby boom" generation, who were born between 1946 and 1964, today represent about one-third of the American population, and their values and lifestyles have had a dramatic impact on cultural trends in American society. As they entered adolescence and adulthood during the turbulent 1960s and 1970s, they were likely to reject established religious institutions. Many of the "boomers" who dropped out during these years have continued to reject institutional forms of religion, although most embrace a spirituality consistent with the "privatized" religion described above. However, as baby boomers have approached midlife, many have returned to organized religion and are especially likely to view religious institutions as important for "rites of passage"—baptisms, marriages, and funerals. The religious participation of baby boomers who had previously dropped out has been especially affected by their location in the life cycle; in the 1980s, baby boomers were likely to be involved in family formation and parenting. Those who had dropped out of organized religion earlier in their lives were far more likely to have renewed their religious participation if they had children (Roof, 1990; Roozen et al., 1990; Sullivan, 1991; Gessner and LaMagdeleine, 1991; Hutchinson, 1991, p. 136).

However, in a major study of the religious values, practices, and commitments of the baby boom generation, Roof (1993) contends that their religiosity does not simply represent a "return" to traditional forms of religious activity, but rather suggests a "major restructuring" of the American religious landscape. The religiosity of the boomers is especially reflected in their quest for new forms of community, especially in a variety of small-group settings, including "adult education classes, Twelve-Step groups, caucuses, sharing groups, workshops, yoga classes, therapeutic groups..., the men's movement, and scores of special purposes organizations" that provide opportunities for people to explore and "give expression to their deepest feelings and commitments" (Roof, 1993, pp. 252, 257). Many churches and synagogues have explicitly sought to attract the boomer generation by developing a variety of such programs—often initiated after extensive market research—and have "modernized" their religious services by using modern technology and synthesized music in an effort to respond to the boomers' spiritual quest (Clark, 1994).

Changing Role of Women in Religion

One of the major issues that grew out of the "equality revolution" of the 1960s and has since become more pronounced in American religion concerns the role of women. Although women have traditionally been more active participants than men and have played very crucial support roles in most religious organizations in the United States, they have until recently been virtually excluded from formal positions of authority and leadership in most Christian and Jewish congregations. Today women cannot be ordained in the Roman Catholic church, the Eastern Orthodox church, many conservative Protestant denominations, and Orthodox Jewish congregations. However, reflecting the impact of the feminist movement, since the 1970s significant challenges have been brought to the traditional definitions of male and female roles within several religious organizations. Although overall seminary enrollments in recent years have been declining, between 1972 and 1991 female enrollments in Protestant seminaries increased by nearly 400 percent; in 1972 only one-tenth (10 percent) of the country's Protestant seminary students were women, but by 1993 that figure stood at nearly one-third (31 percent) (Bedell, 1995b, p. 280). Moreover, as Table 15–3 indicates, the number of female Protestant clergy nearly doubled between 1977 and 1986. Women clergy were most numerous in certain theologically conservative denominations (for example, Assemblies of God, Salvation Army, Foursquare Gospel Church) and in some theologically liberal denominations (for example, United Methodist, Presbyterian Church, USA, United Church of Christ, Disciples of Christ) (Jacquet, 1988b). The feminist impact has also been reflected in movements within Mor-

Table 15–3   Ten Protestant Denominations with Largest Number of Women Clergy, 1986

Denomination	*Number of Women Clergy*	*Women Clergy as Percentage of Total*
Assemblies of God	3718	13.9
Salvation Army	3220	62.0
United Methodist	1891	5.0
Presbyterian Church, USA	1519	7.8
United Church of Christ	1460	14.5
Episcopal	796	4.5
Christian Church (Disciples of Christ)	743	10.9
International Church of the Foursquare Gospel	666	19.1
Lutheran Church in America	484	5.6
American Baptist Church	429	5.6

Source: Constant H. Jacquet, Jr. *Women Ministers in 1986 and 1977: A Ten Year View.* New York: National Council of Churches, 1988.

monism and within Conservative Judaism to permit women to participate more fully in religious observances and in policy-making bodies (Wuthnow, 1988b, p. 229; Johnson, 1994b). The ordination of women, which is supported by 61 percent of American Catholics, has become increasingly controversial and divisive in the Roman Catholic Church. Responding to the debate over ordination, in 1995 the Vatican, with the approval of Pope John Paul II, announced that Roman Catholics must accept the doctrine that only men can be ordained as priests as "infallible" (Steinfels, 1995).

The increasing presence of women in the clergy and in policy-making positions—primarily in mainstream Protestant denominations—also sparked controversies over other issues related to the status of women. Illustrative of these controversies has been the movement for "inclusive language"—the effort to alter the terminology in which conceptions of the sacred are communicated. Critics of traditional religious discourse argue that the very symbols and language that have been used to describe God in Judaism and Christianity—King, Lord, Master, and Father—not only reflect a tradition of male domination, power, and authority, but also limit and circumscribe conceptions of what is virtually impossible to describe in human terms. The movement for inclusive language seeks "to minimize the male bias reflected in . . . language about human beings and language about . . . God," and reflects one of the major issues in contemporary American religious life (National Council of Churches, 1983, p. 6).

Personal Religious Experience

Religious experiences vary widely in form and intensity. For many whose lives have been secularized, religious interpretations have little meaning. For many others, religion is a purely formal and social obligation that may involve activities such as attending religious services, but otherwise it has little effect on their lives. However, nearly nine of ten (87 percent) people in the United States claim that religion is very important or fairly important in their lives; only 12 percent said that religion was not very important to them (Princeton Religious Research Center, 1995, p. 13). Moreover, a substantial number claim to have had one or more dramatic and intensely personal religious experiences. In 1991 more than half (54 percent) claimed to have been aware of or influenced by a power greater than themselves, while in 1994 36 percent of adults who were questioned described themselves as "born-again" or evangelical Christian (Gallup and Newport, 1991; Princeton Religious Research Center, 1995). Reflecting their generally higher rates of church membership and attendance, African Americans were much more likely than whites to claim that they were "born again" (*Emerging Trends,* 1995, p. 4).

On the basis of extensive research on the diversity of religious experience in American society, Glock and Stark (1965) have developed a typology of religious experience, which we examine in the order of the frequency with which each type of experience occurs. The four types of religious experience are *confirming, responsive, ecstatic, and revelational.*

Confirming Religious Experience

The most frequently reported form of religious experience in contemporary American society is a confirming experience, "a sudden feeling, knowing, or intuition that the beliefs one holds are true" (Glock and Stark, 1965, p. 43). The individual becomes aware of the existence or presence of the sacred. A confirming experience is not a spectacular, overwhelming, or particularly dramatic event. However, it has deep personal meaning and significance to the individual. The sudden intensification of feeling that occurs may take a general form in which the individual experiences a sense of reverence, awe, solemnity, or calmness. Or the individual may have a distinct awareness of the closeness of a divine being, such as may be elicited by the wonders of nature (Hay, 1979). During the mid-nineteenth century Henry David Thoreau described such an experience during his solitude at Walden Pond.

> Once,... in the midst of a gentle rain,... I was suddenly sensible of such sweet and beneficent society in nature, in the very patterning of the drops, and in every sight and sound around my house, and infinite and unaccountable friendliness all at once, like an atmosphere, sustaining me, as made the fancied advantages of human neighborhood insignificant.... Every little pine-needle expanded and swelled with sympathy and befriended me. I was so distinctly made aware of the presence of something kindred to me, that I thought no place could ever be strange to me again (Thoreau, 1854, p. 116).

Responsive Religious Experience

The confirming experience is passive; the individual merely feels aware of the presence of the divine. The responsive experience, on the other hand, is marked by reciprocity; the individual feels that the divine is responding to him or her as well. Rather than merely being made aware of the presence of the divine, individuals sense that the divine has taken special notice of them.

The responsive experience can take a variety of forms. It frequently involves an awareness of an external power controlling and guiding the individual. It can also produce a sense of peace, serenity, and joy, a feeling that the divine has chosen the individual (Hay, 1979). A responsive experience is frequently reported among those who pronounce themselves "born-again Christians." Responsive religious experiences frequently occur during periods of stress (Hay, 1979, p. 176), as when individuals perceive the divine to have helped them in a time of crisis, such as an illness, a miraculous escape or rescue from danger, or a positive turn in one's economic fortune.

Ecstatic Religious Experience

The ecstatic religious experience involves not only awareness of the presence and responsiveness of the divine but also a feeling of an intense and intimate emotional relationship with the sacred. So powerful is the intensity of the ecstatic experience that one of the most prominent features reported about them is the imagery of light or the physical sensation of being electrified. Probably the most famous conversion in Christian tradition was that of the Apostle Paul, whose experience is described in the New Testament: "Now as he journeyed he approached Damascus, and suddenly a light from heaven flashed about him. And he fell to the ground and heard a voice saying to him, 'Saul, Saul, why do you persecute me?'" (Acts 9:3–4).

In his analysis of religious experiences among British graduate students, Hay (1979), within the category of ecstatic religious experiences, has found extrasensory perceptions, out-of-body experiences (in which an individual's soul or mind is reported to have left the body and observed the body from outside), and visions. He reports the following visionary experience.

> A week after I met_____, we were sitting looking at each other's eyes in a bedroom and there began to be a beam passing between our eyes and also a third eye in the middle of our foreheads. This lasted for about two hours and we didn't say a word to each other. Towards the end of the two hours . . . [it] came and went in waves, and we began to know that we had known each other in a previous life. Because we had known each other, we *knew* each other (Hay, 1979, p. 171).

Revelational Religious Experience

The least common type of religious experience, but perhaps the one that receives the most publicity, is the revelational. While other types of religious experiences may involve a sense of the divine speaking, the distinctive characteristic of the revelational experience is that the individual receives "confidential information about the future, divine nature, or plan" (Glock and Stark, 1965, p. 55). Such revelations may be *orthodox*—that is, supportive of the existing religious and social order—or *heterodox*—that is, critical and potentially disruptive of the status quo.

An example of an orthodox revelation is the reported appearance or apparition of the Virgin Mary, a religious experience with a tradition in Christianity dating back to the Middle Ages (Zimdars-Swartz, 1991a). Between 1928 and 1973 more than 200 such encounters were reported to Roman Catholic authorities, and since then apparitions have been reported by devout Roman Catholics in Ireland, France, Yugoslavia, Italy, the Soviet Union, Rwanda, Egypt, Spain, and the United States (Zimdars-Swartz, 1988, 1989a, 1991a, 1991b). Reports of such experiences have frequently had a dramatic public impact. Some have been memorialized by the establishment of sacred shrines, such as that in Lourdes,

France. Reports of appearances by the Virgin Mary have often drawn great crowds. In 1950 an estimated 100,000 people traveled to the Wisconsin farm of Mary Ann Van Hoof to witness messages that were transmitted through her from the Virgin Mary (Zimdars-Swartz, 1989b). In 1988 over 13,000 people from all over the United States gathered in Lubbock, Texas, after three people reported that they were receiving messages of peace and hope from Mary (Pratt, 1988, p. 1; Zimdars-Swartz, 1991a, pp. 17–18). During the 1990s reports of apparitions throughout the United States—in Cold Springs, Kentucky; Marlboro Township, New Jersey; Denver, Colorado; Scottsdale, Arizona; Emmitsburg, Maryland; and Hollywood, Florida—attracted crowds of believers. Tens of thousands of people from all 50 states, Europe, and Mexico made pilgrimages to the town of Conyers, Georgia, for the chance to witness the apparitions claimed by a local woman (Goldman, 1992; Associated Press, 1995).

These experiences of encounters with the Virgin Mary are orthodox in the sense that they usually encourage people to become more devout in their adherence to established religious practices and authority. Heterodox revelations, on the other hand, are important sources of social change, for they provide visions of a new social order and a basis for rejecting and challenging established authority.

Many examples of revelational experiences have been recorded among the world's religions. The Islamic and Christian faiths, as well as many sects in both religions, originated with their founder's claims of having received divine revelation.

One of the most dramatic revelational experiences in American religious history was that of Joseph Smith, from whose experiences the Latter-day Saints (Mormon) churches have developed. As an adolescent, Smith, who had been deeply troubled by the competing claims of truth offered by various denominations, had a striking revelational experience.

> After I had retired...I kneeled down and began to offer up the desires of my heart to God. I had scarcely done so, when immediately I was seized upon by some power which entirely overcame me, and had such an astonishing influence over me as to bind my tongue so that I could not speak. Thick darkness gathered around me, and it seemed to me for a time as if I were doomed to sudden destruction.... just at this moment of great alarm, I saw a pillar of light exactly over my head, above the brightness of the sun, which descended gradually until it fell upon me.... When the light rested upon me I saw two personages, whose brightness and glory defy all description, standing above me in the air. One of them spake unto me, calling me by name, and said—pointing to the other—THIS IS MY BELOVED SON, HEAR HIM (*History of the Church of Latter-day Saints,* 1902, pp. 5–6).

Revelational experiences have frequently provided the inspiration and source of authority for new social movements. Weber called the authority derived from such experience *charismatic.* As noted in Chapter 4, *charisma* refers to qualities of an individual personality that are believed to be exceptional and sometimes of supernatural origin that give the individual authority over others.

Persons with charismatic qualities frequently become the leaders of **revitalization movements:** "deliberate, organized efforts by members of a society to create a more satisfying culture" (Wallace, 1966, p. 626). A revitalization movement provides a new belief system for interpreting and explaining the universe. Faith in a charismatic leader elicits a total commitment among movement followers, which accounts for the extremely well-disciplined nature of many such groups. Throughout the American experience many revitalization movements have developed into organized religions. Among the more successful and enduring are the Mormons, Christian Scientists, and the Black Muslims. More recently, sensational publicity has been directed toward such revitalization movements as the Unification Church, the Children of God, and the International Society for Krishna Consciousness (Hare Krishnas), among others.

Leaving Religion

Religion is always a dynamic, changing phenomenon, and this is especially true in a society such as the United States, where religious participation is voluntary and there is considerable competition among religious groups. Although most people maintain their affiliation with the denominational family in which they were reared, many people change their religious identities during their lifetimes. Many of them will switch to another religious affiliation (Roof and Hadaway, 1979; Nelson and Bromley, 1988), usually within the same broad denominational grouping (for example, liberal, moderate, or conservative Protestant). Since the 1970s, the number of people switching to conservative Protestant denominations and declaring no religious affiliation has increased; liberal and moderate Protestants and Catholics, on the other hand, have been the primary losers among those switching their religious affiliation (Hadaway and Marler, 1993).

Most of our previous discussion of religious experience has focused on processes whereby people affiliate or identify with a religious tradition. However, as the data on religious switchers indicates, people may also become disillusioned with and reject or disaffiliate from organized religions. Therefore, it is necessary to consider the experience of leaving religion.

We noted above that a substantial minority (40 percent) of American adults reported attending religious services regularly. However, an almost equal proportion reported being relatively uninvolved in religious activities. In 1994, 38 percent of adults sampled in a national survey indicated that they "seldom" or "never" attended religious services (Princeton Religious Research Center, 1995). The vast majority of the unchurched report a religious preference but seldom attend religious services. Only a small proportion of Americans—about 8 percent—report no religious preference. Among these are people who never had a religious identity and those who once had a religious identity but rejected it later in life.

In the News

Promise Keepers: A Male Revitalization Movement in Religious Garb

A fascinating example of a revitalization movement during the 1990s has been the "men's movement," which has been fueled especially by publication of books such as Robert Bly's *Iron John* and Sam Keen's *Fire in the Belly*. The broader movement, which has sought to reclaim for modern men a "masculine" identity in a world perceived as increasingly feminized, has featured loosely organized, male weekend retreats and workshops in which participants are encouraged to recapture the essence of their "deep" manhood. Although the men's movement has involved a general spiritual quest for meaning, its largest, most visible, and most dramatic manifestation has been the Promise Keepers (PK), an evangelical Christian movement that has experienced meteoric growth since its founding in 1990 by former University of Colorado football coach Bill McCartney. At its first rally in 1991, 4200 men attended, but by 1995 PK attracted more than 727,000 men to conferences that have packed football stadiums in major cities throughout the country. The organization plans a 1997 rally in Washington, D.C., that will parallel the Million Man March of African American men in 1995.

Other than its avowedly evangelical (although nondenominational) Christian focus, PK is distinctive in several respects. First, one of its most prominent themes is its explicit commitment to racial reconciliation, which is reflected in its racially integrated staff, speakers, and conferences. Second, it emphasizes male responsibilities for maintaining "traditional family values," especially in being loving husbands and fathers and in maintaining leadership of their families, a role that many men are perceived to have abdicated to women. Third, PK is explicitly a male organization; women are encouraged to support the organization but are not permitted to participate in PK conferences themselves, because "women's presence tends to inhibit men."

Many commentators have praised PK's progressive stance on race and its therapeutic effects—its ability to change men's lives and make them more caring and responsible husbands and fathers. However, critics contend that, although PK may condemn spousal abuse and encourage greater male responsibility for their families, they merely reinforce traditional gender relations. "They believe men ought to be good masters, not abusive ones. They don't doubt for a moment that the ultimate responsibility for the world—and men's and women's lives both—is men's. . . . To the Promise Keepers, patriarchal power is legitimate and, in fact, desirable, so long as it is not 'misused.'" Men should "remain at the 'head' of the family, and women behind—so long as men are kind and good."

Gustav Niebuhr. "Men Crowd Stadiums to Fulfill Their Souls." *New York Times*, August 6, 1995.
Donna Minkowitz. "In the Name of the Father." *Ms*, November/December 1995.
Joseph P. Shapiro. "Heavenly Promises." *U.S. News and World Report*, October 1, 1995.

Hadaway and Roof (1988) focused on **apostates,** those who earlier in their lives had had a religious identity but who later came to reject any religious identity. They found that apostates are most likely to be young, single, male, highly educated, politically independent, geographically mobile, more involved socially with friends than with family, urban and suburban residents, and much more accepting of the "new morality" on issues such as drug use and sexual behavior. The peak period of rejection of religion in the post-World War II period occurred during the 1960s and early 1970s, when many young Americans questioned traditional institutions. However, since the early 1970s religious apostasy appears to have declined (Hadaway and Roof, 1988).

The Institutionalization of Religious Experience

The origins of many religious organizations, beliefs, and forms of worship can be located in the religious experiences of a religion's founder, frequently a charismatic leader claiming to speak for the divine. Whenever a new religious movement is founded and dominated by a charismatic leader, the death of that leader threatens the religion's continued existence. Members must adapt to new circumstances if they want to continue the practice of their religion. If charismatic leaders want to ensure the success of the group beyond their lifetimes, some means for governing the religious organization must be created. The authority of the charismatic leader may be transferred to relatives, to trusted colleagues, or to impersonal positions in the organization itself.

The crisis of continuity for a religious organization on the death of a charismatic leader is resolved by the institutionalization of religious experience. Many religious rituals are methods developed to continue the religious experiences of a movement's earliest participants. Thus, a relatively spontaneous and subjective experience becomes institutionalized, patterned, and routine. Institutionalized behaviors and structures become the ways of eliciting, creating, or maintaining religious experience. O'Dea and Aviad (1983) have identified three aspects of the process of institutionalization in a religious movement: cultic activity or religious behavior that involves patterns of worship or ritual; beliefs that are a religious movement's pattern of ideas; and organization, that is, the social organization, or social structure, of a religious group.

Religious Behaviors

Rituals are complex, communally shared, ceremonial forms of religious behavior. They symbolically express spontaneous religious values and experiences that have become standardized and institutionalized over time. Rituals occur during worship services and around events, such as christenings, weddings, and funerals, that mark important stages in the life cycle. In Christianity, for instance, the Mass or Liturgy "became both the representation of the original experience and the way in which the worshippers expressed their relationship to the sacred" (O'Dea and Aviad, 1983, p. 42). Similarly, a Jewish seder at Passover is characterized by a prescribed series of prayers, the recitation of sacred literature, a huge feast, and a congregational gathering that both commemorates the historic experiences of the Jewish people and unites them in a community. As time passes, proper performance of a ritual becomes increasingly important, and any effort to change it is upsetting.

Religiosity can be expressed in a variety of rituals. It would be difficult to describe all religious behaviors because many that are not usually defined as religious actually are manifestations of religious sentiments. For example, for the strongly patriotic who perceive their particular brand of nationalism as deriving from God, standing at attention for the raising of the flag or the playing of the national anthem is a religious behavior. On the other hand, some behaviors that are commonly defined as religious (for example, attending church) may involve nonreligious motivations, such as making social contacts, impressing business associates, or finding a suitable marriage mate for one's child.

Prayer, a form of addressing the sacred, is one of the most widespread forms of religious behavior and is found in virtually all religions. A prayer can take the form of asking the sacred for a favor or giving thanks to the sacred force for a past blessing. It can also serve as an affirmation of faith in the religious system itself.

Another basic religious behavior involves some form of physical exercise. Guttman (1978, p. 16) has pointed out that many societies have "incorporated running, jumping, throwing, wrestling, and even ball playing in their religious rituals and ceremonies." The ancient Olympic games, conducted in honor of the god Zeus, were sacred festivals, an integral part of ancient Greek life. In Iran's national religion, Shi'ism, a branch of Islam, religious activities among the most devout adherents involve an exhausting and arduous athletic ritual designed to purify the minds of participants ("The Sport of Religion," 1972). Sufism, a mystical Islamic tradition that has recently gained increasing numbers of American adherents, uses physical exercises, including breath control, body movement, and dance, to gain control over the senses and achieve a mystical experience (Awn, 1987, p. 119). Similarly, sumo wrestling, Japan's most popular spectator sport, has its roots in Shinto, the national religion. Early sumo contests were part of Shinto religious festivals (Halloran, 1974, p. 10:1). For the Shakers, a communal religious group that flourished in the eighteenth and nineteenth centuries in the United States, physical exercise in the form of an elaborate communal dance was an integral part of their religious ritual (Nordoff, 1875/1971).

Drugs may be used as a means of producing physiological changes in the individual that could induce a spiritual state. Although many religious leaders deny the religious authenticity of a drug-induced experience, drugs have been used for sacramental purposes in many societies. The ancient Greeks, for example, chewed the intoxicating leaves of ivy to induce an ecstatic state. In the Native American Church, a religion that has become popular among North American Indians since the turn of the twentieth century, an elaborate ritual surrounding the use of peyote has developed. A participant in the peyote rites recalled:

> For three days and for three nights I had been eating the peyote and not slept at all. Now I [suddenly] realized that throughout all the years that I had lived, I had never once known a truly holy thing. Now, for the first time, I knew it (Radin, 1926, p. 182).

Drugs or physical exercise are not the only methods by which religious experiences can be elicited. Other methods of physiological inducement of religious feeling include the mortification of the flesh by pain, sleeplessness, or going without food or water. All these methods were employed among the Plains Indians, for whom fasting and self-torture were a necessary prelude to a young male's acquiring a vision or communication with a "guardian spirit," which served as a ritual transition from adolescence to maturity (Benedict, 1922; Powers, 1987).

Religious behavior often involves notions of mana and taboo. **Mana** refers to the power inherent in sacred objects. To a believer, touching sacred objects will cause the powerful qualities of those objects to be transmitted to them or will bring them good fortune. Touching the Western Wall in Jerusalem is a sacred rite for Jews. Many Christians claim miraculous cures by visiting sacred shrines, such as the one in Lourdes, France. On a more mundane level, mana is exemplified in the belief that luck follows from carrying a rabbit's foot or kissing the Blarney Stone.

The converse of the notion of mana is a **taboo,** a religious proscription against having physical contact with certain objects in order to prevent the power embodied by these objects from affecting a person. The Polynesians, for example,

> maintained an elaborate set of taboos on contacts of one kind or another between status groups, particularly between royalty and commoners. The chief's body could not be touched by the body of a commoner; even if the contact were accidental, death would be the result for the commoner. The commoner could not look down upon his chief from a higher elevation (looking is, in a sense, like touching), and so the chief had to sit upon a raised platform and be carried on a raised litter above the shoulders of his subjects (Wallace, 1966, pp. 61–62).

Taboos are often related to food, drink, or other substances that may be taken into the body. Among Orthodox Jews and among Muslims a wide variety of foods are taboo. Similarly, several contemporary religious sects, such as the Hare Krishnas, forbid the use of drugs. Mormons proscribe the use of tobacco, alcoholic beverages, and drinks containing caffeine, such as coffee and tea.

Another type of religious behavior involves the creation and use of various forms of religious symbols or icons. These symbols represent either sacred entities, or the values, relationships, processes, or events associated with the sacred. Examples of religious symbols include the Christian cross or fish, the Jewish Star of David or menorah, and (in civil religion) the flag of the United States.

Religious Belief Systems

Religious belief systems include both myth and theology. A **myth** is a sacred story, a parable, or a graphic way of communicating a basic idea concerning the activities and moral prescriptions of divine beings. It provides a concrete and emotionally charged explanation of the historically significant events in a religious system. To a sociologist, the importance of a myth is not its truth or accuracy, but its ability to bind believers into a common community and to reinforce belief in a society's basic values and social institutions. The Christmas stories of the shepherds, the angels, and the three kings are part of Christian mythology. Their historical accuracy or inaccuracy is irrelevant; their importance lies in uniting Christians into a sacred community for the celebration of Christmas.

Of particular importance are "origin" or "creation" myths, found in many different societies. Creation myths describe the origins of the universe and humans' place in it. They usually include descriptions of the origins of societal norms and values, family organization, law, and government. They are kept alive by periodic recitation. Although such myths persist in contemporary society, recitation today most often takes the form of reading or repeating aloud the basic truths as they are recorded in sacred documents, such as the Old and New Testaments in the Christian tradition.

The belief system of a new religion is born in the experience or inspiration of the religion's founders. The rational and logical development and extension of these ideas is the task of theology. **Theology** applies the process of rationalization to a religious belief system. A theology usually develops when a priestly class is differentiated from lay members of a religion. The more clear the distinctions between clergy and laity become, the more specialized the clergy's functions become, and the more likely it will be that a system of religious ideas, a theology, will become elaborated and rationalized.

Religious Organizations

The process of institutionalization is clearly apparent in the organization or structure of religious groups. An important distinction in religious organization appears in the two ideal types that the German sociologist Ernst Troeltsch (1931) called *sect* and *church*. A further distinction is made between these two forms of religious organization and cults.

Sect. A **sect** is a small, voluntary group of members who join the group of their own conscious choice. A sect is the type of organization that characterizes a religion in the first stage of a revitalization movement. Primary emphasis in a sect is placed on a personal religious experience, and its leadership is usually composed of laypeople with no specialized training. The primary source of guidance for the sect's members is the sacred scriptures or personal inspiration. Rather than accepting the existing society, sect members tend to reject or feel alienated from it. Consequently, membership is often drawn from the lower classes—the "disinherited," who have no vested interests in maintaining the status quo.

Sect members withdraw into their own community, which develops its own rigorous standards of perfection (such as a conversion experience, renunciation of all worldly possessions, or renunciation of "vices," such as smoking, drinking, or gambling). Sects are exclusive religious organizations; they do not admit people who do not conform to their rigorous norms. Membership in a sect is total; the group's code of ethics is uncompromising and absolute, demanding full conformity. This characteristic is reflected in the group's limited interaction with outsiders and its refusal to participate in many societal activities (such as military service, saluting the flag, or medical treatment). Frequently, sects set themselves apart by such things as peculiar dress or dietary restrictions. Sect members may live in territorial isolation from the world, as the Amish do, or within the general society but with limited social interaction with nonmembers, as Hasidic Jews do. (See Chapter 3.)

Church. Distinct from a sect, a **church** is a large, socially acceptable, institutionalized religious group into which one usually is born, rather than converted. No special requirements are prescribed for membership; some members join only for secular or social reasons. While the sect is exclusive, a church is inclusive and often national in scope. It tries to extend its spiritual influence to as many people as possible. A church is characterized by a bureaucratic structure made up of a professional clergy within an established hierarchy. Ritual and belief systems tend to be elaborate and highly prescribed. Because most members are born into a church and do not actively choose membership, a strong emphasis is placed upon education as a means of perpetuating the faith.

One further distinction between a sect and a church is that a church accommodates itself to the secular world, while a sect resists such accommodation and frequently is in tension with it. Churches tend to be relatively larger and more socially inclusive than sects, but sects make stronger demands on and elicit greater commitment from their members (Finke and Stark, 1992). "Churches attempt to regulate or fulfill a few of the activities or needs of large numbers of people; sects attempt to regulate or fill many of the needs of small numbers of people" (Wuthnow, 1988a, p. 495).

That sects elicit greater commitments from their members is reflected by the differences in levels of financial contributions among American Protestant denominations. The eight Protestant denominations listed in the annual *Yearbook of American and Canadian Churches* with over a million members in 1993 averaged $398 per capita in annual contributions. However, as Table 15–4 indicates, the Protestant groups with the highest per capita giving tend to be relatively small in membership. Of the ten groups with the highest per capita contributions, only two—the Wesleyan Church and the Presbyterian Church in America—had a membership exceeding 100,000 (Bedell, 1995, pp. 274–277). Similarly, a national survey found that the level of religious commitment, as measured by

Table 15–4 Differences in Annual per Capita Contributions among American Protestant Churches: Denominations with a Million or More Inclusive Members and the Denominations with Annual per Capita Contributions of More than $1,000, 1992–1993

	Membership	Per Capita Contributions
Largest denominations		
Southern Baptist Convention	15,398,642	$350
United Methodist Church	8,646,595	382
Evangelical Lutheran Church in America	5,212,785	315
Presbyterian Church, USA	3,796,766	530
Lutheran Church, Missouri Synod	2,598,935	354
The Episcopal Church	2,504,682	644
United Church of Christ	1,530,178	406
American Baptist Churches in the USA	1,516,505	263
Highest in Contributions		
Allegheny Wesleyan Methodist Connection	2,043	2,048
Evangelical Mennonite Church	4,228	1,619
Missionary Church, Inc.	28,408	1,386
Independent Fundamental Churches of America	71,672	1,353
The Wesleyan Church (USA)	115,368	1,194
Evangelical Presbyterian Church	56,421	1,135
Primitive Methodist Church in the USA	7,360	1,123
Presbyterian Church in America	239,500	1,091
Evangelical Covenant Church of America	89,511	1,075
Mennonite Church	95,634	1,039

Source: From *Yearbook of American and Canadian Churches, 1995,* edited by Kenneth B. Bedell. Copyright © 1995 by Abingdon Press. Reprinted by permission.

frequency of attendance at religious services, was directly related to contributions to and volunteer activities for *both* religious and other charities; those who were highly involved in religious activities contributed and volunteered much more substantially than those who were only minimally involved or uninvolved. The authors conclude that "generosity with money and time is not so much determined by income as by level of religious commitment" (Hodgkinson, Weitzman, and Kirsch, 1990, p. 109).

Because their appeal is oriented primarily to the middle and upper classes, churches are frequently alien to the lower classes in decorum and social composition. Sects emerge from the dissatisfaction felt toward these established expressions of religiosity. However, the sectarian character of a religious group is almost always short-lived. It is either modified over time, or it ceases to exist.

The transition of an organization from sect to church illustrates the process of routinization or institutionalization, which is a common characteristic of religious movements. As Niebuhr has pointed out, "by its very nature the sectarian type of organization is valid only for one generation" (Niebuhr, 1929, p. 19). Numerous Christian denominations that began as sects appealing to the disinherited, such as Baptists, Methodists, and Quakers, gained social respectability and became churches. Although an individual may join a sect by choice, his or her children are born into the group and do not necessarily share the enthusiasm and fervor that prompted the parent's participation. To convince a new generation, the sect must modify entrance requirements, usually by making them less stringent, and it must emphasize the role of education. If a sect is successful and attracts increasing numbers, an organizational apparatus becomes necessary.

As the organization expands, it begins to develop a life of its own. Those who work within the religious organization develop the need to expand their own power bases, to advertise the good deeds of the organization, and to develop educational techniques to ensure the support of the succeeding generations. All these needs lead to an ever-expanding bureaucratic structure. In addition, the organization develops an interest in its own survival that leads to the support of the status quo. If the group is prospering in its environment, it will resist efforts to change it. Religious routines tend to become less dynamic and spontaneous and more routine. All of these developments signal the loss of characteristics that initially marked the sect. Once the organization becomes institutionalized, it tends to become rigid and formal. Inevitably some people find that its prescribed formulas do not meet their religious needs. Sectarian groups that are able to respond to this dissatisfaction are likely to grow. Thus religious organizations that began as sects may be subject to the same kinds of disaffection, change, and revitalization that originally led them to grow. Finke and Stark (1992) have recently argued that the sect–church process is the primary dynamic that has characterized the history of American religion, which accounts for the continuous vitality of religion in American life; "the sect–church process is always under way" (Finke and Stark, 1992, p. 237).

Cults.* The basic distinction between a church and a sect is that a church accepts the status quo while a sect rejects it. However, Stark and Bainbridge (1979) have argued that sects should be distinguished from cults, even though both stand in tension with their surrounding sociocultural environment. **Cults** are small, voluntary, and exclusive religious groups that have created new religious systems. These two types of religious organizations are distinguished primarily by their origins—the manner in which they begin.

Sects are the result of schisms; they break off from existing religious organizations. Founders of a sect do not seek to create a new religious body but to realize what they perceive as the "original" beliefs and practices of the organization from which they have split. They begin as internal factions of a religious body. They are religious conservatives, seeking to reestablish the "true faith," which they claim the established religious body has abandoned. For example, many Protestant denominations in the United States were organized not as efforts to establish new religious faiths but as attempts to realize more fully the essence of the Christian church.

Cults, on the other hand, are not schismatic; they are not splinter groups breaking away from an established religious tradition. With no previous organizational attachment to an existing religious body, they represent a new religious tradition altogether. Because they introduce new religious beliefs or practices that may be completely alien to an established religious tradition, founders of cults are religious radicals. Cults may take the form of either religious innovations, which are based on new revelations or insights, or importations, which involve acceptance of a tradition or faith well established in another society but new and different in the receiving society. Examples of innovative cults include the early Mormons and the Unification Church of the Reverend Sun Myung Moon, the founders of which both claimed to be introducing new doctrines that fulfilled traditional Christianity. Among recent imported cults are several groups drawn from Eastern religions, such as various Muslim and Buddhist sects.

Summary

Religion is one of the most pervasive and complex of all human activities. The sociology of religion is concerned with understanding the role that religion plays

*In popular usage, the term cult has today come to have an extremely unfavorable and pejorative meaning—referring to an authoritative, manipulative, religiously radical group that seeks aggressively to indoctrinate members. As a consequence, some scholars (for example, Richardson, 1993) have suggested that the term should be abandoned. However, because of the long history of the term in the sociology of religion and the important distinction it provides in comparing the origins of religious organizations, we have retained it here while simultaneously rejecting the negative connotations that have popularly been attached to it.

in society and the influence of social factors upon religious activity. Religion is what is socially defined as sacred, encompassing entities that evoke a sense of awe, mystery, respect, and honor. For many people the sacred involves supernatural entities. It can also include a variety of other phenomena, such as political ideologies or even scientific systems, that provide a system of ultimate meaning.

Religion has several social consequences, both positive and negative, depending upon one's individual perspective. By providing an explanation and interpretation of the universe, religion deals with the problems of meaning that are inherent in the precariousness of human existence. It serves as a source of strength, comfort, and consolation for the individual, a means of warding off uncertainty. It provides a sense of individual and group identity. Religion also often functions to legitimate the existing social order. By interpreting society as something other than a human creation that is difficult, if not impossible, to change, religion reinforces the status quo. However, religion also frequently performs a critical function by providing a basis from which to criticize and challenge society. Many revitalization movements, which are efforts to create a more satisfying society, have their origins in a religious impulse.

Religion in American society has been characterized by three basic features: pervasiveness, secularism, and denominational pluralism. From colonial times to the present, religion has been a prominent feature of American life. Yet, despite this pervasive attachment to religion, the authority of religious beliefs, values, and practices has declined. Religious diversity, or denominational pluralism, has characterized religion in America. It is a result of social class, racial, and ethnic factors, and the spontaneous creation of new religious groups within American society.

Religion involves several different but related features: personal experiences, behaviors, beliefs, and organizations. Personal religious experience takes many forms. New religions or religious revitalization movements often are based on a charismatic leader's claim of having had a revelational experience. New religious movements can take the form of sects or cults. Sects are offshoots of existing religious organizations, while cults represent religious innovations or importations. Once new religious movements are founded, they attempt to institutionalize the religious experience of their founders. This involves the development of rituals, beliefs, and organizational structures. As a group's organizational structure becomes established, new movements, with different social bases, may emerge to start the process again. Thus, change in religious organizations is a dynamic and recurring process.

CRITICAL THINKING

1. Is religion a source of social stability or social change? Give examples to support each viewpoint.
2. Why are sociologists so interested in the role of religion in society? Use Max Weber's study on the Protestant ethic to show how religion and economics might be intertwined.
3. How can sociologists who believe in the scientific method study a subject that is associated with "faith" rather than "facts"?
4. What is religion? Why is it considered by sociologists to be a social phenomenon?
5. What aspects of religious behavior in the United States are relatively unchanging?
6. What is "liberation theology"? With which part of the world is it most commonly associated? How does the existence of liberation theology show that religion is a social phenomenon that affects other parts of society?
7. Describe the major social functions of religion and give examples to illustrate each function. Does religion provide social stability or promote social change?
8. What is secularization? How is secularization related to other major trends in American society such as industrialization, urbanization, bureaucratization, and rationalization?
9. In what ways is religion "marketed" in American society? How does this trend show religion to be social behavior related to other aspects of society? Is this a positive or negative trend?
10. Describe civil religion in the United States. Speculate as to the nature of civil religion in an "atheist" society such as the former Soviet Union.
11. What is privatized religion and why is it on the rise in the United States? In what ways does such religion circumvent the traditional functions ascribed to religious behavior?
12. Compare and contrast the various types of religious organizations mentioned in the chapter. What function might each serve in society?

16

Political Life

The political system of the United States was designed to give people a strong voice in determining what their government should do. Voting for political leaders is an important way for people to express their will. In contrast to many democracies, however, especially those in Western Europe, a comparatively small percentage of the population participates in the voting process. For example, in the 1992 presidential election only about 55 percent of those eligible to vote bothered to cast a ballot. The youngest eligible voters in the population are least likely to vote—those between 18 and 29 years of age. The paradox is that young people have the greatest stake in political elections. If elected leaders get the country into a war or undertake other military adventures, young people will most likely do the fighting and dying. Young people have the longest time to live, and political decisions made now (for example, increasing the national debt) are apt to have a great effect on them for many years.

Even among older age groups, from one-third to one-half of eligible voters in the United States do not vote in presidential and congressional elections. Although Americans give great lip service to democracy, their voting behavior is very low compared to other democratic nations (Piven and Cloward, 1988). Americans think of their government as the most democratic in the world, but large numbers of them do not participate, even in the simple act of voting.

Power, the State, and Government

The central concern of the political institution, or polity, is power—the ability to control other people's behavior and carry out one's will despite resistance. Obviously there are some situations in which people comply more willingly to the imposition of power than others. As we saw in Chapter 4 in our discussion of bureaucracy, the German sociologist Max Weber (1918/1946) distinguished between legitimate and illegitimate power. Legitimate power, or **authority,** is power exercised by leaders that is generally approved or accepted as appropriate by members of a group or society. Although they may strongly disagree with laws that their elected officials enact, most people in the United States accept the right of those officials to pass such laws and hence accept them as legitimate.

On the other hand, there are circumstances in which people do not recognize the power exerted over them as legitimate and do not comply willingly to its exercise; they comply only because they are forced to do so. **Coercion** is power based on the threat or use of force, and is therefore considered illegitimate by the people who are forced to act against their will.

The State and Government

The **state** is the dominant political institution in modern societies (Lehman, 1988). The state is the sole source of legitimate physical force (Weber, 1918/1946); it is the only institution that can impose taxes, declare war, and imprison law violators.

The enormous power of the state appears in the variety of functions it performs (Weber, 1921/1978, p. 905):

1. The enactment of law (legislative function).
2. The protection of personal safety and public order (police).
3. The protection of vested rights (administration of justice).
4. The cultivation of hygienic, educational, social-welfare, and other cultural interests (the various branches of administration).
5. The armed protection against outside attack (military administration).

Sociologists sometimes use the term **nation-state** when referring to a state that has power over people living in a distinct geographical area known as a nation. The nation-state developed in Europe only about 500 years ago, and it has emerged in most Asian and African societies during this century. However, the nation is not found in all societies. Some preindustrial societies in Africa and Asia exist without clearly defined state structures. In fact, in the African nation of Somalia there is, as of this writing, *no* functioning state structure.

The principal organization of the state is the government. Governments can be organized in a number of different ways and can take different forms. Governments typically take one of three major forms: autocracy, totalitarianism, or democracy.

Autocracy.   In an **autocracy,** ultimate power is held by a single person. An autocrat may gain the position through heredity (an absolute monarch) or by rule of force (a dictator). Among the most recognizable autocratic rulers in the world today is Mu'ammar Gadhafi of Libya. Autocrats rely on their ability to control the military and police systems of their countries, and to maintain the unquestioning loyalty of large numbers of their subjects. Criticism of the government and the autocrat is usually prohibited. The government often censors the media and sometimes uses terror to stifle public dissent. However, an autocracy tends to separate the private and public lives of its subjects, allowing individuals some degree of freedom in private matters of family and religion.

Totalitarianism.   **Totalitarianism** is a form of government involving state control and regulation of all major institutions in a society. The state is represented by a small ruling clique that relies on physical force and terror to maintain social order. A totalitarian government exerts total control over a nation and makes little distinction between public and private concerns. A totalitarian regime seeks to control family life as well as economic and political institutions. Friedrich and Brzezinski (1965) have suggested six elements of totalitarian rule:

1. *A single political party.* Totalitarian states are one-party governments led by dictators or by a ruling clique. The one political party is the only legal party in the state.
2. *Control of the economy.* Totalitarian states exercise control over virtually all portions of the economy. The state may set goals for economic production, establish prices and supplies for goods, and dissolve private ownership of either industry or farms.
3. *Control of media.* Totalitarian states control television, radio, newspapers, and magazines. They deny a public forum to dissenting opinions so that only the official party position is communicated to the people.
4. *Control of weapons.* Totalitarian states monopolize the use of weapons, denying the individual the right to own arms.
5. *Ideology.* Totalitarian states use an elaborate ideology to explain virtually every aspect of social life. Social goals and values are described in simple terms, and distortions are often made about the state's enemies.
6. *Terror.* Totalitarian states rely on terror to maintain social control. Secret police, torture, and punishment without trial are common in totalitarian states.

Nazi Germany is a major example of totalitarian rule in this century. Antisemitic ideology, concentration camps for Jews and others, and the terror of the Gestapo (Hitler's secret police) were key elements of Nazi Germany's totalitarian power. Many of these features also characterized the former Soviet Union and its onetime client states in Eastern Europe.

Democracy.   The word *democracy* is derived from the Greek roots *demos,* which means people, and *kratia,* which means rule. Literally, then, democracy means rule by the people.

In everyday conversation the political system of the United States is usually referred to as a **democracy.** A democracy is a form of government in which there are periodic opportunities for the people being governed to retain or replace governing officials. A country is democratic when a large part of the population is able to "influence major decisions by choosing among contenders for political office" (Lipset, 1963a, p. 28). By this criterion it appears that the United States is a democratic society. We do have periodic elections to select the president, senators, representatives, governors, mayors, and other elected officials. In choosing among aspirants to political office, voters are presumably able thereby to influence the programs and policies of the government.

Three Views of the Political System of the United States

Considerable controversy exists among sociologists concerning the extent to which the U.S. political system is actually democratic. There are three different views of the U.S. political system: pluralist, neo-Marxian, and elitist. Of these three views, only the pluralist is consistent with characteristics of a democratic system. The neo-Marxian perspective emphasizes how power is held by those who control the economic system. The elitist view also contends that power is held by a relatively small group, but that group is not limited to capitalists controlling the economic system.

Pluralist View

Pluralism describes a society that is made up of a number of competing interest groups (Rose, 1967). These competing groups serve to disperse power in a pluralistic society (Wasburn, 1982, p. 299). Such groups may represent the interests of business, labor, education, medicine, sports, or others. Each group has power within its own realm, and exerts power and influence over the federal government. Although the government is not a pawn in the hands of various interest groups, it is seen as directed and influenced by each of these powerful interests. Which interest group, or coalition of interest groups, wins out on a particular issue depends upon which one is most powerful at a given time in a particular sphere. Since each group can exert greater power on some issues than on others, no single interest group ever fully realizes its goals and dominates other groups. In a pluralistic society the political process is not run by a single powerful elite but is characterized by shifting patterns of interest-group influence. In fact, in the pluralist view, the balance of power among interest groups makes the United States a democratic society (Dahl, 1967).

An ideal pluralistic system operates under four basic conditions (Gamson, 1975). First, everyone must accept the norms and values of constitutional democracy. Second, there must be a set of groups whose interests overlap so that individuals are linked to a variety of groups in which they encounter people with different orientations. This prevents people from developing a single image of what should be done in society. Thus, a given individual is likely to be a member of a wide array of very different groups, including family, community, work, religion, ethnic, and social class. Third, in a pluralistic political system, access to the political arena should be open so that any group has the opportunity to receive a fair hearing for its point of view. Fourth, a balance of power must exist among competing groups so that no one group can dominate on all issues and so that coalitions among groups can shift, depending on the issue.

A Theory of Power Based on a Pluralist View.   David Riesman (1961) advanced a pluralist view of power based on the notion of veto groups. A **veto group** is a special interest group that attempts to protect itself by blocking the actions of other groups. Riesman suggests that the U.S. has two levels of power, an upper level of competing veto groups and a lower level of the unorganized public. Veto groups compete for dominance on particular issues and they seek public support in their efforts. An example of veto group competition is the fight over handgun regulation between the National Rifle Association (opposed) and Handgun Control, Inc. (in favor). In Riesman's view, power is diversified among the plurality of veto groups, and no single group dominates political decision making. The emergence of veto groups has been an important political development. Indeed, Riesman suggests that the "only leaders of national scope left in the United States today are those who can placate the veto groups" (Riesman, 1961, p. 213).

Political Action Committees.   In recent years political action committees, usually simply called PACs, have emerged as influential veto groups (Clawson, Neustadtl, and Scott, 1992; Stern, 1988). PACs are political organizations that operate independently of political parties, channeling money from special-interest groups into the election campaigns of political candidates. The special-interest groups are sometimes representatives of some portion of the political spectrum, such as conservatives or liberals, but more often they represent some special economic or demographic group.

Let us look, for example, at the role of PACs in the 1992 elections. Through June 30, 1992, PACs had contributed a total of approximately $73 million to congressional campaigns and about $38 million to the presidential campaign (Babcock, 1992). Democrats had received about twice as much money ($73.3 million) as Republicans ($38 million). Interestingly, PACs supported incumbents to an

In the News

Is Canada Disintegrating?

A major news item in 1995 was the October 30 referendum on whether Quebec voters favored sovereignty. The vote constituted the culmination, at least for the time being, of a long-term effort to win independence for the predominantly French speaking province of 7.25 million people. The referendum was narrowly defeated by only 50,000 votes—50.6 to 49.4 percent. This was clearly a moral victory for the separatists and is likely to fuel further efforts to gain independence. In fact, a poll conducted toward the end of 1995 indicated that a majority of those polled (55 percent) favored independence and a separate nation of Quebec. Relatedly, there seems to be some decline in the feeling outside Quebec about keeping it part of the nation (Reuters, 1995a). Furthermore, a majority of Canadians are now pessimistic about the possibility of keeping the nation together. In fact, almost a third (and almost half of all Quebeckers) felt that the nation as we know it would cease to exist by the turn of the century (Reuters, 1995b). When the new premier of Quebec, Lucien Bouchard, took office in early 1996, he contended that Canada was becoming resigned to separation. Furthermore, Bouchard contended, "Canada is divisible because it is not a real country. Here are two people, two nations and two territories. And this one is ours" (Trueheart, 1996, p. A11).

While the rift between Quebec and the rest of Canada is well known, there are other divisions that threaten the nation. There are profound economic differences between the westernmost provinces (British Columbia and Alberta), the prairie provinces (Saskatchewan and Manitoba), Ontario, and the Maritime Provinces. The prairie and Maritime Provinces are less well off than the rest and are being subsidized by them. The more economically successful provinces might well consider going it alone, and some of them might even favor integration with the United States (Brimelow, 1995). Even if that seems far-fetched, the fact is that it is not just the Quebec issue that threatens the future of Canada; there are also severe economic strains between the regions of the country.

And then there is a growing right-wing separatist movement based in the western part of Canada. This movement is centered in Calgary and headed by the Reform Party. Among its stated objectives is a dramatic cut in federal spending and an increase of control by the provinces over such things as health care and education. Most generally, it feels that central government in Ottawa is meddling in its affairs. Furthermore, it feels Ottawa spends too freely and is squandering the resources it drains from the region.

One of the things that irritates the western separatists is the fact that they historically have paid far more in taxes than they have gotten in return in services. According to one estimate, since 1961, Alberta has paid in excess of

$100 billion to the federal government, while Quebec has received approximately $125 billion more in benefits than it has paid in taxes (Symonds, 1995). It is such practical economic matters, to say nothing of hostility toward Quebec over its long-term and continuing efforts to secede, that fuels the interest in independence in Western Canada. Were Quebec to win independence at some point in the future, the reform party has made several positions quite clear. For example, it would challenge Quebec's control over its northern areas, which are rich in resources. It has also threatened to veto any effort by Quebec to enter NAFTA (North American Free Trade Agreement).

Given the closeness of the 1995 referendum, it seems clear that there will be another such referendum in the not-too-distant future. A lot can happen between now and then, but, given current sentiments, it is not unlikely that such a referendum would be approved at some future date. A movement toward independence in Quebec would likely set in motion a series of reactions throughout the country that might, as has already been predicted, lead to the dissolution of Canada as it is currently constituted.

BRIMELOW, PETER. "Four Canadas?" *Forbes,* December 4, 1995.
REUTERS. "Poll Finds Majority of Quebeckers Back Independence." December 30, 1995a.
REUTERS. "Canadians Pessimistic about Country's Future—Poll." December 18, 1995.
SYMONDS, WILLIAM C. "The Call of the Wild in Western Canada." *Business Week,* December 18, 1995.
TRUEHEART, CHARLES. "Bouchard Takes Office as Premier of Quebec." *Washington Post,* January 30, 1996.

overwhelming degree, $91.6 million versus $8.2 million to challengers and $12.3 million to open-seat candidates (*Washington Post,* 1992). On support for incumbents, the director of a nonpartisan organization said that it "isn't a surprise to many of us inside the Beltway, but it's a cynical example of how Washington works.... It shows the most important thing to these groups isn't which party you belong to but whether you're in office" (Babcock, 1992, p. A19). Incumbents are supported to such a large degree because history shows that there is a very high probability that they will be reelected.

The definitive analysis of the role of PACs, in particular those representing corporations, in the political sector is Clawson, Neustadtl, and Scott's (1992) *Money Talks: Corporate PACs and Political Influence.* Money has always "talked" in politics, but it "talks" more than ever today because large sums of it are more necessary than ever before. This is the case because of the high costs of many of the key elements of modern political campaigns—expensive TV spots, political consultants, and media experts. Thus, in 1992 the average winning candidate for the House spent $543,000 (versus $201,000 for the loser) and for the Senate $3.9 million (versus $2.0 million for the loser) (Bonifaz, 1994). Furthermore, politics has become a kind of endless race and money is needed for each new election. Thus, successful politicians are almost continually in the business of raising money and "the champion money raiser wins almost regardless of the merits" (Clawson, Neustadtl, and Scott, 1992, p. 8).

Six PACs—three labor organizations (for example, the National Education Association PAC) and three trade associations (Realtors PAC, for example)—contributed more than $1 million to federal campaigns in the first half of 1992; the top corporate PAC (AT&T's) had contributed over $800,000 (*Washington Post,* 1992). Nevertheless, Clawson, Neustadtl, and Scott focus on corporate PACs because there are many more of them and collectively they represent the single most concentrated source of money (more than $50 million in the 1988 elections) for politicians. (The others are trade-membership-health PACs [less than $40 million], labor [less than $35 million], and unconnected [less than $20 million].) According to Bonifaz (1994), business PACs outspent labor PACs by a three to one margin in the 1992 congressional elections. Adding to the economic clout of corporate PACs is the fact that trade PACs often follow their lead. Furthermore, individual corporate leaders also contribute large sums of money on their own. Corporate PACs are also the focus of attention because they exercise disproportionate power in the society as a whole and because they have the capacity to raise far larger sums of money if needed and desired. Corporate PACs are distinguished from other PACs because of their ability to coerce people, especially employees, gently and not so gently, into donating to the PAC. Thus, unlike most other PACs, corporate PACs are *not* democratic.

Most PACs adopt a pragmatic, rather than an ideological, approach to donations to political candidates. They give most of their money to the politicians who are best able to help them and further their interests. Clawson, Neustadtl, and Scott argue that the money given to candidates is neither an outright bribe nor a disinterested donation, but should rather be seen as *gifts*. As such, they are "intended to create a feeling of obligation" on the part of those receiving the money (Clawson, Neustadtl, and Scott, 1992, p. 54). These gifts involve the "norm of reciprocity" (Gouldner, 1960). That is, because candidates have received money, they have incurred an obligation to reciprocate in some, at the time undetermined, way. Thus, PACs operate far more subtly than is commonly assumed.

The influence of PACs on political decision making is also far more subtle than is generally assumed, but it is nonetheless of great consequence. It is a myth to think that PACs are able to buy politician's votes on high-visibility issues. However, on low-visibility issues, such as securing a seemingly insignificant tax loophole (that could mean millions or billions of dollars to business), PACs do have considerable impact that is not available to others in society.

However, political incumbents and candidates are often not as subtle as PACs. PACs are frequently inundated with requests for money and pressured by politicians and their representatives for donations. For example, a lobbyist said of

Senator Alfonse D'Amato (R–NY) and his staff, "Nothing is enough. It's continuous pressure. If you don't contribute, they don't return your calls" (Clawson, Neustadtl, and Scott, 1992, p. 60).

In 1992, when the average campaign cost $4.3 million, D'Amato spent $15 million (over $10 million more than the average for senatorial campaigns), two-and-a-half times the amount spent by his challenger. Those who contributed large sums to his campaign often had dealings with the Senate committee D'Amato now heads, Banking, Housing, and Urban Affairs (Schwinn, 1995).

Together, the not-so-subtle demands of politicians and the subtler effects of PACs on political decision making led Clawson, Neustadtl, and Scott to see a major problem here, but one that will not be solved by the kinds of piecemeal reforms generally put forth. Rather, they argue for a major reform that would replace the current system of campaign financing (including PACs) with public financing of election campaigns (see also Bonifaz, 1994). Such financing would eliminate the substantial advantage that the current system gives to various interest groups, most notably corporate PACs.

Neo-Marxian View

Neo-Marxian theory is derived from Karl Marx's idea that the legal and political systems are built upon, and are a reflection of, the economic base of the society. Neo-Marxians generally accept this idea but have often modified it to correspond with contemporary realities in capitalist countries. Some neo-Marxists have taken an even more extreme view of these matters than Marx did. They have seen the state as *wholly* determined by economic forces. Lenin, for example, saw the state as simply a tool used by one social class to oppress another. Thus, he felt that if economic inequality were ended, it would lead to a withering away of the state, at least as an instrument of oppression. Of course, the history of the former Soviet Union after the revolution of 1917 indicated anything but a withering away of the state. The Soviet state became huge, powerful, and often oppressive, guilty of murdering millions in what Solzhenitsyn (1973) called the "Gulag Archipelago."

Most modern neo-Marxists no longer accept this simplistic view of the relationship between the state and the economy. At one time, neo-Marxists argued that in American society the state was simply a tool of the capitalist class, but such a view is no longer considered tenable. A moderate neo-Marxist view is that the state is not dominated by economic interests, but it still usually protects the interests of the capitalists (Poulantzas, 1973).

Military–Industrial Complex.   A good example of the continued applicability of the neo-Marxian perspective is found in the idea of a military–industrial complex. The **military–industrial complex** refers to the close alliance between the military establishment and the industries that make a major share of their profits from producing military equipment (Dye, 1983; Marullo, 1993).

The two sectors—the military and industrial—tend to foster the interests of each other. It is in the economic self-interest of the military-weapons industry to support the military; conversely, it is in the interest of the military to support industries that enhance its power and ensure its existence. Critics of the military–industrial complex charge that it adversely affects the military, industry, and the society as a whole.

Although the idea of a military–industrial connection had been recognized some years before by sociologist C. Wright Mills (1956), public awareness was increased greatly when President Dwight D. Eisenhower, in his farewell address, warned of the dangers of this connection. Eisenhower told the nation that the combined influence of the military establishment and the industries that benefitted from producing weapons could become too powerful. With too much power the military–industrial complex could "endanger our liberties and democratic processes" (Eisenhower, 1972, pp. 31–32).

In the years since Eisenhower's warning, both the military and the industries supplying the military have grown immensely. Weapons systems and defense systems have been created, only to be abandoned when they became obsolete, leading to the expenditure of billions of dollars. The 1992 military budget was nearly $284 billion (McManus and Mann, 1992, p. A16). Serious questions have been raised about many costs within the military system, especially because of repeated scandals that revealed waste, corruption, and crime.

The most obvious examples of a large and uncontrolled military/industrial complex have involved industries' overcharging the government for military materials. For example, in late 1985 several executives of General Dynamics, the third largest military contractor, were indicted for improperly billing the government for $7.5 million. This incorrect billing was, however, only a small part of a larger scandal. The billing was related to DIVAD, the name of a prototype for a General Dynamics gun (later known as the Sergeant York) that was supposed to protect troops from air attack. A contract for its production had been awarded in 1981. By 1985, following the expenditure of almost $2 billion, the DIVAD project was scrapped because this anti-aircraft gun had repeatedly failed to perform satisfactorily. It was the close connection between the military establishment and defense contractors that explains how such a vast amount of money could have been spent on a failed weapons system (Rasor, 1985). Investigations have now revealed that for many years the Pentagon withheld information from Congress that would have revealed the ineffectiveness of the gun under combat conditions. It seems that within the military the program managers for any weapons system have a vested interest in keeping the procurement process going once it has been started. Of course, the latter is clearly in the interests of the weapons makers. A Pentagon watchdog describes the situation this way:

> Because of the high stakes created each year by a $100 billion procurement budget, the system puts tremendous pressure on each individual [military program manager] to not rock the boat and then places him in a position to become very cozy with the contractor (Rasor, 1985, p. 137).

Military officers who are in charge of procuring weapons for the Defense Department are often well rewarded if they remain "cozy" with defense contractors. Upon retirement from military duty, many high-ranking officers join the same corporations whose products they have been purchasing and approving (Rasor, 1985). This practice is so widespread that it has been called the "revolving door." It is good business for the defense contractors to hire former military officers because the knowledge they bring to the company can greatly aid in retaining present contracts and gaining new ones.

This close connection between military people and industrialists enhances the possibilities for corruption and crime. With billions of dollars to be made from Defense Department contracts, defense industry executives and military officials can be tempted. For example, in 1989 a former top executive with the Unisys Corporation (a major electronics firm) pleaded guilty to bribing an assistant secretary of the Navy. During the same period that the bribes were made, the Unisys Corporation received two Navy contracts totaling over $300 million. This incident is only one in a series of corrupt and illegal actions described as the military procurement scandal (Murphy, 1989).

When military purchases are influenced by bribes, corruption, and various levels of collusion, it is not surprising that many purchases made by the military are outrageously priced. Among the examples of exorbitant prices paid by the military, it is difficult to find a case that exceeds the boxes of tools the Gould Corporation sold to the Navy for $10,168.56 each. When Congressman Berkley Bedell's staff went to a hardware store and bought the same tools, the cost was $119.23 (Rasor, 1985, p. 164). The Navy audit system found the tools overpriced but concluded that the costs were "legal." The Navy then negotiated with the Gould Corporation, which returned 10 percent of the overcharge. The Navy held a press conference when the refund check was received from Gould, apparently feeling that this represented "a big victory" (Rasor, 1985, p. 166).

The most recent example of exorbitant costs (as well as cost overruns) is NASA's new toilet for its space shuttle. The price tag for the toilet is $30 million, 900 percent above its original price tag (Sawyer, 1993).

In spite of the end of the Cold War and contrary to expectations in a declining market for military hardware, the number of fraud cases (this includes not only overcharges but also things like defective equipment) and the amount paid in fines by errant defense contractors has been increasing rapidly. While defense spending declined by about 70 percent between 1986 and 1995, the amount collected in such fines and civil recoveries increased elevenfold. Almost 70 percent of the 100 top defense contractors were under investigation in 1995. Said a U.S. assistant attorney, "As military budgets shrink, we see more and more companies trying to maintain profits by cutting corners and committing fraud.... There were a lot of people who thought that defense downsizing would result in fewer instances of fraud, but that has not been the case" (Vartabedian, 1995). However, there are those who argue that this increase is traceable to overly zealous investigators and defense contractors who would rather settle quickly than experience prolonged criticism in the press.

The military–industrial complex constitutes a huge economic bloc that wields substantial power and strongly influences U.S. policies and actions. This exceptional power lends support to the neo-Marxian view that the political and social aspects of a society will be shaped by its most powerful economic interests.

Elitist View

The third approach to the state emphasizes the existence of a political **elite,** or a small group of people who come to power and dominate the population. Proponents of this approach also dispute the pluralist idea that the United States is democratic. Elite theorists developed their orientation in direct opposition to the Marxian belief that it is possible under communism to develop a society characterized by political, social, and economic equality. In their view, an elite evolves to govern any and every form of society.

Elite theorists believe that political systems are run by a small elite. One elite theorist describes the United States this way: "Great power in America is concentrated in a tiny handful of people" (Dye, 1983, p. 3). However, elite theorists sometimes differ in their evaluation of this condition. Some favor the concentration of power in the hands of the elite rather than in the hands of the masses (Ortega y Gasset, 1932). This group of elite theorists is fearful of democratic rule and favorably disposed toward control by a small elite. Others who subscribe to elitist political theory tend to be critical of elites and to see them as having a negative effect on society.

The Power Elite.   C. Wright Mills (1956) suggested such a negative elitist model of power, which he called the "power elite." The **power elite** is a small group of influential persons who occupy key positions in large corporations, the executive branch of government, and the military. Members of the power elite share common interests and goals; many have attended the same colleges, and many know one another personally. The members of the power elite are powerful not because of extraordinary personal skills and abilities but because they occupy important bureaucratic positions:

> No one, accordingly, can be truly powerful unless he has access to the command of major institutions, for it is over these institutional means of power that the truly powerful are, in the first instance, powerful. Higher politicians and key officials of government command

such institutional power; so do admirals and generals, and so do the major owners and executives of the larger corporations (Mills, 1956, p. 9).

Mills suggests three basic levels of power in the United States. At the top, of course, is the power elite. Interest group leaders, legislators, and local opinion leaders compose the middle level. The bottom level consists of the mass of unorganized citizens who are controlled by the "higher-ups" and are often unaware of how important political decisions have been made.

G. William Domhoff (1967; 1978; 1983) presents an elitist model of power based on the idea of a "ruling class":

> the ruling class is socially cohesive, has its basis in the large corporations and banks, plays a major role in shaping the social and political climate, and dominates the federal government through a variety of organizations and methods (Domhoff, 1983, p. 1).

Membership in the governing class is based on an individual's being listed in the *Social Register,* attending a prestigious preparatory school, belonging to an exclusive men's club, or being a millionaire. Domhoff estimates that the governing class consists of not more than 0.5 percent of the population, or about 1 out of every 200 people. This uppermost social class is extremely wealthy and exerts control over the executive branch of government, major corporations, the military, the mass media, major regulatory agencies, and boards of trustees of major universities. Through its control of these organizations and institutions, the ruling elite is able to formulate political and economic policies that will be of greatest benefit to their interests. This policy-planning process begins in the boardrooms of the largest corporations in the United States, and it extends into policy-discussion organizations where the issues of the day, such as "foreign aid, tariffs, taxes and welfare policies," are discussed (Domhoff, 1983, p. 84).

Another useful mechanism of the ruling class for establishing policy is the nonprofit foundation. Foundations are tax-free institutions that are "an upper-class adaptation to inheritance and property taxes. They provide a means by which wealthy people and corporations can in effect decide how their tax payments will be spent, for they are based on money that otherwise would go to the government in taxes" (Domhoff, 1983, p. 84). The most famous and influential of the "old money" foundations are those created by the Ford, Rockefeller, and Carnegie fortunes.

After the ruling elite has established which political and economic policies are most advantageous, the next step is to get them implemented. This goal is accomplished, in part, by shaping public opinion through the public schools, churches, and voluntary associations. Opinions, beliefs, and attitudes of the people are also shaped through "movies, television programs, books, pamphlets, speakers, advice and financial support" (Domhoff, 1983, p. 99).

However, the ruling elite, according to Domhoff, need not rely heavily on shaping public opinion, because policy objectives can be attained much more effectively by affecting the operations of the government directly. One method for doing this is to influence the candidate selection process of the major political parties. The method of the ruling elite is simple and direct: "large campaign donations that far outweigh what other classes and groups can muster" (Domhoff, 1983, p. 117). But even this method can be unstable and unreliable as a way of influencing policy. A more direct approach is to influence the elected officials after they are in office, regardless of who they may be. This effort is accomplished through a variety of lobbying and influence groups.

Domhoff's notion of a ruling class closely parallels Mills's "power elite" model. Both views see the masses as unorganized and powerless. Both models suggest that Congress has relatively little power compared to the executive branch, and, most important, both argue that power resides with a small and cohesive group of individuals who share similar social backgrounds. The major difference in the models is that Mills considers the military leadership and the executive branch more or less coequals with the corporate rich, while Domhoff views the upper social class as completely dominant; it controls the power elite.

There is no certain way of judging whether the pluralist, the neo-Marxian, or the elitist view of politics is the best description of the U.S. political system or any other political system. All three views provide insights into the workings of political systems, and thus they help us to understand the political process, both in our own country and elsewhere. As each new political issue arises, we can observe whether the pluralist, the neo-Marxian, or the elitist view provides the best explanation of the outcomes.

Changes in American Politics

American politics has changed dramatically in recent years. These changes are especially clear in elections for the presidency and presidential politics, but some of the same changes have occurred at other political levels as well.

Money and Presidential Elections

One outcome of the Watergate scandal was the revelation that Richard Nixon, in his 1972 election campaign, had received huge, illegal, corporate contributions. In addition, large sums had come from individuals, some of whom were later rewarded with ambassadorships. The result was a 1974 law limiting individual and corporate contributions to presidential (and congressional) campaigns, and establishing public financing of presidential campaigns. Once nominated by his or her party, a candidate gets a set sum from the government and is not allowed to take private contributions. As a result of this dictum, the two parties waged the 1976 presidential campaign on roughly equal economic footing. A Commission on National Elections concluded that the reforms had worked and that public financing had "clearly proved its worth in opening up the process, reducing undue influence of individuals and groups and virtually ending corruption in presidential election finance" (Ignatius, 1988, p. D5). However, Congress soon made some changes in the law that subverted its effectiveness.

The 1979 changes to the law re-created the potential for imbalances in future elections. For example, state and local party organizations were allowed to spend unlimited sums for voter registration and efforts to get out the vote. An individual or corporation could give enormous sums (now called "soft money") to state or local drives aimed at helping elect a presidential candidate. In terms of its effect, this money worked in a way similar to giving it directly to the presidential candidates. Thus, the 1974 law was circumvented; huge contributions could again be made, albeit indirectly, to presidential campaigns (Drew, 1983).

The issue of money and politics was never clearer than in Ross Perot's self-financed bid for the presidency in 1992. It is clear that Perot never would have been a serious candidate and never would have been able to garner the votes that he did were it not for the fact that he was a billionaire who was willing to spend $60 million on his own campaign (Cloud, 1992, p. 69).

In the 1996 campaign for the Republican nomination for the presidency, a political unknown, Malcolm S. "Steve" Forbes, Jr., made himself a force to be reckoned with by spending a not insignificant portion (about $20 million dollars *before* the first primary) of his estimated $439 million net worth on his campaign, mostly on television commercials (Fineman and Hosenball, 1996). He was asked by one television reporter, "Are you trying to buy this nomination?" (Kurtz, 1996b, p. Al). Although it may not have bought him the Republican nomination, it certainly brought him national attention that he otherwise would never have received. Forbes's campaign manager has argued that the political power structure is not happy about the impact of Forbes's money and that if he is not elected president "they will reform the campaign-finance laws to make sure this doesn't happen again" (Gibbs, 1996, p. 27). Time will tell, but it would be ironic if a reversal of the trend toward the increasing role of money in presidential politics was set in motion by one of its most extreme manifestations.

Of course, money is a problem not only in presidential politics, but in elections at every level in this country. In fact, John Bonifaz and Jamin Raskin have created a term to describe this problem, the "wealth primary":

> The wealth primary is that exclusionary process, leading up to every party primary and every general election, in which those with money or access to money, by means of their campaign contributions, choose the candidates who almost invariably go on to govern. Those who do not raise enough money—that is, those who lose the wealth primary—almost always do not win office (Bonifaz, 1994).

The result is that most Americans are effectively shut out of the process of choosing their elected officials. Candidates without wealth have a difficult time being elected, and voters without wealth have no influence over who the candidates who will represent them will be.

The Increasing Role of Television

Television is clearly playing a key role in politics, especially at the presidential level. The political candidate who controls the news broadcasts is almost certain to win the election. President Ronald Reagan was able to dominate the news media (Hertsgaard, 1988). Through television, Reagan overrode the stars of network news (Dan Rather, Tom Brokaw, and others). "He stepped right past these stars and took his place alongside the Americans in their living rooms, and together they paid no great mind to what these media were saying" (Schram, 1987, p. 27). The key to Reagan's success was an emphasis on visual rather than verbal impact. Writer Martin Schram calls this "The Great American Video Game." Presidential advisors were able to create great visual scenes (for example, Reagan with World War II veterans on the beach in Normandy) with the president in the forefront in order to manipulate the electronic media into building stories around the photo opportunities. Because television by its nature is a visual medium, the visual image tends to create a more powerful impression than verbal communication. The candidate who can control visual imagery has the significant advantage in a campaign.

Visual images certainly played a key role in the 1992 presidential campaign, for example, Bill Clinton's saxophone playing on the Arsenio Hall show, Admiral James Stockdale's (Ross Perot's running mate) spectacularly inept performance in the vice-presidential debate, including turning off his hearing aid so that he was unable to hear a question aimed at him, and even *Saturday Night Live*'s Dana Carvey's imitation and skewering of both George Bush and Ross Perot. Furthermore, new ground was broken as the candidates went beyond appearing on hard news programs such as *Meet the Press* and were frequently seen on more entertainment-oriented programs such as the *Phil Donahue* show. Then, of course, the presidential and vice-presidential debates made for good television viewing. And the candidates continued to create visuals solely for the purpose of hoping they would be used on the evening news. For example, when George Bush was to sign a bill easing credit for small businesses, he was whisked 50 miles by helicopter to Fredericksburg, Virginia, so that he could sign the bill in front of a picturesque 1950s pharmacy. Said a local businessman, "Hey, this'll make nice pictures on the national news.... Isn't that what it's all about today?" (Turan, 1992, p. A5).

However, it did appear that the media were less inclined to focus as much attention on visuals preplanned and prestaged by the candidates. And it appeared that many voters, deeply troubled by the long-running recession, wanted to see less and hear more about the issues. As a result, the networks, especially ABC, focused less on staged appearances. Here is what ABC anchor Peter Jennings said about the issue:

> None of this is brain surgery or utterly original.... We must resist today and not be seduced by pictures as we've been so easily seduced in the past. I don't think any of us

ever wants to be in the flag factory [a staged appearance by George Bush in the 1988 campaign aimed at surrounding himself in patriotic symbols] situation again (Kurtz, 1992a, p. A10).

NBC tried to keep the visuals, but to use them in a more serious way. Thus, NBC's Washington bureau chief said, "We're trying to use the campaign photo ops as ways into more serious pieces without losing the texture of the campaign.... It shouldn't just be the food fight" (Kurtz, 1992a, p. A10).

Of course, moving away from visuals and doing more reporting leads to the possibility of another kind of bias, that what reporters say about the candidates will be slanted in one way or the other. In fact, one study showed that the commentaries on evening news shows were biased against George Bush. The study showed that fully 71 percent of the comments about Bush were negative (compared to 55 percent of the comments about Perot and 48 percent about Clinton) (Kurtz, 1992b). The director of the center doing the study felt that reporters were on a "slippery slope toward partisan reporting" (Kurtz, 1992b, p. A7). However, network representatives attributed the bias to such things as the "rotten" economy, government scandals, and Bush's poor campaign. The executive producer of *CBS Evening News* countered, "we had trouble finding people, even Republicans, who would say nice things about George Bush" (Kurtz, 1992b, p. A7).

The importance of television visuals continued to be manifest in 1996 presidential elections. For example, in the campaign for the New Hampshire primary, Republican candidate Lamar Alexander insisted on having a press conference outdoors because a television camera team was present. This in spite of the fact that it was a frigid and snowy morning. Said an Alexander campaign aide, "'We need the visual of a New Hampshire winter'" (Kurtz, 1996a, p. A10). Recognizing how absurd it was to be outdoors rather than in the warm town hall, Alexander told assembled and shivering reporters, "'I promise to be brief. That way we won't freeze to death'" (Kurtz, 1996a, p. A10).

To take another example, Bob Dole was far in front for the Republican presidential nomination, at least until he delivered the Republican response to Bill Clinton's 1996 State of the Union address. Whatever the merit of the substance of what he had to say, Dole was described by friends and foes alike as "'dour'" and "'cadaver-like'" during his televised speech (Freund, 1996). The result was that Dole's ratings in the presidential polls took a nosedive.

Increasing Attention to Campaign Advertising

Intimately related to the accelerating importance of television imagery is the increasing significance of campaign advertising, especially television ads, which, of course, depend heavily on their visual component (Jamieson, 1984). Television ads are important for several reasons. First, they build name recognition for the candidate. Second, they allow the candidates to frame precisely, in whatever way they want, the issues that they consider central to the election. Third, they allow the candidates to expose their temperaments and their talents in the most favorable light. Fourth, they are short (usually a minute) and therefore are in line with the limited attention devoted to such matters by most television viewers.

Critics have generally argued that not only is campaign advertising growing more common and more important, it is also growing increasingly negative. That is, instead of portraying the candidate in a positive way, the ads portray opposing candidates negatively. Again, the 1996 campaign by Steve Forbes for the Republican presidential nomination illustrates this point. Two-thirds of the many millions spent by Forbes early in the campaign were on advertising that was negative in character. Of the front runner, Senator Robert Dole, Forbes's ads said such things as: Bob Dole was losing ground in the polls, was being deceptive, or was showing increasing desparation (Kurtz, 1996c). The media advisor to Republican candidate Lamar Alexander accused Forbes of running the most "cynical" campaign he had ever seen. He further accused Forbes of spending more money on negative advertising than any presidential candidate before him (Kurtz, 1996c).

The Changing Nature of Political Speeches

In *Eloquence in an Electronic Age,* Kathleen Jamieson (1988b) has related the impact of television to the transformation of political speechmaking. Jamieson writes that the increasing role of television is reducing the importance of memorable words and speeches. Instead, as mentioned earlier, the visual image matters most. "Television has changed public discourse dramatically. Increasingly, eloquence is visual, not verbal" (Jamieson, 1988b, p. 44). Even when television does report on the speeches themselves, the emphasis in newscasts is on the "15-second sound bite." Jamieson (1988b, p. 9) reports a study that found that the average number of seconds a candidate for president was shown speaking on a network news segment in the 1984 campaign was slightly less than 15 seconds. By the 1988 campaign reports indicated that speaking time had been reduced to nine seconds (Kalb, 1988). Because political campaign speeches are tailored for television coverage and *not* the immediate audience, they have grown shorter, less than 20 minutes on the average, including time for applause. The focus in candidates' speeches and campaign appearances is on the limited, 15-second portion that is apt to be picked up by the national television networks. Since this 15 seconds will be seen by many times more than the number of people witnessing the speech or appearance, most of the attention of presidential advisors is lavished on producing just the right snippet for the TV news.

On this, and many other issues related to the media, something of a counter-reaction set in in the 1992 elections. For example, ABC anchor Peter Jennings said, "There will be less attention to . . . sound bites designed exclusively for television" (Kurtz, 1992a, p. A10). ABC did take the lead on this, but the other networks lagged behind, and it remains to be seen whether 1992 was merely an aberrant year and whether we will be back to even shorter sound bites in subsequent elections.

In fact, the sound bites were back in 1996. In the campaign for the Republican presidential nomination, candidates repeated tried and true sound bites over and over in speech after speech. Some of them included

"I will put Bill Clinton in the crossfire [a reference to a television program Buchanan had co-hosted] and we will send him and Hillary back to Arkansas" (Pat Buchanan).

"We should expect less from Washington and more from ourselves" (Lamar Alexander).

Steve Forbes on the tax system: "Scrap it, kill it, bury it and hope it never rises again" (Kurtz, 1996a, p. A10).

Said one reporter who was forced to listen to such one liners over and over again at different speeches, "'You get tired of listening to the same spiel'." (Kurtz, 1996a, p. A10).

In addition to the decline of televised reports of speeches, televised speeches have undergone a similar decline. Prior to the advent of television, political speeches on radio were at first usually an hour in length, but by the 1940s the norm had dropped to 30 minutes. In the early years of television, speeches were that same length, but they rapidly decreased to 5 minutes, and by the 1970s the speech itself had been replaced by the 60-second, and even 30-second, advertisement (Ansolabehere and Iyengar, 1995). A tremendous decline in information transfer has occurred in this historical process, and complex ideas have given way to simple assertions. In addition, the brevity of contemporary speeches leads to increased use of hyperbole to catch the audience's attention.

Again, a counterreaction occurred in the 1992 elections. The most important was the great success of Ross Perot's set of half-hour political ads. The first of these, essentially a half-hour speech on the economy, drew higher ratings than the baseball playoff game that it preceded. In fact, all Perot's ads drew higher than expected audiences. A media critic concluded that this was "proof that voters will sit still for a straightforward [and lengthy] discussion of issues" (Zoglin, 1992, p. 70). Also of importance were the appearances of the candidates on talk shows like *Larry King Live,* which often involved extended discussions of various issues. Again, we will need to wait to see whether this reversal of the tendency toward progressively shorter speeches holds for later elections.

Debates between candidates for elected office have also grown shorter. In contemporary televised debates, if they can really be called that, candidates have a minute or two to offer their position on a given issue. "By contrast, in each of their seven senatorial debates of 1858, Lincoln and Douglas spoke for ninety minutes each on a single topic: the future of slavery in the territories" (Jamieson, 1988b, p. 11).

Another development has been the increasing differentiation between speech writer and speech giver. Instead of writing their own speeches or daring to speak extemporaneously, today's politicians rely on texts written for them by professional speech writers. Hence, the successful modern politician needs to be good only at reading speeches and not at creating artful prose.

The Rise of Political Consultants

Another reality of contemporary presidential politics is the increasing use of a wide array of political consultants. Several types of consultants are employed. Polling consultants are experts brought in to conduct various polls to tell the candidates how they are doing, what is working, what is not, how the opposition is doing, and so on (Barone, 1988). Media consultants are hired to help candidates get more media exposure and to be sure that the correct message comes across. The importance of media consultants was underscored when President-elect Jimmy Carter wrote to his media consultant, Gerald Rafshoon, "I'll always be grateful that I was able to contribute in a small way to the victory of the Rafshoon agency" (Sabato, 1981, p. 112). In addition, direct-mail fund-raising consultants are needed, whose expertise lies in the techniques necessary to raise the huge amount of money needed to finance a national political campaign. The danger in all these high-powered, high-priced consultants is that they are anxious to mold a candidate into an image that will win; the candidate may go along with these efforts, even if the image runs counter to who he or she "really" is (Sabato, 1981).

At no time were political consultants more visible than in the 1992 elections. In part, this was because James Carville played such a central role in Bill Clinton's successful presidential campaign and, in part, because of the love affair between Carville and George Bush's Deputy Campaign Manager Mary Matalin. Undaunted by her relationship with Carville, Matalin talked of "Boy Clinton" and described his (and implicitly Carville's) campaign as "lower-than-a-snake's-belly" (Grove, 1992a, p. D1).

Carville is known as a no-holds-barred political consultant who warned, "When [the Republicans] come after you...you have to answer them and tear their heads off" (Grove, 1992b, p. D2). And the Republicans knew that their attacks would be met with equally vicious responses. Carville was also reputed to have a "great gut" for the crucial issues to the middle class and for remaining doggedly focused on them. Thus, early in the campaign he defined the poor economy as *the* central issue ("It's the Economy, Stupid") and refused to allow the Clinton campaign to lose that single-minded focus. In the minds of most people it was that issue and his continual exploitation of it that won the election for Clinton. As a result of this success, it is likely that Carville will be even more in demand in future elections. More generally, his contributions and success further solidify the position of political consultants in the American political system.

In fact, Carville was back as a consultant to Bill Clinton for the 1996 presidential campaign (Keller, 1995). Most of the presidential candidates in the 1996 election were spending heavily on consultants. For their part, consultants were eager to be involved in this campaign. Said one consultant, "Every political consultant on the planet needs a presidential campaign on his résumé" (Keller, 1995).

The Increasing Role of Women in Politics

The election of 1992 was supposed to be the widely heralded "Year of the Woman." In fact, there were eleven female candidates for Senate seats and five of them were elected, including the first black woman senator, Carol Moseley Braun from Illinois. The number of female members of the House of Representatives also increased dramatically. Behind these very visible gains has been the slow and steady growth of women's political groups like the National Organization of Women (founded in 1966 and now with 270,000 members) and the National Women's Political Caucus (founded in 1971, 35,000 members) (Manegold, 1992). These organizations have also been able to develop significant war chests to be used to fund female candidates. Although smaller than the organizations mentioned above, an organization known as Emily's List (22,000 members) had by far the largest sum of money, $6 million, to distribute to female candidates. [EMILY stands for "early money is like yeast" (Manegold, 1992, p. D21).] Organizations like these dedicate their efforts to the ultimate objective that female political representation reflects the proportion of women in the population as a whole. And these organizations have helped not only in the dramatic cases of senators and congresswomen mentioned above, but in a series of steady gains throughout the full range of the political system.

While there have been gains for women in politics, it is abundantly clear that there is a long way to go before women achieve parity with men in the political arena. For example, even with the recent gains, women constitute only 6 percent of the Senate and 11 percent of the House (Ehrenreich, 1992). This proportion lags far behind not only the proportion of women in the United States, but also female representation in European legislatures. Although plans are finally being developed to rectify the situation, as of the end of 1992 the Senate, quite symbolically, still lacked a women's bathroom. This led to the following tart observation: "Future archaeologists, studying the pipes and bathroom fixtures of Capitol Hill, may conclude that late-20th century America was a fortress of patriarchy on a par with Saudi Arabia" (Ehrenreich, 1992, p. 61).

The Coming Revolution in Cyberpolitics

While its impact is just starting to be felt, it seems clear that the computer and the Internet are beginning to have a profound effect on political campaigns and elections. Among other things, these technologies allow us to instantly compare the records of candidates, to hear and even view speeches, and to receive mail from the candidates at virtually no cost to them. In the not too distant future we will be able to ask questions and get personal responses, and we may even someday be able to vote via computer (Haase, 1995).

All but one of the candidates for the Republican nomination for president in 1996 had web sites. A major attraction to candidates is that they can reach voters directly without having to go through the news media. Furthermore, the people that candidates reach in this way seem highly likely to vote; thus, efforts on them are less likely to be wasted. Another is that cost is extremely low, a great inducement in an era in which escalating campaign costs are a major problem and public issue. While voters still have far more mailboxes, telephones, and television sets than they do computers, the number of computers and people who are computer literate is growing rapidly. Said a communications consultant, "It's startling. It's a virtual certainty that on-line campaigning will move ahead at warp speed, driven by voter demand and the low cost of the medium" (Matthews, 1995). The 1996 presidential election is likely to be the true starting point for the coming revolution in cyberpolitics.

The Voters in Democratic Societies

The Apathy of Voters in the United States

As we noted at the beginning of this chapter, elections in the United States in the twentieth century have had relatively low voter turnouts. During the nineteenth century, American voter participation was much higher, with a peak of approximately 85 percent of those eligible to vote casting ballots during the presidential election of 1876 (see Figure 16–1). During the early years of the twentieth century, however, voter participation substantially declined: the rate of voter participation (43 percent) in 1920 was about half of what it had been in 1876. Since 1920, the high point of voter participation occurred in the Kennedy–Nixon contest of 1960, in which 63 percent of those eligible to vote cast ballots (see Table 16–1). Voter participation consistently declined until 1984, when the Reagan–Mondale contest attracted slightly more than half (53 percent) of those eligible to vote and ended a 20-year decline in the presidential-year voter turnout rate.

In the 1988 Bush–Dukakis election, the decline continued, and quite dramatically, as only 50.2 percent of eligible voters cast ballots. Furthermore, the total number of people voting was several million less than in 1984, the first time since 1944 that the total number of voters declined from one presidential election to the next.

However, in the 1992 elections, there was a big increase in voter turnout, with about 55 percent of the electorate voting, far above the 1988 turnout. Of course,

Figure 16–1.   Voter Turnout: 1789–1992. (*Source:* William Casey and Jeannette Belliveau, "Voter Turnout over the Years." *Washington Post,* November 6, 1992, p. A25.)

1992 was an unusual year with the third-party candidacy of Ross Perot and a long and persistent recession making the electorate restless. Again, we will need to see whether 1992 marks the beginning of a reversal or merely a blip in the otherwise long-term decline in voter turnout.

Table 16–1   Percentage of Persons Eligible to Vote Who Voted in Presidential and Congressional Elections, 1920–1992

	Percentage of Those Eligible to Vote Who Voted	
Year	*President*	*Representatives*
1920	43	. . .
1922	. . .	32
1924	44	. . .
1926	. . .	30

(*continued*)

Table 16–1   *Continued*

	Percentage of Those Eligible to Vote Who Voted	
Year	*President*	*Representatives*
1928	52	. . .
1930	. . .	34
1932	52	. . .
1934	. . .	41
1936	57	. . .
1938	. . .	44
1940	59	. . .
1942	. . .	33
1944	56	. . .
1946	. . .	37
1948	51	. . .
1950	. . .	41
1952	62	. . .
1954	. . .	42
1956	60	. . .
1958	. . .	43
1960	63	. . .
1962	. . .	45
1964	62	. . .
1966	. . .	45
1968	61	. . .
1970	. . .	44
1972	56	. . .
1974	. . .	36
1976	54	. . .
1978	. . .	35
1980	52.6	. . .
1982	. . .	38
1984	53.3	. . .
1986	. . .	33.4
1988	50.2	. . .
1990	. . .	33
1992	55.0	. . .
1994	. . .	36

Source: Data from U.S. Bureau of the Census, *Statistical Abstract of the United States,* 93rd ed. Washington, D.C.: U.S. Government Printing Office, 1972; and 105th ed. Washington, D.C.: U.S. Government Printing Office, 1985; 109th ed. Washington, D.C.: U.S. Government Printing Office, 1988h; 1990 data from *Congressional Quarterly Almanac,* Vol. XLVI. Washington, D.C.: Congressional Quarterly Inc.: 901; 1992 data from William Casey and Jeannette Belliveau, "Voter Turnout over the Years." *Washington Post,* November 6, 1992, p. A25; U.S. Bureau of the Census, *Statistical Abstract of the United States, 1995.* Washington, D.C.: U.S. Government Printing Office, 1995.

This relatively low rate of voter participation in the United States contrasts sharply with the situation in other modern democracies. Since World War II, voter participation in Italy and Belgium has exceeded 90 percent. In Portugal, the former West Germany, and Norway, from 80 to 85 percent of those eligible actually vote, and from 70 to 80 percent of Canadians, Greeks, and Japanese vote (Glass, Squire, and Wolfinger, 1984). Overall, the average turnout in other industrialized countries is 80 percent of the eligible electorate (Powell, 1986, p. 16). "During the 1980s, the United States ranked 19th out of 20 Western industrial nations in turnout" (Casey and Belliveau, 1992, p. A25).

In contrast to the low voter turnout, however, there is one sense in which Americans appear to be more politically involved than the citizens of other democracies (Powell, 1986). In comparison with seven other industrial nations, U.S. citizens are most likely to feel that they have a say in what the government does, and that they have at least some interest in politics. These views of Americans are borne out by some of their political activities: Americans are most apt to discuss politics with others and to have worked for a party or candidate during an election. Thus, on a variety of attitudinal and behavioral measures, Americans are highly involved in the political process. If this is the case, then why the low voter turnout in U.S. elections?

Some important structural and institutional conditions in the United States make the average voter turnout relatively low. First, some industrialized nations invoke legal penalties if a citizen does not vote, but the United States does not mandate voter participation. Second, in many nations the government takes the initiative to get people to register to vote, but in the United States registration is left largely to the individual. Other aspects of the registration process inhibit voting in the United States such as the absence in most states of day-of-voting registration. Often it is inconvenient to get to registration sites during their hours of operation. If a person moves, he or she must reregister. Since almost half the population might move in a five-year period, a large portion of the electorate must make the *double effort* of registering *and* voting. In fact, a post-1988 election survey indicated that 37 percent of nonvoters did not vote because they were not registered. Two-thirds of these people indicated that they would have voted if they could simply have shown up on election day without prior registration. Three-quarters of these people think the election laws should be changed to allow easier registration (Dionne, 1988b). In recognition of the barriers to registration, during the 1992 presidential campaign Ross Perot (and others) supported legislation designed to make it easier to register to vote.

Another factor inhibiting voting in the United States is the electoral college system, which gives all of a state's votes to the winning candidate. With this system, neither political party will make an effort to get out the vote in states where the outcome appears to be a foregone conclusion.

Finally, voting in the United States is hampered by the fact that, unlike many European countries, there is no strong tie between belonging to certain groups (occupational, religious) and partisan political activity. Such a strong linkage between one's social group and one's political party seems to lead to a higher voter turnout.

Even in light of these structural and institutional barriers, a large number of U.S. citizens still choose not to vote in presidential and congressional elections. In contrast, in some state and local elections turnout has been very high (Gans, C., 1988). Perhaps the issues of national elections are too remote for most people. Or it may be that citizens are "turned off" by excessively long political campaigns and the self-serving actions of the political candidates. With presidential campaigns now sometimes extending over a two-year or three-year period, many people often say that they are tired of the candidates' charges and counter-charges.

Beyond barriers to voting and legitimate reasons for not voting, people in a democratic society still have a responsibility to exercise their vote. Primarily through their votes they can shape and influence governmental policy and action. Yet substantial evidence shows that many people in the United States, particularly the young, simply do not care enough and are not interested enough to participate in elections.

Various plans have been suggested and efforts made to increase voter participation in elections. In a particularly notable one, on January 30, 1996, Oregon held a special election to fill its vacant senatorial seat and voters were permitted to use a mail-in ballot (Claiborne, 1996a; Knickerbocker, 1995). In fact, more than 65 percent of registered voters participated in the special election (only slightly less than participated in the 1994 general election), far more than the expected 40 to 50 percent turnout (Claiborne, 1996b). It is also estimated that vote-by-mail saved the state a million dollars in poll-station costs. While mail-in elections may save money and serve to increase voter participation, they are not without their critics: "In many ways Americans are already 'absentees' in political life. The old election rallies have been replaced by televised debates and dueling commercials. Politics has become a spectator sport, and Americans couch potato constituents" (Goodman, 1995).

The End of Militarism?

With the end of the Cold War, there is a great debate taking place over the future of the American military (Betts, 1996). There are those who see this as a great opportunity to downsize the military and to save huge sums of money. On the other side are those who feel that such cuts will leave us unprepared to handle future military threats and will cost us more money in the long term to rebuild a depleted military at highly inflated prices. The military is clearly on the defensive in an era when there are powerful efforts to balance the budget and lower the national debt, as well as because there is no longer any major enemy like the Soviet Union in existence or on the horizon. However, the defense budget remains

Cross-national Perspectives

Peru's Shining Path Guerrillas

With the demise of communism in Russia and Eastern Europe and with China drifting toward capitalism, at least economically if not politically, it would appear that this would not be a good time for communists bent on overthrowing a capitalistically oriented government. While this is true in general, there are a few exceptions. The most notable of these exceptions is the Maoist Shining Path movement in Peru (Robinson, 1992).

The Shining Path began what it defined as an all-out war against the Peruvian government in 1980, and since then an estimated 26,000 people have died as a result of its activities. It also caused approximately $22 billion in damages. It has used traditional guerrilla tactics of murdering those who oppose it and terrorizing target groups within the society. In spite of, or perhaps because of, these tactics, the Shining Path and its 8000 fighters is not likely to win control of Peru any time soon. This seemed especially true when its leader, Abimael Guzman, was captured and imprisoned in September 1992, and a period of disarray and internal conflict followed. One police official said, "Guzman was a god and what he said was the law so that no one would oppose him. . . . There is no one now who can re-create that mystique" (Nash, 1992, p. A3).

The Shining Path did not disappear following the capture of Guzman. In late 1995, Peruvian police reported that it was reorganizing under a new leader, Oscar Alberto Ramirez, and it expected the group to carry out a wide range of guerrilla actions (UPI, 1995). In a preemptive strike undertaken at the end of 1995, the Peruvian army launched a wide-scale attack on the Shining Path stronghold in the Amazon jungle (Agence France Presse, 1995). The strike was prompted by guerrilla acts and by the ambush and murder of seven soldiers. It is not clear how successful the military action was, but it seems certain the Shining Path activities will continue, if not accelerate.

Nevertheless, at least some peasants are returning to the villages that they were forced to flee by the Shining Path. Said one village leader, "Now the guerrillas have gone, we want to return to our old ways" (Scrutton, 1996). It remains to be seen whether they will be able to live safely in their villages, or whether they will be forced to flee again in the face of increased guerrilla activity by the Shining Path.

The lesson of the Shining Path and its continuing success is that the economic roots of communist movements remain in place in many parts of the world. Poverty has long been a breeding ground for dissident groups. Since it is unlikely that poverty is going to be eliminated anytime soon in Peru, or in the rest of the world, the roots of communist movements remain.

There is an ongoing debate among Marxists today about their role in the world after the demise of the Soviet Union (Burawoy, 1990; Jones, 1990). The continuing success of the Shining Path indicates one arena in which they have a role to play. More generally, as more and more of the world embraces capitalism as the only viable economic path, we are likely to see more of the great differences in wealth that characterize capitalistic societies. Those great disparities will also provide a fertile ground for communist movements. Thus, in the wake of the demise of Soviet communism, it may be that we have been overly hasty in declaring the collapse of communism as a whole. In light of its past failures, communism may need to devise new forms and approaches, but poverty and great disparities in wealth will continue to provide the movement, or something very much like it, with fertile ground on which to develop.

AGENCE FRANCE PRESSE. "Peru Launches New Military Campaign against Shining Path." December 20, 1995.

BURAWOY, MICHAEL. "Marxism as Science: Historical Challenges and Theoretical Growth." *American Sociological Review* 55, 1990.

JONES, GARETH STEDMAN. "Marx after Marxism." *Marxism Today,* February 1990.

NASH, NATHANIEL C. "Shining Path Reeling in Wake of Chief's Capture." *New York Times,* November 20, 1992.

ROBINSON, EUGENE. "Peru's Guerrillas Pose New Threat." *Washington Post,* February 16, 1992.

ROSENAU, WILLIAM. "Is the Shining Path the "New Khmer Rouge"? *Studies in Conflict and Terrorism,* 17, 1994.

SCRUTTON, ALISTAIR. "War-weary Peruvian Peasants Find They Can Go Home Again." *Tampa Tribune,* January 7, 1996.

UPI. "Peru Rebels Rebuilding Capacity." August 14, 1995.

huge, higher than that of all the other great powers combined. New high-tech weapons systems are enormously expensive, as are peace missions such as the one undertaken in Bosnia.

Various efforts have been undertaken to reduce dramatically military costs in the post-Cold War era. For example, efforts were made to reform the way weapons and equipment are acquired. For another, cuts have been made in infrastructure, such as the closing of military bases. However, in the main these efforts have not made much of a dent in defense spending.

Compared to the heyday of the Cold War, the U.S. military faces an uncertain future. While it may have been fraught with potential dangers, the Cold War had some predictability. Now the United States has no clear idea where its next major threat might come from. A revived Soviet Union? A newly militant Russia? China? Regional problems in the Middle East? A combination of confrontations in places like North Korea and Iraq? Given such unpredictability, it is difficult to plan future military expenditures. Too much would likely lead to enormous waste; too little might leave the United States unprepared for unforeseen military problems.

One thing does seem sure: the military–industrial complex will fight to keep defense expenditures as high as it possibly can. It will have more difficulty attaining its goals with the end of the Cold War, but its history of success should lead us to be wary of confidently predicting that defense expenditures are likely to be reduced substantially in the coming years. The need for new high-tech technology for the digitized battlefield of the future, especially given the desire to reduce military personnel, will certainly help to fuel the military–industrial complex. In addition to new technologies, arguments being made by the military–industrial complex include the danger of allowing the defense industry to founder, the greater costs of having to rebuild that industry in the future, and paying for weapons systems with future inflated dollars rather than buying them now at comparatively lower cost.

The U.S. military needs to be prepared for at least two major contingencies in the future. One is being able to respond to one threat (say from North Korea), while being tied up dealing with another (say Iraq). The second is a larger-scale international threat (say from China with its huge military force and nuclear arms). We can be sure that the military–industrial complex will use these and other potential threats to keep defense spending as high as the world situation will permit.

Sam Marullo (1993) contends that the five decades of the Cold War left the United States with cultural, economic, and political forces that serve to sustain militarism and an unnecessarily high probability of war.

Marullo first deals with the cultural forces that fuel militarism in American society. For one thing, various American values promote militarism. For example, the valuing of efficiency and our faith in technology leads to the continual search for ever-more efficient and sophisticated weapons systems. Then, there are values that are more specific to the military sector that also contribute to militarism. For example, we believe there is such a thing as a "just war;" that is, "it is sometimes necessary to use force, and even to kill, in order to defend ourselves or other innocents from victimization" (Marullo, 1993, p. 112). Thus, for example, in the Persian Gulf War Saddam Hussein was portrayed as a modern-day Hitler and the war against the Iraqis was, as a result, defined as a just war. In addition, the mass media often play a key role in communicating cultural meanings that serve to fan the flames of militarism (Gamson and Stuart, 1992).

Second, it is in the economic interest of various organizations associated with the previously discussed military–industrial complex to be sure that large sums of money continue to be poured into military undertakings, such as acquiring new weapons, maintaining operational readiness and the military's infrastructure, supporting the standing army, and research into and development of future weapons. Marullo argues that there are five groups that have a vested interest in high levels of military spending:

1. *Defense contractors* are obviously the most dependent on military expenditures for their survival, and they will continue to press for defense expenditures in order to continue to be viable.
2. *Scientists, engineers, and policy analysts* in universities, laboratories, and think tanks depend on military research for their livelihood.
3. *Organized labor,* representing many of those who work in the defense industries, wants to keep those people on the job.
4. The *Department of Defense* owes its existence and its power to the continued existence of a large and powerful military.
5. The *senators and members of the House of Representatives* who are involved in defense policy and expenditures would lose their power and influence if there were a substantial decline in military spending.

The third factor contributing to the continuation of military spending and militarism is the organizational structure of the state, or the "national security state." This involves mainly elements of the executive, representative, and judicial branches of the state that have a vested interest in military matters. It is a huge structure with enormous resources. One example of this is the lack, at least thus far, of a "peace dividend" derived from money no longer needed for defense purposes. This money was supposed to be used for such things as cutting the federal budget deficit or improving the nation's infrastructure. Innumerable committee meetings have been devoted to the issue. The secretary of defense urged Congress not to cut military spending. Some members of Congress grew afraid that cutting defense would lead to such things as base closings in their districts that would hurt their reelection chances. In the end, after interminable discussions, there was little more than a negligible peace dividend.

Thus, an array of cultural, economic, and political forces coexist and are likely to continue to impel us in the direction of militarism even with the apparent end of the Cold War. To stop this trend, we need to understand how these forces operate. That understanding then needs to be used by a reinvigorated peace movement to be sure that there is a substantial peace dividend and that it is, in fact, invested in peaceful rather than warlike undertakings.

Summary

Political sociology is primarily concerned with the distribution and exercise of power, which is the ability to control other people's behavior and to carry out one's will. Legitimate power, or authority, involves acceptance of the exercise of power by members of a society or group, while illegitimate power, or coercion, is power that relies solely on force to achieve its objectives. The dominant political institution in modern societies is the state, which claims a monopoly over the legitimate use of force.

The United States is nominally a democracy, but three different views exist about the degree to which the nation is, in fact, democratic. The pluralist view emphasizes the existence of many competing interest groups. The give-and-take among these groups produces a relatively democratic system because no one group gains control. The neo-Marxist perspective stresses the way in which the dominant economic groups in the society hold the most political power. One major special interest group predominates in the United States: the military–industrial complex. This huge economic interest group can exert extraordinary influence on government policies. The dominance of this coalition supports a neo-Marxist view of political power in the United States. The elitist view also perceives that power is held by a relatively small group but sees this group as not limited to the economic elite.

Politics in the United States in general, and more specifically presidential politics, are changing dramatically. In spite of laws designed to limit individual contributions to presidential campaigns, ways have been found to funnel huge sums of money into them. This puts the presidency on the "auction block" and opens the possibility that huge contributors will be rewarded by the victor in various ways. Television news is playing an increasingly central role in presidential campaigns, with the emphasis more and more on visual images rather than substance. In a related area, advertising, especially on TV, is key to a presidential victory. Political speeches are growing shorter and less substantive, with emphasis shifting to the generation of the "correct" 10-second or 15-second "sound bite" for the evening news. Political consultants (for example, media advisors) are more and more important to presidential (and many other) campaigns. Although they have a very long way to go, women have made recent gains in the political sector.

A revolutionary change in the making is the coming age of cyberpolitics. That is, the Internet will change, perhaps even revolutionize, politics in the not-too-distant future.

Evidence shows increasing voter apathy in presidential elections. The 1992 election was an exception, but we need to see whether this was merely an isolated exception to a general rule. Americans continue to be involved in various other ways in political activities.

Concerns about war and peace dominate the international political scene. With the demise of the Soviet Union and the end of the Cold War, significant steps have been taken toward a more peaceful relationship between the United States and the former Soviet Republics, most notably Russia. Nevertheless, there are important cultural, economic, and political forces that continue to push the United States (and other countries) in the direction of militarism.

CRITICAL THINKING

1. In what ways does a state wield power over its citizens? What means might be used to assure the continuation of power? What is the basis of governmental power in the United States?
2. Describe the three major forms of governments listed in the chapter and give a contemporary example of each.
3. What explanations would you offer for why the youngest voters in the United States have the lowest percentage voting in elections?
4. What is the military–industrial complex? In what ways does this interest group exert influence on government policy? What does this example teach you about the nature of power in our political system?
5. Is the U.S. political system truly democratic? Compare and contrast the three major sociological views of the U.S. political system: the pluralist, the neo-Marxist, and the elitist. What evidence can you muster to support each viewpoint? How do PACs reflect the pluralist view?
6. Assess the impact of campaign finances, television, campaign advertising, political speeches, and political consultants on presidential elections. Does the picture presented conform to society's notion of the ideal democracy?
7. Outline as many changes in political campaigns that you can think of that are likely to result from the coming revolution in cyberpolitics. Are these changes likely to be more for the good? or the bad?
8. The United States is stereotyped as the greatest democracy in the world. How does U.S. voting behavior contradict this stereotype? Compare U.S. voting behavior with that in other Western democracies.
9. Use conflict theory and structural functionalism to analyze the end of the Cold War.
10. What forces continue to impel the United States, in spite of the end of the Cold War, in the direction of militarism?

Part IV   Social Change

17

Population and Urbanization

Every four days a million people are added to the world's population (Population Reference Bureau, 1995). This growth in numbers is being added largely to the urban places of the world (United Nations, 1995). The growth of the world's population and the ever-increasing numbers of people living in urban places are two of the major influences on societies in the twentieth century. This chapter will describe both of these trends and their implications for social life.

The scientific study of population is called **demography** (Daugherty and Kammeyer, 1995). Demographers study why and how populations grow and decline by examining the three basic processes that determine population size. The first process is **fertility,** a term used by demographers to indicate the actual childbearing behavior of people. The second is **mortality,** which refers to deaths and death rates of a specific population. The third is **migration,** which is the permanent (or semipermanent) change of one's place of residence. In addition to studying these dynamic features of populations, demographers also consider the characteristics of the population (called **population composition**). The most frequently considered characteristics of a population are age and sex.

570

Fertility

Having children is fundamentally a social behavior since it is profoundly influenced by the social contexts in which people live. These contexts may be as large scale as the economic or political times or as small scale as the particular couples who are making decisions about whether to have a baby. Even if, as some people believe, there is a human "instinct" or genetic "drive" to have children, this explanation would not reveal why some people have many children, others have only a few, and some have none.

Just as individuals (or couples) vary greatly in the number of children they have, so do groups or categories of people. As an extreme example, the Hutterites, a fundamentalist religious group living in the plains states of the northern Midwest and southern Canada, have the record for the highest fertility ever reliably recorded for any population. As recently as the 1950s, Hutterite women had an *average* of nearly 11 children. The Hutterites oppose any methods of controlling childbearing, they marry in their late teens or early twenties, and they do not allow divorce. Among the Hutterites all property is owned in common and children are cared for communally. Because of these particular social arrangements and cultural values the Hutterites have what population scientists believe to be the maximum level of fertility (Stockwell and Groat, 1984). This maximum level of uncontrolled childbearing is called **natural fertility** (Bongaarts, 1987).

As an interesting contrast to the Hutterites, there were two U.S. religious groups of the nineteenth century for which fertility was almost nonexistent. The Shakers and the Rappites, both located in the eastern United States, prohibited sexual intercourse for most of their members. The only way these religious groups could grow in size was to recruit new members and to adopt children. Today the Rappites have completely disappeared, and only a handful of Shaker women survive (Kephart, 1976; Muncy, 1973).

The fertility extremes of the Hutterites on the one hand, and the Shakers and Rappites on the other, illustrate very well how social contexts influence childbearing. In contemporary American society differences in fertility still exist between some societal groups and categories, but the differences are not great, and they are less pronounced today than they were in the past. Some differences in fertility among religious, racial, and socioeconomic groups will be considered after we examine some general trends in fertility in the United States.

Childbearing in the United States, over the last 20 years, has been at its lowest level in history. At the time of the founding of the country the average woman had just under eight births. Today the number of births per woman is slightly over two (2.06) (U.S. Bureau of the Census, 1995b). The birth rate went down steadily through the entire nineteenth century and for nearly half of the twentieth. Then, after World War II, the birth rate went up substantially and remained high during the 1950s. This period between 1946 and 1960 is called the *baby boom.*

Fertility in this post-World War II period actually reached its peak in 1957. For nearly two decades after the peak, the U.S. birth rate declined steadily. Since the mid-1970s the birth rate has been relatively stable, although there were some modest increases in the late 1980s (U.S. Bureau of the Census, 1995b).

Social Factors Related to Fertility Rates

The influence of social factors on childbearing is demonstrated by comparing the birth rates of various categories in the society. For example, fertility differs by occupational categories, education, income, and religion (Daugherty and Kammeyer, 1995). We will examine religion first.

Religion. Because the Roman Catholic church disapproves of mechanical and chemical methods of birth control (including sterilization), it is often assumed that the Catholic birth rate is much higher than the birth rates of other religious groups. That is not the case in the United States, however (Mosher and Bachrach, 1996). For the last two decades, Catholic fertility has been virtually the same as non-Catholics (Westoff and Jones, 1979).

A recent national survey of American women aged 15 to 39 shows Catholic women having *fewer* children than Protestant women (Mosher et al., 1992). Among non-Hispanic whites, Catholic women are averaging about one-quarter of a child less than Protestants (1.64 babies versus 1.91). The apparent reason for the lower fertility among Catholic women is their later entry into marriage. This same survey shows that Catholic women expect to have more children in the future than do the Protestant women, but previous studies have shown that unmarried Catholic women overestimate the number of children that they will have (Mosher et al., 1992).

The fact that Catholic fertility is no higher than Protestant fertility (and is actually lower in the national survey just described) is not too surprising when one understands that there are no longer differences between Catholic and non-Catholic contraceptive use (Goldscheider and Mosher, 1991). American Catholics generally use the same contraceptive measures as non-Catholics, and the overall pattern of contraceptive use by Catholics and Protestants is very similar. The major difference is that Catholic women are somewhat less likely to use sterilization as a method of contraception (Goldscheider and Mosher, 1991).

Across the entire spectrum of religious–ethnic groups there are some groups that fall at the extremes. The lowest fertility in the United States is found among whites who have *no* religious affiliation; Jews have the next lowest fertility. The highest levels of fertility are found among Hispanic Catholics, fundamentalist Protestants, and Mormons (Mosher et al., 1992).

The high Mormon and fundamentalist Protestant fertility may be related to other research evidence showing that women who participate more in religion are likely to have higher fertility. The effect of church attendance is especially pronounced among Protestants. Protestant women who attend religious services weekly have an average of 2.24 children, while Protestant women who attend less often have only 1.75 children (Mosher et al., 1992). A similar pattern was found in a Rhode Island study, in which Catholic fertility was higher than non-Catholic fertility, but almost all the difference was produced by the greater church attendance of Catholic women (Williams and Zimmer, 1990). When infrequent church attenders were compared, non-Catholic women actually had more children than the Catholic women (Williams and Zimmer, 1990).

Race and Ethnicity.   Racial and ethnic groups in the United States continue to have differences in fertility levels, but they are not exceptionally large. The differences may be seen by examining the number of *children ever born* to women aged 35 to 44 (both married and unmarried). While some children may yet be born to the women in this age group, the numbers will probably not change greatly when they have completed childbearing. White women aged 34 to 44 have an average of just under two children per woman (1.93). Black women in this age group average 2.24 children, and Hispanic women average 2.60 children (U.S. Bureau of the Census, 1991b).

While Hispanic women have the highest level of fertility, there are significant differences among Hispanics. Cubans have the lowest fertility among Hispanics, while Mexicans have the highest. Asian Americans generally have lower fertility than other Americans, although again there are important differences: Japanese Americans have lower fertility than whites, while Vietnamese in the United States have higher fertility than whites (Westoff, 1986).

Socioeconomic Status.   Most people accept the precept that socioeconomic status is related to fertility. In sociological terms, "lower socioeconomic status is associated with higher fertility." This is consistent with the old cliché that ends, "and the poor get children." Although these statements are somewhat true, qualifications are necessary. For example, the opposite is the case in traditional peasant societies, where wealthier land-owning couples may have more children than those less well off. Studies from India, Bangladesh, Iran, Nepal, the Philippines, and Thailand show some tendency for higher-status landowners to have higher fertility than other farm families. In these societies, owning land increases the demand for children and provides greater security for old age (World Bank, 1984).

In Western societies during the twentieth century, however, the relationship between socioeconomic status and fertility has usually been negative. But this negative relationship was strongest in the early part of the twentieth century, as the middle and upper middle classes started using family limitation methods that were not yet available to the lower classes.

In present-day American society, regardless of whether socioeconomic status is measured by educational level, occupational status, or income, higher-status women have fewer children. Of these three indicators of socioeconomic status, the educational attainment of a woman is the strongest variable. Among married women aged 25 to 34 years, those with less than a high school education have an average of 2.1 children, while women of the same age with four years of college have an average of about 0.8 of a child. Of course, some of these college-educated women who are still in their twenties are likely to have more children before they complete childbearing years. Figure 17–1 shows the average number of children per woman aged 35 to 44 years (an age group that has probably completed most of its childbearing) at various educational levels. For this age group, there is more than a one-child difference between women who did not complete high school and women who completed college. Although this figure does show the expected relationship with socioeconomic status, the difference is less than one child between the lowest education group and college-educated women.

Mortality

Death is obviously a biological event, since every death is ultimately due to a biological cause. Nonetheless, social factors do contribute to differences in death rates among different groups and categories in society. Two distinctive aspects of social life are related to mortality differences: (1) the positions that people have in the social structure and (2) lifestyles.

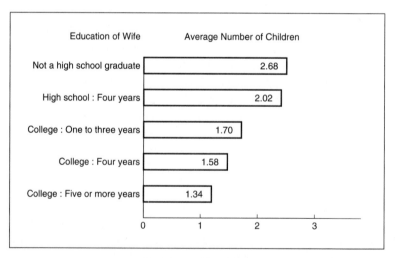

Figure 17–1. Average Number of Children Born to Wives Aged 35 to 44 Years in Married-couple Families, by Education of Wife, 1994. (*Source:* U.S. Bureau of Census, *Fertility of American Women: June 1994, Current Population Reports,* P-20, No. 482, 1995.)

Position in the social structure refers to the way some groups or categories have lower (or higher) places in some ranking system of the society. Life-style refers to the choices people make in the conduct of their daily lives. This includes how they eat, use alcohol or drugs, exercise, and so on (Rogers, 1995). Life-style is not a precise scientific concept, but a number of causes of death are clearly associated with the choices people make about their lives. We begin our examination of the way in which these social factors influence mortality by considering some examples of how position in the social structure influences death rates and longevity.

Position in the Social Structure

In Chapter 8 we saw how the position one has in the stratification structure of a society can influence length of life. People in the lower socioeconomic classes have higher death rates and a shorter life expectancy. As a general principle we may say that people who are in lower or disadvantaged positions in a society (or social structure) will have higher death rates and shorter lives (Christenson and Johnson, 1995).

This principle is also illustrated by comparing the life expectancies of black and white Americans. At birth a black female has a life expectancy that is 5.9 years less than a white female (black, 73.9 years versus white, 79.8 years). Black males are even more disadvantaged compared to white males since white males can expect to live 8.2 years longer (National Center for Health Statistics, 1995a).

Gender Roles and Mortality.   In Chapter 10 we saw that the feminine gender role, especially in traditional, patriarchal societies, places women in subordinate positions to men. It follows, therefore, that females should have higher death rates or lower life expectancy than males. In fact, females in the contemporary world generally have a longer life expectancy than males, but that may be due to a biological advantage of females over males. We know, for example, that the death rate among male fetuses is higher than female fetuses during pregnancy, and that males have a higher death rate than females during the first four weeks of life. Both of these facts suggest that the female organism is more viable than the male organism, since social and cultural factors could not account for the lower death rates of females.

Yet societies do exist in which females do not survive as long as males, or they have only a slight advantage over males; these are often the same societies in which males have distinctly dominant positions in the social structure. A World Bank report shows only three countries of the world (India, Pakistan, and Bhutan) in which female life expectancy is less than male life expectancy (World Bank, 1984). In the two large Asian countries, females generally hold a status subordinate to that of males (Miller, 1981; Preston, 1982).

Often these same countries have an excess of males over females in their populations, whereas in European countries and the United States the opposite is true (Coale, 1991). In European countries and the United States, the surplus of females is generally attributed to the higher death rates of males at all ages. In countries where there is a shortage of females, not a surplus, the shortage is caused by the unequal treatment of women, which leads to higher, not lower, death rates for females. Analysts are now estimating that from 60 to 100 million women of the world's population are "missing" (Coale, 1991; Sen, 1989). The countries that have the most significant shortages of women are China, India, Pakistan, Bangladesh, Sri Lanka, Egypt, and others in the western part of Asia (Coale, 1991).

The females of these countries have higher death rates during infancy, often, it is believed, because female infanticide is practiced.[1] China, because of its population policy that encourages and pressures couples to have only one child, has an especially high female infant mortality rate (Arnold and Zhaoxiang, 1986; Johansson and Nygren, 1991; Riley, 1996). In the Punjab state of India, where parents often do not want female children, the childhood death rate of females is twice as high as that of males (Das Gupta, 1987). This study also found that females under 5 years *who had older sisters* had a death rate twice that of males under 5. This suggests that parents who already have female children do not want any more. A recent study of 350 districts in India reveals that the cultural under-evaluation of females continues to produce higher death rates for Indian girls, compared to Indian boys, especially in Northern India (Kishor, 1993).

Lifestyles and Mortality

Lifestyle, as we noted earlier, refers to the choices people make in the conduct of their daily lives. Today, in a country such as the United States, heart disease, cancer, and accidents are major causes of death, and all appear to be greatly influenced by the choices people make in their daily lives (Rogers, 1995). The significance of lifestyle choices on mortality is vividly illustrated by the use of tobacco and tobacco products. Most of the world lived without any knowledge and therefore use of tobacco until it was discovered by Columbus and his men in Cuba in 1492. Even then it took nearly 100 years before tobacco was successfully introduced to most Europeans (Ravenholt, 1990).

---

[1]There is also evidence that more female babies than male babies are aborted in some countries. News reports describe the use of ultrasound prenatal examinations in India to determine if the fetus is male or female. If the fetus is female, it is much more likely to be aborted (CBS, *"60 Minutes,"* January 24, 1993).

Cross-cultural Perspectives

Infanticide and the Preference for Male Children

In societies around the world there is a preference for male babies over female babies. Parents in virtually every society candidly admit that they prefer their first child to be a male, and, in general, they prefer a larger number of sons than daughters (Williamson, 1978). This widespread cultural preference has often led to female infanticide, in which female babies are killed, or allowed to die, after they are born. While most examples of infanticide are historical, there is evidence that even in the contemporary world female babies are sometimes allowed to die because they are not wanted by their parents. Contemporary India, China, and Japan all provide illustrations of female infanticide.

In Japan the year 1966 was called the year of the Fiery Horse. According to traditional Japanese beliefs, a girl born in the year of the Fiery Horse was ill fated. Some Japanese parents apparently accepted this belief, because in 1966 a larger proportion of female babies died in the first month of life than would have been expected from the records of previous, or subsequent, years. While this could be a confirmation of the validity of the folklore, a more likely possibility is female infanticide (Kaku, 1975).

There is also much evidence of infanticide in India's history. Before the British outlawed the practice in 1870 with the passage of the Infanticide Act, female infanticide was openly practiced. In the nineteenth century the following dialogue occurred between a British official and an Indian landholder:

'It is the general belief among us, Sir, that those who preserve their daughters never prosper; and, that the families into which we marry them are equally unfortunate.'

'Then you think that it is a duty imposed upon you from above, to destroy your infant daughters; and that the neglect and disregard of that duty brings misfortunes upon you?'

'We think it must be so, Sir, with regard to our own families or clan!' (Miller, 1981).

In fact, the practice of female infanticide in some areas of India was so common that visitors noticed, and later censuses confirmed, that there was a shortage of females.

Why was female infanticide practiced so often in certain parts of India prior to 1870? Pride and money appear to be important factors. Fathers wanted to marry their daughters into families of equal or higher status, and a prestigious marriage required the payment of a large dowry. In addition, it was considered shameful to have unmarried daughters at home. Thus, if parents had many daughters or few resources, economics and pride would lead them to consider killing some as infants.

While open infanticide is no longer condoned in India, it may still be practiced in a more subtle manner. One researcher found that, in families where mothers expressed a preference for no more children, there was a higher rate of female infant deaths. Male infant deaths were also higher in such families, but not to the same degree as females (Simmons et al., 1982).

One observer of contemporary India has said:

> The actual murder of little girls has in great measure ceased, but it has been replaced . . . by a degree of carelessness hardly less criminal (Miller, 1961).

In modern China, also, there is circumstantial evidence of some female infanticide. When China's one-child policy is rigidly enforced, a higher percentage of female first-children die than would normally occur (Hull, 1990; Johansson and Nygren, 1991).

Even in contemporary England, the fourth or fifth child of a family has a 25 percent greater chance of dying in infancy than a child who is the first born (Weeks, 1989). Although not indicating a preference for male children, or female infanticide, such evidence suggests that infanticide may be occurring, even in developed countries with modern medical systems.

HULL, TERRANCE H. "Recent Trends in Sex Ratios at Birth in China." *Population and Development Review* 16, 1990.

JOHANNSSON, STEN, AND NYGREN, OLA. "The Missing Girls of China: A New Demographic Account." *Population and Development Review* 17, 1991.

KAKU, KANAE. "Were Girl Babies Sacrificed to Folk Superstition in 1966 in Japan?" *Annals of Human Biology* 2, 1975.

MILLER, BARBARA D. *The Endangered Sex: Neglect of Female Children in Rural North India.* Ithaca, N. Y.: Cornell University Press, 1981.

SIMMONS, G., SMUCKER, C., BERNSTEIN, S., AND JENSEN, E. "Post-neonatal Mortality in Rural India: Implications of an Economic Model." *Demography* 19, 1982.

WEEKS, JOHN R. *Population: An Introduction to Concepts and Issues,* 4th ed. Belmont, CA: Wadsworth Publishing Co., 1989.

WILLIAMSON, NANCY E. "Boys or Girls? Parents' Preferences and Sex Control." *Population Bulletin* 33, 1978.

Since the latter part of the sixteenth century, however, human beings in great numbers around the world have chosen to smoke, sniff, and chew tobacco. The massive numbers of deaths produced by tobacco use has led one scholar to describe it as "Tobacco's Global Death March" (Ravenholt, 1990, p. 213). Worldwide, 5 trillion cigarettes are smoked annually and millions of tons of tobacco are consumed in other forms. The deaths resulting from the use of tobacco will rival those of the Black Death, smallpox, malaria, yellow fever, Asiatic cholera, and tuberculosis. The major difference between the deaths caused by tobacco and those caused by the other epidemics is that people choose to use tobacco. The worldwide death toll from tobacco use is estimated at 3 million annually. More than 50 million people will die during this century because of their choice to use tobacco (Ravenholt, 1990).

For specific examples of how the use of tobacco, along with other lifestyle choices, influence death rates we have the results of research on two religious groups in the United States: Mormons and Seventh-Day Adventists.

Mormons and Seventh-Day Adventists.   Both of these religions have doctrinal restrictions on the use of both tobacco products and alcohol. The Mormons also restrict the use of coffee, tea, and addictive drugs, while the Seventh-Day Adventists are urged to abstain from coffee, tea, other caffeine beverages, and meat (Enstrom, 1978; Phillips et al., 1980). Studies of the adherents of these two religious groups, plus other selected populations who practice "healthy" lifestyles, have persistently shown them to have large advantages in mortality when compared to the general population (Manton et al., 1991). Samples of Mormons, both high priests in the Church and others who practiced the healthy lifestyles dictated by their religion, have repeatedly shown them to have exceptionally high life expectancies—well over 85 years (Enstrom, 1989). A study of Seventh-Day Adventist physicians found that they had a mortality rate 44 percent lower than the U.S. male white population (reported in Manton et al., 1991). In this last case, the physicians had both their higher socioeconomic status (position in the social structure) and their apparently healthy lifestyles giving them a mortality advantage.

Migration

Migration is the movement of individuals or groups from one place of residence to another when they have the intention of remaining in the new place for some substantial amount of time. By this definition it is not migration if someone simply travels someplace for a visit and returns. Even temporarily living in another place, as one might do at a summer vacation home, is not migration. The key to migration is that a new residence is being established. Sometimes that new residence may be a different house in the same neighborhood or community, but at the opposite extreme, the new residence may be in a different country. The term *immigration,* which we discussed in Chapter 9, refers to migration from one nation or country to another.

Migration in the United States

In the United States today, about 18 percent of Americans change residences (migrate) each year (U.S. Bureau of the Census, 1991c). Throughout the history of the United States, migration from one state, or one region, to another has been an important factor in determining the growth and development of the country. Historically the two major migration trends in the United States have been from rural to urban places, and from east to west. (Later in this chapter we will focus on migration from rural to urban places and, in particular, on the continuing growth of metropolitan areas.)

Migration to the Sun Belt. A general westward migration has characterized much of U.S. history, and it continues, but in recent decades that trend has been modified by a southward movement as well. The new migration pattern is toward the Sun Belt—the states in the southern and western parts of the United States that have mild climates. The 1990 census revealed a continuation of this trend toward the south and west. Every state on the southern perimeter of the United States grew by at least 15 percent except Louisiana, Mississippi, and Alabama (they grew, but only slightly) (U.S. Bureau of the Census, 1991b). The big gainers, in percentages and numbers, were Florida (33 percent), California (26 percent), and Texas (19 percent). Florida, in particular, continues to grow rapidly because of migration, due to a combination of retirees migrating from the North and Hispanic immigrants. (Prud'homme, 1991).

Some states are expected to lose population in the next two decades, in part because of out-migration. These states are located primarily in the upper Midwest but also include some western, eastern, and border states. Specifically, the states expected to lose population in the next two decades include Montana, Wyoming, North Dakota, Nebraska, Iowa, Wisconsin, Illinois, Michigan, Indiana, Kentucky, Ohio, West Virginia, and Pennsylvania (U.S. Bureau of the Census, 1991b).

World Population Growth

The term **population explosion** has been widely used to describe the rapid growth of the world's population in the twentieth century. Although this is not a technical demographic term, it is an apt description of how much the population of the world has grown in the last 50 years. In comparison with the rest of human history, there has been an explosion in the number of the earth's inhabitants.

In the long history of human life on earth, which some archaeologists and anthropologists estimate to be as much as 2 million years, the human population did not grow very rapidly. It is estimated that even after the world was well into the Christian era, 1000 A.D., there were fewer than 300 million people (Durand, 1977). It took all the preceding thousands of years for the population of the earth to reach 300 million people, but in our time it takes less than 4 years to add that many people to the world's population.

In all likelihood, the world first achieved a population of 1 billion people in the early part of the 1800s. By 1930 the size of the population had reached 2 billion;

the third billion was added in just 30 years, by 1960. The fourth billion was added in about 13 years, in 1973. Since then, the rate of growth has slowed down a little, but with a larger population base, it now takes only about 12 years to add a thousand-million people (a billion). Every 4 days 1 million more people are added to the earth's population (Moffet, 1994).

Let us be clear on this point. A million people are added to the world's population every four days, despite the high death rates that prevail in many countries, despite high rates of infant mortality, despite deaths caused by wars, starvation, natural disasters, and disease. In other words, the number of births occurring each year exceeds the number of deaths, and thus the world's population grows by more than 85 million people each year.

Some people say that there is no population explosion or that talk about a population explosion is an exaggeration or scare tactic. Since the term has no precise definition, these charges are difficult to evaluate. However, two things can be said with certainty. First, the number of people being added to the earth's population each year is many times greater than ever before in human history. Second, the current 1.5 percent growth rate doubles the earth's population every 45 years; this level of growth cannot go on indefinitely. These facts have led most people to conclude that steps must be taken to slow down or stop the rate of population growth. But first we must understand why the earth's population, after hundreds of thousands of years of relative stability, started growing in the seventeenth century and has been growing especially fast in the last 50 years. It will help us if we first consider an important idea of demography: the demographic transition.

The Demographic Transition

The **demographic transition** can be described as a three-stage process of population change that occurs as societies change from agricultural to more industrialized, urban economies. The agricultural stage typically has a balanced population with a high death rate and a high birth rate. The transition stage has a growing population with a high birth rate and a decreasing death rate. And the final stage of a transition has a much lower population growth rate because the birth rate has dropped to a level roughly equal to that of the death rate. The three stages of the demographic transition and the levels of population growth are shown in Table 17–1.

An understanding of the demographic transition can help us to understand why the world's population is currently growing so fast. The recent dramatic increases in population growth, especially in developing countries, have been produced by *declines in death rates,* while birth rates have remained high. Many people erroneously believe that birth rates have been rising rapidly in many countries, thus producing rapid population growth. This is not true; the populations of many countries have "exploded" because of declines in their death rates, with no corresponding declines in birth rates.

Table 17–1 The Three Stages of the Demographic Transition

Stage	Death Rate	Birth Rate	Population Growth Rate
1. Agricultural	High	High	Low
2. Transition	Low	High	High
3. Final	Low	Low	Low

The demographic transition has been experienced, though in varying ways, by most countries of northern and western Europe. By the beginning of the eighteenth century, as the countries of this region began the process of economic development, their death rates started to decline. The birth rates in these countries, which had traditionally been high, remained at that level for some time. The result, of course, was population growth during the transition period. Although exceptions to this pattern have been found in some European countries, they do not outweigh the far greater number of cases where mortality started declining at the beginnings of economic development, to be followed considerably later by declines in fertility (Beaver, 1975).

Economic development also brings about a decline in birth rates, but this decline usually comes later than the decline in death rates. One reason why birth rates go down after death rates is that the characteristics of childbearing are very different from the characteristics of mortality. This is especially the case with respect to the positive value that most societies place on life (both producing it and keeping it going). Whereas lowering the death rate is completely consistent with the positive value placed on life, lowering the birth rate is not. Producing new life by having children, in society after society, is an act that is praised and greeted with joy. If fertility is to go down, it is necessary to some degree for individual couples to act contrary to this valued act. Even when it might be advantageous for an individual couple to refrain from having children, the prevailing values, supported by customs and norms, act as strong pressures for them to have children anyway.

Nonetheless, as the process of economic development continues, and especially as societies become primarily urban instead of rural, the birth rates do go down. This is the final stage of a demographic transition, and usually means that population growth slows down greatly or stops completely. Today almost all European countries (as well as the United States, Canada, Australia, and New Zealand) have stopped growing at a rapid rate because their birth rates have declined to levels almost as low as their death rates. Indeed, the entire European continent now has a death rate that exceeds its birth rate and is not, therefore, growing at all (Population Reference Bureau, 1995). Russia's death rate is at 16 per 1000, while its birth rate is at 9 per 1000; these two rates mean that Russia's population is declining by .6 percent per year.

For European countries, the transition from high birth and death rates to low birth and death rates took about 200 years. The declines in the death rates came about because of changes and advances that evolved gradually. The entire demographic transition, as experienced in Europe, is shown in Figure 17–2.

The demographic experience of the developing countries in the past 50 years has been similar to the European experiences in the transition stage, although one part of the process has been much more rapid. In the developing countries, representing 75 to 80 percent of the world's population, the decline in the death rate has been very fast. It has taken only a few decades for the death rates in these countries to drop because of the importation of medical, technical, and scientific advances from the developed countries. Since the birth rates have often remained high, the gap between births and deaths is great, and the resulting growth rate is extraordinary. In some areas of the world with huge populations, the birth rate remains very high, while the death rate is as low as that in the developed countries. For example, all of Latin America has a birth rate of 26 per 1000, while the death rate is seven per 1000. The growth rate for Latin America is 1.9 percent, which means that the present population of 481 million will double every 36 years if the current rate of growth continues (see Figure 17–3).

The African continent, with a population of 720 million, has a growth rate even greater than that of Latin America (2.8 percent). However, in much of Africa the death rate is not as low, remaining at about 13 per 1000, while the birth rate is

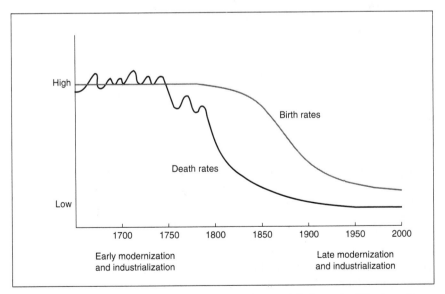

Figure 17–2. The Demographic Transition (as modeled on the Western European experience).

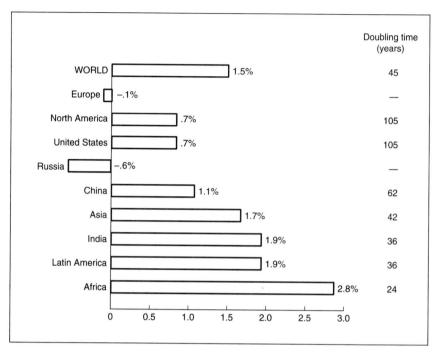

Figure 17–3.   Growth Rates and Doubling Times for the World, the Five Continents, and Major Countries. (*Source:* Population Reference Bureau, 1995, *World
Population Data Sheet.* Washington, D.C.: Population Reference Bureau, Inc.,
1995.)

estimated at a very high 41 per 1000. Asia, with a population of 3.5 billion people, has a death rate of 8 per 1000 and a birth rate of 24 per 1000, for a 1.7 percent
increase per year (Population Reference Bureau, 1995).

Seen from the perspective of the demographic transition, the current rate of
world population growth is largely due to the fact that the developing countries
have reduced their death rates far more quickly than their birth rates. Birth rates
remain high because of the value that societies place on producing life. Death
rates have declined fairly quickly because people are likely to adopt the means for
controlling death soon after they become available. Lowering birth rates, however, runs counter to the value placed on producing life, so methods of controlling
birth are not so quickly adopted. Many, many individual couples have to modify
their orientations toward childbearing before the birth rate begins to go down.
Generally, this takes a considerable period of time, during which the population
grows very rapidly.

This point raises the question about whether decreases in fertility can be
brought about more quickly so that population growth will be less rapid. Much of

the debate about population growth centers around the question of how fertility can be lowered in populations where it remains high. We consider some major points of view about this question next.

Approaches to Reducing Fertility

Some specialists on population have argued that it is not necessary to make any special efforts to lower fertility levels and slow population growth (Simon, 1981). However, this view is clearly in a minority; the broad consensus is that it would be better for individual countries and the world in general if the growth of population could be slowed. Three different views about reducing fertility can be identified: economic development, voluntary family-planning programs, and societal change.

Economic Development.   The following slogan is often heard from the advocates of this view: *Economic development is the best contraceptive.* The assumption is that developing countries, which are now experiencing the highest growth rates, will experience a lowering of fertility when their economies become more urban, industrialized, and modernized. Economic development in these countries is expected to have the same effects on fertility as it did in Europe, the United States, and other developed countries. This view reflects a faith that the demographic transition will take its course, just as it did in the societies that modernized in the nineteenth and early twentieth centuries.

A recent study in India found that, while lower levels of gender inequality are related to lower fertility, so also is economic development (Malhotra et al., 1995). When districts of India have higher economic development, their fertility is also lower, which lends support to the view that economic development can be a good "contraceptive."

Voluntary Family Planning.   *Family-planning programs* have three basic elements: providing knowledge and information about reproductive physiology and contraceptive techniques; (2) providing contraceptive techniques; and (3) conducting a propaganda campaign that supports the small family ideal and the acceptability of contraception.

This approach is voluntary because the aim is not to coerce or force people to use contraception or limit their family size. In fact, in some countries, there is evidence that a substantial number of couples want fewer children than they have. There is evidence that with a well-run, comprehensive family-planning program, the reduction in fertility rates will come from fewer births of unwanted children (Freedman, 1990; Mauldin, 1983).

Societal Change.   A number of demographers have pointed to the limitations of family-planning programs alone, arguing that without some basic societal changes, it will be difficult or impossible to reduce fertility. These advocates point out that most societies, especially many of the developing ones, have social institutions and cultural values that make large families both advantageous and desirable (Davis, 1967; Demerath, 1976).

The social institutions of many societies are arranged in such a way that children have economic value for parents. In many societies, even young children are able to contribute to the economic well-being of the family. This is especially true of children who live in rural areas who work in the fields, tend livestock, and take care of smaller children while their parents are working. Even in the urban areas of many Third World countries children begin working beside their parents at an early age (Weiner, 1991). Later in life, children are economically beneficial because they will care for their elderly parents (Caldwell, 1982; Nugent, 1985).

Advocates of societal change argue that, in addition to family-planning programs, there must be reductions in these economic motivations for having children. Two very important societal changes that do reduce fertility are compulsory mass education and laws prohibiting child labor. Both of these actions have the effect of reducing fertility because children are less economically valuable to their parents. Cross-national studies have shown that the larger the proportion of children in school, the smaller the number of children born to women in the society (London, 1992).

Changes in the role of women in society can also be a factor that will reduce fertility levels. When women are isolated from participating in activities outside the home, their status (or worth) rests largely on their ability to bear and rear children. Under these societal and cultural conditions, where the primary role for women is motherhood, fertility is likely to remain high. To decrease fertility, societal changes can be made that will improve the status of women. Studies have shown that when women are given greater educational and employment opportunities, fertility declines (Malhotra et al., 1995; World Bank, 1984; Youssef, 1974).

Can Population Growth Be Slowed or Stopped?

Demographers have identified key ways of reducing fertility—through economic development, family-planning programs, and societal change—but the question still remains as to whether these solutions can be made to work in the real world. Many observers doubt that deeply embedded social institutions and cultural values can be changed among people who live in poverty, who are poorly educated, and who are bound by custom, superstition, and tradition. Although the efforts required to reduce fertility in many developing countries are difficult, accumulating evidence shows that when family-planning programs are combined with strategic societal changes, reduction can be accomplished.

Several countries that had high fertility rates 30 or 40 years ago, and were then considered less-developed countries, now have fertility levels similar to those of the United States and some European countries. Taiwan, South Korea, and Singapore are examples of countries that have lowered fertility through a combination of family-planning programs, some societal changes, and economic development. But the most important example is China, which, in the space of 40 years, has lowered its fertility to a level that would not have been anticipated in 1949. Between 1970 and 1979, for example, the Chinese birth rate declined more than 50 percent, from 34 per 1000 population to 18 per thousand (Tien et al., 1992). This decline occurred before the widely discussed "one-child" policy. In 1995 the Chinese birth rate is estimated to be about 18 per thousand (Population Reference Bureau, 1995).

The Chinese reduction of fertility occurred, in part, because the government undertook extensive family-planning programs. The first program was started in 1954, and although it produced some decline in the birth rate, the most important family-planning program has been the well-publicized one-child program of the 1980s. But in addition, again going back to the 1950s, the Chinese made some societal changes that had the potential for reducing fertility (Greenhalgh, 1990). These included efforts to improve the status of women and laws to raise the age of marriage.

The one-child policy of China has often had a near-mandatory family-planning component, with close supervision of the contraceptive practices of couples and some penalties for disregarding the regulations. However, the one-child policy also includes some rewards, and these are consistent with what we have described as societal changes. Couples who agree to have only one child are given greater monthly stipends, better housing, preferred status for their children in schools, and supplemental pensions when parents reach old age (Chen and Kols, 1982). These rewards, in combination with the family-planning program, have been most effective in the major cities of China and somewhat less effective in the rural areas (Greenhalgh et al., 1994; Hardee-Cleveland and Banister, 1988; Whyte and Gu, 1987).

Since 1983 the Chinese government has sometimes modified its enforcement of the one-child program, but the government still has the aim of keeping its growth rate at less than 1.5 percent until at least the year 2000. The important point to be drawn from the Chinese experience is that fertility can be lowered to the levels of Western societies, even before a substantial amount of economic development has been achieved (Freedman, 1990; Greenhalgh, 1990; Li, 1995; Whyte and Gu, 1987).

The Chinese experience, combined with those of a number of other developing countries, shows that the present rate of population growth in the world can be reduced in a relatively short period of time. But it can be done only with family-planning efforts, societal changes to reduce motivations for fertility, and, to the extent possible, economic development.

All these efforts are most easily and successfully undertaken in cities and urban environments, as we have seen in the Chinese case. In the remainder of this chapter we examine the urbanization process, both in the United States and in other countries of the world.

Urbanization

The rise of cities has been one of the most dramatic and momentous developments in human history. Most of the classic European sociological theorists discussed in this book (Durkheim, Marx, Weber, Simmel, and others) focused much of their attention on efforts to understand the changes transforming Western civilization during the nineteenth and early twentieth centuries. One of their central concerns was to analyze the unprecedented social changes accompanying the process of urbanization.

Key Concepts in Urbanization

Several key terms and concepts help to develop a sociological understanding of our increasingly urban society. First, we need to identify what we mean by the term *urban*. Often people consider the adjective *urban* to carry the same meaning as the noun *city*. However, the two terms need to be distinguished. A **city** can be defined as a relatively large, permanent, and spatially concentrated human settlement with a population far more economically interdependent and occupationally diverse than in agriculturally oriented rural areas.

There are several bases for classifying a geographically defined area and its population as urban. The definitions developed by national census agencies generally focus solely on the numbers of persons living in a specified area. In the United States, any town, municipality, or other politically defined place with a population of 2500 or more residents is classified as **urban** by the U.S. Census Bureau. However, this number differs substantially in other nations. For example, in Greece only areas with populations exceeding 10,000 are defined as urban; in Denmark, villages with only 250 residents are defined as urban; in Canada, the official definition of an urban place is one with 1000 or more residents. In light of the confusion generated by such different standards, the United Nations has recommended a standard of 20,000 residents as the level of population necessary to characterize an area as urban. Sociologically this number makes sense, because an urban place is one that has a complex array of social, economic, political, and cultural characteristics that are unlikely to emerge in places with only a few hundred or a few thousand residents.

A third concept, **urbanization,** refers primarily to the process by which an increasing percentage of a society's population comes to be located in urban areas. Thus, at any given time the extent of urbanization in a society is reflected by the proportion of the total population living in urban places. Urbanization occurs largely as a result of migration of formerly rural residents within a society to urban areas, or as a result of urban settlement patterns among immigrants from other societies. The resulting concentration of population in urban centers, in turn, contributes to an expansion of the scope of urban influence in modern societies. Indeed, the term *urbanization* is also used to refer to the concentration of economic activity, political administrative organization, communication networks, and political power in urban centers.

Urbanism refers to the "way of life" associated with urban residence. Much of the field of urban sociology has focused on ways in which living in urban places may affect the life-styles, attitudes, and social relationships exhibited by urban dwellers. As noted later in this chapter, sociologists continue to debate whether urban life is characterized by negative or positive features. However, there is little doubt that the unique experiences associated with the urban environment do contribute to ways of life that are very different from those in rural areas and small towns.

World Urbanization

The first cities appear to have been established during the period from 3000 to 5000 B.C. Until very recently, however, only a small proportion of the world's people were city dwellers. In 1800, only six metropolitan areas—Tokyo, London, Paris, Naples, Constantinople-Istanbul, and Beijing—had half a million residents; today 287 metropolises have 1 million or more (Gottman and Harper, 1990; United Nations, 1995, p. 167). As late as 1850, only 2 percent of the world's population lived in cities of more than 100,000 persons. Less than two centuries later, this situation has changed dramatically. Today about 45 percent of the world population resides in urban places, and the urban population is growing three times more rapidly than the rural population. As a consequence, the percentage of people living in urban areas is expected to increase by more than one-half by the year 2005 (United Nations, 1995, p. 20).

The emergence of early urban settlement patterns seems to have depended upon two developments. The first was the existence of a surplus supply of food and other staples. The cultivation of grain, domestication of animals, and development of rudimentary agricultural technologies combined to create the **Agricultural Revolution.** These developments contributed to a shift from nomadic living patterns to residential stability, and allowed a family to produce more than it needed for its own survival. The second development, related to the first, was the emergence of forms of social organization other than those based solely on family and kinship ties.

Until recently, most cities were very small by modern standards. Cities of more than 100,000 people were extremely rare, although some, such as Rome in the second century A.D., were substantially larger.

A major factor underlying the development of an urban world occurred in the late 1700s and early 1800s with the **Industrial Revolution.** As we noted in Chapter 13, the Industrial Revolution occurred when machines were substituted for hand tools, and when inanimate sources of energy (water, steam, coal, oil) were used for power instead of humans or animals. The development of machines for production and the use of new energy sources greatly increased productivity and gave rise to the factory system. Large numbers of workers were needed to work in the factories, as well as to distribute and sell the manufactured products. At the same time, improvements in agricultural technology made it possible for fewer farmers to supply the needs of an expanding population.

World urban growth has been especially rapid since World War II. The world's urban population grew from 738 million in 1950 to 2.6 billion in 1995, and it is projected to exceed 5 billion by 2025 (United Nations, 1995, pp. 86–87). As Figure 17–4 indicates, the increase in the percentage of people living in urban areas has been equally as dramatic, especially in less developed countries in Asia, Latin America, and Africa. The number of cities with over 1 million inhabitants has increased by more than six times since 1950; in 1950, only 53 urban centers

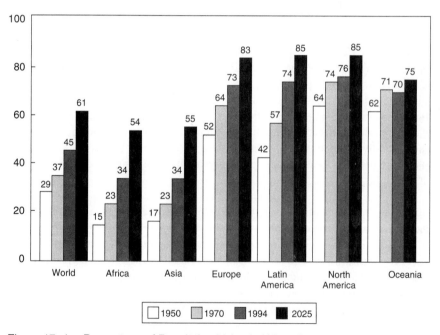

Figure 17–4.   Percentage of Population Living in Urban Areas, 1950, 1970, 1994, and 2025. (*Source:* United Nations, *World Urbanization Prospects: The 1994 Revision.* New York: United Nations, 1995, pp. 21, 78–85.)

had more than 1 million inhabitants, but by 1995 more than 325 metropolises exceeded this size (United Nations, 1995, p. 167). Moreover, the number of *megacities,* which are defined by the United Nations as cities with 8 million or more residents, has increased dramatically. In 1950 there were only two mega-cities—New York and London—in the world. By 1994, this number had increased to 22, and it has been estimated that by the year 2000 there will be 25, more than three-fourths of them in less developed countries (United Nations, 1995, p. 6). Thus, the last half of the twentieth century has witnessed "the greatest flowering of cities and urban life in world history" (Hall, 1984).

As Table 17–2 shows, the world's largest urban areas are found today on every inhabited continent except Australia. They are located in both developed countries, such as the United States and Japan, and in developing countries, such as Mexico, Indonesia, India, and China. By the year 2015, two-thirds of the world's urban population and 13 of 15 of the world's largest urban areas will be located in developing countries. Dramatic increases in growth are projected for Third World cities such as Mexico City; Sao Paulo and Rio de Janeiro, Brazil; Shanghai, Beijing, and Tianjin, China; Bombay, Calcutta, and Delhi, India; Seoul, Korea; Jakarta, Indonesia; Lagos, Nigeria; Karachi, Pakistan; Dhaka, Bangladesh; and Manila, Philippines (see Table 17–2).

Urban Development in the United States

In 1790, when the first U.S. Census was taken, only one in twenty Americans (5 percent) was an urban resident. Since that time, the urban proportion of the population has increased in every decade except one (1810–1820), but it was not until 1920 that a majority of the American people lived in urban areas (Schneider, 1991, p. 2335). By 1990, three-fourths (75.2 percent) of the population was urban (see Figure 17–5) (U.S. Bureau of the Census, 1992f). The U.S. population has become so concentrated that by 1990 urban residents occupied less than 2 percent of the nation's land.

Preindustrial Cities

The urban proportion of the U.S. population remained quite low well into the nineteenth century. Preindustrial cities were usually quite small, and they were predominantly commercial and shipping centers. The largest cities were East Coast seaports; Boston, for example, led the country in size and importance in 1743 with a population of slightly more than 16,000. In 1775, just before the American Revolution, Philadelphia's population of 40,000 made it the nation's largest city. In 1800, only six cities in the United States had more than 8000 residents (Bridenbaugh, 1938; Gist and Fava, 1974, p. 63).

Table 17–2   World's Fifteen Largest Urban Areas, 1950, 1994, and 2015

Urban Area	Population
1950	
New York, United States	12.3
London, United Kingdom	8.7
Tokyo, Japan	6.9
Paris, France	5.4
Moscow, USSR	5.4
Shanghai, China	5.3
Essen, Germany	5.3
Buenos Aires, Argentina	5.0
Chicago, United States	4.9
Calcutta, India	4.4
Osaka, Japan	4.1
Los Angeles, United States	4.0
Beijing, China	3.9
Milan, Italy	3.6
Berlin, Germany	3.3
1994	
Tokyo, Japan	26.5
New York, United States	16.3
Sao Paulo, Brazil	16.1
Mexico City, Mexico	15.5
Shanghai, China	14.7
Bombay, India	14.5
Los Angeles, United States	12.2
Beijing, China	12.0
Calcutta, India	11.5
Seoul, Republic of Korea	11.5
Jakarta, Indonesia	11.0
Buenos Aires, Argentina	10.9
Osaka, Japan	10.6
Tianjin, China	10.4
Rio de Janeiro, Brazil	9.8
2015	
Tokyo, Japan	28.7
Bombay, India	27.4
Lagos, Nigeria	24.4
Shanghai, China	23.4
Jakarta, Indonesia	21.2
Sao Paulo, Brazil	20.8
Karachi, Pakistan	20.6
Beijing, China	19.4
Dhaka, Bangladesh	19.0

Urban Area	Population
Mexico City, Mexico	18.8
New York, United States	17.6
Calcutta, India	17.6
Delhi, India	17.6
Tianjin, China	17.0
Metro Manila, Philippines	14.7

Source: United Nations, *World Urbanization Prospects: The 1994 Revision.* New York: United Nations, 1995, pp. 4–5.

Industrial Cities

By the beginning of the twentieth century the United States had become the foremost industrial nation in the world, and the rapid urbanization of the country paralleled its increasing industrialization. The urban-industrial period between 1850 and 1920 marked the era of America's most dramatic urban growth. The urban portion of the total population rose from less than one-sixth (15 percent) in 1850

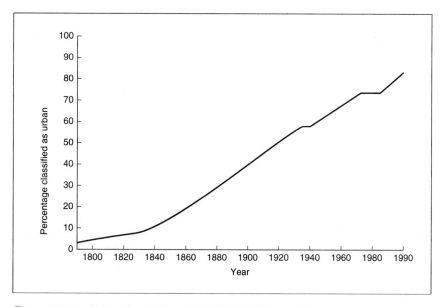

Figure 17–5.   Urban Population of the United States: 1790–1990. (*Sources:* U.S. Bureau of the Census, *Statistical Abstract of the United States, 1961 and 1972,* pp. 14, 16; U.S. Bureau of the Census, *U.S. Commerce Dept. News,* Aug. 13, 1981; May 29, 1992.)

In the News

Population, Progress, and Pollution in Mexico City— An "Ecological Disaster"

"Whether the weather is cold or hot, one thing is usually certain [in Mexico City]: it snows" (Uhlig, 1991, p. 1). "Snow" is the word for the fine white chemical powder that each morning covers everything in Mexico City and its vast, sprawling suburbs. The problems of air pollution that afflict Mexico City today illustrate those confronting most of the rapidly expanding urban areas in the developing world.

In 1950, Mexico City had a population of about 3 million, which grew to 15 million in 1980. It is estimated that its population will reach 26 million by 2000, making it the largest urban area in human history. As Mexico City approaches this position as the world's largest megacity, it has also acquired the dubious distinction of having the most polluted air of any major metropolitan area in the world. The city's level of contaminants, said one of the country's leading environmentalists, is an "ecological disaster."

A combination of human waste, industrial emissions, smoke, and, especially, vehicle exhausts, the pollution in Mexico City exceeds by as much as four times the World Health Organization's maximum limits. These conditions have contributed to numerous illnesses, ranging from skin disorders, respiratory ailments, eye irritation, and increased susceptibility to heart attacks to infectious diseases such as salmonella and hepatitis. So severe are the health risks that officials at the American School, a prestigious preparatory school, cancelled all outdoor sports activities because they concluded that the harmful effects of vigorous exercise in Mexico City outweighed its benefits.

But it is not simply the dramatically increasing numbers of people living in Mexico City that has created this environmental crisis. First, Mexico City is located in a geological basin that traps pollutants and prevents winds from dispersing many of the contaminants, and its elevation—7280 feet—limits the oxygen needed for burning fuel. Equally important, however, is that the Mexican government's efforts to reduce pollution in Mexico City have been limited and ineffective. Few effective restrictions have been placed on emissions from vehicles and industries, which release 4.35 million tons of pollutants annually. Moreover, about 30 percent of the city's residents lack effective methods for disposing of human waste, which is carried both in the city's dust or is transported into the air as harmful gases. Increasingly, environmental crises such as that confronting Mexico City will represent major challenges to political leadership throughout the world; such challenges are likely to be especially acute as pressures for urban and economic growth increase in developing countries.

HALL, PETER. The World Cities, 3rd ed. London: Weidenfeld and Nicolson, 1984. "Megacities." *Time,* January 11, 1993.
UHLIG, MARK A. "Mexico City: The World's Foulest Air Grows Worse." *New York Times,* May 12, 1991.

to over half (51.2 percent) by 1920. By 1920, New York City had more than 5.5 million inhabitants, and Philadelphia, nearly 2 million. Chicago grew from less than 4000 in 1830 to over 2 million in 1910.

Several factors contributed to this dramatic spurt in the urbanization of the United States. First, transportation improvements such as the construction of extensive inland canal systems and the building of transcontinental railroads made it easier to ship both raw materials and agricultural products. Second, manufacturing grew as the basis of urban economies. Unlike handicrafts and other home-based economic activities of the preindustrial city, manufacturing required the employment of large numbers of people in factories. The demand for unskilled factory labor attracted many residents from rural areas into the major industrial cities. By 1910, at least one-third of the total urban population consisted of native-born Americans who had migrated from rural areas.

As industrial growth continued, factory operators turned to European immigrants to provide an abundant and cheap labor supply. During the first decade of the twentieth century about 1 million immigrants entered the United States each year. The influx of foreign-born residents created in most U.S. cities a mosaic of immigrant neighborhoods, located in distinct areas where cheap housing was within walking distance of work.

Newcomers of each immigrant wave moved from one urban neighborhood to another as their social and economic status changed. Areas deserted by one ethnic group were often quickly taken over by members of another. For example, in the years following the Civil War, the Irish and Germans of New York moved from the Lower East Side to areas of north Manhattan and Brooklyn. Italians moved into the old Irish neighborhoods, while Russian and Polish Jews occupied the formerly German districts (Glaab and Brown, 1967, p. 139). **Invasion–succession** is the term used by sociologists to identify the process whereby one group moves to a different area and is replaced by another.

Although immigrant neighborhoods frequently contained a high proportion of one particular ethnic group, they were never homogeneous and invariably contained a diversity of ethnic groups. Moreover, immigrant neighborhoods were seldom enduring or long-lived; as second generation European ethnic groups became increasingly culturally and structurally assimilated into American society, they tended to settle in different areas of the metropolitan area. In contrast, urban African American neighborhoods, which grew rapidly in the twentieth century, tended to be much more homogeneous and permanent. Social restrictions on geographical and social mobility for African Americans contributed to the emergence of racially distinct cities within cities, where proportions of black residents reached as high as 95 percent. By 1930, the enduring black ghetto had become firmly established in most U.S. cities, especially in the North. The process of ghettoization of American cities was heightened during the 1930s, 1940s, and 1950s as the Great Migration of African Americans out of the rural South intensified (Massey and Denton, 1993).

Urban Differentiation.   As cities grew in size and diversity, areas within them became increasingly specialized and differentiated. Rather than locating residential and commercial properties in the same neighborhood, cities came to be characterized by a business district, a wholesale district, a manufacturing district, and so on.

During the first four decades of the twentieth century, numerous sociologists worked to develop general theories to explain the patterns of urban differentiation that they saw emerging. Among the most prominent in the effort to comprehend the dynamics of city life in the first half of the twentieth century were scholars associated with the Department of Sociology at the University of Chicago, whose distinctive focus on urban life became identified as the "Chicago School" of sociology. One of the most important early efforts to conceptualize the processes of urban differentiation was the **concentric zone model** advanced by Robert E. Park (Park et al., 1925). This model suggested that urban differentiation occurred through the development of unique zones of land-use types, organized in successive rings around the city center. As indicated in Figure 17–6, this approach identified a central business district at the core of the city, representing the economic center in which retail stores, theaters, hotels, banks, and office buildings were concentrated. Adjacent to this was the zone of transition, an area of older warehouses, factories, and the deteriorating residential neighborhoods in which immigrant populations were initially concentrated. Next came the zone of workingmen's homes, an area characterized by neighborhoods often populated by second-generation and third-generation immigrant families. The fourth zone, called the residential zone, was characterized primarily by middle-class residential neighborhoods. Finally, at the outer edge of the city were the upper-class residential areas and the commuter zone, representing the earliest suburbs, in which upper-middle-class and upper-class populations resided.

Although the concentric zone model appeared to provide a fairly accurate depiction of urban differentiation in Chicago during the early twentieth century, sociologists who focused on other urban settings discovered that in many instances urban development patterns exhibited different characteristics. One attempt to account for such differences was the **sector model** (Hoyt, 1939), which focused on the importance of major transportation arteries such as streets and trolley lines as key determinants of development patterns, resulting in the appearance of wedge-shaped areas of unique land uses (see Figure 17–5). A third approach, the **multiple nuclei model** (Harris and Ullman, 1945), suggested that in many cities a number of distinct centers of activity and land use may develop. As Figure 17–6 illustrates, this approach focused on the importance of several different nuclei, rather than one main urban core, as the center for development patterns.

The Metropolis

As U.S. cities expanded and became differentiated, they also became increasingly intertwined with the outlying areas that surrounded them. In the process, urban

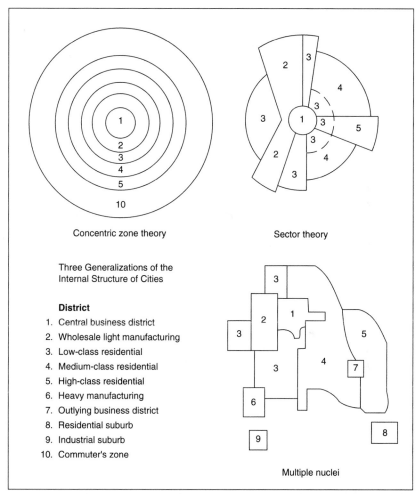

Concentric zone theory

Sector theory

Three Generalizations of the
Internal Structure of Cities

District

1. Central business district
2. Wholesale light manufacturing
3. Low-class residential
4. Medium-class residential
5. High-class residential
6. Heavy manufacturing
7. Outlying business district
8. Residential suburb
9. Industrial suburb
10. Commuter's zone

Multiple nuclei

Figure 17–6.   Patterns of Urban Spatial Differentiation. (*Source:* Chauncy Harris and Edward Ullman, "The Nature of Cities," *Annals of the American Academy of Political and Social Sciences* 242, November 1945, p. 13.)

areas became decentralized—that is, spread over a much broader geographic area. The **metropolis**—a large urban area containing a central city and surrounding communities that are economically and socially linked to the central city—is an urban form that has emerged in American society since approximately 1920. During the metropolitan period cities have been restructured and have become increasingly decentralized as both people and many of the cities' basic activities have been relocated.

Recognizing that many central cities and their adjacent communities have become integrated economically and socially, the United States Bureau of the Census has adopted a measure called a Metropolitan Statistical Area. A **Metropolitan Statistical Area (MSA)** is a geographic area (usually a county or series of counties) of at least 100,000 residents that includes a center city of 50,000 or more people. Presently, more than three-fourths (77.5 percent) of the United States population lives in the nation's 284 MSAs (U.S. Bureau of the Census, 1991h, p. 2). In 1990, for the first time in American history, a majority of the American people lived in metropolitan areas of 1 million or more (Hughes and Sternberg, 1993, p. 5; Ames et al., 1992, p. 199). Table 17–3 shows the twenty largest metropolitan areas in the United States in 1990.

In several parts of the country, MSAs have grown so large that the outer ring of one MSA expands and ultimately overlaps with the outer ring of a neighboring one. The result is an unbroken chain of urban and suburban development, sometimes stretching for hundreds of miles. This concentration of dense population

Table 17–3   The Twenty Largest Metropolitan Areas in the United States, 1990

		Rank	
Metropolitan Area	*Size (millions)*	*1990*	*1980*
New York CMSA	18.1	1	1
Los Angeles CMSA	14.5	2	2
Chicago CMSA	8.0	3	3
San Francisco CMSA	6.3	4	5
Philadelphia CMSA	5.9	5	4
Detroit CMSA	4.7	6	6
Boston CMSA	4.2	7	7
Washington, D.C. MSA	3.9	8	8
Dallas CMSA	3.9	9	10
Houston CMSA	3.7	10	9
Miami CMSA	3.2	11	12
Atlanta MSA	2.8	12	16
Cleveland CMSA	2.8	13	11
Seattle CMSA	2.6	14	18
San Diego MSA	2.5	15	19
Minneapolis–St. Paul MSA	2.5	16	17
St. Louis MSA	2.4	17	14
Baltimore MSA	2.4	18	15
Pittsburgh CMSA	2.2	19	13
Phoenix MSA	2.1	20	24

Source: U.S. Bureau of the Census. "Half of the Nation's Population Lives in Large Metropolitan Areas." *United States Department of Commerce News,* CB91-66, February 21, 1991.

over an entire region, which Gottmann has termed a **megalopolis,** has become a worldwide phenomenon (Gottmann, 1961; Gottmann and Harper, 1990). As of 1986, the Census Bureau had identified 21 megalopolitan areas in the United States. The largest—familiarly known as the "Boston–Washington corridor"— stretches along the northeastern seaboard and encompasses more than 53,000 square miles from southern New Hampshire to northern Virginia. The trend toward contiguous urban development has also been pronounced near the Pacific and Atlantic coasts (Frey, 1990) and, to a lesser degree, around the Great Lakes. Although sociologists and urban planners find it difficult to predict accurately future urban patterns, they have projected that by the year 2000 the United States will have at least 25 megalopolitan areas (see Figure 17–7).

Thus, today the vast majority of Americans live, work, and shop within metro-politan areas. Gottdiener (1994) contends that these expanding urban regions, which he terms **multinucleated metropolitan regions,** represent a new form of settlement space in human history. Characterized by a diverse mixture of cities, suburbs, towns, and exurbs spread over a wide geographic area, a multinucleated metropolitan region "is the first really new way people have organized their living and working arrangements in 10,000 years" (Gottdiener, 1994, p. 5).

Suburbanization and Its Consequences

Decentralization—of population, business, and industry—has, therefore, been the distinguishing feature of metropolitan America. This decentralization has usually been associated with the growth of **suburbs,** which are satellite urban areas adjacent to, but outside the political boundaries of, large central cities. Although suburbs began to emerge in some areas before the turn of the twentieth century, suburban growth has been most pronounced since World War II. Since then the suburban population has grown much more rapidly than the population of central cities. In 1940, only about 17 percent of Americans lived in suburbs; by 1990, almost half (48 percent) of the U.S. population resided in suburban areas. This demographic shift has a wide range of implications, one of the most noteworthy of which has been its political impact. Today the American suburbs, which in the past have voted heavily Republican, have become the new power base in American politics (Schneider, 1991). Recognizing this, during the 1992 presidential campaign, Bill Clinton adopted a strategy designed to appeal to suburban voters and their interests.

A prominent feature of the residential expansion into areas formerly at the periphery of central cities has been the selectivity of the suburbanization process: it has been primarily a middle-class phenomenon. Prompted by problems of urban decay and pollution, increasing concern over urban violence, and conflicts and tensions between minority groups and the white majority, many urban dwellers fled to suburbia in search of cleaner air, lower crime rates, better schools, and affordable single-family housing (Ames et al., 1992).

1.	Metropolitan Belt	7.	North Georgia-	14.	Central Oklahoma-	21.	Nashville Region
1A	Atlantic Seaboard		South East Tennessee		Arkansas Valley	22.	East Tennessee
1B	Lower Great Lakes	8.	Puget Sound	15.	Missouri-Kaw Valley	23.	Oahu Island
2.	California Region	9.	Twin Cities Region	16.	North Alabama	24.	Memphis
3.	Florida Peninsula	10.	Colorado Piedmont	17.	Blue Grass	25.	El Paso-Ciudad Juarez
4.	Gulf Coast	11.	St. Louis	18.	Southern Coastal Plain		
5.	East Coast Texas-Red River	12.	Metropolitan Arizona	19.	Salt Lake Valley		
6.	Southern Piedmont	13.	Willamette Valley	20.	Central Illinois		

Figure 17–7. Megalopolis in the Year 2000. (*Source:* Presidential Commission on Population Growth and the American Future. *Population Growth and the American Future.* Washington, D.C.: United States Government Printing Office, 1972, p. 33.)

However, the rapid post-World War II suburbanization of the United States was greatly aided by both private enterprise and government programs. For example, use of the automobile, which sparked the suburbanization of modern America, as the primary means of transportation (instead of mass transit systems) reflected the impact of certain interest groups on public policy (Gottdiener and Feagin, 1988, p. 181). Other factors influencing metropolitan expansion included cheap energy, the investments of billions of federal dollars in massive urban expressways and interstate highway systems, and the provision of federally supported, low-interest mortgage programs that encouraged new suburban housing developments.

Policies that facilitated suburbanization also increased racial and class polarization. As a result of "white flight" from the central cities, suburbs have generally been overwhelmingly white and middle-class, while the central cities have increasingly been left to racial and ethnic minorities—African Americans, Hispanics, and, recently, Asians. Moreover, the poor among these populations have been increasingly concentrated in central cities, especially in the nation's largest metropolitan areas (Sassen, 1990, p. 481). This poverty concentration, especially of blacks, has resulted from several factors, foremost among which has been racial segregation (Massey, 1990). Despite laws that should ensure fair housing practices, African Americans have been prevented from entering the suburbs by deliberate exclusionary housing practices, exclusionary zoning ordinances, and the persistence of a stratification system that has blocked their social mobility. In 1991, more than half (56 percent) of African Americans lived in urban central-city areas. In contrast, only about one-quarter (26 percent) of white Americans lived in central cities (U.S. Bureau of the Census, 1992g). However, as a consequence of the recent increase in immigration from Third World countries (see Chapter 9), many central cities have become racially and ethnically more diverse, and immigrants have often made up for the continuing loss of the white population (Espiritu and Light, 1991; Frey, 1990, pp. 32–34; Sassen, 1994, p. 103; Kleniewski, 1994). New York City, for example, experienced an overall population increase of 3.5 percent during the 1980s, despite a 10.2 percent decline in its white population. Between 1980 and 1989, New York took in 850,000 immigrants, mainly from Asia, the Caribbean, and Latin America (Fiske, 1991, p. A18).

Although suburbs have frequently been portrayed simply as places where people live, business and industry have also moved out of the central cities. This trend was a crucial aspect of the restructuring of the U.S. economy (Sassen, 1990; Hughes and Sternberg, 1993; Kephart, 1991). Although the movement of jobs from central cities to the suburbs had begun prior to 1970, it was especially pronounced during the economic restructuring of the U.S. city that has occurred since the 1970s. Deindustrialization and the exodus of jobs abroad and to the suburbs have led to the decline of numerous central-city manufacturing, retail, and wholesale enterprises, especially in cities in the Northeast and Midwest (Kephart, 1991). For example, between 1976 and 1986, two-thirds of all employment growth (8 million of 11.8 million jobs) occurred in the suburbs. Moreover, whereas central cities experienced a decline of over a quarter of a million (288,000) manufacturing jobs between 1980 and 1986 alone, suburban manufacturing jobs increased by 353,000 (Hughes and Sternberg, 1993, pp. 10–11).

Because of the loss of manufacturing jobs, many central-city manufacturing districts have become virtual wastelands of empty buildings and closed stores. Moreover, as discussed in Chapters 8 and 9, the loss of manufacturing jobs has greatly increased central-city unemployment and contributed to the increasing concentration of poverty and its related social dislocations—increased crime, welfare dependency, and family disruption (Wilson, 1987, 1991; Taylor, 1991).

Today the majority of people who live in suburbs also work there (Baldassare, 1992, p. 477). Facilitated especially by interlocking expressways and advances in communications technology, twice as many workers in 1982 commuted *between* suburbs than commuted from suburbs to central cities (Leinberger and Lockwood, 1986). Industrial parks, real estate developments, shopping malls, and business offices have spread over the landscape of suburban and even outlying nonmetropolitan areas.

Some of the decentralization of urban populations has seen residents moving into small towns beyond metropolitan areas. This occurred especially during the 1970s, when areas outside of existing metropolitan areas grew more rapidly than either central cities or suburbs; those metropolitan areas that did grow during the 1970s were relatively small (under 250,000) and were located primarily in the South and the West (Frey, 1990, pp. 8–9). However, during the 1980s the growth of metropolitan areas once again exceeded that of nonmetropolitan areas, and by 1990 more than three-fourths of Americans were metropolitan residents (Ames et al., 1992). Moreover, most rural workers are employed in urban-type occupations. Indeed, agricultural employment today represents less than 10 percent of all nonmetropolitan jobs (Frisbie and Kasarda, 1988).

Recent Countertrends.　As manufacturing has fled the central city, however, a recent countertrend of growth has developed in highly skilled, managerial, professional, and technical information-processing occupations. The result has been the transformation of many cities from goods-producing and -processing centers to information-producing and -processing centers. As a result, while blue-collar and relatively unskilled jobs have declined significantly, white-collar, information-processing jobs requiring substantial education have increased. For example, by 1980 the cities of New York and Boston had more people employed in knowledge-intensive, information-processing occupations than in manufacturing, construction, retail, and wholesale industries combined, a dramatic change from 30 years earlier, when the traditional urban industries outnumbered information-processing occupations by three to one (Kasarda, 1985). Most clearly exemplifying this trend have been **global** or **world cities,** such as New York, Los Angeles, and Miami, which have become financial and trading centers—"transnational market 'spaces'"—in the international economy (Sassen, 1994). Together with cities such as Tokyo, Paris, London, Sao Paulo, Hong Kong, and Frankfurt, global cities have increased their dominance as centers of international finance, headquarters for transnational corporations, and the locale for highly technical services (Frey, 1990; Sassen, 1994; Ames, 1993). The preeminence of global cities has become especially pronounced during the past 20 years as a consequence of revolutions in telecommunications and in international finance that have produced increasing centralization of top-level management and control of international economic activities. Because "national and global markets, as well as globally integrated operations, require central places where the work of globalization gets done ... and a vast physical [and personnel] infrastructure" (Sassen, 1994, p. 1), global cities have acquired a unique and strategic position among urban centers throughout the world. Indeed, Sassen contends that global cities today have more in common with each other than with regional cities in their own countries (Sassen, 1994).

Some observers interpret these trends as indications that the fortunes of the city will soon improve. Massive urban redevelopment projects, including large hotels, offices, civic centers, entertainment areas, restaurants, and retail shopping areas, sometimes within one "megastructure," have appeared in a number of cities. Boston's Quincy Market, Baltimore's Inner Harbor, San Francisco's Ghirardelli Square, Detroit's Renaissance Center, and Chicago's Water Tower Palace illustrate such urban revitalization.

The growth of high-rise administrative buildings constructed during the 1970s and 1980s symbolizes the recent growth in information-processing service occupations. Manufacturing, wholesale trade, and retail activities, which provided the economic base for cities in an earlier period, required large areas for the work of their employees. These space requirements could be met only with buildings spread horizontally over large areas. Information-processing enterprises, on the other hand, can be carried out efficiently in small spaces. "Thus people who process information can be stacked, layer after layer, in downtown office towers with resulting proximity actually increasing the productivity of those whose activities require an extensive amount of nonroutine, face-to-face interaction" (Frisbie and Kasarda, 1988, p. 636).

In addition to the development of some massive urban commercial complexes, other factors have contributed to changes in the social composition of American cities. First, the social composition of the suburbs is changing. The most rapid period of suburban development coincided with the post-World War II baby boom. Young couples moved to the suburbs to raise their children in a more "wholesome" and socially homogeneous environment. Moreover, the suburban life-style strongly emphasized traditional male and female gender roles. Today, however, more young women are rejecting the traditional role of housewife in favor of white-collar and professional occupations. Declines in the birth rate and in household size make large suburban homes both impractical and unattractive for many people. Increasing numbers of young adults are choosing to live in high-density settings such as condominiums and central city apartments, rather than in single-family dwellings.

People working in professional, managerial, administrative, and information-processing jobs in central city office complexes often seek housing close to their work. Moreover, such people are particularly attracted to the way of life offered by the city. The amenities of urban life, including its restaurants, clubs, parks, zoos, theaters, cultural activities, and sporting events, provide a stimulating and exciting range of opportunities often unavailable in the suburbs. Seeking to capitalize on these amenities, an "urban gentry" of young, affluent, business and professional people have, in some instances, moved into declining urban neighborhoods and restored their deteriorating stock of housing. This process of urban residential revitalization of older neighborhoods is known as **gentrification** (Zukin, 1987).

However, many central-city residents, especially minorities, have not benefited from these changes in U.S. cities. First, although service sector jobs have grown, many central-city residents lack the educational qualifications to take advantage of them. Instead, a mismatch has developed between the educational qualifications required for the knowledge-intensive jobs being created in the service sector and the educational skills of the minorities who make up an increasing proportion of the population of central cities. The situation in today's central cities is much different from that in central cities in the industrial period when widespread opportunities existed for those with little education and few skills. This mismatch between increasing educational requirements for urban employment and the educational attainments of central-city residents represents one of the major dilemmas for urban social policy today (Kasarda, 1989).

Second, despite highly publicized revitalization efforts, the prospects for an urban renaissance are at best uncertain. Between 1968 and 1979 gentrification affected only a small fraction—less than 1 percent—of central-city housing units. Nearly three-fourths of those who moved into restored housing units were intra-city movers, not suburbanites who had moved to the city (Kasarda, 1980).

Third, urban redevelopment efforts, including the creation of urban megastructures and gentrification, have contributed to the displacement of substantial numbers of urban elderly and low-income residents (LeGates and Murphy, 1984; LeGates and Hartman, 1986; Sassen, 1990). The result has been the disruption of long-established and socially integrated neighborhoods, forcing many residents to experience financial distress as they look for new homes in housing markets characterized by an increasingly short supply of low-income housing (Hopkins, 1985; Sassen, 1990). In a study of the effects of gentrification in ten major U.S. cities, Nelson (1988) found that in most cities poor residents were displaced from gentrifying areas into lower-class areas, contributing to new concentrations of poverty.

The preceding discussion of the historic patterns of urban growth and development in the United States has centered primarily on patterns of population, technological, and economic growth and change and has not focused extensively on the social inequality and conflict among interest groups—local, national, and global—that have typically characterized cities. Moreover, it has not addressed the broader political and economic contexts within which modern cities have developed. Recently a "new urban sociology" (Gottdeiner and Feagin, 1988; Gottdeiner, 1994; Hutchinson, 1993; Sassen, 1994) has emerged that emphasizes the ways in which urban "processes and structures produce advantages for some groups and disadvantages for others." Proponents of this "new urban sociology" are concerned especially with "how political economic systems work, about which groups tend to monopolize power, and who is likely to benefit or suffer from the status quo in cities" (Smith, 1995, p. 433). Moreover, they seek to examine the development of cities and the process of urbanization in the context of the broader global capitalist economy. In other words, they are interested in identifying the ways in which the structure and functioning of cities are affected by political and economic interests and decisions—national and, especially, transnational—far beyond immediate city boundaries.

The Impact of Urban Life

Negative Views

Earlier we discussed the changes accompanying the rapid urbanization of Western society, in particular of the United States during the late nineteenth and early twentieth centuries. We noted that modern sociology emerged from the work of people who tried to understand and explain these changes. Most sociologists who considered the impact of increasing urbanization did not respond to it merely as disinterested social scientists. They themselves were products of societies being rapidly transformed, and in many instances they tended to view the passing of traditional society with nostalgia. The negative view of urban life, which for many years dominated sociological perspectives on the city, reflected in many respects the preference for a rural society that the early sociologists saw being undermined by the forces of modernization—by industrialization, bureaucratization, and urbanization.

As noted in Chapter 4, Ferdinand Toennies used the terms *gemeinschaft* and *gesellschaft* to distinguish the social relations characteristic of rural, traditional societies and modern, urban societies. *Gemeinschaft* communities are characterized by personalized, face-to-face relationships such as those in the family, the rural village, and the small town. *Gesellschaft* societies, in contrast, are associated with impersonal and distant relationships, the kind we associate with urban life. In *gemeinschaft* communities, social relationships are valued as ends in themselves. In *gesellschaft* communities, social relationships are little more than means to other ends; for example, people associate only with those who reward them with money, goods, or services (Toennies, 1857/1957).

One of the earliest and most influential sociological analyses of the city was made by the German sociologist Georg Simmel (1903/1971). Primarily concerned with the psychological effects of urban society on individuals, Simmel observed that life in cities (as contrasted with life in small towns and rural areas) exposes people to a greater variety and intensity of stimuli. He argued that the more hectic pace and intensity of city life produce more psychological stress than the slower, less hectic, and more relaxed pace of rural life.

Simmel concluded that the greater psychic stress of urban life affects the emotional and intellectual character of urban residents. In attempting to adapt to and protect themselves from stresses created by the profusion of people and environmental stimuli about them, urban residents may suppress their emotions and follow only their intellect in deciding how to act. As a consequence, urban dwellers develop an emotional restraint or insensitivity in their dealings with others. They develop rational standards of calculation, punctuality, and exactness so that some semblance of order can be maintained within a chaotic array of events and social contacts. In Simmel's view, the more leisurely pace and more intimate nature of social life in rural areas enable people to be more spontaneous and less calculating in their personal relations than is characteristic of urbanites. Moreover, as urbanites are subjected to a barrage of stimuli, events, and individual differences, they become less likely to be shocked or excited by new, unusual, and bizarre events.

Simmel also recognized that cities allow a greater expression of personal freedom than do rural communities. Rural communities are apt to have restrictive social norms and conservative attitudes about social diversity, may severely restrict the expression of individual differences, and insure that those people who do not conform to the norms will feel social isolation from those who do. However, Simmel did not feel that the increased freedom in urban settings necessarily enhanced the quality of human life. On the contrary, he contended that increased individual freedom tends to heighten the urbanite's feelings of social isolation and loneliness in the midst of a social milieu characterized by impersonality and anonymity, rather than intimacy and primary group ties.

Simmel's essentially negative view of urban life has been shared by several prominent American sociologists. Robert E. Park, who was instrumental in the development of the Chicago School of sociology, was greatly influenced by Simmel. Through Park's influence, the Chicago School focused especially on urban life during a period (the 1920s and 1930s) when American cities were still experiencing a substantial rural-to-urban migration. In 1938, one of Park's colleagues at the University of Chicago, Louis Wirth, published an essay, "Urbanism as a Way of Life" (Wirth, 1938) that summed up many of the contrasting themes of urban and rural life that Simmel had expressed and reflected much of the basic orientation of the Chicago School's urban research.

Wirth contended that the city is characterized by three features: relatively greater size, population density, and social diversity. He emphasized that these factors produce a greater division of labor, a growth in formal communications (such as newspapers, magazines, and radio), increased specialization and differentiation among different areas of the community, and a growth in specialized organizations and associations. Wirth felt that the city's greater population density leads to more impersonal social relationships among urban residents and that the city's social diversity encourages indifference to others, depersonalization, and the weakening of social bonds. Urban areas adversely affect society by encouraging "the substitution of secondary for primary contact, the weakening of bonds of kinship and the declining significance of the family, the disappearance of the neighborhood and the undermining of the traditional basis of social solidarity" (Wirth, 1938).

In addition to producing social disorganization, Wirth also argued that the city has negative effects on the personalities of city dwellers, producing increases in "personal disorganization, mental breakdown, suicide, delinquents, crime, corruption, and disorder" (Wirth, 1938). The ultimate result is *anomie,* weakened social norms, and an absence of moral consensus among the city's heterogeneous population.

Challenges to the Negative View

Numerous studies have confirmed that urban residents are more tolerant of and express more permissive *attitudes* toward a range of deviant or unconventional behavior—the use of alcohol and marijuana, divorce, gambling, abortion, premarital sex, marital infidelity, and homosexuality—than do residents of smaller communities; permissiveness toward the unconventional increases with greater community size (Wilson, 1995). However, permissive attitudes do not necessarily mean that urbanism promotes unconventional behavior. In a survey of sexual behavior, Wilson (1995) found that community size was unrelated to the frequency of premarital sex, cohabitation, and marital infidelity.

Thus, in recent years an increasing number of sociologists have argued for a more complex and balanced assessment of the effects of urban life. Two closely related perspectives—the compositional and the subcultural—have challenged the idea that cities inevitably produce psychological distress, social disorganization, and other dehumanizing effects (Fischer, 1984).

The **compositional theory of urbanism** emphasizes the positive aspects of the cosmopolitanism and diversity that characterize city life. Compositionalists view the city as a mosaic of different social worlds based on kinship, neighborhood, ethnicity, occupation, common interests, and lifestyle. The presence of these social worlds allows intimate, primary group relations to exist independently of the broader urban environment, affording protection against the city's anonymity and the psychological stresses emphasized by Simmel.

From the compositional perspective, behaviors and experiences of urbanites are shaped not so much by the size, density, or social diversity of the urban population as by the characteristics—including social class position, stage in the life cycle, and ethnic identity—of those who live there.

Even in the largest cities people create and live within communities—"urban villages"—that prevent them from feeling socially isolated. The traditional negative perspective of urbanism fails to distinguish how people act in public settings and how they act in more private contexts. Claude Fischer (1981) has suggested that in the "public world," urbanites are confronted by numerous others who are strangers and who are often perceived as "strange" because of the cultural diversity of the urban milieu. Therefore, in public contexts, most urban dwellers do tend to feel and act like anonymous, detached individuals.

In the "private world" of interactions among family and friends, however, social relations characterized by primary associations and mutual support and assistance tend to flourish. Indeed, the "personal communities" provided by the networks of association among urban dwellers appear to provide a majority of urbanites with greater opportunities for social attachments than may exist among small-town and rural dwellers (Fischer, 1982; Wellman, 1979).

The **subcultural theory of urbanism** argues that a city's size, density, and diversity do affect the urban experience, but in a positive way. Intimate social worlds are *created* and *enhanced* in an urban milieu, not broken down, as the critics of urban life argue. The urban environment provides opportunities to create a variety of meaningful subcultures (for example, ethnic, artistic, religious, gay–lesbian, literary, intellectual) that could not develop in smaller communities because there would not be a sufficient number—a critical mass—of similarly interested individuals. For example, although he found that urbanism had no effect on sexual behavior generally, Wilson discovered that homosexual behavior was reported more frequently in urban areas. He contends that this finding is consistent with subcultural theory because "open homosexuals are likely to find supportive subcultures only in large communities, where the critical mass of homosexuals needed to insure the viability of the homosexual subculture can be found" (Wilson, 1995). Thus, urbanism can foster unconventional and deviant behavior not because an impersonal city produces anomie and undermines social bonds and social control, but because it provides an environment in which subcultures identified as deviant by the larger society can be created and thrive. The subcultural and compositional perspectives differ slightly in their focus, but both demonstrate ways in which personal relationships are sustained and fostered in an urban environment.

In conclusion, the negative view of the city reflects a general tendency among both the American public and social scientists to exaggerate and romanticize the virtues of a rural existence, to which cities are often contrasted. Urban life certainly has its problems, but so do suburban and rural life. To assess accurately the effects of urbanism, we must examine them carefully and systematically.

Summary

Demography is the scientific study of population. The three basic processes of population are fertility (childbearing), mortality (death), and migration (change of residence). Age and sex are the two major demographic characteristics of population.

Fertility is a socially motivated behavior, as the extremes in childbearing behavior (the Hutterites, the Shakers, and the Rappites) illustrate. Childbearing in the United States today is at its lowest rate in history. Differences in fertility can still be found between religious, racial, ethnic, and socioeconomic status groups.

Mortality is influenced by one's social position and personal life-style. Migration shapes the growth and development of different parts of the country, and has generally been from rural to urban places, and from east to west in the United States. Today, much migration is toward the South.

The most far-reaching population issue today is the rapid growth of the world's population. The "population explosion" is a recent phenomenon in demographic history, having begun with the economic development of various European states in the seventeenth and eighteenth centuries and accelerated greatly in the twentieth century. Demographic transitions have already occurred in the economically developed countries. Generally, the demographic transition involves a declining death rate while the birth rate remains high. The rapid rate of the world's population growth today stems from the fact that the death rates in many of the developing countries have dropped while the birth rates remain high or very high.

Responses to the rapid growth of the world's population are varied. One view is that "economic development is the best contraceptive," so emphasis should be placed on development, and fertility declines will follow. A second view is the family-planning approach, which emphasizes contraception, education, and propaganda as ways of reducing fertility. A third view would combine the family-planning approach with societal changes to reduce motivations for childbearing. Contemporary China is an exemplar of the latter approach to reducing fertility.

Cities are a relatively recent form of human organization, although some did appear soon after the Agricultural Revolution. In more recent times the Industrial Revolution sparked the growth of cities. The pace of urban growth has been especially pronounced since World War II. Recent urban growth has been most rapid in Third World countries.

In the United States, industrialization in the nineteenth and early twentieth centuries led to urbanization. The process of suburbanization has seen the growth of primarily white suburbs and the abandonment of the central cities to minority residents and the poor. Business and industry have also been part of the flight to the suburbs, creating severe economic problems for the central cities. As suburban metropolitan fringes have moved farther away from central cities, they have overlapped with the fringes of other metropolitan areas, creating a continuous metropolitan complex known as a megalopolis.

Recently, countertrends to the decentralization of American urban areas have been noted. Urban redevelopment projects in many cities have produced massive office buildings in which to conduct the growing number of central-city service jobs. Some cities have also experienced gentrification, but this process has not benefited all city residents, especially minorities and the poor.

The long-standing negative perception of urban life is being challenged today. Sociologists who emphasize a more balanced portrait of the city argue that the city's anonymity has not led to social anarchy and personal isolation. Instead, the city offers a "mosaic of social worlds," opportunities for the creation of intimate associations and communities based on kinship, neighborhood, ethnicity, occupation, or life-style.

CRITICAL THINKING

1. Explain how a demographic phenomenon, such as the baby boom, can have an effect on a variety of factors in a society.
2. What general trends in fertility are evident in the United States? The developed world? The developing world?
3. What factors might influence the rate of fertility in a given society? Give examples to support your ideas.
4. What three basic processes determine population size? Explain how each is affected by social factors.
5. What is the population explosion? Explain how this phenomenon is unprecedented in human history. Why should it concern you?
6. Speculate on the social effect of population measures such as the one-child policy in China. How would such measures affect social institutions, such as the family, education, and the economy?
7. Distinguish among the terms *urban, urbanization,* and *urbanism.*
8. Why is the Industrial Revolution considered to be a major factor in the development of urbanization?
9. Where are the ten largest urban areas in the world concentrated? In your opinion, is this a positive or negative phenomenon?
10. Describe the general history of urbanization in the United States. What general theories exist to explain the patterns of urban spatial differentiation? Which best describes the urban area closest to you?

18

Social Change, Collective Behavior, and Social Movements

"You can't teach an old dog new tricks." "Can a leopard change its spots?" "The more things change, the more they stay the same." Such folk sayings suggest that change is difficult and relatively rare. But, as we have seen throughout this book, change is pervasive. Indeed, our experience of the world teaches us that we live in the midst of ongoing change.

We have only to ask our parents or grandparents to describe life when they were growing up. Their descriptions of work, education, entertainment, and technology are apt to be very different from what we experience today. We can also compare a current map of Africa with one published in 1950, where we will see that many of today's countries were not in existence 40 years ago. As we saw in Chapter 16, relations between the United States and the former Soviet Union (and now the Commonwealth of Independent States) have undergone dramatic changes in the last decade. The cold war, which has threatened our existence over the last 40 years, is over. As a result, the pace of international change is, at the moment, almost dizzying. Rather than living in a relatively changeless world, it appears at times that we live in an age in which everything that had been nailed down is coming loose.

In this chapter—building on prior discussions of social theory, bureaucracy, and culture—we look more closely at the nature of social change, at social movements, and at people's experiences of change.

The Meaning of Change

Social Change Defined

We define **social change** as variations over time in the relationships among individuals, groups, cultures, and societies. Social change is pervasive; all "of social life is continually changing" (Lauer, 1982, p. 4; Harper, 1989). In the family, for example, recent changes include the surge of married women and mothers into the labor force, and the increasing proportion of nontraditional living arrangements (such as an unmarried couple's living together). At the societal level, crime rates, population statistics, distribution of income, and level of technological development register measurable shifts. At the global level, trade patterns, political alliances, and the distribution of wealth take new shapes over time (Chirot, 1994).

The Changing Nature of Street Gangs: An Example

It would be useful at this point to offer a specific example of social change focusing on the changing nature of street gangs in the United States (and the street gang is largely an American phenomenon). Prior to the 1970s, youths joined street gangs to gain a sense of identity. Contrary to popular opinion, they did not join to engage in crime, although that may have eventually occurred as a result of gang membership. The crime that did occur tended to be minor forms, such as vandalism or petty theft. Most of the time spent with the gang was rather boring, including "eating, sitting around, walking the streets looking for each other, checking out the local school or park, cruising in someone else's car" (Klein, 1992, npi). When violence did occur, it tended to be aimed at members of other gangs. The kinds of gangs that come to mind in thinking about these early forms are the comparatively benign gangs depicted in the movie and play *West Side Story.*

Clearly, today's gangs are far different from the relatively harmless forms described above (Howell, 1994). Let us briefly look at the situation in Los Angeles, widely regarded as the gang capital of the United States with its famous gangs like the Bloods and the Crips. It is estimated that the city has 1,142 gangs and approximately 150,000 gang members (Monmaney, 1995; *Austin American-Statesman,* 1995). Over one-quarter of the more than 27,000 murders committed in Los Angeles between 1979 and 1994 was linked to gangs. While the proportion of killings due to gang violence was 18 percent in 1979, it increased to 43 percent in 1994. The vast majority (94 percent) of the victims are Hispanic and black; it is not unusual for children to be among the victims of gang violence. These numbers indicate that today's gangs are quite different from those that were depicted in *West Side Story*.

Klein argues that there are six major areas in which today's gangs are very different from those of the past. First, gang members tend to be older. In the past, gang members averaged about 16 years of age. Today, the average is about 20 and, in addition, there are large numbers of members in their late twenties and even early thirties.

Second, the organizational form has changed. In the past, gangs tended to involve a series of loosely organized, age-based subgroups with each having its own leadership structure. Gangs today tend to be heterogeneous in age, smaller in size, and largely independent from one another. Because there are more of them and they are more flexibly organized, Klein believes that they have a much greater potential for growth than the older gangs.

Third, while gangs in the past have been largely black and Hispanic, we are now witnessing a rapid increase in the number of Asian South Pacific Islander gangs, as well as other ethnic gangs (Tanton and Lutton, 1993). Another new type of gang is the white supremacist, or "skinhead," gang.

Fourth, it seems clear that, while there is considerable variation among subtypes, today's gangs are more violent [gang members are 60 times more likely to be murdered than people in general (LaSalandra, 1995)], have more sophisticated weapons (sometimes more advanced than the police), and are more likely to kill or injure nongang members.

In his study of gangs, Jankowski (1991) differentiates between individual violence and organizational gang violence. In terms of the former, he argues that, in fact, a substantial portion of gang violence is the result of individual members operating on their own. Violence also often occurs as a result of directives from the gang (organizational gang violence). In either case, violence takes six basic forms: violence against fellow gang members, attacks on members of other gangs, assaults on community residents, attacks on those outside the community, and assaults on property both inside and outside the community.

Fifth, and a major factor that has led to increasing national interest and concern about gangs, is the fact that gangs are no longer restricted to a few large cities. As of 1992, Klein (1995, p. 91) found that 766 cities had gangs (up from 54 prior to 1961). Many towns with less than 10,000 people now report a gang presence.

Finally, and the other major reason why so much attention is being devoted these days to gangs, is the growing relationship between gangs and drugs. In the past, drug use was fairly common among gang members. What is different today is that gangs are increasingly in the business of distributing drugs. Interestingly, in a later work, Klein downplayed the significance of drugs. Although many gang members may use drugs, Klein (1995, p. 42) concludes, "Gangs are lousy mechanisms for drug distribution."

Thus, in a variety of ways, gangs have changed dramatically and, in the process, they have become a much greater problem for society.

Patterns of Change

Change is not a purely haphazard process, but rarely are its patterns represented by smooth lines or curves. Patterns of change fall into three broad categories: a general trend (upward or downward), cyclic variations, and irregular or random variations. A general trend designates a long-term tendency to increase or decrease. Cyclic variations may occur around seasons or over periods of years or even centuries. Irregular variations are often tied to particular events, such as natural disasters, wars, or inventions. The U.S. economy, for example, has grown over the past century (an upward trend), has had a series of booms and recessions (cyclic variations), and has also had some short-term reversals and sudden surges (irregular and random variations).

At every level of human life (family, society, and the world), then, trends, cycles, and variations help us to identify changes that have occurred, changes that are currently occurring, and changes likely to occur in the future. Change is pervasive.

Theories of Change

In Aldous Huxley's *Brave New World,* one of the leaders of the Western world calls change a "menace." In the novel, the rulers of the society did not want any change. Wary of any invention or innovation, they cherished stability above all else. They believed that maintaining the social order as it was would keep them secure and happy. Had Huxley's characters understood history, they would have known that they could never bring human society into a state of changeless stability. Societies change as inexorably as the ocean tide comes in.

How do we account for the multitude of changes at the various levels of social life? Sociologists as well as other social scientists try to answer this question. Economists, political scientists, anthropologists, and psychologists tend to focus on a particular segment of society—the economy, political institutions, culture, or individual personalities. Sociologists try to understand the totality—how the social structure and culture change over time. They tend to look at change in terms of the social factors involved. They explore such factors as internal systemic strains and contradictions, interpersonal and intergroup processes such as conflict, technological developments, and institutional arrangements.

To begin to understand social change, some theorists have looked at the broad sweep of history. Others have focused on structure and process in the social order. In Chapter 1 we discussed the Marxist perspective that identifies inherent conflicts in the social order as the driving mechanism of change throughout human history. We also looked at structural–functionalism, which posited more stability than change in social systems. Functionalists acknowledge that social systems change, but generally they argue that the forces tending toward stability are stronger than the forces tending toward change. In addition to these two perspectives, three other theories of change have been influential in sociology—cyclic theory, evolutionary theory, and conflict theory. We examine each type through representative theorists.

Cyclic Theory

Cyclic theory conceptualizes change as an ongoing series of cycles rather than as a process with some kind of direction. The Greeks, Romans, and Chinese, among others, viewed history in terms of great cycles rather than in terms of progress or decline.

Pitirim Sorokin, a sociologist who formulated a cyclic theory of change, investigated the whole field of human culture, including art, science, literature, technology, philosophy, and law. He concluded that culture is composed of a series of parts that are unified around a fundamental principle and a basic value (Sorokin, 1941, p. 17). In any given age, more than one society can exhibit the same principle or basic value. The United States, Canada, and Western Europe could be one "culture" in Sorokin's terms because all of these societies are essentially materialistic. In a materialistic culture, science, art, literature, and all other cultural areas will be materialistic. Sorokin called the materialistic culture *sensate*. A **sensate culture** is one pervaded by the principle that the material or sensory world is the true reality and value. A second type is the **ideational culture,** pervaded by the principle that a supersensory or nonmaterial world is the true reality and the highest value. The third type, the **idealistic culture,** combines the other two in an integrated blend of the supersensory and the sensory (nonmaterial and material). Sorokin argued that medieval Europe, with its belief that the sensory world is only a transitional step on the way to the eternal City of God, typified an ideational culture, while the modern West typifies the sensate culture.

All of history, according to Sorokin, is a cyclic variation among the three types of cultures. Cultures grow and decline, and give way to one of the other types of culture. Our own Western system, he insisted, is not only sensate but an "over-ripe" sensate culture, ready to give way to an ideational or idealistic type. In the late 1930s, Sorokin (1957, pp. 699–701) forecast a number of dire developments that would signal the downfall of our sensate culture. Among them were an increasing loss of moral sensitivity, a mechanistic view of humans, the use of force and deception to maintain social order, the disintegration of the family, an obsession with quantity rather than quality, and an increase in such things as suicide, mental illness, and crime. In his analysis, these lamentable developments do not mean the demise of civilization but merely the transition to an ideational or idealistic culture, and a new period of growth and development in a more spiritual world.

Cyclic theory contributes to our understanding of change by identifying one important pattern of change in social life. Cyclic variations occur at every level of life, from the individual to the global. At the individual level, for example, cyclic variations appear in physiological functions, such as diurnal variations in body temperature and blood pressure. A great variety of social phenomena have been charted and shown to vary cyclically over time, including wars, crime, marriage and birth rates, and religious and scientific activity.

Cyclic theory, however, does not account for all of the important factors in change. Sorokin, in particular, fails to consider social–psychological factors. His theory casts people as virtual pawns of the massive sociocultural cycles in human history. Moreover, broad descriptions of cycles in social life fail to capture qualitative differences in different phases of the cycles. For example, to describe both the modern West and the Greco-Roman world at the birth of Christ as sensate cultures may be accurate, but it does not illuminate essential differences in the two cultures. There is more to change than cyclic variations.

Evolutionary Theory

In contrast to the cyclic theory, **evolutionary theory** gives direction to change (Dietz, Burns, and Buttel, 1990). Gerhard and Jean Lenski (1982) have developed one of the more influential discussions of evolutionary change. Not all change, they argue, is evolutionary; some is cyclic, and some is unpatterned and random. But evolutionary change is the predominant pattern and differs from the others because it is a "process of cumulative change" (Lenski and Lenski, 1982, p. 56). Organic and sociocultural evolution are similar in some ways (Lopreato, 1990; van den Berghe, 1990), including the fundamental fact that both are cumulative change based on systems of encoded information. Organic evolution is based in part on the information encoded in the DNA molecule. Sociocultural evolution is based on symbol systems, or language.

The Lenskis define sociocultural evolution as "the process of change and development in human societies that results from cumulative change in their stores of cultural information" (Lenski and Lenski, 1982, p. 60). Cumulative change occurs through the twin processes of innovation and selection. Innovation produces new variations, and selection produces decisions about which variations to retain and which to reject.

Inventions, discoveries, alterations of existing cultural elements, and diffusion from one society to another constitute the basic forms of innovation. More than anything else, however, technological developments provide the driving mechanism of change. New technologies help satisfy human needs more completely or more efficiently. Needs here refer to socially and culturally derived needs as well as to subsistence needs. We *need* to have esthetic satisfaction and to find self-fulfillment as well as to obtain food, clothing, and shelter. In the course of seeking satisfaction of such needs, people continually develop new technologies. Those technologies, in turn, alter social life by opening up new options for people. The dramatic changes in the shifts from simple hunting-and-gathering societies through agricultural and industrial societies to today's world highlight the impact of technological developments upon the social order. The store of cultural information in a computer society is vastly different from that in the stone-tool, plow, or steam-engine societies.

According to the Lenskis, the processes of innovation and selection occur at two different levels: in individual societies and in the world system. At the level of the individual society, the variations produced are cultural elements, some of which are retained while others are rejected. Those retained shape the character of the evolving social order. At the level of the world system, the variations produce entire societies. Those with the greater amount of technological information will survive and shape the character of the evolving world system. The world system has evolved from one in which the dominant social order was hunting and gathering, through systems dominated by the horticultural and the agrarian society, to a system dominated by an industrial society.

And where is evolution leading us? The Lenskis assert that human culture has been highly successful as an adaptive mechanism, for the human race has not only survived but has flourished in terms of sheer numbers. If we go beyond numbers and ask about progress toward such values as freedom, justice, and happiness, however, we find a complex situation. Technological developments have certainly raised the upper level of freedom, in the sense that those in the upper strata in industrial societies have a far greater range of options than those who had the most options in agrarian societies. The freedom of the average person is more debatable; industrial societies offer fewer physical and biological restraints but more social restraints. People in advanced societies today, for example, have far fewer problems with health than in former years, but they have more governmental restrictions.

Dealing with justice, the Lenskis point out that the amount of inequality in societies changes as we move from one type of society to another. Inequality increases in the shift from a hunting-and-gathering to a horticultural and agrarian society. The surplus of goods increases, but that surplus is invariably distributed unequally among the population. Industrial societies initially maintain this trend toward increasing inequality, but the trend finally reverses as industrialization continues.

The Lenskis raise important issues about equality, justice, and happiness that we cannot resolve here. Generally, they portray the course of evolution as one of progress for the human race. Evolutionary theory also underscores the fact that certain factors, such as technology, are far more crucial to the process of change than other factors. On the other hand, although evolutionary theory may be useful in explaining large-scale, long-term trends, it is not useful in accounting for the smaller-scale, shorter-term alterations in social life, such as alterations in social institutions or public attitudes. Nor is evolutionary theory useful for explaining the significant differences in societies at the same level of evolutionary development. In fact, some older evolutionists argued that the process of evolution demands that all societies evolve along the same lines toward the same kind of social order. Clearly, that has not happened. What else, then, is going on in social life that is crucial to our understanding of social change? For some theorists, the answer is conflict.

Conflict Theory

Conflict theory of change, as we have seen throughout, views change as the inevitable result of inherent conflicts between groups with diverse interests. In a statement representative of conflict theory, Dahrendorf (1959, p. 208) comments: "I would suggest . . . that all that is creativity, innovation, and development in the life of the individual, his group, and his society is due, to no small extent, to the operation of conflicts between group and group, individual and individual, emotion and emotion within one individual." The origin of social conflict, according to Dahrendorf, is the dominance relations that prevail in societies. Conflict is generally a struggle over the legitimacy of authority relations (Collins, 1990).

Dahrendorf develops four propositions to highlight the nature of conflict and its role in social change:

1. Every society is at every point subject to processes of change; social change is ubiquitous.
2. Every society displays at every point dissensus and conflict; social conflict is ubiquitous.
3. Every element in a society renders a contribution to its disintegration and change.
4. Every society is based on the coercion of some of its members by others (Dahrendorf, 1959, p. 162).

Change is inevitable because authority relationships are pervasive, and there will always be conflict over authority relationships.

The analysis of bureaucracy (Chapter 4) provided specific illustrations of conflict as a force for change in industrial organizations. Many case studies have documented struggles between employees and management. In Dahrendorf's analysis, conflict will occur regardless of the nature of management, whether management is composed of owners, stockholders, or the government. Whether managers try to fashion a participatory system or a restrictive bureaucracy, conflict will still exist because it is rooted in the contradictory interests embedded in authority relationships. Conflict and its outcome—social change—are inevitable.

Conflict, like technology, is an important part of social change. Nevertheless, conflict does not explain all change, and it can sometimes impede change. In some Third World nations, such as Burma and the Sudan, intergroup conflict has been so intense that progress toward a modern, constitutional state has been stifled. Furthermore, some change occurs without conflict. As James G. March (1981, p. 563) points out, organizations may change "routinely, easily, and responsively." Many businesses have changed their internal structure and processes in an effort to enhance productivity or to adapt to a changed environment, and they have implemented the changes without conflict.

Conflict and Terrorism.   In contemporary world conflicts, we find many militant groups that engage in terrorism. **Terrorism** can take many forms, but it can be defined as the systematic or threatened use of murder, injury, or destruction in order to achieve some political end (Laqueur, 1987, p. 72; Reich, 1990). By their actions, terrorists seek to create tensions that can ultimately lead to the changes they desire.

Over the years we have all heard of terrorist acts committed by such groups as the Irish Republican Army (IRA) (Heskin, 1994), Hamas, the Palestinian Liberation Organization (PLO), the Red Brigades (Italy), and others. Terrorists engage in a wide range of activities, including plane hijacking, kidnapping, embassy bombings, car bombings, and other violent acts.

And terrorism is no longer something that occurs only in far-off places. There are now major examples of terrorism in the United States, especially in the bombing of the World Trade Center in New York City on February 26, 1993 (six deaths and about 1,000 injuries; a cost of $300 million) and of the Alfred P. Murrah Federal Building in Oklahoma City on April 19, 1995 (169 dead; hundreds of injuries; eleven buildings destroyed and more than 300 damaged; over $100 million in damages). It is not only the location of these bombings that is important, but also their huge scale. They reflect the fact that we have entered, at least in the view of one observer, the era of "superterrorism" (Kitfield, 1995). The fear is that even these bombings will seem puny when and if terrorists are able to get their hands on things like the lethal Sarin gas used in the two attacks (June 27, 1994, and March 20, 1995) in Tokyo subways and, most importantly, nuclear weapons. Given the chaotic state of Russia today and its possession of vast stores of nuclear weapons, there is a far greater likelihood that terrorists will be able to obtain such weapons.

We are all familiar with the terrorism of groups like the IRA and the PLO, but let us take the recent example of a terrorist bombing in Colombo, Sri Lanka, in which at least 72 people were killed and over 1,000 injured (Cooper, 1996a, b). Blame for the attack was placed on Tamil separatists who have been fighting for more than a decade for an independent homeland within Sri Lanka. The Tamils, who are Hindu, make up 18 percent of the population of Sri Lanka, while the dominant Sinhalese (Buddhists) constitute almost three-quarters of the nation's population. To further their cause, the Tamils have been accused of many acts of terrorism over the last decade, including blasting a train in 1985, bombing a plane in 1986, exploding a car bomb at Colombo's central bus station in 1987, and assassinating the deputy defense minister of Sri Lanka and the former premier of India in 1991 and the president of Sri Lanka in 1993. The bombing in Colombo in early 1996 is part of an acceleration of terrorist attacks by Tamils; 1995 had witnessed a number of bombings and other terrorist activities.

The Tamils may have been heartened by the seeming success of other terrorist groups. In the 1940s the activities of Jewish terrorists associated with groups like Irgun and the Stern gang contributed to the ouster of the British from Palestine. More recently, the British seem more willing to negotiate with Irish separatists in part because of IRA activities, and the recent Israeli concessions and negotiations with the Palestinians may be linked to the terrorism of the PLO and the even more radical Hamas. While terrorist actions are rarely decisive, they sometimes do contribute to the achievement of political goals. We are likely to continue to see terrorist acts in various parts of the world in the coming years, and they are likely to take many different, and perhaps some new, forms (Cetron and Davies, 1994).

Although all the types of theory are useful, no one adequately explains all change. Perhaps a future theorist will utilize elements of the various theories to fashion a more complete explanation of social change than is now available.

Sources of Change

Various change theories stress differing sources of change. Sorokin saw change as a normal outcome of the functioning of the social system. Marx pointed to inherent contradictions in the larger society, while conflict theorists stress the role of the struggle between groups with opposed interests. Functionalists identify many sources of change, both internal (such as strain in the system) and external (such as changes in the physical environment or war with another society). The functionalists correctly point out the multiple sources of change. All the factors noted by the theorists, in fact, are part of the process of social change. We now discuss three of the more important factors: technology, ideologies, and competition/conflict.

Technology

Our earlier discussion of culture pointed to the importance of technology (Wallace, 1989)—materials, tools, machines, skills, and procedures—in a society. An examination of Ogburn's (1964) view of **cultural lag** established that change occurs first in material culture and that rapid technological change causes maladjustment because the old norms, roles, and, in some cases, values no longer seem to apply to the situation created by the new technology. The maladjustment, in turn, stimulates people to address the resulting problems. Thus change is ongoing as people must continually seek to adapt their nonmaterial culture to the material.

As an example of cultural lag, the development of nuclear armaments has made it irrational for nations to wage wars with these weapons in order to achieve political goals. And yet some national leaders, even in the post-Cold War era, talk about potential wars, or they even threaten wars, as if we were in a pre-nuclear missile age.

In a recent study, Evans (1993) examined the issue of cultural lag as it applies to children with birth defects, specifically spina bifida, and the availability of technology to keep the children alive. He found that, although technology had advanced, the ability to deal with the health problem rationally had not kept pace.

How Technology Causes Change. Ogburn identified one of the ways in which technology causes change—by creating social problems that require people's action. But technology also leads to change in a second way—by increasing our alternatives. Consider, for example, the options opened up by the computer (Turkle, 1984). In many cases, the computer has radically altered the nature of the workplace (Zuboff, 1988), changing the kind and number of workers needed and the kind and amount of information that can be kept and used. The computerization of an office may mean that fewer workers are required, and that those who are needed will have to possess different skills (for example, the ability to work at the computer terminal) than those who previously worked there. On the other hand, that office force can handle much more information (facts about inventory, production and clients, and forecasts about the future) than could the noncomputerized group. Largely because of the computer, the number of workers in the information field—those engaged in collecting and analyzing various kinds of data pertinent to an operation—has dramatically increased in modern nations. The computer's impact can be seen in virtually every human endeavor. New methods of education, such as computer-assisted instruction, are available. Health care can be individualized in a way not possible before; a hospital patient can be hooked up to a computer that will continually monitor his or her physical status or make analyses to facilitate an accurate diagnosis and treatment. Computers allow people to shop from their homes.

Of course, the options are not all desirable. Through computerized job surveillance, corporations are able to invade the privacy of their employees (Rule and Brantley, 1992). Computers can also be used to commit crime and to wage war. Criminals have learned to use the computer to "break in" to the operations of a company and steal information or materials. The military has used the computer to create frightening new weapons that can kill more people with greater accuracy at longer distances. The options opened up by the computer are enormously varied, but not all are conducive to human well-being.

Perhaps the most pervasive problem associated with computers is the threat they pose to our right to privacy (Rule, 1992). For example, the computers of the nation's credit bureaus hold over 200 million files on people and their creditworthiness. Information pours into those files every time we apply for a credit card, a mortgage, or a personal loan. This information is updated every time we use any of these sources of credit. Thus, the credit bureaus possess, and share, a great deal of information about us (Ritzer, 1995). But information about us is stored in many other computer systems as well. For example, the government possesses lots of information about us in, among other places, our income tax records. This information is supplemented whenever, for example, we commit a crime and that information is entered into the FBI's computerized data bank, the *National Crime Information Center.* Any one of these data banks poses a threat to our privacy, but taken together there is the potential for the elimination of much of our privacy.

The third way in which technology leads to change is by altering interaction patterns—new technologies frequently lead to new interaction patterns. For instance, one study has shown that a robot installed in a machine plant drastically altered the workplace (Goleman, 1983, pp. 40–41). In essence, the robot did the work previously done by a human, and the human ran the robot. Workers agreed that the robot had eliminated physical stress, but they noted other stresses that were added because the robot required the full attention of the worker. The joking and bantering of pre-robot days were gone. As one worker put it, "I don't have time to talk with anyone. I don't want them breaking my concentration." The robot changed interaction patterns in the factory. In other cases, a new technology does not demand, but may result in, changed patterns. The automobile and television are examples of technologies that an individual can use to change his or her interaction patterns, although neither requires those changes. That is, one need not break off friendships or cut down on interaction with family members in order to use an automobile or television. In fact, the automobile can help one to maintain existing interaction patterns even after a move to a different location; television can be a shared experience with friends or family members. Most technologies do not require us to alter interaction patterns, but they give us the option to do so.

Ideology: Impediment or Facilitator of Change?

As we saw in Chapter 8, an **ideology** is a set of ideas that explains reality, provides directives for behavior, and expresses the interests of particular groups. An ideology may be elaborate, such as the ideologies of Marxism, capitalism, or Catholicism. Or the ideology may be focused on a specific issue, such as the ideologies of the prochoice and antiabortion groups. In either case, the ideologies fulfill several functions. For instance, groups in this controversy each have an ideology that explains their position on abortion; among other things, the ideologies take a position on whether the fetus is a living human. Antiabortionists argue that the fertilized egg is a human. From a biological point of view, they say, the fertilized egg is a unique, genetic entity. The Catholic church agrees, and adds that the fertilized egg must be considered a human because it has human potential, because "if you are conceived by human parents, you are human" (*Time,* 1981, p. 23). On the other hand, those who favor a woman's right to abortion argue that human life does not technically begin until some time after conception. For example, one biologist argues that fertilization is not the beginning of human life, but a "highly significant step in its continuity," since the egg and sperm are both living human cells. The fertilized egg lacks some of the important characteristics we attribute to people, including a nervous system and the ability to respond to stimuli. One may also consider a human as someone with self-awareness. But during the first three months, the fetus "lacks an adequate neural foundation for minimal subjective experience, let alone self-awareness" (Grobstein, 1982, p. 14).

For those opposed to abortion, however, the act is one of killing a human being, regardless of how soon the abortion occurs after conception. As a legislative aide put it, "We must do everything we can under our constitutional system to stop the killing of unborn children. We're talking about life and death" (*Time,* 1981, p. 20). For those who favor women's choice in the matter, the issue is one of a woman's right to have control of her body and her general well-being. A woman's right to self-determination is threatened, they say, by antiabortion efforts.

These ideologies also provide directives for behavior; each group actively lobbies and propagandizes in an effort to win public and governmental support. Each group tries to marshal support for political candidates who support their position. Antiabortionists mobilize supporters to picket (or disrupt) abortion clinics. And the ideologies clearly reflect the interests of the two groups; those who argue for choice in the matter feel that such choice is important to maintain the rights of women, while those who argue against abortion feel that the sanctity of human life generally, and of their quality of life in particular, is being threatened. In addition to serving the various functions for groups holding them, ideologies affect change in a number of ways.

Ideology as an Impediment to Change.   Although change is inevitable, some people who benefit enough from the existing order will always vigorously resist change. In some cases, people use ideologies to impede or block change. During the Middle Ages, the clergy used religious ideology to gain more power for themselves and to impede certain economic developments. For instance, they inhibited the development of economic surplus by defining usury as sinful. They diverted whatever surplus wealth there was from economic enterprises by stressing the insignificance of worldly gain and the crucial importance of spiritual works. Consequently, people tended to use their energies and resources to build religious monuments and secure greater favor with God. The large number of religious holidays and festivals similarly consumed people's time and energies, and diverted them from such things as economic development.

Nonreligious ideologies can also inhibit change. In the United States, people have used the ideology of equality of opportunity to resist changes that would benefit minorities. After all, they argue, if every person in the United States truly has the same opportunity as every other person, why do we need such things as affirmative action laws?

Ideology as a Facilitator of Change.   If ideology impedes change, it can also be used to facilitate change. Many changes in the United States are related to the ideology that technology will resolve all of our problems. Ideology has also facilitated action in social movements. In the women's movement, the ideology of female–male equality has led to the demand for female participation in areas formerly believed to be appropriate only for males. Women have entered the military academies, become a part of construction crews, and opted for careers in engineering—all considered unsuitable for women only a few years ago. Similarly, homosexuals have "come out" in large numbers and have begun to win such rights as the adoption of children in some states. The pursuit of these rights was stimulated by the ideology that gays and lesbians are as normal as anyone else and deserve, therefore, the same rights as heterosexuals.

The Role of Competition and Conflict in Change

Competition and conflict have stimulated so much change that some sociologists would argue that all change is the result of these two forms of interaction. Although this view overstates the case, it is true that they are fundamental and pervasive aspects of social change.

Competition.   The importance of competition in change is well illustrated by the progress of science. While science is supposed to be governed by the norms of sharing, cooperation, and openness, in reality, fierce competition is more typical. For instance, three researchers won the 1977 Nobel Prize in physiology or medicine for their research on the role of hormones in the chemistry of the body. Two of the men—Roger Guillemin and Andrew Schally—were bitter enemies (Wade, 1981). At one time they were colleagues, but each formed his own team and set out to win the prize. In the course of the race, the two scientists often ignored the norms that supposedly govern science. For instance, they tried to avoid acknowledging each other's work. Guillemin left out Schally's work when he wrote review articles. Schally told members of his team not to talk to "the enemy." The two researchers even refused to report some of their advances at scientific meetings for fear that the other might pick up on the information and jump ahead in the race. Ultimately, they had to share the prize for discovering and characterizing the hormones that the brain uses to control various bodily functions. Their rivalry was intense, leading them to work fiercely toward the goal. For our analysis, the important point is that the goal was achieved, and that the competition facilitated the achievement by impelling the scientists to intensive work.

Conflict. Conflict is a potent factor in change at all levels of life, including in organizations, communities, and whole societies. The conflict between workers and management, between ideological factions in communities and the nation, between individuals who dislike each other in an organization, between representatives of various social institutions such as religion and government—all are examples of the multitude of different conflicts that pervade societies.

The changes resulting from the conflict between students and college and university administrators in the 1960s illustrates the kind of shifts that can occur in organizations as a result of conflict (Kriesberg, 1982, pp. 248–249). The conflicts were ideologically based and centered on diverse goals. One conflict, for instance, focused on the role of the schools in national and local matters. Liberal and left-wing students protested such things as the contribution of university research to war generally and to the war in Vietnam in particular; the investments made by colleges and universities in corporations that students defined as exploiting the poor or contributing to international tensions and exploitation of Third World nations and the expansion of school property that resulted in a displacement of the poor. Students and administrators also had conflict over such academic matters as the relevance of certain subjects for study and over such practical matters as dormitory rules.

The conflicts produced significant changes in a number of areas of college life. Rules about dormitory living were liberalized throughout the country, including the broadening or elimination of rules about curfews, drinking, and entertaining members of the opposite sex in dormitory rooms. There were curriculum changes, with many schools instituting programs of black studies and women's studies. Grade inflation occurred, and many schools gave students more pass–fail options for courses in lieu of grades. Some schools even ended their research affiliation with the military. Finally, as noted above, administrators in many schools agreed to student participation in the decision-making process. By the end of the 1970s, a survey of colleges and universities showed that students participated on the boards of trustees for 20 percent of the schools and on faculty curriculum committees in 58 percent of the schools (Kriesberg, 1982, pp. 248).

Many of those changes have been reversed as a new generation of students showed less interest in participating in the administration of their schools, and administrators did nothing to encourage continued participation. By the late 1980s, students may have realized what they had lost, for conflict reemerged as students on campuses around the nation sought to convince their trustees and administrators to withdraw investments in South African enterprises (Hirsch, 1990). Many students felt morally outraged by the fact that they attended schools that supported apartheid through investments, but they often discovered that they had little or no official influence.

Collective Behavior and Social Change

Collective behavior is behavior expressed as part of a collectivity (such as a crowd), focused on a particular phenomenon or event (such as a concert or fight), in a situation of relative change, conflict, or uncertainty. Below we look at four types of collective behavior: crowds, rumors, disasters, and social movements.

Crowds

Turner and Killian (1972) distinguish among acting, expressive, diffuse, and conventionalized crowds. An **acting crowd** is a large number of people who are attempting to change something in their environment. A riot is an example (Turner, 1994). The bloody 1992 riot in Los Angeles is only the most recent of a long history of American riots. In 1991, a riot broke out in Washington, D.C. when a citizen was wounded by a police officer. The riot was attributed to the fact that the Hispanic community felt it did not have a say in the largely black D.C. government. In 1980, blacks in Miami rioted for three days after an all-white jury acquitted four white policemen in the beating death of a black businessman (Ladner, Schwartz, Roker, and Titterud, 1981). Over two-thirds of the participants who were surveyed said that they believed the riots would get people to pay more attention to the needs of the black community, and nearly half said that the riots would somehow make things better for the community. More generally, rioters hope to change their economic and political situation by dramatizing the extent of their grievances.

An **expressive crowd** is one in which there are intense displays of feelings and emotions, often accompanied by some kind of exuberant physical behavior. A religious revival meeting may become an expressive crowd when the members of a congregation engage in spontaneous singing, shouting, speaking in tongues, waving arms, and moving the body rhythmically. The fans at concerts often become expressive crowds when the music brings them to their feet in a frenzy of dancing, clapping, and singing.

A **diffuse crowd** is composed of dispersed individuals who follow a particular kind of behavior or experience a particular sentiment. Fads and crazes are forms of the diffuse crowd. Numerous fads and crazes of all kinds dot U.S. history, including an infatuation with certain games (Nintendo), with celebrities (the "mania" over the Beatles and some contemporary rock stars such as Michael Jackson and Madonna), with physical activities (piano-wrecking or running), with magical schemes (chain letters), and with daredevil activities (skateboarding). Fads occur in the arts and sciences as well as in everyday affairs. Experts in childrearing at times have extolled the virtues of breastfeeding infants and at other times have lauded the superiority of bottle-feeding.

Finally, the **conventionalized crowd** is a collectivity gathered for a particular purpose and acting in accord with established norms. The people in the conventionalized crowd expect to experience mutual influence; they are not merely an assemblage of isolated individuals. A theater audience and fans at a sporting event are examples of conventionalized crowds. The fact that they are not merely a gathering of isolated individuals is underscored by such things as rhythmic clapping and chanting.

Emergent norm theory suggests that, when collective behavior such as crowds occurs, new norms, social relationships, communications patterns, and values often emerge, especially in response to unforeseen events. In other words, collective behavior is not just random, uncontrolled behavior; instead, it has some degree of social organization (Aguirre et al., 1988).

One tragedy involving a conventionalized crowd that panicked provides support for the emergent norm theory. In 1979, 11 people were killed as they tried to enter a rock concert. The British rock group The Who was scheduled to perform at a stadium in Cincinnati. As crowds massed outside the gates, attempting entry, many people closest to the entry points were crushed. In contrast to widespread interpretations by the mass media that this event was the result of unregulated, callous competition by young "barbarians" for good seats, Johnson (1987a, 1987b) found little evidence to support this interpretation. Instead, Johnson's study found many reports of people trying to help others endangered by the crush. They were not indifferent; they were physically unable to help. In addition, the study found that traditional gender-role behavior remained in effect as men took the lead in trying to help those in danger. Johnson's study also found that most members of the crowd were part of small, primary groups following established norms and values. Thus, Johnson concludes that, as emergent norm theory suggests, the social structure did not break down in Cincinnati.

Rumor

A **rumor** is unverified information that diffuses through a collectivity as a result of people's attempts to understand something. People need to make sense of their world. But many aspects of life are ambiguous, and the evidence is not clearly available for a meaningful interpretation. Rumors provide the information necessary for understanding. Thus, a rumor is a form of problem solving.

Rumors are likely to appear, then, whenever people lack the information necessary to make sense out of something. For instance, why does a young woman at work suddenly appear so cheerful? If nothing about her life circumstances suggests an answer, a rumor could resolve the issue—she knows that she is getting the job for which two other people in the office have applied. Or, to take an incident from the news, what is the meaning of the well-known Procter & Gamble logo, the human face in the quarter moon looking out at thirteen stars? Why would a soap company select such a logo? In 1980, a rumor began to circulate that answered the question—the symbol is satanic. Moreover, the rumor claimed that Procter & Gamble executives had admitted on television programs that they supported devil worship. Fundamentalist religious groups began to call for a boycott of all Procter & Gamble products. The company took the rumor and the boycott threats seriously, publicly denying any connection with Satan worship and filing defamation suits against three people known to have helped spread the rumor. Actually, there never were any executives on television discussing the logo, and the logo itself dates back to 1852. The thirteen stars symbolized the original thirteen colonies, and the face in the moon was simply a popular image at the time. Lacking such information, many people accepted the rumor as truth.

Thus, one of the important functions of a rumor is to reduce ambiguity, to make sense out of the world or some part of the world. As such, rumors can reduce anxiety because a world that cannot be understood is a threatening world. Rumors also legitimate and motivate certain kinds of behavior. The Procter & Gamble rumor led some fundamentalists to boycott the products. Race riots in the United States have frequently crystallized around, or been fanned by, rumors (Rosnow and Fine, 1976). When leaders of a movement are jailed, rumors of mistreatment may lead people to take action of various kinds. In an organization, rumors may circulate of an impending "shake-up," leading people to act to protect their own positions. Such rumors may be true or false. In either case, they help people make sense out of their situation and lead them to act accordingly.

Disasters

Much of the research on collective behavior in recent decades has focused on disasters (Kreps, 1989). A disaster may be a natural phenomenon, such as a flood or earthquake, or the result of human action and activity, such as a fire or an airplane crash. Research has shown that there are some common misconceptions about disasters (Wenger, Dykes, Sebok, and Neff, 1975). First, many people believe that disasters almost always create panic and flight. Actually, such behavior is rare. Disasters are more likely to involve convergence behavior—people converge toward the disaster. Some are residents who fled when the disaster first occurred, some are anxious friends or relatives, some are curious or desirous of helping, and some want to exploit the situation.

A second false belief is that looting typically occurs. Frequently rumors of looting spread widely, and police and National Guard often are called on to prevent looting (again, the rumor leads to the behavior). But verified cases of actual looting are limited.

Cross-national Perspectives

Disasters in Florida and Bangladesh: A Comparison

Disasters recur with great regularity. By the time you read this brief essay, new disasters will almost certainly have befallen various parts of the world. The goal here is to compare the effects of, and responses to, two recent disasters in very different parts of the world—a hurricane (Andrew) that buffeted the southern part of Florida in the United States on August 24, 1992, and a cyclone that struck Bangladesh on April 30, 1991.

The Florida hurricane hit with sustained winds of 140 miles per hour. As one journalist put it, "Modern America has never seen a natural disaster like Hurricane Andrew" (Booth, 1992a). Then-president Bush said it may have been "the worst natural disaster this country has ever seen" (Jordan, 1992, A18). An area of 165 square miles, the size of eight Manhattan Islands, was the most adversely affected. Whole towns, such as Florida City with a population of about 6000 people, were leveled. Forty-one deaths were attributed to the storm. Overall, the hurricane destroyed 85,000 homes and caused $30 billion in property damage. Approximately 250,000 people were displaced from their homes (Navarro, 1995). Many people were hurled back into the Stone Age, foraging for whatever food and water they could find. People were forced to live outside or in tents. They complained of dead animals littering the streets; of an invasion of flies, rats, and snakes; of looters; and of the lack of air conditioning and ice cubes because of the absence of electricity. Said one woman, "We can't stand this heat any longer.... The heat is killing us. My husband had open-heart surgery. I had a heart attack in November. We can't take this" (Booth, 1992a, p. A18).

In the immediate aftermath of the hurricane, there were criticisms about the lack of response from the federal government. Three days after the hurricane struck, the director of emergency management services in one of the affected counties said, near tears, "'Where the hell is the cavalry on this one?'" (Lippman, 1992, p. A21). President Bush, in the midst of a presidential campaign and fearful of being criticized for mishandling the crisis, finally reacted, and the next day the first of 7000 troops were on their way to the disaster site. By the following day, many more troops were dispatched, helping to bring the eventual total to about 20,000.

Four months later, the area was still described as resembling the "Third World" or an "undeveloped world," with tens of thousands still homeless and sleeping in tents or cars or in their gutted houses (Booth, 1992b). Even two years later, in addition to the thousands of homes that have yet to be rebuilt, many other reminders of Hurricane Andrew remain: shattered buildings and signs, businesses that never reopened, houses still with spray-painted signs asking for help from the insurance companies, and people who are still unable to move out of federal trailer parks and back to their homes (Silver, 1994).

Lest we think that Florida moved quickly to be able to deal better with hurricane disasters, a fierce hurricane season in 1995 revealed the following problems: an insurance market that is still in crisis in the wake of Hurricane Andrew (several companies went bankrupt and others' rates increased dramatically), poorly constructed buildings, the continued increase in population in the coastal areas most prone to hurricane damage, which makes evacuation more difficult and increases insurance risk, and continued problems in disaster planning (Navarro, 1995).

While the Florida hurricane was certainly a disaster, it hardly compares to the disaster that struck a "real" Third World country—the 1991 Bangladesh cyclone in which over 138,000 people were killed and perhaps 10 million (!) people were left homeless (Ahmed, 1995; Crossette, 1991). The cyclone hit with slightly more force (145 miles per hour) than the Florida hurricane and was accompanied by devastating, 18-foot waves that hit an area that is barely above the sea level. Here is the way an aid worker for CARE described the scene:

> It's as though the whole country was a sandcastle and a huge wave just washed it away.... Whole villages are gone. Bridges are wiped out. Bodies are everywhere.... Islands that used to be inhabited are now devoid of life.... They're just under water (Drogin, 1991, p. A1).

As bad as this may seem, such cyclones are not unusual in Bangladesh. In fact, the country has been hit by six cyclones in the last three decades. Furthermore, this last cyclone was far from the worst. A 1970 cyclone killed 300,000 people.

The cyclone hit a desperately poor nation ill-equipped to handle a disaster of that magnitude. For example, compare the response to the Florida hurricane with the fact that the entire nation of Bangladesh had only six functioning helicopters at its disposal to respond to the crisis. Television and radio stations in and around Miami undoubtedly have more helicopters than the nation of Bangladesh. The extreme poverty of the people before the hurricane meant that a far larger proportion of them, as compared to the Floridians who experienced the hurricane, were not going to survive the disaster and its aftermath, which included wide-scale destruction of crops that were ready to be harvested. Farther down the road are the consequences of the fact that land flooded with salt water may be unworkable for 2 to 3 years. Also adversely affecting the future food supply was the fact that shrimp farms and fishing fleets were destroyed. Homes, schools, and hospitals were demolished, leaving large numbers of people vulnerable to the elements of a country noted for its hot and humid climate. Victims of this disaster, unlike their counterparts in Florida, are unlikely to complain about the absence of air conditioning and ice cubes since they undoubtedly didn't have either of them in the first place. Some storm shelters have been built in the years after the storm, and some volunteers have been recruited to warn people of impending storms, but the efforts seem meager, especially if Bangladesh should experience a cyclone of the magnitude that hit in 1991.

While the intent here is not to denigrate the hardships caused by the Florida hurricane, it is clear that its effects were minuscule when compared with the impact of the Bangladesh cyclone. Furthermore, the smaller Florida hurricane was met with a massive federal response, while the capacity of the Bangladesh government to react was puny by comparison. The victims of the Bangladesh cyclone were, in the main, left as they had been for decades to cope as best they could with the devastation. And as has also been true for decades, many were unable to cope, and they died as a result. Natural disasters cannot be avoided, but the wealth of a nation is a big factor in its ability to respond to and cope with such disasters.

AHMED, ANIS. "Bangladesh Tries to Learn from 1991 Disaster." *Reuters,* April 30, 1995.

BOOTH, WILLIAM. "Hurricane's Fury Left 165 Square Miles Pounded into the Ground." *Washington Post,* August 30, 1992.

BOOTH, WILLIAM. "After Andrew, a Trail of Squalor." *Washington Post,* December 13, 1992.

CROSSETTE, BARBARA. "Bangladesh Reports Toll from Storm near 40,000; Says It May Exceed 100,000." *New York Times,* May 3, 1991.

DROGIN, BOB. "New Storms Slow Aid to Bangladesh." *Los Angeles Times,* May 4, 1991.

JORDAN, MARY. "As Life Resumes, Protecting What's Left and Wondering Why." *Washington Post,* August 30, 1992.

KERR, PETER, "Survey Doubles Hurricane Loss Estimate." *Washington Post,* December 12, 1992.

LIPPMAN, THOMAS W. "Hurricane May Have Exposed Flaws in New Disaster Relief Plan." *Washington Post,* September 3, 1992.

NAVARRO, MIREYA. "Fierce Hurricane Season Exposes Florida's Flaws." *Commercial Appeal* (Memphis), October 15, 1995.

SILVER, VERNON. "Two Years after Hurricane, Reminders and Renewal in South Florida." *New York Times,* November 26, 1994.

Washington Post. "$500 Million Tax Fund for Relief, Insurance Bailout Approved." December 13, 1992.

Third, most people believe that citizens will readily evacuate an area when warned about an impending disaster (such as a flood or hurricane). The people most likely to leave, however, are transients and visitors. Residents tend to stay, and some refuse to leave until they are forced by authorities.

Finally, most people believe that victims are in a state of shock, unable to fend for themselves immediately after the disaster occurs. But with a few exceptions, various needs are cared for and services provided by the victims themselves with some assistance from others in the immediate vicinity. Overall, people are more likely to deal with disasters rationally than irrationally (Kreps, 1984).

Mileti and O'Brien (1992) have studied the way people reacted to the 1989 earthquakes that struck California, specifically the cities of San Francisco and Santa Cruz. The focus of concern was what people did after the main shock and after they were warned that there would be damaging aftershocks. San Francisco had less damage from the original shock than Santa Cruz, but it elicited more media coverage, largely because the media were there to cover the World Series. Santa Cruz had more damage but attracted far less media attention. The issue of concern is the relationship between these two factors, amount of damage and media attention, and public response to the warnings about aftershocks.

The main finding of the study was that, although the vast majority of those studied in both cities heard warnings about the aftershocks from the media, the residents of Santa Cruz were more likely to believe that an aftershock would cause additional injury, and they perceived an aftershock to be a greater risk. More importantly, they were far more likely than San Franciscans to take various actions, such as making household items safer, developing emergency plans, and making their dwellings more structurally sound. Thus, while the influence of the media is important, it is actual exposure to the damage of earthquakes that is likely to alter peoples' perceptions and to lead them to take preventive action.

What are the consequences of disasters? They may bring about both short- and long-term change. The short-term change is likely to be disruption of various kinds. Long-term consequences may be either positive or negative. Research into the effects of a 1974 tornado that killed 33 and injured 1200 in Xenia, Ohio, reported that some of the survivors discovered that they had more internal resources than they realized (Taylor, 1977). They handled the crisis well, and their self-esteem was enhanced. On the other hand, a study of those caught in a 1972 flood in a Pennsylvania town showed that after five years the disaster victims, compared to people in nearby towns that had not flooded, had a greater incidence of various kinds of physical illness and more problems of emotional health (Logue et al., 1981).

Social Movements

Social movements are a key type of collective behavior. By definition, they are integrally tied to change because they are collective efforts to resist or to bring about some kind of change. We focus here on the way social movements intersect with social change.

Why are social movements important? As individuals, we are limited in our ability to make the societal changes we would like. There are massive social forces that make change difficult; these forces include the government, large and powerful organizations, and the prevailing values, norms, and attitudes. As individuals going to the voting booth, we have minimal power. As individuals protesting to officials, we have minimal power. As individuals standing against the tide of public opinion, we have little hope of exerting influence. As individuals confronting a corporate structure, we are doomed to frustration and failure. But if we combine with others who share our convictions, organize ourselves, and map out a course of action, we may be able to bring about numerous and significant changes in the social order. Through participation in a social movement, we can break through the social constraints that overwhelm us as individuals.

Types of Social Movements. Sociologists have classified four different types of social movements according to their relationship to social change: *revolutionary, regressive, reform,* and *expressive* (Rush and Denisoff, 1971). A **revolutionary movement** is an attempt to create a new social order. It aims at radical change, though not always by radical methods. Some radical groups see the violent overthrow of the government as the only realistic way to bring about the changes they desire. Libertarians in the United States, on the other hand, advocate laissez-faire capitalism and stress the efficacy of educating people to accept their ideology. Once the ideology is accepted, they argue, people will act on it to change the society accordingly (Lauer, 1976). In any case, a revolutionary movement always seeks to alter the power structure of the society.

Jack Goldstone (1992; 1993) has recently suggested a *process* model of revolutions. There is no single cause of a revolution; several factors are often involved. One factor that frequently exists is a series of popular grievances. People do not usually set out to start a revolution. Rather, they are interested in expressing their dissatisfaction with various things and seeking changes in the sources of their grievances. Thus, the peasants who supported the French Revolution did not want to overthrow the monarchy, but merely wanted more land at lower cost. Another element is the fact that revolutions tend to be led by elite individuals and groups, that is, those who already have high status and much power. For example, it was disenchanted nobles who took the lead in the French Revolution. Still another factor is the political and economic strength of the state. Those states that are weak in both areas are most vulnerable to revolution. For example, in the late 1980s the Soviet Union and its allies in Eastern Europe were bad off economically and lacked popular political support. As a result, they were highly vulnerable to the revolutions that dismantled their communist regimes. Finally, international pressures often affect revolutions. For example, when the Soviet Union reduced its military presence in Eastern Europe in 1989, revolutions ensued.

Once a revolution occurs, it is a process that may encompass several different stages. The most obvious is an outbreak of widespread violence, although revolutions can occur with little or no violence. Another element is the building of a revolutionary coalition. Various groups may be opposed to the government for very different reasons. A key to the success of a revolution is that they be able to put aside their differences and cooperate with one another to overthrow the government. If they are unable to do that, internal differences and squabbling may doom a revolution. Another key element in the revolutionary process is the development of an ideology, a simple set of ideas, around which revolutionaries can rally. For example, "forging an Islamic Republic" was an ideological rallying cry during the Iranian Revolution. Finally, the wars that often result from revolutions frequently lead to large numbers of casualties. Furthermore, if a revolutionary group is victorious, it often engages in state terror against its opponents that leads to additional casualties.

What of the outcomes of revolutions? First, new revolutionary governments are generally stronger politically than their predecessors because they are likely to enjoy the support of much of the population. Second, the population is likely to be instilled with a great deal of national pride in the revolution and its results. Third, revolutions have generally been less successful in resolving the economic (for example, the need for economic expansion) and political (for example, the need to reduce inequality) problems that led to their development in the first place. This makes them vulnerable to later revolutionary movements. Fourth, while revolutions generally promise democracy, they often fail to deliver. This failure is generally caused by the need to militarize and retain centralized control to fight off counterrevolutionary forces. The result is that, instead of democracy, revolutions often lead to dictatorships or one-party states. Finally, one of the most unfortunate aspects of most revolutions is the massive numbers of refugees who, as a result of the revolution, are forced to flee a country or who find themselves in hideous refugee camps.

Thus, revolutions often create as many, or more, problems than they solve. However, they persist because the underlying causes remain and because new revolutionaries continue to believe that *their* revolution will be different.

A **regressive movement** attempts to restore a past or passing social order on the grounds that the past order is preferable to any other. For example, the long-standing battle over the teaching of evolution in the schools took on new intensity in the 1980s. The battle arrayed those who stood for "scientific creationism" against those who affirmed evolution. The former argued that the Book of Genesis gives an adequate account of the beginning of the world, that the universe is no more than roughly 7000 to 10,000 years old, and that the action of God rather than some impersonal evolutionary process is responsible for the existence of the world as we know it. Those who supported evolutionary theory, itself diverse, accepted the idea of a slow process of change requiring billions of years for the world to reach its present stage. The evolutionary process involved the gradual emergence of humans from lower forms of life. Creationists wanted textbooks to reflect their view, or at least to give it equal weight with evolutionary theory.

In 1980, creationists were able to influence eleven state legislatures to consider bills that would require the teaching of scientific creationism in any biology class where evolution was taught. Texas had already established laws in 1974 that set guidelines for the content of textbooks, which made the teaching of evolution difficult. In 1981, Arkansas passed a law that required equal time for the two perspectives. Creationists also were able to persuade some textbook publishers to modify the way their books treated evolution and the age of the earth. But a series of court cases defeated the antievolutionists. A 1981 California court ruling held that the teaching of evolution without giving any attention to creationism did not infringe on the right of freedom of religion. The Arkansas law was ruled unconstitutional in 1982. In 1984, Texas repealed its antievolution textbook selection rules. In 1985, an appeals court upheld a ruling against Louisiana's "balanced treatment" approach to the issue. The creationist movement had been soundly defeated, but its members continue their efforts to restore a past social order.

Reform movements aim at alterations in the existing order to make it more acceptable. Typically, reform movements seek to make the existing order more effective or more equitable for more people. That may mean extending certain rights to people to whom they have been denied (such as occupational opportunities for women or equal housing and job opportunities for minorities). New legislation, rather than a radically altered power structure, may suffice to bring about such changes. Various AIDS groups may be thought of as reform movements seeking, among other things, greater access to treatment facilities and available drugs and a larger investment of time and money in AIDS research (Gamson, 1989).

Expressive movements seek to change individuals, who will then either change the social order or adapt better to the existing order. Religious movements exemplify the expressive social movement. One movement is the charismatic or Pentecostal movement, stressing the experience of "speaking in tongues." Those who have the experience, according to the ideology of the movement, have a supreme spiritual experience as well as concrete evidence of the presence of the Holy Spirit. The movement tends to operate independently of established churches, but has secured the commitment of many members of those churches.

Sociological Approaches to Social Movements

We can identify three broad sociological approaches to the study of social movements, especially to the relationship between social problems and social movements. The first is the **grievance approach,** which sees social problems as objective facts that give rise to social movements (Koopmans and Duyvendak, 1995). For example, a nuclear accident like the one at Chernobyl in 1986 would have been expected to lead to antinuclear social movements, especially in the nations affected by the disaster. Koopmans and Duyvendak sought to ascertain whether, in fact, this was the case. They found that, while there were no substantial differences in the degree to which Western European nations were affected by Chernobyl, there were great differences in the degree of reaction to the disaster. Clearly, objective grievances alone cannot account for the rise of social movements.

The second broad approach is **social constructivism** (Miller and Holstein, 1993). The focus here is not on objective issues or grievances, but the way in which they come to be defined as problems that people ought to mobilize to do something about. Of central importance is not only the way that people, but also social movements, define and construct social problems. And key to this is the "framing" process (Snow et al., 1986; Jenness, 1995). Social movements attempt to frame social conditions; that is, they assign meaning to them and interpret them. The goal of such framing is to incite social change by, among other things, mobilizing people to become involved in the social movement. For example, "environmental justice" is such a frame and it has been used, among other places, to lead a local community to mobilize against toxic contamination (Capek, 1993). Thus, social constructivism in general and more specifically "frame analysis" focus on cognitive processes, not objective conditions. The concern is with the cognition of individuals, the way in which social movements frame social problems, as well as with the process by which the two are brought into alignment. In terms of the latter, the goal of a social movement is to get people to see things the way the movement does.

A third approach focuses not on problems or their definition, but on the objective capacities of the social movement and its organization. The best known of these approaches focuses on what is known as resource mobilization (Jenkins, 1983). **Resource mobilization** refers to the idea that protest movements form not so much because of grievances or social constructions, but in response to available resources and the effective mobilization of these resources (Gerhards and Rucht, 1992; Khawaja, 1994). Grievances, deprivation, and definitions are usually sufficient to allow some groups to engage in protests. However, for an actual social movement to arise, adequate resources must be available, as well as an organization (Staggenborg, 1989) and leadership to exploit those resources.

Three resources are particularly worthy of note—*members,* a *communication network,* and *leaders* (McAdam, McCarthy, and Zald, 1988). All social movements need members and usually recruit them through established lines of interaction. Second, social movements need a communication network to succeed. For example, the women's movement was aided by a communication network consisting of women involved in the Presidential and State Commissions on the Status of Women, established under President John F. Kennedy, and feminists working within the Equal Employment Opportunity Commission (Freeman, 1983). Well aware of the inequities that they and other women faced, these women had contact with each other through their participation in the governmental organizations. Third, the leaders are usually drawn from preexisting groups.

Other resources may also be important, such as support from well-to-do people, and institutional resources obtained from government agencies, private foundations, the mass media, and corporations (McCarthy and Zald, 1977). Resources may also be mobilized through the actions of professionals who, as part of their mobilization efforts, may aim to raise the consciousness of people to develop a clientele. The environmental and consumer rights movements, for example, were developed largely by professional organizers who educated people on the necessity of the movements.

Kleidman (1994) has recently studied the impact of paid professionals on three major peace campaigns. He found that, while such professionals can play a positive role by facilitating volunteer activism, they can also serve to reduce that activism and even become a substitute for it. Of central importance are the resources available to them as well as their values and strategies. One-time activists, still interested in promoting grass-roots activism, make particularly good professional leaders of such social movements.

Rosenfeld and Ward have supplemented resource mobilization theory with competition theory to explain the rise of the women's movement. The basic premise of *competition theory* is that the success of a social movement is based on its ability to compete "for scarce resources in the same environment" in which other movements are found (Rosenfeld and Ward, 1991, p. 472; Estenberg, 1994). And the ability of a social movement to compete successfully is, in turn, based on its capacity to mobilize organizational resources.

The basic thesis of the Rosenfeld and Ward study is that, as women began to compete with men, at least some of them began to organize around their identity as women. As the competition increased, so did these organizations and, as a result, the women's movement in general grew. They found that, after World War II, women, impelled by various demographic changes (for example, changes in women's family position, which pushed them into the labor force in greater numbers), began competing with men to a larger extent in the occupational and educational sectors. This competition was supplemented at the organizational level by the growth of, and increasing competition with, antifeminist organizations. While social movements are often in conflict with one another, there are also times when they complement one another. That is, the success of one aids another. For example, the experience obtained and networks developed by the civil rights and peace movements were of great help to the development of the women's movement. These complementary relationships, but more importantly the competition mentioned above, "led to increases in the numbers of people holding attitudes favoring sex equality, in membership of organizations associated with the women's movement, and in frequency of demonstrations and meetings" (Rosenfeld and Ward, 1991, p. 496). In other words, competition played a key role in the rise of the women's movement.

Organizations are usually treated as entities that help people involved in a social movement attain their objectives. That is, preexisting organizations provide those involved with needed resources and solidarity. However, Conell and Voss (1990) have shown that a preexisting organization can also serve as an impediment to the achievement of the goals of a social movement. For example, a preexisting organization could serve to reinforce old identities while the existing situation requires that those involved develop new identities. More generally, organizations and other social phenomena that might be resources in one context can turn out to be impediments to a social movement in another context.

While social movement organizations are often in competition with one another, they can also cooperate in various ways and also have positive effects on one another [although that is not always easy, as Lichterman (1995) has shown]. Meyer and Whittier (1994) examined the relationship between the peace movement of the 1980s and the modern women's movement with its roots in the 1970s. They found that the women's movement had a variety of positive influences on the peace movement (and the latter had its beneficial influences on the former), including the adoption of some its ideologies (for example, seeing the arms race as linked to patriarchy), use of some of its tactics (for example, "peace camps"), the accession of women to leadership positions within the peace movement, and the development of organizational structures that, among other things, sought to minimize hierarchical differences. These positive effects came about as a result of such things as coalitions between organizations and the sharing of personnel. Thus, it would be a mistake to take the position that competition alone defines the relationship between social movements.

As in the case of the peace movement, new recruits can come from preexisting social networks, but it is also necessary for social movements to recruit outsiders. Jasper and Poulsen (1995) have found that what they call "moral shocks" were important in the recruitment of people to the animal rights movement. Said one activist,

> But I went by a table one day and saw these terrifying pictures. *That's* what goes on inside our country's best, most scientific labs? There was a tabby [cat] that looked just like mine, but instead of a skull it had some kind of electrodes planted in its head. . . . I decided, that's gotta stop (Jasper and Poulsen, 1995, p. 506).

Michaelson (1994) argues that we have tended to focus on movements that engage in conflict not only with other social movements, but also with the larger environment. He argues that we have tended to ignore "consensus movements," that is, organizations that experience widespread support and scant, if any, organized opposition. He uses Kenya's Green Belt Movement (GBM) to illustrate the idea of a consensus movement. With roots in the late 1960s and early 1970s, GBM has as its broad goals the protection and improvement of the natural environment and improving human skills and self-images, especially among women. Thus, because it focused on social and environmental issues *and* it had no overt political agenda, it was able to avoid open confrontation and conflict with a repressive political regime, at least in its early years. As a result of its nonconfrontational approach, GBM was able to increase tree growing in an effort to ward off desertification and to help to increase the income of people. It also served to empower many Kenyans and to give them greater self-confidence and social consciousness.

Approaches to the Study of International Social Change

Over the years, sociologists have adopted a number of different approaches to the study of change at the international level. One approach is **modernization theory,** which focuses on the degree to which developing countries follow the model of the West—the degree to which they have become Westernized (Tiryakian, 1991). Westernization generally means industrialization, as well as the adoption of Western social and cultural innovations (Harper, 1989). In recent years, modernization theory has come under attack, primarily because of its ethnocentric bias that Western practices ought to be followed by the rest of the world.

For a time, modernization theory was superseded by **development theory,** which may be defined as a general process of economic growth (in production, consumption, per capita income, and so on), but it does not necessarily mean that manufacturing industries must be emphasized. Economic development can be spearheaded by advances in mining, fishing, or agriculture. Emphasis lies not just on improvement in material well-being but also in the quality of people's lives. Societies can grow larger and more complex without copying the Western model. Saudi Arabia is a good example of a country that has developed substantially *without* following the West.

Among the earliest critics of modernization theory were those who accepted dependency theory (Frank, 1969). According to **dependency theory,** the developed countries did not represent the salvation of developing countries but were instead the *cause* of their underdevelopment. The West had grown rich on the basis of its exploitation of poor nations; its development required the underdevelopment of other nations. Modernization theory led developing countries to seek internal changes (for example, to develop manufacturing), but the real changes, according to dependency theory, had to be made in the relationships between developing and developed nations. Dependency theory was a forerunner to world-system theory.

World-system Theory

World-system theory is an attempt to comprehend contemporary processes of development and underdevelopment (Wallerstein, 1974, 1979, 1980, 1989). Using the entire world as the unit of analysis, **world-system theory** stresses the economic and power inequalities of the present international order. The world is viewed as a stratified system shaped by the world economy. In a geographical division of labor within the world economy, certain nations exploit the labor of others. In the core (richer) nations, free labor engages largely in skilled labor. In the peripheral (poorer) nations, there exists a preponderance of coerced and unskilled labor. Since the core nations are the major benefactors of the cheap goods and materials produced by the laborers in the poor nations, the situation is essentially one of exploitation.

World-system theorists argue that the gap between the rich and the poor nations is growing. A minority of the world's people are living well at the expense of the majority. How can such a system be maintained? Wallerstein identifies three mechanisms. The superior military power of the core nations minimizes the probability of a forceful alteration of the system by the poorer nations. Moreover, leaders of both rich and poor nations have an ideological commitment to the system; most leaders try to convince their people that progress can be made by working within the system rather than by rebelling against it and trying to establish a different system. Finally, a group of nations is midway in terms of affluence between the core and the periphery—the semiperiphery. The semiperiphery has a function similar to the middle class within a nation—symbolizing to the poorer nations the possibility of progress. It appears to demonstrate that the world situation is not simply one of an impervious core and a relatively powerless and exploited periphery. The existence of such a middle group, therefore, keeps the world from being polarized into two camps which could, ultimately, lead to the rebellion of the periphery and a worldwide war that would force alterations in the system.

A substantial amount of research supports world-system theory (Borg, 1992; Smith and White, 1992). The research underscores the significance of such things as world trade patterns and multinational corporations in constraining the development of the poorer nations. Essentially, the development of the poorer nations is tied up with processes in advanced capitalist societies. Changes have occurred in the economies of the developing nations like Venezuela over time, but those changes can be understood only in terms of the nation's linkage with the world capitalist economy (Roseberry, 1983).

Not only are the economies of the poorer nations dependent upon policies and practices of the rich nations, but the latter frequently work to the detriment of the former. For example, one factor that inhibits development in poorer countries is overurbanization—too heavy a concentration of the population in the urban areas and too much employment in service rather than manufacturing occupations. Both agriculture and industry suffer when there is overurbanization. Studies of the problem suggest that overurbanization is not simply the outcome of internal processes of a nation but is related to the nation's dependence on foreign capital (Timberlake and Kentor, 1983). The more a nation's economy depends on foreign capital, the more the nation tends to suffer from overurbanization. And as overurbanization increases, per capita economic growth tends to decline.

In the News

The "De-Development" of Zaire

When we think of development, we generally conceive of it as a one-way process—nations develop; they grow increasingly modern. However, it is possible for the process to go the other way, as is being demonstrated today in Zaire. Zaire is a large country; there are about 44 million people in an area about the size of the United States east of the Mississippi River. It has a wealth of natural resources, including diamonds, copper, and other minerals. And it has been the centerpiece of much strategic planning about the future of Africa. Its president, Mobutu Sese Seko, was once considered by the United States and other western nations to be one of the most important leaders in Africa (he used to be called simply "the Guide" by his people). His anti-Communism attracted western support and economic aid. However, he has now been in power for over 30 years, and his ability and honesty have come to be questioned by many. He is rarely in the capital city and shows little interest in helping the country to function better.

In spite of its many advantages, on a variety of dimensions life in Zaire seems to be regressing rather than progressing. Consider the following, for example:

- The jungle is retaking many of the roads.

- With the roads deteriorating, travel is coming once again to depend on what it always did—the rivers.

- Many buses don't run. Open trucks are often used to transport people, and it is not unusual for them to crash.

- Many phones don't work. They don't work because, according to the U.S. ambassador, at least in part "money to be used for maintenance has been stolen.... Instead of laying the cables, they stole the money" (Duke, 1996a, p. 40A) . Those who can afford them depend on cellular phones for communication.

- The national treasury is being looted by politicians. As much as two-thirds of the nation's currency in the early 1990s was counterfeit. Inflation is rampant, running at about 300 percent (Duke, 1996b).

- Education has collapsed in many places because, among other things, teachers have not been paid. To compensate, parents have had to start their own schools.

- Ambulances are scarce, and when a disaster like a plane crash occurs, victims have to be transported to hospitals by private automobile.

- Basic services and amenities are lacking.

- Life expectancy is about 47 years.

- AIDS represents an enormous health problem.

- The city of Kikwit recently experienced a serious outbreak of the dreaded Ebola virus.

- Fertility is high; women have, on average, six children. Thus, the population is booming as the standard of living is declining.

- So many officials are on the take that the nation has been called a "kleptocracy" (Duke, 1996a).

- The copper mines, which accounted for 70 percent of export earnings, are now producing less than a tenth of what they once did.

- The United States has halted all foreign aid to Zaire because of problems like those listed here and because the nation is so far behind in its payment of past loans.

Given these realities and the fact that on many fronts things seem to be growing worse, not better, it is likely that Zaire will continue on a path of de-development or de-modernization for many years to come.

DUKE, LYNNE. "Zairians Create New Coping Skills to Survive in Collapsed Country." *Dallas Morning News,* February 4, 1996.
DUKE, LYNNE. "Kinshasa, When the Sun Goes Down." *Washington Post,* February 5, 1996.
LIPPMANN, THOMAS. "GOP Activists Join Push for Mobutu Visa; Opponents Say Zairian Leader Wants U.S. Travel Ban Lifted to Sanitize Image, Boost Power." *Washington Post,* August 6, 1995.

Even foreign aid has done little to change the advantage of the developed nations. In fact, both investments and aid have frequently resulted in worsening some aspects of the situation in developing nations. Bornschier et al. (1978, p. 652) summarized the results of a number of studies based on data from 1950 to 1970 by saying, "foreign investment and aid have the long-term effect of decreasing the rate of economic growth and of increasing inequality."

World-system theory has recently been used to help explain the decline of the U.S. economy on the world scene (Smith and White, 1992; Boswell and Bergeson, 1987). The world system has two long-term characteristics. First, periods of economic boom are followed by periods of economic stagnation. Second, a cycle of the rise and fall of a core nation comes to dominate the world system. From this point of view, the problems of the U.S. economy are traceable to the fact that these two cycles are currently intersecting. That is, the world economy is stagnating *and* the United States is simultaneously losing its dominant position in the world economy to Japan and other nations.

World-system theory is derived from Marxian theory, but it has been criticized by Marxists for failing to emphasize the importance of social classes. To most Marxists the key issue is not the relationship between the core and the periphery but rather the relationship between social classes within given societies. A compromise position would be that *both* relationships between core and periphery *and* class relationships within society are of great importance (Bergeson, 1984). Others have criticized world-system theory for its oversimplification: reducing a complex world into a simplistic core–semiperiphery–periphery model.

Globalization Theory

World-system theory was a forerunner to what is now called globalization theory. Today, world-system theory is but one type of globalization theory. In fact, **globalization theory** has emerged as a central concern in sociology (Robertson, 1990, 1992; Featherstone, 1990; Waters, 1995). It is distinguished from the other theories discussed in this section by the fact that it does not give priority to any one nation or part of the world. While there are significant differences among globalization theorists, most if not all would accept the idea that sociologists should focus on the study of the world as a whole. This means a concern with global processes that operate more or less autonomously of processes that occur at the societal level.

Globalization theorists see the global order as defined by continuing struggles to gain control over at least part of it. There are many competitors for predominance, with the result that the global order is seen as being "up for grabs." There is little prospect of unity at the global level. While unity is unlikely, we are witnessing a process of "the compression of the world" and "the intensification of consciousness of the world as a whole" (Robertson, 1992, p. 8). That is, it seems to many that the world is growing smaller and more interrelated. Furthermore, more people are thinking about global issues. A rather distinctive aspect of the globalization process is the emergence of third cultures within the global system (Robertson, 1992). These are partially autonomous cultures that transcend national boundaries and exist on a global basis. Appadurai (1990) has identified several third cultures. For example, there is the global "finanscape" dealing with the "movement of megamonies through national turnstiles at blinding speed" (Appadurai, 1990, p. 298). Another is the "ethnoscape," involving the movement of large numbers of people around the world via tourism. And yet a third is the "technoscape," involving technologies that girdle the globe. All three, and others, are global processes that cut across national boundaries.

Unlike modernization, dependency, and world-system theorists, who tend to focus on economic and political factors, globalization theorists give special attention to cultural factors and to the emergence of a "global culture" (Robertson, 1992, p. 114). However, to Robertson (1992, p. 135), this global culture is not normatively binding on people around the world, but simply a "general mode of discourse about the world as a whole and its variety." A key aspect of global culture is the internationalization of consumption, or of the "consumer society" (Friedman, 1994). For example, eating is a central component of all cultures as well as of the consumer society. Thus, for example, the spread of fast-food restaurant chains around the world contributes to both a global culture and the internationalization of consumption.

The above represent some of the positive ideas that stand at the heart of globalization theory, but an even better way to get a handle on this theory is to focus on some of the things that it rejects:

1.   A focus on any single nation-state
2.   A focus on the West in general or the United States in particular, as well as on the impact of the West (Westernization) or the United States (Americanization) on the rest of the world
3.   A concern with homogenization (rather than heterogeneization)

Let us look at each of these.

1. The focus on the globe as the unit of analysis is generally coupled with a rejection of a focus on the nation-state (and related phenomena). This is a result of a sense, derived from the work of Emile Durkheim, of emergence, or the view that the globe is more than the sum of the parts, especially the nations, that make it up (Beyer, 1994, p. 14). Therefore, globalization theory involves a shift in the unit of sociological analysis from the nation to the globe. Put more negatively, the unit of analysis in globalization theory is not the nation, state, or region (Beyer, 1994, p. 2).

This change in the unit of analysis is sometimes seen as a result of the fact that there has been a historical shift, and the nation-state is no longer the major player on the globe (Smith, 1990, p. 174). This major social change is seen as leading to a shift in the main focus of sociology away from the society and to the globe (Archer, 1990, p. 133). Indeed, classical and contemporary sociology are often criticized for their near single-minded concern with the nation to the exclusion of an interest in global processes. Globalization theorists seem intent on righting this wrong by moving our focus away from the nation and to the globe. While globalization theorists may be right about a traditional imbalance in sociological concerns and the contemporary importance of global processes, that is not to say that the nation-state has ceased to be of great, if not paramount, importance in the contemporary world.

In a related, but more general, argument, Appadurai (1990, p. 301) contends that deterritorialization "is one of the central forces in the modern world." In such a deterritorialized world, "money, commodities and persons are involved in ceaselessly chasing each other around the world" (Appadurai, 1990, p. 303). Thus, the focus should be on these processes and *not* on a particular territory.

Sassen (1994), too, downplays the importance of the nation and focuses on transnational processes. However, she devotes special attention to what she calls "global cities," such as New York, Tokyo, London, Sao Paulo, and Hong Kong. While these cities exist in particular nations, they have more in common with each other than with other areas within their own nations. They have become transnational market spaces. **Global cities** have three basic characteristics; they are

(1) command points in the organization of the world economy;

(2) key locations and marketplaces for the leading industries of the current period, which are finance and specialized services for firms; and

(3) major sites of production for these industries, including the production of innovations (Sassen, 1994, p. 4).

While Sassen is concerned with these particular cities, she shares with globalization theorists an interest in transnational processes and the view that the nation-state is of declining importance.

While generally rejecting a focus on such units of analysis as territories and nations, globalization theorists *do,* in fact, have a great deal to say about territories and nation-states, but they tend to be *different* territories (like Sassen's world cities) and states than those of interest in traditional sociology. That is, to use the concepts of world-system theory, while traditionally sociologists have focused on "core" nations (and territories) and their impact on "peripheral" nations, globalization theorists are much more interested in peripheral nations and the way that they resist or modify what emanates from the core nations (Smart, 1994).

Thus, as even many globalization theorists implicitly acknowledge, the nation-state remains important today. However, it is certainly not just the peripheral nations that are of significance; core nations like the United States remain of great, if not overwhelming, importance. Thus, in their rush to focus on the globe, globalization theorists sometimes lose sight of the importance of nation states, *both* core *and* periphery.

2. Globalization theorists also reject a focus on the United States or the West in general, as well as on the processes of Americanization or Westernization (Robertson, 1992; Friedman, 1994). For example, there has in the past been a tendency to equate the consumer society with the United States and therefore to see the spread of consumerism as a manifestation of the growing global power of the United States. Relatedly, this universal consumer culture is seen as destroying local ways of consuming (Featherstone, 1991, p. 127). Instead, globalization theorists see a shift away from the dominance of the United States and the West. Globalization theorists not only reject a focus on the West, but also on the process of westernization (Pieterse, 1994, p. 163). Much thinking about international processes has, in the past, been biased in the direction of America and the west: Americanization and Westernization. Globalization theorists argue that such perspectives were misguided and ethnocentric.

Furthermore, even if globalization theorists are willing to admit (and they aren't) that Americanization and westernization adequately described the past, they argue that the world has changed, has become more "compressed" and increasingly subject to multidimensional and multidirectional processes. One key factor in all this is the growth of global telecommunications systems that allow information to move easily in all directions (Smith, 1990, p. 177). Another important factor has been the demise of communism. The result has been the breakdown of the global order dominated by the United States and the former Soviet Union. More generally, the result has been "declining centers of the world system" (Friedman, 1994, p. 99). Thus, from the point of view of globalization theorists, a focus on America and the West, or Americanization and westernization, would be both far too restrictive and out of touch with contemporary global realities.

3. In the past, the emphasis was on the degree to which the world was growing increasingly homogeneous. However, most globalization theorists argue that we are now witnessing far greater heterogeneization [what Featherstone (1991) calls the "globalization of diversity"] than homogenization. It may be better to think of the world as a global "melange" undergoing a process of hybridization. As examples of such hybridization, Pieterse (1994, p. 169) offers the following: "Thai boxing by Moroccan girls in Amsterdam, Asian rap in London, Irish bagels, Chinese tacos and Mardi Gras Indians in the United States." In fact, of course, it is possible for *both* things to be true. That is, we can have the greater homogenization of some aspects of our lives along with the greater heterogeneization of other aspects (Giddens, 1990, p. 64). Robertson (1992, p. 132) takes this position: "it is possible for there to be an equal emphasis upon societal uniqueness, on the one hand, and the commonality of mankind, on the other." In a specific setting, King (1990, p. 410) concludes that the world's cities are growing simultaneously more "similar to, and different from, each other." In fact, it could be argued that it is homogenization that tends to bring forth heterogeneization as a response to it. That is, for example, local communities, upset by the influx of fast-food chains, may come to emphasize the indigenous cuisine and local restaurants. Thus, one observer argues that "the local is itself a global product" (Friedman, 1994, p. 198).

More generally, Robertson is correct in pointing to the global importance of factors such as ethnicity, nationalism, race, and gender. These can and do serve to retard the progress of westernization and Americanization. At the same time, the forces behind the latter processes actively seek to neutralize such factors by co-opting them into the system. For example, advertisements are tailored to the needs and interests of different ethnic and national groups, different races, and both genders. The result is greater homogenization.

McDonaldization, McWorld, Americanization, and Jihad

However, not all social analysts have jumped on the globalization bandwagon. For example, Ritzer (1993; 1996a) has argued that "McDonaldization" is a major social change sweeping not only across the United States, but throughout the world. The fast-food restaurants, chains, and most generally the principles that lie at the base of their success are of increasing importance and influence throughout the world. This is a global process in the sense that many areas of the world are involved in the creation and dissemination of these structures and principles. However, it is much better thought of as a process of Americanization rather than globalization. That is, these are structures and principles that are to a large extent American innovations and American exports to the rest of the world. The flow of these things out of the United States and to the rest of the world dwarfs their return flow. Much the same thing can be said about another American innovation, the credit card (Ritzer, 1995). This view stands in contrast to globalization theory in a number of ways, including its emphasis on the nation-state (especially the United States) and its privileging of the influence of the United States on the rest of the world.

In *Jihad vs. McWorld,* Barber (1995) has picked up some of these themes under the heading of "McWorld" and juxtaposed them with the very different, albeit related, idea of "Jihad." In his view these two developments and their inter-relationship are serving to define a large part of the world today. They are serving to both bring us together and to tear us apart. Most importantly, from Barber's point of view, they are both serving to undermine the chances of democracy throughout the world. While Barber sees both of these forces as important, he makes it clear that in the long run McWorld will overwhelm Jihad, bringing about, in Ritzer's terms, the "McDonaldization of Society."

McWorld is a metaphor for a series of American innovations that are serving to homogenize the world, tying it together "by communications, information, entertainment and commerce" (Barber, 1995, p. 4). Obviously, McDonald's is part of McWorld, but other central creators and components of McWorld are Disney, Macintosh, MTV, CNN, Blockbuster Video, Coca-Cola, television, movies, Home Shopping Network, shopping malls, and the Internet. These are to an extraordinary extent American creations, and they are rapidly transforming the world; that is, they are bringing American monoculture to the world.

Jihad is Barber's metaphor for all those forces that oppose McWorld and universalism in general. Included are local, tribal, racial, and religious groups that are seeking to reemphasize their importance and significance while resisting incursions from without, especially from McWorld.

While pitted against one another, Barber sees a tight linkage between McWorld and Jihad. For example, Jihad needs McWorld to have something to fight against. For its part, McWorld imperils Jihad by threatening to swamp it in a sea of uniformity. Furthermore, each uses the other. Jihad uses the techniques of McWorld, telecommunications for example, in order to bring its messages to large numbers of people. As Barber (1995, p. 83) puts it, "Jihad itself can be commodified." The greater interdependence brought about by McWorld allows Jihad to spread its message faster and farther. McWorld uses the dangers of Jihad to sell its universalistic message. And it is to Jihad that McWorld must constantly adapt.

Most important from Barber's point of view is the fact that neither McWorld nor Jihad respect the nation-state. Indeed, the actions of both tend to erode it. McWorld emphasizes the universal over the nation, while Jihad privileges the local over the national. In addition, both stand as threats to democracy. Jihad tends toward tyranny, while McWorld focuses on free global markets and opposes national efforts to protect its citizens economically. As Barber (1995, p. 223) puts it, "Neither Jihad nor McWorld cares a fig about citizens."

Summary

Social change refers to variations over time in the relationships among individuals, groups, cultures, and societies. Because social change is patterned, we can distinguish trends, cyclic variations, and irregular or random variations.

A variety of theories attempt to explain change. Cyclic theorists, exemplified by Sorokin, view change as an ongoing series of cycles rather than as a process with direction. Evolutionary theorists view change as a directional process; Lenski and Lenski, key exponents of this approach, see technological developments as the major determinants of change. Conflict theorists, exemplified by Dahrendorf, view change as the inevitable result of inherent conflicts between groups with diverse interests.

Technology, one of the most important sources of change, brings about change by increasing our alternatives, altering interaction patterns, and generating social problems (for example, the use of computerized data banks to invade privacy). Ideologies affect change in diverse ways, sometimes acting as impediments or barriers, sometimes as facilitators. Competition and conflict have stimulated much change, especially in scientific developments.

Collective behavior frequently arises from change, or it may produce change. Crowds may have the specific purpose of bringing about some kind of change in their immediate environment. Rumors help people resolve ambiguity in their situations and may be used to legitimate certain behavior, such as rioting. Disasters may result in both short- and long-term changes.

Social movements, collective efforts to promote or resist change, can be classified as revolutionary, regressive, reform, or expressive. One explanation for movements is the resource mobilization perspective, which stresses the importance of mobilizing sufficient resources to redress the grievances always present in a population.

There are various approaches to the study of social change at the international level. Some earlier approaches include modernization, development, and dependency theories. A variant of the latter that has a considerable following today is world-system theory. This theory focuses primarily on the relationship between core and peripheral nations, especially the ways in which the core nations exploit the peripheral nations. However, the dominant approach today is probably globalization theory, with its focus on the globe as a unit of analysis and on the changing nature of global processes. Others see the importance of global processes, but they see the United States as the central player in the world today. They focus on the issue of homogenization through processes like McDonaldization and Americanization, although they recognize that there are a variety of countervailing forces (Jihad, for example).

CRITICAL THINKING

1. Discuss the ways in which contemporary gangs differ from their predecessors.
2. In general, how successful is terrorism in promoting social change? Think of recent examples of terrorist incidents described in the newspapers or on television. To what degree were these efforts at change successful?
3. How do sociologists account for the multitude of changes at various levels of life? Give a brief explanation of the perspectives of the following schools of thought: cyclic, evolutionary, and conflict theory. Compare and contrast the theories in terms of their usefulness in explaining various types of social change.
4. In what ways does the introduction of new technology in society cause change? Are these changes positive or negative? What happens when a society's old norms, roles, or values no longer apply to the situation created by new technology?
5. In what ways does ideology facilitate or impede change in society? Give specific examples to support your ideas.
6. Many people view conflict in a negative light. In what ways is conflict useful in promoting social change? In what ways has competition been useful in promoting social change?
7. What stereotypes exist about people's behavior during disasters? Are these stereotypes supported by the evidence presented in this chapter?
8. Compare and contrast the different types of social movements presented in the chapter. Which have been evident in U.S. history? How important is resource mobilization in determining the success of a social movement?
9. Describe the world-system theory of development. What evidence supports this viewpoint?
10. What is McDonaldization? How do the models of "McWorld" and "Jihad" relate to one another?

REFERENCES

ABRAMOWITZ, MICHAEL. "Primary Health Care Lacking for D.C.'s Poor, Study Shows." *Washington Post,* August 3, 1988.

ACKER, JOAN R. "Women and Stratification: A Review of the Literature." *Contemporary Sociology* 9, 1980.

ADLER, PATRICIA A., and ADLER, PETER. *Backboards and Blackboards.* New York: Columbia University Press, 1991.

ADLER, PATRICIA A., and ADLER, PETER. "Observational Techniques." In Norman K. Denzin and Yvonna S. Lincoln (eds.), *Handbook of Qualitative Research.* Newbury Park, Calif: Sage, 1994.

ADLER, PATRICIA A., KLESS, STEVEN J., and ADLER, PETER. "Socialization to Gender Roles: Popularity among Elementary School Boys and Girls." *Sociology of Education* 65, 1992.

Agence France Presse. "Asians Puff Their Way Towards World's Largest Cigarette Market." February 15, 1994.

Agence France Presse. "European Non-Smokers Meet in Sweden to Defend Their Rights." August 3, 1995.

AGUIRRE, B. E., QUARANTELLI, E. L., and MENDOZA, JORGE L. "The Collective Behavior of Fads: The Characteristics, Effects, and Career of Streaking." *American Sociological Review* 53, 1988.

AHLBERG, DENNIS A., and DE VITA, CAROL J. "New Realities of the American Family." *Population Bulletin* 47, 1992.

AHRONS, CONSTANCE R. "The Continuing Coparental Relationship Between Divorced Spouses." *American Journal of Orthopsychiatry* 51, 1981.

AHRONS, CONSTANCE, R., and RODGERS, ROY H. *Divorced Families: A Multidisciplinary Developmental View.* New York: W.W. Norton & Company, 1987.

AIDS Weekly. "Conference Coverage (APHA): AIDS among Drug Users in Amsterdam on Decline." November 13, 1995.

AIKEN, LINDA H., GUYTHEN, MARNI, and FRIESE, CHRISTOPHER R. *Statistical Bulletin—Metropolitan Life Insurance Company,* 76, January 1995.

AKERS, RONALD L., and COCHRAN, JOHN K. "Adolescent Marijuana Use: A Test of Three Theories of Deviant Behavior." *Deviant Behavior* 6, 1985.

ALDOUS, JOAN. "Birth Control Socialization: How to Avoid Discussing the Subject." *Population and Environment* 6, 1983.

ALEXANDER, JEFFREY C., and COLOMY, PAUL. "Neofunctionalism Today: Reconstructing a Theoretical Tradition." In George Ritzer (ed.), *Frontiers of Social Theory.* New York: Columbia University Press, 1990.

ALEXANDER, KARL L., ECKLAND, BRUCE K., and GRIFFIN, LARRY J. "The Wisconsin Model of Socioeconomic Achievement: A Replication." *American Journal of Sociology* 81, 1976.

ALEXANDER, KARL L., ENTWISLE, DORIS R., CADIGAN, DORIS, and PALLAS, AARON. "Getting Ready for First Grade: Standards of Deportment in Home and School." *Social Forces* 66, 1987a.

ALEXANDER, KARL L., ENTWISLE, DORIS R., and THOMPSON, MAXINE S. "School Performance, Status Relations, and the Structure of Sentiment: Bringing the Teacher Back In." *American Sociological Review* 52, 1987b.

ALLEN, CRAIG M. "On the Validity of Relative Validity Studies of 'Final Say' Measures of Marital Power." *Journal of Marriage and the Family* 46, 1984.

ALLEN KATHERINE R. "The Dispassionate Discourse of Children's Adjustment to Divorce." *Journal of Marriage and the Family* 55, 1993.

ALIC, JOHN A., and JONES, MARTHA CALDWELL. "Employment Lessons from the Electronics Industry." *Monthly Labor Review* 109, 1986.

ALWIN, DUANE F. "College Effects on Educational and Occupational Attainments." *American Sociological Review* 39, 1974.

AMATO, PAUL R. "Family Structure, Family Process, and Family Ideology." *Journal of Marriage and the Family* 55, 1993.

AMATO, PAUL R., and BOOTH, ALAN. "Consequences of Parental Divorce and Marital Unhappiness for Adult Well-being." *Social Forces* 69, 1991.

AMATO, PAUL R., and KEITH, BRUCE. "Parental Divorce and Adult Well-being: A Meta-analysis." *Journal of Marriage and the Family* 53, 1991a.

AMATO, PAUL R., and KEITH, BRUCE. "Parental Divorce and the Well-being of Children: A Meta-analysis." *Psychological Bulletin* 110, 1991b.

AMBERT, ANNE-MARIE, ADLER, PATRICIA, ADLER, PETER, and DETZNER, DANIEL F. "Understanding and Evaluating Qualitative Research." *Journal of Marriage and the Family* 57, 1995.

AMERICAN COUNCIL ON EDUCATION. *One Third of a Nation.* Washington, D.C.: American Council on Education, 1988.

AMES, DAVID L., BROWN, NEVIN C., CALLAHAN, MARY HELEN, CUMMINGS, SCOTT B., SMOCK, SUE MARX, and ZIEGLER, JEROME M. "Rethinking American Urban Policy." *Journal of Urban Affairs* 14, 1992.

ANDERSON, CYNTHIA D., and TOMASKOVIC-DEVEY, DONALD. "Patriarchal Pressures: An Exploration of Organizational Processes That Exacerbate and Erode Gender Earnings Inequality." *Work and Occupations* 22, 1995.

ANDERSON, MARGARET. *Thinking about Women: Sociological Perspectives on Sex and Gender.* New York: Macmillan, 1988.

ANDERSON, STEPHEN A., RUSSELL, CANDYCE S., and SCHUMM, WALTER R. "Perceived Marital Quality and Family Life Cycle Categories: A Further Analysis." *Journal of Marriage and the Family* 45, 1983.

ANSOLABEHERE, STEPHEN, and IYENGAR, SHANTO. *Going Negative: How Political Advertisements Shrink and Polarize the Electorate.* New York: The Free Press, 1995.

ANTONOVSKY, AARON. "Social Class, Life Expectancy and Overall Mortality." *Milbank Memorial Fund Quarterly* 45, 1967.

APGAR, WILLIAM C., JR., and BROWN, H. JAMES. *The State of the Nation's Housing.* Cambridge, Mass.: Joint Center for Housing Studies of Harvard University, 1988.

APPADURAI, ARJUN. "Disjunction and Difference in the Global Cultural Economy." In Mike Featherstone, (ed.), *Global Culture: Nationalism, Globalization and Modernity.* London: Sage, 1990.

APPLEBOME, PETER. "U.S. Prisons Challenged by Women behind Bars." *New York Times,* November 30, 1992.

APPLEYARD, BRYAN. *Understanding the Present: Science and Soul of Modern Man.* New York: Doubleday, 1992.

ARCHER, MARGARET S. *Culture and Agency: The Place of Culture in Social Theory.* New York: Cambridge University Press, 1988.

ARCHER, MARGARET S. "Theory, Culture and Post-Industrial Society." In Mike Featherstone, (ed.), *Global Culture: Nationalism, Globalization and Modernity.* London: Sage, 1990.

ARIÉS, PHILLIPE. *Centuries of Childhood.* New York: Random House, 1962.

ARLUKE, ARNOLD, KENNEDY, LOUANNE, and KESSLER, RONALD C. "Reexamining the Sick-Role Concept: An Empirical Assessment." *Journal of Health and Social Behavior* 20, 1979.

ARMSTRONG, THOMAS. *The Myth of the A.D.D. Child.* New York: Dutton, 1995.

ARNETT, JEFFREY J. "Reckless Behavior in Adolescence: A Developmental Perspective." *Developmental Review* 12, 1992.

ARNETT, JEFFREY J. "Broad and Narrow Socialization: The Family in the Context of a Cultural Theory." *Journal of Marriage and the Family* 57, 1995.

ARNEY, WILLIAM RAY. *Power and the Profession of Obstetrics.* Chicago: University of Chicago Press, 1982.

ARNOLD, FRED, and ZHAOXIANG, LIU. "Sex Preference, Fertility, and Family Planning in China." *Population and Development Review* 12, 1986.

ARONSON, RONALD. *After Marxism.* New York: Guilford Press, 1995.

ARROW, MARTIN, and KING, ELIZABETH. (eds.). *Globalization, Knowledge and Society: Readings from "International Sociology."* Newbury Park, Calif.: Sage, 1990.

ARUM, RICHARD, and SHAVIT, YOSSI. "Secondary Vocational Education and the Transition from School to Work." *Sociology of Education* 68, 1995.

ASCH, SOLOMON. *Social Psychology.* Englewood Cliffs, N.J.: Prentice-Hall, 1952.

ASSAEL, M., and GERMAN, G. A. "Changing Society and Mental Health in Eastern Africa." *The Israel Annals of Psychiatry and Related Disciplines* 8, 1970.

ASSOCIATED PRESS. "Believers Find Visions of Mary Everywhere." *Lawrence Journal-World.* October 16, 1995.

ASTONE, NAN M., and McLANAHAN, SARA S. "Family Structure, Parental Practices and High School Completion." *American Sociological Review* 56, 1991.

ATKINSON, ANTHONY B., RAINWATER, LEE, and SMEEDING, TIMOTHY. *Income Distribution in OECD Countries.* Paris: Organization for Economic Co-operation and Development, 1995.

ATKINSON, PAUL, and HAMMERSLEY, MARTYN. "Ethnography and Participant Observation." In Norman K. Denzin and Yvonna S. Lincoln (eds.), *Handbook of Qualitative Research.* Thousand Oaks, CA: Sage Publications, 1994.

Atlanta Journal and Constitution. "Bush Promises Escalation of Anti-Drug War." January 27, 1992.

AUGUST, MARK. "With Elders, Clinton Killed the Messenger." *Tampa Tribune,* December 14, 1994.

Austin American-Statesman. "Murders Plague L.A.," October 10, 1995.

AWN, PETER J. "Sufism." In Mircea Eliade (ed.), *The Encyclopedia of Religion.* New York: Macmillan, 1987.

BABCOCK, CHARLES, R. "In Donating $230 Million, Interests Favored Bush, Hill Democrats." *Washington Post,* October 23, 1992.

BACHARACH, SAMUEL B., and BAMBERGER, PETER. "Contested Control: Systems of Control and Their Implications for Ambiguity in Elementary and Secondary Schools." *Work and Occupations* 22, 1995.

BACHMAN, JERALD G., JOHNSTON, LLOYD D., O'MALLEY, PATRICK M., and HUMPHREY, RONALD H. "Explaining the Recent Decline in Marijuana Use: Differentiating the Effects of Perceived Risks, Disapproval, and General Lifestyle Factors." *Journal of Health and Social Behavior* 29, 1988.

BACHMAN, JERALD G., WALLACE, JOHN M., O'MALLEY, PATRICK M., JOHNSTON, LLOYD D., KURTH, CANDACE L., and NEIGHBORS, HAROLD W. "Racial/Ethnic Differences in Smoking, Drinking, and Illicit Drug Use among American High School Seniors, 1976–89." *American Journal of Public Health* 81, 1991.

BAHR, STEPHEN J. "Marital Dissolution Laws: Impact of Recent Changes for Women." *Journal of Family Issues* 4, 1983.

BAILEY, WILLIAM C., and PETERSON, RUTH D. "Murder, Capital Punishment, and Deterrence: A Review of the Evidence and an Examination of Police Killings." *Journal of Social Issues* 50, 1994.

BAKER, RAY STANNARD. *Following the Color Line: American Negro Citizenship in the Progressive Era.* New York: Harper Torchbooks, 1964.

BALDASSARE, MARK. "Suburban Communities." *Annual Review of Sociology,* 18. Palo Alto, Calif.: Annual Reviews, 1992.

BARAN, PAUL A., and SWEEZY, PAUL M. *Monopoly Capital: An Essay on the American Economic and Social Order.* New York: Modern Reader Paperbacks, 1966.

BARBER, BENJAMIN R. *Jihad vs. McWorld.* New York: Times Books, 1995.

BARKER, IRWIN R., and CURRIE, RAYMOND F. "Do Converts Always Make the Most Committed Christians?" *Journal for the Scientific Study of Religion* 24, 1985.

BARKER-BENFIELD, G. J. *The Horrors of the Half-Known Life: Male Attitudes Toward Women and Sexuality in Nineteenth-Century America.* New York: Harper & Row, 1976,

BARLOW, PHILIP L. *Mormons and the Bible: The Place of the Latter-day Saints in American Religion.* New York: Oxford University Press, 1991.

BARNETT, ROSALIND C., and BARUCH, GRACE K. "Determinants of Fathers' Participation in Family Work." *Journal of Marriage and the Family* 49, 1987.

BARON, JAMES N., and BIELBY, WILLIAM T. "Organizational Barriers to Gender Equality: Sex Segregation of Jobs and Opportunities." In Alice S. Rossi (ed.), *Gender and the Life Course.* New York: Aldine, 1985.

BARON, JAMES N., MITTMAN, BRIAN S., and NEWMAN, ANDREW E. "Targets of Opportunity: Organizational and Environmental Determinants of Gender Integration within the California Civil Service, 1979–1985." *American Journal of Sociology* 96, 1991.

BARONE, MICHAEL. "The Power of the President's Pollsters." *Public Opinion,* September/October, 1988.

BARR, STEPHEN. "The Thickening of Bureaucracy." *Washington Post,* February 1, 1995.

BARRETT, DAVID B. "Adherents of All Religions by Eight Continental Areas, mid-1990." *1991 Britannica Book of the Year.* Chicago: Encyclopædia Britannica, 1991.

BARRINGER, FELICITY. "Census Shows Profound Change in Racial Makeup of the Nation." *New York Times,* March 11, 1991.

BARRINGER, FELICITY. "Census Reveals a City of Displacement." *New York Times,* May 15, 1992.

BASSUK, ELLEN L. "Homeless Families: Single Mothers and Their Children in Boston Shelters." In Ellen L. Bassuk (ed.), *The Mental Health Needs of Homeless Persons.* San Francisco: Jossey-Bass, 1986.

BASTIAN, L. D. and TAYLOR, B. M. *School Crime: A National Crime Victimization Survey Report.* Washington, D.C.: U.S. Department of Justice, 1991.

BAZEMORE, GORDON. "Delinquent Reform and the Labeling Perspective." *Criminal Justice and Behavior* 12, 1985.

BEACH, FRANK A., (ed.). *Human Sexuality in Four Perspectives.* Baltimore: The Johns Hopkins University Press, 1977.

BEAN, FRANK D., and TIENDA, MARTA. *The Hispanic Population of the United States.* New York: Russell Sage Foundation, 1987.

BEAVER, STEVEN E. *Demographic Transition Theory Reinterpreted.* Lexington, Mass.: Lexington Books, 1975.

BECKER, GARY. *A Treatise on the Family.* Chicago: University of Chicago Press, 1991.

BECKER, GAY, and NACHTIGALL, ROBERT D. "Eager for Medicalisation: The Social Production of Infertility as a Disease." *Sociology of Health and Illness* 14, 1992.

BECKER, HOWARD S. *Outsiders: Studies in the Sociology of Deviance.* New York: The Free Press, 1963.

BECKER, HOWARD, and GEER, BLANCHE. "The Fate of Idealism in Medical School." *American Sociological Review* 23, 1958.

BECKETT, KATHERINE. "Setting the Public Agenda: Street Crime and Drug Use in American Politics." *Social Problems* 41, 1994.

BECKWITH, CAROL. "Niger's Wodaabe: People of the Taboo." *National Geographic,* October 1983.

BEDAU, HUGO A. "American Populism and the Death Penalty: Witnesses at an Execution." *Howard Journal of Criminal Justice* 33, 1994.

BEDELL, DOUG. "Panelists Say Lesbian Issue Simple to Address: They Say Common-sense." *Dallas Morning News,* May 21, 1995a.

BEDELL, KENNETH B. *Yearbook of American and Canadian Churches, 1995.* Nashville, TN: Abingdon Press, 1995b.

BELL, DANIEL. *The Coming of the Post-Industrial Society: A Venture in Social Forecasting.* New York: Basic Books, 1973.

BELLAH, ROBERT N. "Civil Religion in America." *Daedalus,* Winter, 1967.

BELLAH, ROBERT N., and HAMMOND, PHILLIP E., (eds.). *Varieties of Civil Religion.* New York: Harper & Row, 1980.

BELLAH, ROBERT N., MADSEN, RICHARD, SULLIVAN, WILLIAM M., SWIDLER, ANNE, and TIPTON, STEVEN M. *Habits of the Heart.* New York: Harper & Row, 1985.

BENEDICT, RUTH. "The Vision in Plains Culture." *American Anthropologist* 24, 1922.

BENET, SULA. *Abkhasians: The Long Living People of the Caucasus.* New York: Holt, Rinehart & Winston, 1974.

BENIN, MARY, and KEITH, VERNA M. "The Social Support of Employed African American and Anglo Women." *Journal of Social Issues* 16, 1995.

BENNETT, NEIL G., BLOOM, DAVID E., and MILLER, CYNTHIA K. "The Influence of Nonmarital Childbearing on the Formation of First Marriages." *Demography* 32, 1995.

BERGER, ARTHUR A. "Introduction." In Arthur A. Berger (ed.), *Television in Society.* New Brunswick, N.J.: Transaction Books, 1987.

BERGER, BENNETT. *An Essay on Culture: Symbolic Structure and Social Structure.* Berkeley, CA: University of California Press, 1995.

BERGER, PETER. *The Sacred Canopy: Elements of a Sociological Theory of Religion.* Garden City, N.Y.: Doubleday, 1967.

BERGER, PETER, and LUCKMANN, THOMAS. *The Social Construction of Reality.* Garden City, N.Y.: Anchor Books, 1967.

BERGESON, ALBERT. "The Critique of World-System Theory: Class Relations or Division of Labor?" In Randall Collins (ed.) *Sociological Theory—1984.* San Francisco: Jossey-Bass, 1984.

BERK, RICHARD A., CAMPBELL, ALEC, KLAP, RUTH, and WESTERN, BRUCE. "The Deterrent Effect of Arrest in Incidents of Domestic Violence: A Bayesian Analysis of Four Field Experiments." *American Sociological Review* 57, 1992.

BERK, RICHARD A., LENIHAN, KENNETH J., and ROSSI, PETER H. "Crime and Poverty: Some Experimental Evidence from Ex-Offenders." *American Sociological Review* 45, 1980.

BERKE, RICHARD L. "Experts Say Low 1988 Turnout May be Repeated." *New York Times,* November 13, 1988.

BERNARD, JESSIE. *The Female World from a Global Perspective.* Bloomington, Ind.: Indiana University Press, 1987.

BERNHARDT, ANNETTE, MORRIS, MARTINA, and HANDCOCK, MARK S. "Women's Gains or Men's Losses? A Closer Look at the Shrinking Gender Gap in Earnings." *American Journal of Sociology* 101, 1995.

BERNSTEIN, RICHARD. "A Growing Islamic Presence: Balancing Sacred and Secular." *New York Times,* May 2, 1993.

BERRYMAN, PHILLIP. *The Religious Roots of Rebellion: Christians in Central American Revolutions.* Maryknoll, New York: Orbis Books, 1984.

BETTELHEIM, BRUNO. "Punishment vs. Discipline." *The Atlantic* 256, 1985.

BETTS, RICHARD K. "The Coming Defense Train Wreck and What to Do about It." *Washington Quarterly* 19, 1996.

BEYER, PETER. *Religion and Globalization.* London: Sage, 1994.

BIELBY, WILLIAM T., and BARON, JAMES N. "Men and Women at Work: Sex Segregation and Statistical Discrimination." *American Journal of Sociology* 91, 1986.

BIGGART, NICOLE. *Charismatic Capitalism: Direct Selling Organizations.* Chicago: University of Chicago Press, 1989.

BILLY, JOHN O. G., TANFER, KORAY, GRADY, WILLIAM R., and KLEPENGER, DANIEL H. "The Sexual Behavior of Men in the United States." *Family Planning Perspectives* 25, 1993.

BIRENBAUM, ARNOLD, and SAGARIN, EDWARD. *Norms and Human Behavior.* New York: Praeger, 1976.

BIRON, LOUISE L., BROCHU, SERGE, and DESJARDINS, LYNE. "The Issue of Drugs and Crime among a Sample of Incarcerated Women." *Deviant Behavior* 16, 1995.

BISHOP, KATHERINE. "Malibu to Maui, It's Surfspeak U.S.A." *New York Times,* August 30, 1991.

BLACK, MERLE, and REED, JOHN SHELTON. "Perspectives on the American South." In *Annual Review of Society, Politics and Culture* 2. New York: Gordon & Breach, Science Publishers, 1984.

BLANCHARD, FLETCHER A., LILLY, TERI, AND VAUGHN, LEIGH ANN. "Reducing the Expression of Racial Prejudice." *Psychological Science* 2, 1991.

BLAU, JOEL. *The Visible Poor: Homelessness in the United States.* New York: Oxford University Press, 1992.

BLAU, PETER M. *The Dynamics of Bureaucracy.* Chicago: University of Chicago Press, 1963.

BLAU, PETER M. *Exchange and Power in Social Life.* New York: John Wiley, 1964.

BLAU, PETER M., and MEYER, MARSHALL W. *Bureaucracy in Modern Society,* 3d ed. New York: Random House, 1987.

BLAUNER, ROBERT. *Alienation and Freedom.* Chicago: University of Chicago Press, 1964.

BLINDE, ELAINE M., and TAUB, DIANE E. "Women Athletes as Falsely Accused Deviants: Managing the Lesbian Stigma." *Sociological Quarterly* 33, 1992.

BLOOD, ROBERT O., JR. *Love Match and Arranged Marriage.* New York: Free Press, 1967.

BLOOD, ROBERT O., JR. and WOLFE, DONALD M. *Husbands and Wives: The Dynamics of Married Living.* New York: The Free Press, 1960.

BLOOM, HAROLD. *The American Religion: The Emergence of the Post-Christian Nation.* New York: Simon and Schuster, 1992.

BLUESTONE, BARRY. "The Inequality Express." *The American Prospect,* Winter, 1995.

BLUESTONE, BARRY, and HARRISON, BENNETT. *The Deindustrialization of America.* New York: Basic Books, 1982.

BLUESTONE, BARRY, and HARRISON, BENNETT. "The Great American Job Machine: The Proliferation of Low Wage Employment in the U.S. Economy." Study Prepared for the Joint Economic Committee of the Congress. Washington, D.C., 1986.

BLUM, LINDA, and SMITH, VICKI. "Women's Mobility in the Corporation: A Critique of the Politics of Optimism." *Gender and Society* 13, 1988.

BLUMBERG, ARTHUR, and BLUMBERG, PHYLLIS. *The School Superintendent: Living with Conflict.* New York: Teachers College Press, 1985.

BLUMBERG, RAE L. "A General Theory of Gender Stratification." In Randall Collins (ed.), *Sociological Theory—1984.* San Francisco: Jossey-Bass, 1984.

BLUMBERG, RAE L. "Income under Female Versus Male Control: Hypotheses from a Theory of Gender Stratification and Data from the Third World." In Rae Lesser Blumberg (ed.), *Gender, Family, and Economy: The Triple Overlap.* Newbury Park, Calif.: Sage, 1991.

BOAS, FRANZ. *Handbook of American Indian Languages.* Washington, D.C.: U.S. Government Printing Office, 1911.

BOCK, E. WILBUR, BEEGHLEY, LEONARD, and MIXON, ANTHONY J. "Religion, Socioeconomic Status, and Sexual Morality: An Application of Reference Group Theory." *The Sociological Quarterly* 24, 1983.

BOCK, KENNETH. *Human Nature and History: A Response to Sociobiology.* New York: Columbia University Press, 1980.

BOHANNAN, PAUL. "The Six Stations of Divorce." In Paul Bohannan (ed.), *Divorce and After.* New York: Doubleday, 1970.

BOLTON, CHARLES D., and KAMMEYER, KENNETH C. W. *The University Student.* New Haven, Conn.: College & University Press, 1967.

BONACICH, EDNA. "A Theory of Ethnic Antagonism: The Split Labor Market." *American Sociological Review* 37, 1972.

BONGAARTS, JOHN. "Why High Birth Rates Are So Low." In Scott W. Menard and Elizabeth W. Moen (eds.), *Perspectives on Population: An Introduction to Concepts and Issues.* New York: Oxford University Press, 1987.

BONIFAZ, JOHN. "Losing Our Vote in the WEALTH PRIMARY." *Legal Times,* October 24, 1994.

BOODMAN, SANDRA G. "What Do Babies Know—And When Do They Know It?" *Washington Post Health,* October 6, 1992.

BOONE, LOUIS E., KURTZ, DAVID L., and FLEENOR, C. PATRICK. "The Road to the Top." *American Demographics* 10, 1988.

BOOTH, ALAN, and EDWARDS, JOHN N. "Age at Marriage and Marital Stability." *Journal of Marriage and the Family* 47, 1985.

BOOTH, ALAN, EDWARDS, JOHN N., and JOHNSON, DAVID R. "Social Integration and Divorce." *Social Forces* 70, 1991.

BORDEWICH, FERGUS M. "Colorado's Thriving Cults." *New York Times Magazine,* May 1, 1988.

BORG, MARIAN J. "Conflict Management in the Modern World-System." *Sociological Forum* 7, 1992.

BORJAS, GEORGE J. "The Economics of Immigration." *Journal of Economic Literature* 32, 1994.

BORNSCHIER, VOLKER, CHASE-DUNN, CHRISTOPHER, and RUBINSON, RICHARD. "Cross-National Evidence of the Effects of Foreign Investment and Aid on Economic Growth and Inequality: A Survey of Findings and a Reanalysis." *American Journal of Sociology* 84, 1978.

BOSE, CHRISTINE E., and ROSSI, PETER H. "Gender and Jobs: Prestige Standings of Occupations as Affected by Gender." *American Sociological Review* 48, 1983.

BOSK, CHARLES L. *Forgive and Remember: Managing Medical Failure.* Chicago: University of Chicago Press, 1979.

BOSWELL, TERRY, and BERGESON, ALBERT. "American Prospects in a Period of Hegemonic Decline and Economic Crisis." In Terry Boswell and Albert Bergeson (eds.), *America's Changing Role in the World System.* New York: Praeger, 1987.

BOTTOMORE, T. B. *Classes in Modern Society.* New York: Pantheon Books, 1966.

BOULTON, MARY, et al. "Social Class and General Practice Consultation." *Sociology of Health and Illness* 8, 1986.

BOURDIEU, PIERRE, and WACQUANT, LOIC J. D. "The Purpose of Reflexive Sociology (The Chicago Workshop)." In P. Bourdieu and L. J. D. Wacquant (eds.), *An Invitation to Reflexive Sociology.* Chicago: University of Chicago Press, 1992.

BOUVIER, LEON F. "Immigration at the Crossroads." *American Demographics* 3, 1981.

BOUVIER, LEON F., and GARDNER, ROBERT W. "Immigration to the U.S.: The Unfinished Story." *Population Bulletin* 41, 1986.

BOWLES, SAMUEL, and GINTIS, HERBERT. *Schooling in Capitalist America: Educational Reform and the Contradictions of Economic Life.* New York: Basic Books, 1976.

BOWLES, SCOTT. "Police Search of AOL Files Divides the On-line World." *Washington Post,* January 16, 1996.

BRACEY, GERALD W. "U.S. Students: Better Than Ever." *Washington Post,* December 22, 1995.

BRAITHWAITE, JOHN. "The Myth of Social Class and Criminality Reconsidered." *American Sociological Review* 46, 1981.

BRAITHWAITE, JOHN. "White Collar Crime." In Ralph H. Turner and James F. Short, Jr. (eds.), *Annual Review of Sociology* 11. Palo Alto, Calif.: Annual Reviews, Inc., 1985.

BRAUNSEN, ELS. "Has Menstruation Been Medicalised? Or Will It Never Happen?" *Sociology of Health and Illness* 14, 1992.

BRAVERMAN, HARRY. *Labor and Monopoly Capital: The Degradation of Work in the Twentieth Century.* New York: Monthly Review Press, 1974.

BREAULT, K. D. "Suicide in America: A Test of Durkheim's Theory of Religious and Family Integration, 1933–1980." *American Journal of Sociology* 92, 1986.

BRIDENBAUGH, CARL. *Cities in the Wilderness: The First Century of Urban Life in America.* New York: Ronald Press, 1938.

BRIMHALL-VARGAS, MARK. "Hispanic Elected Officials, 1994." Washington, DC: National Association of Latino Elected Officials Fund, 1994.

BROAD, WILLIAM J. "Ridden with Debt, U.S. Companies Cut Funds for Research." *New York Times,* June 30, 1992a.

BROAD, WILLIAM J. "Clinton to Promote High Technology, with Gore in Charge." *New York Times,* November 10, 1992b.

BRODERICK, CARLFRED B. "How to Rewrite Your Marriage Script So It Works." *Redbook,* February 1979.

BRODERICK, CARLFRED B. *Marriage and the Family,* 3d ed. Englewood Cliffs, N.J.: Prentice Hall, 1989.

BRODY, JANE E. "Children of Divorce: Actions to Help Can Hurt, Studies Find." *New York Times,* July 23, 1991.

BROWN, DAVID. "Smoking Deaths Seen Climbing." *Washington Post,* May 22, 1992.

BROWN, DAVID. "Clot-dissolving Drug Offers New Hope for Victims of Stroke; More May Have Full Recovery." *Washington Post,* December 14, 1995.

BROWN, L. K., DICLEMENTE, R. J., and BEAUSOLEIL, N. I. "Comparison of Human Immunodeficiency Virus Related Knowledge, Attitudes, Intentions, and Behaviors among Sexually Active and Abstinent Young Adolescents." *Journal of Adolescent Health* 13, 1992.

BROWNE, IRENE. "The Baby-Boom and Trends in Poverty, 1967–1987." *Social Forces* 73:3, March 1995.

BROWNMILLER, SUSAN. *Against Our Will: Men, Women and Rape.* New York: Simon and Schuster, 1975.

BRUBAKER, ROGER. *The Limits of Rationality: An Essay on the Social and Moral Thought of Max Weber.* London: George Allen & Unwin, 1984.

BRUCE, STEVE. *Pray TV: Televangelism in America.* London: Routledge, 1990.

BRUSH, LISA D. "Violent Acts and Injurious Outcomes in Married Couples: Methodological Issues in the National Survey of Families and Households." *Gender and Society* 4, 1990.

BRYANT, CLIFTON D. *Sexual Deviancy and Social Proscription: The Social Context of Carnal Behavior.* New York: Human Sciences Press, 1982.

BUECHLER, STEVEN M. "Beyond Resource Mobilization? Emerging Trends in Social Movement Theory." *Sociological Quarterly* 34, 1993.

BUMPASS, LARRY L., SWEET, JAMES A., and CHERLIN, ANDREW. "The Role of Cohabitation in Declining Rates of Marriage." *Journal of Marriage and the Family* 53, 1991.

BUMPASS, LARRY L., SWEET, JAMES A., and MARTIN, TERESA CASTRO. "Changing Patterns of Remarriage." *Journal of Marriage and the Family* 52, 1990.

BURAWOY, MICHAEL, and KROTOV, PAVEL. "The Soviet Transition from Socialism to Capitalism: Worker Control and Economic Bargaining in the Wood Industry." *American Sociological Review* 57, 1992.

BURGESS, JOHN. "Television Takeover." *Washington Post-Business,* May 26, 1991a.

BURGESS, JOHN. "TV-Maker Zenith Will Move Assembly Operations to Mexico." *Washington Post,* October 30, 1991b.

BURGESS, ROBERT G. *In the Field: An Introduction to Field Research.* London: George Allen & Unwin, 1984.

BURRIDGE, KENELM O. L. "A Tangu Game." *Man,* 1957.

BURT, MARTHA. *Over the Edge: The Growth of Homelessness in the 1980s.* Washington, DC: Urban Institute Press, 1992.

BUSH, DIANE MITSCH, and SIMMONS, ROBERTA G. "Socialization Processes Over the Life Course." In Morris Rosenberg and Ralph H. Turner (eds.), *Social Psychology: Sociological Perspectives,* new ed. New Brunswick, N.J.: Transaction, 1990.

Business Week. "Delivering What Make Up Only Promises." February 8, 1988.

BUZAWA, EVE S., and BUZAWA, CARL G. (eds.). *Do Arrests and Restraining Orders Work?* Thousand Oaks, CA: Sage, 1996.

CAHAN, ABRAHAM. *The Rise of David Levinsky.* New York: Harper Torchbooks, 1966. Originally published 1917.

CALAVITA, KITTY, and PONTELL, HENRY N. "'Other People's Money' Revisited: Collective Embezzlement in the Savings and Loan Industry." *Social Problems* 38, 1991.

CALDWELL, JOHN C. *Theory of Fertility Decline.* New York: Academic Press, 1982.

CALHOUN, A. W. *A Social History of the American Family.* 3 vols. New York: Barnes & Noble Books, 1945.

CALIFORNIA ASSEMBLY OFFICE OF RESEARCH. *California 2000: A People in Transition.* Sacramento: Assembly Office of Research, 1986.

CAMPBELL, ANNE, and MUNCER, STEVEN. "Them and Us: A Comparison of the Cultural Context of American Gangs and British Subcultures." *Deviant Behavior* 10, 1989.

CAMPBELL, ERNEST Q. *Socialization: Culture and Personality.* Dubuque, IA: William C. Brown, 1975.

CAMPBELL, ROBERT A., and JAMES E. CURTIS. "Religious Involvement across Societies: Analyses for Alternative Measures in National Surveys." *Journal for the Scientific Study of Religion* 33, 1994.

CANDELARIA, MICHAEL R. *Popular Religion and Liberation: The Dilemma of Liberation Theology.* Albany, N.Y.: State University Press of New York, 1990.

CANNER, GLENN B., and SMITH, DELORES S. "Home Mortgage Disclosure Act: Expanded Data on Residential Lending." *Federal Reserve Bulletin,* November 1991.

CAPEK, STELLA M. "The 'Environmental Justice' Frame: A Conceptual Discussion and an Application." *Social Problems* 40, 1993.

CAPLOW, TED. "Contrasting Trends in European and American Religion." *Sociological Analysis* 46, 1985.

CAPPEL, CHARLES L., and GUTERBOCK, THOMAS M. "Visible Colleges: The Social and Conceptual Structure of Sociology Specialties." *American Sociological Review* 57, 1992.

CARLSON, BONNIE E. "Wife Battering: A Social Deviance Analysis." In Josefina Figueira-McDonough and Rosemary Sarri (eds.), *The Trapped Woman: Catch-22 in Deviance and Control.* Beverly Hills, Calif.: Sage, 1987.

CARTER, BILL. "Children's TV, Where Boys Are King." *New York Times,* May 1, 1991.

CARTER, DEBORAH J., and WILSON, REGINALD. *Ninth Annual Status Report: Minorities in Higher Education.* Washington, D.C.: American Council on Education, 1991.

CARTER, DEBORAH J., and WILSON, REGINALD. *Minorities in Higher Education.* Washington, DC: American Council on Higher Education, 1995.

CASEY, WILLIAM, and BELLIVEAU, JEANNETTE. "Voter Turnout over the Years." *Washington Post,* November 6, 1992.

CASPER, LYNNE M., McLANAHAN, SARA S., and GARFINKEL, IRWIN. "The Gender–Poverty Gap: What We Can Learn from Other Countries." *American Sociological Review* 59, 1994.

CENTER FOR DEMOGRAPHY AND ECOLOGY, UNIVERSITY OF WISCONSIN. "Publication of Data from the National Survey of Families and Households (NSFH)." Madison, WI: unpublished report, 1995.

CENTERS FOR DISEASE CONTROL, *HIV/AIDS Surveillance Report,* October 1995.

CETRON, MARVIN J., and DAVIES, OWEN. "The Future Face of Terrorism." *Futurist* 28, 1994.

CHAFETZ, JANET SALTZMAN. "The Gender Division of Labor and the Reproduction of Female Disadvantage." In Rae Lesser Blumberg (ed.), *Gender, Family, and Economy: The Triple Overlap.* Newbury Park, Calif.: Sage, 1991.

CHAGNON, NAPOLEON A. *Yanomamo: The Fierce People.* New York: Holt, Rinehart & Winston, 1968.

CHAGNON, NAPOLEON A. "Life Histories, Blood Revenge, and Warfare in a Tribal Population." *Science* 239, 1988.

CHAMBLISS, WILLIAM J. "A Sociological Analysis of the Law of Vagrancy." *Social Problems,* 1964, 12.

CHAMBLISS, WILLIAM J. "Policing the Ghetto Underclass: The Politics of Law and Law Enforcement." *Social Problems* 41, 1994.

CHARON, JOEL M. *Symbolic Interactionism: An Introduction, an Interpretation, an Integration,* 3d ed. Englewood Cliffs, N.J.: Prentice Hall, 1988.

CHARON, JOEL M. *Symbolic Interactionism: An Introduction, an Interpretation, an Integration,* 4th ed. Englewood Cliffs, N.J.: Prentice Hall, 1992.

CHEN, P. C., AND KOLS, A. "Population and Birth Planning in the People's Republic of China." *Population Reports,* Series J, No. 25. Baltimore, Md.: Johns Hopkins University, 1982.

CHERLIN, ANDREW J. "Remarriage as an Incomplete Institution." *American Journal of Sociology* 84, 1978.

CHERLIN, ANDREW J. *Marriage, Divorce, Remarriage* (revised and enlarged edition). Cambridge, MA: Harvard University Press, 1992.

CHERLIN, ANDREW J., and McCARTHY, JAMES. "Remarried Couple Households: Data from the June 1980 Current Population Survey." *Journal of Marriage and the Family* 47, 1985.

CHERLIN, ANDREW J., FURSTENBERG, FRANK F., CHASE-LANSDALE, P. L., KIERNAN, K. E., ROBINS, P. K., MORRISON, D. R., and TEITLER, J. O. "Longitudinal Studies of the Effects of Divorce on Children in Great Britain and the United States." *Science* 252, 1991.

Chicago Tribune. "Problems Persist in Voter Bill." May 21, 1991.

CHIRA, SUSAN. "Bias Against Girls Is Found Rife in Schools, with Lasting Damage." *New York Times,* February 12, 1992.

CHIROT, DANIEL. *How Societies Change.* Thousand Oaks, CA: Pine Forge Press, 1994.

CHOMSKY, NOAM. *Language and Mind* (Enlarged edition). New York: Harcourt Brace Jovanovich, 1972.

CHOMSKY, NOAM. *Rules and Representations.* New York: Columbia University Press, 1980.

CHRISTENSON, BRUCE A., and JOHNSON, NAN E. "Educational Inequality in Adult Mortality: An Assessment with Death Certificate Data from Michigan." *Demography* 32, 1995.

CHRISTIE, NILS. *Crime Control as Industry.* London: Routledge, 1993.

CHRONICLE OF HIGHER EDUCATION. *The Almanac of Higher Education, 1991.* Chicago: The University of Chicago Press, 1991.

CHURCH OF JESUS CHRIST OF LATTER-DAY SAINTS, Media Relations Department. Personal communication. December 28, 1995.

CIARDI, JOHN. *A Browser's Dictionary and Native's Guide to the Unknown American Language.* New York: Harper & Row, 1980.

CIMINI, MICHAEL. "Collective Bargaining in 1990: Search for Solutions Continues." *Monthly Labor Review,* January 1991.

CITIZENS FOR TAX JUSTICE. "A Far Cry from Fair." Washington, D.C.: 1991.

CLAIBORNE, WILLIAM. "Democrats Hail Oregon Win as Rejection of GOP Agenda." *Washington Post,* February 1, 1996a.

CLAIBORNE, WILLIAM. "Oregon Election Officials Tout Mail-in Ballot Result." *Washington Post,* February 2, 1996b.

CLARK, CHARLES S. "Religion in America." *CQ, Researcher* 4 November 25, 1994.

CLARK, JOHN. "Presidential Address on the Importance of Our Understanding of Organizational Conflict." *The Sociological Quarterly* 29, 1988.

CLARK-NICOLAS, PATRICIA, and GRAY-LITTLE, BERNADETTE. "Effect of Economic Resources on Marital Quality in Black Married Couples." *Journal of Marriage and the Family* 53, 1991.

CLARKE, SALLY C., and WILSON, BARBARA F. "The Relative Stability of Remarriages: A Cohort Approach Using Vital Statistics." *Family Relations* 43, 1994.

CLAWSON, DAN, NEUSTADTL, ALAN and SCOTT, DENISE. *Money Talks: Corporate PACS and Political Influence.* New York: Basic Books, 1992.

CLINTON, WILLIAM J. "An American Renewal." *New York Times,* January 21, 1993.

CLOUD, STANLEY W. "The Lessons of Perot." *Time,* November 16, 1992.

CLOWARD, RICHARD, and OHLIN, LLOYD. *Delinquency and Opportunity: A Theory of Delinquent Gangs.* New York: The Free Press, 1960.

COALE, ANSLEY J. "Excess Female Mortality and the Balance of the Sexes in the Population: An Estimate of the Number of 'Missing' Females." *Population and Development Review* 17, 1991.

COCHRAN, JOHN K., BEEGHLEY, LEONARD, AND BOCK, E. WILBUR. "Religiosity and Alcohol Behavior: An Exploration of Reference Group Theory." *Sociological Forum* 3, 1988.

COCKERHAM, WILLIAM C. *Medical Sociology,* 3d ed. Englewood Cliffs, N.J.: Prentice-Hall, 1986.

COCKERHAM, WILLIAM C. *This Aging Society.* Englewood Cliffs, N.J.: Prentice-Hall, 1991.

COCKERHAM, WILLIAM C., et al. "Social Stratification and Self-Management of Health." *Journal of Health and Social Behavior* 27, 1986.

COHEN, ALBERT K. *Delinquent Boys: The Culture of the Gang.* Glencoe, Ill.: The Free Press, 1955.

COHEN, ARTHUR M., and BRAWER, FLORENCE. *The American Community College.* San Francisco: Jossey-Bass, 1982.

COHEN, ROBIN. *Endgame in South Africa?* Paris: Unesco Press, 1986.

COHEN, ROGER. "Amid Growing Crime, Zurich Closes a Park It Reserved for Drug Addicts." *New York Times,* February 11, 1992.

COHEN, ROGER. "Yugoslavia's Ethnic Conflict Threatens Europe's Stability." *New York Times,* November 26, 1994.

COLBURN, DON. "Medicine, Losing Its Appeal." *Washington Post—Health,* August 30, 1988.

COLBURN, DON. "Drug Prices: What's Up?" *Washington Post—Health,* December 15, 1992a.

COLBURN, DON. "A Vicious Cycle of Risk." *Washington Post—Health,* July 28, 1992b.

COLCLOUGH, GLENNA, and TOLBERT, CHARLES M., II. *Work in the Fast Lane.* Albany, N.Y.: SUNY Press, 1992.

COLE, STEPHEN. "Why Sociology Doesn't Make Progress Like the Natural Sciences." *Sociological Forum* 9, 1994.

COLE, STEWART G., and COLE, MILDRED WISE. *Minorities and the American Promise.* New York: Harper & Row, 1954.

COLESANTO, DIANE, and DeSTEFANO, LINDA. "Public Image of TV Evangelists Deteriorates." *The Gallup Report,* 288. 1989.

COLLINS, RANDALL. "A Conflict Theory of Sexual Stratification." *Social Problems* 19, 1971.

COLLINS, RANDALL. *Sociology of Marriage and the Family: Gender, Home and Property,* 2d ed. Chicago: Nelson-Hall, 1988.

COLLINS, RANDALL. "Conflict Theory and the Advance of Macro-Historical Sociology." In George Ritzer (ed.), *Frontiers of Social Theory.* New York: Columbia University Press, 1990.

COLOMY, PAUL, ed. *Functionalist Sociology.* Brookfield, VT.: Elgar Publishing, 1990.

COLTRANE, SCOTT. "Theorizing Masculinities in Contemporary Social Science." In Harry Brod and Michael Kaufman (eds.), *Theorizing Masculinities.* Thousand Oaks, CA: Sage, 1994.

COMPUTER AUDIT UPDATE. "Italy New Computer Crime Law." March 1994.

COMSTOCK, GEORGE, with PAIK, HAEJUNG. *Television and the American Child.* New York: Academic Press, 1991.

CONELL, CAROL, and VOSS, KIM. "Formal Organization and the Fate of Social Movements: Craft Association and Class Alliance in the Knights of Labor." *American Sociological Review* 55, 1990.

CONGRESSIONAL BUDGET OFFICE. *The Changing Distribution of Federal Taxes: 1975–1990.* Washington, D.C., 1987.

CONRAD, PETER. "The Discovery of Hyperkinesis: Notes on the Medicalization of Deviant Behavior." *Social Problems* 23, 1975.

CONRAD, PETER. "Problems in Health Care." In George Ritzer (ed.), *Social Problems,* 2nd ed. New York: Random House, 1986.

CONRAD, PETER, and SCHNEIDER, JOSEPH W. *Deviance and Medicalization: From Badness to Sickness.* St. Louis: Mosby, 1980.

CONVERSE, JEAN M., and PRESSER, STANLEY. *Survey Questions: Handcrafting the Standardized Questionnaire.* Beverly Hills, Calif.: Sage Publications, 1986.

COOK, KAREN S., O'BRIEN, JODI, and KOLLOCK, PETER. "Exchange Theory: A Blueprint for Structure and Process." In George Ritzer (ed.), *Frontiers of Social Theory.* New York: Columbia University Press, 1990.

COOK, T. D., and CAMPBELL, D. T. *Quasi-Experimentation: Design and Analysis Issues for Field Settings.* Chicago: Rand-McNally, 1979.

COOLEY, CHARLES H. *Human Nature and the Social Order.* New York: Charles Scribner's, 1902.

COOLEY, CHARLES H. *Social Organization: A Study of the Larger Mind.* New York: Charles Scribner's, 1909.

COOPER, KENNETH. "Bomb Kills 60 in Sri Lanka's Capital." *Washington Post,* February 1, 1996a.

COOPER, KENNETH. "Police Say Terrorists Used 2 Bombs in Sri Lanka Attack That Killed 72." *Washington Post,* February 2, 1996b.

CORNFIELD, DANIEL. "Union Decline and the Political Demands of Organized Labor." *Work and Occupations* 16, 1989.

CORNWALL, MARIE, HEATON, TIM B., and YOUNG, LAWRENCE A. *Contemporary Mormonism: Social Science Perspectives.* Urbana: University of Illinois Press, 1994.

CORSARO, WILLIAM A. "Interpretative Reproduction in Children's Peer Cultures." *Social Psychology Quarterly* 55, 1992.

COSE, ELLIS. *The Rage of the Privileged Class.* New York: HarperCollins, 1993.

COSER, LEWIS A. *The Functions of Social Conflict.* Glencoe, Ill.: The Free Press, 1956.

COTTER, DAVID, DEFIORE, JOANN M., HERMSEN, JOAN M., KOWALEWSKI, BRENDA M., and VANNEMAN, REEVE. "Occupational Gender Desegregation in the 1980s." *Work and Occupations* 22, 1995.

COUSART, FELICIA. "Group's Visit Clocks Rise in National Debt; Each Family's Share Grew to $79,340 Since Group's Last Stop in Fresno." *Fresno Bee,* July 21, 1995.

COX, GARY W. "Closeness and Turnout: A Methodological Note." *Journal of Politics* 50, 1988.

CRAWFORD, CHRISTINE. *Mommie Dearest.* New York: William Morrow, 1978.

CRIPPEN, TIMOTHY. "Old and New Gods in the Modern World: Toward a Theory of Religious Transformation." *Social Forces* 67, 1988.

CRISPELL, DIANE. "Dual-Earner Diversity." *American Demographics* 17, July 1995.

CROSSETTE, BARBARA. "India's Descent." *New York Times Magazine,* May 19, 1991.

CROUCH, BEN M., and ALPERT, GEOFFREY P. "The American Prison Crisis," in Craig Calhoun and George Ritzer (eds.), *Social Problems.* New York: McGraw-Hill, 1992.

CURRIE, ELLIOTT, DUNN, ROBERT, and FOGARTY, DAVID. "The Fading Dream: Economic Crisis and the New Inequality." In Jerome H. Skolnick and Elliott Currie (eds.), *Crisis in American Institutions.* Glenview, Ill.: Scott Foresman and Company, 1988.

CURTISS, SUSAN. *Genie: A Psycholinguistic Study of a Modern-Day "Wild Child."* New York: Academic Press, 1977.

DAHL, ESPEN. "Social Inequalities in Ill Health: The Significance of Occupational Status, Education and Income—Results from a Norwegian Study." *Sociology of Health and Illness* 16, 1994.

DAHL, ROBERT. *Pluralist Democracy in the United States: Conflict and Consent.* Chicago: Rand McNally, 1967.

DAHRENDORF, RALF. *Class and Class Conflict in Industrial Society.* Stanford, Calif.: Stanford University Press, 1959.

DAS GUPTA, MONICA. "Selective Discrimination Against Female Children in Rural Punjab, India." *Population and Development Review* 13, 1987.

DAUGHERTY, HELEN GINN AND KAMMEYER, KENNETH C. W. *An Introduction to Population* (2nd ed.). New York: Guilford Press, 1995.

DAUNER, JOHN T. "Man Gets Prison for Racial Attack." *Kansas City Times,* February 3, 1987.

DAVENPORT, WILLIAM H. "Sex in Cross-Cultural Perspective." In Frank A. Beach (ed.), *Human Sexuality in Four Perspectives.* Baltimore: The Johns Hopkins University Press, 1977.

DAVIDSON, JAMES D., PYLE, RALPH E., and REYES, DAVID V. "Persistence and Change in the Protestant Establishment." *Social Forces* 74, 1995.

DAVIES, SCOTT. "Leaps of Faith: Shifting Currents in Critical Sociology of Education." *American Journal of Sociology* 100, 1995.

DAVIS, DONALD. "Portrayals of Women in Prime-time Network Television: Some Demographic Characteristics." *Sex Roles* 23, 1990.

DAVIS, JAMES A. "What's Wrong with Sociology?" *Sociological Forum* 9, 1994.

DAVIS, JAMES A., and SMITH, TOM W. *The NORC General Social Survey: A User's Guide.* Newbury Park, Calif.: Sage, 1992.

DAVIS, KINGSLEY. "Extreme Isolation of a Child." *American Journal of Sociology* 45, 1940.

DAVIS, KINGSLEY. "Final Note on a Case of Extreme Isolation." *American Journal of Sociology* 50, 1947.

DAVIS, KINGSLEY. "Population Policy: Will Current Programs Succeed?" *Science* 158, 1967.

DAVIS, KINGSLEY. "Wives and Work: Consequences of the Sex Revolution." *Population and Development Review* 10, 1984.

DAVIS, KINGSLEY, and MOORE, WILBERT E. "Some Principles of Stratification." *American Sociological Review* 10, 1945.

DAVIS, SHELLEY J. "The 1990–1991 Job Outlook in Brief." *Occupational Outlook Quarterly* 34, 1990.

DAY, JENNIFER C. "Population Projections of the United States, by Age, Sex, Race, and Hispanic Origin: 1993 to 2050." U.S. Bureau of the Census, *Current Population Reports,* P25-1104. Washington, DC: U.S. Government Printing Office, 1993.

DEBUONO, BARBARA A., SINNER, STEPHEN H., DAAMEN, MAXIM, and McCORMACK, WILLIAM M. "Sexual Behavior of College Women in 1975, 1986, and 1989." *The New England Journal of Medicine* 322, 1990.

DE CREVECOEUR, J. HECTOR ST. JOHN. *Letters from an American Farmer.* New York: Penguin Books, 1782/1981.

DEDMAN, BILL. "Blacks Turned Down for Home Loans from S&Ls Twice as Often as Whites." *Atlanta Constitution,* January 22, 1989.

DEGLER, CARL N. *In Search of Human Nature: The Decline and Revival of Darwinianism in American Social Thought.* New York: Oxford University Press, 1991.

DELAMATER, JOHN and MACCORQUODALE, PATRICIA. *Premarital Sexuality.* Madison: University of Wisconsin Press, 1979.

DELL'ANGELA, TRACY. "In Immigrant Families, Kids Have the Critical Voice." *Chicago Tribune,* Nov. 17, 1995.

DEMAUSE, LLOYD, (ed.) *The History of Childhood.* New York: The Psychohistory Press, 1974.

DEMERATH, NICHOLAS J. *Birth Control and Foreign Policy: The Alternatives to Family Planning.* New York: Harper & Row, 1976.

DEMERATH, N. J., III, and WILLIAMS, RHYS H. "Civil Religion in an Uncivil Society." *The Annals of the American Academy of Political and Social Science* 480, 1985.

D'EMILIO, JOHN, and FREEDMAN, ESTELLE B. *Intimate Matters: A History of Sexuality in America.* New York: Harper & Row, Publishers, 1988.

DEMO, DAVID H., and ACOCK, ALAN C. "The Impact of Divorce on Children." *Journal of Marriage and the Family* 50, 1988.

DEMOTT, BENJAMIN. *The Imperial Middle: Why Americans Can't Think Straight about Class.* New York: William Morrow, 1990.

DENTLER, ROBERT A., and ERIKSON, KAI T. "The Functions of Deviance in Groups," *Social Problems* 7, 1959.

DENZIN, NORMAN K. *The Recovering Alcoholic.* Beverly Hills, Calif.: Sage, 1986.

DENZIN, NORMAN K. *The Alcoholic Self.* Beverly Hills, Calif.: Sage, 1987.

DENZIN, NORMAN K., and LINCOLN, YVONNA S. *Handbook of Qualitative Research* (eds.). Thousand Oaks, CA: Sage, 1994.

DeSTEFANO, LINDA. "Church/Synagogue Membership and Attendance Levels Remain Stable." *Gallup Poll Monthly* 292, 1990.

DeSTEFANO, LINDA, AND COLASANTO, DIANE. "Unlike 1975, Today Most Americans Think Men Have It Better." *Gallup Poll Monthly,* February 1990.

DE TOCQUEVILLE, ALEXIS. *Democracy in America,* Vols. 1 and 2. New York: Schocken Books, 1961.

DIETZ, THOMAS, BURNS, TOM R., and BUTTEL, FREDERICK. "Evolutionary Theory in Sociology: An Examination of Current Thinking." *Sociological Forum* 5, 1990.

DINGES, WILLIAM D. "Catholic Traditionalism." In Joseph H. Fichter (ed.), *Alternatives to American Mainline Churches.* New York: Rose of Sharon Press, 1983.

DINGES, WILLIAM D., and HITCHCOCK, JAMES. "Roman Catholic Traditionalism and Activist Conservatism in the United States." In Martin E. Marty and R. Scott Appleby (eds.), *Fundamentalisms Observed.* Chicago: University of Chicago Press, 1991.

DINNERSTEIN, LEONARD, and REIMERS, DAVID M. *Ethnic Americans: A History of Immigration and Assimilation.* 3rd edition. New York: Harper & Row, 1987.

DIONNE, E. J., JR. "'Solid South' Again, but Republican." *New York Times,* November 13, 1988a.

DIONNE, E. J., JR. "If Nonvoters Had Voted: Same Winner, but Bigger." *New York Times,* November 21, 1988b.

DIPRETE, THOMAS A., and SOULE, WHITMAN T. "Gender and Promotion in Segmented Job Ladder Systems." *American Sociological Review* 53, 1988.

DOBASH, RUSSELL P., DOBASH, R. EMERSON, WILSON, MARGO, and DALY, MARTIN. "The Myth of Sexual Symmetry in Marital Violence." *Social Problems* 39, 1992.

DOMHOFF, G. WILLIAM. *Who Rules America Now?* Englewood Cliffs, N.J.: Prentice-Hall, 1983.

DORRIS, MICHAEL, A. "The Grass Still Grows, the Rivers Still Flow: Contemporary Native Americans." *Daedalus* 110, 1981.

DOTTER, DANIEL L., and ROEBUCK, JULIAN B. "The Labeling Approach Re-examined: Interactionism and the Components of Deviance." *Deviant Behavior* 9, 1988.

DRAPER, PATRICIA. "!Kung Women: Contrasts in Sexual Egalitarianism in Foraging and Sedentary Contexts." In R. Reiter (ed.), *Toward an Anthropology of Women.* New York: Monthly Review Press, 1975.

DREW, ELIZABETH. *Politics and Money: The New Road to Corruption.* New York: Macmillan, 1983.

DROZDIAK, WILLIAM. "Dutch Drugs Irks Neighbors: Coffee-House Marijuana Now Crossing Europe's Lax Borders." *Washington Post,* November 4, 1995.

DUBERMAN, LUCILE. *The Reconstituted Family: A Study of Remarried Couples and Their Children.* Chicago: Nelson-Hall, 1975.

DUFF, JOHN B. *The Irish in the United States.* Belmont, Calif.: Wadsworth, 1971.

DUKE, LYNNE. "N.Y. Black, Jewish Tension Not Seen as Indicative of Groups' Relations." *Washington Post,* December 27, 1992.

DUNCAN, GREG J., SMEEDING, TIMOTHY M., and RODGERS, WILLARD. "The Incredible Shrinking Middle Class." *American Demographics,* May 16, 1992.

DUNCAN, GREG J., et al. *Years of Poverty: Years of Plenty: The Changing Economic Fortunes of American Workers and Families.* Ann Arbor, Mich.: Institute for Social Research, 1984.

DUNN, JUDY, and PLOMIN, ROBERT. *Separate Lives: Why Siblings Are So Different.* New York: Basic Books, 1990.

DUNNING, ERIC, MURPHY, PATRICK, and WILLIAMS, JOHN. "Spectator Violence at Football Matches: Towards a Sociological Explanation." *The British Journal of Sociology* 37, 1986.

DURAND, JOHN D. "Historical Estimates of World Population." *Population and Development Review* 3, 1977.

DURKHEIM, EMILE. *Suicide.* New York: The Free Press, 1951. Originally published 1897.

DURKHEIM, EMILE. *The Division of Labor in Society.* New York: The Free Press, 1964. Originally published 1895.

DURKHEIM, EMILE. *The Elementary Forms of Religious Life.* New York: The Free Press, 1965. Originally published 1912.

DURKIN, KEITH F., and BRYANT, CLIFTON D. "'Log on to Sex': Some Notes on the Carnal Computer and Erotic Cyberspace as an Emerging Research Frontier." *Deviant Behavior* 16, 1995.

DWORKIN, ANTHONY GARY. *Teacher Burnout in Public Schools.* Albany, N.Y.: State University of New York Press, 1987.

DYE, THOMAS R. *Who's Running America? The Reagan Years,* 3d ed. Englewood Cliffs, N.J.: Prentice-Hall, 1983.

ECK, DIANA L. "Challenge to Pluralism." *Nieman Reports.* Summer 1993.

ECKHOLM, ERIK. "Frayed Nerves of People without Health Coverage." *New York Times,* July 11, 1994.

Economic Report of the President. Washington, D.C.: U.S. Government Printing Office, 1983.

The Economist. May 13, 1985.

EDER, DONNA. "Ability Grouping as a Self-Fulfilling Prophecy: A Micro-Analysis of Teacher Student Interaction." *Sociology of Education* 54, 1981.

EDSALL, THOMAS BYRNE, with EDSALL, MARY D. *Chain Reaction: The Impact of Race, Rights, and Taxes on American Politics.* New York: Norton, 1992.

EDWARDS, JOHN N. "New Conceptions: Biosocial Innovations and the Family," *Journal of Marriage and the Family* 53, 1991.

EDWARDS, RICHARD. *Contested Terrain: The Transformation of the Workplace in the Twentieth Century.* New York: Basic Books, 1979.

EHRENREICH, BARBARA. "What Do Women Have to Celebrate?" *Time,* November 16, 1992.

EHRLICH, HOWARD J. *Campus Ethnoviolence and Policy Options.* Baltimore: National Institute Against Prejudice and Violence, 1990.

EISENHOWER, DWIGHT D. "Liberty Is at Stake." In Herbert I. Schiller and Joseph D. Phillips (eds.), *Super-State: Readings in the Military-Industrial Complex.* Urbana: University of Illinois Press, 1972.

EISENSTADT, S. N. "The Japanese Historical Experience—Comparative and Analytical Dimensions." *Qualitative Sociology* 18, 1995.

EKEH, PETER. *Social Exchange Theory: The Two Traditions.* Cambridge, Mass.: Harvard University Press, 1974.

ELLER, T. J. "Household Wealth and Asset Ownership: 1991." U.S. Bureau of the Census. *Current Population Reports,* P70-34. Washington, DC: U.S. Government Printing Office, 1994.

Emerging Trends. "Religion a Driving Force for Most Black Americans." 17, October 1995.

ENGELS, FRIEDRICH. *The Origin of the Family, Private Property and the State.* New York: International Publishers, 1972. Originally published 1884.

ENGLAND, PAULA. "Work for Pay and Work at Home: Women's Double Disadvantage." In Craig Calhoun and George Ritzer (eds.), *Social Problems.* New York: McGraw-Hill, 1992.

ENGLAND, PAULA, and McCREARY, LORI. "Gender Inequality in Paid Employment." In Beth B. Hess and Myra Marx Ferree (eds.), *Analyzing Gender: A Handbook of Social Science Research.* Beverly Hills, Calif.: Sage, 1987.

ENGLAND, PAULA, FARKAS, GEORGE, KILBOURNE, BARBARA, and DOU, THOMAS. "Explaining Occupational Sex Segregation and Wages: Findings from a Model with Fixed Effects." *American Sociological Review* 53, 1988.

ENGLISH, KIM. "Self-reported Crime Rates of Women Prisoners." *Journal of Quantitative Criminology* 9, 1993.

ENNIS, JAMES G. "The Social Organization of Sociological Knowledge: Modeling the Intersection of Specialties." *American Sociological Review* 57, 1992.

ENSMINGER, MARGARET E., AND SLUSARCICK, ANITA L. "Paths to High School Graduation or Dropout: A Longitudinal Study of a First-grade Cohort." *Sociology of Education* 65, 1992.

ENSTROM, JAMES E. "Cancer and Total Mortality Among Active Mormons." *Cancer* 42, 1978.

ENSTROM, JAMES E. "Health Practices and Cancer Mortality among Active California Mormons." *Journal of the National Cancer Institute* 81, 1989.

ENTWISLE, DORIS R., and HAYDUK, LESLIE ALEC. "Lasting Effects of Elementary School." *Sociology of Education* 61, 1988.

ERDRICH, LOUISE, and DORRIS, MICHAEL. "Who Owns the Land?" *New York Times Magazine,* September 4, 1988.

ERIKKSON, BJORN. "The First Formulation of Sociology: A Discursive Innovation of the 18th Century." *Archives of European Sociology* 34, 1993.

ERIKSON, KAI. "Notes on the Sociology of Deviance." In Howard S. Becker (ed.), *The Other Side: Perspectives on Deviance.* New York: The Free Press, 1964.

ESCOBAR, GABRIEL. "Washington Area's 703 Homicides in 1990 Set Record." *Washington Post,* January 2, 1991.

ESPIRITU, YEN LE, and LIGHT, IVAN. "The Changing Ethnic Shape of Contemporary America." In Mark Gottdiener and Chris G. Pickvance (eds.), *Urban Life in Transition.* Newbury Park, Calif.: Sage, 1991.

ESTERBERG, KRISTIN G. "From Accommodation to Liberation: A Social Movement Analysis of Lesbians in the Homophile Movement." *Gender and Society* 8, 1994.

ETZIONI, AMITAI. *A Comparative Analysis of Complex Organizations.* New York: The Free Press, 1961.

EVANS, DARYL. "Cultural Lag, Economic Scarcity, and the Technological Quagmire of 'Infant Doe'." *Journal of Social Issues* 49, 1993.

Evans-Prichard, E. E. "Sexual Inversion Among the Azande." *American Anthropologist* 72, 1970.

FACELIERE, R. *Love in Ancient Greece.* Translated by James Cleugh. New York: Crown, 1962.

FACIONE, NOREEN. "Role Overload and Health: The Married Mother in the Waged Labor Force." *Health Care for Women International* 15, 1994.

FALUDI, SUSAN. "The Money Shot." *New Yorker,* October 30, 1995.

FANTASIA, RICK. "The Assault on American Labor." In Craig Calhoun and George Ritzer (eds.), *Social Problems.* New York: McGraw-Hill, 1992.

FANTE, JOHN. "The Odyssey of a Wop." In Oscar Handlin (ed.), *Children of the Uprooted.* New York: George Braziller, 1966.

FARHI, PAUL. "Study Finds Real Harm in TV Violence." *Washington Post,* February 6, 1996.

FARLEY, REYNOLDS, and ALLEN, WALTER R. *The Color Line and the Quality of Life in America.* New York: Russell Sage Foundation, 1987.

FARLEY, REYNOLDS, and FREY, WILLIAM H. "Changes in the Segregation of Whites from Blacks during the 1980s: Small Steps toward a More Integrated Society." *American Sociological Review* 59, 1994.

FARNSWORTH, MARGARET, and LEIBER, MICHAEL J. "Strain Theory Revisited: Economic Goals, Educational Means, and Delinquency." *American Sociological Review* 54, 1989.

FARSON, RICHARD. *Birthrights.* New York: Macmillan, 1974.

FAUPEL, CHARLES E. "Heroin Use, Street Crime, and the 'Main Hustle': Implications for the Validity of Official Crime Data." *Deviant Behavior* 7, 1986.

FEAGIN, JOE C. "The Continuing Significance of Race: Antiblack Discrimination in Public Places." *American Sociological Review* 56, 1991.

FEAGIN, JOE R., and SIKES, MELVIN P. *Living with Racism: The Black Middle Class Experience.* Boston: Beacon, 1994.

FEATHERSTONE, MIKE. "Global Culture: An Introduction." In Mike Featherstone, (ed.), *Global Culture: Nationalism, Globalization and Modernity.* London: Sage, 1990.

FEATHERSTONE, MIKE. *Consumer Culture and Postmodernism.* London: Sage, 1991.

FELMLEE, DIANE, and EDER, DONNA. "Contextual Effects in the Classroom: The Impact of Ability Groups on Student Attention." *Sociology of Education* 56, 1983.

FERNANDEZ, JOHN P. *Child Care and Corporate Productivity: Resolving Family/Work Conflicts.* Lexington, Mass.: Lexington Books, 1986.

FERNANDEZ, R.M., PAULSON, R., and HIRANO-NAKANISHI, M. "Dropping Out among Hispanic Youth." *Social Science Research* 18, 1989.

FERREE, MYRA M. "The View from Below: Women's Employment and Gender Equality in Working Class Families." *Marriage and Family Review* 7, 1984.

FERREE, MYRA M. "She Works Hard for a Living: Gender and Class on the Job." In Beth B. Hess and Myra Marx Ferree (eds.), *Analyzing Gender: A Handbook of Social Science Research.* Beverly Hills, Calif.: Sage, 1987.

FERREE, MYRA M. "Beyond Separate Spheres: Feminism and Family Research." *Journal of Marriage and the Family* 52, 1990.

FIELD, DAVID. "Getting There Safely: Road Fatalities Down, But Can Drop Continue?" *Washington Times,* September 3, 1995.

FINE, GARY A. *With the Boys: Little League Baseball and Preadolescent Culture.* Chicago: University of Chicago Press, 1987.

FINE, GARY A. "Symbolic Interactionism in the Post-Blumerian Age." In George Ritzer (ed.), *Frontiers of Social Theory.* New York: Columbia University Press, 1990.

FINEBERG, HARVEY V. "The Social Dimensions of AIDS." *Scientific American* 259, 1988.

FINEMAN, HOWARD, and HOSENBALL, MARK. "Buying Power" *Newsweek,* January 29, 1996.

FINKE, ROGER, and STARK, RODNEY. *The Churching of America, 1776–1990: Winners and Losers in Our Religious Economy.* New Brunswick, N.J.: Rutgers University Press, 1992.

FINKELHOR, D., HOTALING, G., LEWIS, I. A., AND SMITH, C. "Sexual Abuse in a National Survey of Adult Men and Women: Prevalence, Characteristics, and Risk Factors." *Child Abuse and Neglect* 14, 1990.

FINLEY, MERRILEE K. "Teachers and Tracking in a Comprehensive High School." *Sociology of Education* 57, 1984.

FINNEGAN, WILLIAM. "The Sporting Scene: Playing Doc's Games—II." *The New Yorker,* August 31, 1992.

FIREBAUGH, GLENN, and DAVIS, KENNETH E. "Trends in Antiblack Prejudice 1972–1984: Region and Cohort Effects." *American Journal of Sociology* 94, 1988.

FISCHER, CLAUDE S. "The Public and Private Worlds of City Life." *American Sociological Review* 46, 1981.

FISCHER, CLAUDE S. *To Dwell Among Friends: Personal Networks in Town and City.* Chicago: University of Chicago Press, 1982.

FISCHER, CLAUDE S. *The Urban Experience,* 2nd ed. New York: Harcourt Brace Jovanovich, 1984.

FISHER, MARC. "Germany's Health System: Model for America or Plan in Crisis?" *Washington Post,* December 28, 1992.

FISHER, SUE. "Doctor–Patient Communication: A Social and Micro-Political Performance." *Sociology of Health and Illness* 6, 1984.

FISHER, SUE, and GROCE, STEPHEN B. "Doctor–Patient Negotiation of Cultural Assumptions." *Sociology of Health and Illness* 7, 1985.

FISKE, EDWARD B. "New York City's Population Gain Attributed to Immigrant Tide." *New York Times,* February 22, 1991.

FLAIM, PAUL, O. "New Data on Union Members and Their Earnings." *Employment and Earnings* 32, 1985.

FLAIM, PAUL O. "Population Changes, the Baby Boom, and Unemployment," *Monthly Labor Review* 113, 1990.

FLANAGAN, WILLIAM G., and McMENAMIN, BRIGID. "The Playground Bullies Are Learning How to Type." *Forbes,* December 21, 1992.

FLYNN, CLIFTON P.. "Regional Differences in Attitudes toward Corporal Punishment." *Journal of Marriage and the Family* 56, 1994.

FONOW, MARY MARGARET, RICHARDSON, LAUREL, and WEMMERUS, VIRGINIA A. "Feminist Rape Education: Does It Work?" *Gender and Society* 6, 1992.

FORISHA, BARBARA LUSK. *Sex Roles and Personal Awareness.* Glenview, Ill.: Scott, Foresman, 1978.

FORREST, JACQUELINE DARROCH and SINGH, SUSHEELA. "The Sexual and Reproductive Behavior of American Women, 1982–1988." *Family Planning Perspectives* 22, 1990.

FORSYTH, CRAIG J., and BENOIT, GENEVIEVE M. "'Rare, Ole, Dirty Snacks': Some Research Notes on Dirt Eating." *Deviant Behavior* 10, 1989.

FORSYTH, CRAIG J., and MARCKESE, THOMAS A. "Thrills and Skills: a Sociological Analysis of Poaching." *Deviant Behavior* 14, 1993.

FOX, A. J., and ADELSTEIN, A. M. "Occupational Mortality: Work or Way of Life." *Journal of Epidemiology and Community Health* 32, 1978.

FOX, GREER LITTON. "The Mother–Adolescent Daughter Relationship as a Sexual Socialization Structure: A Research Review." *Family Relations* 29, 1980.

FOX, GREER LITTON, and INAZU, JUDITH K. "Patterns and Outcomes of Mother-Daughter Communications About Sexuality." *Journal of Social Issues* 36, 1980.

FOX, NICHOLAS J. "Discourse, Organisation and the Surgical Ward Round." *Sociology of Health and Illness* 15, 1993.

FRANCE, ANATOLE. *Crainqueville.* Freeport, N.Y.: Books for Libraries, 1922.

FRANK, ANDRE GUNDER. *Capitalism and Underdevelopment in Latin America: Historical Studies of Chile and Brazil.* New York: Monthly Labor Review Press, 1969.

FRANK, ROBERT H., and COOK, PHILIP J. *The Winner-Take-All Society.* New York: Free Press, 1995.

FRANKL, RAZELLE. *Televangelism: The Marketing of Popular Religion.* Carbondale and Edwardsville: Southern Illinois University Press, 1987.

FRANKLIN, JAMES C. "The American Workforce: 1992–2005; Industry Output and Employment." *Monthly Labor Review,* November 1993.

FREEDMAN, RONALD. "Family Planning Programs in the Third World." *Annals of the American Academy of Political and Social Science* 510, 1990.

FREEMAN, JO. "On the Origins of Social Movements." In Jo Freeman (ed.), *Social Movements of the Sixties and Seventies.* New York: Longman, 1983.

FREEMAN, RICHARD B., and MEDOFF, JAMES L. *What Do Unions Do?* New York: Basic Books, 1984.

FREIDSON, ELIOT. *Doctoring Together.* New York: Elsevier, 1975.

FREUND, CHARLES P. "Portrait of a Double Standard." *Washington Post,* February 4, 1996.

FREY, WILLIAM H. "Metropolitan America: Beyond the Transition." *Population Bulletin* 45, 1990.

FRIEDMAN, EMILY. "The Uninsured: From Dilemma to Crisis." *Journal of the American Medical Association* 265, 1991.

FRIEDMAN, JONATHAN. *Cultural Identity and Global Process.* London: Sage, 1994.

FRIEDMAN, THOMAS L. "Kahane Appeal to Oust Arabs Gains in Israel." *New York Times,* August 5, 1985.

FRIEDRICH, CARL J., and BRZEZINSKI, ZBIGNIEW. *Totalitarian Dictatorship and Autocracy,* vol. 2. Cambridge, Mass.: Harvard University Press, 1965.

FRISBIE, W. PARKER, and KASARDA, JOHN D. "Spatial Processes." In Neil J. Smelser (ed.), *Handbook of Sociology.* Beverly Hills, Calif.: Sage, 1988.

FRYE, ALTON. "The ZBM Solution: Let's Get Rid of All Ballistic Missiles." *Washington Post,* January 3, 1993.

FULLER, THEODORE, EDWARDS, JOHN N., SERMSRI, SANTHAT, and VORAKITPHOKATORN, SAIRUDEE. "Gender and Health: Some Asian Evidence." *Journal of Health and Social Behavior* 34, 1993.

FULLERTON, HOWARD N., JR. "Labor Force Projections: The Baby Boom Moves on." *Monthly Labor Review,* November 1991.

FULLERTON, JR., HOWARD N. "Another Look at the Labor Force." *Monthly Labor Review,* November, 1993.

FURLONG, MICHAEL J., CHUNG, ANNIE, BATES, MICHAEL, and MORRISON, RICHARD. "Who Are the Victims of School Violence? A Comparison of Student Non-Victims and Multi-Victims." *Education and Treatment of Children* 18, 1995.

FURSTENBERG, FRANK F., JR. "The Social Consequences of Teenage Parenthood." In Frank F. Furstenberg, Jr., Richard Lincoln, and Jane Menken (eds.), *Teenage Sexuality, Pregnancy and Childbearing.* Philadelphia: University of Pennsylvania Press, 1981.

FURSTENBERG, FRANK, MORGAN, S. PHILIP, MOORE, KRISTIN A. and PETERSON, JAMES L. "Race Differences in the Timing of Adolescent Intercourse." *American Sociological Review* 52, 1987.

The Gallup Report. "Religion in America." Report No. 259, 1987.

GALLUP, GEORGE, JR., and HUGICK, LARRY. "Racial Tolerance Grows, Progress on Racial Equality Less Evident." *Gallup Poll Monthly* 297, 1990.

GALLUP, GEORGE JR., and NEWPORT, FRANK. "Almost Half of Americans Believe Biblical View of Creation." *Gallup Poll Monthly,* November 1991.

GAMSON, JOSH. "Silence, Death, and the Invisible Enemy: AIDS Activism and Social Movement 'Newness'." *Social Problems* 36, 1989.

GAMSON, WILLIAM A. *The Strategy of Social Protest.* Homewood, Ill.: The Dorsey Press, 1975.

GAMSON, WILLIAM A., and STUART, DAVID. "Media Discourse as a Symbolic Contest: The Bomb in Political Cartoons." *Sociological Forum* 7, 1992.

GANS, CURTIS. "No Wonder Turnout Was Low." *Washington Post,* November 11, 1988.

GANS, HERBERT J. *Middle American Individualism.* New York: The Free Press, 1988.

GANS, HERBERT J. "Deconstructing the Underclass." *Journal of the American Planning Association* 56, 1990.

GANS, HERBERT J. "Some Virtues of Sociology." *Footnotes* 20, November 1992.

GARBARINO, JAMES, and SHERMAN, DEBORAH. "High-Risk Neighborhoods and High-Risk Families: The Human Ecology of Child Maltreatment." *Child Development* 51, 1980.

GATES, BILL. *The Road Ahead.* New York: Viking, 1995.

GATES, HENRY L., JR. "Thirteen Ways of Looking at a Black Man." *New Yorker,* October 23, 1995.

GECAS, VIKTOR. "Contexts of Socialization." In Morris Rosenberg and Ralph H. Turner (eds.), *Social Psychology: Sociological Perspectives,* new edition. New Brunswick, N.J.: Transaction, 1990b.

GECAS, VIKTOR, and BURKE, PETER J. "Self and Identity." In Karen S. Cook, Gary Alan Fine, and James S. House (eds.), *Sociological Perspectives on Social Psychology.* Boston: Allyn & Bacon, 1995.

GEDYE, ROBIN. "Dopeheads Put a Match to Old German Values." *Sunday Telegraph,* October 23, 1994.

GEHRIG, GAIL. *American Civil Religion: An Assessment.* Monograph Series, 3. Storrs, Conn.: Society for the Scientific Study of Religion, 1979.

GELLES, RICHARD J. *Family Violence,* 2nd ed. Beverly Hills, Calif.: Sage, 1987.

GERBER, JURG, and SHORT, JAMES F., JR. "Publicity and the Control of Corporate Behavior: The Case of Infant Formula." *Deviant Behavior* 7, 1986.

GERHARDS, JURGEN, and RUCHT, DIETER. "Mesomobilization: Organizing and Framing in Two Protest Campaigns in West Germany." *American Journal of Sociology* 98, 1992.

GERTH, HANS, and MILLS, C. WRIGHT, (eds.) *From Max Weber: Essays in Sociology.* New York: Oxford University Press, 1958.

GESSNER, JOHN C., and LaMAGDELEINE, DONALD R. "The Impact of the Baby Boom Cohort on U.S. Religious Denominations: Theoretical and Research Directions." In Monty L. Lynn and David O. Moberg (eds.), *Research in the Social Scientific Study of Religion,* 3. Greenwich, Conn.: JAI Press, 1991.

GIALLOMBARDO, ROSE. *The Social World of Imprisoned Girls: A Comparative Study of Institutions for Juvenile Delinquents.* New York: John Wiley, 1974.

GIAMO, BENEDICT, and GRUNBERG, JEFFREY. *Beyond Homelessness: Frames of Reference.* Iowa City: University of Iowa Press, 1992.

GIBNEY, FRANK. "The Strange Ways of Staphorst." *Life,* September 27, 1948.

GIDDENS, ANTHONY. *The Consequences of Modernity.* Stanford, CA: Stanford University Press, 1990.

GIDDENS, ANTHONY. *The Constitution of Society: Outline of the Theory of Structuration.* Berkeley: University of California Press, 1984.

GIELE, JANET Z. "Introduction: The Status of Women in Comparative Perspective." In Janet Z. Giele and A. C. Smock (eds.), *Women: Roles and Status in Eight Countries.* New York: Wiley-Interscience, 1977.

GIELE, JANET Z. "Gender and Sex Roles." In Neil J. Smelser (ed.), *Handbook of Sociology.* Beverly Hills, Calif.: Sage, 1988.

GILBERT, DENNIS, and KAHL, JOSEPH A. *The American Class Structure: A New Synthesis.* Belmont, Calif.: Wadsworth, 1993.

GILGUN, JANE F. "We Shared Something Special: The Moral Discourse of Incest Perpetrators." *Journal of Marriage and the Family* 57, 1995.

GILL, VIRGINIA T., and MAYNARD, DOUGLAS W. "On 'Labeling' in Actual Interaction: Delivering and Receiving Diagnoses of Developmental Disabilities." *Social Problems* 42, 1995.

GIST, NOEL P., AND FAVA, SYLVIA FLEIS. *Urban Society,* 6th ed. New York: Thomas Y. Crowell, 1974.

GLAAB, CHARLES N., and BROWN, THEODORE A. *A History of Urban America.* New York: Macmillan, 1967.

GLADWELL, MALCOLM. "City, Suburbs Battle for Scanning Device." *Washington Post-Health,* August 23, 1988.

GLADWELL, MALCOLM. "Public Health Experts Turn to Economic Ills." *Washington Post,* November 26, 1990.

GLADWELL, MALCOLM. "Why Canada's Health Plan Is No Remedy for America." *Washington Post,* March 22, 1992.

GLASS, DAVID, SQUIRE, PEVEREILL, and WOLFINGER, RAYMOND. "Voter Turnout: An International Comparison." *Public Opinion,* December/January 1984.

GLAZER, NATHAN, and MOYNIHAN, DANIEL P. *Beyond the Melting Pot: The Negroes, Puerto Ricans, Jews, Italians, and Irish of New York City.* Cambridge, Mass.: The MIT Press, 1963.

GLENN, NORVAL. "Quantitative Research on Marital Quality in the 1980s: A Critical Review." *Journal of Marriage and the Family* 52, 1990.

GLENN, NORVAL D., and SHELTON, BETH ANN. "Regional Differences in Divorce in the United States." *Journal of Marriage and the Family* 47, 1985.

GLOCK, CHARLES V., and STARK, RODNEY. *Religion and Society in Tension.* Chicago: Rand McNally, 1965.

GOFFMAN, ERVING. "The Moral Career of the Mental Patient." *Psychiatry* 22, 1959a.

GOFFMAN, ERVING. *The Presentation of Self in Everyday Life.* Garden City, N.Y.: Anchor Books, 1959b.

GOFFMAN, ERVING. *Asylums: Essays on the Social Situation of Mental Patients and Other Inmates.* Garden City, N.Y.: Anchor Books, 1961.

GOFFMAN, ERVING. *Stigma: Notes on the Management of Spoiled Identity.* Englewood Cliffs, N.J.: Prentice-Hall, 1963.

GOLDBERG, STEVEN. *The Inevitability of Patriarchy.* New York: William Morrow, 1973.

GOLDFIELD, MICHAEL. *The Decline of Organized Labor.* Chicago: University of Chicago Press, 1987.

GOLDMAN, ARI L. "When Mary Is Sighted, a Blessing Has Its Burdens." *New York Times,* September 6, 1992.

GOLDSCHEIDER, CALVIN, and MOSHER, WILLIAM. "Patterns of Contraception Use in the United States: The Importance of Religious Factors." *Studies in Family Planning* 22, 1991.

GOLDSCHEIDER, FRANCES K., and WAITE, LINDA J. *New Families, No Families?* Berkeley: University of California Press, 1991.

GOLDSTEIN, PAUL J., and BROWNSTEIN, HENRY H. *Understanding the Relationship between Violence and Drugs.* New York: Lexington Books, forthcoming.

GOLDSTONE, JACK. "Revolution." In Craig Calhoun and George Ritzer (eds.), *Social Problems.* New York: McGraw-Hill, 1992.

GOLDSTONE, JACK A. "Predicting Revolutions: Why We Could (and Should) Have Foreseen the Revolutions of 1989–1991 in the U.S.S.R. and Eastern Europe." *Contention: Debates in Society, Culture, and Science* 2, 1993.

GOLEMAN, DANIEL. "The Electronic Rorschach." *Psychology Today,* February 1983.

GONZALEZ, DAVID. "Hispanic Voters Struggle to Find the Strength in Their Numbers." *New York Times,* May 26, 1991.

GOODE, ERICH, (ed.), *Marijuana.* Chicago: Aldine, 1969.

GOODE, ERICH. "The Use of Alcohol and Drugs." In Craig Calhoun and George Ritzer (eds.), *Social Problems.* New York: McGraw-Hill, 1992.

GOODE, WILLIAM J. "The Theoretical Importance of Love." *American Sociological Review* 24, 1959.

GOODMAN, ELLEN. "Oregon Brings the Ballot to the Couch Potato." *Newsday,* November 7, 1995.

GORDON, DAVID M. "Class and Economics of Crime." *Review of Radical Political Economies* 3, 1981.

GORDON, MICHAEL, and SHANKWEILER, PENELOPE. "Different Equals Less: Female Sexuality in Recent Marriage Manuals." *Journal of Marriage and the Family* 33, 1971.

GORDON, MILTON M. *Assimilation in American Life: The Role of Race, Religion and National Origins.* New York: Oxford University Press, 1964.

GOTTDIENER, MARK. *The New Urban Sociology.* New York: McGraw-Hill, 1994.

GOTTDIENER, MARK, and FEAGIN, JOE R. "The Paradigm Shift in Urban Sociology." *Urban Affairs Quarterly,* 24, 1988.

GOTTDIENER, MARK, and PICKVANCE, CHRIS G. (eds.), *Urban Life in Transition.* Newbury Park, Calif.: Sage Publications, 1991.

GOTTMAN, JEAN. *Megalopolis: The Urbanized Northeastern Seaboard of the United States.* New York: Twentieth Century Fund, 1961.

GOTTMAN, JEAN, and HARPER, ROBERT A. *Since Megalopolis: The Urban Writings of Jean Gottman.* Baltimore, Md.: Johns Hopkins University Press, 1990.

GOULD, STEPHEN JAY. *Ever Since Darwin.* New York: W.W. Norton, 1977.

GOULD, STEPHEN JAY. *The Mismeasure of Man.* New York: W.W. Norton, 1981.

GOULDNER, ALVIN W. *Patterns of Industrial Democracy.* Glencoe, Ill.: The Free Press, 1954.

GOULDNER, ALVIN W. "The Norm of Reciprocity." *American Sociological Review* 25, 1960.

Gove, Walter (ed.). *The Labelling of Deviance: Evaluating a Perspective,* 2nd ed. Beverly Hills, Calif.: Sage, 1980.

GOVE, WALTER R. "Is Sociology the Integrative Discipline in the Study of Human Behavior?" *Social Forces* 73, 1995.

GRACEY, HAROLD. "Learning the Student Role: Kindergarten as Academic Boot Camp." In Dennis Wrong and Harold Gracey (eds.), *Readings in Introductory Sociology.* New York: Macmillan, 1967.

GRANFIELD, ROBERT. *Making Elite Lawyers: Visions of Law at Harvard and Beyond.* New York: Routledge, Chapman and Hall. 1992.

GRANFIELD, ROBERT, and KOENIG, THOMAS. "Learning Collective Eminence: Harvard Law School and the Social Production of Elite Lawyers." *Sociological Quarterly* 33, 1992.

GRAY, DAVID E. "Perceptions of Stigma: The Parents of Autistic Children." *Sociology of Health and Illness* 15, 1993.

GREELEY, ANDREW M. *Ethnicity in the United States: A Preliminary Reconnaissance.* New York: John Wiley, 1974.

GREELEY, ANDREW M. "The Ethnic Miracle." *The Public Interest* 45, 1976.

GREENBERG, DANIEL S. "Finding Time to Produce." *Washington Post,* March 6, 1979.

GREENBERG, EDWARD, and GRUNBERG, LEON. "Work Alienation and Problem Alcohol Behavior." *Journal of Health and Social Behavior* 36, 1995.

Greenfeld, Lawrence A., and Minor-Harper, Stephanie. "Women in Prison." *Bureau of Justice Statistics Special Report.* Washington, D.C.: U.S. Department of Justice, 1991.

GREENHALGH, SUSAN, CHUZHU, ZHU, and NAN, LI. "Restraining Population Growth in Three Chinese Villages, 1988–1993." *Population and Development Review* 20, 1994.

GREENWALD, JOHN. "What Went Wrong?" *Time,* November 9, 1992.

GRIFFIN, LARRY J. "How Is Sociology Informed by History?" *Social Forces* 73, 1995.

GROBSTEIN, CLIFFORD. "When Does Human Life Begin?" *Science* 82, 1982.

GROSBY, STEVEN. "Introduction: The Tasks of Historical Sociology." *Qualitative Sociology* 18, 1995.

GROVE, LLOYD. "The Bush Women, Calling the Shots." *Washington Post,* August 18, 1992a.

GROVE, LLOYD. "The Double-fidget Campaign Whiz." *Washington Post,* January 23, 1992b.

GRUSKY, DAVID B., and HAUSER, ROBERT M. "Comparative Social Mobility Revisited: Models of Convergence and Divergence in 16 Countries." *American Sociological Review* 49, 1984.

GUNTER, B. G., and GUNTER, NANCY C. "Leisure Styles: A Conceptual Framework for Modern Leisure." *Sociological Quarterly* 21, 1980.

GUSFIELD, JOSEPH R., and MICHALOWICZ, JERZY. "Secular Symbolism: Studies of Ritual, Ceremony, and the Symbolic Order of Modern Life." In Ralph H. Turner and James F. Short, Jr. (eds.), *Annual Review of Sociology* 10. Palo Alto, Calif.: Annual Reviews, 1984.

GUTTMAN, ALLEN. From Ritual To Record: *The Nature of Modern Sports.* New York: Columbia University Press, 1978.

GUTTMAN, MONIKA. "Kids and Pills: The Ritalin Generation." *USA Weekend,* October 29, 1995.

HAASE, DAVID L. "How the Campaign Trail Is Merging with Information Superhighway." *Indianapolis Star,* December 10, 1995.

HABERMAN, CLYDE. "Flow of Turks Leaving Bulgaria Swells to Hundreds of Thousands." *New York Times,* August 15, 1989.

HABERMAN, CLYDE. "Turks Say Hussein Plotted to Drive Out the Kurds." *New York Times,* April 12, 1991.

HABERMAS, JURGEN. *The Theory of Communicative Action, Vol. 2, Lifeworld and System: A Critique of Functionalist Reason.* Boston: Beacon Press, 1987.

HADAWAY, C. KIRK, and MARLER, PENNY L. "All in the Family: Religious Mobility in America." *Review of Religious Research* 35, 1993.

HADAWAY, C. KIRK, and ROOF, WADE CLARK. "Apostasy in American Churches: Evidence From National Survey Data." In David G. Bromley (ed.), *Falling From the Faith.* Beverly Hills, Calif.: Sage, 1988.

HADDAD, YVONNE Y. *The Muslims of America.* New York: Oxford University Press, 1991.

HADDEN, JEFFREY K., AND SHUPE, ANSON. *Televangelism: Power and Politics on God's Frontier.* New York: Henry Holt & Company, 1988.

HAFFERTY, FREDERIC, and LIGHT, DONALD W. "Professional Dynamics and the Changing Nature of Medical Work." *Journal of Health and Social Behavior,* Extra Issue, 1995.

HAGE, JERALD (ed.). *Futures of Organizations: Innovating to Adapt Strategy and Human Resources to Rapid Technological Change.* Lexington, Mass.: Lexington Books, 1988.

HAINES, HERB. "Flawed Executions, the Anti-Death Penalty Movement, and the Politics of Capital Punishment." *Social Problems* 39, 1992.

Hak, Tony. ''The Interactional Form of Professional Dominance." *Sociology of Health and Illness* 4, 1994.

HALL, DAVID R., and ZHAO, JOHN Z. "Cohabitation and Divorce in Canada: Testing the Selectivity Hypothesis." *Journal of Marriage and the Family* 57, 1995.

HALL, ELAINE. "Smiling, Deferring, and Flirting: Doing Gender but Giving 'Good Service'." *Work and Occupations* 20, 1993.

HALL, PETER. *The World Cities,* 3d ed. London: Weidenfeld and Nicolson, 1984.

HALLORAN, RICHARD. "Notes of a Sumo Wrestling Fan." *New York Times,* January 6, 1974.

HALPERN, SYDNEY A. *American Pediatrics: The Social Dynamics of Professionalism, 1880–1980.* Berkeley: University of California Press, 1988.

HALPERN, SYDNEY A. "Dynamics of Professional Control: Internal Coalitions and Crossprofessional Boundaries." *American Journal of Sociology* 97, 1992.

HAMILL, PETE. "Facing Up to Drugs: Is Legalization the Solution?" *New York,* August 15, 1988.

HAMMOND, JUDITH. "Biography Building to Insure the Future: Women's Negotiation of Gender Relevancy in Medical School." *Symbolic Interaction* 3, 1980.

HANAWALT, BARBARA A. "Historical Descriptions and Prescriptions for Adolescence." *Journal of Family History* 17, 1992.

HARDY, ANN M. "AIDS Knowledge and Attitudes for January–March 1991." *Advance Data from Vital and Health Statistics; No. 216,* Hyattsville, Md.: National Center for Health Statistics, 1992.

HARPER, DOUGLAS. *Good Company,* abridged edition. Chicago: University of Chicago Press, 1989.

HARRINGTON, MICHAEL. *The New American Poverty.* New York: Penguin Books, 1984.

HARRIS, ALLEN C. "Ethnicity as a Determinant of Sex Role Identity: A Replication Study of Item Selection for the Bem Sex Role Inventory." *Sex Roles* 31, 1994.

HARRIS, CHAUNCEY, and ULLMAN, EDWARD. "The Nature of Cities." *Annals of the American Academy of Political and Social Science* 242, 1945.

HARRIS, DAVID. "The 1990 Census Count of American Indians: What Do the Numbers Really Mean?" *Social Science Quarterly* 75, 1994.

HARRIS, JEAN. *Stranger in Two Worlds.* New York: Macmillan, 1986.

HARRIS, LIS. "Holy Days—I." *The New Yorker,* September 16, 1985.

HARRIS, LIS. *Holy Days: The World of a Hasidic Family.* New York: Summit, 1986.

HARRIS, MARVIN. *Cows, Pigs, Wars, and Witches: The Riddles of Culture.* New York: Vintage Books, 1974.

HARRIS, MARVIN. *America Now: The Anthropology of a Changing Culture.* New York: Simon and Schuster, 1981.

HARTWIG, M. C. "Aborigines and Racism: An Historical Perspective." In F. S. Stevens (ed.), *Racism: The Australian Experience,* vol. 2. New York: Taplinger, 1972.

HATCH, NATHAN O. "The Puzzle of American Methodism." *Reflections,* Summer–Fall, 1993.

HAUG, MARIE R., and FOLMAR, STEVEN J. "Longevity, Gender and Life Quality." *Journal of Health and Social Behavior* 27, 1986.

HAUGHEN, STEVEN E., and MEISENHEIMER, JOSEPH R., II. "U.S. Labor Market Weakened in 1990." *Monthly Labor Review* 114, 1991.

HAURIN, R. J., and MOTT, F. L. "Adolescent Sexual Activity in the Family Context: The Impact of Older Siblings." *Demography* 27, 1990.

HAY, DAVID. "Religious Experience Amongst a Group of Post-Graduate Students—A Qualitative Study." *Journal for the Scientific Study of Religion* 18, 1979.

HAYGHE, HOWARD W., "Rise in Mother's Labor Force Activity Includes Those with Infants." *Monthly Labor Review* 109, 1986.

HAYGHE, HOWARD W., and BIANCHI, SUZANNE M. "Married Mothers' Work Patterns: The Job–Family Compromise." *Monthly Labor Review,* June 1994.

Hearn, Frank (ed.). *The Transformation of Industrial Organization.* Belmont, Calif.: Wadsworth, 1988.

HEATH, JULIA A., and BOURNE, W. DAVID. "Husbands and Housework: Parity or Parody?" *Social Science Quarterly* 76, 1995.

HEATH, THOMAS. "In a Mafialess City, Some Las Vegans Don't Like Their Odds." *Washington Post,* December 26, 1995.

HEFFERNAN, ESTHER. *Making It in Prison: The Square, the Cool, and the Life.* New York: Wiley-Interscience, 1972.

HEILBRON, JOHAN. "August Comte and Modern Epistemology." *Sociological Theory* 8, 1990.

HELLER, JOSEPH. *Catch-22.* New York: Dell, 1955.

HENLEY, NANCY M., and THORNE, BARRIE "Womanspeak and Manspeak: Sex Differences and Sexism in Communications, Verbal and Nonverbal." In Alice G. Sargent (ed.), *Beyond Sex Roles.* St. Paul, Minn.: West, 1977.

HERBERG, WILL. *Protestant, Catholic, and Jew.* Garden City, N.Y.: Anchor Books, 1955.

HERNANDEZ, DONALD J. *America's Children: Resources from Family, Government, and the Economy.* New York: Russell Sage Foundation, 1995.

HERRNSTEIN, RICHARD J. and MURRAY, CHARLES. *The Bell Curve: Intelligence and Class Structure in American Life.* New York: The Free Press, 1994.

HERSHBERG, THEODORE, BURSTEIN, ALAN N., ERICKSEN, EUGENE P., GREENBERG, STEPHANIE, and YANCEY, WILLIAM L. "A Tale of Three Cities: Blacks, Immigrants, and Opportunity in Philadelphia: 1850–1880, 1930, and 1970." In Norman R. Yetman, (ed.), *Majority and Minority: The Dynamics of Race and Ethnicity in American Life,* 5th ed. Boston: Allyn and Bacon, 1991.

HERSHEY, ROBERT D., JR., "Bias Hits Hispanic Workers." *New York Times,* April 27, 1995.

HERTSGAARD, MARK. *On Bended Knee: The Press and the Reagan Presidency.* New York: Farrar Straus Giroux, 1988.

HESKIN, KEN. "Terrorism in Ireland: The Past and the Future." *Irish Journal of Psychology* 15, 1994.

HESS, BETH B., and FERREE, MYRA MARX. "Introduction." In Beth B. Hess and Myra Marx Ferree (eds.), *Analyzing Gender: A Handbook of Social Research.* Beverly Hills, Calif.: Sage, 1987.

HESS STEPHEN. "Why Great Men Are Not Chosen Presidents." *Society,* July/August 1988.

HETHERINGTON, MAVIS E., COX, MARTHA, and COX, ROGER. "The Aftermath of Divorce." In J. H. Stevens, Jr., and M. Matthew (eds.), *Mother–Child, Father–Child Relations.* Washington, D.C.: National Association for the Education of Young Children, 1978.

HEWITT, JOHN P. *Self and Society: A Symbolic Interactionist Social Psychology,* 3d ed. Boston: Allyn and Bacon, 1984.

HEWLETT, SYLVIA ANN. *When the Bough Breaks: The Cost of Neglecting Our Children.* New York: Basic Books, 1991.

HEYDERBRAND, WOLF V. "New Organizational Forms." *Work and Occupations* 16, 1989.

HICKS, ALEXANDER. "Is Political Sociology Informed by Political Science?" *Social Forces* 73, 1995.

HICKS, JONATHAN. "Companies Working out of the Recession with No Added Jobs." *New York Times,* July 5, 1992.

HILL, MICHAEL R. Review of *Auguste Comte: An Intellectual Biography, Vol. 1* by Mary Pickering. *Contemporary Sociology* 24, 1995.

HINDS, MICHAEL DECOURCY. "Feeling Prisons' Costs, Governors Weigh Alternatives." *New York Times,* August 7, 1992.

HIRSCHMAN, CHARLES, and WONG, MORRISON G. "The Extraordinary Educational Attainment of Asian-Americans: A Search for Historical Evidence and Explanations." *Social Forces* 65, 1986.

History of the Church of Latter-Day Saints. Salt Lake City: Deseret News Press, 1902.

HOCHSCHILD, ARLIE R. *The Managed Heart: Commercialization of Human Feeling.* Berkeley: University of California Press, 1983.

HODGKINSON, HAROLD L., with OUTTZ, JANICE HAMILTON, and OBARAKPOR, ANITA M. *The Demographics of American Indians: One Percent of the People; Fifty Percent of the Diversity.* Washington, D.C.: Center for Demographic Policy, 1990.

HODGKINSON, VIRGINIA A., WEITZMAN, MURRAY S., AND KIRSCH, ARTHUR D. "From Commitment to Action: How Religious Involvement Affects Giving and Volunteering." In Robert Wuthnow, Virginia A. Hodgkinson, and associates, (eds.). *Exploring the Role of Religion in America's Voluntary Sector.* San Francisco: Jossey-Bass, 1990.

HODSON, RANDY, and ENGLAND, PAULA. "Industrial Structure and Sex Differences in Earnings." *Industrial Relations* 25, 1986.

HOFFERTH, SANDRA L., KAHN, JOAN R., and BALDWIN, WENDY. "Premarital Sexual Activity Among Teenage Women Over the Last Three Decades." *Family Planning Perspectives* 19, 1987.

HOFFMAN, SAUL D., and DUNCAN, GREG J. "What *Are* the Economic Consequences of Divorce?" *Demography* 25, 1988.

HOFFMAN, SHIRL J., (ed.), *Sport and Religion.* Champaign, IL: Human Kinetic Books, 1992,

HOGE, DEAN R., and ROOZEN, DAVID A. *Understanding Church Growth and Decline: 1950–1978.* New York: Pilgrim Press, 1979.

HOGE, R. D., and RENZULLI, J. S. "Exploring the Link between Giftedness and Self-concept." *Review of Educational Research* 63, 1993.

HOLLINGER, RICHARD C., and LANZA-KADUCE, LONN. "The Process of Criminalization: The Case of Computer Crime Laws." *Criminology* 26, 1988.

HOLLINGSHEAD, AUGUST B., and REDLICH, FREDERICK C. *Social Class and Mental Illness.* New York: John Wiley, 1958.

HOMANS, GEORGE C. *Social Behavior: Its Elementary Forms,* rev. ed. New York: Harcourt Brace Jovanovich, 1974.

HOOYMAN, NANCY R., and KIYAK, H. ASUMAN. *Social Gerontology: A Multidisciplinary Perspective,* 2d ed. Boston: Allyn and Bacon, 1991.

HOPKINS, ELLEN. "The Dispossessed." *New York,* May 13, 1985.

HOPKINS, KEITH. "Brother–Sister Marriage in Roman Egypt." *Journal for Comparative Study of Society and History* 22, 1980.

HOUBOLT, JAN. "An Empirical Critique of Blauner's Concept of Powerlessness on the Automobile Assembly Line." Paper presented at the 53rd Annual Meeting of the Eastern Sociological Society, Philadelphia, Pa. 1982.

HOUSE, JAMES S., LEPKOWSKI, JAMES M., KINNEY, ANN M., MERO, RICHARD P., KESSLER, RONALD C., and HERZOG, A. REGULA. "The Social Stratification of Aging and Health." *Journal of Health and Social Behavior* 35, 1994.

HOUT, MICHAEL. "More Universalism, Less Structural Mobility: The American Occupational Structure in the 1980s." *American Journal of Sociology* 93, 1988.

HOUT, MICHAEL, and GREELEY, ANDREW M. "The Center Doesn't Hold: Church Attendance in the United States, 1940–1984." *American Sociological Review* 52, 1987.

HOWELL, JAMES C. "Recent Gang Research: Program and Policy Implications." *Crime and Delinquency* 40, 1994.

HOYT, HOMER. *The Structure and Growth of Residential Neighborhoods in American Cities.* U.S. Federal Housing Administration. Washington, D.C.: U.S. Government Printing Office, 1939.

HUBER, JOAN. "Trends in Gender Stratification, 1970–1985." *Sociological Forum* 1, 1986.

HUBER, JOAN. "A Theory of Family, Economy, and Gender." In Rae Lesser Blumberg (ed.), *Gender, Family, and Economy: The Triple Overlap.* Newbury Park, Calif.: Sage, 1991.

HUBER, JOAN, and FORM, WILLIAM H. *Income and Ideology.* New York: The Free Press, 1973.

HUCKSHORN, KRISTIN. "Poverty Stereotypes Wrong, Study Says." *Kansas City Star,* June 3, 1991.

HUDELSON, RICHARD. "Has History Refuted Marxism?" *Philosophy of the Social Sciences* 23, 1993.

HUDSON, WINTHROP. *Religion in America.* New York: Charles Scribner's, 1973.

HUGHES, DAVID. "When Nurse Knows Best: Some Aspects of Nurse/Doctor Interaction in a Casualty Department." *Sociology of Health and Illness* 10, 1988.

HUGHES, MARK ALAN, and STERNBERG, JULIE E. *The New Metropolitan Reality: Where the Rubber Meets the Road in Antipoverty Policy.* Washington, D.C.: Urban Institute, 1993.

HUGHES, GERALD and DEGHER, DOUGLAS. "Coping with a Deviant Identity." *Deviant Behavior* 14, 1993.

HULT, CHRISTINE A. *Researching and Writing across the Curriculum.* Boston: Allyn & Bacon, 1996.

HUMAN RIGHTS WATCH. *War Crimes in Bosnia–Herzegovina.* New York: Human Rights Watch, 1992.

HUMMEL, RALPH P. *The Bureaucratic Experience.* New York: St. Martin's Press, 1977.

HUMMEL, RALPH P. *The Bureaucratic Experience,* 3d ed. New York: St. Martin's Press, 1987.

HUMPHREYS, LAUD. *Tearoom Trade: Impersonal Sex in Public Places,* enlarged ed. Chicago: Aldine, 1975.

HUNT, GEOFFREY, RIEGEL, STEPHANIE, MORALES, THOMAS, and WALDORF, DAN. "Changes in Prison Culture: Prison Gangs and the Case of the 'Pepsi Generation'." *Social Problems* 40, 1993.

HUNT, JENNIFER. "The Development of Rapport through the Negotiation of Gender in Field Work Among Police." *Human Organization* 43, 1984.

HUNT, JENNIFER. "Police Accounts of Normal Force." *Urban Life* 13, 1985.

HUNTER, JAMES D. *Cultural Wars: The Struggle to Define America.* New York: Basic Books, 1991.

HUNTER, JAMES D. *Before the Shooting Begins: Searching for Democracy in America's Culture War.* New York: Free Press, 1994.

HURLBERT, JEANNE S., and ROSENFELD, RACHEL A. "Getting a Good Job: Rank and Institutional Prestige in Academic Psychologist's Careers." *Sociology of Education* 65, 1992.

HURYN, JEAN SCHERZ. "Giftedness as Deviance: A Test of Interaction Theories." *Deviant Behavior* 7, 1986.

HUSTON, ALETHA C. *et al. Big World, Small Screen: The Role of Television in American Society.* Lincoln: University of Nebraska Press, 1992.

HUTCHINSON, WILLIAM R. "Forum: The Decline of Mainline Religion in American Culture." *Religion and American Culture* 1, 1991.

HYER, MARJORIE. "'Sin' of Gender Discrimination Denounced." *Washington Post,* December 8, 1985.

IGNATIUS, DAVID. "What's Left of Big Steel?" *Washington Post-Outlook,* March 20, 1988.

ILG, RANDY E. "The Changing Face of Farm Employment." *Monthly Labor Review,* April, 1995.

INKELES, ALEX, and ROSSI, PETER H. "National Comparisons of Occupational Prestige." *American Journal of Sociology* 61, 1956.

IRVINE, JANICE M. "Cultural Differences and Adolescent Sexualities." In Janice M. Irvine (ed.), *Sexual Cultures and the Construction of Adolescent Identities.* Philadelphia: Temple University Press, 1994.

IRWIN, JOHN, and JAMES AUSTIN. *It's about Time: America's Imprisonment Binge.* Belmont, CA: Wadsworth, 1994.

ISHIDA, HIROSHI, MULLER, WALTER, and RIDGE, JOHN M. "Class Origin, Class Destination, and Education: A Cross-National Study of Ten Industrial Nations." *American Journal of Sociology* 101, 1995.

IUTCOVICH, JOYCE, and IUTCOVICH, MARK. *The Sociologist as Consultant.* New York: Praeger, 1987.

JACKALL, ROBERT. *Moral Mazes: The World of Corporate Managers.* New York: Oxford University Press, 1988.

JACKSON, LINDA A., HODGE, CAROLE N., and INGRAM, JULIE M. "Gender and Self-concept: A Reexamination of Stereotypic Differences and the Role of Gender Attitudes." *Sex Roles* 30, 1994.

JACKSON, PETER W. "Passive Smoking and Ill-Health: Practice and Process in the Production of Medical Knowledge." *Sociology of Health and Illness* 16, 1994.

JACOBS, JERRY A., (ed.) "Sex Segregation and Gender Stratification." Special Issue of *Work and Occupations* 19, 1992.

JAQUET, CONSTANT H., JR. *Women Ministers in 1986 and 1977: A Ten Year View.* New York: National Council of Churches, 1988.

JAQUET, CONSTANT H., JR., (ed.) *Yearbook of American and Canadian Churches, 1990.* Nashville: Abington Press, 1990.

JAMESON, SAM. "Roh Takes Over, Vows End to Repression in S. Korea." *Los Angeles Times,* February 25, 1988.

JAMIESON, KATHLEEN HALL. *Packaging the Presidency: A History of Presidential Campaign Advertising.* New York: Oxford University Press, 1984.

JAMIESON, KATHLEEN HALL. *Eloquence in an Electronic Age: The Transformation of Political Speechmaking.* New York: Oxford University Press, 1988.

JANKOWSKI, MARTIN SANCHEZ. *Islands in the Street: Gangs and American Urban Society.* Berkeley: University of California Press, 1991.

JASPER, JAMES M., and POULSEN, JANE D. "Recruiting Strangers and Friends: Moral Shocks and Social Networks in Animal Rights and Anti-Nuclear Protests." *Social Problems* 42, 1995.

JAYNES, GERALD DAVID, and WILLIAMS, ROBIN M., JR. *A Common Destiny: Blacks and American Society.* Washington, D.C.: National Academy Press, 1989.

JEFFRIES, VINCENT, and RANSFORD, EDWARD. *Social Stratification: A Multiple Hierarchy Approach.* Boston: Allyn and Bacon, 1980.

JENCKS, CHRISTOPHER. "Is the American Underclass Growing?" In Christopher Jencks and Paul E. Peterson, (eds.) *The Urban Underclass.* Washington, D.C.: The Brookings Institution, 1991.

JENCKS, CHRISTOPHER. "Housing the Homeless," *New York Review of Books,* May 12, 1994a.

JENCKS, CHRISTOPHER. *The Homeless.* Cambridge, MA: Harvard University Press. 1994b.

JENCKS, CHRISTOPHER. "The Homeless." *New York Review of Books,* April 21, 1994c.

JENCKS, CHRISTOPHER, and PETERSON, PAUL E., (eds.) *The Urban Underclass.* Washington, D.C.: The Brookings Institution, 1991.

JENKINS, C. DAVID. "Social Environment and Cancer Mortality in Men." *New England Journal of Medicine* 308, 1983.

JENNESS, VALERIE, "Social Movement, Growth, Domain Expansion, and Framing Processes: The Gay/Lesbian Movement and Violence against Gays and Lesbians as a Social Problem." *Social Problems,* 42, 1995.

JENSEN, ARTHUR A. "How Much Can We Boost I.Q. and Scholastic Achievement?" *Harvard Educational Review* 39, 1969.

JENSEN, GARY F. "Functional Research on Deviance: A Critical Analysis and Guide for the Future." *Deviant Behavior* 9, 1988.

JOHANSSON, STEN, and NYGREN, OLA. "The Missing Girls of China: A New Demographic Account." *Population and Development Review* 17, 1991.

JOHNSON, CATHRYN. "Gender, Legitimate Authority, and Leader–Subordinate Conversations." *American Sociological Review* 59, 1994.

JOHNSON, CLIFFORD M., MIRANDA, LETICIA, SHERMAN, ARLOC, and WEILL, JAMES D. *Child Poverty in America.* Washington, D.C.: Children's Defense Fund, 1991.

JOHNSON, DAVID R., AMOLOZA, TEODORA O., and BOOTH, ALAN. "Stability and Developmental Change in Marital Quality: A Three Wave Panel Analysis." *Journal of Marriage and the Family* 54, 1992.

JOHNSON, DIRK. "Growing Mormon Church Faces Dissent by Women and Scholars." *New York Times,* November 2, 1994a.

JOHNSON, DIRK. "Economies Come to Life on Indian Reservations." *New York Times,* July 3, 1994b.

JOHNSON, JEFFREY C. *Selecting Ethnographic Informants.* Newbury Park, Calif.: Sage Publications, 1990.

JOHNSON, MICHAEL P. "Patriarchal Terrorism and Common Couple Violence: Two Forms of Violence Against Women." *Journal of Marriage and the Family* 57, 1995.

JOHNSON, NORRIS R. "Panic and the Breakdown of Social Order: Popular Myth, Social Theory, Empirical Evidence." *Sociological Focus* 20, 1987a.

JOHNSON, NORRIS R. "Panic at 'The Who Concert Stampede': An Empirical Assessment." *Social Problems* 34, 1987b.

JOHNSON, T. C. "Child Perpetrators—Children Who Molest Other Children: Preliminary Findings." *Child Abuse and Neglect* 12, 1988.

JOHNSON, T. C. "Children Molesting Children." *Preventing Sexual Abuse* 2, 1990.

JOHNSTON, LLOYD D., O'MALLEY, PATRICK M., BACHMAN, JERALD G. *Drug Use, Drinking, and Smoking: National Survey Results From High School, College, and Young Adult Population, 1975–1988.* Rockville, Md.: National Institute on Drug Abuse, 1989.

JOINT CENTER FOR POLITICAL STUDIES. Personal Communication, 1992.

JONES, A. E., and PLACEK, PAUL. "Teenage Women in the USA: Sex, Contraception, Pregnancy, Fertility and Maternal and Infant Health." In Theodora Ooms (ed.), *Teenage Pregnancy and Family Impact: New Perspectives on Policy.* Philadelphia: Temple University Press, 1981.

JONES, FAUSTINE C. "External Crosscurrents and Internal Diversity: An Assessment of Black Progress, 1960–1980." *Daedalus* 110, 1981.

JORDON, MARY. "Two More Suicides Spotlight Pressures on Japanese Students." *Washington Post,* January 28, 1996.

JORDON, MARY, and SULLIVAN, KEVIN. "Anguish Grows in Japan over School Bullies." *Washington Post,* November 26, 1995.

JOSEPH, NATHAN. *Uniforms and Nonuniforms: Communication Through Clothing.* Westport, Conn.: Greenwood Press, 1986.

JOURNAL OF THE AMERICAN MEDICAL ASSOCIATION, 265, 1991.

JOY, LESLEY A., KIMBALL, MEREDITH M., and ZABRACK, MERLE L. "Television and Children's Aggressive Behavior." In T. M. Williams (ed.), *The Impact of Television: A Natural Experiment in Three Communities.* Orlando, Fla.: Academic Press, 1986.

JUDD, ELEANORE PARELMAN. "Intermarriage and the Maintenance of Religio-Ethnic Identity, A Case Study: The Denver Jewish Community." *Journal of Comparative Family Studies* 21, 1990.

KABEL, MARCUS. "Zurich Warns Major 'Needle Park' Could Return." *Reuters World Service,* March 15, 1995.

KAHN, JANET R. "Speaking across Cultures within Your Own Family." In Janice M. Irvine (ed.), *Sexual Cultures and the Construction of Adolescent Identities.* Philadelphia: Temple University Press, 1994.

KAHN, JOAN R., KALSBEEK, WILLIAM D., and HOFFERTH, SANDRA L. "National Estimates of Teenage Sexual Activity: Evaluating the Comparability of Three National Surveys." *Demography* 25, 1988.

KAHN, ROBERT L., WOLFE, DONALD M., QUINN, ROBERT P., SNOEK, J. DIEDRICK, in collaboration with ROSENTHAL, ROBERT A. *Organizational Stress: Studies in Role Conflict and Ambiguity.* New York: John Wiley, 1964.

KAIN, JOHN F. "The Spatial Mismatch Hypothesis: Three Decades Later." *Housing Policy Debate* 3, 1992.

KALB, MARVIN. "TV, Election Spoiler." *New York Times,* November 28, 1988.

KALBERG, STEPHEN. "Max Weber's Types of Rationality: Cornerstones for the Analysis of Rationalization Processes in History." *American Journal of Sociology* 85, 1980.

KALLEBERG, ARNE L. "Sociology and Economics: Crossing the Boundaries." *Social Forces* 73, 1995.

KALMIJN, MATTHIJS. "Shifting Boundaries: Trends in Religious and Educational Homogamy," *American Sociological Review* 56, 1991.

KALMIJN, MATTHIJS. "Mother's Occupation and Children's Schooling." *American Sociological Review* 59, 1994.

KAMMEYER, KENNETH C. W. "The Feminine Role: An Analysis of Attitude Consistency." *Journal of Marriage and the Family* 26, 1964.

KAMMEYER, KENNETH C. W. "The Dynamics of Population." In Harold Orel (ed.), *Irish History and Culture: Aspects of a People's Heritage.* Lawrence, Kans.: The University of Kansas Press, 1976.

KAMMEYER, KENNETH C. W. "The Decline of Divorce in America." Paper presented at the annual meeting of the Midwest Sociological Society, Minneapolis, Minn., 1981.

KAMMEYER, KENNETH C. W. *Marriage and Family: A Foundation for Personal Decisions.* Boston: Allyn and Bacon, 1987.

KAMMEYER, KENNETH C. W., and GINN, HELEN L. *An Introduction to Population.* Chicago: The Dorsey Press, 1986.

KANDO, THOMAS M. *Leisure and Popular Culture in Transition,* 2d ed. St. Louis: C.V. Mosby, 1980.

KAPLAN, BERNARD D. "French Turning up Noses on Move to Ban Smoking." *Times-Picayune,* April 24, 1994.

KASARDA, JOHN D. "The Implications of Contemporary Distribution Trends for National Urban Policy." *Social Science Quarterly* 61, 1980.

KASARDA, JOHN D. "Urban Industrial Transition and the Underclass." *Annals of the American Academy of Political and Social Science* 501, 1989.

KATZ, HARRY C. *Shifting Gears: Changing Labor Relations in the U.S. Automobile Industry.* Cambridge, Mass.: The MIT Press, 1985.

KATZ, MICHAEL B. *The Irony of Early School Reform.* Cambridge, Mass.: Harvard University Press, 1968.

KATZ, MICHAEL B. *Class, Bureaucracy and Schools: The Illusion of Educational Change in America.* New York: Praeger, 1971.

KATZ, MICHAEL, B. *Reconstructing American Education.* Cambridge, Mass.: Harvard University Press, 1987.

KELLER, AMY. "The Carvilles of 1996: Big Bucks and Cachet Lure Consultants to Next Year's Presidential Campaigns." *Roll Call,* December 14, 1995.

KELLEY, JONATHAN, and EVANS, M. D. R. "The Legitimation of Inequality: Occupational Earnings in Nine Nations." *American Journal of Sociology* 99, 1993.

KELLEY, JONATHAN, and EVANS, M. D. R. "Class and Class Conflict in Six Western Nations." *American Sociological Review* 60, 1995.

KELLY, DEAN M. *Why Conservative Churches Are Growing.* New York: Harper & Row, 1972.

KEMPTON, MURRAY. "Quality of Milken Mercy." *Newsday,* September 27, 1990.

KENNEDY, JOHN W. "Redeeming the Wasteland." *Christianity Today,* October 2, 1995.

KENNICKNELL, ARTHUR, and SHACK-MARQUEZ, JANICE. "Changes in Family Finances from 1983 to 1989." *Federal Reserve Bulletin,* January 1992.

KEPHART, GEORGE. "Economic Restructuring, Population Distribution, and Migration in the United States." In Mark Gottdiener and Chris G. Pickvance (eds.), *Urban Life in Transition.* Newbury Park, Calif.: Sage Publications, 1991.

KEPHART, WILLIAM M. *The Family, Society and the Individual,* 5th ed. Boston: Houghton Mifflin, 1981.

KEPHART, WILLIAM M., and ZELLNER, WILLIAM W. *Extraordinary Groups: The Sociology of Unconventional Life-Styles,* 4th ed. New York: St. Martin's Press, 1991.

KERBO, HAROLD R. *Social Stratification and Inequality.* New York: McGraw-Hill, 1983.

KERCKHOFF, ALAN C., CAMPBELL, RICHARD T., and WINFIELD-LAIRD, IDEE. "Social Mobility in Great Britain and the United States." *American Journal of Sociology* 91, 1985.

KHAWAJA, MARWAN. "Resource Mobilization, Hardship, and Popular Collective Action in the West Bank." *Social Forces* 13, 1994.

KILGORE, SALLY B. "The Organizational Context of Tracking in Schools." *American Sociological Review* 56, 1991.

KIMBALL, MEREDITH M. "Television and Sex-Role Attitudes." In Tannis M. Williams (ed.), *The Impact of Television: A Natural Experiment in Three Communities.* Orlando, Fla.: Academic Press, 1986.

KING, ANTHONY. "Architecture, Capital and the Globalization of Culture." In Mike Featherstone, ed., *Global Culture: Nationalism, Globalization and Modernity.* London: Sage, 1990.

KING, MARTIN LUTHER, JR. *Why We Can't Wait.* New York: Harper & Row, 1963.

KINGSNORTH, RODNEY, and JUNGSTEN, MICHAEL. "Driving Under the Influence: The Impact of Legislative Reform on Court Sentencing Practices." *Crime and Delinquency* 34, 1988.

KINSEY, ALFRED C., POMEROY, WARDELL B., and MARTIN, CLYDE E. *Sexual Behavior in the Human Male.* Philadelphia: W.B. Saunders, 1948.

KINSEY, ALFRED C., POMEROY, WARDELL B., MARTIN, CLYDE E., and GEBHARD, PAUL H. *Sexual Behavior in the Human Female.* Philadelphia: W.B. Saunders, 1953.

KINZER, STEPHEN. "A Pro-Drug Ruling Stirs the Pot in Germany." *New York Times,* March 3, 1992.

KIRKLAND, MICHAEL. "Executions Set Post-1976 High." *UPI,* December 12, 1995.

KISHOR, SUNITA. "May God Give Sons to All: Gender and Childhood Mortality in India." *American Sociological Review* 58, 1993.

KITAGAWA, EVELYN, and HAUSER, PHILIP M. "Education Differentials in Mortality by Cause of Death, United States 1960." *Demography* 5, 1968.

KITFIELD, JAMES. "The Age of Superterrorism." *Government Executive,* July 1995.

KITSON, GAY C. *Portrait of Divorce: Adjustment to Marital Breakdown.* New York: Guilford Press, 1992.

KITSON, GAY C., and MORGAN, LESLIE A. "The Multiple Consequences of Divorce: A Decade Review." *Journal of Marriage and the Family* 52, 1990.

KLEIDMAN, ROBERT. "Volunteer Activism and Professionalism in Social Movement Organizations." *Social Problems* 41, 1994.

KLEIN, MALCOLM W. "Labeling Theory and Delinquency Policy: An Experimental Test." *Criminal Justice and Behavior* 13, 1986.

KLEIN, MALCOLM. "Street Gangs." In Craig Calhoun and George Ritzer (eds.), *Social Problems*. New York: McGraw-Hill, 1992.

KLEIN, MALCOLM. *The American Street Gang: Its Nature, Prevalence, and Control.* New York: Oxford University Press, 1995.

KLENIEWSKI, NANCY. "Immigration and Urban Transformations." *Urban Affairs Quarterly* 30, 1994.

KLINE, MARSHA, JOHNSTON, JANET R., and TSCHANN, JEANNE M. "The Long Shadow of Marital Conflict: A Model of Children's Postdivorce Adjustment." *Journal of Marriage and the Family* 53, 1991.

KLUEGEL, JAMES R., and BOBO, LAWRENCE. "Opposition to Race-Targeting: Self-interest, Stratification Ideology, or Racial Attitudes?" *American Sociological Review* 58, 1993.

KNICKERBOCKER, BRAD. "Electing a Mail-order Senator." *Christian Science Monitor,* September 19, 1995.

KOHLBERG, L. "A Cognitive-Development Analysis of Sex-Role Concepts and Attitudes." In Eleanor Maccoby (ed.), *The Development of Sex Differences.* Stanford, Calif.: Stanford University Press, 1966.

KOHN, MELVIN L. *Class and Conformity: A Study of Values,* second ed., with a reassessment. Chicago: University of Chicago Press, 1977.

KOHN, MELVIN L. "Cross-National Research as an Analytic Strategy." *American Sociological Review* 52, 1987.

KOHN, MELVIN L., (ed.) *Cross-National Research in Sociology.* Newbury Park, Calif.: Sage Publications, 1989a.

KOHN, MELVIN L. "Cross-National Research as an Analytic Strategy." In Melvin L. Kohn (ed.), *Cross-National Research in Sociology.* Newbury Park, Calif.: Sage Publications, 1989b.

KOHN, MELVIN L., and SCHOOLER, CARMI. "Occupational Experience and Psychological Functioning." *American Sociological Review* 38, 1973.

KOHN, MELVIN L., with MILLER, JOANNE, MILLER, KAREN A., SCHOENBACH, CARRIE, and SCHOENBERG, RONALD. *Work and Personality: An Inquiry into the Impact of Social Stratification.* Norwood, N.J.: Ablex, 1983.

KOMAROVSKY, MIRRA. "The Concept of Social Role Revisited." *Gender & Society* 6, 1992.

KOOPMANS, RUUD, and DUYVENDAK, JAN W. "The Political Construction of the Nuclear Energy Issue and Its Impact on the Mobilization of Anti-Nuclear Movements in Western Europe." *Social Problems* 42, 1995.

KOSMIN, BARRY A., and LACHMAN, SEYMOUR P. "The National Survey of Religious Identification, 1989–90." Research Report. New York: The Graduate School and University Center of the City University of New York, 1991.

KOSMIN, BARRY A., and SEYMOUR P. LACHMAN. *One Nation under God: Religion in Contemporary American Society.* New York: Harmony Books, 1993.

KOSS, M. P., GIDYCZ, C. A., and WISNIEWSKI, N. "The Scope of Rape: Incidence and Prevalence of Sexual Aggression and Victimization in a National Sample of Higher Education Students." *Journal of Consulting and Clinical Psychology* 55, 1987.

KOWALSKI, GREGORY S., and FAUPEL, CHARLES E. "Heroin Use, Crime and the 'Main Hustle'." *Deviant Behavior* 11, 1990.

KOZOL, JONATHAN. "A Nicely Decorated Poorhouse." *The Kansas City Star,* April 9, 1989.

KOZOL, JONATHAN. *Savage Inequalities: Children in America's Schools.* New York: Crown Publishers, 1991.

KREPS, GARY A. "Sociological Inquiry and Disaster Research." In Ralph H. Turner and James F. Short, Jr. (eds.), *Annual Review of Sociology 10.* Palo Alto, Calif.: Annual Reviews, 1984.

KREPS, GARY A. "Future Directions in Disaster Research: The Role of Taxonomy." *International Journal of Mass Emergencies and Disasters* 7, 1989.

KRIEGER, LISA. "HIV Infects 19.5 Million Worldwide." *San Francisco Examiner,* December 6, 1995.

KRIESBERG, LOUIS. *Social Conflicts,* 2d ed. Englewood Cliffs, N.J.: Prentice-Hall, 1982.

KULKA, R. A., and WEINGARTEN, H. "The Long-Term Effects of Parental Divorce in Childhood on Adult Adjustment." *Journal of Social Issues* 35, 1979.

KUO, WEN H. "Coping with Discrimination: The Case of Asian-Americans." *Ethnic and Racial Studies* 18, 1995.

KURDEK, L. A., BLISK, D., and SIESKY, A. E. "Correlates of Children's Long-Term Adjustment to Their Parents' Divorce." *Developmental Psychology* 17, 1981.

KURTZ, HOWARD. "Media Notes." *Washington Post,* May 27, 1991.

KURTZ, HOWARD. "Media Alter Approach to Campaign Coverage." *Washington Post,* September 11, 1992a.

KURTZ, HOWARD. "Networks Stressed the Negative in Comments about Bush, Study Finds." *Washington Post,* November 15, 1992b.

KURTZ, HOWARD. "Sound-bite Zingers Prevail over Substance." *Washington Post,* January 15, 1996a.

KURTZ, HOWARD. "Forbes Leaps out of Pack and into the Media's Glare." *Washington Post,* January 22, 1996b.

KURTZ, HOWARD. "Mild-mannered Forbes's Hard-edged Ads." *Washington Post,* February 1, 1996c.

KURZMAN, CHARLES. "A Dynamic View of Resources: Evidence from the Iranian Revolution." *Research in Social Movements, Conflicts and Change* 17, 1994.

KUTNER, NANCY G. "Issues in the Application of High Cost Medical Technology: The Case of Organ Transplantation." *Journal of Health and Social Behavior* 28, 1987.

KUTSCHER, RONALD E. "Overview and Implications of the Projections to 2000." *Monthly Labor Review* 110, 1987.

LADNER, ROBERT A., SCHWARTZ, BARRY J., ROKER, SANDRA J., and TITTERUD, LORETTA S. "The Miami Riots of 1980: Antecedent Conditions, Community Responses and Participant Characteristics." In L. Kriesberg (ed.), *Research in Social Movements, Conflicts and Change,* vol. 4. Greenwich, Conn.: JAI Press, 1981.

LAFRANIERE, SHARON. "In Maine, Prison Crowding Had Fatal Consequences." *Washington Post,* February 21, 1992.

LAQUEUR, WALTER. *The Age of Terrorism.* Boston: Little, Brown, 1987.

LARCEN, DONNA. "Wrinkle-fighting Acids Winning Doctors' Approval." *Chicago Sun-Times,* October 8, 1995.

LARDAS, JOHN H. "Graceland: An Analysis of Sacred Space on the American Religious Landscape." Paper presented at the American Academy of Religion, November 1995.

LAROSSA, RALPH. "And We Haven't Had Any Problems Since: Conjugal Violence and the Politics of Marriage." In Murray A. Straus and Gerald T. Hotaling (eds.), *The Social Causes of Husband–Wife Violence.* Minneapolis: University of Minnesota Press, 1980.

LAROSSA, RALPH. "The Transition to Parenthood and the Social Reality of Time." *Journal of Marriage and the Family* 45, 1983.

LASALANDRA, MICHAEL. "Study: Gang Members at High Risk of Violence." *Boston Herald,* October 4, 1995.

LASLEY, JAMES R. "New Writing on the Wall: Exploring the Middle-class Graffiti Writing Subculture." *Deviant Behavior* 16, 1995.

LASTER, LEONARD. "Do Doctors Give a Damn? The Other Health Care Crisis." *Washington Post,* August 23, 1992.

LAUMANN, EDWARD O., GAGNON, JOHN H., MICHAEL, ROBERT T., and MICHAELS, STUART. *The Social Organization of Sexuality: Sexual Practices in the United States.* Chicago: University of Chicago Press, 1994.

LAWLER, JOHN J., and WEST, ROBIN. "Impact of Union-Avoidance Strategy in Representation Elections." *Industrial Relations* 24, 1985.

LAZARSFELD, PAUL. "Notes on the History of Quantification in Sociology—Trends, Sources, and Problems." In Harry Woolf (ed.), *Quantification: A History of the Meaning of Measurement in the Natural and Social Sciences.* New York: Bobbs-Merrill, 1961.

LECHNER, FRANK J. "The Case against Secularization: A Rebuttal." *Social Forces* 69, 1991.

LEE, FELICIA R. "Poor Record Seen on Immunizations." *New York Times,* October 16, 1991.

LEE, SHARON M. "Poverty and the U.S. Asian Population," *Social Science Quarterly* 75, 1994.

LEE, SHARON M., and EDMONSTON, BARRY. "The Socioeconomic Status and Integration of Asian Immigrants." In Barry Edmonston and Jeffrey S. Passel, (eds.), *Immigration and Ethnicity.* Washington, DC: Urban Institute Press, 1994.

LEGATES, RICHARD T., and HARTMAN, CHESTER. "The Anatomy of Displacement in the United States." In Neil Smith and Peter Williams (eds.), *Gentrification of the City.* Boston: George Allen & Unwin, 1986.

LEGATES, RICHARD T., and MURPHY, KAREN. "Austerity, Shelter, and Social Conflict in the United States." In William K. Tabb and Larry Sawers (eds.), *Marxism and the Metropolis.* New York: Oxford University Press, 1984.

LEHMAN, EDWARD W. "The Theory of the State Versus the State of Theory." *American Sociological Review* 53, 1988.

LEHMANN, JENNIFER M. "Durkheim's Theories of Deviance and Suicide: A Feminist Reconsideration." *American Journal of Sociology* 100, 1995a.

LEHMANN, JENNIFER M. "The Questions of Caste in Modern Society: Durkheim's Contradictory Theories of Race, Class, and Sex." *American Sociological Review* 60, 1995b.

LEICHT, KEVIN T., WALLACE, MICHAEL, and GRANT, DON S. "Union Presence, Class, and Individual Earnings Inequality." *Work and Occupations* 20, 1993.

LEIKER, JASON J., TAUB, DIANE E., and GAST, JULIE. "The Stigma of AIDS: Persons with AIDS and Social Distance." *Deviant Behavior* 16, 1995.

LEINBERGER, CHRISTOPHER B., and LOCKWOOD, CHARLES. "How Business Is Reshaping America." *The Atlantic Monthly,* October 1986.

LEMERT, EDWIN. *Human Deviance, Social Problems, and Social Control.* Englewood Cliffs, N.J.: Prentice-Hall, 1967.

LEMERT, EDWIN. *Human Deviance, Social Problems, and Social Control,* 2d ed. Englewood Cliffs, N.J.: Prentice-Hall, 1972.

LENNON, MARY C., and ROSENFIELD, SARAH. "Relative Fairness and the Division of Housework: The Importance of Options." *American Journal of Sociology* 100, 1994.

LENSKI, GERHARD, and LENSKI, JEAN. *Human Societies,* 4th ed. New York: McGraw-Hill, 1982.

LEO, RICHARD A. "Trial and Tribulations: Courts, Ethnography, and the Need for an Evidentiary Privilege for Academic Researchers." *American Sociologist* 23, 1995.

LE PLAY, FREDERIC. *Les Ouvriers Europeens.* Paris: Imprimerie Royale, 1855.

LERNER, GERDA. "The Lady and the Mill Girl: Changes in the Status of Women in the Age of Jackson." *Midcontinent American Studies Journal,* Spring 1969.

LESTER, DAVID. *Emile Durkheim: Le Suicide—One Hundred Years Later.* Philadelphia: Charles Press, 1994.

LEVINE, DANIEL H. "On Premature Reports of the Death of Liberation Theology." *Review of Politics* 57, 1995a.

LEVINE, JEFF. "Smokeless Tobacco Carries High Levels of Carcinogens." *CNN,* December 19, 1995b.

LEVY, FRANK. *Dollars and Dreams: The Changing American Income Distribution.* New York: Russell Sage Foundation, 1987.

LEWIN, TAMAR. "High Medical Costs Hurt Growing Numbers in U.S." *New York Times,* April 28, 1991.

LEWIS, DARRELL, HEARN, JAMES, and ZILBERT, ERIC. "Efficiency and Equity Effects of Vocationally Focused Postsecondary Education." *Sociology of Education* 66, 1993.

LEWIS, NEIL, A. "Police Brutality Under Wide Review by Police Department." *New York Times,* March 15, 1991.

LEWIS, NEIL A. "President Foresees Safer U.S.: Others See Crime Bill as Symbolic." *New York Times,* August 27, 1994.

LI, JIALI. "China's One-child Policy: How and How Well Has It Worked? A Case Study of Hebei Province, 1979–88." *Population and Development Review* 21, 1995.

LICHTERMAN, PAUL. "Piecing Together Multicultural Community: Cultural Differences in Community Building among Grass-roots Environmentalists." *Social Problems* 42, 1995.

LIEBERSON, STANLEY, and BELL, ELEANOR O. "Children's First Names: An Empirical Study of Social Taste." *American Journal of Sociology* 98, 1992.

LIEBERT, ROBERT M., and SPRAFKIN, JOYCE. *The Early Window: Effects of Television on Children and Youth,* 3rd ed. New York: Pergamon Press, 1988.

LIEBMAN, ROBERT C., and WUTHNOW, ROBERT. *The New Christian Right.* New York: Aldine, 1983.

LIGHT, DONALD. "Health Care." In Craig Calhoun and George Ritzer (eds.), *Social Problems.* New York: McGraw-Hill, 1992.

LIGHT, PAUL C. *Thickening Government: Federal Hierarchy and the Diffusion of Accountability.* Washington, DC: Brookings Institute, 1995.

LIN, NAN, and XIE, WEN. "Occupational Prestige in Urban China." *American Journal of Sociology* 94, 1988.

LIND, MICHAEL. "To Have and Have Not: Notes on the Progress of the American Class War." *Harper's,* June 1995.

LINK, BRUCE. "Reward System of Psychotherapy: Implications for Inequities in Service Delivery." *Journal of Health and Social Behavior* 24, 1983.

LINK, BRUCE G., CULLEN, FRANCES T., STRUENING, ELMER, and SHROUT, PATRICK E. "A Modified Labeling Theory Approach to Mental Disorders: An Empirical Assessment." *American Sociological Review* 54, 1989.

LIPPY, CHARLES H. *Being Religious, American Style: A History of Popular Religiosity in the United States.* Westport, CT: Greenwood, 1994.

LIPSET, SEYMOUR M. *The First New Nation.* New York: Basic Books, 1963.

LIPSET, SEYMOUR M. "Comparing Canadian and American Unions." *Society,* January/February 1987.

LIPSET, SEYMOUR M., TROW, MARTIN, and COLEMAN, JAMES. *Union Democracy.* Garden City, N.Y.: Anchor Books, 1962.

LITTLE, ROGER. "Buddy Relations and Combat Performance." In Oscar Grusky and George A. Miller (eds.), *The Sociology of Organizations.* New York: The Free Press, 1970.

LOCK, MARGARET. "Protests of Good Wife and Wise Mother." In Edward Norbeck and Margaret Lock (eds.), *Health, Illness, and Medical Care in Japan.* Honolulu: University of Hawaii Press, 1987.

LOFLAND, LYN. "Social Life in the Public Realm: A Review." *Journal of Contemporary Ethnography* 17, 1989.

LOGAN, JOHN R., and SCHNEIDER, MARK. "Racial Segregation and Racial Change in American Suburbs, 1970–1980." *American Journal of Sociology* 89, 1984.

LOGUE, JAMES N., HANSEN, HOLGER, and STRUENING, ELMER. "Some Indicators of the Long Term Health Effects of a Natural Disaster." *Public Health Reports* 96, 1981.

LONDON, BRUCE. "Dependence, Distorted Development, and Fertility Trends in Noncore Nations: A Structural Analysis of Cross-national Data." *American Sociological Review* 53, 1988.

LONDON, BRUCE. "School-enrollment Rates and Trends, Gender, and Fertility: A Cross-national Analysis." *Sociology of Education* 65, 1992.

LONDON, BRUCE, and HADDEN, KENNETH. "The Spread of Education and Fertility Decline: A Thai Province Level Test of Caldwell's 'Wealth Flows Theory'." *Rural Sociology* 54, 1988.

LOPREATO, JOSEPH. "From Social Evolutionism to Biological Evolutionism." *Sociological Forum* 5, 1990.

LORBER, JUDITH. "Deviance as Performance: The Case of Illness." *Social Problems* 14, 1967.

LORBER, JUDITH. *Women Physicians.* New York: Tavistock, 1984.

LORD, WALTER. *A Night to Remember.* New York: Henry Holt, 1955.

Los Angeles Times. "Modern Anxiety: What to Do When Smut Rides Internet?" June 16, 1995.

LOSH-HESSELBART, SUSAN. "Development of Gender Roles." In Marvin B. Sussman and Suzanne K. Steinmetz (eds.), *Handbook of Marriage and the Family.* New York: Plenum Press, 1987.

LOWENBERG, JUNE S., and DAVIS, FRED. "Beyond Medicalisation–Demedicalisation: The Case of Holistic Health." *Sociology of Health and Illness* 16, 1994.

LOWENSTEIN, DOUGLAS, and LOWENSTEIN, ROCHELLE. "The Baby and Us." *The Washington Post Magazine,* October 16, 1983.

LUCAL, BETSY. "The Problem with 'Battered Husbands'." *Deviant Behavior* 16, 1995.

LUMSDEN, C. J., and WILSON, E. O. *Promethean Fire.* Cambridge, Mass.: Harvard University Press, 1983.

LUXENBERG, STAN. *Roadside Empires: How the Chains Franchised America.* New York: Viking, 1985.

LYE, DIANE N., and BIBLARZ, TIMOTHY J. "The Effects of Attitudes toward Family Life and Gender Roles on Marital Satisfaction." *Journal of Family Issues* 14, 1993.

LYON, DAVID. "From 'Post-Industrialism' to 'Information Society': A New Social Transformation?" *Sociology* 20, 1986.

MACCOBY, E. E., and JACKLIN, C. N. *The Psychology of Sex Differences.* Stanford, Calif.: Stanford University Press, 1974.

MACCOUN, ROBERT J., KAHAN, JAMES P., GILLESPIE, JAMES, and RHEE, JEEYANG A. "A Content Analysis of the Drug Legalization Debate." *Journal of Drug Issues* 23, 1993.

MACDONALD, KEITH. *The Sociology of the Professions.* London: Sage, 1995.

MACKEY, WADE. *Fathering Behaviors: The Dynamics of the Man–Child Bond.* New York: Plenum Press, 1986.

MALCOLM X. *The Autobiography of Malcolm X.* New York: Grove Press, 1966.

MALHOTRA, ANJU, VANNEMAN, REEVE, and KISHOR, SUNITA. "Fertility, Dimensions of Patriarchy, and Development in India." *Population and Development Review* 21, 1995.

MALINOWSKI, BRONISLAW. *Magic, Science, and Religion and Other Essays.* New York: Anchor Books, 1955. Originally published 1925.

MANEGOLD, CATHERINE S. "Women Advance in Politics by Evolution, Not Revolution." *New York Times,* October 21, 1992.

MANTON, KENNETH G., and MYERS, GEORGE C. "Recent Trends in Multiple-Caused Mortality, 1968–1982: Age and Cohort Comparisons." *Population Research and Policy Review* 6, 1987.

MANTON, KENNETH G., STALLARD, ERIC, and TOLLEY, H. DENNIS. "Limits of Human Life Expectancy: Evidence, Prospects, and Implications." *Population and Development Review* 17, 1991.

MAR, DON, and KIM, MARLENE. "Historical Trends." In Paul Ong, (ed.), *The State of Asian Pacific America: Economic Diversity, Issues and Politics.* Los Angeles: LEAP Asian Pacific American Public Policy Institute and UCLA Asian American Studies Center, 1994.

MARCH, JAMES G. "Footnotes to Organizational Change." *Administrative Science Quarterly* 26, 1981.

MARE, ROBERT D. "Five Decades of Assortative Mating." *American Sociological Review* 56, 1991.

MARGOLIN, LESLIE. "Goodness Personified: The Emergence of Gifted Children." *Social Problems* 40, 1993.

MARKOFF, JOHN. "How a Need for Challenge Seduced Computer Expert." *New York Times,* November 6, 1988.

MARRIOTT, MICHEL. "Fervid Debate on Gambling: Disease or Moral Weakness?" *New York Times,* November 21, 1992.

MARSH, HERBERT W., CHESSOR, DANUTA, CRAVEN, RHONDA, and ROCHE, LAWRENCE. "The Effects of Gifted and Talented Programs on Academic Self-concept: The Big Fish Strikes Again." *American Educational Research Journal* 32, 1995.

MARSHALL, VICTOR W. *Last Chances: A Sociology of Aging and Dying.* Monterey, Calif.: Brooks/Cole, 1980.

MARTIN, TERESA CASTRO, and BUMPASS, LARRY L. "Recent Trends in Marital Disruption." *Demography* 26, 1989.

MARTY, MARTIN E. "Transpositions: American Religion in the 1980s." *The Annals of the American Academy of Political and Social Science* 480, 1985.

MARTY, MARTIN E. "Two Years That Shook the World." *1991 Britannica Book of the Year.* Chicago: Encyclopædia Britannica, 1991.

MARULLO, SAM. "Political, Institutional and Bureaucratic Fuel for the Arms Race." *Sociological Forum* 7, 1992.

MARULLO, SAM. *Ending the Cold War at Home: From Militarism to a More Peaceful World Order.* New York: Lexington Books, 1993.

MARX, KARL. *The Economic and Philosophic Manuscripts of 1884.* Dirk J. Struik, (ed.), New York: International Publishers, 1964. Originally published 1932.

MARX, KARL. *Capital: A Critical Analysis of Capitalist Production,* vol. 1. New York: International Publishers, 1967. Originally published 1867.

MARYANSKI, ALEXANDRA, and TURNER, JONATHAN H. "The Offspring of Functionalism: French and British Structuralism." *Sociological Theory* 9, 1991.

MASHETER, CAROL. "Postdivorce Relationships between Ex-spouses: The Roles of Attachment and Interpersonal Conflict." *Journal of Marriage and the Family* 53, 1991.

MASON, KAREN OPPENHEIM, and LU, YU-HSIA. "Attitudes Toward Women's Familial Roles: Changes in the United States, 1977–1985." *Gender & Society* 2, 1988.

MASSEY, DOUGLAS S. "American Apartheid: Segregation and the Making of the Underclass." *American Journal of Sociology* 96, 1990.

MASSEY, DOUGLAS S., and DENTON, NANCY A. "Trends in the Residential Segregation of Blacks, Hispanics, and Asians: 1970–1980." *American Sociological Review* 52, 1987.

MASSEY, DOUGLAS S., and DENTON, NANCY A. "Suburbanization and Segregation in U.S. Metropolitan Areas." *American Journal of Sociology* 94, 1988.

MASSEY, DOUGLAS S., and DENTON, NANCY A. *American Apartheid: Segregation and the Making of the Underclass.* Cambridge, Mass.: Harvard University Press, 1993.

MATHEWS, JESSICA. "Lessons from Asian Schools." *Washington Post,* November 30, 1992.

MATSUEDA, ROSS L. "Reflected Appraisals, Parental Labeling, and Delinquency: Specifying a Symbolic Interactionist Theory." *American Journal of Sociology* 97, 1992.

MATTHEWS, JON. "New Campaign Soapbox." *Sacramento Bee,* November 24, 1995.

MAULDIN, W. PARKER. "Population Programs and Fertility Regulation." In Rodolfo A. Bulatao and Ronald D. Lee (eds.), *Determinants of Fertility in Developing Countries,* vol. 2. New York: Academic Press, 1983.

MAUSS, ARMAND L. "Sociological Perspectives on the Mormon Subculture." In Ralph H. Turner and James F. Short, Jr. (eds.), *Annual Review of Sociology* 10. Palo Alto, Calif.: Annual Reviews, Inc., 1984.

MAYER, JOHN E., and ROSENBLATT, AARON. "Encounters with Danger: Social Workers in the Ghetto." *Sociology of Work and Occupations* 2, 1975.

MAYER, KURT B., and BUCKLEY, WALTER. *Class and Society*, 3d ed. New York: Random House, 1970.

MAYNES, MARY J. *Schooling in Western Europe*. Albany: State University of New York, 1985.

MCADAM, DOUG, MCCARTHY, JOHN D., and ZALD, MAYER N. "Social Movements." In Neil J. Smelser (ed.), *Handbook of Sociology*. Beverly Hills, Calif.: Sage, 1988.

MCANENY, LESLIE, and SAAD, LYDIA. "Strong Ties Between Religious Commitment and Abortion Views." *The Gallup Poll News Service,* April 27, 1993.

MCBRIDE, DUANE C., and MCCOY, CLYDE B. "The Drugs–Crime Relationship: An Analytic Framework." *Prison Journal* 73, 1993.

MCCARTHY, JOHN D., and ZALD, MAYER N. "Resource Mobilization and Social Movements: A Partial Theory." *American Journal of Sociology* 82, 1977.

MCCARTNEY, ROBERT J. "Milken Gets 10-Year Prison Sentence." *Washington Post,* November 22, 1990.

MCCOWN, SCOTT. "Jail Crowding: Excess Prison Space Is Actually an Illusion." *Dallas Morning News,* March 27, 1994.

MCCURDY, DAVID W., and SPRADLEY, JAMES P. (eds.), *Issues in Cultural Anthropology: Selected Readings*. Boston: Little, Brown, 1979.

MCGUIRE, JACQUELINE. "Gender Stereotypes of Parents with Two-Year-Olds and Beliefs about Gender Differences in Behavior." *Sex Roles* 19, 1988.

MCKEOWN, THOMAS. "A Historical Appraisal of the Medical Task." In G. McLachlan and T. McKeown (eds.), *Medical History and Medical Care: A Symposium of Perspectives*. New York: Oxford University Press, 1971.

MCKEOWN, THOMAS. *The Modern Rise in Population*. London: Edward Arnold, 1976.

MCKEOWN, THOMAS. *The Role of Medicine: Dream, Mirage, or Nemesis?* Princeton, NJ: Princeton University Press, 1979.

MCKINLAY, JOHN, and MCKINLAY, SONJA. "The Questionable Contribution of Medical Measures to the Decline of Mortality in the United States in the Twentieth Century." *Milbank Memorial Quarterly/ Health and Society* 55, 1977.

MCKINNEY, WILLIAM. "Forum: The Decline of Mainline Religion in American Culture." *Religion and American Culture* 1, 1991.

MCMANUS, DOYLE, and MANN, JIM. "Big 3 Tested: Will Economic Rivalry Break up the Allies?" *Los Angeles Times,* June 9, 1992.

MCMILLEN, MARILYN M. "Differential Mortality by Sex in Fetal and Neonatal Deaths." *Science* 204, 1979.

MCMILLEN, MARILYN M., KAUFMAN, PHILLIP, and WHITENER, SUMMER D. *Dropout Rates in the United States: 1993*. Washington, DC: U.S. Government Printing Office, 1994.

MCNEIL, LINDA M. *Contradictions of Control: School Structure and School Knowledge*. New York: Routledge & Kegan Paul, 1986.

MEAD, GEORGE H. *Mind, Self and Society*. Chicago: University of Chicago Press, 1962. Originally published 1934.

MEAD, MARGARET. *Sex and Temperament in Three Primitive Societies*. New York: Mentor Books, 1935.

MEAD, MARGARET. *Culture and Commitment: A Study of the Generation Gap*. Garden City, N.Y.: Natural History Press/Doubleday, 1970.

MEAD, MARGARET. *Blackberry Winter.* New York: William Morrow, 1972.

MEEKER, BARBARA F., and LEIK, ROBERT K. "Experimentation in Sociological Social Psychology." In Karen S. Cook, Gary Alan Fine, and James S. House (eds.), *Sociological Perspectives on Social Psychology*. Boston: Allyn & Bacon, 1995.

MEHAN, HUGH. "Understanding Inequality in Schools: The Contribution of Interpretive Studies." *Sociology of Education* 65, 1992.

MEHTA, STEPHANIE N. "Declining Power of Picket Line Blunts New York Maintenance Workers' Strike." *Wall Street Journal,* January 17, 1996.

MELLEN, S. L. *The Evolution of Love*. San Francisco: W.H. Freeman, 1981.

MELTON, J. GORDON. *The Encyclopedia of American Religions,* 2d ed. Detroit: Gale Research Company, 1987.

MELTON, JAMES VAN HORN. *Absolutism and the Eighteenth Century Origins of Compulsory Schooling in Prussia and Austria*. Cambridge, England: Cambridge University Press, 1988.

MELTZER, BERNARD N. "Mead's Social Psychology." In Jerome Manis and Bernard N. Meltzer (eds.), *Symbolic Interaction: A Reader in Social Psychology,* 3d ed. Boston: Allyn and Bacon, 1978.

MENARD, SCOTT. "A Developmental Test of Mertonian Anomie Theory." *Journal of Research in Crime and Delinquency* 32, 1995.

MENNERICK, LEWIS A., and NAJAFIZADEH, MEHRANGIZ. "Observations on the Missing Linkage Between Theories of Historical Expansion of Schooling and Planning for Future Educational Development." *International Review of Education* 33, 1987.

MEREDITH, PHILIP. "Patient Participation in Decision-making and Consent to Treatment: The Case of General Surgery." *Sociology of Health and Illness* 15, 1993.

MERNISSI, FATIMA. *Beyond the Veil: Male–Female Dynamics in Modern Muslim Society.* Bloomington, Ind.: Indiana University Press, 1987.

MERTON, ROBERT. "Social Structure and Anomie." *American Sociological Review* 3, 1938.

MERTON, ROBERT. *Social Theory and Social Structure,* rev. ed. New York: The Free Press, 1957.

MERTON, ROBERT. *Social Theory and Social Structure,* 3d ed. New York: The Free Press, 1968.

METHVIN, EUGENE H. "The Anti-Crime Solution: Lock up More Criminals." *Washington Post—Outlook,* October 27, 1992.

MEYER, DAVID S., and WHITTIER, NANCY. "Social Movement Spillover." *Social Problems* 41, 1994.

MEYER, JOHN W., RAMIREZ, FRANCISCO O., and SOYSAL, YASEMIN NUHOGLU. "World Expansion of Mass Education, 1870–1980." *Sociology of Education* 65, 1992.

MEYER, LAWRENCE. *Israel Now: Portrait of a Troubled Land.* New York: Delacorte Press, 1982.

MEYER, MARSHALL W., STEVENSON, WILLIAM, and WEBSTER, STEPHEN. *Limits to Bureaucratic Growth.* New York: de Gruyter, 1985.

MICHAELSON, MARC. "Wangari Maathai and Kenya's Green Belt Movement: Exploring the Evolution and Potentialities of Consensus Movement Mobilization." *Social Problems* 41, 1994.

MICHELS, ROBERT. *Political Parties: A Sociological Study of the Oligarchical Tendencies of Modern Democracy.* New York: The Free Press, 1962. Originally published 1915.

MIDDLETON, RUSSELL. "Brother–Sister and Father–Daughter Marriage in Ancient Egypt." *American Sociological Review* 27, 1962.

MILETI, DENNIS S., and O'BRIEN, PAUL W. "Warnings during Disaster: Normalizing Communicated Risk." *Social Problems* 39, 1992.

MILGRAM, STANLEY. *Obedience to Authority.* New York: Harper & Row, 1974.

MILLER, B. D. *The Endangered Sex.* Ithaca, N.Y.: Cornell University Press, 1981.

MILLER, BRENT C., and BINGHAM, C. RAYMOND. "Family Configuration in Relation to the Sexual Behavior of Female Adolescents." *Journal of Marriage and the Family* 51, 1989.

MILLER, GALE, and HOLSTEIN, JAMES A. "Constructing Social Problems: Context and Legacy." In Gale Miller and James A. Holstein, (eds.), *Constructivist Controversies: Issues in Social Problems Theory.* Hawthorne, NY: Aldine, 1993.

MILLER, STEPHEN. "The Social Base of Sales Behavior." *Social Problems* 12, 1964.

MILLER-LOESSI, KAREN. "Comparative Social Psychology." In Karen S. Cook, Gary Alan Fine, and James S. House (eds.), *Sociological Perspectives on Social Psychology.* Boston: Allyn & Bacon, 1995.

MILLING, KINARD E., and REINHERZ, HELEN. "Effects of Marital Disruption on Children's School Aptitude and Achievement." *Journal of Marriage and the Family* 48, 1986.

MILLMAN, MARCIA. *The Unkindest Cut: Life in the Backrooms of Medicine.* New York: William Morrow, 1977.

MILLMAN, MARCIA. *Such a Pretty Face: Being Fat in America.* New York: W.W. Norton, 1980.

MILLS, C. WRIGHT. *The Power Elite.* New York: Oxford University Press, 1956.

MILLS, C. WRIGHT. *The Sociological Imagination.* New York: Oxford University Press, 1959.

MIN, PYONG G. *Asian Americans: Contemporary Trends and Issues.* Thousand Oaks, CA: Sage Publications, 1995.

MIRANDE, ALFREDO. *Gringo Justice.* South Bend, Ind.: Notre Dame University Press, 1987.

MIRANNE, ALFRED C., III, and GRAY, LOUIS N. "Deterrence: A Laboratory Experiment." *Deviant Behavior* 8, 1987.

MIROWSKY, JOHN, and ROSS, CATHERINE. "Belief in Innate Sex Roles: Sex Stratification Versus Interpersonal Influence in Marriage." *Journal of Marriage and the Family* 49, 1987.

MISCHEL, LAWRENCE, and BERNSTEIN, JARED. *The State of Working America.* Washington, D.C.: Economic Policy Institute, 1992.

MISCHEL, LAWRENCE, and FRANKEL, DAVID M. *The State of Working America: 1990–91 Edition.* Armonk, N.Y.: M. E. Sharpe, 1991.

MITOFSKY, WARREN J., and PLISSNER, MARTIN. "Low Voter Turnout? Don't Believe It." *New York Times,* November 10, 1988.

MITZMAN, ARTHUR. *The Iron Cage: An Historical Interpretation of Max Weber.* New York: Grosset & Dunlap, 1969.

MIYAHARA, KOJIRO. "Inter-College Stratification: The Case of Male College Graduates in Japan." *Sociological Forum* 3, 1988.

MODEL, SUZANNE. "The Economic Progress of European and East Asian Americans." In Norman R. Yetman (ed.), *Majority and Minority: The Dynamics of Race and Ethnicity in American Life,* 5th ed. Boston: Allyn and Bacon, 1991.

MOFFATT, MICHAEL. *Coming of Age in New Jersey.* New Brunswick, N.J.: Rutgers University Press, 1989.

MOFFETT, GEORGE D. *Critical Masses: The Global Population Challenge.* New York: Penguin Books, 1994.

MOHAN, MARY L. *Organizational Communication and Cultural Vision: Approaches for Analysis.* Albany, NY: State University of New York Press, 1993.

MOLM, LINDA D., and COOK, KAREN S. "Social Exchange and Exchange Networks." In Karen S. Cook, Gary Alan Fine, and James S. House (eds.), *Sociological Perspectives on Social Psychology.* Boston: Allyn & Bacon, 1995.

MONK-TURNER, ELIZABETH. "The Occupational Achievements of Community and Four Year College Entrants." *American Sociological Review* 55, 1990.

MONMANEY, THOMAS. "Medical Researchers Call Gang Killings 'Epidemic' in County." *Los Angeles Times,* October 4, 1995.

MONROE, PAUL. *Founding of the American Public School System.* New York: Macmillan, 1940.

Monthly Labor Review. "Current Labor Statistics." October 1992.

MOORE, CHARLES A. "Taming the Giant Corporation? Some Cautionary Remarks on the Deterrability of Corporate Crime." *Crime and Delinquency* 33, 1987.

MOORE, R. LAURENCE. *Selling God: American Religion and the Marketplace of Culture.* New York: Oxford University Press, 1994.

MOORE, MOLLY. "In Far Northeast India, Mountain Tribes Meet the World." *Washington Post,* Dec. 26, 1992.

Morbidity and Mortality Weekly Report. "Sexual Behavior among High School Students," 40, 1992.

MORGAN, EDMUND. *Visible Saints: The History of a Puritan Idea.* Ithaca, N.Y.: Cornell University Press, 1963.

MORGAN, LESLIE A. *After Marriage Ends: Economic Consequences for Midlife Women.* Newbury Park, Calif.: Sage Publications, 1991.

MORGAN, S. PHILIP, LYE, DIANE, and CONDRAN, GRETCHEN. "Sons, Daughters, and the Risk of Marital Disruption." *American Journal of Sociology* 94, 1988.

MORIN, RICHARD. "A Distorted Image of Minorities." *Washington Post,* October 8, 1995a.

MORIN, RICHARD. "Unmarried Moms around the World." *Washington Post,* July 16, 1995b.

MORINAGA, YASUKO, FRIEZE, IRENE H., and FERLIGOJ, ANUSKA. "Career Plans and Gender–Role Attitudes of College Students in the United States, Japan, and Slovenia." *Sex Roles* 29, 1993.

MOSHER, WILLIAM D., and BACHRACH, CHRISTINE A. "Understanding U.S. Fertility: Continuity and Change in the National Survey of Family Growth, 1988–1995." *Family Planning Perspectives* 28, 1996.

MOSHER, WILLIAM, WILLIAMS, LINDA B., and JOHNSON, DAVID P. "Religion and Fertility in the United States: New Patterns." *Demography* 29, 1992.

MOTT, FRANK L., and HAURIN, R. JEAN. "Linkages Between Sexual Activity and Alcohol Use Among American Adolescents." *Family Planning Perspectives* 20, 1988.

MOUZELIS, NICOS. "The Interaction Order and the Micro-Macro Distinction." *Sociological Theory* 10, 1992.

MUNCY, RAYMOND L. *Sex and Marriage in Utopian Communities: 19th Century America.* Bloomington, Ind.: University of Indiana Press, 1973.

MUNNELL, ALICIA H., BROWNE, LYNN E., McENEANEY, JAMES, and TOOTELL, GEOFFREY M. B. "Mortgage Lending in Boston: Interpreting HMDA Data." Boston: Federal Reserve of Boston, Working Paper 92–7, 1992.

MURDOCK, GEORGE P. "Comparative Data on the Division of Labor by Sex." *Social Forces* 15, 1937.

MURDOCK, GEORGE P., and PROVOST, CATRINA. "Factors in the Division of Labor by Sex: A Cross-Cultural Analysis." *Ethnology* 12, 1973.

MURPHY, CARLYLE. "Former Executive, 2 Others in Defense Probe Plead Guilty." *Washington Post,* March 10, 1989.

MURRAY, CHARLES. *Losing Ground: American Social Policy 1950–1980.* New York: Basic Books, 1984.

MUTCHNICK, ROBERT J., and BERG, BRUCE L. *Research Methods for the Social Sciences.* Boston: Allyn & Bacon, 1996.

NAJAFIZADEH, MEHRANGIZ, and MENNERICK, LEWIS A. "Worldwide Educational Expansion from 1950 to 1980: The Failure of the Expansion of Schooling in Developing Countries." *The Journal of Developing Areas* 22, 1988.

NAKONEZNY, PAUL A., SHULL, ROBERT D., and RODGERS, JOSEPH L. "The Effect of No-fault Divorce Law on the Divorce Rate across the 50 States and Its Relation to Income, Education, and Religiosity." *Journal of Marriage and the Family* 57, 1995.

NANDRAM, SHARDA S., and KLANDERMANS, BERT. "Stress Experienced by Active Members of Trade Unions." *Journal of Organizational Behavior* 14, 1993.

NAOI, ATSUSHI, and SCHOOLER, CARMI. "Occupational Conditions and Psychological Functioning in Japan." *American Journal of Sociology* 90, 1981.

NASAR, SYLVIA. "Those Born Wealthy or Poor Usually Stay So, Studies Say." *New York Times,* May 18, 1992a.

NASAR, SYLVIA. "More College Graduates Taking Low-wage Jobs." *New York Times,* August 7, 1992b.

NASAR, SYLVIA. "U.S. Output per Worker Is Growing." *New York Times,* November 27, 1992c.

A Nation at Risk: The Imperative for Educational Reform. Washington, D.C.: The National Commission on Excellence in Education, 1983.

NATIONAL CENTER FOR HEALTH STATISTICS. *Health, United States, 1987.* Washington, D.C.: U.S. Government Printing Office, 1988.

NATIONAL CENTER FOR HEALTH STATISTICS. *Health, United States, 1989.* Washington, D.C.: U.S. Government Printing Office, 1990.

NATIONAL CENTER FOR HEALTH STATISTICS. *Health, United States, 1991.* Washington, D.C.: U.S. Government Printing Office, 1992a.

NATIONAL CENTER FOR HEALTH STATISTICS. *Health, United States, 1993.* Washington, D.C.: U.S. Government Printing Office, 1994.

NATIONAL CENTER FOR HEALTH STATISTICS. *Monthly Vital Statistics Report,* Vol 40. Washington, D.C.: U.S. Government Printing Office, 1992b.

NATIONAL CENTER FOR HEALTH STATISTICS. "Annual Summary of Births, Marriages, Divorces, Deaths: United States, 1991." *Monthly Vital Statistics Report,* 41, Washington, D.C.: U.S. Government Printing Office, 1992c.

NATIONAL CENTER FOR HEALTH STATISTICS. "Advance Report on Final Mortality Statistics, 1988." *Monthly Vital Statistics Report,* 41. Washington, D.C.: U.S. Government Printing Office, 1993.

NATIONAL CENTER FOR HEALTH STATISTICS. "Advance Report on Final Mortality Statistics, 1992." *Monthly Vital Statistics Report,* 43. Washington, DC: U.S. Government Printing Office, 1995a.

NATIONAL CENTER FOR HEALTH STATISTICS. *Health, United States, 1994.* Washington D.C.: U.S. Government Printing Office, 1995b.

NATIONAL COUNCIL OF CHURCHES. *An Inclusive Language Lectionary.* Philadelphia: Westminster Press, 1983.

National Criminal Justice Reference Service. "The Nation's Prison Population Grew Almost 9% Last Year." Washington, DC: U.S. Department of Justice, 1996.

NAUGHTON, JIM. "The Devil and Duffy Strode." *The Washington Post,* August 29, 1988.

NAVARRETTE, RUBEN, JR. *A Darker Shade of Crimson: Odyssey of a Harvard Chicano.* New York: Bantam Books, 1993.

NAVARRO, VICENTE. "Race or Class versus Race and Class: Mortality Differentials in the United States." *Lancet,* November 17, 1990.

NAVARRO, VICENTE. "Class and Race: Life and Death Situations." *Monthly Review* 43, 1991.

NELSON, KATHRYN P. *Gentrification and Distressed Cities: An Assessment of Trends in Intrametropolitan Migration.* Madison, Wisc.: University of Wisconsin Press, 1988.

NELSON, LYNN D., and BROMLEY, DAVID G. "Another Look at Conversion and Defection in Conservative Churches." In David G. Bromley (ed.), *Falling From the Faith.* Beverly Hills, Calif.: Sage, 1988.

NETTLETON, SARAH, and HARDING, GEOFF. "Protesting Patients: A Study of Complaints Submitted to a Family Health Service Authority." *Sociology of Health and Illness* 16, 1994.

New York Times. "Life Term Is Upheld in Theft of $120.75." March 19, 1980.

NEW YORK TIMES/CBS NEWS POLL. "Portrait of the Electorate." *New York Times,* November 10, 1988.

NEWACHECK, PAUL W., et al., "Income and Illness." *Medical Care* 18, 1980.

NEWHOUSE, JOHN. "Profiles (Margaret Thatcher) The Gamefish." *The New Yorker,* February 10, 1986.

NEWMAN, WILLIAM M. *American Pluralism: A Study of Minority Groups and Social Theory.* New York: Harper & Row, 1973.

NEWPORT, FRANK. "Half of Americans Believe in Creationist Origin of Man." *The Gallup Poll Monthly,* September 1993.

Newsweek, "What Color Is Black? Science, Politics and Racial Identity." February 13, 1995a.

Newsweek, "Whites vs Blacks." October 16, 1995b.

NEWTON, GERALD. *The Netherlands: A Historical and Cultural Analysis.* Boulder, Colo.: Westview, 1978.

NIEBUHR, GUSTAV. "More Than a Monument: The Spiritual Dimension of These Hallowed Walls." *New York Times,* November 11, 1994.

NIEBUHR, H. RICHARD. *The Social Sources of Denominationalism.* New York: Henry Holt, 1929.

NIMMO, DAN. "Elections as Ritual Drama." *Society,* May/June 1985.

NORDOFF, CHARLES. *The Communistic Society of the United States.* New York: Schocken Books, 1971. Originally published 1875.

NORTON, ARTHUR J., and MILLER, LOUISA F. "Marriage, Divorce, and Remarriage in the 1990s." *Current Population Reports,* P-23, #180. Washington, DC: U.S. Government Printing Office, 1992.

NORTON, ROBERT. "Measuring Marital Quality: A Critical Look at the Dependent Variable." *Journal of Marriage and the Family* 45, 1983.

NOVAK, MICHAEL. *The Joy of Sports.* New York: Basic Books, 1976.

NUGENT, JEFFREY B. "The Old-age Security Motive For Fertility." *Population and Development Review* 13, 1985.

OAKES, GUY. *The Soul of the Salesman.* Atlantic Highlands, N.J.: Humanities Press International, 1990.

OAKES, JEANNIE, "Classroom Social Relationships: Exploring the Bowles and Gintis Hypothesis." *Sociology of Education* 55, 1982.

OAKES, JEANNIE. *Keeping Track: How Schools Structure Inequality.* New Haven, Conn.: Yale University Press, 1985.

OAKES, JEANNIE and GUITON, GRETCHEN. "Matchmaking: the Dynamics of High School Tracking Decisions." *American Educational Research Journal* 32, 1995.

OBERSTAR, JAMES. "Ban Smoking on International Flights." *Congressional Press Releases,* February 20, 1995.

O'BRIEN, WILLIAM V. "International Crimes." In David L. Sills (ed.), *International Encyclopedia of the Social Sciences.* New York: Macmillan, 1968.

O'DEA, THOMAS F, and AVIAD, JANET O'DEA. *The Sociology of Religion,* 2d ed. Englewood Cliffs, N.J.: Prentice-Hall, 1983.

OGBU, JOHN U. "Minority Status and Literacy in Comparative Perspective." *Daedalus* 119, 1990.

OGBURN, WILLIAM F. *Social Change.* New York: The Viking Press, 1964. Originally published 1922.

OGLE, LAURENCE, and ALSALAM, NABEEL (eds.), *The Condition of Education: 1990 Edition.* Washington, D.C.: U.S. Government Printing Office, 1990.

O'HARE, WILLIAM P. and FELT, JUDY C. "Asian Americans: America's Fastest Growing Minority Group." *Population Trends and Public Policy.* Washington, D.C.: Population Reference Bureau, 1991.

OKAMI, PAUL. "'Child Perpetrators of Sexual Abuse': The Emergence of a Problematic Deviant Category." *Journal of Sex Research* 29, 1992.

OKIE, SUSAN. "Study Links Cancer, Poverty." *Washington Post,* April 17, 1991a.

OKIE, SUSAN. "South American Cholera Epidemic Among Worst." *Washington Post,* April 26, 1991b.

OLIVER, MARY BETH, and SEDIKIDES, CONSTANTINE. "Effects of Sexual Permissiveness on Desirability of Partner as a Function of Low and High Commitment to Relationship." *Social Psychology Quarterly* 55, 1992.

OLIVER, MELVIN L., and SHAPIRO, THOMAS M. "Wealth of a Nation: A Reassessment of Asset Inequality in America." *American Journal of Economics and Sociology* 48, 1989.

OLSON, DAVID H., and CROMWELL, RONALD E., (eds.), *Power in Families.* New York: John Wiley, 1975.

OMANG, JOANNE. "A-Worker Exposure Soars, Group Says." *Washington Post,* September 5, 1981.

ORTEGA Y GASSET, JOSÉ. *The Revolt of the Masses.* New York: W.W. Norton, 1932.

OSMOND, M. W., and THORNE, B. "Feminist Theories: The Construction of Gender in Families and Society." In Pauline Boss, W. J. Doherty, R. LaRossa, W. R. Schumm, and Suzanne K. Steinmetz (eds.), *Sourcebook of Family Theories and Methods: A Contextual Approach.* New York: Plenum, 1993.

OTTENHEIMER, MARTIN. "Lewis Henry Morgan and the Prohibition of Cousin Marriage in the United States." *Journal of Family History* 15, 1990.

OUCHI, WILLIAM. *Theory Z.* New York: Avon, 1981.

OUTLER, ALBERT. *Library of Protestant Thought: John Wesley.* New York: Oxford University Press, 1964.

OWENS, TIMOTHY J. "Two Dimensions of Self-esteem: Reciprocal Effects of Positive Self-worth and Self-deprecation on Adolescent Problems." *American Sociological Review* 59, 1994.

PADILLA, FELIX M. *The Gang as an American Enterprise.* New Brunswick, N.J.: Rutgers University Press, 1992.

PAGET, MARIANNE A. *The Unity of Mistakes: A Phenomenological Interpretation of Medical Work.* Philadelphia: Temple University Press, 1988.

PARELIUS, ANN PARKER, and PARELIUS, ROBERT J. *The Sociology of Education.* Englewood Cliffs, N.J.: Prentice-Hall, 1978.

PARK, ROBERT E., BURGESS, E. W., and MCKENZIE, RODERICK D. (eds.), *The City.* Chicago: University of Chicago Press, 1925.

PARSONS, TALCOTT. *The Social System.* Glencoe, Ill.: The Free Press, 1951.

PARSONS, TALCOTT. "The School Class as a Social System: Some of Its Functions in American Society." *Harvard Educational Review* 29, 1959.

PATE, ANTHONY M., and HAMILTON, EDWIN E. "Formal and Informal Deterrents to Domestic Violence: The Dade County Spouse Assault Experiment." *American Sociological Review,* 1992.

PATERNOSTER, RAYMOND. *Capital Punishment in America.* New York: Lexington Books, 1991.

PATTERSON, JAMES T. *The Dread Disease: Cancer and Modern American Culture.* Cambridge, Mass.: Harvard University Press, 1987.

PEAR, ROBERT. "Health-care Costs up Sharply Again, Posing New Threat." *New York Times,* January 5, 1993.

PEARLSTEIN, STEVEN. "Big Retailers Rewrite Rules of Competition." *Washington Post,* November 13, 1995a.

PEARLSTEIN, STEVEN. "Reshaped Economy Exacts Tough Toll." *Washington Post,* November 12, 1995b.

PECK, JANICE. *The Gods of Televangelism.* Cresskill, NJ: Hampton Press, 1993.

PEERS, MARTIN. "Is Milken Mulling Moguldom?" *Variety,* March 13–March 19, 1995.

PENCE, ELAINE, and PAYMAR, MICHAEL. *Education Groups for Men Who Batter: The Duluth Model.* New York: Springer, 1993.

PERL, PETER. "Lower Pay for Women Blamed on Job Barriers." *Washington Post,* December 15, 1985.

PERROW, CHARLES. *Complex Organizations: A Critical Essay,* 3d ed. New York: Random House, 1986.

PERSELL, CAROLINE HODGES. *Education and Inequality: A Theoretical and Empirical Synthesis.* New York: The Free Press, 1977.

PESCOSOLIDO, BERNICE A., and GEORGIANA, SHARON. "Durkheim, Suicide, and Religion: Toward a Network Theory of Suicide." *American Sociological Review* 54, 1989.

PETERS, JOHN F. "Adolescents as Socialization Agents to Parents." *Adolescence* 20, 1985.

PETERSON, GARY W., and ROLLINS, BOYD C. "Parent–Child Socialization." In Marvin B. Sussman and Suzanne K. Steinmetz (eds.), *Handbook of Marriage and the Family.* New York: Plenum Press, 1987.

PETERSON, RICHARD A., SCHMIDMAN, JOHN T., and ELIFSON, KIRK W. "Entrepreneurship or Autonomy? Truckers and Cabbies." In Phyllis L. Stewart and Muriel G. Cantor (eds.), *Varieties of Work.* Beverly Hills, Calif.: Sage, 1982.

PETERSON, TROND, and MORGAN, LAURIE A. "Separate and Unequal: Occupation–Establishment Sex Segregation and the Gender Wage Gap." *American Journal of Sociology* 101, 1995.

PETROW, STEVEN. *Dancing Against Darkness: A Journey Through America in the Age of AIDS.* Lexington, Mass.: Lexington Books, 1990.

PFEIFFER, JOHN. "Girl Talk—Boy Talk." *Science* 85, January/February, 1985.

PHEYSEY, DIANA C. *Organizational Cultures: Types and Transformations.* London: Routledge, 1993.

PHILLIPS, KEVIN. *The Politics of Rich and Poor.* New York: Random House, 1990.

PHILLIPS, KEVIN. "Down and Out: Can the Middle Class Rise Again?" *New York Times Magazine,* January 10, 1993.

PHILLIPS, ROLAND L., KUZMA, J. W., BEESON, W. LAWRENCE, and LOTZ, TERRY. "Influence of Selection Versus Lifestyle on Risk of Fatal Cancer and Cardiovascular Disease Among Seventh-Day Adventists." *American Journal of Epidemiology* 112, 1980.

PIETERSE, JAN N. "Globalisation as Hybridisation." *International Sociology* 9, 1994.

PIFER, ALAN, and BRONTE, D. LYDIA. "Introduction: Squaring the Pyramid." *Daedalus* 115, 1986.

PIKE, E. ROYSTON. "The Natural History of the Kiss." In Charles C. Hughes (ed.), *Custom-Made: Introductory Readings for Cultural Anthropology,* 2d ed. Chicago: Rand McNally, 1976.

PIVEN, FRANCES FOX, and CLOWARD, RICHARD. *Why Americans Don't Vote.* New York: Pantheon, 1988.

PLUNKERT, LOIS. "The 1980's: A Decade of Job Growth and Industry Shifts." *Monthly Labor Review* 113, 1990.

POLLACK, ANDREW. "Medical Technology 'Arms Race' Adds Billions to the Nation's Bills." *New York Times,* April 29, 1991.

POLLACK, ANDREW. "After Stall, Koreans See Need for Economic Reform, Too." *New York Times,* December 15, 1992.

POMERLEAU, ANDREE, BOLDUC, DANIEL, MALCUIT, GERARD, and COSSETTE, LOUISE. "Pink or Blue: Environmental Gender Stereotypes in the First Two Years of Life." *Sex Roles* 22, 1990.

POPE, LISTON. *Millhands and Preachers.* New Haven: Yale University Press, 1942.

POPENOE, DAVID. "Beyond the Nuclear Family: A Statistical Portrait of the Changing Family in Sweden." *Journal of Marriage and the Family* 49, 1987.

POPULATION REFERENCE BUREAU. "World Population Data Sheet, 1991." Washington, D.C.: Population Reference Bureau, 1991.

POPULATION REFERENCE BUREAU. "World Population Data Sheet, 1992." Washington D.C.: Population Reference Bureau, 1992.

POPULATION REFERENCE BUREAU. "World Population Data Sheet, 1995." Washington, DC: Population Reference Bureau, 1995.

PORTELLO, JACQUELINE Y., and LONG, BONITA C. "Role Orientation, Ethical and Interpersonal Conflicts, and Conflict Handling Styles of Female Managers." *Sex Roles* 31, 1994.

POULANTZAS, NICOS. *Political Power and Social Classes.* London: NLB and Sheed and Ward, 1973.

POUSSAINT, ALVIN F. "A Negro Psychiatrist Explains the Negro Psyche." In Norman R. Yetman and C. Hoy Steele (eds.), *Majority and Minority: The Dynamics of Racial and Ethnic Relations.* Boston: Allyn and Bacon, 1971.

POWELL, DAVID E. "Soviet Society Today." In Uri Ra'anan and Charles M. Perry (eds.), *The USSR Today and Tomorrow: Problems and Challenges.* Lexington, Mass.: Lexington Books, 1987.

POWELL, G. BINGHAM. "Voter Turnout in Comparative Perspective." *American Political Science Review* 80, 1986.

POWERS, WILLIAM K. "Indians of the Plains." In Mircea Eliade (ed.), *The Encyclopedia of Religion.* New York: Macmillan, 1987.

PR Newswire."New American Factories Sparked Auto Industry Renaissance: International Automaker Leader Calls for Equal Treatment." May 18, 1994.

PRATT, BETH. "Many Profess to Feel Holy Presence." *Lubbock Avalanche-Journal,* August 16, 1988.

PREBISH, C. S. "Heavenly Father, Divine Goalie. Sport and Religion." *Antioch Review* 42, 1984.

PRESSER, STANLEY. "Informed Consent and Confidentiality in Survey Research." *Public Opinion Quarterly* 58, 1995.

PRESTHUS, ROBERT VANCE. *The Organizational Society,* rev. ed. New York: St. Martin's Press, 1978.

PRESTON, SAMUEL H. *Biological and Social Aspects of Mortality and the Length of Life.* Leige: Ordina, 1982.

PRESTON, SAMUEL H. "Children and the Elderly: Divergent Paths for America's Dependents." *Demography* 21, 1984.

PRIGERSON, HOLLY G. "Socialization to Dying: Social Determinants of Death Acknowledgment and Treatment among Termally Ill Geriatric Patients." *Health and Social Behavior* 33, 1992.

PRINCETON RELIGIOUS RESEARCH CENTER. *The Unchurched American.* Princeton: Princeton Religious Research Center and the Gallup Organization, 1978.

PRINCETON RELIGION RESEARCH CENTER. "Religion in America: 1995 Supplement." Princeton, NJ: 1995.

PRITCHARD, LINDA K. "Religious Change in Nineteenth-Century America." In Charles Y. Glock and Robert N. Bellah (eds.), *The New Religious Consciousness.* Berkeley: University of California Press, 1976.

PROSEN, ROSE MARY. "Looking Back." In Michael Novak (ed.), *Growing Up Slavic in America.* Bayville, N.Y.: EMPAC, 1976.

PRUD'HOMME, ALEX. "A Nation on the Move." *Time,* April 29, 1991.

RADIN, PAUL (ed.), *Crashing Thunder: The Autobiography of a Winnebago Indian.* New York: D. Appleton, 1926. Published in 1920 as Part 1 of the autobiography.

RAINES, HOWELL. *My Soul Is Rested.* New York: Bantam Books, 1978.

RAINWATER, LEE. "The Lower Class: Health, Illness and Medical Institutions." In Irwin Deutscher and Elizabeth J. Thompson (eds.), *Among the People: Encounters with the Poor.* New York: Basic Books, 1968.

RASOR, DINA. *The Pentagon Underground.* New York: Random House–Times Books, 1985.

RAVENHOLT, R. T. "Tobacco's Global Death March." *Population and Development Review* 16, 1990.

RAWLINGS, STEVE W., and SALUTER, ARLENE. *Household and Family Characteristics: March 1994.* Current Population Reports, P-20, No. 483. Washington, DC: U.S. Government Printing Office, 1995.

READ, KENNETH E. *The High Valley.* New York: Columbia University Press, 1980.

REED, EVELYN. "Is Biology Woman's Destiny?" *International Socialist Review,* 1971.

REEDER, LEO G. "The Patient-Client as a Consumer: Some Observations on the Changing Professional-Client Relationship." *Journal of Health and Social Behavior* 13, 1972.

REICH, ROBERT B. *The Work of Nations.* New York: Random House, 1992.

REICH, ROBERT B. "Class Anxieties." *Harper's,* February 1995.

REICH, WALTER (ed.), *Origins of Terrorism: Psychologies, Ideologies, Theologies, States of Mind.* New York: Cambridge University Press, 1990.

REID, T. R. "The Puckering Stops Here." *Washington Post,* November 8, 1994.

REIMAN, JEFFREY H. *The Rich Get Richer and the Poor Get Prison.* New York: John Wiley, 1979.

REINHOLD, ROBERT. "In the Middle of L.A.'s Gang Warfare." *New York Times Magazine,* May 22, 1988.

REINHOLD, ROBERT. "Aloft Without Nicotine: Can Smokers Cope?" *New York Times,* February 26, 1990.

REINISCH, JUNE M., SANDERS, STEPHANIE A., HILL, CRAIG A., and ZIEMBA-DAVIS, MARY. "High-risk Sexual Behavior among Heterosexual Undergraduates at a Midwestern University." *Family Planning Perspectives* 24, 1992.

REISS, IRA L. *The Social Context of Premarital Sexual Permissiveness.* New York: Holt, Rinehart, and Winston, 1967.

REISS, IRA L. *Family Systems in America.* New York: Holt, Rinehart and Winston, 1980.

REISS, IRA L. *Journey into Sexuality: An Explanatory Voyage.* Englewood Cliffs, N.J.: Prentice-Hall, 1986.

REISS, IRA L., and LEE, GARY R. *Family Systems in America,* 4th ed. New York: Holt, Rinehart & Winston, Inc., 1988.

REMINI, ROBERT V. *Andrew Jackson and the Course of American Democracy, 1833–1845.* New York: Harper & Row, 1984.

RENSBERGER, BOYCE. "African Women Save Energy Using Head for Heavy Loads." *Washington Post,* February 23, 1986.

RENSBERGER, BOYCE. "Sexual Competition and Violence." *Washington Post,* February 29, 1988.

RESKIN, BARBARA F., and HARTMAN, HEIDI (eds.), *Women's Work, Men's Work: Sex Segregation on the Job.* Washington, D.C.: National Academy Press, 1986.

RESKIN, BARBARA F., and PADOVIC, IRENE. *Women and Men at Work.* Thousand Oaks, CA: Pine Forge Press, 1994.

RESKIN, BARBARA F., and ROOS, PATRICIA A. (eds.), *Job Queues, Gender Queues.* Philadelphia: Temple University Press, 1990.

RICH, SPENCER. "Surgeon General Sees Oral Cancer Epidemic." *Washington Post,* December 11, 1992.

RICHARDSON, LAUREL. *The New Other Woman: Contemporary Single Women in Affairs with Married Men.* New York: The Free Press, 1985.

RICHARDSON, JAMES R. "Definitions of Cult: From Sociological–Technical to Popular–Negative." *Review of Religious Research.* 34, 1993.

RICHEY, RUSSELL E., and JONES, DONALD G. *American Civil Religion.* New York: Harper & Row, 1974.

RIDGEWAY, CECILIA, and WALKER, HENRY A. "Status Structures." In Karen S. Cook, Gary Alan Fine, and James S. House (eds.), *Sociological Perspectives on Social Psychology.* Boston: Allyn & Bacon, 1995.

RIDING, ALAN. "Some Suave Fumeurs Putting Their Packs Away." *New York Times,* November 9, 1992.

RIESMAN, DAVID. *The Lonely Crowd.* New Haven, Conn.: Yale University Press, 1961.

RILEY, MATILDA WHITE, FONER, ANNE, and WARING, JOAN. "Sociology of Aging." In Neil J. Smelser (ed.), *Handbook of Sociology.* Beverly Hills, Calif.: Sage, 1988.

RILEY, NANCY E. "China's 'Missing Girls': Prospects and Policy." *Population Today* 24, 1996.

RITZER, GEORGE. "The Permanently New Economy: The Case for Reviving Economic Sociology." *Work and Occupations* 16, 1989.

RITZER, GEORGE. *Metatheorizing in Sociology.* Lexington, Mass.: Lexington Books, 1991.

RITZER, GEORGE. *The McDonaldization of Society.* Newbury Park, Calif.: Pine Forge Press, 1993.

RITZER, GEORGE. *Expressing America: A Critique of the Global Credit Card Society.* Thousand Oaks, CA: Pine Forge Press, 1995.

Ritzer, George. *The McDonaldization of Society,* rev. ed. Thousand Oaks, CA: Pine Forge Press, 1996a.

Ritzer, George. *Sociological Theory,* 4th ed. New York: McGraw-Hill, 1996b.

Ritzer, George, and Walczak, David. *Working: Conflict and Change,* 3d ed. Englewood Cliffs, N.J.: Prentice-Hall, 1986.

Ritzer, George, and Walczak, David. "Rationalization and the Deprofessionalization of Physicians." *Social Forces* 66, 1988.

Roberts, Elizabeth, Kline, David, and Gagnon, John. *Family Life and Sexual Learning: A Study of the Role of Parents in the Sexual Learning of Children.* Cambridge, Mass.: Population Education, 1978.

Robertson, Roland. "Mapping the Global Condition: Globalization as the Central Concept." In Mike Featherstone (ed.), *Global Culture: Nationalism, Globalization and Modernity.* London: Sage, 1990.

Robertson, Roland. *Globalization: Social Theory and Global Culture.* London: Sage, 1992.

Rockett, Ian R. H. "Population and Health: An Introduction to Epidemiology." *Population Bulletin* 49, 1994.

Rodgers, Joseph L., and Rowe, David C. "Influence of Siblings on Adolescent Sexual Behavior." *Developmental Psychology* 24, 1988.

Rodgers, Joseph L., Rowe, David C., and Harris, David F. "Sibling Differences in Adolescent Sexual Behavior: Inferring Process Models from Family Composition Patterns." *Journal of Marriage and the Family* 54, 1992.

Roethlisberger, Fritz, and Dickson, William J. *Management and the Worker.* New York: John Wiley & Sons, 1964. Originally published in 1939.

Rogers, Jackie K. "Just a Temp: Experience and Structure of Alienation in Temporary Clerical Employment." *Work and Occupations* 22, 1995.

Rogers, Richard G. "Sociodemographic Characteristics of Long-lived and Healthy Individuals." *Population and Development Review* 21, 1995.

Rogers-Dillon, Robin. "The Dynamics of Welfare Stigma." *Qualitative Sociology* 18, 1995.

Rollins, B. C., and Galligan, R. "The Developing Child and Marital Satisfaction of Parents." In R. M. Lerner and G. B. Spanier (eds.), *Child Influences on Marital and Family Interaction.* New York: Academic Press, 1978.

Romero, Mary. *Maid in the U.S.A.* New York: Routledge, 1992.

Roof, Wade C. "Return of the Baby Boomers to Organized Religion." In Constant H. Jacquet, Jr., (ed.), *Yearbook of American and Canadian Churches 1990.* Nashville: Abington Press, 1990.

Roof, Wade C. *A Generation of Seekers: The Spiritual Journeys of the Baby Boom Generation.* New York: HarperCollins, 1993.

Roof, Wade C., and Hadaway, C. Kirk. "Denominational Switching in the Seventies: Going Beyond Stark and Glock." *Journal for the Scientific Study of Religion* 18, 1979.

Roof, Wade C., and McKinney, William. *American Mainline Religion: Its Changing Shape and Future.* New Brunswick, N.J.: Rutgers University Press, 1987.

Roozen, David A., McKinney, William, and Thompson, Wayne. "The 'Big Chill' Generation Warms to Worship: A Research Note." *Review of Religious Research* 31, 1990.

Roscigno, Vincent J., and Kimble, M. Keith. "Elite Power, Race, and the Persistence of Low Unionization in the South." *Work and Occupations* 22, 1995.

Rose, Arnold. *The Power Structure.* New York: Oxford University Press, 1967.

Rose, Peter I. (ed.), *Socialization and the Life Cycle.* New York: St. Martin's Press, 1979.

Roseberry, William. *Coffee and Capitalism in the Venezuelan Andes.* Austin: University of Texas Press, 1983.

Rosecrance, John. "Compulsive Gambling and the Medicalization of Deviance." *Social Problems* 32, 1985.

Rosen, Sherwin, and Taubman, Paul. "Changes in the Impact of Education and Income on Mortality in the U.S." In Linda DelBene and Foritz Schueren (eds.), *Statistical Uses of Administrative Records with Emphasis on Mortality and Disability Research.* Washington, D.C.: U.S. Department of Health, Education and Welfare, 1979.

Rosenbaum, Emily, and Kandel, Denise B. "Early Onset of Adolescent Sexual Behavior and Drug Involvement." *Journal of Marriage and Family* 52, 1990.

Rosenbaum, James E. *Making Inequality: The Hidden Curriculum of High School Tracking.* New York: John Wiley, 1976.

ROSENBERG, MORRIS. *Conceiving the Self.* New York: Basic Books, 1979.

ROSENBERG, MORRIS. "The Self Concept: Social Product and Social Force." In Morris Rosenberg and Ralph H. Turner (eds.) *Social Psychology: Sociological Perspectives,* new edition. New Brunswick, N.J.: Transaction, 1990.

ROSENBERG, MORRIS, and TURNER, RALPH H. "Introduction to the Transaction Edition." In Morris Rosenberg and Ralph H. Turner (eds.), *Social Psychology: Sociological Perspectives,* new edition. New Brunswick, N.J.: Transaction, 1990.

ROSENBERG, MORRIS, SCHOOLER, CARMI, SCHOENBACH, CARRIE, and ROSENBERG, FLORENCE. "Global Self-esteem and Specific Self-esteem: Different Concepts, Different Outcomes." *American Sociological Review* 60, 1995.

ROSENFELD, RACHEL A., and WARD, KATHRYN B. "The Contemporary U.S. Women's Movement: An Empirical Example of Competition Theory." *Sociological Forum* 6, 1991.

ROSENTHAL, ELISABETH. "Health Problems of Inner City Poor Reach Crisis Point." *New York Times,* December 24, 1990.

ROSENTHAL, ELISABETH. "In Canada, a Government System that Provides Health Care to All," *New York Times,* April 30, 1991.

ROSENTHAL, NEAL H. "The Nature of Occupational Employment Growth: 1983–93." *Monthly Labor Review,* June 1995.

ROSNOW, RALPH L., and FINE, GARY ALAN. *Rumor and Gossip.* New York: Elsevier, 1976.

ROSS, CATHERINE E., and BIRD, CHLOE E. "Sex Stratification and Health Lifestyle: Consequences for Men's and Women's Perceived Health." *Journal of Health and Social Behavior* 35, 1994.

ROSS, CATHERINE E., and DUFF, RAYMOND S. "Returning to the Doctor: The Effect of Client Characteristics, Type of Practice, and Experience with Care." *Health and Social Behavior* 23, 1982.

ROSS, CATHERINE E., MIROWSKY, JOHN, and HUBER, JOAN. "Dividing Work, Sharing Work, and In Between: Marriage Patterns and Depression." *American Sociological Review* 48, 1983.

ROSS, H. LAURENCE. *Confronting Drunk Driving: Social Policy for Saving Lives.* New Haven, Conn.: Yale University Press, 1992.

ROSSI, ALICE S. "Naming Children in Middle-class Families." *American Sociological Review* 30, 1965.

ROSSI, PETER. *Without Shelter: Homelessness in the 1990s.* New York: Priority Press, 1992.

ROTELLO, GABRIEL. "Gay Place in Sports Routinely Dismissed." *Arizona Republic,* May 23, 1995.

ROTH, JULIUS A. *Timetables: Structuring the Passage of Time in Hospital Treatment and Other Careers.* Indianapolis: Bobbs-Merrill, 1963.

ROTH, JULIUS A. "Treatment of the Sick." In J. Kosa, Aaron Antonovsky, and Irving Kenneth Zola (eds.), *Poverty and Health.* Cambridge, Mass.: Harvard University Press, 1969.

ROTHMAN, DAVID. *The Discovery of the Asylum: Social Order and Disorder in the New Republic.* Boston: Little, Brown, 1971.

ROTHSTEIN, STANLEY W. *Schools and Society: New Perspectives in American Education.* Englewood Cliffs, NJ: Prentice Hall, 1996.

ROWAN, BRIAN, and MIRACLE, ANDREW W., JR. "Systems of Ability Grouping and the Stratification of Achievement in Elementary Schools." *Sociology of Education* 56, 1983.

ROY, DONALD. "Efficiency and the 'Fix': Informal Intergroup Relations in a Piecework Machine Shop." *American Journal of Sociology* 60, 1954.

ROY, DONALD. "Banana Time: Job Satisfaction and Informal Interaction." *Human Organization* 18, 1959–1960.

RUBIN, LILLIAN B. *Worlds of Pain: Life in the Working Class Family.* New York: Basic Books, 1976.

RUBIN, LILLIAN B. *Erotic Wars: What Happened to the Sexual Revolution?* New York: Farrar, Straus & Giroux, 1990.

RUBINSON, RICHARD, and RALPH, JOHN. "Technical Change and the Expansion of Schooling in the United States, 1890–1970." *Sociology of Education* 57, 1984.

RUDIN, A. J. "America's New Religion." *The Christian Century* 89, 1972.

RULE, JAMES. "The Need to Know versus the Right to Privacy." In Craig Calhoun and George Ritzer (eds.), *Social Problems.* New York: McGraw-Hill, 1992.

RULE, JAMES, and BRANTLEY, PETER. "Computerized Surveillance in the Workplace: Forms and Distributions." *Sociological Forum* 7, 1992.

RUMBAUT, RUBEN G. "Origins and Destinies: Immigration to the United States Since World War II." *Sociological Forum* 8, 1994.

RUMBERGER, RUSSELL W. "Chicano Dropouts: A Review of Research and Policy Issues." In R. R. Valencia (ed.), *Chicano School Failure and Success: Research and Policy Agendas for the 1990s.* New York: Falmer, 1991.

RUMBERGER, RUSSELL W. "Dropping Out of Middle School: A Multilevel Analysis of Students and Schools." *American Educational Research Journal* 32, 1995.

RUSH, GARY B., and DENISOFF, R. SERGE. *Social and Political Movements.* New York: Appleton-Century-Crofts, 1971.

RUSHING, WILLIAM A. "The Supply of Physicians and Expenditures for Health Services with Implications for the Coming Physician Surplus." *Journal of Health and Social Behavior* 26, 1985.

RUSSELL, CHRISTINE. "What Do You Know About AIDS?" *Washington Post Health,* February 5, 1991.

RYAN, KEVIN. "Technicians and Interpreters in Moral Crusades: The Case of the Drug Courier Profile." *Deviant Behavior* 15, 1994.

RYAN, WILLIAM. *Blaming the Victim.* New York: Pantheon Books, 1971.

RYDER, NORMAN R. "What Is Going to Happen to American Fertility?" *Population and Development Review* 16, 1990.

RYMER, RUSS. "Annals of Science: A Silent Childhood—II," *The New Yorker,* April 20, 1992.

RYMER, RUSS. *Genie: An Abused Child's Flight from Silence.* New York: HarperCollins, 1993.

RYSCAVAGE, PAUL, and HENLE, PETER. "Earnings Inequality Accelerates in the 1980's." *Monthly Labor Review* 113, 1990.

SABATO, LARRY J. *The Rise of Political Consultants: New Ways of Winning Elections.* New York: Basic Books, 1981.

SACHAR, HOWARD M. *A History of Israel, Volume II, From the Aftermath of the Yom Kippur War.* New York: Oxford University Press, 1987.

SADKER, MYRA, and SADKER, DAVID. "Sexism in the Schoolroom of the '80s." *Psychology Today,* March 1985.

SAFILIOS-ROTHSCHILD, C. "Study of Family Power Structure: 1960–1969." *Journal of Marriage and the Family* 32, 1970.

SALOME, LOUIS J. "Dutch Tolerate Drug Use in Effort to Control Abuse." *Courier-Journal,* July 3, 1994.

SANDAY, PEGGY REEVES. *Female Power and Male Dominance.* New York: Cambridge University Press, 1981.

SANDEFUR, GARY D., and TIENDA, MARTA. *Divided Opportunities: Minorities, Poverty, and Social Policy.* New York: Plenum Press, 1988.

SASSEN, SASKIA. "Economic Restructuring and the American City." *Annual Review of Sociology* 16, 1990.

SASSEN, SASKIA. *Cities in a World Economy.* Thousand Oaks, CA: Pine Forge Press, 1994.

SAUNDERS, DANIEL G. "When Battered Women Use Violence: Husband-Abuse or Self-Defense?" *Violence and Victims* 1, 1986.

SAVETH, EDWARD N. *American Historians and European Immigrants.* New York: Columbia University Press, 1948.

SAWYER, KATHY. "NASA's New Space Toilet: $30 Million up the Drain?" *Washington Post,* January 5, 1993.

SAXE, LEONARD, and FINE, MICHELLE. *Social Experiments: Methods for Design and Evaluation.* Beverly Hills, Calif.: Sage, 1981.

SCANZONI, JOHN. *Sexual Bargaining: Power Politics in the American Marriage.* Englewood Cliffs, N.J.: Prentice-Hall, 1972.

SCANZONI, JOHN. "Social Processes and Power in Families." In Wesley R. Burr, Reuben Hill, F. Ivan Nye, and Ira L. Reiss (eds.), *Contemporary Theories About the Family: Research-Based Theories,* Vol. 1. New York: The Free Press, 1979.

SCARCE, RIK. "(No) Trial (But) Tribulations: When Courts and Ethnography Conflict." *Journal of Contemporary Ethnography* 23, 1994.

SCHAEFER, WALTER E., OLEXA, CAROL, and POLK, KENNETH. "Programmed for Social Class: Tracking in High School." *Trans-Action* 7, 1970.

SCHMIDT, STEVE. "ADD Traced to Brain in New Studies." *San Diego Union-Tribune,* December 18, 1995a.

SCHMIDT, STEVE. "Puzzling over the Furies in Children Attention Deficit Disorder Torments Parents, Schools." *San Diego Union-Tribune,* December 18, 1995b.

SCHNEIDER, WILLIAM. "Rule Suburbia." *National Journal* 39, September 28, 1991.

SCHOEN, ROBERT, and WEINICK, ROBIN M. "The Slowing Metabolism of Marriage: Figures from 1988 U.S. Marital Status Life Tables." *Demography* 30, 1993.

SCHRAM, MARTIN. *The Great American Video Game: Presidential Politics in the Television Age.* New York: William Morrow, 1987.

SCHULTZ, JAMES H., BOROWSKI, ALAN, and CROWN, WILLIAM H. *Economics of Population Aging: The "Graying" of Australia, Japan, and the United States.* New York: Auburn House, 1991.

SCHUMAN, HOWARD, STEEH, CHARLOTTE, and BOBO, LAWRENCE. *Racial Attitudes in America: Trends and Interpretations.* Cambridge, Mass.: Harvard University Press, 1985.

SCHUMM, WALTER R., and BUGAIGHIS, MARGARET A. "Marital Quality over the Marital Career: Alternative Explanations." *Journal of Marriage and the Family* 48, 1986.

SCHUR, EDWIN M. *Crimes Without Victims: Deviant Behavior and Public Policy.* Englewood Cliffs, N.J.: Prentice-Hall, 1965.

SCHUR, EDWIN M. *The Americanization of Sex.* Philadelphia: Temple University Press, 1988.

SCHWALBE, MICHAEL L. *The Psychosocial Consequences of Natural and Alienated Labor.* Albany, N.Y.: State University of New York Press, 1986.

SCHWARTZ, HILLEL. *Never Satisfied: A Cultural History of Diets, Fantasies and Fat.* New York: The Free Press, 1986.

SCHWINN, ELIZABETH. "D'Amato's Fund Raising Legendary." *San Diego Union-Tribune,* May 29, 1995.

SCOTT, BILL. "Don't Bite off More Than You Can Chew." *Idaho Falls Post Register,* December 3, 1995.

SCOTT, DANIEL T. *Technology and Union Survival: A Study of the Printing Industry.* New York: Praeger, 1987.

SECCOMBE, KAREN, and AMEY, CHERYL. "Playing by the Rules and Losing: Health Insurance and the Working Poor." *Journal of Health and Social Behavior* 36, 1995.

SEDLAK, MICHAEL W., WHEELER, CHRISTOPHER W., PULLIN, DIANA C., and CUSIK, PHILIP A. *Selling Students Short: Classroom Bargains and Academic Reform in the American High School.* New York: Teachers College Press, 1986.

SEN, AMARTYA. "More Than 100 Million Women Are Missing." *New York Review of Books,* December 1989.

SENNETT, RICHARD, and COBB, JONATHAN. *The Hidden Injuries of Class.* New York: Vintage Books, 1972.

SEUBERT, VIRGINIA R. "Sociology and Value Neutrality: Limiting Sociology to the Empirical Level." *American Sociologist* 19, 1991.

SEWELL, WILLIAM H. "Inequality of Opportunity for Higher Education." *American Sociological Review* 36, 1971.

SHAIKEN, HARLEY. *Work Transformed: Automation and Labor in The Computer Age.* Lexington, Mass.: Lexington Books, 1986.

SHANK, SUSAN E. "Women and the Labor Market: The Link Grows Stronger." *Monthly Labor Review* 111, 1988.

SHANNON, LYLE W. "Assessing the Relationship of Adult Criminal Careers to Juvenile Careers." In C. Abt (ed.), *Problems in American Social Policy.* Cambridge, Mass.: Abt Books, 1980.

SHAPIRO, CONSTANCE H. "Sexual Learning: The Short-Changed Adolescent Male." *Social Work* 25, 1980.

SHAVIT, YOSSI, and BLOSSFELD, HANS-PETER (eds.). *Persistent Inequality.* Boulder, CO: Westview, 1993.

SHAVIT, YOSSI, and FEATHERMAN, DAVID L. "Schooling, Tracking, and Teenage Intelligence." *Sociology of Education* 61, 1988.

SHAW, LINDA. "Psychologist's New Book Questions Diagnosis of Attention-deficit Disorder." *Seattle Times,* October 2, 1995.

SHEFFIELD, CAROLE J. "Sexual Terrorism: The Social Control of Women." In Beth B. Hess and Myra Marx Ferree (eds.), *Analyzing Gender: A Handbook of Social Science Research.* Beverly Hills, Calif.: Sage, 1987.

SHEHAN, CONSTANCE L., and SCANZONI, JOHN H. "Gender Patterns in the United States: Demographic Trends and Policy Prospects." *Family Relations* 37, 1988.

SHEHAN, CONSTANCE L., BOCK, E. WILBUR, and LEE, GARY R. "Religious Heterogamy, Religiosity, and Marital Happiness: The Case of Catholics." *Journal of Marriage and the Family* 52, 1990.

SHELL, ELLEN RUPPEL. "The Getting of Respect." *The Atlantic,* February 1988.

SHEPHERD, GORDON, and SHEPHERD, GARY. *A Kingdom Transformed: Themes in the Development of Mormonism.* Salt Lake City: University of Utah Press, 1984.

SHERIF, MUZAFER. "A Study of Some Social Factors in Perception." *Archives of Psychology* 27, 1935.

SHERIF, MUZAFER. *Groups in Harmony and Tension.* New York: Harper & Brothers, 1953.

SHERMAN, LAWRENCE W., and BERK, RICHARD A. "The Specific Deterrent Effects of Arrest for Domestic Assault." *American Sociological Review* 49, 1984.

SHERMAN, LAWRENCE W., and COHN, ELLEN G. "The Impact of Research on Legal Policy: A Case Study of the Minneapolis Domestic Violence Experiment." *Law and Society* 23, 1989.

SHERMAN, LAWRENCE W., and SMITH, DOUGLAS A. "Crime, Punishment, and Stake in Conformity: Legal and Informal Control of Domestic Violence." *American Sociological Review* 57, 1992.

SHORTER, EDWARD. *A History of Women's Bodies.* New York: Basic Books, 1982.

SIGNORIELLI, NANCY. "Television and Conceptions about Sex Roles: Maintaining Conventionality and the Status Quo." *Sex Roles* 21, 1989.

SILVER, MARC L. *Under Construction: Work and Alienation in the Building Trades.* Albany, N.Y.: State University of New York Press, 1986.

SILVESTRI, GEORGE T. "Occupational Employment: Wide Variations in Growth." *Monthly Labor Review,* November 1993.

SILVESTRI, GEORGE T., and LUKASIEWICZ, JOHN M. "A Look at Occupational Employment Trends to the Year 2000." *Monthly Labor Review* 110, 1987.

SILVESTRI, GEORGE T., LUKASIEWICZ, JOHN M., and EINSTEIN, MARCUS E. "Occupational Employment Projections Through 1995." *Monthly Labor Review* 106, 1983.

SIMMEL, GEORG. "The Dyad and the Triad." In Kurt Wolf (ed.), *The Sociology of Georg Simmel.* Glencoe, Ill.: The Free Press, 1950.

SIMMEL, GEORG. "The Metropolis and Mental Life." In Donald Levine (ed.), *Georg Simmel: Individuality and Social Forms.* Chicago: University of Chicago Press, 1971. Originally published 1903.

SIMMONS, J. L. "Public Stereotypes of Deviants." *Social Problems* 13, 1965.

SIMMONS, J. L., and McCALL, GEORGE J. *Social Research: The Craft of Finding Out.* New York: Macmillan, 1985.

SIMON, DAVID R. and EITZEN, STANLEY D. *Elite Deviance,* 3rd ed. Boston: Allyn and Bacon, 1990.

SIMON, JULIAN L. *The Ultimate Resource.* Princeton, N.J.: Princeton University Press, 1981.

SIMON, RITA, and LANDIS, JEAN. *The Crimes Women Commit, The Punishments They Receive.* Lexington, Mass.: Lexington Books, 1991.

SIMPSON, GEORGE EATON, and YINGER, J. MILTON. *Racial and Cultural Minorities: An Analysis of Prejudice and Discrimination,* 5th ed. New York: Plenum, 1985.

SIMPSON, SALLY. "Corporate Crime." In Craig Calhoun and George Ritzer (eds.), *Social Problems.* New York: McGraw-Hill, 1992.

SINGH, J. A. L., and ZINGG, ROBERT M. *Wolf Children and Feral Man.* New York: Harper & Row, 1942.

SITU, YINGYI, AUSTIN, TIMOTHY, AND LIU, WEIZHENG. "Coping with Anomic Stress: Chinese Students in the USA." *Deviant Behavior* 16, 1995.

SKLAIR, LESLIE. *Sociology of the Global System.* Baltimore: Johns Hopkins University Press, 1991.

SLOMCZYNSKI, KAZIMIERZ M., MILLER, JOANNE, and KOHN, MELVIN L. "Stratification, Work, and Values: A Polish-United States Comparison." *American Sociological Review* 46, 1981.

SMART, BARRY. "Sociology, Globalisation and Postmodernity: Comments on the 'Sociology for One World' Thesis." *International Sociology* 9, 1994.

SMITH, ADAM. *The Wealth of Nations.* New York: The Modern Library, 1937.

SMITH, ANTHONY D. "Towards a Global Culture." In Mike Featherstone (ed.), *Global Culture: Nationalism, Globalization and Modernity.* London: Sage, 1990.

SMITH, CHRISTIAN. *The Emergence of Liberation Theology: Radical Religion and Social Movement Theory.* Chicago: University of Chicago Press, 1991.

SMITH, DANIEL S. "The Dating of the American Sexual Revolution." In Michael Gordon (ed.), *The American Family in Social Historical Perspective,* 2nd ed. New York: St. Martin's Press, 1978.

SMITH, DAVID A. "The New Urban Sociology Meets the Old." *Urban Affairs Review* 30:3, January 1995a.

SMITH, DAVID A. and WHITE, DOUGLAS R. "Structure and Dynamics of the Global Economy: Network Analysis of International Trade 1965–1980." *Social Forces* 70, 1992.

SMITH, DAVID N. "The Genesis of Genocide in Rwanda: The Fatal Dialectic of Class and Ethnicity." *Humanity and Society* 19, 1995b.

SMITH, DOUGLAS A., and GARTIN, PATRICK R. "Specifying Specific Deterrence: The Influence of Arrest on Future Criminal Activity." *American Sociological Review* 54, 1989.

SMITH, JAMES D. "Trends in the Concentration of Personal Wealth in the United States, 1958 to 1976." *Review of Income and Wealth* 30, 1984.

SMITH, LEEF. "Gangs Continue to Terrorize L.A. Residents." *Washington Post,* September 16, 1992.

SMITH, SALLY E. "The Great Diet Deception." *USA Today* (Magazine), January 1995c.

SMITH, VICKI. "Braverman's Legacy: The Labor Process Tradition at 20." *Work and Occupations* 21, 1994.

SNELL, JOEL, GREEN, DONALD, and WAKEFIELD, BILL. "Criminal Justice Education: Textbook Criminal Typologies and Merton's Paradigm." *Journal of Instructional Psychology* 21, 1994.

SNIPP, C. MATTHEW. "American Indians and Natural Resource Development." *American Journal of Economics and Sociology* 45, 1986.

Snow, David A., Rochford, E. Burke, Jr., Worden, Steven K., and Benford, Robert. "Frame Alignment Processes, Micromobilization, and Movement Participation." *American Sociological Review* 51, 1986.

Soldo, Beth J., and Agree, Emily. "America's Elderly." *Population Bulletin* 43, 1988.

Sollie, D., and Miller, B. "The Transition to Parenthood as a Critical Time for Building Family Strengths." In N. Stinnet and P. Knaub (eds.), *Family Strengths: Positive Models of Family Life.* Lincoln: University of Nebraska Press, 1980.

Solon, Gary. "Intergenerational Income Mobility in the United States." *American Economic Review,* June 1992.

Solorzano, Daniel G. "The Chicano Educational Experience: Empirical and Theoretical Perspectives." In Stanley W. Rothstein (ed.), *Class, Culture, and Race in American Schools: A Handbook.* Westport, CT: Greenwood Press, 1995.

Solzhenitsyn, Alexander I. *The Gulag Archipelago.* New York: Harper & Row, 1973

Sommer, Robert, Burstein, Emily, and Holman, Sandy. "Tolerance of Deviance as Affected by Label, Act, and Actor." *Deviant Behavior* 9, 1988.

Sommers, Ira, Baskin, Deborah R., and Fagan, Jeffrey. "Getting out of the Life: Crime Desistance by Female Street Offenders." *Deviant Behavior* 15, 1994.

Sonenstein, Freya L., Pleck, Joseph H., and Ku, Leighton C. "Sexual Activity, Condom Use and AIDS Awareness Among Adolescent Males." *Family Planning Perspectives* 21, 1989.

Sorensen, Glorian, et al. "Sex Differences in the Relationship Between Work and Health: The Minnesota Heart Survey." *Journal of Health and Social Behavior* 26, 1985.

Sorokin, Pitirim A. *The Crisis of Our Age.* New York: E.P. Dutton, 1941.

Sorokin, Pitirim A. *Social and Cultural Dynamics.* Boston: Porter Sargent, 1957.

Sosin, Daniel M., Koepsell, Thomas D., Rivara, Frederick P., and Mercy, James A. "Fighting as a Marker for Multiple Problem Behaviors in Adolescents." *Journal of Adolescent Health* 16, 1995.

South, Scott. "Sex Ratios, Economic Power, and Women's Roles: A Theoretical Extension and Empirical Test." *Journal of Marriage and the Family* 50, 1988.

South, Scott J., and Spitze, Glenna. "Housework in Marital and Nonmarital Households." *American Sociological Review* 59, 1994.

Southern Poverty Law Center. "'Move-in' Violence: White Resistance to Neighborhood Integration in the 1980s." Montgomery, Ala.: Southern Poverty Law Center, 1987.

Sowell, Thomas. *Ethnic America: A History.* New York: Basic Books, 1980.

Spanier, Graham B. "Measuring Dyadic Adjustment: New Scales for Assessing the Quality of Marriage and Similar Dyads." *Journal of Marriage and the Family* 38, 1976.

Spanier, Graham B., and Furstenberg, Frank F., Jr. "Remarriage and Reconstituted Families." In Marvin B. Sussman and Suzanne K. Steinmetz (eds.), *Handbook of Marriage and the Family.* New York: Plenum Press, 1987.

Spector, Malcolm. "Legitimizing Homosexuality." *Society,* July/August 1977.

Spindler, George D., and Spindler, Louise. "Anthropologists View American Culture." *Annual Review of Anthropology* 12, Palo Alto, Calif.: Annual Reviews, Inc., 1983.

"The Sport of Religion: The Ritual Athletes of Iran." CBS television program, February 9, 1972.

Sprecher, Susan, Barbee, Anita, and Schwartz, Pepper. "'Was it Good For You Too?': Gender Differences in First Sexual Intercourse Experiences." *The Journal of Sex Research* 32, 1995.

Sprecher, Susan, McKinney, Kathleen, and Orbuch, Terri L. "Has the Double Standard Disappeared?: An Experimental Test." *Social Psychology Quarterly* 50, 1987.

Stacey, Judith, and Thorne, Barrie. "The Missing Feminist Revolution in Sociology." *Social Problems* 32, 1985.

Stack, Steven. "The Effect of the Decline in Institutionalized Religion on Suicide, 1954–1978." *Journal for the Scientific Study of Religion* 22, 1983.

Stack, Steven. "New Micro-level Data on the Impact of Divorce on Suicide, 1954–1980: A Test of Two Theories." *Journal of Marriage and the Family* 52, 1990a.

Stack, Steven. "The Effect of Divorce on Suicide in Denmark, 1951–1980." *The Sociological Quarterly* 31, 1990b.

Stack, Steven. "Execution Publicity and Homicide in Georgia." *American Journal of Criminal Justice* 18, 1994.

Stafford, Mark, and Gibbs, Jack. "A Major Problem with the Theory of Status Integration and Suicide." *Social Forces* 63, 1985.

STAFFORD, MARK, and GIBBS, JACK. "Change in the Relation Between Marital Integration and Suicide Rates." *Social Forces* 66, 1988.

STAGGENBORG, SUZANNE. "Stability and Innovation in the Women's Movement: A Comparison of Two Movement Organizations." *Social Problems* 36, 1989.

STARK, RODNEY, and BAINBRIDGE, WILLIAM SIMS. "Of Churches, Sects, and Cults: Preliminary Concepts for a Theory of Religious Movements. " *Journal for the Scientific Study of Religion* 18, 1979.

STARR, PAUL. *The Social Transformation of American Medicine.* New York: Basic Books, 1982.

STAUDOHAR, P., and BROWN, H. *Deindustrialization and Plant Closings.* Lexington, Mass.: D.C. Heath, 1987.

STEEMI, FEHMIDA. "Higher Settlements in 1989 End Innovative Decade." *Monthly Labor Review* 113, 1990.

STEIN, LEONARD I. "Male and Female: The Doctor-Nurse Game." In James P. Spradley and David W. McCurdy (eds.), *Conformity and Conflict: Readings in Cultural Anthropology,* 2d ed. Boston: Little, Brown, 1974.

STEINBERG, LAURENCE, and SILVERBERG, SUSAN B. "Influences on Marital Satisfaction During the Middle Stages of the Family Life Cycle." *Journal of Marriage and the Family* 49, 1987.

STEINBERG, STEPHEN. *The Ethnic Myth: Race, Ethnicity, and Class in America.* Boston: Beacon, 1989.

STEINFELS, PETER. "Vatican Says the Ban on Women As Priests Is 'Infallible' Doctrine." *New York Times,* November 19, 1995.

STEINMETZ, SUZANNE K. "Family Violence." In Marvin B. Sussman and Suzanne K. Steinmetz (eds.), *Handbook of Marriage and the Family.* New York: Plenum Press, 1987.

STEPP, LAURA S. "A Wonder Drug's Worst Side Effect." *Washington Post,* February 5, 1996.

STERN, PHILIP M. *The Best Congress Money Can Buy.* New York: Pantheon, 1988.

STERNGOLD, JAMES. "Japan's Health Care: Cradle, Grave and No Frills." *New York Times,* December 28, 1992.

STETS, JAN E. "Cohabiting and Marital Aggression: The Role of Social Isolation." *Journal of Marriage and the Family* 53, 1991.

STEVENS, ROSEMARY. *American Medicine and the Public Interest.* New Haven, Conn.: Yale University Press, 1971.

STOCKWELL, EDWARD G., and GROAT, H. THEODORE. *World Population: An Introduction to Demography.* New York: Franklin Watts, 1984.

STOLZENBERG, ROSS M. "Educational Continuation by College Graduates." *American Journal of Sociology* 99, January 1994.

STONE, CAROL L. "Estimates of Muslims Living in America." In Haddad, Yvonne Y. (ed.), *The Muslims of America.* New York: Oxford University Press, 1991.

STRAUS, MURRAY A. "Victims and Aggressors in Marital Violence." *American Behavioral Scientist* 23, 1980.

STRAUS, MURRAY A., and GELLES, RICHARD J. "Societal Change and Change in Family Violence from 1975 to 1985 As Revealed by Two National Surveys." *Journal of Marriage and the Family* 48, 1986.

STRAUS, MURRAY A., and GELLES, RICHARD J. (eds.), *Physical Violence in American Families.* New Brunswick, NJ: Transaction, 1990.

STRAUS, MURRAY A., GELLES, RICHARD J., and STEINMETZ, SUZANNE K. *Behind Closed Doors: Violence in the American Family.* Garden City, N.Y.: Anchor/Doubleday, 1980.

STRAUSS, VALERIE. "Disparity between City, Suburban Schools Put at $440 a Student." *Washington Post,* September 28, 1994.

STRICKLAND, W. P. (ed.), *Autobiography of Peter Cartwright, The Backwoods Preacher.* New York: Carlton and Porter, 1856.

STRODTBECK, FRED L. "Family Interaction, Values, and Achievement." In Marshall Sklare, ed., *The Jews: Social Patterns of an American Ethnic Group.* New York: The Free Press, 1958.

STRYKER, SHELDON. "Symbolic Interactionism: Themes and Variations." In Morris Rosenberg and Ralph H. Turner (eds.), *Social Psychology: Sociological Perspectives,* new edition. New Brunswick, N.J.: Transaction, 1990.

SULLIVAN, DEIDRE. "Targeting Souls." *American Demographics,* October 1991.

SULLIVAN, KEVIN. "Red-blooded Romantics." *Washington Post,* December 29, 1995.

SULLIVAN, RONALD. "Milken's Sentence Reduced by Judge; 7 Months Are Left." *New York Times,* August 6, 1992.

SUMNER, WILLIAM GRAHAM. *Folkways: A Study of the Sociological Importance of Usages, Manners, Customs, Mores, and Morals.* Boston: Ginn, 1906.

SUNDET, JON MARTIN, MAGNUS, PER, KVALEM, INGELA LUNDIN, SAMUELSON, SVEN OVE, and BAKKETEIG, LEIV S. "Secular Trends and Sociodemographic Regularities of Coital Debut Age in Norway." *Archives of Sexual Behavior* 21,1992.

SUPLEE, CURT "The Electronic Sweatshop." *Washington Post-Outlook,* January 3, 1988.

SUSSER, MERVYN W., HOPPER, KIM, and RICHMAN, JUDITH. "Society, Culture, and Health." In D. Mechanic (ed.), *Handbook of Health, Health Care, and the Health Professions.* New York: The Free Press, 1983.

SUTHERLAND, EDWIN H. *Principles of Criminology,* 4th ed. Chicago: Lippincott, 1947.

SWEET, JAMES, BUMPASS, LARRY, and CALL, VIRGINIA. "The Design and Content of the National Survey of Families and Households." Madison: University of Wisconsin, Center for Demography and Ecology, 1988.

Swiss Review of World Affairs. "Zurich and Other Cities Losing Drug War." September 1, 1994.

SWOBODA, FRANK. "AFL-CIO Membership Is Shifting." *Washington Post,* October 31, 1991.

SWOBODA, FRANK. "Labor Loses the Strike as a Weapon." *Washington Post,* July 5, 1992a.

SWOBODA, FRANK. "In Omaha, the Underside of a Jobs Promise." *Washington Post,* October 25, 1992b.

SYME, S. LEONARD, and BERKMAN, LISA F. "Social Class, Susceptibility, and Sickness." In Peter Conrad and Rochelle Kern (eds.), *The Sociology of Health and Illness.* New York: St. Martin's Press, 1981.

SZINOVACZ, MAXIMILIANE. "Family Power." In Marvin B. Sussman and Suzanne K. Steinmetz (eds.), *Handbook of Marriage and the Family.* New York: Plenum Press, 1987.

TAKAHASHI, DEAN. "Convicted Hacker Had Worked for Intel Security." *Austin American-Statesman,* September 18, 1995.

TALESE, GAY. *Thy Neighbor's Wife.* New York: Doubleday, 1980.

TANNEN, DEBORAH. *You Just Don't Understand. Women and Men in Conversation.* New York: Ballantine Books, 1990.

TANTON, JOHN and LUTTON, WAYNE. "Immigration and Criminality in the U.S.A." *Journal of Social, Political and Economic Studies* 18, 1993.

TAYLOR, RALPH B. "Urban Communities and Crime." In Mark Gottdiener and Chris G. Pickvance (eds.), *Urban Life in Transition.* Newbury Park, Calif.: Sage Publications, 1991.

TAYLOR, VERTA. "Good News About Disaster." *Psychology Today,* October 1977.

TEACHMAN, JAY D. "Who Pays? Receipt of Child Support in the United States." *Journal of Marriage and the Family* 53, 1991.

TEITELBAUM, MICHAEL S., and WINTER, JAY M. *The Fear of Population Decline.* New York: Academic Press, 1985.

TERKEL, STUDS. *Working.* New York: Pantheon Books, 1974.

TEWKSBURY, RICHARD. "'Speaking of Someone with AIDS...': Identity Constructions of Persons with HIV Disease." *Deviant Behavior* 15, 1994.

THIO, ALEX. *Deviant Behavior.* Boston: Houghton Mifflin, 1978.

THOITS, PEGGY A. "Self-Labeling Processes in Mental Illness: The Role of Emotional Deviance." *American Journal of Sociology* 91, 1985.

THOITS, PEGGY A. "Social Psychology: The Interplay between Sociology and Psychology." *Social Forces* 73, 1995.

THOMPSON, CYNTHIA A., and BLAU, GARY. "Moving beyond Traditional Predictors of Job Involvement: Exploring the Impact of Work–Family Conflict and Overload." *Journal of Social Behavior and Personality* 8, 1993.

THOMPSON, LARRY. "The AIDS Statistics: Despite Prevention Efforts, HIV Continues to Spread." *Washington Post Health,* April 3, 1990.

THOMPSON, LINDA, and WALKER, ALEXIS J. "The Place of Feminism in Family Studies." *Journal of Marriage and the Family* 57, 1995.

THOMPSON, SHARON. "Putting a Big Thing into a Little Hole: Teenage Girls' Accounts of Sexual Initiation." *The Journal of Sex Research* 27, 1990.

THOMPSON, WILLIAM E. "Handling the Stigma of Handling the Dead: Morticians and Funeral Directors." *Deviant Behavior* 12, 1991.

THOMPSON, WILLIAM E., and HARRED, JACKIE L. "Topless Dancers: Managing Stigma in a Deviant Occupation." *Deviant Behavior* 13, 1992.

THOREAU, HENRY D. *Walden: Or, Life in the Woods.* Boston: Ticknor and Fields, 1854.

THORNBERRY, TERENCE P., and FARNSWORTH, MARGARET. "Social Correlates of Criminal Involvement: Further Evidence on the Relationship Between Social Status and Criminal Behavior." *American Sociological Review* 47, 1982.

THORNTON, ARLAND, and CAMBURN, DONALD. "Religious Participation and Adolescent Sexual Behavior and Attitudes." *Journal of Marriage and the Family* 51, 1989.

THORNTON, RUSSELL. *American Indian Holocaust and Survival.* Norman: University of Oklahoma Press, 1987.

TIEN, H. YUAN, et al. "China's Demographic Dilemmas." *Population Bulletin* 47. Washington D.C.: Population Reference Bureau, 1992.

TIGER, LIONEL. *Men in Groups.* New York: Random House, 1969.

TIMBERLAKE, MICHAEL (ed.), *Urbanization in the World-Economy.* New York: Academic Press, 1985.

TIMBERLAKE, MICHAEL, and KENTOR, JEFFREY. "Economic Dependence, Overurbanization, and Economic Growth: A Study of Less Developed Countries." *The Sociological Quarterly* 24, 1983.

Time. "The Battle over Abortion." April 6, 1981.

Time. "Racism on the Rise." February 2, 1987.

Time. "A Move to the Right." November 14, 1988.

Time. "The Changing Face of America." Special Issue, Fall 1993.

TIRYAKIAN, EDWARD A. "Pathways to Metatheory: Rethinking Presuppositions of Macrosociology." In George Ritzer (ed.), *Metatheorizing.* Newbury Park, Calif.: Sage, 1992.

TITTLE, C. R., VILLEMEZ, W. J., and SMITH, D. A. "The Myth of Social Class and Criminality: An Empirical Assessment of the Empirical Evidence." *American Sociological Review* 43, 1978.

TOCQUEVILLE, ALEXIS DE. *Democracy in America.* New York: Random House, 1835/1954.

TODD, ALEXANDRA DUNDAS. *Intimate Adversaries: Cultural Conflict between Doctors and Patients.* Philadelphia: University of Pennsylvania Press, 1989.

TOENNIES, FERDINAND. *Community and Society.* New York: Harper Torchbooks, 1957. Originally published 1887.

TOLMAN, DEBORAH L. "Daring to Desire: Culture and the Bodies of Adolescent Girls." In Janice M. Irvine (ed.), *Sexual Cultures and the Construction of Adolescent Identities.* Philadelphia: Temple University Press, 1994.

TOREN, NINA. "The Bus Driver: A Study in Role Analysis." *Human Relations* 26, 1973.

TORNQUIST, CYNTHIA. "Priests Imported to Meet U.S. Demand." Cable News Network, October 29, 1995.

TRAEEN, BENTE and LEWIN, BO. "Casual Sex among Norwegian Adolescents." *Archives of Sexual Behavior* 21, 1992.

TREAS, JUDITH. "Older Americans in the 1990s and Beyond." *Population Bulletin* 50, 1995.

TREIMAN, DONALD. *Occupational Prestige in Comparative Perspective.* New York: Academic Press, 1977.

TRICE, HARRISON M. "The Outsider's Role in Field Study." In William J. Filstead (ed.), *Qualitative Methodology: Firsthand Involvement with the Social World.* Chicago: Markham, 1970.

TRICE, HARRISON M., and BEYER, JANICE M. *The Cultures of Work Organizations.* Englewood Cliffs, N.J.: Prentice Hall, 1993.

TRICE, HARRISON M., and ROMAN, PAUL. "Delabeling, Relabeling and Alcoholics Anonymous." *Social Problems* 17, 1970.

TRILLIN, CALVIN. "Black or White." *The New Yorker,* April 14, 1986.

TROELTSCH, ERNST. *The Social Teachings of the Christian Churches.* New York: Macmillan, 1931.

TROVATO, FRANK. "A Longitudinal Analysis of Divorce and Suicide in Canada." *Journal of Marriage and the Family* 49, 1987.

TSCHETTER, JOHN. "Producer Services Industries: Why Are They Growing So Rapidly?" *Monthly Labor Review* 110, 1987.

TUCK, BRYAN, ROLFE, JAN, and ADAIR, VIVIENNE. "Adolescents' Attitude toward Gender Roles within Work and Its Relationship to Gender, Personality Type, and Parental Occupation." *Sex Roles* 31, 1994.

TUCKER, MARC, and MARSHALL, RAY. *Thinking for a Living: Education and the Wealth of Nations.* New York: Basic Book, 1992.

TUMIN, MELVIN M. *Social Stratification,* 2d ed. Englewood Cliffs, N.J.: Prentice-Hall, 1985.

TURAN, KENNETH. "President Looks Every Bit the Part." *Los Angeles Times,* September 5, 1992.

TURKLE, SHERRY. *The Second Self: Computers and the Human Spirit.* New York: Simon and Schuster, 1984.

TURNER, JONATHAN H., SINGLETON, ROYCE, JR., and MUSICK, DAVID. *Oppression: A Socio-History of Black–White Relations in America.* Chicago: Nelson-Hall, 1984.

TURNER, MARGERY AUSTIN, FIX, MICHAEL, and STRUYK, RAYMOND J. "Opportunities Denied, Opportunities Diminished: Discrimination in Hiring." Washington, D.C.: The Urban Institute, 1991.

TURNER, RALPH H. "Race Riots Past and Present: A Cultural–Collective Behavior Approach." *Symbolic Interaction* 17, 1994.

TURNER, RALPH H., and KILLIAN, LEWIS M. *Collective Behavior,* 2d ed. Englewood Cliffs, N.J.: Prentice-Hall, 1972.

UDRY, J. RICHARD. "Sociology and Biology: What Biology Do Sociologists Need to Know?" *Social Forces* 73, 1995.

UNITED NATIONS. *World Population Trends and Policies, 1987 Monitoring Report.* Population Studies No. 103. New York: United Nations, 1987.

UNITED NATIONS. *World Urbanization Prospects: The 1994 Revision.* New York: United Nations, 1995.

UNITED NATIONS DEPARTMENT OF INTERNAL ECONOMIC AND SOCIAL AFFAIRS. "National Accounts Statistics: Compendium of Income Distribution Statistics." *Statistical Papers.* Series M. No. 79. New York: United Nations. 1985.

UNIVERSITY OF MICHIGAN. "Drug Use Rises Again in 1995 among American Teens." News and Information Services, press release, December 11, 1995.

UNIVERSITY OF MICHIGAN, SURVEY RESEARCH CENTER. "Many Forms of Drug Use Decline Among American High School and College Students." News and Information Services, press release, January 25, 1992.

U.S. BUREAU OF JUSTICE STATISTICS. *Report to the Nation on Crime and Justice: The Data.* Washington, D.C.: U.S. Government Printing Office, 1983.

U.S. BUREAU OF JUSTICE STATISTICS. *Crime in the United States: 1987, Uniform Crime Reports for the United States.* Washington, D.C.: U.S. Government Printing Office, 1988a.

U.S. BUREAU OF JUSTICE STATISTICS. *Prisoners in 1987.* Washington, D.C.: U.S. Government Printing Office, 1988b.

U.S. BUREAU OF JUSTICE STATISTICS. *Prisoners in 1991.* Washington, D.C.: U.S. Government Printing Office, 1992.

U.S. BUREAU OF JUSTICE STATISTICS. *Crime in the United States: 1993, Uniform Crime Reports for the United States.* Washington, DC: U.S. Government Printing Office, 1994.

U.S. BUREAU OF JUSTICE STATISTICS. *Sourcebook of Criminal Justice Statistics—1994.* Washington, DC: U.S. Government Printing Office, 1995a.

U.S. BUREAU OF JUSTICE STATISTICS. *Crime in the United States: 1994, Uniform Crime Reports.* Washington, D.C.: U.S. Government Printing Office, 1995b.

U.S. BUREAU OF THE CENSUS. *Population, Part 1. U.S. Summary.* Washington, D.C.: U.S. Government Printing Office, 1984.

U.S. BUREAU OF THE CENSUS. "Rural and Urban Farm Population: 1987." *Current Population Reports.* Series P-27, No. 61. Washington, D.C.: U.S. Government Printing Office, 1987.

U.S. BUREAU OF THE CENSUS. "Poverty in the United States: 1986." *Current Population Reports.* Series P-60, No. 160. Washington, D.C.: U.S. Government Printing Office, 1988a.

U.S. BUREAU OF THE CENSUS. "Projections of the Population of States, by Age, Sex, and Race: 1988 to 2010." *Current Population Reports.* Series P-25, No. 1017. Washington, D.C.: U.S. Government Printing Office, 1988b.

U.S. BUREAU OF THE CENSUS. "School Enrollment—Social and Economic Characteristics of Students: October 1986." *Current Population Reports.* Series P-20, No. 429. Washington, D.C.: U.S. Government Printing Office, 1988c.

U.S. BUREAU OF THE CENSUS. "The Hispanic Population of the United States." *Current Population Reports.* Series P-20, No. 418. Washington, D.C.: U.S. Government Printing Office, 1988d.

U.S. BUREAU OF THE CENSUS. "Household Wealth and Asset Ownership: 1988." *Current Population Reports.* Series P-70, No. 22. Washington, D.C.: U.S. Government Printing Office, 1990.

U.S. BUREAU OF THE CENSUS. "Fertility of American Women: June 1990." *Current Population Reports.* Series P-20, No. 454. Washington, D.C.: U.S. Government Printing Office, 1991a.

U.S. BUREAU OF THE CENSUS. No. 456, "Geographical Mobility: March 1987 to March 1990." *Current Population Reports.* Series P-20. Washington D.C.: U.S. Government Printing Office, 1991b.

U.S. BUREAU OF THE CENSUS. "Half of the Nation's Population Lives in Large Metropolitan Areas." *United States Department of Commerce News,* February 21, 1991c.

U.S. Bureau of the Census, *Statistical Abstract of the United States: 1991.* Washington, D.C.: U.S. Government Printing Office, 1991d.

U.S. Bureau of the Census. "Marital Status and Living Arrangements, March, 1991." *Current Population Reports.* Series P-20, No. 461. Washington, D.C.: U.S. Government Printing Office, 1992a.

U.S. Bureau of the Census. *Minority Economic Profiles.* July 24, 1992b.

U.S. Bureau of the Census. "Money Income of Households, Families, and Persons in the United States: 1991." *Current Population Reports.* Series P-60, No. 180. Washington, D.C.: U.S. Government Printing Office, 1992c.

U.S. Bureau of the Census. "Poverty in the United States: 1991." *Current Population Reports.* Series P-60, No. 181. Washington, D.C.: U.S. Government Printing Office, 1992d.

U.S. Bureau of the Census. "The Black Population in the United States: March 1991." *Current Population Reports.* Series P-20, No. 464. Washington, D.C.: U.S. Government Printing Office, 1992e.

U.S. Bureau of the Census. "The Nation's Economic, Social, and Housing 'Portrait' Drawn from 1990 Census Long Form." *U.S. Department of Commerce News,* May 29, 1992f.

U.S. Bureau of the Census. "Workers with Low Earnings: 1964 to 1990." *Current Population Reports.* Series P-60, No. 178. Washington, D.C.: U.S. Government Printing Office, 1992g.

U.S. Bureau of the Census. "Hispanic Americans Today, 1993." *Current Population Reports.* Series P-23, No. 183. Washington, DC: U.S. Government Printing Office, 1993.

U.S. Bureau of the Census. *Statistical Abstract of the United States: 1994.* Washington, DC: U.S. Government Printing Office, 1994a.

U.S. Bureau of the Census. "The Hispanic Population in the United States: March 1993." *Current Population Reports.* Series P-20, No. 475. Washington, DC: U.S. Government Printing Office, 1994b.

U.S. Bureau of the Census. "Marital Status and Living Arrangements, March, 1993." *Current Population Reports,* Series P-20, No. 478. Washington, D.C. Government Printing Office, 1994c.

U.S. Bureau of the Census. "Income, Poverty, and Valuation of Noncash Benefits: 1993." *Current Population Reports,* Series P60, No. 188. Washington, DC: U.S. Government Printing Office, 1995a.

U.S. Bureau of the Census. *Statistical Abstract of the United States, 1995.* Washington, DC: U.S. Government Printing Office, 1995b.

U.S. Bureau of the Census. "Statistical Tables for the Hispanic Origin Population from the March 1994." *Current Population Survey.* Washington, DC: U.S. Government Printing Office, 1995c.

U.S. Centers for Disease Control. "Premature Mortality by Income Level—Multnomah County, Oregon, 1976–1984." *Morbidity and Mortality Weekly Report* 37, 1988.

U.S. Commission on Civil Rights. *The Economic Status of Americans of Asian Descent.* Washington, D.C.: U.S. Government Printing Office, 1988.

U.S. Commission on Civil Rights. *Intimidation and Violence: Racial and Religious Bigotry in America.* Washington, D.C.: U.S. Government Printing Office, 1990.

U.S. Commission on Civil Rights. *Civil Rights Issues Facing Asian Americans in the 1990s.* Washington, DC: U.S. Government Printing Office, 1994.

U.S. Department of Agriculture. *Budget Estimates for the United States Department of Agriculture.* Washington, D.C.: U.S. Government Printing Office, 1986.

U.S. Department of Education, National Center for Educational Statistics. *The Conditions of Education, 1995.* Washington, D.C.: 1995.

U.S. Immigration and Naturalization Service. *Statistical Yearbook of the Immigration and Naturalization Service, 1990.* Washington, D.C.: U.S. Government Printing Office, 1991.

U.S. Immigration and Naturalization Service. *Statistical Yearbook of the Immigration and Naturalization Service, 1993.* Washington, DC: U.S. Government Printing Office, 1994.

U.S. News and World Report. "When Blocks Battle to Stay Lily-White." December 9, 1985.

Useem, Elizabeth L. *Low Tech Education in a High Tech World: Corporations and Classrooms in the New Information Society.* New York: The Free Press, 1986.

Useem, Michael, and Karabel, Jerome. "Pathways to Top Corporate Management." *American Sociological Review* 51, 1986.

van den Berghe, Pierre. "Why Most Sociologists Don't (and Won't) Think Evolutionarily." *Sociological Forum* 5, 1990.

Vartabedian, Ralph. "Cases of Defense Fraud Boom amid Cutbacks; Military: Weapon Purchases Have Plummeted, Yet Criminal Fines and Civil Recoveries are Soaring." *Los Angeles Times,* March 26, 1995.

VEBLEN, THORSTEIN. *The Theory of the Leisure Class: An Economic Study of Institutions.* New York: Macmillan, 1899.

VENER, A. and STEWART, C. "Adolescent Sexual Behavior in Middle America Revisited, 1970–1973." *Journal of Marriage and the Family* 36, 1974.

VERBRUGGE, LOIS M. "Females and Illness: Recent Trends in Sex Differences in the United States." *Journal of Health and Social Behavior* 17, 1976.

VERBRUGGE, LOIS M. "Gender and Health: An Update on Hypotheses and Evidence." *Journal of Health and Social Behavior* 26, 1985.

VERBRUGGE, LOIS M. "The Twain Meet: Empirical Explanations of Sex Differences in Health and Mortality." *Journal of Health and Social Behavior* 30, September 1989.

VEROFF, JOSEPH, SUTHERLAND, LYNEE, CHADIHA, LETHA, and ORTEGA, ROBERT M. "Predicting Marital Quality with Narrative Assessments of Marital Experience." *Journal of Marriage and the Family* 55, 1993.

VOBEJDA, BARBARA. "Home Alone, Glued to the TV." *Washington Post,* December 10, 1992.

VOYDANOFF, PATRICIA. "Work Role Characteristics, Family Structure Demands, and Work/Family Conflict." *Journal of Marriage and the Family* 50, 1988.

WADE, NICHOLAS. *The Nobel Duel.* Garden City, N.Y.: Anchor Books, 1981.

WAITE, LINDA J., and HARRISON, SCOTT C. "Keeping in Touch: How Women in Mid-life Allocate Social Contacts among Kith and Kin." *Social Forces* 70, 1992.

WAITE, LINDA, HAGGSTROM, GUS, and KANOUSE, DAVID. "The Consequences of Parenthood for the Marital Stability of Young Adults." *American Sociological Review* 50, 1985.

WAITZKIN, HOWARD. "Information Giving in Medical Care." *Journal of Health and Social Behavior* 26, 1985.

WALDO, GORDON, and GRISWOLD, DAVID. "Issues in the Measurement of Recidivism." In Lee Sechrest, Susan O. White, and Elizabeth D. Brown (eds.), *The Rehabilitation of Criminal Offenders.* Washington, D.C.: National Academy of Sciences, 1979.

WALDRON, INGRID. "Sex Differences in Illness Incidence, Prognosis and Mortality: Issues and Evidence." *Social Science & Medicine* 17, 1983.

WALKER, BLAIR. "Racial Aspect of Case Is a Charged Issue." *USA Today,* July 6, 1994.

WALKER, H. M., COLVIN, G., and RAMSEY, E. *Antisocial Behavior in School: Strategies and Best Practices.* Pacific Grove, CA: Brooks/Cole, 1995.

WALLACE, ANTHONY F. C. *Religion: An Anthropological View.* New York: Random House, 1966.

WALLACE, MICHAEL. "Brave New Workplace: Technology and Work in the New Economy." *Work and Occupations* 16, 1989.

WALLERSTEIN, IMMANUEL. *The Modern World-System.* New York: Academic Press, 1974.

WALLERSTEIN, IMMANUEL. *The Capitalist World Economy.* Cambridge, England: Cambridge University Press, 1979.

WALLERSTEIN, IMMANUEL. *The Modern World-System II: Mercantilism and the Consolidation of the European World-Economy, 1600–1750.* New York: Academic Press, 1980.

WALLERSTEIN, IMMANUEL. *The Modern World-System III: The Second Era of Great Expansion of the Capitalist World-Economy, 1730–1840.* New York: Academic Press, 1988.

WALLERSTEIN, JAMES S., and WYLES, CLEMENT J. "Our Law-Abiding Law-Breakers." *Probation* 25, 1947.

WALLERSTEIN, JUDITH S., and BLAKESLEE, SANDRA. *Second Chances: Men, Women, and Children a Decade after Divorce.* New York: Ticknor and Fields, 1990.

WALLERSTEIN, JUDITH S., and KELLY, JOAN B. "The Effects of Parental Divorce: Experiences of the Preschool Child." *The Journal of the American Academy of Child Psychiatry* 14, 1975.

WALLERSTEIN, JUDITH S., and KELLY, JOAN B. "Effects of Parental Divorce: Experience of Children in Later Latency." *American Journal of Orthopsychiatry* 46, 1976.

WALLIS, ROY, and BRUCE, STEVE. "Secularization: Trends, Data, and Theory." In Monty L. Lynn and David O. Moberg (eds.), *Research in the Social Scientific Study of Religion,* 3. Greenwich, Conn.: JAI Press, 1991.

WALSH, ANTHONY. "Twice Labelled: The Effect of Psychiatric Labeling on the Sentencing of Sex Offenders." *Social Problems* 37, 1990.

WALSH, DIANA CHAPMAN. *Corporate Physicians: Between Medicine and Management.* New Haven: Yale University Press, 1987.

WALTERS, VIVIENNE. "Company Doctors' Perceptions of and Responses to Conflicting Pressures from Labor and Management." *Social Problems* 30, 1982.

WARD, DAVID A. and CHARLES R. TITTLE. "Deterrence or Labeling: the Effects of Informal Sanctioning." *Deviant Behavior* 14, 1993.

WARNER, R. STEPHEN. "Work in Progress toward a New Paradigm for the Sociological Study of Religion in the United States." *American Journal of Sociology* 98, 1993.

WARNER, W. LLOYD, and LUNT, PAUL S. *The Social Life of a Modern Community.* New Haven, Conn.: Yale University Press, 1941.

WARR, MARK. "Age, Peers, and Delinquency." *Criminology* 31, 1993.

WARSHAW, R. *I Never Called It Rape.* New York: Harper & Row, 1988.

WASBURN, PHILO C. *Political Sociology: Approaches, Concepts, Hypotheses.* Englewood Cliffs, N.J.: Prentice-Hall, 1982.

WASH, DARREL PATRICK, and BRAND, LESLIE E. "Child Day Care Services: An Industry at a Crossroads." *Monthly Labor Review* 113, 1990.

Washington Post. "Pope Emphasizes Motherhood Role." January 11, 1979.

Washington Post. "More Money for Male Doctors." February 16, 1988a.

Washington Post. "Why Nurses Quit: The Frustration Behind the Shortage." July 12, 1988b.

Washington Post. "Tuesday's Turnout." November 13, 1988c.

Washington Post. "For the Record." June 9, 1988d.

Washington Post. "Top 50 PACS in Contributions to Federal Campaigns." September 18, 1992.

Washington Post. "FBI Data Show 12 Percent Decline in Murder, Biggest Drop in Decades." December 18, 1995a.

Washington Post. "Prison Population Grows at Record Pace." December 4, 1995b.

WATERS, MALCOLM. *Globalization.* London: Routledge, 1995.

WATERS, MARY C. *Ethnic Options: Choosing Identities in America.* Berkeley: University of California Press, 1990.

WATTENBERG, BEN. *The First Universal Nation: Leading Indicators and Ideas about the Surge of America in the 1990s.* New York: Free Press, 1991.

WAX, ROSALIE. *Doing Field Work.* Chicago: University of Chicago Press, 1971.

WEBER, MAX. *From Max Weber: Essays in Sociology.* H. H. Gerth and C. Wright Mills (eds.). New York: Oxford University Press, 1946. Originally published 1918.

WEBER, MAX. *The Methodology of the Social Sciences.* New York: The Free Press, 1949. Originally published 1903–1917.

WEBER, MAX. *The Protestant Ethic and the Spirit of Capitalism* (Talcott Parsons, trans.). New York: Oxford University Press, 1958. Originally published 1904–1905.

WEBER, MAX. *Economy and Society: An Outline of Interpretative Sociology,* 3 vols. Guenther Roth and Claus Wittich (eds.). New York: Bedminster Press, 1968. Originally published 1921.

WEED, FRANK J. "Organizational Mortality in the Anti-Drunk-Driving Movement: Failure Among Local MADD Chapters." *Social Forces* 69, 1991.

WEGMANN, ROBERT. "Classroom Discipline: An Exercise in the Maintenance of Social Reality." *Sociology of Education* 49, 1976.

WEINBERG, MEYER. *The Search for Quality Integrated Education.* Westport, CT: Greenwood, 1983.

WEINER, MYRON. *The Child and the State in India: Child Labor and Education Policy in Comparative Perspective.* Princeton, N.J.: Princeton University Press, 1991.

WEISMAN, STEVEN R. "Broken Marriage and Brawl Test a Cohesive Caste." *New York Times,* February 21, 1988.

WEISS, ROBERT S. *Marital Separation.* New York: Basic Books, 1975.

WEISS, ROBERT S. *Going It Alone: The Family Life and Social Situation of the Single Parent.* New York: Basic Books, 1979.

WEISS, ROBERT S. *Learning from Strangers: The Art and Method of Qualitative Interview Studies.* New York: The Free Press, 1995.

WEITZ, ROSE, AND SULLIVAN, DEBORAH. "License Lay Midwifery and the Medical Model of Childbirth." *Sociology of Health and Illness* 7, 1985.

WEITZMAN, LENORE J. *Sex Role Socialization: A Focus on Women.* Palo Alto, Calif.: Mayfield, 1979.

WEITZMAN, LENORE J. *The Divorce Revolution: The Unexpected Social and Economic Consequences for Women and Children in America.* New York: The Free Press, 1985.

WELLMAN, BARRY. "The Community Question: The Intimate Networks of East Yorkers." *American Journal of Sociology* 84, 1979.

WELTER, BARBARA. "The Cult of True Womanhood: 1820–1860." *American Quarterly,* Summer 1966.

WELCH, CHARLES E. III, and PRICE-BONHAM, SHARON. "A Decade of No-fault Divorce Revisited: California, Georgia, and Washington." *Journal of Marriage and the Family* 45, 1983.

WENGER, DENNIS E., DYKES, JAMES D., SEBOK, THOMAS D., and NEFF, JOAN L. "It's a Matter of Myths: An Empirical Examination of Individual Insight into Disaster Response." *Mass Emergencies* 1, 1975.

WERTZ, RICHARD W., and WERTZ, DOROTHY C. "Notes on the Decline of Midwives and the Rise of Medical Obstetricians." In Peter Conrad and Rochelle Kern (eds.), *The Sociology of Health and Illness: Critical Perspectives 1986.* New York: St. Martin's Press, 1986.

WEST, CANDACE. "When the Doctor Is a 'Lady': Power, Status, and Gender in Physician–Patient Encounters." *Symbolic Interaction* 7, 1984.

WEST, CANDACE, and FENSTERMAKER, SARAH. "Power, Inequality, and the Accomplishment of Gender: An Ethnomethodological View." In Paula England (ed.), *Theory on Gender/Feminism on Theory.* New York: Aldine De Gruyter, 1993.

WESTOFF, C. F., and JONES, E. F. "The End of 'Catholic' Fertility." *Demography* 16, 1979.

WESTOFF, CHARLES F. "Fertility in the United States." *Science* 234, 1986.

WHITE, LYNN, and BOOTH, ALAN. "The Transition to Parenthood and Marital Quality." *Journal of Family Issues* 6, 1985.

WHITE, LYNN K., BOOTH, ALAN, and EDWARDS, JOHN N. "Children and Marital Happiness: Why the Negative Correlation?" *Journal of Family Issues* 7, 1986.

WHITE, RICHARD W. *Rude Awakenings: What the Homeless Crisis Tells Us.* San Francisco: ICS Press, 1991.

WHYTE, MARTIN KING, and GU, S. Z. "Popular Response to China's Fertility Transition." *Population Development and Review* 13, 1987.

WHYTE, WILLIAM F. *Participant Observer: An Autobiography.* Ithaca, NY: ILR Press, 1994.

WIERSMA, UCO J. "A Taxonomy of Behavioral Strategies for Coping with Work–Home Role Conflict." *Human Relations* 47, 1994.

WILLETS-BLOOM, MARION C., and NOCK, STEVEN L. "The Influence of Maternal Employment on Gender Role Attitudes of Men and Women." *Sex Roles* 30, 1994.

WILLIAMS, CHRISTINE L. *Gender Differences at Work: Women and Men in Nontraditional Occupations.* Berkeley: University of California Press, 1989.

WILLIAMS, CHRISTINE L. "The Glass Escalator: Hidden Advantages for Men in the 'Female' Professions." *Social Problems* 39, 1992.

WILLIAMS, GREGORY H. *Life on the Color Line: The True Story of a White Boy Who Discovered He Was Black.* New York: Dutton, 1995.

WILLIAMS, LINDA B., and ZIMMER, BASIL G. "The Changing Influence of Religion on U.S. Fertility: Evidence from Rhode Island." *Demography* 27, 1990.

WILLIAMS, ROBIN M., JR. *American Society: A Sociological Interpretation,* 3rd ed. New York: Alfred A. Knopf, 1970.

WILLIAMS, TERRY, and MAJOR, TED. *The Secret Language of Snow.* New York: Sierra Club/Pantheon Books, 1984.

WILLIAMS, TERRY, DUNLAP, ELOISE, JOHNSON, BRUCE D., and HAMID, ANSLEY. "Personal Safety in Dangerous Places." *Journal of Contemporary Ethnography* 21, 1992.

WILLIAMSON, JEFFREY G., and LINDERT, PETER H. *American Inequality.* New York: Academic Press, 1980.

WILLIAMSON, LISA. "Union Mergers: 1985–1994 Update." *Monthly Labor Review,* February 1995.

WILLS, GARRY. "The New Revolutionaries." *New York Review of Books* 42, August 10, 1995.

WILSON, E. O. *Sociobiology: The New Synthesis.* Cambridge, Mass.: Harvard University Press, 1975.

WILSON, FRANKLIN D., TIENDA, MARTA, and WU, LAWRENCE. "Race and Unemployment: Labor Market Experiences of Black and White Men, 1968–1988." *Work and Occupations* 22, 1995.

WILSON, KENNETH G., and DAVISS, BENNETT. *Redesigning Education.* New York: Henry Holt and Company, 1994.

WILSON, THOMAS C. "Urbanism and Unconventionality: The Case of Sexual Behavior." *Social Science Quarterly* 76, 1995.

WILSON, WILLIAM J. *The Declining Significance of Race.* Chicago: University of Chicago Press, 1978.

WILSON, WILLIAM J. *The Truly Disadvantaged: The Inner City, the Underclass, and Public Policy.* Chicago: University of Chicago Press, 1987.

WILSON, WILLIAM J. "The Cost of Racial and Class Exclusion in the Inner City." *Annals of the American Academy of Political and Social Sciences* 501, 1989a.

WILSON, WILLIAM J. (ed.), "The Ghetto Underclass: Social Science Perspectives." *The Annals of the American Academy of Political and Social Science* 501, 1989b.

WILSON, WILLIAM J. "Studying Inner-City Social Dislocations: The Challenge of Public Agenda Research." *American Sociological Review* 56, 1991.

WIRTH, LOUIS. "Urbanism as a Way of Life." *American Journal of Sociology* 44. 1938.

WOLFE, ALAN. "Has There Been a Cognitive Revolution in America?" In Steven Fraser, ed., *The Bell Curve Wars: Race, Intelligence, and the Future of America.* New York: Basic Books, 1995.

WOLFF, EDWARD N. "Estimates of Household Wealth Inequality in the United States, 1962–1983." *The Review of Income and Wealth* 33, 1987.

WOLFF, EDWARD N. "Changing Inequality of Wealth." *American Economic Review* 82, May 1992a.

WOLFF, EDWARD N. "The Rich Get Increasingly Richer." *Economic Policy Institute Briefing Paper,* 1992b.

WOLFF, EDWARD N. *Top Heavy: A Study of the Increasing Inequality of Wealth in America.* New York: Twentieth Century Fund Press, 1995a.

WOLFF, EDWARD N. "How the Pie Is Sliced: America's Growing Concentration of Wealth." *American Prospect* 22, 1995b.

WOLFINGER, NICHOLAS H. "Passing Moments: Some Dynamics of Pedestrian Interaction." *Journal of Contemporary Ethnography* 24, 1995.

WOLFSON, MARK. "The Legislative Impact of Social Movement Organizations: The Anti-Drunken Driving Movement and the 21-Year-Old Drinking Age." *Social Science Quarterly* 76, 1995.

WOLINSKY, FREDRIC D. *The Sociology of Health: Principles, Practitioners, and Issues,* 2d ed. Belmont, Calif.: Wadsworth, 1988.

WOLINSKY, FREDRIC D., MOSELY, RAY R., II, and COE, RODNEY. "A Cohort Analysis of the Use of Health Services by Elderly Americans." *Journal of Health and Social Behavior* 27, 1986.

WOLPE, PAUL ROOT. "The Maintenance of Professional Authority: Acupuncture and the American Physician." *Social Problems* 32, 1985.

WOOLFOLK, ALAN. "A House Divided? Diagnosing the American Kulturkampf." *Qualitative Sociology* 18, 1995.

WORLD BANK. *World Development Report 1984.* New York: Oxford University Press, 1984.

WORLD BANK. *World Development Report 1988.* New York: Oxford University Press, 1988.

WRIGHT, ERIC OLIN, SHIRE, KAREN, HWANG, SHU-LING, DOLAN, MAUREEN, and BAXTER, JANEEN. "The Non-effects of Class on the Gender Division of Labor in the Home: A Comparative Study of Sweden and the United States." *Gender and Society* 6, 1992.

WRIGHT, JAMES D. *Address Unknown: The Homeless in America.* New York: Aldine de Gruyter, 1989.

WRIGHT, LAWRENCE. "One Drop of Blood." *New Yorker.* July 25, 1994.

WRONG, DENNIS. "The Oversocialized Conception of Man in Modern Sociology." *American Sociological Review* 26, 1961.

WUTHNOW, ROBERT. "Sociology of Religion." In Neil J. Smelser (ed.), *Handbook of Sociology.* Beverly Hills, Calif.: Sage Publications, 1988a.

WUTHNOW, ROBERT. *The Restructuring of American Religion: Society and Faith Since World War II.* Princeton, N.J.: Princeton University Press, 1988b.

WYLIE, C. *Village in the Vaucluse,* 2d ed. Cambridge, Mass.: Harvard University Press, 1961.

XIAOHE, XU, and WHYTE, MARTIN KING. "Love Matches and Arranged Marriages: A Chinese Replication." *Journal of Marriage and the Family* 52, 1990.

XU, WU, and LEFFLER, ANN. "Gender and Race Effects on Occupational Prestige, Segregation, and Earnings." *Gender and Society* 6, 1992.

YARROW, M. R., CLAUSEN, J. A., and ROBBINS, P. R. "The Social Meaning of Mental Illness." *Journal of Social Issues* 11, 1955.

YENCKEL, JAMES. "Smoke: In the Air and on the Ground." *Washington Post,* June 5, 1988.

YETMAN, NORMAN R. (ed.), *Majority and Minority: The Dynamics of Race and Ethnicity in American Life,* 4th ed. Boston: Allyn and Bacon, 1985.

YETMAN, NORMAN R. (ed.), *Majority and Minority: The Dynamics of Race and Ethnicity in American Life,* 5th ed. Boston: Allyn and Bacon, 1991.

YINGER, J. MILTON. "Contraculture and Subculture." *American Sociological Review* 25, 1960.

YOUSSEF, NADIA HAGGAG. *Women and Work in Developing Societies.* Westport, Conn.: Greenwood Press, 1974.

ZACHARY, G. PASCAL. "Unions Talk Tough But Face Big Hurdles." *Wall Street Journal,* January 22, 1996.

ZEFFANE, RACHID, and MACDONALD, DUNCAN. "Uncertainty, Participation and Alienation: Lessons for Workplace Restructuring." *International Journal of Sociology and Social Policy* 13, 1993.

ZELLNER, WILLIAM W. *Countercultures: A Sociological Analysis.* New York: St. Martin's Press, 1995.

ZELNIK, MELVIN, and SHAH, FRAIDA K. "First Intercourse Among Young Americans." *Family Planning Perspectives* 15, 1983.

ZHANG, LENING, and MESSNER, STEVEN F. "The Severity of Official Punishment for Delinquency and Change in Interpersonal Relations in Chinese Society." *Journal of Research in Crime and Delinquency* 31, 1994.

ZHOU, XUEGUANG. "Unorganized Interests and Collective Action in Communist China." *American Sociological Review* 58, 1993.

ZIMDARS-SWARTZ, SANDRA L. "The Virgin Mary: Mother as Intercessor and Savior of Society." In Sharon S. Brehm (ed.), *Seeing Female: Social Roles and Personal Lives.* Westport, Conn.: Greenwood Press, 1988.

ZIMDARS-SWARTZ, SANDRA L. "Popular Devotion to the Virgin: The Marian Phenomena at Melleray, Republic of Ireland." *Archives de Sciences Sociale des Religions,* 1989a.

ZIMDARS-SWARTZ, SANDRA L. "Religious Experience and Public Cult: The Case of Mary Ann Hoof." *Journal of Religion and Health* 28, 1989b.

ZIMDARS-SWARTZ, SANDRA L. *Encountering Mary: from La Salette to Medjugorje.* Princeton: Princeton University Press, 1991a.

ZIMDARS-SWARTZ, SANDRA L. "Visions and Visionary Experience in Religion." *Religion* 28, 1991b.

ZIMMERMAN, SHIRLEY. "The Welfare State and Family Breakup: The Mythical Connection." *Family Relations* 40, 1991.

ZINN, MAXINE BACA. "Family, Race, and Poverty in the Eighties." *Signs* 14, 1989.

ZOGLIN, RICHARD. "It Just Wasn't That Simple." *Time,* November 16, 1992.

ZORZA, JOAN. "The Criminal Law of Misdemeanor Violence, 1970–1990." *Journal of Criminal Law and Criminology* 83, 1992.

ZORZA, VICTOR. "When Brothers Share Wives, Age Counts." *Washington Post,* May 2, 1982.

ZUBOFF, SHOSHANA. *In the Age of the Smart Machine: The Future of Work and Power.* New York: Basic Books, 1988.

ZUKIN, SHARON. "Gentrification: Culture and Capital in the Urban Core." *Annual Review of Sociology* 13. Palo Alto, Calif.: Annual Reviews, Inc., 1987.

ZUO, JIPING, and BENFORD, ROBERT D. "Mobilization Processes and the 1989 Chinese Democracy Movement." *Sociology Quarterly* 36, 1995.

Glossary

Acculturation   *See* Cultural assimilation.

Achieved status   A status that people acquire through their own efforts.

Acting crowd   A large number of people trying to change some aspect of their immediate environment.

Adult socialization   Those occasions in life when adults learn the new behaviors expected of them as they enter new occupations, professions, work settings, institutions, or life stages.

Age stratification   A system of social definitions based on age; giving people in different age categories certain rights but also placing limits on their behavior.

Ageism   An attitude that limitations and restrictions can be based on a person's age.

Agricultural revolution   The shift from hunting-and-gathering subsistence patterns to the cultivation of grains and domestication of animals.

Alienation   Breakdown of the natural connections between people and their work, other people, and the natural world.

Anglo-conformity   The American concept of assimilation that assumes that minorities should adopt traits of the dominant group.

Anomie   A state of normlessness; situations in which individuals are uncertain about the norms of society.

Anticipatory socialization   The process of learning what will be expected of one in a status before entering that status.

Apartheid   The South African legal system of "separate development" that perpetuated white power and privilege.

Apostates   People who early in their lives have a religious identity but later come to renounce or reject it.

Applied research   Research designed and conducted to answer a specific practical question or solve a particular social problem.

Arranged marriage   Marriages in which parents select marriage partners for their children.

Ascribed status   A status into which individuals move, or are placed, irrespective of their efforts or capacities.

Assimilation   The integration or incorporation of a minority into the mainstream of a society.

Attitudinal discrimination   Discrimination that stems from prejudicial attitudes and usually involves direct and overt forms of behavior.

Attitudinal objectivity   Scientists maintaining an attitude of fairness and honesty when planning and conducting their research.

Authority   Legitimate power; the exercise of power that is accepted by those over whom it is exerted.

Autocracy   A form of government in which ultimate authority is vested in a single person.

Basic research   Research designed and conducted to test hypotheses derived from theories.

Blended *or* reconstituted families   Remarried families when one or both partners bring children to the marriage.

Bureaucracy   An organization that has a division of labor, hierarchical authority, rules and procedures, impersonality in relations among members, and selection and promotion based on competence and expertise.

Bureaucratic personality   The tendency of bureaucrats to conform slavishly to organizational rules, with the result that the rules are more important than the task or objective of the organization.

Capitalism   Economic system that emphasizes the private ownership of property and the means of production (raw materials, factories, machines, and equipment).

Capitalists   Marx's term for the owners of the means of production in a capitalist economic system.

Caste system   The most rigid and closed of stratification systems in which one's status is inherited and fixed, and people are prohibited from marrying members of other strata.

Catch-22   A situation in which the rules of a bureaucracy are in conflict in such a way as to block action.

Charisma   Extraordinary qualities, often believed to be supernatural, that give a leader authority over others.

Church   A large, socially acceptable, institutionalized religious group.

City   A relatively large, densely populated, and diverse settlement of people.

Civil religion   The system of symbols, beliefs, values, and practices that have sacred meaning for a nation and a people.

Class   Social ranking in a stratification system based on one's relationship to the means of production; more commonly, social ranking based on economic factors such as income and wealth.

Closed class system   A system of stratification in which people's positions are fixed and there is little possibility of social mobility.

Coercion   Power that is based on the threat or use of force and is therefore considered illegitimate by the people who are forced to do what they do not wish to do.

Coercive organization   An organization that uses force to control those at the bottom of the structure.

Cohabitation   Unmarried couples living together.

Collective behavior   Behavior that is expressed as part of a collectivity, focused on a particular phenomenon or event, involves a situation of change, conflict, uncertainty, or ambiguity, and is relatively unconstrained by well-established social patterns.

Commercialization of sex   Sex that is bought and sold just like any other commodity in the marketplace.

Common couple violence   Violence that is the product of conflicts that occur in many couple relationships.

Communicable disease   Disease that can be transmitted to people in a variety of ways, including other people, animals, other organisms, food, and water.

Community property laws   Laws holding that earnings and property accumulated during a marriage are owned jointly by the couple.

Community divorce   The changes in relationships with friends, relatives and associates because of divorce.

Competitive capitalism   Capitalist system in which no one capitalist, or small group of capitalists, can gain complete or uncontested control over the market.

Compositional theory of urbanism   A model of urban life that emphasizes the importance of social class, ethnicity, and life-cycle stage in determining urban social relationships.

Computer abuse   Unauthorized entry into someone else's computer data and altering, stealing, or sabotaging it.

Concentric zone model   A model of urban development emphasizing differences in urban land use involving a series of successive rings surrounding a central business district.

Concept   A word or phrase that summarizes some meaningful part of the social world.

Conflict theory   A view of society as constantly in a state of imbalance and conflict, in which social groups or societies are composed of units that are often engaged in a struggle for power.

Conflict theory of change   Change seen as a result of conflicting interests between groups.

Conformists   People who accept cultural goals and conventional means to achieve them.

Conspicuous consumption   Acquiring things simply to display them and to show that one can afford them.

Control group   Subjects in an experiment who are not exposed to the experimental variable.

Convenience sample   Research subjects who are conveniently available to complete questionnaires or to be interviewed.

Conventionalized crowd   A collectivity gathered for a particular purpose and acting in accord with established norms.

Co-parental divorce   The stage of divorce when issues of child custody, visitation rights, and child support are determined.

Correlation   A measure of how much two variables are co-related or associated; indicated by a correlation coefficient, expressed as a decimal fraction from -1.00 to $+1.00$, that summarizes the degree and direction of the relationship between the variables.

Counterculture   A societal group that is consciously in opposition to the widely held norms and values of the dominant culture.

Crime   Deviant behavior that violates the law and is subject to formally sanctioned punishment by the larger society.

Crimes against people (violent crime)   Crimes involving the threat of injury, or threat (or use) of force, against victims.

Criminology   The subfield of sociology devoted to the study of crime, criminal behavior, and the treatment of criminals.

Cross-cultural studies   Often anthropological reports and descriptions of other (often small) nonliterate societies and their cultures.

Cross-national research   The collection of similar types of data in two or more societies so that results can be compared.

Cults   Small, voluntary, and exclusive religious groups that have created a new religious system.

Cultural assimilation (*or* acculturation)   A process by which members of subcultures and minorities acquire cultural characteristics (including values, beliefs, language, and behaviors) of the dominant group.

Cultural explanations of social inequality   Explanations of social inequality that see a group's social status and attainments as a consequence of its cultural characteristics: the values, attitudes, beliefs, and behaviors learned in the family and community.

Cultural lag Social and cultural practices that are no longer appropriate when technological change occurs faster than social systems can adapt.

Cultural norms Rules for what should and should not be done in given situations.

Cultural relativism An approach that evaluates the behavior of the people of other societies, not on the basis of the evaluator's own culture, but in terms of the culture under consideration.

Cultural values A key component of culture, the standards of desirability, of rightness, and of importance in a society.

Culture The entire complex of ideas and material objects that people of a society (or group) have created and adopted for carrying out the necessary tasks of collective life.

Cyclic theory The theory of social change in which change is seen as an ongoing series of recurring cultural emphases rather than as a process with some kind of direction.

Deindustrialization The decline of U.S. industry through plant shutdowns, layoffs, and downsizing.

Delabeling A process by which a deviant label is shed and replaced by a socially acceptable label.

Democracy A form of government in which there are periodic opportunities for the people being governed to retain or replace governing officials.

Demographic transition A three-stage process of population change that occurs as societies develop economically.

Denominational pluralism A situation in which different religious groups coexist in a society, with no single group dominating.

Dependency theory A theory that argues that the developed countries are not the salvation of developing countries, but the cause of their underdevelopment.

Dependent variable A variable that is changed or influenced by an independent variable.

Depersonalization of sex Sexual interaction that is impersonal and self-interested.

Descriptive statistics Statistics used to communicate information about numerical data.

Descriptive survey A survey designed to obtain some basic information about a population, for example, surveys of attitudes and behavior, opinion polls, and market surveys.

Development The general process of economic growth, not necessarily emphasizing manufacturing.

Deviance Any behavior that most members of a society or social group consider a violation of group norms.

Differential association theory A sociological theory that sees deviance as learned by individuals being socialized by a group of people who engage in and accept deviant behavior.

Diffuse crowd A large number of dispersed individuals who follow particular kinds of behavior or who experience a particular sentiment, for example, fads and crazes.

Direct expulsion Use of laws and government policies to expel minorities.

Discreditable stigma A negative characteristic of a person that is neither known about by those present, nor immediately perceived by them.

Discredited stigma A negative characteristic of a person that is known about already or is evident to any observer.

Discrimination Unfavorable treatment of people because of their group membership.

Division of labor by gender Society-wide assignment of different work tasks to males and females.

Dominant group *See* Majority group.

Double standard   A set of norms that gives males more sexual freedom than females.

Downsizing   Permanent cuts in American industry of large numbers of both white- and blue-collar workers.

Dramaturgy   Performances by individuals aimed at manipulating situations in ways favorable to themselves.

Dyad   Two people engaged in interaction.

Dysfunction   The detrimental consequence for a society of some social structure.

Economic divorce   A stage of divorce when money and property are divided and levels of economic support are established.

Economy   The social institution involved in the production and exchange of a wide range of goods and services.

Elite deviance   Deviant or criminal acts committed by the wealthy and powerful members of society.

Elite   A small group of people who come to power and dominate the population.

Emergent norm theory   In collective behavior, a theory that emphasizes the similarity between collective behavior and institutionalized social life. When some form of collective behavior occurs, new norms, social relationships, communication patterns, and values emerge.

Emotional divorce   An early stage of divorce when there is a recognition that the emotional relationship with one's spouse is deteriorating and the marriage is ending.

Empiricism   The act of experiencing something with one's senses, in contrast to imagination and speculation.

Ethnic group   A group that is socially defined on the basis of its cultural characteristics. Members of an ethnic group consider themselves, and are considered by others, to be part of a distinct culture or subculture.

Ethnicity   The sense of belonging to and identifying with a particular ethnic group.

Ethnocentrism   The view held by the people of a society that they are of central importance in the universe and therefore their ways of doing things are the right ways.

Evolutionary theory   A theory of social change in which change is seen as directional, a process of cumulative change.

Exchange theory   (*See* Social exchange theory)

Exclusion   Policies and practices that seek to maintain a society's cultural homogeneity by refusing to admit culturally different groups.

Experimental group   Subjects in an experiment who are exposed to the experimental variable.

Experiments   Research method in which the independent variable is under the control of the researcher so that its impact on a dependent variable can be observed directly.

Explanatory surveys   Surveys attempting to find independent variables that relate to or account for differences in behaviors or attitudes.

Expressive crowd   A group of people displaying intense feelings, emotions, and exuberant physical behavior.

Expressive movements   A social movement aimed at changing individuals, who will then either change the social order or adapt better to the existing order.

Expulsion   Practices and policies that seek to move minorities from areas controlled by the dominant group.

Extended family   Family units made up of three or more generations living in the same household or very close together.

Extermination (*or* genocide) Practices and policies that seek to reduce, destroy, or eliminate a minority population.

External explanations of social inequality Explanations of social inequality that see a group's social status and attainments as a consequence of factors outside the group, over which it has little or no control.

Family of orientation The nuclear family into which one is born.

Family of procreation The nuclear family that one creates by marrying and having children.

Felonies Serious crimes, punishable by a year or more in prison.

Feminization of poverty The increasing number of families in poverty who are headed by women.

Feral children Wild children; children who have allegedly been reared in the wild by animals.

Fertility The term used by demographers to indicate the actual childbearing behavior of people.

Field experiments Experiments conducted in settings that are natural and involve activities that are relatively normal.

Folkways Rules that generally govern everyday conduct, such as the rules for eating.

Fourth quarter of life The years between 75 and 100.

Function According to structural–functional theory, a positive purpose or consequence necessary for the continued existence of a society (or some other social system).

Functional theory *See* Structural–functionalism.

Game stage Mead's final stage of a child's social development in which the child simultaneously assumes the roles of a number of other people and responds to the expectations made of him or her by these people.

***Gemeinschaft* societies** Toennies's term for societies characterized by personal, face-to-face relationships, such as those in families, rural villages, and perhaps small towns.

Gender A term used to indicate the social definitions attached to males and females.

Gender gap in wages The tendency for women to receive lower monetary rewards than men even when they are in the same occupational categories.

Gender identity The recognition of one's gender and an acceptance of the characteristics typically associated with that gender.

Gender roles The expectations that prevail in a society about the activities and behaviors that may and may not be engaged in by males and females.

General deterrence The threat of punishment having the intention that people will not commit crimes because they fear they will be caught and punished.

Generalized other The internalization of the norms of the larger social group or society by an individual.

Genocide *See* Extermination.

Gentrification The process in which affluent people move into and restore previously declining older urban neighborhoods.

***Gesellschaft* societies** Toennies's term for a society characterized by impersonal and distant social relationships; people interact with each other, but in very limited ways, and for what the relationship may provide in terms of calculated self-interest. Associated with urban life.

Global cities   Cities that are major centers of international finance, headquarters for transnational corporations, and the locales for the distribution of highly specialized technical services in the global economy.

Globalization theory   The view that the world must be studied as a whole; global processes today operate autonomously of individual societies.

Grievance approach   An approach that sees social problems as objective facts that give rise to social movements.

Group   A relatively small number of people who interact with one another over time and thereby establish patterns of interaction, group identity, and rules or norms governing behavior.

Historical-comparative method   The examination and comparison of the events and histories of whole societies, or of the events and histories of major components of societies (for example, religious systems).

Homogamy   Marriage between two people with very similar social characteristics.

Horizontal mobility   Movement from one social position to another of equal rank.

Hypothesis   A statement about how various phenomena are expected to be related to each other.

Ideal culture   Values and norms that most people are aware of and accept, but do not necessarily live up to.

Ideal type   A logical, exaggerated, and "pure" model of some phenomenon one is studying or wishes to analyze.

Idealistic culture   Culture that blends the supersensory and sensory (nonmaterial and material) worlds.

Ideational culture   Culture dominated by the principle that a supersensory or nonmaterial world is the only true reality and the highest value.

Ideology   A set of ideas used to legitimate and justify the existing social order; also a set of ideas that explains reality, provides directives for behavior, and expresses the interests of particular groups.

In-group   A group with whom members are involved and with whom they identify.

Income   The economic resources that people receive or obtain during a specified period of time.

Income sufficiency   The amount of money needed to purchase the basic necessities of life.

Independent variable   A variable that is thought to produce a change in some other variable.

In-depth interviews   (*See* **Qualitative interviews**)

Index offenses (street crimes)   Crimes against people and property crimes.

Indicators   Observable phenomena that indicate the presence or absence, or level, of a concept.

Indirect expulsion   Use of harassment, discrimination, and persecution to force minorities to leave an area or nation.

Individualism   The importance placed on the rights, freedoms, and responsibilities of every person.

Industrial Revolution   In the nineteenth century, a rapid major social and economic change marked by the use of power-driven machinery; the rise of the factory system.

Inferential statistics   Techniques that assist in making statements about a population from a sample.

Innovators   People who accept cultural goals but reject conventional means.

Institution   A set of groups and organizations, with norms and values, that attend to the basic needs of a society.

Institutional discrimination   Rules, policies, practices, procedures, and laws that appear to be neutral but have a negative effect on minorities.

Institutional sexism   The day-to-day operations, rules, and policies of organizations and institutions that result in the discriminatory treatment of women.

Intergenerational mobility   Differences between the social-class position of children and the social-class position of their parents.

Internal explanations of social inequality   Explanations of social inequality that see a group's social status and attainments as a consequence of the distinctive traits, abilities, qualities, or characteristics that each group possesses.

Intersender role conflict   Situation in which two or more people have conflicting expectations of a person in a given role.

Interrole conflict   Situation in which expectations attached to one role are in conflict with expectations of another role.

Interview   Questions asked by an interviewer or researcher, in person or by telephone.

Intragenerational (*or* career) mobility   Movement in the class structure by individuals during their lifetimes.

Invasion–succession   The process whereby one identifiable group moves to a different part of an urban area and is replaced by another group.

Isolation   A condition resulting from a feeling of not belonging to one's workplace or other settings; a dimension of alienation.

Juvenile delinquency   Illegal or antisocial behavior on the part of a minor.

Knowledge and beliefs   A body of information created and accepted by the people of a society that influences their behavior.

Labeling theory   A sociological theory that focuses on the process by which some people in society are able to label other individuals as deviant.

Laboratory experiments   Experiments conducted in specially designed rooms that are equipped with one-way mirrors, audio systems, and video recording equipment.

Lancaster system   A highly structured school system of the nineteenth century that emphasized rote memorization of facts and enforced strict discipline.

Latent function   A less obvious, unanticipated, or unexpected consequence of a social structure.

Laws   The norms that are written and enforced by the government.

Legal divorce   A stage of divorce when the state's requirements for ending a marriage are learned and carried out.

Liberation theology   A contemporary Christian religious doctrine emphasizing social justice for the poor and dispossessed.

Life expectancy   The average number of years that people in a social or demographic category will live on average.

Life chances   The likelihood of realizing a certain standard of living or quality of life as it is affected by one's position in a stratification system.

Looking-glass self   The image of oneself that is a reflection of how others respond to one.

Macroscopic sociology   The sociological study of the larger social units—groups, organizations, cultures, and societies.

Majority group   A group that occupies a position of superior power, prestige, and privilege, and is able to realize its goals and interests even in the face of resistance.

Mana   The force or power believed to be inherent in a sacred object.

Manifest function   The intended and well-recognized purpose or consequence of a social structure.

Marital quality   A general term referring to an individual's satisfaction with a marriage and with the relationship between marital partners.

Mass production   Production system in which products are standardized, parts are interchangeable, the production process yields high volume, the flow of materials is synchronized, and the entire process is as continuous as possible.

Master status   A position so important that it dominates or overrides all other statuses, both for the person and for all other people.

Material culture   The artifacts, objects, and tools used by the members of a particular society.

Materialism   A preoccupation with acquiring more and more possessions and property.

McDonaldization   The adoption of the operating principles of the fast-food industry—efficiency, predictability, control, and quantification—by more and more sectors of the American and world economies.

Mean   A numerical average of a set of numbers, obtained by adding all the numbers in a set and dividing the sum by the total number of cases in the set; a measure of central tendency.

Meaninglessness   A condition in which one cannot see one's place and significance in the broader scheme of things; a dimension of alienation.

Median   The middle number of a distribution of numbers arranged from lowest to highest; a measure of central tendency.

Medicalization of society   The tendency to exaggerate the importance of medicine and to call something an illness that was not previously thought of in this way.

Megacities   Cities of 8 million or more residents.

Megalopolis   An area of continuous urban and suburban settlement formed when the outer rings of adjacent metropolitan areas merge.

Melting pot   A description of the process of assimilation in which many different ethnic groups contribute elements of their distinctive cultures to the creation of a new and different culture.

Meritocracy   An ideology that justifies social inequality by emphasizing equality of opportunity for everyone in a society.

Meritocratic ideology   An ideology that justifies social inequality by emphasizing equality of opportunity and that differences of individuals' social rank are a consequence of their own merit.

Metropolis   A large urban area containing a central city and the surrounding communities that are economically and politically linked to the central city.

Metropolitan Statistical Area (MSA)   A United States designation for a geographic area (usually a county or series of counties) of at least 100,000 residents that includes a center city of 50,000 or more people.

Migration   The term demographers use to describe the permanent (or semipermanent) change of one's place of residence.

Microscopic sociology The sociological study of the smallest social units—individuals, their thoughts, and actions.

Military–industrial complex The informal but closely knit cooperation between military and industrial sectors that tends to foster the mutual interests of each.

Minority group A group that occupies an inferior or subordinate position of prestige, power, and privilege; is excluded from full participation in the life of the society; and is the object of discrimination by the majority group.

Misdemeanors Minor crimes punishable by less than a year in prison.

Mode The most frequently observed number in a set of numbers; a measure of central tendency.

Modeling Children observing the behavior of same-sex significant others and imitating that behavior.

Modernization The degree to which less developed countries follow the model of the developed countries of the West.

Monopoly capitalism Modern capitalist system in which one or a few capitalists control a given sector of the economy.

Moral function of education The educational system teaching children the norms and values of the society.

Mores Rules relating to serious behaviors and moral standards, such as stealing, robbing, killing, espionage.

Mortality The term used by demographers to refer to death or death rates of a population.

Multiple nuclei model A model of urban development emphasizing that cities have several distinct centers of activity.

Multinucleated metropolitan region A regional settlement pattern characterized by a mixture of cities, suburbs, towns, and exurbs spread over a wide geographic area.

Myth A sacred story that communicates the moral prescriptions of divine beings and binds believers into a community and a belief system.

Nation-state A state that has power over people living in a distinct geographical area known as a nation.

Natural fertility The maximum level of uncontrolled childbearing.

Natural selection A theory that states that the fittest members of any species will be allowed to survive and to spread their traits throughout the population.

Neo-Marxian theory A sociological theory in which legal and political systems are seen as being built upon, and are a reflection of, a society's economic base.

Net financial assets Household wealth after equity in homes and vehicles has been deducted.

Net worth Household wealth based on the difference between assets and liabilities.

"New" immigration Immigrants of the late nineteenth and early twentieth century who were drawn primarily from southern and eastern Europe (for example, Poland, Italy, Greece, Russia).

Nonverbal symbol A physical display that has social meaning.

Norm of reciprocity A standard that calls for two interacting people to give one another things of equal or almost equal value.

Normative, *or* voluntary, organization An organization that controls participants by its norms and values.

Norms *See* **Cultural norms**
Nuclear family A family unit made up of a husband, wife, and children.

Objectivity In science, conducting research in a way that personal, subjective views do not influence research results.

Observational studies Systematic and purposive observations of human behavior in natural settings.

"Old" immigration The wave of immigrants from northern and western Europe (for example, Great Britain, Germany, Ireland, and Scandinavia) who came to the United States primarily between 1820 and 1895.

Old-old Elderly persons over seventy-five years of age, often in chronic ill health or with infirmities.

Oligarchy A small, powerful, controlling group at the top of an organization having almost all of the control and power.

Open class system A system of stratification in which there are few obstacles to people's moving up or down in the system.

Oppression The exploitation of a minority group by excluding it from equal participation in a society.

Organization A deliberately constituted collectivity aimed at achieving specified goals, with clearly delineated statuses, roles, and rules.

Organized crime Self-perpetuating, structured, and disciplined associations in which profits are obtained wholly or in part through illegal means.

Out-group From the point of view of in-group members, a group to which outsiders belong.

Overclass A contemporary elite social class whose members are characterized by the possession of highly specialized technical skills and are adept at problem solving and manipulating information in a complex global economy.

Participant observation A research method that typically involves the researcher directly in the lives and events of the people being studied; the researcher is both a participant and an observer.

Patriarchal terrorism Violence almost exclusively initiated by men as a way of gaining and maintaining total and absolute control over their women partners.

Patriarchy The dominance of husbands and fathers in family life.

Person-role conflict Conflict between the expectations associated with a particular role and a person's moral and personal values.

Personal control The idea that individuals cannot be made to do things that they do not want to do by social, political, or economic forces.

Personal values The values individuals use to make decisions about their personal lives and how they will respond to public issues.

Play stage Mead's second stage of a child's social development in which the child evaluates himself or herself from the point of view of significant others.

Pluralism (1) A system in which different ethnic or racial groups can coexist equally and be preserved. (2) A political situation in which a number of competing interest groups exert power, with no single group able to control all situations.

Political action committees (PACs)   Political organizations that operate independently of political parties, channeling money from special-interest groups into the election campaigns of political candidates.

Political crime   Misconduct and crime committed within or against a political system.

Population composition   The term demographers use to describe the characteristics of a population (age and sex, for example).

Postindustrial society   A society that was formerly industrial, but is now primarily producing services and information, rather than manufactured goods.

Poverty index   The federal government's estimate of the annual income necessary to meet minimal living costs in the United States.

Poverty rate   The percentage of the population below the poverty line.

Power   The ability of an individual or group to realize its interests and to impose its will upon others, despite resistance.

Power elite   A small group of nationally influential persons who occupy key positions in large corporations, the executive branch of government, and the military.

Powerlessness   A condition of being dominated by another individual or by circumstance; a dimension of alienation.

Prejudice   A set of rigidly held negative attitudes, beliefs, and feelings toward members of another group.

Preparatory stage   Mead's first stage of a child's social development in which the young child engages in a primitive form of interaction.

Prestige   The esteem, honor, and social approval accorded to an individual or a social status.

Primary deviance   Early, nonpatterned acts of deviance.

Primary socialization   Socialization by parents (or caregivers) that lays the foundation for personality development.

Primary groups   Groups characterized by intimate face-to-face association and cooperation, typically small and close-knit.

Procedural objectivity   Performing and reporting all research tasks so that any interested person will know how the research was conducted.

Procreative view of sex   The idea that sex is only for reproduction.

Profane   Those things socially defined as everyday, commonplace, utilitarian, and ordinary; contrasts with the sacred.

Progressive taxes   Taxes based on the ability to pay; the percentage of income one pays increases as one's income increases; the wealthier are taxed at higher rates than the poor.

Proletariat   As used by Marx, the masses of workers, the subordinate, propertyless members of a capitalist society who must sell their labor to capitalists in order to survive.

Property crime   Crimes aimed at gaining or destroying property unlawfully.

Prophetic function of religion   Circumstances in which a religious impulse provides the basis for critically examining, challenging, and changing the existing social or religious order.

Proportional taxes   Taxes in which all people, regardless of income, pay the same percentage of income in taxes.

Protestant ethic   A system of beliefs and actions involving a moral commitment to hard work, frugality, self-denial, acquisitiveness, and systematic calculation.

Psychic divorce   The process of regaining an individual identity and autonomy after a divorce.

Qualitative interviews (*or* in-depth interviews)   Questions asked in face-to-face situations in which the interviewer uses an interview guide or loosely organized questions.

Qualitative research   Sociological studies that use verbal descriptions and analysis, often done by those who claim that the subject matter of sociology cannot be reduced to mathematical formulas and statistical techniques.

Quantitative research   Sociological studies that use numerical measurement and statistical analysis as a way of conducting research.

Questionnaire   Written set of self-administered questions delivered to respondents by hand or mail.

Race   A group that is socially defined on the basis of physical characteristics.

Racism   Belief in the inherent superiority of one racial group and the inherent inferiority of others.

Random sample   A sampling procedure giving every person in a population an equal chance of being selected in the sample.

Rational–legal authority   Legitimization of authority by the rule of law; authority derived from the rules and regulations of the system rather than from personal qualities of individuals or tradition.

Rationality   A form of human action based primarily on efficiency; goals and objectives set and achieved in the most efficient way possible.

Real culture   The everyday conduct of people, which may differ from the ideal culture.

Rebels   People who reject both cultural goals and means and substitute new goals and means.

Recidivism   Reimprisonment for new crimes committed after having previously served time in prison.

Reciprocity   The socially accepted idea that if you give something to someone, he or she must give you something of equal or near equal value in return.

Reference groups   Groups that a person takes into account when evaluating his or her actions or characteristics.

Reform movement   A social movement aimed at altering the existing social order to make it more acceptable.

Regressive movement   A social movement aimed at restoring a past or a passing social order on the grounds that the past order is preferable to any other.

Regressive taxes   Taxes in which the percentage of income paid in taxes decreases as income increases; the poor are taxed at higher rates than the wealthy.

Religion   An institutionalized system of symbols, beliefs, values, and practices dealing with those things believed to be sacred and with questions of ultimate meaning.

Remarried couple household   A household maintained by a married couple, one or both of whom have been previously married.

Replication   Redoing studies or experiments to see if the findings of an original study can be duplicated.

Resocialization   The process of unlearning old norms, roles, and values, and learning new ones required by a new social environment.

Resource mobilization   The idea that protest movements arise as a result of the existence of available resources and the effective mobilization of those resources.

Resource theory   A theory that explains the distribution of marital power in terms of the resources brought into the marriage by each of the spouses.

Retreatists   People who reject both cultural goals and conventional means of conduct.

Reverse socialization   When people who are normally the ones being socialized are instead doing the socializing.

Revisionist view of the history of education   The economic and social elites will develop an educational system that meets their needs more than the needs of the masses of people.

Revitalization movements   Social movements involving deliberate, organized efforts by members of a society to create a more satisfying culture.

Revolutionary movement   A social movement aimed at creating a new social order.

Rituals   Complex, communally shared, ceremonial expressions of religious experience that have become institutionalized.

Ritualists   People who cannot achieve cultural goals but continue to adhere strictly to conventional means of conduct.

Role   Behavior generally expected of one who occupies a particular status.

Role conflict   Situation in which a person who holds a position is confronted with conflicting or contrary expectations so that compliance to one makes compliance to the other difficult.

Role making   The ability of individuals to modify their roles, at least to some degree.

Role orientation   An individual's emphasis on specific aspects of a role.

Role overload   Situation in which an individual in a role is confronted with a large number of expectations and finds it difficult, if not impossible, to satisfy all of them in a given time period.

Routinization of charisma   The process of passing on the qualities associated with an individual leader and incorporating them into the characteristics of a group or organization.

Rule creators   Those who devise society's rules, norms, and laws.

Rule enforcers   Those who attempt to maintain social control and order through the threat or actual application of undesirable labels.

Rumor   Unverified information that diffuses through a collectivity as a result of people's attempting to understand something.

Sacred   Those entities and objects that people define and act toward with reverence, respect, mystery, awe, and sometimes fear.

Sanctions   Punishments for violation of mores.

Sapir–Whorf hypothesis   The idea that perceptions of reality are shaped by words and language.

Secondary analysis   The reanalysis of survey data sets collected by other researchers.

Secondary deviance   Forms of deviance that persist in individuals and cause them to organize their lives and personal identities around their deviant status.

Secondary groups   Groups that are typically large and impersonal; members do not know each other as intimately or completely as do the members of a primary group.

Sect   A small, voluntary, and exclusive religious group that has broken away from an existing religious organization.

Sector model   A model of urban development that emphasizes the influence of transportation paths (waterways, railways, and highways) in determining patterns of urban land use.

Secularization   A decline in the authority of religious beliefs, values, and practices.

Self-concept   An individual's thoughts about and evaluations of himself or herself.

Self-esteem   The degree to which people have positive views of themselves.

Self-estrangement   A condition of not being able to express one's abilities, potentialities, and personality in one's work or other settings; a dimension of alienation.

Self-fulfilling prophecy   An initial expectation, even when false, can produce the behavior that makes the original expectation come true. In schools, teachers may have expectations about certain students that will make the expectations come true.

Sensate culture   Culture dominated by the principle that the sensory or material world is the only true reality and the highest value.

Separatism   A system in which minorities voluntarily choose to be isolated from the majority group.

Sex segregation   The unequal allocation of occupations and professions to men and women.

Sexual coercion   Sex through force or rape.

Sick role   The role of sick people in society with respect to how they are supposed to act when ill.

Significant other   People close to an individual whose views shape an individual's self and provide definitions of other social objects; most common examples are parents, family members, friends, marriage partners, fellow workers, and the like.

Social change   Variations over time in the relationships among individuals, groups, cultures, and societies.

Social constructivism   An approach to social movements that places the emphasis on how social problems come to be defined.

Social control   Process by which a group or society enforces conformity to its demands and expectations.

Social epidemiology   The study of the frequency and pattern of a disease within a particular population.

Social exchange theory   A theory emphasizing that motivations for human behavior are found in its costs and rewards; that a person will repeat behaviors that have been rewarded and will stop behaviors that have been costly.

Social gerontology   The study of the impact of social and cultural conditions on the process of aging, and also the social consequences of age changes in the populations of a society.

Social integration   Belonging to, or being part of, social groups or society.

Social mobility   Movement of people from one position in a system of stratification to another.

Social movements   Collective efforts to resist or bring about some kind of social change.

Social stratification   The hierarchical structure of social inequalities that are institutionalized; the manner in which scarce resources and social rewards are distributed among different social categories.

Social structure   A regular pattern of social interaction and persistent social relationships, for example, the socioeconomic status system.

Social survey   Collecting information from a sample of people through questionnaires or interviews.

Socialization   The process by which a person learns and generally accepts the ways of a particular social group or society.

Society   A population of people living in a given territory, who share a culture and have a system of patterned interaction—a social structure.

Sociobiology A theory that posits that human behavior reflects genetically inherited traits that have been acquired through the evolutionary process of natural selection.

Sociological theories Theories that explain a wide range of human behavior and a variety of social and societal events.

Sociology of religion The study of the social manifestations of religions, including experiences, behaviors, beliefs, social roles, and organizational structures.

Specific deterrence The actual punishment of an individual is supposed to deter him or her from committing other crimes in the future.

State The dominant political institution in modern societies and the sole source of legitimate physical force.

Statistics Techniques used to process numbers produced by research and measurement.

Status A position or place within a set of social relationships; also used in stratification to denote social ranking on the basis of prestige.

Stereotype A belief that a certain category of people has a particular set of personal characteristics.

Strain theory A sociological theory that sees deviance as being caused by lack of congruence between institutional means and cultural goals.

Structural assimilation The integration of minorities into primary and secondary social relations with the dominant group.

Structural–functional theory A theory emphasizing that every societal pattern (structure) makes some positive or negative contribution to the society.

Structural mobility Social mobility resulting from changes in a society's occupational structure.

Subcultural groups (*or* **subcultures**) Societal groups that differ significantly from the dominant culture.

Subcultural theory A sociological theory that sees deviant behavior as conformity to the norms and values of a subculture that are different from those of the larger society.

Subcultural theory of urbanism An interpretation of urban life that emphasizes how the city's size, density, and diversity create a variety of subcultures that provide meaningful social settings for its inhabitants.

Subordinate group *See* **Minority group.**

Suburbs Urban areas adjacent to but beyond the political boundaries of a city.

Symbolic interactionism A theory that views social phenomena primarily through interaction among individuals at the symbolic level.

Symbols Words, gestures, and objects that communicate meaning because people agree on and recognize what they represent.

Taboo A religious proscription against physical contact with objects.

Technology The complex interplay of machines, equipment, tools, skills, and procedures for carrying out tasks.

Terrorism Systematic, or threatened, use of murder, injury, or destruction in order to achieve some political end.

Theology The rational and logical development of religious belief systems.

Theory A set of ideas that provides explanations for a broad range of phenomena.

Third quarter of life The years between age 50 and 75.

Total institution A closed organization that is set apart from the rest of society, forms an all-encompassing social environment, and serves as the only source of meeting the needs of its members.

Totalitarianism   A form of government involving state control and regulation of all major institutions in a society.

Tracking   Grouping children by their ability level in schools.

Tradition   The ways things have been done for a long time in a society or social group; as a source of authority it comes primarily from the position into which one is born.

Traditional view of the history of education   The American democratic political system requires an educated and an informed population, which the educational system provides.

Triad   Three people engaged in interaction.

Underclass   The most impoverished segment of American society for whom poverty is relatively permanent.

Urban   A place in which population exceeds a specific number of residents. The U.S. Bureau of the Census identifies as urban all towns and municipalities having more than 2500 residents.

Urbanism   The ways of life characteristic of urban residents.

Urbanization   The process by which the population of a society becomes concentrated in cities; also refers to the concentration of economic activity, political-administrative organization, communication networks, and political power in urban centers.

Utilitarian organization   An organization that uses money to control those at the bottom of the structure.

Values   *See* **Cultural values.**

Variables   Objects or phenomena that can change from one size, state, or degree to another.

Verbal symbols   Verbal utterances that are part of the spoken or written language of a society.

Vertical mobility   Movement upward or downward in social rank.

Veto group   A special interest group that attempts to defend itself by blocking the actions of other groups.

Victimless crime   Crimes in which it is difficult to identify a victim; participants choose to be involved in the activities.

Wealth   The accumulated economic resources that people possess or have acquired over time.

White ethnics   Contemporary descendants of the "new" immigrants.

White-collar crime   Crime committed by upper-status people in the course of their occupations.

World-system theory   A theory that stresses the economic and power inequalities of the present international order.

World Cities   *See* **Global cities**

Name Index

Subject Index